THE CAMBRIDGE HISTORY OF

TWENTIETH-CENTURY ENGLISH LITERATURE

This new Cambridge History is the first major history of twentieth-century English literature to cover the full range of writing in England, Scotland, Wales and Ireland. The volume also explores the impact of writing from the former colonies on English literature of the period and analyses the ways in which conventional literary genres were shaped and inflected by the new cultural technologies of radio, cinema and television. In providing an authoritative narrative of literary and cultural production across the century, this History acknowledges the claims for innovation and modernisation that characterise the beginning of the period. At the same time, it attends analytically to the more profound patterns of continuity and development which avant-garde tendencies characteristically underplay. Containing all the virtues of a Cambridge History, this new volume is a major event for anyone concerned with twentieth-century literature, its cultural context and its relation to the contemporary.

LAURA MARCUS is Professor of English at the University of Sussex, and co-director of its Centre for Modernist Studies. She has published widely on nineteenth- and twentieth-century literature and culture. Her publications include *Auto/biographical Discourses: Criticism, Theory, Practice* (1994/8) and *Virginia Woolf* (1997/2004), and, as editor, *Sigmund Freud's 'The Interpretation of Dreams': New Interdisciplinary Essays* (1999) and *Close Up 1927–33: Cinema and Modernism* (1998).

PETER NICHOLLS is Professor of English and American Literature at the University of Sussex, and co-director of its Centre for Modernist Studies. He is the editor of *Textual Practice*. He is the author of *Politics, Economics and Writing: A Study of Ezra Pound's 'Cantos'* (1984), *Modernisms: A Literary Guide* (1995) and of many articles and essays on twentieth-century literature and theory. He has recently co-edited *Ruskin and Modernism* (2001).

THE NEW CAMBRIDGE HISTORY OF

ENGLISH LITERATURE

The New Cambridge History of English Literature is a programme of reference works designed to offer a broad synthesis and contextual survey of the history of English literature through the major periods of its development. The organisation of each volume reflects the particular characteristics of the period covered, within a general commitment to providing an accessible narrative history through a linked sequence of essays by internationally renowned scholars. The History is designed to accommodate the range of insights and fresh perspectives brought by new approaches to the subject, without losing sight of the need for essential exposition and information. The volumes include valuable reference features, including extensive bibliographies and a full index.

The Cambridge History of Medieval English Literature
EDITED BY DAVID WALLACE

The Cambridge History of Early Modern English Literature
EDITED BY DAVID LOEWENSTEIN AND JANEL MUELLER

The Cambridge History of English Literature 1660–1780
EDITED BY JOHN RICHETTI

The Cambridge History of Twentieth-Century English Literature
EDITED BY LAURA MARCUS AND PETER NICHOLLS

In preparation
The Cambridge History of English Romantic Literature
EDITED BY JAMES CHANDLER

THE CAMBRIDGE HISTORY OF TWENTIETH-CENTURY ENGLISH LITERATURE

*

Edited by
LAURA MARCUS
and
PETER NICHOLLS

CAMBRIDGE
UNIVERSITY PRESS

PUBLISHED BY THE PRESS SYNDICATE OF THE UNIVERSITY OF CAMBRIDGE
The Pitt Building, Trumpington Street, Cambridge, United Kingdom

CAMBRIDGE UNIVERSITY PRESS
The Edinburgh Building, Cambridge CB2 2RU, UK
40 West 20th Street, New York, NY 10011-4211, USA
477 Williamstown Road, Port Melbourne, VIC 3207, Australia
Ruiz de Alarcón 13, 28014 Madrid, Spain
Dock House, The Waterfront, Cape Town 8001, South Africa

http://www.cambridge.org

First published 2004

Printed in the United Kingdom at the University Press, Cambridge

Typeface Dante MT 10.5/13 pt *System* LaTeX 2ε [TB]

A catalogue record for this book is available from the British Library

Library of Congress Cataloguing in Publication data

The Cambridge History of Twentieth-Century English Literature / edited by
Laura Marcus and Peter Nicholls.
p. cm. – (The New Cambridge History of English Literature)
Includes bibliographical references and index.
ISBN 0 521 82077 4 (hardback)
1. English literature – 20th century – History and criticism. 2. Great Britain – Intellectual life – 20th century. I. Marcus, Laura. II. Nicholls, Peter, 1950– III. Series.
PR471.C36 2004
820.9′0091 – dc22 2004045922

ISBN 0 521 82077 4 hardback

Contents

PART FIVE
TOWARDS THE MILLENNIUM, 1970–2000

Contributors

Jane Aaron	University of Glamorgan
Ann L. Ardis	University of Delaware
Tim Armstrong	Royal Holloway, University of London
David Ayers	University of Kent at Canterbury
Elleke Boehmer	Royal Holloway, University of London
David Bradshaw	Worcester College, Oxford
Peter Brooker	University of Nottingham
Ronald Bush	St John's College, Oxford
Gerard Carruthers	University of Glasgow
Robert L. Caserio	Temple University
Bryan Cheyette	University of Southampton
Steven Connor	Birkbeck College, University of London
Nate Dorward	Independent scholar
Paul Edwards	Bath Spa University College
Regenia Gagnier	University of Exeter
Maggie B. Gale	University of Birmingham
David Glover	University of Southampton
Trevor R. Griffiths	University of North London
Ken Hirschkop	University of Manchester
Michael Levenson	University of Virginia
Alison Light	Independent scholar
John Lucas	Nottingham Trent University
Roger Luckhurst	Birkbeck College, University of London
Scott McCracken	Sheffield Hallam University
Ronan McDonald	University of Reading
Laura Marcus	University of Sussex
Rod Mengham	Jesus College, Cambridge
Peter Middleton	University of Southampton
Tyrus Miller	University of California at Santa Cruz

Julian Murphet	University of Sydney
Susheila Nasta	Open University
Peter Nicholls	University of Sussex
Michael North	University of California at Los Angeles
Patrick Parrinder	University of Reading
Deborah Parsons	University of Birmingham
Adam Piette	University of Sheffield
Max Saunders	King's College London
Simon Shepherd	Central School of Speech and Drama
Vincent Sherry	Tulane University
Morag Shiach	Queen Mary College, University of London
Lyndsey Stonebridge	University of East Anglia
Keith Tuma	Miami University, Ohio
Patricia Waugh	Durham University
Keith Williams	University of Dundee
Tim Woods	University of Aberystwyth

Acknowledgements

We would like to thank Christopher Gregory-Guider for his enormous contribution as Editorial Assistant. His energy and attention to detail played a substantial part in bringing this volume to completion. We are grateful, too, to Peter Boxall for his specialist advice and input, and to Ray Ryan, our editor at Cambridge University Press, for inviting us to undertake this project, and for his advice and support throughout. Thanks are also due to Nikki Burton and Alison Powell at the Press, and to Margaret Berrill for her scrupulous copy-editing. Finally, we are very grateful to our contributors for bringing to our narrative construction of the century their own challenging perspectives.

Introduction

LAURA MARCUS AND PETER NICHOLLS

As the first *Cambridge History of Twentieth-Century English Literature*, this volume has a difficult brief. The last century has yet to compose itself definitively as a 'period', and our volume has to reckon with the fact that the concluding phases of the century will often prompt provisional comment rather than a sense of summative closure. The volume also covers a period in which questions of history and nation are particularly volatile, and while taking its place in an extended series of literary histories, recognises that for its precursors 'English' has generally been a less contentious term than it is now. In this *History*, 'Englishness' is not merely a given attribute of the literature under discussion, but a cultural condition in which complex questions of identity and location are constantly at stake.

It is also important to note here that the volume is intended as a history rather than as a Companion or as an anthology of essays on the period. In that sense it reflects a particular self-consciousness in the period itself about historical change and the changing relation of cultural forms. The *History* thus recognises the claims for cultural innovation and modernisation that characterise the beginning of the period at the same time as it attends analytically to the more profound patterns of continuity and development which avant-garde tendencies characteristically underplay. Along with this tension between change and continuity – and perhaps another version of it – is the troubled relation of internationalist perspectives to nationalist ones. British Modernism was an exilic phenomenon (hardly 'English' at all) and at its height mounted a radical attack on British society and government in their most settled and conservative forms. England and Englishness were criticised from the outside as avant-gardism was increasingly equated with cosmopolitanism. This particular tension is one that informs the *History* as a whole; indeed, it provides one of its principal armatures. After the High Modernist phase of the twenties, we find an increasing attraction to forms of localism and regionalism, and consequently a redefined sense of what constitutes 'Englishness' and 'Britishness'. While a strand of Modernist cosmopolitanism outlived the Modernist moment itself, it frequently existed alongside a literature concerned more directly with local specificities of class and place. We may detect, in fact, an increasing and related concern with national identities, as a coherent idea(l) of 'Englishness' fragmented under pressure from the devolved communities of Northern Ireland, Wales and Scotland. The process of dispersal gained further momentum from emerging concepts of postcolonial identity and from a renewed 'cosmopolitanisation' of British literature by writers with roots in the Commonwealth nations and the Caribbean.

As this example suggests, the tendency in the cultural scene that this volume explores is towards a greater complexity that resists easy categorisation and clear-cut chronological phases. The volume provides an extended history of the literature of the twentieth century, but one whose linear structure is complicated by cross-connecting themes and topics, different viewpoints and often overlapping chronologies. The *History* is also attentive to the fact that the chronologies of literary production and reception have their own distinctive forms, and that the impact of historical events on creative activities is often indirect and inflected by the imaginative processes of reconstruction. The volume is, of course, itself one such process, marked in particular by the continuing sense of the twentieth century's proximity to our own present, and this in turn is complicated by the fact that the century's temporal boundaries may be at odds with its defining cultural moments. So while the volume is broadly concerned to situate the works it discusses in a familiar unfolding history, cultural periodisation often cuts against that grain. We begin not in 1900 but with a section on 'Writing Modernity', which traces responses to modern life through late nineteenth-century Decadence and explores the generation of writers whose work crosses the century divide. The closing chapters of the volume are for their part necessarily provisional in their presentation of a cultural scene whose contours are yet to acquire full definition.

Movements, phases, influences – these are the usual currency of cultural histories and they are much in evidence in this volume. At the same time, though, our narrative acknowledges the increasingly multifaceted nature of the literary scene as it reveals tensions between high and low culture, between avant-gardism and tradition, between the national and the international and so on. The volume is inevitably much preoccupied with the question of what constitutes the 'literary' and is for that reason increasingly attuned to the ambiguous borders between genres. This is a period, of course, that saw the rise of new technologies of representation and communication. Cinema, along with other new and emergent media, provided crucial contexts for understanding developments in literary Modernism and, more broadly, the cultural debates of the period – debates, for example, over mass and minority culture and the reception of culture. The volume also examines the construction and representation of literary culture by the new media and the ways in which forms of voice and vision shaped literary expression. Radio produced a new kind of drama, while television film led to the return of a theatrical naturalism which also strongly influenced developments in the novels of the 1950s and 60s. In the last decades of the century the Postmodern work often borrowed from film, television, video, music and performance, media which interacted with and newly shaped the possibilities of textual representation.

Popular fictions have an important place in this literary history, and several chapters investigate the phenomenon of the bestseller and twentieth-century developments in genre or niche publishing, demonstrating an increasing interchangeability between journalism, consumer culture and popular fiction. The volume explores the cultural and historical determinants of the 'anti-Modernisms' of the middle decades of the century, considering the part played by the media – in particular, literary journalism and radio – in shaping the dominant image of 'literary culture', and the extent to which the new class fraction of literary producers reacted against an 'elitist' avant-gardism. There was a perception, too, of a widening split between the professional critic and the common reader. The 1930s saw the emergence of a vociferous, non-bellettristic, literary criticism that propelled the academic study of literature in significant new directions and claimed a renewed Arnoldian centrality for literary texts. In the post-war period, this redefinition of the role of writers and intellectuals continued but with a new consciousness of working-class cultures. These years also witnessed a resurgence of national self-consciousness which was simultaneously contested by a new cosmopolitanism, fuelled in its turn by resurgent continental philosophies of existence. That philosophy should thus consort with imaginative writing indicates the growing proximity of 'theory' to the creative arts. In the period after 1970, the influence of European thought reached increasingly beyond the academy. Ideas drawn from Post-Structuralism, Deconstruction and psychoanalysis were absorbed by writers and artists, and led to radical reappraisals of concepts of language, subjectivity and ideology. The impact of theory on literary criticism instigated controversies over the canon, the 'death of the author', and other anti-metaphysical conceptions of the literary work. The legacy of these controversies continues to be felt in criticism and in academic study, notably in recent discussions of Post-modernism. The volume presents no singular and conclusive account of these developments, seeking rather to register their complexity and to understand them as part of an ongoing and unresolved critical debate. At the same time, it does now seem clear that Modernism must be seen not simply as a movement belonging to the early decades of the century, but as a tendency that lives a rich and discontinous life across the period as a whole. The notion of the Postmodern, in apparent violation of its own terms, has not proven to be an efficient periodising concept that clearly situates us in a context distinct from modernity; rather, it affirms a continuing and troubled relation to a modernity that we cannot evade. A number of our contributors, writing on the last decades of the century, have found Postmodernism to be a useful, if not unavoidable concept, while others have attended to the persistence of Modernist strands late into the century. Others have sought different categories altogether, particularly in writing of postcolonial literatures and the literatures of diaspora.

We begin with Part I, 'Writing Modernity', which discerns traces of Modernism's pre-history in *fin-de-siècle* Decadence, presenting this older generation as to some degree preparing the way for the more self-consciously experimental work of the Modernist writers. This first section of the *History* explores a number of major themes whose subsequent manifestations will be traced in later chapters: concepts of identity, private and public; the changing relation of literature to nationalism; the redefinition of style and its opposition to 'rhetoric' in *fin-de-siècle* writing; the characterisation of the aesthetic as a kind of autonomous realm; empire fictions and their interactions with Modernist writing; the cultural interchange between Britain and France; the post-Romantic response to scientific developments; the impact of anthropology at the turn of the century; the response to commodification and the developing literary marketplace; the significance of a gendered aesthetic and of a modernity whose newness was encapsulated in models of an evolving and progressive femininity.

Part 2, 'The Emerging Avant-garde', considers what is arguably the second phase of Modernism's pre-history, exploring the ambiguous positioning of Edwardian and Georgian writers on the divide between realism and Modernism. The *History* begins a multifaceted examination of the century's new aesthetic, tracing its formation as an avant-garde tendency and examining the political and economic conditions which gave it its definitive character. Here contributors reconstruct the London of the period, analysing the different forms of interaction that sustained an avant-garde grouping of writers and artists, deriving from very different social and national backgrounds. The question of class and 'classlessness' is important here, for it is arguably the case that in the rigidly defined pre-1914 class system foreign intellectuals had a particular kind of class mobility that allowed them to move relatively easily between, for example, the Lyons Corner House and the literary salon. Separate chapters are devoted to an account of 'the arts of publicity' in the period before the war, exploring the vital role played in the dissemination of the new Modernism by little magazines, some of which (like *The New Freewoman*) had clearly marked political agendas that did not necessarily accord with the primarily aesthetic aims of this phase of avant-garde activity. Exploration of 'the political scene' further opens this set of questions, especially with regard to suffragism and its contradictory relations to a predominantly male avant-garde. The section closes with a historical account of the Great War, gauging its impact on cultural activity in Britain, and opening up the category of war-writing beyond combatant literature in order to examine the ubiquity of war-consciousness in the texts of the period.

The *History* then moves in Part 3, 'Modernism and its Aftermath, 1918–1945', to an exploration of developments in prose writing after the cessation of hostilities, deploying the concept of 'trauma' to trace the movements of remembering and repetition that characterise so much post-war writing. It examines the ways in which the literature of this period was shaped by acts of confrontation with and evasion of the immediate past, focusing on narrative and psychological experiments with time. This concern with temporality informed the major work of such Modernists as Joyce, Woolf, Ford, Conrad, Lawrence and Lewis, issuing in an increasing preoccupation with the phenomenology of consciousness. This is in many ways the best-known aspect of the period's writing, at least insofar as that is represented by the products of High Modernism. At the same time, the volume recognises the achievement of novelists situated outside and, at times, in opposition to Modernist aesthetics and is alert to connections between different groupings. The medium of satire offers perhaps the most powerful example of such permeability between categories of writer that are normally held to be exclusive, bringing into conjunction such different novelists of modern life as Wyndham Lewis and Evelyn Waugh.

The section moves to a more extended consideration of the new poetics and its engagement with modernity on the one hand, and with myth and tradition on the other. This double temporality was at the heart of psychoanalytic thinking, the emergence of which variously affected writing in this period, opening possibilities of a new language for the unconscious. Biography and autobiography had a particular significance in the first decades of the century as conduits through which psychoanalysis entered cultural life, bringing into being the concept of a distinctively modern subjectivity. At the same time, the 'New Biography' was an aspect of the burgeoning cultures of publicity and public life in the 1920s. Developments in popular fiction, theatre and cinema were indissolubly linked with the articulation of a newly politicised culture during the 1930s, as writers and intellectuals sought to negotiate aesthetic questions in relation to the contesting ideologies of the time. Thirties writing here connected briefly and problematically with European avant-gardism in the work of the English Surrealists. The section closes with World War II, considered from two angles and from a number of locations. Travel writings of the immediate pre-war period portrayed a world of contested and closed borders, making familiar maps opaque and uncertain. The writing of World War II emerged not only from the experiences of international theatres of war, but from London as a city under siege, its ruins opening it up to a buried past and an uncertain future.

Writing the history of the second half of the twentieth century raises central questions about continuity and change. To answer these, Part 4 of the *History*, 'Post-war Cultures, 1945–1970', investigates the role of writers and intellectuals in the project of cultural reconstruction. Questions of class and education assumed a new importance as traditional images came under pressure from movements of devolution and migration that reassigned relations between centre and so-called peripheries. A further tension in the period was once again between the demands of nationalism and internationalism, played out in the cultural sphere as a new set of arguments for and against Modernism. With questions of national and regional identity high on the agenda, the varied responses to these frequently determined writers' handling of the Modernist legacy.

Part 5, 'Towards the Millennium', explores the literature and culture of the last thirty years of the century. 'Culture' becomes all-pervasive, appearing in one guise as the pernicious vehicle of capitalist ideology, and in another as the utopian expression of an alternative society. The example of American society, with its ostentatious commitment to newness and opportunity, offered a powerful alternative to what was frequently thought of in the period as British provincialism and laid the foundations for what would soon be much talked about as Postmodernism. The period saw at once the rapid expansion of genre fiction and the rise of new publishing initiatives, particularly through feminist presses. New spaces also opened in the sphere of theatrical performance, with the resurgence of a 'theatre of cruelty', the celebration of the weakening of censorship and the relaxing of laws against homosexuality in the late 1960s.

This sense of a culture poised for radical change was fuelled by a growing awareness of thriving cultures outside a narrowly conceived English tradition, with writing from Ireland, Scotland and Wales articulating at once their relations to the 'centre', and their own particular internal divisions of language and literature. These increasingly prominent literatures were notable for their combination of experiment with a renewed sense of national history. If this seems at odds with the dominant paradigm of Postmodernism, it is nonetheless the case that in many exemplary instances of 'depthless' Postmodern style, writers have still shown a consistent investment in questions of history, memory and ethics. This highly charged relation to the past has also been expressed in the literatures of confession, witness and testimony that contribute to the expanding field of life-writing.

Much Postmodern literature and theory exploits a generic hybridity that takes on a sharper cultural and political edge in the literatures and theories of postcolonialism. Part 5 of the *History* addresses not only the very wide range of literatures that has recently been gathered under the postcolonial umbrella, but the significance, and the limitations, of the term itself. The section explores the ways in which contemporary postcolonial writing inscribes the clash of cultures alongside the representation and testing of 'multiculturalism'. In this field, the pressures of cultural, ethnic and national diversity render suspect the very category of 'English literature'. Yet as the volume shows, while 'English' has obviously lost its neutrality as a descriptive term, it still provides a sensitive register of the fictions and fantasies of national identity which literature continues to articulate. The screw tightens, of course, when 'literature' itself is called in question, though the challenge to the primacy of literature from media and the new technologies has proven a spur rather than a curb to innovation. The resulting literary scene is one that escapes neat summation; this *History* comes to its close, recognising that it must be complexity rather than completion that has the final word.

ONE

*

WRITING MODERNITY

I

Science and knowledge at the beginning of the twentieth century: versions of the modern Enlightenment

PATRICK PARRINDER

Ursula Brangwen in the laboratory

In his multi-generational novel *The Rainbow* (1915), D. H. Lawrence shows his early twentieth-century heroine Ursula Brangwen as a biology student at Nottingham university college. During her final year of study Ursula has a conversation with a woman doctor of physics, Dr Frankstone, a materialist who believes that there is no special mystery to life. Life is simply a 'complexity of physical and chemical activities, of the same order as the activities we already know in science'.[1] As scientific research continues, there is no reason why we should not come to know everything. But the conversation ends on a note of uncertainty – Dr Frankstone is, after all, only restating the conventional outlook of nineteenth-century scientific Positivism – and Ursula, for one, is not convinced.

Positivism has been defined as 'a collection of prohibitions concerning human knowledge, intended to confine the name "knowledge" or "science" to the results of those operations that are observable in the evolution of the modern sciences of nature'.[2] There is, then, a distinct circularity involved in the claim that we can come to know everything through scientific research, since science itself has been allowed to prescribe what counts as knowledge. Dr Frankstone is speaking for the so-called 'classical' Victorian physics, which would be fundamentally challenged in the early twentieth century by Einsteinian relativity, quantum theory and Heisenberg's Uncertainty Principle. Classical physics derives from Newton, but in the late nineteenth century its most influential figure was Lord Kelvin, whose Laws of Thermodynamics had led to a conception of the physical universe in which everything could be charted and everything

1 D. H. Lawrence, *The Rainbow* (Harmondsworth: Penguin, 1949), p. 440.

2 Leszek Kolakowski, *Positivist Philosophy: From Hume to the Vienna Circle*, trans. Norbert Guterman (Harmondsworth: Penguin, 1972), p. 18.

was predictable. In what H. G. Wells mockingly called the 'Universe Rigid', a universal space–time diagram was theoretically possible in which all past and future events would find their appointed place. To picture the Positivist conception in this way was, however, to demonstrate its absurdity.

But there was a powerful alternative to the view of the physical universe associated with the Laws of Thermodynamics. While Lawrence's Dr Frankstone is anxious to assimilate biology to physics, Charles Darwin's *The Origin of Species* (1859) had suggested that 'life' had its own laws of reproduction and variation, leading to an endless prospect of dynamic change. Thus Wells, a Darwinian and a former biology teacher, argued in 'Scepticism of the Instrument' (1905) that logical analysis could never keep pace with the natural world's ability to throw up new and surprising forms. The philosopher T. E. Hulme accused the scientific Positivists of trying to 'hold water in a wire cage'. The universe was not a 'chess-board', but a 'chaotic cinder heap'; and Hulme cited the radical scepticism of Friedrich Nietzsche, who had argued that 'What can be conceived is necessarily a fiction.'[3] Ursula Brangwen, too, rejects the physical materialist outlook in which everything can be reduced to matter and energy, like the movements of billiard balls. But she goes further than this. Studying an organism under the microscope, she cannot believe that its 'life' is a mere blind struggle to adapt and survive, as Darwin's evolutionary theory had seemed to imply. Like her creator D. H. Lawrence, Ursula is drawn towards religious mysticism rather than philosophical scepticism or some form of biological materialism. She has a moment of revelation in the botany laboratory:

> Suddenly in her mind the world gleamed strangely, with an intense light, like the nucleus of the creature under the microscope. [. . .] She could not understand what it all was. She only knew that it was not limited mechanical energy, nor mere purpose of self-preservation and self-assertion. It was a consummation, a being infinite.[4]

Ursula is searching for an apprehension of the meaning of life beyond the bounds of any scientific discipline, but her conception of infinity is post-Christian as well as post-scientific. For Lawrence and for other modern writers such as W. B. Yeats, science was no longer opposed to orthodox religion as it had been in the nineteenth century. No single religion could claim a monopoly of truth, any more than the scientific universe could; there might, however, be mystical truths at once hidden by, and latent within, the traditional religions. The notion of latency is a pervasive aspect of early twentieth-century

[3] T. E. Hulme, 'The New Philosophy', *New Age*, n.s. 5, 10 (1 July 1909), p. 198.
[4] Lawrence, *The Rainbow*, p. 441.

thought, as we shall see. But it is also significant that Lawrence locates Ursula's rejection of nineteenth-century forms of scientific certainty within a vividly realised portrayal of the experience of modern higher education.

The university or 'academy' embodies nineteenth-century attitudes to knowledge, both in its technical and liberal aspects. It accommodates both sides of the 'science' versus 'culture' debate, which had been initiated in England in the 1880s by T. H. Huxley and Matthew Arnold. At the same time, the university was rapidly becoming the dominant intellectual institution of the new century. Ursula, like the great majority of women students in her time, attends one of the new civic universities where she is accepted as a full member of the student body. She has entered the university as a trainee schoolteacher (teaching was the only graduate profession fully open to women before World War I), but she has switched from a general arts course to an honours degree in botany.

The provincial, 'redbrick' English universities mostly began as strictly technical and vocational institutions, but their original purpose was rapidly diluted in pursuit of the more prestigious activities of liberal education associated with Oxford and Cambridge. At the same time, the rapid specialisation of knowledge and its separation into scientific and humanistic disciplines split the university into competing faculties and departments, each with its own compelling sense of mission. Ursula's college is a sham-Gothic edifice, its architecture deliberately recalling the ethos of the medieval universities. Her conversation with the physicist Dr Frankstone shows her, however briefly, as a member of an interdisciplinary community of scholars and seekers after truth. But Ursula has already concluded that the university's attempt to invoke the ancient virtues of scholarship is largely fraudulent. The place she is attending is not a temple of knowledge but an offshoot of industrial society, a 'little side-show' to the mills and factories of Nottingham.[5] Typically, she makes an exception for her chosen discipline of plant science – a specialised research environment which does, apparently, retain some of the ancient virtues. On the afternoon when Lawrence shows her looking through the microscope she is a final-year student examining a new preparation which the professor himself is excited about; she is, as we say, pushing at the frontiers of knowledge. But a few weeks later she herself will sit, and fail, a public examination for her BA, for which she has to travel to London.

Since 1858 London University degrees had been open to anyone regardless of institutional affiliation, in sharp contrast to the pastoral education provided

[5] Ibid., p. 434.

under the tutorial system at Oxford and Cambridge and, to a lesser extent, by Ursula's fledgling university of Nottingham. Ursula in the laboratory works under the professor's eye, like a trusted apprentice, but her London University examination defines education in starkly Positivist terms, as the mastery of a body of knowledge.[6] It was precisely this view of knowledge that had been denounced by the defenders of culture against science. In the mid-twentieth century the literary critic F. R. Leavis, echoing the Arnold–Huxley debate, would use D. H. Lawrence's writings as a touchstone in his attack on C. P. Snow's advocacy of scientific and technological education.[7] From the Leavisian point of view, Ursula's failure in an examination which simply measured the acquisition of technical skills and a body of approved knowledge appears as a vindication for the opponents of Positivism. But Ursula's experience in the laboratory also shows that a scientific education could force the student to question the ultimate meaning of life, perhaps far more effectively than a classical or literary education would have done. Thus Lawrence, even if unwittingly, offers strong support to Huxley and Snow as well.

The 'science of man' and the 'Key to All Mythologies'

For all its self-contradictions there was no obvious alternative to the university, either as a location for what was increasingly known as 'research' or as a training-ground for young minds. The university aspired to be open to any qualified person regardless of class, race or gender, though in practice (and much more in England than in Scotland) access long remained highly restricted. It also stood for the pursuit of knowledge as a narrowly professional calling, though educationists continued to prize the virtues of the generalist and the gifted amateur. Governments were increasingly aware that a modern higher education system was needed in the interests of national prosperity and competitiveness; at the same time, university extension was a response to the popular demand for a better life. It was no longer acceptable to be learned and erudite without taking part, in one way or another, in the educational mission of modern democratic society. The extent of the change can be seen if we recall the gentlemanly scientists and intellectuals portrayed in George Eliot's novel *Middlemarch*, published in 1871–2 but set some forty years

[6] See R. D. Anderson, *Universities and Elites in Britain since 1800* (Basingstoke: Macmillan, 1992), p. 17.

[7] F. R. Leavis, *Two Cultures? The Significance of C. P. Snow* (London: Chatto & Windus, 1962), esp. pp. 22–3.

earlier. Lydgate, a provincial doctor, is working at cell-theory; Farebrother, a clergyman, is a keen spare-time entomologist and butterfly-hunter; while his fellow-clergyman Casaubon is a classicist intent on discovering the 'Key to All Mythologies'. From an educational standpoint all this knowledge is wasted. In the real world Charles Darwin, the greatest of nineteenth-century scientists, was also perhaps the last of the great independent scholars. Huxley, his friend and champion, who became Professor of Biology and Dean of the Normal School of Science (soon to be incorporated into Imperial College, England's leading technological university) was a much more modern figure.

Supposing that he ever finds it, Casaubon's 'Key to All Mythologies' is not, apparently, expected to unlock the door of the Anglican religion which he dutifully preaches every Sunday. The late nineteenth century, however, saw the establishment of the new 'Science of Man', anthropology, whose most influential practitioners followed Darwin in linking humanity to the biological kingdom. No sooner had they attained academic recognition than the anthropologists launched what could be seen as a concerted attack on theology, the once undisputed 'Queen of the Sciences' which had now become intellectually moribund. The new 'Key to All Mythologies' clearly was expected to account for the Christian religion. Colonel Lane Fox Pitt-Rivers had given his magnificent collection of ethnographic specimens to Oxford University in 1881, and shortly afterwards E. B. Tylor was appointed as the nation's first anthropology lecturer. Pitt-Rivers wanted his collection to demonstrate the 'general principle of evolutionary improvement' across all human culture and history; 'history' and 'evolution' were, he thought, synonymous terms.[8] The 'Key to All Mythologies' would thus link archaeology to anthropology and the physical to the social sciences. It entailed a search for origins and a hypothesis of universal, more or less linear, development from simpler to more complex forms. The result was a way of mapping the universe owing far more to the idea of a genealogical tree than a diagram of forces. Darwin's two great works were *The Origin of Species* and *The Descent of Man* (1871); the latter was much discussed in anthropological circles. All human history, it now seemed, was contained in embryo in what W. H. Auden in 'Spain 1937' would call 'the classic lecture / On the origin of Mankind'.

E. B. Tylor, often regarded as the founding father of British anthropology, had argued in *Primitive Culture* (1871) that culture and religion were virtually identical in tribal societies. What Tylor called 'animism' was the fundamental

[8] Dan Smith, 'Evolution and Culture: the Pitt Rivers Museum, Oxford', *things*, 14 (Summer 2001), p. 17; Lt-Gen. A. Lane Fox Pitt-Rivers, in *The Evolution of Culture and Other Essays*, ed. J. L. Myres (Oxford: Clarendon Press, 1906), p. 24.

principle of all religions. The most unforgettable claim to have discovered the 'Key to All Mythologies' came, however, not from the anthropology school at Oxford but from J. G. Frazer of Trinity College, Cambridge. Frazer's massive, inspired treatise *The Golden Bough* (1890–1915) linked the 'barbarous' and 'savage' customs of tribal peoples all over the world to the Christian beliefs that he summed up, in a concluding image, by evoking the 'church bells of Rome'.[9] Frazer divided human development into three progressive stages – the magical, the religious and the scientific. His aim was to write the epitaph of the religious age and to usher in the age of science. Frazer's theory of universal progress, however, is contradicted by his tendency to regard the transition from magic to religion as one involving intellectual degeneration rather than progress.[10] Magical ceremonies, in his view, were experimental attempts by primitive people to change the natural conditions to which they were subjected. These experiments usually failed, but they continued to be repeated because their failure was not apparent. Successful experiments became part of humanity's technological inheritance; failed experiments turned into rituals kept up 'from force of habit', while an increasingly elaborate religious mythology was invented in order to explain and justify these rituals. Frazer was content to dismiss the history of religion as a long attempt to 'reconcile old custom with new reason, to find a sound theory for an absurd practice'.[11]

Frazer typifies the 'armchair anthropologist' who views the world from one of the metropolitan centres of civilisation and has no direct contact with tribal peoples. His outline of human development set out in the second edition of *The Golden Bough* in 1900 remained unmodified despite the welter of new examples added for the purpose of illustration as his treatise eventually swelled to twelve volumes.[12] *The Golden Bough* might be seen as the harbinger of a new globalisation of culture, justifying the 'civilising mission' of European imperialism but without the national flag-flying and the Christian proselytisation usually associated with imperialism. Frazer drew much of his ethnographic evidence from missionaries sent out to redeem the 'backward' portions of the globe. Ultimately, his aim was to convert both missionaries and subject peoples to the scientific world-view that his comparative anthropology so monumentally embodied.

[9] Sir James George Frazer, *The Golden Bough: A Study in Magic and Religion*, abridged edn, 2 vols. (London: Macmillan, 1957), II, p. 934.

[10] On this point see Steven Connor, 'The Birth of Humility: Frazer and Victorian Mythography', in Robert Fraser, ed., *Sir James Frazer and the Literary Imagination: Essays in Affinity and Influence* (Basingstoke: Macmillan, 1990), esp. p. 67.

[11] Frazer, *The Golden Bough*, pp. 424, 626. [12] Connor, 'The Birth of Humility', p. 76.

Frazer's world-embracing rationalism could hardly be uncontroversial. Critics such as Andrew Lang argued that a scientific theory of the origins of religion was premature and perhaps unattainable. Beyond the world of anthropology, *The Golden Bough*'s evocations of tribal magic and primitive myth rapidly proved irresistible to novelists and poets; at the same time, Frazer's contempt for the religious stage of human development exposed what many of his readers regarded as the unacceptable face of scientific materialism.

Already in the nineteenth century, the rise of scientific and technical education had been opposed by the institution of Catholic universities in many European countries. In Ireland, for example, University College, Dublin, which James Joyce attended, was designed to counter the British government's 'godless colleges' at Belfast, Galway and Cork. (Galway and Cork later came under heavy Catholic influence.) In Joyce's autobiographical fictions we see how the student intellectual life of the Catholic university is sometimes discreetly, sometimes overtly censored by the authorities. When Joyce's hero sets out to devise an aesthetic theory, he has learnt his lesson so well that his theory is 'applied Aquinas', a scholarly reinterpretation of a canonical medieval text. Opposition to materialism and modern science also found expression in the mushroom growth of movements such as spiritualism, occultism, theosophy, religious transcendentalism and vitalism around the turn of the century.[13] Perhaps more lasting in its intellectual influence was the 'Neo-Christian' literary movement, beginning with G. K. Chesterton and Hilaire Belloc in the Edwardian period; its later expressions include the poetry and criticism of T. S. Eliot as well as the writings of the scholarly fantasists C. S. Lewis and J. R. R. Tolkien. The Neo-Christians typically sought to expose the 'scientism' of their opponents as a form of quasi-religious (and necessarily heretical) dogma. They were certainly right in arguing that to reject Christianity was not necessarily to escape from its shadow. Frazer's *The Golden Bough*, like Yeats's *A Vision*, Freud's later writings, and some of Lawrence's novels, owes much of its fragile grandeur to the attempt to write a Bible or sacred book for modern, post-religious humanity. In Frazer's work, the classic lecture on the origin of mankind had become a new spiritual history for the human race.[14]

The search for a 'Key to All Mythologies' exemplifies a pervasive ambition which links together all the so-called 'grand theories' of the nineteenth and

[13] For a good survey of these movements see Tom Gibbons, *Rooms in the Darwin Hotel: Studies in English Literary Criticism and Ideas 1880–1920* (Nedlands, WA: University of Western Australia Press, 1973), chapter. 1.

[14] On the notion of the 'modern Bible' cf. Robert W. Maslen, 'Towards an Iconography of the Future: C. S. Lewis and the Scientific Humanists', *Inklings-Jahrbuch für Literatur und Ästhetik*, 18 (2000), p. 226.

twentieth centuries – that of laying bare the deep structures below surface appearances, and of revealing the latent beneath the manifest. Psychoanalysis, Structuralism, semiotics and the Marxist critique of ideologies all follow this approach. It has been claimed that it is fundamental to the anthropological study of culture, and that it has its roots in evangelical sermons. (The argument neatly reproduces the methodology of the discipline it sets out to analyse.)[15] The American philosopher and psychologist William James complained that in materialist philosophy 'what is higher is explained by what is lower',[16] but this was perhaps inevitable at a time when geological and archaeological discoveries had done so much to identify the idea of excavation with the quest for knowledge. The belief that what is 'lower down' is more important and more fundamental is an almost inevitable consequence of conceiving scientific and scholarly work as a genealogical exploration or a quest for origins. The power of the primitive can be seen in the archaeologists' search for the so-called 'missing link' between the apes and *homo sapiens*, which led in 1912 to the notorious hoax of Piltdown Man. The most celebrated archaeological discoveries of the time all tended to be at spectacularly 'early' sites: Sir Arthur Evans's excavations at Knossos, Howard Carter's opening of Tutankhamen's tomb, and the Palaeolithic cave paintings unearthed in France and northern Spain.

In anthropology, the publication in 1922 of Bronislaw Malinowski's *Argonauts of the Western Pacific* has been taken to symbolise a decisive shift from universal evolutionary narratives to the functional analysis of specific societies studied in detail. The functionalists abandoned all speculations about 'origins' or 'primeval states', arguing that they were mere flights of the imagination with no genuine scientific content.[17] Archaeology and anthropology had earlier been linked by their joint concern with human origins; but after Malinowski all that remained was a much more tenuous link between two disciplines based on (very different kinds of) scientific fieldwork. There was, however, another kind of anthropology at the turn of the century, the so-called 'classical anthropology' concerned not with gathering ethnographic data but with studying archaeological excavations and reinterpreting ancient texts. Frazer could be said to have begun this, since at the start of *The Golden*

[15] Christopher Herbert, *Culture and Anomie: Ethnographic Imagination in the Nineteenth Century* (Chicago and London: University of Chicago Press, 1991), esp. pp. 17, 254, 256.

[16] William James, *Pragmatism and Other Essays*, intro. Joseph L. Blau (New York: Washington Square, 1963), p. 11.

[17] See Bronislaw Malinowski's 'Special Foreword' to *The Sexual Life of Savages in North-Western Melanesia*, 3rd edn (London: Routledge, 1932), pp. xxiii, xxv, and Stefan Collini, *English Pasts: Essays in History and Culture* (Oxford University Press, 1999), pp. 280–7.

Bough he discussed the rule for the succession to the priesthood at Nemi under the Roman Empire. Frazer's most distinguished scholarly successor was Jane Ellen Harrison, author of *Prolegomena to the Study of Greek Religion* (1903) and *Themis* (1912).

In *Themis*, Harrison's account of the 'social origins of Greek religion' is built around a commentary on a single text, the *Hymn of the Kouretes*, newly discovered by archaeologists. This hymn, like the shrine at Nemi, belonged to the late classical period, but for Harrison it contained material which was self-evidently 'primitive' and which, therefore, pointed to the earliest state of Greek religion. She regarded religion as a reflection of the community in which it arose, though she did not share Frazer's hostility to the religious impulse. Harrison, a Cambridge don patiently working through the agenda first sketched out in Nietzsche's *The Birth of Tragedy*, would later be portrayed by Virginia Woolf in *A Room of One's Own* as the archetypal early twentieth-century woman scholar, famous yet socially marginalised, a formidable blue-stocking dressed in the shabbiest of frocks. We may, however, see her not just as a pioneer of women's mental emancipation but as, like Frazer and Sigmund Freud, a pioneer in the shift of epistemological attention from the natural to the social sciences, and from discovery to interpretation or reinterpretation as the dominant paradigm of intellectual enquiry. Freud's *The Interpretation of Dreams* (1900) sets out to distinguish the repressed or 'latent' (that is, the more powerful and primitive) contents from the manifest contents of dreams. His later ventures into anthropology in *Totem and Taboo* (1913) and *Moses and Monotheism* (1939) draw heavily on Frazer and his contemporaries. Moreover, Freud's recourse to the Oedipus myth to explain the fundamental structure of the psyche is a remarkable testimony to the continuing importance both of the classical world and of classical anthropology as a means of understanding the modern predicament.

The social sciences and twentieth-century Britain: industry and empire

It may seem paradoxical to speak of a shift in attention from the natural to the social sciences in the early twentieth century, since (as we have seen) this was the time of a revolution in physics unparalleled since the age of Newton. Yet relativity, quantum mechanics and the Uncertainty Principle all contrived to make physical science far more esoteric than it had been in the nineteenth century. Ordinary people's lives at the turn of the century were profoundly affected by the advent of the internal combustion engine, electric lighting, the telephone, radio and the aeroplane. Nuclear weapons and nuclear energy – though forecasted in Frederick Soddy's popular lectures on *The Interpretation of Radium* (1908) – remained the stuff of science fiction until August 1945, when the hitherto secret process of atomic fission was unleashed on Hiroshima and Nagasaki. Moreover, science fiction, the literary genre concerned with 'discovery' and its effects, became after the age of Verne and Wells a minority interest aimed, for the most part, at a loyal but restricted readership. It was the detective story and the spy thriller – forms of popular fiction foregrounding interpretation rather than discovery – that were read by almost everyone. The new scientifically and technically trained elite never became a political force, and remained largely invisible; their influence was greatest in wartime when they were known, significantly, as 'back-room boys'. Sociologists and economists, by contrast, played an increasingly prominent role in politics and government. When in 1910 the *New Age*, a radical political weekly, published a special supplement on 'Science', the articles (assembled by the geographer Patrick Geddes) covered the fields of sociology, social anthropology, economics, education and eugenics. The physical sciences were unrepresented.[18]

Anthropology apart, the social sciences in early twentieth-century Britain were for the most part practically and locally oriented. Poverty, unemployment, childcare and the treatment of the insane were major concerns. Graham Wallas's *Human Nature in Politics* (1908), a discussion of the political effects of advertising, is a pioneering text in both social psychology and media studies. Wallas attacks 'intellectualist fallacies' in thinking about politics, and his own bias is heavily empirical. British sociology, too, was notoriously lacking in the theoretical stimulus that Jane Harrison, for example, found in contemporary French thinkers such as Emile Durkheim. During his lifetime (he died in 1929) the nation's only professor of sociology was L. T. Hobhouse, a figure who pales by comparison with the great European sociologists Durkheim and Max Weber. Unlike them, Hobhouse retained an essentially Victorian belief in the necessary connection between scientific knowledge and social progress. His *Morals in Evolution* (1906) argues that in modern civilisation the evolution of human intelligence has become a 'purposive, self-directed movement'; moreover, the emergence of sociological science is prime evidence for this evolution.[19] Hobhouse did not live to see the full extent of the corruption of public morals in the twentieth century under Communism and Fascism. His son recorded, however, that World War I struck directly at the foundations of his thought.

18 *New Age*, 7, 1 (5 May 1910).

19 L. T. Hobhouse, *Morals in Evolution: A Study in Comparative Ethics* (London: Chapman & Hall, 1906), 2 vols., II, pp. 278, 280.

Far from continuing to expect global evolution to reach ever-greater moral heights, Hobhouse came to doubt whether humanity had the moral wisdom needed for its own survival.[20]

Between 1906 and 1920 Hobhouse contributed articles to the *Nation*, the leading organ of the collectivist Liberalism associated with the founding of the welfare state in the UK. The welfare state came about partly as a result of democratic and humanitarian concerns, but it was also a response to social-evolutionist warnings about the need to improve 'national efficiency' by raising the standard of the workforce. The term 'eugenics' had been invented by Francis Galton to denote the so-called science of human breeding. The Eugenics Education Society, founded in 1907 to disseminate Galton's ideas, became a forum for hard-line eugenicists who dreamed of human stud farms in which compulsory sterilisation and guided mating would bring about a race of supermen. The Society had no direct political impact, and the form of eugenics it tried to propagate was widely denounced as a pseudo-science. Indirectly, however, it helped to foster the climate of opinion that led to Nazism.

During the Edwardian period, however, the language of eugenics was far from being confined to Galton and his circle. The more moderate eugenicists believed in introducing maternity benefits and voluntary contraception, as well as improvements in natal care, nutrition, public health and pre-school education. Their belief that these were eugenic measures was sustained by the ambiguity of the idea of 'breeding', which denotes nurture and upbringing as well as nature and genetic endowment. For example, in *Cities in Evolution* (1915) Patrick Geddes claimed that there was a 'necessary association' between eugenics and 'civics' – between the future development of the human race, that is, and its social and built environment. Geddes, one of the pioneers of modern town planning, foresaw that the urban squalor of the era of coal and steam-power would give way to the clean and rational cities of the 'Second Industrial Revolution' fuelled by oil and electricity. Adapting the vocabulary of prehistoric archaeology, he welcomed humanity's passage from the 'paleotechnic' to the 'neotechnic' age.[21]

It might be objected that Geddes's use of eugenic ideas was largely extraneous to his main argument. The same could not be said of another response to the 'Second Industrial Revolution', *Woman and Labour* (1911) by the South African novelist and feminist Olive Schreiner. Schreiner described her book as a

[20] Peter Weiler, 'The New Liberalism of L. T. Hobhouse', *Victorian Studies*, 16, 2 (December 1972), pp. 159–60.

[21] Patrick Geddes, *Cities in Evolution* (London: Routledge/ Thoemmes Press, 1998), pp. 59, 63–4, 376.

fragment of a much longer, unfinished study of gender differences and their role in the biological evolution of species. She found the key to humanity's future development in the imminent disappearance of the traditional forms of female domestic labour, due to the spread of labour-saving machinery and advances in medicine. The choice facing modern women was between 'sex-parasitism' leading to racial decadence, and entry into the full range of occupations in the male labour market. Schreiner's work itself promotes a view of human life in which gender equality is of the essence, since 'labour' denotes both economic activity and the task of biological reproduction. Her horror at the waste of women's lives in luxury and prostitution is equalled only by her admiration for the 'mighty labouring woman', who is the 'most productive toiler known to the race'.[22] Moreover, she warns of the inevitability of national and imperial decline if women's demands for intellectually satisfying work are not met. Her parasitic women are, typically, those of the Roman (and, by analogy, the British) Empire; her 'virile', labouring females belong to the Teutonic tribes that overcame the Roman Empire, and to their modern descendants such as the Boer women of South Africa.[23]

In the Edwardian period, socialists as well as feminists found intellectual justification in a social-evolutionary perspective in which parasitism and wastage were destined to be swept away by the new standards of efficiency made possible by modern technology. Marxism's claims to offer a scientific theory of social progress had little appeal in Britain until the 1930s, when scientists of the calibre of J. B. S. Haldane and J. D. Bernal were attracted to the cause.[24] The British form of 'scientific socialism' was found in the Fabian Society, which deeply influenced both the collectivist Liberals and the emergent Labour Party. Under the leadership of Sidney and Beatrice Webb, the Fabians turned away from the insurrectionary model of socialism as typified by the short-lived Paris Commune of 1871. Fabian socialism was to be brought about gradually by administrative measures capable of winning cross-party support – by evolution, that is, rather than revolution. This meant that socialism depended on the prior accumulation of a library of scholarly work in political science, including the Webbs' own studies of the poor law, trade unionism and local government. It also depended on the training of a new cadre of supposedly impartial administrative

[22] Olive Schreiner, *Woman and Labour* (London: Virago, 1978), p. 103.

[23] Ibid., esp. pp. 92, 93n., 281.

[24] As early as 1896, Bertrand Russell was arguing that Marxism should be regarded as a new religion rather than a social science. Russell, *German Social Democracy* (London: Allen & Unwin, 1965), pp. 6 ff. On Marxism and British scientists in the 1930s see Gary Werskey, *The Visible College: A Collective Biography of British Scientists and Socialists of the 1930s* (London: Free Association, 1988).

experts, and on the building of political alliances. In 1895 the Webbs founded the London School of Economics, staffed with social scientists from across the political spectrum. In 1902 they instituted a dining club known as the 'Co-efficients', with members from each of the main political parties. The club's declared purpose was to study 'the aims, policy and methods of imperial efficiency at home and abroad'.[25] Sidney Webb would later serve as Colonial Secretary in the second Labour Government of 1929–31. In 1931 the Webbs visited Soviet Russia, where they became uncritical admirers of Stalin's bureaucratic autocracy. Much earlier than this, however, the Fabians had made common cause with the more 'efficient' and 'enlightened' forms of British imperialism.

The Coefficients Club was formed immediately after the end of the South African War of 1899–1902, in which, after many setbacks, the British army defeated the insurgent Dutch farmers, rounded them up and put them in the world's first concentration camps. Although it was fought between two groups of colonists, the 'Boer War' was in some respects the century's first anti-colonial conflict. It was also the last major war that Britain would undertake on its own. The British victory sustained imperial pride and (it was argued) demonstrated the ability of a modern, mechanised army to impose its will on a backward group of colonists, however distant from the home country. The war was far from universally popular in Britain, but, in the view of the Webbs and others, it owed its moral justification to the Empire's modernity and efficiency. (For very similar reasons the Webbs opposed Home Rule for Ireland.)[26] In much the same spirit Gerald Crich, the coal-owner and Boer War veteran in D. H. Lawrence's *Women in Love*, ruthlessly imposes principles of scientific management on his workforce in order to make his mines more profitable. Thanks to the doctrine of social evolution, the more efficient believed it was their duty to impose their will on the less efficient.

One of the more remarkable intellectual by-products of the Boer War was the science of geopolitics, inaugurated in a 1904 paper by Halford J. Mackinder, a member of the Coefficients, director of the London School of Economics, and future Conservative member of parliament. Mackinder realised that the 'Columbian epoch' of Western exploration and discovery was now over, so that geography had become the study of a closed system. Noting that the South African War coincided with the Russian intervention in Manchuria (which led

[25] Quoted in W. H. Parker, *Mackinder: Geography as an Aid to Statecraft* (Oxford: Clarendon Press, 1982), p. 30.

[26] Shirley Robin Letwin, *The Pursuit of Certainty* (London: Cambridge University Press, 1965), p. 367.

to the Russo-Japanese War of 1904–5), Mackinder concluded that Europe, Asia and Africa formed, for political purposes, a single 'World-Island' which could eventually be unified by a combination of land-power and sea-power. Germany was busily creating a naval fleet to rival Britain's, and, if Germany were to form an alliance with Russia, the 'empire of the world' would be in sight.

Mackinder believed that 'Britain's only salvation as a great power lay in consolidating round the mother country a united Empire.'[27] Like all writers on the British Empire since the historian Sir John Seeley's *The Expansion of England* (1883), he drew a sharp distinction between the 'first empire', consisting largely of the white-settler countries which were rapidly becoming independent democracies, and the 'second empire' of British rule over alien peoples in India and Africa. He believed that the second empire could be ruled justly, without economic exploitation or racial oppression. Empire, in any case, was the natural and inevitable outcome of the 'grouping of lands and seas, and of fertility and natural pathways', and the world divided between rival European imperialisms must eventually give place to a single world-empire.[28] It is not clear whether he envisaged that Britain alone could be the basis of such an empire. After World War I, when the victory of a democratic alliance of Britain, the British dominions, France and the United States led to the setting-up of the League of Nations, Mackinder published a full statement of his ideas in *Democratic Ideals and Reality* (1919). Mackinder's doctrines were, however, taken up by Karl Haushofer, a geographer and military strategist destined to become president of the German Academy under Hitler. As a British journalist noted in August 1939, the Nazi policy of world-domination was, in part, 'stolen from the intellectual arsenal of British Imperialism'.[29] Later in World War II Mackinder's work came to the notice of American global strategists, and in the 1990s *Democratic Ideals and Reality* was brought back into print by the Institute for National Strategic Studies, an arm of the US Government.

For Mackinder, the driving-force of empire was political and geographical. For his Liberal contemporary J. A. Hobson, however, it was economic. At the close of the Boer War Hobson published *Imperialism: A Study* (1902), a book that influenced both Keynes and Lenin. A freelance journalist who never held an academic post, Hobson held that the underlying truth of imperialism was that of the capitalist exploitation of foreign markets. What was hidden by the pseudo-scientific rhetoric of 'social efficiency' was the need to invest surplus

27 Parker, *Mackinder*, p. 60.

28 Rt. Hon. Sir Halford J. Mackinder, *Democratic Ideals and Reality: A Study in the Politics of Reconstruction* (Washington, DC: National Defense University Press [1996]), esp. pp. 2, 192.

29 *New Statesman* (26 August 1939), quoted in Parker, *Mackinder*, pp. 158–9.

capital overseas because of under-consumption at home. If the national standard of living were to be raised by redistributing income to the working classes, then overseas investment with its military and political accompaniments would no longer be necessary. Hobson's argument that imperialism was a 'depraved choice of national life', brought about by self-seeking investors, thus carried the implication that a state could opt out of its imperial commitments without damaging national prosperity.[30] Sir John Seeley had famously argued that Britain seemed to have 'conquered and peopled half the world in a fit of absence of mind'.[31] Hobson maintained that an enlightened nation ought to show the presence of mind to get rid of its empire. And this, half a century later, was what successive British governments found themselves having to do.

From Decadence to modernity

In retrospect it might seem that there was a clear connection between the Positivist aim of universal scientific knowledge and the political vision of a single world-empire.[32] Both, as we have seen, treat the world as a closed system. For most early twentieth-century intellectuals, however, the question was whether the world-system was expanding and evolving, or contracting and subject to entropy. J. A. Hobson was one of the optimists. In 1909 he published *The Crisis of Liberalism*, a title reflecting the short-lived parliamentary uproar caused by the House of Lords' rejection of Lloyd George's tax-raising Budget. Hobson's outlook in this book was remarkably insouciant, with few, if any, intimations of the impending political changes which in the next decade would all but destroy the Liberal Party. Instead, he looked forward to a period of social and intellectual reconstruction animated by a 'new and common spirit' of realism. Above all, the 'new spirit' interpreted nature as a 'psycho-physical process', not in terms of mechanical materialism: 'Man is the maker of the Universe', Hobson wrote. In literature and art, the prospect of reconstruction showed that 'Wagner, Millet, Whistler, Nietzsche, Tolstoy, Whitman, Ibsen, have not laboured in vain.'[33]

Such a list of late nineteenth-century harbingers of what has sometimes been called a New Enlightenment would have been familiar enough to

30 J. A. Hobson, *Imperialism: A Study*, 3rd edn (London: Allen & Unwin, 1968), pp. 155, 368.

31 Sir J. R. Seeley, *The Expansion of England: Two Courses of Lectures*, 2nd edn (London: Macmillan, 1897), p. 10.

32 See, for example, Thomas Richards, *The Imperial Archive: Knowledge and the Fantasy of Empire* (London and New York: Verso, 1993).

33 J. A. Hobson, *The Crisis of Liberalism: New Issues of Democracy* (London: King, 1909), pp. 273–5.

Hobson's readers, however strange it sounds today. It reflects the progressivism of the early 1890s, when Hobson's contemporary Henry Havelock Ellis wrote *The New Spirit*, a series of critical essays on Tolstoy, Whitman, Nietzsche and others. Bernard Shaw at about the same time was writing *The Quintessence of Ibsenism* and *The Perfect Wagnerite*. Havelock Ellis went on to become the pioneer of sexology and author of the multi-volume *Studies in the Psychology of Sex* (1897–1928). The first volume in the series, *Sexual Inversion*, was the earliest book in English to treat homosexuality as neither a crime nor a disease. (Published by the so-called 'University Press of Watford', it was rapidly put on trial for obscenity.) Ellis's work is a reminder that the Victorian narrative of social progress inspired by scientific knowledge continued to sustain the campaign for sexual liberation, just as it sustained the birth control movement (in which Ellis, oddly, took rather little interest), long after the disillusionments of the two World Wars. Sexual liberation, too, was the one progressive cause that was close to the heart of Modernist writing; it sparked some of the energy behind the experiments of Lawrence, Joyce, Djuna Barnes, Virginia Woolf and others. Nevertheless, for many observers, it was degeneration rather than reconstruction that summed up the prospect for the new century.

The 1890s were the Decadent decade, when (as Yeats put it) poets drank absinthe, joined the Catholic Church, or committed suicide. Oscar Wilde, imprisoned for homosexuality, petitioned the Home Secretary for release on the grounds that his homosexuality was a type of degenerate sexual madness – a disease that, he argued, was peculiar to the literary or artistic temperament. Wilde was, in fact, one of numerous writers who were accused of pathological abnormalities in Max Nordau's *Degeneration* (1892), an international bestseller purporting to analyse the contemporary arts from the standpoint of psychiatric medicine. For all its absurdity, Nordau's work is in some sense an anticipation of Freud's almost equally reductive analysis of artistic creativity. In the words of one recent scholar, 'If Nordau had spoken of degenerate compulsions, Freud spoke of neurotic ones.'[34] Nor were 'degenerate' tendencies to be found only in modern art. On pseudo-Darwinian grounds it could be (and was) easily argued that democracy, feminism, socialism and industrialism must all have dire consequences for the human race. In 1911 the *New Age* held a 'Symposium on Racial Development', in which leading biologists and anthropologists were presented with a five-point questionnaire. The first question was, 'Have recent events, in your opinion, shown an evolution towards racial, i.e. biological

[34] William Greenslade, *Degeneration, Culture and the Novel 1880–1940* (Cambridge University Press, 1994), pp. 120–33; the quotation is from p. 129.

degeneration?'[35] Even though a majority of the respondents answered this question in the negative, the episode strongly suggests the public's need for reassurance in the face of prophecies of degeneration.

Physics, even more than biology, offered grounds for pessimism about humanity's future. Kelvin's Second Law of Thermodynamics, the famous law of entropy, revealed that the sun was eventually destined to burn out, leaving the earth and the rest of the solar system incapable of supporting human life. This grimly eschatological vision of an 'utter final wreck and tragedy' was, as William James wrote, of the essence of scientific materialism.[36] The 'running-down universe' continued to set an absolute limit to human aspirations in such popular expositions of astronomical physics as Sir James Jeans's *The Universe Around Us* (1930), yet it did not pass uncontested. The discovery of thermonuclear energy by Ernest Rutherford and Frederick Soddy meant, in Soddy's words, that 'Our outlook on the physical universe has been permanently altered. We are no longer the inhabitants of a universe slowly dying from the physical exhaustion of its energy, but of a universe which has in the internal energy of its material components the means to rejuvenate itself perennially over immense periods of time.'[37] Formerly, the sun had been considered as a kind of immense coal-fire; now it was a nuclear fusion reactor. Yet even fusion reactors must eventually burn down, so that the principle of ultimate entropy remained the same. Bertrand Russell, reviewing the law of entropy from a humanist standpoint in 'A Free Man's Worship' (1903), could only come up with an attitude of stoic, cosmic pessimism. In the light of materialist eschatology, human aspirations appeared meaningless, and there could be no cosmic or supernatural sanction for whatever meaning we might choose to give them.

One of the unforeseen consequences of materialist eschatology was the questioning of the idea of truth as it was embodied in scientific enquiry. Might not, say, a belief in an all-powerful God be more helpful to mankind – and therefore in some sense more 'true' – than the feelings of nihilism and despair brought about by the ultimate truths proposed by the scientific outlook? In the seventeenth century this had been known as 'Pascal's wager', leading to an opportunist decision to conform with the Christian religion – Christianity offered at least the chance of salvation, whereas the atheist had no hope. Robert Browning's poem 'Bishop Blougram's Apology' had restated this dilemma for

[35] Huntly Carter, 'A Symposium on Racial Development', *New Age*, 9, 5 (1 June 1911), pp. 105–7.

[36] James, *Pragmatism*, pp. 47–8.

[37] Frederick Soddy, *The Interpretation of Radium: Being the Substance of Six Free Popular Experimental Lectures Delivered at the University of Glasgow*, 3rd edn (London: Murray, 1912), p. 248.

the mid-Victorians. In Edwardian England, the majority of educated Christians no longer believed in a literal Heaven and Hell, so Pascal's wager had lost its force. Metaphysical scepticism, however, led not just to the rejection of theological absolutes but to the reformulation of the scientific idea of truth. In the Pragmatist philosophy outlined most influentially by William James, truth became an instrumental, not an absolute category. Ideas were held to be true if they served humanity better than false ideas. The British philosopher F. C. S. Schiller argued that truths should be judged by their survival-value, since they were subject to evolution like everything else. There was a process of natural selection among truths.[38] The Pragmatist view of truth is irreparably self-contradictory – equating truth with expediency, as it were – but it arose from the need for a scientific philosophy to fill the breach left by the collapse of nineteenth-century Positivism.

In 1900 the established alternative to scientific Positivism was still the tradition of Hegelian idealism associated with T. H. Green (who had died nearly twenty years earlier) and his pupils. The young T. E. Hulme welcomed William James's version of Pragmatism, not as a satisfactory position in itself but at least as a counterweight to the English Hegelians. For Hulme Pragmatism pointed the way to modern continental philosophy, notably that of Henri Bergson. Bergson like James was a post-Nietzschean 'anti-intellectualist', the philosopher of an untidy and unpredictable world – the universe not as a chess-board but as a cinder-heap. Hulme went on to argue in somewhat Wildean fashion that philosophy was an 'art' and not a 'science', and that it should be judged not by its correctness but by its beauty.[39] When in 1911 he travelled to Bologna for a philosophy congress, he was amazed to find that the philosophers were rated important enough for a full-scale civic reception. He was certainly not the last British theorist to cross the Channel and bring back the news that the modern European mind was far in advance of philistine England. Hulme's testimony should remind us, however, that Pragmatism was the last movement in Anglo-American philosophy whose doctrine was readily accessible to the ordinary reader. William James had trained as a doctor, and taught physiology and psychology at Harvard before his appointment to a chair in philosophy. Hulme was killed in action in Belgium in 1917; Bertrand Russell's later, more popular philosophical works never equalled his intensely difficult pre-World War I work on mathematical logic; and thereafter the field was left, more or

38 On Schiller, see Frederick Copleston, S J, *A History of Philosophy*, 8 vols. (New York: Image, 1967), VIII, pp. 105–7.

39 Hulme, 'The New Philosophy', p. 198; 'Searchers after Reality: Jules de Gaultier', *New Age*, n.s. 6, 5 (2 December 1909), p. 108.

less, to professional academics who pursued a remarkably esoteric discourse about the meaning and virtues of ordinary language.

If, as the Pragmatists claimed, all truths were provisional, then classical artistic canons must also be subject to change. At the same time, the doctrine of evolutionism implies that art, however revolutionary and avant-garde, must always remain linked to its origins. Preferably it should be more 'primitive' and more fundamental than the art that came immediately before it. Like the *Hymn of the Kouretes* in Jane Harrison's analysis, it should be both intrinsically 'early' and chronologically late. For this reason, far from abandoning the classics, Modernist writing specialises in startling reinterpretations of them. The 'Classicism' proclaimed by Hulme, Eliot, Pound, Joyce and others plays on the manifold ambiguities of that term, and thus is hard to pin down. But these writers' critical manifestoes tend to portray Classicism as being more technically demanding, more rigorously objective and (by implication) more scientific than the Romanticism which is its opposite.

In his essay 'Tradition and the Individual Talent' (1919), T. S. Eliot's version of Modernist Classicism focuses on the artist's relationship to the 'mind of Europe'. The European mind, Eliot writes, is a 'mind which changes'; but this development (or evolution) 'abandons nothing *en route*'; it 'does not superannuate either Shakespeare, or Homer, or the rock drawing of the Magdalenian draughtsmen'.[40] Here Eliot's notion of the artistic canon extends to the latest archaeological discoveries of palaeolithic art, which he had just seen in southern France and which had been unknown to every previous age of European culture. Palaeolithic cave paintings posed a crucial challenge to anthropological theory and to evolutionism more widely. They were at once highly complex and supremely simple; they were instantly comprehensible to the eye, and yet almost wholly resistant to interpretation. They showed an aesthetic skill that modern artists could only acquire after years of study and practice. We will never know what the cave paintings meant for the people who made them. Their appearance in Eliot's argument, however, undermines what might otherwise be read as an impeccably orthodox appeal to a continuous European tradition. The rock drawing of the Magdalenian draughtsmen was both something immeasurably ancient, and something completely new. In 'Tradition and the Individual Talent', as in Eliot's poem *The Waste Land*, we find a direct link between the 'classic lecture / On the origin of Mankind' and the most innovative aspects of twentieth-century writing.

[40] T. S. Eliot, *Selected Essays*, 3rd edn (London: Faber & Faber, 1961), p. 16.

2

The Victorian *fin de siècle* and Decadence

REGENIA GAGNIER

The modern roots of Decadence were in 1830s American Gothic and late Romanticism. Edgar Allan Poe elevated disease, perversity and decay to new heights of artistic expression. Alfred Tennyson's *Poems* of 1832, the poems of languor rather than of politics – 'The Lady of Shalott', 'The Lotus-Eaters' and 'The Palace of Art' – evoked a philosophy of Inaction that would later be elaborated in Oscar Wilde's *Intentions* (1891) and in the American Ralph Cram's *The Decadent: The Gospel of Inaction* (1893). Although Poe's success in the United States was trivial until he was discovered by Charles Baudelaire, his perversity and Tennyson's celebrity – in the words of the latter's Ulysses 'I am become a name' – were the two touchstones of Decadence: the naturalistic uniqueness of the individual psyche and the recognition of 'brand' or personal commodification that would be central to modern consciousness. Baudelaire took up the first in *Les Fleurs du Mal*, censored by the French state in 1857, and the latter in the figure of the Dandy in *The Painter of Modern Life* (1863). Baudelaire began translating Poe (culminating in 5 volumes) in 1848, and thereby turned from Romantic nature to urban perspectives and personalities. His successor, Stéphane Mallarmé, known as the founder of French Symbolism, took up objects as well, and infused them with non-material properties as a counter to a too-materialistic age.

In his 'Further Notes on Edgar Poe' (1857), Baudelaire reappropriated the intentionally negative phrase of his critics, 'a literature of decadence', in a revolutionary, affirmative way to describe a literary *progress* (ironically parodying the great theme of the age) from infancy, through childhood and adolescence, towards a mature Decadence. He then asked why he should be blamed for 'accomplishing the mysterious law' and 'rejoicing in our destiny'. Baudelaire figured the Decadence as a sunset, grand couturier:

> That sun which a few hours ago was crushing everything beneath the weight of its vertical, white light will soon be flooding the western horizon with

> varied colours. In the changing splendours of this dying sun, some poetic minds will find new joys; they will discover dazzling colonnades, cascades of molten metal, a paradise of fire, a melancholy splendour . . . And the sunset will then appear to them as the marvellous allegory of a soul, imbued with life, going down beyond the horizon, with a magnificent wealth of thoughts and dreams.[1]

In 'The Decadent Movement in Literature' (*Harper's* Nov. 1893) and *The Symbolist Movement in Literature* (1899), Arthur Symons divided the Decadence between the Symbolist poets Baudelaire and Mallarmé seeking the truth of appearance to the soul, and prose Impressionists such as the Goncourt Brothers, Edmond and Jules, seeking the truth of appearance to the senses. Their qualities included an intense self-consciousness, restless curiosity in research, an over-subtilising refinement, spiritual and moral perversity. Decadence was 'a disease', but nonetheless a disease of 'truth', reflecting the scientific spirit of the age. In a backlash that would have epochal consequences for the art world, the physician and writer Max Nordau in *Degeneration* (1893 in German, 1895 in English) used the same writers as exempla, adding Wilde and Friedrich Nietzsche for their egoism, Ibsen for his feminism and Zola for his naturalism. Taking the disease literally, Nordau institutionalised the pathologisation of the art world that would progressively desublimate art in the twentieth century. Culture could henceforth be attacked as an index of the social diseases of modernity. Specifically, health, muscularity and masculinity were opposed to a decadent, feminine Art.

Decadent authors were allegedly too wedded to the aesthetic, i.e., to the image without critical distance on the whole, as in Poe's short story 'Berenice' (1835), whose protagonist turns his monocle on his own obsession, via his victim's teeth:

> Then came the full fury of my monomania, and I struggled in vain against its strange and irresistible influence. In the multiplied objects of the external world I had no thoughts but for the teeth. For these I longed with a frenzied desire . . . They alone were present to the mental eye, and they, in their sole individuality, became the essence of my mental life.[2]

The more isolated the image, the clarity of depiction, the more it reflected the psyche of the beholder.

1 Charles Baudelaire, 'Further Notes on Edgar Poe', *Selected Writings on Art and Literature*, trans. P. E. Charvet (London: Penguin, 1992), p. 189.

2 Edgar Allan Poe, 'Berenice', in *The Second Dedalus Book of Decadence: The Black Feast*, ed. Brian Stableford (Cambridgeshire: Dedalus, 1992), p. 232.

Modern Decadence was identified as the choice and fantasy of the individual psyche, detaching it from the social whole. Even when sex was the apparent cause of the Decadence, as in so much literature on the subject, in the 1890s it was characteristically sex in thought rather than in action: the dream of sexual freedom (as in Wilde's "The Portrait of Mr. W. H." [1889]), or freedom from gender constraints, or freedom from reproduction (as in the so-called New Woman literature). This state of reflection, obsession or critique was the necessary component of Decadence, a philosophy of inaction in an age of industry.

Thomas Mann invoked his own magisterial *Buddenbrooks* (1901) in *Reflections of a Nonpolitical Man* (1918) as describing the degeneration of a bourgeois way of life into the subjective–artistic.[3] For Mann, those born around 1870 were compelled into a Decadence that could be described by the two faces of Nietzsche: Nietzsche *militans* and Nietzsche *triumphans*. Nietzsche *militans* was critical, psychological, post-Christian; but those who were then young would transcend the introspective moment and adopt Nietzsche *triumphans*'s anti-Christian and anti-spiritual – in fact, traditionally aristocratic – notions of nobility, health and beauty. They would have the 'emancipatory will' to reject Decadence and nihilism.

In his *Autobiographies: The Trembling of the Veil* (1922), W. B. Yeats captured the reflective quality of the Decadents that led them intently to criticise the Establishment, but, as Mann said, lent them equally the imaginative will to transcend it. Yeats wrote of the 'Tragic Generation': 'Why should men who spoke their opinions in low voices as though they feared to disturb the readers in some ancient library, and timidly as though they knew that all subjects had long since been explored . . . live lives of such disorder and seek to rediscover in verse the syntax of impulsive common life? Was it that we lived in what is called "an age of transition" and so lacked coherence, or did we but pursue antithesis?'[4] Yeats accused them of too much introspection. Their artist Aubrey Beardsley of *The Yellow Book* died at twenty-six; the psychological author Hubert Crackanthorpe at thirty-one; the poets Ernest Dowson and Lionel Johnson at thirty-two and thirty-five respectively; John Davidson committed suicide, and their brave publisher Leonard Smithers died of an overdose. Wilde, as essentially a 'man of action' for Yeats, was peripheral to his 'Tragic Generation,' and exceeded their rhyming in his mastery of many genres (society comedies, biblical spectacle, fiction, criticism, prose poems

[3] Thomas Mann, *Reflections of a Nonpolitical Man*, trans. Walter D. Morris (New York: Ungar, 1983).

[4] W. B. Yeats, *Autobiographies: The Trembling of the Veil* (London: Macmillan, 1995), pp. 303–4.

and poetry). Nonetheless he was dead at forty-six after public humiliation and imprisonment, and subsequent critics have included him among the tragic victims or martyred heroes.

Decadence was thus a pan-European and trans-Atlantic phenomenon that entailed a falling away from or a rejection that could also be a creative repudiation. In Baudelaire and Walter Pater it was overheard as a dying fall or cadence. In Nietzsche, it was a saying no to the status quo, or a transvaluation of values. In Wilde, it was a dandiacal strategy of self-differentiation. What is essential is the non-absolute value of this usage. Creative repudiation can mean creative destruction or war as easily as critique. Death can imply rebirth. As Baudelaire's figure suggested, the dominant organic metaphor of decay and degeneration could turn seamlessly into a cross-fertilisation of amazing light and colour. Decadence and Progress could be the same thing.

Between the one and the many: the dandy

Amazing light and colour were also what Baudelaire associated with the dandy. 'Dandyism is a sunset; like the declining daystar, it is glorious, without heat and full of melancholy.'[5] Baudelaire interpreted dandyism in socio-political terms as a 'cult of the self' arising from 'the burning need to create for oneself a personal originality' before 'the rising tide of democracy levels everything'.[6] Appearing in periods of transition, when the aristocracy is impotent and before the people have become the masses, men of natural abilities arise, whose gifts are those that work or money are unable to bestow. Declining with mass society, torn between a God that he is too materialist to believe in and a humankind too materialist for him to respect, he glitters alone among the crowd in icy splendour.

The dandy was the human equivalent of art under aestheticism. He was removed from life, like the Duke in Max Beerbohm's *Zuleika Dobson* (1910), a living protest against instrumentality and vulgarity, or the creation of mass needs and desires. Like the dandies in Wilde's comedies, he provided a commentary on a society he despised in the form of wit at its expense. This wit, technically the inversion of the language of popular sentiment, was the major form of the dandy's participation in society. In the early periods of Beau Brummell and the Count D'Orsay, he had patrons, but by the *fin de siècle* dandies used their wit to be both critical and commercially competitive, ironically commodifying

5 Baudelaire, 'The Painter of Modern Life', *Selected Writings*, p. 421.
6 Ibid., p. 420, p. 422.

themselves as products in a utilitarian economy. Socially central, yet politically marginal and financially vulnerable, their position was often compared to that of women, who were limited in their ability to be dandies by the social constraints upon their ability to be commercial. (Yet see Anthony Trollope's Madame Max Goesler, the greatest of the female dandies [*Pallisers* series, 1865–80], who was able to achieve this status due to her marginal nationality and independent wealth.) Demonstrating the superiority of his individual style, articulating a creed of disinterestedness and often languor, the dandy affronted the masculine and bourgeois ideology of equality, energy, duty and sincerity.

In *Du dandysme et de George Brummell* (1844), Jules Barbey d'Aurevilly had observed that dandyism arose within a wealthy society's contradictions between the luxury and power of the Establishment and its ensuing boredom, or ennui. The conventions, constraints and tedium of high society are counterparts to the scarcity and monotony of working-class life. The dandy accepts for his own benefit and others' amusement the materialism of affluent society, while he mocks its superficiality, its knowing (as Wilde would say) the price of everything and the value of nothing. Applying to Brummell a *mot* from Edward Bulwer Lytton's silver-fork novel *Pelham* (1828), 'he displeased too generally not to be sought after', Barbey likened society's worship of the dandy to 'the wish to be beaten of powerful and licentious women'.[7] Wilde called one of his dramatic dandies 'the first well-dressed philosopher in the history of thought'.[8] The dandy was the first to make style the basis of philosophy, of the only philosophy consistent with modern materialist life.

Dandyism declined with Aestheticism after 1895. Like the dream of autonomous art, dandies were pure. They entertained without belonging. When his trials for homosexuality made out that Wilde was *not* a dandy – dandies, wrote Baudelaire approvingly in *Mon Cœur mis à nu* (1862), did not have erections – the public that he had amused for a season deserted him, as it had deserted Brummell and others whose vulnerability was traced to the social and financial insecurity that Baudelaire had theorised (Wilde was also Irish). Given that Wilde's private life was all too *engagé*, contradicting his public aesthetic code of disinterestedness, the aestheticism that he had helped to promote fell in the public mind from its height of dandiacal purity to a shameful bohemianism that was to be associated with the art world for decades to come. Yet in his heyday, the dandy was the ironic conscience of mass society. Ostentatiously

[7] Jules Barbey D'Aurevilly *Of Dandyism and of George Brummell* trans. Douglas Ainslie (London: J. M. Dent, 1897), p. 102.

[8] See Oscar Wilde, *An Ideal Husband* (1895), in *The Complete Works of Oscar Wilde* (London and Glasgow: Collins, 1990), p. 522.

brilliant, he could still distinguish between value and price. Aloof and critical, he still retained a desire for community, for the approval of others. He showed the Establishment gentleman what he had sacrificed in the age of privacy and mass production: individuality, community, beauty.

Progress and Decadence

'Progress and Decadence are interchangeable terms', wrote Clive Bell in *Civilisation: An Essay* (1928), in which the modern emphasis on individualism was both progressive and decadent. It was progressive in the sense that Herbert Spencer intended in his evolutionary psychology, and it was decadent in that its focus on the distinct moods, tastes and perspectives of individuals isolated them from the group, collective or mass. For Spencer, all Progress was progress towards individuation through increasing differentiation. Increasing differentiation described the division of labour in political economy; the origins of different species in biology; racial difference in physiology; psychological realism and fragmentation in literature. 'Progress, therefore', Spencer wrote, in the classic statement of Victorian optimism of 1857,

> is not an accident, but a necessity . . . As surely as the tree becomes bulky when it stands alone, and slender if one of a group; as surely as the same creature assumes the different forms of cart-horse and race-horse, according as its habits demand strength or speed; as surely as a blacksmith's arm grows large, and the skin of a labourer's hand thick; as surely as the eye tends to become long-sighted in the sailor, and short-sighted in the student; . . . as surely as a passion grows by indulgence and diminishes when restrained; as surely as a disregarded conscience becomes inert, and one that is obeyed active; as surely as there is any efficacy in educational culture, or any meaning in such terms as habit, custom, practice; so surely must the human faculties be moulded into complete fitness for the social state; so surely must the things we call evil and immorality disappear; so surely must man become perfect.[9]

Yet by the end of the century this increasing differentiation threatened the integrity of the whole. Through most of the nineteenth century, *Reason* had meant the mind's ability to improve the world. Only towards its end and in the twentieth century did *rationality* come to mean an individual's chosen path to get what he or she wanted irrespective of the quality of the choice. The Good, the True, and the Beautiful as universal or collective consensus could give way

[9] Herbert Spencer, 'Progress: Its Law and Cause', in *Essays, Scientific, Political, and Speculative*, 2 vols. (London: Williams & Norgate, 1883), vol. 1, p. 58.

to individual choice as taste, or mood, or lifestyle. The individual choice or preference could be seen as monomania, as in Wilde's *Picture of Dorian Gray* (1891) or *Salomé* (1893). The psychologist Havelock Ellis analysed Decadence in 1889 as when the individuation of parts led to the disintegration of the whole, and a Decadent style in literature as an anarchistic style in which everything was sacrificed to the development of the individual parts.[10] The poet Ernest Dowson refined further in 1891. In English literature, Decadence described 'an age of afterthought, of reflection. Hence come one great virtue, and one great vice: the virtue of much and careful meditation upon life, its emotions and its incidents: the vice of over subtlety and of affectation, when thought thinks upon itself, and when emotions become entangled with the consciousness of them.'[11] The article was followed by Dowson's 'Non Sum Qualis Eram Bonae sub Regno Cynarae', in which the poet introspects on whether he has been faithful to his lover, concluding that it depends on his own mind: 'I have been faithful to thee, Cynara, in my fashion.' Many, like Matthew Arnold in 'On the Modern Element in Literature' (1869), followed Georg Wilhelm Friedrich Hegel and Johann Christoph Friedrich von Schiller in worrying about the cost of this self-reflection in 'a state of feeling unknown to less enlightened but perhaps healthier epochs – the feeling of depression and the feeling of ennui. Depression and ennui; these are the characteristics stamped on how many of the representative works of modern times.'[12] Nerves, rather than the more Romantic–Victorian Senses, characterised the Decadence.

The Decadent was the opposite of the primitive, or Noble Savage: urban, introspective, individuated, enervated. The New Woman writer George Egerton (Mary Chavelita Dunne) summed it up in presenting half of her essentially modern couple in *Keynotes* (1893): 'I was analysing, being analyzed, criticising, being criticized.'[13] The New Woman literature was composed of complex, self-reflective relations between men and women, but the women authors' emphasis on relatedness distinguished them from the isolation or independence of the male Decadents.[14] The latter were described by the philosopher Vernon Lee (Violet Paget) in her tale 'The Virgin of the Seven Daggers' (1889),

10 Havelock Ellis, 'A Note on Paul Bourget', *Pioneer* (October 1889) cited in R. K. R. Thornton, *The Decadent Dilemma* (London: Edward Arnold, 1983), pp. 38–9.

11 Ernest Dowson, 'A Note upon the Practice and Theory of Verse at the Present Time Obtaining in France', *Century Guild Hobby Horse* (April 1891), cited in Thornton, *Decadent Dilemma*, p. 41.

12 Cited in Thornton, *Decadent Dilemma*, p. 4.

13 In *A New Woman Reader*, ed. Carolyn Christensen Nelson (Toronto: Broadview, 2001), p. 30.

14 See Regenia Gagnier, 'Individualism from the New Woman to the Genome: Autonomy and Independence', in *Partial Answers*, Ii (January 2003), 103–28.

in which Lee parodies the male egoism of Don Juan. Here the independent hero–male can only be saved by the blessed mother, a model of interdependence. As in so much of the Decadence, the issue is not whether Don Juan sleeps with men or women, but whether he ever escapes his own mind to connect with others at all, the kind of mind that Pater called in the 'Conclusion' to *The Renaissance* (1893) 'that thick wall of personality through which no real voice has ever pierced . . . keeping as a solitary prisoner its own dream of a world'.[15]

Modern literature is arguably the dialogue between individual independence and interdependence with others, from Leopold Bloom's disintegration, to Molly's integration; from Eliot's solipsism in *The Wasteland* (1922) ('I have heard the key / Turn in the door once and turn once only / We think of the key, each in his prison, / Thinking of the key'), to Gertrude Stein's intersubjective *Autobiography of Alice B. Toklas* (1933). Like individuals, states could reside in peaceful coexistence with other states or present themselves as essentially different, competitive or at war. Ironically it was the United States rather than Old Europe that represented Decadence for Baudelaire in 1857: 'A nation begins in decadence and starts in fact where others end up . . . Young and old at one and the same time, America chatters and drivels away with astonishing volubility.'[16] We shall return to the idea of national literatures in the section on 'Nation and Communication', in this chapter.

The mirror and the (street) lamp

In Thomas Hardy's early novel *A Pair of Blue Eyes* (1873), on church restoration in Cornwall, Hardy contrasts the village artificer in stone with the London social atom: 'In common with most rural mechanics, he had too much individuality to be a typical "working-man" – a resultant of that beach-pebble attrition with his kind only to be experienced in large towns, when metamorphoses the unit Self into a fraction of the unit Class.'[17] Hardy attributed the decline of individualism to the reification of socio-economic class in the division of labour. Alternatively, W. E. Henley used precisely the division of labour in his *In Hospital* (1888) and *London Types* (1898) to characterise the diversity of types in London that distinguished them from what Karl Marx had called in *The Communist Manifesto* (1848) the lack of differentiation in the country, or 'the idiocy of rural life'. The *fin de siècle* saw a series of volumes of poetry celebrating the multiplication of types in London: Amy Levy's *A London*

15 Walter Pater, *The Renaissance: Studies in Art and Poetry*, ed. Donald L. Hill (Berkeley: University of California Press, 1980), pp. 187–8.
16 Baudelaire, 'Further Notes on Edgar Poe', p. 189.
17 Thomas Hardy, *A Pair of Blue Eyes*, ed. Alan Manford (Oxford University Press, 1985), p. 87.

Plane-Tree (1889); Henley's *In Hospital*, *London Voluntaries* (1893) and *London Types*; Lawrence Binyon's series of *London Visions* (1896 and 1899); Ernest Rhys's *A London Rose* (1894); John Davidson's *Fleet Street Ecologues* (1893); and Arthur Symons's *London Nights* (1895). Henley used these types' class-based idioms in dramatic lyrics and monologues; throughout the 1890s he also compiled and edited a dictionary of *Slang and Its Analogues* (1890–1904), a groundbreaking work in lexicography, using language to differentiate the geography of the metropolis.

Yet the Literature of the Pavement, as Arthur Machen and others called it, remained as much about introspection as interpersonal exchanges. In 'Jenny' (1881), Dante Gabriel Rossetti's persona began by objectifying the street-walker ('Lazy, laughing languid Jenny / Fond of a kiss and fond of a guinea'), but ended objectifying himself ('And must I mock you to the last / Ashamed of my own Shame – aghast').[18] There is a line in *De Profundis* (1897), Wilde's long letter to Alfred Douglas from prison, which objectifies Wilde's comparable self-scrutiny and self-contempt, when he describes the way that he and Douglas, after having flaunted bourgeois morality, appealed to bourgeois law in conversations with their solicitors: 'when in the ghastly glare of a bleak room you and I would sit with serious faces telling serious lies to a bald man'.[19] In Arthur Symons's 'White Heliotrope' (1897), the couple regard each other through their mutual self-absorption (that thick wall of personality through which no real voice has ever pierced):

> The mirror that has sucked your face
> Into its secret deep of deeps,
> And there mysteriously keeps
> Forgotten memories of grace;
> And you, half dressed and half awake,
> Your slant eyes strangely watching me,
> And I, who watch you drowsily,
> With eyes that, having slept not, ache.

In Symons's 'Stella Maris' (1897), the 'Juliet of a night' whose 'heart holds many a Romeo' is matched only by the speaker who has 'sought on many a breast / The ecstacy of love's unrest'. He does not even know why he recalls her, she being but a serial lover, 'neither first nor last of all'. Yet, unlike Eliot's awful

[18] Dante Gabriel Rossetti, *Poems* (London: Dent, 1968), p. 72.

[19] *The Portable Oscar Wilde*, ed. Richard Aldington and Stanley Weintraub (London: Penguin, 1981), p. 626.

daring of a moment's surrender that an age of prudence can never retract, Symons does not repent with North American Puritan shame but endlessly repeats in his mind the anonymous pleasures:[20]

> Child, I remember, and can tell
> One night we loved each other well,
> And one night's love, at least or most,
> Is not so small a thing to boast . . .
> That joy was ours, we passed it by,
> You have forgotten me, and I . . .
> Won an instant from oblivion.

The division of labour that produced diversity of type also produced regularity, reproduction of type and mechanical rhythms of subjectivity. The sexual promiscuity so celebrated in the 1890s also induced the ennui of the mechanical lover – the 'love-machine' – of Swinburne's 'Faustine' (1862). Swinburne's mechanical metre was beaten into his young body by Classics tutors at school.[21] Subjective rhythm matches the subjective transformation of the public sacramental image in Swinburne's 'Triumph of Time' (1866), in which life is wrung dry as a wafer, and broken as bread, but no body and no blood is transubstantiated, just offered up in obsessively metrical sacrifice of self to lover:

> I had wrung life dry for your lips to drink,
> Broken it up for your daily bread:
> Body for body and blood for blood,
> As the flow of the full sea risen to flood
> That yearns and trembles before it sink,
> I had given, and lain down for you, glad and dead.

The second generation Arts and Craftsmaster John Paul Cooper perceived the mechanical rhythms of modern life as threats to the movement's individualism: 'art is intuition and intuition is individuality, and individuality can never be repeated'.[22] The duality of Progress (later called the Dialectic of Enlightenment) was epitomised in the 1896 Olympic Games in Athens. '*Citius, altius,*

[20] For the tensions between Symons's posture of the Artist and his Cornish family's Methodism, see R. Gagnier, 'Art, Elitism, and Gender: the Last of the Aesthetes', in *Review*, 12 (Charlottesville: University Press of Virginia, 1990), pp. 107–17.

[21] Yopie Prins, *Victorian Sappho* (Princeton University Press, 1999), p. 119–22.

[22] N. Natasha Kuzmanović, *John Paul Cooper: Designer and Craftsman of the Arts and Crafts Movement* (Phoenix Mill: Sutton, 1999), p. 155.

fortius' – faster, higher, stronger – the motto signified a European dream of individual perfection through perfect competition, Spencer's progress. Yet as the means – perfect competition – were mechanised, the end result was the Taylorisation of the athlete. F. W. Taylor began his career in sport, and Taylorism culminated in the 'totalization of sport', in which wealthy nations produced athletes through sophisticated and expensive technical intervention. Henning Eichberg has studied the 'Anthropology Days' of the 1904 Olympics, which pitted indigenous peoples against one another with the consequence that they failed to prove themselves competitive.[23]

The rapid interface of technologies and subjectivities characterises the period: the rise of the giant corporation, mass production and mass consumption; the development and distribution of electrical energy (see Richard Le Gallienne's 'iron lilies of the Strand' in 'Ballad of London' (1895), in which the metropolis is the 'Great City of Midnight Sun', not for its northern lights but for its streetlamps); aviation and motor vehicles (see John Davidson's 'ever-muttering, prisoned storm / the heart of London beating warm' ('London,' 1894)); the emergence of mass politics, mass media and mass sport, by way of which the body of ordinary people, denoted as 'the masses', was growing into a major participant in public affairs; popular culture and leisure activities; the birth of quantum mechanics, relativity physics and the beginning of the systematic study of genetics.[24] In his extensive work on Victorian mass media, Patrick Brantlinger has written of the flourishing of sociological theory between 1880 and 1914: Ferdinand Tönnies's analysis of *Gemeinschaft* and *Gesellschaft*, Emile Durkheim's of 'anomie' and suicide, Georg Simmel's of the marketplace and exchange, Vilfredo Pareto's of elites versus masses.[25] These developments and analyses revealed the division of labour that both individuated and reproduced types, that brought freedom as well as anomie and bureaucracy. They offered individuals unprecedented scope and choice, so that progress was towards individualism. However, the same techniques, as Hardy had said, tended to mechanise, routinise, massify. As crowd psychology grew, Sigmund Freud's *Civilization and Its Discontents* (1930) turned Spencer on his head. Freud, who it is increasingly clear should be recognised as the philosopher of the Decadence, feared that Individualism, as a socio-biological drive towards self-assertion, would be overwhelmed. All

23 Henning Eichberg, 'Forward Race and the Laughter of Pygmies: on Olympic Sport', in Mikulas Teich and Roy Porter, eds., *Fin de Siècle and Its Legacy* (Cambridge University Press, 1990), pp. 115–31.

24 See Teich and Porter, eds., *Fin de Siècle and Its Legacy*.

25 Patrick Brantlinger, 'Mass Media and Culture in Fin-de-siècle Europe', in Teich and Porter, *Fin de Siècle and its Legacy*, pp. 80–97.

progress and civilisation were away from individualism towards the herd or mass.[26]

Art and life, and death

If the Decadence is characterised by socio-psychological tensions between the one and the many, Aestheticism is characterised by the tensions between art and life. While women of all classes were moving into public- or work-space, male 'designers' were beginning to colonise the home, displacing the less pretentious home decorators of an earlier era.[27] Some women responded to this colonisation of the domus by out-heroding Herod, with a formalist aesthetic as Aesthetic as the men's. Thus Rosamund Marriott Watson, who ran a fashion column in the *Pall Mall Gazette*, perfected the idea of woman as consumer, whose taste reflected her choices and preference. Marriott Watson referred exclusively to the form, not function, of women's wear, making no reference to the woman who might wear the garment, but only to its contrast of line and colour, and turning the dress away from human wear and tear (and dirt) towards the functionlessness of sculpture: she refers not to the hem of the gown that trails on the ground but the *foot*, like a pedestal. Marriott Watson does not write as John Ruskin or Henry Mayhew had done, of textile and couture production in conditions of exploitation, but rather she aestheticises with the timelessness of the mythic Orient: '[The] gown reminds you of Japan, of course, as all good decoration must.'[28] The woman of Taste must be able to interpret such distinctions, to 'read' the garment and exercise judgement.

Even more parodically, Mariott Watson analysed the *ascesis* (the much-praised aesthetic economy of discipline and restraint) of mourning as a 'poetics of clothing', a Whistlerian palette of black, grey, lavender and white, which, like the rigid forms of the Sonnet, simultaneously confined and expressed great feeling. She analysed formal mourning as 'the poetry of sorrow' and embroidered the phrase as 'the shadow of consolation in the language of variegated woolens',[29] 'that dawn of comfort (in heliotrope and grey) to which the deep night of sables has perforce to give place'.[30] Like Symons's Symbolist poets, she interpreted broken patterns as expressing emotional fragmentation: the

[26] Sigmund Freud, *Civilization and Its Discontent* in *The Standard Edition of the Complete Psychological Works of Sigmund Freud*, trans. James Strachey, 24 vols. (London: Hogarth Press, 1961), XXI, pp. 140–1.

[27] See Talia Schaffer, *The Forgotten Female Aesthetes: Literary Culture in Late-Victorian England* (Charlottesville: University Press of Virginia, 2000).

[28] Ibid., p. 115. [29] Ibid., p. 116. [30] Ibid., p. 117.

cloud of black skirt bewails the relative, while the silver-lined bodice rejoices in the legacy.[31] Marriott Watson can express laughter between the tears because formal mourning is not about grief but the *performance* of grief. She uses aesthetic form to distance herself from the everyday woman's world of cleaning, clothing and grieving.

Another female aesthete, Alice Meynell, employed the formal properties of art – metre and colour – to aestheticise everyday life. An industrious woman, Meynell ran a literary writing and publishing partnership with her husband, raised seven children, and in the 1890s while serving the Catholic Revival also wrote a weekly column for the *Pall Mall Gazette*. 'The Rhythm of Life' (1893) is a lyrical meditation on recurrence in the day-to-day repetitions in life with children, the elderly and the ailing; in the cycles of reproduction and domesticity; in the life of emotions and the metricality of disease.[32] It is a critique of linearity and progress as profound as that of the Modernists Virginia Woolf and James Joyce. In 'The Colour of Life' (1896) Meynell again vivifies a formal property, in this case colour rather than metre. She opposes the red of bloodshed – of life violated – to the colour of life:

> Red has been praised for its nobility as the colour of life. But the true colour of life is not red. Red is the colour of violence, or of life broken open, edited, and published. Or if red is indeed the colour of life, it is so only on condition that it is not seen . . . It is one of the things the value of which is secrecy, one of the talents that are to be hidden in a napkin. The true colour of life is the . . . modest colour of the unpublished blood.[33]

Meynell laments that for months together London cannot see the colour of life for people go darkly covered, which introduces the London boy stripping down for an illicit dip in the Serpentine, whose nakedness returns to off-season London the colour of life: 'At the stroke of eight he sheds . . . the hues of dust, soot, and fog, which are the colours the world has chosen for the clothing of its boys – and he makes . . . a bright and delicate flush between the grey-blue water and the grey-blue sky.'[34] The passage shows the formalist distinctions of the connoisseur as in Marriott Watson: the reduction of the boy to 'figure' and the emergence of colour and character through contrast and juxtaposition. The boy is so entirely aestheticised, so absorbed into the landscape, that we are surprised when Meynell suddenly gives him voice: 'All the squalor is gone

31 Ibid.

32 All citations from Alice Meynell, *Prose and Poetry Centenary Volume*, ed. Vita Sackville-West (London: Jonathan Cape, 1947).

33 Ibid., p. 219. 34 Ibid., p. 220.

in a moment, kicked off with the second boot, and the child goes shouting to complete the landscape with the lacking colour of life. You are inclined to wonder that, even undressed, he still shouts with a Cockney accent.'[35]

We may contrast Meynell's emphasis on the reproduction of metre and colour in life and art, and her ethics of interdependence, with an equal countertendency in the literature of the *fin de siècle*. This is the masculine notion – very different in tendency – of life as Will. Life as Will is also about continuous movement or motion but this is motion as continuous violence, sometimes called 'creative destruction'. John Davidson's persona in the dramatic monologue 'Thirty Bob a Week' (1894) anticipated not just T. S. Eliot's Prufrock, Sweeney, Gerontian, and the masses of clerks pouring over London Bridge in *The Waste Land*, but also Joyce's demotic *Ulysses* (1922). Eliot wrote of the poem's 'complete fitness of content and idiom', while the clerk writes of survival of the fittest on thirty bob a week. Too experienced in the school of hard knocks to believe in Progress, but too proud to believe in social determinism, the clerk opts for individual will and Darwinian struggle ('complete fitness of content and idiom'):

> And it's this way that I make it out to be:
> No fathers, mothers, countries, climates – none;
> Not Adam was responsible for me,
> Nor society, nor systems, nary one:
> A little sleeping seed, I woke – I did, indeed –
> A million years before the blooming sun.
> I woke because I thought the time had come;
> Beyond my will there was no other cause . . .
>
> I was the love that chose my mother out;
> I joined two lives and from the union burst;
> My weakness and my strength without a doubt
> Are mine alone for ever from the first.[36]

This is voluntarism with a self-hating vengeance, an insistence on independence not just from society and parents but at the level of the sperm. Yet while the clerk's class has adopted this Smilesian self-help verging on Nietzschean will, his is no paean to Progress. He knows that there is no reason on the part of his class for Reason, that there is nothing 'proper' – his own – or fitting about his life on thirty bob a week. The poem concludes with a mere mechanical

[35] Ibid.

[36] John Davidson, 'Thirty Bob a Week', in R. K. R. Thornton and Marion Thain eds., *Poetry of the 1890s* (London: Penguin, 1997), pp. 89–93.

struggle for survival, as pointless and doomed as the trenches would be for the next generation (by which time Davidson will have thrown himself off the cliffs at Penzance).

> It's a naked child against a hungry wolf;
> It's a playing bowls upon a splitting wreck;
> It's walking on a string across a gulf
> With millstones fore-and-aft about your neck;
> But the thing is daily done by many and many a one;
> And we fall, face forward, fighting, on the deck.

Davidson's profoundly empathic insight into the Darwinian struggle for working-class men eventually took possession of him in an unflinching materialism that saw itself as a will to power as knowledge. In his 'Testament of a Vivisector' (1901–2), heavily influenced by Arthur Schopenhauer, Charles Darwin and Nietzsche's ideas of will via Havelock Ellis, the protagonist has been abandoned by wife and children and pursues his trade in rapt isolation.[37] The vivisector sees carving up living creatures as the 'zest' of scientific inquiry: matter is thought achieved, unconscious will. The desire to escape from it is matter warring with itself, the dialectics of nature, of Enlightenment. Initially the vivisector 'began to hew the living flesh, / I seemed to seek . . . The mitigation of disease'. He soon begins to 'study pain' for its own sake, until there is only pain, pain as knowledge, whether in the heat of the sun or the contractions of maternity. Davidson does not perceive Meynell's dulcet rhythm of recurrence but the eternal destruction of Will to knowledge. Davidson's next poem would be the posthumously published 'Testament of John Davidson'.

The idea of Will as biological instinct, like the force that drives the plant to grow or the cancer to spread or the species to multiply, was profoundly linked to Victorian ideas of knowledge and science. The meticulous, even obsessive, transcriptions and analyses that did not distinguish between health and disease defined empirical science and its literary offshoot Naturalism. Indeed it was this lack of distinction between health and disease as both equally the subject of knowledge that made progress and Decadence, or, in scientific terms, Degeneration, interchangeable. Brian Stableford, who has collected the most extreme literature of Decadence, sees syphilis as the key cause of the movement, as many of its writers suffered and died from the disease. Where most saw health and Progress the Decadents saw disease, which they clinically, or, in literary terms, Naturalistically, transcribed. They were thus the forerunners

[37] John Davidson, 'Testament of a Vivisector', in *The Second Dedalus Book of Decadence* pp. 210–17.

of the pathology of everyday life of Freudian psychology. The most extreme Decadent literature aestheticises the nervousness of dying as an intense form of living, and knowledge itself.

In Joris-Karl Huysmans's *A Rebours* (1884), the so-called 'breviary of the Decadence' (Symons), 'it all comes down to syphilis in the end'.[38] The Decadent protagonist Duc Jean Floressas des Esseintes enjoys self-imposed isolation in order to construct highly personal canons of language, literature, clothing and cosmetics. He has prepared a Black Feast, and in this, as in his canon-construction, he nods to Decadence in its classical sense of 'coming after'. Yet whereas the Roman Black Feast or funereal dinner party was moralised as exposing the decadence of the guests or politicised as displaying the power of the host, i.e., as producing the *social* effects of cathartic pity and fear, Des Esseintes's invitations merely request spectators at 'a funeral banquet in memory of the host's virility'.[39] Whereas Black Feasts in Petronius, Seneca, Domitian and Tacitus are all action and violence, in Huysmans they are all contemplation and morbidity. In Huysmans, Decadence is a category of Taste, the construction of a private canon or gesture that defines the self, as in Nietzsche's Hellenism or Pater's highly idiosyncratic Renaissance, that reaches from twelfth-century France to eighteenth-century Germany. As in Wilde's astonishing lists in *Dorian Gray* or 'The Sphinx' (1894), these private canons often interpellated specific audiences, which interpellations annoyed those of the mass-oriented Nordau's persuasion.

However, the Will to knowledge was not necessarily a death-wish. The Spencerian Individualists defined Energy of Will as self-originating force, 'the soul of every great character', and the basis of the self-governing state.[40] Along with the political philosophers who made up the Individualists were the clerks themselves, who rejected Davidson's and Dostoevsky's combative and resentful clerks, Forster's Leonard Bast, or Eliot's hordes going to work over London Bridge. Submerged in the mass, they worked well and taught themselves. According to Jonathan Rose in *The Intellectual Life of the British Working Classes* (2001), the authors of so many clerks' autobiographies 'were not isolated or alienated: they depict themselves as part of a large and lively community of philosopher–accountants'.[41] Far from Eliot's city of faceless masses, London

[38] J. K. Huysmans, *Against Nature*, trans. Robert Baldick (New York: Penguin, 1982), p. 101.
[39] Ibid., p. 27.
[40] For the Individualists, see Regenia Gagnier, 'The Law of Progress and the Ironies of Individualism in the Nineteenth Century', in *New Literary History*, 31, 2, pp. 315–36. Special issue on *Economics and Culture*.
[41] Jonathan Rose, *The Intellectual Life of the British Working Classes* (New Haven: Yale University Press, 2001), p. 407.

offered these office workers unequalled scope for identity and liberty. V. W. Garratt, migrating to London from Birmingham after World War I, found that the city's crowds stimulated individuality by giving poor men access to art, literature and music not available in the village.[42]

These autodidacts saw the North American Modernists as deracinated, imitating hypersophisticated European Decadents. Admirers of Wilde like F. Holland Day and Ralph Cram in New England educated boys at Day's farm Little Good Harbour in the ways of European culture, a paideuma that produced the author of *The Prophet* (1923), Kahlil Gibran. Yet Richard Church (b. 1893), the son of a postman, raised and educated in South London, judged T. S. Eliot's style the 'dreadful self-consciousness of so many *déraciné* Americans, aping the hyper-civilised European decadent. [It] has always given me the sensation of being in the presence of death, of flowers withered because the plant has been torn from its taproot in a native soil. Even the novels of Henry James have for me this desiccated atrophy, unsimple and pretentious.'[43] These are the people whom Eliot, Forster, Davidson and James himself in *The Princess Cassamassima* (1886) reduced to their function in the division of labour.

When working-class autodidacts like Aneuran Bevan did fear the 'abominable brutality of the majority'[44] that would overrun individual dignity they turned to A. R. Orage's *New Age* and the Modernist journal *The Egoist: An Individualist Review*. They responded enthusiastically to Nietzsche and the Uruguayan philosopher José Enriqué Rodo, who combined economic egalitarianism with intellectual elitism. Edwin Muir (b. 1887) wrote: 'The idea of a transvaluation of all values intoxicated me with a feeling of false power. I, a poor clerk in a beer-bottling factory, adopted the creed of aristocracy, and happy until now to be an Orkney man somewhat lost in Glasgow, I began to regard myself somewhat tentatively as a "good European."'[45]

Nation and communication

Nietzsche's image of the Good European, who would transcend national, ethnic, and racial boundaries by way of a communicative cosmopolitanism, was one expression of the period's complex geopolitical vision. The local and rooted could have two faces: the 'blood and soil' that could culminate in Fascism or the ethnic pride that resisted domination. Cosmopolitanism as

[42] Ibid., p. 411. [43] Ibid., p. 416. [44] Ibid., p. 423. [45] Ibid., p. 428.

a progressive vision of transnational communication and cultural exchange was distinguished from international trade, or globalisation, which was often resisted as colonisation and domination.

The Irish Literary Renaissance countered a materialistic and global Englishness by way of a chthonic Irish literature and theatre, including models of heroism, epic vision, classlessness and emotion connected with the land. Kasturi Chaudhuri has compared Yeats's anti-political, or spiritual, nationalism with that of Rabindranath Tagore, who 'valued the inner life or soul of the people' more than the political concept of the nation.[46] This comparative context could certainly be developed in relation to the European concept of the *Volk*.

Scott Ashley has contextualised the morbidity of the European Decadence with the postcolonial decline of the Atlantic 'Celtic Fringe'.[47] Edward Tylor's anthropology after 1871, Andrew Lang's *Custom and Myth* (1884) and James Frazer's *Golden Bough* (1890) linked the decimation of Ireland and other colonial peoples to Degeneration at home (see Stevenson's *The Beach of Falesá* (1892) and *In the South Seas* (1896), which were parallel to his planned but unwritten work *The Transformation of the Scottish Highlands*). Ireland, the Scottish Highlands, Wales and Brittany had suffered depopulation, famine and linguistic persecution since the late eighteenth century. Cornwall, still clinging to the last relics of its language in 1700, had seen it bleed to death with remarkable rapidity by 1800. By the 1890s Irish, Gaelic, Breton, Welsh and Manx were with good evidence being described as dying languages by both their champions and their detractors, and during the last decades of the nineteenth century several attempts were made to reverse the rapid erosion of Celtic speakers, perhaps the most famous of which was the founding of the Gaelic League in 1893. Yet despite these institutional efforts, all non-native speaker revivals were posited on images of decay and death. Hence the Irish Literary Renaissance is also known as the Celtic Twilight.

Collecting ballads and folklore in Brittany from rural labourers and artisans marginalised by industrialisation at the *fin de siècle*, Anatole Le Braz talked of the 'songs turned to sighs'. In 1896, Elisabeth and William Sharp, creators of the Hebridean peasant–visionary 'Fiona Macleod', published *Lyra Celtica*:

46 Kasturi Chaudhuri, 'Synge and the Irish Literary Renaissance', (PhD Thesis, University of Calcutta, New Delhi, 2000), p. 68.

47 Scott Ashley, 'Primitivism, Celticism and Morbidity in the Atlantic *Fin de Siècle*', in Patrick McGuinness, *Symbolism, Decadence and the Fin de Siècle: French and European Perspectives* (University of Exeter Press, 2000), pp. 175–93.

An Anthology of Representative Celtic Poetry, which duly inspired the pan-Celtic vision of W. B. Yeats, John Millington Synge and Augusta Gregory. True to the Symbolist roots of his early poetry, Yeats saw in the everyday existence of the people symbols to move Ireland to action. Synge invested much of his adult life studying Irish in Dublin and Paris, spending part of his summers among Irish speakers on Aran (1898–1902) and in the Kerry Gaeltacht and the Blasket Islands (1903–5). He was initially disappointed by the triviality of indigenous speech rather than what he pursued as 'the real spirit of the island'. Yet witnessing mourners at a funeral, he came to understand, as Samuel Beckett would with a vengeance, that 'talk of the daily trifles veils them from the terror of the world': 'In this cry of pain the inner consciousness of the people seems to lay itself bare for an instant.'[48] What Synge saw in the indigenous peoples was a tragic vision comparable to that in the Greek myths of the wild Peloponnesus. And so it was to tragedy that the Irish Renaissance returned: the inward-looking soul of a people expressed in song against Weber's mechanised iron cage.

British writers had to make a similar choice between internationalism and ethnicity. William Morris and Edward Carpenter expressed in the 1880s an ethnic idealism that might have converged with the murderous masculinism evoked by Davidson in Britain and the Freikorps in Germany, replete with icons of priapic labour and desire for the labouring body of the proletariat. But there were two crucial distinctions between the Morris–Carpenter vision and the German Volk's. The first was not gendered: the virile body in service of protecting others was ultimately chivalric, aristocratic, rather than mass, and it was equally accessible to women: as with Yeats's and Lady Gregory's Cathleen ni Houlihan (Ireland), women in Morris, as in our current popular fantasies, are as virile as the men, and men are as protective of the weak as are women. And, second, it was precisely labour that constituted the transformative power of the biological will in Morris and Carpenter, not the sterile reflective thought – the scientific will to knowledge – that drove the Vivisector and Nietzsche himself to destruction. The labouring body in Morris and Carpenter is more akin to the maternal figures in Meynell than the Freikorps soldier–male: rigid, independent, terrified of absorption in the mass even while his identity is only in the armoured millipede of the phalanx.

The duality was crystallised in Morris's socialist romance *Pilgrims of Hope* (1885), in which voice and speech uniting the generations are breathed from the virile bodies of father and mother, and the folk (in this case the French

[48] Ibid., p. 191.

Communards) are poised between the beloved soil and the socialist International. The mother who will die on the barricades addresses her infant son:

> Then mayst thou remember hereafter . . . this tale of thy mother's voice
> As oft in the calm of dawning I have heard the birds rejoice,
> As oft I have heard the storm-wind go moaning through the wood,
> And I knew that earth was speaking, and the mother's voice was good.

The next century would see the struggle between the identity politics of emerging national literatures / mother-tongues and cosmopolitanism, or, in more negative, economic, terms, globalisation.

3

Empire and modern writing

ELLEKE BOEHMER

The Indian-born Rudyard Kipling (1865–1936), who throughout his career wrote from a sense of being un-English and 'unhomely', although himself a writer in English, was one of the first openly to recognise that British culture and literature were shot through and through with the experience and the perceptions of empire. This chapter, 'Empire and Modern Writing', aims to expand on some of the implications of Kipling's thought. It will suggest that understanding British society at the turn of the nineteenth into the twentieth century in all its fissiparous uncertainty, its fears of degeneration coupled with its convictions of cultural superiority, entails placing that society inside the complicated context of its longstanding colonial engagements. Here lie many of the sources of its chronic paranoia; here is located the contact zone with those other cultures in relation to which it understood itself.[1] This was a time when the British Empire had reached its greatest geographic extent ever, even as British industrial power was for the first time feeling the pinch of competition from Germany and the United States. Whether they were writing swashbuckling adventure tales, or probing inner structures of feeling, writers were not unaware of this impress of the rest of the world not only on the British Isles, but on the millions of miles of its imperial borders. As Kipling himself memorably put it in a poem calling for a greater imperial awareness in Britain: 'And what should they know of England who only England know?'[2]

At about the same time Kipling began to publish in Lahore the Indian short stories that made his name, another colonial writer, the South African feminist Olive Schreiner (1855–1920), too, explored from her own alienated vantage point feelings of absurdity and suppressed terror at the project of dominating other peoples. In particular, her work dramatises how Enlightenment ideas of

[1] On cultural and linguistic contact zones, see Mary Louise Pratt, *Imperial Eyes: Travel Writing and Transculturation* (London: Routledge, 1992).

[2] Rudyard Kipling, 'The English Flag', *The Definitive Edition of Rudyard Kipling's Verse* (London: Hodder & Stoughton, 1989), p. 221.

rational, progressive development, which fuelled nineteenth-century science and social thinking as well as the imperial project itself, were rendered useless and destructive when they failed to take account of the cultural mentalities with which that project brought them into contact. Empire, stripped of its pomp, finery and manifold hypocrisy, and viewed in relation to its oppressed, in fact made a very poor moral show. Some twenty-five years later Leonard Woolf (1880–1969) glossed what he saw as the bankrupting of liberalism by empire in this way: 'Theoretically everyone is told that he is equal with everyone else, while practically we try to be paternal, despotic.'[3]

Schreiner's 1883 iconic first novel *The Story of an African Farm* represents colonial settler society in microcosm in the form of a small farm community isolated on the arid plains of the South African hinterland.[4] Within the surrogate family that makes up this community, greed, fear and shapeless yearning are the governing emotions, in relation to which inherited moral structures, just like the maps brought over from Europe, have little purchase. Nothing that is created on the farm comes to fruition and natural generation has been curtailed: the children are orphans, the 'New Woman' Lyndall dies in childbirth, the 'wild boy' Waldo's carefully designed machine is destroyed. In spite of Schreiner's own Social Darwinist language, the suspicion arises that if the colonial characters were only able to address the outside world of the desert and the natives who populate it, whose art scores the rocks round about, they might break out of their deadly introversion. This would, however, mean changing their social character entirely, and giving up their autocratic power. Significantly, those who converse most easily, or who most successfully translate *between* the monadic personalities of the farmstead, are either African or white children.

As Schreiner's example demonstrates, far more intensely so than in the middle nineteenth century, late nineteenth- and early twentieth-century literature not only registered but reflected upon the profound social, political, cultural and epistemological impacts of colonialism, and its formal incarnation, imperialism.[5] It is an observation that applies not only to the so-called colonial writing produced in the British Empire by native-born Europeans, such as Kipling and Schreiner (whose careers were, however, made in London), but, as will be seen, to metropolitan writers like D. H. Lawrence and Virginia Woolf also. In a world

3 Leonard Woolf, Letter to Lytton Strachey (3 March 1907), in *The Letters of Leonard Woolf*, ed. Frederic Spotts (London: Bloomsbury, 1990), pp. 124–5.

4 Olive Schreiner, *The Story of an African Farm*, 'Foreword' by Doris Lessing (London: Hutchinson, 1987).

5 In brief, imperialism may be defined as the process of controlling land one does not possess and forcing governance upon the people who live there.

seemingly made smaller by speeded-up travel and communications systems (the commercial steamship, the telegraph),[6] the commodities, artefacts and even presences of other cultures, far-flung and nearby, and variously interpreted either as vital and alarming, or primitive and fear-inducing, inevitably became knitted deep into British society. This was a time when, as Lyn Innes among others has observed, Britain played host to an increasing number of Indian, African and Caribbean 'visitors' from the colonies. These included students like Sarojini Naidu, Cornelia Sorabji and Jawaharlal Nehru; reformers like J. J. Thomas and Pandita Ramabai; travellers like A. B. C. Merriman Labour.[7] Agitated by the repeated political failure to achieve Home Rule, Irish writers, too, such as W. B. Yeats, J. M. Synge and James Joyce, responded to their particular experience of Ireland's colonisation by Britain when in their work they sought to supply their nation with cultural self-definitions of its own. The Irish, Joyce wrote, had to 'stamp' upon the English language 'the mark of their own genius' in order that the language might bear the burden of an Irish colonial awareness.[8]

Even those British authors and cultural commentators whose attitudes remained resolutely of an imperial stripe, such as the writer of adventure fiction H. Rider Haggard or Robert Baden-Powell, founder of the worldwide Scout Movement, were occasionally given to expressing respect for so-called primitive cultures, Native American and Zulu in particular.[9] Despite their delight in imperial adventure and success, despite their undisguised triumphalism, they saw in these cultures evidence of social and military discipline and survival skills which, in appropriated form, they believed might prove the salvation of a west believed to be degenerating even as it was expanding. The West's decadence, in fact, was the corrosive threat that lay at the heart of all imperial endeavour. As in the case of Rome, so, too, of Britain – empire, overextending itself, might end in ruins.[10] Or as in Kipling's poem 'Recessional': 'Lo, all our pomp of yesterday is one with Nineveh and Tyre.' Especially around the time of the disastrous Anglo-Boer war (1899–1902), the British in Kipling's view were in danger of losing their redeeming imperial idealism, their belief in Duty and

[6] In 1900, with the laying of the cross-Pacific cable between Australia and Canada, the imperial communications network had in fact become global in its reach.

[7] See C. L. Innes, *A History of Black and Asian Writing in Britain, 1700–2000* (Cambridge University Press, 2002), for example, pp. 126–41.

[8] Richard Ellman, *James Joyce* (Oxford University Press, 1965), p. 26.

[9] See H. Rider Haggard, *King Solomon's* Mines (1885; Oxford World's Classics, 1989) and *She* (1887; Oxford World's Classics, 1991); and Robert Baden-Powell, *Scouting for Boys*, ed. Elleke Boehmer (Oxford World's Classics, 2004).

[10] Baden-Powell, *Scouting for Boys*, pp. 295–6.

Law, and their empire with it.[11] Native 'savagery' and vitality thus represented at once a major threat to the Empire's stability, and, in appropriated form, a possible source of its salvation. As regards the general pressure of the margins upon the centre, therefore, chroniclers of colonial experience like Haggard or Conrad prepared the ground for the admission of the simultaneous fascination and threat of *difference* among a younger, more culturally and ethically uncertain group of writers, such as the early Modernists. The 'other', or 'contending native', in the imperial historian J. R. Seeley's phrase, even if labelled by and contained within racist stereotypes, offered new ways of seeing to artists already pondering the implications of the subjective, relativising gaze. As the proto-Modernist, Polish-born Joseph Conrad (1857–1924) expressed it in 'An Outpost of Progress' (1896), a curtain-raiser for his tenebrous indictment of colonial brutality in *Heart of Darkness* (1899): 'The contact with primitive man and primitive nature brings sudden and profound trouble into the heart.'[12] What that trouble entailed, essentially, was a sense of the extreme foreignness yet intense recognisability of 'primitive nature'. The white man was attempting to distance as 'other' that which he at the same time partially conceded was fundamental to himself.[13]

It is the narrator Marlow's suspicion at the start of *Heart of Darkness* that Europe exposes its own primitive heart in the very act of 'civilising' other peoples, which leads him to utter his well-known assertion: London, too, 'has been one of the dark places of the earth'. The contemporary shock factor of this statement is most clearly perceived when we remember that the effort to bring 'backward peoples' into the light of progress (represented either by commerce or by Christianity, or both), constituted a major justification for the imperial mission in the first place. Imperial ideology dictated that the 'lesser breeds' of Kipling's 'Recessional', for example, should be saved from themselves, although never fully so, not to the extent of their becoming part of the white colonial elect. However, in a world of collapsing certainties, as Marlow's perception reveals, it became the more difficult to disguise the contradiction that lay at the very heart of the colonial project: the simultaneous

11 Kipling, 'Recessional' (1897), *The Definitive Edition*, p. 328.

12 Joseph Conrad, 'An Outpost of Progress', in *Tales of Unrest* (London: T. Fisher Unwin, 1898); rpt. in *Empire Writing: An Anthology of Colonial Literature 1870–1918* (Oxford University Press, 1998), pp. 248–70. See also Joseph Conrad, *Heart of Darkness* (London: Penguin, 1995).

13 The masculinity of the imperial project is conventionally taken as axiomatic. White women, of course, played important roles in colonialism as wives, nurses, missionaries and, occasionally, explorers and reformers, but their gender placed them in a secondary position in relation to the core structures and definitions of imperial power. See, for example, Kumari Jayawardena, *The White Woman's Other Burden* (London: Routledge, 1995).

appeal to, and denial of, the humanity of colonised people. Although slow to concede a basic articulacy to oppressed Africans, Conrad's scepticism with regard to the benefits of progress in *Heart of Darkness*, as also in *Nostromo* (1904), brought him close to an acknowledgement that the position of the white man in the colonies was morally indefensible. Ultimately, as Leonard Woolf also realised, colonial oppression might thus become impossible practically to sustain.[14]

The unsettling resonances of the imperial encounter had the effect, too, of amplifying the other shocks sustained by the British social and political body in the 'Age of Empire' (1875–1914), in Eric Hobsbawm's term.[15] These embraced, in no particular order, the rise of socialism, the emergence of the New Woman, the failure of religion among intellectuals, and the unease created by national rivalries within Europe. Indeed, as against the many interpretations of Modernism as an 'Anglo-Saxon' or northern phenomenon – most notoriously in Fredric Jameson's essay 'Modernism and Imperialism' – such emergent political, social and cultural movements internal to Europe were probably seen as the more disruptive due to that 'profound trouble' brought by colonial contact. New explorations in psychoanalysis, too, complemented by developments in anthropology, unsettled the boundaries of the known, familiar world by proposing that savagery's primary residence lay within the unconscious, not in the far recesses of the Empire.[16] As also in experiments with so-called primitive art forms at this time, like those of Paul Gauguin, Pablo Picasso or Mark Gertler, the conventional divides between reason and unreason, as between metropolis and colony, were rendered mobile, porous and constantly shifting. The contact with native cultures raised difficult, if not unanswerable questions about the certainty and stability of Western social, national and spiritual orders, which, as I will show, were translated into the new inconclusiveness and formal incompletions of art.

Quite contrary to prevailing colonial assumptions, therefore, that Britain had firmly placed its imprint on the Empire, colonised cultures in fact helped to mould the modern formation of the British nation and its culture, and, as Simon Gikandi and Jonathan Schneer have argued, shaped its image of

[14] Joseph Conrad, *Nostromo*, ed. Martin Seymour-Smith (London: Penguin, 1983).

[15] Eric Hobsbawm, *The Age of Empire 1875–1914* (Harmondsworth: Penguin, 1987).

[16] See Fredric Jameson, 'Modernism and Imperialism', *Nationalism, Colonialism and Literature* (Minneapolis: University of Minnesota Press, 1990), pp. 43–68. It is worth noting here that Sigmund Freud's *The Interpretation of Dreams*, his account of his initial forays into the unconscious, was published in 1899, the same year as *Heart of Darkness*. In Conrad's novella, Kurtz's imposing rhetoric, which masks the brutality of his practices, interestingly, is said to partake of the terrific suggestiveness of words heard in dreams (p. 107).

itself.[17] Responding to the pervasive sense of cultural dishevelment and loss of control, artists and intellectuals began to rifle through the symbolic systems of other societies to find alternative sources of meaning and creative energy. For a number of mainstream Modernist writers – including D. H. Lawrence (1885–1930) in *Kangaroo* (1923) and *The Plumed Serpent* (1926), and Katherine Mansfield (1888–1923) in her New Zealand short stories – other cultural presences, Mexicans or Maoris, represent the intriguing *plus ultra*, the ultimate test case, to the central tenets of their work. These tenets include their ideas of character and characterisation, and conventions around narrative perspective and the omniscient eye. Tradition, it was felt, had to be remade from scratch, with a new respect for intuition, ritual and ceremony, and for subjective awareness. That Lawrence and Mansfield were both themselves social outsiders – Lawrence as a class exile, Mansfield as a settler colonial – no doubt contributed to the deep sense of cultural relativity that informs their work.

The postcolonial critic Edward Said in his monumental study *Culture and Imperialism* (1993) – more conclusively so than in *Orientalism* (1978) – makes the compelling point that cultural forms, such as the novel, are important not only in registering but in supporting and reinforcing 'imperial attitudes, references, and experiences'.[18] Expanding on the tentative remarks of Raymond Williams concerning the influence of 'peripheral' cultures on the colonial centre, Said's observations relate to the imaginative works of the early twentieth century as much as to, his primary focus, the 'great novels' of the nineteenth century.[19] Modernist writing, too, is an expression of 'the relationship between culture and empire', although a relationship felt to be less secure than was earlier the case. Imperialism was for a period of time, up until about 1947, *the* primary pattern of domination and governance for the world. Writers like Conrad, T. S. Eliot and Lawrence who worked in this period, therefore, Said contends, helped consolidate, shore up, justify, if also occasionally question, that pattern of domination.

Indeed, as Said specifically recognises, a growing awareness of the 'delusions' involved in ruling over others – such as the imperial conviction of permanent rule or of infallible knowledge of the 'other' that undergirds it – is powerfully communicated in Modernism at a variety of levels. It is registered, for

17 See Simon Gikandi, *Maps of Englishness: Writing Identity in the Cultures of Colonialism* (New York: Columbia University Press, 1996); Jonathan Schneer, *London 1900: The Imperial Metropolis* (New Haven: Yale University Press, 1999).

18 Edward Said, *Culture and Imperialism* (London: Chatto & Windus, 1993), p. xii.

19 Raymond Williams, *The Country and the City* (Oxford and New York: Oxford University Press, 1973). See also his discussion of Modernism in *The Politics of Modernism: Against the New Conformists*, ed. Tony Pinkney (London: Verso, 1989).

example, not merely in the widespread preoccupation with decline, invasion and internal collapse, but also in the nostalgic fascination, formally registered, with closed systems and patterned geometric structures, as in the overarching mythic frameworks of James Joyce's *Ulysses* or T. S. Eliot's *The Waste Land* (1922). By deploying their myth systems in these texts, it is as if the writers were attempting to assert at a formal, metatextual level certainties that were crumbling in the real world. As social hierarchies, too, came increasingly under threat, as centre and periphery were in danger of being tumbled about, as Yeats's 'The Second Coming' (1920) anticipates, aesthetic form offered to writers like Eliot and Yeats compensatory distinctions, divisions and structures through which to order chaos.[20]

Indicatively, Bram Stoker's *fin-de-siècle* novel *Dracula* (1897), which represents Britain under the threat of invasion by eastern European forces that debilitate its men and penetrate its women, too, can be read as the outpouring of an imperialism which feels itself to be overstretched and insecure.[21] Although not generally recognised as Modernist, Stoker's novel, that ur-text of vampire fiction, published in the same year as 'Recessional', is equally, even classically, a nationalist introjection of anxieties about excessive geographic expansion, as well as, of course, about the miscegenation or racial mixing that such expansion might occasion. The narrative is also formally, and again indicatively, densely structured, a choreographed mix of first-person accounts and eye-witness reportage which has the effect at one and the same time of seeming to diversify the threat of the bloodsucking Dracula, even while also gradually closing in upon him from all sides.

With an eye on *Dracula*'s prescient symbols, the aim in the rest of this essay is to examine in more detail how Modernist writing, which is generally seen as introverted and aesthetically circumscribed in relation to, say, the Victorian realist novel, responded to the shocks and revelations of empire. Remembering Schreiner's pessimistic vision of fatal claustrophobia on the veldt, how did the relationship between culture and empire in the period *circa* 1900–20 express itself, through which images and structures? In particular, I will suggest, it is in its characteristic truncations of form, and splits and disruptions of narrative language, as much as in its preoccupation with systems, that the writing of this period reverberates both discordantly and creatively with the echoes of 'darkness'. Moreover, this impact is demonstrated not

[20] W. B. Yeats, *The Collected Poems*, ed. Richard J. Finneran (London: Macmillan, 1993), p. 187.

[21] Bram Stoker, *Dracula*, ed. Maud Ellman (Oxford University Press, 1996). See also Rod Edmond, 'Degeneration in Imperialist and Modernist Discourse', in Howard Booth and Nigel Rigby, eds., *Modernism and Empire* (Manchester University Press, 2000), pp. 39–63.

only in these disruptions themselves, but also in how they ramify globally. Across the expanding cities of the increasingly interconnected imperial world, the fragment, with all that it signified of irresolution and incertitude, was proliferating as the expressive mode of choice. Modernist writing registered the innovating presence of immigrants like Pound, Eliot and Mansfield to the metropolis, as Raymond Williams acknowledges, yet insofar as it was also manifested, even if in embryonic form, in Sydney, Calcutta and Rio de Janeiro, for example, it was also a globally 'efflorescent' phenomenon.[22]

Like the imperial railway, which became a network of exchange and trade wherever it was established, so, too, the collage poem or the 'mythic method' might be adapted to suit local structures of feeling. Across the Empire fragmented, recognisably Modernist forms registered how the apparent viability of other cultures, once declared savage or obsolete, had everywhere brought the elevated values and vocabularies of the civilising mission into crisis (as demonstrated, too, in the new anthropology of Edward Tyler or J. G. Frazer, among others). Across the Empire, native intellectuals and thinkers, the Indian poet and seer Aurobindo Ghose, the African activists and writers J. E. Casely-Hayford and Solomon T. Plaatje, used layered, multi-voiced, typically 'Modernist' styles to appeal to their different social and political constituencies, native and non-native. Through the medium of these forms they reflected upon their divided sense of themselves while at the same time working to retrieve and restore their own cultural myths and legends. In the early years of the twentieth century, eclecticism and cultural mixing, again significantly, became the keynotes of the formal poetry of the Caribbean Claude McKay as of the Bengal art movement led by Rabindranath Tagore and Sister Nivedita. Taking into account these different modes of Modernist response in different colonial spaces, it then becomes possible to speak of a *world Modernism* as a simultaneous, layered and uneven combination of developments, with moments of emergence here and periods of retraction and abeyance there.[23] In effect, the whole combination can be seen as a tangled skein of creative trajectories, all preoccupied, however, with the collapse of cultural and spiritual certainty and the rise of an atomising modernity right the way across the colonial world. That said, it is important to remember that such appeals to otherness, and negotiations between colonial and native systems, as well as the structural

[22] See Elleke Boehmer, *Colonial and Postcolonial Literature: Migrant Metaphors*, rev. edn (Oxford University Press, 2004), p. 130; Tom Standage, *The Victorian Internet; The Remarkable Story of the Telegraph* (Weidenfeld and Nicolson, 1998).

[23] See Patrick Williams's useful essay, 'Theorising Modernism and Empire', in Booth and Rigby, eds., *Modernism and Empire*, pp. 13–38.

admissions of doubt on the part of European and American writers, were by and large contained within the epistemological systems of the West. After all, settler and native intellectuals and artists tended to be educated in colonial schools and colleges. So, while writers may have cited the carvings, chants, cicatrices and ceremonies of the native by way of challenging their own cultural assumptions, the threat that these represented was ultimately either elided or recuperated back into European frameworks of reference – frameworks over which the rational, Enlightenment self presided. Symptomatically, the shard of Sanskrit that appears at the end of *The Waste Land*, although it seems to shadow forth the presence of another cultural universe, ultimately becomes, within the context of the whole poem, only a fragment among other fragments, self-consciously quoted as one of its many cosmopolitan voices.[24]

As this implies, Modernism's characteristic multi-voicedness, even if viewed as globally diversified, is simultaneously a demonstration of the new cultural relativity of the period, *and* a powerful means of reconciling the Empire's newly emergent subjectivities within the controlling sphere of the aesthetic. So the 'many voices' of *The Waste Land* are ultimately contained within the framework of a poem of structured fragments, and the hieratic poetic authority which informs it, by analogy with how the implied shape of a guitar, say, organises the newspaper cut-outs of a Cubist work of art. So, too, Virginia Woolf, like her colleagues James Joyce and Eliot, approached the problem of representing the numinous envelope of subjective consciousness, and of intersubjective relationship in particular, structurally, by moving her narrative focus rapidly between and through different streams-of-consciousness. In novels like *Mrs Dalloway* (1924) or *The Waves* (1931), characters in interaction emerge as so many intertwined thought-fragments, where none is more authoritative or conclusive than the other. Ultimately, however, these seemingly random intercuttings are gathered together into the resolving shape of the work of art, that hard, crystalline structure that for Woolf subtends the cotton wool of day-to-day perception.[25]

Significantly, Virginia Woolf's vision of the changing state of Britain, and its crises in national and imperial confidence, was profoundly informed by her husband Leonard's disillusioning imperial experience as a colonial officer in Ceylon, as well as by her family's Raj connections. Memories of empire, 'of India, or even Ceylon', like characters with imperial experience – Peter Walsh,

[24] T. S. Eliot, *The Complete Poems and Plays* (London: Faber & Faber, 1969), p. 75.

[25] Virginia Woolf, *Mrs Dalloway* (Harmondsworth: Penguin, 1982); *The Waves*, ed. Kate Flint (Harmondsworth: Penguin, 1992); and 'A Sketch of the Past' in *Moments of Being* (Harmondsworth: Penguin, 1976).

Percival – have the habit of irrupting, at times almost at random, into the train of thought or action of Woolf's narrative, like so many permanently disruptive reagents.[26] In harmony with Leonard Woolf's deepening anti-imperialism, empire in Virginia Woolf is almost invariably associated with self-delusion, moral bewilderment and a sense of incipient failure. In Leonard Woolf's own profoundly Conradian short story, 'Pearls and Swine' (1921), as in his novel, *The Village in the Jungle* (1913), the white man in the colonies is tellingly represented as out of place and morally adrift.[27] Social order in both texts relentlessly descends into entropy despite the colonial state's presiding authority. Here it is worth noting that, political differences aside, Leonard Woolf's conviction that all that stood between the colonial ruler and total disorder were the structures of administrative hierarchy was one he shared with Kipling, as in stories like 'The Conversion of Aurelian McGoggin' or 'His Chance in Life'.[28]

As an enactment of relativity – whether cultural, religious or otherwise – the many-voiced narrative or poem thus manifested in effect as another type of inconclusiveness: it refused to offer a final meaning, a conclusive utterance. A similar open-endedness – of the nature of those 'inconclusive experiences' associated with Marlow's mode of narration in *Heart of Darkness* – characterises the short stories of not only Kipling but Katherine Mansfield, too. Interestingly, both Kipling and Mansfield, though otherwise so divergent in taste and perspective, evoked the strangeness and partial inadmissibility of their colonial experience by drawing on journalistic and snapshot techniques they had developed living by their pens as jobbing writers in the imperial capital. Inconclusiveness, disjunction and suggestiveness appear in Mansfield stories like 'A Dill Pickle' or 'The Garden Party' as a means of translating her cultural and psychic displacement, as they do in Kipling's 'The Madness of Private Ortheris', for example.[29]

In conclusion, it is appropriate to turn back to that picture of Modernism-within-empire evoked earlier, that is, of early twentieth-century Modernist writing not only as an aesthetic and cultural product of empire, but as itself a globally constellated phenomenon. As he intimates in 'Recessional' and 'His Chance in Life', as elsewhere in his work, it was Kipling's fear and fascination that the colonial project would 'loose wild tongues' to flout British moral

[26] See Woolf, *Mrs Dalloway*, pp. 195–6.

[27] Leonard Woolf, 'Pearls and Swine', in *Stories of the East* (London: Hogarth Press, 1921); and *The Village in the Jungle* (London: Hogarth Press, 1961).

[28] See Rudyard Kipling, *Plain Tales from the Hills*, ed. Andrew Rutherford (Oxford University Press, 1987), pp. 59–64 and 81–5, respectively.

[29] Katherine Mansfield, *The Collected Short Stories* (Harmondsworth: Penguin, 1982); Kipling, *Plain Tales from the Hills*, pp. 207–14.

precepts because it taught 'lesser breeds' language (as Prospero does Caliban). The ironic outcome of educating the native was to shift the axes of the stable colonial world. His xenophobia aside, Kipling was right in surmising this insofar as one of the fundamental transformations of modern British culture in the early decades of the twentieth century was brought about through the involvement and input of native artists and writers. When, from the 1910s onwards, colonial writers began appropriating the English language and metropolitan forms to express their own cultural points of view, modern art and writing became, literally, multi-voiced. 'Settlers' like Mansfield and Jean Rhys, and Indian, Caribbean and African authors like Mulk Raj Anand, Claude McKay, Aimé Cesaire, Solomon Plaatje and others, subversively perforated English literature with the quixotic hesitations and recalcitrant gaps of their intentionally incomplete translations of their cultural worlds. As Edward Said writes, colonised peoples took over received forms and used them 'to assert their own identity and the existence of their own history'.[30] To reuse and remake an aesthetic mode that itself claimed to be 'making new', or to be 'doing many voices', was both to enact plurality, and powerfully to upset conventional ideas of cultural authority.

With regard to this potential of the imperial 'other' to disturb the centre, it is significant, finally, how many imperial returnees and human relics of empire, as well as characters who have 'gone native', wander through the pages of Modernist narrative. Conrad's Kurtz and Almayer, R. L. Stevenson's Wiltshire in 'The Beach of Falesa' (1892), Leonard Woolf's White in 'Pearls and Swine', even Lawrence's Mellors in *Lady Chatterley's Lover* (1928), appear as uncomfortable reminders of the enticing and destructive other worlds which colonialism had opened to the West. Like the jagged inconclusiveness of the Modernist fragment itself, they stand as indices of the irreversible historical changes that the imperium had visited even upon its rulers.

[30] Said, *Culture and Imperialism*, p. xii.

4

The gender of modernity

ANN L. ARDIS

'Modernity' is a relatively new term in literary scholarship on the turn of the twentieth century.[1] Sociologists organise their research around issues of 'modernisation' unique to this period: the Taylorisation of industrial production, the professionalisation of science and the organisation of the modern research university, the development of new mediums and media for both mass transportation and mass communication, and the impact on the conceptualisation of a public sphere of women's and non-whites' advocacy for an extension of the rights of citizenship to previously excluded populations. Sociologists focus as well on the 'dramatic transformations of worldviews and philosophies' encompassed by the still broader term 'modernity' (290). By contrast, literary scholars typically have mapped late nineteenth- and early twentieth-century history in terms of a neat, clean and emphatically teleological succession of literary movements, charting a 'progress' from realism to either naturalism or aestheticism and Decadence and then to Modernism. Rather than entertaining the possibility that these aesthetic modes can exist simultaneously in the same text,[2] or that they were produced and marketed for different audiences throughout this period,[3] the emphasis until quite recently has been placed on

[1] As noted in Rita Felski, 'Afterword', in Ann L. Ardis and Leslie W. Lewis, eds., *Women's Experience of Modernity, 1875–1945* (Baltimore and London: Johns Hopkins University Press, 2002), p. 290. Further references given in parenthesis in the text.

[2] For an excellent overview of such arguments, see Lynne Hapgood and Nancy L. Paxton's 'Introduction' to *Outside Modernism: In Pursuit of the English Novel, 1900–30* (London: Macmillan; New York: St Martin's Press, 2000).

[3] See Kevin J. H. Dettmar and Stephen Watt, eds., *Marketing Modernism: Self-Promotion, Canonization, Rereading* (Ann Arbor: University of Michigan Press, 1996); Joseph Kelly, *Our Joyce: From Outcast to Icon* (Austin: University of Texas Press, 1998); Gail McDonald, *Learning to Be Modern: Pound, Eliot, and the American University* (Oxford University Press, 1993); Lawrence Rainey, *Institutions of Modernism: Literary Elites and Public Culture* (New Haven: Yale University Press, 1998); Ian Willison, Warwick Gould and Warren Chernaik, eds., *Modernist Writers and the Marketplace* (London: Macmillan; New York: St Martin's Press, 1996); and Joyce Piell Wexler, *Who Paid for Modernism? Art, Money, and the Fiction of Conrad, Joyce, and Lawrence* (Fayetteville: University of Arkansas Press, 1997).

literary Modernism's success in 'extricat[ing] itself and our epoch from the *fin de siècle*'.[4] That is to say, artists and literary critics claiming Modernism to be *the* aesthetic of modernity first established its position front-and-centre in the cultural landscape by putting other aesthetic paradigms either 'behind' it or 'below' it (or both).

Rather than merely displacing such literary periodisation, scholarship's recent turn towards a focus both on Modernism's relationship to modernity and on the gender of modernity[5] is exposing what Raymond Williams has termed 'the machinery of selective tradition', by means of which a 'highly selected version of the modern' comes to stand in 'for the whole of modernity'.[6] How must our conceptualisation of the early history of literary Modernism change as we explore its deep and complex entanglements in *fin-de-siècle* cultural debates rather than reproducing its moves to 'extricate' itself from them? What has been hidden from history both through an exclusive appreciation of formally self-conscious, experimental and anti-mimetic writing and through Modernism's classic 'narrative[s] of rupture'?[7] How would our understanding of modernity be changed if, for example, 'feminine phenomena, which are often seen as having a secondary or marginal status, were given a central importance in the analysis of the culture of modernity?'[8] What is 'the narrative function of "the modern" in our collective histories', and how might this change as scholarship begins to tell 'an entirely different kind of story', a story written 'outside the terms and tropes of the so-called "Great Divide" [between] Modernist high seriousness and everyday life?'[9] Questions such as these, which now animate turn-of-the-twentieth-century studies, position literary Modernism as one aspect – but only one aspect – of modernity. They fuel recovery work on specific authors obscured from the historical record as literary Modernism claimed aesthetic hegemony. And they fuel work on the early history of English studies as a discipline. It is with the latter that this

4 'Extricate' is Hugh Kenner's phrasing, as used in *The Pound Era* to explain how this monumental study was to function (*The Pound Era* (Berkeley and Los Angeles: University of California Press, 1971), p. xi).

5 'The gender of modernity' is Rita Felski's phrase, as used first in her important book by that title (Cambridge, MA: Harvard University Press, 1995).

6 Raymond Williams, *The Politics of Modernism: Against the New Conformists* (London and New York: Verso, 1989), p. 33.

7 Tamar Katz, *Impressionist Subjects: Gender, Interiority, and Modernist Fiction in England* (Champagne–Urbana, IL: University of Illinois Press, 2000), p. 7.

8 Felski, *The Gender of Modernity*, p. 10.

9 Julian Yates, 'Shift Work: Observing Women Observing, 1937–1945', *Women's Experience of Modernity*, p. 272.

chapter begins, for an understanding of the way in which literature and the study of literature were conceptualised in gendered terms at the turn of the century can usefully precede a survey of turn-of-the-century novels, poetry and drama that addresses the gendered dimensions, and contradictions, of 'modern' life.

Bringing English studies to order, 1870–1921

In the mid-nineteenth century, creative writers both enjoyed and exercised a great deal of cultural authority: novelists such as Charles Dickens not only were immensely popular, their cultural commentary also commanded great respect. With the rise of a culture of professionalism, the reorganisation of the human sciences in the 'modern' research university, and the expansion of the education system to reach the entire populace, however, literature's place in the hierarchy of discourses about culture came into question in the closing decades of the century. As Chris Baldick has argued, Matthew Arnold initiated a bold offensive against literature's main competitors – religion, philosophy and science – in the 1860s and 70s by attempting to 'quarantine' science. By characterising science as nothing more than the gathering of data in works such as *Schools and Universities on the Continent* (1868), 'On Poetry' (1879), and 'The Function of Criticism at the Present Time' (1865), Arnold sought to reduce its threat to the cultural authority of humane letters.[10] Faced in the 1880s with the increasing institutional and educational status of science, he went still further. Co-opting the authority of science for humanists in key works such as 'Literature and Science' (1882), for example, he counters claims that the 'modern' university's curriculum should be centred on training in science by characterising all 'genuine' humanism as 'scientific'. The chief limitation of work in the natural sciences, he insists, is its willingness to ignore what he terms 'the facts' of human nature, specifically 'our instinct' for 'beauty' and 'conduct'.[11]

Arnold's insistence on the cultural authority of the arts, the scientific method of humanistic study and the universality of aesthetic value are largely unacknowledged but nonetheless profound influences on the work of influential

[10] Chris Baldick, *The Social Mission of English Criticism, 1848–1932* (Oxford: Clarendon Press, 1983), p. 41.

[11] Matthew Arnold, 'Literature and Science' (1882); as rpt. in Miriam Allot and Robert H. Super, eds., *Matthew Arnold* (Oxford University Press, 1986), pp. 459, 471.

Modernist artist–critics such as Ezra Pound and T. S. Eliot, both of whom played key roles not only in promoting literary Modernism but in establishing 'the frontiers of literary criticism' in the early twentieth century.[12] In spite of the fact that Eliot, for example, was vehemently opposed to Arnold's secular humanism, both Eliot and Pound employ Arnoldian scientific conceits extensively in manifestoes such as 'The Serious Artist' and 'Tradition and the Individual Talent' to articulate the cultural value of 'serious' art – and to distinguish it, with absolute confidence, from the reading matter enjoyed by what Pound terms 'the half-educated simpering general', that is, the newly (and, as far as he's concerned, inadequately) literate populace in Britain created after the 1870 Education Act and the establishment of board schools, workingmen's institutes and women's colleges.[13] Arnold's influence over the New Critics who secured the credibility of both literary Modernism and English studies in the 1930s and 40s is equally profound. What disguises this intellectual continuity, obscures it in the face of much more obvious and striking differences, is the gendered rhetoric by means of which English was 'fashion[ed]' into a 'serious' discipline at the turn of the twentieth century.[14]

Terry Eagleton's account of this disciplinary history in *Literary Theory: An Introduction* is still one of the best. As he notes, English as an academic subject in England was first institutionalised not at Oxford and Cambridge but in the Mechanics' Institutes, working men's colleges and extension lecture circuits. 'English was literally the poor man's Classics – a way of providing a cheapish liberal education for those beyond the charmed circles of public school and Oxbridge' (27). The rise of English studies in England ran parallel as well to the 'gradual, grudging admission of women' to higher education: 'since English was an untaxing sort of affair, concerned with the finer feelings rather than with the more virile topics of *bona fide* academic "disciplines"', it was a 'convenient sort of non-topic to palm off on the ladies, who were in any case excluded from science and the professions' (28).

But if English as a discipline of study was initially feminised, it quickly acquired a masculine character as it was put to use in the service of empire and charged with exemplifying 'the human spirit concealed and revealed in

[12] Michael Coyle, *Ezra Pound, Popular Genres, and the Discourse of Culture* (University Park: Pennsylvania State University Press, 1995), p. 19.

[13] Ezra Pound, 'The New Sculpture', *Egoist*, 1, 4 (16 February 1914), p. 68; as rpt. in Lea Baechler, A. Walton Litz and James Longenbach, eds., *Ezra Pound's Poetry and Prose, Contributions to Periodicals* (New York and London: Garland, 1991), p. 221.

[14] Terry Eagleton, 'The Rise of English Studies', *Literary Theory: An Introduction* (Minneapolis: University of Minnesota Press, 1983), p. 31. Further references given in parenthesis in the text.

a great artist's work'.[15] What came to be at stake in English studies 'was less English *literature* than *English* literature' (Eagleton, 28). A 'new patriotism' was fostered at the turn of the century through the pursuit of English language and literature studies in a movement to transform the curriculum that culminated with the publication of the Newbolt Report in 1921.[16] A key example of this are changes in William Shakespeare's characterisation after the 'crises of sexual identity and male privilege' of the 1890s that culminated in Oscar Wilde's trials in 1895.[17] In the early 1890s, in the context of intense public debates about the circulating libraries' stranglehold on the literary marketplace, Shakespeare was valued as a writer who speaks – more 'candidly' than late Victorian writers could, given the constraints of the literary marketplace – about 'sexual relationship *as it is*', as Thomas Hardy noted.[18] And Shakespeare was known, in some circles at least, as a man of intensely 'bi-social' attachments: a man who loved Willie Hughes *and* the dark lady of the *Sonnets*.[19] By contrast, in influential critical studies published after 1895 such as Georg Brandes's *William Shakespeare* (1898), Sydney Lee's *A Life of William Shakespeare* (1898), and Edmund Gosse's *English Literature: An Illustrated Record* (1903), critical debate about Shakespeare's homo- or hetero-sexuality was erased from the scholarly record and the search for autobiographical information in literary texts was dismissed as 'misinterpretation of Elizabethan publishing transactions'.[20] Functioning as an exemplum of the way in which great works of art rise above the temporal and material specificities of history, Shakespeare was promoted as Britain's highest literary achievement because he 'transmute[s] his personal

15 Georg Brandes, *William Shakespeare* (London: William Heinemann, 1898), p. 1.

16 Stephen Ball, Alex Kenny and David Gardner, 'Literacy, Politics, and the Teaching of English', in Ivor Goodson and Peter Medway, eds., *Bringing English to Order: The History and Politics of a School Subject* (New York, London, and Philadelphia: Faber Press, 1990), p. 52. Other excellent sources on this topic include: Robin Morgan, 'The Englishness of English Teaching', *Bringing English to Order*, pp. 187–241; Brian Doyle, 'The Invention of English', in Robert Colls and Phillip Dodd, eds., *Englishness: Politics and Culture, 1880–1920* (London: Croom Helm, 1986), pp. 89–115; Doyle, *English and Englishness* (London and New York: Routledge, 1989); and Janet Batsleer, Tony Davies, Rebecca O'Rourke and Chris Weedon, eds., *Rewriting English: Cultural Politics of Gender and Class* (London and New York: Methuen, 1985), pp. 13–40.

17 Richard Dellamora, *Masculine Desire: The Sexual Politics of Victorian Aestheticism* (Chapel Hill: University of North Carolina Press, 1990), p. 217.

18 Thomas Hardy, 'Candour in English Fiction', *New Review*, 2 (1890), pp. 15–21, 20, emphasis added.

19 Margaret Stetz, 'The Bi-Social Oscar Wilde and "Modern" Women', *Nineteenth-Century Literature*, 55, 4 (2001), pp. 515–37.

20 Sydney Lee, *A Life of William Shakespeare: A Critical Study* (London: Macmillan, 1898), p. 92. For further discussion, see Ardis, 'Inventing Literary Tradition, Ghosting Oscar Wilde and the Victorian Fin de Siècle', *Modernism and Cultural Conflict, 1880–1922* (Cambridge University Press, 2002), pp. 45–77.

and private agonies into something rich and strange, something universal and impersonal'.[21]

It is on the basis of these kinds of both universalising and highly nationalistic claims that English studies first achieved professional and disciplinary credibility in the early twentieth century. If it was, as Eagleton notes, 'desperately unclear' in the early 1920s 'why English was worth studying at all', by the early 1930s 'it had become a question of why it was worth wasting your time on anything else': 'English was not only a subject worth studying, but *the* supremely civilizing pursuit, the spiritual essence of the social formation' (31). It was not 'just one discipline among many but the most central subject of all, immeasurably superior to law, science, politics, philosophy, or history'; it was 'less an academic subject than a spiritual exploration coterminous with the fate of civilization itself' (32). In launching *Scrutiny* in 1932, F. R. and Q. D. Leavis launched not a journal but a 'moral and cultural crusade':

> its adherents would go out to the schools and universities to do battle there, nurturing through the study of literature the kind of rich, complex, mature, discriminating, morally serious responses . . . which would equip individuals to survive in a mechanized society of trashy romances, alienated labour, banal advertisements and vulgarizing mass media. (33)

That Eagleton's list of the low-brow cultural forms against which *Scrutiny*'s crusaders set themselves to battling begins with 'trashy romances' is telling. As this passage suggests and as scholars such as Suzanne Clark, Bruce Robbins and Antony Easthope have argued, the study of literature was professionalised through the articulation of proper methods and objects of study – and the latter's differentiation from what it is not, namely 'trashy romances': popular, low-brow forms enjoyed by the *female* 'half-educated simpering general [public]' (to paraphrase Pound).[22] Although in many other regards the Modernist avant-garde and the first generations of professional literary critics are direct and obvious inheritors of an Arnoldian project of arts education, the hostile, hyper-heterosexualised rhetoric with which they constructed their domain of expertise distinguishes their defence of the arts from that of the

[21] T. S. Eliot, 'Tradition and the Individual Talent', *Selected Essays of T. S. Eliot* (New York: Harcourt, Brace & World, 1964), p. 117.

[22] Suzanne Clark, *Sentimental Modernism: Women Writers and the Revolution of the Word* (Bloomington and Indianapolis: Indiana University Press, 1991), Bruce Robbins, *Intellectuals: Aesthetics, Politics, and Academics* (Minneapolis: University of Minnesota Press, 1990), Robbins, *Secular Vocations: Intellectuals, Professionalism, and Culture* (London and New York: Verso, 1993) and Antony Easthope, *Literary Into Cultural Studies* (London and New York: Routledge, 1991).

Victorians. The edge and the energy in their sexualised rants against 'effeminate' art (e.g., *fin-de-siècle* aestheticism) and a feminised mass culture, together with their dismissive characterisations of writing by women as 'sentimental' ('indifferent to intellectuality' was John Crowe Ransom's phrasing),[23] registers their anxious defensiveness about the cultural work and value of literature and the study of the literature in the face of fragmentations of the public sphere much severer than anything Arnold had anticipated.

It is with an interest in charting turn-of-the-century literary history with what might be termed 'a-Modernist' co-ordinates, then, that this chapter will now survey those writings depicting women's experience of modernity that were never 'filtered through the sieve of those definitions of the literary which emerged with the development of institutionalised literary studies in the twentieth century'.[24]

'Woman's experience' and the literary marketplace, 1880–1914

'Woman's experience' was an important rallying cry for women – both advocates of social reform and defenders of the Victorian status quo – at the turn of the century. It was a means of making an enormous variety of claims both for and against women's right of access to the public world: as voters, as paid labourers and professionals, as political activists functioning in a (feminist or black counter-) public sphere, as both the subject and the creators of high-, low- and middle-brow art. At the same time, however, 'woman's experience' was also a source of great divisiveness among women, as such claims about the universality of 'woman's experience' unravelled to reveal the biases and ideological investments of their proponents. The focus here will be on the way this cultural debate played out in the literary marketplace.

When Olive Schreiner published her first novel, *The Story of an African Farm*, in 1883, the circulating libraries dominated the literary marketplace. Literary production and distribution were both fairly tightly controlled and contained by what George Moore, in his three-penny pamphlet *Literature at Nurse; or Circulating Morals* (1885), would lambaste as 'the illiterate censorship' of the circulating libraries.[25] A symposium on 'Candour in English

23 John Crowe Ransom, 'The Poet as Woman', *Southern Review*, 2 (Spring 1937), pp. 783–806, 784.
24 Lynn Pykett, *Engendering Fictions: The English Novel in the Early Twentieth Century* (London: Edward Arnold, 1995), p. 5.
25 George Moore, *Literature at Nurse; or, Circulating Morals*, ed. Pierre Coustillas (Sussex: Harvester Press, 1976), p. 32.

Fiction' published by the *New Review* in 1890 exemplifies this vein of criticism: '[T]he magazine in particular and the circulating library in general', Thomas Hardy complains, 'do not foster the growth of the novel which reflects and reveals life.' As a result of the circulating libraries' 'censorship of prudery', he goes on to note, contemporary fiction cannot rise to the heights of tragedy, 'lest we should fright the ladies out of their wits' with 'the crash of broken commandments' (18). The novel as a form can be made 'honest' once again, he warns, only if it can be allowed to end with something other than 'the regulation finish that "they married and were happy ever after"' (17); it will rise among the hierarchy of art forms only when it is allowed to portray real tragedy: 'catastrophes based on sexual relationship as it is' (17).

In 1885, 195 three-volume novels were published by Mudie's Select Library and circulated to a quarter of a million readers. By 1895 the number of triple-deckers had dwindled to fifty-two, the circulating libraries no longer controlled the literary marketplace, single-volume novels had replaced the triple-decker as the standard format for longer fiction, the short story was emerging as a distinct genre, and a number of other factors were altering considerably the relations among authors, publishers and readers. The increasingly frequent use and effectiveness of literary agents in brokering contracts, and the Society of Authors' efforts to professionalise / unionise gave established writers (if not those attempting to break into the market) new means of advocacy. Both changes in international copyright law and the establishment of any number of new venues for publication (publishing firms as well as journals) were also altering the dynamics of competition among publishers fairly significantly.[26]

As Margaret Stetz has argued, an upstart young publisher such as John Lane was more than willing, in the early 1890s, to turn a neat profit on his 'stable' (his term) of women writers, whom he introduced to the reading public in *The Yellow Book* and through the Bodley Head Press's 'Keynotes' fiction series (which was named after the first volume of short stories published under his imprint by George Egerton (Mary Chavelita Dunne)).[27] W. H. Heinemann and T. Fisher Unwin were similarly eager to risk associating themselves as publishers with the literary controversies of the day as they sought to lure

[26] Guinevere Griest, *Mudie's Circulating Library and the Victorian Novel* (Bloomington and London: Indiana University Press, 1970), p. 208. See also Peter Keating, *The Haunted Study: A Social History of the English Novel, 1875–1914* (London: Secker & Warburg, 1989); John Sutherland, *Victorian Novelists and Publishers* (London: Athlone Press, 1976); and Joseph McAleer, *Popular Reading and Publishing in Britain, 1914–50* (Oxford: Clarendon Press, 1992).

[27] Margaret D. Stetz and Mark Samuels Lasner, *England in the 1890s: Literary Publishing at the Bodley Head* (Washington, DC: Georgetown University Press, 1990), pp. 39–42.

authors and readers alike away from established publishing houses such as Smith, Elder, John Murray, George Bentley and Macmillan's. In his autobiography, Grant Richards, for example, notes with admiration that Sarah Grand (Frances Elizabeth McFall)'s *The Heavenly Twins* (1893) was 'an abominably printed three-volume novel that no one could read in comfort' before Heinemann 'took it over' and 'link[ed] it up with the cause of revolting women, an equal moral law for both sexes, social purity, the Contagious Diseases Act and all that kind of stuff'.[28] Although many of the most venerable Victorian publishing firms continued to wield considerable power well into the early twentieth century, they did so by mimicking the acquisition and marketing practices of these new firms rather than by operating as conservative forces in the literary marketplace. Not unlike Lane and Heinemann, they took significant risks on unknown writers; they brokered equally effectively the perceived needs and interests of both an increasingly literate populace and the literary establishment's counter-moves to preserve the autonomy and authority of a non-commercialised sphere of high culture.[29]

Gaye Tuchman and Nina Fortin have argued that women were 'edged out' of the literary marketplace at the end of the nineteenth century. While their findings certainly hold true for Macmillan's, the publishing firm whose records they have mined so very thoroughly and carefully, their conclusion does not hold more generally. 'Woman's experience' was a rallying cry for both experimentation with literary form in the 1880s and early 1890s and expansion of the literary marketplace – and women as well as men were able to take advantage of the public's willingness to engage 'The Woman Question' in literary as well as political venues.

Fifteen years ago, the body of scholarship on 'New Women' – that is, women who challenged both the conventions of Victorian sexual ideology and the orthodoxies of the marriage plot in a variety of ways and for a variety of reasons – was extremely limited. Moreover, it made extremely limited claims about her role in turn-of-the-twentieth-century literary and cultural history. Since 1990, however, the Victorian *fin de siècle* has emerged as the most exciting arena

[28] Grant Richards, *Author Hunting, by an Old Literary Sports Man* (New York: McCann, 1934), p. 143.

[29] As Anthea Trodd notes, 'in the Edwardian period and thereafter publishers were torn between two particular models for their relations with their writers. One was that of the traditional paternalist, who nurtured his stable of talent, exemplified by John Murray's hopes for Rose Macaulay . . . The other model was that of the risk-taker backing a hunch on an unknown writer, as Fisher Unwin did when they gambled on the often rejected manuscript of Ethel M. Dell's *The Way of an Eagle* (1912)' (*Women's Writing in English: Britain 1900–1945* (London and New York: Longman, 1998), p. 33). See also Ian Norrie, *Mumby: Publishing and Bookselling in the Twentieth Century*, 6th edn (London: Bell & Hyman, 1982).

of study within Victorian studies, and the New Woman has been recognised once again as a central figure in turn-of-the-twentieth-century debates about gender, race, class, national identity and the 'progress' of modernity. Scholars draw attention now not only to the sheer volume of writing by and about women during this period but also to its aesthetic diversity and its ideological and thematic heterogeneity.

More than one hundred novels were published at the turn of the century on the New Woman. Some of these novels were by established writers such as Grant Allen, Rhoda Broughton, George Gissing, Thomas Hardy, Iota (Kathleen Mannington Caffyn), Henry James, D. H. Lawrence, Eliza Lynn Linton, George Moore, Mark Rutherford (William Hale White), H. G. Wells and Virginia Woolf.[30] Other writers either made a splashy entrance into the literary marketplace with their short stories and novels about New Women or saw their sales and literary reputations crest in this context. Among the latter would be writers such as Mona Caird, Mary Cholmondeley, Victoria Cross (Vivian Cory), Ella D'Arcy, Gertrude Dix, Ella Hepworth Dixon, Menie Muriel Dowie, George Egerton, Sarah Grand (Frances Elizabeth McFall), Violet Hunt, Arabella Kenealy, Dorothy Leighton, George Paston (Emily Morse Symonds), C. E. Raimond (Elizabeth Robins), Olive Schreiner, Evelyn Sharp, Netta Syrett, John Strange Winter (Henrietta Strange) and Mabel Wotton.[31]

The aesthetic diversity of New Woman fiction is a point of emphasis in current scholarship. On the one hand, a writer such as George Egerton 'found the proto-Modernist form of the short story, with its focus on individual psychological "moments", a useful vehicle for giving a voice to that *terra incognita* of womanhood which had arguably yet to be described'. On the other hand, a writer such as Olive Schreiner 'used a multitude of literary forms – the political tract, the realist novel, the allegory, the dream and the utopia – to give voice to her feminism'.[32] Most New Woman writers, however, simply turned the conventions of traditional narrative realism inside out, so to speak. Rather than promoting the stylistic experimentalism of literary Modernism or working in a range of genres, they challenged Victorian novelistic conventions of plotting

[30] As this list suggests, 'high-brow' and 'low-brow' popular novelists were equally engaged in and by the literary and social debate about New Women. As I have argued in *New Women, New Novels: Feminism and Early Modernism* (New Brunswick, NJ: Rutgers University Press, 1990), New Women writings ignore the high/low culture 'divide' in interesting ways.

[31] See *New Women, New Novels*, pp. 205–12, and Ann Heilmann, *New Woman Fiction: Women Writing First-Wave Feminism* (London: Macmillan, and New York: St Martin's Press, 2000), pp. xi–xviii, for useful bibliographies.

[32] Sally Ledger, *The New Woman: Fiction and Feminism at the Fin de Siècle* (Manchester University Press, 1997), p. 181.

and characterisation without questioning linguistic representationalism in any fundamental way. Thus, while some scholars have yoked the recovery of turn-of-the-century feminist writers to the prehistory of literary Modernism, others have argued for the importance of their contribution to realist traditions. As Sally Ledger has emphasised, for example, narrative realism was a far more effective vehicle for social critique at the turn of the century than we have typically credited it with being.

The ideological heterogeneity of these short stories and novels is another point of emphasis in current scholarship on the period. Some New Woman writings foreground issues of sexuality and offer a critique of Victorian marital conventions. Others focus largely on the professional ambitions of middle-class women, inviting readers to imagine that daughters of educated men (to borrow Virginia Woolf's phrasing) can and should have a right to pursue non-domestic vocations. Still others set even more ambitious social agendas, attempting to reimagine gender, class and race relations in England and the broader world. Brief discussion of several examples of each of these three thematic foci will provide a sense of the ideological range at play here.

George Egerton's *Keynotes* (1893), Sarah Grand's *The Heavenly Twins* (1893), and Grant Allen's *The Woman Who Did* (1895) were centre-stage in heated public debates about New Woman writers' presentation of sexual passion as the 'main-spring' of human action.[33] The protagonist of Egerton's short story, 'A Cross Line', daydreams about dancing on an ancient stage, arms 'clasped with jewelled snakes', and 'hundreds of [male] faces upturned towards her' in the amphitheatre – and she dismisses her lover quite unceremoniously once she realises she is pregnant (though we never learn whether the child is his or her husband's). While Grand's heroine scandalised bourgeois society by critiquing male sexual hedonism, Allen's violated convention by entering into a 'free union' – a non-marital but nonetheless monogamous heterosexual relationship. These and other New Woman writings about sexuality not only sparked extensive debate in the periodical literature. They also prompted other writers to provide counter-examples of New Womanly behaviour. Allen's heroine, for example, refuses to marry her lover for fear that a legal tie would change the character of their relationship. By contrast, the heroine of Lucas Cleeve (Adelina G. I. Kingscote)'s *The Woman Who Wouldn't* (1895) is a bride who refuses to have sex with her husband because she does not want to confuse spiritual love with physical passion. 'If one young girl is kept from a

[33] James Ashcroft Noble, 'The Fiction of Sexuality', *Contemporary Review*, 67 (1895), pp. 135–49, 493.

loveless, mistaken marriage, if one frivolous nature is checked in her career of flirtation by the remembrance of Lady Morris [her heroine], I shall perhaps be forgiven by the public for raising my feeble voice in answer to "The Woman Who Did"', Cleeve writes in her preface.[34] Within months of the publication of both these texts, Victoria Cross provided yet another counter-representation of the New Woman's sexuality in *The Woman Who Didn't* (1895). While intertextuality this overt is somewhat unusual among New Woman writings, the point to emphasise here is that the treatment of sexuality in these works is quite diverse: while some New Woman writers celebrated women's 'discovery' of their sexual and/or maternal desires, others were social purity campaigners, valuing chastity within as well as external to marriage.

Still other New Woman writers critique compulsory heterosexuality as it was deployed by late Victorians to curtail female ambition, challenging Victorian readers to allow women to realise their professional ambitions, not their erotic fantasies. Novels such as Mary Cholmondeley's *Red Pottage* (1899), Gertrude Dix's *The Image-Breakers* (1900), and Edith Johnstone's *A Sunless Heart* (1894), for example, provide their female protagonists with both a male romantic interest and a passionate female friendship. These woman-centred friendships initially seem to be peripheral to the main plot; ultimately, however, they displace the central male/female dynamic of the novels. For it is their female friends, not their male lovers, who endorse these New Women's efforts to reject traditional gender-based divisions of labour, providing them with the encouragement and emotional support that sustains them as they seek to establish themselves as, respectively, writers, political activists and visual artists. In each of these novels, sexuality is not contained in private relationships. Instead, given the encouragement provided by other women, women commit themselves – passionately – to women's rights activism, to socialism, to art, to all manner of behaviour once deemed 'unwomanly' and 'sterilising'. The energy that Victorian society would have these women channel into private life is redirected into a wide range of cultural activities.

The criticisms of Victorian cultural conventions offered in novels such as the above is notably limited, however, in comparison with the broader challenges to class and race as well as gender ideologies developed by a New Woman writer such as Olive Schreiner. As Carolyn Burdett has suggested, Schreiner's feminist critique of modernity was a 'road not taken' by either most of her contemporaries or later feminists.[35] Emphasising points of substantial

[34] Lucas Cleeve, *The Woman Who Wouldn't* (London: Simpkin, Marshall, 1895), p. vi.

[35] Carolyn Burdett, *Olive Schreiner and the Progress of Feminism: Evolution, Gender, Empire* (Basingstoke: Palgrave, 2001). Further references given in parenthesis in the text.

contention rather than consensus among *fin-de-siècle* feminists, Burdett describes Schreiner as one of the most significant figures in the 'Woman Debate' at the turn of the twentieth century because, as a British citizen born in South Africa, 'she increasingly understood, and sought to represent, the connections between the anticipatory claims being made by middle-class women in the "dominant" West, and the impact on the peoples elsewhere of that domination (particularly in the form of imperialism)' (6). Unlike many of her feminist contemporaries, Schreiner never universalises female experience. Instead, works such as the allegorical *Trooper Peter Halket of Mashonaland* (1897) and the non-fiction essays on Boer life she wrote after her return to South Africa in the early 1890s are increasingly sensitive to the 'cost' of modernity for non-white, non-English populations. 'More and more strongly', Burdett argues, Schreiner 'came to see the issue of women's emancipation as inseparable from that of colonization, as both are bound together in a larger question about the nature and meaning of progress in the modern world' (114).

Whether or not other New Woman writers followed Schreiner's lead in this regard, all of the writers mentioned above believed in the cultural work of fiction. That is, they viewed the aesthetic realm as an integral component of the political and economic order, not as a separate and subordinate sphere. And they wrote a multiplicity of stories about 'modern' women that 'opened up a gynocentric space in culture and literature for the discursive interrogation and experimentation with new female subjectivities' (Heilmann, 195).

It would be wrong, however, to assume that all women writing at the turn of the twentieth century were always or necessarily proffering their challenges to Victorian gender ideology in the name of feminism. As Talia Schaffer and Kathy Psomiades argue in the 'Introduction' to *Women and British Aestheticism*, for example, current historical recovery work focused on New Woman writing 'often seems to include all of the women writers of the period'. Yet in actuality it 'tends to discuss only those with strong feminist or political credentials. This selection effect drastically skews our sense of the period, for it tacitly ignores the majority of late-Victorian women writers whose writing does not fit twentieth-century activist criteria.'[36] The latter includes writers such as Alice Meynell, E. Nesbit, Gertrude Jekyll, Lucas Malet (Mary St Leger Kingsley Harrison), Ada Leverson, Vernon Lee (Violet Paget), Marie Corelli, Graham R. Tomson (Rosamund Marriott Watson), Sarojini Naidu, Laurence Hope (Adela Nicolson) and Michael Field (Katherine Bradley and Edith Cooper), all

[36] Talia Schaffer and Kathy Psomiades, 'Introduction', *Women and British Aestheticism* (Charlottesville and London: University of Virginia Press, 1999), p. 15.

of whom found fascinating ways to manipulate the discourses of aestheticism to explore art's relationship to commodity culture, to experiment with the representation / articulation of non-normative sexuality and to critique male aesthetes' conduct towards women. Working in fiction, poetry and a multiplicity of non-fiction prose genres aimed at both 'high' and 'low' audiences (the advice-book, travel literature, garden writing and the scholarly essay) and employing 'a variety of experimental literary styles', women aesthetes 'constitute an impressive group of women writers who enjoyed strong sales and critical acclaim' (16).

Critical reception of both New Woman writing and female aestheticism was varied, as one might imagine. At one end of the spectrum, critics such as Edmund Gosse praised the innovations of New Woman writers as a fortunate fall. In *Questions at Issue* (1893), he writes: 'The public has eaten of the apple of knowledge and will not be satisfied with mere marionettes. Whatever comes next, we cannot return, in serious novels, to the inanities and impossibilities of the old well-made plot, to . . . the madonna-heroine, and the god-like hero, to the impossible virtues and melodramatic vices.' Fiction, he goes on to announce with satisfaction, 'has taken its place among the arts'.[37] At the other end of the spectrum lie comments such as the following by the *Athenaeum*'s editors, who viewed the new 'candour in English fiction' with great scepticism in their 'Year in Review' essay for 1893: 'Not so very many years ago Mr George Moore was the only novelist in England who insisted on the novelist's right to be true to life, even when life is unpleasant and immoral; and he was attacked on all sides. Now every literary lady is "realistic", and everybody says, "How clever! how charming!"' In the context of the scandals of 1895 centred around Oscar Wilde's trials, such sarcasm intensified into outright condemnation: 'Women's pictures, women's plays, women's books. What is it that makes them temporarily so successful, and eternally so wanting?' A. G. P. Sykes complains in the *Westminster Review*. Writing for *Blackwood's* in June of 1895, Hugh E. M. Stufield blames not only women writers but also male aesthetes and decadents for the recent 'degeneration' of British literature and culture. Although most of his article, 'Tommyrotics', focuses on 'the wom[en] of the new Ibsenite neuropathic school', his carefully curt references to both Wilde's trials and the homosexual subculture of the 1890s link women writers with 'the true inwardness' (read homoeroticism or sexual 'invertedness') of modern aesthetic Hellenism – and associate both with what yet another conservative reviewer terms the 'socio-literary portents' of 'anarchy' in *fin-de-siècle* British literature

[37] Edmund Gosse, *Questions at Issue* (London: W. Heinemann, 1893), p. 22.

and culture.[38] In certain limited regards, the conservative backlash that both produced and followed Wilde's trials actually created new opportunities for women writers and artists. As Stetz and Mark Samuels Lasner have noted, for example, John Lane's decision to fire Aubrey Beardsley as *The Yellow Book*'s chief illustrator in the wake of Wilde's trials in 1895 offered women illustrators and writers a chance to step into that vacuum.[39] For the most part, however, women writers were discredited and disenfranchised by what Sally Ledger has termed 'the reaction formation' that supported the promotion of literary Modernism to a position of cultural centrality.[40] The wagons of high culture were circled so as not to include either feminised/effeminate literary productions or the women who, as Henry James suggests to William Dean Howells, recently seem to have 'taken universal possession' of the literary marketplace.[41] James's phrasing of his concerns in 'The Future of the Novel' is more subtle than William Courtney's in *The Feminine Note in Fiction* (1904) or Harold Williams's in *Modern English Writers* (1925), but his point is the same: the cultural legitimacy of literature, of the novel in particular, was very much perceived to be at risk in the late 1890s, and was to be reclaimed only by rising 'above' the social and political controversies associated with Wildean Decadence and New Women.

The impact of this conservative backlash on women playwrights was also considerable. While Henrik Ibsen's work was initially a *cause célèbre* for women such as Janet Achurch and Elizabeth Robins, women playwrights were often disappointed by their difficulties in finding financial support for original productions and by conservative critical responses to their work. While recovery efforts of contemporary feminist scholars are unearthing fascinating details about the lives and professional theatrical careers of women such as Achurch, Elizabeth Baker, Githa Sowerby and Cecily Hamilton, it is also the case that we are learning more about the theatrical careers of women such as Robins and Netta Syrett, both of whom *quit* writing plays for West End theatres and turned either to other genres or to other venues of production when confronted by the hostility of critics and West End theatre stage-manager/producers.[42]

38 'The Year in Review', *Athenaeum* (6 January 1894), pp. 17–18; A. G. P. Sykes, 'The Evolution of the Sex', *Westminster Review*, 143 (1895), p. 397; Hugh E. M. Stutfield, 'Tommyrotics', *Blackwood's*, 157 (1895), p. 833.

39 Stetz and Samuels Lasner, *England in the 1890s*, pp. 57–8.

40 Ledger, *The New Woman*, p. 179.

41 Henry James, 'The Future of the Novel', in Leon Edel, ed., *The Future of the Novel* (New York: Vintage, 1956), p. 40.

42 For further discussion of Robins and Syrett, see Kerry Powell, *Women and Victorian Theatre* (Cambridge University Press, 1997). On Robins, see also Penny Farfan, 'From *Hedda Gabler* to *Votes for Women*: Elizabeth Robins's Early Feminist Critique of Ibsen', *Theatre Journal*, 48, 1 (March 1996), pp. 59–78; Joanna Gates, *Elizabeth Robins, 1862–1951:*

Again, though, rather than simply find evidence in this of the ways in which women were edged out of the literary marketplace in the backlash against 'tommyrotics' that followed in the wake of Wilde's trials, I would emphasise women's resourcefulness in finding new ways to carve out careers for themselves as writers. Not unlike Thomas Hardy, who abandoned the novel and devoted his energy exclusively to poetry after *Jude the Obscure* was reviewed so scathingly in the months following Wilde's trials, Robins, for example, turned first to alternative theatre and then to street theatre and novel-writing in the context of the Edwardian suffrage campaign. Sarah Grand's career follows a similar trajectory: having been stage-centre of the cultural and literary debate about New Woman fiction in the early 1890s, she focused her time and energy after 1898 on feminist political activism rather than fiction- or play-writing. Other women whose writing careers had flourished in the midst of the social and literary controversies of the early nineties turned different corners in their writing lives at the century's end. After publishing a number of novels in the 1890s, George Paston turned her hand to writing non-fiction, mainly on the eighteenth century, after 1900. Known for her wonderfully witty parodies of Wilde and aestheticism during the 1890s, Ada Leverson published only fiction after 1900, pushing the envelope of the middle-brow 'women's novel' to include all manner of unconventional behaviour – but doing so without engaging in the edgy oppositional politics practised by both late Victorian male aesthetes and the Modernist avant-garde. She kept company in this regard with Netta Syrett, who returned to fiction-writing late in the first decade of the new century, but had also worked below the critics' radar screen, so to speak, for more than five years, publishing only children's fiction and historical popularisations after Clement Scott, the influential reviewer for the *Daily Telegraph*, trashed her play *The Finding of Nancy* (1902) on the basis of its allegedly autobiographical sexual content. Not unlike the aspiring young science writer Beatrix Potter – who wasn't allowed to present her research to the Linnaean Society but found success redirecting her skills as a naturalist in writing for children – Syrett found the undervalued field of children's literature a fertile ground for her creative efforts until she could once again make novel-writing 'a sure thing'.[43] In spite, then, of the increasing conservatism of the critical establishment, women found success in a variety of aesthetic modes and venues of literary

Actress, Novelist, Feminist (Tuscaloosa, AL: University of Alabama Press, 1994). See also Katherine E. Kelly, ed., *Modern Drama by Women 1880s–1930s: An International Anthology* (London and New York: Routledge, 1996); and William W. Demastes and Katherine E. Kelly, eds., *British Playwrights, 1880–1956: A Research and Production Sourcebook* (Westport, CT, and London: Greenwood Press, 1996).

43 Netta Syrett, *The Sheltering Tree* (London: G. Bles, 1939), p. 119.

and cultural production as they negotiated the 'rhetorics of sexuality and the "modern" in a changing world'.[44]

Of special interest in this regard are women's innovative collaborations at the turn of the twentieth century: their co-authorship under male pseudonyms; their efforts to facilitate other writers' efforts through their work as editors of periodicals and independent presses; and their establishment of a feminist counter-public sphere in the context of the Edwardian suffrage campaign. As Holly Laird and Bette London have argued, the writing careers of authors such as Michael Field (Katherine Bradley and Edith Cooper), Somerville and Ross (Edith Somerville and Violet Martin), E. D. Gerard (Emily and Dorothy Gerard) and Mary and Jane Findlater present unique challenges for contemporary scholars committed to feminist recovery work. Laird notes: 'greatness in art, which has long been largely contingent on single, identifiable authorship, carries inconsistent but all the more powerful associations with innate, semidivine genius and with a democratic ideal of noble, free individualism'. And yet, despite 'an increasingly entrenched mythology of solitary authorship', collaboration 'persisted in the nineteenth and twentieth centuries' – and even 'became more common at the turn of the century'. It has, however, rarely 'been acclaimed and rarely earned both partners equal honor'.[45] While early feminist scholarship contributed to rather than challenged this dis-valuation of collaborative writing, scholars such as Laird and London are now inviting us to expand our appreciation of women's writing practices to include the 'contradictory legacies' (Laird's phrasing) of turn-of-the-century women's co-authors: their 'risky, self-compromising, though occasionally thrilling struggle for identity (for name and fame)'; their 'still undecided battle with the Romantic myth of single, canonized (male) authorship' (93); and their efforts (especially in the case of the aesthete Michael Field) to gain control of the material production of their work.

Attention is given elsewhere in this volume to the impact of women editors on the production and marketing of literary Modernism. It is with consideration of the efforts of women to establish and sustain a feminist counter-public sphere through the alternative publishing venues associated with the women's suffrage campaign that this chapter concludes.

44 Claire Buck, '"This Other Eden": Homoeroticism and the Great War in the Early Poetry of H. D. and Radclyffe Hall', *Women's Experience of Modernity*, p. 77.

45 Holly Laird, *Women Coauthors* (Urbana and Chicago: University of Illinois Press, 2000), p. 85. Further references given in parenthesis in the text. See also Bette London, *Writing Double: Women's Literary Partnerships* (Ithaca and London: Cornell University Press, 1999), pp. 91–118.

As scholars such as Wendy Mulford, Barbara Green and Lisa Tickner have discussed at length, the semi-underground economy of woman-centred literary production and reception sustained during the Edwardian suffrage campaign by organisations such as the Women Writers' Suffrage League, the Women's Social and Political Union (WSPU), the National Union of Women's Suffrage Societies (NUWSS) and independent publishers operated completely outside of the literary mainstream. Entirely without benefit of institutionally based evaluative practices (e.g., reviews in mainstream periodicals, influential works of literary criticism, school curricula), suffrage campaigners deployed creative writing as well as non-fiction prose in their efforts to educate a broad range of readers. Plays, masques, farces, short fiction, novels, poetry: all manner of literary materials were produced and displayed in suffrage shops alongside essays, pamphlets and other non-fiction texts produced by the WSPU, the NUWSS and independent publishers. Not unlike the way in which H. D.'s poetry and fiction circulated in an activist women's community long before her work was reclaimed by academic feminism and made available again commercially, suffrage literature played 'a significant role in the developing politicisation of women'.[46] As Kate Flint has argued, it 'created and consolidated a community of women readers, who could refer to these works as proofs of their psychological, social, and ideological difference from men', and who viewed their reading of literary works as both an impetus for and a major component of their social and political activism.[47]

The fact that literary critics writing today concern themselves mainly with the appreciation and evaluation of the individual text, and the individual great writer's work, makes it easy to ignore the historical impact of the suffrage writers, whose texts are arguably less impressive individually than in the aggregate, as Mulford notes. The point to emphasise here as well, though, is that, in tandem with turn-of-the-century socialists such as Robert Blatchford (editor of the *Clarion* and author of bestselling novels such as *Merrie England*), H. M. Hyndman and A. R. Orage (editor of the *New Age*), suffrage writers resisted the rarification of the aesthetic sphere and the professionalisation of literary study that the Modernists better known to us today – though problematically identified as 'representative' early twentieth-century figures – were quite anxiously promoting in an effort to secure the cultural authority of both a particular literary aesthetic and the discipline of English studies.

[46] Wendy Mulford, 'Socialist–Feminist Criticism: a Case Study, Women's Suffrage and Literature, 1906–1914', in Peter Widdowson, ed., *Re-Reading English* (London: Methuen, 1982), p. 186.

[47] Kate Flint, *The Woman Reader, 1837–1914* (Oxford: Clarendon Press, 1993), p. 305.

Mary Poovey has argued that literary historical recovery work raises thorny theoretical questions: questions that speak to 'our profession's current indecision about the role and nature of literary criticism'; questions that jeopardise 'the foundational claims of our entire discipline'.[48] And she positions archival research on uncanonised women writers antithetically to the work on disciplinary history that she views as taking precedence in the new millennium. This chapter's argument instead has been that archival recovery work and disciplinary self-reflection are most productively pursued simultaneously. In one sense, the goal of studies such as this *History* is to capture, memorialise and lend a sense of permanency to a particular reading of its subject-matter, in this case, twentieth-century history. By contrast, however, one might hope to replace Raymond Williams's mechanistic image of the 'machinery of selective tradition' with a more dynamic modelling of what Rita Felski has termed 'the inevitable partiality of our perspective(s) on the past'. As she suggests in her 'Afterword' to a recent volume on women and modernity, 'the experience of modernity in the late nineteenth and early twentieth century is both uncannily like and uncannily unlike our own' experience of modernity in the new millennium. Felski concludes that '[i]t is out of such a dialectical movement, which simultaneously respects and bridges the otherness of the past', that the most interesting work on the gender of modernity is emerging (298).

[48] Mary Poovey, 'Recovering Ellen Pickering', *Yale Journal of Criticism*, 13, 2 (2000), p. 451.

TWO

*

THE EMERGING AVANT-GARDE

5

Edwardians to Georgians

ROBERT L. CASERIO

King Edward VII's reign is a rebellious era, establishing a libertarian agenda for subsequent decades. 'What [makes] it a new age', writes J. B. Priestley of the Edwardian period, 'is not the . . . conformity it carried over from Victorian England but . . . all the attempts . . . to push forward into a freer atmosphere.' The forward push was enacted by 'rebels from the middle classes' who shared 'a common platform – a belief that . . . society might be rationally transformed',[1] might lead to a socialist state, women's liberation from patriarchy, and dissolution of the Empire. Edwardian writers explored that rebellious common platform.

Priestley emphasises the common platform's rational aims. But the era's writers also liberated passions of the mind and body that did not always co-operate with the goals of rational transformation. Moreover, the writers sought an avant-garde autonomy for art: art's liberty to develop free of responsibility to reflect the world 'realistically'; free even of responsibility to immediate political relevance. That search for autonomy links Edwardian literature with Modernism and with the post-Edwardian Georgians (so called after King George V). Pursuing artistic freedom, Edwardians, Modernists and Georgians experiment with literary forms and genres. They experiment with realism, and they experiment with romance, understood as a contrast to realism and as a marker of art's independence. But that experimentation is not pursued for its own sake exclusively: it refers back, however indirectly, to the Edwardian agenda for change. It is possible to argue that, for Edwardians, Modernists and Georgians, both realism and romance have a libertarian reference; and that for them romance largely promotes empire's dissolution, in contrast to the Victorians' version, which often promoted imperialist adventure.

The Edwardian platform is tied to romance even in John Galsworthy and Arnold Bennett, whose names have been bywords for a photographic realism

[1] J. B. Priestley, *The Edwardians* (New York: Harper & Row, 1970), pp. 84, 108, 89.

that merely records facts. Certainly, Galsworthy's novels and plays apply realism to Edwardian platform issues: husbands' abuse and rape of wives; conflicts between capitalists and unions; inhuman machinery of law. Yet Galsworthy also combines realism and progressivism with anti-realist components. A character in *Fraternity* (1909) is writing 'The Book of Universal Brotherhood', a shadow *Fraternity*. That book within a book reveals England as an abattoir, wherein equality has been slaughtered by individualism, property, and sexual jealousy. The author of 'The Book of Universal Brotherhood', despite being a scientist, is not a realist, but a Blakean visionary. He doubles Galsworthy, whose realism is epiphenomenal upon visionary romance. Galsworthy equates visionary romance in *The Dark Flower* (1913) with erotic passion that undermines bourgeois marriage – and reality itself. 'The dark flower' of passion represents what reality, or what even progressive social order, cannot encompass.

Bennett pairs 'realist' attacks on property and marriage with evocations of desire and liberty that suggest supra-human possibility – and that therefore evoke romance. Of course, Bennett's historical realism, attached to the common platform, is one of his modes. His realist hit play *Milestones* (1912) shows three generations of an English industrial family undergoing historical change; by 1912, the modern father faces his ultimate milestone when the family's women have become feminists who support union organisation against their patriarchs. Bennett's Clayhanger novels (1910–15) include Hilda Lessways's story, and use realism to recover the history of Hilda's struggle for independence as a New Woman, and to underwrite the suffrage movement. There is another Bennett, however, who transcends realism. Hilda Lessways and Edwin Clayhanger's good marriage is damaged by its partners' secret, disjunctive histories. In regard to those disjunctions realism works ambiguously. It reveals the secrets, and fills in the gaps. At the same time, realism, by dedicating fiction to persons or forces that escape documentation, suggests realism's potential – and a potential of political platforms – for remaining permanently distant from truth.

Art's reach therefore must exceed realism. Accordingly, Bennett produces, hand in hand with his realism, works of fantasy or romance. 'The Death of Simon Fuge', in *The Grim Smile of the Five Towns* (1907), is about the late Fuge, an under-appreciated artist who has been, according to rumour, a remarkable sexual adventurer. A London museum curator travels to Fuge's native Five Towns, where the curator meets Fuge's acquaintances, including two sisters the artist is rumoured to have seduced one fabled evening. The curator discovers banal facts behind Fuge's legend; yet he also discovers, in the person of one of the fabled sisters, that banal facts have an uncanny way of restoring 'the empire of romance'. His research thereby puts him in touch with the truth about Fuge's work: although Fuge believed himself to be 'exclusively preoccupied with . . . the authentic', his pictures transform authentic reality into 'the romance of the authentic'.[2] Through Fuge's story Bennett dramatises his own impulse to reinvent realism as romance.

E. M. Forster's work evokes romance in order to criticise oppressive conventions and subvert realism. In *The Longest Journey* (1907) conventional married manhood suffocates Rickie Elliot; just as, he discovers, marriage suffocated his mother. She committed adultery, and bore another son. Rickie discovers in his half-brother (an atheist who contemns marriage) a fearless vitality that has more dignity than any marital relation can bestow. Rickie can see his brother's distinction because Rickie imagines him in mythological or romance terms, in line with stories that Rickie writes and that his wife and brother-in-law scorn for not being 'realistic'. 'Gods and fairies [are] far nearer to reality', Rickie thinks, than anything quotidian.[3] He ecstatically imagines his brother as Pan, and enshrines him in a collection of stories, *Pan Pipes*. Consistent with *The Longest Journey* and *Pan Pipes*, Forster's posthumously published *Maurice* (written in 1913–14), representing male homosexual and inter-class union as an ultimate alternative to bourgeois marriage, locates that union in 'the greenwood', a 'romance wild' suited to Pan.[4]

Forster's inspiration for *Maurice* was Edward Carpenter, an open advocate of homosexuality who helped found the Labour Party. Carpenter came from an older generation of radical intellectuals: Samuel Butler, for one. To begin a survey of Edwardian tradition with Galsworthy, Bennett and Forster is to start in medias res. Fabian socialists in the 1890s initiated Edwardian writing's 'attempts to break away' from the past by founding the Stage Society. The Society desired a venue for commercially non-viable plays, especially because the Fabian George Bernard Shaw's plays – for example, *Mrs Warren's Profession* (1894), wherein the decent rationality of a sex-worker turned madam is presented without censure – were not granted licences for performance. Shaw's *Man and Superman* (1903) typifies the cutting edge of the Stage Society's development. That play rejects Victorian identifications of democracy with 'reform' in favour of permanent revolution in all spheres of life. *Man and Superman* also advances Shaw's experimentation in dramatic genre: the play introduces myth, dream and romance into Shaw's realism, in a way

[2] Arnold Bennett, *The Grim Smile of the Five Towns* (Harmondsworth: Penguin, 1946), pp. 170, 161.

[3] E. M. Forster, *The Longest Journey* (New York: Alfred A. Knopf, 1922), p. 189.

[4] E. M. Forster, *Maurice* (New York: W. W. Norton, 1971), p. 250.

that calls attention to realism as itself an artifice, and identifies truth with fantasy.

The Stage Society set a standard of rebellion for a younger generation of artists. One sees a complement of the Society's aims in the London Rebel Art Centre's circle of writers – Wyndham Lewis, Ezra Pound, Ford Madox Ford, Rebecca West – who in 1914 created the artistic movement called Vorticism, and the journal *Blast*, an epitome of 'all the attempts to push forward into a freer atmosphere'. Literary history classifies *Blast*'s collaborators as Modernists, in contrast with Edwardians; it keeps Galsworthy, Bennett, Shaw, H. G. Wells and even Forster sealed off from the likes of Pound and Lewis. Whatever the usefulness of compartmentalising, even the Rebel Art Centre group did not practise it in the wholesale way of later criticism. West in 1912 celebrates the Edwardian Stage Society playwright, actor and producer Harley Granville Barker as the strongest contemporary exponent of 'fierce refusal to leave things as they are'.[5] That fierce refusal perhaps results from Barker's embrace of romance in tandem with progressive-minded realism. He realistically reproduced a suffrage rally on stage for Elizabeth Robins's *Votes for Women!* (1907); but in his own plays he dissolves realism into an experimental collage of perspectives. His experimentation is complemented by such ventures into romance as his and Laurence Houseman's *Prunella* (1904), and his 'post-Impressionist' production of Shakespeare's *The Winter's Tale* in 1912. Facile oppositions, whether between realism and romance, or between Barker's generation and West's, obscure the substantial as well as temporal convergence of Edwardians and Modernists. Facile oppositions also obscure the convergence of Edwardian Modernists with writers born as far back as the 1830s and 1840s: Thomas Hardy and Henry James.

The younger generation sees in Hardy and James links among progressive platforms, experiments in literary form, and romance modes. Pound's retrospect of Hardy in 1938 celebrates Hardy's critical social conscience in the poetry Hardy published during the Edwardian and Georgian years. Pound joins Hardy with 'H. James': 'they stand together . . . in disgust with the social estimates of their era, in rebellion against the sordid matrimonial customs of England. And between 'em they bred a generation that . . . carried their disbelief into action.'[6] In the light of Pound and the Edwardian platform, Hardy's late novels are social protests more than they are demonstrations of crushing fate. Hardy himself opposed characterisations of his work as pessimistic,

[5] Jane Marcus, ed., *The Young Rebecca: Writings of Rebecca West 1911–17* (London: Macmillan, 1982), p. 20.

[6] Ezra Pound, *Guide to Kulchur* (New York: New Directions, 1938), p. 287.

and insisted (in a 1922 reiteration of his 1911 preface to the Wessex edition of his novels) that his work be considered 'only "questionings" in the exploration of reality, and . . . the first step towards . . . betterment'. For Hardy, poetry's vocation is progressive, and he looked to poetry to reconcile religion and 'complete rationality' by means of poetry's 'breath and finer spirit of all knowledge'.[7]

That finer spirit's ties to the progressive platform do not depend on realism. Neither Hardy's practice nor Pound's is solely realist, any more than Galsworthy, Bennett, or Forster's is. In *The Spirit of Romance* (1910) Pound declared poetry to be a sort of 'inspired mathematics . . . equations for the human emotions'. Most important among emotions for which poetry seeks expression are ecstasy and wonder. Modern poetry's pursuit of prose-like clarity results from 'a sceptical age', which 'hungers after the definite, . . . something it can pretend to believe. The marvelous thing [must be] made plausible.' The plausibility of representations equated with literary realism might fulfil that hunger. But Pound insisted that one way to make the marvellous plausible, and to stir ecstasy, is to heighten thought, so that ecstasy becomes 'a function of . . . intellect'.[8] Vorticism was announced as a mode of passionately apprehended ideas, of ecstatic intellect. Not reality, and not any mere imitation of reality, but ideas about reality, was the purpose of Vorticist poetics. For Pound it was art's forms, abstracting ideas from reality, which opened the gate to ecstasy. The origin of Vorticist ecstasy is Pound's meditation on romance.

If one looks to Hardy from the vantage point of Pound's aesthetics one finds in the older writer a similar bias against realism, and a proto-Modernist advocacy of form. Hardy mocks realism, 'an artificiality . . . which has been assumed in some places to mean copyism, and in others pruriency'. Hardy insists on art as a selective construction that abstracts from fact, and rules over it. 'With an eye to being more truthful than truth (the just aim of Art)', the most devoted realist 'transforms himself' from a mimeticist 'into a technicist' – an impersonal manipulator of representational or structural techniques.[9] Hardy's last novel, *The Well-Beloved* (1897), which Hardy added to the Wessex edition in 1912, and classified as a romance, moves the novelist's representation of marriage and extra-marital sex beyond realism. His romance's technicist construction allows Hardy to satirise copyism; and allows him to handle erotic material that, keeping faith with Edwardian and Modernist rebellion,

[7] *Collected Poems of Thomas Hardy* (New York: Macmillan, 1925), pp. 526, 531.
[8] Ezra Pound, *The Spirit of Romance* (New York: New Directions, 1968), pp. 14–15, 91.
[9] Thomas Hardy, *Life and Art* (New York: Greenberg, 1925), pp. 87, 86.

unsettles differences between promiscuity and 'the world-wide fond superstition' of monogamy.[10]

In enlisting James alongside Hardy for the push forward, Edwardian–Georgian Modernists were obliged to wrestle with fiction's potentially autonomous relation to politics and morality. Pound's case for James's political impact assumed that James's rebellious portrayal of social and national forces required of James an unparalleled 'comprehension of the novel as a "form"'.[11] But James's attention to form appeared increasingly to sink his comprehension of everything else. James's other canonisers, Ford and West, found James apolitical – and amoral; and they accordingly found themselves unsettled as well as admiring. West mocked James's indifference to political or ethical values when she argued that James hadn't noticed that his novel *The Golden Bowl* (1905) was merely 'an ugly . . . story about . . . people who are sexually mad' because technique preoccupied him. Certainly James brought into fiction a belief (shared by many Edwardian platform allies) in heightened intelligence, including intelligent use of art, as an autonomous value, transcending conventional ideas of 'good' and 'bad'. And yet West, despite her mockery, mostly rejoices in James's aesthetic autonomy. James, West declares, is the one triumphant product of 1890s aestheticism, which inspired him to cultivate apolitical, amoral subjects and techniques. One such technique is his formal equivalent for *blessed are the pure in heart*: James, West says, 'demonstrated [that beatitude] in no spirit of moral propaganda, but for the technical reason' that a selfless, relatively impersonal consciousness illuminates a situation better than a self-centred one does.[12]

James's last book of stories, *The Finer Grain* (1910), represents a 'finer grain' of characters, who exemplify James's merger of 'technical reasons' with selfless consciousness. In *The Finer Grain*'s 'The Bench of Desolation', a man suffers because of a woman's breach of promise suit against him. But even while he suffers, the woman is impersonally sacrificing herself to a self-disciplined plot that will save him from suffering. Her plotting allegorises James's 'technicist' art, which requires an impersonal disinterestedness that, submitting life to art's reworking, uses heightened intellection to rescue life from a fallen state. Such rescue, perhaps an instance of Pound's ecstasy fostered by intellect, refers itself to romance as well as to technique. *The Finer Grain* begins with 'The Velvet Glove', a story that opposes identifications of fiction with real life. Real life is fiction's inspiration, it is even a kind of romance; nevertheless, the

[10] Thomas Hardy, *The Well-Beloved* (London: Macmillan, 1975), p. 54.
[11] T. S. Eliot, ed., *Literary Essays of Ezra Pound* (New York: New Directions, 1968), p. 337.
[12] Rebecca West, *Henry James* (London: Nisbet, 1916), pp. 110, 95.

story suggests, fiction is not copyism, but rigorous formal construction – an adventure in the passion of technique, an alternative romance.

James's art borrows from the wonder of romance rather than from the ordinariness of reality so that it can become an autonomous construction. But fiction cannot become autonomous without paying for its liberty. That payment, enacted by James's fine-grained characters, shows sorrow and loss inherent in triumph. The heroine of *The Golden Bowl* wins autonomous agency for herself when out of her passion for her husband she devises a strategy that wins him back from an affair with her stepmother; but she pays for her victory with the loss of her passionately loved father, from whom she must separate permanently. Her passions suffer desolation even as they succeed. In James, passion painfully compromises agency, indeed fetters it. Intelligence and technique as well as agency in James all turn out to be subject to constraint.

James's representation of constrained agency heightened the difficulty his Modernist canonisers felt when recruiting him for politics. Ford met the difficulty by insisting that James's aesthetic disinterestedness is actually a political boon: it provides, Ford says, 'the very matter upon which we shall build the theory of the new body politic'.[13] Ford would have had to make the same claim about his sometime-collaborator Joseph Conrad (with whom Ford co-wrote a science fiction, *The Inheritors* [1901], and a historical novel, *Romance* [1903]). Passion and constrained agency pervade Conrad's work, even though Conrad believes in art's autonomy, and believes literary artists should be, at least in regard to 'technicist' invention, powerful agents. Himself an agent of formal innovations, Conrad develops 'impressionism' (a use of prose to evoke immediacy of sensations in a reader), which he employs alongside Jamesian impersonality of observation, and with a narrative technique that continually disrupts a story's chronological continuity. Conrad uses his new forms to serve both realist and romance modes of fiction. It is the presence of romance in his work that especially resists attempts to enlist Conrad for the Edwardians' 'new body politic'. For Conrad inherited from Victorian fiction a species of romance called 'imperial romance': stories that support imperialism by glorifying British agency at the expense of those foreign 'others' who fall victim to Empire's adventures. Readers argue whether Conrad's *Heart of Darkness* (1902) is ultimately another imperialist romance (like H. Rider Haggard's or John Buchan's) that glamorises empire's runaway agency and superiority; or whether it is a blend of realism and romance that shows the hollowness of

[13] Ford Madox Hueffer, *Henry James* (New York: Boni, 1915), p. 48.

imperialism (in the vein of the explicitly anti-imperialist romancer Robert Louis Stevenson). The answer might lie in Conrad's elevation of passionate suffering, whenever he employs romance, in relation to adventurous agency. By inhibiting the effectiveness of agency in his romances, Conrad tips them towards realism, while still preserving romance conventions (quests for redemption; noble conduct; disguises; startling coincidences); he thereby uses romance to hollow out the pride of agency on which world powers, or would-be world powers, stake their will to domination.

Conrad's *Under Western Eyes* (1911), a realist fiction that is also a dark version of romance adventure, suggests the political moral of constrained agency in Conrad. The story is about terrorist attacks on Russian autocracy; and about a student, Razumov, whose ability to act freely is destroyed when he betrays a terrorist assassin to the police. The police coerce Razumov into disguising himself as a revolutionary who will spy on a nest of terrorists in Geneva. But Razumov the secret agent has little power of action, and never gains more: his life ends as a passion of unrequited suffering – and unrequited love for the assassin's sister, Nathalie. Given the harshness of Razumov's fate, it appears that Conrad's political moral is to point up the equal horrors of Russian imperialism and Eastern terrorism. That appearance gains credibility from the way Conrad's narrator, a liberal English Westerner, presents autocratic empire, terrorism and Razumov's passion as alien, inferior to his own rationality and free agency. But Conrad's experimental narrative structure casts doubt on the narrator's invidious distinctions between East and West, including his distinction between Eastern passion and Western action. Those distinctions serve imperialist perspectives; and the narrator's imperialist cast of mind prevents him from admitting that his own passion for Nathalie binds his story, and his identity, to Razumov's. East and West are factitious constructs. The men are doubles; and Conrad's experimentation with narrative form in *Under Western Eyes* makes it possible for readers to see that the men also are doubles for a 'town peasant' in the story whose fate is controversial: is the peasant (or Razumov, or the narrator) a deliberate political agent surmounting passion, or a figure representing agency's defeat by passion? Conrad's narrative refuses the question's alternatives, for his novel resists the idea that agents or actions can secure liberty by getting an upper hand over passion, or by dividing action from passion. That idea, Conrad suggests, leads to a hypertrophy of action that inspires imperialists and terrorists alike to beat their victims, and their victims' passions, into submission. Politically, then, Conrad arguably is on the side of whatever 'new body politic' will not sacrifice passions to a morbid idealisation of agency. The romance elements Conrad retains in all his fiction – elements that Ford's 1924 memoir of Conrad testifies Conrad could not separate from art, history, politics or life – serve idealism and a quest for liberty, but do not subordinate passions to either.

Readers who want fiction to celebrate political freedom of action will insist on divorcing Conrad from Edwardian–Georgian movements for social transformation. Justifiable as that insistence might be, Conrad's emphasis on passions is continuous with a like emphasis in George Bernard Shaw, who assigns passions a prominence that limits agency; and who requires politics, including the most progressive, to accommodate that limit. At first glance, however, Shaw's experiments with form mask the role of passion in his dramas, and their romance elements as well. Shaw names his experiments 'problem plays', and equates their heightened intellectual aspect with anti-realistic abstraction. A problem play instances 'the resistance of fact and law to human feeling'.[14] Early reviews of Shaw complained that Shaw's 'civic ardour' made him value a dialectic of ideas above emotions or emotional plausibility.[15] Indifferent to such complaints, Shaw estimated 'real' emotion as merely an artefact of theatrical convention. His vocation was to overturn conventions of audience emotional response, as well as of playwriting and acting, in order to undermine capitalist social order.

But even as Shaw undermines conventions regulating emotion, his work values feeling's resistance to fact and law. Shaw presents passionate feeling as a creative outer limit of dialectics. Dialectics regulate only the first acts of the anti-imperialist play *John Bull's Other Island* (1904), Shaw's breakthrough success with the public (and King Edward). In the play's exposition antithetical characters, English and Irish, come to inhabit positions that synthesise their opposed identities. Such synthesised identifications mock national character and nationalist (and religious) antagonisms. Excoriating those antagonisms, Shaw's preface to his play declares there is 'no greater curse to a nation than a nationalist movement' – except imperialism. A recent British massacre of Egyptian Muslims makes Shaw insist that there is 'no more sacred and urgent political duty on earth than the disruption, defeat and suppression of the Empire'.[16] Rational transformation of society cannot proceed without a recognition that nationalism and imperialism mask global capitalism's exploitations.

[14] Bernard Shaw, *Plays Unpleasant* (Harmondsworth: Penguin, 1988), p. 198.
[15] Max Beerbohm, *Around Theatres* (London: Rupert Hart-Davis, 1953), p. 193.
[16] Bernard Shaw, *John Bull's Other Island* and *Major Barbara* (New York: Brentano's, 1908), p. lix.

Yet anti-nationalist, anti-imperialist economic realism, *John Bull's Other Island* concedes, is only a temporary solution.

The play assigns to a minor character, a defrocked Catholic priest, a major visionary statement that protests against capitalism and realism alike. The ex-priest's vision instances a passion for which no current dialectic offers adequate terms. Hence the ex-priest expresses his passion in paradoxes. The note of such paradox was first struck by the romance-mode extravagance of *Man and Superman*'s third act. Characteristically, Shaw's plays bring their rational dialectics (their ecstatic intellection) towards an expression of paradoxical, impersonal passions. In Shaw's address to 'sordid matrimonial customs', *Getting Married: A Disquisitory Play* (1908), the heroine openly avows her promiscuity, as well as her fidelity to her husband. In the course of the play, as she takes a new lover, she falls into a trance, wherein she utters an impersonally passionate monologue about women's baffled place in gender's long history. If marriage is to have a future, it will need to articulate the meaning of her passion better than she can, and better than current revolutionary programmes or dramatised disquisitions can.

Shaw and the Stage Society's rebellious aim for drama was partly inspired by the efforts of W. B. Yeats, Lady Augusta Gregory and J. M. Synge to establish an anti-imperialist Irish national theatre. Yeats's anti-imperialist political motives explain the inspiration he drew from Robert Bridges's verse drama *The Return of Ulysses* (1890). *The Return of Ulysses* is a romance (derived from the archetypal romance, *The Odyssey*) about a man's recovery of his country from imperialists: Penelope's suitors. To overthrow them, Ulysses must mask himself, making improvised theatre his instrumental strategy. Yeats adapts that Ulyssean instrument, transforming traditional dramatic elements – will and action – into 'lyrical and meditative ecstasies', which 'enable . . . us to pass . . . into a deep of the mind that had hitherto been too subtle for habitation'. That deep is an elsewhere of 'vast passions', not a realist's copy of life.[17] The passions staged by Yeats's plays dwarf, and destroy, imperialist agencies. *Cathleen NiHoulihan* (1902) lyricises passionate revolt against empire and quotidian restraint (marriage); *The King's Threshold* (1904), about the aftermath of a king's decision to exile poets from state power, shows that the passion of exile becomes a poet's capacity to laugh at the vulnerability of imperial domination. Yeats's theatre remains in touch with its anti-imperialist roots via a populist impulse, inhering in the Irish vulgate of Yeats and Lady Gregory's plays, and inspiring Yeats's devotion to Synge.

[17] W. B. Yeats, *Essays and Introductions* (New York: Macmillan, 1961), pp. 201, 225, 243.

Yeats's praises Synge's 'living speech', the language of the people, for conveying an 'emotion of multitude' that is derived from social reality.[18] The intensity of Synge's realism shocked Dublin audiences, inciting them to riot in protest. Yet Synge too cuts free from copyism. In his *The Well of the Saints* (1905) a blind couple figures an ecstatic turn inward to a human darkness that shatters the outward world's simple assumptions about what is real. Even the realism of Synge's *The Playboy of the Western World* (1907) attaches itself to romance. The Playboy's fantasies typify the aggression of all Synge's dramas, which employ realist elements in order simultaneously to subvert realism and undermine figures of authority.

Edwardian writing's pursuit of autonomy, its fascination with passions and its generalised rebelliousness are consummated in the Georgian–Modernist *Blast*'s appearance in June 1914. At the same time, Ford's contribution – 'The Saddest Story' (opening chapters of Ford's novel *The Good Soldier* [1915]) – appears to disrupt technicist experiment's alliance with passion, social progress and modes of romance. 'The Saddest Story', about promiscuity and hatred in the lives of 'perfect' couples, claims that real passion is anti-progressive. Eros and aggression, Ford's narrator confesses, hollow out 'the big words, courage, loyalty, honour, constancy' – hallmarks of romance. 'There is nothing to guide us . . . It is all a darkness.'[19] The narrator's 'darkness', possibly satirising James's 'finer grain' of intelligence, also results from Ford's projection onto it of Conrad's disjunctive storytelling. Ford's narrator pulverises straightforwardly intelligible narration, confounding plain readers who expect life, and art, to make sense.

Ford's text points towards history – an unconcluded struggle between Protestantism and Catholicism – as what might make sense of the sexual and moral madness that conjoins Ford's spouses and lovers. But historical sense in Ford is never far from romance. Ford wrote a trilogy of historical novels about Henry VIII and modernity's first attack on marital institutions. In *The Fifth Queen Crowned: A Romance* (1908) Henry's fifth queen Katherine Howard lives amid allegations about her that make it hard to tell history apart from fictive invention: romance in the worst sense. There must be an escape, Ford suggests, from unbridled invention, even if that invention goes by the name of historical reality. An alternative realism is not the solution. Katherine's desire to restore Catholicism in England, in opposition to England's male initiators of modern capitalism, pursues an ideal of civic virtue derived from her Latin

[18] Ibid., pp. 301, 215–16.
[19] Wyndham Lewis, ed., *Blast 1* (Santa Barbara: Black Sparrow Press, 1981), pp. 94, 89.

books about *res publica*. Ford uses Katherine to enlist romance in the sense of 'matter of Rome' to figure the Edwardian platform cause of an ideal anti-capitalist public realm, a *collective* good life that remains out of reach of the modern state.

In *Mr Apollo: A Just Possible Story* (1908) Ford again employs romance as a reform-inspiring alternative to historical realism. In *Mr Apollo* the Greek god Apollo, arriving in contemporary London, condemns English economic injustice; he also criticises a circle of socialists. Ford's brief in his novel is on behalf of art's power to transform the world. Art can do so, apparently, only if it has Apollo's autonomy; only if art can be trusted even when it criticises the socio-political avant-garde. To be sure, in the light of 'The Saddest Story', Ford looks wary of refashioning reality in the names of art and of 'just possible' romance. Yet after *Blast* a reversion to romance, in connection with experimental techniques, is a constant of Ford's career.

There remain two writers of the era who significantly employ and vary romance. Rudyard Kipling's variant, rooted in Victorian imperial adventure, and explicitly distant from the progressive platform, presents an ultimate test case for the political bearings of romance in Edwardian–Georgian–Modernist usage: is the genre an eligible ally for *any* political agenda, but especially for Kipling's (and Buchan's) imperialist one; or does romance's post-Victorian use exhibit a libertarian bias?

Kipling's *Actions and Reactions* (1909) contains stories that nakedly avow the good of the British Empire for colonial peoples, especially in Africa. 'Little Foxes' dramatises an Ethiopian village's happy collaboration between natives and English rulers. The natives, opposing anti-imperialist reformers in Parliament, are insiders, at home with their white men, who are also at home with them; it is the reformers who are suspicious aliens. Democracy is suspect too. Express opposition to it in *Actions and Reactions* appears in 'With the Night Mail', a romance – and a science fiction – set in 2000 AD, when the world is ruled by a small organisation of 'semi-elected' persons who co-ordinate global transport and communication. That co-ordination has supplanted '"autonomous institutions", "local self-government", and the rest of the archaic lumber devised in the past for the confusion of human affairs'.[20]

The politics of 'With the Night Mail' may be distasteful from a progressive Edwardian perspective, but Kipling's technicist treatment of the story compels attention. An account of a night on a nuclear-powered airship, the story is accompanied by Kipling's version of pages from the journal in which the

[20] Rudyard Kipling, *Actions and Reactions* (Garden City, NY: Doubleday, Page, 1915), p. 137.

account appears. Those pages, in various typefaces, predict the collage layouts (inspired by advertising) of *Blast*. Kipling's reactionism thus assumes an avant-garde character, which is facilitated by formal experiments he identifies with fantasy or romance. That experimentation possibly facilitates more. Despite Kipling's projection of imperialism's know-it-all superiority, it is never very clear which side of rule Kipling is on. He has a penchant for becoming a critic of his own side – an outsider after all. In *Actions and Reactions* 'The Puzzler' and 'A Deal in Cotton' subvert imperialist hierarchy. A poem in the collection lambasts the English for being 'undemocratic', and for adjudicating problems by 'hinting' at 'a matter's inwardness', rather than by making openly public decisions.[21] In his historical fictions – for example, in *Rewards and Fairies* (1910) – romance intensifies Kipling's hostility to imperialism, allowing him to recover the lives of colonial subjects whom empire and history have obliterated. Puck in *Rewards and Fairies* is a romance muse applauding wily strategies of subalterns in response to powers that oppress them; he does not much applaud wily conduct at the top of the heap. A story and poem about 'Gloriana', at the start of *Rewards and Fairies*, deflates the Empire.

Kipling's use of romance, or its use of him, instances art's tricky autonomy in relation to realism, or to programmatic purposes, including imperialist ones. Wells's use of romance asserts his independence from realism; but Wells insists that art must not be autonomous, that *Modernist* romance must advance rational social transformation. Wells's insistence suggests his alliance with the Edwardian platform; nevertheless, Wells thought Edwardian radicalism fell short of its aims. Speaking for Wells, a scientist hero in Wells's *Marriage* finds 'the general field of social reform,' including radical political organisations, 'a mere stop-gap . . . There's no clear knowledge – no clear purpose.'[22] Clear purpose for Wells meant a propaganda effort to convert all classes to socialism, hence meant rejecting socialist orthodoxy about inevitable class conflict. Collective responsibility and planning; and collectivity defined as a world community in global, rather than in national, class, party or local terms became Wells's programme in 1906. Dedicating his novels thereafter to his propaganda, Wells attacks Shaw and Kipling for their brands of 'stop-gap' politics, and blasts James and Conrad for thinking art more important than a new world order.

Despite Wells's dissociation from his fellow writers, romance forges similarities between him and them. Like James in 'The Velvet Glove', Wells uses romance as a hinge between an individual's impressions (impressions which

[21] Ibid., p. 209. [22] H. G. Wells, *Marriage* (New York: Duffield, 1912), pp. 420–1.

James, Conrad and Ford constructed as a component of 'realism') and something more objectively 'Real'. *Marriage* formulates that hinge when its scientist writes a manifesto he calls 'From Realism to Reality'. That title describes the trajectory of Wells's fiction, which evokes realism, but then becomes speculative romance in order to express authentic Reality. In Wells's '"scientific romances" or "futurist romances"', Wells experiments formally and thematically with differences between individual impressions and Real knowledge of the world. The hero of *The War in the Air* (1908), Bert Smallways, has a passion for motors and planes, and is an uncritical pro-imperialist patriot. When he unwittingly becomes involved in a German air assault on the towers of Manhattan that begins a world war, Wells's narrator demonstrates a fatal gap between Bert's impressions (decent and likable though Bert is) and the objective, collective Reality to which Bert's delight in machines, and his knee-jerk patriotism, contribute. 'Produced by imperial and international politics',[23] both Bert's sensuous self-centredness and his patriotism turn Bert into an inadvertent agent of global holocaust. To have prevented his fate, Bert should have developed powers of impersonal consciousness and observation that James and Wells, *pace* their differences, use the romance of fiction to model.

Wells's involvement of a new world order with romance modes also brings Wells and Kipling to a point of convergence. Wells complements Kipling's opposition to democracy; that complementarity suggests there might be a more sympathetic collective-minded logic underlying Kipling's stance than at first appears. In Wells's *The World Set Free* (1914), which like *The War in the Air* looks back on history from the twenty-first century, Wells notes that as late as the 1950s, when 'a man could carry about in a handbag an amount of latent [nuclear] energy sufficient to wreck half a city', no collective regulation controlled nuclear arms and nuclear waste. The politics of representative democracy precluded regulation. But when in *The World Set Free* 'the last war' realises an ultimate destruction, new ideas about the body politic emerge. The need for world order supersedes suffrage and rights. '"We'll contrive a way for anyone interested to join in"', says one post-nuclear holocaust thinker: '"That's quite enough in the way of democracy."' '"Lawyers live on rights . . . We've done with that way of living."'[24] What is needed, besides an end to nuclear armaments, is an international economic administration that permits no 'economic disadvantage' to any peoples on the globe, and that facilitates a happy diaspora of the world's multiple cultures. An international organisation will

[23] H. G. Wells, *The War in the Air* (Thirsk, North Yorkshire: House of Stratus, 2002), pp. i, 85.
[24] H. G. Wells, *The Last War* [*The World Set Free*] (Lincoln: University of Nebraska Press, 2001), pp. 61, 89.

supervise that diaspora to counter any return to cultural or religious nationalisms. A similar generous hope about internationalism, one might argue, is encapsulated in the 'semi-elected' committee to promote global communication and transport in 'With the Night Mail'. Although Kipling and Wells are established as antithetical figures in literary history, imperialist artist and anti-imperialist anti-artist, apparently too reactionary and too advanced for a common platform, perhaps they are fellow-travellers on a progressive path laid down by romance.

Unexpected conjunctions characterise the era before the first global war, and during it. One last intermingling of Edwardians, Georgians and Modernists, under the rubric of 'Georgian poetry', is noteworthy. Edward Marsh, Private Secretary to Winston Churchill, co-operated with bookshop owner and poet Harold Monro to publish a semi-annual anthology calling attention to the work of younger writers. *Georgian Poetry*, in five appearances between 1912 and 1922, featured Rupert Brooke, Walter de la Mare, D. H. Lawrence, Robert Graves, Siegfried Sassoon and others. The anthologies seemed in later decades to be antithetical to Modernism, but Lawrence and Graves's place in them suggests no neat opposition. Simultaneous with Lawrence's appearance in *Georgian Poetry*, Lawrence's poems were published alongside Pound's and Ford's in showcases for Imagism, a precursor to Vorticism. And Lawrence the Georgian, like Pound the Vorticist, was inspired by Hardy, to whom Marsh dedicated *Georgian Poetry 1918–1919*.

The technical experiments and the passions of Edwardian–Georgian Modernism saturate Brooke's and Lawrence's careers. Brooke epitomises Edwardian progressivism, and avidly mimes its literary avant-gardism. A Fabian at Cambridge, Brooke starred in undergraduate theatricals, perhaps inspired by Granville Barker's celebrity. Brooke's experimental practice of verse includes his revival, as in his *Georgian Anthology* poem 'Heaven,' of a seventeenth-century metaphysical style that became a hallmark of Modernist taste. His letters express love of Hardy; a wish for companionship with Yeats; and identifications with Forster's characters, with Bennett's Clayhanger, with 'a minor character in a Kipling story,' with Conrad's characters and with Robert Louis Stevenson. 'Romance! Romance!' he exclaims en route to Samoa in 1913.[25]

Lawrence seems less 'literary' than Brooke; yet Lawrence's passions and judgements derive from Edwardian literary radicalism. Two of Lawrence's poems in *Georgian Poetry 1913–1915* become segments of *Look! We Have Come Through!* (1917), a volume that echoes (often in Imagist style) anti-marital,

[25] Edward Marsh, *Rupert Brooke* (New York: Dodd, Mead, 1922), p. 106.

amoral, and anti-nationalist stances of Galsworthy, Forster, Shaw and Wells. And Georgian–Modernist Lawrence furthers Edwardian technicist innovation by subordinating forms of art to what he considered vital passions. His novelty is free verse, which in letters to Marsh Lawrence defends on the ground that life never can be crystallised into regular measures. However, although Lawrence's lyric immediacy expresses antagonism to art's autonomy, *Look! We Have Come Through!* evokes mythological or romance realms wherein Lawrence's real-life passions are impersonally transmuted.

The mythological and romance elements one finds in Lawrence pervade the Georgian anthologies. Marsh, perhaps influenced by Yeats and Pound, selects work which emphasises England as a mythical place or romance landscape. That vague, fairy-tale or romance England in the anthologies adheres to one of Brooke's impulses: on his way to war he said he wanted to write a long poem 'about the existence – and non-locality – of England', an abstract, timeless idea of a nation, rather than a real one.[26] Graves's 'Rocky Acres' in the 1918–19 volume executes Brooke's idea. And when realism arrives in the anthologies – in Graves's and Sassoon's war poetry – their subject-matter is subordinated to an impersonalising formal decorum. Graves's *Fairies and Fusiliers* (1917), from which Marsh reprints poems, juxtaposes realism about misery at the front with poems that refer contemporary war to distant archetypes; and Graves supplements that juxtaposition with lyrics (often in antiquated verse forms) about 'fairy' matters. Refusing to give the front pride of place, or to emphasise novelty or contemporaneity, Graves practises a poet's autonomous sovereignty in his choice of objects and techniques.

But the Edwardian common platform's dedication to progress is missing in Marsh and Graves. Graves and Laura Riding's *A Survey of Modernist Poetry* explains that absence. *A Survey* celebrates Modernism's technical experiments and impersonality, but it rejects the programmatic or platform aspects of Modernism, both political and aesthetic. Even the Georgian anthologies, Graves and Riding say, had a programme: 'Their [the Georgians'] voice should avoid all formally religious, philosophic or improving things in reaction to Victorianism; and all sad, wicked café-table themes in reaction to the 'nineties. It was to be English yet not . . . imperialistic; pantheistic rather than atheistic; and as simple as a child's reading book.' That programme did not succeed: Georgian poetry came rather to 'be praised for what it was not than for what it was'. What it was tied it to its time, as well as to its programme. But neither programmatic ties, nor poets who 'write as a period', Graves and Riding explain, can

[26] Ibid., p. 175.

produce genuine poetry, or genuine Modernists. A poet who believes 'in one way of writing poetry as against another [has] the attitude of a quack rather than a scientist towards [his] art'; and for a poet to write in the service of a programme or platform, no matter how civilised, is for a poet to gainsay originality. 'The Modernist poet' – the one who will keep Modernism alive – 'assumes that his readers owe no trite emotional allegiance to any religious or social or national institution, even that they have emerged from the combative stages of mere "doubt" or "naughtiness" ... [Poetry] is a broader intellectual exercise than before'. It is also a less passionate exercise than before, because it enacts a habitual cynicism about both gloomy and happy possibilities of life. It accompanies that cynicism with self-mockery and 'formal clownishness'.[27] Modernism in Graves and Riding sounds already like Postmodernism.

It is no longer necessary to repudiate aspects of Edwardian or Georgian Modernism as decidedly as Graves and Riding did. It even might be important to recover our ties to an era when progressive collective politics, realist *and* romance modes of writing, formal innovation and unruly passions shared, however uneasily, a liberating agenda. The Edwardian–Georgian–Modernist effort in which Graves participated establishes precisely the assumption, vital to Modernism or Postmodernism, and equally vital to radical platforms, that readers 'owe no trite emotional allegiance to any religious or social or national institution'. Literary art's ecstatic heightening of thought, its liberation of passion and its blurring of oppositions between realism and romance contributed to making that assumption a matter of common agreement.

[27] Robert Graves and Laura Riding, *A Survey of Modernist Poetry* (London: Heinemann, 1929), pp. 119, 155, 117, 199, 229.

6

The avant-garde, bohemia and mainstream culture

TYRUS MILLER

Between the artistic avant-garde and that cultural stratum called, since the 1840s, 'bohemia', there is a historical relationship that is almost self-evident yet difficult precisely to characterise. Both avant-garde and bohemia depend on a stance of separation from the putative mainstream of culture, a conservative, moralising, middle-brow taste of the 'bourgeois', the 'philistine', or 'man in the street'. Both seek programmatically to break down barriers between art and life and to fuse them in a integral aestheticisation of everyday life; this, in turn, should invest art with greater existential intensity than in its traditional forms. Both are marked by ambiguous ties to popular culture and more generally to the commercial market in cultural goods; they appear alternately to repel and invite success in the monetary terms of capitalist societies. Indeed, both appear to have their origins in a particular historical matrix: the broad social front of progressive, oppositional elements of the middle-classes in France up to the 1848 uprisings. This social milieu had aspects of both a political and cultural vanguard, and only later, in the course of the reaction that followed the suppression of the mid-century revolutions, would the avant-garde artist proper precipitate out as a distinct social identity. It is a commonplace of cultural history, and by no means a merely banal one, that the avant-garde and bohemia occupy overlapping cultural spaces and exhibit parallel gestures; that the avant-garde, indeed, emerges in some way within the milieu of bohemia and lends the figure of the bohemian a new, reinvigorating stamp.

Nevertheless, when one seeks to determine more closely the nature of this oft-remarked affinity, the evidence becomes contradictory and confusing. The avant-garde has used its relation to bohemia to define its own identity, and that use involves both identification with bohemia and distinction from it. In general, it has proved difficult to grasp the avant-garde's simultaneous socio-cultural dependency on the existence of a bohemian milieu and its regular impulse to differentiate itself from that milieu in the name of an authentic, serious, innovative and truly revolutionary artistry. Accordingly, from Gustave Flaubert's ironic characterisations of the bohemian milieu in *A Sentimental Education* to Karl Kraus's parodies of Vienna's café literati in *Demolished Literature*, to the parodies of the 'bourgeois bohemia' of modern times in Ezra Pound's *Hugh Selwyn Mauberley* and Wyndham Lewis's *Tarr* and *The Apes of God*, to Gilbert Sorrentino's Postmodernist satire of the New York bohemia of the 1960s in *Imaginative Qualities of Actual Things*, the literary avant-garde has sought to prise itself free from its bohemian shadow, while the avant-garde artist nonetheless exploits as artistic material his intimate, first-hand knowledge of bohemian life. Literary and art historical studies of the English avant-garde movements have, accordingly, linked them to the broader bohemian social and cultural milieu, both as a native presence in London and as an exotic import from Paris. William Wees's ably researched study *Vorticism and the English Avant-Garde* dedicates its early chapters to reconstructing the broader bohemian milieu from the turn of the century on and documents in detail the network of cafés, salons, studios and clubs that germinated and supported avant-garde groups. Wees, moreover, is sensitive to the connections between the artistic coteries of the 1890s, the pre-World War I bohemia of London, and the avant-garde tendencies that had a brief flourishing from about 1910 to 1918. These included the Omega Workshops directed by Roger Fry; the Camden Town group meetings led by Walter Sickert; Ezra Pound's Imagist evenings; the gatherings at Ford Madox Ford's and Violet Hunt's 'South Lodge' villa in Kensington; Ethel Kibblewhite's Soho salon, dominated by T. E. Hulme; Hulme's Tuesday evening lectures and discussions; Stuart Gray's socialist-leaning Ormand Terrace parties; favourite artist restaurants and cafés such as the Sceptre, Bellotti's, the Eiffel Tower, the Dieudonné, the Florence, the Dieppe, the Vienna and various other cafés and teashops; the Rebel Art Centre, headquarters of the secession from the Omega Workshops that Wyndham Lewis had orchestrated; the Poetry Book Shop of Harold Monro; and the Cave of the Golden Calf nightclub, filled with works of Modernist artists and run by Madame Frida Uhl Strindberg, August Strindberg's second wife.[1] Drawing a direct link between the modern artists of London and an earlier Parisian bohemia, Ford Madox Ford referred to the group of rebel artists and writers that assembled at his house as *les jeunes*, alluding to Théophile Gautier's 1833 collection of parodic stories about the extravagances of the young romantics

[1] William C. Wees, *Vorticism and the English Avant-Garde* (University of Toronto Press, 1972), pp. 41–52.

of Paris, *Les Jeunes-France*, a witty riposte to more earnest journalistic attacks on this proto-bohemian milieu.[2]

Wees also insightfully notes the complex relations of mimicry and rivalry towards 'mainstream' commercial culture in the publicity strategies of the rebel artists, which culminated in the loud typography and boisterous rhetoric of the first issue of the Vorticists' journal *Blast*. He suggests that the main dynamics of the avant-garde movements internalised, reworked, and confrontationally exaggerated the ways these movements were (usually hostilely) presented in journalism. In turn, however, they were, in his view, drawn into the same temporality of fashion and obsolescence of all commercialised culture. This dialectic that Wees describes is thus characterised by a paradoxical rupture between avant-garde and journalism and, at the same time, the avant-garde's internalisation of the main features of journalistic culture: its sensational rhetoric, its emphasis on public impact and effect, its ephemerality and need for continual renewal.[3]

Since the appearance of Wees's book in the early 1970s, scholars have devoted considerable theoretical and historical attention to the topics of the avant-garde and of bohemia, as well as to the relationship of these oppositional cultures to mainstream academic and popular cultures. Drawing on earlier work by theorists such as Walter Benjamin, Theodor Adorno and Guy Debord, more recent Marxist critics such as Peter Bürger, Fredric Jameson, T. J. Clark, Andreas Huyssen and Thomas Crow have similarly stressed the strong interdependencies of 'high' and 'low' cultures, avant-garde and popular cultures, though with a new twist. These critics have tended to see in Modernist and avant-garde art an ideologically distorted reflection of that interdependency. The dynamism and innovative energy of the avant-garde, they claim, feeds off of its resistance to a commercialised, popular, 'mainstream' culture. Yet in their view, this very process of differentiation, by which the avant-garde defines itself, also obscures its roots in the same underlying social and political forces that define the mainstream, the political, economic and cultural evolution of bourgeois society. With specific reference to the English avant-garde, art historian David Peters Corbett concurs with this general theoretical conclusion and argues that the radical Modernism that seemed to take hold in English art in the years 1914–18 proved a chimera. Even as radical and critically self-conscious an artist, critic and writer as Wyndham Lewis was, in Corbett's

[2] Ibid., p. 44; Mary Gluck, 'Theorizing the Cultural Roots of the Bohemian Artist', *Modernism/Modernity*, 7, 3 (2000), pp. 366–8.

[3] Wees, *Vorticism*, p. 40.

view, ideologically blindsided by his temporary success as the inspirer and impresario of *Blast*.[4]

Bohemia, as a cultural concept, its ideological and social function in society as a whole, has been subject to a similar critical re-examination. Beginning with César Graña's 1964 study *Bohemian Versus Bourgeois* and continuing in more recent work such as T. J. Clark's study of Courbet, *The Image of the People*, Jerrold Seigel's *Bohemian Paris*, Marilyn R. Brown's *Gypsies and Other Bohemians*, and Mary Gluck's 'Theorizing the Cultural Roots of the Bohemian Artist', scholars have attempted to account for the social roots and function of the bohemian milieu in nineteenth-century French society. Clark's position has been especially influential, and it bears some kinship to a criticism of bohemianism generated from within the avant-garde, that of the later Wyndham Lewis.

In defining bohemia, Clark argues, one must take care to distinguish the mythology of 'la vie de Bohème', elaborated by Henri Murger, Puccini and countless others, and its material reality in the urban life of mid-nineteenth-century Paris. Clark situates this authentic bohemia not among bourgeois students of the Latin quarter, but rather among the *déclassés* composed of indigent, unemployed, often criminal elements who could not be assimilated by the capitalist production system or else had already fallen victim to it. This was a seething, rebellious mob that had a key point of affinity with the intellectuals: their lack of clear social identity, hence lack of definite political representation, within the bourgeois class system. Yet, Clark argues, bohemia was not only a 'social situation', it was a chosen 'life-style', a stylisation of social uselessness in terms of the values of bourgeois society: 'It meant a dogged refusal to abandon the aims of Romanticism, a manic and self-destructive individualism, a "cult of multiple sensation".'[5] The bohemian took up as elements of his lifestyle the values of the once-radical bourgeoisie – especially the value of individual freedom – and turned them, like a utopian mirror, on the actual bourgeois who had betrayed the revolutionary past.

Two things are notable in Clark's account. First is that, parenthetically, he suggests that 'the British variants' of bohemia were failures, presumably because British society lacked a powerful revolutionary past from which to draw critical ammunition against the bourgeoisie of the present. Putting it in a formula, we might say that if Clark identifies bohemia with a socially dangerous

[4] David Peter Corbett, *The Modernity of English Art, 1914–30* (Manchester University Press, 1997), p. 25.

[5] T. J. Clark, *Image of the People: Gustave Courbet and the 1848 Revolution* (Princeton University Press, 1973, 1982), p. 24.

mobilisation of style in mid-nineteenth-century Paris, in the British variant he sees predominantly style and little danger. Second is that Clark divides bohemia in two: a true bohemia, aligned with the dangerous classes and thoroughly withdrawn from bourgeois society; and the false or corrupt bohemia that only wanted to play in the margins for a while, perhaps to return to conventional bourgeois life enriched by elements of style learned in the cultural hothouse of bohemian life. Yet this latter 'false' bohemia is not merely a negative fact for Clark, but rather a key index of how 'popular culture' worked to integrate the new professional classes that rose to prominence in the latter part of the nineteenth century. The sentimentalised involvement of the bourgeoisie in bohemia, mediated through novels, theatre and opera, he implies, is a special instance of a more general process wherein class identities get articulated through culture. In his celebrated study *The Painting of Modern Life*, Clark stages this argument not through a nineteenth-century Parisian example, but, significantly, through T. S. Eliot's 1923 'London Letter', a memorial tribute to the dance-hall comedian and singer Marie Lloyd.[6]

At first glance, the subject-matter of Eliot's essay seems a rather unlikely publication by the poet of *The Waste Land*, written, indeed, in the same *annus mirabilis* as that poem appeared. Yet the particular argument of 'Marie Lloyd' belies this initial improbability. Eliot presents Lloyd as having 'represented and expressed that part of the English nation which has perhaps the greatest vitality and interest', namely, the working class.[7] Eliot briefly alludes to Lloyd's precise acting style and contrasts her to other, more broadly parodic performers such as Nellie Wallace and Little Tich. Yet, as he himself admits, his comments are more 'moral' than 'artistic'; they are no less than a set of reflections on the potential for culture to express and represent a social class as a distinct moral community. If Marie Lloyd therefore is unique – and Eliot at the very outset expresses his surprise in discovering how unique a figure she was – it is not first and foremost because of her artistic talent. It is rather because the middle class and the aristocracy, the other two social groups that might articulate a distinct morality and give rise to a representative artistic figure like Lloyd to express it, have become corrupted. The middle class, he argues, depends for its moral values on the aristocracy, which it mimics poorly. The aristocracy, for its part, is increasingly absorbed into the middle class and is becoming indistinguishable from it, not just in economic, but also in cultural

6 T. J. Clark, *The Painting of Modern Life: Paris in the Art of Manet and His Followers* (Princeton University Press, 1984), pp. 216 ff.

7 T. S. Eliot, 'Marie Lloyd', in *Selected Essays* (New York: Harcourt, Brace, 1932), p. 405.

and moral terms. Even the lower classes are threatened. The cinema, the revue and the technological life-form represented by the motorcar, radio and gramophone will, Eliot suggests, not only lower the level of culture. More consequentially, it will abolish the final residues of distinct class cultures and moralities, a distinction that only persisted in the spontaneous aspirations of the working class to consciously be working-class and not some less well-heeled version of a middle-class, consumer culture. Eliot's conclusion is apocalyptic, and very much in tune with the imagery of infertility and extinction that characterise *The Waste Land*. Citing the psychologist W. H. R. Rivers, from an essay about the depopulation of Melanesia of its native peoples, Eliot postulates that under the influence of an imported and alien Western 'civilization' the population of 'that unfortunate archipelago' lost interest in life and starting dying out 'from pure boredom'. No less a fate may await the last 'primitive' natives of the British Isles, the lower-class audience of Marie Lloyd's performances, along with their declining superiors.[8]

Clark moves back into the nineteenth-century French correlates of Eliot's argument in order to understand how a sentimentalised image of the popular, of which the pseudo-bohemian was another representative, served to solidify the still uncertain identity of an emergent class, the lower professional class of clerks, functionaries, petty bureaucrats: that anonymous, but increasingly numerous class of typists and young men carbuncular, we might, with Eliot, say. Clark, however, turns Eliot on his head. The middle classes' putative identification with popular culture, an identification that Eliot himself is performing with self-conscious ideological ends, is precursor to and path-breaker for that generalised culture industry that Eliot laments. Similarly, the creators of the sentimental myth of bohemia, from Henri Murger on, offer the middle classes a consumable set of stylistic signs of social distinction in place of the genuine risk of true bohemian existence.

Eliot, however, was clearly not one of Clark's petty employees, but rather, for all his occasional masquerade as a humble bank clerk, a Harvard-educated man of letters from a wealthy family, with an impressive philosophical and literary culture and, by 1923, an estimable if small corpus of published works. Nor, despite his occasional forays, could he really be said to be an expert in popular culture in the way that his French contemporary Blaise Cendrars or a present-day writer such as Salman Rushdie genuinely could. It is true that Eliot uses popular culture in this instance to define a particular social role

[8] Ibid., p. 408.

for the intellectual, but it is less to hold out the prospect of social integration than to win ironic distance from the present and its forms of life. Eliot's approach is only in its premise a positive appreciation of the form of popular culture represented and expressed by Lloyd; its real energies are negative, setting in perspective and attacking that form of culture which Lloyd did not represent: the post-war culture industry. Rhetorically, Eliot sets the reigning disarray of cultural value in relief, contrasting the morally noble low culture of Lloyd with the morally base culture that has been embraced by the middle and upper classes. Moreover, insofar as Eliot does positively identify with Lloyd as an artist, he invests her with a very partial set of traits, making her represent a kind of Modernist ethos *in nuce*, despite her particular social location. Her work, he argues, sublimates popular life to a 'kind of art', 'expressing the soul of the people'.[9] She manifests perfection in her acting style, while to the end rejecting the 'money-making' temptation of cinema. Like an imagist poet or a Flaubertian searcher for the *mot juste*, she never stoops to the grotesque, but relies on 'selection and concentration'.[10] With the careful observation of a skilled realist novelist, she knows exactly what a middle-aged charwoman would have in her handbag and finds a perfect tone in which to enumerate its contents to her audience.

Eliot's rhetorically complex placement of the Modernist intellectual in this occasional essay suggests a structure that might be extended more generally to the avant-garde's relation to the bohemian milieu. Bohemia functioned for the avant-garde as a source of style by which it might signal its rejection of middle-class society and its values. Undoubtedly, for instance, the major figures of the avant-garde *were* bohemians in performing this rejection, as Mary Gluck argues, 'through gestures, clothes, lifestyle, and interior decoration . . . by dressing up in outrageous costumes'.[11] We can see this concern with external presentation in Ezra Pound's response in 1915 to James Joyce's request for a photograph of his correspondent, whom he had not yet met in person. Pound writes:

> I solemnly swear that I will someday send you a photograph, at present I am torn between conflicting claims. I have an excessively youthful and deceptive photograph (very rare edition). I have several copies of a photo of a portrait of me, painted by an amiable jew who substituted a good deal of his own face for the gentile parts of my own. I have the seductive and sinister photograph by

[9] Ibid., p. 406. [10] Ibid.

[11] Gluck, 'Theorizing the Cultural Roots of the Bohemian Artist', p. 356.

> Coburn which I expect to have photograved in order to sell my next book of bad poems. It is like a cinque, or quattrocento painting . . . Dante . . . mentions a similar predicament about presenting one's self at a distance. It is my face . . . I enclose, my face as immortalized by vorticist sculpture, which I enclose, this bust is monumental, but it will be no use to the police, it is hieratic, phallic, even, if you will consider the profiles not shown in the photograph. No, I will either, get a new photo, or send you the photogravure in good time.[12]
>
> (35)

Pound refers here to Coburn's fractured cubist photograph of the poet and to Gaudier-Brzeska's Vorticist sculpture of him, for a time set up in the garden of Ford's villa and later transported to Rapallo by Pound. Symptomatically, the bohemian problem of oppositional self-stylisation and the avant-garde forms of artistic abstraction converge in Pound's jovial remarks. But he instinctively identifies the common ground between the two: the 'predicament about presenting one's self at a distance'. Pound intuits that the resources of ironic, critical distance learned amid bohemia can be turned to good professional use by the 'serious artist' (as he would call one of his essays of 1913). In both cases, the expressions of the genuinely individual self, those emotions, passions, angers and loves that exceed middle-class moral norms, are to be 'presented at a distance': controlled through the discipline of style and transformed into the material of art.

Nevertheless, the potential affinity and identification between bohemian and artist also creates the possibility of a dangerous confusion and rivalry. In England, the need to differentiate artist and bohemian was made even more urgent by the association of the bohemian figure with France and with the specifically Francophile and feminised aspect of the English Aestheticist and Symbolist literature and above all, with the popular image of an effete, frivolous Oscar Wilde. Aspirants of the avant-garde, as I have already suggested, also saw it necessary to draw a clear line between themselves, as the virile representatives of true art, and those who were merely playing at being artists in order to enjoy the bohemian lifestyle, often with implications of sexual ambiguity or homosexuality. The cutting-edge of this division was a vehement assertion of professional ethos, rigour of style and form, serious dedication to craft, knowledge of tradition, ostentatious erudition and disenchanted hard work. It could even take the form of an avant-garde, counter-bohemian self-stylisation, an exaggerated code of belonging to an efficient, hard-working,

[12] Forrest Read, ed., *Pound/Joyce: The Letters of Ezra Pound to James Joyce* (New York: New Directions, 1967), p. 35.

sober, technically knowledgeable professional class. As Wees reports, 'In reaction against the Romantic capes and sombreros, a few artists, like the Italian Futurists on their periodic invasions of England, dressed in dark business suits – a mode Wyndham Lewis adopted in 1914, and tried to impose on the artists regularly in attendance at the Rebel Art Center.'[13] One can understand T. S. Eliot's deliberately wan countenance and understated bank clerk's elegance as a similar performative gesture of adherence to non-bohemian norms. Even the normally foppish and extravagant Pound – notorious for his beards, his exaggerated American drawl, his excitability, his earrings and his macaronic sense of evening wear – could play at this game of adopted conventionality, at least formally, as when he suggested that he and Eliot should don the mantle of tradition and return to the discipline of the rhymed quatrain to counter the corruptions of bad imagist *vers libre*. In fact, in his book *Gaudier-Brzeska*, Pound would explicitly state that the old, nineteenth-century social division of bourgeois and bohemian had been replaced by a new professional division: 'We have our segregation amid the men who invent and create, whether it be a discovery of unknown rivers, a solution of engineering, a composition in form, or what you will. // These men stand on one side, and the amorphous and petrified and the copying, stand on the other.'[14] The most essential cleavage, then, gathers together serious professionals such as the scientist, engineer and serious artist, setting them against the drone-like worker, the conservative philistine and the would-be artist content to imitate in order to adopt the artist's 'lifestyle'.

Wyndham Lewis, as the most emphatically avant-gardist of the English writers and artists, was also the most programmatic in his satirical attacks on the confusion of bohemia with art. His early literary sketches and stories, the gallery of grotesquery collected in *The Wild Body*, came out of his experience as an Augustus John-like wanderer in Brittany, an enthusiast of turn-of-the-century British artistic 'gypsies' in search of cheap accommodation, picturesque landscapes and primitive rustic types. His first novel *Tarr*, begun before the outbreak of war and published in 1918, is an even more direct confrontation with the classical bohemia of Paris, though with English and German characters at its centre. In Lewis's bohemian Paris:

> Art is the smell of oil paint, Henri Murger's 'Vie de Bohème,' corduroy trousers, the operatic Italian model. But the poetry, above all, of linseed oil and

[13] Wees, *Vorticism*, p. 38.

[14] Ezra Pound, *Gaudier-Brzeska: A Memoir* (New York: New Directions, 1970), p. 122.

> turpentine. The Knackfus Quarter is given up to Art. == Letters and other things are round the corner. == Its rent is half paid by America. Germany occupies a sensible apartment on the second floor.[15] (21)

At the outset of his novel, thus, Lewis established a contiguity of the English art scene of his own present day, represented by the Lewis-like eponymous artist–hero Tarr, and the now-decadent historical roots of Parisian bohemia in the mid-century fusion of criminal underworld, political radicalism, impoverished intellectuals, immigrants and aspiring artists. In 1920, reviewing Lewis's writing, Ezra Pound discarded even the veil of its fictional setting and read the novel as a direct satire of *London*'s bohemian milieu. Pound claims that though the scene is 'nominally, in Paris', it does not matter whether we take it to be Paris or London. He goes on to say that Lewis's four main characters move

> lit by the fare of restaurants and cafés, against the frowsy background of 'Bourgeois Bohemia', more or less Bloomsbury. There are probably such Bloomsburys in Paris and in every large city.[16]

The value of Lewis's book, as Pound sees, lies not in its 'style', but rather in the very vigour with which it performs its work of differentiating the genuine and the fake artist, of setting apart the serious labour of art from mere bohemian horseplay. 'It *is* due to the fact that we have a highly-energized mind performing a huge act of scavenging', Pound writes, 'cleaning up a great lot of rubbish, cultural, Bohemian, romantico-Tennysonish, arty, societish, gutterish.'[17] This satirical break with bohemia sufficed, it seems, to justify Lewis's book as a serious work of art, despite those technical flaws Pound notes in contrast to Joyce's *Portrait of the Artist as a Young Man*, 'a triumph of actual writing'.[18]

In *Time and Western Man* (1927), Lewis retrospectively took stock of the avant-garde and its cultural environment, from the perspective of over ten years' distance from the heady events leading up to the publication of *Blast* in 1914–15. He filled the first part of this lengthy treatise with attacks on former comrades-in-arms such as Pound ('A Man In Love with the Past') and Joyce ('An Analysis of the Mind of James Joyce'), other Modernist writers ('The Prose-Song of Gertrude Stein'), fashionable popular writers such as Anita Loos, author of

15 Wyndham Lewis, *Tarr: The 1918 Version*, ed. Paul O'Keefe (Santa Rosa, California: Black Sparrow Press, 1990), p. 21.
16 Ezra Pound, 'Wyndham Lewis', in T. S. Eliot, ed., *Literary Essays of Ezra Pound* (London: Faber & Faber, 1954), p. 428.
17 Ibid., p. 429. 18 Ibid., p. 425.

Gentlemen Prefer Blondes, and the silent-film clown Charlie Chaplin. Together, Lewis argued, these figures, however different their talents and specific work, all represented examples of a Modernism that focused on subjective feeling and lived time, breaking down individuality into a flux of uncertain experiences and sensations. He also saw in this tendency a correlative softening of masculinity, a convergence of bodily image upon a soft, androgynous ideal.

Notable in this regard, however, is another chapter included in this opening part of Lewis's treatise: 'The Russian Ballet the Most Perfect Expression of the High-Bohemia'. Lewis saw in Sergei Diaghilev, the producer of the Ballets Russes, the very type of the pseudo-revolutionary exploiter of the arts. Promising the risk and danger of truly innovative art, Diaghilev carefully concocted a mixture of mythicising and fashionable elements in a blend calculated to attract the upper classes. Lewis argues that the early Russian ballet was 'merely archaeological and romantic', the recent work (of the 1920s) cunningly modish:

> All the earlier Russian Ballets consist of reconstructions of the Past and especially of barbaric times, principally Russian or Asiatic. The Ballet, thus, to start with, was a Scott novel, or a Tarzan of the Apes, in a sensuous, spectacular, choreographic form. It had nothing whatever to do with any artistic experiment specifically of the present period. And as to Diagileff's more recent troupes, they reflect, as I have said, that phase of feminism expressed in the gilded Bohemia of the great capitals by the epicene fashion.[19]

Moreover, Lewis links the effeminacy and regressiveness of the Ballet directly to Francophile English artists of the 1890s, against which the avant-garde had directed some of its noisiest rhetoric. In the title manifesto *Blast*, 'THE BRITANNIC AESTHETE / Cream of the snobbish earth' had been blasted 'with expletive of whirlwind,' and shortly after that, the whole period between 1837 and 1900 was blasted.[20] In *Time and Western Man*, Lewis associates the Russian Ballet, the High-Bohemia (an imitative and nostalgic, but well-heeled one) and nineties Decadence: 'The Russian Ballet is the Nineties of Oscar Wilde and Beardsley staged for the High-Bohemia, evolved by the constellations of wars and revolutions of the past ten years.'[21] Moreover, Lewis's analysis was not even a new one among the avant-gardists in his circle. At the time of the original Ballet Russe performances in Britain, Diaghilev had been careful not to alienate more conservative British tastes and, for example, he excluded the ballets of

19 Wyndham Lewis, *Time and Western Man*, ed. Paul Edwards (Santa Rosa: Black Sparrow Press, 1993), p. 33.
20 Wyndham Lewis, ed., *Blast 1* (Santa Rosa: Black Sparrow Press, 1992), pp. 15, 18.
21 Lewis, *Time and Western Man*, p. 33.

Stravinsky from the programme at their British debut in 1911.[22] For their part, the avant-garde had been relatively diffident and only the Bloomsbury circle had shown great enthusiasm. Ezra Pound made fun of the fanfare around the Russian Ballet in his poem 'Les Millwin' (published in *Poetry*, November 1913), which parallels the bland incomprehension of the wealthy Millwin family to the enthusiasm of 'The turbulent and undisciplined host of art students – / The rigorous deputation from 'Slade' [the art school]': 'With arms exalted, with fore-arms / Crossed in great futuristic X's, the art students / Exulted, they beheld the splendours of *Cleopatra*.'[23]

By any standards, Pound's poem is a slight one. Yet the symptomatic value of its satiric juxtapositions, its 'ideogrammic' concatenation of cultural facts 'worthy of record', should not be overlooked. The poem refers to the orientalist exoticism of Michel Fokine's ballet *Cléopâtre*, which had taken Paris by storm in 1909. This success made Diaghilev decide emphatically to follow the exoticist strain of the Ballets Russes at the expense of its neo-Romantic repertoire. In a description of the Paris performance, the Comtesse Anna de Noailles captures something of the lush, symbolistic orientalism of the ballet: 'Everything that could dazzle, intoxicate, seduce, arrest seemed to have been dredged up and brought to the stage to luxuriate there . . . [T]he kings of India and China, . . . appeared in the enormous luxury of palm trees spreading their greenery against indigo skies. Their costumes . . . [were] gold with heavy embroideries.'[24] Notably, however, the rhetoric of the Comtesse's description is not so different from that of another 'dance' poem that Pound had published in *Poetry* eight months earlier than 'Les Millwin', the Swinburnian exercise entitled 'Dance Figure': 'Gilt turquoise and silver are in the place of thy rest. / A brown robe, with threads of gold woven in patterns, hast thou gathered about thee / O Nathat-Ikanaie, "Tree-at-the-river".'[25] One might see this poem as Pound's attempt to move towards an abstraction of subject-matter in a self-reflexive focusing of the poem upon its own metrical patterning: 'There is none like thee among the dancers; / None with swift feet' (91). The vehicle of this metrical abstraction, however, the exotic revelling in Egyptian splendour, the lush sounds and colours, the ostentatious 'oriental' sensuality makes this poem very much an artefact of the same modish cultural milieu as that which would greet *Cléopâtre* with enthusiasm. Though initially pleased with

22 S. I. Grigoriev, *The Diaghilev Ballet, 1909–1929* (London: Penguin, 1960), p. 67.

23 Ezra Pound, 'Les Millwin', in Ezra Pound, *Personae: Collected Shorter Poems* (New York: New Directions, 1971), p. 93.

24 Comtesse Anna de Noailles, quoted in Lynn Garafola, *Diaghilev's Ballets Russes* (Oxford University Press, 1989), p. 46.

25 Pound, 'Dance Figure', in *Personae*, p. 91.

the poem, Pound would ultimately reject in 'Dance Figure' all but its rhythm, its metrical experiment shorn of its uncomfortable similarity to the exotica of the Ballets Russes. Pound still awaited new ways of appropriating the performative energies of the dance for poetry, only finding them later in the static/dynamic tensions of Vorticist art and in the Noh dramas as a model for an extensive, yet allusive poetic form.

Cléopátre came to London first in June 1911. During the début years of the Ballets Russes in England, it was very much a high-society affair, a setting for upper-class display.[26] Yet the taste of this fashionable milieu was still more conservative than its Parisian counterpart, particularly with respect to the more racy, sexual side of performances. As Diaghilev's *régisseur* S. L. Grigoriev notes in his memoir, unlike in Paris, 'It became clear indeed during this season that the London public preferred our romantic ballets to such works as *Cléopâtre* and *Schéhérazade*.'[27] This combination of ruling-class fashion and conservatism, of social power and aesthetic inexpertise, forms the background to Pound's satirical verse 'Les Millwin'. The 'mauve and greenish souls' of the Millwins, Pound writes, lie 'along the upper seats'. Their souls are thus only fashionable clothes, donned and shed according to the occasion; yet at the same time, they are pale and lacking in passion by comparison to either the enthusiastic bohemian art students in the audience or to the bespangled, sensual performers. While the Millwins are putting themselves on display to fashionable society, the art students below are as much a part of the exotic spectacle as the Russian dancers. In fact, with the word 'host' to describe them and the implication of a mass ornament in the figure of the 'great futuristic X' they collectively describe, Pound hints that the bohemian audience is enslaved to the spectacle of the ballet like the Egyptian slaves that serve Cleopatra and Caesar (the Futurists being the new conquerors of the UK coming over the seas from Italy).

In an essay of 12 September 1912, Pound would make explicit that the enthusiasm of the bohemians for such putatively Modernistic and shocking spectacles was, in fact, retrograde. It was not merely that *Cléopâtre* had already had its moment of fashion in France a few years earlier and now came to the UK already a little stale. Rather, Pound suggests, the bohemians' very propensity to enthuse about the Ballets Russes merely repeats in degraded form the reception of French Symbolism by the generation of Wilde, Symons and the young Yeats. This earlier reception, in turn, was fundamentally shaped by late Victorian Aestheticism: 'The Russian dancers present their splendid, luxurious paganism, and everyone with a Pre-Raphaelite or Swinburnian education is

[26] Garafola, *Diaghilev's Ballets Russes*, p. 300. [27] Grigoriev, *The Diaghilev Ballet*, p. 67.

in raptures.'[28] Hence, Pound implies, the 'advanced' taste of the bohemians is, covertly, as recrudescent as that of the scandalised bourgeois sitting in the boxes. The improbable and merely superficial 'francophilia' of the otherwise conservative upper classes, marked by the ridiculous moniker 'Les Millwin' and their wide-eyed surprise at the exotic orgy on the stage and down in the orchestra-pit seats, finds its exact complement of the slavish bohemian enthusiasm of the Slade students. Both 'mainstream' and 'bohemian' culture are thus ironised by the avant-garde poet, who merely registers these 'facts' with bemused distance. Pound sees two ways forward from the degraded Symbolist poetics of the Ballets Russes, two paths for the serious artist to follow in differentiating himself from the merely fashionable postures of the bourgeois and the slavish, but ultimately retrograde enthusiasms of the bohemian. The first is the abandonment of Symbolism for the Vorticist aesthetic: a hardening of the line and form, so that motion becomes captured in terse, spare, intense geometrical patterns. Wyndham Lewis's drawings of the Russian ballet and Kermesse painting could be seen as a step in this direction, but Pound especially sees Gaudier-Brzeska's 'Red Stone Dancer' of 1913 as a significant exemplum of this direction. In 1918, thus, in his preface to the Leicester Galleries memorial exhibition of Gaudier-Brzeska (London, May–June 1918), Pound wrote of the taut interaction between the triangle and the circle in Gaudier-Brzeska's 'Red Stone Dancer'.

> The triangle moves towards organism it becomes a spherical triangle (the central life-form common to both Brzeska and Lewis). These two developed motifs work as themes in a fugue . . . The "abstract" or mathematical bareness of the triangle and circle are fully incarnate, made flesh, full of vitality and of energy. The whole form-series ends, passes into stasis with the circular base or platform.[29]

Gaudier-Brzeska thus shows the way to internalise performative energy as formal tension, which entails both precision of craft and austerity of artistic idiom. Guaranteeing both is the commitment of the serious artist to concentrate all his powers on the intensive perfection of the artwork itself.

The second solution that Pound offers is a more moderate one with respect to tradition and even to the immediate Symbolist past. It represents not so much a rejection of the Symbolist legacy, as a distilled reduction and concentration of it. In connection with W. B. Yeats and with the background of imagist

[28] Pound, quoted in K. K. Ruthven, *A Guide to Ezra Pound's Personae (1926)* (Berkeley and Los Angeles: University of California Press, 1969), p. 168.

[29] Pound, *Gaudier-Brzeska: A Memoir*, pp. 137–8.

poetics in mind, Pound proposed the Japanese Noh drama as a model for Modernist writing. For the plays themselves, Pound drew on the translations and notebooks of the scholar Ernest Fenollosa (also the source of his *Cathay* Chinese poems and the 'ideogrammic' poetics outlined in *The Chinese Written Character as a Medium for Poetry*). Pound saw in the Noh drama both a technical model and a social model for art centred on allusiveness: they reduced the narrative to essential signs that suggest much vaster contents, and in turn, they demanded an audience 'trained to catch the allusion'.[30] Such training would entail at once deep knowledge of tradition and acute sensitivity to nuance. The Noh drama thus demands both a cultural inheritance and an aesthetic education, which are necessarily the privilege of an elite. W. B. Yeats, in his introduction to Pound's published volume *Certain Noble Plays of Japan* (1916), was even more explicit about this elitist and intimist aspect of the model. Pound's work on the Noh drama helped to nudge forward the reductive, anti-naturalistic stage conception Yeats had already tentatively developed on the basis of Maurice Maeterlinck's Symbolist dramas, the critical writings of his friend Arthur Symons, and the dramatic theories of Gordon Craig. The first concrete result was the staging of Yeats's Cuchulain drama *At the Hawk's Well* as a private performance in the drawing room of Lady Cunard in Cavendish Square, London, on 2 April 1916. The production included the use of masks and had choreography and dancing by the Japanese dancer Michio Ito. In his text for the first performance, Yeats programmatically advocates the turn of modern art away from the public towards a private space in which an aesthetic–social elite can 'concentrate'. This turn is an epochal necessity, Yeats argues:

> We must recognize the change as the painters did when, finding no longer palaces and churches to decorate, they made framed pictures to hang upon a wall. Whatever we lose in mass and in power we should recover in elegance and in subtlety. Our lyrical and our narrative poetry alike have used their freedom and have approached nearer, as Pater said all the arts would if they were able, to 'the condition of music'; and if our modern poetical drama has failed, it is mainly because, always dominated by the example of Shakespeare, it would restore an irrevocable past.[31]

With this declaration, Yeats seems to accept historical necessity and reject nostalgic attempts to heal the rupture of public and private that is characteristic of modernity. Yet as other statements suggest, the private space of advanced art

30 Ezra Pound and Ernest Fenollosa, *The Classic Noh Theatre of Japan* (New York: New Directions, 1959), p. 4.

31 W. B. Yeats in David. R. Clark and Rosalind E. Clark, eds., *The Collected Works of W. B. Yeats, Volume II: The Plays* (New York: Scribner, 2001), p. 692.

must also be carefully policed against the popular representatives of modernity. To arts patron John Quinn he wrote: 'No press, no photographs in the papers, no crowd. I shall be happier than Sophocles. I shall be as lucky as a Japanese dramatic poet at the Court of the Shogun.'[32] In his Introduction to Pound's Noh volume, Yeats is even less measured in spelling out the social implications of 'being lucky as a Japanese court poet' and the class nature of the spiritual elite projected by his plays: 'In fact, with the help of these plays . . . I have invented a form of drama, distinguished, indirect and symbolic, and having no need of mob or press to pay its way – an aristocratic form.'[33] Here is Yeats's aggressive complement to Eliot's nostalgic celebration of true working-class popular culture: the aesthetic and moral revalidation of an aristocracy in eclipse.

In both cases, in Pound's celebration of Gaudier-Brzeska's skilful concentration of energies in the Vorticist artefact and in Yeats's attempt to revive a culturally conscious aristocracy around works of poetry, there is a shared strategy, a common attempt to retain the value of art and its makers in the face of a crisis of value. Art must sacrifice in its extensive dimension, relinquishing a measure of its public and communicative efficacy, in order to gain intensity of form and intimacy of reception. This sacrificial economy is characteristic of Modernist art in general and has been much discussed by critics and theorists. What makes Pound's and Yeats's version of it notable is their situating of it in the theatrical context, where audiences and spaces of reception are literal, immediate, even technical facts.

It should not be implied, however, that all of Pound's and Yeats's avant-garde compatriots accepted their turn towards the intimate, intensive dimension as the appropriate space for modern art. There was a 'third way' adumbrated by Lewis, which, however, remained largely a road not taken. That way was indicated by the radically confrontational idiom and format of Lewis's expressionistic drama *Enemy of the Stars*, as it first appeared in the début issue of *Blast* in 1914. A veritable snarl sounds in the opening stage instructions:

> Type of characters taken from broad faces where Europe grows arctic, intense, human and universal.
>
> 'Yet you and me: why not from the English metropolis?' – Listen: it is our honeymoon. We go abroad for the first scene of our drama. Such a strange thing as our coming together requires a strange place for initial stages of our intimate ceremonious acquaintance.[34]

32 Yeats in *The Collected Works of W. B. Yeats, Volume II*, p. 871.

33 Yeats, 'Introduction to *Certain Noble Plays of Japan* by Pound and Fenollosa', in Pound and Fenollosa, *The Classic Noh Theatre of Japan*, p. 151.

34 Wyndham Lewis, *Enemy of the Stars*, in *Blast 1*, p. 59.

Though Lewis's play precedes Yeats's Noh drama essay and drawing-room performance of *At the Hawk's Well* by two years, its reference to estrangement and intimacy seems almost to parody in advance the Irish poet's conclusion about the artificially intensified, private, symbolistic world of the plays for dancers. 'One realized anew', Yeats wrote, 'at every separating strangeness, that the measure of all arts' greatness can be but in their intimacy.'[35] Lewis, in contrast, displaces the drama of modern art not to a London drawing-room, nor to the formally intensive manifold of geometrical designs, but rather to an aggressively primitive, violent terrain that is at once an archaic, cosmic space and the immediate stage of the continental avant-gardes. Trapped in insular complacency, Lewis implied, England needs to be torn from its cultural sleep, stripped bare, and subjected to extraterritorial, nomadic violence. Significantly, however, though Lewis's drama seemed in 1914 to hold out the possibility of a revolutionary avant-garde in Britain, it remained an isolated product. Not even Lewis himself, whose cultural–political stance was greatly altered by his experience as a World War I combatant and by his reaction to the post-war stabilisation, was much inclined to develop this artistic programme. That which would emerge on the continent under the banners of radical Expressionism and Dadaism – a utopian insurrection of the arts in public – would only flash prematurely in Britain and fade, not to reappear in any strength until the 1960s.

[35] Yeats, 'Introduction to *Certain Noble Plays of Japan* by Pound and Fenollosa', p. 153.

7

'Our London, my London, your London': the Modernist moment in the metropolis

PETER BROOKER

It has become something of a truism to observe that Modernism emerged in tension both with the forces of modernisation and tendencies in social, economic and political modernity. The example of London was to bear this out, especially through the complex cultural and political sea-change of World War I. By 1920 Ezra Pound had given up on London and had already drafted the Hell Cantos which took London as their subject. Ford Madox Ford retreated after the war to the country and thence to Paris and the USA. Lewis went underground, then shifted to the USA and Canada. Only Eliot of the canonic men of 1914 found ways to negotiate the post-war conservatism which had driven others from the capital. This antagonism between Modernist culture and modern metropolitan society was an expression of relations between the individual artist and the social mass, new regimens of work, and the apparatuses of mass production and consumption, but it was expressed in another way, too, by London's relation to the cities positioned historically, geographically and mythologically either side of it.

Paris, the 'capital of the nineteenth century', was in this scheme of things a city of European sophistication and advanced artistic culture; New York, on the other hand, was a brazen emblem of the new, the coming city of the twentieth century, and already in the 1900s an emerging finance capital and model of consumerism whose cultural life, at least in the eyes of its expatriate artists, was at best embryonic. Though a different kind of metropolis from either city, London performed a complex translation service across old and new worlds. Its long relation with Paris had meant that the semiology of that city had entered its own psyche and physical make-up. London was not Paris but could not shake, nor, for many, compete with this counter-image. Such at least was the conviction of Arthur Symons, devotee of the Café Royal and of the Empire Music Hall and the major conduit of French Symbolist verse into England. 'Only Soho is Bohemia', Symons declared, though 'not in the literal sense' for 'Bohemia exists only in Paris.'[1] New York, on the other hand, was rejected or patronised. For Pound, following Henry James and James McNeill Whistler across the Atlantic, London was the 'intellectual capital of America' and home of the highest art.[2] Of course there were artists who resisted this view and were ready to see the USA and pre-eminently New York as an image of the future. In the event, the myth of both cities had to compete with the actuality. By the 1920s, too, something had changed. European and American cities were discovering new configurations and alliances, and Modernism in its new transatlantic phase passed between Paris and New York, cutting London out of the circuit.

The irresistible image for London's Modernist years is that of the Vortex, 'from which and through which, and into which, ideas are constantly rushing'.[3] To put a date to it, Modernist London spun into most vibrant social and artistic existence in 1914–18, only for its energies to dissipate in the aftermath of war. The longer Modernist period in London has its well-known markers, of course: 1910 and 1922, planted respectively by Virginia Woolf and Eliot's *The Waste Land*. The latter date marks the advent, I suggest, of a textual, transnational Modernism when Modernist works, in a now fitful association with actual metropolitan locations, assumed a separated status. The promise of a London-based, cosmopolitan Modernism had evaporated.

We can find an earlier date than 1910, of course. 1908, for example, the year Pound arrived in London from Venice and Lewis and Hulme returned respectively from France and Germany. They had all met by the end of the following year: Pound and Hulme, with others, at the Tour Eiffel Restaurant, Lewis and Pound at the Vienna Café, and all three probably at Hulme's Tuesday evenings in Frith Street. Thus a pattern of social and artistic relations among a younger generation of thinkers and artists was early established in and around Soho. If this was not Paris, the Tour Eiffel, which was to have a long association with London Bohemia, was run by a French restaurateur, Rudolf Stulik, and had been decided on as a venue for the Poets' Club because it more nearly resembled the intense café society of Verlaine and his companions.[4] When Lewis and Pound met at the Vienna Café they were sorting out their artistic destinies, as much in their adopted manners and costume as in their art. Lewis was a latter-day dandy, an 'idle student', he said, who 'bought his clothes in

[1] Arthur Symons, *The Café Royal And Other Essays* (London: Beaumont Press, 1924), p. 4.

[2] Ezra Pound, *Certain Radio Speeches*, ed. William Levy (Rotterdam: Cold Turkey Press, 1975), n.p.

[3] Ezra Pound, *Gaudier-Brzeska: A Memoir* (New York: New Directions, 1970), p. 92.

[4] F. S. Flint, 'Book of the Week', *New Age* (11 February 1909), p. 327.

Savile Row or Brook Street'.[5] Pound presented a piebald scholar–gypsy whose 'transatlantic bohemianism' had struck Douglas Goldring from the beginning.[6] Lewis saw only a 'cowboy songster'.[7] He was himself 'morose' though he saw Pound's difficulty clearly enough: that as an American and suspected Jew he was at odds with the British Museum mandarins who were Lewis's companions. He assessed rightly that Pound would need a go-between such as Ford if he were to survive in London. As editor of *The English Review* and as host with Violet Hunt at teas, tennis and garden parties at South Lodge, Kensington, Ford served exactly this function. Thus Pound joined London literary society: Kensington was 'SWARming with artistic types'; soon he knew 'all the Swells'; he was 'by way of falling into the crowd that does things here'.[8] With Ford he talked about poetry and learned the hard lesson of writing verse in a direct, unadorned spoken idiom. The problem was 'English', the language, and the social and moral codes which held middle-class Kensington society together. This he encountered more directly through Olivia Shakespear, her titled friends and her daughter Dorothy whom he was to marry in 1914. Dorothy, commented Agnes Bedford, was 'very *Kensington*'; she was 'very English' and not 'awakened', said Hilda Doolittle.[9]

Pound had not come to London to join this society. Nor was it to learn from Ford. London was 'the place for poesy' not Imagist poetics, and its greatest poet in residence was the last Romantic, W. B. Yeats. In other words, London was a literary before it was a social or physical place, a cultural rather than an imperial capital whose new buses and underground, suffrage demonstrations, crowded streets, office-workers and suburbs were a forgettable background. Pound was 'drunk with . . . Dowson's "Cynara"'[10] and aching to meet Yeats, but his Baedeker did not take him to the Cheshire Cheese pub where the Rhymers had met. At first his London meant the route between the British Museum and Elkin Matthews's bookshop in Vigo Street. Matthews provided introductions to Ernest Rhys, Laurence Binyon, May Sinclair and so to Ford Madox Hueffer. Hence Pound's move in 1910 to a room in Kensington to be 'nearer to most

5 Wyndham Lewis, *Blasting and Bombardiering* (London: John Calder, 1982), pp. 272, 273.

6 Douglas Goldring, *South Lodge* (London: Constable, 1943), p. 47.

7 Lewis, *Blasting*, p. 274.

8 Humphrey Carpenter, *A Serious Character: The Life of Ezra Pound* (London: Faber & Faber, 1988), p. 130; D. H. Lawrence quoted in Noel Stock, *The Life of Ezra Pound* (London: Penguin, 1970), p. 97; D. D. Paige, ed., *Selected Letters of Ezra Pound* (New York: New Directions, 1971), p. 7.

9 Hugh Kenner, 'D. P. Remembered', *Paideuma*, 2, 3 (Winter 1973), p. 493; J. J. Wilhelm, *Ezra Pound in London and Paris* (University Park and London: Pennsylvania State University Press, 1990), p. 151.

10 Ezra Pound, *Literary Essays* (London: Faber & Faber, 1960), p. 367.

of my friends'.[11] Olivia Shakespear introduced him to Yeats, who had rooms in Bloomsbury. Pound attended Hulme's evenings and meetings at the Tour Eiffel, but never ventured further east, he said, than Cursitor Street;[12] that is to say, beyond the offices of the *New Age* and the ABC tearooms in Chancery Lane where contributors met once a week before moving off back into Soho for the music hall or Café Royal. Pound therefore inhabited a delimited London. If it contained any divisions these too were firstly literary and only secondarily social or geographical. Thus he recalled spending his afternoons with Ford and his evening at Yeats's.[13] The two masters never dined together, he said, and were in their ideas and example 'in diametric opposition': Ford was direct; Yeats associative.[14] The first was to prove more decisive, but if Pound learned this from Ford it was from his conversation. Ford didn't understand Pound's verse and barely followed his Philadelphian accent. Pound did not much read novels. Nevertheless they put together the working principles of Imagism, setting Pound on a course which would both distance him from his own earlier verse and from the combined social decorum, literary taste and Englishness of Edwardian Kensington.

It's unlikely that Pound bothered much with the twenty-five books Ford had written before 1909, among them the popular *Soul of London* (1905). All the same, much as in his thoughts on the virtues of good prose, Ford sets out some of the thematics that inform Pound's London career and those of fellow London Modernists. Ford responds in *Soul of London* to two developments in the city: the changes in population and transport, the growth of the suburbs, commerce and an administrative class which had made London a world city, and the discourse of statistics and factual report introduced to literally map and monitor these changes. Ford was determined to respond to the experience of London with the telling anecdote rather than the statistical or systemic account. His was the discourse of the imaginative artist and storyteller who sought out the 'personal image'.[15] The presiding note of London is 'alone-ness', he argues.[16] The impersonality of the city has fragmented both the city and its citizens who can only know London in part and never as a whole. Identity is splintered while the differences of ethnic peoples and of rich and poor are rubbed down to 'the dead level of democracy'.[17] Thus Ford joins other

[11] Carpenter, *Serious Character*, p. 127.

[12] Patricia Hutchins, *Ezra Pound's Kensington* (London: Faber & Faber, 1965), p. 18.

[13] Donald Hall, 'The Art of Poetry v. Ezra Pound: an Interview' *Paris Review*, 28 (1962), p. 36.

[14] Hutchins, *Pound's Kensington*, p. 94; Ezra Pound, 'Status Rerum', *Poetry* (January 1913), p. 125.

[15] Ford Madox Ford, *The Soul of London* (1905; London: Everyman, 1995), p. 3.

[16] Ibid., p. 9. [17] Ibid., p. 12.

commentators on the theme of the mental life of the metropolis, though, unlike them, he pits the novelistic detail of the inner life against the levelling forces of modernity. Typically he catches the characterful incident on the move in a way reminiscent of Baudelaire's passer-by, though less now as leisurely stroller than bus or railway passenger. His sketches are perforce strung in a loose series without a plot, since neither he nor we can pursue the narrative he glimpses. The illuminated incident passes into a hazy blur, ironically reinforcing the incomprehensibility of the 'illimitable' city[18] and those same abstract processes which had undermined its narrative and cognitive wholeness.

In effect, Ford advances the impressionist aesthetic of Whistler's *Nocturnes* and Symons's poems of lamp-lit Piccadilly. Symons's own prose accounts of London invoke Baudelaire and the French Symbolists, Whistler and Whitman – figures in both Eliot's and Pound's literary and cultural imaginary. That Pound came to London to learn from Yeats and not Symons, Yeats's friend and fellow Rhymer, is a measure of the contradictory aspects of his own London. For it confirmed how famously out of touch Pound was, both with the modernising metropolis and the Symbolist verse which had taken the tones of modern urban life as its subject. Paradoxically, however, this same aloofness was to prove him the more uncompromising international Modernist whose sights were no more set on local colour or ordinary people's lives than they were upon an exclusively national literature. Ford, meanwhile, was left behind by what he started. For if Impressionism led to Imagism, the Imagist(e) Pound sought precision not precise realism, an impersonal not 'personal image'. Respected still by Pound, Ford was ignored by Eliot and written off by Lewis. The youngish trio met, fittingly enough, in the Vorticist space of the Pounds' triangular room at Holland Place Chambers. Not only did they know partial Londons; they were to ask the city itself to play a different part.

Legend tells how in a Kensington teashop Pound took a blue pencil to poems by Hilda Doolittle to declare her 'HD Imagiste'. The place was English, its leading exponent was an American and the poems were sent to *Poetry* (Chicago) as a first instalment on an American 'Risorgimento'. The Frenchified collection *Des Imagistes* whose contributors were mostly American followed. Pound's own Imagist poems in *Cathay* (1915) and *Lustra* (1916), were creative translations from the Chinese; his most famous Imagist poem, 'In a Station of the Metro', had a Parisian setting and borrowed the methods of Kandinsky. Ford struggled to get the word 'car' into the poem 'On Heaven', hailed by

18 Ibid., p. 15.

Pound for being 'in the "twentieth-century fashion,"'[19] but his own poem on a bus is the French 'Dans un Omnibus de Londres'. London was a pretext, therefore, an ideological place from which to launch an international campaign. This set him and a notion of Modernist art against and above the local and parochial. Thus he sidelines Joyce's Irishness in favour of his Modernist hardness.[20] Some were baffled, some suspicious. Pound's project was all of a piece, however, insofar as a patchwork can be: a developing *œuvre* which included translations from Provençal, Anglo-Saxon, Latin, Japanese and Chinese in the chameleon personae of the Yankee troubadour. It's not surprising he fell foul of the niceties of being English in Kensington.

Pound didn't in fact read the codes of English conduct nor of literary culture at all fluently. He 'really must *not* in London wear that turn down collar, with a black coat', said Olivia Shakespear; 'Dorothy *must* marry' and he wouldn't do; people didn't understand his 'American ways'.[21] Ford's famous roll on the floor at his old-fashioned verse helped him make the break both from this society and 'the arthritic milieu that held control of the respected British critical circles'.[22] The volume *Canzoni* which doubled Ford up with laughter was dedicated to Olivia and Dorothy Shakespear. In marrying Dorothy, Pound 'had *married* England', says Donald Davie.[23] Rejecting 'her book' was tantamount, therefore, to a divorce from her world, including the kind of artist she had taken him to be. Pound thenceforth shifted into the Modernist phase of Imagism and Vorticism and shifted his venues from South Lodge and Miss Ella Abbot's teashop in English Kensington to weekly gatherings in Belotti's Ristorante Italiano in cosmopolitan Soho.

In September 1908, when Pound arrived in London, Arthur Symons had just departed for Venice. He was to return home mentally unbalanced and in October was declared insane. The possibility that, in other circumstances, Symons might have introduced Pound to Yeats and to contemporary French poetry was now cancelled absolutely. Meanwhile, in Harvard in the same year, T. S. Eliot discovered Symons's *The Symbolist Movement in Literature* and this took him onto the poetry of Tristan Corbière and Jules Laforgue. They taught him that there was a way to write about the ordinary dreariness of

19 Hugh Kenner, *A Sinking Island: The Modern English Writers* (London: Barrie & Jenkins, 1988), p. 91–2.

20 Pound, *Essays*, pp. 399–402.

21 Omar Pound and A. Walton Litz, eds., *Ezra Pound and Dorothy Shakespear: Their Letters 1909–1914* (London: Faber & Faber, 1984), pp. 92, 153, 154.

22 William Cookson, ed., *Ezra Pound: Selected Prose 1909–1965* (London: Faber & Faber, 1973), p. 432.

23 Donald Davie, *Studies in Ezra Pound* (Cheadle: Carcarnet Press, 1991), p. 233.

the American cities of St Louis and Boston which in phrases and fragments ('yellow evening', 'sparrows in gutters', 'vacant lots') would serve for London too.[24] He had 'modernised himself', Pound marvelled.[25] In a sense this meant Eliot took on the problem of disconnection presented by both Impressionist and Imagist method, and thus the task of reconciling the parts of modernity first identified by Baudelaire: 'the ephemeral, the fugitive, the contingent' with 'the eternal and the immutable'.[26] Ford's answer lay in the loose assemblage of descriptive prose and reminiscence or the controls of fictional narrative. But mere description was anathema to Pound and the age of the novel, said Eliot, was over.[27]

Eliot's remarks appeared in his reflections on Joyce's *Ulysses*, whose size and sprawl had presented him, he said, with the problem of artistic form. The answer he found and adopted for his own purposes in *The Waste Land* was the 'mythic method' which gave shape to the 'panorama of futility and anarchy which is contemporary history'.[28] If we remember the simple fact that Joyce's fiction is set in and is about the city of Dublin, the materials Eliot views as uncontrolled anarchy (and which Pound dismissed as merely parochial) were those of the – hardly advanced – modern city. The city is thereby associated with a distracting novelistic particularity and a threatening formlessness. The latter, in an animated vocabulary of floods and monsters, had long been a way, too, of seeing the urban crowd. Eliot's own first response to the people of the streets of Bloomsbury was quite different; he was responsive to an evident ethnic and linguistic variety.[29] In *The Waste Land*, however, the crowd becomes the uniform mass of city workers, pitched into limbo, or the sketchily ominous 'hooded hordes', both drained of variety and reference. Reading *Ulysses* we might feel that the materials of a day in the life in the city provide the pleasure rather than pain of the novel, and reading *The Waste Land* that its fragments defeat the attempt to put them in order. But this is to say, as many have, that Eliot's poem contradicts its avowed purpose to render art impersonal: the exact cause in Ford's eyes of the plight of the modern city.

Eliot arrived in London at the moment of *Blast*. Lewis's Modernist *samizdat* appropriated the large format and headlining style of the popular press

[24] T. S. Eliot, *Inventions of the March Hare: Poems 1909–1917*, ed. Christopher Ricks. (London: Faber & Faber, 1996), p. 107.

[25] Paige, ed., *Letters*, p. 40.

[26] Charles Baudelaire, *The Painter of Modern Life and Other Essays*, ed. Jonathan Mayne (London: Phaidon Press, 1964), p. 13.

[27] Eliot in Vassiliki Kolocotroni, Jane Goldman and Olga Taxidou, eds., *Modernism: An Anthology of Sources and Documents* (Edinburgh University Press, 1998), p. 372.

[28] Ibid., p. 373.

[29] T. S. Eliot, *The Letters of T. S. Eliot. Vol. I, 1898–1922* (London: Faber & Faber, 1988), p. 55.

and advertising, to see off Impressionism and outgun Futurist sloganeering in the name of an uncompromisingly abstract art. Its lists of those 'Blasted' and 'Blessed' were violently discriminating, anti-establishment, arbitrary and comic. The magazine was a sensation and Lewis was lionised by the class he for the most part despised – perhaps because *Blast* was thought a grand lark, perhaps because its acclaim for England's industrial and seafaring might ('BLESS ALL PORTS . . . BLESS ENGLAND, industrial island machine') and national character (Shakespeare's 'bitter Northern Rhetoric', 'the separating, ungregarious BRITISH GRIN') could be read as boosting patriotic sentiment.[30] Shortly before the issue of *Blast*, Lewis had decorated the dining room of Lady Drogheda's Belgravia home and earlier made a significant contribution to the décor of the Cave of the Golden Calf, 'the first English Artists' Cabaret'[31] opened by Mme Frida Strindberg in Heddon Street in 1912. Later, in 1915, he was to paint a Vorticist Room at the Tour Eiffel Restaurant. Vorticism therefore presented a London based avant-garde for Londoners, taken beyond the gallery and studio into its homes and cafés. The brochure for the Cabaret Club, designed by Lewis, expressed this confidence: 'We do not want to Continentalise, we only want to do away, to some degree, with the distinction that the word "Continental" implies, and with it the necessity of crossing the Channel to laugh freely and to sit up after nursery hours.'[32] With fatal irony, therefore, London was coming into its own as a cosmopolitan capital ('LONDON IS NOT A PROVINCIAL TOWN', *Blast* insisted) at the very moment when Vorticism's militarised antics were dwarfed by the reality of actual combat.

By early 1914 Pound had caught up with Lewis. He contributed the name 'Vorticism' to the commitment to abstraction across the arts and was active in promoting new work with patrons and in little magazines. *Blast* both intensified his own development and, in its aftermath, especially in his being banished by G. W. Prothero from the pages of the *Quarterly Review*, spurred his departure from London. These few years were full of contrary directions, however. For if Pound felt increasingly frustrated at the hands of the English literary establishment, this was also the period of the *Egoist* and the productions of the Egoist Press. Iris Barry remembers the latter years of the war as the 'Ezra Pound Period' when at weekly meetings in Belotti's, Pound orchestrated a new generation in the fight for liberty and justice.[33] The metropolis was vital

[30] Wyndham Lewis, ed., *Blast 1* (1914; Santa Rosa: Black Sparrow, 1997), pp. 23, 26.

[31] Richard Cork, *Art Beyond the Gallery* (New Haven and London: Yale University Press, 1985), p. 61.

[32] Ibid., pp. 101–3.

[33] Iris Barry, 'The Ezra Pound Period', *Bookman* (October 1931), p. 163.

to this project and Pound envisioned a cultural axis connecting Paris, London and New York.[34] By the end of decade, however, London had failed him. He responded bitterly to Prothero's symbolic rejection and bade London farewell, turning to the one civilised alternative that remained – Paris.

'Civilisation is individual' declared Pound.[35] And *Blast*, Lewis proclaimed, presented 'an art of individuals'.[36] For Lewis this implied an armour-plated individualism, the silent, energy-packed place of the artist 'at the heart of the whirlpool'.[37] 'Vorticism was what I, personally, did and said in a certain period', Lewis later notoriously claimed.[38] It needed the delayed imaginative reconstruction by William Roberts in his painting of 1961–2, 'The Vorticists at the Restaurant de la Tour Eiffel: Spring 1915', to return Vorticism to a fuller sense of the individuated contributions to this collective project. Roberts's painting sets Lewis at the centre of the picture with fellow artists, including himself and Pound, to either side. Entering late and in the background are Helen Saunders and Jessica Dismorr. Both had illustrations included in the second issue of *Blast* and Dismorr also contributed a set of prose poems. The third of these, 'June Night', reports on the precarious and jagged excitement of the metropolis from the top of a crowded bus. She separates from her boring escort to risk the 'mews and by-ways', 'the unplumbable depths' and 'widening circles of alarm' in the city.[39] The sense in this text of places out of reach or out of bounds and in Dismorr's 'London Notes' of the city's inner, hidden places genders the city feminine. In both her own and Saunders's painting the representation of figures is machine-like and anonymised according to the dictates of Modernist impersonality, though, by the same token, 'de-gendered' away from a binary registration of sexual difference.[40] The prose poems do something else, however. For here, in 'Monologue' and 'June Night', the speaker and the figures are embodied in sexualised urban landscapes in ways that combine Modernist form with more overt expressions of female sexuality.

The texts of 'High Modernism' tend to match a display of kinetic energy with a contrasting stasis which frames the inner activity of the work and so confers form upon matter. Like the 'taxi, throbbing waiting' in Eliot's *Waste Land*; 'the human engine' has its motor running, is ready to depart, but stands

34 Pound, *Essays*, p. 356. 35 Ibid., p. 344. 36 Lewis, *Blast 1*, n.p.

37 Goldring, *South Lodge*, p. 65.

38 Wyndham Lewis, 'Introduction' to 'Wyndham Lewis and Vorticism' (London: Tate Gallery, 1956), p. 3.

39 Wyndham Lewis, ed., *Blast 2* (1915; Santa Barbara: Black Sparrow Press, 1981), p. 68.

40 Jane Beckett and Deborah Cherry, 'Reconceptualizing Vorticism: Women, Modernity, Modernism', in Paul Edwards, ed., *Blast: Vorticism 1914–1918* (Aldershot: Ashgate, 2000), pp. 70–1.

immobile. One alternative in the period was the speeding automobile of Futurism though this had been discredited by London's Vorticists. Another was not to speed up the Modernist text but slow it down; to dwell upon the moment of the passing impression or precise image, to write beyond the structured unity of the Modernist epic and to go on writing. Such was the method of Dorothy Richardson's *Pilgrimage*, a sequence of twelve novels published between 1915 and 1938 (a thirteenth unfinished novel was published in 1967) which take the life of Miriam Henderson from 1891–1912, principally in Bloomsbury, as their core subject. In 1916, reading the second volume *Backwater*, Bryher (Annie Winifred Ellerman) recognised it as 'a precursor of the cinema . . . the Baedeker of all our experiences' 'as we rode down a London street, like Miriam, on top of a bus'.[41] Richardson demonstrates at once the persistence of mimetic narrative and of the local, seemingly cancelled or transcended by classic international Modernism. Her answer to the question of structure was an open-ended, autobiographical fiction coincident with a life, whose associations with the feminine and with the flow of time was of the kind which Lewis had pilloried in the renegade Joyce.[42] Richardson's sustained, precisely referenced London novel not only questioned the forms and assumptions of Modernist abstraction, however, but differed from Ford's localism in *Soul of London*.

Pilgrimage confirms, first of all, Ford's sense that 'knowing' London implied the intimate knowledge of a demarcated region; the area, in this case, of Bloomsbury between the British Museum and the Euston Road, and Tottenham Court Road and Judd Street. However, where Ford had set the stories of the inner life against a discourse of facts and figures, and where he had seen a levelling down and resignation in the face of inequalities, Richardson sees private and public spheres as gendered physical and cognitive spaces and moves her character and text with a sense of active enquiry and wonder across these worlds. Also, whereas Ford apprehends urban modernity as a speeding passer-by, Richardson means to delay cognition in a collaborative exchange between author and reader. She tends, therefore, to dwell within a confined space upon the lineaments of the individuated object and a single mental life in deliberate slow-motion. Syntax is stretched out – in what Virginia Woolf termed, 'the psychological sentence of the feminine gender'.[43] Hence the characteristic length of the novels' descriptive passages and the ongoing narrative life of the series,

41 Quoted in Laura Marcus, 'Continuous Performance: Dorothy Richardson', in James Donald, Anne Friedberg and Laura Marcus, eds., *Close Up 1927–1933: Cinema and Modernism* (London: Cassell, 1998), pp. 152–3.

42 Julian Symons, ed., *The Essential Wyndham Lewis* (London: André Deutsch, 1989), pp. 202–4.

43 Virginia Woolf, *A Woman's Essays*, ed. Rachel Bowlby (London: Penguin, 1992), p. 51.

which stretches across autobiography and fiction to connect with discourses on the family, national morality, philosophy, economics and ecology in a broad intertextual and public context. The result is less an itemised list or series of impressions or events than an oscillating movement which swings both inwards and outwards on what we might term the 'psychological sentence' of the city. Richardson therefore simultaneously investigates and opens a single feminine consciousness to a diverse archive of contemporary knowledges in the busy world of the capital. Is it too much to think of this as a slow-turning vortex? If so, it is quite differently gendered from the masculinised model, to the point of gendering the city itself, so Jean Radford suggests, as a loving maternal figure.[44]

What is especially striking about Richardson's London, however, is her valorisation of silence. Thus both reader and writer join in an unspoken conversation across the novel text, and the individual woman, Miriam Henderson, enters an internalised dialogue traversing the city, especially in those places which combine private and public spheres in wordless communion: the church, the Quaker meeting house and the cinema. The cinema for Richardson meant primarily the silent cinema on which she was to write several notices for the journal *Close Up*. Ford identifies loneliness as the dominant note of London. For Richardson solitude is not loneliness since it enables this kind of rapt attention and internal dialogue with a wider world. In the cinema's silent communal space, women, seeking respite and fantasy, could become citizens of the world, joined in a mode of 'collective seeing' and there, so Laura Marcus ventures, be educated for modernity.[45] Cinema was in short 'a civilising agent'.[46] One thinks how this contrasts with the mantra 'civilisation is individual', but Richardson was faced with a difficult choice of her own, between silent and sound film. The latter she saw as fulfilling a 'masculine destiny . . . of planful becoming rather than of purposeful being'.[47] In 'The Film Gone Male' she finds a way of welcoming the prospect of sound film 'turning the world into a vast council-chamber',[48] but this is in the expectation, in an intrepid essentialism, that 'the unconquerable, unchangeable eternal feminine' will claim a powerful role in this chamber.[49]

One wonders at these gendered distinctions. For Lewis and others the city crowd is associated with the flow and formlessness of matter which art would master and separate from itself. 'Is the crowd feminine?' he asked?[50] 'Is the crowd male' then for Dorothy Richardson, associated in its turn with sound

[44] Jean Radford, *Dorothy Richardson* (London: Harvester, 1991), p. 61.
[45] Marcus, 'Continuous Performance', pp. 155, 152. [46] Ibid., p. 153.
[47] Ibid., p. 206. [48] Ibid., p. 207. [49] Ibid. [50] Lewis, *Blasting*, p. 78.

and speech and the 'Uncertainty, noise, speed, movement' of a too rapidly changing world?[51] Hence the pleasure she finds, we might think, in wandering upon a season of silent films at the Scala cinema in a place 'of London's former quietude'.[52] *Pilgrimage*, we should remember, though, ends in 1912 at the point when London Modernism begins with Imagism, and when 'The Bloomsbury Group' was already emerging under the signature of the Woolfs, Lytton Strachey, Clive Bell, Roger Fry and others. If Richardson treasured Bloomsbury as a place of quiet female solitude, it became with 'Bloomsbury' a place of acerbic talk and active socialising, of frank exchange and sexual tolerance among familiars. Bloomsbury defied Victorianism with its bohemian ways, but it was a select circle whose nonconformity attracted Eliot because it was expressed, suggests Ackroyd, at the expense of a culture 'to which they nevertheless firmly belonged'.[53] Compared with the other contemporary London Modernisms, Bloomsbury was a remarkably homogeneous and stable grouping – in terms of the shared Cambridge background of its men, the family connections, class attitudes, liberal positions on social and economic issues, and common artistic taste of its members. When Woolf famously declared 'that on or about December 1910 human character changed'[54] she had in mind the new assertiveness of her cook and, it is usually thought, the first Post-Impressionist exhibition organised at the Grafton Gallery by Roger Fry. Neither Pound, nor Lewis, nor Joyce had servants (the Eliots had one, but this is a mark of their unique participation in both worlds). Nor is it likely that Pound or Lewis would have conceded that Fry's exhibition meant more than some date in the Imagist or Vorticist calendar. After all, Lewis had fallen out with Fry almost immediately on joining his Omega Workshop in 1913 and had gone on to set up his own short-lived rival in the 'Rebel Arts Centre'.[55] This too was in Bloomsbury but 'Bloomsbury' – whose actual location came to embrace houses in Richmond and Sussex – henceforth became associated, for the expatriate moderns Pound and Lewis, with effete English art.

Ford's picture of the metropolis as composed of the estranged individual and the crowd failed to anticipate this intermediary world of shifting and antagonistic artistic communities and coteries. In this sphere patrons, allies, rivals, lovers and friends existed as variegated groupings inside and in defiance of the public life of bourgeois imperial London – in much the same way that they

[51] Marcus, 'Continuous Performance', p. 204. [52] Ibid., p. 200.
[53] Peter Ackroyd, *T. S. Eliot* (London: Abacus, 1984), p. 74.
[54] Woolf, *Woman's Essays*, p. 70.
[55] William C. Wees, *Vorticism and the English Avant-Garde* (Toronto and Buffalo: University of Toronto Press, 1972), pp. 59–66.

sought a niche market within mainstream commercial markets for the independent publications (the *Egoist*, *Blast*, the Woolfs' Hogarth Press). A social–symbolic map of these groupings across the city gives a sense of subcultural rather than individually experienced Londons. They were noisier (we think of *Blast*) and more gregarious than Richardson's Bloomsbury, internally fractious and in the case of Bloomsbury and most of 'the Men of 1914', violently and lastingly antipathetical (if Lewis was adamant that Fry was 'vulgar, nasty, mean', Woolf 'hated' Pound, found Lewis 'detestable', Joyce indecent and remained fearful of Eliot).[56]

The animus of such views reveals how much was at stake: no less than the nature of modern art and a notion of the 'civilised' life. Arguably too, the very tension within and across groups energised the artistic experiment and experimental lives that would realise these doctrines. The London venues and symbolic geography of respective parts of the city played their part in this, too. Life at Gordon Square, Bloomsbury, was innovative in its easy liaisons and in the equality it allowed women – though Virginia Woolf's bouts of depression hardly suggest this select society was free of anxiety. The less well-defined cosmopolitan Modernist groups in and around Soho were mixed by social class, ethnicity and gender – though here, too, it needed a special boldness on the part of Iris Tree and Nancy Cunard to enter the Café Royal in 1914.[57] William Roberts's painting of the Vorticists at the Tour Eiffel, too, neatly shows how women artists were positioned in the background of the restaurant as of the artistic movement. All the same, Nancy Cunard and Nina Hamnet became regulars there and at the Café Royal. And at Belotti's, as recalled by Iris Barry, the company embraced artists of different generations and included Harriet Shaw Weaver to whom all were deferential, along with senior figures such as Violet Hunt and May Sinclair and younger women such as H.D., Mary Butts, Dorothy Pound and Barry herself. London café society, therefore, threw up a picture of contested boundaries and the collective life along with disarray and jarring hierarchies, as did Modernist art itself.

With the exception of Eliot, the wall between the 'Men of 1914' and Bloomsbury remained solid. Woolf and the others, and Eliot, elected to remain in London, therefore declaring a cultural allegiance to a nation which by the end of the decade Pound, for one, found irredeemably provincial and moribund. But if London failed some of the 'Men of 1914', their international

56 Wees, *Vorticism*, p. 63; Hermione Lee, *Virginia Woolf* (London: Vintage, 1997), pp. 406, 439.

57 Hugh David, *The Fitzrovians: A Portrait of Bohemian Society 1900–55* (London: Michael Joseph, 1988), p. 112.

Modernism was bedevilled by its own insistent, gendered binaries and strategies of containment and expulsion. Our present perspective on this project is inevitably retrospective and contemporary to ourselves. We tend to prefer moments of self-critique, surplus and hybridity to affirmations of order; to see the metropolis as the site of coexistence and difference, of process and provisionality rather than the either/or of chaos and permanent form. We posit, that is to say, a dialogic aesthetic and dialogic cosmopolitanism for our own and – less confidently perhaps – for earlier times. Sometimes, however, a seeming contemporary perspective is forthcoming from unexpected quarters in the period itself. It's doubtful, for example, that John Cournos is much read now. His novel *Babel*, published in 1922, is the story of how a young Russian-born American Jew, much like Cournos himself, travels to France and to London to fulfil his ambition to become a writer. He dreams of London, and on arriving is enchanted by his bus ride across the city. In the course of time he meets its established and newer writers and becomes aware of the Imagists and Vorticists. In the character who represents Gaudier-Brzeska he discovers an art which embraces opposites: 'the primitive, savage spirit incarnated in mechanics . . . a Maori spear and the French machine gun',[58] the two extremes coexisting across the ages as in the compendious brain of the British Museum. His own brain rings out a 'medley of discordant tunes'.[59] He is a Jewish Russian–American, a 'monk and roué'[60] at war with himself, pulled between domesticity and the romance of art. Other analogies suggest themselves, with the London crowd and with jazz. He is struck by the taken-for-granted variety of the city's population and realises, listening at Speakers' Corner in Hyde Park, that the tolerance of difference and disputation was 'the by-product of a complex, many-tongued civilisation'.[61] The Babel of 'multiple faced' modern London is tottering into the false unity of war but its jagged chorus of harmonious and querulous voices combines, for now, in a cosmopolitan jazz improvisation: 'a many-tuned medley . . . an ultra modern music shaped out of discords'.[62]

A second surprising advocate of dialogue and difference is Ezra Pound. In essays on Henry James and Remy de Gourmont in 1918 and 1920, Pound had set the metropolitan civilisation of both Paris and London against prejudice, dogma and conformity. This entailed, he said, in words that have an unexpectedly contemporary ring, 'not a leveling' or 'elimination of differences' but 'a recognition of differences, and the right of differences to exist'.[63] In 1938

[58] John Cournos, *Babel* (New York: Boni & Liveright, 1922), p. 346. [59] Ibid., p. 37.
[60] Ibid., p. 62. [61] Ibid., p. 124. [62] Ibid., pp. 328, 89. [63] Pound, *Essays*, p. 298.

he wrote to Ronald Duncan, remembering the creative activity of the earlier period, 'After all there *were*, in London dining circles or a *weekly* meeting of us and periphery . . . It was a sort of society or social order or dis-order.'[64] Later Pound advised Patricia Hutchins against tipping all the writers into 'one "period" attitude'.[65] Instead, he suggests we think of an irregular shape, a 'literary rhomboid or whatever non-form or aggregate existed'.[66] The problematics of order or dis-order ran through Pound's career. But if Modernism felt bound to adjudicate on the either / ors of matter and form, the fragment and the abstract whole, the local and the international, this effort now seems less interesting than the balancing act astride such terms and their double application to art and the art of life Pound is remembering. It is instead, I suggest, Cournos's 'medley of discordant tunes', his 'complex, many-tongued civilisation' and Pound's rhomboid social 'dis-order' which make the years of Modernism's formation in this London still a compelling place to visit.

64 Paige, *Letters*, p. 306. 65 Hutchins Papers, British Library, 11 September 1953, n.p.
66 Ibid., 1 March 1957, n.p.

8

Futurism, literature and the market

PAUL EDWARDS

I

'On or about December 1910, human character changed.' Virginia Woolf's famous formulation has always conveniently served to mark the beginning of real Modernism in England, separating it from the more tentative anticipations of the Edwardian era. But Woolf was pointing also to a more general social change, visible to her, for example, in the friendly insubordination of domestic servants. The contemporary cook would be 'in and out of the drawing room . . . to borrow the *Daily Herald*'. Insubordination of various kinds, amounting to a militant unwillingness to know one's place and stay in it, was by 1914 to bring Britain to the brink of civil war in Ireland, and to the brink of a possible revolution, triggered by a likely general strike in the same year. The House of Commons showed its own lack of subordination to the Lords by passing the Parliament Act in 1911, after two general elections caused by the Lords' obstructiveness after the 'People's Budget' of 1909. Henceforth the upper house had no power to alter money bills, and its right to veto other bills was restricted to two successive sessions of Parliament. But Parliament no longer commanded much respect. Woolf's cook would have found in the *Daily Herald* she borrowed from her employer that parliamentary debates were reported under the heading 'The House of Pretence'.[1] The *Herald* was founded in 1911, aimed at the working-class; part of Woolf's point about change was that it was the mistress of the household who subscribed to this working-class paper.

Parliament appeared to be discrediting itself by its behaviour in debate: when the Commons debated the Lords' amendments to the Parliament Bill in July 1911, the Prime Minister, Herbert Asquith, was heckled and shouted down by a furious opposition, with cries of 'Traitor', while the Irish members

[1] Donald Read: *England 1868–1914: The Age of Urban Democracy* (London: Longman, 1979), p. 498.

quarrelled loudly among themselves over some unidentified dispute.[2] It was these Irish members that Asquith was relying on to ensure the rejection of the amendments and return of the bill to the Lords, for the two major parties were evenly represented in the House after the general election of December 1910, and the price of Irish support was a promised bill to bring about Irish Home Rule. In practice all Asquith offered was a minor devolutionary measure, but it was fiercely opposed by the Conservatives, while in Ulster, Unionists under the leadership of Sir Edward Carson (erstwhile prosecutor of Oscar Wilde) began arming a militia to resist any change in the constitution. Nearly 25,000 pledged themselves to fight. The 'Curragh Mutiny' of 1914 (actually the threatened resignation of British Army officers) showed that the Army could not be relied on to enforce government policy in Ireland. They had been encouraged in this by the Leader of the Opposition, Bonar Law. In a speech given in Dublin in November the previous year, he urged a parallel with 1688, when the army of James II 'refused to fight for him' when William of Orange landed and ejected the legitimate sovereign.[3] In July 1914 a conference of the main political leaders was held in Buckingham Palace to avert civil war in Ireland. It broke down, and what *The Times* called 'one of the greatest crises in the history of the British race'[4] was averted (or rather postponed) only because of the outbreak of a wider European war on 4 August.

1910 also saw the escalation of militancy in the campaign for women's suffrage, after a bill that would have enfranchised a million women was lost (apparently with Asquith's connivance) during the wind-up of government business before the first of the general elections occasioned by the quarrel with the Lords. On 'Black Friday' (18 November), women protesters were beaten up by the police and public; demonstrations continued in Downing Street the following day, leading to a total of 280 arrests over the two days. During the next year militants attacked government buildings, and in 1912 went on a shop-window-smashing spree in the West End, causing thousands of pounds' worth of damage to property. Women prisoners on hunger strike were forcibly fed, with great brutality. A campaign of arson, damage to post-boxes and golf courses followed. Thanks once more to Asquith's manoeuvrings in 1913, a bill that would have granted the vote to 5 million women (through an amendment

[2] George Dangerfield, *The Strange Death of Liberal England* (1935; London: McGibbon & Kee, 1966), pp. 56–8. My account of civil unrest is derived from this book and Read's *England 1868–1914*. I am indebted to W. C. Wees's groundbreaking *Vorticism and the English Avant-Garde* (Manchester University Press, 1972) for his recognition of the connections between the events recorded in Dangerfield's book and the artistic ferment of the time.

[3] Dangerfield, *The Strange Death of Liberal England*, p. 120.

[4] Read, *England 1868–1914*, p. 508.

to a Male Suffrage bill) was withdrawn over a technicality. Militancy and violence increased: empty mansions were burnt down, paintings were slashed, bombs left outside the Bank of England and elsewhere (Lloyd George's house was badly damaged by one, and two exploded in Westminster Abbey); the government's response (including the infamous 'Cat and Mouse bill', allowing the release of weakened prisoners on hunger strike and their rearrest on recovery) was brutal and scarcely constitutional. The campaign continued in 1914: 107 buildings were burnt before the outbreak of war, attacks were made on Sir Edward Carson's house, Velasquez's *Rokeby Venus* was slashed, and a demonstration at Buckingham Palace was violently suppressed by truncheon-wielding police. By July 1914 the government appeared to have backed down but, again, it was the outbreak of war that extinguished civil strife.

The final major field of strife was industry. Trade unions vastly increased their membership during the period, in line with increasing discontent. The worst year of strikes was 1912, when nearly 41,000 working days were lost (compare 1907, when the figure was just over 2,000),[5] but trouble had started in 1910. Miners struck in South Wales over a demand for a minimum wage. Rioting was quelled by police and troops. In 1912 a million miners struck nationally. The first national rail strike took place in August 1911, and the same year there was a strike of seamen and dockers, bringing London to a standstill. It happened again in 1912, and though 1913 saw a reduction in the number of days lost, the actual number of disputes and stoppages increased. The labour unrest of the period was unpredictable and haphazard, and union officials were unable to keep track of demands and negotiate for their members. And the government was ineffective in its interventions. Miners' strikes were motivated at least in part by political objectives. The syndicalist theory and tactics of Georges Sorel were known to have inspired some leaders of the unrest: the state would be abolished and workers would control all production, which would be planned by a central committee. More exciting than the objective, however, was the means of achieving it: through violence and the General Strike. Sorel was a follower of Henri Bergson, the philosopher of vitalism and anti-rationalist intuitionism. He envisioned a breakdown of all established order that would be simultaneously a breakthrough into a new order of life and political organisation. The random and frequent stoppages of 1913 could be interpreted as a build-up to precisely such a breakthrough, to be achieved by a general strike. To an establishment with such fears, the formation of the 'Triple Alliance' of miners, transport and port workers in September that

[5] Ibid., p. 495.

year was ominous. By the summer of 1914 it seemed likely that the combined workers were indeed about to embark on such a strike, prompted by Scottish coal-owners' declaration that they could no longer pay the minimum wage. Again, it was war that prevented the forthcoming violence and disorder.

II

Virginia Woolf's statement about the change in human character is usually seen not in the context of the beginning of this period of violent social unrest and breakdown, but as tied to a particular cultural event, Roger Fry's exhibition, 'Manet and the Post-Impressionists', staged at the Grafton Galleries in Bond Street from 8 November 1910 to 13 January 1911. The truth is that it is only in the visual arts that any transformation of high culture at all equivalent to the social ferment of the time can really be traced. And it had its impact partly because visual art could be cheaply reproduced for the public in illustrated magazines such as the *Tatler*, the *Sketch* and the *Illustrated London News*.[6] The next major exhibition in London was the March 1912 'Italian Futurist Painters' at the Sackville Gallery, followed in October by the 'Second Post-Impressionist Exhibition' (again at the Grafton Gallery), which ran until January 1913. All attracted profuse press comment and public controversy.[7] Many of the articles were serious attempts at critique, others apoplectic expressions of outrage by traditionalists. Some specifically linked the 'new' art (many of the works in the first Post-Impressionist exhibition were not new at all, of course) with the ideology they took to be threatening social stability: 'they are the analogue of the anarchical movements in the political world, the aim being to reduce all institutions to chaos; to invert all accepted ideas on all subjects . . . ' The writer of this in some respects absurd diatribe points also to the role of cheap illustrations in the process he describes: 'We are suffering from a surfeit of fine art; and from the democratisation of art by reproductive processes . . . '[8] Leaving aside the initial production of artworks by painters like Van Gogh or Matisse, and the conditions and significance of their initial entry into the marketplace, we can say that what was happening to these works in 1910 as they entered the new public sphere through reproduction was that they became

[6] For examples, see Anna Gruetzner Robins, *Modern Art in Britain 1910–1914* (London: Merrell Holbertson in association with Barbican Art Gallery, 1997), figs. 2, 8, 18, 27 and 28.

[7] For a full account and a generous selection of articles, see J. B. Bullen, ed., *Post-Impressionists in England* (London: Routledge, 1988).

[8] Ebenezer Wake Cook, 'The Post-Impressionists', *Morning Post* (19 November 1910), rpt. *Post-Impressionists in England*, pp. 118, 119.

colonised by the divided and mutually antagonistic general culture they were being taken to represent. They were high art no longer.

The avant-garde consciously repeats this originally somewhat fortuitous process, so that it becomes not so much a factor in the reception of art, but actually intrinsic to the work itself. The cheap products of the popular press that have appropriated high art (and to some extent imposed a new cultural role on it) are themselves in turn appropriated, reappearing 'within' the visual artwork in the form of collaged newsprint, oilcloth, wallpaper or bus tickets. Its participation is now, however ironically, direct.[9] It was part of the genius of Filippo Tommaso Marinetti, the founder and chief activist of the Futurist movement, that he understood and exploited this strategy more variously, inventively and thoroughly than anyone else, completely breaching the boundary between the 'work' and the culture into which it was now entirely interpellated. It is no accident that Futurism made its first appearance on the public scene through a newspaper feature in *Le Figaro*, on 9 February 1909.

It should be remembered, however, that there was also another strategy for Modernism, one that involved instead the negation of the cheap, exploitative commercial culture that was colonising it. This strategy was to wall high culture more securely in a restricted area of 'purity' of spirit that it could preserve uncontaminated by traffic with the world. The aesthetic of this strategy was formulated in England by two of the foremost champions of 'Post-Impressionism', Roger Fry and Clive Bell. For them, visual art, at least, became virtually a platonic realm of 'pure form' created by the elements of painting, and not a representation or incorporation of the culture of its time. As such, of course, it had a cultural function of opposition, and it had its aesthetic equivalent in a certain strain of literary Modernism. Conveniently, the clearest example of this strategy in literature is the declared aesthetic of Virginia Woolf (associated with Fry, and influenced by his ideas). Woolf was not concerned so much with the achievement of 'pure form' in literature as in locating within the psychological experience of her characters something that was negated by the 'materialism' of modern life as represented in the work of Edwardian realists. In her case the rejection of everyday experience is so total (at least avowedly, in her aesthetic) that she aspires instead to reach back behind the material world to where the categories of experience that are its complement (space, time, subject, object) have not yet emerged.

[9] An excellent and suggestive account of this process, to which I am indebted, is in Thomas Crow, 'Modernism and Mass Culture in the Visual Arts', in his book, *Modern Art in the Common Culture* (New Haven and London: Yale University Press, 1996), pp. 3–37.

To take for a moment these two strategies – of rejecting the culture of capitalism in favour of an uncontaminated region of form (or psychology, or even geography) and the other one, of appropriating that culture and making art out of it – it can readily be seen that both may express a variety of relationships with history. As protests against a dominant ideology, both have their risks. The first may be little more than ivory-tower aestheticism or escapism, while the second may become indistinguishable from a passive consumerism. For a cultural historian of Marxist orientation, who knows where history has been and where it is going, there is therefore great scope for subtle discrimination in identifying elements that are dominant, residual or emergent at any particular crucial moment. This scope is increased by the fact that in actual cultural products neither strategy is ever kept entirely separate from its antithesis. But it is not my purpose to make such discriminations here. Marinetti is fascinating partly because he moved abruptly from the first strategy to the second. He began his poetic career squarely in the Symbolist tradition of a wilful alienation from the everyday. In his early poems Marinetti piled Pelion on Ossa; not only did he express a self-lacerating yearning for an impossible infinite, symbolised by the stars ('O Stars! Stars! For ever shall you be the despair of our burdensome nights of fever! For ever shall you be our ideal pain! Oh! to break our moorings and depart with you, towards the shores of the Infinite!'), he also attributed a similar yearning to the stars themselves: 'Dream that all the Stars weep for being wept for, vainly, weep for loving without hope, a Star that cannot be!'[10] The yearning reaches a scale of cosmic destruction in *La conquête des étoiles*, his epic of 1902, a sort of *Prometheus Unbound* as visualised by Gustave Moreau.[11] But in developing Futurism, Marinetti avowedly spurned this Decadent past: 'We Abjure our Symbolist Masters, the last Lovers of the Moon' was the title of one of his manifestoes.

Marinetti's crucial realisation was that an extreme, neo-Romantic anti-Positivism and anti-rationalism no longer required the stage-properties of Decadence. The founding manifesto signalled immediately Futurism's affinity with the contemporary apocalyptic and irrationalist current of thought associated with the names of Max Stirner, Friedrich Nietzsche, Georges Sorel

[10] 'Etoiles! Etoiles! vous serez à jamais / le désespoir de nos pesantes nuits de fièvre! / Vous serez à jamais notre idéale douleur! / . . . Oh! rompre les amarres et partir avec vous, vers les plages de l'Infini!'; 'Songez que toutes les Etoiles / pleure d'être pleurées, vainement, / pleurent d'aimer sans espoir, une impossible Etoile!' F. T. Marinetti, 'Etoiles! Etoiles!', *La revue blanche*, 25, 195 (1 July 1901), pp. 437–8.

[11] *La conquête des étoiles* (1902), rpt. F. T. Marinetti, *Scritti Francesi*, vol. 1, ed. Pasquale A. Jannini (Milan: Arnoldo Mondadori, 1983), pp. 51–129.

and Henri Bergson.[12] Each of these thinkers sought alternatives to the Kantian–Newtonian world of positive science, in which everything was calculable and subject to the iron laws of cause and effect. The intellectual and material structures that were the concomitants of this world replicated this dual character of human power: they are the result of calculation and knowledge but also subject humanity to the oppressed condition of being a determinate part of a finite, closed system (no matter how nominally 'progressive' it proclaims itself to be). The most instructive comparison is with Bergson, for it was particularly against machines and mechanical determinism that he opposed his transcendent life-force. Marinetti was able to change from one artistic strategy to another because he had the brilliant idea of seeing the mechanical not as oppressive but precisely as the vehicle of achieving a Bergsonian transcendence:

> We stand on the last promontory of the centuries! . . . Why should we look back, when what we want is to break down the mysterious doors of the Impossible? Time and Space died yesterday. We already live in the absolute, because we have created eternal, omnipresent speed.[13]

Transcendence comes through driving fast; the limited world of Kantian common sense is vitalised as effectively as any Bergsonian could desire, but through a perceptive manifold rendered fluid by speed. In psychological terms the return to that pre-Oedipal stage where subject and object are fused is achieved when, in the framing narrative of the manifesto, the speeding car crashes and pitches its occupants into the effluent from a factory:

> Oh! Maternal ditch, almost full of muddy water! Fair factory drain! I gulped down your nourishing sludge; and I remembered the blessed black breast of my Sudanese nurse.[14]

Futurism embraces modern technological and capitalist culture as a delighted consumer, seeing it as a vehicle of a Nietzschean (as much as Bergsonian) transcendence of human limits. The violent cultural and political transformations that England appeared to undergo almost unconsciously from 1910 to 1914 were consciously celebrated in its manifestoes: Sorelian revolt, nationalism, war ('the world's only hygiene'), the end of woman as a vehicle of male

[12] Still one of the most illuminating studies of this current of thought is John Caroll, *Break-out from the Crystal Palace: The Anarcho-psychological Critique: Stirner, Nietzsche, Dostoevsky* (London: Routledge & Kegan Paul, 1974).

[13] F. T. Marinetti, 'Manifesto of Futurism', in R. W. Flint, ed., *Marinetti: Selected Writings* (New York: Farrar, Straus & Giroux, 1972), p. 41.

[14] Ibid., p. 40.

fantasy,[15] the destruction of past culture in museums and galleries, the beauty of struggle.

It was only with the 1912 exhibition of Futurist paintings that the movement impinged on the general consciousness in Britain. Valerio Gioè's valuable bibliography of Futurism in England records forty-six magazine and newspaper articles about the exhibition, as well as a spate of general articles about the movement in that year.[16] Roger Fry's own review of the exhibition confirmed his position above the fray by pointing to what he saw as the lesson of the paintings on display, that they served to show that 'it is not necessary that the images of a picture should have any fixed spatial relation to one another except that dictated by the needs of pure design'.[17] Given the subjects of many of these paintings (indicated by such titles as *The Rising City*, *The Funeral of the Anarchist Galli*, *Rebellion* and *Train at Full Speed*) this austere observation is almost wilfully perverse, but it is consistent with the alternative strategy for Modernism. It was also consistent with the slightly blasé condescension with which Futurism was received by those who were not 'outraged' by it.

III

Marinetti made his first visit to London in March 1910, giving two lectures at the Lyceum Club. These went unreported in the press. The first was most likely a rendition of the founding manifesto of Futurism, while the second (given in April) was specifically tailored to his audience, a 'Futurist Speech to the English'. He praised the English for their cult of sport and physicality, for their bellicose patriotism and love of liberty. But he complained of their lack of interest in ideas, the hypocrisy that condemned Oscar Wilde, and the

15 'The end of woman as a vehicle of male fantasy' presents Futurist gender-politics as a great deal less problematic and more acceptable to feminism than they actually are. The manifesto famously advocates 'scorn for women'; but the suffragette vandalism of the *Rokeby Venus* is not so far from the demand of Futurist painters for a moratorium on the salacious motif of the nude in painting: 'We fight . . . against nudity in painting as nauseous and tiring as adultery in literature' ('Manifesto of the Futurist Painters'; flyer issued in English by *Poesia*, Milan (n.d.; probably for the Futurist Exhibition of 1912).

16 Valerio Gioè, 'Futurism in England: a Bibliography', *Bulletin of Bibliography*, 44, 3 (September 1987), pp. 175–6, 179. For studies of the influence of Futurism in England, see Giovanni Cianci, 'Futurism and the English Avant-Garde: the Early Pound between Imagism and Vorticism', *Arbeiten aus Anglistik und Amerikanistik*, 6, 1 (1981), pp. 3–39 and 'Un Futurismo in panni neoclassici: sul primo Wyndham Lewis vorticista', *Wyndham Lewis: Letteratura / Pittura*, ed. Giovanni Cianci (Palermo: Sellerio, 1982), pp. 25–66.

17 Roger Fry, 'Art: the Futurists', *Nation* (9 March 1912), rpt. *Post-Impressionists in England*, p. 301.

pervasive snobbery of English society. He concluded by hitting out at Ruskin as an epitome of English *passéism*:

> With his morbid dream of primitive rustic life, with his nostalgia for Homeric cheeses and legendary wool-winders, with his hatred for the machine, steam, and electricity, that maniac of antique simplicity is like a man who, after having reached full physical maturity, still wants to sleep in his cradle and feed himself at the breast of his decrepit old nurse in order to recover his thoughtless infancy.
>
> Ruskin would certainly have applauded those passéist Venetians who wanted to rebuild the absurd Bell Tower of San Marco, like offering a baby girl who has lost her nurse a little cloth and cardboard doll as a substitute.[18]

Though unreported in the press, the lecture had one significant echo. On 5 May in the *New Age*, the painter–writer Wyndham Lewis published an article entitled 'Our Wild Body' taking up Marinetti's critique (without mentioning it) and adapting his positive points so that they do the English less credit. The English have only cultivated sport and physical fitness as a way of 'taming the body, and the spirit as well' as part of their system of insulating themselves from real life in a world of artifice and make-believe:

> In conclusion, who ever saw a woman who nursed her baby one half hour, and a wax-doll the next? When she gets old enough to have a baby she discards her doll. And yet one may see any day of the week men of all ages guilty of an absurdity of this nature.[19]

The repetition of Marinetti's image of the doll (albeit in a less 'offensive' context) clinches what is in any case deducible from the general spirit of the piece, that Lewis was among Marinetti's audience on this occasion. 'Our Wild Body' was intended as a preface to a collection of Lewis's writings celebrating the 'primitive' vigour and comic absurdity of the lives of the peasants, fishermen and innkeepers he had encountered over the previous few years in his travels in Brittany and Spain. Hearing Marinetti had evidently decided him to attempt to enlist these writings in a quasi-Futurist critique of English complacency. On the face of it, the attempt was absurd; the travel writings, with their gentle humour and spirit of bemused detachment, are closer to W. H. Hudson than they are to Marinetti. Lewis had not yet learned the avant-garde strategy of

[18] R. W. Flint, ed., 'Futurist Speech to the English', in *Marinetti: Selected Writings*, pp. 64–5. Compare the image with that of the return to 'the black breast of my Sudanese nurse' in the framing narrative of the founding Manifesto, quoted above. Ultimately it is Ruskin's strategy that is under attack more than the ambition Marinetti attributes to him, despite the scornful tone.

[19] Wyndham Lewis, 'Our Wild Body', *New Age* (5 May 1910), p. 9.

incorporating mass-culture within the work of art (either in his writing or his painting). The same incongruity is evident in the first publication of Futurist manifestoes in the British press in August: abridged versions of the founding manifesto and 'Futurist Venice', in *The Tramp*, a magazine celebrating hiking and the open-air life. They are preceded by book reviews (*Highways and Byways in Buckinghamshire* by Clement Shorter) and followed by 'Kit Notes' on travelling in Europe by Edith A. Browne ('Shall I go as a Tramp?': 'you must be willing to live as a native, partake of native fare, travel in native style').[20]

Marinetti visited England again in 1912, to launch the Futurist exhibition, and gave a lecture at the Bechstein Hall on Futurism in Literature and Art. He also, accompanied by the painter Umberto Boccioni and an unidentified man (probably an Italian journalist), paid a visit to an English journalist to complain of his disrespectful coverage of the Italian campaign against Turkey at Tripoli the previous year.[21] Further visits coincided with exhibitions in 1913 and 1914. Futurism had now definitely arrived in England, and from 1912 until the outbreak of war it was rarely out of the public press. Gioè's bibliography records over 250 articles about it in newspapers and magazines during the period. This excitement over Futurism was part of the general excitement about bohemia. Marinetti read at the Cabaret Theatre Club (The Cave of the Golden Calf), which was decorated with avant-garde art by Jacob Epstein and Wyndham Lewis (among others). In England, at least, Futurism provided new forms for the rich to indulge in a bourgeois–bohemian Saturnalia in the run-up to the anticipated war or revolution. The Futurist painters attended a ball at the Albert Hall in March 1912, and in December 1913 a 'Picture Ball' was held at the same venue, organised by Lady Muriel Paget. A highlight of the evening was a tableau in which Edward Marsh and Sir Denis Anson paraded in 'Futurist' costumes designed by Wyndham Lewis. The designs were reproduced in the *Daily Mirror*, and photographs of them were reproduced after the ball.[22] In June 1914 another Futurist exhibition was held, and Marinetti lectured at Cambridge University and at the Coliseum Music Hall, with demonstrations of Futurist

[20] 'Futurism', *Tramp: An Open Air Magazine* (August 1910), pp. 487–8. The *Tramp* was edited by Douglas Goldring, an associate of Ford Madox Hueffer's from the *English Review*. The August 1910 issue also contained 'A Breton Innkeeper', by Lewis (pp. 411–14). 'Futurism' prints a letter from Marinetti to the editor ('in its quaint English . . . It is such fun!'); it is certainly possible that Futurism made its first press appearance here through the influence of Lewis.

[21] See Wees, *Vorticism and the English Avant-Garde*, pp. 94–6.

[22] 'Living Pictures at the Night's Ball: What the Futurists will Look Like', *Daily* Mirror (3 December 1913); see Paul O'Keeffe, *Some Sort of Genius: A Life of Wyndham Lewis* (London: Jonathan Cape, 2000), pp. 140–2. The designs and photographs are reproduced by O'Keeffe between pp. 218 and 219.

music on Luigi Russolo's 'noise-tuners'.[23] Futurism also became a convenient reference point by which political commentators (of all persuasions) could characterise the social upheavals of the day. The anonymous 'Musings without Method' that appeared in *Blackwood's Magazine* in January 1914, having mocked Marinetti's poetic ('He attempts to prove himself original by breaking the laws imposed upon his craft by far greater men than he') and compared its results unfavourably with the speech of Alfred Jingle from *Pickwick*, went on to call Herbert Asquith 'the Marinetti of the House of Commons' for destroying the constitution by limiting the powers of the Lords: 'it was prophesied in this Magazine, even before the Home Rule Bill was introduced, that Civil War would be the logical result of the Parliament Act'.[24] Cartoonists in particular used the new pictorial style to convey the chaos of the time. 'A "Futurist Picture" of the Coal Strike, by Natura! A Synthesis of the States of Mind of Miners and Owners!' in March 1912 was the first of many.[25]

IV

As I have suggested, whatever the fascination with Futurism in England, its effect on literature remained virtually non-existent, and when it did have an effect on actual writing it did so only in the wake of its unquestionable influence in forming a visual avant-garde in England, the Vorticists, christened as such in 1914 in an attempt to claim for themselves a crucial difference from the Futurists (a difference that was not readily discernible to any but themselves). A form of Cubo-Futurist painting by English artists was already visible in the second Post-Impressionist exhibition, but there was no equivalent assimilation of Futurism to writing. Instead, and most comprehensively in 1913, there were printings of manifestoes and commentaries on Futurist ideas about writing. In September, Harold Monro edited a special Futurist issue of *Poetry and Drama*. It contained translations of poems by Marinetti himself, by Paolo Buzzi and Aldo Palazzeschi. They are all from the transitional stage of Futurism, free verse rather than full 'words-at-liberty'. Monro declared that he too was a Futurist, and announced his Futurist resolutions, which were framed in the spirit of Nietzsche's 'I love those that know not how to live except as down-goers, for

[23] For a subtle and suggestive (as well as exhaustively researched) account of the Coliseum lectures, see Lawrence Rainey, 'The Creation of the Avant-Garde: F. T. Marinetti and Ezra Pound', chapter 1 of *Institutions of Modernism: Literary Elites and Public Culture* (New Haven and London: Yale University Press, 1998.)

[24] 'Musings without Method', *Blackwood's Magazine* (January 1914), pp. 138–39, 140, 142.

[25] *Sketch* (20 March 1912), p. 335. The allusion is to Boccioni's series of paintings of 'states of mind' in the Futurist exhibition.

they are over-goers . . . I love those who . . . sacrifice themselves to the earth, that the Earth of the superman may hereafter arrive':[26]

> I. To forget God, Heaven, Hell, Personal Immortality, and to remember, always, the earth.
> II. To lift the eyes from a sentimental contemplation of the past, and, though dwelling in the present, nevertheless, always, to *live*, in the future of the earth.[27]

The pious tone of these resolutions hardly fitted the spirit of the 'new Futurist manifesto' concerning literature that the magazine also printed, 'Wireless Imagination and Words at Liberty'. Marinetti demands

> Condensed Metaphors. – Telegraphic images. – Sequences of analogies. – Colour-equilibriums. – The dimensions, weights, measures and speed of sensations. – The plunge of the inevitable word into the water of consciousness, without the concentric circles which the word produces around itself. – Pauses of the intuition. – Movement in two, three, four, five time. – Analytical and explanatory poles sustaining the wires of intuition.

He calls for the abandonment of normal syntax and its replacement by mathematical signs, the replacement of metaphor by unconnected and apparently remote images and analogies and a typographical revolution against bibliographical good taste:

> Our revolution is directed against the so-called typographical harmony of the page, which is opposed to the flux and reflux, the jerks and bursts of style that are represented on it. We shall use, therefore, in the same page, *three or four different colours of ink*, and, if necessary, even twenty different forms of type. *Italics*, for instance, for one series of similes and equally rapid sensations, SMALL CAPITALS for violent onomatopoeia.[28]

Later in the same issue, F. S. Flint contributed a 'French Chronicle' in which he treated these ideas with scepticism, declaring that they were 'likely to ruin futurism'.[29] Flint was associated with Imagism; he had welcomed Futurism the previous year, and asked rhetorically whether English poetry did not need the greater part of the Futurist programme outlined in the founding manifesto.[30] In a 1914 issue of *Poetry and Drama*, Monro was to make his rejection of Futurism

[26] Friedrich Nietzsche, *Thus Spake Zarathustra*, vol. IV of *Complete Works*, ed. Oscar Levy (Edinburgh and London: T. Foulis, 1910), 'Zarathustra's Prologue', section 4.
[27] Harold Monro, 'Varia', *Poetry and Drama*, 1, 3 (September 1913), p. 262.
[28] 'Wireless Imagination and Words at Liberty: the New Futurist Manifesto' trans. Arundel del Re, *Poetry and Drama*, 1, 3, pp. 319–25.
[29] F. S. Flint, 'French Chronicle', *Poetry and Drama*, 1, 3, p. 357.
[30] F. S. Flint, 'F.-T. Marinetti and "Le Futurisme" ', *Poetry Review* (August 1912), p. 411.

even clearer. Futurism was fine for Italy but 'it is essential for us to be allowed to solve our own problems in our own manner'. He goes on to announce with pride the publication later in the issue of a new poem 'by the new Laureate, Mr Robert Bridges'. An only slightly warmer welcome for Marinetti's technical ideas would be given by Henry Newbolt, in the *Fortnightly Review* in May the same year.[31]

What had really impressed Monro about futurist poetry was its phenomenal sales, not its radicalism: 'for us . . . Marinetti's most interesting attitude is rampant with his 35,000 copies of the *Book of the Futurist Poets*'. These huge sales (in Italy) were more important for him than any technical transformation of poetry. Mindful also, no doubt, of the omnipresence of Futurism in the popular press, Monro declared that 'our present hope lies rather in circulation than innovation. We desire to see a public created that may read verse as it now reads its newspapers.'[32] But the only poetry that could hope to fulfil that desire and emulate the sales of the Futurist anthology was by such writers as Kipling, William Watson, Newbolt or Alfred Noyes. On a lower level, C. K. Stead records, John Oxenham's *Bees in Amber* went though fourteen printings within a year of publication in June 1914. Newbolt republished a book of verse in 1914 after the outbreak of war and achieved sales of 70,000.[33]

V

Monro's wistful yearning for an infinite circulation comparable with what the great media empires of Newnes, Harmsworth and Pearson achieved was faintly echoed in the running of what is now seen as England's most important Modernist periodical, *The Egoist*.[34] The importance of the *Egoist* to literary history is its role in publishing Ezra Pound and the Imagists, serialising Joyce's *A Portrait of the Artist as a Young Man* (and some of *Ulysses*) and Wyndham Lewis's *Tarr*. It also published T. S. Eliot's 'Tradition and the Individual Talent' in its

[31] Henry Newbolt, 'Futurism and Form in Poetry', *Fortnightly Review* (May 1914), pp. 804–18. In the course of his discussion, Newbolt gives an amusing Futurist translation of Keats's 'Ode to a Nightingale': 'Death = ease + richness + jug-jug-jug-bubble-bubble, = ecstasy deafness, requiem sod', etc. (p. 813).

[32] Harold Monro, 'Futurist Poetry' and 'Broadsides and Chap-Books', *Poetry and Drama*, 1, 3, pp. 264, 265. The confused thinking about poetry and the market that Monro's moderation led him into is analysed well in C. K. Stead, *The New Poetic: Yeats to Eliot* (Harmondsworth: Penguin, 1967), pp. 59–60.

[33] Stead, *The New Poetic*, pp. 65, 90.

[34] For a detailed and perceptive study of the relationship between *The Egoist* (including its earlier incarnations, *The Freewoman* and *The New Freewoman*), and the marketplace, see Mark Morrisson, 'Marketing British Modernism: *The Egoist* and Counter-Public Spheres', *Twentieth-Century Literature*, 43, 4 (Winter 1997), pp. 439–69.

final issue: a signpost to the future. Like the more successful *New Age*, the paper included advanced literature as only one of its areas of interest. Despite the abundant signs of social and political unrest, its 'advanced' position on such issues did not make it a rallying post where a whole counter-culture might unite, guaranteeing for itself a viable circulation. On the contrary, its anti-suffrage feminism made it less attractive to the women's movement, and it lost many of its female readers as it changed its focus to anarcho-syndicalism and to a variety of 'individualism' that, like Stirner's (upon which it was modelled) distrusted 'causes' and collective action.[35] Imagism, while theoretically compatible with Stirnerian egoism, hardly shared its ethos, and tended to alienate readers who were its adherents.

In its drive for circulation, the *Egoist* emulated on a small scale the tactics of the successful popular press, with advertising, discussion groups, poster campaigns and sandwich-board men. As *The Freewoman* in 1911 it carried advertisements from companies marketing goods likely to appeal to middle-class women. Mark Morrisson notes 'advertisements for new national brand name products, like Horrocks's "flanalette" and Adori soap . . . alongside ads for women's patent medicines'.[36] Beginning with a print-run of 2,000, it rapidly dropped to 1,500 and again to 1,000 by September 1913. At its demise in 1919 only 400 copies were being printed.[37]

As Lawrence Rainey has ingeniously suggested, far from being the first avant-garde in Anglo-American literature, Imagism is better understood as 'the first anti-avant-garde.'[38] Its connection with the culture that Futurism embraced is almost entirely negative. Morrisson notes its negative portrayal of cinema, the Tube (underground railway) and popular press. The *Egoist*'s 'Imagist Number' (May 1915) published a poem by Flint in which a swan in a London park is sullied by the black scum of newsprint from a discarded newspaper caught underneath it as it swims.[39] Flint's discouragement ('Friend, we are beaten') could not be further from the avowed exultation of Marinetti as he gulped the nourishing mud and effluent into which his speeding car had pitched him. Imagism adopted the first of the two strategies outlined above for engaging with the culture and products of modernity, which it rejected in favour of an uncontaminated region of form or beauty. Ezra Pound's most famous Imagist poem, 'In a Station of the Metro', while ostensibly admitting modernity into itself (the underground railway) in accordance with Futurist

35 Ibid., p. 456. 36 Ibid., p. 444. 37 Ibid., p. 466 (n. 42).
38 Rainey, *Institutions of Modernism*, p. 30.
39 F. S. Flint, 'Easter', *Egoist* (May 1915), p. 75; discussed by Morrisson, 'Marketing British Modernism', pp. 447–8.

and avant-garde practice, actually confirms the formalist nature of Imagist strategy, for the crowd it represents is merely a background for the petal-like faces of the few, and these faces themselves have no social definition. They are apparitions from an ancient underworld or formalist 'splotches of colour' as they might appear in a painting by Kandinsky.[40]

Pound, however, was about to join forces with a genuinely avant-garde movement, that of the advanced English painters inspired by Futurism and other European Modernist art movements. Pound even supplied a name for the group and their movement, Vorticism, but his own transition to an avant-garde strategy was uneasy and not successful, at least in the poems that flowed from it.[41] Much has been written in exploration of the aesthetic differences between Vorticism and Futurism (not least by Pound and Wyndham Lewis), and in some contexts these differences are certainly of great importance to an understanding of the movements' different artistic products.[42] But it is reasonable to consider Vorticism in its main features as a Futurist avant-garde movement.[43] The title, Vorticism, was not invented until the movement's magazine, *Blast*, was already in production.[44] The movement itself had emerged out of a small-scale 'industrial dispute', when Wyndham Lewis and three other workers walked out of their employer's workshop (the employer was Roger Fry, the workshop the Omega Workshops) over a commission to decorate a room for the *Daily Mail* 'Ideal Home' exhibition in 1913. The artists allied themselves to Marinetti, set up their own 'Rebel Art Centre', planned their

[40] Ezra Pound, 'In a Station of the Metro' (1913), rpt. *Collected Shorter Poems* (London: Faber & Faber, 1968), p. 119. Pound's explanation of the composition of the poem is in his 1914 essay, 'Vorticism', rpt. Ezra Pound, *Gaudier-Brzeska: A Memoir* (1918), rpt (New York: New Directions, 1970), pp. 86–9.

[41] For example, 'Salutation the Third' ('Let us deride the smugness of "The Times": / GUFFAW!', *Blast 1*, p. 45) or 'The New Cake of Soap' that 'glistens . . . like the cheek of a Chesterton' (p. 49).

[42] See, for example, Wees, *Vorticism and the English Avant-Garde*, Michael Durman and Alan Munton, 'Wyndham Lewis and the Nature of Vorticism', *Wyndham Lewis: Letteratura / Pittura*, pp. 111–18, and Reed Way Dasenbrock, *The Literary Vorticism of Ezra Pound and Wyndham Lewis: Towards the Condition of Painting* (Baltimore and London: Johns Hopkins University Press, 1985).

[43] The definitive history of Vorticism is Richard Cork, *Vorticism and Abstract Art in the First Machine Age*, vol. I: *Origins and Development*, vol. II: *Synthesis and Decline* (London: Gordon Fraser, 1976).

[44] See Paul O'Keeffe, 'The Troubled Birth of *Blast*: December 1913–June 1914', *ICSAC Cahier 8/9: Vorticism*, ed. Andrew Wilson (December 1988), pp. 43–57. Traces of the movement before its christening may be found in *Blast* itself: 'Of all the tags going, "Futurist", for general application, serves as well as any for the active painters of to-day' (Wyndham Lewis, 'The Melodrama of Modernity', *Blast*, *1* (June 1914), facsimile rpt ed. Bradford Morrow (Santa Barbara: Black Sparrow Press, 1981), p. 143.

magazine and finally adopted their new name when they broke with Marinetti and Futurism before publication on the grounds of Marinetti's misappropriation of their trademark 'Rebel Art Centre' address.[45]

Blast, the Vorticists' magazine, was printed in outsize format on cheap spongy paper with liberal use of large sans serif type (mixed with underlined type and type of varying point-sizes, and serif faces for many areas of the text) on page layouts that, in their inventive spacing, produced a visual effect that served an expressive, tonal and syntactic purpose. It reproduced and to some extent anticipated the typographical grammar of popular newspapers, following as far as possible (given limited resources) some of the ideals set forth in Marinetti's 'Wireless Imagination', though it eschewed the mathematical signs and onomatopoeic effects that had been derided in English discussions of Futurist literary theories.[46] The manifestoes and commentaries that opened the magazine were thoroughly imbricated with the public culture of the day, and reproduced within themselves its antagonisms and aggressions. Edward Carson and Captain Craig are blessed, as are the militant suffragettes Frieda Graham and Lillie Lenton. Music-hall artists like George Robey and Harry Weldon as well as boxers, art critics (and James Joyce) were also blessed. C. B. Fry (standing in for Roger), cod-liver oil and Bergson were blasted, castor oil and Charlotte Corday were blessed. The 'Blast' and 'Bless' pages that opened the magazine were playful and witty, but they also situated the Vorticists fairly precisely in relation to the public culture of the day.[47]

Wyndham Lewis, who was the chief writer and designer of *Blast*, as well as its editor, had in the years since his first encounter with Marinetti achieved a reputation as a painter rather than a writer (though he continued working on his novel, *Tarr*, written largely in 1911 and to be revised and completed in

[45] A concise account of the emergence of Vorticism can be found in the 'Introduction' to Paul Edwards, ed., *Blast: Vorticism 1914–1918* (London: Ashgate, 2000). Lisa Tickner, *Modern Life and Modern Subjects: British Art in the Early Twentieth Century* (New Haven and London: Yale University Press, 2000) traces the presence of popular commercial culture in Lewis's 1912 painting, *Kermesse*. Marinetti and the 'English Futurist' C. R. W. Nevinson made the 'unauthorised use' in their manifesto 'Vital English Art', *Observer* (7 June 1914). In a spirit of surrender hardly Futurist, in a reprint of the manifesto as a pamphlet (n.d., but shortly afterwards), references to Lewis and other painters were dropped, and addresses in Milan and Hampstead were substituted.

[46] See Michael E. Leveridge, 'The Printing of *Blast*', *Wyndham Lewis Annual* 2000, 7, 21–31, and, for an analysis of the typographical effects, Wees, *Vorticism and the English Avant-Garde*, chapter 10.

[47] Appendix B of *Vorticism and the English Avant-Garde* gives a useful account of the blasted and blessed. See also Alan Windsor, 'Wyndham Lewis's "Blast and Bless" ', *Wyndham Lewis: Letteratura / Pittura*, pp. 86–100, where the influence of Guillaume Apollinaire's *L'antitradition futuriste* is also discussed.

1915). There was, he realised in 1914, no avant-garde writing being produced in England suitable for inclusion in *Blast*. In 1910 he had been unsure what form such writing should take, but was now confident enough to supply it himself: 'My literary contemporaries I looked upon as too bookish and not keeping pace with the visual revolution. A kind of play, "The Enemy of the Stars" . . . was my attempt to show them the way', he later recalled.[48] The title of the piece recalls Marinetti's *Conquête des étoiles*, but apart from sharing with that work an esoteric Gnosticism (in which the stars are 'Archons', agents of a vengeful God in his enslavement of the human soul), it bears no resemblance to that Decadent epic.[49] It is, rather, a violent fable in which a protagonist (Arghol) and his antagonistic disciple (Hanp) act out the conflict between the pristine spiritual self and the 'false' version of that self that is created in the traffic and exchange of participation in bourgeois urban culture. It recuperates, in other words, precisely the dialectic of the two artistic strategies for engaging with the marketplace that have been the backdrop to this chapter.

Enemy of the Stars incorporates the products of modernity in its medium (even if it does so less extensively that do the manifesto pages of the magazine): 'A gust, such as is met in the corridors of the Tube, makes their clothes shiver or flap, and blares up their voices.' There are references to cinema, to caustic Reckitts stain, and the sky is an 'immense bleak electric advertisement of God'. Mostly it is simply the phrasal style, in which the relation between phrases is indeterminate, that evokes a Futurist aesthetic:

> Port-prowler, serf of the capital, serving its tongue and gait within the grasp and aroma of the white, matt, immense sea. Abstract instinct of sullen seafarer, dry-salted in slow acrid airs, aerian flood not stopped by shore, dying in dirty warmth of harbour-boulevards.[50]

[48] Wyndham Lewis, *Rude Assignment: A Narrative of My Career Up-to-date* (London: Hutchinson, 1950), p. 129.

[49] See Massimo Carrà, 'Religion', Pontus Hulten, ed., *Futurism* (London, Thames & Hudson, 1986), pp. 552–3.

[50] Wyndham Lewis, *Enemy of the Stars*, *Blast*, 1, pp. 60, 66, 62, 64, 69 (spelling and punctuation corrected; *Blast* was mocked for its errors of this kind. Ford Madox Hueffer defended it on the grounds that Shakespeare had similar 'problems'). For discussions of the style of *Enemy of the Stars* see Dasenbrock, *The Literary Vorticism of Ezra Pound and Wyndham Lewis*, chapter 4, 'Lewis's *Enemy of the Stars* and Modernism's Attack on Narrative', and David Graver, 'Vorticist Performance and Aesthetic Turbulence in *Enemy of the Stars*, *PMLA*, 107, 3 (May 1992), pp. 482–96; for a discussion of its meaning and some of its esoteric dimension, see Paul Edwards, *Wyndham Lewis: Painter and Writer* (New Haven and London: Yale University Press, 2000), chapter 5, 'The Modernism of *Enemy of the Stars*'.

In scene 6 of Lewis's strange dream-play (at this moment the narrative is literally in Arghol's dream), for a moment the fanatical protagonist seems to have achieved his ambition of return to uncontaminated purity:

> He was Arghol once more.
>
> Was that a key to something? He was simply Arghol.
>
> 'I am Arghol'.
>
> He repeated his name – like sinister word invented to launch a new Soap, in gigantic advertisement – toilet-necessity, he, to scrub the soul.[51]

The moment of realisation is figured through an image from consumer culture that for the 1914 reader inevitably familiar with advertising posters (or the adverts for Adori soap in the *Freewoman*) immediately negates what it so precisely vivifies. What happens in Lewis's writing here is something more complex and less definable than irony, though irony begins to impinge in the parody of the pretentious vocabulary of advertising copy ('toilet-necessity'). At the least, what is signalled is an interdependence of cultural spheres that from now on cannot be escaped.[52]

But *Blast* and Vorticism did not succeed in opening a space in British culture for the avant-garde. On the title page it is announced as having been published by John Lane, and three pages of advertisements at the back for the firm's other publications (sets of *The Yellow Book*, books by Wilde, Vernon Lee and Richard Le Gallienne, books on Whistler and Charles Conder) promised a cultural success that the magazine never achieved. As was the case with so much in this period, it was deferred and finally rendered impossible by the arrival of war a month after publication. In fact, the involvement of Lane had not been quite what it seemed. He did not finance publication; for £50 worth of advertising he became entitled to 1,000 copies without charge (probably about a third of the print-run).[53] Much of the money for Vorticism came from the investor-cum-patron-cum-artist, Kate Lechmere, and much of this was lost in the venture. It was, besides, impossible to find a niche in British culture for an avant-garde magazine like *Blast*. It was received with tired, superior yawns, only A. R. Orage, having dismissed it in the *New Age* one week as 'not

[51] *Blast*, 1, p. 80.

[52] Mark Morrisson, in *The Public Face of Modernism: Little Magazines, Audiences, and Reception, 1905–1920* (Madison: University of Wisconsin Press, 2001), p. 131, plausibly sees this moment in the play as indicating an embrace of publicity and marketing as a way forward for Lewis.

[53] O'Keeffe, *Some Sort of Genius*, p. 151.

worth understanding', conceding the next that *Enemy of the Stars* 'contains ideas of an almost grandiose dimension, though felt rather than thought'. 'But for the present', he added, 'the movement appears to me to be the very devil.'[54] There was to be no place for an avant-garde literature in England. Modernism would 'succeed' through the po-faced strategy of T. S. Eliot in his respectable magazine, *The Criterion*. His own attempt at a full-blooded avant-garde strategy, *Sweeney Agonistes*, would come to nothing.

VI

D. H. Lawrence also responded to Futurism and Marinetti, and voiced his thoughts in two letters to A. W. McCleod and Edward Garnett.[55] His reading of Marinetti enabled him to articulate to himself his objective as a novelist in writing what would become *The Rainbow*. Marinetti's Bergsonian desire to penetrate behind the phenomenal barriers of perception to a more intuitive level underlies Lawrence's famous statement that he is concerned not with the 'old stable ego' but a deeper one that 'passes through . . . allotropic states which it needs a deeper sense than any we've been used to exercise, to discover are states of the same single radically unchanged element'.[56] *The Rainbow* was hardly an avant-garde work; it may be thought that its closest link with Futurism is a shared assumption that destruction is a midwife to creation. At any rate, it was suppressed for obscenity in November 1915. James Joyce and Wyndham Lewis both had novels that Ezra Pound was trying to place with mainstream publishers at about the same time. *A Portrait of the Artist as a Young Man* and *Tarr* are not by today's standards especially avant-garde or shocking, yet even with the efforts of Joyce's agent, J. B. Pinker, neither could achieve publication in the mainstream of British publishing. John Lane, who had 'published' *Blast*, found *Tarr* 'too strong a book', and Werner Laurie and Martin Secker also declined the risk. Both novels were serialised in the *Egoist* and then published in volume form by Harriet Shaw Weaver under the *Egoist* imprint (in 1916 and 1918 respectively).[57] T. S. Eliot's *Prufrock and Other Observations*

[54] A. R. Orage, 'Readers and Writers', *New Age* (9 and 16 July 1914), rpt. Wallace Martin, ed., *Orage as Critic* (London: Routledge & Kegan Paul, 1974), pp. 137–8.

[55] Lawrence to McLeod, 2 June 1914; Lawrence to Garnett, 5 June 1914, nos. 731 and 732 in *The Letters of D. H. Lawrence*, 8 vols. vol. II, ed. G. J. Zytaruk and J. T. Boulton (Cambridge University Press, 1981).

[56] *Letters of D. H. Lawrence*, II, p. 183. Giovanni Cianci has made the fullest study of Lawrence's attitude to Futurism: 'D. H. Lawrence and Futurism/Vorticism', *Arbeiten aus Anglistik und Amerikanistik*, 8, 1 (1983), pp. 41–53.

[57] See the publication history given in Paul O'Keeffe's 'Afterword' to his edition of Wyndham Lewis, *Tarr: The 1918 Version* (Santa Rosa: Black Sparrow Press, 1990).

(1917) also depended on Weaver for publication. Despite the excitement of Futurism, there was as yet virtually no niche in the marketplace for Modernist writing. From this perspective, Lewis's often-quoted 1937 judgement that 'We are the first men of a Future that has not materialized' seems an accurate conclusion.[58]

[58] Wyndham Lewis, *Blasting and Bombardiering* (London: Eyre & Spottiswoode, 1937), p. 258.

9

Literature and World War I

VINCENT SHERRY

'As swimmers into cleanness leaping':[1] the image in which Rupert Brooke projected the high aims of early autumn 1914 remains vivid in cultural memory, among other reasons, for the profound irony it affords in historical retrospect. To greet the hideous futility of four years of trench warfare as a cleansing pleasance of late summer? The gesture magnetises our attention in the same way that the impact of an accident seems to be caught most powerfully when, looking back, we see an expression of unsuspecting happiness immediately preceding it. Just so, however, the pattern of contrast that Brooke forms might be dismissed as a heuristic, really just a useful fallacy, insofar as it allows us to feel a meaning in history that may not be borne out by the facts. As any detailed account of English political and cultural history will indicate, the years preceding the outbreak of the Great War resist assimilation to that myth of the 'Golden Summer of 1914'. In *The Strange Death of Liberal England*, for instance, George Dangerfield proposes that the war, far from shaking the foundations of English society, actually helped to preserve the status quo by diverting the energies of a social revolution being threatened by the workers' and women's movements, not to speak of the steadily escalating menace in Ireland.[2] The 'Golden Summer' theory may be met with equal scepticism when it is applied to literary history: the decorous measures that Brooke presents in his exemplary instance of Georgian poetics were being countered as a prevailing standard, most notably by an increasingly robust avant-garde – a term that signals a militarisation of culture already under way *avant-guerre*. Yet the larger outlines of political and cultural history are formed by relative sizes, proportionate masses. The majority status that the Liberal Party enjoyed establishes a framework of social values and political practices that comprise a mainstream attitude. A similarly representative strength may be found in

[1] 'Peace', in *The Collected Poems of Rupert Brooke* (1915; New York: Dodd, Mead, 1925), p. 7.
[2] George Dangerfield, *The Strange Death of Liberal England* (1935; New York: Putnam's, 1980), passim, esp. pp. 408–25.

the literary sensibility of a group of poets who take their name from the reigning English king. Georgian Liberalism remains a valid, practicable frame of reference for assessing what was at issue and at stake in August 1914, and an account of the fate its representative poetry met in the trenches may begin to focus the difference the war made in relevant aspects of English national life.

The sonnets gathered in 1915 in Brooke's *1914* (the title-date already frames the *early* war as the moment of high emotional occasion) find a tonic chord in 'The Soldier'. The speaker foresees his death in a 'foreign' war and idealises the experience, striking the deep keynote of Georgian nationalism:

> If I should die, think only this of me:
>   That there's some corner of a foreign field
> That is for ever England. There shall be
>   In that rich earth a richer dust concealed;
> A dust whom England bore, shaped, made aware,
>   Gave, once, her flowers to love, her ways to roam,
> A body of England's, breathing English air,
>   Washed by the rivers, blest by suns of home.[3]

Euphemism is fluent, including among its obvious improvements the 'richer dust' of a decaying corpse but asserting as well some essential continuity between the beautified conditions of arcadian 'England' (the word recurs six times, in varying formations, over the short course of a fourteen-line poem) and the 'foreign' circumstance of this continental war. Brooke thus extends the imaginative claim of Georgian nationalism to its revealing extreme, a verge and limit at which its establishing outlook is at once exaggerated and typified.

At this ideal extremity, Brooke's poem opens the space in which the realities of war will intervene – inevitably, in subsequent years. Ivor Gurney offers his riposte in 'To His Love', an elegy uttered as a sort of Georgianism *manqué*. A strategic use of rhetorical negatives indicates all in English pastoral that does *not* accommodate the untoward event of the subject's death in alien lands:

> He's gone, and all our plans
>   Are useless indeed.
> We'll walk no more on Cotswold
>   Where the sheep feed
>   Quietly and take no heed.
>
> His body that was so quick
>   Is not as you

[3] Brooke, 'The Soldier', in *Collected Poems*, p. 111.

Knew it, on Severn river
Under the blue
Driving our small boat through.

You would not know him now . . .

While Gurney can dub his 'not's and 'no's into the idiom of Georgianism, its topographies control the poetic feeling in the piece, even – or especially – in being forgone. The dominant voice holds its greatest potential for expression, then, when its tongue is tied. The military interment service of the final stanza begins thus with nervous words, exclamatory stammering:

Cover him, cover him soon!
And with thick-set
Masses of memoried flowers –
Hide that red wet
Thing I must somehow forget.[4]

The enjambment in the final line brings the heavy stress of that building rhythm down hard on 'Thing' – a word that offers its ultimate subject, the loved body of the fallen soldier, its generic non-specificity, which is remarkably, shockingly, movingly inadequate.

What has failed as Georgianism, of course, is a stylised, idealised product – the air-brushed, country-day Englishness of the high-gloss coffee-table book. This sensibility stems from conditions that include cultures genuinely lived in, however, a real *gens*, local habitations and their names. If these inward continuities of place are generalised outward into the Englishness of Georgian nationalism, their memory is present in one of the convention's unconventional representatives, an Anglo-Welsh fellow-traveller. Edward Thomas is the radical who returns to the root, who testifies to the greater depths of his British tradition, and, in doing so, witnesses the profounder crisis its spirit meets in the current circumstance.

Thomas's 'A Private' recasts the poetic location of 'The Soldier', repeating the situation of an Englishman dead in an alien land but extending its commemoration in a homelier poetic dialect:

This ploughman dead in battle slept out of doors
Many a frosty night, and merrily
Answered staid drinkers, good bedmen, and all bores:
'At Mrs Greenland's Hawthorn Bush', said he,

[4] In P. J. Kavanagh, ed., *Collected Poems of Ivor Gurney* (Oxford University Press, 1984), p. 41.

'I slept'. None knew which bush. Above the town,
Beyond 'The Drover', a hundred spot the down
In Wiltshire. And where now at last he sleeps
More sound in France – that, too, he secret keeps.[5]

The differences from Brooke's sonnet extend from the particularised realities of the landscape to the living form of the poem: an oral historian's anecdote, it 'turns back' on itself at the end like a good countryman's joke. Yet the two pieces show a common method and aim. Superimposing the topographies of the foreign field and the native terrain, Thomas is also attempting to establish some continuity between his character's English background and his distant death. In this way he offers his own writ, some silent warrant, for the event that occasions the poem. The rationale is indeed 'secret' – the wordplay on 'Private', combining with the military rank's official character, capitalises this motif and raises it to an entitled prominence. This quiet confidence draws upon the resources of a most intimate dominion, the England of the mind that Thomas has built out of his own closely local knowledge.

This ideal Englishness speaks a whispery, nearly mystic idiom, however, and its limiting condition may be witnessed when Thomas attempts to extend it into the discursive circumstances in which the ideological war was actually fought. In 'This is No Case of Petty Right or Wrong', he addresses the mass media of this first mass conflict. He disclaims the totalisations that total war enforced on the discourse – the exaggerations that stimulate the required popular involvement, the hate campaigns, the cartoon enmities, all in all, the mechanism of oppositional thinking and the bogus extremities it effected:

I hate not Germans, nor grow hot
With love of Englishmen, to please newspapers.
Beside my hate of one fat patriot
My hatred of the Kaiser is love true:–
A kind of god he is, banging a gong.

Overriding those false dichotomies of demagogic politics, Thomas disables the claims of the 'versus habit' in the first line of his finale, where he offers his own apologia for the English cause:

But with the best and meanest Englishmen
I am one in crying, God save England, lest
We lose what never slaves and cattle blessed.

[5] In R. George Thomas, ed., *The Collected Poems of Edward Thomas* (Oxford: Clarendon Press, 1978), p. 67.

The ages made her that made us from dust:
She is all we know and live by, and we trust
She is good and must endure, loving her so:
And as we love ourselves we hate her foe.[6]

Running most of the rhyme words on through enjambment, Thomas mutes the closural effect of the couplet and avoids the ring and resonance of any rhetorical peroration. He moves his poetic appeal away from forum oratory and towards the sort of quiet in which his Private's secret would speak its deeper truth. All the earnest effort Thomas evidences in expressing the inwardness of the Englishness he fights for, however, serves to measure the stronger force of its opponent, the England of tabloid politics. The antithesis in the last line bristles with oppositional thinking, which Thomas brokers in the totalised categories of the emotions invoked. Does hate, moreover, derive rightly from love? The apparently logical proposition Thomas balances across this line suggests the specious reasoning of a preconceived, easy-to-consume, daily-journalism sort of rationale. This disparity – between the absolute purity of a spiritual England, to which Thomas alludes as the establishing condition of his cause, and the contingent, coerced and coercive word of the vulgar tongue – bespeaks at once the reality of the current circumstance and the sadness of a casualty that is more than abstract.

How the language of literature is co-opted by politics is a story that begins in early September 1914, when C. F. G. Masterman, acting as director of an office newly created by the War Government, the Department of Information, convened the major novelists and poets of the moment. In effect, he commissioned them to propagandise the English cause in the war. A surplus of patriotic verse and nationalistic fiction followed the influential lead of authors such as Robert Bridges, John Masefield, G. K. Chesterton.[7] This 'authorised version' varied in style and sophistication, ranging from placarded caricatures of the barbaric Hun and poster images of English beauty spots to nuanced critiques of Germanic philology, statism or Hegelianism. The unity of view these arguments produced, however, precluded much beyond the wearily predictable certitudes of cultural nationalism that they began with. Nonetheless, the consensus understanding this literature reflects may be remembered as a prevailing standard, one that establishes the substantial challenge writers find in fashioning a language adequate to an individual apprehension.

6 In ibid., p. 257.
7 See Samuel Hynes, *A War Imagined: The First World War and English Culture* (New York: Atheneum, 1991), 'The Arts Enlist', pp. 25–56.

Wilfred Owen testifies to the meaning of his own combat experience in a lyric realism of fiercely detailed immediacy. While this appreciation is featured routinely – and rightly – in literary histories, the achievement of his mature poetry also shows a special, steady intensity of address to the public, political constructions of the war. This imperative accounts for one of the stronger rhetorical personalities in the major work of the last year of the war. Here he assumes the role of reporter, who orients his witnessing force to the standard, presumptive misunderstandings, of which he will disabuse his readership. In 'Dulce et Decorum Est', for instance, the narrative account of a gas attack modulates into a direct address to the audience – the 'you' Owen accuses in his rhetorically forceful, masterfully contoured, finale:

> If in some smothering dreams you too could pace
> Behind the wagon that we flung him in,
> And watch the white eyes writhing in his face,
> His hanging face, like a devil's sick of sin;
> If you could hear, at every jolt, the blood
> Come gargling from the froth-corrupted lungs,
> Obscene as cancer, bitter as the cud
> Of vile, incurable sores on innocent tongues, –
> My friend, you would not tell with such high zest
> To children ardent for some desperate glory,
> The old Lie: Dulce et decorum est
> Pro patria mori.[8]

The double periodic construction of subordinate clauses suspends the arrival of the main clause and then intensifies its impact, its dominance in the grammatical structure, when it comes. The speaker thus rather overwhelms the level familiarity Owen assigns his reader, as 'My friend'. This personage retains some memory of Jessie Pope, whom Owen named in a mock-dedication to an earlier draft of the poem. She had gained her fame from the noisily jingoistic poetry she published so widely.[9] Its voluble demagoguery has required Owen himself to turn up the poetic volume. Even his courageously angry answer shows the powerful determinants, the really coercive forces, in the verbal culture of mass war.

In these conditions, some of the most important poems are those that get beyond the well-established, all-too-embattled strategies of argument for or against the war. 'The Poetry is in the pity', Owen proposed (in his preface to a

[8] In C. Day Lewis, ed., *The Collected Poems of Wilfred Owen* (1963; London: Chatto & Windus, 1972), p. 55.
[9] See ibid.

collection of war verse not published in his lifetime). He would penetrate to a dimension of feeling that he understands to be somehow deeper, cleaner, more powerfully and genuinely affective than polemic. He follows this directive in his own exemplary instance in 'Strange Meeting', a dream scenario in which his speaker meets the ghost of the German soldier he has killed. They exchange words of (shared) suffering, and this act of imaginative compassion establishes the basis for the poem's major formulation on the import of (this) war: 'I mean the truth untold, / The pity of war, the pity war distilled.'[10] Whether or not poetry can be lifted away from the fury and mire of an ideologically driven history, it is a true measure of the heavy expense of war fought for ideas no longer believed in that the poets of major record seek to reserve an alternative sphere for verse. The poetry Owen models relocates its centres of imaginative attention to a level of elementary, apparently unprepossessed feeling, where the bleaker truths of the human condition, seen as suffering in the image of war, are newly expressed.

In these circumstances, the poetry of Isaac Rosenberg achieves its special representative status. A painter by profession, Rosenberg *sees* the war through a frame of reference that appears immune or indifferent to nationalist, partisan discourses. As a Jew, he understands his experience through a vision formed strongly in accord with the historical and prophetic books of Hebrew scripture, whose ancient fatalism appears timely indeed in face of the current war's incomprehensible eventuality. 'On Receiving News of the War' establishes this Jewish painter's angle of view on the emergent event:

Snow is a strange white word.
No ice or frost
Has asked of bud or bird
For Winter's cost.

Yet ice and frost and snow
From earth to sky
This Summer land doth know.
No man knows why.[11]

'Snow is a strange white word': the logical assertion devolves its verbal constituents to colour spots on the artist's palette. In the vacuum left by the absence of rationale Rosenberg catches the impact of the advent of war, again in 'August 1914', where a language of primary emblematic substances – 'Iron,

[10] Ibid., pp. 31, 35.

[11] In Gordon Bottomley and Denys Harding, eds., *The Collected Poems of Isaac Rosenberg* (1937; New York: Schocken, 1974), p. 124.

honey, gold' – shifts the consideration from any rationalistic grammar to the vivid and impending register of these images:

> Iron are our lives
> Molten right through our youth.
> A burnt space through ripe fields
> A fair mouth's broken tooth.[12]

The shock is as solid as the provocation is bare, unaccommodated by a syntax of statement and any of the expected explanations.

Not that Rosenberg's poetry withholds suppositions about the causes or consequences of war. The scheme of the seasons in 'On Receiving News' provides a temporal conception in which the event takes its designated place, but strangely, since the natural pattern seems aberrant: Winter comes in Summer, devastating war in plentiful August. Any cognisance of the sense this system makes seems to be reserved, suspended in a dimension beyond the poet's ken. 'No man knows why', after all,

> Some spirit old
> Hath turned with malign kiss
> Our lives to mould.[13]

'Some spirit old': the reference plays for associations through the Genesis legends of the Hebrew Wisdom books, which mythologise variously that spirit of original malignity. It is not with the force of a moral hortative, however, that Rosenberg invokes such aboriginal calamity. The antique mysteriousness of that spirit appears as its most compelling element, for him and his reader. It is a quality that frames and fables the special incomprehensibility of this particular war.

Rosenberg's importance may be sized in ratio to the immense efforts the mainstream culture of Britain undertook to make its war acceptable. The breach Rosenberg's poetry opens in the scheme of received meanings and reasons locates the creative space of much of the major work of the English war. The circumstances under which those consensus understandings were constructed may be rehearsed, then, with a view to establishing the occasion in which this literature of essential record assumed its resistant shape, its exceptional significance.

By the intellectual values of its partisan tradition, the War Government of the Liberal Party was compelled to provide moral rationales for any military action. This imperative stemmed from its Victorian precedents, most notably

[12] Ibid., p. 70. [13] Ibid., p. 124.

from Prime Minister W. E. Gladstone. The code had been broken by the most influential members of the War Cabinet, however. Prime Minister H. H. Asquith and his Foreign Secretary Sir Edward Grey conceived British needs strategically, primarily, and, since 1906, had moved Britain into a series of continental alliances. Their agreements had to be kept secret, however, due to the ongoing hegemony of Gladstonian standards in the public discussion of policy. These agreements would nonetheless necessitate British involvement in a European war, when it eventuated, but the strategic motives would then need to be replaced, at least in public, with ethical rationales. The lack of valid matter here resulted in case-making efforts of the most strenuous kind. The grandiosity of these hortative formulations – a moral War for Civilisation, for Progress, for Democratic Tolerance, for the Rights of Small Nations, and so on – exposed the holiness of cause as the hollowest of logics.[14] The crisis of those majority values and practices represents a condition in which all the work of substantial and lasting record participates. This connection may be evidenced first in the best-known examples of the English war memoir, which, in the documentary quality the genre features, adds historical memory to personal recollection and, in this expanded awareness, relives the import of the war in political and cultural history as well as individual experience.

Robert Graves's *Good-bye to All That* (1929) frames its war-story (roughly, its middle third) within an autobiography that offers a background narrative and a record of subsequent developments. What Graves takes through the trenches with him is the officer- and governing-class orientation of his generation, which has been formed in the long heyday of British Liberalism. But Graves's personal temperament positions him at the off-angle to standard liberal values: in his youth he avidly – and defiantly – consumes Samuel Butler's *Erewhon*, a distopia (making an anagram from the *nowhere* of *u-topos* as its title lead) that belies any belief in progress through scientific rationalism, that particularly liberal faith,[15] the one which the unforeseeable atrocity of mass technological war would discredit so heavily. Accordingly, and especially in memory, Graves orients the younger version of himself towards the war as the defining crisis of Liberalism. The first casualty he names takes on the loaded

[14] Government documents reveal the existence of the secret agreements; see E. D. Morel, *Truth and the War* (London: National Labour Press, 1916), esp. pp. 273–300. The verbal construction of the war by the Liberal Government, in particular the establishment of the ethical case and the elaboration of its rationalistic language, is followed through the partisan journalism by Irene Cooper Willis, *How We Went into the War: A Study of Liberal Idealism* (Manchester: National Labour Press, 1918), esp. 'The Holy War', pp. 86–141.

[15] Robert Graves, *Good-bye to All That* (1929), 2nd edn (1957; New York: Doubleday, 1989), p. 69.

associations of a strong partisan legacy: 'a Liberal M.P., Second-Lieutenant W. G. Gladstone . . . a grandson of old Gladstone, whom he resembled in feature, and Lord-Lieutenant of his county'. The fate Gladstonian Liberalism suffers in the history Graves prefigures with this initial death is detailed further in an adjacent passage, where he pauses over the preserved antiquity of his regiment's name: '"Welch" referred us somehow to the archaic North Wales of Henry Tudor and Owen Glendower and Lord Herbert of Cherbury, the founder of the Regiment; it dissociated us from the modern North Wales of chapels, Liberalism, the dairy and drapery business, slate mines, and the tourist trade'.[16] The commitment to prosperity in the commercial middle class avowed nineteenth-century Liberalism's confidence in material progress, and Graves's report of this social code (including the probity of its Gladstonian, 'chapels' morality) includes a testament of the reverse turn his own experience will take. The zoning of emotional associations in regimental history in particular, in general a shift to the pre-modern past as the centre of affective attention: this frame of reference replaces the forward orientations of rational 'progress'. The undoing of this machinery of received meanings lends Graves's record of his experience its exceptionally representative strength.

'The Illogical Element in English Poetry', the BA paper Graves went on to write after his return in 1919 to Oxford (published subsequently as *Poetic Unreason*), claims the importance of a sub-rational language for literature.[17] This is the mature youth's scholarly riposte to the majority values of English Liberalism, which have authored the moral reasoning for the war in documents whose logic has been disproved. Out of the ruins of that strained and degraded rationalism, Graves is attempting to renew the language of literature. But the trouble in coming up with a speech for unreason can hardly be gainsaid. Graves's own prose seems incapable of being deflected from the impeccable measures of its own neo-Classical *sanitas*. This fact does not discredit his critique, but it raises the issue of the ownership of the literary idiom by established values and, in this way, underscores the real challenge in talking back.

This difficulty finds its most indicative instance perhaps in the work commonly regarded as the exemplary equal of Graves's work in the genre, Siegfried Sassoon's *Memoirs of an Infantry Officer* (1930). This novel–memoir (middle entry in the trilogy *The Memoirs of George Sherston*) rises to the crisis of its author's own great climacteric – the public statement which Sassoon's process of disillusionment with the war, recorded as the main story in this narrative, has led

[16] Ibid., pp. 74, 85–6. [17] Ibid., p. 320.

him to make. Its occasion is arranged through a series of well-placed acquaintances, beginning with the editor of the liberal literary weekly the *Nation*, here the unambiguously renamed *Unconservative Weekly*. Sherston meets this Mr Markington at a club Sassoon labels 'the Mecca of the Liberal Party', and he is led thence into the more heavily mentoring presence of Thornton Tyrrell, who is Bertrand Russell, doyen and philosophical powerhouse of Liberal pacifism.[18] Here is the intellectual elite of a dissident wing of political Liberalism, whose long-deliberated case and carefully fashioned language exert an irresistible influence on Sassoon's personage, who, in turn, takes over the wording of their resistance position. The manifesto is not unfelt, nor inexpressive: the case it makes against the war as an effort lacking strategic reasoning as well as moral rationale conveys the great indignation its author has earned in his service to the causes he disavows here. In the process of its making, however, the statement leaves Sherston feeling as though he were attempting to memorise a foreign language, and its alien bearing to the witness he wishes to give is an insistent, growing, lasting recognition.[19] For it is a language committed to the values and practices of rationalism. And where it misses the inner gestalt of Sherston's combat reality, it also reveals its pre-emptory command over the external, public circumstance of political discourse. It owns both the policy logic of the partisan war and the record of its most devoted, professional objection.

In this situation Edmund Blunden's *Undertones of War* (1928) recovers the urgency of an attempt to listen for meanings 'beneath' the audible range of those normative discourses. In this effort to represent an inherently – and increasingly – 'reasonless' war,[20] Blunden develops an idea he draws from classical antiquity: the Roman Mars, before his service as a war god, was originally a fertility spirit. This double function of creation and destruction reflects an understanding that defies the usual attitudes towards war in liberal modernity, which tends to regard organised violence as a regrettable exception to the otherwise benign, perfectible potential of humankind. (The special 'case' – *casus*, 'fall' – that this lapse from the ideal represents to a liberal sensibility occasions the need to provide some overriding ethical reason for it.) Blunden's anthropological scholarship gives him an imaginative language in which he can approach an awareness otherwise unspeakable in his day, at least to its reigning Liberal deities.

18 Siegfried Sassoon, *Memoirs of an Infantry Officer* (1930; London: Faber & Faber, 1965), pp. 193, 195, 199 ff.
19 Ibid., pp. 200 ff., esp. pp. 202, 211, 218.
20 Edmund Blunden, *Undertones of War* (1928; New York: Harcourt Brace, 1965), 'Introduction' (1965), p. 6.

'[T]he *red* god Mars' is too 'often worshipped, or at least made obeisance to',[21] Blunden protests in his 'Introduction', signalling the obvious prominence of bloody war under this god's patronage. This divinity's coincidence with the green spirit, however, locates the imagery and substance of the difficult recognition to which Blunden's speaker must accede. A Georgian Liberal idealist (of sorts), he initially resists the recognition by remarking, for instance, how 'the lizard ran warless in the warm dust', or how the 'green fields and plumy grey-green trees' of a back area reveal the *matériel* of war as a 'trifling interruption' only. But he is compelled soon to conclude that the sanctuary is phantasmal, that 'the defence of a country must be miles in depth'.[22] This recognition adduces one stunning image after another, as scenes of vegetal abundance appear, even – or especially – in their extreme virulence, all too complicit with the deathly energy of war: 'Over Coldstream Lane, the chief communication trench, deep red poppies, blue and white cornflowers and darnel thronged the way to destruction.' The 'pilgrim' motif Blunden assigns his counterpart moves this character-in-voice through a typical coming-of-age fable, but the development includes a special recognition of green childhood's convergence on bloody adulthood, of playfield on battle plain: 'but put back the blanket, a garden gate, opening into a battle field'.[23]

Blunden's rhetorical art conveys the impression that his speaker reaches these illiberal truths in the solitude of pastoral meditation. A number of textual references, however, confirm his place within a broader culture of scepticism about the partisan war. These titles provide a record of the crisis – the really critical condition – into which the dominant logic of the majority attitude has passed.

C. E. Montague's memoir *Disenchantment* (1922) draws upon the author's pre-war career as leader-writer for the Liberal *Manchester Guardian*. This background gives his expression of 'disenchantment' the condensed, bitter eloquence of a betrayed member of the partisan faithful. 'There's reason in everything', Montague rues with mournful irony in his heckling echo of the formulas of rationalisation that the Liberal leadership applied to the war.[24] The 'reason' through which its causes were spoken had ceased to mean anything recognisable, as the consequences reached areas of the previously unthinkable, the unimaginably sordid. Montague's inwardness with the tradition

[21] Ibid., p. 8. For the double character of Mars, see W. Warde Fowler, *The Religious Experience of the Roman People: From the Earliest Times to the Age of Augustus* (1911; New York: Cooper Square, 1971), pp. 131–3.

[22] Blunden, *Undertones of War*, pp. 28, 39. [23] Ibid., pp. 48, 77.

[24] C. E. Montague, *Disenchantment* (1922; London: Chatto & Windus, 1934), pp. 194, 196, 205. Blunden refers to Montague's memoir in *Undertones*, p. 179.

being compromised speaks sometimes in partisan code. 'Our Moderate Satanists', for instance, title of the chapter in which he addresses those party intellectuals who have turned to support the war, recalls 'Our Liberal Practicioners', the summary chapter in Matthew Arnold's *Culture and Anarchy*: the 'reason and justice' refrain of Victorian Liberalism provides the words of Arnold's – also an ex-Liberal's – vindictive mimicry.[25] This parody language of Liberal rationality has established itself so extensively, however, that Montague does not confine his views to a cryptic script. He spells them out angrily in his round-up account of war-time writing: oddly straitened logic, daffily rationalised statistics, bizarre novelties of argument and case-making – these are now routine atrocities in the Liberal press.[26]

Another reference in *Undertones* identifies Blunden as a reader of the *Cambridge Magazine*. University humorists took on the logical folly of the war party with a remorselessly mordant wit. They 'took off' the official lingo on a range of policy issues, most notably those of relevance to young men of military age – conscription, for chief instance, where the contradiction inherent in an attempt to make 'compulsion' compatible with freely reasoned choice received the rebuking spoof it was due.[27]

If Blunden's citations measure the extent of informed dissent in Liberal Britain, these references also acknowledge – in the constant topic of their riposte – the encompassing power of that dominant, majority consciousness. The tenacity with which its fundamental assumptions are maintained over the course of the war may be sensed in the work of the leading literary Liberal, H. G. Wells, most notably in *Mr Britling Sees It Through* (1916). This eponymous hero centres a fictional history of Britain at war that is, also, Wells's quintessentially Liberal apology for the policy.

Opposed beforehand, like Wells and many other Liberals, who initially rejected the ethical reasons as superficial, Britling is converted, like most British Liberals, and promotes the pro-war case with a passionate rationalism. This residual uncertainty is compensated for in Britling's formulation of Liberal policy in a fashion equally representative and revealingly extravagant: this is a document indicative of a common party predicament, outrageously (as usually) addressed. An attempt to explain and justify the war thus brings

[25] Matthew Arnold, *Culture and Anarchy*, ed. J. Dover Wilson (1932; Cambridge University Press, 1969), pp. 223–4, 254.
[26] Montague, *Disenchantment*, esp. p. 120.
[27] See, for example, 'The Duty of Suicide – Fiat Justitia Ruat Caelum', *Cambridge Magazine*, 18 November 1916, p. 143. Blunden refers to the journal in *Undertones*, p. 169.

Britling – Wells – to write 'An Anatomy of Hate', an exercise in the genre of scientific positivism that is conducted to rigorous standards of linear, propositional logic. The notion this treatise proposes, however, is fetched from possibilities – like the war being argued for – far from the centre of the old Liberal conscience. '"Is there not", [Britling] now asked himself plainly, "a creative and corrective impulse behind all hate? Is not this malignity indeed only the ape-like precursor of the great disciplines of a creative state?"'[28] This argument represents in substance and method a cartooning parody of the twin liberal standards of creative evolution and progressive reason. Wells's Britling reinscribes the highest principles of liberal tradition in a manner consistent, nonetheless, with their current animadversion. It is an accurate travesty. Wells's unwillingness to admit the comic downturn of his intellectual tradition, however, measures the embedded strength of Liberalism, at least on this level of presumptive understandings.

While the logical folly in Wells's book constitutes a kind of sombre, involuntary comedy of contemporary Liberalism, this consciousness is framed as the aim and target of the Anglo-German Tory, Ford Madox (Hueffer) Ford, in his sequence of war novels, *Parade's End*. The political drama revolves around Ford's protagonist and (sometime) counterpart, the *déclassé* English aristocrat Christopher Tietjens. His (precariously) landed values are countered by the designs of a typical arriviste figure, here the cartoon character of a timely and opportunistic Liberalism, Vincent Macmaster, who begins the series in the typical Liberal position of resisting the imminent war. His conversion is swift, complete and much to his benefit. By the end of the first novel he has been knighted, and by the beginning of the third Sir Vincent Macmaster has become 'Principal Secretary to H. M. Department of Statistics'.[29] The triumph *Vincent Macmaster* scores as the unsubtle, doubled significance of his name has been won along the standard Liberal way: his work in the Department of Statistics echoes to the background sound of falsified reports, pseudo-logic and sham rationale that characterised partisan justifications of the war effort.

Add this record of the Liberal hegemony to the chronicles of Montague and the *Cambridge Magazine*, then to the monumental confidence of Wells. The conventional sensibility reveals its summary dimensions. This moment in

[28] H. G. Wells, *Mr Britling Sees It Through* (1916; London: Hogarth Press, 1985), pp. 284 ff., 296.

[29] Ford Madox Ford, *Parade's End* (New York: Knopf, 1992), p. 549; this volume contains the texts of the four war novels, *Some Do Not* (1924), *No More Parades* (1925), *A Man Could Stand Up* (1926) and *The Last Post* (1928).

political and cultural time defines a crisis in traditional values as sizable as the opportunity it affords is daunting. It is the substantial challenge that Graves and Sassoon locate in their own underdeveloped projects, which would consolidate some alternative to the established language of Liberal rationalism. A literary idiom in which reason speaks against itself? A new usage, where the standards and practices of rationalism collapse into some expression of unlikely sense? Not in Ford's novel, which, in the main, remains true to a fairly standard syntactic logic. But Ford's double identity in literary history – a sort of half-Modernist, an elder member of the generation whose advance awareness he does not always complement with a correspondingly experimental temper – may be reclaimed usefully and revealingly here. For Ford presents the recognition his younger contemporaries will turn into a verbal art that distinguishes the most representatively 'modernist' work of this moment.

If the suffix in Modern*ism* signifies anything, it means being 'modern' in more than a chronological way. It suggests a more intense present, some heightened because self-conscious awareness of this modernity, which hinges on a feeling of *difference* from what has gone before. The interruption the Great War represents in the mainstream traditions of liberal modernity is uttered in the language of London Modernism, in the physical body and semiological tissue of its literary usage, which is conceived to the timeliest of conceits: all in all, a sort of reasonable nonsense. Far from trivial in its iteration, this idiom echoes to the background of a civilisation collapsing, all too rationally.[30]

This is the novel prosody the major Modernist poetry of the moment develops concurrently, in 1917, in Ezra Pound's *Homage to Sextus Propertius* and T. S. Eliot's quatrain verse. Their work finds its consonance in an all too logical *folie*, a wry *jouissance* of reason gone awry. Eliot's quatrain art concocts a rhetorical fiction of particularly sagacious high-jinks, sententious absurdity. His tautly formed stanzas employ normative syntax and mechanical metre to create a feeling of reasoned meditation that dissolves constantly, however, into imponderable propositions, unpronounceable words. As in 'Mr Eliot's Sunday Morning Service':

> Polyphiloprogenitive
> The sapient sutlers of the Lord
> Drift across the window-panes.
> In the beginning was the Word.

[30] This argument is developed through the several contexts of literary and political history by Vincent Sherry, *The Great War and the Language of Modernism* (New York: Oxford University Press, 2003).

In the beginning was the Word.
Superfetation of τὸ ἕν,
And at the mensual turn of time,
Produced enervate Origen.[31]

Pound's Roman poet responded to the literary politics of his own Augustan day, exhibiting a kind of resisting reciprocity with its commissioned idioms. Pound's creative translation cues his riposte to the wit he signals in the invocation of his particular, timely, muse:

> Out-weariers of Apollo will, as we know, continue their Martian generalities,
> We have kept our erasers in order.[32]

The wording is almost wholly interpolated; the joke is all Pound's: Apollo, the god of logic (as well as poetry and music), has been wearied and worn out in this war, but not by generals, rather by the 'generalities' of Mars. These are the political discourses of Liberal conflict – statements that wear a hole in the language, in the logos, in the very logic of words. Pound's critical perception resonates as poetic usage in this heroic catalogue, for typical instance, where the first (interpolated) word injects a note of reasoned sequence, which the rest of the recitation hardly bears out:

For Orpheus tamed the wild beasts –
        and held up the Thracian river;
And Citheron shook up the rocks by Thebes
        and danced them into a bulwark at his pleasure,
And you, O Polyphemus? Did harsh Galatea almost
Turn to your dripping horses, because of a tune, under Aetna?
We must look into the matter.[33]

Pound is using the idiom of his contemporary persona, the logic of his own parole, to assume some ready and available meaning for those obscure classical allusions that are the basic imaginative language of the poem. This knowingness is as concocted as the rhetorical question in which Pound concentrates this note of meaning- and reason-seemingness. A tone new to his developing range, as it is to Eliot's, it locates the timely element in the major Modernist poetry of the moment.

31 T. S. Eliot, *Collected Poems*, 1909–1962 (1963; London: Faber & Faber, 1974), p. 57; first published in September 1918.
32 Ezra Pound, *Personae: Collected Shorter Poems of Ezra Pound* (1926), rev. edn, ed. Lea Baechler and A. Walton Litz (New York: New Directions, 1990), p. 205; first published serially through 1919.
33 Pound, *Personae*, p. 206.

The use Virginia Woolf will make of this opportunity may be projected from a reconnaissance she takes in April 1917, in 'The Mark on the Wall'. Musing on the activities of 'novelists in future', she interrupts herself thus:

> – but these generalisations are very worthless. The military sound of the word is enough. It recalls leading articles, cabinet ministers – a whole class of things indeed which as a child one thought the thing itself, the standard thing, the real thing, from which one could not depart save at the risk of nameless damnation. Generalisations bring back somehow Sunday in London, Sunday afternoon walks, Sunday luncheons . . .[34]

Echoing Pound's 'Martian generalities', Woolf's 'generalisations' present the new idiom of total war, a context 'the military sound of the word' specifies. This usage echoes in particular to the language of official rationales; of policy documents and partisan briefs; of 'leading articles' and 'cabinet ministers'. Whereas the Anglo-American poets relate to this linguistic situation strategically, with the opportunism of ex-colonials, a constellation of objects known and rituals remembered revolves for Woolf around the words now ceasing to cohere. For Virginia Stephen Woolf had been born, as Sir Leslie Stephen's daughter, if not to the preferred gender, at least within the clerisy of cultural liberalism. The 'nameless damnation' she fears as punishment for transgressing that former order is indeed the damnation of namelessness, the fate she must face as one raised in the formidable traditions of rationalist language. In advance, she claims the major ambition and dare of the Modernist project she consummates – the nerve and courage of her own emergent attempt to speak reason against itself.

In her major linguistic inventions of the 1920s, Woolf evolves a prosody of the *mock*-logical, a grammar of the *pseudo*-propositional. A typical, prefiguring instance occurs in the opening sentence of her 1922 narrative, her first modern*ist* novel, *Jacob's Room*. '"So of course", wrote Betty Flanders, pressing her heels rather further in the sand, "there was nothing for it but to leave."'[35] 'So of course': the gesture of logical conclusion that opens this novel includes already a sense of its ending, the death in the Great War of Betty *Flanders*'s son Jacob, an immanence projected from the beginning of this family-chronicle novel through a name that goes to one of the most charged, valorised sites of the recent conflict. The one matter of narrative and logical course in this novel is the inevitability of an event otherwise, however, mainly unnamed in

[34] In Susan Dick, ed., *The Complete Shorter Fiction of Virginia Woolf*, 2nd edn (San Diego: Harcourt Brace Jovanovitch, 1989), p. 86; first published in July 1917.

[35] Virginia Woolf, *Jacob's Room* (1922; San Diego: Harcourt Brace Jovanovitch, 1990), p. 7.

the story. The War is presented ever at the oblique angle of the extreme trope, or in moments of apparently chance evocation like a family name. 'And then, here is Versailles',[36] goes the whole of a one-sentence paragraph in the midst of the continental tour Jacob undertakes in *early* summer 1914, where the forward import of the war, formally concluded in the Versailles Treaty of 1919, can hardly be claimed in narrative time. What the novel traps again and again is the inadequacy of language to the salient fact of the war, specifically of the rationalistic language it puts forward in so conspicuous and exposed a position at its outset, or through a usage like 'Versailles', the monument of a first Age of Reason involved now in the collapse of a second. A parsing of the syntax in the especially expressive passages in *Mrs Dalloway* (1925) and *To the Lighthouse* (1927), her other major novels of the decade, reveals a steady pressure being exerted against the constraints of the rationalistic language her sentences otherwise observe on their surfaces. These narratives enact a verbal ceremony of the ongoing end of that major value of liberal modernity – an end she centres with ostensible and insistent references to the war, not only to its human victims but also to its constructions in the political culture of Liberalism.

Woolf's representations of the war's Liberal character(s) find a summary instance in her depiction of the events of early August 1914, in *Jacob's Room*, which recounts her perception of the gendered dimension of the political enterprise. This Whitehall scene features 'the sixteen gentle*men*, lifting their pens or turning perhaps rather wearily in their chairs', who 'decreed that the course of history should shape itself this way or that way, being *man*fully determined, as their faces showed, to impose some coherency upon Rajahs and Kaisers and the mutterings in bazaars'.[37] The crisis that an identifiably (or self-assigned) 'male' reason meets in rationalising this war shows most locally and affectively, in Woolf's literary record, in *Mrs Dalloway*, in her representation of the combat experience of her male protagonist. In these martial circumstances, and in response to conventional expectations, Septimus Warren Smith 'developed manliness'; in reacting to the death of his officer and friend, Evans, Smith 'congratulated himself upon feeling very little and very reasonably. The War had taught him. It was sublime'.[38] The inadequacy of this rationalist attitude is manifest, and its extravagant failure goes as well, and most notably, to an unravelling of its establishing personality of 'manliness'. This incident offers a signal instance of a widely working influence in the social culture of the English war, all in all, a reimagining and recasting of conventional gender identities.

36 Ibid., p. 128. 37 Ibid., p. 172.

38 Virginia Woolf, *Mrs Dalloway* (1925; rpt San Diego: Harcourt Brace Jovanovitch, 1990), p. 86.

The intimation elsewhere of a homoerotic quality in the bond between Smith and Evans may be taken as an indication of a new range of expressive revelation, in the literary record of the war, of male sexual affection. The representation of these feelings included homosexual as well as homoerotic elements, that is, manifestations through overt sexual behaviour as well as expressions of sheer physical appeal, bodily fondness, etc. While attraction could be exerted by characters 'manly' by customary signs, the various circumstances of the war, ranging from the 'unmanning' of its rhetorical authority to the 'feminising' of soldiers in the intimate, day-by-day situation of stationary warfare, all contributed to an opening of areas of male feeling previously closed by conventional proscription. Memories of tenderness new to the experience of their recorders appear frequently on the pages of unpublished letters and diaries, variously from the officer class and soldiers of other ranks, in the archives of the Imperial War Museum. Clarified, intensified, eroticised or sexualised to differing degrees, these feelings of male attraction also generate a literature as extensive as the list of major names in the canon of British war writing: Graves, Sassoon, Owen, Brooke, Gurney and David Jones, among others. The purity of the pathos of foregone love between men, the condition establishing the vocal character and expressive value of Gurney's 'To His Love', may contrast manifestly with the register in Owen's poetry, say, where a thwarted, self-censoring force often contorts the erotic impulse into a laborious ceremonial of dead, or deathly, sexuality. 'Red lips are not so red / As the stained stones kissed by the English dead'.[39] Even the beauty of epicene youth in Owen's 'Arms and the Boy' presents an attraction that is magnified by the countermanding, reprimanding voice, which punishes or threatens this affection, seemingly, by menacing the body of a love still unable to speak its name: 'Let the boy try along this bayonet-blade / How cold steel is, and keen with hunger of blood'.[40] But if the resistance indicated here also measures the pressure of the instigation, a fair assessment may be taken of the demand these newly realised feelings were making for more direct expression.

The opportunities the war afforded women in the way of new work eventuated, it is well known, in the acquisition of their long-sought right of suffrage and, in the franchise, the capacity of potentially meaningful social representation. Self-representation in writing is also occurring with a new breadth and exceptional depth of literary activity by women. Whether or not the 'combat status' of a writer authorises his or her record in some exceptional way (it does not), the representation women made of their work in the war effort has drawn

[39] Owen, 'Greater Love', *Collected Poems*, p. 41. [40] Ibid., p. 43.

steadily increasing attention from literary historians. What may be featured here is the critical witness some women were giving to the existing political discourses which, until 1918, and at least so far as the vote was concerned, still officially excluded them. The externality of perspective their outsider status conferred on them (as on the Anglo-American poets, Woolf's fellow Modernists) also provided the advantaging circumstance for this critique.

Founding editor of the *Freewoman* (1911), subsequently the *New Freewoman* (1913) and the *Egoist* (from 1914), Dora Marsden took her perspective on English politics from the vantage of a sometimes radical feminism. Her critique of the Liberal hegemony worked diversely, most searchingly in her analysis of the assumptions of its rationalist language, which, in her perception, exhibited the worst proclivities of Nominalism. The Liberal era was, for her, 'the verbal age', and the possibilities to which it consecrated its monuments of hope and policy were the projections of a wholly linguistic way of thinking. When the old Liberal testament of a sheerly verbalist reason comes undone under the burden of the war, Marsden registers its defeat with the eloquent concision of her own vindication. Thus on 1 September 1914 she hears the expression of the official 'Reasons for this War' as just so much 'cant'. She expands this understanding two weeks later, calculating the extent of the damage done to the language of rationalism by the agents of this latter-day Gladstonianism. Rehearsing the now established moralistic arguments for the war, she repeats the response to the question 'Why We English Fight?' by Lord Rosebery: '"To maintain", he proposed, "the sanctity of international law in Europe"'. She expatiates: '"Mumbo-jumbo, Law and Mesopotamia" can always be relied on to work all the tricks, and cloak all the spoof.'[41] Her parody of this Liberal imperialist is clarifying as well as caricaturing: his is the non-sense logic in which a long-endowed, well-established male rationalism uttered the antic rant of its collapse. It is a critical perception shared and augmented in the account of Irene Cooper Willis. She conducted a searching archaeology of the contemporary record, ranging from daily journalism to diplomatic correspondence, collecting and analysing these materials in *How We Went into the War: A Study of Liberal Idealism* (1918).[42]

Marsden's *Egoist*, the journal of Anglo-American Modernism in its nascent day, represents a staging area for reactions, at once intellectual and imaginative, to this breakdown in the traditions of public reason in liberal modernity. Even within London Modernism, however, the response was composite, various. Wyndham Lewis, premier representative of the English avant-garde in his

[41] Dora Marsden, 'Views and Comments', *Egoist*, 1 September 1914, p. 324; 'Views and Comments,' *Egoist*, 15 September 1914, p. 344.

[42] See n. 14.

work as Vorticist and editor of *Blast*, drew an energy of self-presentation from the resources of cultural and political nationalism, like many artists in the European avant-garde; like many Futurists, he compounded this persona with the masculinist values being hazarded, Woolf was correct in observing, with the collapse of rationalism: he appears unwilling to exploit the critical condition of 'male' reason in English Liberalism.[43] David Jones, whose *In Parenthesis* (1937) models itself on the already accomplished Modernism of Eliot, presents a rich and dense evocation of the author's service on the Western Front; its verse-with-prose experiment hardly seems second-hand, but this neo-Modernist work witnesses no evident attention to Liberal England's disability – as an instigating condition of new writing.[44] The novel quality in Modernist response to this extraordinary moment in history is fostered by a sense of *difference*, an awareness in particular of the disabled claims of the formerly majority values of Liberal rationalism. The male ownership of that language helps to make female Modernist writing a register equally rare and fine of this timely difference.

Rebecca West's *Return of the Soldier* (1918) takes the story its title announces as the occasion for her male character's experience of personal estrangement from the England he left in 1914. The 'dissociation' or 'memory fugue' from which Captain Chris Baldry is suffering has shifted his centre of remembered value from Baldry Court, the ancestral demesne in which he lived before the war with his wife. He recovers an earlier and humbler love, one whose authenticity lies in its being unscripted to the customs dominating the quasi-public character of life at Baldry Court. That locale shows its emblematic quality in his wife Kitty, whose beauty, which compels men to ever greater exertions in order to please her, is described as a 'civilizing' force,[45] the same value for which Chris has fought in England's Great Liberal War. His inability to recognise the image of this now forgone authority registers the difference the war actually made in the code of meanings that dominated the mainstream experience of Liberal political culture. The salient value of 'reasonableness' in that convention appears in West's extraordinarily perceptive record as the weird, eerie reasonableness of a former norm now unrecognised, its once presumptive authority a memory unremembered. The lie the Great War for English Civilisation gave to the Liberal standard of reason in all things is the truth to which West gives her own exemplary testament as a female Modernist.

43 Lewis censors the practice of pseudo-logic in 'T. S. Eliot: the Pseudo-Believer', in *Men without Art* (London: Cassell, 1934), pp. 65–100.

44 David Jones, *In Parenthesis* (1937; London: Faber & Faber, 1982).

45 Rebecca West, *The Return of the Soldier* (1918), 2nd edn (1980; New York: Carroll & Graf, 1990), p. 154.

THREE

*

MODERNISM AND ITS AFTERMATH, 1918–1945

10

Trauma and war memory

DEBORAH PARSONS

'We should have done well, I think, to be satisfied with the aspect of peace', Virginia Woolf wrote from Richmond on 12 November 1918, describing the grey, wet day that met the armistice of World War I with weary solemnity. Arriving in London, however, the euphoria of the loud and drunken crowds carousing in the rain struck her as nervy and strained. 'There was no centre, no form for all this wandering emotion to take', she noted, 'in everyone's mind the same restlessness and inability to settle down, & yet discontent with whatever it was possible to do.'[1] For those who had survived the conflict, jubilation would quickly give way to a growing sense of dislocation and indeterminacy. The confident Edwardian world that had approached war in 1914 had by now dissolved into myth, and, surveying its ruins, modern society faced a crisis of belief and identity.

The disintegration of nineteenth-century assumptions of progress, order and the stability of self and nationhood had, of course, been heralded well before. In the years immediately prior to the conflict, the avant-garde movements of Futurism, Imagism and Vorticism were vociferous in proclaiming their determined dissociation from the past, condemning the enervating effect of bourgeois tradition and rejecting historical consciousness for the immediacy of the modern. Recalling the creative energy of the London literary scene of the time in his memoir *Return to Yesterday*, for example, Ford Madox Ford depicts the young artist 'D.Z.' (a caricature of Wyndham Lewis), exultingly announcing to the older writer: 'Finished! Exploded! Done for! Blasted in fact. Your generation has gone. [. . .] You stand for Impressionism. It is gone. [. . .] This is the day of Cubism, Futurism, Vorticism. What people want is me, not you.'[2] It was one thing to protest against the weight of history when its power and influence was oppressively evident, however, and quite another to do so

[1] Virginia Woolf, *The Diary of Virginia Woolf*, ed. Anne Olivier Bell, 5 vols. (London: Hogarth Press, 1977–84), vol. 1, *1915–1919* (1977), p. 217.

[2] Ford Madox Ford, *Return to Yesterday* (1931; Manchester: Carcanet Press, 1999), p. 311.

when it seemed irretrievably lost. The moment when 'Ezra and his gang of young lions raged through London' was brief. Ford's reminiscences end with the retrospective knowledge that 'louder Blasts soon drowned them out and put back the hands of the clock to somewhere a good deal the other side of mere Impressionism'.[3] With the onset of war Edwardian England was made acutely aware of the aggressive forces of modernity and had little sympathy for the violent idiom of Futurist or Vorticist radicalism.

Patriotic rhetoric at the beginning of the war depended on a generation brought up with abstractions of heroism and glory that would fight for its threatened 'Englishness'. By the disillusionment of 1916, however, and the losses of the Somme and Passchendaele, the seeds of destruction were being recognised within the blind moribundity of 'cultured, leisured Europe before the war' itself.[4] Nevertheless, it was the war that undoubtedly represented the culmination of such change, and came to stand for the point of shattering rupture with a previous era. 'Adult lives were cut sharply into three sections – pre-war, war, and post-war', Richard Aldington recalled; 'It is curious – perhaps not so curious – but many people will tell you that whole areas of the pre-war lives have become obliterated from their memories.'[5] Estranged from its recent history by the social and psychological chasm of the war years, post-war Europe became pathologically preoccupied with its ability (and inability) to forget and to remember. 'Never again, for me and my generation', Vera Brittain observed in *Testament of Youth*, sounding the prevalent tone of these years, 'was there to be any festival the joy of which no cloud would darken and no remembrance invalidate.'[6]

National reconstruction, social and cultural as well as economic, was high on the post-war political agenda. Its principles were at once recovery and revision; a re-establishment of the past status quo, alongside a reconception of that past from the perspective of a reformed present. Acts of official commemoration and closure endeavoured to give shape and form to public grief, integrating the war into a historical narrative of heroism, patriotism and sacrifice in the service of a higher cause. This all-but hopeless task was characterised by a new impulse towards national historiography, and at the same time a profound scepticism towards its success, exemplified by E. M. Forster's complaint against H. G. Wells's determinedly reconstructionary and immensely popular *Outline of History* (1920) that: 'Our "own times" as they are ironically termed,

[3] Ibid., p. 312.
[4] George Bernard Shaw, *Heartbreak House* (1919; London: Penguin, 1964), p. 7.
[5] Richard Aldington, *Death of a Hero* (1929; London: Hogarth Press, 1964), p. 224.
[6] Vera Brittain, *Testament of Youth* (1933; London: Virago, 1978), p. 91.

are anything but ours; it is as though a dead object, huge and incomprehensible, had fallen across the page, which no historical arts can arrange, and which bewilders us as much by its shapelessness as by its size.'[7] It was not until the end of the decade, marked by a flush of memoirs including Aldington's *Death of a Hero*, Robert Graves's *Goodbye to All That* (1929), Irene Rathbone's *We That Were Young* (1932) and Brittain's *Testament of Youth* (1933), that the war and all that it had destroyed seems able to have been narrated and mourned as past. These works, as their titles and others like them indicate, swiftly consolidated the generational myth of the Great War, an elegiac and acutely classed narrative of radiant youth sent to its death by the 'botched civilization' of an older social order.[8] In the meantime, however, the war and its aftermath remained a gap or absence in history that resisted representation. The early post-war years, dominated by psychological bewilderment and social and economic uncertainty, were a limbo period in which the intensity of horror and loss could not be integrated into normal understanding. 'Those who have attempted to convey any real war experience, sincerely, unsentimentally, avoiding any ready-made attitudes (pseudo-heroic or pacifist or quasi-humorous)', Aldington observed in 1926, 'must have felt the torturing sense of something incommunicable.'[9]

Fragmentation and reconstruction

The haunting legacy of the war on the processes of memory and representation was integral to the emerging cultural identity and imagination of the 1920s. Resisting representation in conventional historical narrative, its trauma demanded expression in new writerly forms and strategies. By 1918 both the neo-Romantic pastoralism of the Georgians and the protestations of the avant-garde were giving way to a new cultural and literary mood. The short-lived but suggestively titled journal *New Paths*, for example, was tellingly dedicated to artists and writers who had been lost to the war, 'those gallant gentlemen who, but for having died in the service of their country, would have been pioneers along the new paths of literature and art', a list headed by Rupert Brooke and the Vorticist sculptor Henri Gaudier-Brzeska.[10] But Brooke and Gaudier-Brzeska, along with T. E. Hulme, were now gone, and Siegfried Sassoon's angry verses were being dismissed by critics as deserving of sympathy as

7 E. M. Forster, 'Mr Wells' "Outline"', *Athenaeum*, 19 November 1920, p. 690.

8 Ezra Pound, *Hugh Selwyn Mauberley*, in *Collected Shorter Poems* (London: Faber & Faber, 1968), p. 208.

9 Richard Aldington, Review of Herbert Read, *In Retreat*, *Criterion*, 4 (April 1926), p. 363.

10 Quoted in Samuel Hynes, *A War Imagined: The First World War and English Culture* (London: Bodley Head, 1990).

the work of a soldier, yet not of praise as the work of an artist.[11] In their place were already new pioneers and different directions, and with the lifting of wartime travel restrictions (when Pound, Lawrence and H. D. all left London for the continent), a new literary geography. With the exception of Ford, who enlisted in 1915 and fought at the Somme, the main proponents of post-war Modernism would be non-combatants (Pound, James Joyce, T. S. Eliot, Virginia Woolf), of whom only Eliot and Woolf were largely permanent in London. The tenor of change, moreover, from now on would be crisis rather than revolution, rebellious iconoclasm shifting to a stylistic innovation that, as David Peters Corbett argues, exemplified the 'retreat, evasion, and concealment of modernity's impact'.[12]

Corbett's choice of words here is illuminating. The war is not so much disregarded as *dissociated* in post-war writing. Too close and too incomprehensible to be imagined, its traumatic effect appears indirectly through the characteristic fragmentation of subject and narrative. In his 'Foreword' to *Women in Love* (1920), D. H. Lawrence states that the novel, written and revised during the summer of 1916, 'took its final shape in the midst of the period of war, though it does not concern the war itself', and goes on to explain that he yet wanted 'the time [in which it is set] to remain unfixed, so that the bitterness of the war may be taken for granted in the characters'.[13] Trauma resists temporal definition, Lawrence here implies, and the war would impact catastrophically on modern consciousness far beyond the space and time of actual fighting. If the war itself is absent from *Women in Love*, its scars are nevertheless to be felt in the mechanical self-defensiveness of its tortured characters, in their will to destruction, in their social and psychological dislocation and their desperate desire for meaning. They are also to be found in the spiritual and emotional wastelands, emasculated anti-heroes and anguished detachment from the past that are pervasive in literature of the period more generally.

No centre, no form; the sense of the incomprehensibility and meaninglessness of the post-war world that Woolf observed in the armistice crowds, and the consequent attempt to both evoke and give order to the fragmentation and flux that newly characterised experience, have become the accepted tenets of literary Modernism. But they are also indicative of the trauma of what T. S. Eliot described as the 'immense panorama of futility and anarchy'

[11] See, for example, J. Middleton Murry, 'Mr Sassoon's War Verses', *Nation*, 23 (13 July 1918), p. 398.

[12] David Peters Corbett, *The Modernity of English Art 1914–1930* (Manchester University Press, 1997), p. 1.

[13] D. H. Lawrence, *Women in Love* (1920; London: Penguin, 1995), p. 485.

of its contemporary history.[14] The key experimental techniques with which Modernist writers sought to express such instability – introspective narratives full of temporal dislocations, associative images and ellipses – compare strikingly, for example, with the symptoms of war neuroses and hysteria (amnesia and repetitive memory disorders, fragmented consciousness, paralysis or loss of speech, hypersensitivity and emotional apathy). 'The memory throws up high and dry / A crowd of twisted things', Eliot declared in 'Rhapsody on a Windy Night' in 1917. It would take another five years, and the writing of *The Waste Land*, before he could begin the gathering together of those distorted fragments in the effort of shoring up the ruins of belief and identity. The Modernist project may have insisted on the aesthetic autonomy of art, but it was deeply shaped by the broad fissures of World War I; from its compulsive re-enactments of social, physical and psychic fragmentation, to its gradual reconstruction of the past across the abyss of lost time, through narratives of mourning and remembrance.

Traumatic memories, Judith Herman elucidates, are typically experienced as 'vivid sensations and images' rather than 'a verbal, linear narrative'.[15] For Ford Madox Ford, the disconnected snapshots of his war memories presented a problem of articulation that would continue well beyond the end of the war as a symptom of lingering war neurosis. Serving with the Welsh Regiment and stationed close to the front line at Ypres, an exploding shell in the summer of 1916 had left him with severe concussion and amnesia. In 'A Day of Battle', an essay written shortly after rejoining his battalion, Ford ponders his inability to write about his experience: 'I have asked myself continuously why I can write nothing – why I cannot even think anything that to myself seems worth thinking – about the psychology of that Active Service of which I have seen my share.'[16] Despite this disavowal, 'A Day of Battle' is in actual fact extremely lucid about the psychological repression that war demands, and the soldier's necessary detachment of consciousness from the events around him. Ford notes, for example, that although his mind has retained intense visual images of his experiences, he can in no way record them in words:

> Today, when I look at a mere coarse map of the Line, simply to read 'Ploegsteert' or 'Armentières' seems to bring up extraordinarily coloured and exact pictures behind my eyeballs – little pictures having all the brilliant minuteness

[14] T. S. Eliot, 'Ulysses, Order and Myth' (1923), in Peter Faulkner, ed., *A Modernist Reader: Modernism in England 1910–1930* (London: Batsford, 1986), p. 103.

[15] Judith Herman, *Trauma and Recovery* (New York: Basic Books, 1992), pp. 38, 37.

[16] Ford Madox Ford, 'A Day of Battle', in *The Ford Madox Ford Reader*, ed. Sondra J. Stang (Manchester: Carcanet Press, 1986), pp. 456–61 (p. 456).

> that medieval illuminations had – of towers, and roofs, and belts of trees and sunlight; or, for the matter of these, of men, burst into mere showers of blood and dissolving into muddy ooze; or of aeroplanes and shells against the translucent blue. – But as for putting them – into words! No: the mind stops dead, and something in the brain stops and shuts down.[17]

If Ford's experiences of 1916 prompted his exploration of the impact of war on the unconscious, they also therefore, as Max Saunders notes, posed 'new *aesthetic* problems', significantly 'the question of how to *render* his impressions of war – and how to transform them into narrative'.[18]

During the 1920s Ford would return again and again to his traumatic war memories, re-enacting and reworking them in fiction in an attempt to impose form on the shards of his personal and cultural history. When the narrator of *No Enemy*, for example (written shortly after the end of the war but not published until 1929), asserts to the reader that 'This is a Reconstructionary tale', it is with both heavy irony and a desperate optimism: 'For it struck the writer that you hear of the men that went, and you hear of what they did when they were There. But you never hear how It left them. You hear how things were destroyed, but seldom of the painful processes of Reconstruction.'[19] Ford's post-war writings pay testimony to those persistent 'painful processes', struggling to give narrative form to raw memory, and emphasising the disjunction between abstract political ideals of regeneration and the individual struggle against psychological fragmentation and its aftermath. The result of this conjunction of psychological and professional self-questioning, Malcolm Bradbury argues, was 'the most important and complex British novel to deal with the overwhelming subject of the Great War', and 'a central Modernist novel of the 1920s', Ford's quasi-autobiographical tetralogy *Parade's End*.[20]

In his pre-war novel, *The Good Soldier* (1915), Ford had portrayed the English gentleman and officer, 'full of the big words courage, loyalty, honour, constancy', struggling with the clash of his human passions and his chivalric ideals.[21] *Parade's End* explores the fate of this character-type after 1914, taking him from the pre-war setting of *Some Do Not* in 1924, through the psychological disintegration of the two war volumes *No More Parades* (1925) and *A Man Could*

[17] Ibid., p. 456.

[18] Max Saunders, *Ford Madox Ford: A Dual Life, Vol. II, The After-War World* (Oxford University Press, 1996), p. 15.

[19] Ford Madox Ford, *No Enemy: A Tale of Reconstruction* (1929; Manchester: Carcanet Press, 2002), pp. 11, 7.

[20] Malcolm Bradbury, 'Introduction' to Ford Madox Ford, *Parade's End* (London: Everyman's Library, 1992), pp. xii, xv.

[21] Ford Madox Ford, *The Good Soldier* (1915; Oxford University Press, 1990), p. 33.

Stand Up (1926), to the reconstructionary pastoralism of his post-war life in *The Last Post* (1928). Christopher Tietjens, the 'last Tory', is introduced travelling in a railway carriage towards Rye with his friend Macmaster, in 1912. The train, with its luxurious upholstery and 'admirable varnish', epitomises the comfortable self-assurance of a society built on the principles of class and tradition, but also, as *Some Do Not* soon indicates, what is merely the polished façade of an Edwardian society disintegrating amid political self-advancement, materialism and social unrest.[22] Tietjens's marriage is already a domestic battlefield, his wife Sylvia an adulteress who takes sadistic pleasure in flaunting her infidelities and who has borne him a possibly illegitimate son. With civilisation seemingly collapsing around him, however, Tietjens clings desperately to his principles of duty and allegiance and thus will not expose her. His increasingly fragile mind may retain the memory of Valentine Wannop, but his survival depends on the tight maintenance and control of his pre-war values and behavioural codes. When asked by Colonel Campion, for example, why he refuses to divorce Sylvia, the question precipitates a period of mental instability reflected by the suddenly fragmentary and staccato form of his internal narrative. As he declares to the crazed Captain Mackenzie: 'If you let yourself go, you may let yourself go a tidy sight further than you want to.'[23] What makes *Parade's End* so powerfully compelling is Ford's articulation of this mental tension, manifest in Tietjens's determined impassivity with his men, his wife and in moments of danger, and by contrast the nightmares, hallucinatory visions, halting speech and crumbling memory that trouble him at rest.

The prevalence of mental disturbances among soldiers during World War I had encouraged a resurgence in psychoanalytic methods for the treatment of neurosis, hitherto rejected by the contemporary medical profession. Famously asserting in *Studies of Hysteria* (1895) that '*Hysterics suffer mainly from reminiscences*', Freud and Breuer's early case studies had suggested that neurotic illness was typically caused by a traumatic event, too catastrophic to be integrated by conscious understanding, which the mind had consequently repressed.[24] Such repressed experiences, they argued, although seemingly forgotten, were re-experienced instead in the form of repeated and overpowering symptoms (such as nightmares, flashbacks, convulsions or sleep-walking). The aim of the psychoanalyst, through hypnotic suggestion, was to encourage the

[22] Ford Madox Ford, *Parade's End* (1924–8; Manchester: Carcanet Press, 1997), p. 3.
[23] Ibid., p. 302.
[24] Josef Breuer and Sigmund Freud, *Studies on Hysteria* (1895), in *The Standard Edition of the Complete Psychological Works of Sigmund Freud*, trans. James Strachey, 24 vols. (London: Hogarth Press, 1957), II p. 7.

patient to reproduce the original traumatic experience and thus bring about its catharsis. While wartime psychotherapists such as William Brown and W. H. Rivers recognised the value of the cathartic technique for the rehabilitation of shell-shock victims, however, they fundamentally disagreed with Freud's post-seduction-theory focus on the psychosexual origins of hysteria, arguing instead for the specificity of war trauma. If the effects of World War I thus played an important part in establishing psychoanalysis as a therapeutic strategy, they also forced a reconsideration of this main tenet of Freud's thought, leading to his speculative exploration of the mental response to danger and fear, a defence of his theory of the function of dreams, and the conception of self-preservative and aggressive instincts that are distinct from the phantasies of the pleasure principle.

Traumatic neuroses, Freud observes in *Beyond the Pleasure Principle* (1920), are typically the result of the mind's reaction to a sudden fright or threat to life, one that has usually *not* ended in physical injury, but that produces nightmares in which the experience is compulsively repeated. While the conscious mind protected itself from the shock of danger – few patients, Freud noted, were 'much occupied in their waking lives with memories of their accident', being instead 'more concerned with not thinking of it' – the individual relived the frightening event in the form of flashbacks or traumatic dreams.[25] Central to Freud's argument here, however, is his emphasis on the traumatic dream or memory as the experience in the *present* of an event that the shocked mind had been unable to register consciously when it actually took place in the past. As Cathy Caruth explains, 'trauma is not locatable in the simple violent or original event in the individual's past, but rather in the way that its very unassimilated nature – the way it was precisely not known in the first instance – returns to haunt the survivor later on'.[26] Traumatic experience is thus defined by its deferral or delay. It is the mind's attempt, Freud argued, 'to master the stimulus retrospectively, by developing the anxiety whose omission was the cause of the traumatic neurosis'.[27]

In *Parade's End* the dissociation of horror and fright, and the deferral of emotional reaction, is evident in Tietjens's psychic response to the war. This is most overt in his guilt over the death of one of his men, O Nine Morgan, to whom Tietjens has refused leave in an attempt to protect him from his wife's violent lover. At the sight of his obliterated body, Tietjens's immediate reaction

[25] Sigmund Freud, *Beyond the Pleasure Principle* (1920), *Standard Edition*, XVIII, p. 13.
[26] Cathy Caruth, *Unclaimed Experience: Trauma, Narrative, and History* (Baltimore: Johns Hopkins University Press, 1996), p. 4.
[27] Freud, *Beyond the Pleasure Principle*, p. 32.

is one of removed, aesthetic contemplation: 'In the bright light it was as if a whole pail of scarlet paint had been dashed across the man's face on the left and his chest. It glistened in the firelight – just like fresh paint, moving! [. . .] The red viscousness welled across the floor; you sometimes so see fresh water bubbling up in sand.'[28] O Nine Morgan's death becomes an abstraction, as Tietjens's mind dissociates the scene from its horror. The image will return repeatedly to haunt him, however, prompted by the pre-war trauma of his father's suicide, or on other occasions when the demand for mental constraint denies any immediate emotional response. When a German soldier descends into the trenches in *A Man Could Stand Up*, for example, the military mind takes over and he draws his knife with cool detachment. It is only later, during a nightmare in which he sees again the face of the dead O Nine Morgan, that he is suddenly overcome by delayed terror: 'Fear possessed him! He sat up in his flea-bag, dripping with icy sweat. "By Jove, I'm for it!" he said. He imagined that his brain was going; he was mad and seeing himself go mad. He cast about in his mind for some subject about which to think so that he could prove to himself that he had not gone mad.'[29] It is during the nightmare, and on waking, that Tietjens experiences the delayed fright of the trenches. It is not only the threat to life but also the incomprehensibility and guilt of his survival that constitutes the trauma.

Over the past decade, historians and literary critics have begun to discover the lost voices and memories of those working alongside soldiers within the militarised zone, notably the women who volunteered as field nurses, ambulance drivers and army domestic staff, who were also subject to the severe physical and psychological shocks that could result in traumatic symptoms. Rathbone's *We That Were Young* and Brittain's *Testament of Youth*, for example, reveal the effects of the war on the lives of young middle-class women in 1914, both the social and economic freedoms that it enabled and the emotional losses that it demanded, and provide detailed social documentaries of the daily life of women's war service in YMCA recreation camps, for the WAAC, in munitions factories and as Voluntary Aid Detachment nurses. Both, moreover, present clear indictments of the position of women *returning* from active service, accustomed to a degree of equality and self-sufficiency upon which post-war society was keen to renege. The feminist and socialist politics of Rathbone's and Brittain's texts, however, are ultimately subordinated to the purpose of facilitating in writing a process of mourning, remembrance and reconstruction, through an elegy of collective generational loss. 'Perhaps, after all', Brittain

[28] Ford, *Parade's End*, p. 307. [29] Ibid., p. 564.

writes at the end of *Testament of Youth*, 'the best that we who were left could do was to refuse to forget.'[30]

The form of this refusal moderates, through the passage of time, both the horrors and individual pain of war. Brittain's and Rathbone's memoirs thus act as a process of writing out the trauma of their war experiences, while at the same time acting as safeguards against raw and angry memory, rather in the way that Joan Seddon, the semi-autobiographical protagonist of *We That Were Young*, develops a mental shock-absorber against the gruesome daily realities of her work at the First London General Hospital in 1916: 'With unconscious wisdom she let down a sort of safety-curtain between her mind and the sights before her, keeping them at bay, preventing their full significance from penetrating.'[31] Brittain too, remembers the shock of the death of her fiancé Roland Leighton as 'a series of pictures, disconnected but crystal clear', the visual precision of her detached consciousness similar to that described by Ford of his memories of Ypres in 1916.[32] By the end of the war, she has become an automaton, existing within 'a deep, nullifying blankness, a sense of walking in a thick mist which hid all sights and muffled all sounds'.[33] With the passing of a decade retrospection provides a different form of detachment and strengthens the possibility of romanticising the memory of all that has been, and is perceived to have been, lost. E. M. Delafield notes in her 'Preface' to *We That Were Young* that war breeds sentimentality, 'for sentimentality is one of the most powerful narcotics in the world'.[34] Channelling individual bereavement and anger into a narrative of collective mourning, the generational elegy serves both to give form and structure to the social and psychological fragmentation of the Great War, and to endow its memory with what Joan can still feel in 1928 as its 'ghastly glamour'.[35]

Rathbone would write a more cynical condemnation of the political conduct of the war and its aftermath in her later, far more stylistically experimental novel *They Call it Peace* (1936). Her ambivalence is yet already hinted at in the final section of *We That Were Young*, when the pacifist history-master Philip Nicol, who had fought throughout the war suffering from shell-shock, commits suicide in 1928, bitterly disillusioned by the sham promises and failed ideals of the Armistice. The raw events of the war reawakened in Joan's memory by Philip's death, she finds herself exasperated at the annual two-minute silence of

[30] Brittain, *Testament of Youth*, p. 645.

[31] Irene Rathbone, *We That Were Young* (1932; New York: Feminist Press, 1989), p. 195.

[32] Brittain, *Testament of Youth*, p. 239. [33] Ibid., p. 458.

[34] E. M. Delafield, 'Preface' to Rathbone, *We That Were Young*, p. viii.

[35] Rathbone, *We That Were Young*, p. 465.

the Armistice commemorations: 'the ceremony was [. . .] a species of let-off. "Remember for two minutes; you can then forget, and resume." As though one wanted to remember – in that fashion; as though one wanted to forget.'[36] Her mind is instead jolted from the numb limbo of the post-war years by a different remembering, 'something inward and unexpected – something which broke her completely up, and which there was no resisting', a form of traumatic memory that is symptomatic of the memoir's very form.[37] For interrupting Rathbone's and Brittain's generally retrospective narratives are the stark descriptions and raw impressions of the nursing episodes, the result of recourse to original diaries and letters, and moments that register the memory of extreme shock and fear, as in Rathbone's description of the Zeppelin raids over London in 1917: 'Raids, raids, raids. Nights of broken sleep. Nights of strange vigils in cellars. Nights while the skies detonated. Jangled nerves. Ruined buildings. Deaths.'[38] Into the carefully constructed memorial to a lost past break the unassimilable fragments of traumatic experience.

It is the very violence of traumatic memory that characterises perhaps one of the most striking accounts of women's war service, Helen Zenna Smith's *Not So Quiet . . . Stepdaughters of War* (1930). Helen Zenna Smith was the pseudonym of Evadne Price, a popular and prolific writer who had been asked by the publisher Albert Marriott to write a riposte to Erich Maria Remarque's *All Quiet on the Western Front* (1929). Unlike Rathbone or Brittain, however, she drew not on her own memories filtered by time, but from the more direct experience of war as recorded in the diaries of Winifred Young, an ambulance driver at the Front. The result is a vivid exposition of the harsh physical conditions and psychological torment these women faced, and a bitter indictment of the propagandist rhetoric of the recruiting platform that had sent them to war. Field ambulance volunteers, like VADs, were typically recruited from the upper and middle classes, 'sheltered young women who smilingly stumbled from the chintz-covered drawing-rooms of the suburbs straight into hell'.[39] The angry monologue of Nell Smith ('Smithy') savagely reveals the ugly realities of their role; the disillusionment, danger and horrors that remained unspoken in cheery letters home, and that were silenced after the war by a society that refused in shame to acknowledge them. England, her mother writes to her on lilac notepaper, 'is proud of her brave daughters, so very proud', yet it also proves swift to disown the psychological casualties that they become. 'It takes nerve to carry on here', Georgina Toshington ('Tosh') the aristocratic leader

[36] Ibid., p. 463. [37] Ibid. [38] Ibid., p. 343.

[39] Helen Zenna Smith, *Not So Quiet . . . Stepdaughters of War* (1930; New York: Feminist Press, 1989), p. 165.

of Nell's team tells her when she first arrives at the convoy headquarters, 'but it takes twice as much to go home to flag-crazy mothers and fathers.'[40]

Although taking up a similar focus as the wartime episode in Radclyffe Hall's *The Well of Loneliness*, published the previous year, *Not So Quiet* . . . thus offers a representation of the ambulance women's experiences that is in many ways ideologically opposed. It is undoubtedly heavily homophobic, Helen Zenna Smith's depiction of the 'yellowy' lesbian Skinny in comparison with the strength and courage of the Amazonian Tosh, with her 'breasts of a nursing mother', in explicit contrast to Hall's romantic celebration of the mannish lesbian at war in the figure of Stephen Gordon, who is decorated for heroism.[41] For Hall the war released the manly woman from a life of frustrated self-disavowal: 'War and death had given them a right to life, and life tasted sweet, very sweet to their palates.'[42] A significant but only brief moment within the novel, Hall notes with bitter awareness the experience of lesbian women in the war's aftermath, when 'the very public whom they had served was the first to turn round and spit upon them', a theme that she would take up again in the short story 'Miss Ogilvy Finds Herself' (1934).[43] Yet *The Well of Loneliness* nevertheless romanticises the war in its glorifying of patriotism as enabling the recognition and liberation of the lesbian, and in its celebration of the values and attributes of masculinity, both an idealism and a politics that *Not So Quiet* . . . furiously counters.

As in Ford's *Parade's End*, Nell's experience of war in *Not So Quiet* . . . , as she turns from initial outrage, to doubt, to psychological paralysis and finally to the point of insanity, is strikingly 'Modernist'. The narrative is constantly interrupted by fragments of interior monologue, dreams and nightmares, flashbacks, shards of memory and letters that are themselves broken up by the censor. Nell's consciousness spews images of grotesque, polluted, dying bodies, with vivid clarity, challenging and assaulting the reader in the foul language that the nation's young ladies swiftly learn as more appropriate to their understanding of war than their parents' patriotic cant about England's 'Splendid Young Women', 'doing their bit' for the cause.[44] In a conspiracy of silence with regard to the male instigators of the conflict, the blood-baying civilian nation in *Not So Quiet* . . . is embodied in the monstrous maternal figures of Nell's mother and her friend and rival Mrs Evans-Mawnington, vying over how many of their offspring they can sacrifice for the greater good of the

40 Ibid., p. 13. 41 Ibid., p. 17.
42 Radclyffe Hall, *The Well of Loneliness* (1928; London: Virago, 1982), p. 275.
43 Ibid., p. 412. 44 Ibid., p. 96.

country. Their voices break into the fragmentary montage of mutilated bodies in Nell's nightmares:

> Mrs Evans-Mawnington, scowling, furious-mouthed, jealous . . . Mother smug, saccharine-sweet . . . shelves of mangled bodies . . . filthy smells of gangrenous wounds . . . shell-ragged, shell-shocked men . . . men shrieking like wild beasts inside the ambulance until they drown the sound of the engine . . . *'Nellie loves to be really in it'* – no God to pray to because you know there isn't a God – how shall I carry on? . . . *'Proud to do her bit for the old flag.'* Oh, Christ! Oh Christ![45]

The shattered 'shell-shocked' monologue, with its ellipses, hallucinations and passionate interjections, contrasts violently with the more conventional narrative style of Brittain, Rathbone or Hall from the same period.

Mary Borden's *The Forbidden Zone* (1929), a collection of sketches, stories and poems written during and after her service as a nurse with the French army, is more conscious in its radical aesthetics. Borden was the daughter of a Chicago millionaire and had moved in avant-garde intellectual circles prior to the war, for a time intimate with and patron to Wyndham Lewis. *The Forbidden Zone* both draws upon the experimental strategies of the pre-war avant-garde, and critiques the naïvety of its rhetoric celebrating technology, dehumanisation and the destruction of the past. Taking her title from *la zone interdite*, the space immediately behind the Front Line, Borden presents the war scene as surreal and apocalyptic, the scarred, broken wasteland of Belgium haemorrhaging mud. The war distorts understanding; 'What does it mean?' Borden's autobiographical narrator asks again and again, as prayers are made to 'War, world without end, amen'.[46] An aeroplane, a violent 'messenger from heaven', drops bombs before which men fall 'on their faces like frantic worshippers'; limousines 'meant to carry ladies to places of amusement' transport 'generals to places of killing'; in the field-hospitals doctors and nurses heal the wounded, their purpose only to return them to slaughter.[47] This is the warped logic of war, Borden argues in the short story 'Conspiracy', for '[e]verything is arranged. It is arranged that men should be broken and that they should be mended.'[48]

'To those who find these impressions confused', Borden writes in her Foreword to *The Forbidden Zone*, 'I would say that they are fragments of a great confusion. Any attempt to reduce them to order would require artifice on

45 Ibid., p. 33. 46 Mary Borden, *The Forbidden Zone* (London: Heinemann, 1929), p. 58.
47 Ibid., pp. 6, 8; p. 14. 48 Ibid., p. 117.

my part and would falsify them. To those on the other hand who find them unbearably plain, I would say that I have blurred the bare horror of facts and softened the reality in spite of myself.'[49] Confusion, incoherence and the determined, self-protective blunting of sensibility are the dominant reaction to war experience. Daily horrors are again articulated with a tone of indifferent clarity, as when Borden removes a man's head bandage only to find that his brain has come away with it. She recounts the event in a tone devoid of expression, distancing the gruesome physicality of the man's mutilated body from her mental comprehension, mechanical action required for the purposes of sanity. In this world of broken, impotent men, the gender distinctions of war, as in the battle zone of *Not So Quiet*... become meaningless: 'There are no men here, so why should I be a woman?' Borden asks. 'There are heads and knees and mangled testicles. There are chests with holes as big as your fist, and pulpy thighs, shapeless; and stumps where legs once were fastened', there is nothing that resembles the body of a man.[50] The deadened sensibility of the nurses unites them with the corpses they attend: 'She is no longer a woman', Borden states. 'She is dead already, just as I am.'[51]

'What is to become of us when the killing is over?', Nell Smith, contemplating her persistent nightmares, asks of the war-shocked woman in *Not So Quiet*... :

> 'Whenever I close my aching red eyes a procession of men passes before me: maimed men; men with neither arms nor legs; gassed men, coughing, coughing, coughing; men with dreadful burning eyes; men with heads and faces half shot away; raw, bleeding men [. . .] I fear these maimed men of my imaginings as I never fear the maimed men I drive from the hospital trains to the camps. The men in the ambulances scream, but this ghostly procession is ghostly quiet. I fear them, these silent men, for I am afraid they will stay with me all my life, shutting out beauty till the day I die.[52]

Writing about his shell-shock in a letter to C. F. G. Masterman in 1917, Ford admitted:

> I suppose that, really, the Somme was a pretty severe ordeal, though I wasn't conscious of it at the time. Now, however, I find myself suddenly waking up in a hell of a funk – & going on being in a hell of a funk till morning. And that is pretty well the condition of a number of men here. I wonder what the effect of it will be on us all, after the war – & on national life and the like.[53]

[49] Ibid., p. i. [50] Ibid., p. 60. [51] Ibid., p. 59. [52] Smith, *Not So Quiet*..., pp. 167, 163.
[53] Ford Madox Ford to C. F. G. Masterman, 5 January 1917, *Letters of Ford Madox Ford*, ed. Richard M. Ludwig (Princeton University Press, 1965), pp. 81–3.

'Not then was the evil hour, but now', Siegfried Sassoon notes in his fictionalised memoir of the post-war years; 'now, in the sweating suffocation of nightmare, in paralysis of limbs, in the stammering of dislocated speech.'[54] Tietjens too continues to suffer from traumatic memories after the war, believing himself responsible for both O Nine Morgan's death and the young soldier Arunjuez's lost eye: 'It's a sort of monomania', he explains to Valentine Wannop, 'It recurs. Continuously.'[55]

Remembering and moving on

'The objects of this autobiography', Robert Graves wrote in an early draft of *Good-bye to All That*, 'are simple enough: an opportunity for a simple goodbye to you and to you and to me and to all that; forgetfulness because once all this has been settled in my mind and written down and published it need never be thought about again.'[56] In 'Mourning and Melancholia' (1917), Freud describes mourning as a form of painful goodbye; 'the reaction to the loss of a loved person, or to the loss of some abstraction which has taken the place of one, such as one's country, liberty, an ideal'.[57] In some cases, however, particularly those in which individuals felt ambivalently towards the lost object, Freud found that mourning was substituted by the condition of melancholia, marked by pathological symptoms of self-hatred. In melancholia, he concluded, the individual suffers both grief and guilt, feeling responsible for the death of the ambivalently loved and hated object of loss. If mourning is a necessary and therapeutic process, through which the individual gradually comes to accept his or her loss, in melancholia the individual remains haunted by the past, unable to mourn and move on. At what point, however, does melancholia become mourning and is trauma overcome?

Key to Breuer and Freud's early treatment of neurotic patients had been the catharsis or abreaction of the disturbing memory trace through its telling, eliminating the impulse to its traumatic repetition through the distancing effect of narration. In Pierre Janet's work on memory and trauma, for example, similar to but also rivalling that of Freud, normal memory is dependent on our ability to situate ourselves in the present while we perform an act of self-representation in telling the story of our past. Overcoming trauma involves making a transition from the unconscious reproduction *of* the past (traumatic memory), to its conscious acceptance, assimilation and representation *as* past

[54] Siegfried Sassoon, *Sherston's Progress* (London: Faber & Faber, 1936), p. 71.
[55] Ford, *Parade's End*, p. 659. [56] Quoted in Hynes, *A War Imagined*, p. 429.
[57] Sigmund Freud, 'Mourning and Melancholia' (1917), *Standard Edition*, XIV, p. 243.

(narrative memory).[58] Remembering, in other words, is necessary in order to forget. The problem, however, remains exactly how the trauma victim is able to narrate a past event they are unable to consciously remember. As Herman explains, trauma is characterised by a central dialectic of denial and compulsive repetition, which manifests itself in fragmentary or disguised modes of expression. Incomprehensible and unspeakable, trauma refuses representation. The task that post-war literary Modernism took up was exactly that of aesthetic expression and reconstruction out of the ambivalent remembering and forgetting of its recent history.

Max Saunders suggests that a fundamental element of *Parade's End* is 'its Proustian project of recovering lost time: the lost era of Edwardian innocence; the lost years of the war; the lost weeks of shell-shock'.[59] Yet where Marcel's extraordinary act of narrative recollection in *A la recherche du temps perdu* would seem to epitomise a faith in the total and authentic recall of past experience, Ford's depiction of broken memory is less optimistic of the possibility of such continuity. Proust's archival model of memory is that of a vast store in which every experience remains lodged, and the aim of *A la recherche* is thus to access and reread its dusty records. Ford, however, is more wary of the recurrence of the past in the present in this way. For while Proust celebrates the epiphanic significance of involuntary recollection, Ford is all too aware that such memories are just as likely to be destructively traumatic. In an unpublished piece of autobiographical fiction from shortly after the end of the war, he writes of the irruption of traumatic memory as overpowering and uncontrollable: 'His past came back to him in waves. It came back to him in waves of an extraordinary intensity; it was if they took hold of him and overwhelmed him.'[60] *Parade's End* ultimately attempts to reconfigure the past *as past*; it is about how to forget as much as how to remember. 'Cut it out, and join time up . . . It *can* be done' (284), Tietjens exclaims to Valentine on the eve of his leaving for the Front in *Some Do Not*. In so assembling and transforming the autobiographical fragments of his earlier post-war writings into fictional narrative in *Parade's End*, Ford perhaps finds in aesthetic form the means to order and reconstruct his traumatic memories.

'Hitherto, she had thought of the War as physical suffering only', Ford writes of Valentine Wannop, observing Tietjens's shattered psyche on Armistice Day, 'now she saw it only as mental torture. Immense miles and miles of anguish

[58] See Ruth Leys, 'Traumatic Cures: Shell Shock, Janet, and the Question of Memory', *Critical Inquiry*, 20 (1994), pp. 623–62.
[59] Saunders, *Ford*, p. 277.
[60] 'True Love & a G.C.M.', quoted in Saunders, *Ford Madox Ford*, p. 9.

in darkened minds. That remained' (659). The Armistice may announce an official end to the war, Valentine realises, but in the haunted memories of ex-combatants and civilians alike it would never be over. In Rebecca West's *Return of the Soldier* (1919), which Saunders suggests might itself have been based on Ford's shell-shock, amnesia is presented as an ambiguous relief from the trauma of war memory.[61] Chris Baldry, a wealthy landowner married to the exquisite yet doll-like Kitty, returns from the Front suffering from severe loss of memory. The struggle of his assimilation into contemporary life is told through the eyes of his cousin, Jenny, allowing West both a relatively conventional narrative style, and a female perspective on war neurosis and the breakdown of masculine norms and values that it popularly implied. Expecting to return to the woman he had been in love with fifteen years before, Chris is unable to recognise his wife or to remember the deaths of either his father or his baby son. West, far more explicitly than Ford, thus again maps war trauma onto an earlier domestic trauma, against which Kitty has constructed a façade of upper-class ease and satisfaction, a model of the English country house, filled with 'beautiful brittle things'.[62] Amid the elegance, luxury and taste of the renovated Baldry Court of his marriage, Chris would seem to have been content. 'Here we had made happiness inevitable for him', Jenny declares, and she longs to restore him to its safety. If the house, is 'the core of his heart' as Jenny believes, however, at its centre remains the child's nursery, its toys left as if ready for play, a haunted and haunting space which Chris has refused to have altered.[63] In his amnesiac state his mind represses not only the experiences of wartime, but also the entire period of his life since his father had sent him to Mexico to manage the failing family assets, bringing to an end his youthful romance. When he does return to Baldry Court, it is not to the 'green pleasantness' that Kitty and Jenny have carefully created, but to the memory of a turn-of-the-century idyll embodied by the plain and artless physicality of the lost Margaret Allington.[64]

With the deaths of Chris's father and then his heir, Baldry Court represents an Edwardian world already in decline by the outbreak of war, desperately concealing and postponing its imminent collapse. Unburdened by traumatic remembrance, however, and reunited with Margaret, Chris regains a youthful vivacity, at least until reminded of the social realities of the forgotten present. Jealous of their bond, Jenny nevertheless recognises that when contrasted with the poorer woman's simple kindnesses, Kitty appears 'the falsest thing

[61] Saunders, *Ford Madox Ford*, p. 29.
[62] Rebecca West, *The Return of the Soldier* (1918; London: Virago, 1980), p. 15.
[63] Ibid., p. 19. [64] Ibid., p. 13.

on earth'.[65] Recalling with radiance his courtship of the younger Margaret during dusky summer evenings next to the Thames, for example, Chris describes an impressionistic scene of meadow flowers, rose and amber sunsets and the scent of walnut trees, a natural paradise from which he is sharply drawn by the intruding images of war: 'a hateful world where barbed-wire entanglements showed impish knots against a livid sky full of booming noise and splashes of fire'.[66] His loss of memory, Jenny realises, is in fact 'a triumph', madness lying as much in the realities that he refuses as in his delusionary amnesia. The Freudian-minded doctor that Kitty turns to in a final attempt for a cure agrees as much. 'One forgets only those things one wants to forget', Dr Anderson asserts, dismissing the hypnotism employed by previous physicians as 'a silly trick'.[67] Comprehending in Chris's condition a mental phenomenon comparable with that Freud termed *Nachträglichkeit*, in which the traumatic meaning and consequent repression of one event or set of events is only triggered by a second, he recognises in the dead child the key to his memory. Margaret's task, and her moral dilemma, thus becomes the telling of this tragedy, forcing Chris back into traumatic consciousness and in so doing losing him to a heedlessly overjoyed Kitty. If West's soldier has physically come home, psychologically he has returned to the trenches, 'that No Man's Land where bullets fall like rain on the rotting faces of the dead'.[68]

'We do not like the war in fiction', Woolf had written in March 1917, only a year before West's explicit case-study of shell-shock in *Return of the Soldier*, '[t]he vast events now shaping across the Channel are towering over us too closely and too tremendously to be worked into fiction without a painful jolt in the perspective'.[69] It was of exactly this refusal to register the effects of war in her writing, however, that Katherine Mansfield complained forcefully to John Middleton Murry on reading Woolf's *Night and Day* in 1919. 'My private opinion is that it is a lie in the soul', Mansfield declared:

> The war has never been: that is what the message is. I don't want (G forbid!) mobilisation and the violation of Belgium but the novel cant just leave the war out. There *must* have been a change of heart. It is really fearful to me the 'settling down' of human beings. I feel in the *profoundest* sense that nothing can ever be the same – that as artists we are traitors if we feel otherwise: we have to take it into account and find new expressions new moulds for our new thoughts and feelings.[70]

[65] Ibid., p. 181. [66] Ibid., p. 86. [67] Ibid., pp. 165, 166. [68] Ibid., p. 187.

[69] Quoted in Hermione Lee, *Virginia Woolf* (London: Chatto & Windus, 1996), p. 343.

[70] Katherine Mansfield to J. Middleton Murry, 10 November 1919, in *The Collected Letters of Katherine Mansfield*, ed. Vincent James O'Sullivan and Margaret Scott, 4 vols. (Oxford: Clarendon Press, 1984–96), vol. III (1993), p. 97.

Mansfield herself had suffered personal loss as a result of the war, her brother killed at Ploegsteert in October 1915. In her critique of *Night and Day*, Mansfield demands a literature that recognises that the late-Victorian world had vanished for ever, and that expresses the influence of the trauma of war on human character, not just in its subject-matter but in its very style and form. She is not advocating 'realist' depictions of the trenches – far from it. The social and psychological conditions of the post-war period, she argues, posed a challenge to the conventions of representation that it was the obligation of art to meet. '[W]e have died and live again' Mansfield continues in a letter to Murry a week later:

> How can that be the same life? It doesn't mean that life is the less precious or that 'the common things of light and day' are gone. They are not gone, they are intensified, they are illumined. Now we know ourselves for what we are. In a way it's a tragic knowledge: it's as though, even while we live again, we face death. But *through Life*: that's the point.[71]

Without direct representation of the war scene, her writing afterwards was deeply touched by a concern to illuminate the present through the memories of the past, to acknowledge life through the acceptance of death.

Night and Day was in many ways a novel that Woolf had to write before she could embark on that jolt of perspective that she had foreseen that the war entailed, its conventional style part of a necessary therapeutic process after her mental breakdown of 1913–15. 'I was so tremblingly afraid of my own insanity that I wrote Night and Day mainly to prove to myself that I could keep entirely off that dangerous ground', she later admitted.[72] The novel also provided a means by which Woolf could work through her intense if ambivalent relationship with her Victorian literary inheritance. When Leonard Woolf described the novel as 'melancholy', she wrote in her diary that 'the process of discarding the old, when one is by no means certain what to put in their place, is a sad one', implying at once the recognition of the end of the Victorian era, and the struggle to relinquish its potent influence.[73]

It was this process of putting away the past that Woolf embarked upon in her next novel, *Jacob's Room* (1922). Her first novel in experimental style, *Jacob's Room* offers an elegy to pre-war England, to the lost promise of its energetic young men, and to a social world suddenly aborted, yet, as if in response to

71 Katherine Mansfield to J. Middleton Murry, 16 November 1919, in ibid., p. 97.

72 Virginia Woolf to Ethel Smyth, 16 October 1930, in *The Letters of Virginia Woolf*, ed. Nigel Nicolson, 6 vols. (London: Hogarth Press, 1975–80), vol. IV, *A Reflection of the Other Person, 1929–1931*, p. 231.

73 Virginia Woolf, 27 March 1919, *Diary* I, p. 259.

Mansfield's criticism, from the perspective of a changed present, in which post-war nostalgia mixes with an equally pervasive post-war doubt. Through the impressions and fragmentary glimpses of those around him Woolf presents the figure of Jacob Flanders, from a small boy playing on the beach, through his years at Cambridge and within the London arty bohemia of the 1910s, to his death in the Great War. Jacob himself, however, remains a ghostly absence throughout, the product and casualty of a patriarchal belief system whose own rhetoric, as the poppy petals pressed between the leaves of his Greek dictionary at Cambridge imply, will lead it to destruction. 'What did he expect? Did he think he would come back?' his friend Bonamy wonders at the end of the novel, as he surveys the everyday disorder of his vacant lodgings. For a moment, surrounded by letters, invitations, a bill for a riding crop, the past seems to return, captured in the atmosphere of leisured listlessness that the room evokes. But then the noise of the street breaks through the reverie, signalling the disjunction of the present: '"Such confusion everywhere!"' Jacob's mother exclaims.[74]

By the end of writing *Jacob's Room*, Woolf was reading Proust and finding herself excited and stimulated by his sensual prose. Although she would ultimately take up a deeply Proustian understanding of remembrance, however, writing of the past in 1939 as 'an avenue lying behind; a long ribbon of scenes, emotions', and of memory as 'only a question of discovering how we can get ourselves again attached to it', her writings of the early post-war years, like those of Ford, suggest a far less serene confidence in the recovery of the past, and a more questioning exploration of traumatic memory.[75] Like West, Woolf, in her next novel, *Mrs Dalloway* (1925), explored the narrow limits of sanity and insanity, through the construction of the shell-shocked soldier Septimus Warren Smith and the society hostess Clarissa Dalloway as alter egos. Septimus is a poetic young man who had volunteered for war service, eager to defend an England of poetry and Shakespeare. Decorated for bravery in action, by 1923 he has yet become an uncomfortable reminder of war in a society keen to forget the atrocities with which it was complicitous. Embracing the insights of his madness, Septimus becomes a compulsive writer, attempting to convey messages from the dead, 'about war; about Shakespeare; about great discoveries; how there is no death'.[76] His narrative of trauma is a tale, however,

74 Virginia Woolf, *Jacob's Room* (1922; London: Grafton, 1976), p. 173.
75 Virginia Woolf, 'A Sketch of the Past', in *Moments of Being* (London: Grafton, 1989), pp. 74, 75.
76 Virginia Woolf, *Mrs Dalloway* (1925; Oxford University Press, 1992), p. 183.

that nobody wants to hear or to remember, and when faced with an authoritarian medical profession determined to restore his 'sense of proportion', he commits suicide. If Septimus chooses psychological fragmentation and death over reconstruction, however, Clarissa does not, called back from empathy with his trauma by the striking of a clock to the social confines of her party.

For Woolf, the break with the past that the war made apocalyptically evident, paradoxically seems to have enabled the narrative reconstruction of previously inexpressible traumatic memories from her own personal history; of her brother Thoby Stephen, who died of typhoid in 1906, in *Jacob's Room*, and of her own suicidal depression in *Mrs Dalloway*. It was in *To the Lighthouse* (1927), however, that she felt that she had finally managed to work through the haunting affect of the past on her self and writerly identity. Wary of what she regarded as the reductiveness of Freudian accounts of mental illness, Woolf was nevertheless conversant with the concepts and terminology of psychoanalytic techniques, and declared of *To the Lighthouse*: 'I suppose I did for myself what psycho-analysts do for their patients. I expressed some very long felt and deeply felt emotion. And in expressing it I explained it and laid it to rest.'[77] Here the traumas of the past are again projected onto the period of the war, which stands at the structural and symbolic heart of the novel as the catalyst of change from the Victorian to modern worlds. Woolf wrote that she intended the central 'Time Passes' section to signify, 'Hopeless gulfs of misery. Cruelty. The War. Change. Oblivion'.[78] A break in the continuity of time, it represents a social and emotional void, in which death appears only in parentheses, as if unrepresentable within the flow of narrative. Set against the context of a cyclical natural world, however, as 'time passes' violence and destruction gives way to reconstruction and rebirth. When the Ramsay family returns to the lighthouse in the final section of the novel, it is to complete the journey that they had never made, and in so doing to perform an act of mourning and moving on from the demands of the past. For the artist Lily Briscoe, it is to complete a portrait that assimilates and transforms memory into art, a process of registering the past *as past* that she recognises asserts her own aesthetic identity.

If *Night and Day* was an expression of Woolf's melancholia for a lost yet haunting late Victorian era, can we then read *To the Lighthouse* as a narrative of mourning, as Woolf herself claimed? Psychological trauma, as studies from the late nineteenth century to our own post-Holocaust era attest, presents a

[77] Woolf, 'A Sketch', p. 90. [78] Quoted in Lee, *Virginia Woolf*, p. 342.

fundamental challenge to conventional understanding of memory and identity, and to issues of knowledge, ethics and representation. Post-war literary Modernism, faced with the void of history between a world of accepted values and beliefs, confident in its own endurance, and a world of disillusionment and loss, put its faith in the power of aesthetic reconstruction. As the tensions between its fragmentary, allusive narratives and structuring impulse reveal, however, the resolution of trauma perhaps never entirely surmounts the impact of its articulation.

11

The time–mind of the twenties

MICHAEL LEVENSON

> When you thought of Time in those days your mind wavered impotently like eyes tired by reading too small print.
>
> Ford Madox Ford, *A Man Could Stand Up*[1]

> It takes it out of you, certainly, Time.
>
> Wyndham Lewis, *The Childermass*[2]

> This extraordinary discrepancy between time on the clock and time in the mind is less well known than it should be and deserves fuller investigation.
>
> Virginia Woolf, *Orlando*[3]

The British Modernist novel did not discover time in the years after the World War I. Before Modernism, outside Britain, and in other genres, the mysteries of temporality had disclosed themselves. Within the English novel, Sterne's *Tristram Shandy* and Emily Brontë's *Wuthering Heights* are luminous and unforgettable precedents. But there can be little doubt that in the first post-war decade, at a moment of vaulting ambition in the High Modernist novel, time became such a dominant concern that it can be taken as a cultural signature. In the years after the war, it ceased to be a background for literary events, an invisible medium surrounding the enactment of a plot. It became rather a fully thematised subject in its own right – a fact that can be seen in the epigraphs to this chapter, where time becomes an upper-case abstraction, indeed a protagonist as real as the fictive human agents.

At the outset we need to distinguish three aspects of the problem: (1) the time of modernisation that surrounds and permeates the literary experiments; (2) the representation of temporality within the fictional world; and (3) the

1 Ford Madox Ford, *A Man Could Stand Up*, vol. III of *Parade's End* (1926; New York: Vintage Books, 1979), p. 517.
2 Wyndham Lewis, *The Childermass* (London: Chatto & Windus, 1928), p. 96.
3 Virginia Woolf, *Orlando* (1928; New York: Harcourt Brace Jovanovich, 1956), p. 98.

forms and structures of narrative time. All three elements are indispensable, and they must be kept in close relation to one another. The extra-literary historical realm of novelty – the experience of rapid modernisation in technologies, social relations, religious beliefs, philosophic principles – entered the literary universe, providing the subject-matter for the novel of time. But the deployment of these time-subjects was not merely achieved through new narrative structures; it was in large part modified and constituted by the forms themselves. Just as events in the social world circulated within the thematic world of Modernist fiction, so did the labour of form modify the experience of time.

How shall we describe the temporal world of the early twentieth century? We might begin by saying that both the *sensation* of living in new times and the *theory* of time are inevitable features of modernity. We know that any dating of the modern is itself an unworthy fiction. But where time is concerned, we can plausibly follow Reinhart Koselleck, who has argued that by the year 1800 Europeans became conscious of living within 'new times', *neue Zeit*. The present was experienced not as a stable historical period, the latest in a succession of periods, but as something unprecedented and distinctive, 'a period of transition' characterised by 'the expected otherness of the future and, associated with it, the alteration in the rhythm of temporal experience: acceleration, by means of which one's own time is distinguished from what went before'. The result was that 'lived time was experienced as a rupture, a period of transition in which the new and the unexpected continually happened'.[4]

This broader understanding of modernity as *neue Zeit* is a necessary context for any approach to literary time. Through the later nineteenth century, a chronic sense of novelty had been stimulated by the growth of cities, the speed of transportation and by such technological wizardry as the telephone and the automobile. The consciousness of change was heightened by the turn of the century followed soon after by the death of Queen Victoria. But the sense of transition, rupture and acceleration underwent a radicalisation in the post-war years. In major part, this was a response to the slaughter in the trenches: young death on an unprecedented and unassimilable scale. But wartime death was not only a brute *thing*; it was also a *sign*. It indicated the reach of new technologies, including the technology of violence; even through death, the war established the terms of mass society: individual atoms absorbed within the surge and swarm of groups.

[4] Reinhart Koselleck, *Futures Past: On the Semantics of Historical Time*, trans. Keith Tribe (Cambridge, MA: MIT Press, 1985), pp. 251–2, 257.

In the 1920s within the cities of Modernism, there were more anodyne reflections of *neue Zeit*. The opening sequence of Virginia Woolf's *Mrs Dalloway* – with its shoppers moving through crowded streets, while an aeroplane flies overhead – gives a tableau of the self-consciously transitional urban modernity. Woolf's Peter Walsh strolls through London on the first day of his return from India, stirred by his recognition of passing time:

> Those five years – 1918 to 1923 – had been, he suspected, somehow very important. People looked different. Newspapers seemed different. Now, for instance, there was a man writing quite openly in one of the respectable weeklies about water-closets. That you couldn't have done ten years ago – written quite openly about water-closets in a respectable weekly. And then this taking out a stick of rouge, or a powderpuff, and making up in public.[5]

This is the double recognition in the 1920s: the sense of rupture brought by a catastrophic war, and then the perception of a peace that is not a return to pre-war years but a passage into another strangeness, in which five years can measure the overturning of a world. As Peter Walsh's ruminations make clear, the consciousness of time appears on the micro as well as the macro plane: the image of 'new times' includes the smallest change in speech and fashion, as well as large changes in the relations between men and women, believers and sceptics, owners and managers.

The most fruitful way to think of the conjuncture of the 1920s may be to see it as an acceleration within an acceleration, as a heightening of the sense of rupture and transition that had accompanied modernity since at least the beginning of the nineteenth century. The war forced a recognition of terrifying novelty, and the peace created the uncanniness of a return that was also a discontinuity. Taken together, these events prepared for the remarkable encounters with time undertaken by the authors under consideration here. In approaching the fiction, however, we come upon a different though related question, namely, the temporality of literary careers. These, too, unfold in time, and English Modernism possessed a notable generational character. Those fiction writers who were dominant figures in the Modernist canon of the 1920s were born within relatively few years of one another – Ford (b. 1873), Richardson (b. 1873), Forster (b. 1879), Joyce (b. 1882) Lewis (b. 1882), Woolf (b. 1882), Lawrence (b. 1885) – and their first significant efforts each appeared within the decade before the war. The philosopher Alfred Schutz has followed Dilthey in offering a theory of generational unity, in which the 'community of time'

[5] Virginia Woolf, *Mrs Dalloway* (1925; Harmondsworth: Penguin Books, 1973), p. 80.

defining a generation is bound by a sense that 'we are growing old together.'[6] In the case of these Modernists, a collective consciousness of maturing as artists accompanies a memory of having been young together in the uncertain pre-war period. The writings of the 1920s, then, were conceived within the longer trajectory of Modernism, and their engagement with time unfolds against the background of developing vocations/professions with their own time-sense and the shared resolve to build more ambitious works at this stage in their careers.

Within this generational matrix Ford Madox Ford played a distinctive role, and his fictional tetralogy, *Parade's End*, gives us a convenient entry to the problem. Older than the fierce artists whom he liked to call *les jeunes*, Ford identified with his predecessors, Henry James (b. 1843) and Joseph Conrad (b. 1857), and partly through the accident of his age, and partly through his efforts in criticism and personal ambassadorship, he helped to bring James and Conrad into the generational unity of Modernism. Of the two, the relationship with Conrad was the more sustained and substantial, and that connection offers an approach to the time-conscious fiction of the 1920s.

* * *

Conrad's invention of his narrator Marlow, first in 'Youth' and then more notably in *Heart of Darkness* and *Lord Jim*, marks a threshold in the staging of the 'narrating instance'. This is a term developed by Gérard Genette to denote the scene of narrating itself, the activity of storytelling at the moment of utterance. Genette seeks to identify the fictional 'enunciating' act that lies behind the record of events, an enunciation that is always presupposed and that must be rigorously distinguished from biographical authorship. All narrative implies the enunciation of a narrator. And yet despite this discursive truth, the realist tendency in novel-writing often worked to obscure the traces of a constituting voice. So, for instance, Henry James, despite his attention to the workings of subjectivity, still enshrined a third-person standpoint, which would fix the consciousness of characters from the outside, and which in the last great phase (*The Ambassadors*, *The Wings of the Dove* and *The Golden Bowl*) studiously avoids the questions, Who narrates this novel?, when?, and where? Conrad, on the other hand, finds these richly attractive questions. *Heart of Darkness* begins with an unnamed narrator locating Marlow's scene of storytelling – on the yacht *Nellie* anchored in the Thames estuary at dusk – and the tale is

[6] Alfred Schutz, *The Phenomenology of the Social World*, trans. George Walsh and Frederick Lehnert (Evanston: Northwestern University Press, 1967), p. 163.

regularly interrupted by reminders of the present moment and the strain of communication: 'This is the worst of trying to tell . . . You can't understand? How could you –.'[7] In *Lord Jim*, too, the narrating instance repeatedly displays itself, at once breaking the spell of Jim's history and forcing attention to the labour of tale-bearing.

The staging of the narrative instant, as it is developed in the device of 'Marlow', has profound implications for fictive temporality, implications extending beyond the Conradian device itself. The recognition that the act of telling has conditions independent of the represented world – this breaks the hegemony of the event. One way to understand the nineteenth-century development from Realism towards Naturalism is to see it in terms of an increasingly rigorous logic of incidents. Partly this is due to an absorption in the world of action that gave little value to subtle acts of storytelling, and partly it's due to the ascendancy of causal theories derived from the new sciences. The logic of plot that one finds in Gissing, Zola and later Hardy invited a view of fiction as the strict unfolding of inner necessities. But once the fabricating work of a narrator becomes fully audible, then the time of fiction need no longer follow the time of causally linked events, time's straight arrow: it can now follow the more uncertain arc of memory and speech.

Ford's *The Good Soldier*, published just as the war was beginning, offers one epitome of an emancipated narrative, which radicalises the methods of Conrad to create a novel that fully defeats the logic of event. In his writings on Impressionism, Ford held that the goal of fiction was to create not the 'rounded annotated record' but the 'impression of the moment', 'the impression not the corrected chronicle'.[8] John Dowell, the narrator of *The Good Soldier*, writes that 'The whole world for me is like spots of colour in an immense canvas', and given this disorderly perception of the world, Dowell is left to narrate in 'a very rambling way'.[9] With an extravagant negligence, *The Good Soldier* disregards chronology, leaping backwards and forwards in time, invoking one event only to leave it for another, acknowledging no dictate more supreme than the will of the narrating mind at the instant of narration. In all these respects, the book

7 Joseph Conrad, *Heart of Darkness*, ed. Robert Kimbrough (New York: W. W. Norton, 1988), pp. 48–9. Of course, Conrad never elaborates the 'narrating instance' of the unnamed speaker who provides the frame tale that surrounds Marlow's. Conrad is far from systematic in working out his narrative principles, and the invention of Marlow is less an aesthetic deduction (as in Genette) than an instinctive response to a fictional challenge.

8 Ford Madox Ford, 'Impressionism and Fiction', *Critical Writings of Ford Madox Ford*, ed. Frank MacShane (Lincoln, NE: University of Nebraska Press, 1964), p. 41.

9 Ford Madox Ford, *The Good Soldier: A Tale of Passion* (1915; New York: Vintage, 1955), pp. 14, 183.

is a decisive moment within the history traced here: it liberates time from causality and tests the reach of a roving, darting, looping memory.

This is the context in which we can turn to *Parade's End*, the series of four novels published between 1924 and 1928, a grandly ambitious project that aims at once to consolidate the practice of Impressionism and to confront the trauma of war. Strikingly, Ford sets aside the device of the dramatised narrator (a Marlow or Dowell) and pays no attention to the scene of narration. And yet, in deeply challenging ways the work sustains the project begun in the pre-war years, the act of emancipation from the causal nexus. Ford later reflected on the course of the Impressionist experiment conducted with Conrad.

> That we did succeed in finding *a* new form I think I may permit myself to claim, Conrad first evolving the convention of a Marlow who should narrate, in presentation, the whole story of a novel just as, without much sequence or pursued chronology, a story will come up into the mind of a narrator, and I eventually dispensing with a narrator but making the story come up in the mind of the unseen author with a similar want of chronological sequence.[10]

He is describing here the method of *Parade's End*, but what the account leaves to one side is the relationship between the 'new form' and a new subject-matter. The tetralogy begins with a modern battle between the sexes. Christopher Tietjens is estranged from his strong-willed wife, Sylvia, and at their moment of crisis he meets the athletic young suffragette, Valentine Wannop, fair and freckled, with whom he will fall in love. All through these episodes in the first novel, *Some Do Not*, Ford plays a virtuoso match against time. The slow crumbling of Tietjens's universe – the confusions of his marriage and his new desire, the disaffection from his government position (in the Imperial Department of Statistics), the demoralising spectacle of his striving friend McMaster – invites all those strategic dislocations refined over the last decade. Chronology is given no pre-eminence; time is supple and reversible; characters appear, only to be named and introduced many chapters later. A rude phrase drops onto the page and is only belatedly placed in an intelligible context. It's not simply that the narrative moves back and forth through months and years; it is even willing to retreat 'four minutes before'.[11]

Yet it seems fair to say that *Parade's End* only finds its shape when the war between the sexes becomes entangled within the war against the Germans. In Part II of *Some Do Not* the novel reaches the third year of the war. What had

[10] Ford, 'Techniques', *Critical Writings of Ford Madox Ford*, p. 68.
[11] Ford Madox Ford, *Parade's End* (New York: Alfred A. Knopf, 1979), p. 95.

been the patient inevitability of change now becomes the violence of rupture. Important events are elided, referred to glancingly, sometimes elaborated, sometimes not. From this point on, *Parade's End* assumes the form of Trauma and Return. Certain extreme incidents – Sylvia leaving home at dawn, Tietjens asking Valentine to be his mistress in the night before he leaves for combat – exist as wounds in time. The first appearance is almost incidental, since what counts is their recurrence as signs of an unforgettable breach. Then beyond this personal realm stands the war. In one aspect, the war itself makes an irrecoverable breach in the continuity of history – 'What changes in the world! What cataclysms! What revolutions!' (Ford, *Some Do Not*, 522) – that brings a definitive end to a period of history: 'No more Hope, no more Glory, no more parades' (307). But in another aspect, the war is not only a massive event that concludes an age, but is also the very type and symbol of the new time that it inaugurates.

The time of war is that of waiting and death, of interminably slow time and the time of sudden violence. The second volume of *Parade's End* turns on the awful pivot of one soldier's death, the demise of O Nine Morgan, a Welsh soldier under Tietjens's command. With the resource of the mature Impressionist, Ford presents the event within the chaos of subjective apprehension: the reader, like Tietjens, is slow to understand the meaning of the broken body, the viscous blood, the desperate gesture. The immediacy of violence is disrupted by stray memories and incoherent emotions. But the further significance of this death shows itself only later. What it exemplifies is the awful rhythm of war's time. Especially within the third novel, *A Man Could Stand Up*, narrative time loses pace; incidents take many pages to form; and the very notion of event seems to lose its hold. There is 'the eternal waiting that is War', 'those eternal hours when Time itself stayed still' (569). Then, after the endless waiting, comes the noise, the flash, the death – which will then be remembered and reimagined as the novel returns to its long rhythms and slow movements.

In this way the rhythm of the war becomes the basis for Modernist temporality as such. All of experience in *Parade's End* enacts the periodicity of duration and eruption. The romance between Tietjens and Valentine Wannop is defined by its endless incipience: for six or seven years, they remain absorbed by a love that neither would ever mention, until suddenly, in a few convulsive hours on Armistice Day, all is said, felt, resolved. 'Then one day – after thirteen years' – 'in those ten minutes you found you thought out more than in two years': these are characteristic formulae. In the moment of his disarray in the trenches, we are told of Tietjens that 'He had lost all sense of chronology'

(*No More Parades*, 486), and one might say that this is the state towards which all of *Parade's End* is tending. People suffer from the disorder of time, which shatters the continuity of their lives, but they also see opportunity in the wreckage. The destruction of continuous time breaks the stifling entrenchments of bad marriages, bad government and bad wars, and as the tetralogy comes to an end in *The Last Post* it offers a tableau of a chaotic post-war world where the best chances lie in twisting a new life out of the odd strands of tradition and modernity loosened in the acts of destruction.

* * *

For Ford, as for Conrad before him, the reinvention of narrative time was precisely a question of the *narrator's* time. When we consider 'how stories are actually told' by real people in actual circumstances, then we recognise that they follow no order or sequence, but simply come up in the mind as it skips and stalls, stumbles and recovers. The great provocation is addressed to sequence and the continuity of events. Yet in another major phase of Modernism, the questions of narrator and chronology recede in favour of the problem of temporal experience. Not time as narrated but time as lived – this is the second current that we need to follow.

A way to broach the issue is to recognise that the experiments of Ford came out of a coherent fictional tradition, beginning with Flaubert and continuing through Maupassant, Crane, James and Conrad. But a rival lineage emerged from modern lyricism, specifically the lyrics composed out of a single perception. 'Imagism' was Pound's name for the new concentrated forms, but in fact the pertinent literary examples emerge from a wider field, including the shorter narrative forms of the 1890s. When Joyce developed his notion of the 'epiphany' in writing *Stephen Hero*, he was also contributing to the new lyricism. Whether in poetry or prose, the decisive gesture was the concentration upon instantaneous (or at least brief) experience. The prominence of the new experiments in the fine arts was a further influence in this direction. The break with Victorian narrative painting and the growth of pictorial formalism offered examples of the self-sufficiency of the momentary tableau: the card-players of Cézanne, the decorated rooms of Matisse, the guitars of Picasso.

All these gestures had implications for the representation of narrative time. The challenge to narrative lay in the implication that a brief moment was itself long enough to constitute a work of art. The relation between the resonant instant and the unfolding novel became pointed and urgent. Throughout the 1920s, a number of novelists attempted to build large novelistic forms while preserving the power of instants. This was a complex negotiation, nowhere more strenuously performed than in the work of Joyce, who began his career by refining the power of short forms: in the poems of *Chamber Music*, in the stories of *Dubliners*, and in the epiphanies catalogued in his notebooks.

When Joyce published *Ulysses* in 1922, he completed a movement from the epiphany to the epic, and he did so by reimagining the structure of time. His early perception had been that even a mean object – the clock on the Ballast Office – possessed the power of intrinsic meaning: a 'whatness' that 'leaps to us from the vestment of its appearance' until 'the soul of the commonest object . . . seems to us radiant. The object achieves its epiphany.'[12] In the spirit of austerity, he aimed to delineate sharp frames around these objects. But his later, riper thought was that 'whatness' was infinitely dense and that any scene, every object, was open to massive elaboration. The most conspicuous formal gesture in *Ulysses*, the enlargement of a single day to contain the sweep of epic, depends on this deepening sense of temporal density. The world of experience is now so thick with perception that no single epiphany, no self-contained perception, can be faithful to the great parade. Here is Leopold Bloom in the Dublin street.

> By lorries along Sir John Rogerson's quay Mr Bloom walked soberly, past Windmill lane, Leask's the linseed crusher's, the postal telegraph office. Could have given that address too. And past the sailors' home. He turned from the morning noises of the quayside and walked through Lime street. By Brady's cottages a boy for the skins lolled, his bucket of offal linked, smoking a chewed fagbutt. A smaller girl with scars of eczema on her forehead eyed him, listlessly holding her battered caskhoop.[13]

The prodigious dilation of the present tense – this is the first great temporal act of *Ulysses*. The world before us is a swarming host, whose smallest details are composed of those even in smaller. The ceremony of the present demands our endless absorption, curiosity, fascination. Unlike Conrad or Ford, Joyce is not concerned to free events from the sequence of chronology; on the contrary, *Ulysses* is meticulous in charting the march of hours through the day. But there is another logic to resist: namely, the conventional scale of event – the kiss, the stroll, the song – and here the great predecessor is Sterne. By refusing to accept limits on the degree of attention owed to any happenstance, by composing the record of a day that requires far more than a day to read, Joyce creates a narrative present that is potentially expansive without end. The celebrated device of 'stream of consciousness' is not simply a means to let time flow

[12] James Joyce, *Stephen Hero* (New York: New Directions, 1955), p. 213.
[13] James Joyce, *Ulysses* (New York: Random House, 1961), p. 71.

through subjectivity: it is equally a way to obstruct and impede the flow of time, to let the present become viscous and slow.

A question for *Ulysses*, and for the device of 'stream of consciousness', is how it permits modalities other than the present to enter the mental space. A short answer is that consciousness not only views the parade of the world; it also views its own pomp and spectacle. Joycean subjectivity occupies a vanishing point, from which it registers the movement of objects and people, and equally its own fantasies and aversions, ideas and images. What this 'transcendental' standpoint uncovers is that the temporality of memory and desire are always ready to change the valence of the present, to turn it backwards or forwards. So Bloom's mind, with luminous economy, tastes a drop of wine on his palate, recalls a day of romantic joy with Molly, and then thinks wearily, 'Me. And me now' (176).

This turn to the past is exemplary in *Ulysses*. It is true that much of the epic day is spent in anticipation: Molly projecting her afternoon with Boylan, and Bloom dreading that tryst, even as he idly dreams of Martha Clifford and Gerty MacDowell. But acts of anticipation in *Ulysses* are consistently shown to be thin and dangerous. To project a desire – especially a sexual desire – is to become tangled in fantasy. The real labour of time is to recover what has been forgotten, to prise away the phantasmal structure of desire and to reorient consciousness towards the past. On the verisimilar plane of incident, memory is the recovery of early married life and still earlier individual history (Molly's life in Gibraltar, Stephen and his mother, Bloom and his father). On the mythic plane, the movement is less that of conscious memory (though in Stephen's case it is characteristically that) than unconscious participation in the history of archetypes: Bloom as Elijah and Odysseus, Molly as Gea-Tellus.

Futurity is a temptation and a lure. A long patient effort of *Ulysses* is to heal the present by recovering the heft of the past. In this, as in little else, Joyce is congruent with Proust. Their manner and their fictive communities could hardly be more different, but they meet in the vocation of memory. Proust, too, follows the circuit of anticipations – Swann for Odette, Marcel for Gilberte and Albertine – but the work of desire is overwhelmed by the subtlety of recollection. It would be too much to claim that these great works ignore the future, but it seems fair to say that they suspend its urgency, in favour of an orientation towards the past. The dialectic of past and present gives the formal principle of both works.

In the revelation during the party for the Princess de Guermantes, Marcel receives a celebrated series of sensations: feelings of certainty, safety and intense happiness. As he works to understand the apparently insignificant incidents that excite the feelings – 'the sensation of the uneven paving-stones, the stiffness of the napkin and the taste of the madeleine'[14] – he comes to see that the revelatory power depends on an alignment of two different phases of time. His 'felicity' occurred 'in the present moment and at the same time in the context of a distant moment' (222). To become lost in the present or to assume a merely intellectual attitude towards the past is to miss the moment of vision.

> But let a noise or a scent, once heard or once smelt, be heard or smelt again in the present and at the same time in the past, real without being actual, ideal without being abstract, and immediately the permanent and habitually concealed essence of things is liberated and our true self, which seemed – had perhaps for long years seemed – to be dead but was not altogether dead, is awakened and reanimated as it receives the celestial nourishment that is brought to it. (224)

This is what Marcel recognises as the vocation of his art, its 'spiritual' meaning (1001): the disclosure of the 'essence of things' that can be achieved in rare moments when past and present coincide and fuse. Strikingly, these ecstatic instants overcome 'anxiety on the subject of my death' (223). Marcel is now 'unalarmed by the vicissitudes of the future' (223). Past and present come into alliance against the future.

The discovery of Marcel's vocation arrives with the disclosure of the essence of time. Moreover, what Marcel achieves within the fiction, the published novel, unfolding slowly through the years, enacts within the wider culture. That Proust could sustain a novel for so long, that its events could elongate and return, that the plot of novel could resolve in the naming of time as its great protagonist – all this confirmed Time-consciousness as an inescapable topos of Modernism.

In England the way had been prepared by the philosophy of Henri Bergson, which had such a significant influence on Proust. Bergson's lectures became celebrated; his early publications developed a committed following. The telling event was the translation of the early work, *Essai sur les données immédiates de la conscience*, published in France in 1889, appearing in English in 1910 as *Time and Free Will*. It was closely followed by the translations of *Matiére et mémoire, essai sur la relation du corps avec l'esprit* (1896, translated 1910). Together these books offered not only an accessible philosophy of time, but also one suited to the formal experimentation of Modernist fiction.

[14] Marcel Proust, *In Search of Lost Time*, trans. Andreas Mayor and Terence Kilmartin, rev. D. J. Enright, 6 vols. (London: Chatto & Windus, 1992–6), vol. VI, *Time Regained*, p. 220. Further references in parenthesis in the text.

Bergson's celebrated insight was that we are creatures who chronically distort the truth of our experience. Living in a world of material objects, and struggling to find concepts that will comprehend this outer world, we devise a system of understanding based on space and spatial relations. Even when we believe that we have an idea of development or succession – as in the case of numbers – a close look reveals that we rely on a spatial image, the juxtaposition of units within an ideal expanse: 'every clear idea of number implies a visual image in space'.[15] Science is founded on the distinctness of discrete numbers in spatial array.

What happens, asks Bergson, when we look away from numbers and objects, and back to the inwardness of the psyche? Then we discover that many mental states, especially our sense of duration, resist understanding in spatial terms. As opposed to the 'extensive' multiplicity of the world – discrete objects distributed side by side – the 'intensive' multiplicities of consciousness defy a spatial grasp. They resist separation into distinct entities that can be spatially organised. The telling and influential claim is that there are 'two different kinds of reality' (97) and that if we can avoid 'the trespassing of the idea of space upon the field of pure consciousness' (98), then we will recognise the compelling specificity of temporal experience. On the surface of our lives, we look to organise existence within the clarity of space; we conform to the demands of social clarity; we accept the hegemony of science. But the 'fundamental self' lives in the depths, reaching an experience 'confused, ever changing, and inexpressible, because language cannot get hold of it without arresting its mobility or fit[ting] into its common-place forms' (129). For Bergson the decisive aspect of the deep self is its sense of living-through-time, not as a series of separate events within a homogeneous volume, but as a layered heterogeneity, a mix of temporal valences, overlapping and interpenetrating until in a state of 'pure duration', the 'ego lets itself *live*'. It no longer separates the present from earlier states of mind, but instead 'forms both the past and the present states into an organic whole, as happens when we recall the notes of a tune, melting, so to speak, into one another' (100).

Proust's many volumes owe much to such a Bergsonian understanding of both life in time and story in time. In *Narrative Discourse*, Gérard Genette takes the Proustian *œuvre* as a vast cabinet of temporal devices: the 'recall' and 'advance mention', the 'singulative' and 'iterative', the 'pause' and 'ellipsis', indeed all the mechanisms of order, frequency and duration. Yet to the English

[15] Henri Bergson, *Time and Free Will: An Essay on the Immediate Data of Consciousness* (rpt. 1889, *Essai sur les données immédiates de la conscience*) trans. F. L. Pogson (London: George Allen & Unwin, 1950), p. 79. Further references given in parenthesis in the text.

writers on the other side of the Channel, Proust represented a distant and inimitable monument, at once exemplary and extreme.

* * *

Dorothy Richardson, an early and admiring reader of Proust, can be taken as his closest English cousin. She herself notes the coincidence between the appearance of the first volume of *A la recherche du temps perdu* and the beginning of her work on *Pilgrimage*. 'An unprecedentedly profound and opulent reconstruction of experience focused from within the mind of a single individual'[16] – this is how she describes the Proustian revolution. But more even than Proust, Richardson performs the aggressive act of focalisation: the world of *Pilgrimage* is coextensive with the consciousness of its protagonist, Miriam Henderson.

Within fiction written in English, the nearest contemporary parallel is Joyce's *A Portrait of the Artist as a Young Man*. But though they share the vocation of consciousness at a decisive moment in Modernism, their differences are illuminating. Joyce, too, exploited the power of restriction. The mobility of Stephen Dedalus's mind – its wreathing and unfolding – is vivified by the narrow compass of the novel. And yet, Joyce's resolve is always to measure a distance from the intensely focalised consciousness. Through local irony and large-scale narrative patterning, the work of the mind is qualified and enclosed, located within a portrait, kept from the privileges of sovereignty.

Richardson, on the other hand, accepts the risk of sovereignty. Her Miriam is a consciousness liberated from irony and from the qualifications of point of view. In an early and influential reading of the first three volumes of *Pilgrimage*, May Sinclair outlined the principles of Richardson's method: 'She must not be the wise, all-knowing author. She must be Miriam Henderson. She must not know or divine anything that Miriam does not know or divine; she must not see anything that Miriam does not see.'[17] And Sinclair recognises that from this commitment there follows an austere result.

> In this series there is no drama, no situation, no set scene. Nothing happens. It is just life going on and on. It is Miriam Henderson's stream of consciousness going on and on. And in neither is there any grossly discernible beginning or middle or end. (59)

This is the earliest critical use of the phrase 'stream of consciousness', and it's appropriate that Richardson's work should be the first to receive the epithet.

16 Dorothy Richardson, 'Foreword', *Pointed Roofs*, vol. 1 of *Pilgrimage* (New York: Popular Library, 1976), p. 10.

17 May Sinclair, 'The Novels of Dorothy Richardson', *Egoist*, 5, 4, p. 58.

And yet part of what Sinclair recognises here is that the sovereignty of consciousness unsettles the structure of narrative time. If the metaphor of the stream suggests a directed temporal flow, then it is misleading when applied to *Pilgrimage*, as Richardson seems to have noticed. The most distinctive feature of time in the early volumes of *Pilgrimage* is that it tends to become the time of a perpetual present. Events never accumulate into a structure of experience; brief vignettes end abruptly; and each situation strikes Miriam Henderson with the force of novelty. 'She loved the day that had gone', we read in *Pointed Roofs*, 'and the one that was coming.'[18] Each new phase of time has the same claim of freshness. Her life, as she puts it in *The Tunnel*, 'would be perpetually beginning now. Nights and days were all one day; all hers, unlimited.'[19] The present is endlessly absorptive. It's not that the past disappears, rather that it loses its distance and becomes another part of the immediate spectacle. As she would put it much later in *March Moonlight*: 'The whole of what is called "the past" is with me, seen anew, vividly. No, Schiller, the past does not stand "being still". It moves, growing with one's own growth.'[20] In the years during and just after the war, Richardson maintained the rigour of her experiment and produced the most strongly marked convergence of sovereign consciousness and the present tense.

* * *

Like Dorothy Richardson, Virginia Woolf was concerned to preserve the brio of the present, its irreducible plenitude and uproar. And yet, she is even more interested in the fullness of temporal experience. Immediate experience in Woolf is not absorptive, but is always fractured by the other tenses. Paul Ricoeur is right to say that Woolf's art 'lies in interweaving the present, with its stretches of the imminent future and the recent past, and a recollected past, and so making time progress by slowing it down'.[21] The alternating rhythm of long and short temporalities is what strikes Ricoeur, but to develop the thought we need to look further back in the phenomenological tradition – towards Edmund Husserl who was developing his philosophy of time in the early years of the twentieth century.

Husserl, having placed the question of time at the centre of his new phenomenology, found himself returning repeatedly to a central conundrum. We

[18] Richardson, *Pointed Roofs*, p. 111.
[19] Richardson, *The Tunnel*, vol. II of *Pilgrimage*, p. 30.
[20] Dorothy Richardson, *March Moonlight*, vol. IV of *Pilgrimage*, p. 657.
[21] Paul Ricoeur, *Time and Narrative*, trans. Kathleen McLaughlin and David Pellauer, 3 vols. (University of Chicago Press, 1984–8), III, p. 133.

hold to the immediacy of the present, the certainty of our direct encounter with the 'now'. And yet the 'now' continually slips away. How then can we speak of perception if its object is continually disappearing? The instant of our encounter with the world seems too flickering to be the basis for experience. In patient thought about this problem Husserl came to develop a theory of 'retention', which attempts to describe the duration inherent in so-called immediate experience. A colour is glimpsed, a tone is heard, but even as we move to the next perceptual moment, we retain a consciousness of the 'just-having-been, of just-having-experienced'.[22] Without this trace of the elapsed sensation, we would be helpless in the face of successive stimuli. We would never hear a melody, only a string of tones, replacing one another in the position of this-now. In fact, all experience fades into the past leaving a 'comet's tail' (Husserl, *Internal Time*, 37) behind, and sensory life always contains a 'steady continuum of memories'.

Husserl offers a root distinction between the primary memory of retention, the perpetual sense of a 'just-having-been', and recollection proper. The latter corresponds to our customary sense of memory as the retrieval of something lost to experience, while 'retention' indicates the penumbral quality of a perpetually fading present. Apart from its philosophic force, the distinction elucidates the difficulty of Proust, Joyce and Woolf. At the end of her triumphant dinner party, we read that as Mrs Ramsay 'left the room, it changed, it shaped itself differently; it had become, she knew, giving one last look at it over her shoulder, already the past'.[23] Attention to Husserl's distinction helps us to see what distinguishes the temporality of much Modernist narrative: not the formal act of memory, but the play between the now-fading present and the distant past.

Husserl developed the complement to 'retention', namely the sense of an imminent future, which he called 'protention'. Our movement through time involves 'expectation–intentions whose fulfilment leads to the present'.[24] The 'temporal fringe' that surrounds the present contains anticipations of imminence as well as penumbral memory. But Husserl never gave the same weight to 'protention', partly because any bearing towards the future remains uncertain.[25] Like Joyce and Proust, Husserl remained most concerned not with the blank future, but with the vast, intricate expanse of the past. Virginia Woolf,

[22] Edmund Husserl, *On the Phenomenology of the Consciousness of Internal Time*, trans. John Barnett Brough (Dordrecht: Kluwer, 1991), p. 169.

[23] Virginia Woolf, *To the Lighthouse* (New York: Harcourt Brace, 1981), p. 111.

[24] Husserl, *On the Phenomenology of the Consciousness of Internal Time*, p. 54.

[25] Paul Ricoeur notes how Husserl favours 'memory to such an extent at the expense of expectation', and remarks that because of his emphasis on perception, Husserl was incapable of 'dealing directly with expectation . . . Only Heidegger's philosophy, anchored

on the other hand, turns precisely to the blank future, the featureless region of the time to come. Like her great contemporaries, of course, Woolf remains attentive to the elaborations of memory. Her novels of the twenties depend on acts of mourning – for Jacob in *Jacob's Room*, Septimus in *Mrs Dalloway*, Mrs Ramsay in *To the Lighthouse*, Percival in *The Waves* – that require a continuous encounter with the past. And yet, what gives force to the mourning is that beyond what it expresses for the dead, it presupposes a future for the living: they will forget, and then they too will die. Woolf broaches not only the inevitability of death, but also its 'protentive' imminence, in the sense that death is always waiting and lurking. Even before it arrives, it signals its imminence with the little losses of experience, the forgettings, failures and departures.

Not Husserl, but Husserl's student Martin Heidegger, offers the philosophic context for Woolf's fiction of death. That our lived experience is bound up with care, anticipation and dread; that our finitude presses upon us from the future; that the prospect of death is the informing vista of an authentic life – these momentous Heideggerian themes were of course not influences upon Woolf, but they were parallel crystallisations that help to elucidate her project. In *Being and Time*, Heidegger radicalised the temporality of Husserl's phenomenology; he inscribed temporal experience within our 'inmost' being; he understood our situation, our *Dasein*, as an essential structure of anticipation and care. All the modalities of time receive their authentic meaning from the careful anticipation of a futurity that is a 'Being-towards-death'. Everyday life always disguises the significance of our care. But in the 'moment of vision', *Dasein* confronts its 'authentic future'.[26] Anticipation brings *Dasein* 'face to face with the possibility of being itself . . . in an impassioned *freedom towards death*' (Heidegger, *Being and Time*, 311). The resolute consciousness can pierce the evasions of the everyday and understand that the essence of its being is a temporal projection towards death.

The suddenness of mortality in Woolf – whether through war, suicide or illness – enforces its imminence in all her work of the twenties. Despite the labour of memory within *Mrs Dalloway*, its greatest provocation is the swing round from past to future – from the warmth of recollection to the bite of inevitable death: Clarissa in her attic room, forced into consciousness of her age, her weakening body, her fear. The novels typically build a closed circuit of continuities – through minute attention to acts of expectancy and recall – and

directly in care and not in perception, will be able to do away with the inhibitions that paralyze the Husserlian analysis of expectation.' *Time and Narrative*, III, pp. 36–7.

[26] Martin Heidegger, *Being and Time*, trans. John Macquarrie and Edward Robinson (New York: Harper & Row, 1962), p. 388.

then they interrupt the flow of this micro-phenomenology. Clarissa Dalloway recoils, 'What business had the Bradshaws to talk of death at her party?' (203). This is the shudder which breaks through everyday consolation and demands a radical response.

Ricoeur has recorded a long history of the philosophic struggle to comprehend time. On one side, the side of Aristotle, time has been understood as the time of the cosmos, understood in terms of the motion of objects, the whirl of events independent of the work of consciousness. On the other side, the side of Augustine, time is the unfolding of mental elaboration, *distentio animi*, concerned not with the movement of objects but with the rhythm of expectation and memory. The Modernists confronted their version of this ancient quarrel, encouraged in significant ways by the 'cosmological' research of the new physics, most notably the theories of Einstein, and also the new 'soulful' temporalities offered in one form by Bergson and in another by Freud.

Woolf developed her own understanding of the struggle between lived time and the time of the universe. *Orlando*, in its light comic course through the centuries, plays a virtuoso game with time. And in *To the Lighthouse*, Woolf took the dare of her friends, breaking the rhythmic norm of her novel – slow movements through a single day – and writing a lyric hymn to destructive cosmos under the heading, 'Time Passes'. The abruptly enlarging perspective at the centre of the book is nothing less than an effort to think of time beyond the reach of human purposes: characters whose smallest gestures had once been recorded are now left to die within brackets. But when it returns to a daily focus in its last section, the novel enshrines a will-to-meaning even within the acknowledgement of careless, neglectful cosmic time. Woolf's celebrated figure of 'the moment' – the radiant instant when 'Life stands still here' and through an act of responsiveness, coherence can be seized, 'making of the moment something permanent' (*To the Lighthouse*, 161) – offers itself as an art of living within the consciousness of death. Through the arrangement of household objects, the disposition of human beings around a table, or the composition of masses in a painting, a mere mortal deed can redeem time.

***

For Wyndham Lewis it was all a distraction and a mysticism. In a series of related works in the later twenties Lewis offered a sour but significant account of the Modernist 'time-cult'. A special virtue of his polemic was that it forced the thematics of time into prominence; it denied the inevitability of a new dispensation; and it denaturalised certain root commitments of Modernism. Lewis's *The Childermass* is one of the least-read books of the decade, but for all its provoking difficulty, it remains indispensable to any account of Modernist time. This is in part because Lewis is determined to devise a counter-temporal novel, a book that at once develops an oppositional theory and an alternative narrative method. The novel keeps its commitment to an adversarial Modernism while setting aside all those devices that had become distinctive marks of a literary movement: non-linear plotting, the phenomenology of consciousness, prose lyricism, the vocation of memory.

The Childermass is set in a modern limbo, where the dead subsist in a torpid afterlife while they wait to be ushered over the mountains into heaven. Following the aimless circuit of two dull clowns – Pullman and Satterthwaite – the novel offers no plot, no causal or logical succession of incident. Instead it presents fitful action within a condition of stasis. Its two puppets twitch and quiver; nothing is fixed in place; the landscape wavers; time shrinks and then distends. Life is over, but heaven is no nearer. The bitter joke of the first part of *The Childermass* is that in waiting for their ascension, these characters in fact perform the fallen condition of modernity, as Lewis sourly and satirically understands it – a world of weak half-emancipated figures dominated by bullying leaders, all occupying an Einsteinian zone of space–time, a Freudian world of decentred personalities and an empiricist universe of sense-data.

In its second half, with all time, motion or progress suspended, the book settles into a long dialogue between the impresario of this limbo, the Bailiff, and a group of insurgents who gather around Hyperides, a representative of 'classical pre-Christian intelligence'.[27] The Bailiff is precisely the modern leader as showman, a leering, teasing, joky performer, who sees through the littleness of modern emancipation and offers himself as the necessary precipitate of the modernising regime – 'we of the jazz-age who have . . . enthroned sensible sex, who have liberated the working-mass and gutted every palace within sight making a prince of the mechanic' (261). Against this prim up-to-datedness, Hyperides speaks back in Lewis's own accents.

> That Time-factor that our kinsman the Greek removed and that you have put back to obsess, with its movement, everything – to put a jerk and a wriggle, a tic and a grimace, everwhere [sic] – what is that accomplishing except the breaking-down of all our concrete world into a dynamical flux, whose inhuman behests we must follow, instead of it waiting on us? (153)

Pressed hard, the Bailiff gleefully concedes the fatal point: 'Eternity is in love with the productions of Time! . . . Time is the mind of Space – Space is the

[27] Wyndham Lewis, *The Childermass* (London: Chatto & Windus, 1928), p. 310. Further references given in parenthesis in the text.

mere body of Time. Time is life, Time is money, Time is all good things! – Time is God!' (227). The bloated Bailiff contains the entire history of a disgregation: the austerity of life lapsing into the flabby mind of time. Or as he blithely concedes 'personality is really the main factor in the whole thing' (208). The decadent alliance between the fetish of time and the assertion of personality – this is the point of convergence in Lewis's relentless critique.[28]

* * *

D. H. Lawrence comes late in this discussion, in part because he too separates himself from what we may call the temporal consensus of English Modernism: the commitment to time as a sustained thematic occasion, a formal discipline and a phenomenology. No less than Lewis, Lawrence refuses the canon of experiment pursued by his contemporaries: neither 'delayed decoding' nor the vocation of memory attract his regard.

Yet unlike Lewis, all of Lawrence's central conceptions remain determined by categories of time. The failure of the present, as Lady Chatterley understands, is that 'moments followed one another without necessarily belonging to one another':[29] 'Time went on as the clock does, half-past eight instead of half-past seven' (*Lady Chatterley's Lover*, 19). The impulse towards freedom – which becomes both more insistent and convulsive in the later works – is an impulse towards a not yet created, a still unborn future. Indeed, what rankles bitterly with Lawrence is any turn towards the past that looks for pleasure or distraction in the memory of what human beings have made, and felt, and done. Here is the critique of Gudrun and the Decadent avant-gardist Loerke in *Women in Love*: 'They played with the past, and with the great figures of the past, a sort of little game of chess, or marionettes, all to please themselves . . . As for the future, that they never mentioned except one laughed out some mocking dream of the destruction of the world by a ridiculous catastrophe of man's invention . . .'[30] This is the nadir of temporal Decadence for Lawrence, this turning towards the past in idle detachment and curiosity.

As he writes his way out of the wartime catastrophe, Lawrence demands the risk of apocalypse. Agitated by the failure of modernity, he is willing to project its total catastrophe, in the hope, as he puts it in *Kangaroo*, that it will

[28] The polemic of 1927 *Time and Western Man* had indicated the reach of Lewis's animus. The bilious attack not only descends upon leading literary contemporaries such as Pound, Stein and Joyce; it also turns to the philosophy of Bergson and Alexander, the metaphysical history of Spengler and the physics of Einstein.

[29] D. H. Lawrence, *Lady Chatterley's Lover*, ed. Michael Squires (Cambridge University Press, 1993), p. 17.

[30] D. H. Lawrence, *Women in Love* (1920; Harmondsworth: Penguin, 1979), p. 444.

be possible 'to send out a new shoot in the life of mankind . . . to grow into new forms'.[31] Ursula Brangwen 'wanted to have no past' (*Women in Love*, 399), and in the last paragraphs of the novel Rupert Birkin looks with equanimity beyond the human world.

> If humanity ran into a cul-de-sac, and expended itself, the timeless creative mystery would bring forth some other being, finer, more wonderful, some new, more lovely race, to carry on the embodiment of creation. The game was never up. The mystery of creation was fathomless, infallible, inexhaustible, for ever. Races came and went, species passed away, but ever new species arose, more lovely, or equally lovely, always surpassing wonder. (470)

Birkin's speculation stands out as the projection of an anti-humanist, non-Christian futurity, and as such it serves as one epitome of Modernist hope. Suppose it were possible just to cut away the past and to take the dare of an unknown future? Suppose a confidence in the 'creative mystery' were enough to carry one through the failures of the present tense, secure in the thought that splendid novelty would greet the days to come?

But Lawrence understood and recorded the confusing valences of time. Everywhere alongside the confident projection into the future stood the instances of demoralisation and resignation, the disbelief in any redemptive course for a fallen modern humanity. And then perhaps most interesting are those characteristic Lawrentian moments of mixed temporal modes. Often, as he tries to imagine a liveable future, he looks back to a long-suppressed, long-forgotten past, as in his evocation of 'older gods, older ideals, different gods: before the Jews invented a mental Jehovah, and a spiritual Christ' (*Kangaroo*, 206). What has been lost long ago may hold the secret for a redeemed future. The time before may guide us towards the time to come.

* * *

In the last pages of *Parade's End*, the aging Christopher Tietjens has separated from his wife, Sylvia; he is living with the woman he loves, Valentine Wannop; and they reside in the neighbourhood, though not in the grounds, of the ancient Tietjens estate. When Ford was not calling his protagonist a man of the eighteenth century, he was naming him a man of the seventeenth. But here he lives in an openly unsanctified marriage, daring to test progressive ideals. This mixing of temporalities – Tietjiens as the Tory progressive, the seventeenth-century personality as the man of the future – conforms to the Lawrentian

[31] D. H. Lawrence, *Kangaroo*, ed. Bruce Steele (1923; Cambridge University Press, 1994), p. 69.

doubleness. Indeed, the harking back to some distant past – whether in the intimacy of childhood or in public history – is often the condition for any glimpse into a future. Molly Bloom recollecting the proposal on Howth, Lily Briscoe mourning for Mrs Ramsay, Proust's Marcel remembering the madeleine – these are the ancient signs of a world to come, and they stand alongside the examples from Ford and Lawrence to suggest a common disposition in High Modernist narrative.

To call this a synthesis or an equilibrium would be to claim too much. The work of the twenties did not bring the problem of time to any resting place. In the decades to follow, altered circumstances changed the literary enactment of time. One way to put this is to say that time lost its aura, that it was absorbed back into history. But before that occurred, the Modernist 'time–mind' of the 1920s, including its negative image in Wyndham Lewis, forced temporality to occupy a place arguably more conscious and conspicuous than it had ever held before.

12

Modern life: fiction and satire

DAVID BRADSHAW

The epoch between the end of World War I and that of World War II is framed by two of the landmark prose satires of the century. However, while Wyndham Lewis's *Tarr* (1918) is an uncompromising product of the Modernist avant-garde, George Orwell's *Animal Farm* (1945) employs the traditional form of the fable to put across its complex critique of revolutionary socialism with almost populist clarity, the epitome, in every way (apart from its brevity) of all that High Modernism spurned. Other satires of note appeared in the interim, so although the 1918–45 period is most strikingly an era of ambitious rebuilding in Anglo-Irish fiction, with Joyce and Woolf as its leading architects, it is hardly less boldly a time of demolition (both of the certainties of the past and the enthusiasms of the present), with Lewis, Aldous Huxley and Evelyn Waugh as its foremost iconoclasts. Moreover, although the type of social satire with which these three novelists are associated largely dies out by the mid-1930s (before resurfacing, *mutatis mutandis*, in the 1950s novels of Kingsley Amis and Angus Wilson), a satirical spirit pervades the period's literature and is evident, for example, in *Ulysses*, *Jacob's Room*, *The Waste Land*, *Orlando*, *Finnegans Wake* and *Between the Acts*. 'I much doubt that any young person of our time can be impressed by a poem, a painting, or a piece of music that is not flavored with a dash of irony', the cultural critic José Ortega y Gasset remarked in 1925.[1]

It was widely accepted at the time and the critical consensus remains that 'the war was the soil out of which both wartime and post-wartime satire grew. And it was in satire that post-war culture found its particular bitter voice.'[2] If this tone is most audible in the novels of Huxley and Waugh and the poetry of T. S. Eliot, it is discernible everywhere, 'as though disenchantment was a

[1] José Ortega y Gasset, 'The Dehumanization of Art' (1925), rpt. in *The Dehumanization of Art and Notes on the Novel*, trans. Helene Weyl (Princeton University Press, 1948), pp. 3–54; quotation from p. 48.

[2] Samuel Hynes, *A War Imagined: The First World War and English Culture* (London: Bodley Head, 1990), p. 242.

disease, contracted in the trenches but transmittable to persons who had not been there'.[3] We hear it, for example, in *Eminent Victorians* (1918) by Lytton Strachey, a caustic depreciation of Florence Nightingale and other nineteenth-century cynosures, and *Potterism* (1920) by Rose Macaulay, a satire on humbug and the new power of the popular press. It is also perceptible in the novels of William Gerhardie, such as *The Polyglots* (1925) and *Jazz and Jasper* (1928, later retitled *My Sinful Earth*), as well as in *Triple Fugue* (1924) and *Before the Bombardment* (1926) by Osbert Sitwell. 'We live today in a world that is socially and morally wrecked', Huxley wrote in 1922, in words which might stand as a statement of belief for all the authors mentioned so far and many more besides. 'Between them, the war and the new psychology have smashed most of the institutions, traditions, creeds, and spiritual values that supported us in the past . . . The new synthesis that will reassemble, in an artistic whole, the shattered values of our post-war world . . . will surely be a comic synthesis. The social tragedy of these last years has gone too far and in its nature and origin is too profoundly stupid to be represented tragically.'[4]

Wyndham Lewis wrote more about satire than any of his contemporaries, yet the satirical fiction he produced is so demanding and writerly (in comparison with the work of Huxley and Waugh), that while his place in the Modernist canon remains incontestable, he is equally indisputably the social satirist of the 1918–45 period whose fiction is least read. *Tarr*, Lewis's first novel, begun as early as 1907 but only completed around the time of the second and final number of his Vorticist *Blast* magazine (1914–15), is an exacting read not least because he:

> wanted at the same time for it to be a novel, and to do a piece of writing worthy of the hand of the abstractist innovator . . . to eliminate anything less essential than a noun or a verb. Prepositions, pronouns, articles – the small fry – as far as might be, I would abolish. Of course I was unable to do this, but for the purposes of the *novel*, I produced a somewhat jagged prose.[5]

A satire on bohemian life in Paris, in which Lewis gives full rein to his sense of the essential mechanism of human beings and in which the title character, an English painter, is a mouthpiece for many of his own views, Lewis brought out a heavily revised version of *Tarr* in 1928 in which he reinstated 'the small fry' and made numerous additions and syntactic adjustments to the text. In

3 Ibid., p. 389.

4 Aldous Huxley, 'The Modern Spirit and a Family Party' (1922), rpt. in Robert S. Baker and James Sexton, eds., Aldous Huxley, *Complete Essays*, 6 vols. (1920–5; Chicago: Ivan R. Dee, 2000), I pp. 32–8; quotation from p. 33.

5 W. K. Rose, ed., *The Letters of Wyndham Lewis* (London: Methuen, 1963), pp. 552–3.

his preface to the new edition, Lewis described the ur-*Tarr*, justifiably, as 'the first book of an epoch in England', while Pound praised it in 1920 as 'the most vigorous and volcanic English novel of our time'.[6]

Lewis's next work of fiction, *The Wild Body*, a collection of short stories, did not appear until 1927 and the following year he published his second novel, *The Childermass*, an abstruse satirical epic, set on the threshold of a mysterious heavenly city, with the dead ranged before a grotesque and shadowy interrogator called the Bailiff, who controls entrance to it. Eventually, this novel would form the first part of a trilogy called *The Human Age* (the last two volumes, *Monstre Gai* and *Malign Fiesta*, both appeared in 1955). The publication of *The Childermass*, in which Lewis satirised Joyce (just as he pilloried the work of Proust, Gertrude Stein and Joyce in *Time and Western Man*, also published in 1927), more or less coincided with the launch of his third and last magazine, *The Enemy* (1927–9). Lewis had thrived on being a cantankerous cultural pariah for the past decade or so and a couple of years later, revelling in his notoriety, he announced in the *Daily Herald* 'that his average day began with a breakfast of blood oranges, raw meat, and vodka. Thus refreshed, he would dial a random telephone number and abuse whoever happened to answer. Then he would hit the streets to glare at innocent passersby.'[7]

This is the studiedly alarming and abrasive figure who published *The Apes of God* to considerable acclaim and no little outrage in 1930. By some margin the period's most voluminous satire, Lewis's 625-page, 250,000-word third novel targeted the Sitwell and Bloomsbury coteries in particular and metropolitan artiness in general. It showcases some of the most extraordinary prose of its era while being at the same time unrelentingly offensive. 'Lewis disguised his puppets enough to escape libel suits', Robert T. Chapman has written, 'but not too much to hinder identification; yet the value of the novel is not as a *roman à clef*, the "apes" are merely symptomatic of a wider *malaise* and it is this which Lewis explores in the "broadcasts"',[8] set-piece diatribes, such as the 'Extract from Encyclical addressed to Mr Zagreus', in which, *inter alia*, Lewis assails the '[t]he general rabble that collects under the equivocal banner of ART'.[9] Richard Aldington had attempted something similar in his *Death of a Hero* (1929),

6 Ezra Pound, 'Wyndham Lewis'; rpt. in *Literary Essays of Ezra Pound*, ed. T. S. Eliot (London: Faber & Faber, 1954), pp. 424–30, quotation from p. 424.

7 Quoted in Timothy Materer, *Wyndham Lewis the Novelist* (Detroit: Wayne State University Press, 1976), p. 11.

8 Robert T. Chapman, *Wyndham Lewis: Fictions and Satires* (London: Vision Press, 1973), p. 94.

9 Wyndham Lewis, *The Apes of God* (1930; Santa Barbara, Black Sparrow Press, 1981), pp. 118–25; quotation from p. 122.

but *The Apes* is a satirical *battue* on an altogether more epic and thunderous scale.

Lewis's satire is assiduously superficial. 'For *The Apes of God*,' he wrote, 'it could, I think, quite safely be claimed, that no book has ever been written that has paid more attention to the *outside* of people. In it their shells, or pelts, or the language of their bodily movements, come first, not last.'[10] In adopting this externalist approach to his characters, Lewis not only developed the notion of human beings as automata first adumbrated in *Tarr*, but also entrenched himself more deeply in opposition to the likes of Joyce and Stein, whose fiction was contaminated (he believed) by post-Romantic constructions of subjectivity. 'Satire is very *cold*', Lewis insisted in 1934. '... There is nothing of the hot innards of Freud-infected art ... about Satire ... The surface of the visible machinery of life alone is used ... All is metallic – all is external.'[11] In conceiving of satire in such terms, Lewis's anti-Joycean method 'may be folded into the broader neoclassicist discourse of the Modernist period, whose high priest was T. E. Hulme and whose legacies can be traced through high Modernism in the valorization by Pound, Eliot, and others of impersonality, intellection, coldness, hardness, concreteness, stasis, order, and related antiromanticist principles'.[12] Characteristically, Lewis's satire is both stridently anti-Modernist and Modernist to the core.

His '*cold*' and mechanical technique is exemplified in the following extract from *The Apes*, in which Lady Fredigonde Follett, an aged symbol of all Lewis despised, gets up from a chair:

> The unsteady solid rose a few inches, like the levitation of a narwhal. Seconded by alpenstock and body-servant (holding her humble breath), the escaping half began to move out from the deep vent ... The socket of the enormous chair yawned just short of her hindparts. It was a sort of shell that had been, according to some natural law, suddenly vacated by its animal. But this occupant, who never went far, moved from trough to trough – another everywhere stood hollow and ready throughout the compartments of its elaborate animal dwelling.[13]

10 Wyndham Lewis, *Satire and Fiction: Preceded by The History of a Rejected Review*, Enemy Pamphlets No. 1 (London: Arthur Press, 1930), p. 46.

11 Wyndham Lewis, 'Studies in the Art of Laughter' (1934); rpt. in C. J. Fox, ed., Wyndham Lewis, *Enemy Salvoes: Selected Literary Criticism* (London: Vision Press, 1975), pp. 41–9; quotation from p. 44.

12 James F. English, 'Imagining a Community of Men: Black(shirt) Humor in *The Apes of God*', in *Comic Transactions: Literature, Humor, and the Politics of Community in Twentieth-Century Britain* (Ithaca and London: Cornell University Press, 1994), pp. 67–97; quotation from p. 74.

13 Lewis, *The Apes of God*, pp. 22–3.

There is no fictional prose quite like this in Britain either in its own period or, indeed, between 1900 and 2000. *The Apes of God* is *sui generis*, the unmatched *Ulysses* of inter-war social satire, pulsing with luxuriant imaginative energy while also 'mannered, virulent, congested, sometimes obscure, and belligerent both towards other contemporary art and towards broader cultural developments'.[14] The function of satire in classical literature and in the hands, say, of Jonson, Swift and Pope, is to censure vice and to ridicule those whose conduct deviates unacceptably from established norms, but Lewis rejected this view and maintained that for him satire had no ethical purpose at all: 'for no dogmatic moralist sanction seems to me required to play the critic and the artist in one – which is to be a *satirist* – any more than a man has to take out a licence to be a landscape-painter'.[15] 'I am a satirist . . . ,' he reiterated in *Men Without Art* (1934). 'But I am not a moralist . . . And it is these two facts, taken together, which constitute my particular difficulty.'[16]

It may be argued, however, that for all Lewis's focus on exteriority and coldness and his disavowal of ethical purpose, he was an inveterate moralist; the dehumanising detachment of his method is always counter-balanced (and generally overwhelmed) by his conscientious, fiercely personal disgust. His major polemics of the 1920s, *The Art of Being Ruled* (1926), *Time and Western Man* and *The Lion and the Fox* (1927), are strenuously moralistic and, despite his protestations to the contrary, Lewis's fiction is at heart no different. This is clear not only in *Tarr* and *The Apes*, but also in his next, rather less significant novel, *Snooty Baronet* (1932) and, especially, *The Roaring Queen*, his mid-1930s satire on the world of books and reviewing (which was withdrawn before publication in 1936 for fear of libel charges and only appeared in 1973) and *The Revenge for Love* (1937), a hybrid of anti-leftist satire and the conventional novel of action which some critics consider his best work of fiction. It is explicit, furthermore, in *The Mysterious Mr Bull* (1938), where Lewis informs us that '[t]he satirist sets out to destroy what he considers bad, or undesirable, so that what is good, and desirable, may take its place . . . The satirist is an artist in destruction: one whose purpose is a more reasonable and beautiful social system.'[17]

[14] Mark Perrino, *The Poetics of Mockery: Wyndham Lewis's 'The Apes of God' and the Popularization of Modernism* (Leeds: W. S. Maney for the Modern Humanities Research Association, 1995), p. 2.

[15] Fox, ed., *Enemy Salvoes*, pp. 44–5.

[16] Wyndham Lewis, *Men Without Art* (London: Cassell, 1934), p. 106.

[17] Wyndham Lewis, *The Mysterious Mr Bull* (London: Robert Hale, 1938), pp. 144–5.

Eliot hailed Lewis as 'the most fascinating personality of our time' and 'the greatest prose master of style of my generation',[18] and his writings were deeply admired by Yeats and even Joyce, but in trying to explain his comparative neglect by both the academy and the common reader Mark Perrino has argued that Lewis's 'antagonistic stance towards the prevailing Modernist aesthetic' is at least partly responsible, but, more importantly, that the

> heavy element of satire in Lewis's fiction is fundamentally at odds with the romantic, subjectivist aspect of Modernism. Besides being offensive to many humanist sensibilities, radical satire, with its mixture of topicality, didacticism and fantasy, does not often satisfy the ideal of an autonomous, 'organically' unified work of art propounded by the school of American New Criticism which shaped the modern canon.[19]

While his satire is nothing like as 'radical' as Lewis's, this observation also holds true for Huxley's social satires. Taking the novels of Peacock as his principal model, Huxley assembles a house-party of oddballs in his first novel, *Crome Yellow* (1921), and simply lets his characters talk. In so doing, relativity, psychoanalysis, spiritualism, birth-control, the popular *Bildungsroman* and other fads of the moment are sent up. Indeed, one of the characters, Scogan, could be describing much of the appeal of *Crome Yellow* itself when he pinpoints the attractions of the imaginary *Tales of Knockespotch* in chapter 14. 'Fabulous characters shoot across his pages . . . An immense erudition and an immense fancy go hand in hand. All the ideas of the present and of the past . . . smile gravely or grimace a caricature of themselves, then disappear to make place for something new. The verbal surface of the writing is rich and fantastically diversified. The wit is incessant . . . '[20]

But as well as seeking to amuse his readers, Huxley channelled his abhorrence of the war and the Established Church into his portrait of Mr Bodiham, a bellicose cleric. 'He was the man in the Iron Mask . . . iron folds, hard and unchanging, ran perpendicularly down his cheeks; his nose was the iron beak of some thin, delicate bird of rapine . . . round [his eyes] the skin was dark, as though it had been charred . . . His voice . . . when he raised it in preaching, was harsh, like the grating of iron hinges when a seldom-used door is opened' (76–7). Huxley's second novel, *Antic Hay* (1923), opens in a similarly anti-clerical

[18] He made the first comment in 1916 and the second in 1955. Both are quoted in Perrino, *Poetics of Mockery*, p. [1].

[19] Perrino, *Poetics of Mockery*, p. 2.

[20] Aldous Huxley, *Crome Yellow* (London: Chatto & Windus, 1921), pp. 151–2. Further references given in parenthesis in the text.

vein with Theodore Gumbril musing in a chapel with his eyes fixed on 'the vast window opposite, all blue and jaundiced and bloody with nineteenth-century glass . . . about the existence and the nature of God'.[21] His thoughts prove unproductive, but Gumbril does come up with the concept of inflatable trousers to counteract the hardness of ecclesiastical stalls, having previously recalled the death of his mother in a way which is closely indebted to the circumstances surrounding the death of Huxley's own mother in 1908. When his father remonstrated with him about the novel, Huxley was conciliatory, but also explained that it was 'intended to reflect . . . the life and opinions of an age which has seen the violent disruption of almost all the standards, conventions and values current in the previous epoch',[22] and this sense of radical upheaval is shared by a number of his characters. 'The Black and Tans harry Ireland', Scogan remarks in *Crome Yellow*, 'the Poles maltreat the Silesians, the bold Fascisti slaughter their poorer countrymen: we take it all for granted. Since the war we wonder at nothing' (163). Calamy, on the other hand, in Huxley's third novel, *Those Barren Leaves* (1925), in which the country house setting has been relocated to Italy, believes that it would not 'be possible to live in a more exciting age . . . The sense that everything's perfectly provisional and temporary – everything, from social institutions to what we've hitherto regarded as the most sacred scientific truths – the feeling that nothing, from the Treaty of Versailles to the rationally explicable universe, is really safe . . . why, it's all infinitely exhilarating.'[23]

Huxley's early novels throng with men and women who not only talk a lot but talk only on one topic. In *Crome Yellow*, sanitation is the sole concern of Sir Ferdinando Lapith; Henry Wimbush is only interested in the history of Crome he is writing; his wife, Priscilla, is enraptured by astrology to the exclusion of all else and Barbecue-Smith can connect with very little besides spiritualism. Likewise, in *Antic Hay* there are characters who are preoccupied with kidneys (Shearwater), sex (Coleman) and their own unrecognised genius (Lypiatt). As a Menippian satirist, the development of rich and rounded characters held scant appeal for Huxley. Instead, his focus is on 'mental attitudes. Pedants, bigots, cranks, parvenus, virtuosi, enthusiasts . . . [all] handled in terms of their occupational approach to life as distinct from their social behaviour.'[24] 'We are apt to see but a single aspect of reality', Huxley wrote in 1919, 'the aspect

[21] Aldous Huxley, *Antic Hay* (London: Chatto & Windus, 1923), p. 3.
[22] Grover Smith, ed., *Letters of Aldous Huxley* (London: Chatto & Windus, 1969), p. 224.
[23] Aldous Huxley, *Those Barren Leaves* (London: Chatto & Windus, 1925), p. 34. Further references given in parenthesis in the text.
[24] Northrop Frye, *Anatomy of Criticism: Four Essays* (Princeton University Press, 1957), p. 309.

in which we personally are most interested, and to imagine that the single facet which is before our eyes is the whole truth . . . It is the business of the philosopher, standing apart from the world of things . . . to look on reality as a whole and as it exists in all its possible modes of being.'[25] It is from this 'philosophical' position that Huxley satirises the untalented painters, third-rate writers, crotcheteers and sundry monomaniacs who frequent his early fiction. Men such as Lord Tantamount in Huxley's fourth and most ambitious novel of the 1920s, *Point Counter Point* (1928), who, despite his avowed vitalism, is no more than a hard-line mechanist, curious to know, among other things, what might happen if the tissue of a newt's tail is grafted onto the stump of one of its amputated forelegs.

As well as satirising aspects of the present day, *Antic Hay* provides the first glimpse of the more mystically inclined novelist into which Huxley would develop. 'One reality', Lypiatt booms, 'there is only one reality' (64), while Gumbril at one point senses the tantalising proximity of a 'crystal world' of truth (188). Similarly, *Those Barren Leaves* concludes with Calamy pursuing a life of contemplative retirement, utterly persuaded that 'reality exists and is manifestly very different from what we ordinarily suppose it to be' (369). Huxley was satisfied, initially, that he had made plain in his third novel what had only been implied in his second, but almost immediately after its publication he came to the conclusion that *Those Barren Leaves* was 'jejune and shallow and off the point'.[26] He had now entered a D. H. Lawrentian phase (the two men were close friends in the late 1920s) and in *Point Counter Point* he puts all his authorial weight behind the blatantly Lawrentian Rampion, and non-human reality, as reified in the music of Beethoven, is, for the time being, associated with waywardness. (This turn away from mysticism to life-worship is even more pronounced in Huxley's next book, the non-fictional *Do What You Will* (1929).) *Point Counter Point* is primarily a novel of ideas (a genre which is defined in chapter 22: 'The character of each personage must be implied, as far as possible, in the ideas of which he is the mouthpiece . . .')[27] rather than a social satire and it was not to everyone's taste. Lewis, for example, put the first page to what he called 'The Taxi-Cab-Driver Test' in *Satire and Fiction* and found the result 'terribly decisive: for no book opening upon this tone of vulgar complicity with the dreariest of suburban library-readers could . . . change its skin, in the course of its 600 long pages, and become anything but a

[25] Aldous Huxley, 'Lord Haldane as a Philosopher', *Athenaeum* (4 July 1919), p. 558.
[26] Smith, ed., *Letters of Aldous Huxley*, p. 242.
[27] Aldous Huxley, *Point Counter Point* (London: Chatto & Windus, 1928), p. 409.

dull and vulgar book',[28] a judgement (typically) which is both severe and acute.

Brave New World, Huxley's most celebrated novel, appeared in 1932. In many ways a return to the satirical mode which had brought him success in the early 1920s, the primitivism of Lawrence (who had died in 1930) is now lampooned (in Huxley's treatment of the New Mexico Savage Reservation) alongside New Deal economics, Soviet-style planning, Fordism and other contemporary vogues. Traditionally bracketed with Orwell's *Nineteen Eighty-Four* (1949) as a dystopia, a novel in which Huxley inscribes his forebodings about the future and biological engineering, this way of reading *Brave New World* has been problematised in recent years following the rediscovery of Huxley's non-fiction and radio broadcasts from the early 1930s.[29] These indicate that much of what Huxley is presumed to have feared – such as the state use of eugenics, planning and propaganda – he actually embraced as desirable at the time he wrote the novel. In fact, Huxley was a vehement anti-democrat until the mid-1930s, when he committed himself to absolute pacifism. His next novel, *Eyeless in Gaza* (1936), turned out to be a fictionalised chronicle of his life to date, charting his journey through the wilderness of the inter-war years to the higher ground of his new convictions. This was not quite the end of Huxley the satirist, however. Domiciled in the United States from 1937 until his death, Huxley published *After Many a Summer* in 1939, which is in part a satire on the hubristic extravagance of William Randolph Hearst, the newspaper magnate and original of Orson Welles's *Citizen Kane* (1940). *Time Must Have a Stop* (1945) marks the beginning of a palpable decline in Huxley's fiction, and none of his later novels compares favourably with his early work. By abandoning satire in favour of seriousness, Huxley signalled a growing sense of purpose in his life and work, but he had deserted his true forte once and for all.

Another social satirist whose second novel shows clear signs of his eventual turn away from satire is Evelyn Waugh. Prior to *Vile Bodies* (1930), however, Waugh published *Decline and Fall* (1928), one of the undoubted comic masterworks of English literature. Conceived in the fantastic, 'Knockespotchian' mode of *Crome Yellow*, it traces the misadventures of Paul Pennyfeather, an ineffectual Oxford undergraduate, who is sent down after being debagged (his assailants are not even reprimanded) and who is then caught up in a round of absurd events including his unjust imprisonment, apparent death, miraculous recovery and readmission, only thinly disguised as his cousin, to the same

[28] Lewis, *Satire and Fiction*, p. 60.

[29] See David Bradshaw, ed., *The Hidden Huxley: Contempt and Compassion for the Masses 1920–36* (London: Faber & Faber, 1994).

college from which he was expelled. Despite the Gibbonian and Spenglerian nuances of its title, *Decline and Fall* is for the most part an uproarious debunking of modernity, and, more than any other novel of the period, it typifies the 'remarkable revival or reinvention of comic forms in fiction' in the 1920s noted by Malcolm Bradbury, 'as if they offered an ideal means for coping with a postwar world in which disorder seems notably prevalent, value historically extracted, chaos come again, as a direct result of the war and its disorientations and dehumanizations'.[30]

From the beginning of the novel, however, the reader becomes aware that two kinds of sensibility are in play, the *farceur*'s and the moralist's. Waugh's more censorious point of view is 'detectable only as a tonal effect here or as an allusion, a significant juxtaposition there. This is Waugh . . . the guardian of civilised values, full of unspoken disparagement . . . who cannot be ignored, for he silently orders the events of the novel and shapes its outcome.'[31] This side of Waugh is perhaps most noticeable in the 'King's Thursday' chapter. The original King's Thursday was a Marian manor house, but its destruction by Margot Beste-Chetwynde, and her subsequent razing of the house she had built in its place in order to put up an ultra-modern dwelling, stands as testimony to 'the grim cyclorama of spoliation' which, according to Waugh, 'surrounded all English experience' in the twentieth century.[32] Professor Otto Silenus, the architect of the latest King's Thursday, an alienating pile of glass, aluminium, vulcanite and black glass, is a spare and tormented continental whose only qualification for the job is 'the rejected design for a chewing-gum factory which had been reproduced in a progressive Hungarian quarterly'.[33]

Perhaps the most distinctive quality of *Vile Bodies* is its minimalist use of plot and dialogue. Indeed, very little happens at all in the novel besides talking and socialising. Waugh's chief models in this respect were Ronald Firbank, especially such novels as *Valmouth* (1919) and *Sorrow in Sunlight* (1924), the Eliot of 'A Game of Chess' (the second part of *The Waste Land*) and the numerous short stories and novels which P. G. Wodehouse had brought out by 1930. Despite

30 Malcolm Bradbury, 'The Modern Comic Novel in the 1920s: Lewis, Huxley, and Waugh', *Possibilities: Essays on the State of the Novel* (London and Oxford: Oxford University Press, 1973), pp. 140–63; quotation from p. 144.

31 Jeffrey Heath, *The Picturesque Prison: Evelyn Waugh and his Writing* (London: Weidenfeld & Nicolson, 1982), p. 63.

32 Evelyn Waugh, *A Little Learning: The First Volume of an Autobiography* (London: Chapman & Hall, 1964), p. 33.

33 Evelyn Waugh, *Decline and Fall* (1928; London: Chapman & Hall, 1962), p. 141. Further references given in parenthesis in the text.

its content, however, *Vile Bodies* is a less detached novel than its predecessor. In 1929, Waugh spoke of the 'social subsidence' following the war which had left 'a generation of whom 950 in every thousand are totally lacking in any sense of qualitative value'[34] and this comes out in the pointless, repetitive and nausea-inducing activities which many of the characters are involved in, such as Agatha Runcible's dreams in chapter 12 of her fast set 'driving round and round in a motor race'[35] until they all crash, and Nina Blount, in the same chapter, looking down on the sprawling ugliness of England from an aeroplane and feeling sick (197). 'I am relying on a sort of cumulative futility for any effect [*Vile Bodies*] may have', Waugh told a friend.[36] His own recent experience had also left its mark on the novel. Waugh had married in 1928, but about half-way through writing *Vile Bodies* his wife (also called Evelyn) left him and the novel was finished, in his own words, 'in a very different mood from that in which it was begun. The reader may, perhaps, notice the transition from gaiety to bitterness.'[37] Like Graham Greene, Waugh converted to Roman Catholicism in 1930 and his changed values were to become increasingly prominent from then on. At the conclusion of *Vile Bodies*, in a chapter entitled 'Happy Ending', two characters engage in foreplay in the back seat of a car amid the devastation of 'the biggest battlefield in the history of the world' (p. 217) and the sound of renewed hostilities.

Vile Bodies was a huge commercial success and Waugh followed it up with a novel in the same broad vein. Drawing on his experiences in Ethiopia and other African countries in 1930–1, *Black Mischief* (1932) is set mainly in an imaginary island state called Azania, ruled by the Oxford-educated Emperor Seth, a fanatical exponent of progress. It is this gospel, in the form of women's suffrage, birth-control, planning, community singing, compulsory Esperanto and other destabilising imports, which eventually leads, following Seth's murder, to his Minister of Modernisation and co-protagonist, Basil Seal, eating his girlfriend, Prudence, at the funeral feast for Seth which Basil himself has organised. As with *Decline and Fall*, Waugh's treatment of race and class makes uncomfortable reading for a contemporary audience, but as Douglas Lane Patey has commented, 'Waugh invites laughter at the spectacle of natives in

34 Evelyn Waugh, 'The War and the Younger Generation'; rpt. in Donat Gallagher, ed., *The Essays, Articles and Reviews of Evelyn Waugh* (London: Methuen, 1983), pp. 61–3; quotation from p. 62.

35 Evelyn Waugh, *Vile Bodies* (1930; London: Chapman & Hall, 1965), p. 186. Further references in parenthesis in the text.

36 Mark Amory, ed., *The Letters of Evelyn Waugh* (London: Weidenfeld & Nicolson, 1980), p. 39.

37 Waugh, 'Preface', *Vile Bodies*, p. 7.

top hats and tails, at barefoot savages given the titles earl and viscount; but he insists even more on European barbarity.'[38]

This theme is yet more pronounced in his next and perhaps finest novel, *A Handful of Dust* (1934). The story of Tony Last's betrayal by Brenda, his wife, the novel concludes with Last held captive in the jungle and forced to read the works of Dickens for the rest of his days to his captor, the sinister Mr Todd. For this part of the novel Waugh drew on his memories of travelling in British Guiana and Brazil during the winter of 1932–3, later recalling that the idea for the ending of his novel came from 'visiting a lonely settler' in the jungle and 'reflecting how easily he could hold me prisoner'. Waugh's first response was to write a short story called 'The Man Who Liked Dickens' but, he explained, 'after the short story was written and published, the idea kept working in my mind. I wanted to discover how the prisoner got there, and eventually the thing grew into a study of other sorts of savage at home and the civilized man's helpless plight among them.'[39] Waugh said that he was 'trying to deal with normal people instead of eccentrics'[40] in *A Handful of Dust*, but the latter make a triumphant reappearance in his next novel, *Scoop* (1938), a spoof on the press based on his time as a war correspondent in Ethiopia. Critics praised it, but in his subsequent novel, *Put Out More Flags* (1942), set in the phoney war before the real one, and in which his ageing cast of Bright Young People finally take their bow, the satire is distinctly more muted. *Brideshead Revisited* (1945), which he also wrote in uniform, was the most successful of his novels financially, if not critically. An explicitly Catholic novel, written in an ornate and stately prose, Waugh acknowledged that it was 'steeped in theology'[41] and warned on the dust jacket that it was 'not meant to be funny. There are passages of buffoonery, but the general theme is at once romantic and eschatological . . . an attempt to trace the workings of the divine purpose in a pagan world.'[42]

Afternoon Men (1931), by Anthony Powell, chronicles the antics of a similar Mayfair set to the Bright Young People of *Vile Bodies*, and, in William Atwater, features the same kind of hopelessly weak, anti-heroic leading man as *Crome Yellow*'s Denis Stone, *Antic Hay*'s Gumbril, Walter Bidlake (*Point Counter Point*), Bernard Marx (*Brave New World*), Paul Pennyfeather, Adam Fenwick Symes (*Vile Bodies*) and Tony Last. Powell went on to publish *Venusberg* (1932), *From a View to a Death* (1933), *Agents and Patients* (1936) and *What's Become of Waring?*

38 Douglas Lane Patey, *The Life of Evelyn Waugh: A Critical Biography* (Oxford: Blackwell, 1998), p. 99.

39 Evelyn Waugh, 'Fan-fare' (1946); rpt. in Gallagher, ed., *Essays, Articles and Reviews*, pp. 300–4; quotation from p. 303.

40 Amory, ed., *Letters of Waugh*, p. 84.

41 Ibid., p. 185.

42 Quoted in Patey, *Life of Waugh*, p. 224.

(1939), a novel with a much more developed plot than its predecessors and a clear precursor of his major post-war sequence, *A Dance to the Music of Time* (1951–75). Half the text of *Afternoon Men* comprises terse, banal dialogue and all five of Powell's 1930s novels, in differing degrees, reveal how much closer he was in spirit to Firbank, Wodehouse and Waugh than he was to Lewis and Huxley. Yet with Powell we do not feel a sense of latent values behind the gossip and the futile partying as we do, for example, in *Decline and Fall* and *Vile Bodies*. In fact, Powell's dry, detached fictions, so exclusively concerned with the brittle surface of life, might best be viewed as the nearest thing to Lewisian non-moral satire the period has to offer, outside (probably including) Lewis's own work. Other writers of the time who explored the satirical possibilities of the upper classes are Nancy Mitford, especially in her fifth novel and first commercial success, *The Pursuit of Love* (1945), and Henry Green, the pseudonym of Henry Vincent Yorke. This is especially true of *Party Going* (1939), in which Green (like his friend Waugh in *Vile Bodies*) communicates a vivid sense of the inter-war era of weekending, hedonism and inconsequentiality coming to an apocalyptic end.

Some of the most interesting innovations in dialogue in this period are found in the novels of Ivy Compton-Burnett, especially *Brothers and Sisters* (1929), *More Women than Men* (1933), *A House and its Head* (1935) and *A Family and a Fortune* (1939). Although she is not strictly a satirist, Compton-Burnett contests Englishness, sexuality, patriarchy and gender through a deft use of fantasy, flippancy and other comic modes. More mainstream in its appeal, *The Diary of a Provincial Lady* by E. M. Delafield, a humorous account of rural conservatism and small-mindedness, was published to great applause in 1930, while *Cold Comfort Farm* (1932), the first novel of Stella Gibbons, satirises the sentimentalisation of rural life epitomised by such novels as Mary Webb's *Precious Bane* (1924). *The Rock Pool* (Paris, 1936; London, 1947), by Cyril Connolly, is a send-up of Decadence on the French Riviera, but social satire as a genre had practically died out by the mid-1930s. A key reason for this, as Auden later wrote, is that '. . . satire cannot deal with serious evil and suffering. In an age like our own, it cannot flourish except in intimate circles as an expression of private feuds; in public life the evils and sufferings are so serious that satire seems trivial and the only possible kind of attack is prophetic denunciation.'[43] But if prose satire dwindled in significance, verse satire maintained its prominence. Indeed, in 1934, Lewis argued that 'Messrs. T. S. Eliot, Roy Campbell,

[43] W. H. Auden, 'Notes on the Comic' (1952), rpt. in *The Dyer's Hand and Other Essays* (London: Faber & Faber, 1963), pp. 371–85; quotation from p. 385.

Auden . . . are satirists first and foremost. *The Hippopotamus*, *The Waste Land*, *Sweeney Agonistes*, *The Wayzgoose*, *The Georgiad*, *The Orators* are all works of Satire pure and simple',[44] and he could have added works by Basil Bunting, Hugh MacDiarmid, Siegfried Sassoon and others to his list.

Modernism and satire were in many ways incompatible, even adversarial. While a novel such as *Jacob's Room* engages mischievously with the concept of narratorial omniscience, for instance, Lewis, Huxley and Waugh are apparently untroubled by the convention. They intrude into their novels without a qualm, either directly or in the guise of patently autobiographical characters, and they show little (if any) interest in the representation of consciousness, being almost exclusively focused on the exposure of folly. 'The farce, for each writer, is a different one', Malcolm Bradbury has observed, 'presented with different degrees of involvement and urgency. Nonetheless these fictional worlds – distorted, oblique, abundantly rich in indifference, mechanism, generational struggle, and insecure identity, and so leading to a state of affairs in which all quests are suspect, all virtues unestablishable – are sufficiently like the prevailing world outside to be more than amusing.'[45]

But Modernism and satire could also be strange bedfellows. As well as the externalist similarities between Lewis, Eliot and Pound discussed above, there are other affinities to be noted. In attacking a culture as dead as mutton in *The Apes of God*, for example, stuck in '[t]he social decay of the insanitary trough between the two great wars',[46] Lewis anticipates Woolf's central concern in the lengthy 'Present Day' section of *The Years* (1937) and her use of stains, shabbiness and underdone mutton to press home her point of view. Technically and politically, Lewis and Woolf could not have been more dissimilar, but in their criticism of English society they had more in common in the 1930s than they may have been willing to concede.

[44] Fox, ed., *Enemy Salvoes*, p. 44. [45] Bradbury, 'The Modern Comic Novel', p. 146.
[46] Wyndham Lewis, *Rude Assignment: A Narrative of My Career Up-to-date* (London: Hutchinson, 1950), p. 199.

13

Modernist poetry and poetics

RONALD BUSH

Between the 1830s, when the words 'cliché' and 'stereotype' were coined as technical terms for cheap and unchanging page-casts of type – the revolutionary publishing technology that would put a newspaper in every home – and the 1890s, when 'cliché' acquired its figurative sense of a stock or hackneyed expression, the first wave of a literary revolution with deep social and philosophical roots shook the foundations of European poetics.[1] Like painters rebelling against the expectations of an audience smitten with the easy verisimilitude of photography, poets revolted against the way that mass journalism habituated a vastly enlarged European reading public to a glib utilitarian rationalism that short-circuited complex thought and feeling. In the words of Ezra Pound (who spoke for the second wave of that revolution), 'the newspaper criterion that "an article must run straight through from start to finish" . . . is almost pure kinesis designed not to make the reader think, but to make him accept a certain conclusion'. 'Literature and philosophy', he added, differ by a need to 'constantly diverge from this groovedness, constantly throw upon the perceptions new data, new images, which prevent the acceptance of an over facile conclusion'. Between the two, Pound concluded, there was a 'war', and if newspapers won the war Europe would find itself in 'an order of things in which there would be no art, no literature, no manners, no civilisation'.[2] The battleground on which this war was waged was the cliché, and the stakes involved not just style, but what Pound calls here 'civilisation' and elsewhere 'life'.

In 1859 the poet and art critic Charles Baudelaire observed how the fad for photography had already paralysed art, causing it to 'prostrate itself before [an] external reality' that had little to do with 'nature in its entirety' and everything to do with the 'triviality of material reality', and he foresaw the way poetry and

[1] See, for example, George A. Kubler, *A New History of Stereotyping* (New York: Little & Ives, 1941).

[2] Ezra Pound, 'Pastiche: the Regional. XIV,' *New Age* xxv. 26 (23 October 1919), 432.

painting were to evolve in reaction to the pressure of commercial technology. A painter at the present moment, he wrote, must paint 'what he dreams' not 'what he sees' since painting now has its 'value' primarily in 'the sphere of the intangible and the imaginary'– a sphere whose 'significance' resides not in an 'identity' with external nature but in matters of 'colour, contour . . . analogy and metaphor'.[3] And just as painters feel compelled to transcend the mechanical realism of photography by emphasizing the effects of form and texture, so, Baudelaire suggested, poets now need to overcome the degradations of mass journalism by liberating language and its associated habits of thinking and feeling. Thus it was that from the mid-nineteenth century poetry attempted to remove itself from an easy legibility and gravitated towards the ideal realms of Baudelaire's 'dream', 'analogy' and 'metaphor'.

Baudelaire also, in a famous essay called 'The Painter of Modern Life', explained that artists no longer believe in timeless beauty. Instead, modernity requires that every age recreate beauty in a new 'historical envelope'. It is the duty therefore of the artist not only to master form but to recognise those conventions that have become outmoded, and to invent new ones. And since that demands understanding the history of style, it means that art belongs not to the amateur but to the connoisseur–practitioner who can understand the 'form[s] of modernity'.[4]

These attitudes were shared by the most sophisticated poets of the turn of the twentieth century, but not all poets who adhered to them were comfortable with their anti-democratic implications, and fewer still felt happy with the way the obscurity of poetry's self-conscious dreams cut them off from the new reading public. Such ambivalences would propel their work into diverse and sometimes contradictory engagements with the social and political worlds.

Moreover, modern poetry's resistance to easy legibility had to do with more than a revulsion from mass literacy and mass journalism. This itself was only a symptom of something deeper still – philosophy's critique of Enlightenment reason and progress, which involved exploring the irrational motives behind not only newspaper prose but all logical discourse. In this vein, Nietzsche in an 1873 essay called 'Truth and Falsity in an Unmoral Sense' portrays faith in logical argument as one of the self-deceptions of human reason. Reason,

[3] See Charles Baudelaire, 'The Salon of 1859', esp. part two: 'The Modern Public and Photography' and part three: 'The Queen of the Faculties'. My translations are drawn from *Baudelaire: Selected Writings on Art and Artists*, ed. P. E. Charvet (Cambridge University Press, 1972). See esp. pp. 294–9.

[4] See Charles Baudelaire 'The Painter of Modern Life', in *Selected Writings on Art and Artists*, pp. 390–435, esp. pp. 402–3.

Nietzsche argues, is not an autonomous and transcendent faculty primarily involved with the disinterested pursuit of truth, but a secondary faculty whose purpose is to serve our needs and vanities. In this service, it is aided by language, which masquerades as the adjunct of reason but derives from the flights of the imagination and then, pressed into public discourse, degenerates into abstract and empty conventions. 'What', Nietzsche asks, 'therefore is truth? A mobile army of metaphors . . . [which] after long usage seems to a nation fixed, canonic, and binding; truths are illusions of which one has forgotten that they *are* illusions; worn out metaphors which have become powerless to affect the senses; coins which have their obverse effaced and are no longer of account as coins but merely as metal.'[5] Nietzsche, associating reason with the corruption of the marketplace, here not only invokes the way concepts, like coins, wear smooth with use, but subliminally calls up the way newspaper clichés wear out in mass production. There is no progress here, only a cycle of imagination and decay.

It might be said, of course, that this literary and philosophical resistance to Enlightenment progress was the cutting edge of a turn against modernity itself – a possibility that has caused some critics to brand modern art and poetry as simply 'reactionary'. Yet the truth of this assertion is complicated by the fact that the nineteenth century frequently recoiled against earlier forms of social and philosophical modernity in the name of a *more sophisticated modernity*.[6] So Flaubert's *Madame Bovary* (1856) casts a cold eye on the French Revolution's legacy of intellectual and social verities not out of love of the past but in the name of an Art at one with philosophy's ongoing scepticism about progress that is not progressive enough. Stéphane Mallarmé formulated the most sophisticated version of these nineteenth-century ideas in a summary essay of 1896 entitled 'The Crisis of Poetry', which holds not only that human utterance is distorted in itself by social and utilitarian pressure, but that at the present moment in Western society public discourse has become so contaminated by the language of journalism that it can only function 'with the same facility and directness as does money'. Narrative, instruction, description and even speech itself, Mallarmé concludes, have in the current social crisis of language become, like the 'silent exchange of money', vehicles fit only for 'vulgar or immediate purposes'. The first three have been reduced to 'that universal *journalistic style*', which characterises all kinds of contemporary writing with the 'exception of

[5] Geoffrey Clive, ed., *The Philosophy of Nietzsche* (New York: Meridian, 1965), p. 508.

[6] See, for example, Robert B. Pippin, *Modernism as a Philosophical Problem: On the Dissatisfactions of European High Culture* (Oxford: Blackwell, 1991).

literature', and the fourth has become 'no more than a commercial approach to reality'.[7]

By the time Mallarmé published his essay, moreover, similar ideas had coloured advanced thinking on both sides of the English Channel. As early as 1873 Walter Pater, in his once notorious 'Conclusion' to *The Renaissance* (1873), invokes a horror of 'stereotype' and admonishes his readers that 'our failure is to form habits: for, after all, habit is relative to a stereotyped world' and is the equivalent of a 'sleep before evening'. Philosophical systems represent the same danger, he adds, since 'the theory or idea or system which requires of us the sacrifice of any part [of] experience, in consideration of some interest into which we cannot enter, or some abstract theory we have not identified with ourselves, or of what is only conventional, has no real claim upon us'.[8]

But it was Pater's admirer, Arthur Symons, who in *The Symbolist Movement in Literature* (1899) put Mallarmé's assertion that 'poetry is the language of a state of crisis' on the lips of every aspiring poet and inspired the next generation to pursue a 'revolt against exteriority, against rhetoric, against a materialistic tradition'.[9] In an emblematic recollection that would mark the coming century's definitive break with Victorian poetics, Symons even gave the new century its rallying cry: '"Take eloquence and wring its neck!" said Verlaine in his *Art Poétique*; and he showed, by writing it, that French verse could be written without rhetoric.' Verlaine's poems, Symons adds, 'can only be compared, in modern poetry, with a poem for which Verlaine had a great admiration, Tennyson's *In Memoriam*. Only, with Verlaine, the thing itself, the affection or the regret, is everything; there is no room for meditation over destiny, or search for a problematical consolation.'[10]

Symons's anecdote stands as the founding statement of English Modernist poetics. T. S. Eliot, for example, who said that 'Arthur Symons's book on the French Symbolists was of more importance for my development than any other book', paraphrases it at the heart of his most important statement about modern poetry. ('Tennyson and Browning are poets, and they think; but they do not feel their thought as immediately as the odour of a rose . . . Keats

[7] *Mallarmé: Selected Prose Poems, Essays, and Letters*, trans. Bradford Cook (Baltimore: Johns Hopkins University Press, 1956), pp. 42, 40. The original can be found in Henri Mondor and G. Jean-Aubrey, eds., *Mallarmé: Œuvres complétes* (Paris: Gallimard, 1945), pp. 368, 366.

[8] Walter Pater, *The Renaissance: Studies in Art and Poetry*, 1873; rpt. ed. Louis Kronenberg (New York: New American Library, 1963), pp. 158–9.

[9] Arthur Symons, *The Symbolist Movement in Literature* (1899, rev. 1908; New York: Dutton, 1958), p. 5, 66, 74.

[10] Ibid., pp. 46, 51.

and Shelley died, and Tennyson and Browning ruminated.')[11] And behind Eliot stands Yeats, the friend to whom Symons had dedicated *The Symbolist Movement in Literature*, and who elaborated Symons's history in at least three influential accounts of the development of modern poetry over the course of his long career, perhaps most vividly in the 'Introduction' to *The Oxford Book of Modern Verse: 1892–1935*.

The revolt against Victorianism meant to the young poet a revolt against irrelevant descriptions of nature, the scientific and moral discursiveness of *In Memoriam* – 'When he should have been broken-hearted', said Verlaine, 'he had many reminiscences' – the political eloquence of Swinburne, the psychological curiosity of Browning, and the poetical diction of everybody. Poets said to one another over their black coffee – a recently imported fashion – 'We must purify poetry of all that is not poetry', and by poetry they meant poetry as it had been

> written by Catullus, a great name at that time, by the Jacobean writers, by Verlaine, by Baudelaire. Poetry was a tradition like religion and liable to corruption, and it seemed that they could best restore it by writing lyrics technically perfect, their emotion pitched high, and as Pater offered instead of moral earnestness life lived as 'a pure gem-like flame' all accepted him for master.[12]

From the generation of the nineties onwards, Yeats, his contemporaries and near-contemporaries would seek somehow to produce what Symons calls 'the thing itself' – the intensity of pure poetry, without the suspect combination of abstract ideas, high-minded sententiousness, and prose commonplace. But how does one write uncontaminated by public speech and remain intelligible? Modern poetry's first response was to limit its practice to finely crafted lyrics. This was the project of the poems of the nineties, with their artificial polish and their accent on sonority, and then in another idiom the ambition of the rude sincerity of the poems that Edward Marsh began to collect in his Georgian Anthologies starting in 1912. Both assumed the answer to Victorian fuzz was straightforward and could be supplied by rigorously lyric poems constructed

[11] Eliot's 1936 remark on Symons is reprinted in Christopher Ricks, ed., *T. S. Eliot: Inventions of the March Hare: Poems 1909–1917* (London: Faber & Faber, 1996), p. 395. His comment on Tennyson can be found in his essay, 'The Metaphysical Poets' (1921), rpt. *Selected Essays* (New York: Harcourt Brace, 1960), pp. 247–8.

[12] W. B. Yeats, 'Introduction' to *The Oxford Book of Modern Verse: 1892–1935* (New York: Oxford University Press, 1936), p. ix. See also Yeats's essay 'Modern Poetry' (1936 but based on a 1910 lecture, 'Friends of My Youth'), *Essays and Introductions* (London: Macmillan, 1969), pp. 491–508, esp. 494–5; and *The Autobiography of William Butler Yeats* (New York: Macmillan, 1965), p. 229.

out of simpler language, more supple forms or less academic subject-matter.[13] The most gifted of the poets Marsh published (and the one who would most successfully outgrow the manner of the Georgians) was D. H. Lawrence, who, in the 'Preface' to the American edition of his *New Poems* (1918), disdained the 'fixed, set, static' and praised the energies of 'the moment, the quick of all change and haste and opposite'. At first adhering to traditional poetic forms, Lawrence later produced more supple constructions, such as 'Snake' (1923), which complements the thoroughgoing self-questioning with powerful close observation of natural violence.

Yeats, however, and after him Pound, who moved to London to learn from Yeats and became his unofficial secretary, soon came to sense that the crisis of poetry went beyond subject-matter or specific poetic forms. At first both inclined towards the dramatic lyric, in which (as in Villon and Dante) ideas might escape from the abstract rigidity of system and stereotype by being infused with a personal significance and urgency. Long into his career Yeats would continue to insist that 'I have tried to make my work convincing with a speech so natural and dramatic that the hearer would feel the presence of a man thinking and feeling.'[14] Emulating his example, Pound wrote to his college friend William Carlos Williams that 'to me the short so-called dramatic lyric . . . is the poetic part of a drama the rest of which (to me the prose part) is left to the reader's imagination or implied or set in a short note. I catch the character I happen to be interested in at the moment he interests me, usually a moment of song, self-analysis, or sudden understanding or revelation. And the rest of the play would bore me and presumably the reader.'[15]

Yet Yeats was intensely uneasy with drama of a purely social or realistic kind. He would write that 'I hated and still hate with an ever growing hatred the literature of the point of view', in part because it was tied to socially debased 'words in common use', in part because it suggested the kind of originality ('talk to me of originality and I will turn on you with rage') and social carapace encouraged by the sort of mass 'education that enlarges the separated, self-moving mind [and has] made our souls less sensitive'.[16] Yeats's early work at its most radical, therefore, strives to transcend social utterance by attempting a version of Mallarmé's purification of poetry from the individual voice. So, in his essays of the 1890s and associated volumes of verse – *The Rose* (1893) or *The*

[13] See Robert H. Ross, *The Georgian Revolt 1911–1922* (Carbondale: Southern Illinois Press, 1965), esp. chapter 1.
[14] Allan Wade, ed., *The Letters of W. B. Yeats* (New York: Octagon, 1980), p. 583.
[15] D. D. Paige, ed., *The Letters of Ezra Pound 1907–1941* (New York: Harcourt Brace, 1950), pp. 3–4.
[16] Yeats, *Essays and Introductions*, pp. 41, 511, 521, 522.

Wind Among the Reeds (1899) – he attempts an English version of Mallarmé's 'pure' poetry, in which 'the poet's voice must be stilled and the initiative taken by the words themselves, which will be set in motion as they meet unequally in collision. And in an exchange of gleams they will flame out like some glittering swath of fire sweeping over precious stones, and thus replace the audible breathing in lyric poetry of old – replace the poet's own personal and passionate control of verse.'[17] In poems like 'The White Birds', Yeats fashions a slow heavy organic rhythm to purge his poem of a strong personal voice and, as he put it in the contemporary essay 'The Symbolism of Poetry', 'to keep us in that state of perhaps real trance, in which the mind liberated from the pressure of the will is unfolded in symbols'.[18] 'Liberated' from that public discourse which is associated with what Yeats here calls 'the will' and Freud would call the 'ego', the poem fashions an artificial discourse whose utterance, as Mallarmé says, takes on meaning like a 'glittering swath of fire sweeping over precious stones'. Still motivated by a horror of what language has become, this goes well beyond the aspirations of the dramatic monologue or the pared-down lyric. Like Mallarmé's own verse, it wishes to become a poetry so averse to statement that it amounts to a discourse of silence.

In the event, Yeats's 'The White Birds' had more to do with Swinburne's incantation than Mallarmé's opacity. It shared with Mallarmé's more obdurate verse, however, the problem that attempting to remove the poem's utterance from ordinary speech and the poet's words from ordinary language opened poetry to the appearance of being removed from the world (the old worry of Tennyson's 'The Palace of Art'). More, Yeats had much too strong a commitment to the speaking voice ever willingly to submit himself to the astringency of pure poetry for long. Note that even in the citation from 'The Symbolism of Poetry' just quoted, his phrase 'the mind liberated from the pressure of the will is unfolded in symbols' suggests a link between the symbol on the page and the pressure of a mind or sensibility embodied in speech. Whereas Mallarmé had concluded that the contamination of the self by the language of journalism forced poetry to abjure *any* 'personal and passionate' utterance, Yeats tried to push through the problem by anchoring dramatic poetry in a kind of buried self beneath the social self, apparent in pre-logical and pre-linguistic expressions associated with rhythm, image and symbol, and with the body rather than the cliché-ridden ego. (The sense that a public self – whether we call it the 'character', 'personality' or 'will' – might be so utterly clichéd as to

[17] *Mallarmé: Selected Prose Poems, Essays, and Letters*, pp. 40–1.

[18] W. B. Yeats, 'The Symbolism of Poetry'(1900), rpt. in *Essays and Introductions* (London: Macmillan, 1961), p. 159.

require a kind of poetic 'impersonality' to express what we really think and feel would also be one of the core paradoxes of T. S. Eliot's poetics.)

In lectures of 1910, which Yeats said articulated his 'convictions over the last ten or twenty years', he offered his justification of a post-Mallarméan poetics that would unite 'literature once more to personality'.[19] The first part of this involved a recuperation of the speaking self, or 'personality', which, Yeats explained, was detached from the death-like conventions of 'character' (a man's 'habits retained' or his socially conditioned self) and had to do with 'a certain kind of charm and emotional quality . . . a certain gift of passion and desire' (pp. 16, 38–9). Later, Yeats would identify this desire with an impulse or energy emanating from the 'blood, imagination, intellect, running together' and 'from the entire hopes, memories, and sensations of the body'.[20] Ultimately these notions stem from Pater's earlier assertion that 'our one chance' for genuine existence in 'a stereotyped world' comes from that 'quickened sense of life' we gain from 'great passions'; and from Nietzsche's insistence that life and creativity were rooted in the body's instinctual energy.[21] Like Nietzsche, Yeats remained wary of the way the will constantly reappropriates and domesticates this passion, rendering it inadequate to either life or art. And so, like Nietzsche, he began to insist that poets, rather than attempting to *realise* themselves in their lives and verse, constantly battle to *overcome* themselves through the aid of a deliberately created theatrical mask – a projected image of the passionate self. 'The poet makes his genius', he said, 'out of the struggle in his soul.'[22] Or, as he would immortalise the idea in *Per Amica Silentia Lunae*, 'We make out of the quarrel with others, rhetoric, but of the quarrel with ourselves, poetry.'[23]

This intuition that the only truth of the self involved portraying the perpetual conflict between its buried impulses made Yeats's new poems 'dramatic' in yet another way: Yeats would play off one version of the self against another in his poetry and associate each with a 'truth' ('not abstract truth,' but an embodied 'vision of reality which satisfies the whole being') or a 'belief' that

19 See Robert O'Driscoll, 'Yeats on Personality: Three Unpublished Lectures', in Robert O'Driscoll and Lorna Reynolds, eds., *Yeats and the Theatre* (Toronto: Maclean-Hunter, 1975), pp. 4–59, esp. p. 4.

20 See Yeats, *Essays and Introductions*, pp. 266, 292–3.

21 Pater, *The Renaissance*, pp. 158–9. On Yeats and Nietzsche, see John Foster, *Heirs to Dionysus: A Nietzschean Current in Literary Modernism* (Princeton University Press, 1981), pp. 119–20; Denis Donoghue, *William Butler Yeats* (New York: Viking, 1971), pp. 52–69; David Thatcher, *Nietzsche in England, 1890–1914: The Growth of a Reputation* (University of Toronto Press, 1970), pp. 139–74; and Otto Bohlmann, *Yeats and Nietzsche* (Totowa, NJ: Barnes and Noble, 1982).

22 O'Driscoll, 'Yeats on Personality', p. 34.

23 William Butler Yeats, *Mythologies* (New York: Macmillan, 1959), p. 331.

serves as a personal myth – something that can engage our unconscious and activate our largest selves.[24] In the last letter he ever wrote, Yeats put it this way: 'When I try to put all into a phrase I say, "Man can embody truth but he cannot know it."'[25]

In his great poems from "Ego Dominus Tuus" (first draft 1912) through "Among School Children" (1926) and beyond, this transformed poetics of the self renewed dramatic verse's hold on modern poetry and validated Yeats's authority to speak. To quote Thomas Parkinson, by the poetry of the 1920s, Yeats had been able to create the impression of 'a profound dramatic centre', inhering in the tensions of a self at cross-purposes that remains somehow mysteriously whole.[26] Yeats's anchoring of his poems in deep images, his masterful energising of poetic syntax (with an emphasis on ambiguity and open questions), and his ability in poetic suites like 'In Memory of Robert Gregory' to mime the evolving conflicts of a self removed his greatest poems from the ambit of the nineties and established the first body of genuinely modern poetry in English.

Following Yeats's ambivalence about public discourse but heavily reinforced by critical and philosophical currents from other quarters, starting in 1912 Ezra Pound began his own experiments with embodied speech. Two years later, this is the way he summarised his progress in extending modern poetry's techniques of dramatising the conflicts of the self:

> In the 'search for oneself', in the search for 'sincere self-expression', one gropes, one finds some seeming verity. One says 'I am' this, that, or the other, and with the words scarcely uttered one ceases to be that thing.
>
> I began this search for the real in a book called *Personae*, casting off, as it were, complete masks of the self in each poem. I continued in long series of translations, which were but more elaborate masks.
>
> Secondly, I made poems like 'The Return', which is an objective reality and has a complicated sort of significance . . . Thirdly, I have written 'Heather', which represents a state of consciousness, or 'implies' or 'implicates' it.
>
> A Russian correspondent, after having called it a symbolist poem, and having been convinced that it was not symbolism, said slowly: 'I see, you wish to give people new eyes, not to make them see some particular thing.'

24 *The Letters of William Butler Yeats*, ed. Allan Wade (New York: Octagon, 1980), p. 588.

25 Ibid., Wade, ed., p. 922.

26 Thomas Parkinson, 'W. B. Yeats', in Bernard Bergonzi, ed., *The Twentieth Century*, in *History of Literature in the English Language*, II vols. (London: Barrie & Jenkins, 1970), II p. 65. (For a more extended discussion of modern poetry's engagement with dramatic verse, see Robert Langbaum, *The Poetry of Experience: The Dramatic Monologue in Modern Literary Tradition* (New York: Norton, 1957) and *The Mysteries of Identity: A Theme in Modern Literature* (New York: Oxford, 1977).

> These two latter sorts of poem are impersonal, and that fact brings us back to . . . absolute metaphor. They are Imagisme.[27]

To explicate, one might begin with the way Pound's extensive background in European literature (he was an early PhD student – though he never completed his degree – in Romance languages, and one of the first to study the newly rediscovered literature of the troubadours) enabled and encouraged him to 'resurrect . . . forgotten model[s]' in an effort to get beyond ways of thinking and writing derived 'from books, convention and *cliché*, and not from life'.[28] Pound's numerous translations were largely devoted to this aim and provided many of the 'masks' he used to create new voices and new selves for the twentieth century.

'Giving people new eyes' goes further, and seems to have been associated with Pound's discussions, first during 1909 and then in 1911–12 with the autodidact philosopher–poet–critic T. E. Hulme. Hulme had for a while in 1911–12 devoted himself to the philosophy of Henri Bergson and was much taken with Bergson's emphasis on equating consciousness with intuition rather than abstract reason. The core of this for Hulme was Bergson's Nietzschean admonition to supersede intellectual and literary conventions in thought and in life. As Hulme explained, in lectures that Pound attended and praised in the closing months of 1911, what we think, hear, see, and say corresponds to no more than a 'practical simplification of reality . . . We only see stock types. We tend to see not *the* table but only *a* table.'[29] In its way, Hulme told his audience, this process is both natural and useful – without it we would be overwhelmed by the complexity of experience. But because it tends constantly to degrade perception and thought into simple counters, it would soon render language and consciousness unreal were it not for the iconoclasm of artists, who not only see things freshly but are driven by a need to express that freshness to revolutionise the tools we use to think, see and speak. As philosopher, Hulme was most interested in the renovation of words, the tools of thought, and so he focused especially on the power of poetry. Like Nietzsche, he held that

27 Ezra Pound, 'Vorticism'. Originally published in the *Fortnightly Review* for September 1914 and reprinted in *Gaudier-Brzeska: A Memoir* (1916; rpt. in expanded form, New York: New Directions, 1970). See p. 85.

28 Ezra Pound, 'Credo', originally 1912 but republished under the rubric 'A Retrospect', first in *Pavannes and Divisions* (1918) and subsequently in *Literary Essays*, ed. T. S. Eliot (New York: New Directions, 1968). See *Literary Essays*, p. 11.

29 The details of Pound's attendance and reaction to the lectures can be found in Noel Stock's *Life of Ezra Pound* (New York: Pantheon, 1970), pp. 106–7. The lectures themselves are reprinted in T. E. Hulme, *Speculations: Essays on Humanism and the Philosophy of Art*, ed. Herbert Read (1924; London: Routledge & Kegan Paul, 1958), pp. 141–214 as 'Bergson's Theory of Art' and 'The Philosophy of Intensive Manifolds'. See pp. 158–9.

language evolves out of metaphors that 'soon run their course and die'.[30] In associated notes he went further still and claimed that 'thought' consists only in 'the discovery of new analogies' and that these analogies are not relational in an Aristotelian sense, but merely consist 'in the simultaneous presentation to the mind of two different images'.[31] It is because poetry, being true thought, deals principally in 'imagery' rather than logic, therefore, that it can convey 'something which ordinary language and ordinary expression lets slip through':[32] 'The fallacy [is] that language is logical, or that meaning is . . . Very often the idea, apart from the analogy or metaphor which clothes it, has no existence . . . the analogy is the thing, not merely decoration . . . Thought is prior to language and consists in . . . the discovery of new analogies.' 'Two visual images form what one may call a visual chord. They unite to suggest an image which is different to both.'[33] If this describes the current function of poetry, Hulme argues in his 'Lecture on Modern Poetry', we should realise that its characteristic methods are no longer as they were. Poetry, Hulme insists, has transformed itself over time. Once it had to do with the transmission of wisdom through 'religious incantation: it was made to express oracles and maxims in an impressive manner, and rhyme and metre were used as aids to the memory'. However, as modern philosophers 'no longer believe in absolute truth . . . [or] in perfection, either in verse or in thought', and as poetry is no longer chanted but read, rhyme and metre are no longer necessary. Following the 'contours' of modern thought, then, modern poetry in English could and should be (as in the case of recent French *vers libre*) free from metrical regularity, 'oscillating [its length] with the images used by the poet . . . to use a rough analogy, it is clothes made to order, rather than ready-made clothes'. What is most important, Hulme asserts, is that poetry be, in its 'direct language', different from the 'conventional language' of prose:

> The direct language is poetry, it is direct because it deals in images. The indirect language is prose, because it uses images that have died and become figures of

[30] T. E. Hulme, *Speculations*, p. 151.

[31] T. E. Hulme, *Further Speculations*, ed. Samuel Hynes (Lincoln: University of Nebraska Press, 1955). See 'Notes on Language and Style', pp. 77–100, esp. p. 84.

[32] T. E. Hulme, *Speculations*, p. 163.

[33] Ibid., see pp. 83–4, 73. Hulme's insights would be replicated in succeeding years by similar and more famous formulations, such as Hart Crane's call for 'a "logic of metaphor," which antedates our so-called pure logic, and which is the genetic basis of all speech, hence consciousness and thought-extension' and T. S. Eliot's affirmation that 'there is a logic of the imagination as well as a logic of concepts'. (See Hart Crane, 'General Aims and Theories', *The Complete Poems and Selected Letters and Prose of Hart Crane* (New York: Anchor Books, 1966), p. 221, and T. S. Eliot's 'Preface' to his translation of St John Perse's *Anabasis* (1930; New York: Harcourt Brace, 1949), p. 10.)

> speech. The difference between the two is, roughly, this: that while one arrests your mind all the time with a picture, the other allows the mind to run along with the least possible effort to a conclusion . . . One might say that images are born in poetry. They are used in prose, and finally die a long lingering death in journalists' English. Now this process is very rapid, so that the poet must continually be creating new images, and his sincerity may be measured by the number of his images.[34]

With Hulme, Pound became convinced that only by utilising free-verse rhythms and stripping away rhetoric from a play of images could poetry find a place in modern culture. By April 1912, when he published an essay entitled 'The Wisdom of Poetry', he had translated this into a theoretical statement: 'the function of an art is to strengthen the perceptive faculties and free them from . . . such encumbrances, for instance, as set moods, set ideas, conventions'; 'thought is perhaps important to the race, and language, the medium of thought's preservation, is constantly wearing out. It has been the function of poets to new-mint the speech, to supply the vigorous terms for prose.'[35]

Pound's definition of poetry as iconoclasm, no less than Yeats's emphasis on escaping the pressure of the will or Mallarmé's insistence that poems allow words to break free from 'the poet's voice', roots poetry in the pre-logical and the somatic. But it escapes from a poetics of reverie and passivity and isolation that after Wilde's 1895 public shaming had become stigmatised as insufficiently masculine. In the new definition of Pound and Hulme, modern poetry asserts its affiliation not with dreaming but with 'thought' – in fact with that most muscular of modern intellectual pursuits, science. ('Now that mechanical science has realized [man's] ancient dreams of flight and sejunct communication', Pound wrote, '[the poet] is [its] advance guard.' Even more than philosophy, poetry is grounded in experiment, so that 'that which the philosopher presents as truth, the poet presents as that which appears as truth to a certain sort of mind under certain conditions . . . his observations rest as the enduring data of philosophy. He grinds an axe for no dogma.')[36] What Pound calls 'absolute metaphor' or (in a 1911 observation on the Italian poet Cavalcanti, a 'precise interpretive metaphor') he means us to

[34] The lecture was given originally in 1908 or 1909 and then in 1914, but not published until 1938 as an appendix to Michael Roberts, *T. E. Hulme* (London: Faber & Faber). It is republished in *Further Speculations*, where the citations in this paragraph can be found on pp. 73, 71, 70, 74–5.

[35] The essay was originally published in *Forum* (New York) and is reprinted in Pound's *Selected Prose: 1909–1965* (London: Faber & Faber, 1973), pp. 329–32. See pp. 330–1.

[36] Pound, *Selected Prose*, p. 331.

understand as the foundation of new thought, capable of 'giving people new eyes'.[37]

But Pound's theory would have meant little had it not been accompanied by a genius for manifesto and a creative gift almost unmatched among the poets of his generation. As propagandist, he conflated his and Hulme's stress on images with the purifying prescriptions of Yeats, and with a set of like-minded poets he produced the prescriptions for what Eliot was later to call the *point de repère* and 'the starting-point of modern poetry' – 'Imagism'.[38] Imagism produced its own anthologies, analogous to Marsh's, and included in them the American Poet H. D. (Hilda Doolittle), whose success as an inventor of the Imagist lyric and a practitioner of the Imagist long poem would be enmeshed with Pound's own.[39] In its core statement of principles, the group attempted its own version of Symons's admonition to concentrate on 'the thing itself': '1. Direct treatment of the "thing" whether subjective or objective. 2. To use absolutely no word that does not contribute to the presentation. 3. As regarding rhythm: to compose in the sequence of the musical phrase, not in sequence of a metronome'.[40] But Imagism's real power came from formulations which harked back to Hulme's assertion that the pre-logical bases of thought were analogies formed by two images that 'unite to suggest an image which is different to both': so Pound emphasised the 'intellectual' component of poetry when he wrote that 'An "Image" is that which presents an intellectual and emotional complex in an instant of time ... It is the presentation of such a "complex" instantaneously which gives that sense of sudden liberation; that sense of freedom from time limits and space limits; that sense of sudden growth, which we experience in the presence of the greatest works of art.'[41] Elsewhere, he observed that poetry of this kind is a 'sort of knowing. ... The "one image poem" is a form of super-position, that is to say, it is one idea set on top of another.'[42]

Because Pound placed it at the centre of several self-narratives about the discovery of Imagism, the classic example in his poetry of such a poem is the two-line 'In a Station of the Metro'(1913), in which a contemporary scene in a Paris metro station in the first line is 'superposed' onto an image of natural mutability in the second to create both a sensation of liberation from the

[37] Pound argued that his notion of a 'precise interpretive metaphor' predated Hulme's contributions. See *The Literary Essays of Ezra Pound*, p. 162.

[38] T. S. Eliot, 'American Literature and the American Language'(1953). See *To Criticize the Critic* (New York: Farrar, Straus & Giroux, 1965), p. 58.

[39] For H. D.'s crucial role in creating the Imagist idiom, see Cyrena N. Pondrom, 'H. D. and the Origins of Imagism', in *Sagetrieb*, 4 (1985), pp. 73–100.

[40] Ezra Pound, 'A Retrospect', in *Literary Essays*, p. 3. [41] Ibid., p. 4.

[42] 'Vorticism', in *Gaudier-Brzeska: A Memoir*, pp. 88, 89.

evanescent into the universal and a new composite 'image' of transitory human life.[43] But the understanding that a succession of images may dramatise the ongoing process of minting new perceptions soon drove Pound to experiment with longer sequences and in 1915–19 to begin *The Cantos*, the long poem which absorbed all his poetic energies after 1921. The crucial perception here was to emphasise not just images but the ongoing mental flux from which they emerged, and to present them as stages in an authentic poetry that plunged below the appearances of 'self' or 'character' and participated in what Hulme, with reference to Bergson, called 'the stream of the inner life', and which Pound, (using an electromagnetic figure) called the 'VORTEX, from which and through which, and into which, ideas are constantly rushing'.[44]

The modern long poem which emerged from Pound's experiments can be said to constitute the principal innovation and fundamental medium of twentieth-century verse. As flexible as the free-verse lyric but more capacious, the form at once suggests the immediacy of perception and opens itself up to many different kinds of explicit or implied mental progression, ranging from the severities of Pound's sometimes opaque images to the 'moods' of reverie, the play of memory in free association, the shifting inflections of unconscious sensibility, the stages and configurations of response to difficulty or puzzlement or love or inspiration or belief, a meditation on the significance of a drama or a narrative (or the fragments of a drama or narrative), the play of 'ideas' in the formal sense of rhythmic phrases, or the progression of 'ideas' in the more ordinary sense of conceptual moments in an ongoing wrestle with some pervasive concern.

When ideas in this last kind of progression take on the form of logical statements, the critic I. A. Richards writes in *Science and Poetry* (1926), we should not confuse them with the statements of science or philosophy. They are rather what Richards calls 'pseudo-statements' – never to be judged according to their 'truth', but only as symbols or fictions which organise a stream of 'interests' which are the real masters of what appear to be our 'pure thought[s]'.[45] Thus does modern poetry redefine statements and assertions – no longer things

43 The poem was first published in *Poetry* for April 1913 and then in *Lustra* (1916) and subsequent versions of Pound's collected shorter poetry. For the narratives in which he narrates the composition of the poem to illustrate the principles of Imagism, see 'How I Began' in *T. P.'s Weekly* (6 June 1913), p. 707, and 'Vorticism', in *Gaudier-Brzeska: A Memoir*, pp. 86–9.

44 See Hulme, 'Bergson's Theory of Art', *Speculations*, p. 149, and Pound's 'Vorticism', in *Gaudier-Brzeska: A Memoir*, p. 92.

45 I. A. Richards, *Poetries and Sciences* (1935; New York: Norton, 1970), pp. 57 ff, 25. (*Poetries and Sciences* was a republication, slightly revised and with additional commentary, of *Science and Poetry*, 1926.)

whose sense is to be judged on their own, but something more like a 'theme' or 'motif' in a piece of music, where significance depends on changing context. The result is – quite paradoxically – that, staying true to Pater's and Mallarmé's strictures about restoring literature to the condition of music, modern poetry managed to reconnect with public discourse by absorbing blocks of quotidian material – historical or documentary prose, even journalism – into an essentially lyric modality, the post-Imagist long poem.

No one was more pleased about this development than Pound, who had long wished to re-engage the tradition of the epic that poetry had relinquished to the novel during the nineteenth century, and who, once he started his long poem, never again wrote in any other form except for translations. His best definition of *The Cantos* was a 'poem including history' – and during the fifty-odd years he worked on it he managed to include historical material from the letters of Renaissance condottieri to the records of the American republic.[46] Other poets, however, used the demotic and the 'impure' registers of the long poem intermittently, to complement and energise their shorter work. The same drive that produced Pound's *Cantos* also produced – driven by quite other sets of linguistic, cultural and ideological interests – poems as different as Hugh MacDiarmid's *A Drunk Man Looks at the Thistle* (1926; a Scots response to *The Waste Land*) and the adopted Welshman David Jones's *In Parenthesis* (1937), a poem about the Great War. Deliberately transgressing the pastoralism of Georgian poetry and the lyric refinement of the early phase of Imagism, these works open poetry up to the complexity of twentieth-century reality in a way almost unimaginable at the beginning of the century.

Nor was this turn towards documentary, history and the epic the only paradoxical connection that Modernist poets forged with the world of public discourse. As an outgrowth of the poet's mission to new-mint cliché, Pound and Eliot pre-eminently came to see themselves as 'conservators of the public speech' (or as Eliot put it in an essay entitled 'The Social Function of Poetry', the guardians of national culture whose job it was to refresh 'the speech and the sensibility of the whole nation').[47] And at a time when Europe was entering World War I, such ambitions could not help but become embroiled in matters of history and politics, giving poetry a gravity it had not had since the time of the French revolution. Pound, for example, reading another Nietzschean, Remy de Gourmont, in early 1912, repeatedly cited Gourmont's contention

46 Ezra Pound, *ABC of Reading* (1934; New York: New Directions, 1960), p. 46.

47 Ezra Pound, 'The Wisdom of Poetry'(1912), *Selected Prose: 1909–1965*, p. 331. T. S. Eliot, 'The Social Function of Poetry'(1945), in *On Poetry and Poets* (New York: Farrar, Straus & Giroux, 1961), p. 12.

that, without the intervention of literature, 'most men think only husks and shells of the thoughts that have been already lived over by others' – husks and shells that constitute 'the system of echoes, of the general vacuity of public opinion'[48] (for which, read war propaganda).[49]

Pound's poetry and criticism therefore become preoccupied not only with creating modern lyric beauty, but with the novelist's task of exposing dangerous social clichés. He champions Flaubert's and Henry James's and, in his own generation, Joyce's efforts to analyse the political clichés of national hostility, 'which chemicals too little regarded have in our time exploded for want of watching', and he repeats Flaubert's admonition that if Europe had read his *Education Sentimentale*, the War of 1870 'wouldn't have happened'.[50] More and more an active engagement with the language of journalism seems to Pound the necessary occupation of the poet in a time of war and the analytic procedures of the realist tradition the only school for wartime poetry. His own verse turns to satire, where the 'instinct' for prose ('the detailed, convincing analysis of something detestable') produces an 'assertion' of lyric desire 'inversely, i.e. as of an opposite hatred'.[51] The ultimate product of these concerns is the suite 'Hugh Selwyn Mauberley', whose syncopated ironising of the literary and journalistic culture of the Great War represents one of the high-water marks of Modernist poetry.

Pound was turning towards prose, moreover, at the moment he met T. S. Eliot, who arrived in England in the summer of 1914. Eliot encapsulates their collaborative concerns in a semi-satirical sketch published in 1917, in which he and Pound, under the pseudonyms 'Eeldrop and Appleplex' reinforce each other's horror of public 'labels'. Eliot's little dialogue is extraordinary in the way it quotes Mallarmé on the false coinage of public discourse even as it reverses its thrust. Now, rather than something to be lamented, the fact that 'the majority of mankind live on paper currency: they use terms which it merely good for so much reality, they never see actual coinage' (here attributed to Appleplex–Pound) supplies the core material for poetry: '"I should go even

48 Ezra Pound, *Literary Essays*, pp. 371–2. Pound's source was Gourmont's *The Problem of Style*. See Glenn S. Burne, ed., *Remy de Gourmont: Selected Writings* (Ann Arbor: University of Michigan Press, 1966), p. 115, and also Richard Sieburth's commentary in *Instigations: Ezra Pound and Remy de Gourmont* (Cambridge, MA: Harvard University Press, 1978), pp. 67 ff.

49 Vincent Sherry, in *The Great War and the Language of Modernism* (New York: Oxford University Press, 2003), explores important implications of this moment, and traces Modernism's attempt to discredit the liberal tradition and the liberal rhetoric that was used to justify the war. (A part of Modernism's conservative politics can be traced to its sense of betrayal by the liberal tradition out of which it emerged.)

50 Ezra Pound, *Literary Essays*, p. 301, 297.

51 Ibid., p. 324.

further than that." said Eeldrop [Eliot]:

> The majority not only have no language to express anything save generalized man; they are for the most part unaware of themselves as anything but generalized men. They are first of all government officials, or pillars of the church, or trade unionists, or poets, or unemployed; this cataloguing is not only satisfactory to other people for practical purposes, it is sufficient to themselves for their 'life of the spirit.' Many are not quite real at any moment.[52]

It is the solemn task of the poet, Eliot suggests, to expose that unreality.

Eliot's wartime poetry, like Pound's, focuses on the cultural clichés that support the 'unreality' of 'generalized' men and women. First in free verse and then in satirical quatrains, the irony of his poetic machines ('Cousin Nancy', 'Burbank with a Baedecker; Bleistein with a Cigar', 'Sweeney Agamemnon') spotlights the cant that justified the war. Building on the philosophical ironies of his early verse, though, Eliot's engagement with cliché has a pessimism and a subtlety all its own.

Eliot had founded his mature style on the practice of the French poet Jules Laforgue, and on Arthur Symons's account of Laforgue's 'surprising irony of cosmical vision'.[53] The speakers of Eliot's dramatic monologues, like Laforgue's, employ a deliberately obtrusive diction, ranging from scientific or intellectual jargon to the sentimental images of romantic verse, which marks their statements with knowing irony. So, in Eliot's 'La Figlia Che Piange' a speaker says he should have found 'Some way incomparably light and deft' to separate a pair of doomed lovers, and in the unexpectedly arch multisyllable 'incomparably' creates scare quotes around the remark that imply he too is aware of its cynicism. The large implications of this characteristic gesture are fundamental and far-reaching. In this kind of poetry it is irony rather than the preconscious that provides an alternative to cliché – but the alternative is no escape, for in the poetry of Laforgue and Eliot no expression, no truth, no wholeness is allowed to remain unquestioned. So conceived, literature cannot escape the crisis of language but can only exist as a vehicle for self-conscious reflection upon its impossible condition.

This ironic sophistication suffused Eliot's early successes ('The Love Song of J. Alfred Prufrock', 'Portrait of a Lady', 'La Figlia Che Piange'), and, having inspired Pound (who, thinking not only of Laforgue and Eliot but of Mina Loy and Marianne Moore, called it 'logopoeia' – 'the dance of the intellect

52 T. S. Eliot, 'Eeldrop and Appleplex I'(1917); rpt. in Margaret Anderson, ed., *The Little Review Anthology* (New York: Horizon Press, 1953), pp. 104–5.

53 Symons, *The Symbolist Movement*, pp. 57, 59, 58.

among words')[54] helped produce the greatest achievements of Modernist poetry, among which any list must contain Pound's 'Homage to Sextus Propertius' and Eliot's *The Waste Land*. Ironically reflexive dramas of language, poetry, and history, both answer to Mallarmé's 'Crisis of Poetry'. Pound's suite addresses the situation of modern writing obliquely, adopting as his mask a figure from a comparable moment in history, who speaks through a translation that is not quite a translation. Using Propertius' resistance to the clichés of Augustan propaganda and Augustan poetry as a substitute for his own situation, Pound (as he says of Laforgue) functions as 'nine-tenths of him, critic – dealing for the most part with literary poses and *clichés*, taking these as his subject matter', and finally suggesting by the intensity of his struggle 'his own very personal emotions . . . his own unperturbed sincerity'.[55] As in many of Pound's translations, a voice from another time, another place, another language, provides him with just enough distance to sound the limitations of his own discourse. The result exemplifies what is perhaps the greatest strength of Modernist verse – its exquisite ear for outdated or pretentious diction and its preternatural skill for registering the social nuances of speech.

But it was Eliot's *The Waste Land* that, as Pound said, was the 'justification' of 'our modern experiment, since 1900'.[56] Combining the musical procedures of the long poem that Pound had helped develop with the sophisticated irony of Eliot's early verse, *The Waste Land* presents an orchestrated series of vignettes that displays all the complexities of modern verse – a critical awareness of the history of literature combined with a thorough-going scepticism about literature's ability to achieve a status more profound than speech; a psychologically intense drama of the mind combined with a critical analysis of the clichés of twentieth-century culture; a lyric poem of great poignancy combined with an epic presentation of the manners of the modern city. In the poem, Eliot's narrator repeatedly tries to establish the validity of a remembered moment of ecstasy (the moment in the hyacinth garden) by finding a form of expression

[54] Pound at first uses Remy de Gourmont's phrase, 'verbalism' to describe Laforgue in 'Irony, Laforgue, and Some Satire' (1917; see Ezra Pound, *Literary Essays*, pp. 280–4), then uses his own term 'logopoeia' first in reference to Moore and Loy in 'A List of Books', *Little Review*, 4, 11 (March 1918), pp. 56–8, rpt. in Bonnie Kime Scott, ed., *The Gender of Modernism: A Critical Anthology* (Bloomington: Indiana University Press, 1990), pp. 365–6. (*The Gender of Modernism* also includes a shrewd account of Mina Loy's work written by Carolyn Burke – see pp. 230–8). Finally, in 'How to Read' (1929; see *Literary Essays*, p. 25), Pound defines 'logopoeia' as something that 'employs words not only for their direct meaning, but it takes count in a special way of habits of usage, of the context we *expect* to find with the word . . . and of ironical play'.

[55] Pound, 'Irony, Laforgue, and Some Satire', p. 283.

[56] Paige, ed., *Letters of Ezra Pound*, p. 180. To Felix E. Schelling, 8 July 1922.

adequate to its power. But no form suffices, nor does attempting to validate the experience by reference to the most important historical, legendary and religious narratives of his culture. Along the way of this nightmarishly compulsive inquest, every instrument that the narrator uses to alleviate his doubt is itself questioned and found wanting. Ringed round by the poem's ironies, no authority remains: religion may be illusion, history may be lies, memory may be a fabrication, the rambling self may be but an artificial construct, sensation may be hallucination, literature may be rhetoric, even language may be nothing more than empty words. To such extremes had a horror of cliché driven modern poetry.

After a poem like *The Waste Land*, to write without such self-consciousness was to risk ridicule. Modernism's assault on cliché, however, probably reached its apogee in the period during and immediately following the Great War. Afterwards, the jazz-like rhythms of a poem like Edith Sitwell's 'Aubade' (1923) or the mysterious landscapes of W. H. Auden's 'The Watershed' (1927) reabsorbed and refined selected elements of the Modernist repertory for their own, slightly different, purposes, and later still the whole repertory was to be several times remixed, as for example in the Surrealist verse of the thirties and forties. Meanwhile the Modernists of the teens and twenties – Yeats, Pound, Eliot, H. D. and the rest – went on wrestling with a condition of crisis that was rooted in the first two decades of the century.

14

Modernity and myth

STEVEN CONNOR

We are perhaps entitled to assume that the words 'myth' and 'modernity' named sharply antithetical things. Myths are thought to be primordial and universal. Modernity, along with its cultural and artistic complement, Modernism, is both urgently present and geopolitically particular. Myths and mythical thinking are what modern culture has gone beyond and, whether willingly or unwillingly, left behind. The effort to understand, engage with or revive myth is an effort on the part of modern writers and artists to enter into habits of thought, belief and feeling that are nothing if they are not not-modern. The point of myth is precisely that it is not modern, and the pursuit of myth is therefore a form of the effort to 'think the unthought' that seems to be a definitional part of Modernist cultural aspiration.

Modernity is sometimes identified with the ideal of Enlightenment that grew up in the late seventeenth and early eighteenth centuries. But the Enlightenment relationship to myth is much simpler than that of Modernism. For early Enlightenment thinkers such as Bernard de Fontenelle, myth was part of the apparatus of superstition, credulity and ignorance from which reason was attempting to unpick itself. Myth was, in a sense, the past itself, insofar as the past came to be thought of, not merely as different from the present, but as darkness, error, infancy, impediment, in short, as the antagonist of the present as it strove to realise itself. But the capacity of reason to free itself from myth could also be a proof of its self-corrective capacity. '[L]et us not look for anything in the fables except the history of the errors of the human mind', wrote Fontenelle in his *Of the Origin of Fables* (1724), but added that

> The human mind is the less subject to error to the degree that it knows how much and in how many different ways it is subject to error. It is not science to have one's head filled with the extravagances of the Phoenicians and the

> Greeks, but it is science to understand what led the Phoenicians and Greeks to such extravagances.[1]

The desirability, and even the possibility, of establishing a clear separation between the mythological past and the clear-thinking present came to seem less assured as the eighteenth century wore on. For Giambattista Vico, writing as early as 1744, myth was the expression of 'a metaphysics not rational and abstract like that of learned men now, but felt and imagined as that of these first men must have been, who, without power of ratiocination, were all robust sense and vigorous imagination'.[2] Vico's ideas were transmitted to German writers later in the century, especially Gottfried Lessing, J. G. Herder, Christian Gottlieb Heyne, Karl Moritz and the two Schlegel brothers, A. W. Schlegel and Friedrich Schlegel. For these writers, myth was the evidence not of what must be excoriated from human culture and consciousness, but the promise of what might still be available to it. Romantic writers began to think of myth, not just as foolish or flatulent fables, but as a vital resource for a new age. Herder wrote: 'Let us study the mythology of the ancients as poetical heuristics, to become inventors ourselves.'[3] Myth played an important part in the growing suspicion that reason abstracted knowledge from experience, making the world knowable by striking it dead. Myth promised a new, more vital way of knowing the world. Friedrich Schlegel went further than others in calling for a reawakening of a mythopoeic sensibility and a remaking of myth. Schlegel wrote in 1800 that the task of all poetry was 'to cancel the progression and laws of rationally thinking reason, and to transplant us once again into the beautiful confusion of imagination, into the original chaos of human nature, for which I know as yet no more beautiful symbol than the motley throng of the ancient gods'.[4]

Nineteenth-century investigations of myth oscillated between these two traditions, of the eschewal and the renewal of myth. While maintaining a Romantic idealisation of the primitive sensibility and responsiveness to the divine in nature, the philologist Friedrich Max Müller also saw the dangers of myth for rational thought, seeing myths as the product of misunderstanding

[1] Bernard de Fontenelle, *De l'origine des fables*, ed. J.-R. Carré (Paris: Félix Alcan, 1932), pp. 39–40.

[2] Giambattista Vico, *The New Science*, trans. Thomas Godard Bergin and Max Harold Fisch (Ithaca: Cornell University Press, 1968), p. 116.

[3] Johann Gottfried Herder, 'Of Contemporary Uses of Mythology' ('Vom neuern Gebrauch der Mythologie'), *Ueber di neuere deutsche Litteratur*, 2 vols. (Riga: J. F. Hartknoch, 1767), Dritte Sammlung, II. 5, vol. II, p. 158. My translation.

[4] Friedrich Schlegel, *Dialogue on Poetry and Literary Aphorisms*, trans. Ernst Behler and Roman Stuc (University Park: Pennsylvania State University Press, 1968), p. 100.

and the mind led astray by the 'disease of language'. With the rise of anthropology, as evidenced in E. B. Tylor's *Primitive Culture* (1871) and, late in the century, in J. G. Frazer's *The Golden Bough* (first edition 1890), myth was shifted somewhat from the centre of attention. The doctrine that contemporary tribal peoples preserved 'survivals' of primitive belief meant that myth was no longer the principal evidence for the nature of primitive culture. Rather than myth being the key to understanding primitive culture, an understanding of primitive culture was necessary to make sense of myth.

All these different traditions were entertained by Modernist artists and writers, in a strange, asynchronous medley. On the one hand, even writers who were suspicious of many aspects of the modern world, like T. S. Eliot and Ezra Pound, shared an aspiration to absolute newness and self-making that has affinities with Enlightenment modernity. Things would be much simpler if Modernists simply sought a retreat or reprieve from modernity in the alleged universals of myth. But Modernism also retained many aspects of the Romantic effort, not just to retrieve myth, but also to transform it for the modern world. Modernist culture sought to establish a 'modern myth', and the modernity of Modernism is in large part defined by the complex and paradoxical relationship it establishes to what it thinks of as myth. This essay will attempt to characterise some of these paradoxes.

When the bough breaks: Frazer and mythical method

Modern writers derived much of their information regarding myth from the work of ethnologists, mythographers and psychologists. But they are characterised by an extraordinary aptitude for reading such scholarly and scientific interpretations of myth against the grain. The most conspicuous objects of this process are the works of Frazer and Freud.

Frazer's *The Golden Bough* served many writers and artists as a huge sourcebook both for myths and legends, and ideas about their nature and function. The latter is somewhat surprising, since the book is not really intended as a study of myth as such. Rather, it is an attempt to use the evidence of myths, alongside rituals and religious practice and beliefs from a huge range of cultures, to establish a history of human understanding. Frazer thought that human culture passed universally through three stages, the magical, the religious and the scientific. In the magical stage, primitive man believes he can control the world through the manipulation of relations of likeness and association. Frazer thought of magical thinking as a kind of incipient but imperfect scientism, since it depended on a conception of nature as bound by universal and impersonal laws (the wrong ones, though). This phase of human culture shows no sign of a religious conception, which is to say a conception that the operations of nature are controlled by powerful, superhuman beings. This phase only supervenes at the point at which the mistaken science of magic begins to be revealed as unreliable. Myth seems to belong for Frazer to this religious phase, and to share in the apologetic or explanatory function of religion: the world does not obey the magician because it is ruled by the caprice of gods, who need to be nagged, flattered and wheedled into guaranteeing human well-being. For all his sentimental appreciation of the poetry and prettiness of myths, Frazer was essentially an Enlightenment rationalist, who saw myths as bound up with the religious impulses and beliefs that had been the source of so much error and cruelty through the ages. In its quiet confidence that religion was in the process of being surpassed by scientific thinking, along with its self-identification as part of that long movement from superstition into enlightened freedom, Frazer's *Golden Bough* is a fundamentally anti-mythological book.

But this antagonism towards myth is only implicit, since, unlike his influential predecessor Friedrich Max Müller, Frazer actually had no strong or consistent theory of myth to offer. Sometimes beliefs are enacted in rituals, sometimes they are projected as fables. Sometimes, they are attempts to patch up or make sense of rituals, the meanings of which have become forgotten or merely habitual. Where Müller saw myths as the engines of thought and belief, usually with damaging effect, Frazer, as the leading representative of what came to be known as the 'anthropological school' saw myths simply as the reflex or vehicle of systems of belief. Thus, Frazer was not inclined towards the idea that myth has any kind of essence, belongs to any particular stage of human development, or has any particular, transhistorical power.[5] And yet writers who turned to *The Golden Bough* seemed regularly to find in it a very different kind of argument, about the powerful and ineradicable persistence of myth through every form of culture, and the dangerous effects of neglecting or suppressing mythical consciousness. This, for example, was how D. H. Lawrence recorded his response to reading Frazer in 1915:

> I have been reading Frazer's *Golden Bough* and *Totemism and Exogamy*. Now I am convinced of what I believed when I was about twenty – that there is another seat of consciousness than the brain and the nerve system: there

[5] See my 'The Birth of Humility: J. G. Frazer and Victorian Mythography', in Robert Fraser, ed., *Sir James Frazer and the Literary Imagination* (London: Macmillan, 1990), pp. 61–80.

> is a blood-consciousness which exists in us independently of the ordinary mental consciousness . . . and the tragedy of this our life, and of your life, is that the mental and nerve consciousness exerts a tyranny over the blood-consciousness.[6]

For all the savagery and violence to which *The Golden Bough* bore witness, it is hard to imagine Frazer ever throwing the idea of 'blood-consciousness' into the conversation at high table in Trinity College. So why, even though *The Golden Bough* was such a continuous presence in English-speaking culture for almost thirty years, during which time it was repeatedly revised, reissued, reviewed, interpreted and criticised, were its central arguments so easy to ignore? There were two features of *The Golden Bough* that may help account for this. The first was the principle of scholarly reserve that Frazer maintained in and about his work. Like Darwin, and unlike some of the more daredevil folklorists of the 1890s, such as Edward Clodd, who made no bones about the analogies he saw between Christian ritual and barbaric cannibal practices, Frazer always carefully avoided religious controversy, preferring to bury himself instead in the details of anthropological affinities and development. The result is that nowhere in *The Golden Bough* does Frazer make explicit the large conclusions about the nature and origin of Christianity or its likely fate in the modern world that the overall structure of his argument might seem to make unavoidable. The second was Frazer's own magpie instinct of aggregation. In order to maintain the consistency of its arguments in the face of so much anthropological evidence, and to defend itself against the growing objections of generations of reviewers, *The Golden Bough* had to get bigger and bigger, a process which itself meant that the arguments could easily get lost in the spreading arborescence of its instances. Certainly readers of *The Golden Bough*, such as W. B. Yeats, T. S. Eliot, Ezra Pound, D. H. Lawrence, and others whom their example encouraged, tended to ignore, or perhaps not even to notice the strong current of rationalism and progressivism which tugged through the work. Since the long story of the emergence of reason from superstition was so episodic and uneven, it seems to have been easy for the attention of Modernist readers to have been captured instead by the local patterns of resonance and recurrence between the different kinds of myths and practices which Frazer continued to amass and collocate.

It was this very 'armchair anthropology' aspect of Frazer's work, which was actually beginning to make it seem quaintly out of date, even at the moment

[6] D. H. Lawrence, letter to Bertrand Russell, 8 December 1915, *The Letters of D. H. Lawrence*, 8 vols., vol. II, ed. George J. Zytaruk and James T. Boulton (Cambridge University Press, 1981), p. 470.

of its triumphant culmination, the appearance of the twelve-volume third edition from 1906 to 1915, which was probably the form in which it came to the attention of modern writers. By this time, other anthropological writers, led by Bronislaw Malinowski, were offering functional rather than poetic accounts of myth and stressing the importance of understanding the systematic interconnection between myth and other aspects of life within individual cultures, rather than the apparently universal structures of belief yielded by the syncretic, generalising methods of 'comparative mythology'. While Frazer's work expanded irresistibly outwards, fieldworkers began to tunnel deeper inwards into individual cultures. Many Modernist writers read *The Golden Bough* alongside, or even, in Yeats's case, through the lens of, H. P. Blavatsky's crazy compendium of occult lore, myth and mystical science fiction, *The Secret Doctrine*, which had appeared two years before it. In its attempt to synthesise magic, myth and science, *The Secret Doctrine* reads like *The Golden Bough* reflected in a funhouse mirror. But Lawrence recommended it to a friend in 1920, in the same breath as he seconded her approval of Frazer: 'I'm sure you like *The Golden Bough*. – Get Blavatskys book one day.'[7]

The reading of Frazer was also accented in England and beyond by the increasing awareness of the work of Nietzsche, especially his *The Birth of Tragedy* (1871), in which he first formulated his ideas about the conflict between the abstract and philosophic Apollonian principle and the violent, ecstatic Dionysian principle in Greek culture. Nietzsche argued that the great founding myths of civilisation, such as the Oedipus myth, had a dark underside: '"The edge of wisdom is turned against the wise man; wisdom is a crime committed on nature": such are the terrible words addressed to us by myth.'[8] With his vision of tragedy as the revenge of the Dionysian impulse upon the sweetly reasonable thing that myth had become in Classical Greece, and his insistence on 'the Greek desire . . . for ugliness . . . their commitment to the tragic myth, image of all that is awful, evil, perplexing, destructive, ominous in human existence',[9] Nietzsche became an important focaliser for those determined to abstract from Frazer's explication of fertility ritual and the cycles of death and rebirth a dark and thrilling vision of the savage impulses seething below the thin crust of modern life.

[7] D. H. Lawrence, letter to Marie Hubrecht, 13 May 1920, *The Letters of D. H. Lawrence*, vol. III, ed. James T. Boulton and Andrew Robertson (Cambridge University Press, 1984), p. 526.

[8] Friedrich Nietzsche, *The Birth of Tragedy and the Genealogy of Morals*, trans. Francis Golffing (New York: Doubleday, 1956), p. 61

[9] Ibid., p. 9.

However, as John Vickery suggests, it may have been the form as much as the content of *The Golden Bough* which had the greatest influence on writers such as Yeats, Eliot, Pound and Joyce. Frazer's extraordinary multiplication of juxtapositions and cross-references, darting from Aztec fertility rituals to Bohemian smoke dances and Swedish weaving-lore, seemed to provide a model for the similar historical syncopations and jump-cut structures evolved in *The Waste Land*, *The Cantos*, *Finnegans Wake* and *The Anathemata*.[10] The classical statement of this procedure is often taken to be Eliot's explication of what he calls the 'mythical method' of Joyce's *Ulysses*, when he reviewed it in 1922.

> In using the myth, in manipulating a continuous parallel between contemporaneity and antiquity, Mr Joyce is pursuing a method which others must pursue after him . . . It is simply a way of controlling, of ordering, of giving a shape and a significance to the immense panorama of futility and anarchy that is contemporary history . . . Psychology (such as it is, and whether our reaction to it be comic or serious), ethnology, and *The Golden Bough* have concurred to make possible what was impossible even a few years ago. Instead of narrative method we may now use the mythical method. It is, I seriously believe, a step towards making the modern world possible for art.[11]

Eliot speaks of 'a continuous parallel', though he must have known that Joyce's use of the *Odyssey* in *Ulysses* really offers no such thing – unless he was among those who took on trust the advance critical publicity that the book had generated, some of it encouraged by Joyce himself. In fact, Joyce allowed himself to be extremely arbitrary in the way in which he built up his concordance between the experiences of a June day in Dublin in 1906 and the years-long wanderings of Ulysses around the Mediterranean. Indeed, far from maintaining a 'continuous parallel' between the two, it might be said that Joyce deliberately cultivated different kinds of discontinuous parallels. The 'Cyclops' episode uses Ulysses' escape from the angry one-eyed giant Polyphemus as an ironic gloss on an unpleasant encounter between Bloom and a bigoted (= one-eyed) nationalist. The 'Aeolus' chapter, by contrast, can scarcely be said to employ parallels between characters and events at all, for it uses the Homeric story of the unloosing of a bag of winds to develop a discussion of rhetoric and journalistic windbaggery. The 'Wandering Rocks' chapter builds an entire sequence out of what is no more than a brief allusion and not an episode at all in the Odyssey.

10 John Vickery, *The Literary Impact of 'The Golden Bough'* (Princeton University Press, 1973), pp. 125–6.

11 T. S. Eliot, '*Ulysses*, Order and Myth', *Selected Prose*, ed. Frank Kermode (London: Faber & Faber, 1975), pp. 177–8.

When he wrote his review of *Ulysses*, Eliot had already evolved his own kind of 'mythical method' in *The Waste Land*, which the creative vandalism of Ezra Pound had turned from a suite of grumpy, sub-Popean squibs on the emptiness and boredom of modern life into a suggestive cross-historical kaleidoscope of images, murmurs and lamentations, all suggestive of a crisis of degeneration and disconnection and an urgent, but inchoate longing for some spiritual transformation or revelation. Neither Joyce's nor Eliot's practice seems all that close to the plump Edwardian orotundity of Frazer's writing, if taken paragraph by rolling paragraph. Their work depended, not upon accretive association, but upon jagged, ironic ragtime, raised from the condition of a technique to that of a world-view.

There is an even more obvious oddity about seeing this kind of technique as 'mythical method'. For, although it may very well resemble and even derive from the kind of roaming, scrapbook syncretism exemplified in *The Golden Bough* – as amplified perhaps by the discontinuous kind of reading given to the book by many writers and artists – the method of either *Ulysses* or *The Waste Land* certainly does not resemble the method, or form of myths themselves, taken singly. Homer's *Odyssey* may be an exception here, but only because the *Odyssey* is itself a literary compendium, rather than an example of myth in its original or primitive state. It is not myths taken singly which exemplify this principle of continuous discontinuity, but mythology seen as a whole, which, at least since the eighteenth century, rationalising mythographers had tended to condemn as an anarchic tangle of contradiction. The mythical method starts to look like a mythotropic method – the mixed voice of a Modernist style turned aside by myth.

Psychoanalysis and myth

The reading of Frazer's work against the grain is paralleled by the use of psychoanalysis by Modernist writers interested in myth. The assumption grew early on that myth had something important to do with the unconscious and that therefore, as the discoverer and principal explicator of the unconscious, Freud must also have something important to say about myth. It is true that Freud had been interested from early in his career in the parallels between neurotic illness and primitive belief, though he had by and large left it to his followers, such as Otto Rank, Karl Abraham and C. G. Jung, to explore these parallels and it was not until the 1920s that he turned his attention seriously to the anthropological study of culture. Nevertheless, by this time there were many who assumed that Freudian psychoanalysis meant the effort to illuminate in the individual a hidden substratum of unconscious thoughts and desires which are the equivalent of the kind of race-unconscious or cultural-unconscious embodied in myth.

In fact, the analogy between these two forms of unconsciousness is very shaky. Myths, or bodies of mythology, can only be said to be 'unconscious' in the sense that they have no obvious authors or carriers of conscious intent. There seems nothing in the least 'unconscious' about the story of Oedipus, in the sense in which Freud assumed a patient might be unconscious of the real meaning of their dreams. In what sense, one wonders, can the themes of the rivalry of father and son, and the incestuous guilt attaching to the desire for the mother possibly be said to be hidden or repressed in the Oedipus story? Indeed, Freud's sparse remarks about particular myths suggest that he saw them, not as embodying the work of repression, which for him was always linked to the unconscious, but rather the blurting out of preoccupations that are otherwise kept out of sight or unavailable to consciousness.

Freud tried to resist, not always successfully, the idea that 'the unconscious' had its own character and destiny. It was Freud's associate and, later, rival, C. G. Jung, who developed the idea that myth embodied a special kind of 'unconscious meaning'. After his split with Freud in 1913 over the question of the prominence of sexuality in psychoanalysis, Jung sought to develop the view that the unconscious was a positive force, always seeking to rise up into, to perfect itself in consciousness. He came increasingly to see myth as the language of this unconscious. Where Freud saw myths as occasionally offering support for the insights of psychoanalysis concerning the individual mind, Jung saw the entire realm of psychic life as mythical. Indeed, it may have been his growing interest in myth and the secret immemorial knowledge that he saw embodied in it that helped prompt his break with Freud over the question of the sexual nature of unconscious fantasy and the origin of the unconscious in repression.

The work of writers like W. B. Yeats, D. H. Lawrence and H. D. (Hilda Doolittle), all of whom came to believe in versions of collective unconscious of which myths gave evidence, resonates with the ideas of Jung. W. B. Yeats seems to have had little direct exposure to the work of Jung when he wrote in 1917 of the 'Anima Mundi', a notion which he had encountered in the work of the seventeenth-century neo-Platonist Henry More, and yet his words seem to confirm the hospitable context that Jung's ideas may have met:

> I have always sought to bring my mind close to the mind of Indian and Japanese poets, old women in Connacht, mediums in Soho, lay brothers

> whom I imagine dreaming in some mediaeval monastery the dreams of their village, learned authors who refer all to antiquity; to immerse it in the general mind where the mind is scarce separable from what we have begun to call 'the subconscious'.[12]

D. H. Lawrence seems to take no account of the work of Jung until 1926, when he wrote that he thought him 'very interesting, in his own sort of fat muddled mystical way'.[13] But the criticism he offers of the Freudian notion of the unconscious in his *Psychoanalysis and the Unconscious* of a few years before suggests that he is reproducing the lines of the Jungian disagreement with Freud: '[t]he Freudian unconscious is the cellar in which the mind keeps is own bastard spawn. The true unconscious is the well-head, the fountain of real motivity.'[14]

The most remarkable example of this displacement among modern writers is furnished by H. D., who underwent sustained analysis with Freud during 1933 and 1934. Her *Tribute to Freud*, written ten years later and first published only in 1956, glows with praise for her analyst in guiding her towards a recognition and acceptance of the importance and power of mythic archetypes. Much of her narrative is taken up with an account of the attention Freud had her pay to a series of semi-visions which she had seen projected on the wall of her apartment in Capri in the 1920s. Her account of her analysis and its interpretation is full of mythic symbols and occult images: a three-legged lampstand, for example, is 'none other than our old friend, the tripod of classic Delphi'.[15] Even as she pays tribute to his intellectual daring, H. D. subjects his work to a fantastic and appropriative transformation, like the other writers who sought to Jungify Freud:

> He had dared to say that the dream came from an unexplored depth in man's consciousness and that this unexplored depth ran like a great stream or ocean underground, and the vast depth of that ocean was the same vast depth that today, as in Joseph's day, overflowing in man's small consciousness, produced inspiration, madness, creative idea, or the dregs of the dreariest symptoms of mental unrest and disease. He had dared to say that it was the same ocean of universal consciousness, and even if not stated in so many words, he had dared to imply that this consciousness proclaimed all men one; all nations and races met in the universal world of the dream; and he had dared to say

[12] W. B. Yeats, 'Anima Mundi', *Mythologies* (London: Macmillan, 1962), p. 343.

[13] D. H. Lawrence, letter to Mabel Dodge Luhan, 23 September 1926, *The Letters of D. H. Lawrence*, vol. v ed. James T. Boulton and Lindeth Vasey (Cambridge University Press, 1989), p. 540.

[14] D. H. Lawrence, *Psychoanalysis and the Unconscious* (London: Heinemann, 1923), p. 26.

[15] H. D., *Tribute to Freud*, ed. Kenneth Fields (Boston: David R. Godine, 1974), p. 46.

that the dream-symbol could be interpreted; its language, its imagery were common to the whole race, not only of the living, but of those ten thousand years dead.[16]

Mythopoeia

The most important aspect of Jung's attitude to myth was the importance in it of the work of mythopoeia. Jung broke with Romantic ideas of myth as primal intuitions of the divine, and with nineteenth-century ideas of myth as explanations of the natural world. The origin and subject of myth was the life of the mind itself:

> So far mythologists have always helped themselves out with solar, lunar, meteorological, vegetal, and other ideas of the kind. The fact that myths are first and foremost psychic phenomena that reveal the nature of the soul is something they have absolutely refused to see until now. Primitive man is not much interested in objective explanations of the obvious, but he has an imperative need – or rather, his unconscious psyche has an irresistible urge – to assimilate all outer sense experiences to inner, psychic events.[17]

In mirroring the struggles of the collective mind to achieve integration and self-awareness, the work of myth is actually for Jung a kind of self-figuring. Where Müller made out in myth references to the sun and weather, where Frazer saw references to a cyclical philosophy of death and renewal, and where Freud saw references to guilt and desire, Jung's analyses of myth construe them as nothing less, or more, than allegories of the power of myth itself. The psyche uses myth to tell the story to itself of its own endless quest for integration through, and with, myth.

Modernist writing offers parallels to this circularity. Myth signifies the power of myth for Modernism itself. As I have tried to show elsewhere, myth is often invoked to signify the mythic power of invocation.[18] When Ezra Pound retells in his second Canto Ovid's story (*Metamorphoses*, II, 580–691) of Bacchus turning the crew of a pirate ship into animals and fish, he is evoking the metamorphic power of myth itself to form and persist amid change, as well as predicting

[16] Ibid., p. 71.

[17] C. G. Jung, *The Archetypes and the Collective Unconscious*, trans. R. F. C. Hull, vol. IX .1 (1959) of the *Collected Works of C. G. Jung*, 20 vols. (London: Routledge & Kegan Paul, 1953–79), pp. 5–6.

[18] Steven Connor, 'Echo's Bones: Myth, Modernity and the Vocalic Uncanny', in Michael Bell and Peter Poellner, eds., *Myth and the Making of Modernity* (Amsterdam and Atlanta, GA: Rodopi, 1998), pp. 213–35.

the sinuous metamorphoses that lie in the future for his own, life-long poem:

> And where there was gunwale, there now was vine-truck,
> And tenthril where cordage had been,
> grape-leaves on the rowlocks,
> Heavy vine on the oarshafts,
> And, out of nothing, a breathing[19]

In an immaculate tautology, myth, conceived as 'mythopoeia', comes to enact Modernism's self-elected power to revive myth and transform it for its own purposes. However, unlike primitive myth, Modernist mythopoeia must needs be intensely conscious of itself. Modernist myth is thus not concerned with maintaining the fabric of belief and social cohesion, which was supposed to be the role of myth in primitive cultures, but with maintaining the special vocation of the Modernist artist to legislate on such things. 'Myth', in fact, becomes another of the many names for 'art' and 'the aesthetic'. Hence the blending of myth with aristocratic, or shamanic occultism. Myth was both universal truth and secret knowledge, available only to the adept or artist. Having evoked the resources uniquely available to the modern artist in ethnology and mythography, Eliot concluded his review of *Ulysses* with the assertion that 'only those who have won their own discipline in secret and without aid' can further the end of making the modern world intelligible and orderly.[20]

This derivation of a 'secret discipline' from the anthropology of Frazer, Jessie Weston and Jane Ellen Harrison is also at the heart of Mary Butts's work, in such novels as *Ashe of Rings* and *The Death of Felicity Taverner*. Butts, like Eliot, was fascinated by the legend of the Sanc Graal, or Holy Grail (that of the cup used by Christ at the Last Supper), which provided the principal focus of her second novel *Armed with Madness*, published in 1928. In an isolated house on the English coast a young woman, Scylla Taverner, lives with her brother Felix: 'They belonged to the house and the wood and the turf and the sea; had no money and the instincts of hospitality; wanted everything and nothing, and were at that moment lying out naked on a rock-spit which terminated their piece of land.'[21] At the opening of the novel a friend, Ross, is staying with them, and they are joined by an American, Carson, and two English friends, Picus and Clarence, who live nearby but come to stay when their well dries up and they are left without water. When cleaning out the well, 'an odd cup of

19 *The Cantos of Ezra Pound* (London: Faber & Faber, 1968), p. 12.
20 Eliot, '*Ulysses*, Order and Myth', p. 178.
21 Mary Butts, *Armed with Madness* (1928; Harmondsworth: Penguin, 2001), p. 4.

some greenish stone' is fished out with a spear, and brought to the Taverners' house. Thus begins what Scylla calls 'the sacred game', as the group play out sexually charged scenes in the presence, and absence, of a possible Grail. When it disappears for a time, 'they passed the morning entering and leaving rooms where the cup was not'. It is later revealed that Picus had stolen the cup from his father and planted it in the well. Yet, as Robin Blaser wrote:

> We never know whether the cup is simply a jade cup, an old altar vessel, an ashtray as it is once used in the novel, a spitting-cup, so used by Picus' father's mistress before her death, as the old man cruelly tells us, a poison cup out of the East – jade is said to detect poison – or the Sanc-Grail. It is of course, all of these in one way or another. In this way, Mary Butts tests the symbol and pursues her imaginative investigation of the condition of the sacred in our century.[22]

Myth and history

Myth always belongs to the past, which is to say that myth is always out of place in the modern world. Myth is always behindhand, returning from, or lingering into a time that is not that of its authentic rising. But what is this time of myth's authentic dawn? This time of this dawn is always indeterminate. According to the nineteenth-century historian of Greece, George Grote, myth belongs to 'a past that has never been present'. But this condition of temporal deracination is precisely what seems to make myth universally accessible and retrievable, a permanent fund (Philip Larkin dismissively called it the 'myth-kitty') on which literature and culture can draw freely without fear of depleting it. So one might say with quite as much justice that myth inhabits a present without a past. Presentless past, or pastless present, myth is neither a part of, nor wholly apart from history.

Perhaps in this myth resembles Modernism itself. For Modernism seems to conceive itself in a similarly ambivalent way. To be modern is to belong to history, in that one feels oneself with a peculiar intensity to be at the leading edge of time, conceives oneself and one's time to be the very work of time, shaping itself into futurity. And yet to be modern also involves the opposite of this, for feeling modern involves feeling oneself plucked out of the one-damn-thing-after-another of habitual time. A modern must feel himself to

22 Robin Blaser, 'Here Lies the Woodpecker Who Was Zeus', in *A Sacred Quest: The Life and Writings of Mary Butts*, ed. Christopher Wagstaff (Kingston, New York: McPherson, 1995), p. 171.

belong to a time in which time itself has the possibility of being redeemed. The analogies between revolutionary Modernism, whether the revolutions were taking place in the political sphere or in the sphere of artistic practice, and religious millenarianism are striking. For both, the present becomes a time out of time, the entering of the timeless into time. The time of myth seems to be an example of a similar intersection.

But Modernism's myth is characterised by another kind of temporal paradox. The premise of any number of books and articles, including, it would seem, this present one, is that Modernism both nurtured and was itself enriched by an intense, widespread and sustained engagement with the idea of myth. Like many of the characterising features of Modernism, this is not a view developed by Modernists themselves – or, at least, not by first-generation Modernists. Like the concept of Modernism itself, this perspective is put together after the event, and more specifically during the years after World War II during which the concept of Modernism was being forged.

As it happens, this was a period when a strong and self-conscious preoccupation with the nature of myth was coming to the fore. Although Jung had been writing throughout the century, it was only during the 1950s that his work came to be most widely known, especially in America. This was due in large part to the efforts of the American Joseph Campbell, who, more than any other writer, established the bond between Modernism and myth. After developing an interest in American–Indian ethnography and mythology, Campbell went to study in Paris and Munich, where he encountered the avant-garde art of Picasso and Joyce, along with the theories of Jung. After his return to the USA, he began to publish a series of works in which he attempted to revive the discipline of comparative mythology which had been waning since the beginning of the century. The first of his works in this vein was *A Skeleton Key to Finnegans Wake* (1944) co-authored with Henry Morton Robinson, a book that read Joyce's work in terms of Jungian patterns of conflict and resolution between male and female mythical figures. This was followed in 1946 by his study of myths of the hero, *The Hero With a Thousand Faces*, followed by *The Masks of God*, which appeared in four volumes from 1959 to 1967. Campbell insists on the deep and inescapable power of myth, and the insights it offers into the essential and eternal unity of mankind. 'The comparative study of the mythologies of the world compels us to view the cultural history of mankind as a unit', he writes.[23] But Campbell attempts to maintain a flexible and

[23] Joseph Campbell, *The Masks of God: Primitive Mythology* (New York: Viking, 1970), p. 3.

open-ended conception of this unity. *The Masks of God*, his own multi-volume *Golden Bough*, offers, not a 'key to all mythologies', or a Jungian call to integration with the archetypes, but rather the challenge of evolving a mythology that will not relapse into the local dogmatisms that have always impersonated universality.

> Communities that once were comfortable in the consciousness of their own mythologically guaranteed godliness find, abruptly, that they are devils in the eyes of their neighbours. Evidently some mythology of a broader, deeper kind than anything envisioned anywhere in the past is now required: some *arcanum arcanorum* far more fluid, more sophisticated, than the separate visions of the local traditions, wherein those mythologies themselves will be known to be the masks of a larger – all their shining pantheons but the flickering modes of a 'timeless *schema*' that is no *schema*.[24]

Literature and art remain at the heart of this enterprise of totalisation, and the idea that mythology consists in masking or dissimulation of the transcendent rather than a direct embodiment of the truth opens the door to the more pluralistic accounts of myth that have begun to flourish during the 1980s and 1990s, as myth has begun to be recruited to the 'postmodern'.

Another of the most important and influential documents of the myth-fifties was Northrop Frye's *Anatomy of Criticism*, a work that shifted the arguments of contemporary comparative mythology into the field of literary criticism, to produce a universal typology of literary modes. Frye is much more circumspect than other myth-critics, and concludes his work by remarking that 'a myth being a centripetal structure of meaning, it can be made to mean an indefinite number of things, and it is more fruitful to study what in fact myths have been made to mean'.[25] In fact, however, Frye's promise is to reunite the centrifugal nature of literary forms with their inaugural, coherence-giving archetypal forms, thus putting the idea of myth at the heart of a project of 're-forging the links between creation and knowledge, art and science, myth and concept'.[26]

In this period, a new conception of myth grew. Myth was now no longer an expression of subjugation to or immersion in primordial truth, but rather a positive form of self-making, the way in which man constructed, not just his relation to the world, but his world as such. The philosopher Ernst Cassirer

[24] Ibid., p. 18.
[25] Northrop Frye, *Anatomy of Criticism: Four Essays* (Princeton University Press, 1957), p. 341.
[26] Ibid., p. 354.

defined myth in terms which allowed it to be taken as a warrant of Modernist self-making:

> [M]yth, art, language, and science appear as symbols; not in the sense of mere figures which refer to some given reality by means of suggestion and allegorical meanings, but in the sense of forces, each of which produces and posits a world of its own.[27]

Myth, it began to be assumed, had much to do with Modernism. In fact, it looks as though the development of the myth of myth, and during this period rather than during the High Modernism of three decades, had much to do with the creation of the myth of Modernism. The role of myth is largely to maintain the myth of the modern. As Robert Ellwood suggests, rescuing the idea of myth from the apparently terminal discredit into which it might seem to have fallen, as a result of the tawdry and revolting excesses of the Nazi era, was important not just in forming the idea of Modernism, but also in preparing for the spreading of myth-theory into popular culture during the 1960s, which required, as he puts it, 'a curious movement of myth, archaism and Jungianism from political right to left in the intellectual spectrum'.[28]

The myth-consciousness which was built into the critical definitions of Modernism that were formed during the 1950s and 1960s, in which studies of the mythical structures of Modernist writing abounded, also encouraged the proliferation of seemingly second-generation Modernist mythopoeia – for example in the work of Ted Hughes – that was really the echo or reflection of the way in which first-generation Modernism was itself being constructed. More recently, the myth business has been given a shot in the arm by post-modernity, which allows some of the attitudes and ideals about myth projected into Modernism after the war to be claimed as part of a Postmodern turn away from the excesses and abstractions of modernity. Here, in other words, Postmodern myth updates and claims as its own the anti-modernity of Modernism. One recent example is a study of what is called the 'radical nostalgia' of J. R. R. Tolkien, one of the writers swept into popular success by the mythicist mindset of the 1950s. Patrick Curry argues that '[D]rawing on the power of ancient Indo-European myth, [Tolkien's works] invite the reader into a compelling and remarkably complete pre-modern world.'[29] The

[27] Ernst Cassirer, *Language as Myth*, trans. Susanne K. Langer (New York: Dover, 1953), p. 8.

[28] Robert Ellwood, *The Politics of Myth: A Study of C. G. Jung, Mircea Eliade, and Joseph Campbell* (Albany: State University of New York Press, 1999), pp. 4–5.

[29] Patrick Curry, *Defending Middle Earth: Tolkien, Myth and Modernity* (London: HarperCollins, 1998), p. 23.

difference between Postmodern myth and Modernist myth, it is claimed, is that, where Modernism sought single and universal truth in myth, postmodernity embraces myth's multiplicity. Michael Bell's more sophisticated rereading of Modernist myth-making as a form of cultural relativism rather than a reactionary retreat into authoritarian or nostalgic fantasy is evidence of the new, Postmodern inflection of myth, as is the work of Marina Warner.[30]

Conclusion

Modernity has always understood itself either as an effort to live without or after myth, or as an effort to recover the lost wholeness of myth. Max Weber's view of modernity as the 'disenchantment of the world' and the view of a more recent historian of myth that modern culture is characterised by an irresistible process of 're-mythification'[31] have in common the idea that modernity is the response to the demise of myth, disastrous or deliberated as it may be. The larger truth may be that there can be no myth before modernity, since modernity always invents myth, and in the process of inventing its relation to myth, invents itself. There must be myth in order for there to be the modernity that spurns or mourns it. This is not precisely what Theodor Adorno and Max Horkheimer meant when they evoked the paradoxical inseparability of myth and Enlightenment: 'Myth is already enlightenment, and enlightenment reverts to mythology.'[32] They meant that the idea of scientific rationality was insufficiently vigilant or self-aware to resist the process of becoming a kind of all-powerful ideology itself, which is to say, a narrative that governs and generates thought rather than being generated and governed by it. Writing in the aftermath of World War II, they clearly have in mind the grotesque alliance of archaic myth and technological rationality in evidence in Nazi Germany. But their formulation offers the suggestion that the very idea of the modern, as an absolute privation of the unity of being evidenced in the mythic condition, might itself be a willed illusion – or myth. If to be modern is to be cut off from, and to yearn once more to be, mythical or mythopoeic, then perhaps, as Bruno Latour suggests, we can never really have been modern, in that modernity has

30 Michael Bell, *Literature, Modernism and Myth: Belief and Responsibility in the Twentieth Century* (Cambridge University Press, 1997).

31 Eleazar M. Meletinsky, *The Poetics of Myth*, trans. Guy Lanoue and Alexandre Sadetsky (New York and London: Routledge, 2000), p. 17.

32 Theodor W. Adorno and Max Horkheimer, *Dialectic of Enlightenment: Philosophical Fragments*, ed. G. S. Noerr, trans. E. Jephcott (Stanford University Press, 2002), p. xviii.

so busily to keep inventing the object of its loss and yearning.[33] The loss and regaining of myth is the great founding, tragic, reparative myth of the modern. For the same reason that we have never been truly modern, we have never been, nor ever could be, 'mythic'. Perhaps we can only ever be, as we have always been (but always differently), between worlds, between times.

[33] Bruno Latour, *We Have Never Been Modern*, trans. Catherine Porter (London and New York: Harvester Wheatsheaf, 1993).

15

Psychoanalysis and literature

LYNDSEY STONEBRIDGE

In January 1939, Sigmund Freud presented Virginia Woolf with a narcissus. The gift, we can suppose, was a token of appreciation from the analyst to his English publishers. Thanks to the Woolfs' Hogarth Press, Freud's writings not only received a British audience, but were also introduced into the heart of the Bloomsbury enterprise. Perhaps unconsciously (or perhaps not) Freud's choice of a narcissus was particularly apposite for a writer who so often put the self at the centre of her work. Narcissus, the self-centred image-lover, speaks eloquently to certain strands of literary Modernism and to the psychoanalytic project. Both put the self at the centre of their enquiries, and both try to find a new language to describe that self or, to be more precise, try to render what is most obscure about that self newly intelligible. Indeed, one way to think about the relationship between psychoanalysis and literature in this period is as a joint venture in forging a new language for the unconscious. From the science of the psyche and the art of the modern writer emerges a distinctly modern materialism for the dreamworld. But, and this is a paradox that lies at the heart of both psychoanalysis and literary Modernism, the self that both return to endlessly in this endeavour is not, as it were, in full possession of itself, but is rather characterised by a recognition of the limits of its own self-knowledge. What the Modernist poet and the free-associating patient both do, the psychoanalyst and critic Adam Phillips has argued, is inject 'something irreducibly enigmatic into the culture, something no one quite knows what to do with'.[1]

The history of the relation between psychoanalysis and English literature is the history of various and diverse attempts to name that enigmatic something. Where some, like the poet H. D. (Hilda Doolittle), found a new poetry of the unconscious in analysis, others, like Woolf herself, defined their work

[1] Adam Phillips, 'The Soul of Man under Psychoanalysis', *Equalities* (London: Faber & Faber, 2002), p. 140.

not only with Freud, but *against* psychoanalysis: indeed for Woolf and others psychoanalysis was all too often not enigmatic enough. Neither were analysts themselves immune from the influence of the work of their contemporaries: as this chapter will suggest, the development of psychoanalysis in early twentieth-century England was also characterised by its own particular engagement with art and literature. Whereas in France the relationship between Surrealism, for example, and the radical psychoanalyst Jacques Lacan defined a kind of avant-garde unconscious for an entire generation, in England a distinctly different kind of pattern emerged. Psychoanalysis was at once received as a science of the new: hence its appeal to socialists, feminists and educationalists, as well as to writers, scientists and philosophers. Yet possibly because it was a distinctively modern type of materialism of the unconscious, psychoanalysis was also appreciated for its power to comprehend not only Eros, the more progressive partner in Freud's famous opposition, but Thanatos, death. Shaped by two world wars, the dialogue between psychoanalysis and literature turned, on the one hand, on the recognition that what is most enigmatic about our natures could also be what is most morbid and destructive and, on the other, on the question of sublimation, of how our enigmatic desires might indeed be named and harnessed to culture and progress.

The age of nerves

In some senses, Freud's work entered British culture under the sign of death. Bizarrely perhaps for this most secular of thinkers, Freud's writings on hysteria were cited as evidence of life after death in 1893 in the work of F. W. H. Myers, President of the Society for Psychical Research, founded in 1882 by a group of Cambridge intellectuals with the aim of developing a 'materialist approach to the immaterial world'.[2] The Society was the intellectual wing of a more widespread interest in the occult. If, the thinking at the turn of the century went, the post-Darwinian soul no longer belonged to God, another way of thinking about death had to be found. Ghosts began to interfere in the everyday life of the new secular age. In this context, Myers's reference to Freud is not as bizarre as it first appears. Drawing a parallel between the states of hysteria, telepathy and clairvoyance, Myers observed that all indicate the presence of something very similar to what Freud at the time was calling the unconscious.[3] Talking to the dead, like listening to the voices of past familial loves in the

[2] Robert Hinshelwood, 'Psychoanalysis in Britain: Points of Cultural Access, 1893–1918', *The International Journal of Psychoanalysis*, 76, 1 (February 1995), p. 136.
[3] Ibid., p. 137.

narratives of hysterics, as Freud and his colleague Josef Breuer were doing in the 1890s, pointed to the existence of a realm well beyond consciousness, a hidden part of the self.

Typically for its time, the Society for Psychical Research adopted a rigorously scientific approach to the occult and to the psyche; and it is this empirical emphasis, as much as the seductive otherworldliness of the spectacle of the hysteric that made Freud attractive to its members, who thought enough of his work to request that he submit a paper to their *Proceedings* in 1912. In that paper, 'A Note on the Unconscious', Freud emphasised how although the unconscious may produce enigmas, it has a set of laws and structures which can make its own mysteries intelligible. For Freud, psychoanalysis was above all a 'natural science', whose aim, he had already stated as early as 1895, was to 'represent psychical processes as quantitatively determined states of specifiable material particles and so to make them perspicuous and void of contradiction'.[4] It was this emphasis on intelligibility, on making the hidden self opaque, that so impressed Leonard Woolf when, in the first non-scientific notice of Freud's work in 1914, he reviewed the American A. Brill's translation of Freud's *The Psychopathology of Everyday Life*:

> It is [Freud's] aim to show that it is the 'dark half' of the mind which in the perfectly normal waking man produces all kinds of trivial errors and slips and forgettings and rememberings, and which under other conditions will, following the same laws, produce the absurd fantasies of sleep or the terrible fantasies of madness.[5]

The unconscious is responsible equally for our daytime bungling and the terrors of the dreamer, the neurotic or psychotic: all are subject to the 'same laws'. For Woolf, then, as for the psychical researchers, Freud was significant not only because he drew attention to the sheer force of the unconscious, but also because he insisted on the value of interpretation. The unconscious can be rendered plain and free from contradiction: that is the promise offered by psychoanalysis – the 'greatest promise', H. G. Wells went so far as to note, 'in the science of the present time'.[6]

[4] Sigmund Freud, 'The Project for a Scientific Psychology' (1895), *The Standard Edition of the Complete Psychological Works of Sigmund Freud*, trans. James Strachey, 24 vols. (London: Hogarth Press, 19xx), I p. 295.

[5] Leonard Woolf, 'Review of Freud's *Psychopathology of Everyday Life*', *New Weekly*, I, 13 (June 1914), p. 412, rpt. in *A Bloomsbury Group Reader*, ed. S. P. Rosenbaum (Oxford: Blackwell, 1993), p. 191.

[6] Quoted in Dean Rapp, 'The Reception of Freud by the British Press: General Interest and Literary Magazines, 1920–1925', *Journal of the History of the Behavioral Sciences*, 24 (April 1988), p. 193.

The more that the psyche becomes subject to science, however, the spookier it seems to get. As Henry James (whose philosopher brother, William, was a member of the Society for Psychical Research) also understood, the empirical study of the psyche – and the psychic – raises a bewildering set of epistemological issues. What precisely is it that spooks the hysteric was Freud and Breuer's question in *Studies in Hysteria* (1895); the same question that James forces us to ask but resolutely refuses to resolve in his psychological gothic classic, *The Turn of the Screw* (1898). Sexual trauma was Freud's first answer to this question; a position that famously he later revised, claiming that our early *fantasies* about sexuality can be not only as significant as any real event, but even more so. When Freud says that hysterics suffer mainly from reminiscences, what he means is that they are bothered by memories of a traumatic sexual nature that cannot be admitted into culture. It is the unspeakable enigma of our earliest desire, in other words, that founds the unconscious itself.

It was one thing, as many writers, thinkers and scientists did, to accept the existence of the unconscious, but quite another to take on Freud's emphasis on seduction and sexuality. Indeed, it was precisely the sexual component of the Freudian enigma that was rejected at the very moment at which psychoanalysis really began to come of age in British culture. World War I witnessed the emergence of the soldier hysteric, the gibbering, war-ravaged, hollow men who began to fill up the field hospitals in France with strange and disturbing symptoms. Originally thought to be suffering from the impact of shelling (hence 'shell-shock') as the war progressed, some began to explore the idea that these men too might be suffering from unbearable memories, that shock might be a form of conversion hysteria. The Cambridge anthropologist W. H. R. Rivers is probably the best-known exponent of Freud from this time, largely thanks to Pat Barker's recent fictionalisation of his relationship with the poets Siegfried Sassoon and Wilfred Owen at Craiglockhart Hospital, Edinburgh, in her *Regeneration* trilogy.[7] Craiglockart, Sassoon later noted, was an 'underworld of dreams haunted by submerged memories of warfare'.[8] By listening to those dreams and interpreting those memories, Rivers began to conclude that although Freud was wrong to insist on the link between sexuality and repression (this is the same Rivers whose own ambivalent sexuality was to play such a part in the creative tension in his relation with Sassoon), he was right about the nature of psychical conflict, and that this aspect of his work might

7 Pat Barker, *Regeneration* (1991), *The Eye in the* Door (1993) and *The Ghost Road* (1995).

8 Siegfried Sassoon, *Sherston's Progress* (1936; London: Faber & Faber, 1988), p. 51.

help unravel the terrors of war neurosis. Rivers's *Instincts and the Unconscious* (1922) was read widely during the immediate post-war period, and his kind of de-sexualised psychoanalysis, like that in the work of Carl Jung, found a receptive audience in post-war English culture. For his part, Freud would later reply to wartime criticisms of his emphasis on the libido, with a hypothesis about a darker and more deadly component of our instincts – the death drive.

It is often claimed that the war marked Freud's definitive arrival in British literary culture, and to a certain extent this is true. However, it is probably more accurate to say that Freud's influence had already begun to be felt by intellectuals and writers by the eve of the war. Brill's translation of *The Interpretation of Dreams* was published in 1913, quickly followed by *The Psychopathology of Everyday Life* (1914). The London Society of Psycho-Analysis was established by Ernest Jones, the most important figure in the foundation of psychoanalysis in Britain, in 1913 (re-established as the British Society of Psycho-Analysis in 1919), as was the more eclectic Medico-Psychological Clinic of London. One year later, the British Society for the Study of Sexology was founded; its leading exponent, Havelock Ellis, was also briefly an admirer of Freud. An early reviewer of Freud and Breuer's *Studies on Hysteria*, Ellis initially saw Freud as an ally in the fight for sexual freedom and introduced his work to figures such as Edward Carpenter, and the writer and feminist, Olive Schreiner, as well as the poet H. D.[9] Later Ellis would dismiss Freud as 'an artist, not a scientist' – precisely the feature of his work that attracted so many writers.

Among those writers who, like Freud and Ellis, understood the extraordinary power of unconscious sexual desire was, of course, D. H. Lawrence. Lawrence came across Freud's work through his German wife, Frieda Weekley, and was also friends with the radical Jewish socialist David Eder (with Jones, the first to practise psychoanalysis in Britain), Edith Eder and Barbara Low (author of the popular *Psycho-Analysis: A Brief Account of the Freudian Theory*, 1920). Lawrence, an early enthusiast for the progressive potential of psychoanalysis, apparently once approached Ernest Jones with the idea of establishing a colony in Mexico to be run on psychoanalytic principles – a sort of utopia devoted to sexual individualism.[10] Like Freud, Lawrence understood how repression turns sexuality into something deadly and lethal, as he was to explore with biting precision in works such as 'The Prussian Officer'('It is lust fermented makes atrocity', Lawrence noted),[11] and 'The Thorn in the Flesh', two

[9] Hinshelwood, 'Psychoanalysis in Britain', p. 138. [10] Ibid., p. 143.

[11] Quoted in Mark Kinkead-Weeks, *D. H. Lawrence: Triumph to Exile, 1912–1922* (Cambridge University Press, 1996), p. 77.

German Soldier short stories published in 1914. Yet precisely because Lawrence embraced the power of sexuality in his writing – it was the unrestricted libidinal economy of Lawrence's prose that later earned him such praise in Felix Guattari and Gilles Deleuze's *Anti-Oedipus* (1977) – he was impatient with what he saw as Freud's conservatism. De-sublimation, not sublimation, is Lawrence's answer to Freud's melancholy insistence on the inevitability of our cultural discontents. Between 1919 and 1920, Lawrence set out his disagreement with psychoanalysis in two works, *Psychoanalysis and the Unconscious* (1921) and *Fantasia of the Unconscious* (1922). The word 'Fantasia' marks the significant difference between the two: Lawrence's unconscious was to be a radically creative force, not something subject to the determining laws of science.

Lawrence was initially sympathetic to psychoanalysis (although his knowledge of Freud was probably only second- or third-hand), because like other writers he saw that Freud was attempting to understand a thoroughly modern dilemma: how can we narrate our life stories when so much happens to us unconsciously; what kind of knowledge is unconscious knowledge and what sort of writing might capture it? How is it possible to rise to the challenge of what a 1917 report on the activities of the Medico-Psychological Clinic of London described as 'this age of "nerves"'?[12] By the war, it was as if people were becoming quite literally sick with modern culture. In 1917, the Clinic was not only treating shell-shocked soldiers, but non-combatants 'suffering from war-panic, overstrain, insomnia and every form of war disaster' too.[13] The brainchild of Dr Jessie Murray, a physician who had worked with Pierre Janet, the Clinic was conceived with the aim of providing access to new forms of therapy, including psychoanalysis, to all who needed it. Like many of the psychoanalytically inspired projects set up at the time, its impulse was radically egalitarian. One of the Clinic's most important patrons and members was the novelist May Sinclair. It was Sinclair who coined the term 'Orthopsychics' to describe the eclectic subject of the Clinic's educational wing, the 'Society for the Study of Orthopsychics', whose students included women who were to become some of the country's most significant psychoanalysts: Ella Freeman Sharpe, Susan Isaacs and Marjorie Brierley. The Society was devoted to the 'study of human character, social and individual', as were indeed, through their growing engagement with psychoanalysis, Sinclair's novels of this period.

[12] Quoted in Theophilus E. M. Boll, 'May Sinclair and the Medico-Psychological Clinic of London', *The Proceedings of the American Philosophical Society*, 106, 4 (1962), p. 319.

[13] Ibid., p. 317.

It is in May Sinclair's writing that psychoanalysis and literary Modernism stage what is perhaps one of their most visible encounters. Sinclair came to psychoanalysis both through her passion for idealism and, following a route that many took and continue to take, through her feminism. Where the first offered the promise of the transformation of the self through thought, the second taught Sinclair how this project was inhibited by gender. Psychoanalysis provided a bridge between the two by, on the one hand, giving an analysis of psychic subjection and, on the other, offering the promise of sublimation. Two late novels, *Mary Olivier: A Life* (1919) and *The Life and Death of Harriett Frean* (1922), retell a familiar story about the subjugation of female passion – a story Sinclair had told before and had worked with in her writing on the Brontë sisters – which engages both with psychoanalysis and, as significantly, with the question of how one might begin to tell a progressive determinist story in a distinctly modern idiom. Sinclair forges a brilliant kind of erotics of subjection in these novels. 'Mamma's breast: a smooth, cool, round thing that hung to your hands and slipped from them when they tried to hold it', is how Sinclair describes Mary Olivier's infant life, for example.[14] For Melanie Klein, who was to arrive in Britain permanently in 1926, as for Sinclair, the discovery was that guilt and inhibition begin in a maternal embrace.

Sinclair was not alone in tracking female subjectivity back to the maternal, the shadowy realm where Freud would only venture hesitatingly and reluctantly. In her account of her analysis with Freud in the 1930s, *Tribute to Freud* (1970), H. D.'s symptom, the hallucinated writing on the wall, is traced back to maternal union ('The Professor translated the pictures on the wall [. . .] as desire for union with my mother').[15] Just as visionary, and just as full of creative potential, is the neo-Platonic scene in Woolf's *To the Lighthouse* (1927) where Lily Briscoe throws her arms around Mrs Ramsay's knees ('What device for becoming like waters poured into one jar, inextricably the same, one with the object one adored? [. . .] Could loving, as people called it, make her and Mrs. Ramsay one?')[16]. But whereas the maternal in both H. D. and Woolf could be read as offering an alternative path for art and subjectivity, for Sinclair, as for Jung, whom Sinclair had begun to study during the war, the desire that binds us to the mother is the cause of our subjection, not an escape from it.[17] Sinclair's characters, to paraphrase a more recent psychoanalytic commentator, love their symptoms as they once loved their mothers.

[14] May Sinclair, *Mary Olivier: A Life* (1919; London: Virago, 1980), p. 4.
[15] Hilda Doolittle (H. D.), *Tribute to Freud* (London: Karnac, 1970), p. 44.
[16] Virginia Woolf, *To the Lighthouse* (1927; Harmondsworth: Penguin, 1992), p. 57.
[17] Suzanne Raitt, *May Sinclair: A Modern Victorian* (Oxford University Press, 2000), p. 228.

In *Mary Olivier* Sinclair offers sublimation, in a notably non-Freudian form, as one answer to a life of oppression and repression. Mary is not, like the Freudian hysteric, bound to her desire: she accepts the life of a dutiful daughter, but finds happiness as a poet. However, nor is she, like the Freudian creative artist or like, indeed, her contemporary, James Joyce's Stephen Dedalus, able to transform perversity into creativity, her daydreams into art. Mary's imagination exists to one side of her sexuality, dynamic, as Jung might say, not drive-bound. With its shifting use of pronouns, *Mary Olivier* experiments with a distinctly modern narrative voice, as does the much thinner, in many senses, *The Life and Death of Harriett Frean*. The later novel presents a life lived without the prospect of sublimation. Harriett exists in a morbid familial rapture, a sort of living death with no prospect of an escape into the life of the mind that redeems Mary Olivier. Compared to Mary's abundance of imagination, Harriett has a parsimonious psychic economy, as Sinclair explores through a tightly restricted use of symbols and images. This is a novel about waste, told with nothing wasted. Read the two novels together, and it is clear that for Sinclair only a willed kind of sublimation keeps us away from a desire that can only *ever* be moribund and self-destructive.

Sinclair's experiments with the image in her fiction were the product of her engagement with both psychoanalysis and Imagism. Despite a similar emphasis on the visual nature of psychic experience, where Imagism insisted on the direct treatment of the thing, psychoanalysis begins with the assumption that images can never directly present any one thing, but rather are always phonetically and semantically contiguous. As Freud argued so forcefully in *The Interpretation of Dreams* (1900), the enigmatic images of the dreamworld are neither random nor mysterious, but articulate the desire of the dreamer through the language of the dreamwork. The dreamworld has a set of 'laws' (to return to Leonard Woolf's review of Freud) which enable us to read the unconscious. It is perhaps no accident that it was two literary critics who were to mine this insight for its full potential. William Empson's extraordinary and exhilarating work on the ambiguity of poetic language owed a marked debt to Freud.[18] Similarly Ella Freeman Sharpe, a former pupil of the Society for the Study of Orthopsychics, literature teacher and analyst (to, among others, Woolf's brother, Adrian Stephen) was intrigued by the possibilities of approaching the mechanisms of dreams through the 'avenue of the accepted

[18] See William Empson, *Seven Types of Ambiguity* (1930; Harmondsworth: Penguin, 1995), and *The Structure of Complex Words* (1951; London: Hogarth Press, 1985).

characteristics of poetic diction'.[19] For Sharpe, it is not so much the symbol that dominates the dream (by contrast it was the Jungian symbol with its balance of opposites that preoccupied Sinclair), but the work of simile and metaphor, metonymy and synecdoche, which she links to Freud's concept of 'displacement'. Anticipating a similar move by Jacques Lacan (for whom, famously, the unconscious is structured like a language), Sharpe was one of the first to build a direct bridge between psychoanalysis and literature. For her, as for Lacan, if the unconscious can be known at all it is because it speaks.

Psychoanalysis, then, like much Modernist literature, set itself the task of finding a language to articulate the muted malaise of the modern soul. Freud's influence had begun to be felt at the turn of the century because it seemed he knew how to speak to modernity's new dead. By the beginning of the 1920s, psychoanalysis had emerged fully, along with cinema, avant-garde poetry and modern fiction, as one of the new sciences of necrophilia, shovelling up corpses with all the decorum of the Modernist poet. Psychoanalysis, noted a hostile reviewer in 1921 in *Outlook*, exemplifies 'the word modern, in its most nauseous form'.[20]

Bloomsbury Freud

Modernist writers themselves, however, did not always recognise any affinity with psychoanalysis. Far from it. The problem with Sinclair's *The Life and Death of Harriett Frean*, wrote T. S. Eliot in a review in the *Dial*, is that 'because the material is so clearly defined (the soul of man under psychoanalysis) there is no possibility of tapping the atmosphere of unknown terror and mystery in which our life is passed and which psychoanalysis has not yet analysed'.[21] Katherine Mansfield agreed: Sinclair's war novel, *The Romantic* (1920), she wrote, is under 'the eclipse of psychoanalysis'.[22] By the 1920s Modernist complaints that psychoanalysis threatened to render the most pressing questions about modern subjectivity as a banal recitation of the comi-tragedy of repressed desire were as common as endorsements of Freud and his work. For some it was possible to know your symptoms all too well and all too tediously, as Virginia Woolf lamented in a 1921 review of J. D. Beresford, 'Freudian Fiction', a point she

[19] Ella Freeman Sharpe, *Dream Analysis: A Practical Handbook for Psychoanalysts* (1937; London: Karnac, 1978), pp. 18–19.

[20] Quoted in Rapp, 'The Reception of Freud', p. 198.

[21] T. S. Eliot, 'London Letter, August 1922', *Dial*, 73 (September 1922), p. 330.

[22] Quoted in Rait, *May Sinclair*, p. 140.

would later drive home in a caricature of Freud's writing in a letter to Molly McCarthy in 1924.[23] But if these writers wanted to establish a distance from Freud, it was not only because psychoanalysis seemed so alien to them, but because it had moved – quite literally – a little too close to home.

In early 1924 James Strachey, younger brother of Lytton, persuaded the Woolfs to publish Freud's writing under the imprint of the International Psycho-Analytic Library. By 1925, four volumes of Freud's *Collected Papers*, translated under the editorship of Ernest Jones, had appeared. Freud had arrived in Bloomsbury. Five years earlier Strachey and his wife, Alix Strachey, had travelled to Vienna to be analysed by Freud himself. (They were following a trend: in 1919 Adrian Stephen and his wife, Karin, the Bergson scholar and niece of Bertrand Russell, had begun analysis with the former President of the Medico-Psychological Clinic, James Glover.) It was to be a propitious meeting. Within weeks, Freud had asked the Stracheys to translate a new paper, Freud's study of the masochistic fantasies that subtend our most sadistic of wishes, 'A Child is Being Beaten', a fittingly punishing choice of text perhaps for, from Freud's perspective, these two most English of Bloomsbury bohemians. As Perry Meisel and Walter Kendrick have suggested, in the Stracheys Freud saw 'the appropriate sensibility for rendering his work into the only tongue besides German to which he deeply responded – the language of his favourite poet, Milton, embellished with the wry urbanity of contemporary aestheticism'.[24] The Stracheys, however wry and urbane in their cultural lives, nonetheless believed that Freud, if he were to be received into English culture, had to be presented foremost as a type of scientist familiar to the English empiricist tradition. As James Strachey was to write much later, in his preface to the monumental *The Standard Edition of the Complete Psychological Works of Sigmund Freud*, he kept before him continually as he translated an 'imaginary model of the writings of some English man of science of wide education born in the middle of the nineteenth century. And I should like to add, in an explanatory and no patriotic spirit, to emphasise the word English.'[25] Out of this

[23] Virginia Woolf, 'Freudian Fiction' (Review of *An Imperfect Mother* (1921), by J. D. Beresford), rpt in *Contemporary Writers* (London: Hogarth Press, 1965), pp. 152–4. 'I glance at the proof and read how Mr A. B. threw a bottle of red ink on to the sheets of his marriage bed to excuse his impotence to the housemaid, but threw it in the wrong place, which unhinged his wife's mind, – and to this day she pours claret on the dinner table.' Letter to Molly MacCarthy, 2 October 1924, *The Letters of Virginia Woolf*, ed. Nigel Nicolson, 6 vols. (London: Hogarth Press, 1975–80), vol. III, *A Change of Perspective*, 1923–1928, pp. 134–5.

[24] Perry Meisel and Walter Kendrick, eds., *Bloomsbury/Freud: The Letters of James and Alix Strachey 1924–25* (London: Chatto & Windus, 1986), p. x.

[25] James Strachey, 'Preface', *The Standard Edition of the Complete Psychological Works of Sigmund Freud*, I, p. xix.

mutual mis-identification of the meaning of 'Englishness', came the version of Freud with which most English-speaking readers are now familiar. As critics of Strachey's translation have long protested, in the process Freud's original prose was deprived of its own wry urbanity and literary sophistication. As eloquent and scrupulous as the translation is, its use of scientific jargon – Strachey's decisions, for example, to render the German *die Seele* or *selisch* (soul) as 'mind' or 'mental'; *der Trieb* (drive) as instinct and *Shaulust* (looking pleasure or voyeurism) as 'scopophilia' – meant that the very contemporary aestheticism Freud might have been looking for was often lost in translation.

The decision to make Freud seem more like a natural scientist than even he had declared himself to be was political as well as cultural. Precisely because psychoanalysis had begun to have a popular currency by the 1920s, for Freud's followers it was imperative that his work be distinguished from the occultism and mysticism of his former acolyte, Carl Jung. The crude reductionism of 'Jungite offshits', as Alix Strachey referred to them, was not to be allowed to contaminate the science of psychoanalysis.[26] Yet it was also because Freud seemed to be offering a materialist account not only of the psyche but, far worse for Modernist aestheticism, of art itself, that his work was criticised by much of Bloomsbury. In 1924, Clive Bell led the attack with the publication of his rebarbative 'Dr Freud on Art' in the *Nation and Athenaeum*, sparking a debate that would go on for some weeks. Earlier in the same year, the artist and critic Roger Fry had elaborated his own formalist aesthetics in opposition to psychoanalysis in an address to the British Psychological Society, later published as a Hogarth Pamphlet, *The Artist and Psycho-Analysis* (1924). For Fry, the problem with Freud was not necessarily that he discovered the origins of sublimation in desire and phantasy, but that while such an account might well suffice for popular forms of art such as romantic fiction and cinema, it fails to appreciate the emotional and psychic significance of pure form. When it comes to art, Fry argues, Freudianism ignores its own strictures about repression: as a consequence the daydreams of the creative artist simply do not seem very interesting. Fry's polemic, then, is another version of the complaint that psychoanalysis is not enigmatic enough about its own enigmas. What if, asks Fry, we start to ask questions about the 'psychological meaning of emotion about forms' instead? What, this question might be rephrased as asking, is the psychic significance of Modernist formalism?[27] A little later, as we will see, a second generation of British analysts will endeavour to answer Fry's question.

[26] Meisel and Kendrick, *Bloomsbury / Freud*, p. 47.

[27] Roger Fry, *The Artist and Psychoanalysis*, Hogarth Essay Series (London: Hogarth Press, 1924), p. 8.

If psychoanalysis seemed unsuited to Bloomsbury aesthetic formalism, it found more luck with another contemporary experimental genre, biography. A keen reader of his work, it may well have been the wry urbanity of Lytton Strachey that Freud hoped he might find in his brother. The famous passage towards the end of his biography of Queen Victoria (1921) where Strachey's narrator enters the head of the dying Queen as she free-associates back to her infancy (a technique that Sinclair will also use in the final pages of *Harriett Frean*), recalls the association between death, the psyche and the language of the unconscious that had attracted some of Freud's earlier admirers. By 1928, Strachey's debt to Freud in *Elizabeth and Essex* (dedicated to James and Alix) had become explicit. As 'a historian', Freud wrote to Strachey, 'you show that you are steeped in the spirit of psychoanalysis.'[28] Similarly steeped were new psychoanalytic attempts at autobiography. On the eve of her analytic training, Marion Milner (writing under the name of Joanna Field) wrote two experimental autobiographies using her psychoanalytic insight: *A Life of One's Own* (1934), with its echoes of Woolf's famous essay, and *An Experiment in Leisure* (1937). In common with other psychoanalytically inspired autobiographical works, Milner's books demonstrate how even as psychoanalysis offers a new language for the self, that very language makes self-knowledge more, not less, elusive. It is as if, once unleashed, the language of the unconscious returns to disrupt the process of self-description. 'A study in the use of masochism', is Milner's subtitle, for example, for her experiment in narrating a modern life of apparent leisure.

Despite their commitment to maintaining Freud's scientific reputation, his translators themselves understood the complexity of the relationship between unconscious phantasy and language better than most. Joan Riviere, one of Freud's most significant and eloquent translators and, like the Stracheys, analysed by Freud himself, was one of the first to draw parallels between literary Modernism and psychoanalysis noting, for instance, the destructive desire underpinning Eliot's *The Waste Land* and the 'concrete realism' of phantasy in Apollinaire's *Alcools*.[29] Similarly, James Strachey, in an extraordinary 1930 paper, pursued the oral, coprophagic and sexual underbelly of the act of reading. Whereas the modern-day mental states of the 'novel-reader, the cinema-goer, the wireless-listener and the rest' suggest 'that their nourishment is liquid and

[28] Quoted in Meisel and Kendrik, *Bloomsbury / Freud*, p. 332.

[29] Joan Riviere, 'The Unconscious Phantasy of an Inner World reflected in Literature', in Melanie Klein, Paula Heimann, R. E. Money-Kyrle, eds., *New Directions in Psycho-Analysis: The Significance of Infant Conflict in the Pattern of Adult Behaviour* (1955; London: Karnac, 1985), pp. 346–69.

that they are sucking it',[30] Strachey argues in this paper, with a characteristically Bloomsbury emphasis on aesthetic discrimination, real reading (like chewing over dense passages of Freud?) is an altogether more ambivalent affair. Reading is an act of cannibalistic aggression: 'And now comes the reader, the son, hungry, voracious, destructive and defiling in his turn, eager to force his way into his mother, to find out what is inside her, to tear his father's traces out of her, to devour them, to make them his own, and to be fertilised by them himself.'[31] To read, implies Freud's translator, is to eat the father's words. As with Riviere's writing, what is so striking in Strachey's article is not just the way that language is imbricated with the drives, but the emphasis on the destructive and violent nature of those drives. In this, both translators are following a slight shift of emphasis in Freud's own work.

The Freud that became 'Bloomsbury Freud' had revised his earlier hypothesis about the pleasure-seeking nature of the libido. Post-war, it was the prospect of a drive that compelled the subject to repeated acts of self-annihilation and which turned outwards to unleash its violence against the world that preoccupied an increasingly pessimistic Freud. By the 1920s, psychoanalysis was concerned with what happens when the enigma of violent death enters the culture at large. When Alix Strachey went to Berlin between 1924 and 1925 to complete her analysis with Karl Abraham, she and her colleagues at the Berlin Polyclinic were confronted with some of Freud's most dark and complex writings: 'Mourning and Melancholia' (1917), *Beyond the Pleasure Principle* (1920), *The Ego and the Id* (1923), 'The Economic Problem of Masochism' (1924) and 'On Negation'(1925). Arguably, the grim intellectual emphasis of the psychoanalysis she returned with was to help inflect the cultural reception of psychoanalysis in the 1920s and 1930s. This was certainly the case with the work of the psychoanalyst Alix Strachey invited back to London with her, Melanie Klein.

The destructive element

In late 1925 Melanie Klein gave a series of lectures on child analysis in Karin and Adrian Stephens's living room. For some of that time, Virginia Woolf was sitting just next door working on the first drafts of *To the Lighthouse*.[32]

[30] James Strachey, 'Some Unconscious Factors in Reading', *International Journal of Psycho-Analysis*, 11 (1930), p. 325.
[31] Ibid., p. 331.
[32] Elizabeth Abel, *Virginia Woolf and the Fictions of Psychoanalysis* (Chicago and London: University of Chicago Press, 1989), p. 13.

'I suppose', Woolf wrote of her novel some years later, 'that I did for myself what psycho-analysts do for their patients. I expressed some very long felt and deeply felt emotion. And in expressing it I explained it and then laid it to rest.'[33] Woolf's emphasis on writing as a kind of mourning chimes with one of Klein's central themes in a way that perhaps neither could have imagined in 1925. Working with children, Klein had discovered that the psychic mechanisms governing our relation to loss and grief that Freud had described so eloquently in 'Mourning and Melancholia' form the bedrock of human subjectivity. A bundle of drives and instincts, the Kleinian infant initially has a paranoid and schizophrenic relation to the outside world. In the first four months of life, there is no stable boundary between inside and outside, love and hate, destruction and persecution, only anxiety exacerbated by the sheer strength of an overwhelmingly destructive drive. As soon as the mother comes into focus as a 'whole object', however, a sort of guilty mourning sets in as the infant begins to fear for the consequences of the damage it has done to the mother in phantasy. The baby becomes a little depressive, anxious to atone for his aggression and make the mother good again. In Klein's work, then, Freud's death-drive found a new role in a profoundly elegiac narrative about the origins of psychic life.

Whereas its mortuary erotics and aesthetics had touched the literary imagination, in Britain psychoanalysis had never really been appreciated for its sexual radicalism (unlike say, in France or Weimar Germany). Similarly, where other literary movements, such as Expressionism and Surrealism, seized on the idea of the unconscious for its potential as a radically expressive force for the self, for Bloomsbury and other British Modernists, the emphasis seemed to be less on the disruptive promise of modern subjectivity than on its melancholic survival within the intricacies of form and language. With her permanent arrival in Britain in 1926, Klein and her emphasis on mourning found a cultural home for psychoanalysis where the themes of death and sublimation could be realised fully. 'All creation', one of Klein's most devoted and lucid followers, Hanna Segal, later wrote,

> is really a re-creation of a once loved and once whole, but now lost and ruined object, a ruined internal world and self. It is when the world within us is destroyed, when it is dead and loveless, when our loved ones are in fragments, and we ourselves in helpless despair – it is then that we must re-create our

[33] Virginia Woolf, 'A Sketch of the Past' (1939–40), *Moments of Being* (1976), ed. Jeanne Schulkind (London: Grafton Press, 1982), p. 94.

> world anew, reassemble the pieces, infuse life into the dead fragments, re-create life.[34]

The immediate reference here is to Proust (without, note, the perversity), but the passage also elegantly summarises Klein's emphasis on the intimate relation between death, guilt and creativity. These are the emotions about form that Roger Fry was looking for, Segal will later argue. Out of 'all the chaos and destruction', the artist 'has created a world which is whole, complete and unified'.[35] 'It is only by putting it into words that I can make it whole', wrote Woolf in a similar vein in her memoir, 'A Sketch of the Past', 'it gives, perhaps, because by doing so I take away the pain, a great delight to put the severed parts together.'[36] And indeed, like Lily Briscoe in *To the Lighthouse*, Kleinian analysands are frequently to be found putting the past to rest by putting a purple triangle there, a line there, in the centre; making formal wholes out of the muddle of memory and desire.

Such an aesthetic is open to the charge that it valorises art over life. As art repairs and improves our relation to our loved objects, those objects themselves start to spin away from the phenomenal world.[37] In this psychoanalysis might be said to share one of the characteristic features of much literary Modernism: it begins with the premise of cultural and psychic violence only to inflate the redemptive power of art itself. Yet in other ways psychoanalysis was used by some as a kind of escape from the more troubling psychic and political implications of literary Modernism. An important figure in this respect is the artist and art critic, Adrian Stokes. Stokes had always been interested in Freud. His two early dense but exuberant works of art history, *The Quattro Cento* (1932) and *The Stones of Rimini* (1935), show a marked debt to Freudian theories of representation. Significantly, these works also bear the traces of Stokes's affinity with the man he had met at a tennis match in Rapallo, Italy, in 1926, Ezra Pound. Quattrocento art, noted Stokes, has an alliance with 'the immediacy of the poet's image':[38] it shares a kind of mastery, an objectivisation or 'carving', to use Stokes's term, of the world remade through the will of the artist. However, a third volume on Italy in which Pound was to figure centrally was abandoned. Instead, Stokes spent the early 1930s in analysis with Melanie

34 Hanna Segal, 'A Psycho-Analytical Approach to Aesthetics', *New Directions in Psychoanalysis*, p. 390.

35 Ibid., pp. 399–400.

36 Virginia Woolf, 'A Sketch of the Past', pp. 83–4.

37 See Leo Bersani, *The Culture of Redemption* (Cambridge, MA: Harvard University Press, 1990).

38 Adrian Stokes, 'Painting, Giorgione and Barbaro', *Criterion*, 9 (April 1930), p. 489.

Klein. Post-Klein, Stokes's writing refigures his earlier aesthetics. 'Carving' is now an act of depressive reparation. The effort to restore the integrity of the object is still there in his writing, but the emphasis on mastery has faded. Psychoanalysis, for Stokes at least, thus becomes an exploration of the ways in which art can teach us to survive loss *without* sacrificing the integrity of the world to our desires.

In common with others writing in 1930s, Stokes's work of this period is laced with forebodings about Fascism and war. For many, it was as if Freud's death-drive and the violent ravages of Kleinian phantasy had slithered off the analytic couch and started to roam the culture as a whole. In 1939 the Hogarth Press published a selection of Freud's writings on war and culture, *Civilisation, War and Death*, in their Epitome series. The volume found a receptive readership. In the same year, Virginia Woolf began to give Freud's writing some serious attention finally, and started to read his *Group Psychology and the Analysis of the Ego* (1921). At the time, Woolf was working on what would be her final novel, *Between the Acts* (1941), in which she explores the unconscious ties that bind together both familial groups and a national culture. Other writers were also testing out the fictional possibilities of group psychology. Katherine Burdekin's *Swastika Night* (1937) and Rex Warner's *The Aerodrome* (1941), for example, both expose the Fascist brutality of group identification with the father that Freud had analysed in his earlier social texts. As war approached, psychoanalysis entered a new political age in British literary culture. The 'something enigmatic' that both the free-associating patient and the Modernist poet had introduced into twentieth-century culture turned savage. Thanks to the same political savagery, Freud's final text was, unusually, first published in English. *Moses and Monotheism* was published by Hogarth in 1939. In this last work, Freud painstakingly uncovers the fictional origins of race and history. Fantasy reconstructs the truth of the past, he argues. This doesn't mean that history lies; merely that ideologies of race and nation are based on a profoundly contingent truth. At the end of his life, newly exiled from Vienna, Freud himself felt the consequences of this kind of history telling all too keenly.

To honour the safe arrival of his precious collection of antiquities in Britain in the autumn of 1938, the poet H. D. sent her former analyst a bunch of gardenias. Anticipating Freud's gift to Woolf a few months later, the flowers were also a tribute to their former analysis and the poetry it had inspired. If Freud had literary culture to thank for the dissemination of his work in Britain, H. D.'s gift might be taken to imply that literature itself also had psychoanalysis to thank for its lessons in how to articulate what is most obscure about modern subjectivity. Both psychoanalysis and modern literature understand how our desires, neuroses, dreams and memories reveal not only a richer self, but also how estranged we are from ourselves. The writer and the analyst each pick at this wound, on the one hand, to better comprehend it and, on the other, to tell us what we are missing about ourselves, to offer us a glimpse of what modern life has made of us. Amid the exchange of floral tributes that must have kept Hampstead florists busy on the eve of Freud's death there was, I think, a mutual recognition of this melancholy affinity between twentieth-century literature and psychoanalysis.

16

Biography and autobiography

MAX SAUNDERS

Life-writing in the twentieth century's era of experiment and modernity has demonstrated that there is still life in its forms. The culture industries have found them persistently lucrative. Lives of royals, generals, politicians and other performers endure on the bestseller lists. Educationalists and clerics may have given way to sports and media 'personalities', but the investment in the biographic remains massive. The 'biopic' emerged as a staple of the film industry in this period. There is enough biographical documentary to programme a Biography Channel for television.

This continued proliferation of the producing and consuming of auto/biography isn't reducible to a single grand narrative of shifts and developments. In part this is because the genres of life-writing are less well-researched than plays, poems or novels – though they have begun to attract more critical attention in the last two decades. But also because, just as realism has flourished in fiction and film alongside and despite other forms (Absurdist, Existentialist, magic realist, supernaturalist, metafictional, Postmodernist), so fundamentally realist biography and autobiography have flourished among more experimental forms of life-writing. This diversity of forms (what we might call 'auto/biodiversity') is arguably part of the condition of postmodernity. How we got there is perhaps best explained in terms of a sequence of challenges – from history, from criticism – to the received forms: challenges which have in turn produced new forms of life-writing and new modes of understanding the genres involved, and generated a new terminology. In this chapter the increasingly common term 'auto/biography' designates autobiography or biography or forms which fuse the two (memoirs, family history).[1] The term 'life-writing' has much broader reference, including all these, and also forms which fragment auto/biography – reminiscences, biographical and

[1] See, for example, Laura Marcus, *Auto/biographical Discourses* (Manchester University Press, 1994).

autobiographical essays and sketches – as well as diurnal modes of writing the self: journals, diaries and letters. The chapter explores a pervasive interfusion of genres throughout the period; but for the sake of clarity discusses biography first, then the autobiographic.

The majority of works discussed will be literary auto/biography; though with 'literary' understood in a broad sense to include biographies about authors; auto/biographies by imaginative writers; and auto/biographies of literary distinction. That is because these works are of the greatest technical interest, as well as being of most interest to specialists in literature. But it should not be forgotten that writers writing about writers represent a small percentage of the total cultural output of life-writing.

Biography

Biography is seen as a quintessentially Victorian genre. But the early twentieth century saw two works which signalled its transformation. Samuel Butler's *The Way of All Flesh* (1903) exemplifies the generic multiplicity that we shall analyse later, being a fictionalised autobiography in the form of a pseudo-biography. At its heart is the portrayal of the conflict between the tyrannical and hypocritical vicar Theo Pontifex and his long-suffering son Ernest. The second work, Edmund Gosse's *Father and Son* (1907), is a more conventional memoir, though it, too, is hybrid, part biography of his father, part autobiography. It, too, charts the son's rejection of his father's faith, and discovery of an alternative vocation: the literary life. Butler and Gosse are significant, then, for their styptic criticism of the Victorian ethos; for a new attitude towards the family, towards religion and towards biography; for marking a break with the past, and the beginnings of a modern subjectivity; and the emergence of what Virginia Woolf was later to call 'The New Biography'.[2]

Woolf and the Bloomsbury Group were at the centre of the New Biography. Her complex involvement in it – as critic, biographer, novelist, diarist, letter-writer – is in part a reaction against her own Victorian father, the historian of ideas, editor and biographer Sir Leslie Stephen, who was also the first editor of the *Dictionary of National Biography*. The *DNB* might be considered the biographical wing of the Establishment: an enterprise dedicated to defining nation and history in terms of the lives of great men, as Carlyle had argued history ought to proceed. Yet Sidney Lee, who edited the

[2] Virginia Woolf, 'The New Biography' (1927), in *The Essays of Virginia Woolf*, vol. IV: *1925–8*, ed. Andrew McNeillie (London: Hogarth Press, 1994), pp. 473–80.

DNB from 1891, himself noted how Edwardian biography had evolved from its Victorian predecessors. In his book *Principles of Biography* (1911) he wrote: 'The aim of biography is not the moral edification which may flow from the survey of either vice or virtue; it is the truthful transmission of personality.' Woolf quoted this comment at the beginning of her essay 'The New Biography'. She had read the book when it came out.[3] So her playfully absurd claim that 'on or about December 1910 human character changed', besides being understood in terms of the end of the Edwardian era, or the mounting of the first Post-Impressionist exhibition in London, should perhaps also be read as reflecting a new concept of the character of biography as well as fiction.[4]

Like the 'New Woman' in the period, 'The New Biography' kept getting newer. If biography had *already* changed by 1910–11, it was to change further thanks largely to the work of the Bloomsbury Group. Woolf's essay was a review of a book by Harold Nicolson, biographer, diarist and author of *The Development of English Biography* (1928). Vita Sackville-West's book about her family and its stately home, *Knole and the Sackvilles*, appeared in 1922, and was followed by two books of saints' lives: *Saint Joan of Arc* (1936) and *The Eagle and the Dove: St Teresa of Avila and St Therese of Lisieux* (1943). Bloomsbury's other major novelist besides Woolf, E. M. Forster, wrote a memoir of the Cambridge political scientist Goldsworthy Lowes Dickinson (1934), which gracefully interrogates the conventions of the genre; a book on his great-aunt: *Marianne Thornton: A Domestic Biography* (1956); and several biographical essays.[5] Woolf's own transformative explorations of life-writing permeate her entire *œuvre*. She too wrote a biography, of her friend Roger Fry (1940).

But it was Lytton Strachey who was the chief Bloomsbury exponent of 'The New Biography'. His landmark volume *Eminent Victorians* appeared in May 1918. Its four studies, of Cardinal Manning, Florence Nightingale, Dr Arnold and General Gordon represent key Victorian professions: the Church; medicine; education; the Army. Nineteenth-century official biographies of such figures frequently ran into multiple volumes to provide 'moral edification'. As Strachey laments in his 'Preface':

[3] Letter to Sidney Lee, 29 July 1911, *The Letters of Virginia Woolf*, ed. Nigel Nicolson, 6 vols. (London: Hogarth Press, 1975–80), vol. I, *The Flight of the Mind, 1888–1912*, p. 473.

[4] Virginia Woolf, 'Character in Fiction' (1924; subsequently rpt. as 'Mr Bennett and Mrs Brown'), *The Essays of Virginia Woolf*, vol. III, ed. Andrew McNeillie (London: Hogarth Press, 1988), pp. 420–38 (p. 421). See Samuel Hynes, *The Edwardian Turn of Mind* (Princeton University Press, 1971), pp. 325–6.

[5] See *Abinger Harvest* (London: Edward Arnold, 1936) and *Two Cheers for Democracy* (London: Edward Arnold, 1951).

> Those two fat volumes, with which it is our custom to commemorate the dead – who does not know them, with their ill-digested masses of material, their slipshod style, their tone of tedious panegyric, their lamentable lack of selection, of detachment, of design? They are as familiar as the *cortège* of the undertaker, and wear the same air of slow, funereal barbarism.[6]

'The art of biography seems to have fallen on evil times in England', he argues. In part the New Biography was an attempt to foster the kind of 'great biographical tradition' that he saw in French literature. 'We have had, it is true, a few masterpieces'; but 'we have had no Fontenelles and Condorcets, with their incomparable *éloges*, compressing into a few shining pages the manifold existences of men'.[7] Strachey's lives were certainly brief. Thomas Arnold gets a mere twenty-five pages in *Eminent Victorians*; and Strachey went on to produce three volumes of what he called 'Characters', or *Portraits in Miniature*. As he explains, he is abandoning 'the direct method of a scrupulous narration' in favour of 'a subtler strategy', which privileges 'a brevity which excludes everything that is redundant and nothing that is significant'.[8] Biography, that is, was to be reconfigured according to Modernist aesthetics. In transforming it from tedious barbarism to an art, he would adopt the methods of modern fiction – selection; obliqueness; indirection – in the name of that 'significant form' that Clive Bell had argued, in his equally iconoclastic 1914 treatise *Art*, was 'the quality shared by all objects that provoke our aesthetic emotions'.[9]

Strachey's strategy wasn't only directed against biographers, however, but against his subjects. He wrote from what he called 'a slightly cynical point of view'.[10] But as he continues his military metaphors in the 'Preface', readers might wonder whether the cynicism didn't go deeper:

> He will attack his subject in unexpected places; he will fall upon the flank, or the rear; he will shoot a sudden, revealing searchlight into obscure recesses, hitherto undivined.[11]

The point of the biographer's detachment – like the impersonality of the Modernist artist – is to ironise the subject, while expressing (as here) the artist's personality. All four subjects emerge as fanatical, ambitious and misguided. This irreverence in part reflected a post-war disillusion with the wisdom and

6 Lytton Strachey, *Eminent Victorians* (Harmondsworth: Penguin, 1986), p. 10.
7 Ibid., p. 10. 8 Ibid., pp. 9–10.
9 Clive Bell, *Art*, ed. J. B. Bullen (Oxford University Press, 1987), p. 8.
10 Letter to Ottoline Morrell, 17 October 1912: quoted in Michael Holroyd, 'Introduction' to *Eminent Victorians*, p. viii.
11 Strachey, *Eminent Victorians*, p. 9.

trustworthiness of figures of authority. Before the war, Strachey had planned to include more figures, some for purposes of praise. He followed the book with a biography of the most eminent Victorian of all, *Queen Victoria* (1921), in which he played with nineteenth-century conventions of romantic fiction and melodrama. His last book, *Elizabeth and Essex* (1928), is another experimental work, combining the structure of an Elizabethan drama with Freudian ideas.

Psychoanalysis was of course a major influence on human character's changing representations. Again Bloomsbury is central to the story of the impact of Freudian ideas on British culture, and to their impact upon biographical and autobiographical writing. The Hogarth Press, founded in 1917 by Leonard and Virginia Woolf, published the papers of the International Psycho-Analytical Institute from 1924.[12] Freud's concepts of the unconscious, the repression or sublimation of sexual wishes, neurosis, dream, fantasy, delusion and the Oedipus complex were all rapidly taken up, with varying degrees of scepticism, by novelists and poets such as D. H. Lawrence, May Sinclair and W. H. Auden. Freud's own narrative forms offered possible models, too, especially to life-writers. His 'Case Histories' are more clinical and theoretical than Strachey's, but they are biographical studies proceeding by comparable criteria: exploring the 'unexpected places' and 'obscure recesses, hitherto undivined'. *The Interpretation of Dreams* is both a masterpiece of theory and an oblique autobiography.

The Bloomsbury Group broke taboos in private; and the New Biography relished the debunking of Victorian moral icons. But its biographies still held back from exemplifying the Freudian vision of the centrality of sexuality to the 'personality' it sought to represent. With the exception of Freud's studies of 'Leonardo Da Vinci and a Memory of His Childhood' (1910), and 'Dostoevsky and Parricide' (1927–8), in Britain it was not until after World War II, and particularly after the sexual liberation of the 1960s, that biographies began explicitly to discuss the sexuality of their subjects. Marie Bonaparte's *Edgar Poe: Etude psychanalytique* (Paris, 1933) was probably the first full-length 'psychobiography', and was not translated into English until 1949.[13]

The New Biography may not have constituted the tradition that Strachey desired. But it produced a new enthusiasm for the form. As Laura Marcus argues, 'The rise in popularity of biographies was linked to the perception that biography had been reinvented for the twentieth century, requiring a

[12] See Perry Meisel and Walter Kendrick, eds., *Bloomsbury/Freud: The Letters of James and Alix Strachey 1924–25* (London: Chatto & Windus, 1986).

[13] Marie Bonaparte, *The Life and Works of Edgar Allan Poe: A Psycho-analytic Interpretation*, trans. John Rodker (London: Imago Publishing, 1949).

new level of critical self-awareness';[14] and she quotes Hesketh Pearson saying in 1930: 'It is the day of the biographer'; and Lord David Cecil arguing in 1936 that biography was 'the only new form' of modern literature. It may seem a paradox that the New Biography's celebration of 'personality' and 'character', however newly presented, coincides with Modernism's doctrine of *im*personality, and its fragmentation of character into a montage of voices. But the relation between them should instead be seen as dialectical. As the New Biography responded to Modernist experiments, the Modernists were reacting against biography in turn (and against Bloomsbury, some of them); and not just its Victorian forms, but the New Biography too. It may have been precisely the sense of a renaissance of the literature of personality that led Eliot to write (in the year following *Eminent Victorians*): 'Poetry is . . . not the expression of personality, but an escape from personality.'[15]

The implications for literary biography were clear. If, as Eliot argued, 'the more perfect the artist, the more completely separate in him will be the man who suffers and the mind which creates', biography of artists who matter can tell us nothing about their creative minds or the art they create.[16] Eliot's ideas were taken up into the American 'New Criticism'. The New Biography thus catalysed a new and substantial challenge to the idea of biography, which had a profound effect on creative writers, critics and teachers. Where a Victorian or Edwardian person of letters would expect to produce biographies as part of an *œuvre*, authors like Joyce, Eliot or Wyndham Lewis did not. Nor did most New Critics. Biography seemed irrelevant to literary studies; a survival from a bellettristic age. This meant both that Modernist writers were often (as we might now say) 'in denial' of the biographic; and also that their critics denied that the Modernists had enough investment in the auto/biographic to be in denial of it. Yet, as we shall see, life-writing is central to Modernism, in ways that have only recently begun to be appreciated. Several writers allied with Modernism wrote biographically: not only Woolf and Forster, but also Ford Madox Ford (on Joseph Conrad, Stephen Crane, Henry James), May Sinclair (on the Brontës), and Richard Aldington (on both D. H. and T. E. Lawrence; Norman Douglas; the Duke of Wellington). Ezra Pound's *Gaudier-Brzeska* (1916) may be formally unconventional – more Vorticist manifesto than memoir of the sculptor – yet it is undeniably a form of life-writing.

14 Laura Marcus, 'The Newness of the "New Biography"', in *Mapping Lives: The Uses of Biography*, ed. Peter France and William St Clair (Oxford University Press, 2002), pp. 193–4.

15 T. S. Eliot, 'Tradition and the Individual Talent' (1919), *Selected Essays* (London: Faber & Faber, 1951), pp. 13–22 (p. 21).

16 Ibid., p. 18.

These ambivalences about life-writing help account for the flourishing of what one might call *biografiction*[17] – fiction *about* biography and biographers. Three strands can be distinguished, though they are sometimes intertwined. First, the *pseudo-biography*, which borrows biographical form to lend verisimilitude. Butler's *The Way of All Flesh*, or Thomas Mann's *Doktor Faustus* (1947), are sustained examples; many novels borrow elements from biographical form. May Sinclair's *Mary Olivier: A Life* (1921) takes not only a biographical-sounding title, but a structure, following the phases of a life in the headings for its five books: Infancy, Childhood, Adolescence, Maturity, Middle Age – each with dates attached. Pseudo-biography can also be written with an ironic purpose (as in Mann's novel, where the plodding biographical specificity is ironised by the intimations of the demonic). Or it can be satirical, as in Richard Aldington's *Soft Answers* (1932), with scathing parodic biographies attacking T. S. Eliot's religiosity ('Stepping Heavenward') and Ezra Pound's megalomania ('Nobody's Baby'). Max Beerbohm's *Seven Men* (1919) combines the two, though the satire is gentler and is directed at types rather than individuals. It might seem surprising to cite Ezra Pound's poem-sequence *Hugh Selwyn Mauberley* (1920) here. But its subtitle – 'Life and Contacts' – intimates that Pound intends some relation to the form of a literary memoir of a minor figure. The poems themselves don't read like biography, of course. But just as Pound said he aimed to condense the Jamesian novel into twenty pages, so he appears here to condense the literary life.[18]

Hugh Selwyn Mauberley is also an example of the second strand, the *mock-biography*, which adopts a pseudo-biographical strategy in order to satirise biographical *form*. Woolf's cunningly sustained *Orlando* (1928) is the best, and best-known, example. Orlando's four-hundred-year life-span and change from man to woman baffle the intrusive figure of the pompous biographer. *Boon* (1915) purports to be 'a First Selection from the Literary Remains of George Boon, Appropriate to the Times, Prepared for Publication by Reginald Bliss . . . with An Ambiguous Introduction by H. G. Wells (Who is in Truth the Author of the entire Book)'. Wells playfully implies the biography of the great author even if he doesn't write it. Vladimir Nabokov's *Pale Fire* (1962) satirises the biographical process, but via the ingenious form of scholarly annotations to a poem which impose upon it the meaning of being the biography of the annotator.

[17] The term is cumbersome, but analogous to the emerging term 'autobiografiction', discussed later. Of the few instances appearing on the Web, most are in French, and few in critical discourse.

[18] *Ezra Pound: Selected Letters: 1907–1941*, ed. D. D. Paige (New York: New Directions, 1971), p. 180.

This shades off into the third strand. Fictional works with biographers as central characters have emerged as an increasingly significant category of Postmodernism. It includes works as diverse as Nabokov's *The Real Life of Sebastian Knight* (1941); Bernard Malamud's *Dubin's Lives* (1979); Julian Barnes's *Flaubert's Parrot* (1984); William Golding's *The Paper Men* (1984); A. S. Byatt's *Possession* (1990) and *The Biographer's Tale* (2000); and Tom Stoppard's plays *Arcadia* (1993) and *Indian Ink* (1995). Like most Postmodern tendencies, however, it has roots in Modernism, which (as the examples from Wells and Woolf suggest) was already exploring the fictionalities of biography. When Ford Madox Ford published his memoir *Joseph Conrad: A Personal Remembrance*, he provocatively described it as a novel, arguing: 'a novel should be the biography of a man or of an affair, and a biography whether of a man or of an affair should be a novel . . .'[19]

Such cross-border migration characterises the relations between fiction and auto/biography in the twentieth century. Harold Nicolson's *Some People* (1927) is a case in point. It is structured as a series of character sketches. These are all characters the narrator has known, and his story emerges as they are told in sequence. That is, the book fuses biography with autobiography. Nicolson's aim was 'to put real people in imaginary situations, and imaginary people in real situations'.[20] It was the book Woolf was reviewing in her essay 'The New Biography'. She, too, picked out this quality, admiring 'his method of writing about people and about himself as though they were at once real and imaginary'. While his 'lack of pose, humbug, solemnity' embody the achievements of the New Biography, Woolf notes that 'the truth of real life' and 'the truth of fiction' are explosively antagonistic. 'Let it be fact, one feels, or let it be fiction; the imagination will not serve under two masters simultaneously.'[21] Yet the twentieth century's literary imagination increasingly did, with Woolf as one of its pioneers. It was perhaps Nicolson's unsettling experiment which precipitated her biographical fantasy *Orlando* about his wife, Vita Sackville-West.

Autobiography

With autobiography, there is a less marked paradigm-shift in the twentieth century than with biography; as becomes clearer when we examine autobiography's anti-genres. The origins of the British novel are inextricable from

[19] Ford Madox Ford, *Joseph Conrad* (London: Duckworth, 1924), pp. 5–6.

[20] Harold Nicolson, *Some People*, 'Introduction' by Nigel Nicolson (London: Constable, 1982), p. vii.

[21] Woolf, 'The New Biography', pp. 475–8.

fabricated autobiographies, such as those of Pamela Andrews, Lemuel Gulliver, Moll Flanders, Tristram Shandy and Roderick Random. Autobiography was early recognised as a potentially dubious form, whether wilfully deceptive, or vitiated by the subject's capacity for self-deception, self-aggrandisement, vanity or insanity. The eighteenth-century novel derives much of its energy from the fictionalising people indulge in when they present themselves; what we might call the psychopathology of everyday life-writing.

Nonetheless, two nineteenth-century developments bear on twentieth-century autobiography. First, a renewal of interest in what autobiography might tell about its author's sanity, or more particularly, insanity. There is a line of nineteenth-century fictions (by Gogol, Tolstoy, Flaubert, Dostoevsky, Strindberg and others) purporting to be life-writings by madmen, which indicate a new kind of anxiety that autobiography might harbour delusion: the dark side of Victorian earnestness, perhaps. Whereas some major autobiographical narratives by Victorian sages turn on mental crises – John Stuart Mill's *Autobiography* (1873); Ruskin's *Praeterita* (1885–9) – in the twentieth century mental patients begin to write autobiographies in which madness is the whole story. Daniel Paul Schreber's *Denkwürdigkeiten eines Nervenkranken* (Memorabilia of a Nerve Patient; 1903) was the book analysed in Freud's celebrated case history of a paranoiac.[22] Autobiography thus becomes increasingly psychological. Second, a more *aesthetic* sense of life and life-writing develops: a tendency not only to see one's own life as a work of art, but also to be conscious of the act of telling it as drawing on the resources of art. Even if they were not aesthetes, autobiographers acquire a new sense of artifice.

Few key members of the Aesthetic movement published autobiography. But their influence is nonetheless pervasive. Twentieth-century autobiographies by writers and artists are generally 'aesthetic', not merely because their authors happened to be artists, but because they investigate how they became artists.[23] The titles of Yeats's two major autobiographic volumes are explicit, both about the development of an aesthetic attitude, and the claim made for his art. *Reveries over Childhood and Youth* (1914): our early daydreams and fantasies might seem things to be outgrown; but for Yeats they are the mature poet's inspiration for poetic reverie. *The Trembling of the Veil* (1922): his life and times, Ireland's

[22] Sigmund Freud, 'Psycho-Analytic Notes on an Autobiographical Account of a Case of Paranoia (Dementia Paranoides)' (1911), in *The Standard Edition of the Complete Psychological Works of Sigmund Freud*, trans. James Strachey, 24 vols. (London: Hogarth Press and the Institute of Psycho-Analysis, 1958), vol. XII.

[23] See Suzanne Nalbantian, *Aesthetic Autobiography: From Life to Art in Marcel Proust, James Joyce, Virginia Woolf and Anaïs Nin* (Basingstoke: Macmillan, 1994).

mythology and nationalism, are the occasions for the poet as mage to attain to quasi-mystical visions.

In the visual arts it is Impressionism which shifts representation from concrete objects to the processes of perception. The term has been found increasingly useful in literature too, to describe work falling between Realism and Naturalism on the one hand, and Modernism on the other. Impressionism presented a radical challenge to autobiography, as Walter Pater realised. His classic account in *The Renaissance* (1873) argues both that it is to individual mental impressions that 'experience dwindles down', and also that these impressions 'are in perpetual flight'. Both representation and analysis of the self are thus deeply problematic, since the self dissolves in the process. Pater talks of 'that continual vanishing away, that strange, perpetual weaving and unweaving of ourselves'.[24] That sense of the evanescent self's weaving and unweaving is the subject of Impressionist autobiography; and suggests one reason why the Aesthetes (like their Modernist heirs) preferred fictionalised displacements of the self to formal autobiography: works like Pater's 'The Child in the House' (1878), or Wilde's *De Profundis* (1905).[25]

Impressionists who did produce volumes of declared autobiography tell the story of the epiphanic impressions which formed the artist. George Moore represents himself as beginning 'apparently with a nature like a smooth sheet of wax, bearing no impress, but capable of receiving any'.[26] His three volumes on the Irish Revival – *Ave* (1911), *Salve* (1912) and *Vale* (1914), collected together as *Hail and Farewell* (1925) – are considered both as his masterpiece, and as unreliable. Anxieties about unreliability have concerned critics of other Impressionist autobiography, such as Joseph Conrad's *The Mirror of the Sea* (1906) and *A Personal Record* (1912).[27]

Henry James's three late volumes of reminiscence, *A Small Boy and Others* (1913), *Notes of a Son and Brother* (1914) and *The Middle Years* (1917), comprise a magnificent elaboration of the Paterian position. James's subject is his consciousness, and what it does with the past, not just in its presence as memory, but in its absence. What he says of a childhood friend is representative: 'He

24 Walter Pater, 'Conclusion', *The Renaissance: Studies in Art and Poetry* (London: Macmillan, 1913), pp. 248–9.

25 Pater's 'The Child in the House' was first published in *Macmillan's*, 1878, and included (with another autobiographical piece, 'Emerald Uthwart'), in *Miscellaneous Studies* (1895). I am indebted to John Stokes for my discussion of the Aesthetic movement.

26 George Moore, *Confessions of a Young Man* (1886), edited and annotated by Moore in 1904 and again in 1916 (London: Heinemann, 1917), p. 1.

27 See my 'Reflections on Impressionist Autobiography: James, Conrad, and Ford', in *Conrad, James, Ford, and Other Relations* in the series 'Joseph Conrad: Eastern and Western Perspectives', ed. Wieslaw Krajka (Lublin and Columbia University Presses, 2003).

vanishes, and I dare say I but make him over, as I make everything.'[28] In an extraordinary image that has been taken up in subsequent discussions of autobiography, James describes his aim as 'to turn nothing less than myself inside out'; and asks: 'What was *I* thus, within and essentially, what had I ever been and could I ever be but a man of imagination at the active pitch?'[29] Ford Madox Ford's autobiographical volumes *Return to Yesterday* (1931) and *It Was the Nightingale* (1934) are also concerned with what makes a man of imagination. Ford is explicit in avowing an even more provocative form of Paterian impressionism. In an earlier autobiographical volume he states:

> This book, in short, is full of inaccuracies as to facts, but its accuracy as to impressions is absolute [. . .] I don't really deal in facts, I have for facts a most profound contempt. I try to give you what I see to be the spirit of an age, of a town, of a movement.[30]

As we have seen, T. S. Eliot's influence produced a devaluation of auto/biography. Many Modernists seem afflicted with what Chekhov diagnosed as 'autobiographobia'.[31] Certainly, we don't have formal autobiography by Eliot, Joyce or Pound, who denigrated it as 'naughtyboyography'.[32] Yet here, too, the dogmas of the New Criticism have obscured the autobiographical energies of many Modernists. English writing may have little to compare with André Breton's surrealist romance *Nadja* (1928); Fernando Pessoa's extraordinary *The Book of Disquietude* – the unfinished, fragmentary, 'factless autobiography' of one of his multiple 'heteronyms', 'Bernardo Soares';[33] or Jean-Paul Sartre's bravura existential self-analysis in *Les Mots* (1964). But British Modernists certainly did write autobiography. Besides those by Yeats and Ford, Wyndham Lewis produced *Blasting and Bombardiering* (1937) and *Rude Assignment* (1950). H. D. wrote memoirs of her relationship with Pound – the journal *End to Torment* (1979) – and her sessions with Freud – *Tribute to Freud* (1970). William Gerhardie's entertaining *Memoirs of a Polyglot* (1931) appeared when its author was a precocious thirty-six. *Everybody's Autobiography* (1937), recounting a lecture tour to America, is one of Gertrude Stein's several significant experiments

[28] Collected into one volume, Henry James, *Autobiography*, ed. Frederick W. Dupee (Princeton University Press, 1983), p. 227.

[29] Ibid., p. 455.

[30] Ford Madox Ford, *Ancient Lights and Certain New Reflections* (London: Chapman & Hall, 1911), pp. xv–xvi.

[31] *Letters of Anton Chekhov*, ed. Avrahm Yarmolinsky (London: Jonathan Cape, 1974), p. 351.

[32] *Pound/Ford: The Story of a Literary Friendship*, ed. Brita Lindberg-Seyersted (London: Faber & Faber, 1983), p. 126.

[33] Fernando Pessoa, *The Book of Disquietude*, published posthumously, ed. Richard Zenith (Manchester: Carnanet, 1996).

with life-writing. Virginia Woolf wrote 'A Sketch of the Past' and other autobiographical pieces collected in *Moments of Being*. Other Modernists wrote autobiographical 'sketches' too, such as May Sinclair, D. H. Lawrence and even, arguably, Joyce, in the essay 'A Portrait of the Artist' (a sketch for what would become *A Portrait of the Artist as a Young Man*, but without the pseudonymity of the protagonist) and the prose poem 'Giacomo Joyce'.[34] In line with the ambivalent relationship of Modernist writers to self-representation in autobiography, Joyce begins his writing career with the ironic detachment of the short stories in *Dubliners* (finally published in 1914) and moves on to the complex blend of self-irony and self-idealisation in the autobiographical novel *Portrait of the Artist as a Young Man* (1916).

Male–Modernist 'impersonality' is a break with the Romantic aesthetic of self-expression. But from another point of view, it is the continuation of the Aesthetic–Impressionist turning inside-out of a personality that is perceived as dissolving. Even those works which seem most remote from formal autobiography are nonetheless often now read as in part autobiographic. The spiritual crisis at the heart of *The Waste Land* owes much to Eliot's mental breakdown and marital crisis – as one of the leading New Critics, William Empson, was to demonstrate subtly in his book *Using Biography* (1984).

Innovative autobiographies were published by early twentieth-century writers who were modern but not Modernist. In Russia, Maxim Gorky, the prime mover of socialist realism, wrote the trilogy *Childhood* (1913), *In the World* (1916) and *My University Years* (1922). When *The Early Life of Thomas Hardy* (1928) and *The Later Years of Thomas Hardy* (1930) were published under the name of his second wife, Florence Emily Hardy, they must have looked like a survival of the Victorian official biography. Yet they had been written in the third person by Hardy himself, to be published posthumously. H. G. Wells's *Experiment in Autobiography: Discoveries and Conclusions of a Very Ordinary Brain (Since 1866)* appeared in two volumes in 1934 – the same year as one of the more formally innovative products of the New Biography, *The Quest for Corvo: An Experiment in Biography* (1934), by A. J. A. Symons. One of the most influential autobiographies of the period was the Romantic, orientalist life by T. E. Lawrence ('of Arabia') *The Seven Pillars of Wisdom* (published privately, 1926; publicly 1937), the account of his role in the Arab revolt against the Turks. A less sentimental version of a life out of Europe is Karen Blixen's *Out of Africa* (1937). E. H. W. Meyerstein's

[34] May Sinclair, 'Autobiographical Sketch', appendix to Suzanne Raitt, *May Sinclair* (Oxford: Clarendon Press, 2000), pp. 269–70. James Joyce, *Poems and Shorter Writings*, ed. Richard Ellmann, A. Walton Litz and John Whittier-Ferguson (London: Faber & Faber, 1991).

Of My Early Life (begun in the late 1930s, but published posthumously in 1957) is striking for the candid yet humorous account of his terror and hatred of his parents; though formally unremarkable, it is the last nail in the coffin of Victorian biographical piety.

World War I presented a new challenge to self-representation. Writers needed to bear witness to their experiences. But the intolerable traumas of violence, danger, anxieties, caused selves to crack up en masse. The war fissured the life-histories of its participants, just as it appeared a 'crack across the table of History' itself.[35] The literary response was to reimagine history as autobiography: first in the rage for poetry, largely testimonial, of the War Poets; then in the mass of memoirs that began to appear about a decade later.[36]

The best-known are by surviving poets. The first volume of Siegfried Sassoon's semi-fictionalised autobiography of 'George Sherston' appeared anonymously as *Memoirs of a Fox-Hunting Man* (1928). It ends (with a disillusion characteristic of many war-memoirs) with his arrival at the Front: 'I remembered that it was Easter Sunday. Standing in that dismal ditch, I could find no consolation in the thought that Christ was risen.' *Memoirs of an Infantry Officer* (1930) recounts Sassoon's war experiences up to his decision to publish a defiant protest against the conduct of the war. *Sherston's Progress* (1936) deals with Craiglockhart mental hospital, and his encounter with the psychologist W. H. R. Rivers. One of the four sections consists entirely of material from Sassoon's diaries. *Siegfried's Journey* (1945) completes his account of this period, describing his friendship with Wilfred Owen at Craiglockhart.

In *Goodbye to All That* (1929), Robert Graves tells how he was erroneously reported as killed in action. This allows him to create an ironic myth of his immortality, while paradoxically writing goodbye to his pre-war self. The book is marked by Graves's cynical detachment from the macabre witnessing of death. Herbert Read's *In Retreat* (1925), describing the German offensive in the Spring of 1918, and *Ambush* (1930), formally more innovative, are comparably detached, if more philosophical. Edmund Blunden's *Undertones of War* (1928) is remarkably understated, approaching equally harrowing experiences through the received language of poetic Romanticism. Ford's *No Enemy* (1929) is disconcertingly oblique about the horrors of war, instead screening them behind intense visual impressionism, whereby traumatic memory is dissolved into a sequence of landscapes and interiors. He is more concerned with the after-effects; and 'the painful processes of Reconstruction', which are the

35 Ford Madox Ford, *Parade's End* (London: Penguin, 2002), p. 510.
36 See Samuel Hynes, *The Soldier's Tale* (London: Pimlico, 1998).

autobiographic processes, too.[37] Again the narrative is semi-fictionalised. Of course the major British fiction of the war was also largely autobiographical: R. H. Mottram's *The Spanish Farm Trilogy* (1924–6); Ford's *Parade's End* (1924–8); Richard Aldington's *Death of a Hero* (1929); and Frederic Manning's *Her Privates We* (1930).

Women who wrote of their experience as wartime nurses include Enid Bagnold (*A Diary Without Dates*; 1918); Florence Farmborough (*Nurse at the Russian Front: A Diary 1914–18*; 1974); Mary Borden (*The Forbidden Zone*; 1929); and Vera Brittain, whose *Testament of Youth* (1933) is one of the greatest women's autobiographies of the century.[38] Its almost unbearably moving account of the deaths of her brother, her fiancé and of their friends is contextualised in terms of her struggle for education, and to grasp the history and politics of the war and its aftermath. She incorporates letters from those she loved, memorialising the dead and their stories. Other soldier–poets were memorialised with posthumous volumes of their letters, such as Charles Hamilton Sorley. Biography is traditionally close to mourning and honouring the dead. In the case of such widespread premature loss, such material is often also autobiographic; as in Helen Thomas's poignant memoirs of her courtship and marriage to Edward Thomas: *As It Was* (1926) and *World Without End* (1931).

The prevalence of such forms of personal testimony reshaped the literatures of memory in two ways. First, twentieth-century autobiographers started writing their lives earlier. Classic autobiography is written towards the end of a life, looking back and trying to see it steadily and see it whole. Literary autobiography in particular is often treated as a kind of afterword to the author's works; a supplement. It is posed as a text outside of the other texts, commenting upon them, trying to make intelligible their origins and development.[39] While it's true that a writer's autobiography may differ from her novels precisely in that the autobiography can discuss those novels, it's also true that the autobiography is another text, another narrative. And, of course, the notion of its being the author's last words on her life is in most cases palpably fictional. Full single-book autobiography thus becomes displaced as the memoir becomes more prevalent. Second, in trying to come to terms with the central historical upheaval of the age, the war memoirs ushered in a new political urgency, as the stress on testimony led to a disillusioned journalistic exposé.

37 Ford Madox Ford, *No Enemy* (New York: Macaulay, 1929), p. 9.

38 See Yvonne M. Klein, ed., *Beyond the Home Front: Women's Autobiographical Writing of the Two World Wars* (Basingstoke: Macmillan, 1997).

39 Compare Marcus, *Auto/biographical Discourses*, pp. 246 ff.

For writers emerging between the wars, the autobiographic challenge was to reconcile psychoanalysis with an increasingly prestigious Marxism which seemed intolerant of expressions of the individual mind. The anti-rhetorical style of Hemingway's Modernism, favouring clarity of concrete *reportage* over linguistic difficulty, paved the way for a new documentary realism. The central figure here is George Orwell. His *Down and Out in Paris and London* (1933) exposed the underclass of the urban homeless and poor. *The Road to Wigan Pier* (1937) recorded working-class poverty and unemployment during the Depression. *Homage to Catalonia* (1938) covers his involvement in the Spanish Civil War. Orwell's technique (analogous to Strachey's, though less archly mandarin) is to undermine the establishment with its own rhetoric: to embody the public-school virtues of honesty and fairness in order to show up hypocrisy and inequity in society. But the effect is to put the figure of the reporter in the centre of the picture; to combine social and political commentary with autobiography.

Thus it should not surprise us that the 'Auden Generation' (if not Auden himself) produced so much autobiographic writing. Not all of it is formal autobiography. Louis MacNeice's *Autumn Journal* (1939) is a verse memoir describing his responses to the outbreak of World War II. Macneice did start a fine autobiography (beginning with an arresting cynicism: 'So what?') immediately afterwards, which was published posthumously as *The Strings are False: An Unfinished Autobiography*. (1965). Most of Christopher Isherwood's work has complex relations to the autobiographic. He takes *fin-de-siècle* play with pseudonymity and fictionalisation a stage further, presenting not only his previous narrated selves but also their author as already fictionalised. *Goodbye to Berlin* (1939) argues: 'Because I have given my own name to the "I" of this narrative, readers are certainly not entitled to assume that its pages are purely autobiographical, or that its characters are libellously exact portraits of living persons. "Christopher Isherwood" is a convenient ventriloquist's dummy, nothing more' (p. 7). One of the most impressive autobiographies of the mid-century is Edwin Muir's *The Story and the Fable* (1940), revised and expanded into *An Autobiography* (1954), recounting Muir's journey through socialism, Nietzschean philosophy and psychoanalysis. Stephen Spender had originally meant to avoid a chronological ordering of his *World Within World* (1951). 'However', he explains: 'after two or three trials, I saw the advantage of having a framework of objective events through which I could knock the holes of my subjective experiences' (p. vii). This image of subjective experiences as gaps in the structure, rather than the thing the structure was there to support, evokes an existential anxiety about the very self that an autobiography sets out to narrate. The traditional oppositions – objective / subjective;

event / experience – seemed pressingly relevant to these autobiographers after the Russian Revolution and world war.

Many of the authors already discussed – James, Ford, Hardy, Orwell, Isherwood – accumulated a series of autobiographic volumes. In some cases – Moore, Gorky, Yeats, Sassoon – a larger sequential autobiographic project is apparent. Though not unprecedented, and related to the *roman-fleuve*, these contribute to a modern sense of autobiography as a potentially all-engrossing project. Sean O'Casey's *I Knock at the Door: Swift Glances Back at Things that Made Me* (1939) was the first of six acclaimed volumes. In the case of Osbert Sitwell, his autobiographies assume a central rather than supplementary role in his *œuvre*. He began them during World War II, publishing five volumes from 1945 to 1950, and another in 1962. Such autobiographical sequences become increasingly important after the war. Major practitioners include Lawrence Durrell, Freya Stark, Arthur Koestler, David Garnett, Leonard Woolf, J. B. Priestley, Compton Mackenzie, Kathleen Raine and Janet Frame.

If some of these works seem like more or less than autobiography (they are also memoirs, works of intellectual history, topographical or travel writing) they indicate the diversity of the 'autobiographic', the definition of which has been transformed by at least four further significant factors. First, women have written unarguably major autobiographies.[40] And the feminist scholarship that recovered women's biographies has rediscovered and celebrated autobiographies by women. Many have already been mentioned (by Brittain, Thomas, Stein). Further examples include Beatrice Webb's *My Apprenticeship* (1926); Ethel Mannin's *Confessions and Impressions* (1930) – the first volume of another sequence; Nina Hamnett's *Laughing Torso* (1932) and *Is She a Lady?: A Problem in Autobiography* (1955); and Elizabeth Bowen's *Seven Winters* (1943).

Second, the discovery, editing and publication of writers' diaries and letters have both augmented the horizons of life-writing and generated a new scholarly interest in these and related forms such as travelogues. Some of the best writing by Joseph Conrad, Katherine Mansfield, Anaïs Nin, D. H. Lawrence, Virginia Woolf or Sylvia Plath appears in their diurnal writing. Its reclamation has been seen as a democratising move, attending not just to authors and celebrities, but ordinary people, as in the establishing of the Mass-Observation archive.

Third, the proliferation of what is increasingly being called *autobiografiction*.[41] The major fiction of the century, especially during the Modernist phase,

40 See Phyllis Rose, ed., *The Penguin Book of Women's Lives* (London: Penguin, 1995).

41 For example, the British Comparative Literature Association held a conference in London in 2003 entitled 'Autobiografictions'. The term 'autofiction' has greater currency, though the majority of uses are in French criticism associated with Serge Doubrovsky

was highly autobiographical. It doesn't only encode the lives of authors and contacts, often in a *roman-à-clef*, but becomes the most productive site for the representation of consciousness, gender identity, education and the inner life. Though the boundaries between fiction and auto/biography have always been blurred, and this in turn has affected the development of autobiography,[42] there are two ways in which the twentieth century could be said to have renegotiated them, to have reinvented 'autobiografiction'. In the eighteenth century, authors use the form of autobiography to present a first-person narrative of someone else's (fictional) experience. Fiction impersonates autobiography and confession. In the twentieth century, by contrast, authors use fictional form and third-person narrative to write about their own experiences. Auto/biography impersonates fiction. The nineteenth century began this shift, in the autobiographical fiction of the Brontës and Dickens, and the development of the *Bildungsroman*. But in the early twentieth century, it's the form of the *Künstlerroman* – the narrative of the education of an artist – which provides many key works of the period: not just the works by Butler and Gosse with which we started, but also Proust's *A la recherche du temps perdu*, Joyce's *A Portrait of the Artist as a Young Man*, Dorothy Richardson's *Pilgrimage*, Lawrence's *Sons and Lovers*, Sinclair's *Mary Olivier*, Woolf's *To the Lighthouse*, Rosamund Lehmann's *Dusty Answer* and H. D.'s *Bid Me to Live.* Fictionalised autobiography evidently offered a space for women as well to enter the mainstream.

Fourth, and finally: just as fiction about biography has proliferated through the twentieth century, so have not only autobiographical novels, but also a variety of fictions *about* autobiography. These don't just represent their author's experience, but are meta-autobiographical: explicitly concerned with the autobiographic process, and the *representation* of auto/biography. Here at least seven types are distinguishable:

1 One *incorporates fictional diary entries or letters within a narrative*, as at the end of Joyce's *Portrait of the Artist as a Young Man*; or in A. S. Byatt's *Possession.*
2 Works entirely in the form of *pseudo-diaries* (as opposed to the older form of epistolary novel) include: Hesketh Pearson, *The Whispering Gallery: Being Leaves from the Diary of an Ex-Diplomat* (1926); and Sartre's *La nausée* (1938), in which the narrator Roquentin turns significantly from trying to write a biography to realising he has to write about himself: to produce the book we have in fact been reading.

[42] Marcus, *Auto/biographical Discourses*, p. 258.

3 *Mock-diaries* mimic the form for humorous purposes. George and Weedon Grossmith, *Diary of a Nobody* (1892) and Mark Twain's *Extracts from Adam's Diary* (1904) and *Eve's Diary* (1906) are hilarious examples. Maurice Baring's *Lost Diaries* (1913) comprises twenty fictional extracts from diaries by mythical, historical and fictional figures including Oedipus, William the Conqueror, Hamlet, the Man in the Iron Mask, Harriet Shelley and Sherlock Holmes.

4 Pseudo-autobiography, in which a formal autobiography is attributed to a fictional persona, appears in two main versions. *Partial pseudo-autobiography* is framed by a narrator, as with *The Autobiography of Mark Rutherford* (1881). Hermann Hesse's *Steppenwolf* (1927) consists mostly of the 'records' left by 'Harry Haller', introduced by a friend. Or it can be presented as fragmentary, as the unconnected reminiscences making up Gissing's *The Private Papers of Henry Ryecroft* (1903).

5 *Full pseudo-autobiography* is a trickier form to instance. Proust's *A la recherche* is a possible candidate insofar as it is fictionalised, though the tentative identification of the narrator as 'Marcel' might seem to blur the distinction between true and pseudo-autobiography. It is at least possible to read Joyce's *Portrait* as not merely Joyce's presentation of Stephen's consciousness, but as Joyce's impersonation of the book Stephen might have written about his experience; in which case it would provide an example of a full pseudo-autobiography. Gertrude Stein's *The Autobiography of Alice B. Toklas* (1933) and Italo Svevo's *Confessions of Zeno* (1923) are the clearest examples.

6 Since pseudo-autobiography ironises the autobiographer, it's hard to draw a line between it and *mock-autobiography*, which ironises the form. The best modern examples have come from Twain again; not only his *Extract from Captain Stormfield's Visit to Heaven* (1909), but also the *Chapters from My Autobiography* (1906–7), which begins with parodic self-justification.

7 There is less *fiction with writing autobiography as its subject* than fiction about writing biography in the period. The works by Proust and Joyce already cited could be seen as instances. While this type appears an ideal Postmodern form, it is relatively unexplored. However, innovative writers (such as Lessing, Spark, Kundera or Coetzee) have continued to work at those frontiers of fiction and auto/biography that have proved such fertile territory in twentieth-century literature.

17

'Speed, violence, women, America': popular fictions

DAVID GLOVER

In a curious incident in *The Apes of God* (1930), Wyndham Lewis's compendious satire on modern intellectual and artistic life, two of the central characters engage in a protracted tussle whose pretext is the fate of popular fiction since World War I. Amid the needling and jockeying for position, a thesis, expressed in a vehement tirade, begins to take shape. By the late 1920s the head of every 'anglo-saxon adult' had become stuffed with 'drugged potions, sawed-off shot-guns, arsenic, hairbreadth escapes, blackmail, armed warders, King's Messengers, pirates and crooks'. 'From station-stall to smart hotel', rich and poor alike were reading Edgar Wallace, whereas before and during 'the Great Massacre' only the upper class were captivated by such bloodthirsty ripping yarns – and certainly not 'the young men' who actually 'fought the Boche'.[1]

Was this view mere fiction? Lewis evidently did not think so, for only a few years earlier he had advanced a similar claim in *The Art of Being Ruled* (1926), his little-read political tract urging the 'segregation of those who decide for the active, the intelligent life' from the rest.[2] As an inventory of the nation's reading, Lewis's argument both registers important truths – the growth of mass literacy, for example, or the uncomfortably close ties between the pre-war spy-thrillers such as those by William Le Queux and debates about national security – while simultaneously simplifying and distorting the structure of the popular-fiction market as a whole. Far from presenting a homogeneous profile, popular literature was becoming increasingly diverse and in many respects rather less conformist than he was ever able to recognise.

Lewis was not alone in linking popular taste with the corrosion of intellect. Q. D. Leavis's assertion that 'the twentieth-century bestseller is concerned with supporting herd prejudices' might almost have been lifted from *The Apes of God*

[1] Wyndham Lewis, *The Apes of God* (Santa Barbara: Black Sparrow Press, 1981), pp. 401–4.
[2] Wyndham Lewis, *The Art of Being Ruled* (Santa Barbara: Black Sparrow Press, 1989), pp. 179–180.

rather than her own, considerably more nuanced, but no less polemical survey *Fiction and the Reading Public* (1932).[3] Jeremiads like these grudgingly testified to a remarkable era in the history of British print culture. *The Apes of God* ends with a depiction of the 1926 General Strike, some three years before the onset of the worst economic depression the country had ever experienced. Yet the trend to which Lewis contemptuously alludes was not halted by the slump: between 1918 and 1945 more people read more often and more widely than in any previous period. Even during World War II when paper was rationed and restrictions on bookselling were introduced, the demand for books remained high. In 1941, the year Hitler invaded the Soviet Union and Japan bombed Pearl Harbor, no fewer than eighty-six new bookshops opened in the UK.[4] As the annual records of books loaned by public libraries vividly show, popular reading increased dramatically throughout the first half of the twentieth century. In 1911 54.3 million library books were issued, a figure that had risen to 85.7 million by 1924. Eleven years later that number had more than doubled to 208 million and by 1939 stood at 247.3 million, reaching a total of 300 million in 1949. The rising curve of book sales tells much the same story, climbing from 7.2 million in 1928 to 26.8 million in 1939.[5]

The origins of this long-term expansion lay in 'the mass production revolution' in publishing from 1875–1914, in which a series of technological innovations in printing and typesetting, combined with increasing use of electrical power, gave an immense boost to the industry's productive capacity.[6] Larger print runs became feasible and competitive advantage shifted decisively towards lower-priced 'Popular Editions', undercutting the expensive three-volume novel and leading to its abandonment by influential middle-class subscription libraries like Mudie's in the mid-1890s. In its place the six-shilling, single-volume novel became the fiction industry's new standard product for the next forty years, but the triple-decker's demise also encouraged greater diversification through cheap reprints, including the triumph of the disposable paper-covered sixpenny edition – the forerunner of the modern paperback – which competed successfully with a thriving magazine trade. As new publishing opportunities opened up, writing became increasingly business-like

3 Q. D. Leavis, *Fiction and the Reading Public* (Harmondsworth: Penguin, 1979), p. 160.

4 Joseph McAleer, *Popular Reading and Publishing in Britain 1914–1950* (Oxford: Clarendon Press, 1992), p. 62.

5 Ibid., p. 49; John Stevenson, *British Society 1914–45* (Harmondsworth: Penguin, 1984), p. 398; H. Cunningham, 'Leisure and Culture', in F. M. L. Thompson, ed., *The Cambridge Social History of Britain 1750–1950*, 3 vols. (Cambridge University Press, 1990), II, pp. 312–13.

6 Simon Eliot, *Some Patterns and Trends in British Publishing, 1800–1919* (London: Bibliographical Society, 1994), pp. 13–14, 106–7.

and professional, with its own distinctive modes of representation and regulation. Literary agents, the system of royalty payments, copyright legislation and special-interest groups like the Society of Authors or the Booksellers' Association were all part of publishing's move into mass production. And, as an integral component of commercial expansion, there was an efflorescence of popular literary and cultural forms to tempt the growing ranks of Board school-educated lower-middle- and working-class readers. By the close of the nineteenth century, concludes Nigel Cross in his study of the late Victorian 'common writer', 'the grid of today's genre fiction had been firmly laid': 'the detective novel, the adventure story, the sex novel, science fiction, even the spy novel' – everything that was once chaotically intermingled in the melodramatic imagination – was ready to go.[7]

Cross's argument poses the question of the continuity between nineteenth-century popular fiction and its twentieth-century successors in the sharpest possible terms, implying that the years from 1918 to 1945 can be construed as a long and largely predictable footnote to the *fin de siècle*. Certainly some of the most enduring successes from the late nineteenth century, like the 'scientific romances' of H. G. Wells or Sir Arthur Conan Doyle's Sherlock Holmes stories, were widely imitated and set an agenda for the future. But care must be taken not to impose too much stability and coherence upon the past. With the highly self-conscious exception of detective fiction, it is far from clear whether systematic genre classification was fully in place until after World War II.[8] A glance at popular inter-war magazines like *The Storyteller* or *The Weekly Tale-Teller*, or their American pulp counterparts like the heady *Weird Tales* (billed as 'a magazine of the bizarre and unusual' and available as a 'Yank mag' from British branches of Woolworth's) reveals that genre markers offered only the loosest or most *ad hoc* indication of narrative content, relying upon lurid visual illustrations to make their gendered pitch to target-readers.[9] Though some niche-marketing began in the USA as early as 1915 with Street & Smith's *Detective Story Magazine*, the 'stirring stories of adventure, mystery, [and] romance' promised in the subtitle of Britain's first attempt to copy the pulp format – Hutchinson's 1922 *Adventure-Story Magazine* – suggests that a miscellany was still considered a safer economic bet. At best, then, the vocabulary of genre was makeshift and evocative, rather than exact.

7 Nigel Cross, *The Common Writer: Life in Nineteenth-century Grub Street* (Cambridge University Press, 1985), p. 221.

8 Clive Bloom, *Bestsellers: Popular Fiction Since 1900* (Basingstoke: Palgrave Macmillan, 2002), p. 87.

9 Tony Goodstone, ed., *The Pulps: Fifty Years of American Pop Culture* (New York: Chelsea House, 1970), pp. 165–6.

If the dividing lines between the various branches of popular fiction were still relatively fluid in the inter-war period, this did not mean that it was immune to the kinds of lapses, lacunae or sudden shifts that occur in any literary field when 'a common reference point or defining model' is rejected or revised and 'supplanted by one that is radically different' as social and economic conditions start to change.[10] Some well-worn exemplars received short shrift after the Great War. Though the type of spiritual romance associated with Hall Caine and Marie Corelli survived the collapse of the triple-decker, it had passed its Victorian peak and neither author was able to recover lost ground after 1914. Corelli, always the more popular of the two, continued to sell well during her lifetime but, like Caine, she lived on chiefly through new editions of her earlier work. Her final novel, *Love – and the Philosopher* (1923), published the year before her death, attempted to restore a sense of the old verities in a characteristically lofty tale of passion and devotion shattered by the impact of the Great War. But her defensive opening sideswipe dismissing psychoanalysis's obsession with the sexual origins of hysteria was a sign that Corelli's writing was beginning to date when set beside the far more frankly transgressive eroticism depicted in Elinor Glyn's *Three Weeks* (1907) or E. M. Hull's *The Sheik* (1919). Despite the determination with which Caine and Corelli were taken to task by Q. D. Leavis for their continuing role in 'the disintegration of the reading public', neither of these corruptors of popular taste had much of a future.[11]

Other Victorian success stories did not so much fade from sight as relocate. Wells wrote very few 'scientific romances' after 1918 – *The Shape of Things to Come* (1933) being a notable exception – and increasingly devoted his time to history, popular science and politics. While his work remained an important inspiration, the most exciting new developments in science fiction in the inter-war years were to be found not in Britain, but in Eastern Europe or in the distinctly more hospitable, if rather steamy, atmosphere provided by American pulp magazines, particularly the fan-centred publications introduced by Hugo Gernsback, who coined the term 'science fiction' in 1929. Perhaps reflecting a certain cultural insularity, coupled with a relative slackening in the pace of technological advance, contributions to the genre from this side of the Atlantic tended to be few and far between. Idiosyncratic figures like Olaf Stapledon or C. S. Lewis were academics, worlds apart from their nickel-a-word American cousins, and it is scarcely surprising that, in his novels *Out of the Silent Planet* (1938) and *Perelandra* (1943) and in his occasional writings,

10 Martin Jordin, 'Science Fiction, Genre and a New Battle of the Books', in Asher Cashdan and Martin Jordin, eds., *Studies in Communication* (Oxford: Blackwell, 1987), p. 157.

11 Leavis, *Fiction and the Reading Public*, pp. 136–9.

Lewis was fiercely at odds with what he saw as the godless imperialism current in much of the genre. Significantly, there was no British magazine specifically directed at science-fiction readers until the publication of the short-lived *Tales of Wonder* in 1937. Thus the period's best-known work in this category, Aldous Huxley's dystopian *Brave New World* (1932), was a mordantly witty satire whose literary acclaim only reinforced its distance from the commercialism of the pulps. However, the absence of a 'King of Science Fiction' to match the duly anointed 'Queen of Crime' (indisputably Agatha Christie – but with Margery Allingham, Ngaio Marsh and Dorothy L. Sayers as heirs apparent) or the 'King of Thrillers' (inevitably the ever-prolific Edgar Wallace) testifies eloquently to the continuing attraction of crime writing among popular audiences. Indeed, it was in the thriller's super-rays and other secret weapons that the imaginary technology of the future was most frequently to be found.

In histories and memoirs the twenties and thirties are regularly fêted as a 'Golden Age' of detective fiction in Britain, but this was also a time when the form itself was subjected to intense scrutiny. Its modern antecedents can be traced back to Edgar Allen Poe's 1841 short story 'The Murders in the Rue Morgue' and by the 1900s the cult status of Sherlock Holmes had made detective fiction into a staple of the paperback reprint market. What was new about the 'Golden Age', however, was the sheer number of new titles that were being produced, the eclipse of the short story by the novel, and the genre's widening social reach. According to a correspondent for the *Observer*, in the first four months of 1938 alone some 200 mysteries had been sent to him for review and it seemed as though 'everyone . . . is writing, or is about to write, or has written a detective novel'.[12] A list of men who began writing mysteries as a sideline would include economists (G. D. H. Cole), poets (Cecil Day Lewis), cultural critics (Christopher Caudwell), scientists (C. P. Snow), barristers (Cyril Hare), and, at least among the ranks of short-story writers, clerics (Monsignor Ronald Knox); while among their less elevated female counterparts there were actors (Ngaio Marsh), advertising copywriters (Dorothy L. Sayers) and, most common of all, schoolteachers (Sayers again, Gladys Mitchell and Josephine Tey, who had been a physical-education instructor). Robert Graves and Alan Hodge's claim that 'low-brow reading was now dominated by the detective novel' registers the extraordinary momentum achieved by this type of writing, yet manages to sidestep the debates and criticism that it engendered.[13] For they fail to acknowledge the extent to which detective fiction actually came to

[12] E. P. Mathers, quoted in E. C. Bentley, *Those Days* (London: Constable, 1940), p. 249.

[13] Robert Graves and Alan Hodge, *The Long Week-end: A Social History of Great Britain 1918–1939* (London: Faber & Faber, 1940), p. 300.

be dominated by the professional middle classes during this period. A certain exclusivity was associated with the idea of the detective story in some circles, especially in comparison with the vulgar crime thriller, and this connoisseurship complicates any notion that it could simply be equated with 'low-brow reading' *per se*.

While detective fiction was obviously designed to divert and to entertain, its practitioners and devotees took their pleasures seriously in two, somewhat antithetical ways. In the first place, while mysteries had to be baffling or challenging, they also had to be fathomable, at least in principle. As a game in which readers pitted their wits against those of the author, a detective novel needs must be orderly, reasonable *and* fair, offering a real opportunity to play Sherlock Holmes, to out-think the fictional investigator. But for this to be possible, urged one influential current of opinion, detective fiction must also be rule-governed. It was, argued T. S. Eliot writing in the *New Criterion* in January 1927, the art of the 'sporting chance': 'a different, and as I think a superior type of detective story' was emerging and consequently 'some general rules of detective technique' could tentatively be formulated, rules whose observance provided the measure of a story's success. Eliot's five rules were only intended as an initial approximation yet, compared to some of his successors, they seem remarkably sober and parsimonious, warning against 'bizarre' or over-fussy plot devices, outlawing 'elaborate and incredible disguises', and urging the avoidance of 'occult phenomena' or far-fetched scientific discoveries. Most important of all was Eliot's insistence upon the *normality* of the criminal's 'character and motives', their accessibility to the ordinary reader, and his closely related stipulation that the detective be 'highly intelligent but not superhuman', a trait exemplified by the growing 'number of competent, but not infallible *professionals* in recent fiction'.[14]

Eliot's austere sense of gamesmanship was a far cry from the rumbustious ceremonies associated with the Detection Club (founded by Anthony Berkeley in 1928) to which so many of the major writers of detective fiction belonged. But this august body required its new members to swear to uphold a similar, if considerably more elaborate, set of rules. Though the language of the oath sounded parodic – candidates had, for example, to 'promise to observe a seemly moderation in the use of Gangs, Conspiracies, Death-Rays, Ghosts, Hypnotism, Trap-Doors, Chinamen, Super-Criminals and Lunatics; and utterly and for ever to forswear Mysterious Poisons unknown to Science' – the

[14] T. S. Eliot, 'Books of the Quarter', *New Criterion*, 5, 1 (January 1927), pp. 139–43. Emphasis in the original.

intention behind it was not.[15]. The rationale for the classic English detective novel hinged upon shedding the last vestiges of the adventure story, still very much present in *The Case-Book of Sherlock Holmes* (1927), and replacing it with what Dorothy L. Sayers once memorably described as 'that quiet enjoyment of the logical which we look for in our detective reading'.[16] When Conan Doyle made one of his villains a foreign scientist whose experimental quest for eternal youth transformed him into a sort of monkey, this Jekyll and Hyde-like twist was clearly a departure from the strict deductive paradigm that Sherlock Holmes had helped to inspire.[17] However, there were perhaps more insidious ways of flouting the reader's powers of reason. The desire for a sensational denouement could sometimes result in an over-dependence upon clever sleights of hand, producing a feeling of having been cheated once the solution to the mystery was in full view. Agatha Christie unquestionably gained many more fans than she lost when she used the fallible narrator as a criminal disguise in her audacious Hercule Poirot mystery *The Murder of Roger Ackroyd* (1926). But even among critics who applauded the brilliance of her trickery, there were those who thought a cautionary note was in order. T. S. Eliot warned a follower of Christie's rule-bending methods: 'you have succeeded, but *don't* do it again'.[18]

Seriousness of a different kind could arise when the detective novel was employed, however covertly, as a vehicle for social or political ideas. The classic English mystery story is often seen as an intrinsically conservative form, but this did not prevent G. D. H. and Margaret Cole, as members of the Fabian Society (and subsequently of the Detection Club), from slanting their work towards a suitably modest brand of socialism. Their series hero Superintendent Wilson was conceived as the perfect analogue for the ordinary man or woman in the street, the actual or desired Labour Party supporter whom they humorously addressed as 'you, [the] stout-hearted, democratic reader'.[19] Unaffected and diligent, 'educated but not highbrow', Wilson is the lower-middle-class scholarship boy who has chosen a police career instead of office work and has

[15] See 'The Detection Club Oath', in Howard Haycraft, ed., *The Art of the Mystery Story* (New York: Simon & Schuster, 1946), pp. 197–9. For a colourful description of a Detection Club meeting, see Ngaio Marsh, *Black Beech and Honeydew: An Autobiography* (London: Collins, 1984), pp. 311–12.

[16] Dorothy L. Sayers, 'Introduction', in Dorothy L. Sayers, ed., *Great Short Stories of Detection, Mystery and Horror* (London: Gollancz, 1928), p. 15.

[17] See 'The Adventure of the Creeping Man', in Arthur Conan Doyle, *The Case-Book of Sherlock Holmes* (London: John Murray, 1927), pp. 203–31. The stories in this collection all date from the 1920s.

[18] T. S. Eliot, 'Books of the Quarter', *Criterion*, 8, 33 (July 1929), p. 760.

[19] G. D. H. and Margaret Cole, *The Death of a Millionaire* (London: Collins, 1925), p. 4.

risen through the ranks. He has a good practical grasp of what makes people tick, a natural air of authority that allows him to handle baronets and shop stewards with equal ease and, most tellingly of all, he has no qualms about asking his wife's opinion when he gets into difficulty. In the Coles' novels, common sense, promoted by the solid virtues of companionate marriage, is always able to cut through the pretensions of class and gender to reveal the sordid human motives beneath, motives that are apt to be pecuniary in origin and are ignored at one's peril. Indeed, a lack of realism about 'human nature' is as much a political as an investigative error, a point that is underscored by Detective Sergeant Gulliver, the working-class Oxford ('Bullbridge') graduate chosen by Wilson to act as his assistant in *Murder at the Munition Works* (1940). A blunt Yorkshireman who describes himself as 'a sort of Socialist', Gulliver has little patience with the type of left-wing idealism that 'thinks you've only got to change the social system to make all men angels' and 'women, too'.[20] Such barbs aside, however, the Coles' forays into sociological observation and political critique were generally urbane and good-humoured. To find an implacably oppositional, even at times bilious, treatment of Britain's ruling classes one would have to look to the opposite end of the political spectrum. As depicted in G. K. Chesterton's *The Man Who Knew Too Much* (1922), Britain is so badly in hock to 'foreign financiers' that it has become prey to an 'infernal coolie capitalism' and stands on the brink of either 'war or ruin'.[21] But behind this corruption lurks a far darker sense of conspiracy charged with a virulent anti-Semitism that has discernable affinities with the rank populist invective of the radical Right and was more commonly to be found in the thriller than among the detective novel's rather casually worn prejudices. At the climax of Chesterton's bleak story the political elite is torn asunder as the immaculately well-connected, if somewhat reluctant, sleuth becomes the killer of his own uncle – a trusted military official who is in the process of betraying the country – in a last desperate attempt to set the world to rights.

For the purist, political matters were, strictly speaking, extraneous to the main business of the detective novel. But the recognition that 'a superior type of detective story' had been created brought its own dangers. As early as 1929, Dorothy L. Sayers noted that there were some indications 'that the possibilities of the formula are becoming exhausted' and that it was quite conceivable that the murder mystery would 'come to an end, simply because the public will have learnt all the tricks'. Interestingly, her own preferred solution to the

[20] G. D. H. and Margaret Cole, *Murder at the Munition Works* (London: Collins, 1940), pp. 36–8.
[21] G. K. Chesterton, *The Man Who Knew Too Much* (New York: Carroll & Graf, 1989), p. 172.

detective story's likely depletion, that of making it less like a crossword puzzle or chess problem and more closely akin to 'the novel of manners', only served to reinforce the pertinence of social and political issues.[22] Writing at a time when the status of women was changing rapidly, while many of the men who had endured the Great War were still struggling with its aftershock, Sayers often used her fiction to comment on the uneasy relations between the sexes. Her third Lord Peter Wimsey mystery, *Unnatural Death* (1927), promoted the sleuthing skills of 'Miss Climpson's Cattery', an organisation staffed by what mass newspapers like the *Daily Mail* had ignominiously dubbed 'superfluous women'. Although she is essentially Wimsey's assistant, Miss Climpson strikingly anticipates the figure of the spinster detective, immortalised by Christie's Miss Marple and Patricia Wentworth's Miss Silver at the end of the decade. However, it was only through the protracted and difficult courtship between Wimsey and the popular novelist Harriet Vane, which began with *Strong Poison* (1930) and reached its resolution in *Gaudy Night* (1935), that Sayers was finally able to produce what she saw as an emotionally literate version of the detective story, a synthesis of mystery and romance. Paradoxically, in transcending the limitations of the genre – and *Gaudy Night*'s painful exploration of the *ressentiment* that fuels an unschooled woman's proto-Fascist hate campaign against an Oxford college goes far beyond the mystery's usually perfunctory treatment of criminal motivation – Sayers effectively wrote herself out of detective fiction. In her later career she abandoned the mystery story for other popular forms, including radio drama and children's books, in order to extend her search for an audience of men and women no longer confined, as she once put it, to 'a single highly-sophisticated and over-sensitive class' nor socially divided between 'the kitchen' and 'the study'.[23]

The notion that it was the writer's duty to advance the literary merits of the detective story and so help to create a new, more discerning breed of common reader was by no means ubiquitous. Some of the most widely read detective novelists like Agatha Christie were content to be known as entertainers. But the worry that the 'superior type' of mystery was increasingly becoming too cerebral or too technical for its own good was matched by a corresponding fear that it was failing to compete with the excitement offered by its rival, the thriller. Much ink was spilled pejoratively contrasting the detective story with the thriller in the 'Golden Age', but in practice reviewers and booksellers tended to use these terms indiscriminately to refer to any work of fiction

22 Sayers, *Great Short Stories*, pp. 42–3.

23 Dorothy L. Sayers, 'The Present Status of the Mystery Story', *London Mercury*, 23, 133 (November 1930), pp. 49–50.

that made use of mystery or suspense. For the true *aficionado* of the detective story, however, the word 'thriller' did not merely designate a class of narrative that broke the rules: it named a type of writing that was so unruly as to be virtually incoherent. Worse still, this reckless unpredictability was just what seemed to make it utterly compelling, even addictive. Much to the distaste of authors like the Coles, the thriller delivered such a surfeit 'of crimes and gangs and secret societies and unknown poisons' that the reader ceased to mind 'whether the plot makes sense or not, provided you are carried along fast enough from one hairbreadth escape to the next'.[24] This is, of course, precisely the fictional miasma against which Wyndham Lewis inveighed in *The Apes of God*: the roller-coaster nightmare dreamed up by Edgar Wallace or Sax Rohmer that threatens to insinuate itself into the waking consciousness of every level of society and create a modern-day bedlam.

The genealogy of the thriller takes in a number of oddly assorted earlier forms: the imperial romance or adventure story, police memoirs and low-life literature, nineteenth-century sensation fiction and – as was also true of many detective novels – a generous serving of Gothic. Their traces linger in the creaky architecture of the modern thriller, which often appears to be fabricated out of the most heterogeneous materials, at once awesome and ramshackle. In this flexible, typically hybrid genre one discovers many mansions: invasion narratives, spy stories, gangster sagas, murder mysteries, pursuit or chase narratives, to cite merely a sample. But what differentiates them from the detective novel, apart from their breakneck pace and primary focus upon action, is an almost imperial sense of scale. In the thriller, crime takes on the dimensions of conquest and ultimately the entire social fabric is at risk. The opening scene of Edgar Wallace's *The Hand of Power* (1925) introduces a heroine who has been forced into an unexplained nocturnal drive across a remote, storm-tossed stretch of Dartmoor only to have the car brought to an abrupt halt by a sinister, hooded figure. But some three hundred pages later, the stakes of the novel have risen astronomically and she is now a passenger on board a hijacked ocean liner that is being steered towards Antarctica with a cargo containing fifty million dollars owed by Britain to the United States. This last detail is not unimportant: *The Hand of Power* has an American hero and ends in New York with a celebration of Manhattan's world-historical skyline, the portent of a decisive shift in the thriller's centre of gravity, which Wallace helped to bring about.

[24] G. D. H. and Margaret Cole, 'Meet Superintendent Wilson', in H. C. Bailey et al., *Meet the Detective* (London: George Allen & Unwin, 1935), p. 106.

Wallace dominated the popular-fiction market long after his death in 1932 and, no matter how exaggerated his fears, Wyndham Lewis was right to highlight the scale of the Wallace phenomenon. Using a dictaphone, Wallace could polish off a 70,000-word novel in a weekend and work on three stories at once, leading to jokes about 'the mid-day Wallace' on sale from railway newsvendors. An erratic working-class journalist with an eye on the main chance, he would turn his hand to virtually any type of writing – including film and theatre – yet always displaying the forceful demotic style that he had learned on the pre-war *Daily Mail*. His first real financial success came with the 'Sanders of the River' series, tales of how 'the British Government' kept 'a watchful eye upon some quarter of a million cannibal folk' in 'West Central Africa' through the offices of an implacable district commissioner, and the spirit of imperial romance continued to haunt many of his books.[25] In this sense, Wallace provides a link with the world of Kipling and Rider Haggard and his early thrillers like *The Four Just Men* (1905) or *Jack O'Judgment* (first serialised in 1919) display something of the same penchant for rough justice, a tendency that he had curbed appreciably by the late 1920s. His remarkable productivity was perfectly attuned to a fiction industry built around a plethora of titles in limited runs with frequent reprinting, but his growing reputation brought him into Hodder & Stoughton's star system in which large printings of new books by well-known names were given maximum publicity. The trademark crimson circle embossed with Wallace's signature was to be seen on two-shilling 'yellow jackets' in bookshops and commercial libraries everywhere, particularly the lower-middle- and working-class 'twopenny libraries' based in newsagents and tobacconists that multiplied so rapidly in the 1930s.

Wallace's success was partly a function of his versatility. If his hasty, feverishly inventive approach to composition occasionally resulted in a slew of inconsistencies and improbabilities, he could also craft tightly plotted mystery stories that would satisfy the most fastidious readers. Indeed, his skill at gathering in a large, socially diverse audience has been compared to that of 'a cautiously egalitarian' innkeeper who surreptitiously removes 'the partition between the saloon and the public bars' at just the right hour when their habituées would be 'too merry to notice that they were mingling'.[26] Unlike many thriller writers, Wallace was able to appeal to women as much as men, since his breezily unmemorable heroes and blankly attractive heroines, set amid a gallery of sub-Dickensian cockneys, crooks and eccentrics, were sufficiently featureless

[25] Edgar Wallace, *Sanders of the River* (London: Ward, Lock, 1911), p. 7.
[26] William V. Butler, *The Durable Desperadoes* (London: Macmillan, 1973), p. 71.

to enable them to be customised by his readers' own fertile imaginations. By contrast, most thrillers by other writers had tended to be abrasively masculine performances, often leavened with a dash of aristocratic *hauteur*. To a twenty-first-century ear, Wallace's rival Sydney Horler came dangerously close to caricature in his complaint that 'there are far too many emasculated twits of various nauseating species' on offer, when what was 'badly wanted in modern fiction' were 'men – *real* men' like his own hero the Hon. Timothy Overbury Standish, son of the Earl of Quorn.[27] Nevertheless, his sentiments are revealing. 'Tiger' Standish was obviously intended as a corrective to Sayers's Lord Peter Wimsey and as an upmarket addition to that line of patriotic derring-do embodied in John Buchan's *The Thirty-Nine Steps* (1915) and 'Sapper' (H. C. McNeile)'s *Bulldog Drummond* (1920), in whose worst-case imaginings Bolsheviks and Jews, frequently portrayed as equivalents, were threatening to pull the nation down. But, tellingly, Horler was insistent that 'Tiger' Standish was also what women readers wanted – a sign that the thriller had begun to change.

Thrillers had always been torn between a grim sense of purpose and a studied nonchalance in the face of danger, the latter a hallmark of the self-possessed gentlemanly amateurs who were supposed to represent the deepest well-springs of British character. But lightness of manner could easily be transmuted into pure exuberance, producing harum-scarum adventures like Agatha Christie's *The Secret Adversary* (1922) that lacked the moral urgency of the pre-World War I invasion narratives of William Le Queux or Erskine Childers. If Christie took the thriller less than seriously, others reacted against its conservatism either by open mockery – Leslie Charteris's 'dago' hero Manrique in *The Bandit* (1929) was a calculated insult aimed directly at the xenophobic 'Sapper' tradition – or, as in the spy thriller, by lending the genre a new kind of seriousness that called its political assumptions into question. W. Somerset Maugham's episodic *Ashenden* (1927) may not have been particularly thriller-like, but its world-weary workaday ethos of sordid manipulation and political expediency showed how the spy novel might be thoroughly de-romanticised, trimmed of any melodramatic excess. By adopting Maugham's tone and reintroducing the element of suspense, Graham Greene and Eric Ambler created a thriller in which a nation's borders are the site of difficulty and confusion rather than a solid line of defence. In Greene's *Stamboul Train* (1932), for example, commitments and desires change destinations against a background of abortive revolution and political intrigue as the Orient Express travels east and

[27] Sydney Horler, 'Meet Tiger Standish', in Bailey, *Meet the Detective*, pp. 60–1.

in Ambler's *The Mask of Dimitrios* (1939) frontiers are merely an opportunity for a murderer to exchange identities and throw his pursuers off the scent. For Ambler especially, the thriller revolves around decency under pressure – the teacher blackmailed into spying by a foreign government, the engineer whose life is endangered by his company's arms deals, the academic detective novelist who gets mixed up with real criminals – and, as often as not, it is market capitalism, in the shape of an amoral corporation or trust, that is the ultimate villain.

Yet for all its iconoclasm, this was a tradition that was still relatively inhospitable to women whether as authors or as characters, even where the latter were more than mere ciphers. Anne Crowder in Greene's *A Gun for Sale* (1936) possesses sympathy as well as pluck, but at the novel's close her remorse at having betrayed the deformed young gunman whose suffering she pitied dissolves into a saccharine vision of tawdry childish pleasures. As though in recognition of the thriller's constricted emotional atmospherics, one increasingly sees a polarisation between male and female taste during the 1930s. These were the years when Mills & Boon began to specialise as a publisher of romantic fiction, rather experimentally at first, but with rising sales between 1935 and 1945. While displaying 'a freer style' than their later reputation would lead one to suspect, the ground rules associated with the firm's novels – narratives told from the perspective of a young, virginal, often orphaned, heroine who is paired with an older, powerful, yet enigmatically difficult 'Alpha male' – were nevertheless starting to fall into place (though their origins can be traced back at least to Charlotte Brontë's *Jane Eyre*).[28] To some extent, Mills & Boon authors like Denise Robins were able to take the greater sexual frankness pioneered by such earlier bestsellers as *The Sheik* as a licence to tackle such taboo subjects as marital rape or divorce, but always from within a firmly moralistic frame, even if this necessitated false marriages, unexpected legacies and other hoary fig-leaves. That there was a real tension here is indicated by the fact that the genre's major triumph in this period, Daphne du Maurier's *Rebecca* (1938), came from outside the Mills & Boon stable. The collusion of the novel's nameless female narrator with its tormented hero around a genuinely guilty secret enacted the romantic bond while breaking the cardinal rule of innocence and forcing the couple into exile to preserve a less than blissfully happy ending. At the same time, du Maurier's choice of a country estate as

[28] Joseph McAleer, *Passion's Fortune: The Story of Mills & Boon* (Oxford University Press, 1999), p. 170.

the scene of crime that must remain hidden at all costs represented a kind of epitaph for the detective novel.

An epitaph of a rather different sort can be seen in local versions of the imported male hard-boiled thriller. In his later novels, Edgar Wallace both reproduced the brutal milieu of the Chicago gangster in *On the Spot* (1931) and also imagined what might have happened *When the Gangs Came to London* (1932). But it was Peter Cheyney who went one better and, in private-eye stories like *The Urgent Hangman* (1938), rewrote London in the image of Dashiell Hammett's San Francisco, creating a strangely sub-American idiolect that by 1944 could sell 1.5 million copies annually. The attempt to beat the Americans at their own game set an agenda that continued through the war years and beyond. The publisher of James Hadley Chase's notorious bestseller *No Orchids for Miss Blandish* (1939) even boasted that the book 'was responsible for improving national morale in 1940', a bizarre claim to make about a tale of unparalleled ferocity in which the eponymous heroine commits suicide after having been raped by a sadistic killer.[29] While Mills & Boon were careful to temper their wartime romances with suitably patriotic passages, Chase was in no doubt about the successful formula underpinning the violent sexuality of his own peculiarly loveless fictional world. What the public wanted, he once opined, was 'speed, violence, women, America'.[30] Ironically, his words were about to acquire a new and arguably more disquieting resonance as, late in 1944, American publishers started to plan the promotion of cheap editions and mass-market paperbacks on a 'global basis.'[31] Just as peace was in sight, another long-term war – this time commercial rather than military – was already on the horizon.

[29] *Bookseller* (31 August 1944), p. 255.

[30] 'James Hadley Chase' in Patricia Burgess, ed., *The Annual Obituary 1985* (London and Chicago: St James Press, 1988), p. 57.

[31] *Bookseller* (7 December 1944), p. 638.

18

Theatre and drama between the wars

MAGGIE B. GALE

Systems of periodisation promise a means of creating useful boundaries and categories of materials to be analysed, but they also contain inherent problems in relation to the processes of analysing those materials. This is especially the case with the period in question, traditionally seen by theatre historians as one in which mainstream drama did not generally reflect social change but, rather, pandered to middle-class tastes and sensibilities.[1] The inter-war theatre industry was made up of a number of interdependent sectors, however, just as the middle classes themselves were widely defined and in a period of social transition.[2] There were clear shifts and developments in the theatre industry and, as a consequence, in the kinds of plays being produced. However, these shifts and developments, although precipitated by it, had already been set in motion before World War I. The growth of the middle classes during the late nineteenth century, the increase in leisure time and the changed social attitudes to theatre and drama as a means of education and social cohesion are as influential upon the developments in British theatre and drama after World War I as are the extraordinary changes in the economic factors controlling the industry as a whole. The theatre of the period, 'reflected many divergent trends and tendencies, and the impact of a number of individuals. It resists simplification.'[3] Many of the theatre critics of the period, highly idiosyncratic and class-conscious as much of their work is, clearly identify the economics of the theatre industry (rises in rent, the formation of management cartels) and a 'new' middle-class audience – often identified implicitly as lower-middle-class – as influencing the kinds of plays that the newly all-powerful managements were

[1] See Jean Chothia, *English Drama of the Early Modern Period: 1890–1940* (London: Longman, 1996) and Andrew Davies, *Other Theatres: The Development of Alternative and Experimental Theatre in Britain* (London: Macmillan, 1987).

[2] See Ross McKibbin, *Classes and Cultures: England 1918–1951* (Oxford University Press, 1998).

[3] Michael Woolf, 'In Minor Key: Theatre 1930–1955', in Gary Day, ed., *Literature and Culture in Modern Britain 1930–1955* (Harlow: Longman, 1997), p. 89.

prepared to put on. For some, the drama of the inter-war years represented a cultural shift similar to that experienced in theatre during the Restoration (a new generation of playwrights, a new audience and an insular theatre world), although this reveals as much about the lack of critical assessment of Restoration drama at the time as it does the drama of the inter-war years. Thus Camillo Pelizzi saw the drama of the late Victorian and Edwardian periods as being the 'last great phase'; for him, drama of the inter-war years reflected the consequences of the crisis which the Great War caused for the middle classes:

> The English middle classes were too great in their period of success not to compel the country now, at the time of reckoning, to go through a period of disorientation and discouragement and, in art, of melancholy and indolence. English present-day drama is proof of this.[4]

For others, such as critic and playwright St John Ervine or chronicler McQueen Pope, the theatre and the drama had lost their identity because of changes in ownership, both in terms of management and in terms of audience. St John Ervine in 1933 felt that drama as an art form was in danger of becoming overrun with political propaganda and more importantly of becoming 'womanised' and, for McQueen Pope, the glamour and 'family run' characteristics of the theatre industry had all but been destroyed.[5]

Such assessments of the state of drama reveal a sense that somehow a great period of dramatic writing had now passed and that the next great phase was yet to come. This is certainly how the inter-war period is traditionally viewed by those who see the next 'great phase' of play-writing as arriving in the mid-1950s. These assessments are also, however, predicated on the belief that 'literary' drama and 'popular' drama can somehow be differentiated in black-and-white terms; this has often been the basis for much criticism of drama of the period. So on the one hand we have the popular drama of Coward, Maugham, Travers and of most of the numerous women writing for the theatre of the period, set up in opposition to the work of Shaw, Auden and Isherwood, O'Casey and so on. Yet the overriding structure of the theatre industry during the inter-war years allowed for many more cross-currents and convergences than such a distinction recognises.

4 Camillo Pellizzi, *English Drama: The Last Great Phase* (London: Macmillan, 1935), p. 301.

5 St John Ervine, *The Theatre in My Time* (London: Rich & Cowan, 1935), p. 135; also see Jim Davis and Victor Emeljanow, '"Wistful Remembrancer": the Historiographical Problem of Macqueen-Popery', *New Theatre Quarterly* 17, 4 (2001), pp. 299–309 (Cambridge University Press).

The structure of the industry is important because it shaped production patterns and, by and large, production patterns influenced the publication of plays. There was no state funding for theatre until the 1940s and the increased level of rents between 1914 and the 1920s meant that the running costs of mounting a production were immeasurably higher than they had been before the 1914–18 war. Very few new theatres were built during the inter-war years and many of the larger theatres, especially outside the West End and in large city centres, had been converted into cinemas by the end of the 1930s. The theatre industry was controlled largely by the commercial interests of a small cartel of businessmen and managers, led by men like Emile Littler and 'Binkie' Beaumont, who saw theatre as a viable and profitable form of investment.[6] As the cost of renting London property in general and theatres in particular rose, so actor–managers who produced their own repertoire, so powerful in the late nineteenth and early twentieth centuries, were by the end of the 1930s few and far between. However, the independent theatre-producing organisations such as those at the Everyman in Hampstead – where Coward had his first play produced – or at the Gate Theatre in Notting Hill – where Peter Godfrey championed Expressionism and was responsible for bringing a great deal of experimental American and European drama onto the English stages – also fed into the commercial system.[7] Transfers into the West End kept small play-producing societies financially afloat and this affected drama originally produced outside of the metropolis. Thus the transfer of the Birmingham Repertory theatre production of Eden Phillpotts's *The Farmer's Wife*, among others, was a great commercial success despite the fact that the Repertory theatres were perceived as catering for a less populist audience.

The Repertory movement saw itself as removed from the star system of actor–managers or the commercial constraints of a theatre concerned only with profit. Equally, models of organisation had been adapted from European practice: a season of plays providing a mixture of the 'classical repertoire' and modern plays or new dramas. The movement to form a National Theatre during the Edwardian period connected with the impetus behind the formation of the Repertory theatre movement. In terms of the development of drama as a form, the Repertory movement and those pressing for the formation of a National Theatre in England were concerned that drama should represent art

[6] Richard Huggett, *Binkie Beaumont: Eminence Grise of the West End Theatre 1933–1973* (London: Hodder & Stoughton, 1989).

[7] See Maggie B. Gale, *West End Women: Women on the London Stage 1918–1962* (London: Routledge, 1996), pp. 38–72 and Norman Marshall, *The Other Theatre* (London: John Lehmann, 1948).

for art's sake and this they shared in common with the independent, subscription and art theatres of the inter-war years for which,

> The studio or art theatre exists to prevent dramatic art from being wiped out by the commercially minded. Unlike ordinary theatre goers, the supporters of art theatres have dramatic convictions.[8]

Subscription or club theatres were beyond the reaches of the censor because they were privately run, through membership or some other kind of financial backing. Through such theatres the works of European and American expressionists such as Ernst Toller, Susan Glaspell and Eugene O'Neill were given production. Although commercial managements were unlikely to produce such financially risqué drama they did take risks in producing other Expressionist work such as Sophie Treadwell's *The Life Machine* (1927 – the original American title is *Machinal*), and the work of other tried and tested playwrights who borrowed from or adapted the Expressionist form, particular examples being Somerset Maugham's *Sheppey* (1933), an everyman 'rags to riches and rejection of capitalist values' play, or the work of J. B. Priestley, where often the obsession with memory and time is framed in an expressionistic context.

Thus, experimental forms of drama existed within the mainstream commercial sector but were small in number. The Repertory and independent theatres could only sustain a certain level of idealism in terms of the economics of theatre production and the inter-war years saw the virtual demise of both, with the Liverpool and Birmingham Repertories being among the few to survive; some historians have seen their demise in terms of the growth of other entertainment industries such as the radio and cinema.[9] The independent theatres both flourished and to some extent collapsed during the period, but their influence upon development in dramatic literature was immense; they were responsible for bringing to the stage writers such as Noel Coward, R. C. Sherriff and Lillian Hellman – whose extraordinary *The Children's Hour* was banned for public production in the mid-1930s – as well as championing lesser produced and frequently censored European playwrights like Ibsen, Strindberg and Capek.[10]

The shape of dramatic output during the period was influenced by economic factors and by the structure of the theatre industry but it was also heavily

8 Phillip Godfrey, *Backstage* (London: Harrap, 1933), pp. 160–70.

9 George Rowell and Anthony Jackson, *The Repertory Movement: A History of Regional Theatre in Britain* (Cambridge University Press, 1984), p. 54.

10 See Steve Nicholson, 'Unnecessary Plays: European Drama and the British Censor in the 1920s', *Theatre Research International*, 20, 1 (1995), pp. 30–6.

influenced by a perceived change in the class make-up of the audience. Ticket prices slowly rose and factors such as the Entertainments Tax of 1924 arguably narrowed accessibility, but clearly after the 1914–18 war, literary theatre was less of an upper-middle-class pursuit than it had once been. The setting up of the Drama League in 1919, an organisation built upon the growing popularity of amateur play production as a form of leisure, formalised the amateur market for drama and in particular for the one-act play. Equally, in the 1920s especially, there was an influx of new playwrights onto British stages – many of those who had experienced success before World War I had all but disappeared from the stage by the late 1930s.

> Writing for the stage . . . has now become so much a woman's business that there were moments in the nineteen thirties when a female stage monopoly seemed in process of creation.[11]

In terms of changes in audience make-up, a number of critics have commented on the influx of female audiences and women dramatists into the professional theatre of the period. The critics, often led by St John Ervine, claimed that in the period immediately after the 1914–18 war, 'flapper' audiences dominated the theatres, and although the angst around this died down a little during the 1920s, St John Ervine was still so determined to berate the 'feminisation of theatre' that in 1933 he suggested:

> Two dangers at present threaten the theatre . . . one that it may become womanised; the other that it may become a machine for party propaganda . . . a prime difference between the man's theatre and a womanised theatre is that women eagerly sought admission to the former and were not happy until they obtained it, whereas men have no wish to enter the latter and increasingly abstain from it . . . Women are less apt in drama than men . . .[12]

Over the period in question, the average percentage of plays in production by women or by male–female partnerships was around 16 per cent: it was often higher than this and rarely lower than 10.8 per cent. Better-known women playwrights such as Clemence Dane, Margaret Kennedy, Gertrude Jennings, Gordon Daviot (Elizabeth Mackintosh), Dodie Smith, Aimée Stuart and Esther McCracken were part of a gender-defined group which also included G. B. Stern, Joan Temple, F. Tennyson Jesse, Joan Morgan, Marie Stopes and many

[11] Rex Pogson, *Theatre Between the Wars (1919–1939)* (Clevedon, Somerset: Triangle Press, 1947).
[12] Ervine, *Theatre in My Time*, pp. 135–6.

others. Many of these playwrights had begun their professional careers as actresses, some were also well-known novelists and others even went into production later in their careers. Of the many women writing for the stage during the period in question, some had other notable careers; G. B. Stern as a novelist, Marie Stopes as a pioneer of the contraceptive movement, Clemence Dane as a film scriptwriter and novelist and Dodie Smith as the author of two of the bestselling works of literature during the mid-twentieth century – *I Capture the Castle* and *One Hundred and One Dalmatians*. Few of the women writing for the theatres of the day experimented with form or had an affiliation with the innovative Modernists – they fed much more in to the popular market but were liked by such Modernist figures as Rebecca West. West's own *The Return of the Soldier* was adapted for the stage by John Van Druten, and other novelists such as Kate O'Brien (*Distinguished Villa* – 1926) and Rosamund Lehmann (*No More Music* – 1939) occasionally turned to the stage as a means of expression. Women playwrights were writing for an emerging 'women's market' as were many of the key Modernist literary figures of the day.[13]

Second-wave-feminist theatre critics have been quick to dismiss the work of these women, suggesting that there was only 'the occasional play about the "woman question"'.[14] Yet a content analysis suggests that although such playwrights were not explicitly feminist in terms of the definition created by the struggle for the vote, many of them wrote from a woman's perspective, using domestic or family settings, representing generational difference among women, the tension between wanting a career and running a family, the consequences of war for women left to manage on the home front and so on. Some plays, such as G. B. Stern's *The Man Who Pays The Piper* (1931), even suggested radical solutions to career angst where traditional gender roles might be reversed and the man run the household. Others specifically focused on women and the relation between gender and the economy during

[13] Bonnie Kime Scott, *Refiguring Modernism, Vol. 1: The Women of 1928* (Bloomington: Indiana University Press, 1995), p. 232. See also Maggie B. Gale, 'Women Playwrights of the 1920s and 1930s', in Elaine Aston and Janelle Reinelt, eds., *The Cambridge Companion to Modern British Women Playwrights* (Cambridge University Press: 2000), pp. 23–37, and Rebecca Cameron, 'Women Playwrights and the Modernist Conception of Genius: Clemence Dane's *Will Shakespeare* (1921) and Gordon Daviot's *The Laughing Woman* (1934)', *Essays in Theatre*, 18, 2 (2000), pp. 161–78, and 'Irreconcilable Differences: Divorce and the Women's Drama before 1945', *Modern Drama*, 44, 4 (2001), pp. 476–90; and Christina Hauck, 'Through A Glass Darkly: *A Game of Chess* and Two Plays by Marie Stopes', *Journal of Modern Literature*, 21, 1 (1997), pp. 109–19.

[14] Michelene Wandor, *Understudies: Theatre and Sexual Politics* (London: Methuen, 1981), p. 10.

the inter-war years. Thus Aimée and Phillip Stuart's *9 Till 6* (1930), where the authors deliberately set the hierarchies of the women working in a fashion shop against the economic dynamics of the retail world, ran for some 259 performances in the West End, and was felt by one commentator to be,

> ... a searching and fair minded ... analysis of women's place in the world of industry. There are those who say that this is a women's counterpart of *Journey's End*; its field of battle is the business world; its privations are the ruthless denials of ease and beauty; its sex problems as incidental.[15]

Some plays, like Clemence Dane's *Bill of Divorcement* (1921) and Fryn Tennyson Jesse's *The Pelican* (1926), dealt with changes to the dynamics of marital relations, such as the liberalising of the divorce laws. Others such as those by Marie Stopes (*Vectia* (1926) and *Our Ostriches* (1923)), brought even more contentious subject-matter, like issues around contraception, to the stage. Although Stopes's Eugenicist ideas around contraception seem reactionary to us today, as a playwright she truly challenged what might and might not be shown and discussed on stage. In her preface to *Vectia*, banned by the official censor, she points out that

> Women have things to say which men have not the ears to hear. Women who think are often like wireless waves without a receiver ... At women as 'lesser men' the critics jibe ... What is the woman dramatist up against today? Men managers, men producers, men theatre owners ... men critics, men censors.[16]

Thus Stopes recognised the gendering of censorship and criticism and despite her own seeming conservatism saw issues around motherhood and childbearing as important and relevant to the audience of the day. Alison Light has pointed to a 'renewed conservatism' in women's writing after World War I,[17] and certainly among the women playwrights of the inter-war period there is little by way of formal innovation but the content of their plays, the areas of discussion brought into the drama and onto the public stage, removed them from the nineteenth-century tradition of commercial-theatre writing to some extent – these were women writing consciously about women's lives. They often used the relatively conservative 'well-made play' formula, or the domestic comedy, but their popularity was discernible as was the concern their presence caused critics.

15 Constance Smedley, from a letter to the editor of the *Sunday Times*, 2 March 1930.
16 Marie Stopes, *A Banned Play (Vectia) and a Preface on Censorship* (London: Bale & Daniellson, 1926), p. 9.
17 Alison Light, *Forever England: Feminism, Literature and Conservatism Between the Wars* (London: Routledge, 1991).

Much of the commercial drama of the age, regardless of the gender of authorship, reflected the conservatism of the society from which it originated – however, a great deal of what was produced challenged socially acceptable ideas about the family, marital relationships, middle-class propriety, the ethics and validity of war and so on. Critics were often concerned about the so-called influx and increased presence of women playwrights and their popularity among female audiences so that even in 1945 the work of such women was seen as lacking drama and sentimental.[18] But the critics, often coming from Oxbridge backgrounds (many of whom tried their hand at playwriting themselves), were also wary of what appears to have been a new generation of younger playgoers. Somerset Maugham, whose success with audiences began to falter the more overt social critique his plays contained, spoke of the enthusiasm of the Gallery audiences and of the fact that 'the best plays appeal to a universal audience; all men and women, whatever their class or education' should be able to enthuse. For him it was no good a play appealing to a 'clique or class', and this is something which many of the critics embroiled in the arguments around the function of theatre found difficult to accept;[19] they yearned for 'plays of ideas' which had appeared to be the new force of drama before World War I. For one audience member of the day, the 'old-time galleryite' was 'hopelessly outnumbered by young men and women with open minds and modern ideas: popular education has had its effects'.[20] Among such audiences the popular playwrights were Noel Coward, Miles Malleson, Frank Vosper, John van Druten, Patrick Hamilton and Harold Harwood. It was many of the above, alongside Emlyn Williams, Ben Travers and Frederick Lonsdale, whose work dominated the theatres of the inter-war period but there are still few critical works on any of these authors. Even Noel Coward has had a limited critical treatment although he was one of the most prolific and influential playwrights of his generation. To some extent this is because the political and poetic drama of the period has received more attention, but more cultural–materialist studies have emerged in recent years.[21]

Clearly specific 'types' of plays were popular during the period; those seen as 'women's dramas' had a certain amount of economic potential for managements as did so-called 'sex plays' such as van Druten's *Young Woodley* (1928) or Miles Malleson's *The Fanatics* (1927), in which an older woman openly discusses her sex life with a younger man. Managements and playwrights alike

[18] Lynton Hudson, *The Twentieth-Century Drama* (London: Harrap, 1946), p. 64.

[19] Fred Bason, *Gallery Unreserved* (London: John Heritage, 1931), p. xvi. [20] Ibid., p. 15.

[21] Clive Barker and Maggie B. Gale, *British Theatre Between the Wars, 1918–1939* (Cambridge University Press, 2000).

were wary of the power of the Censor, who could ban a play late into the process of production, but the process of censorship was never so clear-cut as to ban mention of sex outright.[22] Christa Winslow's moving *Children in Uniform* (1933), a play with an overt lesbian theme, was passed for production as long as the specifically German context of the play was made clear.[23] Such plays were celebrated by a post-war generation desperate to create a different world from that of their parents, wanting to talk about sex and marital relationships in real and modern terms. A good example of this is Michael Egan's *The Dominant Sex* (1935) which had a long West End run; an extraordinarily modern play, in which two sets of couples argue and bicker about where and how they should live. One of the couples has lived together before marrying, much to the disgust of their landlords, who threaten to evict them. A detailed discussion between the two generations about morality and double standards follows. Equally, the lead female forces her husband to admit the chauvinism of his assumption that they should pander to *his* career and that *she* should give up work should they choose to have children. The play makes strong links between gender, marriage and career choices as did other plays of the period such as Aimée and Phillip Stuart's *Sixteen* (1934), G. B. Stern's *The Matriarch* (1931) and van Druten's *London Wall* (1931). Even Coward's worlds of social privilege and acid wit allow for commentary on gender, generation, sexuality and life choices (see *The Vortex* (1925) and *Private Lives* (1930)). Rodney Ackland's *Strange Orchestra* (1932) plays on such interests in an imagined Bohemian Chelsea of the early 1930s. This haunting play is set in the hallway of Vera Lyndon's London flat, the most conspicuous piece of furniture being Vera's divan. Here she holds court while her offspring and tenants go about their daily lives. The hallway plays witness to a range of classes, the London young and the London bohemian, illicit affairs and failed romances. *Strange Orchestra*, written in a style reminiscent of Chekhov, is full of discussions about the meaning and purpose of life in a post-war world, and one of the key moments is the failed suicide of one couple who wanted to kill themselves for fear that life could never be any better than at that moment. The inhabitants of the flat, although touched by poverty, illness and male sexual opportunism, seem somehow to be living in a superficial world of their own, carrying on as if nothing could be more important than the squabbling and discomfort of their own living conditions.

[22] See Steve Nicholson, *The Censorship of British Drama 1900–1968: Vol. 1: 1900–1932* (Exeter University Press, 2003).

[23] See John Deeney, 'Censoring the Uncensored: *Children in Uniform*', *New Theatre Quarterly*, 16, 3 (August 2000), and 'When Men Were Men and Women Were Women', in Barker and Gale, *British Theatre Between the Wars*, pp. 63–87.

Equally if not more popular than so called 'sex' plays, were plays which used the thriller format, full of sexually alluring, cunning but violent heroes such as *Bull Dog Drummond* (1921), or Emlyn Williams's *Night Must Fall* (1935) in which Williams himself played the lead, Dan. Ernest Short argues that Dan, who walks around with the severed head of his first victim in a hat-box, sees *himself* as a victim of life's circumstances and uses his perfected criminal skills to get back at fate and at a society which he feels has failed him. Short recognised the philosophical and psychological complexity underpinning much of the thriller genre, where crime was often framed as an aesthetic activity with its own seductive forms.[24] One reason for the popularity of such thrillers was the fact that particular actors were known for their masterly acting of the thriller hero – actors such as Charles Laughton, Gerald du Maurier and Emlyn Williams, whose *A Murder Has Been Arranged* (1930) also played on the thriller formula. But thrillers also fed into post-war anxiety and the confused or double-sided desire for a new kind of hero. John Stokes has pointed to the ways in which upper-class heroes such as Bulldog Drummond came from an officer class forcefully relocating itself in a post-war world which had clearly betrayed it.[25] Similarly the popularity of such plays as Hamilton's *Rope* (1929) also shows an audience drawn to a cold fascination with murder.

Rope was one of two long-running plays by Patrick Hamilton, and both it and *Gaslight* (1938) were later adapted for film. The play, based on a murder case in America, depicts two men who have murdered another and incarcerated him in a chest on which they later serve tea to friends and acquaintances, one of whom is the dead man's father. Critics were baffled by what appeared to be a motiveless murder but the play concerns the physical strength of one man over another, and the ability of man to murder without actual provocation. To some extent *Rope* hints at the struggle with nihilistic and sado-masochistic urges; it is very much a play which innately reflects post-World War I social angst.[26] Just as the hero of *Rope*, the wounded war hero–poet Rupert, makes a plea for some sort of commitment to personal and social responsibility, so many of the plays of the period worked the thriller and detective format as a means of social commentary. J. B. Priestley, one of the most prolific playwrights of the inter-war years and beyond, often used the detective format and a manipulation of time as a way of taking the audience through the cause and effect of personal, and in

[24] Ernest Short, *Sixty Years of Theatre* (London: Eyre & Spottiswoode, 1951), pp. 320–1.

[25] John Stokes, 'Body Parts: the Success of the Thriller in the Inter-war Years', in Barker and Gale, eds., *British Theatre Between the Wars*, pp. 38–62 (p. 42).

[26] See Michael Kane, *Modern Men: Mapping Masculinity in English and German Literature 1880–1930* (London: Cassell, 1990), and Alan Sinfield, *Out on Stage: Lesbian and Gay Theatre in the Twentieth Century* (New Haven: Yale University Press, 1999).

turn, social action. In *Dangerous Corner* (1932), the meeting in a country house of a group of friends and work colleagues provides the background for revelations about the state of the English middle classes. The events surrounding the death of Robert Caplan's brother Martin slowly reveal the inability of the friends to deal with the truth about their relationships with both Martin and with each other. Martin has had illicit affairs with both Robert's wife Freda and with Gordon and has clearly played them off against each other. The accusation that he had stolen company money, and the family's desire to keep this out of the public eye, has meant that no one has dealt with the truth about his outrageous behaviour and the way in which he has manipulated his relationships with all of them. The family's desire to maintain his honour has meant that each has lied and twisted the truth, the truth about a man they, in actual fact, clearly never knew. Such a deconstruction of the belief in moral sensibility and social responsibility within the middle-class family was at the centre of much of Priestley's work and can be seen most clearly perhaps in *An Inspector Calls* (1945) where Priestley's crafting of the well-made play with manipulations of time and the Expressionist form are perhaps best exemplified.

The idea of social and moral responsibility was situated in the background landscape of many of the plays of the period which used the event of World War I to drive their narrative. There were very few plays which looked directly at war until late into the 1920s. There was an occasional play which mentioned war widows or the disturbance caused by the billeting of army officers in one's home, but it wasn't till plays like van Druten's adaptation of Rebecca West's *The Return of The Soldier* (1928)[27] or Somerset Maugham's *For Services Rendered* (1932) that the effects of war on the soldiers who fought them or on the families destroyed by war came into the public arena provided by live performance. R. C. Sherriff's *Journey's End* (1928) was the first play to bring the trenches onto the stage and as such was a clear condemnation of the war and what it had done to the men who fought it and the world they had left behind. First produced in a private theatre, the play went on to a long run in the West End. Set in a trench near the frontline in France, the world of the play is strangely domesticated. Sherriff creates an all-male world where the rituals of mealtime and watch duty define the rhythm of the action. The characters are constructed as a kind of family, but clearly a middle-class family, with 'uncle' Osbourne and Stanhope as the older brother, heroic in the eyes of the younger officers; the

[27] See Joanna Labon, 'Rebecca West and *The Return of the Soldier*: from Novel to Play', in Maggie B. Gale and Viv Gardner, eds., *Women and Theatre Occasional Papers 4*, University of Birmingham Department of Drama, 1997, pp. 87–96.

'servant' Mason is the only working-class figure on stage, while the others are off stage, waiting to go into battle. The play is a condemnation of the servicing of a fantasy of England and the Empire; playing on the device of a domestication of stage space, Sherriff creates a world of men, imagining taking tea with their families, as they in effect wait to die. The realities of sleep deprivation and poor nutrition puncture the narrative and a questioning of the truth of war – the effects of depressive alcoholism, overbearing fear, frayed nerves, the sound of battle and the fact that the men are given mugs of spirits before going into battle – force upon the audience a picture of war unseen on the stage before this point. After Sherriff there was little to compete on the commercial stages with such overt criticism of war; Coward's expressionistic and strange political play, *Post Mortem* (1931), did not see professional production.

Overt references to political events were rare in the commercial sector and even in many of the independent theatres of the day. Very few plays dealt with the direct effects of economic depression, although there were some exceptions, such as Ronald Gow and Walter Greenwood's *Love on The Dole* (1934), which centred on a Lancastrian family struggling to survive unemployment and social deprivation. Here patriarchy is turned upside-down as the older daughter in the family earns the money and the younger son is caught up in a problematic romance. The hero of the piece, a socialist and political activist, is killed trying to quieten a demonstration and the daughter can only escape the cycle of poverty by going to work for a profiteer as his 'housekeeper'. The play is a bleak depiction of working-class life and the message is not a hopeful one. Other plays, such as Miles Malleson's *Six Men of Dorset* (1934) about the Tolpuddle Martyrs, put political arguments directly onto the stage, but such overt politically driven texts, apart of course from Shaw's plays, which were far more sophisticated in argument, were few and far between. It was outside of the mainstream that political theatre flourished, in Scotland, the North and in the Unity Theatre in London.

Joe Corrie, a Scottish miner, dramatised the effects of the General Strike on a starving community in *A Time o' Strife* (1927), but it was the amateur and semi-professional theatre groups of the Workers' Theatre Movement and Unity Theatre which created and performed political dramas, using agit-prop techniques adapted from Germany and Russia and Living Newspaper techniques from American political theatre of the 1930s.[28] Such organisations as

[28] See Colin Chambers, *The Story of Unity Theatre* (London: Lawrence & Wishart, 1989) and Raphael Samuel, Ewan MacColl and Stuart Cosgrove, *Theatres of the Left 1880–1935*,

came under the banner of the Workers' Theatre Movement were plagued by financial crisis; the American equivalent was substantially funded as the Federal Theatre Project, at one time employing some 12,000 workers – no such funding reached the British Workers' Theatre.[29] Plays such as London taxi-driver Herbert Hodge's *Where's That Bomb?*, Irwin Shaw's *Bury the Dead*, Clifford Odets's *Waiting for Lefty* and Jack Lindsay's *On Guard for Spain* were the staples of many of these political theatre groups. European influences, the impact of which in terms of commercial theatre was not to be felt until the 1950s, came into the British theatrical repertoire through these political groups; thus Brecht and Piscator were to influence the work of Ewan MacColl and Joan Littlewood, both of whom were involved with political theatre in Manchester before setting up Theatre Workshop in East London in the mid-1940s. Plays such as *Johnnie Noble* and *Uranium 235* mixed text, movement, variety and politically astute commentary and analysis; these productions toured countrywide and were often rewritten and adapted for different performances.[30]

The independent theatres in London hosted some experimentation in the form of poetic drama, much of which came out of a movement towards the overt politicisation of literature in the 1930s. Such poetic drama was unattractive to the management monopolies, for whom it presented a potential financial loss; equally the West End theatre managements had little political sympathy with the ideological basis of much of the poetic drama. From 1934 Rupert Doone's Group Theatre, which had begun as an 'actors' co-operative dedicated to the formation of an ensemble, became the home to new left-wing poets seeking wider audiences.[31] Originally concerned with producing drama which incorporated movement and music, Doone was heavily influenced by innovations in ballet and by T. S. Eliot and W. B. Yeats's attempts to create a more theatrically self-conscious drama, one which celebrated community and moved beyond the naturalistic. Although it produced difficult European texts such as Ibsen's *Peer Gynt*, the Group Theatre is best known for its productions of the work of Auden, Isherwood, Louis MacNeice and Stephen Spender.

Workers' Theatre Movements in Britain and America (London: Routledge & Kegan Paul, 1985).

29 Davies, *Other Theatres*, p. 118.

30 See Howard Goorney and Ewan MacColl, eds., *Agit Prop to Theatre Workshop: Political Playscripts 1930–1950* (Manchester University Press, 1986), and Joan Littlewood, *Joan's Book: The Autobiography of Joan Littlewood* (London: Methuen, 1994).

31 Michael Sidnell, *Dances of Death: The Group Theatre of London in the Thirties* (London: Faber & Faber, 1984), p. 60. See, also, William Ostrem, 'The Dog Beneath the Schoolboy's Skin', in James J. Berg and Chris Freeman, eds., *The Isherwood Century: Essays on the Life and Work of Christopher Isherwood* (University of Wisconsin Press, 2001), pp. 162–71.

Auden and Isherwood's *Ascent of F6* (1937) was one of the most successful of the Group Theatre's productions. A 'tragedy in two acts', in which the hero of the piece, based loosely on T. E. Lawrence, while leading a group of mountaineers in a race against a foreign expedition, struggles with his desires for heroism, his feelings about talent being used to fuel the identity of the British Empire and his problematic attachment to his mother, the play is a mixture of philosophy, poetry and political thinking. Auden and Isherwood played with form and with expressionist devices, condensing time, and using a chorus made up of Mr and Mrs A; Everyman-figures who comment on the action, often in a rather simplistic way.

> BOTH: Moments of happiness do not come often,
> Opportunity's easy to miss.
> O, let us seize them, of all their joy squeeze them,
> For Monday returns when none may kiss![32]

Many of the Group Theatre poet–playwrights were concerned to find ways of questioning what they saw as the 'moral bankruptcy of contemporary society',[33] finding ways of presenting a theatre predicated on experiment, which broke with bourgeois conventions and challenged the middle classes to confront the political realities of the late 1930s.

Fabianism and socialist thinking fed the work of one of the most prolific playwrights of the period: George Bernard Shaw was one of the few playwrights whose work was produced through the Edwardian period to beyond the inter-war years. Shaw had been very much part of the struggle against censorship and of the attempts to formulate and sustain an English national theatre. An Irishman by birth, he worked as a critic and then turned to playwriting and was a prolific author of plays demanding intellectual engagement. Shaw's *St Joan* (1923), a chronicle play concerned with re-positioning Joan of Arc within a political narrative, and *The Apple Cart* (1928) were two of the most popular of his inter-war plays. The latter, 'a futuristic high comedy which emphasised Shavian inner conflicts between his lifetime of radical politics and his . . . mistrust of the common man's ability to govern himself', along with his overtly political play *Geneva: A Fancied Page of History* (1938), was the longest-running production of his later plays in London.[34]

32 W. H. Auden and Christopher Isherwood, *'The Ascent of F6' and 'On The Frontier'* (London: Faber & Faber, 1958), p. 43.
33 Chothia, *English Drama of the Early Modern Period*, p. 111.
34 Stanley Weintraub, 'Bernard Shaw', in *Dictionary of Literary Biography, vol. 10: 2* (Ann Arbor: Gale Research Company, 1982), p. 143.

To some extent the influence of Shaw can be seen in the plays of Sean O'Casey, whose early work was produced at the Abbey theatre in Dublin. Originating in 1904 as a means to cultivate national drama, the Abbey became Ireland's first state-subsidised theatre. O'Casey's happy relationship with the Abbey was fairly short-lived but he is seen by some as the man who dramatised the 'birth of the nation'. O'Casey's Dublin trilogy (*The Shadow of a Gunman* (1923); *Juno and the Paycock* (1924); and *The Plough and the Stars* (1926) all foreground the poverty of the dispossessed working classes, life in the tenement slums of Dublin and the socio-political fallout of the struggle for Irish independence.[35] O'Casey mixed lyrical writing with expressionistic influences and a strong sense of the visual potential of theatre and in particular of stage space. *Within The Gates* (1933) for example, originally planned as a film-script for Alfred Hitchcock, is an epic play set in a London park, using music, song and chorus. His experimentation with form, however, lost him favour with the London commercial managements although, interestingly, Broadway productions were often great successes. Always aware of the limitations of naturalism and the well-made play, O'Casey's critical works such as *The Flying Wasp* (1937) were full of condemnation for the way in which critics and managements controlled the theatre and thus the production of new work.

It is clear that British drama underwent significant transformation during the inter-war period. The economics of production and the construction and ownership of the theatre industry, alongside the rise in property rents in London, changed the potential viability of any new play. The period saw a rise in musicals and musical comedy, much derided by the drama critics, but the influence of which could not be ignored. A whole new generation of playwrights was writing for audiences who had witnessed the cultural fallout created by the events of World War I; such audiences appeared to swing between hedonism and a sombre desire to understand how they might change their society so that such a war would never happen again. Many of these new playwrights chose not to experiment with form, but rather to open up the stage to dramatised discussions around issues such as women and the public sphere, the family, masculinity and violence, sexuality and the move away from Victorianism towards an embracing of modern ideas. Although a number of critics complained that the 'free market' – the result of actor–managers no longer holding power over the theatre industry in the way they had before World War I – meant that theatre buildings had lost their identity, a number

[35] Christopher Murray, *Twentieth-Century Irish Theatre: Mirror up to Nation* (Manchester University Press, 1997), p. 88.

were known for productions of specific kinds of plays such as Ben Travers's farces produced through the late 1920s and 1930s at the Aldwych theatre.

Events such as the General Strike of 1926 or the Spanish Civil War had a minimal direct effect on what was produced in theatre, but there were playwrights who directly confronted the social inequality and political developments of the inter-war years; many of these worked successfully outside the mainstream.[36] The reading and performing of plays had become popular pastimes and this is to some extent reflected in the huge number of new plays produced and published. Technological developments such as radio and cinema also affected the development of drama; in terms of buildings, many were converted into cinemas, although these were mostly larger theatres which would have been used for music hall, variety and other forms of non-literary drama. Many playwrights, such as Clemence Dane, Emlyn Williams and Rodney Ackland, found the move into screen writing easy and fairly lucrative. Equally, successful plays, such as Dane's *Bill of Divorcement* (1921) or Williams' *The Corn is Green* (1938), were frequently bought up by studios and adapted for film. Often seen as a threat to theatre as a live art, cinema ironically provided employment and a new form for playwrights of the period. Numbers among the essentially middle-class audience for drama were less affected by cinema than those for more populist forms of live theatre entertainment. Radio, which began broadcasting in the early 1920s, also offered new challenges. Aimed at a wider audience than that found in West End theatre, for example, early radio drama broadcasts made use of well-known classics. Often the forms already popular on stage, such as thrillers, found appreciative radio audiences, as did short sketches by writers like L. du Garde Peach, whose stage works had been mostly mass outdoor celebratory pageants.[37] Although not under the jurisdiction of the Censor or the ideological constraints of sponsorship, Radio was susceptible to the conservatism of its producers, though as an artistic outlet it did help greatly in the development of a number of dramatic forms, especially the documentary drama.

Drama between the two world wars reflected the cultural anxiety of a period of ideological re-examination and political upheaval – not necessarily by direct means, but at times in the ways in which many playwrights chose to

36 John Clark, Margot Heinemann et al., *Culture and Crisis in Britain in the 1930s* (London: Lawrence & Wishart, 1970), p. 219.

37 Chothia, *English Drama of the Early Modern Period*, p. 119, and see also, Mick Wallis, 'Delving the Levels of Memory and Dressing up in the Past', in Barker and Gale, eds., *British Theatre Between the Wars*, pp. 190–214, for more information on the theatre work of L. du Garde Peach.

avoid specific social or political events. The continuing critical debate, about whether the function of theatre and drama was to provide commercial gain and entertainment or to exist for educative and intellectual purposes, seemed to ignore the fact that both kinds of drama and of theatre had always existed in a relation of reciprocity, their participation in the same economic and social system ensuring both diversity and cross-fertilisation.

19

Literature and cinema

LAURA MARCUS

The impact of cinema on early twentieth-century literary and, more broadly, cultural consciousness has, until recently, been neglected. Yet to look back at the period is to find that film consciousness was everywhere. In 1928, Kenneth Macpherson, co-editor of the avant-garde film journal *Close Up*, wrote: 'The cinema has become so much a habit of thought and word and deed as to make it impossible to visualize modern consciousness without it.'[1] In the same year, the poet H. D. (Hilda Doolittle), a fellow contributor to *Close Up*, claimed that 'the world of the film today [. . .] is no longer the world of the film, it is *the* world [. . .] There has never been, perhaps since the days of the Italian Renaissance, so great a "stirring" in the mind and soul of the world consciousness.'[2] She was writing here about 'Russian Films', but the promise of cinema was its internationalism, its creation of a visual language that transcended cultural and linguistic differences, and that, for H. D. as for many other early film enthusiasts, did not survive the transition to sound in the late 1920s and early 30s.

George Bernard Shaw also saw the birth of film as a cultural revolution. 'The cinema', he wrote in 1914,

> is a much more momentous invention than printing was . . . The cinema tells its story to the illiterate as well as to the literate; and it keeps its victim (if you like to call him so) not only awake but fascinated as if by a serpent's eye. And that is why the cinema is going to produce effects that all the cheap books in the world could never produce.[3]

This is in many ways a familiar account of the cinema as a drug of popular entertainment: it is not so much that the spectator looks at the cinema, as

1 Kenneth Macpherson, 'As Is', *Close Up*, 2, 2 (February 1928), p. 8.

2 H. D., 'Russian Films', rpt. in James Donald, Anne Friedberg and Laura Marcus, eds., *Close Up 1927–33: Cinema and Modernism* (London: Cassell, 1998), p. 135.

3 George Bernard Shaw, 'The Cinema as a Modern Leveller', *New Statesman*, 27 June 1914, rpt. in Bernard F. Dukore, ed., *Bernard Shaw on Cinema* (Carbondale and Edwardsville: Southern Illinois University Press, 1997), p. 9.

that the cinema looks at him with its 'fascinating' and deadly 'serpent's eye'. But, in an article written a year later, Shaw wrote of the ways in which theatre would be overtaken by the cinema, which could show aspects of the world unavailable to the stage, and could change scene instantly: 'literally in the twinkling of an eye, sixty times in an hour'.[4] The focus on vision, on seeing, as the condition of modernity was all-encompassing. Reading, Shaw suggested, was largely irrelevant to this modernity but 'all except the blind and deaf can see and hear; and when they begin to see farther than their own noses and their own nurseries, people will begin to have some notion of the world they are living in; and then we, too, shall see: what we shall see'.[5] Modernity created a new perceptual field, and cinema, as Shaw implied, a new form of literacy.

For many writers on the cinema this extended visual realm and capacity was both new – even futuristic – *and* archaic, a double temporality central to Modernist works more generally. The 'new' art of the film was often held to represent or embody a primordial or primitive consciousness, variously denigrated and celebrated. Its animistic powers (on which almost all early cinema played) and 'its yearning for personality in furniture', in the American poet and film theorist Vachel Lindsay's words, were particularly striking to its first commentators, who noted the ways in which the human became the inanimate, the inanimate the human.[6] Avant-garde film theory also explored time in the cinema, taking up the paradoxical relationship between the immobile image and the mobility of the projected film in ways that strongly echoed the philosopher Henri Bergson's early accounts of cinematographic time and movement as models of consciousness, and of time-consciousness in particular.[7]

Photogénie was a key term for French film theorists of the 1910s and 20s; it was variously described as a form of defamiliarisation, as a seeing of ordinary things as if for the first time, as the power of the camera to transform image-objects, and as a temporal category, defined by the film director and theorist Jean Epstein as 'a value on the order of the second', as a sublime instant, though what it flashed up also existed for him in an impossible or illusory time, that of the present.[8] For the art historian Elie Faure, *photogénie*

4 Shaw, 'What the Films May Do to the Drama', *Metropolitan Magazine*, May 1915, rpt. in *Bernard Shaw on Cinema*, p. 15.

5 Ibid., p. 19.

6 Vachel Lindsay, *The Art of the Moving Picture* (1915/1922) (New York: Liveright, 1970), p. 61.

7 See Henri Bergson, *Creative Evolution*, trans. Arthur Mitchell (London: Macmillan, 1911). (Translation of *L'évolution creatrice* (1907).

8 Jean Epstein, *Ecrits sur le cinéma, 1921–1953* (Paris: Seghers, 1974), pp. 179–80.

was both shock or 'commotion' and recognition: 'The revelation of what the cinema of the future can be came to me one day: I retain an exact memory of it, of the commotion that I experienced when I observed, in a flash, the magnificence there was in the relationship of a piece of black clothing to the grey wall of an inn.'[9] Here the aesthetic of film is rendered as visuality and as quite distinct from plot and narrative: the essence of film is pure image, and it inheres in the instant, 'in a flash'. These new ways of seeing and animating the object world entered into and shaped literature in the early decades of the century. The avant-garde's widespread denigration of plot and narrative in cinema (as opposed to vision and movement) is echoed in much Modernist literature of the period, although film in many ways disrupted conventional divisions between high and low culture, avant-gardism and populism. Gertrude Stein, for example, found in Charlie Chaplin's early films the modes of repetition, 'automatism' and the 'continuous present' central to her own Modernist aesthetic; more generally, the French avant-garde's celebration of 'Charlot' was also an embrace of American popular culture.[10]

In Britain, Modernist writers tended to be less receptive to cinema in its first decades. Ezra Pound's *Hugh Selwyn Mauberley*, for example, connects the 'prose kinema' that the 'age demanded' with the mass-produced ornament, 'Made with no loss of time', though later critics have found cinematographic techniques to be paralleled in the fragmentations and juxtapositions of Modernist poetics, including and especially the work of Pound and Eliot. It was the 'Edwardians' – Wells, Bennett, Galsworthy – who had the greatest actual involvement with the cinema, largely because it was their writing that was adapted for film; between 1920 and 1928, Arnold Bennett, for example, signed a dozen contracts for films to be made from his novels, plays and original screenplays, including the 1929 film *Piccadilly.*

H. G. Wells's engagement with film was the most complete and complex of this group of writers, and in many ways his writing career ran parallel to the 'evolution' of the cinema. In October 1895, the year of the Lumière brothers' first films, Robert Paul, the scientific-instrument-maker turned camera- and film-maker, initiated a patent application for a 'Time Machine' based on H. G. Wells's novel of that name. The patent was for an arrangement of mobile platforms on which the members of the audience would sit, and which

[9] Elie Faure, *The Art of Cineplastics*, trans. Walter Pach (Boston: Four Seas, 1923), p. 25.

[10] For discussion of Gertrude Stein and Chaplin, see Julian Murphet, 'Gertrude Stein's Machinery of Perception', in Julian Murphet and Lydia Rainford, eds., *Literature and Visual Technologies* (London: Longman, 2003), pp. 67–81, and Susan McCabe, '"Delight in Dislocation": the Cinematic Modernism of Stein, Chaplin and Man Ray', *Modernism/Modernity*, 8, 3 (September 2001), pp. 429–52.

would 'move towards and away from a screen onto which still and motion pictures were to be projected'; these would appear to carry the audience into the past and the future.[11] The venture was apparently abandoned because of its cost. Robert Paul, however, clearly saw in *The Time Machine* powerful 'cinematic' elements that could be translated onto screen and into spectacle. These elements include both the fascination with the time–space continuum and with the 'fourth dimension', expressed in the novel as philosophical–scientific discussion, as well as the time-traveller's journeys into the future. These journeys would have found simulated expression in Paul's 'time machine'. The novel also suggests the direct influence of early cinema, in particular its play with velocity and with reverse motion. In the third chapter, the time-traveller's housekeeper, walking through the room towards the garden door as the Time-Machine is set in motion, 'seemed to shoot across the room like a rocket'.[12] When the time-traveller returns from the Future, 'I passed again across the minute when she traversed the laboratory. But now every motion appeared to be the direct inverse of her previous one. The door at the lower end opened and she glided quietly up the laboratory, back foremost, and disappeared behind the door by which she had previously entered.'[13]

The Invisible Man, published two years after *The Time Machine*, added a further dimension; the play of absence and presence, and 'the presence of an absence', central to theorisations of filmic ontology. The importance of vision and optics to the story is also striking: 'Light fascinated me', Griffin, the 'invisible man', proclaims, recounting his discovery of the means to make matter transparent and then invisible. Wells also exploited the farcical and, indeed, 'slapstick' possibilities of the invisible man's situation. The proprietors of the rural inn in which he stays (after giving himself the semblance of a material body) enter the stranger's room, believing it to be empty. As the landlady put her hand on the pillow

> a most extraordinary thing happened, the bed-clothes gathered themselves together, leapt up suddenly into a sort of peak, and then jumped headlong over the bottom rail. It was exactly as if a hand had clutched them in the centre and flung them aside. Immediately after, the stranger's hat hopped off the bed-post, described a whirling flight in the air through the better part of a circle, and then dashed straight at Mrs Hall's face . . . She screamed and turned, and the chair legs came gently but firmly against her back and impelled her

[11] See Raymond Fielding, 'Hale's Tours: Ultrarealism in the Pre-1910 Motion Picture', in John F. Fell, ed., *Film Before Griffith* (Berkeley and Los Angeles: University of California Press, 1983), pp. 116–17.

[12] H. G. Wells, *The Time Machine* (London: Everyman, 1995), p. 16.

[13] Ibid., p. 77.

> and Hall out of the room. The door slammed violently and was locked. The chair and bed seemed to be executing a dance of triumph for a moment, and then abruptly everything was still.[14]

The scene has numerous visual counterparts in early cinema's (and the animated cartoon's) exploitations of the new medium's abilities to animate inanimate objects and to move matter through space without visible agency.

Motion and vision also come together in Wells's short story of this period, 'The Crystal Egg', in which the egg, discovered to have curious properties of diffusing light, is subsequently found, when held at a particular angle, to be a lens or window onto 'a wide and peculiar countryside . . . It was a moving picture: that is to say, certain objects moved in it, but slowly in an orderly manner like real things, and according as the direction of the lighting and vision changed, the picture changed also.'[15] The crystal egg, the narrator of the story goes on to reveal, gives a view of a Martian landscape, the egg in this world being 'in some physical, but at present quite inexplicable, way *en rapport*' with one on Mars.[16] The story's emphases on light and its refraction and diffusion, on the angle of vision, and on the actuality of the 'moving picture' bring it into a cinematographic arena of representation. Wells's narrative framings also introduce a number of characters entirely irrelevant (in plot terms) to the central vision of the story: the play of light and the view from one world into another. 'The Crystal Egg' could be read as an allegory of the origins of cinema, the various versions of which frequently contained mysterious figures who emerged to pass on information about and to commission new optical technologies; a proliferation of stories ranged or rayed round the central and fundamental desire for the writing of light.

Wells's speculations on time, space and motion formed part of the broader cultural context in which the technology, philosophy and ontology of cinema developed. For several decades he was seen as one of film's most important prophets. In 1927, Charlie Chaplin wrote of the uncertain future of film and of the motion picture industry: 'A giant of limitless powers has been reared, so huge that no one quite knows what to do with it. I, for one, am hopeful that Mr Wells shall settle the question for us in his next novel.'[17] The novel in question, *The King Who Was a King*, in fact a discursive film scenario which was never

14 H. G. Wells, *The Invisible Man* (London: Everyman, 1995), p. 27.

15 H. G. Wells, 'The Crystal Egg', in *The Complete Short Stories of H. G. Wells*, ed. John Hammond (London: Phoenix Press, 1998), p. 273.

16 Ibid., p. 280.

17 Charlie Chaplin, 'Foreword', in L'Estrange Fawcett, *Films: Facts and Forecasts* (London: Geoffrey Bles, 1927), pp. v–vi.

realised as a film, dented some of the faith in Wells's powers of resolution, but he retained a significant status in relation to this new art and technology, and was indeed quoted at this time as saying, 'I believe that if I had my life over again, I might devote myself entirely to working for the cinema.'[18] He wrote three film shorts – *Bluebottles, Daydreams* and *The Tonic* – in 1928, and in 1936 the film of his 'imaginative history' *The Shape of Things to Come* (1933) was released as *Things to Come*, directed by Alexander Korda: Wells had virtually unprecedented control over the making of the film.

In the 1950s, the British Film Institute produced an experimental film employing a new device called 'The Dynamic Frame', which allowed the screen to be modified to any shape desired. In the course of the shot, they chose as subject, in the director Ivor Montagu's words, 'a highly obscure piece of *fin-de-siécle* symbolism by H. G. Wells (*The Door in the Wall*) and decorated it with such lavishly Protean quick-changes of "expressive" shape to parade the full capacity of the invention that they made certain every prospective magnate and financier would be utterly bemused.'[19] The significant point is that Wells's short story – that of a man who enters another world, an enchanted garden, through the door in the wall – was chosen as the vehicle through which to display the workings of the new device, as if the Wellsian imaginary were still the most appropriate arena for cinematic shape-changing.

Rudyard Kipling had no such history of engagement with the developing art of film, but his 1904 short story 'Mrs Bathurst' is a striking representation of cinema as it appeared to its first spectators. The story is an enigmatic one, and the enigma lies very largely with the Cinematograph. The inaugural 'shock' of the cinema (which 'Mrs Bathurst' represents) has become tied to the Lumière brothers' 1895 film 'Arrival of a Train', in which the train is said to have appeared to its first spectators to be breaking through the screen to run them down; many are reported to have cried out in fear or to have fainted. The account is undoubtedly exaggerated or even apocryphal: as the film theorist Tom Gunning has argued, 'the first spectators' experience reveals not a childlike belief, but an undisguised awareness [of] (and delight in) film's illusionistic capabilities'.[20] Yet it became the founding myth of cinema, a story of the irruption of the new and of an unprecedented encounter with the force and trajectory of the moving image. Kipling reinscribes this inaugural

[18] Quoted on cover of H. G. Wells, *The King Who Was a King: The Book of a Film* (London: Ernest Benn, 1929).

[19] Ivor Montagu, *Film World* (Harmondsworth: Penguin, 1964), p. 84.

[20] Tom Gunning, 'An Aesthetic of Astonishment: Early Film and the (In)credulous Spectator', rpt. in Leo Braudy and Marshall Cohen, eds., *Film Theory and Criticism: Introductory Readings* (Oxford University Press, 1999), p. 832.

moment, sidelining the train, or putting it into a siding – 'The engine come in, head on, an' the women in the front row jumped: she headed so straight' – and makes the true moment of shock that of the recognition of one of its passengers – "Christ! There's Mrs B.!"'[21] Mrs Bathurst, or at least her screen image, heads as straight as the engine, and might indeed be said to take the place of the train in this differently played-out narrative of cinematic shock; one, indeed, in which the interplay of shock and recognition parallels that of the simultaneous 'astonishment and knowledge' ascribed by Gunning to the historical spectator of early cinema.

Kipling turns his narrative attention away from the other circus spectacles and shows of which the pictures are only one part, in contrast to D. H. Lawrence's *The Lost Girl*, in which the moving pictures appear alongside live acrobatic performances. Lawrence, notoriously hostile to film (a hostility which indicates, as Ann Ardis has argued, the extent of Lawrence's anxiety over 'high culture's relative disempowerment in the early post-war period')[22] contrasts, in *The Lost Girl*, the mechanical, lifeless, repetitive nature of the cinema with the marvellous movements of the live human body. The miracles of motion and transformation in the novel are all on the side of the living body, not mechanical reproducibility, though there is irony, too, in his presentation of the live performers:

> Mr May had worked hard to get a programme for the first week. His pictures were: 'The Human Bird', which turned out to be a ski-ing film from Norway, purely descriptive; 'The Pancake', a humorous film: and then his Grand Serial: 'The Silent Grip'. And then, for Turns, his first item was Miss Poppy Traherne, a lady in innumerable petticoats, who could whirl herself into anything you like, from an arum lily in green stockings to a rainbow and a catherine wheel and a cup and saucer: marvellous, was Miss Poppy Traherne.[23]

Miss Poppy's Catherine wheel 'brings down the house'. The Catherine wheel is followed by a film: 'The lamps go out: gurglings and kissings – and then the dither on the screen: "The Human Bird," in awful shivery letters. It's not a very good machine, and Mr May is not a very good operator.'

Here the cinema is represented as appealing to infantile eroticism ('gurglings and kissings'), as 'dither', a word which by the late nineteenth century had become particularly associated with the disturbing vibrations of machinery,

21 Rudyard Kipling, 'Mrs Bathurst' in Andrew Rutherford, ed., *Short Stories*, 2 vols. (Harmondsworth: Penguin, 1971), II, p. 85.
22 Ann L. Ardis, *Modernism and Cultural Conflict 1880–1922* (Cambridge University Press, 2002), p. 86.
23 D. H. Lawrence, *The Lost Girl* (Cambridge University Press, 2002), p. 107.

including the railway, and finally as bad writing or cultural inscription – 'awful shivery letters'. Lawrence was writing about a period in which the cinema was displacing the live performance; Alma (the English spinster who will become 'the lost girl') tells Mr May that the colliers prefer the films to the live performances because 'they can spread themselves over a film, and they *can't* over a living performer. They're up against the performer himself. And they hate it . . . They hate to admire anything that isn't themselves. And that's why they like pictures. It's all themselves to them, all the time.'[24] The distinction here is between the unsettling experience of difference produced by the live performance, and the solipsism – and indeed onanism – of the working-class spectators' identification with the figures on the screen – 'they can spread themselves over a film'. This was echoed in Lawrence's essay 'Pornography and Obscenity', in which he wrote of the 'pornographical' nature of 'the close-up kisses on the film, which excite men and women to secret and separate masturbation', an attack which lies at the heart of his repudiation of the new medium and its singular appeal to the eye.[25]

Lawrence, in reinserting film into the contexts of live performance (and he was writing in 1920, not in the very early years of the cinema, as Kipling was), placed the emphasis on the question of motion, and on the somatic (as in the spreading of the self across the screen) as a cultural 'ooze' through which, here and in other writings, he could represent the contamination of modernity by cinematic vision.[26] Kipling, by extracting the film from the performances that surround it, made the question much more emphatically one of temporality, of the relentless forward movement and irreversibility of cinematic time which, as Mary Anne Doane and others have recently argued, is also modern time,[27] and of the 'shock' of adjustment to the new relations of presence and absence, illusion and reality, represented by the world of the cinema.

There are other Modernist perspectives on cinema in the early decades of the century. In 1909, James Joyce travelled from Trieste, where he had been living since 1904, back to Dublin, in order to establish the first cinema in Ireland. He and his business partners, proprietors of cinemas in Trieste, called

[24] Ibid., p. 116.

[25] D. H. Lawrence, 'Pornography and Obscenity', in *Phoenix: The Posthumous Papers of D. H. Lawrence*, ed. Edward D. McDonald (London: Heinemann, 1936), p. 187. For discussion of Lawrence, film and sexuality, see Linda R. Williams, *Sex in the Head: Visions of Femininity and Film in D. H. Lawrence* (Hemel Hempstead: Harvester Wheatsheaf, 1993).

[26] In 'A Propos of *Lady Chatterley's Lover*' (London: Mandrake Press, 1930), Lawrence writes: 'The radio and the film are mere counterfeit emotion all the time . . . people wallow in emotion: counterfeit emotion. They lap it up: they live in it and on it. They ooze with it.'

[27] See Mary Anne Doane, *The Emergence of Cinematic Time: Modernity, Contingency, the Archive* (Cambridge, MA: Harvard University Press, 2002.)

their new cinema, located in Dublin's Mary Street, the Cinematograph Volta; it opened on 20 December 1909 with a screening of predominantly French and Italian films. Thereafter the programme changed twice weekly, showing a wide range of films, including melodramas, Film d'Arte tragedies, and slapstick comedies. The Volta seems to have been popular and, confident of the success of the enterprise, Joyce returned to Trieste in the New Year. By April 1910, however, his business partners were writing to tell him that the concern was losing money and would have to be wound up, and the Volta was sold that June.[28]

This was the end of Joyce's connections with film exhibition, but by no means the close of his engagement with cinematic representation, which profoundly shaped his fiction, *Ulysses* in particular, as a number of early commentators on his work observed. Harry Levin argued in his 1944 study of Joyce (revised 1960) that Leopold Bloom's mind is a motion picture, cut and edited 'to emphasize the close-ups and fade-outs of flickering emotion, the angles of observation and the flashbacks of reminiscence'. The organisation of the raw material of Joyce's fiction, Levin suggests, entails the operation of *montage*.[29] 'Montage' – which literally means 'editing' – comes to define the way in which film recreates reality, cutting it up and reordering it in ways which create new meanings, connections and juxtapositions. The technique was deployed across Modernist culture, from the collage of the cubists to the fragmentations of T. S. Eliot's poetry.

The German novelist Alfred Döblin, the author of *Berlin Alexanderplatz*, a city novel deeply influenced by Joyce, had defined *Ulysses*, in his 1928 review of the novel, in the terms of cinematic montage: 'The cinema has penetrated the sphere of literature; newspapers must become the most important, most broadly disseminated form of written testimony, everybody's daily bread. To the experiential image of a person today also belongs the streets, the scenes changing by the second, the signboards, automobile traffic.'[30] Walter Benjamin celebrated the use of montage in *Berlin Alexanderplatz*, while at the same time

[28] For discussion of this episode, see Richard Ellmann, *James Joyce* (Oxford University Press, 1959), pp. 310–24.

[29] Harry Levin, *James Joyce: A Critical Introduction* (London: Faber & Faber, 1960), p. 82. Levin adds, however, that, while 'montage' is a useful metaphor, 'Joyce's medium is far less vivid and swift, far more blurred and jerky. His projections, to our surprise, tend to slow down and at times to stop altogether, suddenly arresting the action and suspending the characters in mid-air' (p. 113). In this way, Levin's discussion anticipates recent work on the influence of 'stop-motion' tricks in early films on *Ulysses*.

[30] Alfred Döblin, '*Ulysses* by Joyce', rpt. in Anton Kaes, Martin Jay and Edward Dimendberg, eds., *The Weimar Republic Sourcebook* (Berkeley and Los Angeles: University of California Press, 1994) p. 514.

disallowing it to Joyce, whom he placed in the tradition of the interiorised novel and the 'roman pur', which he called 'pure interiority'. The split, as Benjamin conceived it, was between montage and interior narration.[31] Yet for the Soviet director and film theorist Sergei Eisenstein, the importance of *Ulysses*, which he described as the most significant event in the history of *cinema*, lay in substantial part in the ways in which it confirmed the relationship between montage and 'inner monologue'. For Eisenstein, 'montage form as structure is a reconstruction of the laws of the thought process',[32] and in this way it becomes allied to 'that particular penetration of interior vision which marks the description of intimate life in *Ulysses* and in *Portrait of the Artist* with the aid of the astonishing method of the interior monologue'.[33] It was the coming of sound in the late 1920s, Eisenstein argued, that made possible the 'practical realisation' in film of 'inner monologue', with voice-over representing interior discourse, and in the early 1930s he discussed with Joyce the making of a film of *Ulysses*, although the novel was not in fact filmed until Joseph Strick's version in 1967.

For Joyce, the two possible directors for such a film were Eisenstein himself, and Walter Ruttman, director of the 1927 *Berlin: Symphony of a Great City*, a 'day-in-the-life-of-a-city' film that has strong affinities with both *Ulysses* and Virginia Woolf's *Mrs Dalloway*.[34] Urban consciousness and cinematic consciousness become intertwined in these city fictions, with the deployment of the fictional equivalent of a fixed camera, which records, as pure contingency, everything that passes by it, and of montage techniques represented by contrast and juxtaposition. As Ezra Pound wrote in 1922: 'The life of a village is a narrative . . . In the city the visual impressions succeed each other, overlap, overcross, they are cinematographic.'[35] In the 1930s, 'city symphonies' were widely recreated in the work of writers of the British Left, including John Sommerfield, whose *May Day* (1936) was one of many panoramic and cinematic pictures of contemporary urban life influenced by the work of John Dos Passos and Joyce, by film-makers like Dziga-Vertov and Ruttman, and by montage theories.

31 Walter Benjamin, 'The Crisis of the Novel' (1930), in *Walter Benjamin: Selected Writing Volume II: 1927–1934* (Cambridge, MA: Harvard, 1999), p. 301.

32 Eisenstein, 'Help Yourself', in S. M. Eisenstein, *Selected Works: Volume I Writings, 1922–34*, ed. and trans. Richard Taylor (London: BFI Publishing, 1988), p. 236. See also 'Literature and Cinema', *Selected Works I*, pp. 95–9.

33 Sergei Eisenstein, 'Sur Joyce', *Change* (May 1972), p. 51. (My translation).

34 See Marie Seton, *Sergei M. Eisenstein: A Biography* (London: Bodley Head, 1952), p. 149: 'Joyce told his friend Jolas, the editor of *Transition*, that if *Ulysses* were ever made into a film, he thought that the only men who could direct it would be either Walter Ruttman the German, or Sergei Eisenstein the Russian.'

35 Ezra Pound, 'Paris Letter: December 1921', *Dial*, LXXII. 1 (Jan. 1922), [73]–78.

In recent years, the renewed interest in early cinema has led to work on the more precise and specific relationship between early films and Modernist literature. Joyce's experiences of film-viewing in Trieste in the first decade of the century, and his involvement with films at the *Volta* cinema, are explored in studies of the ways in which early trick and animated films themselves animated *Ulysses*, and in particular the *Circe* chapter of the novel with, in Keith Williams's words, its 'Protean deformation of time, space, body and identity'.[36] The cinematic animism, the endowment of objects with 'intense life', in Jean Epstein's phrase, so celebrated in early film theory and in avant-garde and surrealist writings on film, was most fully embodied in early trick films, with their metamorphoses, transformations and object animations. It seems certain that Joyce was drawing upon such cinematic effects for his own animations of the object world in *Ulysses* – Bloom's singing bar of soap ('We're a capital couple are Bloom and I / He brightens the earth, I polish the sky'), the brothel-madam Bella's erotic talking fan – and, as Williams suggests, for the phonetic deformations of the text, linguistic versions of the visual distortions found in early animated cartoons.[37]

'Early animation', Ian Christie writes, 'often seems, with hindsight, like a popular version of the same concerns that pushed "serious" artists into Modernism.'[38] For the film critic Iris Barry, writing in the mid-1920s, 'the whole tendency of modern painting has been an attempt to fix eternally – that is, in the only way open to a painter – that rhythm of inter-related movement of lively units'. Modern art, she suggested, had turned to the shapes and rhythms of machinery, because 'machines are static lively objects impregnated with internal movement, symbols, that is, of a free motion they do not actually possess themselves'. Cinema, quintessentially an art of movement, 'can take up that part of the modern artist's problem where he is forced to leave off'; the visual quality of film lies in its ability to represent a third dimension, and to revolve its objects before the spectator.[39] Indeed, Barry mused, 'I wonder sometimes why the Montmartre cubists go on cubing when the cinema exists.'[40]

36 Keith Williams, 'Ulysses in Toontown: "vision animated to bursting point" in Joyce's "Circe"', in Julian Murphet and Lydia Rainford, eds., *Literature and Visual Technologies: Writing after Cinema* (Basingstoke: Palgrave Macmillan, 2003), p. 107. See also Austin Briggs, '"Roll Away the Reel World, the Reel World": "Circe" and the Cinema', in Morris Bejma and Shari Benstock, eds., *Coping with Joyce: Essays from the Copenhagen Symposium* (Columbus: Ohio State University Press, 1989), pp. 145–56.

37 Ibid., p. 102.

38 Ian Christie, *The Last Machine: Early Cinema and the Birth of the Modern World* (London: British Film Institute, 1994), p. 85.

39 Iris Barry, *Let's Go to the Pictures* (London: Chatto & Windus, 1926), p. 40.

40 Ibid., pp. 42–3.

In a different but related vein, Aldous Huxley, in an essay published in 1926, 'Where are the Movies Moving?', celebrated the animated cartoon character 'Felix the Cat', describing a scene in which Felix begins to sing, and turns the little black notes that come gushing out of his throat into 'the most ingenious little trolley or scooter', onto which he climbs and rides out of the picture. 'For the dramatist of the screen', Huxley wrote, 'this sort of thing is child's play.' The writer has no such freedom to play with words, he argued, and the Surrealist (or 'Super-Realist', in his terms) writers' attempts to do so fail precisely where the cinema succeeds: 'What the cinema can do better than literature or the spoken drama is to be fantastic.'[41] Where Joyce seems to have fully embraced film as a way of transforming literature, Huxley insisted in his writings on film of the 1920s that 'cinematography differs from literature and drama', its potential dependent on the ways in which it might be developed into something entirely new. Huxley's praise for the animated cartoon and its fantastical aspects as the quintessence of cinema was also a way of demarcating the territories of film and literature respectively and, perhaps, of protecting the established arts of novel and drama from trespass by the new, popular art of the cinema. This position, argued by many writers of the period, overlapped with the views of a number of avant-garde film-makers and theorists, including the Soviet director Dziga-Vertov and the French artist and film-maker Ferdinand Léger, for whom the future of cinema lay in its freeing itself from literary scenarios. Adaptation, it was generally agreed, was the graveyard of cinematic innovation.

The combination of celebration and suspicion in Huxley's essay can be found in Virginia Woolf's 'The Cinema', also published in 1926, during a period in which cinema was providing new terms for theorizing about art and aesthetics. The essay was written while Woolf was working on *To the Lighthouse*, perhaps the most obviously 'cinematic' of her novels, in which she transmuted 'point of view' into the observation of perception itself, looking at people looking and being looked at, and creating a complex interplay of eyelines and sightlines within the text, a form of multiple-shot scenario, in contrast to the representation in 'Mrs Bathurst' of a single, continuous shot. In the first section of *To the Lighthouse*, 'The Window', characters are shown 'looking at' Mrs Ramsay. Some twenty pages into the novel we are told that, from the outset, Mrs Ramsay has been sitting for Lily Briscoe's painting, framed

[41] Aldous Huxley, 'Where are the Movies Moving?', *Essays Old and New* (London: Chatto & Windus, 1926), pp. 182–7.

in the 'window' of the novel's first section. H. D. used a very similar scenario to exemplify the difference between stage and film art. In film, she wrote: 'we are not satisfied with a man and a window, or a woman and a door. We must see a man at a window and then a view of the man from the point of view, for instance, of someone outside that window.'[42]

In the middle section of *To the Lighthouse*, 'Time Passes', Woolf explored the possibilities of a future or potential cinema. Her interest, as articulated in 'The Cinema', lay in abstract film, in which thoughts and emotions could be made visible, 'like smoke pouring from Vesuvius'. In 'Time Passes' she produced a form of cineplay, using visual images to express emotions and animating objects into non-human life, and exploring the play of light and the concept of memory as projection. Her radical experiment in narration in 'Time Passes', in which reality itself is presented as if in the absence of the perceiving subject, is also mirrored in 'The Cinema', in which she described the different 'reality' of screen images: 'We behold them as they are when we are not there. We see life as it is when we have no part in it . . . beauty will continue to be beautiful whether we behold it or not.'[43] This ghostly realism anticipates the film theorist Christian Metz's characterization of the film image as signifying 'the presence of an absence', and suggests something of the risk and the allure of this medium whose world is, as the philosopher and film theorist Stanley Cavell has written, complete without us.

Woolf's essay was highly critical of the cinema when it attempted to usurp what she perceived as the ground of the other arts, and of the novel in particular. Leaving behind the recording of reality – of 'the actual world' and of 'contemporary life' – film-makers had turned to literary texts as their sources, she argued, in disastrous and truly vampiric fashion: 'The cinema fell upon its prey with immense rapacity and to this moment largely subsists upon the body of its unfortunate victim', Woolf wrote of a film of *Anna Karenina*: 'it is only when we give up trying to connect the pictures with the book that we guess from some scene by the way – a gardener mowing the lawn outside, for example, or a tree shaking its branches in the sunshine – what the cinema might do if it were left to its own devices'.[44] In 'The Cinema', she located, indeed, the significant aesthetic of the cinema in that which was not in the film, but a 'blemish' upon its surface, and the accidental and the contingent became

[42] H. D., *Borderline*, in *Close Up 1927–33*, p. 231.

[43] Virginia Woolf, 'The Cinema', in *The Essays of Virginia Woolf*, vol. IV: 1925–8, ed. Andrew McNeillie (London: Hogarth Press, 1994), p. 349.

[44] Ibid., p. 350.

the 'mark' of cinema's aesthetic autonomy. At a screening of *Dr Caligari*, Woolf wrote:

> A shadow shaped like a tadpole suddenly appeared at one corner of the screen. It swelled to an immense size, quivered, bulged, and sank back again into nonentity. For a moment it seemed to embody some monstrous diseased imagination of the lunatic's brain. For a moment it seemed as if thought could be conveyed by shape more effectively than by words. The monstrous quivering tadpole seemed to be fear itself, and not the statement 'I am afraid'. In fact the shadow was accidental and the effect unintentional. But if a shadow at a certain moment can suggest so much more than the actual gestures, the actual words of men and women in a state of fear, it seems plain that the cinema has within its grasp innumerable symbols for emotions that have so far failed to find expression. Terror has besides its ordinary forms the shape of a tadpole; it burgeons, bulges, quivers, disappears. Anger might writhe like an infuriated worm in black zigzags across a white sheet.[45]

The demand here is for a new mode of symbolisation, one not dependent on literature but capable of conveying thought or consciousness in visual terms, and in the form, it is implied, of a hieroglyphics; that mode of representation ('fluttering between word and image') which had become, for early film theorists from the poet Vachel Lindsay to Sergei Eisenstein, the most appropriate way of conceiving the new 'language' of film, and the one that bore the closest relations to a Modernist poetics. 'It has been left', Eisenstein wrote, 'to James Joyce to develop in *literature* the depictive line of the Japanese hieroglyph.'[46] Woolf also deployed the view of film most striking to its early commentators, its power to transform, even to 'annihilate', familiar relations of time and space. 'The most fantastic contrasts', she writes, 'could be flashed before us with a speed which the writer can only toil after in vain.'[47]

In some ways *The Cabinet of Dr Caligari* (produced in 1919, and shown at a London Film Society screening in 1924) was no more than the occasion for Woolf's meditations on the cinema, and she bypassed the film itself in focusing on the accidental shadow on the screen, which became a way of figuring a future language or hieroglyphics of film. Yet *Caligari*, a highly stylised film, with its painted backdrops reminiscent of Expressionist theatre, did have a significant role as the film that 'converted' many intellectuals to the cinema,

[45] Ibid., pp. 350–1.

[46] Sergei Eisenstein, *Film Form: Essays in Film Theory* (New York: Harcourt Brace Jovanovich, 1949), p. 35.

[47] Woolf, 'The Cinema', p. 352.

elevating it from a mass or popular form to the status of high culture. Even the uncompromisingly elitist Clive Bell was prepared to admit cinema to the pantheon of the 'middle country' of art, 'the territory hitherto occupied by those painters and writers who stood between the uncompromising artists and the barbarous horde', after seeing *Caligari*. The film was, he stated, to the best of his knowledge, 'the first attempt to create an art of the cinema': 'There is some appeal to the brain and the eye; there is arrangement and accent; there is a rudimentary, aesthetic intention.'[48]

If at one level *Caligari* is discursively displaced in Woolf's essay, at another level the film becomes central to the emergent aesthetics of cinema. Woolf's representation of the shadow could be equated with a concept of cinematic essence, *photogénie*, conceptualised as a sublime instant; 'For a moment it seemed as if thought could be conveyed by shape more effectively than by words', she wrote of the shadow on the screen. She looked away from the film only to find herself captured, it would seem, by something that was its very essence, the shadow as the metonym for Expressionist cinema, with its shadows, mirrors and doubles – and perhaps for cinema itself. She suggested that 'the art of the cinema is about to be brought to birth', and that it would be seen with a new eye, one brought into being with the apparent supersession of a Kantian aesthetics (such as the Bloomsbury artist and aesthetician Roger Fry's) predicated on 'pure vision abstracted from necessity'. For Woolf, it was the faculty of vision which, currently 'detached from use', would awaken to seize sense impressions at the moment of their fleeting unity. In her account of the cinema she sought to reclaim the ideality of sight – and to mend the split – produced by the technologies of perception – between interiority and the mechanical exteriority of the camera-eye.[49]

Woolf's 'The Cinema' and Iris Barry's *Let's Go to the Pictures* appeared towards the end of the period in which film could be theorised independently of the question of sound; the first sound film (in fact a silent film with sound episodes), Warner Brothers' *The Jazz Singer*, was released in 1927. Sound film brought cinema much more centrally into the sphere of stage drama, whereas critics and theorists had frequently linked silent film to ballet, to painting and to poetry. The poetics of silent film was closely connected for many early commentators with the use of intertitles and subtitles, which, as in Vachel Lindsay's *The Art of the Moving Picture*, were often seen as closest in conception

48 Clive Bell, 'Art and the Cinema', *Vanity Fair* (November 1922), p. 40.

49 See Sara Danius, *The Senses of Modernism: Technology, Perception and Aesthetics* (Ithaca: Cornell University Press, 2002).

to Imagist poetics, and the function and nature of captions and intertitles was much debated in the 1920s, in part as a way of conceptualising the relationship between literature and cinema. Did intertitles represent the intrusion of the literary into what should be an essentially pictorial realm, or were they a valuable authorial signature in a medium otherwise lacking the markers of the individual creative consciousness? Were captions and intertitles speech or writing? Writers on the cinema frequently described these inscriptions as if they possessed an auditory dimension, with the intertitle becoming, or coming to stand in for, the 'voice' of the silent film. As Graham Greene, who began writing film criticism in the mid-1920s, wrote in 1928:

> A phrase can crystallize an emotion which the face is powerless to express. The sub-title must have some of the scorching imagination and brevity of poetry. 'Cover her face: mine eyes dazzle: she died young,' 'Pray you undo this button' – it is on such compressed and poignant outcries that the sub-title should be modelled.[50]

Greene's statement here strongly echoes a passage in *Let's Go to the Pictures*, in which Barry writes:

> At a flash-point of the emotions, the sub-title is needed, unless the actors can let us, by their bearing or by lip-reading, get what their words must inevitably be . . . this cry is . . . an illumination, an amplification, a secret disgorged – and sometimes when that cry does not break out in lettering on the screen, one feels something missing, and the silence of the screen seems for a moment an empty not an eloquent silence.[51]

Among Barry's early publications were the poems that appeared in Harriet Monroe's *Poetry* magazine in 1916, alongside work by Pound and Eliot, and again in 1922. Inspired by Imagism, Barry's poetry from this period provides glimpses of the cinematic shadow-play that would allow her to connect poetry and film; her poems are replete with images of shadows trailing across dream-screens. In *Let's Go to the Pictures*, she defended cinematography as an art, praising the ways in which 'the moving picture speaks direct to the eye': 'So it comes about that even in the crudest films something is provided for the imagination, and emotion is stirred by the simplest things – moonlight playing in a bare room, the flicker of a hand against a window.'[52] In a chapter devoted to subtitles, Barry made an explicit link between poetry and film:

[50] David Parkinson, ed., *Mornings in the Dark: The Graham Greene Film Reader* (Harmondsworth: Penguin, 1995), p. 394.

[51] Barry, *Let's Go to the Pictures*, p. 78. [52] Ibid., p. ix.

> The making of sub-titles might well be held to be a new form of literary style. The sub-title must be crystalline, packed with meaning, allusive, condensed – a work of art and elegance and simplicity, in fact. I think the *vers-librists* would make good title writers: they write fresh active pictorial phrases, they avoid redundancies, elaborations, cliches . . . Brevity would be my motto and eloquence (not flowery eloquence but the small sweet voice) my ambition.[53]

The association of cinema and poetic form was also central to H. D.'s work. In 1927, H. D., one of the most significant figures of the Imagist movement in the 1910s, began to write about the cinema, contributing articles to the film journal *Close Up*, which ran between 1927 and 1933, and was edited from Switzerland by the writer Bryher (Winifred Ellerman) and the young artist Kenneth Macpherson, with whom H. D. was involved in a complex *ménage à trois*. *Close Up* described itself as 'the only magazine devoted to film as an art', and was in part dedicated to bringing to the attention of an English readership an 'international cinema', particularly Soviet and German, and hence to countering the deleterious influence of Hollywood, as it was for the most part perceived, on British films and audiences. The journal, which was also the forum for the first publication of Eisenstein's writings in English, provided an admixture of avant-garde aesthetics and practical work on film production, technologies, distribution and exhibition.

In H. D.'s work and life, cinema and literature combined in a number of ways. She was involved in film-making, both in front of and behind the camera, acting in and helping to edit Macpherson's films, the most significant (and the only surviving one) of which was *Borderline* (1930), in which H. D. appeared with Paul and Eslanda Robeson, and for which she wrote a lengthy explanatory pamphlet. She also wrote extensively on film for *Close Up* in the late 1920s. With the coming of sound, H. D. was no longer drawn to write about films themselves, but she continued to incorporate the modes of vision she had associated with the art of silent film – close-up, symbol, gesture, hieroglyph – into her fiction, her poetry, and her autobiographical writings, including her account of her analysis with Freud in 1933–4. H. D.'s film writings, along with other contributions to the journal *Close Up*, are important dimensions of the imbricated histories of psychoanalysis and cinema, both of them 'technologies', of knowledge and of vision, born at the close of the nineteenth century.

In her autobiographical novel *Bid Me to Live*, which she began writing during the years of World War I, though it was not published until 1958, H. D.'s fictional

[53] Ibid., p. 82.

persona, Julia, visits a cinema packed with soldiers on leave, or waiting to go to the Front. Her surroundings, and the film that is running, seem dangerous, part of the 'frantic maelstrom' of the war years. On the screen, however, there comes 'the answer to everything': 'for surprisingly, a goddess-woman stepped forward. She released from the screen the first (to Julia) intimation of screen-beauty. Screen? This was a veil, curiously embroidered, the veil before the temple . . . Here was Beauty, a ghost but Beauty. Beauty was not dead.'[54] Cinema, and in particular its representations of women's beauty and power, becomes a salvific force against the depredations of (masculine) war, the opposition caught up in H. D.'s habitual polarisation of the culture of Ancient Greece and militaristic Rome.

The same terms and representations are at the heart of H. D.'s film writings for *Close Up*. In the first of her articles, published in 1927, for a three-part series entitled 'Cinema and the Classics', she describes the 'Beauty' of Greta Garbo in G. W. Pabst's *The Joyless Street*, while also defining the medium of cinema itself as a 'goddess'. As she writes in the second of her articles, 'Restraint': 'here is the thing that the Elusinians would have been glad of; a subtle device for portraying of the miraculous . . . The screen is the medium par excellence of movement – of trees, of people, of bird wings. Flowers open by magic and magic spreads cloud forms, all in themselves "classic".'[55] The Hellenism that characterised H. D.'s Imagist aesthetics, and that she continued to develop in her later long poems, *Helen in Egypt* in particular, was also central to her perceptions of film. 'True modernity', she wrote, 'approaches more and more to classic standards.'[56]

During the years of her most intense involvement with cinema, H. D. claimed for film the status of 'the living art, the thing that WILL count', but she saw it as endangered by commercial and popular interests. The novelist Dorothy Richardson, who also wrote extensively for *Close Up*, made no less a claim for the centrality of cinema to modernity, but defended 'the movies' and the significance of film as a popular medium. Her *Close Up* articles, published as a regular series entitled 'Continuous Performance', rarely explored specific films; she focused instead of the conditions of film spectatorship, its different sites (cinema in the West End, cinema in the suburbs, cinema in the slums), and on film techniques (slow motion, film captions, musical accompaniment) and their impact on audiences. Above all, Richardson's concern was with the

[54] H. D., *Bid Me to Live: A Madrigal* (New York: Grove Press, 1960), p. 125.
[55] *Close Up 1927–33*, pp. 112–13. [56] Ibid., p. 112.

cinema-goer's changing, developing relationship to the new art of the film – 'Everyman [made] at home in a new world' by 'the movies': 'The only anything and everything. And here we all are, as never before. What will it do with us?' – and with cinema as a feminised sphere: 'At last the world of entertainment had provided for a few pence, tea thrown in, sanctuary for mothers, an escape from the everlasting qui vive into eternity on a Monday afternoon.'[57]

In one of her film articles, 'This Spoon-Fed Generation', Richardson referred to the film's gifts as 'the awakening of the imaginative power, the gift of expansion, of moving, ever so little, into a new dimension of consciousness'.[58] This account strongly echoes the aesthetic and philosophy of Richardson's novel sequence *Pilgrimage*, the first volume of which was published in 1915, whose narrative is marked by its immersion in her fictional alter ego Miriam Henderson's consciousness, as it moves in and out of encounters and engagements with places, events and people, in a state of flux and process. The centrality of 'cinematic' consciousness to *Pilgrimage* was noted in Bryher's review of its tenth volume, *Dawn's Left Hand*: 'What a film her books could make. The real English film for which so many are waiting . . . And in each page an aspect of London is created that like an image from a film, substitutes itself for memory, to revolve before the eyes as we read.'[59]

In another of her *Close Up* articles, Richardson wrote that 'the right [film] caption at the right moment, is audible, more intimately audible than the spoken word. It is the swift voice within the mind'. Here it is writing that 'speaks'.[60] For many critics of the talkies, sound – or, more accurately, synchronised speech – was represented as a mechanical intrusion into an *essentially* visual medium. While the responses of critics and commentators during the transition period do not divide absolutely along gendered lines, there is a quite marked hostility among women writers to sound technology, and a greater degree of regret for the loss of the silent film; 'the art that died', in Bryher's words. As Richardson wrote in 1932: 'in becoming audible and particularly in becoming a medium of propaganda, [film] is doubtless fulfilling its destiny. But it is a masculine destiny.'[61]

Richardson, like many critics in the transition period, was not opposed to the use of music and sound effects but to dialogue and synchronised speech, which had become identified with an increasing 'staginess' of the cinema and with the hegemony of Hollywood. Silent film, it was argued, had been a universal

57 Ibid., p. 160. 58 Ibid., p. 205. 59 Ibid., p. 210.
60 Ibid., p. 196. 61 Ibid., p. 206.

medium, operating in a kind of visual Esperanto. Moreover, it animated the object world, often in revelatory ways, rather than making the human face and voice its only measure. Sound film, it was argued, produced a destructive competition between eye and ear. The writings of many film aestheticians revealed a hostility to so-called 'hybrid' forms, an insistence that the aesthetic of film was determined by its unity and its visual purity, and a concern about the 'Fall' into linguistic diversity, which it was felt American cinema would use to its own advantage.

The hostility to sound during the transition period expressed by many film theorists also needs to be understood against the background of developments in Soviet cinema; much of Paul Rotha's discussion in *The Film Till Now* (1931), for example, was influenced by the work and theories of Eisenstein. Supporters of montage cinema feared that it would be destroyed by the introduction of sound, in part because an all-too-audible dialogue would drown out 'inner speech', that interiorised ground on which the filmic was said to be figured and which, it was believed, allowed the spectator to make connections between separate shots and to make meaningful the essentially metaphoric nature of visual representation.[62] In fact, like many of his European contemporaries, Eisenstein's fear at this stage was the dominance of synchronised dialogue in the talking film, rather than the sound film in which 'the sound is not used as a naturalistic element and to which, he believed, the future belonged.

In his first sound film, *Blackmail* (1928), Alfred Hitchcock produced an Expressionist manipulation of the sound track, demonstrating the possibility of departure from photographs of people talking which was his own criticism of dialogue in film, and counterpointing sound and image. Graham Greene, in his 1958 'Memories of a Film Critic', recalled that in the 1920s he had been 'a passionate reader of *Close-Up*', and 'horrified by the arrival of 'talkies' (it seemed the end of film as an art form) . . . Curiously enough it was a detective story with Chester Morris which converted me to the talkies – for the first time in that picture I was aware of *selected* sounds; until then every shoe had squeaked and every door handle had creaked.'[63] Greene's critical 'conversion to sound', the phrase identical to that used to describe the film institution's and apparatus's own technological transformations in the late 1920s and 1930s, has as its context the radical impact of sound film on writers. As Greene recalls, with the emergence of 'a selectivity of sound which promised to become as formal as the warning shadow', the writer 'was no longer merely the spectator

[62] See, for example, Boris, Eikhenbaum, 'Problems of Film Stylistics' (1927).
[63] *Mornings in the Dark*, pp. 447–8.

or the critic of the screen. Suddenly the cinema needed him: pictures required words as well as images.'[64]

Greene's involvement with cinema was perhaps the most extensive of any twentieth-century British writer. As a film critic in the twenties and thirties he wrote weekly reviews of an exceptionally wide range of films: the cinema, Greene wrote in 1937, 'has got to appeal to millions; we have got to accept its popularity as a virtue, not turn away from it as a vice'.[65] He was a prolific scriptwriter, whose work in this field included the scripts for five of his own stories. In his novels he experimented with cinematic techniques, most fully, perhaps, in *Stamboul Train* and *It's a Battlefield*, which Greene described as 'intentionally based on film technique'. In interview, Greene stated:

> When I describe a scene, I capture it with the moving eye of the cine-camera rather than with the photographer's eye – which leaves it frozen. In this precise domain I think the cinema has influenced me . . . I work with a camera, following my characters and their movements.'[66]

In the 1930s, a number of British writers travelled to Hollywood, primarily to work as screenplay writers. Costume and historical dramas, and the adaptations of classic British fiction and drama, represented a substantial part of Hollywood production in this period, with the studios exporting British drama to Britain, and writers from England were particularly sought after.[67] Aldous Huxley, Christopher Isherwood, Anthony Powell, J. B. Priestley, P. G. Wodehouse and Evelyn Waugh all spent periods of time in Hollywood, Isherwood finally settling in California permanently. Their fiction also incorporated the filmic medium in a variety of ways. In *Vile Bodies*, Waugh used the vagaries of film-time to represent the chaos, anarchy and inconsequentiality of modern life; in Colonel Blount's film-show, a biographical picture of the life of John Wesley, 'whenever the story reached a point of dramatic and significant action, the film seemed to get faster and faster . . . On the other hand, any scene of repose or inaction . . . seemed prolonged almost unendurably.'[68] Part One of Anthony Powell's *Afternoon Men* (the first volume of his novel-sequence *A Dance to the Music of Time*) is titled 'Montage', although Powell seems to have been borrowing the resonances of the cinematic metaphor rather than engaging with its techniques.

Both Isherwood and Huxley wrote about the worlds of the film studios and film moguls. Huxley's novel *After Many a Summer Dies the Swan* was written

64 Ibid., p. 444. 65 Ibid., p. 414. 66 Ibid., p. xxxii.
67 See David King Dunaway, *Huxley in Hollywood* (New York: Harper & Row, 1989).
68 Evelyn Waugh, *Vile Bodies* (Harmondsworth: Penguin, 2000), p. 178.

during 1938 and 1939, while he was at work in Hollywood on the script for the MGM film *Madame Curie*; the novel is a detective story, at the centre of which is a figure modelled on Randolph Hearst (Huxley's novel was one of the inspirations for Orson Welles's film *Citizen Kane*), and the various subplots were based on Hollywood scandals. Isherwood's autobiographical work *Prater Violet* (the working-title of which had been 'O.K. for Sound'), published in 1945, is set in London in the early 1930s, and recalls his experiences as a scriptwriter to an Austrian émigré film-director whom he calls Friedrich Bergman, the fictional counterpart of the Weimar director Berthold Viertel. Viertel's credits included the street-film *The Adventures of a Ten-Mark Note* (1926), a film set in Berlin in the years of inflation and exemplifying the 'New Objectivity'. Its techniques are echoed in Isherwood's *Goodbye to Berlin*, the first section of which opens with his image of the narrative 'I' as a camera-eye recording a Berlin street scene, in which streets and houses are imaged as 'shabby monumental safes crammed with the tarnished valuables and second-hand furniture of a bankrupt middle class':

> I am a camera with its shutter open, quite passive, recording, not thinking. Recording the man shaving at the window opposite and the woman in the kimono washing her hair. Some day, all this will have to be developed, carefully printed, fixed.[69]

Isherwood's 'camera eye' lays claim to the documentarists' 'objectivity' – he is the 'camera' and not the photographer or the projectionist. Samuel Hynes suggests, however, that beneath the documentary surface, 'it is a personal testament; like Eliot, Isherwood recorded himself in recording his city'.[70] In fact, the absoluteness of the division between objectivity and subjectivity was breaking down in the work of 1930s 'observers', Isherwood included, producing more complex and self-reflexive approaches, as in Charles Madge and Tom Harrisson's account of the 'new method' of Mass-Observation in 1937: 'Ideally, it is the observation by everyone of everyone, including themselves.'[71]

In 1933, Berthold Viertel asked Isherwood to script Gaumont–British's film *Little Friend*, a family drama in the script of which Isherwood was able to suggest themes of repressed and illicit sexuality. In Isherwood's fictionalised

69 Christopher Isherwood, *Goodbye to Berlin* (London: Hogarth Press, 1939), p. 13.
70 Samuel Hynes, *The Auden Generation: Literature and Politics in England in the 1930s* (London: Faber & Faber, 1976), p. 356.
71 Charles Madge and Tom Harrisson, *Mass-Observation* (London: Frederick Muller, 1937), p. 10.

account of his experiences, the film becomes *Prater Violet*, an 'unashamedly corny musical set in pre-1914 Vienna'. The shift serves Isherwood's purpose, as Keith Williams has argued, of pointing to his own complicity and, by extension, that of other writers on the Left, with the political evasions and trivialisations of the mass media with which he and they had become increasingly involved.[72] As *Prater Violet* is filmed, news comes of the crushing of the Social Democrats and the socialists' strongholds in Vienna by Dollfuss's Christian Socialist Party; the film, Bergman states angrily, 'lies and declares that the pretty Danube is blue, when the water is red with blood . . . '.[73]

The function of *Prater Violet* as a text is to reveal both the political events occluded by the historical costume drama and the workings of the film apparatus which must be hidden from the film spectator's view. 'On rare occasions', Isherwood writes, 'the microphone itself manages to get into the shot, without anybody noticing it. There is something sinister about it, like Poe's Raven. It is always there, silently listening.'[74] The shadow in the text of this microphone-shadow (a warning shadow, indeed, to recall Graham Greene's words) which Bergman calls 'the Original Sin of the Talking Pictures', conjures up some of the more dystopian images in 1930s fiction and film of media surveillance. It may also recall Woolf's 'shadow on the screen' and its bodying forth of 'fear itself'. In the *Prater Violet* of 1930s Europe, film and fear are differently but no less fully imbricated, as if a trajectory 'from Caligari to Hitler' were indeed being charted:

> 'Do you know what the film is?' Bergman cupped his hands, lovingly, as if around an exquisite flower: 'The film is an infernal machine. Once it is ignited and set in motion it revolves with an enormous dynamism. It cannot pause. It cannot apologize. It cannot retract anything. It cannot explain itself. It simply ripens to its inevitable explosion.'[75]

Christopher reframes Bergman's statement to his admiring mother and brother, but in doing so turns the account into one of film *speed*: 'There's the film, and you have to look at it as the director wants you to look at it . . . He's started something and he has to go through with it.'[76] Yet the echoes in Bergman's original formulations of the last lines of Auden's *Spain* – 'We are

[72] Keith Williams, *British Writers and the Media 1930–45* (Basingstoke: Macmillan, 1996), p. 174. For discussion of *Prater Violet*, see also Michael Wood, 'Modernism and Film', in Michael Levenson, ed., *The Cambridge Companion to Modernism* (Cambridge University Press, 1999), pp. 218–9.

[73] Christopher Isherwood, *Prater Violet* (London: Minerva, 1997), p. 77. [74] Ibid., p. 64.

[75] Ibid., p. 23. [76] Ibid., p. 25.

left alone with our day, and the time is short and History to the defeated / May say Alas but cannot help or pardon' – is a reminder that the issue was no longer that of the innovation of cinematic time and movement, as it was for cinema's first viewers, but of film as a way of grasping the force and inexorability of history in a state of emergency.

20

The thirties: politics, authority, perspective

ROD MENGHAM

It is not uncommon to refer to various decades in the twentieth century as if they possessed a character of their own, displaying marks of identity not shared by the decades preceding or following them. The 1930s might seem from this point of view the most self-contained decade in the literary history of the last century, bounded on one side by the beginning of the Depression, and on the other by the outbreak of World War II. It is a period deeply marked by the misery of large-scale unemployment, by the rise of Fascism in Europe, and by the Spanish Civil War (1936–9), a conflict that effectively politicised a whole generation and saw the loss in combat of many of its members.

A surprising number of writers active in the 1930s were prepared to take up clear political positions, in a way and to a degree that has never been paralleled in Britain, before or since. When the pamphlet *Authors Take Sides on the Spanish War* was published in 1937, one hundred and twenty seven writers expressed support for the Republican side in the conflict, with five against, and only sixteen placing themselves in the 'neutral' category. Having a political position, and writing from it, was not just a common desideratum; for much of the decade it was felt to be an urgent necessity. Any reading of thirties' literature has to attend to the problems that writers encountered in determining a position and perspective from which to speak. Prompting their sense of urgency was a combination of factors: unignorable facts such as the Depression, widespread unemployment, and growing rearmament; but also the psychological legacy of World War I, during which the generation that subsequently became known as the writers of the 1930s were still at school. They spent their school years anticipating the moment when they would be called up to fight and in all probability be sacrificed for the values of their parents' generation. The expectation of the need for sacrifice – which never came – and the resentment stored up against those who had demanded sacrifice in their own interests, were transformed into a potent psychological inheritance whose conflicting pressures made it easier to accept the alternatives of Fascism and Communism. What Fascism offered was not just the chance of fulfilling the impulse towards self-sacrifice, but of doing it not in support of the dominant culture, not in the service of the parental generation. Fascism showed how to sacrifice oneself in a way that would actually replace the old order, not reinforce it.

But if Fascism follows through the logic of sacrifice, Communism – for these writers, and in this context – founds itself on a logic of betrayal; betrayal being an inverse of self-sacrifice. What Fascism did was to complete a process already at work in the consciousness of these individuals, whereas what Communism did was to give them the means of throwing that same process into reverse. The 1930s was a decade of several very obvious and active betrayals. It was when all the most famous traitors – Philby, Burgess, Maclean, Blunt – were recruited. The conjunction of Communism with spying is not extraneous to the priorities of left-wing writing of the 1930s, but one of its most vivid preoccupations. Particularly in the work of those writers who have been referred to as the Auden 'gang' – including Christopher Isherwood, Stephen Spender, Cecil Day Lewis and Louis MacNeice – it is not often members of the working class who are envisaged as the agents of revolution. Rather it is the spy, as in Auden's poem of January 1928 that was later given the title 'The Secret Agent'. The poem begins:

> Control of the passes was, he saw, the key
> To this new district, but who would get it?
> He, the trained spy, had walked into the trap
> For a bogus guide, seduced with the old tricks.[1]

This poem inhabits a world also populated by poems, stories, novels and plays by authors other than Auden. A number of left-wing writers chose this kind of setting to express their most important concerns. It is a world where the urgency for political action is constantly translated into terms of conspiracy, deceit, secrecy, guilt. It is significant that the spy is an isolated figure, cut off from other people and unable to communicate with them: 'They ignored his wires. / The bridges were unbuilt'; 'They would shoot, of course, / Parting easily who were never joined.' As John Fuller and Edward Mendelson have pointed out,[2] the last line is a straightforward translation of the last line of

[1] W. H. Auden, *The English Auden: Poems, Essays and Dramatic Writings 1927–1939*, ed. Edward Mendelson (London: Faber & Faber, 1977), p. 25.
[2] John Fuller, *A Reader's Guide to W. H. Auden* (1970); Edward Mendelson, *Early Auden* (London: Faber & Faber, 1981).

the Anglo-Saxon poem, 'Wulf and Eadwacer', which is about the parting of two lovers. The allusion confirms that there is a sexual dimension to Auden's poem, whose emphasis on isolation looks even more embattled in the context of its author's social position as a homosexual.

But the line that is most typical of 1930s writing in this poem is the first one, which suggests that the key to everything, the vital clue that will solve the most important problems, is 'control of the passes'. This phrase goes straight to the heart of a body of left-wing writing in the 1930s that was drawn constantly towards such territorial images and that was mesmerised in particular by the idea of journeying from familiar to unknown territory and marking the difference between known and unknown by crossing a threshold, a border, a frontier. This leading motif is present in several of the titles of the era: *On the Frontier* (1938), by Auden and Isherwood, *Journey to the Border* (1938), by Edward Upward, *Across the Border* (title of an unfinished novel by Graham Greene). At only a slight tangent, the most important anthology of left-wing writing in the early 1930s was *New Country* (1933), edited by Michael Roberts. The conception of journeying towards a border that must be crossed in order to reach something new was employed by several writers to dramatise the idea of the inevitable victory of socialism. Society, for them, was journeying in the direction of a new condition, and in order to get there it had to cross the border of revolution.

Critical accounts of the literary writing of the decade have tended either to endorse, or to disapprove of, the judgement that Auden and his associates took a leading role. The authoritative power of Auden's own work, echoed and emulated in that of others, is seen as either a vindication of this judgement or as a political problem in its own right. One of the more curious aspects of this experiment with the language of power is how often it is politically unresolved. In the writings of Spender and Day Lewis – who both became members of the Communist Party – poetry is seldom conceived of as a means of helping to achieve revolution; it is rather an activity whose full scope can be realised only after revolution has taken place. The literature of agitation, produced in considerable quantities especially during the early years of the decade, stems in large part from the uncomfortable awareness of middle-class writers that their work is and must remain socially and politically marginal this side of revolution. Edgell Rickword took Day Lewis to task in just these terms when reviewing the latter's *Noah and the Waters*: 'Day Lewis knows as well as anybody that the poet cannot stand outside the dialectical process, but his poetry is still infected with the feeling that struggle is transitory, and that "afterwards" we shall get down to work.'[3] The necessity for the poet to be reintegrated into the culture from which his work has become estranged is motivated psychologically even while being validated theoretically by the movement of history. The paradox whereby political change is desired in order to release the poet from the burden of politics is detected in Spender's work by Michael Roberts, in his introduction to *New Signatures*, the anthology that consolidated the group identity of the left-wing poets of the 1930s: 'poetry is here turned to propaganda, but it is propaganda for a theory of life which may release the poet's energies for the writing of pure poetry'.[4] Despite this alibi of 'purity', both Day Lewis's and Spender's writings of the early 1930s are dominated by a vocabulary of subversion, conspiracy, political opportunism, guerrilla warfare; by 1933, Day Lewis is clearly mythologising the imagery of crisis developed by Auden, inciting volunteers to 'Break through to blocked galleries below pit-head . . . Men to catch spies, fly aeroplanes.'[5] Spender's work of the same period recycles many of the same gestures, countering social injustice with an absence of political analysis that makes its many exhortations seem to depend on an argument conducted elsewhere.[6]

The crucial alteration in this language of intimidation and overthrow comes with the publication of Spender's *Vienna* in 1934. All the ingredients of revolutionary struggle and heroism can be found in this text, all the already familiar props from the revolutionary scenarios rehearsed in the works of Spender, Auden and Day Lewis. But the difference with this book is that it records an actual uprising, as well as the author's own experience of its aftermath, and as a result there is hardly anything in its language to remind the reader of the usual rhetoric. Auden's own response to genuine conflict, 'Spain 1937', is less profound, even though its eloquence is unparalleled. What is unsettling about this poem is precisely the extent to which it exhibits a formidable degree of formal and intellectual control. The brilliance of Auden's phrase-making is commensurate with the poem's detachment from the effects of political violence. Several critics, including George Orwell, have expressed disgust over the perfunctoriness with which 'necessary murder' is referred to as part of the revolutionary process. Equally telling is the poem's configuration of spatial relations. The crucial moment when the struggle is engaged, marked by the evocation of members of the International Brigades travelling from all over

[3] Edgell Rickword, 'Who is this Noah?', *Left Review*, 2, 7 (April 1936), pp. 339–40.

[4] Michael Roberts, ed., *New Signatures* (London: Hogarth Press, 1934), p. 19.

[5] C. Day Lewis, 'The Magnetic Mountain', in *Collected Poems* (London: Jonathan Cape with the Hogarth Press, 1954), p. 89.

[6] See, for example, poems XXIV and XXVII in *Poems* (London: Faber & Faber, 1933).

Europe, getting closer and closer to their destination, is perceived as if over a distance and from an altitude so immense as to be almost literally astronomical; Spain itself is no more visible than a 'fragment nipped off from hot / Africa'. Auden's own first-hand experience of the Spanish Front (he volunteered as a stretcher-bearer) is almost completely effaced by the repetition of imaginary co-ordinates; and in this respect, the space in which action and perception are grasped is no different from that of Day Lewis's *Transitional Poem* of 1929, where organising movement is characteristically vertical: either downwards to the mines, or upwards to the stars, but hardly ever across the landscapes of ordinary social relations.

The smooth confidence with which the speaker of Auden's poem adjudicates the movement of history is in marked contrast to the unbalanced tones of John Cornford's poetic bulletins from the same war. Cornford, who was a committed Communist, was killed in action at the age of twenty-one. Despite the brevity of his career, his work covers a surprising range of responses to the challenge of war and of ideological conflict. While never seriously doubting the justice of the Communist cause, his best-known works entertain a series of misgivings about his own adequacy in the role he had chosen. 'Full Moon at Tierz: Before the Storming of Huesca' (1936), Cornford's most ambitious poem, is divided almost equally between demonstrations of adherence to the party line and an insidious feeling of personal vulnerability. The decisiveness with which this lack of congruence is exposed to scrutiny is all the more impressive given the extent of Cornford's debt to Auden's style in the poems of his teenage years.

It must be remembered that Auden was later to disavow the position taken up in 'Spain 1937'. He might well feel it was inconsistent with the questioning of external authority that was such a defining feature of much of his poetry during the 1930s. If this essay is to examine the basis of authority in the writing of the period, it needs to query the extent to which Auden's texts should be seen as the source of a dictatorial tendency in left-wing writing. The relevant issues come into focus through a reading of the early poem 'Consider this and in our time' (March 1930) whose first verse paragraph has stimulated controversy:

> Consider this and in our time
> As the hawk sees it or the helmeted airman:
> The clouds rift suddenly – look there
> At cigarette-end smouldering on a border
> At the first garden party of the year.
> Pass on, admire the view of the massif
> Through plate-glass windows of the Sport Hotel;

> Join there the insufficient units
> Dangerous, easy, in furs, in uniform
> And constellated at reserved tables
> Supplied with feelings by an efficient band
> Relayed elsewhere to farmers and their dogs
> Sitting in kitchens in the stormy fens.[7]

A certain orthodoxy has built up in the reception of this poem with regard to the kind of hawk's-eye view that Auden is appealing to in the second line. An almost standard reading has emerged for which this poem more than any other demonstrates an element of totalitarianism in Auden's fascination with 'high-flying, swift-swooping birds of prey, kestrels, Hitlerian and Williamsonian eagles, birds reminiscent of the modern military aeroplane. It's the commanding vision of the "hawk . . . or the helmeted airman" that Auden again and again seeks', in this critical account.[8] Yet the aerial perspective is in fact maintained only for the first few lines. Already in line six, the viewpoint has changed; you cannot actually look through the plate-glass windows at the mountains outside except from inside the hotel. And not only that, the outlook is changed constantly: 'Consider this and *in our time* / As the hawk sees it or the helmeted airman'. It is only in our time that the airman has been enabled to see what the hawk could always see, and what that involves is placing an emphasis not on the position of the perceiving eye, but on all the things that are being perceived. A feeling of dominance is evoked here and there in the poem but what prevails is an awareness of the variety in the scene that is being unfolded: here the garden party, there the Sport Hotel, elsewhere the farmers in kitchens. There have been complaints too that Auden adopts a coercive tone with the reader – 'consider', 'look', 'pass on', 'admire', 'join' – but again, these different instructions don't all share the same value. Several of the predicates are not concerned with simply doing this or doing that, and do not require an element of coercion. In fact the first of them – the first word in the whole poem – encourages the reader to reflect, mull over, think carefully, rather than perform a simple action. We should be careful not to attribute too much peremptoriness to the voice speaking in the poem where a more subtle effect is surely aimed at. Perhaps the voice is primarily testing its readers, taunting us, daring us to join the group, in a way that is actually calculated to warn us off. The limitations of the group in the Sport Hotel are in that sense suggested by the claustrophobic unanimity engendered by the mutual attractions of 'units' / 'uniform',

[7] Auden, *The English Auden*, p. 46.
[8] Valentine Cunningham, *British Writers of the Thirties* (Oxford University Press, 1988), p. 192.

'insufficient' / 'efficient'. The inhumanity of the group's members is hinted at not only in their decision to sit at reserved tables but also in respect of the frosty detachment that makes them appear 'constellated' at reserved tables. The invitation to join these people is accompanied by a sufficient number of signals indicating why we should not want to join them.

The position of the speaker is actually more elusive than it may initially appear, and so is the position of the reader, who is suddenly, at the start of the second verse paragraph, addressed as 'supreme Antagonist', then at the start of the third paragraph as 'Financier', and subsequently as one of a group of 'seekers after happiness'. In the second paragraph, once again, the emphasis is on range and variety: on Cornwall, Mendip and the Pennines, on land and sea, local and universal, and so on. Neither are the imperatives that succeed one another – 'Order the ill . . . visit the ports . . . beckon . . . summon' and the rest – as high-handed as they seem when taken out of context. Put back into their places in the construction of the whole paragraph, they are made to refer to a situation that is the logical outcome of past and present conditions: once, 'long ago', certain things happened which led to the state of affairs we see now – 'You talk to your admirers every day', and so forth – while this in turn makes a certain outcome seem inevitable in the immediate future which does not require the instructions of the poem's speaker in order to be effected.

The poem demonstrates more than one kind of attempt to establish the inevitable connections between events that are separated in time, and one gets a particularly powerful sense of this in what have now become its most famous lines: 'It is later than you think; nearer that day / Far other than that distant afternoon / Amid rustle of frocks and stamping feet / They gave the prizes to the ruined boys.' The intricate relations of distinction and parallelism in these lines – it is later / it is nearer; it is near / it is far; 'Far other than that' / 'It is later than you' – create a sense of the pattern in events by making patterns seem inescapable. And the final mood of the poem is not an imperative but an indicative one: 'To disintegrate on an instant in the explosion of mania / Or lapse for ever into a classic fatigue.' The poem, we might conclude, is not continuously insisting on its command over experience, but offering instead a prognosis of the movement of history.

One characteristic feature of Auden's writing during this period is its mode of address, which communicates the need for decisive action based on the analysis of a general condition, while appearing to confide in an inner circle of conspirators. This aggrandising of the marginalised, appearing to give a secret meaning to the idiom of the socially isolated and politically disempowered, is what energises the homosocial tendencies in the work of this set of young men whose experience of group dynamics is almost entirely confined to that of the all-male societies of certain public schools and certain Oxbridge colleges. No wonder that much of the most socially engaged work of women writers during the decade turns its back on this parade of masonic credentials. The selective morbidity of Auden's northern landscapes is transformed into the realistic settings of regional novels by Phyllis Bentley, Winifred Holtby and Storm Jameson, whose portrayals of industrialised Yorkshire locate their stories of family relationships within the context of long-term historical change. For the most part, these are traditional narratives on domestic and social issues relevant to a wide readership. Even where the theme concerns the development of political consciousness among female characters, as in Sylvia Townsend Warner's *Summer Will Show* (1936), the narrative point of view is inclusive. In the work of those women writers whose involutions of style correspond to a degree of social autism, the pressures on female psychology are related directly to the frustrations of having to struggle with the closed systems of a male-dominated world. Nowhere is this alienation more extreme than in the early novels of Jean Rhys: *Postures* (later re-titled *Quartet*) (1928) and *Voyage in the Dark* (1934).

There is no denying a tendency to cliquish mystification in a poem such as 'Consider this and in our time'. The sense of intrigue aroused is part of what makes it a perfect prototype for what was later to be considered the typical 1930s text, containing as it does many of the features that were to join the decade's repertoire of gestures and obsessions, including: the sense of patterns awaiting events; the elements of fear and anticipation; the presence of guilt; the demand for sacrifice; the feeling of belatedness; the need for disaffiliation; the phantasm of catastrophe; the appeal to conspiracy; the border; forms of constitutional disorder that connect the physical – and the sexual – with the political. What is at issue here is the extent to which the writing of Auden and of others associated with him does not merely reproduce these concerns but explores and tests their bearing and implications. It may be that certain crucial texts actually provide some degree of analytical purchase on those myths of self-definition that they are usually thought to reproduce in an uncritical fashion.

Auden's closest associates at the start of his writing career were Christopher Isherwood and Edward Upward, two valued friends whose sporadic collaboration on a series of stories set in the imaginary landscape of 'Mortmere' was an early influence both on some of Auden's more extravagant formal experiments and on his political awareness. The Mortmere style was wildly subversive, with a savage intensity of focus on the weirdness of English culture. Isherwood's subsequent development as both novelist and autobiographer combined impulses of self-dramatisation and self-deprecation, an unstable mixture whose contradictoriness reflected the disturbance of sexual and political identities experienced by several members of his generation. His first two novels, *All the Conspirators* (1928) and *The Memorial* (1932), are fuelled by resentment of the parental generation, while the subsequent *Mr Norris Changes Trains* (1935) and *Goodbye to Berlin* (1939) include vivid admonitions of the threat posed by Nazism. The desire for disaffiliation from the structures of power is haunted by a countervailing anxiety over the need to find a group to whom one could meaningfully belong.

Upward's trajectory after Mortmere is less well known than Isherwood's reports on the spectacle of Germany in decline. Upward spent much of the decade of the 1930s toiling over his only novel of the period, *Journey to the Border* (1938). Usually thought by critics to illustrate its author's painful, struggling move from fantasy to realism, the text actually does nothing of the sort. It deploys a range of different manners. The one most readily associated with the bizarre world of 'Mortmere' is progressively attached to a form of grotesque naturalism, in a series of hyperbolised close-ups, involving a mesmerised isolating of minute particulars in descriptions of characters' bodies. It is most obviously counterpointed by the long-distance effects of a panoramic sweep which tracks the movement of bodies through landscape. The panoramic and the myopic are held in tension with one another. What is missing is a reassuringly human angle of vision, which the text reaches for but never achieves – the point of view is one that never establishes a proper perspective. The most vivid writing comes from the short-sighted discourse of physicality, which revolves around an obsessive scrutiny of weaknesses, ailments and nastinesses of various kinds. The physical revulsion it produces is linked to the awareness of the protagonist, a middle-class tutor who is supposed to be ready to take up a revolutionary position at the end of the novel.

At one level, that maturing process gradually comes to seem an impossibility, simply because the historically rooted anxieties the tutor is trying to overcome seem to be invested in his very body. It is one thing to change the mind of a spy into the mind of a worker, quite another to effect a similar transformation of the body. The middle-class physique is so saturated with infection and disability in Upward's text, it is as if its owner would have to turn himself physically into an entirely different person in order to be an agent of revolution. The problem in the text is never solved, but disguised by shifting onto other ground. There is another important strain in the writing that is organised less with regard to visual dispositions than in terms of a growing attention to the sound of speech, to the rhythms of a voice that has to articulate very long sentences and take the measure of their overall construction. This is part of a very palpable move towards political oratory in Upward's work which was to intensify considerably during the early 1940s. The problem of inadequacy, given physical representation, is literally disembodied as the writing proceeds to draw strength from the fabrication of a voice. The mismatch of somatic and vocal is brilliantly encapsulated in the behaviour of one of the characters, the charlatan, a trickster who juggles with words: 'Shakespeare, stratosphere, bottled beer'. The charlatan is a figure who operates in terms of rhetorical shaping rather than in terms of semantic coherence, and he is a quintessential figure of disembodiment, being curiously ventriloquial. The movement of his lips does not synchronise with the sound of his words, just as the revolutionary message of the novel is out of synch with its chronic morbidity.

Perhaps the most obvious way in which Upward engages with the mythography of the early thirties is in his play with the imagery of winged creatures – of hawks and helmeted airmen – which his text associates with the aloofness of the panoramic view. In the polemical essay, 'Sketch for a Marxist Interpretation of Literature', Upward forces the point:

> How far do your thoughts give a true picture of the relations actually existing among things? You might think of a man with wings. The man might be real, a friend of yours, and the wings might have belonged to a real swan you had seen in a public park, but the combination in your mind would be nothing more than a contemptible whimsy, a myth.[9]

In *Journey to the Border*, reversion to this imagery of 'men with wings' and to the flight of various kinds of birds – most notably swans – is linked to confirmations of a delusive state. If the critical reception of the hawk's-eye view allows for the prospect of exemption, superiority and freedom from restraint, in Upward's novel this position carries implications of unearthly detachment, of an 'untrue picture of things'. In other words, it is a dehumanising aloofness which is the object of criticism within the text, not a viewpoint it chooses to adopt.

It is precisely the political acuity of those texts whose authors are prepared to interrogate the repertoire of dominant images that renders them suspect in the eyes of those convinced of the need to equate socialism with the literary techniques of socialist realism. The constant revision of motifs can be seen as the reflection of a commitment to rhetorical structure at the expense of verisimilitude. Paradoxically, the incidence of fabular, allegorical or oneiric

[9] Edward Upward, 'Sketch for a Marxist Interpretation of Literature', in C. Day Lewis, ed., *The Mind in Chains: Socialism and the Cultural Revolution* (London: Frederick Muller, 1937).

elements is often proportional to the degree of the writer's political engagement. This makes obvious sense in the case of a writer like Rex Warner (about whom, more shortly) although it fails to square with the elusive style of a writer like Henry Green. Like *Journey to the Border*, Green's *Party Going* (1939) was written over a period of many years, in the course of which several of the defining myths of the thirties were revolved, including an extensive use of bird imagery. The novel actually begins with the death of a pigeon, with the failure of flight:

> She turned and she went back to where it had fallen and again looked up to where it must have died for it was still warm and, everything unexplained, she turned once more into the tunnel back to the station.[10]

The character referred to here, Miss Fellowes, retrieves the bird and washes it, simulating an act of ritual piety. But her motivation is obscure and the meaning of the incident is never explained, despite the text's proclivity to rework certain details of the scene. This portentous moment, seemingly charged with significance but resistant to interpretation, represents a further complexifying of the decade's manner of encoding its concerns. For it is precisely in the use of these figures that have been burdened symbolically in earlier writings that Green insists on their distance from a point of origin and on their loss of vitality. With each return to the imagery of the opening incident, the text provides yet another divergence from the path to knowledge and understanding, rather than further evidence of a gradual progression to meaning:

> 'If he was a bird', he said, 'he would not last long.'[11]

> 'Go on if you like and pick up some bird, alive or dead.' (p. 159)

> That is what it is to be rich, he thought, if you are held up, if you have to wait then you can do it after a bath in your dressing gown and if you have to die then not as any bird tumbling dead from its branch . . . (p. 195)

> Lying in his arms, her long eyelashes down along her cheeks, her hair tumbled and waved, her hands drifted to rest like white doves drowned on peat water . . . (p. 226)

These spasmodic returns to the same basic figure make the writing seem to define itself by the width of its gap between discursive relations and representational reference. Successive layers of obscurity seem to be added to each figure, suspending the expectation of a definitive version of its meaning. This process

[10] Henry Green, *Party Going* (London: Hogarth Press, 1939), p. 7.
[11] Ibid., p. 64. Further references given in parenthesis in the text.

of sublimation is aligned with images of obstruction and inaccessibility, with the interposition of thresholds, veils and frontiers. In *Party Going*, the journey to the border is a process of reading increasingly subject to deceleration, to semantic detours, to a growing realisation that the frustration of meaning is interminable.

A very similar principle underlies the distribution of motifs in Rex Warner's *The Wild Goose Chase* (1937). The title itself encapsulates the manner in which this text elicits moments of estrangement from what is assumed to be familiar. The idiomatic phrase denoting a futile quest is given a haunting resonance in the course of a narrative in which successive waves of explorers journey across the border to become absorbed into the unknown, into what is literally the unhomely. The actual frontier between what is familiar and unfamiliar is impossible to pin down. And on the level of syntactical arrangements, this elusiveness is reflected in a tendency to defer the main clause of the sentence. Every time it seems on the brink of attaining its goal, the sentence redoubles its efforts of protraction:

> Of late the weather had been stormy, though now the sun shone and a stiff breeze blew from the sea, exacerbating the waves in the bay over which, at a great distance from the shore, far from their nesting places, sailing on enormous wings that flashed in their high turnings against the sun, long ribbons of light, or like the rims of metal discs set firm and hardened in the velocity of steep falling, were fishing the great pelagic gannets, seldom to be seen so clearly with the naked eye.[12]

This is, in fact, the first use of bird imagery in a text that finds a special power in the auguries involving geese in particular, but also gannets, gulls, owls and other avians. The appearance of birds is surrounded by superstitious excitement, and by a conflict of interpretations concerning their use as portents. The final clause of this sentence, while bringing them into focus, prepares the reader for disappointment, since birds in this text are seldom – if ever – 'seen clearly'. The main point of the description is its afterthought. Warner was a professional classicist, and it is easy to see the influence of Greek and Latin sentence structure on his carefully contrived periodic prose. But there are other, more far-reaching, ways in which his intellectual training has shaped the design of his narrative. As a translator, his best-known publication was a version of Thucydides for Penguin Classics. But it is another Greek historian, Herodotus, from whom Warner has derived his imaginative structures. The successive groups of three brothers who travel over the border repeat the

[12] Rex Warner, *The Wild Goose Chase* (London: Boriswood, 1937), pp. 15–6.

pattern laid down by several Indo-European myths of origin.[13] The three individuals represent the three estates of priests, warriors and farmers, a division echoed by Warner's distinctions between the scholar, the adventurer and the man of common sense and practical abilities. As in the myths of origin, it is always the youngest brother who succeeds where his elder brothers have failed, in a reversal of primogeniture that would have appealed to Warner's generation. The crucial effect of Warner's sidestepping the example of Thucydides the realist, in a reversion to Herodotus' fascination with the outlandish and the marvellous, is the primacy given to the stories that cultures tell about themselves. Warner's fiction shares the motives of the social anthropologist, intent on the information that cultures give us in their customs and rituals, information that allows us to compare the values and practices of different historical societies. The figure of the anthropological stranger, displacing the familiar points of view, aware of the relative status of social and political conventions, becomes a defining presence in much of the liveliest writing of the period.

One of the most maverick examples is at the centre of Hugh Sykes Davies's curious prose narrative, *Petron* (1935). The picaresque wanderings of its eponymous hero are influenced by the poems of Ariosto, but its methods of construction are primarily Surrealist. Petron encounters a succession of idiots on his journey, figures whose almost complete inarticulacy is replaced startlingly by the balanced antithetical formulae of a neo-Classical decorum. Sykes Davies typically combines two distinct modes of composition: a primary process of composition that generates material whimsically on the model of automatic writing, and a secondary process that renders this material into a condition of rhetorical shapeliness:

> On his way Petron came upon some boys throwing stones at an old twisted tree, and stopped them, saying that it was wrong to inflict harm on any living thing. When the boys had gone away, repentant, hanging their heads, the tree turned to an old man, who thanked Petron fervently for his kindness, and said he hoped to repay him before too long.
>
> Two days later, the old man caught up with our hero, and presented him with a sack full of butterflies, which he had been catching ever since his metamorphosis. Petron received them graciously, but when the old man had gone, 'What on earth,' he said, 'am I to do with all this beauty?' and he pitched the whole sackful down the cliff.[14]

[13] Cf. Herodotus, *The Histories*, trans. Aubrey de Selincourt (Harmondsworth: Penguin, 1954) pp. 102–3.

[14] Hugh Sykes Davies, *Petron* (London: J. M. Dent, 1935), p. 19.

This complete chapter mimics and parodies the textuality of the parable, for which the method of reading has a moralising purpose: every story has a lesson to be learned and applied to the reader's everyday life. But the passage culminates instead with a surrealistic joke at the expense of bourgeois sentimentality. The routinely pious injunction not to destroy life is followed almost immediately with a summary insecticide. The text is also contradictory in a slightly more complicated fashion: its theme of metamorphosis is one of the organising principles of a Surrealism geared to uncovering the hidden life of the everyday; and yet the proposition that the aesthetic transformation of the ordinary, like the development of the caterpillar into the butterfly, involves a refashioning of the ugly into the beautiful, is dismissed as pointless. Metamorphosis is both insisted on and devalued simultaneously.

A later passage examines another defining preoccupation of Surrealism in its testing of the relationship between perception and the world of percepts: between what Breton termed the 'crisis of the subject' and the 'crisis of the object':

> At this point I can imagine you asking, with brow puckered in the irritable and petty attitudes of interrogation: 'What is the size of these adventures? To what may we compare these exploits?'
>
> As a means of seizing the scale of these matters, and placing them against a familiar background, I suggest that you hire a milch cow, in colours as striking as possible, and that you take her to the shore below some cliff of considerable height. There, having tethered her to a boulder, contemplate her until the image is firmly embedded in your mind: so firmly embedded that not even a considerable shock will dislodge it. For it is precisely to such a shock that you must subject the image. Pass another twist of the rope round the rock, make all secure, and then ascend to the top of the cliff. Stand at the edge for a few minutes, concentrating your mind on the image of the cow, and occasionally verifying it by a glance at the real cow below. Then, when you feel quite sure of it, cast yourself over the precipice; head foremost lest your body should impede your view. For you must note as you fall the impression which you have of the cow, outlined upon the rocks where you will so shortly be dashed: note how the cow might be considered to have been so dashed already: note its exact size above all. For that is the size of these adventures of Petron. That is exactly the scale on which we are working.[15]

Changes to the subjective point of view are given an absurdly literal basis as the eye of the observer is moved around from one point to another. At the same time, the impression of the cow to be fixed in the mind's eye is made

[15] Ibid., pp. 27–8.

interchangeable with the image of the cow reflected on the retina of the ordinarily observing eye. The text is constructed around a series of paradoxes. As in the earlier passage, there is a fundamental tension between the presentation of visual data and the language in which it is spoken. On the one hand, the point of view undergoes a violent reversal – a dramatic undermining of the hawk's-eye view – involving loss of security, vertigo, terror. On the other hand, the tone of voice is one of perfect equanimity and detachment, while the syntax exemplifies composure and control. This contrast between voice and point of view is endemic to a great deal of the left-wing writing of the 1930s. It is a defining feature in the work of Edward Upward, but is no less crucial in the prose poetry of Hugh Sykes Davies, Humphrey Jennings and Charles Madge.

Sykes Davies, Jennings and others, including William Empson, had been associated with the Cambridge magazine *Experiment* (November 1928 to Spring 1931), one of the most important early outlets in Britain for Surrealist writing. Cambridge Surrealism, while not immune to the attractions of automatic writing, showed more interest in the political scope of the 'surrealism of everyday life', and focused its attention on the underlying meanings of social conventions and popular culture. Jennings and Madge were to be founder-members of the social survey movement, Mass-Observation, which had its surrealistic beginnings in a letter published in the *New Statesman and Nation* on 30 January 1937, under the title 'Anthropology at Home'. The Mass-Observation project is anticipated in Madge's surrealistic prose poem 'Bourgeois News' (1936). This text is effectively a report on the British, who have been made the object of the kind of scrutiny an anthropologist would bring to bear on the so-called primitive rituals of an exotic tribal culture. An equal measure of attention, more affectionate and more celebratory of British popular culture, is reflected in Jennings's subsequent work as a documentary film-maker.

One of the most significant aspects of the Mass-Observer's point of view is that it contrasts so decisively with that of the hawk or the helmeted airman. I have argued that a dominating perspective is by no means as clearly or as frequently present in Auden's writing as some critics have claimed; but its presence in the reception of the work is what has given it cultural weight and authority. The films of Jennings share with the poetry of Auden a rhetoric of apostrophe, in which the reader or spectator is enjoined to 'observe', 'inspect', or 'look at' the data of English social reality: 'Look, stranger, at this island now' begins one of Auden's most famous poems. But the position of the Mass-Observer, like the point of view in Jennings's films, is never an elevated one; it is that of the figure in the crowd, whose view is frequently obscured, by other passers-by and by traffic; which is shifting, transitory, partial. The anthropological observation in Jennings's work is quite different from that in Auden's early poems: the 'look' of Auden's stranger is associated with spying and surveillance, with an exclusive, Masonic knowledge; the 'look' of the Mass-Observer turns that process of introversion inside out, to display and share with others, the knowledge of a public reality, an understanding of the real meanings of home.

In Julia Strachey's vivacious satire on the English, *Cheerful Weather for the Wedding* (1932), it is precisely in the home that the most exotic discoveries are to be made. The narrative point of view in this energetically paced novella shifts backwards and forwards between members of the Thatcham family and their various guests on the occasion of Dolly Thatcham's wedding to the Hon. Owen Bigham. As the sequence of events leads up to and beyond the wedding ceremony, an alarming accumulation of 'home truths' about the Thatchams renders their façade of gentility completely unsustainable. The chief agent of disclosure in this respect is a student of anthropology, Joseph Patten, who ends the novella seeming to peer at the whole family 'as if through the wrong end of a long telescope'.[16] Joseph's motives are suspect (he is Dolly's jilted lover) and his methods are clumsy (he is still only a student) but his anthropological scrutiny of the English reveals a society whose organising taboos are being systematically flouted. The unfortunate Dolly, who may or may not be the secret mother of two illegitimate children, endures the preparations for the wedding with the help of a bottle of rum. Her confrontation with Joseph follows a bungled attempt to cork this bottle:

> 'For Heaven's sake, what am I to do! What am I to do! I cannot go into the church like this!' she screamed up at him. She held out her skirt towards him; her small hand was dark blue, and upon the white satin was a black stain as big as a tea-pot.
>
> By her toes lay an overturned ink-bottle.[17]

The black stain resists the symbolism of the white wedding-dress, just as shockingly as the bottle of rum supplants the pot of tea the middle-class girl would be expected to handle. The facility with which the Thatchams' poise is undermined, the rapidity with which propriety is dissolved, come to seem inevitable. Just as the word 'stain' is an anagram of 'satin', so the family's disgrace seems to be lurking in their very attempts to secure respectability.

[16] Julia Strachey, *Cheerful Weather for the Wedding* (Harmondsworth: Penguin, 1978), p. 78.
[17] Ibid., p. 50.

Strachey's descriptions of the house in which the action is set conjure up a scenario for the reader entirely different from the one in which all the characters apart from Joseph see themselves:

> Above the writing-table where Dolly sat was an ancient mirror.
>
> This mirror was rusted over with tiny specks by the hundred, and also the quicksilver at the back had become blackened in the course of ages, so that the drawing-room, as reflected in its corpse-like face, seemed forever swimming in an eerie, dead-looking, metallic twilight, such as is never experienced in the actual world outside. And a strange effect was produced:
>
> It was as if the drawing-room reappeared in this mirror as a familiar room in a dream reappears, ghostly, significant, and wiped free of all signs of humdrum and trivial existence. Two crossed books lying flat, the round top of a table, a carved lizard's head on a clock, the sofa-top and its arms, shone in the grey light from the sky outside; everything else was in shadow. The transparent ferns that stood massed in the window showed up very brightly, and looked fearful . . .
>
> To complete the picture, Dolly's white face, with its thick and heavily curled back lips, above her black speckled wool frock, glimmered palely in front of the ferns, like a phosphorescent orchid blooming alone there in the twilit swamp.[18]

What the fictitious mirror shows is what the process of writing uncovers, the familiar made strange, dead meanings brought alive in new and threatening forms. In this alternative universe, the rituals of English life, whether trivial or portentous, drinking tea, choosing socks, offering chocolates, getting married, reappear as viciously competitive, as profoundly deceptive and as inescapable. The more closely the humdrum is examined, the more bizarre and threatening it appears. No wonder Mrs Thatcham is never comforted except by clear days on which it is possible to see two, or even exceptionally, three counties, a burlesque version of the long-sightedness that is critiqued so vigorously in Upward's *Journey to the Border*.

In William Empson's unfinished fable *The Royal Beasts*, written in 1937, but not published until 1986, the anthropological stranger is a member of another species, the creature Wuzzoo, who wanders out of the jungle one day into the office of George Bickersteth, an administrator in the African Crown Colonies. Although ape-like in appearance, Wuzzoo is exceptionally intelligent and artistically gifted, giving rise to multiplying debates in the Western world about

[18] Ibid., pp. 11–12.

the defining characteristics of the human. His acuity and lack of experience of civilisation prompt a series of questions about the rationale for human behaviour, social organisation, politics, religion, law and science. Empson's fable comprises a review of various histories of discrimination, of different criteria employed by different historical groups to determine questions of inclusion and exclusion, of acceptable and unacceptable behaviour. As in *Cheerful Weather for the Wedding*, vital issues concerning what is permissible or impermissible in civilised society are refracted through questions of decorum, of what is polite or impolite behaviour at a tea-party. However, Wuzzoo's membership of a different species gives him the licence to bring up to the surface everything that his human interlocutors repress:

> 'Come back, Mary. You mustn't wince away from me like that. It's bad for my psychology. You had better hold my hand for one minute.'
>
> What Rudyard Kipling described as an unclean dismay descended on the room, as if the lights had gone off. After all, there was fair ground for disapproving, the girl was badly embarrassed. It took the form of being determined to get things clear.
>
> 'It's a misunderstanding, really it is, Mr Wuzzoo. I don't feel like that a bit. I got a kind of shock but it was quite different . . . I'll kiss you if you like.'
>
> 'But my dear girl, you must never kiss an animal on the mouth,' said Wuzzoo, with so effective a smile that the social lights turned on again. 'It may have all *kinds* of germs there. What you want to do is to nudge it under the ears, when you go by.'[19]

Mere embarrassment is subtended to a whole history of discomfort, of the awkwardness that has attended relations between classes, nations and races, of a kind that can be profoundly disturbing when encountered in the work of writers such as Kipling. The diplomacy that constantly euphemises such problems is reduced to a stunned silence by Wuzzoo's physical advance. The relation between male animal and human female is a fantasised version of the sexual encounter between members of different human groups that is clearly responded to with a mixture of fear and bafflement. In many respects this is the most significant frontier in the writing of the 1930s, and the one that is least often crossed. The idea of physical contact between members of different classes is difficult to separate from issues of power and of middle-class disgust.

One of the writers least well-equipped to negotiate this threshold but determined to subject himself to its challenge was George Orwell, several of

19 William Empson, *'The Royal Beasts' and Other Works*, ed. John Haffenden (London: Chatto & Windus, 1986), p. 164.

whose texts report on the experiment of a middle-class sensibility immersed in the physical environment of the *Lumpenproletariat*. After a period in Burma, during which he acted as law-enforcer for the Imperial Office, Orwell returned in 1927 to Europe and actively sought out the company, and shared the living conditions, of the homeless and impoverished. His first book, *Down and Out in Paris and London* (1933), recounts his employment as a *plongeur* in various Paris restaurants and, more remarkably, his achievement of comradeship with Irish tramps living rough in London. A subsequent novel, *A Clergyman's Daughter* (1935), conveys much more powerfully the physical recoil of its heroine from contact with the dispossessed, after an attack of amnesia leads her from a sheltered middle-class existence to the hardships of vagrancy and casual labour. In *The Road to Wigan Pier* (1937), Orwell combines an impassioned protest at living conditions in mining communities afflicted with unemployment, with an unmistakable distaste at the smells and textures of the Wigan households he has to enter to conduct his research. In all his work, there is evidence of a sincere commitment to the defence of the powerless together with intermittent signs of his struggle to assimilate himself to working-class culture. As in the work of Upward, Warner and Sykes Davies, but with a different, more independent, political agenda, Orwell's spokesmanship requires the construction of an adjudicating voice that belies some of its more powerful animating impulses.

The adoption of a stranger's perspective, whether that of airman, spy, anthropologist, Mass-Observer or Left Book Club scribe, is more often than not an intellectual adventure, and a mobilising of creative energies that could go in other directions. The apposition of the homely and the unfamiliar is an invigorating technique that sharpens the analysis of British social and cultural forms during the 1930s. But it is very rarely the case that the perspective of the truly alienated is intrinsic to the focus of novel or poem. One shattering exception to the general rule might be James Hanley's novel *Boy*, first published in 1931. *Boy* catalogues the abuses and degradation endured by a youth forced to leave school at thirteen in order to work, first in the Liverpool docks and then on the high seas. The relentless physical privations and sexual and psychological bullying make for gruelling reading, as does the final episode in which the boy's determination to assert his independence by going to an Egyptian brothel ends in disaster. He contracts syphilis and is smothered by the ship's Captain, who does not even bother to render him unconscious before putting him out of his misery. The use of illness as a literary trope to signify other forms of social and literary malaise has a suggestive power in a number of writings of the decade but not the direct force that Hanley gives it, correlating the vile condition of the youth's body at the end of the novel with the demoralising environment of his home life at the beginning. For Hanley, the sources of alienation are quite precisely, and seemingly ineradicably, 'at home'. The narrative style is expressive, but deliberately shallow, without resonance or allusion. In literary terms, it is disfigured, like an overexposed film. Its display of conditions of labour and sexual practices cannot shelter under any form of literary decorum offering reflections on, or arguments about, anything else. And it may be for this reason that its language has been judged improper. After a limited publication in 1931, the book was judged an obscene libel and withdrawn from circulation in 1935. It was not republished until 1990. Its extraordinary effectiveness is evident from the fact that its supposed libel was not on any person, but on a *place*: Lancashire. Here, clearly, the attempt to see the inexplicable strangeness of English life for what it really was gains power from the very authority it was denied.

21

Literary criticism and cultural politics

DAVID AYERS

This chapter examines the role played in cultural politics between the wars by attempts to address changing configurations of literature and readership, mainly in the creation of new journals and magazines, and also in the emergence of a new, vociferous and non-bellettristic form of literary criticism which would have a major impact on the development of literary studies. Serial publications are an important focus, because they are invariably bids to create a literary or cultural public sphere in a changing cultural climate. The nature of the reader and the role of the artist are put into question in these journals, not only in editorials but also in the editorial decisions which shape their contents. The background to this re-evaluation of writing and readership was the continuing extension of literacy following successive Education Acts, the commercialisation of written and other forms of culture, and a perceived extension of the power and importance of the working class. Serious literary authors and critics, the majority of whom were privately educated and belonged to comparatively wealthy families, were confronted by difficult questions concerning the role of high literature and art, and the meaning and purpose of its relationship to any possible audience. Especially in the 1920s, some writers and editors advocated conservatism and a return to religious and institutional order as an alternative to mass democracy or Communism. By the 1930s, new voices had emerged supporting anti-Fascist struggle and seeking to create an alliance of the cultural upper-middle class and the proletariat. At all times, writers can be found adopting a stance of independence both from the upper-middle class and from the proletariat, outside the Left/Right confrontation which dominated these years. Whether Left, Right or independent, these writers and editors had a common understanding that the nature and purpose of serious culture was both at play and at stake in the broadest political and cultural questions of the day. Q. D. Leavis's *Fiction and the Reading Public* (1932) is an important expression of the pessimism about mass society, and of the attempt to create a strategic alternative to mass culture, which is particularly significant to the creation of modern English studies at Cambridge in the 1920s. This book also has a more general significance as the expression of a widely felt cultural dilemma for those with a literary education, even if Q. D. Leavis's solutions, and her map of the nature of the problem, were only locally shared.

The starting-point of Leavis's analysis is the claim that, while advances in education have made more people literate, the development of individual sensibility, which should be the advantage of literacy, has tended not to take place in the masses. The reason for this is that in the place of a common linguistic and literary culture, such as Leavis claims existed in the Elizabethan period, there has developed a fragmented readership with different literacy levels catered to by newspapers, novels and other cultural forms which stultify individual development. Although Leavis will frequently stress individual 'sensibility', her account makes clear that what she regrets is the loss of culture as a force of social homogeneity in class society. A nation in which the classes are not united by a common culture and a common language will be more susceptible to the language and politics of class war, and the minority of those with a literary education will be unable to exert their former unconscious influence on the masses. According to Leavis, the Elizabethan 'masses' differed from their contemporary counterparts in that they were 'receiving their amusement from above (instead of being specially catered for by journalists, film-directors, and popular novelists as they are now)'. What has been lost is the unconscious education of sensibility which accompanies exposure to the most advanced literary artefacts. Leavis claims that 'education of ear and mind is none the less valuable for being acquired unconsciously', while 'to read Bunyan and Milton for religious instruction, as to attend Elizabethan drama for the "action", is to acquire an education unconsciously'.[1] As well as being prevented from reaching the lower classes, Leavis also claims that the serious cultured minority – designated as 'highbrow' in the vocabulary of the time – is impaired in its ability to reach even its natural constituency by the emergence of a carefully segregated 'middlebrow' culture. According to Leavis, the consumer-oriented *Times Literary Supplement* and the influential reviewer Arnold Bennett typify this new middlebrow culture, which claims for itself in the marketplace the authority of the real cultural elite. Leavis's solution to this is to demand the formation of 'an armed and conscious minority' which will undertake 'educational work in schools and universities' and inculcate in the young the

[1] Q. D. Leavis, *Fiction and the Reading Public* (London: Chatto & Windus, 1965), pp. 85, 97.

'necessity of resistance' to 'such appeals as those made by the journalist, the middleman, the best-seller, the cinema, and advertising'.[2]

Leavis's account drew on reflections on the role of literature and culture which literary journals established in the 1920s had already undertaken. Leavis lists T. S. Eliot's *The Criterion*, John Middleton Murry's *The Adelphi* and Edgell Rickword and Douglas Garman's *The Calendar of Modern Letters* as the most eminent 'highbrow' journals of the period. Although Edgell Rickword would later emerge as a leftist, *The Calendar of Modern Letters* adopted a stance of political independence in the name of defending literary quality, an abstract position which in retrospect can be understood as an attempt to create a breathing space for a literary culture that sought identification with neither Left nor Right. Contributors included D. H. Lawrence, Wyndham Lewis, Iris Barry and Robert Graves. Rickword at this time tended towards the pessimism of Wyndham Lewis, whose critique of modernity in *The Art of Being Ruled* (1926) was compared by Rickword to Matthew Arnold's *Culture and Anarchy*.[3] The tone of the *Calendar* was frequently negative. Wyndham Lewis, who later titled a book *Men Without Art* (1934), bluntly described the contraction of any possible public sphere for art: 'The only *rationale* of the professional artist to-day is to provide the critic with material for criticism.'[4] Rickword lamented that 'verse [now] offers less nourishment to the sophisticated adult than it has done at any time in the last three hundred and thirty years'.[5]

The *Calendar* did not identify any programme for serious literature, which it continued to regard as isolated from any broader social function. T. S. Eliot's *Criterion*, which began publication in 1922, differed sharply in having a definite literary programme organised around the term 'Classicism', and in aligning itself with French Catholic intellectuals and the right-wing Action Française. Eliot had been a vigorous contributor to a number of literary and cultural journals before he founded the *Criterion*, and some of these contributions were gathered together in an influential volume, *The Sacred Wood* (1920). The essays in this volume claimed a centrality and seriousness for poetry and criticism which had resonance in the following decades, even for those who did not share Eliot's developing political agenda. The most famous of these essays, 'Tradition

2 Ibid., pp. 270–1.

3 Edgell Rickword, review of *The Art of being Ruled*, *Calendar of Modern Letters*, 3, 1 (October 1926), pp. 247–50.

4 Wyndham Lewis. 'The Dithyrambic Spectator: an Essay on the Origins and Survival of Art', *Calendar of Modern Letters*, 1, 2 (April 1925), pp. 93–4.

5 'Comments and Reviews', *Calendar of Modern Letters*, 1, 2 (April 1925), p. 153.

and the Individual Talent' (1919)[6], asserted that critical attention should focus on poetry rather than on the biographies of poets. According to Eliot, the poet should be regarded as the impersonal catalyst for poetic activity, and the poem should be assessed in terms of its relation to tradition, not in terms of its novelty. The notion of attending to the work rather than to the author, and the emphasis on the importance of criticism and the critic, had an immediate and continued influence on both academic and extra-academic critics and essayists. More local in its influence was the developing anti-Romantic programme which informed the essay and was carried over into Eliot's own journalistic enterprise, the *Criterion*.

The first issue of the *Criterion* included Eliot's *The Waste Land*, and the numerous prominent contributors included, in the first six issues, May Sinclair, Ezra Pound, Roger Fry, Virginia Woolf, Herbert Read, W. B. Yeats, Wyndham Lewis and Ford Madox Ford. These contributors did not necessarily share Eliot's agenda, but their presence was a powerful endorsement of the *Criterion*'s instant centrality. Eliot sought to cultivate a European standpoint for the journal, by featuring work by German, Italian, French and Russian contributors, including Mallarmé, Valéry, Proust and Dostoevsky. Eliot's own classicist stance, which was to be a dominant theme in a nevertheless diverse journal, was set out in the editorial 'Commentary' of the seventh issue, on the occasion of the publication of a collection of essays by the late T. E. Hulme, *Speculations* (1924). Eliot used Hulme to set out a programme of 'classicism' which would be opposed to belief in progress:

> In this volume he appears as the forerunner of a new attitude of mind which should be the twentieth-century mind . . . Hulme is classical, reactionary and revolutionary; he is the antipodes of the eclectic, tolerant and democratic mind of the end of the last century . . . Classicism is in some sense reactionary, but it must be in a profounder sense revolutionary.[7]

Eliot's Classicism is opposed to Romanticism and humanism; he rejects belief in human progress and the ideal of social revolution. Eliot continued to feature a range of opinion in the *Criterion*, but recommended to his readers the preeminent intellectuals of the French Right (Charles Maurras, Julien Benda and Jacques Maritain). In 'The Values of the Doctrine Behind Subjective Art', Wyndham Lewis provided his own take on Classicism, calling for 'a new, and if necessary shattering critique of modernity', and claiming that all tradition

[6] T. S. Eliot, *The Sacred Wood: Essays on Poetry and Criticism* (London: Methuen, 1960), pp. 47–59.

[7] Eliot, 'Commentary', *Criterion*, 7 (April 1924), p. 231.

which had made art possible in past ages had been destroyed, leaving modern artists as 'the cave-men of the new mental wilderness'. The public sphere had been destroyed, argued Lewis, and artists had failed in their duty to recreate a public language, retreating instead into an art of subjectivism.[8]

John Middleton Murry's *The Adelphi* provided the opposition which *The Criterion* needed to create the sense of a real intellectual war in culture. As much as the *Criterion* was intellectual, Murry's journal was personal, religious and emotional in tone. Inspired and motivated by the death of his wife, the writer Katherine Mansfield, the *Adelphi* adopted Lawrence's rhetorical affirmation of 'life' and featured a great deal of his work. The *Adelphi* sold for much less than the *Criterion* and had a much larger circulation. Although Eliot and Murry used their editorials to exchange remarks on the Classicism / Romanticism debate, Murry was more interested in developing a large and popular readership than in conducting an internecine 'highbrow' war. He advocated the work of Dostoevsky, Tolstoy, Shakespeare and Keats as the great modern Romantics, but tended to refuse the terms of the debate as set by Eliot. Although the *Adelphi* was very much a literary journal and did not imitate the *Criterion*'s move into general cultural theory, it anticipated several of the thirties' journals in its attempt to address a larger readership in a serious fashion, as well as featuring an early example of documentary writing, Roger Dataller's 'From a Miner's Journal'.

The *Criterion* emphasised commentary over artistic practice. Indeed, it found little in contemporary literature to affirm. In a comment on the 'man of letters' *à propos* of Wyndham Lewis, but perhaps applicable to himself, Eliot wrote: 'Mr Lewis is the most remarkable example in England of the actual mutation of the artist into a philosopher of a type hitherto unknown.'[9] Wyndham Lewis had also started a journal in response to his own sense of the decline in meaning and importance of the arts. While other journals sought to address a general literary readership by creating at least a semblance of plurality even where editorial views were already set, Wyndham Lewis used *The Enemy*, published only three times from 1927 to 1929, as a vehicle for his own polemics. The three issues featured extended excerpts from forthcoming books including a satirical critique of Ezra Pound from *Time and Western Man* (1927) and an extended attack on Lawrence from *Paleface* (1929). In *The Enemy* and in the polemical books to which that journal was related, Lewis cast himself as the solitary, outlawed opponent of all forms of contemporary

[8] Wyndham Lewis, 'The Values of the Doctrine Behind Subjective Art', *Criterion*, 6, 1 (July 1927), pp. 9–13.

[9] T. S. Eliot, *Criterion*, 6, 2 (August 1927), p. 98.

art and thought, which he found to be characterised by Romantic subjectivism and naïve sympathy for Bolshevism. His creation of the figure of 'The Enemy' as a public persona was in effect an attempt to use the method of modern publicity to create a public sphere for debate where, Lewis felt, none existed. Lewis provided a bold example of the independent intellectual as seemingly tireless cultural critic, but also demonstrated the limitations of isolation and relentless negativity.

The desire for a central role for poetry and criticism, evidenced in the *Calendar of Modern Letters* and the *Criterion*, began to adopt concrete form at Cambridge University, where the recently founded English Tripos became the vehicle for a radical development of University English studies propelled by a group which included F. R. and Q. D. Leavis, William Empson and I. A. Richards. Several of these figures had a social background which was urban and industrial, and their vigorous and innovative approach differed markedly from that of the wealthy gentleman scholar.[10] I. A. Richards followed Matthew Arnold in advocating poetry as a kind of secular salvation in *Science and Poetry* (1926). Influenced by Richards, and with the model of the short-lived *Calendar of Modern Letters* as a precursor, *Scrutiny* began operations in 1932 under the editorship of L. C. Knights, Donald Culver, Denys Thompson and F. R. Leavis. The journal was an attempt to create a programme for literature and criticism which would be influential in the University and beyond. The broad remit was Arnoldian, in the sense that contributors sought a role for literature, and above all for the practice of reading literature, which would ground culture as the supreme alternative to the contemporary life of a modernity which was seen as degraded. Literary criticism was to be emphatically broadened from its origins in philology and *belles lettres* into the criticism of society, by the cultivation of what was frequently called sensibility, and by the critical articulation of a literary tradition which was seen as the repository of sensibility – in effect, the repository of the mind itself – in a modernity which in its class structure, in its politics, and in its mass-market cultural forms, was at odds with the purpose and meaning of that tradition.

The analysis which supported this project had been set out in Q. D. Leavis's *Fiction and the Reading Public* and in F. R. Leavis's *Mass Civilisation and Minority Culture* (1930). F. R. Leavis and Denys Thompson elaborated their critique of modernity in *Culture and Environment* (1933), emphasising the effects of cultural standardisation, advertising and newspapers on modern readers, who had been transformed from what they believed to be the fulfilled workforce

[10] See Francis Mulhern, *The Moment of 'Scrutiny'* (London: New Left Books, 1979), pp. 22–5.

of the agrarian past into the degraded 'herd' of modern industrial workers. Language was being emptied of its resources by its abuse in newspapers, commercial fiction and advertising, while individuals were denied the richness of experience which alone could give language meaning. The vocabulary and pessimistic outlook reflected Julien Benda's *La trahison des clercs* (1927, translated into English by Richard Aldington as *The Great Betrayal* in 1928), and Wyndham Lewis's *The Art of Being Ruled* (1926), which Rickword had seen as the modern *Culture and Anarchy*. However, the *Scrutiny* project would go beyond the disillusioned polemics of Benda and Lewis in its attempt to formulate a positive alternative to the stance of isolated despair of the lonely intellectual.

The social situation of the 1930s was already very different from that of the later 1920s. The confrontation between Communism and Fascism, and the corresponding leftwards movement of many British intellectuals, meant that *Scrutiny* both had to respond to Marxism and pose itself as an informed alternative. The regard which the *Scrutiny* cadre had for the supposedly organic community evidenced in Elizabethan England might appear merely nostalgic if its essence were not presented as a sufficiently radical alternative to the Marxist vision of the overcoming of class division by Communist revolution. Like the *Criterion* a decade before, *Scrutiny* sought to contest Marxism's right to the 'revolutionary' mantle. *Scrutiny* could not endorse the Marxist notion of the proletariat as the carrier of values opposed to industrial modernity, but instead located 'tradition' as the trans-historical site of opposition to modern social reality.[11] In this way, *Scrutiny* avoided any defence of 'order' or of the 'West' such as could be found in the pages of the *Criterion*, but instead gave a renewed substance to the notion of tradition which Eliot had set out in 'Tradition and the Individual Talent'. Because it adumbrated a particular process of aggressively critical and antithetical reading, and fostered a missionary project based on an expanding community of graduates of the newly formed Cambridge English School, *Scrutiny* can be seen as more than the sum of its parts. The legacy of *Scrutiny* is found in the purposiveness and vigour of a continuing critical project which sees culture as the privileged site where social realities appear and are mediated.

While *Scrutiny* sought to pose itself as an alternative to Marxism, numerous journals of the 1930s reflected the attempt of writers and critics to resist Fascism by adapting their project to the Left in varying degrees. As becomes apparent in retrospect, the process of adaptation was usually incomplete. The journal *New Verse* reveals the uneven nature of this process. Partly because of its connection

[11] Ibid., pp. 72–6.

with Auden, *New Verse* has been mythified as an organ of the cultural Left.[12] The November 1937 issue was indeed an 'Auden Double Number'. However, Geoffrey Grigson's editorial stance was that of the independent intellectual, and his view of art was that it transcended politics, not that it should serve a propagandist function, a position which owed more to Wyndham Lewis, whose journals *Blast* and *The Enemy* offered a declaration of the independence of art which Grigson partially emulated.

Grigson's first editorial claimed that *New Verse* supplied an outlet for serious verse which was otherwise not available, and disclaimed political alignment or any aesthetic programme.[13] However, it seems likely that even from the first issue, which included poems by Auden and Day Lewis, *New Verse* was considered by readers to be a left-wing journal. Grigson reiterated the claim to be independent in his editorial for the second issue, and resisted political identification: 'a reasoned attitude of toryism is welcomed no less than a communist attitude. [. . .] Readers are asked to be aware of this and not to damn NEW VERSE politically where damnation is invalid.'[14] The appearance of Auden, Day Lewis and MacNeice in the first issue had evidently been enough to persuade readers that *New Verse* was run by a left-wing coterie. Grigson used his review of *New Country* (1933) and Day Lewis's *The Magnetic Mountain* (1933) to praise Auden, Spender and Upward as individual artists while denouncing propaganda in art and criticising the claim of the volume's editor, Michael Roberts, that the significance of the writers collected in the volume lay in their shared political feeling: 'Those who feel can only be united, if they wish, in any book, any club, any party; but it disgusts me to find feeling made more than art and the good artist stayed here with sentimentalists or ineffectual propagators.'[15] The contributions of Charles Madge, Gavin Ewart, Kathleen Raine, David Gascoyne and Martin Boldero, with Surrealist and other influences, characterised *New Verse* just as much as the now prominent poetry of the Auden group. Surrealism became a dominant theme of the journal, while events in Germany and Spain had hardly any impact. *New Verse* was attacked in the journal *International Literature* for abandoning its function as a 'major rallying ground' for the Popular Front:

> The publication has entered into a *bloc* with the French Surrealists. It is systematically hounding Day Lewis for what it regards as an excess of Communist loyalty. It has every appearance of becoming a cess-pool of all that is rejected

[12] This discussion is indebted to Adrian Caesar, 'Geoffrey Grigson's *New Verse* and the Myth of English Poetry in the 1930s', *AUMLA*, 73 (May 1990), pp. 39–58.

[13] *New Verse*, 1 (January 1933), pp. 1–2.

[14] *New Verse*, 2 (March 1933), p. 1.

[15] Ibid., p. 15.

> by the healthy organism of the revolutionary movement – a sort of miniature literary Trotskyism.[16]

In response to this, Grigson took the opportunity to reassert the political independence of the journal and to remind readers that he had never claimed to align the journal with the Left. The question of commitment dominated *New Verse* on only two occasions. Issue 11 (October 1934) featured 'Answers to an Enquiry' – a short questionnaire, including questions on political alignment and the influence of Freud, addressed to British and American poets. The results are as often arch as committed, but this issue of *New Verse* is justly famous. More clearly committed is the last number, 31–2 (Autumn 1938), titled 'Commitments'. Grigson acknowledged that 'the aesthetic attitude is now out of place' (2), and the issue featured no poetry: Charles Madge's memorial to Eliot claimed him as '*malgré lui* a revolutionary poet' (19) while Spender and MacNeice discussed the complexity of the demand made on poets that they be political.

In terms of its public profile, *New Verse* was overtaken by the arrival of the overtly political *New Writing* and of the theoretically oriented *Left Review*. *New Writing* (1935–41) was a literary journal, edited by John Lehmann, which sought to capitalise on the success of the *New Country* group and provide a platform for anti-Fascist authors of various nationalities. Notable among the contributions are Christopher Isherwood's stories of Berlin which attempt to develop filmic techniques in quasi-documentary style. The background to this development was the creation of *Left Review*. The formulation of a Popular Front strategy against Fascism led in 1934 to a change of policy regarding liberal and Modernist writers on the part of the Soviet Writers' Congress, which was reflected in Britain by the creation of a broad alliance of Communist, Labour and other left-leaning writers. This new alliance resulted in particular in the creation of *Left Review* (1934–8), a Communist-edited journal set up by the British section of the Writers' International. Its founding members included Edgell Rickword and Douglas Garman, formerly editors of the *Calendar of Modern Letters*. Contributors included Communists, such as Sylvia Townsend Warner, Christina Stead and Hugh MacDiarmid, and non-Communists, such as Auden and Spender.[17] An important achievement of *Left Review* was the founding of a well-informed Marxist cultural criticism in Britain, featuring

[16] Quoted in *New Verse*, 23 (Christmas 1936), p. 24.

[17] All details from Margot Heinemann, '*Left Review*, *New Writing* and the Broad Alliance against Fascism', in Edward Timms and Peter Collier, eds., *Visions and Blueprints: Avant-Garde Culture and Radical Politics in Early Twentieth-Century Europe* (Manchester University Press, 1988), pp. 118–19.

important contributions from Rickword himself, as well as Alick West, Winifred Holtby and others.[18] The nature and status of the intellectual or the bourgeois artist or writer was a recurrent theoretical concern of the journal. Rickword used the first issue to denounce the 'exasperated or plaintive individualism' of Modernist aestheticism, the recourse to religion of Eliot and Murry, and the political inadequacy of Auden's aesthetic. Rickword calls on the 'bourgeois intellectual' to accept the necessity of opposing Fascism.[19] John Strachey was given room to explain his migration from the politics of his 'ruling class' father to those of the workers' revolution in 'The Education of a Communist'.[20] 'Intelligentsia' by D. S. Mirsky, a translated excerpt from *The Intelligentsia of Great Britain*, is a harsh outside voice denouncing the pro-capitalism of Fabians, the 'bohemian, "highbrow" individualistic intelligentsia', and 'bourgeois feminism'.[21] Alick West's response to Mirsky questioned the completeness of his information as well as his simplified model of struggle, a sign that the British Left was uncomfortable with its satellite role and wished for British realities to be properly acknowledged by Soviet theory.[22] Elements of proletarian writing appeared in the journal, Issue 6 featuring 'Nine Workers Describe a Shift at Work'. Initially *Left Review* attracted accusations of incoherence. Montagu Slater attempted to define the purpose of the journal in terms of 'how to win and how present a new view of literature and life'. One of its purposes must be 'to catch up the leeway of forty years stoppage of Marxist theory in England' and in literature it must undertake the task of 'descriptive reporting' of everyday working life. 'We have even invented a jargon name for it, *reportage*.'[23] Although theory rather than reportage would dominate subsequent numbers, Slater's call for *reportage* would find important echoes throughout the decade.

The Surrealist interest of *New Verse* received an innovative inflection from Charles Madge, who used the journal to describe the poetic function of the Mass-Observation movement. Mass-Observation was launched in 1937 as a collaboration between Madge, the ethnographer Tom Harrisson, and the

[18] For a discussion, see David Margolies, ed., *Writing the Revolution: Cultural Criticism from 'Left Review'* (London and Chicago: Pluto Press, 1998), pp. 1–22.

[19] Edgell Rickword, 'Straws for the Wary: Antecedents for Fascism', *Left Review*, 1, 1 (October 1934), pp. 19–25.

[20] John Strachey, 'The Education of a Communist', *Left Review*, 1, 3 (December 1934), pp. 63–9.

[21] D. S. Mirsky, 'Intelligentsia', translated by Alec Brown, *Left Review*, 1, 4 (January 1935), pp. 117–22. Book published as Dmitri Mirsky, *The Intelligentsia of Great Britain* (London: Gollancz, 1935).

[22] Alick West, 'Mirsky's One-Sided Picture', *Left Review*, 1, 8 (May 1935), pp. 324–8.

[23] Montagu Slater, 'The Purpose of a Left Review', *Left Review*, 1, 9 (June 1935), pp. 359–65.

painter and film-maker Humphrey Jennings.[24] Its aim was to document the nature of everyday life in a fashion which would be both scientific and democratic. Mass-Observation commissioned large numbers of participants to produce texts documenting their experience of everyday life. Participants were furnished with a range of questions intended to elicit responses by turns objective, political and unconscious. *May the Twelfth: Mass-Observation Day-Surveys* (1937) which documents Coronation Day was a document assembled from the contributions of numerous participants and resembled a collage of fragmentary viewpoints rather than a single narrative of the Coronation itself. Although it has a scientific, anthropological cast, Mass-Observation patently seeks to find an alternative to both scientific and political hierarchy. The editing of the texts produced is designed to preserve a decentred structure and has features in common with developments in the visual arts and cinema. The evident objective of displacing the monarch from the centre of his own narrative on Coronation Day owes something to the discovery of Joyce's *Ulysses* (1922) and Virginia Woolf's *Mrs Dalloway* (1925) that public figures and events are common points uniting otherwise diverse consciousnesses and histories.

Aesthetically, the movement was also influenced by a reading of literary Surrealism – the example of Louis Aragon's *Paysan de Paris* (1926) and of André Breton's *Manifeste du surréalisme* (1924). However, Madge does not make this connection in his attempt to explain the aesthetic dimension of the project in *New Verse*. In 'Poetic Description and Mass-Observation', Madge argues that the use by Mass-Observation of untrained observers created a poetry 'which is not, as at present, restricted to a handful of esoteric performers' and served 'to devalue considerably the status of the "poet"'.[25] In 'Oxford Collective Poem', Madge describes an experiment in collective writing designed to discover the 'background of social fantasy' underlying individual subjectivity.[26]

The Surrealist component of 'M-O' was left-wing and radical. It looked both to the investigation of existing consciousness and unconsciousness, and to the creation of a new consciousness as a process of this investigation. This element of M-O might have been theoretically developed as an analysis of or contribution to the Marxist project of cultivating the proletariat as the revolutionary collective subject of history, just as in Paris the German–Jewish exile Walter Benjamin was attempting to extend Marxism by studying the nature of collective fantasy and the everyday in his posthumously published *Arcades*

[24] See Laura Marcus, 'Introduction: the Project of Mass-Observation', *New Formations*, 44 (Autumn 2001), pp. 5–19.

[25] *New Verse*, 24 (February–March 1937), p. 2.

[26] *New Verse*, 25 (May 1937), p. 16.

Project. However, by 1939 this more speculative element of M-O practice had receded, and Harrison and Madge began to conform to the emphasis elsewhere on the Left for communication of fact. One chapter of their *Britain by Mass-Observation* (1939) is titled 'Democracy and Facts'. It follows a long section entitled 'Crisis' which focuses on opinion-formation and the relationship between politicians, journalists and electorate. The central issue for Madge and Harrisson is now the failure by press and politicians to keep the electorate informed so that at times of crisis there can be any sense of a democratic integration of the mass of people in the democratic collective process. 'What happens in [the] political sphere obviously affects the sphere of home and work; equally obviously, political developments are affected by the reactions of ordinary people. But between the two there is a gulf – of understanding, of information and of interest. This gulf is the biggest problem of our highly organised civilisation.'[27] The next paragraph goes on, by way of contrast with the intended functioning of a democracy, to mention Hitler and the Nuremberg rallies. Mass-Observation of public opinion, by survey and interview, reveals that people feel generally uninformed and helpless at moments of crisis. The vocabulary of 'fact' and 'crisis' refers to the context of international affairs and the imminence of a European war which is approaching in surges of diplomatic activity and military action. Mass-Observation at this point is principally concerned with the process of democratic integration, although it retains an interest in the collective political unconscious. By 1940 the Mass-Observation team was working for the Ministry of Information and served the war effort by monitoring public opinion and morale.

Literary editors and authors of the 1920s had tended to emphasise their distance from the masses and did not take any responsibility for supplying them with reading material. In their perception, the rapidly expanding lower-middle class and the politically consolidated working class were catered for, as a readership, by an imaginative literature deliberately set at a low intellectual level and cast as escapism and fantasy, and by a press which aimed to manipulate and misinform. On this reading, Communism and socialism seemed to be the ultimate expression of the modern industrial dystopia, an extension of the logic of capitalism rather than its antithesis. Due to the upsurge of Fascism, the later 1930s witnessed a forced convergence of liberal socialists and Communists.[28] In addition, the 1930s saw a general rise in newspaper and book reading, as

[27] *Britain by Mass-Observation* (Penguin: Harmondsworth, 1939), p. 25.

[28] See John Coombs, 'British Intellectuals and the Popular Front', in Frank Gloversmith, ed., *Class, Culture and Social Change: A New View of the 1930s* (Sussex: Harvester Press; New Jersey: Humanities Press, 1980), pp. 70–100.

well as the expansion of other print media – women's magazines, children's comics (*Beano* and *Dandy*), and the new pictorial journalism represented by *Picture Post*.[29] As part of this pattern, the decade saw far more emphasis on addressing and entering into dialogue with the working class on the part of authors and editors who were sympathetic to left-wing politics in spite of their usually privileged backgrounds.

As important as any individual writer are those publishing ventures of the 1930s designed to address the widest possible literate audience. Allen Lane and Victor Gollancz both moved from powerful positions in established publishing houses (Bodley Head and Ernest Benn Ltd) to establish left-leaning imprints which, each in a different manner, addressed the situation of a large reading public. Allen Lane had been involved in acquiring the British publishing rights of James Joyce's *Ulysses* for Bodley Head, an interesting symbolic link to his next venture, the founding of Penguin Books.[30] Lane is perhaps the single most important pioneer of the paperback book. Although Penguin was not the first company to market books at very low prices, the scale of its success puts it at the centre of modern British publishing history. The publishing model was to secure important existing titles at favourable rates and sell them for 6 pence, at that time the cost of ten cigarettes, a business model which Lane imitated from the popular retail chain Woolworth, which at that time sold all its goods for 6 pence or less. The initial launch of ten titles in 1935 included literary works licensed from Agatha Christie and André Maurois. In 1936 Lane launched Pelican, a non-fiction imprint, with the publication of a reissue of George Bernard Shaw's *Intelligent Woman's Guide to Socialism, Capitalism and Sovietism* with additional material by the author. The Pelican series concentrated on political and scientific topics, and the editorial board was left-of-centre. A further left-leaning imprint was created in 1937 – the Penguin Specials. By this date, the emphasis on creating an informed public in the light of growing international crisis led to the publication of such titles as *The Air Defence of Britain*, and *The New German Empire*. *Britain by Mass Observation* was a title in this series and the remarks of Madge and Harrisson represent a left-intellectual response to the challenge of mass literacy and democracy:

> The 250,000 who read a Penguin Special are a drop in the ocean of possible readers, but they represent a big move in the right direction at a time when 'an important book can sell no more than 200 copies'. [. . .] The present position

[29] André Thorpe, *Britain in the 1930s: The Deceptive Decade* (Oxford and Cambridge, MA.: Blackwell, 1992) pp. 108–9.

[30] See J. E. Morpurgo, *Allen Lane: King Penguin. A Biography* (London: Hutchinson, 1979).

> of the Intellectual Few is a relic of the times when the mass of the population could neither read nor write.[31]

While most Penguin Specials sold about 40,000 copies, certain titles did indeed run to 250,000.

Victor Gollancz established the Left Book Club in 1936, with the objective of political education and a business model borrowed from the Collins Crime Club. Although it organised a proletarian novel competition, the emphasis of the club was on political argument and information. Gollancz was the publisher of George Orwell's first book, *Down and Out in Paris and London*. *The Road to Wigan Pier* was published under the Left Book Club imprint and was the club choice for 1937. It is one of the most noted examples of the new factual style, not because of its author's subsequent and continued fame, but because it is stylistically so fully realised. The author's mandate is to live among the workers and unemployed of a northern English town and to describe their lives and conditions with an eye to sociological observation and to human realities. Orwell brings to this mandate touches of Surrealist detail and Dickensian humour:

> The shop was a narrow, cold sort of room. On the outside of the window a few white letters, relics of ancient chocolate advertisements, were scattered like stars. Inside, there was a slab upon which lay the grey flocculent stuff known as 'black tripe', and the ghostly, translucent feet of pigs, ready boiled. It was the ordinary 'tripe and pea' shop, and not much else was stocked except bread, cigarettes and tinned stuff. 'Teas' were advertised in the window, but if a customer demanded a cup of tea he was usually put off with excuses.[32]

The first part of Orwell's book contains a combination of fact and creative observation which its readers found compelling. However, the second half of the book was a direct attack on the middle-class socialists and Communists who would be among its principal readers. Not content with straightforward sociological observation in the descriptive part of his text, Orwell uses the second part to explore his doubts about the unity of middle-class socialists and the working class which left intellectuals were concerned to promote. Victor Gollancz felt it necessary to provide a 'Foreword' addressed to 'members of the Left Book Club' to explain the decision to publish the work and to

[31] *Britain by Mass-Observation*, arranged and written by Charles Madge and Tom Harrisson (Harmondsworth: Penguin, 1939), pp. 10, 11.

[32] George Orwell, *The Road to Wigan Pier*, with a 'Foreword' by Victor Gollancz (London: Victor Gollancz, 1937), p. 7.

counter some of Orwell's claims. Orwell criticises the two groups on whom the literary Left depended. Socialists and Communists of middle-class origin are criticised for their inability to cross class barriers, while the 'young highbrow of proletarian origin' is criticised for creating the fashion for anti-bourgeois '"proletarian" cant'. Orwell singles out *Left Review* and the writers Alec Brown and Philip Henderson as part of this tendency.[33] The controversial second part was withdrawn from the second edition of the book.

The combination in *The Road to Wigan Pier* of observation of the working class with polemical observations on the class structure of the milieu of the cultural Left gives Orwell's text a rare interest. Storm Jameson responded to Orwell in her theoretical discussion of the 'document' as an instrument for socialism published in the journal *Fact*. She criticised the socialist writer who concentrated on 'the emotions, the spiritual writhings, started in him by the sight, smell, and touch of poverty', and praised Orwell for introducing a more objective and documentary style. The writer must visit working communities 'for the sake of *the fact*, as a medical student carries out a dissection'.[34] Jameson argues that such documents, analogous to photographs or to the new documentary film, are needed to lay the foundations of a socialist literature.[35] *Fact* was an attempt to realise this documentary ambition as part of a broader informational approach. The journal was edited by Raymond Postgate, a committed socialist who had been one of the founding members of the Communist Party of Great Britain in 1920 but by this time had returned to the Labour Party. Contributing editors included Margaret Cole (Postgate's sister), George Lansbury (his father-in-law), Leonard Barnes, Storm Jameson, Francis Meynell and Stephen Spender. *Fact* presented its subscribers with 'a sixpenny monograph published on the 15th of every month' and ran from April 1937 to June 1939, publishing twenty-seven numbers in all. *Fact* was hardly a literary journal, but combined writing on politics and economics (such as Margaret Cole's *The New Economic Revolution*), reviews of modern history and current events (including Ernest Hemingway's *The Spanish War*) and documentary surveys of contemporary British life. In the first number the editors boldly compared themselves to Diderot's encyclopedists:

> FACT's editors, in brief, are endeavouring to be the modern Encyclopedists. To-day, all professions, men of all trades, are fairly well aware that the present

[33] Ibid., p. 198. [34] Storm Jameson, 'Documents', in *Fact*, 4 (July 1937), p. 12.

[35] On the connection with documentary film, see John Baxendale and Chris Pawling, *Narrating the Thirties. A Decade in the Making: 1930 to the Present* (Basingstoke: Macmillan, 1996), pp. 17–45.

> system does not *work* [. . .]. But they do not, always, know exactly how much and where it does not work [. . .]. It is our object to show how this is, and from that information to provide knowledge – the knowledge of how to make a much more fundamental change than the French Revolution.[36]

Although most issues of *Fact* were conventional monographs, no. 8 (November 1937) contains a documentary survey by Philip Massey called *Portrait of a Mining Town*. The editorial, titled 'The Four Corners of Britain' proudly announces this as the first part of *Fact*'s 'most ambitious project', 'an attempt to survey typical corners of Britain as if our investigators had been inspecting an African Village' (4). The editorial roundly rebuts the more creative method of Mass-Observation – 'Unselected matter only piles up into a dust heap' (4) – although Massey's social method based on lengthy interviews, his own observation, and a little supplementary research in official papers resembles that of Mass-Observation. However, the result, which maps the basic economic configuration of the Nantyglo-Blaina industrial community in South Wales, presents little in the way of analysis and does little to reproduce the texture of everyday life, despite containing sections on 'Leisure Activities' and 'Homes and Food'. This is the only such number of *Fact*. Following similar attempts in *New Writing* to document the lives of working people in their own words, *Fact* also featured monographs produced by an army private, a former prisoner, a taxi-driver and a miner. Mark Benney's 'The Truth about English Prisons' (no. 12 (March 1938)) is really a social survey of the prison, but Herbert Hodge's *I Drive a Taxi* (22 January 1939) and B. L. Coombes's *I am a Miner* (23 February 1939) contain a large proportion of anecdotal personal history. Not really a journal, *Fact* was an attempt to bring information with a socialist inflection to a wider audience. Part of its work resembled the project of the Left Book Club, and an attempt to emulate *The Road to Wigan Pier* and carry out the project outlined by Jameson. However, the documentary efforts do not rival those of Mass-Observation or of Orwell in colour or interest. After closing *Fact*, Postgate went on to become editor of the left-wing newspaper *Tribune*, a clearer focus for his editorial talents than *Fact*, which in retrospect seems more diffuse than effective.

The period under examination falls between the World Wars and is characterised by continuing uncertainties regarding the legitimacy and viability of the existing form of European society. With increased literacy levels and the accompanying rationalisation of literary consumption, the culturally educated were forced to re-examine the role of the artist and critic in theory and

[36] *Fact*, 1 (April 1937), p. 7.

in practice. The strand which is dominant in the 1920s sees art as isolated and undertakes a defence of 'sensibility' or of the 'West' in the name of an anti-Communist minority. In the 1930s this strain of thought gave way to another, in which the background of Nazism and war led to a call for artists to replace aloofness with political commitment, and a corresponding demand that writing contribute to the democratic process. Whether they align themselves with the Left or the Right, these writers are constantly faced by the question of their own legitimacy and purpose in class society. Not a class in their own right, and conscious of their differences, as individuals and as a sect, from both the ruling class and the proletariat, these authors and editors confront the ambiguity of their position with remarkable energy and honesty.

22

Surrealism in England

PETER NICHOLLS

'It's got here at last!' So Cyril Connolly greeted the appearance in 1935 of David Gascoyne's *A Short Survey of Surrealism* with a degree of surprise we may still share.[1] Why *had* it taken so long for Surrealism to arrive in England? André Breton had, after all, presented the founding manifesto back in 1924 and the first experiment in automatic writing, *The Magnetic Fields*, which he co-produced with Philippe Soupault, had appeared four years before that. The war, of course, had closed borders, literally and metaphorically, and having survived the conflict without suffering invasion or revolution, England in the immediate wake of 1918 would be largely untroubled by the waves of crisis and nihilism which swept most European countries and which generated the newest avant-garde tendency, Dada. While Italian Futurism had launched itself on London in a spectacularly dramatic fashion, Dada would remain an obscurely 'foreign' phenomenon, receiving only patchy mention in literary magazines and never generating sufficient oppositional energy to initiate a parallel English movement in the way that Marinetti had lit the charge for Vorticism.[2]

What was known of the Dada group and the Surrealist tendency it had spawned by 1920 came mostly by way of little magazines rather than from direct personal contact, and the time-lag in picking up on the new movements also meant that it was difficult for most English readers to disentangle Dada, with its poetics of outrage and negation, from Surrealism, with its more affirmative and often prophetic stance. Reception was generally impressionistic, and some of the best critics, such as F. S. Flint, expressed open hostility. Predictably, perhaps, the *Little Review* (1914–29), now based in Paris, offered a more positive view of what was happening, and published work by most of the

[1] Quoted in Michel Remy, 'Introduction' to David Gascoyne, *A Short Survey of Surrealism* (1935; London: Enitharmon Press, 2000), p. 21.

[2] For a detailed account of Dada's non-reception in England, see Alan Young, *Dada and After: Extremist Modernism and English Literature* (Manchester University Press, 1981).

group's leading figures, including André Breton, Paul Eluard, Louis Aragon, Philippe Soupault and Francis Picabia, though it did so without any supporting critical commentary. *This Quarter* (1925–32), also published in Paris, did more to provide much-needed theoretical materials, running a special Surrealism issue in September 1932 in which English readers were able to encounter important statements of principle and intention from Breton, Salvador Dalí, Eluard and Max Ernst.

Even more influential was the Paris-based *transition*, which from 1927 to 1938 established itself as the principal conduit for avant-garde writing in English, while also publicising the work of European Expressionists and Surrealists. Editor Eugene Jolas was fascinated by the workings of the unconscious in language, and his involvement with psychoanalysis and with various forms of irrationalism made *transition* a receptive home for the work of writers like James Joyce and Samuel Beckett who had set their face against British traditionalism. While *transition* was keen to make an impression on the American literary scene, it was also looking for signs of imaginative activity in England and in 1930 published contributions from the Cambridge magazine *Experiment*. These included pieces by Jacob Bronowski, William Empson and Hugh Sykes [Davies], though by general assent the only properly proto-Surrealist item was a short essay on 'Dreams' by Julian Trevelyan in which he concluded that 'TO DREAM IS TO CREATE.'[3]

Such ideas were far from clearly worked out, though their appearance in *transition* signalled a possible alternative to what would soon become the dominant tone in thirties' English writing, that of the Auden circle, urbane, discursive, securely left-oriented. Surrealism offered a very different model of poetic expression, proposing automatic writing as a means to explore dream and unconscious motivation, thus illuminating the operations of chance and contradiction that lay beneath the apparently smooth surface of ordinary communication. Furthermore, by the time the movement began to have an impact in England, Surrealism had also developed political ambitions, bringing together Marxism and psychoanalysis in a conjunction that signalled the possibility of a social transformation grounded in the imaginative power of dream and art. Such a conjunction was immediately attractive to young writers who felt, in David Gascoyne's words, 'a great gap between [the Auden] generation's conception of poetry' and their own.[4] As his contemporary Francis Scarfe put

[3] 'Dreams', *transition*, 19–20 (June 1930), pp. 122. See also Jason Harding, '*Experiment* in Cambridge: "A Manifesto of Young England"', *Cambridge Quarterly*, 27 (1998), pp. 287–309.

[4] David Gascoyne, *Collected Journals 1936–1942*, intro. Kathleen Raine (London: Skoob Publishing, 1991), p. 169 (entry dated 8 August 1938).

it, this younger generation was 'born into one war and fattened for another',[5] and its members' sense of crisis and emergency made them receptive to the strange and the foreign.

Nowhere is this clearer than in the case of Gascoyne himself, who had published his first collection of poetry, *Roman Balcony*, in 1932 at the age of sixteen and who had that same year encountered the work of Breton, Eluard and others in the pages of *This Quarter*.[6] Between 1935 and 1939, Gascoyne spent periods living in Paris, where he managed to meet many of the writers and artists involved in the later phase of Surrealism: Tristan Tzara, Eluard, Breton, Salvador Dalí, Benjamin Peret and others. Gascoyne's close association with this group and his increasingly sophisticated grasp of the French language gave him a deeper understanding of this avant-garde than almost any of his English peers. Not surprisingly, he quickly established himself as a major purveyor of Surrealism to England, publishing his groundbreaking study of the movement – *A Short Survey of Surrealism* (1935) – along with translations of André Breton's *What Is Surrealism?* (1936) and Dalí's *Conquest of the Irrational* (1935). Gascoyne was also responsible for some of the best English versions of Surrealist poetry, including a selection of Benjamin Peret's writings which he co-translated with Humphrey Jennings as *Remove Your Hat* (1936) and a substantial contribution to the volume of translations of Paul Eluard, *Thorns of Thunder* (1936).

While the *Short Survey* has often been criticised for its anecdotal quality, Gascoyne did provide there a clear account of the Surrealist interest in dreams and automatic writing, emphasising in a move unusual for an English observer that 'Surrealism is *not* a style' limited by place and time but rather a way of living shaped by 'a revolution of ideas and not of the forms expressing them'.[7] Gascoyne also armed his readers with Breton's famous definition of Surrealism 'which is by no means so well known in England that I need not quote it here':

> SURREALISM, n. Pure psychic automatism, by which it is intended to express, verbally, in writing, or by other means, the real process of thought. Thought's dictation, in the absence of all control exercised by reason and outside all aesthetic or moral preoccupations. (57)

[5] Francis Scarfe, *Auden and After: The Liberation of Poetry, 1930–41* (London: Routledge, 1942), p.xiii.

[6] David Gascoyne, *Selected Prose 1934–1996*, ed. Roger Smith, intro. Kathleen Raine (London: Enitharmon Press, 1998), p. 134.

[7] Gascoyne, *A Short Survey of Surrealism*, p. 25, p. 42. Further references given in parenthesis in the text.

In this key passage from the first Manifesto, Breton thus defined Surrealism's enduring commitment to 'the omnipotence of dream and . . . the disinterested play of thought'. But, as Connolly had implied, the *Survey* also had some catching up to do, and here again Gascoyne showed an impressive grasp of the internal evolution of the movement, from the so-called 'Period of Sleeping Fits' to 'the new, active, attitude of Surrealism' announced in the Second Manifesto of 1929 (77): 'Without the philosophy of dialectical materialism behind it,' Gascoyne concluded, 'Surrealism could hardly have existed until today and be a living force' (62). Yet this conviction that Surrealism was inseparable from Marxism was not one that Gascoyne could hold unwaveringly. Indeed, in his answers to 'An Enquiry' in *New Verse* (October 1934), for example, he had already observed of the notion of 'writing poems without the control of the reason' that 'The Surrealists themselves have a definite justification for writing in this way, but for an English poet with continually growing political convictions it must soon become impossible.'[8] Gascoyne's engagement with Surrealism would thus prove to be as brief as it was intense. For while the movement provided the model for a political poetry in its mounting of 'an assault on the current conception of reality',[9] poetry at the same time seemed to Gascoyne quite remote from political action. 'The revolution has no need of poetry', he concluded in 1936, 'but poetry has great need of the revolution.'[10] By 1937, he later recalled, 'I was beginning to become a disaffected member of the British branch of the Surrealist movement',[11] a statement which also implies Gascoyne's parallel discontent with English culture, 'where the meaning of revolt has never been understood, where everything is straightaway reduced to banality'.[12] Gascoyne joined the Communist Party in 1936, but the deep interest in matters of the imagination which had drawn him to Surrealism in the first place would lead him ultimately to a mystical Christianity. For this deviation Breton would personally expel him from the movement during one of Gascoyne's later visits to Paris.

Understandably, Gascoyne came to resent 'the label "Surrealist Poet" which was hung around my neck for years and years, long after I had stopped writing automatically',[13] but how close really was his early work to the principles of

[8] Gascoyne, 'Answers to "An Enquiry"' (October 1934), in *Selected Prose*, p. 55.
[9] Gascoyne, 'Poetry and Reality' (May 1936), in *Selected Prose*, p. 75. [10] Ibid., p. 76.
[11] Gascoyne, 'Denis Roche' (1980), in *Selected Prose*, p. 297.
[12] From a letter to Benjamin Fondane (24 July 1937), in 'Meetings with Benjamin Fondane' (1986–7) in Gascoyne, *Selected Prose*, p. 135. Cf. *Collected Journals*, p. 170: 'I belong to Europe before I belong to England' (item dated 8 August 1938).
[13] Gascoyne, 'Interview with Lucien Jenkins' (Spring 1992), in *Selected Prose*, p. 50.

the French movement? Take, for example, the opening lines of his 'And the Seventh Dream is the Dream of Isis', usually taken to be the first Surrealist poem by an English writer:

white curtains of infinite fatigue
dominating the starborn heritage of the colonies of St Francis
white curtains of tortured destinies
inheriting the calamities of the plagues of the desert
encourage the waistlines of women to expand
and the eyes of men to enlarge like pocket-cameras
teach children to sin at the age of five
to cut out the eyes of their sisters with nail-scissors
to run into the streets and offer themselves to unfrocked priests . . . [14]

The poem cuts into a flow of associations almost arbitrarily. There is no punctuation to control the onward movement of the lines, nor is there any predictability to the sequence of items we encounter. We are meant to read this poem literally; as Gascoyne wrote of Eluard's *La rose publique*, 'Every line means exactly what it says: this imagery becomes completely free of symbolism, and refers to nothing but itself. This is a universal language, devoid of all particularities.'[15] This literalism produces some of the most familiar stylistic features of Surrealism: in 'the white curtains of infinite fatigue', for example, the association of curtains with fatigue and the desire for sleep is conventional enough, but instead of merely symbolising fatigue the curtains here turn out to be actual material embodiments of it, the formulaic 'of' (the *x* of *y*) serving to produce the merging of inner and outer which is one of Surrealism's most sought-after effects.[16] As the poem develops, we begin to see that its unexpected juxtapositions and comparisons also serve a more programmatic end, for 'the year is full of unforeseen happenings / and the time of earthquakes is at hand'. This presage of apocalyptic upheaval generates an outpouring of violent imagery in which the particular and the general are disturbingly confused. We may observe here another grammatical mannerism borrowed from Surrealism: the use of the definite article to gesture towards something with which we appear to be familiar but in fact are not – '*the*

[14] First published in *New Verse*, the poem is unaccountably omitted from Gascoyne's *Collected Poems*, ed. Robin Skelton (Oxford University Press, 1965). It is quoted here from *English and American Surrealist Poetry*, ed. Edward B. Germain (Harmondsworth: Penguin Books, 1978), pp. 106–8.

[15] Gascoyne, 'The Public Rose' (February 1935), in *Selected Prose*, p. 355.

[16] Cf. Breton, *What Is Surrealism?*, trans. David Gascoyne (London: Faber & Faber, 1936), p. 49: 'This final unification is the supreme aim of surrealism: interior reality and exterior reality being, in the present form of society, in contradiction . . . '

pavements are covered with needles / *the* reservoirs are full of human hair', and so on. These small words which so often go unnoticed as we hurry to reach the end of a conventionally predictable sentence are here loaded with meaning, effectively situating an imaginary world for the reader. The indefinite article has its part to play, too, creating displacements and metonymies which disembody the human and throw familiar objects into ominously unfamiliar perspectives: 'An eye winks from the shadow of the gallows / A tumbled bed slides upward from the shadow / A suicide with mittened hands stumbles out of the lake . . .'[17]

The unsettling quality of such effects and their way of alluding to a narrative forever out of reach are part of the general subversion of discursive logic which runs through most of Gascoyne's early poems: 'on account of his accent he was discharged from the sanatorium / and sent to examine the methods of cannibals / *so that* wreaths of passion-flowers were floating in the darkness . . .' Actions can be painfully specific – as in the sisters' blinding with nail-scissors – but at the same time they are designedly universal, with the poet speaking of 'children', 'sisters' and 'women' rather than of clearly defined individuals. It is this flight from 'all particularities' (the latter associated from the first with the banal empiricism of realist fiction) that produces the Surrealist interlocking of the absurd and the everyday:

> and the wings of private airplanes look like shoeleather
> shoeleather on which pentagrams have been drawn
> shoeleather covered with vomitings of hedgehogs
> shoeleather used for decorating wedding-cakes . . .

Here the connection of unlike things is enforced, characteristically, through repetition, as we are led from the possible – a similarity in colour, perhaps, between airplane wings and shoeleather – towards the highly unlikely – the use of shoeleather to decorate wedding-cakes. Our attention is held at the level of the line and we are thus prevented from resolving the flow of disparate elements into some propositional whole. The result, of course, is that we focus on particular images, though this also has the disadvantage that it may obscure what Breton had called 'the real process of thought', a tendency compounded by Gascoyne's Surrealist habit of using end-stopped lines.

The priority thus given to the image partly accounts for the number of Gascoyne's poems modelled on the works of painters such as Dalí and Yves Tanguy. One dedicated to René Magritte, 'The Very Image', is a case in point.

[17] Gascoyne, 'The Diabolical Principle', *Collected Poems*, p. 22.

Here the pleasure taken in the incongruities of juxtaposition is given full rein, with each stanza announcing a new image:

> An image of an aqueduct
> with a dead crow hanging from the first arch
> a modern-style chair from the second
> a fir-tree lodged in the third
> and the whole scene sprinkled with snow[18]

As Paul Ray has noted, however, that last line suggests that Gascoyne is describing something objectively seen rather than delving into the workings of the unconscious,[19] and it is frequently the case in these early poems that juxtaposition produces a declaration of mere contiguity rather than the genuine frisson sought by Breton (in its last stanza, Gascoyne brings the various images together by rather coyly arranging them 'like waxworks / in model bird-cages / about six inches high').[20] What we miss here is the darker thrill of the authentic Surrealist image as in Lautréamont's exemplary 'chance meeting of an umbrella and a sewing machine on a dissection table', where beauty consorts with violence in an association at once deadly and mechanical, erotic and absurd. And where the self-reflexiveness of Lautréamont's *Les chants de Maldoror* makes poetic language 'the scalpel of analysis', the violent imagery of Gascoyne's poems seems in comparison conventional, even Victorian, as Ray contends.[21] Gascoyne, we might conclude, misses that aspect of Surrealism that is obsessed with the work of *interpretation*.[22] For while the most notable aspect of Surrealist writing is at first sight its capacity to produce the striking image, we find also, from Lautréamont to Peret, a deeper fascination with the alternative *logic* of the dream and the artwork, a logic which is conceptual rather than primarily visual.

If England's most knowledgeable and skilled reader of French Surrealism tended to miss this dimension of the new aesthetic, it was not surprising that those more clearly on the margins should also partly mistake its aims. As Michel Remy has observed, in England Surrealist painting would always

18 Gascoyne, 'The Very Image', *Collected Poems*, p. 26.

19 Paul C. Ray, *The Surrealist Movement in England* (Ithaca and London: Cornell University Press, 1971), p. 172.

20 An allusion, perhaps, to Duchamp's 'Why Not Sneeze Rrose Sélavy?' (1921), with its birdcage filled with (marble) sugar lumps.

21 Comte de Lautréamont, *Maldoror and Poems*, trans. Paul Knight (Harmondsworth: Penguin, 1978), p. 57; Ray, *The Surrealist Movement in England*, p. 173.

22 See, for example, my *Modernisms: A Literary Guide* (London: Macmillan Press, 1985), pp. 288–9.

be more prominent than Surrealist writing,[23] and the visual emphasis was powerfully reinforced by what was to be the founding event of the short-lived Surrealist Group in London, the 1936 International Surrealist Exhibition. 'Surrealism Has Arrived', declared the poster for the event,[24] and so indeed it must have seemed, with the Exhibition attracting more than twenty thousand visitors to a display of sixty-nine works including contributions from Breton, Ernst, Duchamp, Magritte and de Chirico, presented alongside images and objects by English writers and artists such as Hugh Sykes Davies, Herbert Read, Roland Penrose, Gascoyne, Grace Pailthorpe, Reuben Mednikoff and others. Dalí and Buñuel's notorious *Un Chien Andalou* was also shown. Eluard read his poetry, as did Gascoyne, Humphrey Jennings and George Reavey, presenting their own work and their translations. Most memorable, perhaps, was Dalí's lecture, for which, as Julian Trevelyan recalls, 'He appeared in a diving suit, complete with helmet, leading two enormous white borzois.'[25] Prepared for his dive into the unconscious, Dalí came close to suffocating in the helmet and had to be hurriedly released. More peripheral eccentricities also quickly became part of the legend: Dylan Thomas serving tea cups full of boiled string, for example, and 'surrealist groupie' Sheila Legge wandering about as the Surrealist Phantom, her face completely obscured by roses.[26] The *Daily Mail* found it all 'morbid and disgusting',[27] while everyone else seems to have enjoyed an exciting day out. For a few weeks it seemed that Surrealism really had arrived, and Breton was confident that England could even prove the bridgehead for World Surrealism.[28]

Yet the spectacle was a short-lived one, and the air of 'gentle frivolity' which prevailed in London in the months before the outbreak of the Spanish Civil War both paved the way for the Exhibition's success and contributed to the English movement's ultimate demise.[29] To David Gascoyne it demonstrated that

> In England Surrealism was thought to be something artistic (with a vague revolutionary aspect which was forgotten as soon as possible). Last year there

[23] Michel Remy, *Surrealism in Britain* (Aldershot: Ashgate, 1999), p. 340.

[24] The poster is reproduced in ibid., p. 75.

[25] Julian Trevelyan, *Indigo Days* (London: MacGibbon & Kee, 1957), p. 71. See also the account in Eileen Agar, *A Look at My Life* (London: Methuen, 1988), p. 119. The Exhibition is reviewed in detail in Michel Remy, *Surrealism in Britain*, pp. 73–96.

[26] The phrase 'surrealist groupie' is from George Melly, *Don't Tell Sybil: An Intimate Memoir of E. L. T. Mesens* (London: Heinemann, 1997), p. 35.

[27] See Scarfe, *Auden and After*, p. 148; for the reactions of other newspapers, see Remy, *Surrealism in Britain*, p. 96.

[28] Agar, *A Look at My Life*, p. 117.

[29] 'Gentle frivolity' is from Trevelyan, *Indigo Days*, p. 57.

> was an enormous International Surrealist Exhibition: Can you imagine it, it was madly successful, chic, mildly, faintly, shocking, 'amusing'. I was so fed up that I almost at once joined the Communist Party, and for several months was immersed in political action.[30]

Painter Eileen Agar recalled similarly that 'The problem with the International Surrealist Exhibition was that it was something of a Nine Days' Wonder – the brilliance and momentum of it were impossible to sustain.'[31] Yet some real efforts were taken to build a more lasting base for a definitively English Surrealism. The London Gallery was set up under the directorship of the Surrealist representative for Belgium in the Exhibition, E. L. T. Mesens, who between 1938 and 1940 would also be editor of the *London Bulletin*. Meanwhile, a Surrealist Group was formed, whose membership included the organisers of the Exhibition along with some new recruits: Hugh Sykes Davies, David Gascoyne, Humphrey Jennings, Henry Moore, Paul Nash, Roland and Valentine Penrose, Herbert Read, Roger Roughton, Rupert Lee and Diana Brinton Lee.

The flagship publication of 1936, and one which signalled some of the fundamental problems of a specifically English Surrealism, was the collection of essays edited by Herbert Read as *Surrealism*. The volume shows clearly enough the differences separating English and French contributors. Breton, for example, in his 'Limits not Frontiers of Surrealism' argued for 'Adhesion to the theory of dialectical materialism, which the Surrealists adopt in all its points' and went on to couple this with 'objective humour' as the 'paradoxical triumph of the pleasure principle over real conditions at a moment when they may be considered to be particularly unfavourable'.[32] Georges Hugnet argued for his part that 'Surrealist poetry aims at exteriorising all man's desires, all his obsessions and his despairs: it gives him the means to free himself, to venture forth' (218). In each case, dream and automatism are seen as the means of looking to the future, of releasing a ferocious imaginative energy against the dead weight of both past and present. 'Surrealism', noted Eluard in his contribution, 'Poetic Evidence', 'is a state of mind' (174). For the English contributors Herbert Read and Hugh Sykes Davies, however, Surrealism was less a dynamic state of mind than it was an exciting style, one that, according to them, had been available to English writers long before the appearance of Surrealism. So Hugh Sykes Davies claimed rather disingenuously that 'we, the

[30] Gascoyne, 'Meetings with Benjamin Fondane', in *Selected Prose*, p. 135.
[31] Agar, *A Look at My Life*, p. 126.
[32] *Surrealism*, ed. Herbert Read (London: Faber & Faber, 1936), pp. 102, 103. Further references given in parenthesis in the text.

Surrealists in England, have not heard a message from France in a cloud of fire' and went on instead to derive Surrealism from the work of Coleridge and the English Romantics (90). This tactic, which echoed the claim quoted here from the Exhibition catalogue that 'superrealism [Read's word] in general is the romantic principle in art' (21), might seem to accord with Breton's own acknowledgement in the first Manifesto of Surrealism's English precursors in Romanticism and the Gothic (repeated for more clearly 'political' reasons in his 'Limits not Frontiers' piece). At the same time, though, Davies and Read managed to develop this lineage so as to obscure the avant-garde character of Surrealism and to make it instead something thoroughly domesticated and familiar: 'In all the essentials of romanticism', concluded Davies, 'Surrealism continues the earlier movement', but with this 'advantage', that 'where romanticism was notoriously inchoate, disorderly, intuitive, Surrealism is organised, orderly and conscious' (168).

Francis Scarfe was surely right to call this 'English *neo*-surrealism' in order to distinguish it from the genuine article, though his 'neo-' misses the traditionalist emphasis of Davies's and Read's attachment to 'order' and 'control'.[33] Nowhere perhaps is this clearer than in Read's muddled attempt to explain the poetic effects of the idea of juxtaposition that Breton quotes from Pierre Reverdy in the First Manifesto ('The image is a pure creation of the mind. It cannot be born from a comparison but from a juxtaposition of two more or less distant realities'): first, says Read, 'the dream-thoughts have been condensed into images or symbols . . . Then, to disguise any gaps or incoherency, the conscious mind of the poet has worked over the poem, and given it that smooth façade which is generally demanded by the literary conventions of an age, and which in any case makes for ease of communication' (76). Read's attempt to construe an image from one of his own poems – 'a silhouette hovering like a baffled bird' – as an example of Reverdy's idea of juxtaposition is quite unconvincing and reveals the conventional limits of what is actually mere 'comparison'. And with his talk of the poem's 'smooth façade' and its 'ease of communication', Read shows a complete misunderstanding of Surrealism's aims, as Humphrey Jennings noted in his review of the volume. 'How can one open this book', asked Jennings, 'so expensive, so *well* produced, so conformistly printed . . . and compare it even for a moment with the passion terror and excitement . . . which emanated from *La Révolution Surréaliste* and *Le Surréalisme au Service de la Révolution* . . . ?'[34] Indeed, for all Read's interest in the

[33] Scarfe, *Auden and After*, p. xiii.

[34] *Contemporary Poetry and Prose*, 8 (December 1936), pp. 167–8. Geoffrey Grigson in 'Letter from England', *Poetry*, 49 (November 1936), pp. 101, noted a similar weakness in English

ideas behind Surrealism (his *Reason and Romanticism* [1926], for example, offered an early excursion into psychoanalysis), the editor of the *Burlington Magazine* was not actually about to 'go Surrealist'.[35] His attempt at a Surrealist-inspired novel, *The Green Child* (1935), was in this respect predictably unsuccessful, resulting in an awkward combination of picaresque narrative and sentimental fantasy that showed few traces of authentic Surrealism.

More contradictory was the work of Hugh Sykes Davies, whose short novel *Petron* (1935) occasioned some excitement when it appeared. The book now seems hampered by its own parodic designs, which ultimately bring it closer to Gothic fiction than to Surrealism. For the most part, too, the parody is laboured, reminding us that the light, electric touch of a writer like Peret is conspicuous by its absence from this English 'neo-Surrealism', seeming to surface more clearly in the work of expatriate writers such as Samuel Beckett and Leonora Carrington. *Petron* tells in a deliberately fragmented way of the solitary, Candide-like hero's journey towards 'a country utterly uninhabited'.[36] On the way, a series of violent accidents befall him as he traverses an often hallucinatory landscape. Much of this is told in the idiom of conventional horror: 'upon his horrified senses fell sounds of terror and anguish, increasing sharply in volume as a dim figure stumbled through the gloom with the sound of dripping blood and a clatter of broken bones' (14–15). In his review of *Petron*, Read observed that the work was clearly Surrealist in that here 'The waking life and dreaming life of the poet meet on equal terms.'[37] The 'waking life', though, seems evident only in the ironic authorial voice, while any residual Surrealist elements are confined to moments of fantastic transformation: the giants, for example, whose mouths are suddenly seen to be caverns in the hillside, their legs pine trees, and so on (12). Davies's prose hints at this power of desire to transform the real, though it does so in a litany of images:

> Searching among the rubble, he finds a battered toy that was once his own, but even as he holds it, it stirs in his hand and becomes a grasshopper, then an old man, a monstrous spider, a woman's breast, a bunch of faded grass, a little heap of bones, and so to a lizard which eludes his grasp, and darts away among the sunlit stones. (66)

Surrealism: 'There is our newest cherub, Mr Roger Roughton [editor of *Contemporary Poetry and Prose*], pink from the egg, plodding after tough Eluard and Breton.'

35 According to Michel Remy, *Surrealism in Britain*, p. 348 n. 39, the *Burlington Magazine* 'never mentioned surrealism at all'.

36 Hugh Sykes Davies, *Petron* (London: Dent, 1935), p. 79. Further references given in parenthesis in the text.

37 *New English Weekly*, 8 (November 1935), p. 92.

Occasionally Davies does move beyond the image to a establish a more conceptual approach to his theme, so that a meditation about paths and the injunction from an old hedger that 'people should know where they go' (8) are associated with a signpost on the 'arm' of which Petron inscribes pictures of the hedger. In order to make his point to Petron, the hedger then 'divided each of his fingers with a pruning-bill into a small hand, and subdivided the fingers of these again into smaller hands, and so on until he was possessed of many thousand hands and tens of thousands of fingers' (8). Yet in all this one may find little more than (to use a phrase of Davies's own) 'some faint surrealist whispers behind the arras',[38] and while Davies clearly had a developed interest in Surrealism and met Breton and co. in Paris, the archaising tone of *Petron* finally has more in common with the fairy tale than it does with the urban narratives of the French writers. By way of contrast, Leonora Carrington's stories, while equally fantastic, have a faux-naïf playfulness that situates the extraordinary within the rhythms of the everyday:

> 'Never mind,' I told myself, 'It's only a nightmare.' But then I remembered suddenly that I'd never gone to bed that night, and so it couldn't possibly be a nightmare. 'That's awful.'
>
> Thereupon I left the corpses and went on my way. Walking along I met a friend. It was the horse who, years later, was to play an important part in my life.[39]

Carrington's fiction is closer in feeling and tone to the collages of her one-time husband, Max Ernst, than to Davies's *Petron*, for while the latter, as Gascoyne observed, presents a hero who is 'merely an ingeniously manipulated puppet, made to dance a fantastic tune that Mr Davies once overheard in a library',[40] the constructions of Carrington and Ernst perform the Surrealist trick of making the fantastic an arbiter of the modern.

It is worth repeating that French Surrealism finds in the language of dream and automatism a presage of future freedom, a way to release the imagination from the bonds of the mundane world whose limits we otherwise tend to accept. This aspect of Surrealism rarely seems to travel into English writing, with the result that surrealistic effects are here often associated with madness

[38] Davies applies the phrase to the verse of Nicholas Moore in 'Cambridge Poetry', *Twentieth Century*, 157 (February 1955), p. 156.

[39] Leonora Carrington, *The Oval Lady* (1937–8), in *The House of Fear*, intro. Marina Warner (London: Virago, 1989), p. 62.

[40] Gascoyne, 'On Spontaneity' (December 1935), in *Selected Prose*, p. 356.

and oppression rather than with the open, visionary world conjured up by Breton and his colleagues. Indeed, the Surrealist cult of madness, as exemplified in *Nadja*, could prove difficult to sustain under the pressure of personal experience, as was clear from the darker tones of Carrington's account of her own terrifying descent into insanity, *Down Below* (1944). In England, too, Surrealism had competition from the newly translated works of Franz Kafka, with *Metamorphosis* (under the title *The Transformation*) and *The Trial* available from 1935. Edward Upward in 'The Railway Accident', published under a pseudonym in 1928, for example, had already deployed powerful surrealistic imagery to juxtapose the deranged inner world of the character Hearn with a catastrophic train accident:

> Coaches mounted like viciously copulating bulls, telescoped like ventilator hatches. Nostril gaps in a tunnel clogged with wreckage instantly flamed. A faint jet of blood sprayed from a vacant window. Frog-sprawling bodies fumed in blazing reeds. The architrave of the tunnel crested with daffodils fell compact as hinged scenery. Tall rag-feathered birds with corrugated red wattles limped from holes among the rocks.[41]

The extremism of Upward's imagery – 'Frog-sprawling bodies fumed in blazing reeds' – may be indebted to Surrealism, though its intensity imprisons rather than liberates the self, an idea that acquired a clearly Kafkaesque resonance in Upward's later novel *Journey to the Border* (1938). Here the main character (unnamed) seeks 'some act which would violently break the continuity of his life as a hired tutor', and he is thus easily seduced by the advice of one Gregory Mavors that 'Reason is death . . . Unreason is life . . . Without unreason there can be no thought . . . Unreason is the language of desire.'[42] But the freeing of desire plunges the tutor into a frightening world of hallucination from which he is saved only by an inner voice that counsels him to return to 'the external world' and to seek out the workers' movement.[43] Upward thus draws a stark contrast between an illusory world of surreal desire and one of rational action, a dichotomy we may discern in other explorations of madness in the period such as Emily Holmes Coleman's *The Shutter of Snow* (1930) and Patrick Hamilton's *Hangover Square* (1941), with its premonitory '*Click!*' which announces either George Harvey Bone's punctual descent into madness or his equally sudden emergence from it.

41 Edward Upward, *'The Railway Accident' and Other Stories* (Harmondsworth: Penguin, 1972), pp. 51–2.

42 Ibid., pp. 161–2. 43 Ibid., p. 192.

In cases such as these we can see that a certain Surrealist idiom was absorbed into English writing but was then made to serve ends rather different from those its inventors had intended. It quickly became clear, too, that the two major theoretical dimensions of French Surrealism, Freudian psychoanalysis and Marxism, were not going to have directly aesthetic consequences for their English sympathisers. Just as there was hostility to collaboration and group activity, so there was a robust insouciance in the face of 'theory', a disposition reinforced by the absence of any cheap, popular edition of Freud's work in English.[44] Similarly, many of those drawn to Marxism under the pressure of the Spanish Civil War found themselves abandoning Surrealism for politics, and the series of rather fruitless exchanges which took place in the pages of *Left Review* quickly demonstrated that Surrealism would never establish genuine connections with the English Left.[45] In the absence of a self-conscious avant-garde, the Surrealist fusion of politics and aesthetics seemed impossible to achieve.

All of which suggests not just that the English 'neo-surrealists' were constantly falling short of their continental model, but also that they were finding in the French movement an instigation to return to an older, deeply engrained Romanticism while at the same time appearing to be doing something new and of the time. This at least explains why by 1937, as critic Michael Roberts noted in the *Criterion*, there was 'as yet little poetry to justify the theory as a description of fact'.[46] Of those who, like Gascoyne, had some technical understanding of Surrealism perhaps only Hugh Sykes Davies offers himself as a serious contender. Davies's poems and prose poems (still uncollected) frequently suggest a deliberate working over of psychological material and the imagery has a certain Surrealist density:

> . . . in the stumps of old trees where the hearts have rotted out there are holes the length of a man's arm where the weasels are trapped and the letters of the rook language are laced on the sodden leaves, and at the bottom there is a man's arm. But do not put your hand down to see. . . .[47]

At the same time, other poems seem to co-mingle surrealistic imagery with an irascible address to the reader that is more reminiscent of Dada: 'KEEP YOUR FILTHY HANDS OFF MY FRIENDS USE THEM ON / YOUR BITCHES OR / YOURSELVES

44 See Perry Anderson, *English Questions* (London: Verso, 1992), p. 88.

45 On the generally unsympathetic responses to Surrealism in the *Left Review*, see Ray, *The Surrealist Movement*, pp. 154–9.

46 Quoted in Rob Jackaman, *The Course of English Surrealist Poetry since the 1930s* (Lampeter: Edwin Mellen Press, 1989), p. 70.

47 Roughton, ed., *Contemporary Poetry and Prose*, 7 (November 1936), p. 129.

BUT KEEP THEM OFF MY FRIENDS', and so on.[48] The mixing of registers is more engagingly explored in Roland Penrose's *The Road is Wider than Long*, a book described in the subtitle as 'An Image Diary from the Balkans July–August 1938' and published as no. 1 in the Series of Surrealist Poetry edited by Mesens. Penrose combines photographs with short passages of text printed in a variety of colours and typefaces, surrealistic imagery consorting with the actual sights seen and photographed: '*the monks can lift a man / from water as deep as the eye of a goat / to their dry gardens where a drunken pope / his face consumed by frost / sits alone with religion.*'[49] Penrose's 'Image diary' was attractively experimental in its approach to its material and had about it a serious playfulness that was markedly absent from so many 'neo-surrealist' productions.

There were at the same time several rising talents who were frequently taken to be indebted to the French movement. Of these the most prominent was undoubtedly Dylan Thomas, a writer who then seemed of exceptional promise. Unlike most of the other 'neo-Surrealists', Thomas had discovered *transition* at least as early as December 1933, and he continued to read it and also contributed a short story and a poem.[50] As Dougald McMillan has suggested in his study of the magazine, Thomas would certainly have responded to Eugene Jolas's call for the 'Revolution of the Word' in the June 1929 issue: 'Poetry is a lyrical absolute which seeks an *a priori* reality within ourselves alone', wrote Jolas. 'The literary creator has the right to disintegrate the primal matter of words imposed on him by text-books and dictionaries. He has the right to use words of his own fashioning and to disregard existing grammatical and syntactical laws.'[51] Not everyone associated with *transition* agreed with Jolas's emphasis on neologism (he was, as in almost everything else, thinking of the sections of Joyce's *Finnegans Wake* which appeared there as *Work in Progress*, always *transition*'s prize exhibit), but his advocacy of a 'neo-romanticism' (his term) committed to the 'pre-logical' and to the idea of language not as a medium of representation (the image) but as 'the *universal word*',[52] the key to a Jungian unconscious, were ideas which fused formal avant-gardism with potentially mystical thinking. And while Jolas opened his pages to the Surrealists, he was also critical of them: 'This seems to me also the error of

48 *London Bulletin*, 2 (May 1938), p. 7.

49 Roland Penrose, *The Road is Wider than Long: An Image Diary from the Balkans July–August 1938* (1939; London: Arts Council, 1980), n.p. (the passage is printed in red italic in the original).

50 Dougald McMillan, *Transition 1927–38: The History of a Literary Era* (London: Calder and Boyars, 1975), p. 159.

51 Jolas, 'The Revolution of the Word Proclamation', *transition*, 16–17 (June 1929), p. 1.

52 Jolas, 'Super-Occident, *transition*, 15 (1929), p. 15.

the surrealists', he wrote in the June 1930 issue. 'The surrealist tries to evoke the subconscious in its raw and absolute state "without the intervention of reason". He does not try to organise the symbolic mechanics. He fails to see that there is a difference between the symbols of dream and those of art.'[53]

While some of the poems in Thomas's 1930–2 Notebook suggest experiments in automatic writing,[54] he was for the most part, like Jolas, keen to dissociate himself from Surrealism, arguing that 'The Surrealists . . . put their words down together on the paper exactly as they emerge from chaos; they do not shape these words or put them in order; to them, chaos *is* the shape and order.'[55] Like Jolas, then – and this would become a persistent strain in the increasingly critical view taken of Surrealism in England – Thomas emphasised the need for craft and control. His own work, as it turned out, was more indebted to Blake, Lawrence and the Bible than to Breton and Eluard, but what was initially so striking about it was a certain linguistic density which struck some as Surrealist mainly because it was so unlike the urbane discursiveness now defined as 'Audenesque'. Thomas's early poems did indeed strike the English reader as 'foreign', not just because the poet was Welsh but because the grammar and syntax, let alone the imagery, pulled so fiercely against the linguistic norm:

> The force that drives the water through the rocks
> Drives my red blood; that dries the mouthing streams
> Turns mine to wax.
> And I am dumb to mouth unto my veins
> How at the mountain spring the same mouth sucks.
>
> The hand that whirls the water in the pool
> Stirs the quicksand; that ropes the blowing wind
> Hauls my shroud sail.
> And I am dumb to tell the hanging man
> How of my clay is made the hangman's lime[56]

There are surrealistic images here, 'the mouthing streams', the hand that 'ropes the blowing wind', but what is more striking is Thomas's emphatic way with

[53] Jolas, 'The King's English is Dying', *transition*, 19–20 (June 1930), p. 144.

[54] See, for example, Poem XXIV, in *Poetry in the Making: The Notebooks of Dylan Thomas*, ed. Ralph Maud (London: Dent, 1968), pp. 122–5.

[55] Excerpt from Richard Jones, 'Dylan Thomas's Poetic Manifesto', *Texas Quarterly* (Winter 1961), rpt. in Constantine Fitzgibbon, *The Life of Dylan Thomas* (London: J. M. Dent, 1965), pp. 372.

[56] 'The force that through the green fuse drives the flower', in Dylan Thomas, *Collected Poems 1934–1952* (London: J. M. Dent, 1952), p. 9.

language, the prosody hammered into place with an insistence that seems to compel acceptance of the strangest locutions. In the second line, for example, 'that' usurps the noun ('the force'), gathering up the cumulative energy of the first two lines and delivering it to the deferred verb that opens the third line. Language here has a kind of physicality which is rooted in a view of the world ultimately closer to D. H. Lawrence than to the Surrealists. In a letter of 1933, Thomas referred to this by way of John Donne's *Devotions* as 'earthiness':

> All thoughts and actions emanate from the body. Therefore the description of a thought or action – however abstruse it may be – can be beaten home by bringing it on to a physical level. Every idea, intuitive or intellectual, can be imaged and translated in terms of the body, its flesh, skin, blood, sinews, glands, organs, cells, or senses.[57]

Where Jolas conjures with the idea of somehow overcoming through artifice the 'primal matter' of language, language as it is simply given to us, Thomas wishes to rediscover language as primal, as the 'body' that ensures our continuity with 'nature'. This might not seem so distant from some of Jolas's pronouncements in *transition*, but the difference is greater than at first appears, for the 'revolution of the word' carries within it an inherited distrust of the merely 'natural'. In contrast, Thomas's apocalyptic verse often radiates a sweaty over-excitement, with its rich talk of blood and bone, and its quest for a knowingly archetypal language of 'clay' and 'shroud'. No doubt for this reason contemporary critics such as Francis Scarfe tended to find a stronger Surrealist echo in some of Thomas's short stories.[58] Of these 'The Burning Baby', first published in *New Verse*, is perhaps most frequently cited, though it is arguably less the horror of the story's conclusion than Thomas's way of combining the violent with the everyday that might recall Surrealism: 'They said that Rhys was burning his baby when a gorse bush broke into fire on the summit of the hill.'[59]

The other writer frequently coupled with Thomas in relation to Surrealism is George Barker, whose commitment to poetry as what he called the 'apotheosis of the real' also produced a verse of high emotional intensity, rhetorical, repetitive and emphatic.[60] 'The greatest images are the images of twisted reality', he once observed,[61] and 'The process of the poetic at work on the externally real appears to be a process at once of intensification and

[57] Quoted in Maud, 'Introduction', *Poetry in the Making*, p. 27.
[58] See, for example, Francis Scarfe, *Auden and After*, p. 149.
[59] Dylan Thomas, *The Collected Stories* (London and Melbourne: J. M. Dent, 1983), p. 35.
[60] 'Poetry and Reality' (1937), rpt. in Barker, *Essays* (London: MacGibbon & Kee, 1970), p. 87.
[61] Barker, 'On the Image' (1948), *Essays*, p. 110.

exaggeration.'[62] Yet like Thomas, Barker was more influenced by the English Romantics than by Breton, and in his long poem *Calamiterror* (1937) it was with a vision of Blake over the 'Lincolnshire mountain' that 'I achieved apocalypse.'[63] There are, to be sure, plenty of surrealistic images in the poem – 'The falling cliff that like a melting face / Collapsing through its features, leaves a stare, / The grinning cat'[64] – yet the vision of *Calamiterror*, with its celebration of Blake and Wordsworth (and, perhaps, in these lines, of Lewis Carroll), is ultimately a Romantic rather than a Surrealist one.

It is, significantly, a specifically English apocalypse which Barker urges, and this emphasis on national culture would be reaffirmed by the last grouping of poets to have a tangential relation to Surrealism, the 'New Apocalypse' whose members included J. F. Hendry and Henry Treece (editors of the first anthology of this name), along with G. S. Fraser, Nicholas Moore and Norman MacCaig. These writers were keenly aware of the Surrealist legacy, though by the time their first anthology appeared in 1939 the English group as well as 'the Breton boys' seemed to have exhausted their influence.[65] It was really Thomas and Lawrence who provided the impetus for the 'New Apocalypse' and while Treece acknowledged a surrealistic quality in Thomas's writing he made the usual English move of celebrating craft over automatism: 'It is this discipline of his raw material, this obedience to the dictates of his self-imposed form, which makes Dylan Thomas a superior craftsman to, a truer poet than any of the Surrealists.'[66] G. S. Fraser in an essay in the second of the group's anthologies, *The White Horseman*, reiterated the distinction: 'Apocalypticism, then, unlike Surrealism, insists on the reality of the conscious mind, as an independent, formative principle.'[67] No matter that the French Surrealists had long since complicated their aesthetic beyond mere automatism; the Apocalyptics had their own vision of a future of 'social integration', as Hendry called it, a future liberated from the machine and from the 'mechanistic-materialism'

62 Barker, 'Poetry and Reality', p. 80.
63 Barker, *Calamiterror*, in *Collected Poems 1930–1955* (London: Faber & Faber, 1957), pp. 51, 52.
64 Ibid., p. 31.
65 J. F. Hendry and Henry Treece, eds., *The New Apocalypse* (London: Fortune Press, 1939), p. 58.
66 Henry Treece, 'Dylan Thomas and the Surrealists', *Seven*, 3 (Winter 1938), p. 29. See also Treece, 'An Apocalyptic Writer and the Surrealists', in *The New Apocalypse*, pp. 49–58. The name of the group drew, of course, on Lawrence's *Apocalypse*, though Barker later claimed that he 'was the first chap who had the gumption to use the word "apocalypse"' – see Derek Stanford, *Inside the Forties: Literary Memoirs 1937–1957* (London: Sidgwick & Jackson, 1977), p. 137.
67 J. F. Hendy and Henry Treece, eds., *The White Horseman* (London: Routledge, 1941), p. 5.

of the Auden group,[68] a future which would see an expression of 'collective desire' though 'myth'. The quality of the verse varied, and while Treece had a preference for archaism and Thomasian periphrasis – 'Playing the hour-glass with the living bone'[69] – the limpidity of Nicholas Moore's love-poems contrasted vividly with the barely contained energies of Hendry's radically compacted syntax ('. . . shadows beam the ghost / They shed, forever fast // By shriven marrow- / Blowing bone to trumpet stick / Of eye through sunspot pores').[70] The *New Apocalypse*, of course, was painfully marked by the misery of a new war – this was, indeed, Scarfe's generation 'born into one war and fattened for another' – but the group's careful dissociation of itself from Surrealism could at the same time only serve to highlight its traditionalist qualities. Could one write seriously in 1939 of 'the horny womb of Time', as Treece did, or 'sing sing pretty maid all in a fairy boat' with Nicholas Moore?[71] This sort of thing was after all no better than the degraded surrealistic gestures that also appeared in the *New Apocalypse* ('It was a cardboard morning with galloping panicky breasts', etc.).[72] The Surrealist influence, weak though it clearly was, had actually turned English writing back on itself in a way that paralleled the emergence of neo-Romanticism in painting. And just as many of the painters of the Surrealist Group had become fascinated with biomorphic forms, so the English 'neo-Surrealist' writers tended to find their materials in 'nature' rather than in the modern, *urban* scene that Breton, for example, traversed in *Nadja*.[73]

There was one exception, though it, too, was predictably short-lived: Mass-Observation. Charles Madge and Humphrey Jennings initiated this project to gather extensive information about England's everyday life. Jennings had been one of the organisers of the 1936 Exhibition, and M-O certainly had things in common with Surrealism, especially its interest in what Madge in 1937 called 'mass wish-situations', movements of a collective unconscious that might be catalysed by major events such the Crystal Palace fire and the abdication of

68 J. F. Hendry, 'Introduction: Writer and Apocalypse', *The New Apocalypse*, p. 12.

69 Treece, 'The Shapes of Truth', *The White Horseman*, p. 51.

70 Hendry, 'Apocalypse', *The New Apocalypse*, p. 71.

71 Treece, 'The Shapes of Time', p. 50; Moore, 'Poem', *The New Apocalypse*, p. 75.

72 Dorian Cooke, 'Ray Scarpe', *The New Apocalypse*, p. 42.

73 Cyril Connolly was one of the very few to grasp the urban character of Surrealism, noting in *The Unquiet Grave* (1944; rev. edn 1945; London: Arrow Books, 1961), p. 35: 'Surrealism is a typical city-delirium movement, a violent explosion of urban claustrophobia; one cannot imagine Surrealists except in vast cities . . .' For the biomorphic tendency in English Surrealist painting, see Michel Remy, *British Surrealism*. Remy notes (p. 337) that in contrast to its French and Belgian counterparts, 'British surrealism constantly brought Nature into the dock.' Characteristic is Eileen Agar's comment that 'Surrealism for me draws its inspiration from nature' (*A Look at My Life*, p. 121).

Edward VIII (both in 1936).[74] Developed as a kind of urban anthropology, 'a reading of city inscriptions, of the uncanny in the city',[75] M-O's appetite for detail was omnivorous and for that reason alone it arguably produced its own version of 'a modernist poetics of superimposition',[76] just as its most famous production, *May the Twelfth* (documenting the events of the 1937 coronation of George VI) has been said to resemble the 'great modernist day-books' such as *Ulysses* and *Mrs Dalloway*.[77] Here at first sight was something that might stand comparison with, say, Louis Aragon's *Paysan de Paris* (1926), though on closer inspection the uncanniness of the Passage de l'Opéra is not especially palpable in the pubs and shops of Bolton ('Worktown' as it was called by M-O), just as the 'vertigo' which attaches to Aragon's 'mythology of the modern' is a far cry from the collective sentiments of popular life in England.[78] In this as in so much else one may wonder at the way in which the challenge to reason and logic that Surrealism originally posed tended to fade away in an English climate.[79] As further confirmation of that tendency, M-O was by 1940 lending its services to the Ministry of Information (it would be hard to imagine the Paris Bureau de Recherches Surréalistes delivering itself up to a similar fate).

The war effectively disposed of Surrealism in England, even though the indefatigable E. L. T. Mesens laboured to keep the group in existence, attempting at the very last to forge the collective identity upon which Breton had staked so much.[80] There were expulsions and in-fighting, but these were merely the histrionics of a movement with no real inner core. There would be one final manifesto in 1947, though this was produced only at Breton's insistence and its list of principles turned out to be merely a series of rebuttals of accusations Breton had levelled at the group in a letter.[81] In the same year, Cyril Connolly

[74] Madge, 'Anthropology at Home', *New Statesman and Nation* (2 January 1937), p. 12.

[75] Laura Marcus, 'Introduction: the Project of Mass-Observation', *New Formations*, 44 (Autumn 2001), p. 15.

[76] Rod Mengham, 'Bourgeois News: Humphrey Jennings and Charles Madge', *New Formations*, 44 (Autumn 2001), p. 28.

[77] James Buzard, 'Mass-Observation, Modernism, and Auto-ethnography', *Modernism/Modernity*, 4, 3 (September 1997), p. 111.

[78] Louis Aragon, *Paris Peasant* (1926), trans. Simon Watson-Taylor (London: Picador, 1980), pp. 130, 129; Mass-Observation, *The Pub and the People: A Worktown Study* (London: Victor Gollancz, 1943).

[79] See also Remy, *Surrealism in Britain*, p. 97.

[80] See Denis-J. Jean, 'Was There an English Surrealist Group in the Forties? Two Unpublished Letters', *Twentieth-Century Literature*, 21 (1975), p. 87. For this last phase of English Surrealism, see also Jean Louis Bédouin, *Vingt ans de Surréalisme* (Paris: Denoël, 1961), pp. 59–70. There is a less reverent account in George Melly, *Don't Tell Sibyl*.

[81] Denis-J. Jean, 'Was There an English Surrealist Group in the Forties?', p. 88. For the 'manifesto', see 'Déclaration du Groupe Surréaliste en Angleterre', in André Breton and

would declare that 'such a thing as *avant-garde* in literature has ceased to exist'.[82] Yet, as the example of *transition* showed, the avant-garde had sustained itself in Paris across the thirties, offering not so much a group identity as a space in which risks were encouraged and taken. Equally important, Jolas's 'Revolution of the Word', with its move against the imagistic and the discursive, promoted an interest in internal verbal experience which supported the very different projects of Gertrude Stein, Beckett, Hart Crane, Joyce and the Surrealists. Yet of the texts that appeared in *transition* it was undoubtedly Joyce's *Work in Progress* – finally published in 1939 as *Finnegans Wake* – which reaffirmed the avant-garde spirit most powerfully. Indeed, the *Wake*'s 'alphybettyformed verbage' might seem in retrospect to offer a tacit rebuke to the representational tendencies of 'neo-Surrealism', with Joyce discovering the movements of the unconscious not in visual images but in the workings of language itself. Dream and language here were intersecting worlds we inhabit rather than merely vehicles of self-expression. The English 'neo-Surrealists' had felt the obscure vibration of such possibilities, but in grasping them as merely arbiters of a new literary style they had largely missed the real challenge of the avant-garde.

Marcel Duchamp, eds., *Le Surréalisme en 1947: Exposition Internationale du Surréalisme* (Paris: Maeght, 1947), pp. 45–7.

[82] Connolly, 'Editorial', *Horizon*, 16 (December 1947), p. 299.

23

World War II: contested Europe

ADAM PIETTE

Many key texts of the 1930s, written in grim foreknowledge of World War II, mapped Europe as a psycho-political space of Fascist manipulation, shifting borders and doomed voices demanding just representation before the axe fell. Travel writing, written in response to government appeasement policies, particularly after the failure of the Spanish Civil War and the tragedy of Czechoslovakia, became the key trope and genre for reports from the real and imaginary-future front.

In 1945, Evelyn Waugh distinguished between the innocent age of travel writing, the first half of the 1930s, and the political travel accounts of the run-up to the war. Travel had been a journey to the 'wild lands where man has deserted his post', or to the 'soft breezes and mellow sunshine' of the Mediterranean. But from 1935 onwards, as a war correspondent reporting on Abyssinia, Waugh took on 'the livery of a new age', no longer as 'a free traveller', but as a recruit in the political battleground over the future of Europe.[1] This shift to the political was also played out in the many committed texts about journeys to the Spanish Civil War, a struggle eclipsing 'the Spain that dwells in everyone's imagination'.[2] Its failure initiated a turn inwards in forms and genres of writing which became increasingly psychogeographical, neurotic, mythopoeic.

This shift can be registered even in the orthodox travel accounts that were still being written. Graham Greene's *Journey Without Maps* (1936), an account of his journey to Liberia, is ostensibly a text in the old style,[3] exploiting Liberia as screen for the projection of a Western dream of a primitive lost kingdom. Yet the account begins with a flight over Nazi Berlin, the European heart of

[1] Evelyn Waugh, 'Preface', *When the Going Was Good* (1946; Harmondsworth: Penguin, 1951), p. 8.

[2] George Orwell, *Homage to Catalonia* (1938; Harmondsworth: Penguin, 1989), p. 157.

[3] Graham Greene, *Journey Without Maps: A Travel Book* (1936; London: William Heinemann, 1950). Greene's novel is mentioned by Waugh in his list of innocent texts (p. 8). Further references given in parenthesis in the text.

darkness glimpsed from the air: Greene flies over Fascist Europe and away in a deliberate act of geographical escapism, the writing and journey a 'method of psychoanalysis', 'a long journey backwards without maps' (109), through seedy border-zones towards a lost objectivity (193), the evaded Fascism there as a darkness within the observer's unconscious.

Late thirties' travel writing is a journey to a war, exploring border psychoses in a world both psychoanalytic and political, the Fascist enemy fabulously internalised. The accounts are inward in their compromised retreat into history and psychological roots, troubling the political objectivity of the enemy encountered. Christopher Isherwood's *Goodbye to Berlin* (1939) is typical, a text that travels to Germany by going back in time to Weimar and the host of innocents (sexually independent women, homosexuals, egalitarian working class, Jews) soon to be engulfed in the rise of Fascism. The move back into history is matched by the narrator's passivity ('I am a camera with its shutter open, quite passive, recording, not thinking'), the self-trivialising of Sally Bowles and Otto, and the class entrenchment of the Jewish Landauer family. The documentary force of witness has been replaced by the doom-laden passivity of memory, a passivity which turned politics into psychological fable, as in Edwin Muir's 1937 collection, *Journeys and Places*, where the journey to war is rendered unintelligibly mythopoeic. The voice seems to be sympathising with the victims of Fascism, but they are dressed up as Trojan slaves to their Greek conquerors, slaves who drift 'far inland' in their dreams, seeking 'a kingdom lost' in some nameless unfamiliar place.[4] The legendary historicising is matched by this drift into psychic space, a landscape of the dead, with the Jungian allegorising miming the dreamy indecision of the enslaved mentality. After the perceived failure of political reportage in Spain, travel accounts were also marked by shifts and confusions of genre, documentary objectivity replaced by a generic inwardness matching the shift towards the mythological and psychogeographical. Crossing the border, a familiar 1930s trope in Spanish Civil War writing,[5] had stood for 'crossing the line into committed action', but now signified an abandonment of the political self 'to a powerful, evil fantasy world'.[6]

[4] Edwin Muir, *Journeys and Places* (1937), in *Collected Poems* (London: Faber & Faber, 1984), pp. 57–88. Quotations from 'The Town Betrayed', 'The Unfamiliar Place', pp. 77, 78. Cf. also 'Troy' and 'A Trojan Slave'.

[5] Apart from the poets, these include Orwell, *Homage to Catalonia* (1938); Arthur Koestler, *Spanish Testament* (1937); Claud Cockburn (as Frank Pitcairn), *Reporter in Spain* (1936); Esmond Romilly, *Boadilla* (1937); Tom Wintringham, *English Captain* (1939); Franz Borkenau, *The Spanish Cockpit* (1937); and John Langdon-Davies, *Behind the Spanish Barricades* (1936).

[6] Janet Montefiore, *Men and Women Writers of the 1930s* (London: Routledge, 1996), p. 67.

Stevie Smith's *Over the Frontier* (1938) ponders the neurotic internalisation of Fascist geopolitics by staging the breakdown of the central consciousness, Pompey, caught between English ideological force-fields and Nazi sado-masochism. The final fantasy sequence, where Pompey imagines herself a spy and partisan in a war in Germany, is deliberately suicidal and melodramatic, confessing the melancholy of the subject stripped of all political bearings. The writing destabilises the social and political purposes of the travel narrative, so important in earlier texts such as Naomi Mitchison's *Vienna Diary* (1934) and John Lehmann's *Evil Was Abroad* (1936). It indulges in parody of popular form (its plot mimicking Eric Ambler's 1936 spy thriller *The Dark Frontier*), presenting itself textually as the fantasy diary of a neurotic. In this it resembles Edward Upward's *Journey to the Border* (1938) where the narrator is tempted by the spectacle of individualism, psychoanalysis, Fascism, Lawrentian sexuality. The final homily, that he must discard the escapism of privacy to cross the frontier of political decision and class identification, is counterbalanced by the dominance of the neurotic *journal intime*.[7] The thirties' double attention to Freudian psychoanalysis and Marxist commitments was collapsing inwards.

Fantasy and science fiction became ambiguous vehicles for the journey into Nazi territory, the political parable obscured by the hermetic conventions of the genres. Katherine Burdekin's *Swastika Night* (1937) crossed into Germany through dystopian science fiction, imagining a Nazi-dominated Europe hundred of years after victory in World War II.[8] Rex Warner's *The Wild Goose Chase* (1937) uses fantasy to script the journey across the frontier, the story of three brothers who travel into territory ruled by a totalitarian Town.[9] In both cases, there is a contradiction between the generic dislocation and the rationale of using popular forms to convey political warning. Burdekin aimed to feminise science fiction in order to prove the tight fit between Fascist gender politics and Nazi technology and history, yet the shift into the future confuses the critical gaze of feminism with the alienation of Wellsian scientism. Warner's use of fantasy runs similar risks – though popularising representation of the dangers of totalitarianism, the allegory of the rugby match has a nightmarishly flattening effect generated by the inbuilt commitment of fantasy to dream archetypes.

7 Cf. Patrick Quinn, 'At the Frontier: Edward Upward's *Journey to the Border*', in Patrick Quinn, ed., *Recharting the Thirties* (Selinsgrove: Susquehanna University Press, 1996), pp. 233–46.

8 Written under the pseudonym Murray Constantine.

9 The lame complicity of liberal humanism against Fascism is revisited in *The Professor* (1938), which draws readers over the border into central Europe and into the mind of the ineffectual Prime Minister, prey, like the hapless Judge in Spender's *Trial of a Judge* (1938), to the machinations of Fascists sympathetic to the Nazi state across the frontier.

Generic inwardness is also the net effect of Rebecca West's monumental *Black Lamb and Grey Falcoln* (1942), based on trips to the Balkans before the war.[10] Challenging appeasement, it urged the example of the nascent Yugoslavia's history of resistance to the vicious manipulation of the Turks, Venetians, the Austro-Hungarian Empire, Fascist Germany and Italy. Weaving personal impression, deep history, feminist, cultural and socio-political interpretation, it advocates a left-liberal anti-Fascist politics and the Serbian Yugoslav dream, critiques British imperialism and praises the Serbo-Byzantine peasant cultures that have survived centuries of oppression.[11] *Black Lamb* reassembles the dissected map of the Balkans, as well as of West's own liberal autonomy, revealing the forces that bind the subject to history, geography and culture. In the 'Epilogue', West reviews the disaster that has hit the region since 1939, and inveighs against the 'cataleptic quiet' (1114) of those who stood by and allowed death to rule Europe. The 'appetite for sacrificial self-immolation' (1145) is a death-wish complicit in Fascist refiguration of borders, but can be redeemed by an idea of Europe that is not 'a map of a jungle, in which there range many beasts' (1123), but one which draws energy from the Balkans in its defiance, 'a rock in a shifting world' (1149).[12] It is an extraordinary achievement, but its polemical purposes were disabled by the very means of its success. The heady mix of genres led to a staggeringly long text, militating against its own warnings: 'And what has happened [in South Serbia]? The answer is too long, as long indeed, as this book, which hardly anybody will read by reason of its length' (773). Fascist Germany sought to 'destroy the political and economic centres of ancient states with pasts that told a long continuous story', to impose, once again, upon the Balkans 'History . . . like the delirium of a madman' (1114). West's own long and continuous story and history is caught up in the web of the long 'record of pain and violence and bloodshed' (1126) it sought so bravely to counteract.

There were exceptions to the rule – refugee writing and committed journalism managed to cross the border with eye-witness accounts so necessary to counteract scepticism about atrocity stories. Writing by refugees enabled readers to travel into the darkness of occupied Europe in the company of those who had *seen*. The Austrian novelist Peter Mendelssohn, who had escaped

[10] Rebecca West, *Black Lamb and Grey Falcoln: A Journey through Yugoslavia* (Edinburgh: Canongate, 1993) (1942). Further references given in parenthesis in the text.

[11] See Montefiore, *Men and Women Writers*, pp. 3, 10, 75.

[12] Just as Madrid had been during the Spanish Civil War: Tom Wintringham called Madrid 'the world's "strong point" holding up the war machine of Fascism' (*English Captain* (Harmondsworth: Penguin, 1939), p. 18).

from Vienna to England in 1936, wrote *Across the Dark River* (1939) in English, the story of a group of persecuted Jews from an Austrian village forced across frontiers. The refugee novels reinforced accounts by foreign journalists, such as G. E. R. Gedye's powerful eye-witness reports of Jew-baiting sadism in *Fallen Bastions* (1939). In both kinds of texts, the stillness and inertia of appeasement Britain could be disturbed by the incontrovertible evidence of raw experience, as in West's 'I saw with my own eyes the German hatred of the Slavs' (1099). The act of witness in the Old Testament began as a means of settling a border dispute – a heap of stones marked the border, signifying the eyes of witnesses keeping watch on the covenant that had created the border.[13] Only real human eyes could carry the true reports from the dark border separating Britain from the realities of the fallen cities of Europe, the violation of all human bonds.

If writers of the immediate pre-war found it difficult to confront the enemy except as neurotic symptom, then their predicament prefigures the existential difficulties of artists in the armed forces in the early years of the war. Writers in arms felt the responsibility of their fathers' generation to respond accurately, politically and passionately to war experience, but this was compromised by the long months of the Phoney War, the terrible waiting game after defeat in Norway and Dunkirk, the ideological confusion produced by the Nazi–Soviet pact, and the spectacle of Home Front casualties in the blitzes from the relative safety of countryside camps. The terrible collective urgency of the situation – invasion fears on an isolated island, the desperate mobilisation of everyone and everything in a total war effort, the legitimate pride in resistance and survival written into the myths of the little boats at Dunkirk, the Blitz spirit and the heroism of the Battle of Britain – meant that stories about boot camps and manoeuvres, or personal visions of the bigger picture, seemed not only out of place but self-appeasing betrayals of the common war effort. There was a numbed acceptance of the relative truth of integration propaganda and a sense of shame that men in the army were surviving. Much of the fine work by armed forces writers addresses this uncomfortable truth. Guard-duty poems became a sub-genre to express it, as in Michael Hamburger's 'Sentry Duty', with the box like a coffin, the sentry entering an empty reverie encouraging him to follow the 'Sirens' (signalling blitz as well as mythological creatures) to 'the sweet morgue'.[14] The trance the soldier enters into is the gateway to the morbid other country visited by the neurotic travel writing of the pre-war, a country in guilty relation to the real city under the bombs.

[13] Genesis 32: 44–54.

[14] Michael Hamburger, 'Sentry Duty', in Brian Gardner, ed., *The Terrible Rain: The War Poets 1939–1945* (Methuen, 1983), p. 49.

At issue was the failure of engagement with the real enemy. Instead, the unseen enemy modulated too quickly into the same depth-psychological bogeymen whose repertoire Auden had exhausted with *The Orators*. Auden and Isherwood's abandonment of the country at its time of need (no one seems to have considered the risks they ran as gay intellectuals) very nearly put paid to any serious armed-forces exploration of the enemy within in the Audenesque style. The problematic lack of combat visual experience is played out in many poems about the unseen enemy, as with R. N. Currey's 'Unseen Fire', where the long-range mediation of artillery technology encoded the inhuman ritual of a war fought by ghosts against ghosts; or H. B. Mallalieu's 'State of Readiness' where the soldiers dream of real battle, hoping that 'Tonight the enemy, unseen, / Is real', only to collapse back into reverie: 'Our thoughts resume their island voyages', parody of the journeys to real war.[15] The long months of preparation for combat chimed in with the practice and popularity of apocalyptic and neo-Romantic writing, styles which, though professedly amalgams of Surrealist and social realist modes,[16] continued the inward drift of pre-war mythopoeia. This had its guilty counterpart in the armed forces, as with Sidney Keyes's explorations of the borderlands of violence, fantasy and ritual. In Oxford, Keyes had come under the influence of the Inklings, particularly Charles Williams, and had married Inklings issues of sacrifice, martyrdom and Lawrentian sexual energies with Yeatsian–Jungian abstraction. The preparation for war involved a spiritual appropriation of the figures of the enemy, the victim and the loved one. Victims of war ('Europe's Prisoners'), the loved ones fought for ('Remember your lovers') and the unseen enemies within ('Gilles de Retz', 'Orestes and the Furies') must be acknowledged as psychic personalities before the move to the theatres of war. These are figured in the long poems 'The Foreign Gate' and 'The Wilderness' as Rilkean testing-grounds of the death-wishful imagination, the deserts of North Africa troped as 'the red rock desert / I have dreamt of and desired'.[17] In this he married Williams's cult of sacrifice with contemporary psychology which read the conflict as a projection of the war in the mind: 'wars exist', Charles Berg wrote in 1941, 'because the Id is already at war and wants this dramatisation, projection or mechanism of outward release for its intolerable inner tension and

[15] R. N. Currey, 'Unseen Fire', in John Lehmann, ed., *Poems from 'New Writing' 1936–1946*, p. 156. H. B. Mallalieu, 'State of Readiness', in Brian Gardner, ed., *The Terrible Rain: The War Poets 1939–1945* (London: Methuen, 1987), p. 51.

[16] G. S. Fraser, quoted in Derek Stanford, *Inside the Forties: Literary Memoirs 1937–1957* (London: Sidgwick & Jackson, 1977), p. 84.

[17] Sidney Keyes, 'The Wilderness', *The Collected Poems of Sidney Keyes*, ed. Michael Meyer (London: Routledge, 1988), pp. 115–19 (p. 115).

conflict'.[18] Sidney Keyes was killed after being captured on patrol in Tunisia in 1943.

But there was the possibility of writing for real, too, even in the months of waiting for the move to the fronts, and the potential lay in the new feeling for democracy in the army's uniformed collective. The army recruit, as Alun Lewis saw it in 'Lance-Jack', was 'a migrant, an Arab taking his belongings with him, needing surprisingly little of the world's goods', liberated in the 'sudden *levelling down*', the 'possibility for change' involved in the democratic environment of the new army.[19] Government initiatives fostered this political camaraderie, in particular the work of the Army Bureau of Current Affairs (ABCA) whose fortnightly *Current Affairs* bulletins sent to army units popularised the idea of the citizen–soldier, encouraging discussion of radical post-war reforms, 'the first gesture towards politicizing a British army since Cromwell's day'.[20] The move to North Africa, the first significant front after the defeats in Greece and the Far East, coincided with the entry of the Soviet Union into the war, an event which finally released the anti-Fascist radicalism implicit but repressed in the real Dunkirk spirit. The army became a radical force. As Edward Thompson remembered: 'I recall a resolute and ingenious civilian army, increasingly hostile to the conventional military virtues, which became . . . an anti-fascist and conspicuously anti-imperialist army.'[21]

The internal polarisation – between the soldier's deathward spiritual journey and the post-1941 idea of the citizen–soldier – took its own toll. The entanglement of the personal and the superpolitical characterises Alun Lewis's war work, which advocates the international political engagements of the citizen at the same time as it courts a Rilkean drift towards deep solipsistic release. We can see this in the fine short story 'Ward "O" 3 (b)' which stages complex political debates between wounded soldiers, at the same time as turning metaphorically round a pool in the hospital grounds, figure for inner death wish: 'Circles of water . . . lapped inwards, inwards. He felt the ripples surging against the most withdrawn and inmost ledges of his being, like a series of temptations in the wilderness' (212).[22] Lewis died in Burma of a self-inflicted gunshot wound, hours before engagement with the enemy, as though enacting

[18] Charles Berg, *War in the Mind* (London: Macauley Press, 1941), p. 272.

[19] Alun Lewis, 'Lance-Jack', *Collected Stories*, ed. Cary Archard (Bridgend: Seren Books, 1990), p. 64.

[20] Max Beloff, *Wars and Welfare* (London: Edward Arnold, 1984), p. 264.

[21] 1978 *New Statesman* article quoted in the 'Introduction' to David Edgar and Neil Grant's dramatisation of the Music for All Parliament, *Vote for Them* (London: BBC Books, 1989), p. 5.

[22] Lewis, 'Ward "o" 3(b)', *Collected Stories*, p. 212.

the contradictions of being both a citizen–soldier protecting imperial India, and an inner migrant facing not the Japanese but his own withdrawal into the wilderness of death.

The contradiction pertains in the best writing to come out of the desert war, focusing again on the figure of the enemy. North Africa afforded writers the first real arena where they could stage the similarities and differences between their war and the war their fathers had fought. Trench systems, tanks, massive artillery bombardments in a landscape entirely dominated by war, the proximity of a mad war zone and the carefree civilian zones of Cairo and Alex – the resemblances struck many in the epic series of battles up to Alamein. The writing carefully attended to the dispiriting nature of such repetition, as with Keith Douglas's 'Rosenberg I only repeat what you were saying',[23] at the same time as it signalled differences: this was a new war of incredible technological power and mobility, unprecedented in the deviousness of its deceptions and camouflage, a site of democratic male bonding that even outstripped the camaraderie of the Great War: 'We lived so very much under each other's eyes; our lives were common property', wrote Dan Billany.[24] The visibility of one's own soldiers contrasted with the treacherous and elusive presence of the enemy to the West, and it is in the response to the dead bodies of Italians and Germans killed by artillery and tanks that the contradiction between war as private game and as common humanising effort is revealed. Keith Douglas's poetry and prose stages the soldier's cruelty and power as deranged forces within the trained mind. The tank commander is the new cavalry officer, master of machine and wireless technology; the war's speed, efficiency and long-range killing giving the officer a juvenile boisterousness, an anaesthetising cynical energy disinvesting the infliction of death of humane responses. The poems about the German dead in the desert, 'Vergissmeinnicht', 'How to Kill' and 'Cairo Jag', need to be placed alongside the prose memoir *Alamein to Zem-Zem* to get a real sense of the chilling audacity of Douglas's achievement, for the German dead are there as perverse booty to Douglas's tank commanders. The mobility of the technological warrior is a move into nightmare childhood, a journey through the looking-glass into an unreal world of the game of death. By contrast, Hamish Henderson's astonishing sequence, *Elegies*

[23] Keith Douglas, 'Desert Flowers', *Keith Douglas: The Complete Poems*, ed. Desmond Graham (Oxford University Press, 1987), p. 102.

[24] Dan Billany, *The Trap* (1950; London: Faber & Faber, 1986), p. 254. The desert transformed the very idea of property, as Robert Garrioch argued in 'Property', where the soldier discards all his kit in the battle, except for the bare essentials of water-bottle and groundsheet. In Desmond Graham, ed., *Poetry of World War II: An International Anthology* (London: Chatto & Windus, 1995), pp. 38–9.

for the Dead in Cyrenaica (1948), reads the desert war as a human civil war distorted by the war's 'effect of mirage and looking-glass illusion': the poems undermine all 'blah about their sacrifice' and attend to the common humanity of the dead on both sides, in conscious and necessary recall of World War I tropes.[25] The desert, physically levelling down combatants to the human, deconstructs the rival ideologies of the enemy cultures. As Billany put it: 'in these alien circumstances some of our own tribal gods . . . are seen as comical, romantic and impermanent' (217).

The contradiction between individual introspection and citizen–soldier solidarity is there in the rival groupings in Cairo. The poets gathered around the *Personal Landscape* journal run by Lawrence Durrell, Robin Fedden, Terence Tiller and Bernard Spencer opted for an apolitical poetic, standing back from the war effort to examine the deep histories of precisely 'personal' experiences in wartime. As Roger Bowen has shown, the Landscapers structured their Cairo and Alexandria poems around a bitter contrast between the free mobility of pre-war travel and the enforced stasis of wartime exile, the pre-war mobility darkly recruited and parodied by Panzer Blitzkrieg and Desert Rat tank deployment.[26] Their representative poem, Fedden's 'Personal Landscape', insists on the importance of personal life and values (here figured as a Donne-like aubade) at the same time as it acknowledges that love cannot be disengaged from the ways the human body is being broken by wartime, the military inhabiting the loved one's body (the pun on 'arms'): 'I cannot disentangle your arms / From the body of the day that is breaking.'[27]

The advocacy of lyrical–anarchist individualism at *Personal Landscape* was countered by the many patriotic journals in Cairo gathering poems written by soldiers, notably *Salamander*, which issued the influential Oasis anthologies, run by Keith Bullen and John Cromer. Georgian and Kiplingesque in spirit, the group sought, in Roger Bowen's words, 'to memorialize the soldier as amateur poet and oral historian', to counter what Cromer identified as 'obscurantist modernism', and to celebrate the common purpose and camaraderie of the troops.[28] The extraordinary Music for All Parliament in Cairo in late 1943 and early 1944, a mock parliament which voted for radical post-war

25 *Elegies for the Dead in Cyrenaica* (London: John Lehmann, 1948), pp. 11–12, 36. Cf. also Sorley Maclean's 'Going Westward' (trans. Ian Crichton Smith): 'no rancour in my heart / against the hardy soldiers of the Enemy, / but the kinship that there is among / men in prison on a tidal rock' (Graham, ed., *Poetry of the World War II*, p. 40).

26 Roger Bowen, *'Many Histories Deep': The 'Personal Landscape' Poets in Egypt, 1940–45* (London: Associated University Presses, 1995).

27 Ibid., pp. 46–7.

28 Ibid., p. 47.

democracy, was held in the same services' centre which hosted the Salamander Society.

The contradiction could take place within the individual poem, as with F. T. Prince's 'Soldiers Bathing', which focuses estranging attention on the combatant body, this time one's own men.[29] 'Soldiers Bathing' repeats a common trope of World War I poetry, the soldier revealing the human body, cleansed of the dust of war, in all its naked beauty once stripped of the 'weapons that are lying there'. In its serpentine syntax and its shocking move into Christian symbolism at its close, the poem at once takes delight in the sight of the universal soldier as essential human of all wars in an act of radical Christian democracy, at the same time as it reinterprets First World War homoeroticism in terms of a derangedly inward mystical imagination hungry for sacrifice.

Desert war poetry at its best provides us with sharp and fertile explorations of the clash of psyche and polis, hidden self and outer network, the inner lover/killer and the citizen–soldier, in ways consciously revising the tropes of World War I, importantly representing the new war experiences as entrancingly mediated by technology. The false subjectivity of a world at war experienced through technology began to substitute for an inner life for many in the services. Mary Lee Settle, in *All the Brave Promises* (1984), remembers being a WAAF radio–telephone operator during the war: 'it was hard for the hand not to reach forward to turn the set down, not to recede from it into the dead areas of animal waiting, waiting for the confinement of the closed signals room, the connection by wavelength, even the sense of floating displacement in the state of war itself to be over'.[30] This technologically induced trance is a peculiar feature of the war's long-term effects, particularly in the Forces writing by writers in intelligence, telecommunications, Air Force and Navy, the key areas of combat where location technology dominated.

Alan Ross's poems about war on destroyers are about the ways deception tactics on sea induced trance-like states, minds split into reified dreamers and rootless, mechanical killers. 'Radar' meditates on radar's remoteness of control, the soothing and nightmare ways its feelers multiply 'our eyes for us', lulling feeling with its smooth '[r]otations of power'.[31] 'Destroyers in the Arctic' sees camouflage deception turning the lethal fleet into formal fictions,

[29] F. T. Prince, 'Soldiers Bathing', *Collected Poems 1935–1992* (Manchester: Carcanet Press, 1993), pp. 55–7.

[30] Mary Lee Settle, *All the Brave Promises: Memories of Aircraft Woman 2nd Class 2146391* (London: Pandora, 1984), p. 60.

[31] Alan Ross, 'Radar', *Open Sea* (London: London Magazine Editions, 1975), p. 16.

repetitive, imitative, ruminative, rather than real (11–12). The entrancing nature of technology was reprised in Ross's great narrative poem about the 1942 Battle of the Barents Sea, 'J. W. 51B: A Convoy', written after the war, which links the unreality induced by 'radar / And Asdic and RL 85 slowly revolving' to the image of the crew in deep sleep (26). E. Denyer Cox, in 'Aviator', glimpses the face of the enemy pilot too late, the war an affair of technology controlling the primitive man of action: 'The eye glances along the sights, / The instinctive mind calculates familiar data; / . . . A white blur of face / Storms sickeningly up, confused among dark wings.'[32] The war was being planned and fought by the technicians of these new technologies, moving men thousands of miles locked within so many lethal machines, towards a death unleashed by the same technologies. The fear that the inner mind was not only being entranced but also generated by war technology begins to mark the writing from the services with a deep paranoia, as the huge build-up for the invasion of Europe progressed. G. S. Fraser's 'Journey' relates this paranoia to the travel motif of war – the planners are not only moving men around the world, they are mapping their very insides, inhabiting basic responses with the ghosts summoned within the body by technological forces:

> Mappers of nerves, who graph our play and toil,
> Who aim the rifle, fire, and the recoil
> Hits not their hearts, as our own crimes had done,
> These armoured men, of metal and of steel,
> With rubber hands and fluorescent eyes,
> Who act, but who neither think nor feel,
> Whom we poor poets curse.[33]

The man of war in the body, the 'hot aching man of blood within', in Norman Cameron's phrase, is a creature generated at the contact zone between 'the inner and the outer conflagration'. The journey to the war, as the Allies moved into Italy then Normandy in such numbers so incalculably controlled by war technology and bureaucracy, became a paranoid journey within the body in search of the 'throbbing meshes' the technology controlled.[34]

The paranoia created by the war's power made it difficult for writers to communicate the radical collective energies in the Forces, partly because the paranoia matched so closely the kinds of nausea and suspicion generated by

32 A. Denyer Cox, 'Aviator', in Keidrych Rhys, ed., *Poems from the Forces* (London: Routledge, 1941), pp. 21–2.

33 G. S. Fraser, 'Journey', *Scottish Arts and Letters* 1 (1944), p. 37.

34 Norman Cameron, 'Let Him Loose', *The Complete Poems of Norman Cameron*, ed. Warren Hope (Florence, KY: Barth, 1985), p. 27.

propaganda. Wartime propaganda needed to confuse government and citizen feelings, to court individual assent as dutiful mass response, and had overt ('white') and covert ('black') means to do so. As Jacques Ellul has argued, World War II propaganda was openly discussed to create a 'white' façade which helped to bring public resistance to propaganda out into the open while propagandists 'worked public opinion in entirely different directions, seeking to provoke very different reactions, using even public resistance to white propaganda for their own purposes'.[35] The complex varieties of propaganda, combined with deliberately low-key, sober and informative styles to counteract jaundiced suspicions after World War I, made propaganda an astonishingly powerful weapon in the Second. Individuals felt alienated by the strange new artificial world inhabiting their minds, unsure whether they had *become* another person, or whether they were *obeying* another person (Ellul, 189).

Many writers were drawn into propaganda work during the war. At the Ministry of Information (MoI), they included Graham Greene, Evadne Price, George Orwell, Inez Holden, C. S. Forester, Cecil Day Lewis, E. Arnot Robertson, George Blake, Monica Stirling and Laurie Lee. The Ministry also indirectly influenced public opinion through publishers (using the bait of extra paper), the press, the film industry and the BBC. Writers were mobilised, writes Keith Williams, 'in the biggest exercise in mass-communications ever undertaken by a British government'.[36] The brief of the MoI was to achieve a blend of American advertising techniques, Soviet-style people's war integration propaganda, a democratised version of pre-war imperial discourses, and a low-key display of liberal values. The propaganda aimed abroad was very important to get right, since it had simultaneously to sustain morale in the Forces and to influence opinion in highly volatile civilian populations. The propaganda work created precisely the feelings of paranoid uncertainty about inner and outer worlds that characterises so much of the writing from the Forces. The most striking example of this is George Orwell.

Orwell worked for the BBC's Empire Service as Talks Producer in the Indian Section between 1941 and 1943, broadcasting propaganda to Indian universities to counter nationalist anxieties after the internment of leaders

[35] Jacques Ellul, *Propagandes* (Paris: Armand Colin, 1962), p. 28. (My translation.)

[36] Keith Williams, *British Writers and the Media, 1930–45* (Basingstoke: Macmillan, 1996), p. 182. Cf. also Kenneth Short, ed. (*Film and Radio Propaganda in World War II* (London: Croom Helm, 1983). For a political account of the MoI, cf. Ian McLaine's *Ministry of Morale* (London: George Allen & Unwin, 1979).

such as Nehru, and to justify the need for Indian volunteers.[37] Having predicted the passivity and demise of the liberal writer as war encouraged totalitarian values in 'Inside the Whale' in 1940, Orwell found confirmation in his own easy acceptance of MoI censorship, in his recruitment of poetry and fiction in the talks and readings he organised, and in the devious ways his propaganda work mimicked the totalitarian forms of control he anathematised. In his 1941 article on 'Literature and Totalitarianism', Orwell could very well be describing his own wartime productions: '[Totalitarianism] creates an ideology for you, it tries to govern your emotional life as well as setting up a code of conduct. And as far as possible it isolates you from the outside world, it shuts you up in an artificial universe in which you have no standards of comparison.'[38] Work for the propaganda machine mirrored the contradictions suffered by those in the Forces. 'Only externally', Rom Landau wrote in his diary, 'can private conduct be kept separate from service conduct; spiritually, this is impossible; for the two do not merely overlap but flow into one another, forming a single stream.'[39] Landau's service paranoia, becoming a cog in a machine that recruits private feeling, matches Orwell's dismal sense of the propagandised mind in *Nineteen Eighty-Four*. And just as the contradictions between service paranoia and communal war effort tended to draw the composing mind inwards towards a fake enemy within, so, too, did propaganda have the effect of obscuring the truth about the fate of the victims of Fascism in Europe. The single most devastating effect of MoI censorship was its downplaying of the Final Solution. Arthur Koestler had castigated readers of *Horizon* in late 1943 for disbelieving his 'Mixed Transport' piece on the Chelmno mobile gas-chambers: and this despite the evidence for the *Endlösung* being available since 1941.[40] It was MoI policy to avoid reference to the Jewish victims for fear of atrocity-mongering and because of unease about anti-Semitism in Britain and sensitivity about reactions in the Middle East.[41] Writers in the main acquiesced in this tactical silence, and also to overt censorship of it – as when the MoI requested Koestler to tone down accounts of the concentration camps in his script for the film *Lift*

37 Cf. *Orwell: The War Broadcasts*, ed. W. J. West (London: Duckworth/BBC, 1985).

38 George Orwell, 'Literature and Totalitarianism', *The Collected Essays, Journalism and Letters of George Orwell*, ed. Sonia Orwell and Ian Angus, 3 vols. (London: Secker & Warburg, 1968), II, pp. 134–7 (p. 135).

39 Rom Landau, *The Wing: Confessions of an RAF Officer* (London: Faber & Faber, 1945), p. 317.

40 Cf. the 'Propaganda' chapter in my *Imagination at War* (Basingstoke: Macmillan, 1995), pp. 190–7.

41 Cf. Bernard Wasserstein's *Britain and the Jews of Europe, 1939–1945* (London: Clarendon Press, 1979), Arthur Koestler's 'On Disbelieving Atrocities' in *Yogi and the Commisar* (London: Jonathan Cape, 1945), McLaine's *Ministry of Morale*, pp. 166–70.

Your Heads Comrade.[42] In a very real sense, the attempts by late 1930s writers to raise British consciousness about the plight of the victims of Fascism had been allowed to fail.

As the Allies moved into Europe, they finally discovered the true ferocity of the enemy they had been fighting. But by this time, psychologically, the war had become too big, so vast on all its many fronts that the imagination baulked at the prospect of bearing witness. The war's powers of transformation beggared the attempts of individual artists. Coverage of Normandy, the move into Germany and the discovery of the death camps was dominated by war correspondents, mainly American, and we have to wait until after the war for the small number of texts to attend to this, the final discovery of the reality of the horrors in the enemy's country. But this was done as though incidentally and marginally, as uneasy footnotes to Nuremberg and within the ideological context of denazification, as with Stephen Spender's *European Witness* (1946), which attempts to discover the current state of intellectual life in ruined Germany. 'How many of us to-day', asks Spender, 'are guilty of the hardness of heart and indifference to the fate of others which condoned Nazism?'[43] The question is clumsy, tired and rhetorical, for by this time, Europe and Germany in particular had become the focus of another war, another mysterious system of control and paranoia, the Cold War.

In our reconsideration of the war poetry and fiction of the armed forces during the war, it is difficult not to feel that the desperate good intentions of the 1940s' inward turn in all its manifestations marked a water-shed in twentieth-century British literature. The question was never 'Where are the War Poets?', but how effective their act of witness was to be to the prevailing conditions, in the light of the knowledge of the atrocities being unleashed in Europe. To seek for traces of experimental and committed writing during these years is disingenuous, for most of the writers recruited into the war machine as combatants and propagandists knew that their job was not a formal issue but a frighteningly ethical one. A measure of the sense that writers had failed is there in the list of literary artists who fell silent after 1945: Gascoyne, Rook, Symons, Madge, McFadden, Hendry and, arguably, Empson. It is also there in the shift towards translation as the only means of representing Europe during the war. The best anthology of the war still remains Desmond Graham's extraordinary *Poetry of World War II: An International Anthology*, the last half of which is dominated by translations of poets like Miklós Radnóti, Nelly Sachs, Primo

42 Williams, *British Writers and the Media*, pp. 227–8.

43 Stephen Spender, *European Witness* (London: Hamish Hamilton, 1946), p. 164.

Levi. One long poem by a British writer stands out from Graham's selections for the sections dealing with refugees, genocide, survivor testimonies and liberation: Ruth Pitter's 'Victory Bonfire'. It is a poem of guilt and fear, the victory bonfire unleashing the nightmare images which the inward turn of wartime writing had evaded, internalised and obscured:

> Vast caverns of embers, volcanoes gushing and blushing,
> Whitening wafts on cliffs and valleys of hell,
> Quivering cardinal-coloured glens and highlands,
> Great masses panting, pulsating, lunglike and scarlet,
> Fireballs, globes of pure incandescence
> Soaring up like balloons, formal and dreadful,
> Threatening the very heavens.[44]

It reads like a parody of the Blitz-inspired apocalyptic writing that had marked the beginning of the war, but it is a judgement on the very idea of 'formal and dreadful' incandescent writing; for the bonfire is governed by 'Hitler's ghost', transforming Britain ('White – . . . cliffs', 'glens and highlands') into a landscape saturated with the terrible knowledge of the Holocaust.

The wartime poetry and fiction of the Armed Forces form, nevertheless, a crucial set of documents about the ways the collective imagination fought that war. Do not ask whether the texts are fine and innovative enough to merit attention; but read them as necessary writing that failed, as all imaginations still fail, when lit by the pulsating light of that 'bonfire'. And the collective memory of the war continued to be marked by symptoms of trauma and repression in the Cold War fifties and sixties. Representative texts attempted to tell of the huge changes the war initiated, but repressed both the radicalism of the war and the terrible fate of European victims. The war novels written by Evelyn Waugh, Olivia Manning and Anthony Powell are representative post-war epics of this phase.[45] Waugh's 'The Sword of Honour' trilogy and the wartime sections of Powell's *A Dance to the Music of Time* cover the power-shift from the increasingly eccentric military–aristocratic caste towards the era of common-man social democracy, yet the novels read as deliberately shallow memoirs from a narrow point of view, reducing the massive collective movements either to random, insane acts by isolated individuals (Waugh) or to a history of events observing the leisurely laws of seasonal change (Powell).

[44] Ruth Pitter, 'Victory Bonfire', *Poetry of World War II: An International Anthology*, ed. Desmond Graham (London: Chatto & Windus, 1995), pp. 221–3 (p. 222).

[45] 'Post-war epics' is Alan Munton's phrase. Cf. his *English Fiction of World War II* (London: Faber & Faber, 1989).

Similarly, Olivia Manning's Balkan and Levant Trilogies gainsay their seeming concern for Guy's political engagement by acquiescing in Harriet's self-pityingly dogged focus on their marriage. These post-war epics are products of the Cold War, repressing change by neutralising it within elegiac comedies of manners, dissolving the epic enormity of the war, trivialising the radical energies of the People's War.[46]

Texts that evaded Cold War repression did so because they took the process of repression as their subject, as with Pamela Hansford Johnson's *An Avenue of Stone* (1947), where the revelations of the Holocaust and Hiroshima have caused history to stop, minds to withdraw into bruised fatalism and guilt.[47] The bomb damage wreaked on cities and imaginations was taken as a motif for the repression that had annihilated the wild resistance energies of the war, minds hypnotised by the spectacle of ruins, as in Rose Macaulay's *The World My Wilderness* (1950). Beckett's trilogy, *Molloy*, *Malone Dies* and *The Unnamable*,[48] explores similar bombed-out territory, crossing visions of a compromised neutral space (like De Valera's Eire) with a zone of ruins Beckett had witnessed at St-Lô (where he'd worked at the Irish Red Cross Hospital after the war).[49] The clandestine work he had done in the Resistance is merged with a vision of post-war Europe, a wilderness of ruins peopled by a vagrant population of traumatised displaced persons, outside history, subject to blackouts of memory, dreaming of the peace of death.

It took another generation before British writing could cope more openly with the full range of forces unleashed by the war. By counteracting Cold War distortion, British culture could move towards real contact with the darkness of the war, as if undertaking a retrospective journey into the occupied countries. British Jewish writers could deal powerfully with the complex legacies of the Shoah in modern politics, as did Emanuel Litvinoff in *Falls the Shadow* (1983). The psychosexual godgames, paranoia and sado-masochistic theatricality generated by Nazi history could be addressed, in ways foundational to the Postmodern novel, most notably in John Fowles's *The Magus* (1965) about the German occupation of the Greek islands. Postmodernism was partly

46 Cf. Munton, 'The Post-war Epic', *English Fiction*.

47 Cf. the 'Post-War Post-Script' chapter in Jenny Hartley's *Millions Like Us: British Women's Fiction of World War II* (London: Virago, 1997).

48 *Molloy* (French 1951), *Malone meurt* (1951), *L'innomable* (1953), *Molloy* (English translation with Patrick Bowles 1955), *Malone Dies* (1958), and *The Unnamable* (1959).

49 The Allies had reduced the town to rubble, and it became known as the 'Capitale des Ruines', according to Beckett. Cf. James Knowlson's biography, *Damned to Fame* (London: Bloomsbury, 1996), p. 345.

generated as the delayed reaction to the evil technological mind games inherent in Fascist theatricality, and the paranoid perception that they had not only secretly shaped Cold War power structures, but also the very bases of fictionality. Postmodern deconstructive display of the complicities between power and fiction, J. G. Ballard argues in *Empire of the Sun*, is partly a by-product of the processes by which post-war fictionality was 'brought up', as a child is educated, in and by the war. *Empire of the Sun*, which relates his childhood experiences in an internment camp after the occupation of Shanghai by the Japanese, is about fascination with enemy technology, with the spectacle of mass death and the empire of the atomic sun, as though ambiguously 'in' the enemy's camp, key vectors in the ways the post-war imagination must both construct and suspiciously unmake its own fictional worlds.

By the 1990s, following intense translation work of survivor and witness testimonies, and difficult archival and documentary work coinciding with the fiftieth anniversaries of the war, the Holocaust could begin to be assessed within British writing.[50] True crossover texts gained a place in British culture, as with the bilingual, dual-citizen Rachel Seiffert's *The Dark Room* (2001), based on extensive research into family history, a set of three long short stories that interrogate the burden of the war's history on the children and grandchildren of the Nazis. Though concerned with post-war Germany's amnesia about the Third Reich, the texts are about the unhoused European mind in estranging states of trauma and uncanny mourning, bringing them into line with W. G. Sebald's work, as translated by Michael Hulse and Anthea Bell.

W. G. Sebald's *Austerlitz* (2001) concerns the obliterating processes of history at the same time as it acknowledges that private writing which seeks to explore the dark and terrible histories of the ghettoes and death camps can only do so under a double censoring restraint. Most powerful are the censoring after-effects of collective trauma. The Holocaust, Shoshona Felman argues, 'still functions as a cultural secret, a secret which, essentially, we are still keeping from ourselves through various forms of communal or of personal denial, of cultural reticence or of cultural canonization'.[51] The second-degree witnessing

50 Cf. for instance, Edwin Morgan's translations in *Modern Hungarian Poetry*, ed. Miklos Vajda (1977), Ruth Feldman and Brian Swann's Primo Levi translations, *Collected Poems* (1988), Michael Hamburger's Celan, *Selected Poems* (1988), and Ruth Whitman's translations of Rachel Korn, *Generations: Selected Poems*, ed. Seymour Mayne (1982); Tony Harrison's film-poem for Channel 4, *Shadow of Hiroshima* (1995), Diane Samuels's documentary play *Kindertransport* (1992), and Eva Hoffman's *Shtetl* (1999).

51 Shoshana Felman and Dori Laub, *Testimony: Crises of Witnessing in Literature, Psychoanalysis, and History* (New York and London: Routledge, 1992), p. xix.

of historians can only hope to bring the dead victims alive *as* dead men and women, for that is the ethical imperative of their subject position.[52] Yet historians, as for all generational inheritors of the stories of those barbarous years, are also inflected by the symptoms of trauma that silenced and obliterated the evidence and witness in the first place. Jacques Austerlitz bears a name which resembles the worst death camp of the war, but can get no closer to that unnamable centre than feverishly oblique and ghosting censorship of the horrors of the Terezin ghetto. The writing bears the traces of trauma, with a psychotic dissolution of boundaries of matter, time and space and the terrifying illusion of being possessed by the war dead. As Anne Adelman has shown in her work on the transgenerational evolution of Holocaust narratives, what signifies and constitutes the trauma is a prohibition against naming which 'perpetuates a sense of nameless dread and leaves remnants of unintegratable and unspoken knowledge'.[53] Sebald's *Austerlitz* is written in traumatised prose, haunted by the victims of persecution as if by the nameless dread of their unintegratable and unspoken knowledge.

The second censoring process concerns the monumental archival and museum industries which supposedly memorialise the Holocaust victims, but which actually serve further to obliterate their lives and potential witness by encasing their stories within the very structures of imperial modernity which were used to destroy them. The act of writing, Sebald warns us, may have to be complicit in, even through the act of witnessing against, the archival encrypting of the past, through its comparably obliterating eye of traumatic testimony and mourning. The photographs Sebald weaves through his texts seem to signal the return of the dead, as though approaching a point of contact, yet they also necessarily and uncannily present the past scenes and bodies *as* dead, hopelessly being seen as without being, in an act of intergenerational broken elegy.

For Sebald, the whole of Europe, Britain included, is veiled by the shadow of the dead of that war, rendering every European site and city irredeemably uncanny, strangely familiar because possessed by the absent presences of the dead which the continent can neither fully acknowledge nor deny. In the form of the shadows of the events, scenes and lives its systems of memorialisation seek informationally to bury, Europe has allowed its very unconscious to become

[52] Felman, in Felman and Laub, *Testimony*, p. 216.

[53] Anne Adelman, 'Observations on the Transgenerational Evolution of Narratives of the Holocaust', in Cornelia Berens, ed., *'Coming Home from Trauma': The Next Generation, Muteness, and the Search for a Voice* (Hamburg: International Study Group for Trauma, Violence and Genocide, 1996), pp. 79–93 (p. 79).

secretly identified with those destroyed by the mad politics that constructed, ruined and then rebuilt it. Sebald's work is a foreign discourse, incorporated within the British Isles by the estranging familiarity of translation, that speaks of the terminally traumatised relation of English to the war-generated European cultures at the millennium. As such it is itself a self-obliterating monument to the enduring cycles of traumatic return and repression which must, still, structure the ways we try to forget World War II.

24

World War II: the city in ruins

MICHAEL NORTH

One of the most vivid literary descriptions of World War II occurs at the end of Evelyn Waugh's *Vile Bodies*, which was published in 1930. If this seems a bit premature, it should be noted that prescient British observers had been predicting another war at least since the publication of John Maynard Keynes's *Economic Consequences of the Peace* ten years earlier. Keynes had warned that, unless the peace terms extracted from Germany at Versailles were adjusted, there would be another war, 'before which the horrors of the late German war will fade into nothing, and which will destroy, whoever is victor, the civilization and the progress of our generation'.[1] This conviction of the utter ruin to be brought by another war grew over the next two decades, until it became widely assumed that the next war would mean the virtual collapse of civilisation in the UK, beginning with the physical destruction of British cities. Alexander Korda's 1935 film version of H. G. Wells's *Things to Come* gave a vivid and influential visual form to the assumption that another war would be fought primarily from the air by bombers whose penetration of civil defence perimeters was virtually assured. One military calculation predicted 600,000 civilian dead and 1.2 million wounded in the first six months of aerial bombardment.[2] The use of gas in such attacks would mean, as Waugh has it in 1930, a civilian population going to bed each night in gas masks.

Though such predictions of the effects of German bombardment turned out to be wildly exaggerated, the attention they directed to the consequences of war for civilians was not misplaced. In 1939, a government committee predicted that there would be as many as 3 million to 4 million cases of hysteria or war neurosis so serious as to be incapacitating. Grim visions were offered of a populace so unnerved by aerial bombardment that the dead could not be buried, fires would never be extinguished and the Underground would fill

[1] John Maynard Keynes, *The Economic Consequences of the Peace* (1920; New York: Penguin, 1995), p. 268.

[2] Alfred Price, *Blitz on Britain 1939–45* (Stroud: Sutton, 2000), p. 2.

with refugees unwilling to emerge.[3] Thus civilian morale became a key issue in war preparations, which were undertaken in a spirit so fretfully suspicious that centralised mass shelters were not constructed for fear of encouraging a 'deep shelter mentality' that would turn London's population into a race of modern Morlocks.[4] The guiding light in these efforts was General Giulio Douhet, who taught in *The Command of the Air*, published in 1921, that a civilian population steadily bombed from the air would inevitably crumble and force its leaders to capitulate.[5] As it happened, Douhet was quite right in predicting that civilian morale would be a key issue in the next war, but completely wrong in teaching that civilian weakness would undermine the military effort.

In fact, World War II was over three years old before British military casualties surpassed the number of civilians killed by bombs. In 1940 and 1941, about 43,000 civilians were killed, with another 17,000 dying in the rest of the war.[6] Though the physical destruction wreaked on British cities was nowhere close to the pre-war estimates, it was fearful enough nonetheless. One-sixth of the citizens of London, for example, were made homeless before the end of May 1941.[7] A considerable number of prominent public buildings were destroyed as well, including fifteen Wren churches in the City of London alone.[8] But, as Churchill caustically observed before Parliament in October 1940, it would have taken ten years of bombing at the rate attained during the Blitz to destroy even half the houses in London.[9] And though this war brought many of the horrors of the trenches to the very streets of the UK, so that one fictitious soldier could exclaim incredulously over 'Civilians with shell-shock', there were in fact relatively few of the 'psychiatric air raid casualties' so fearfully expected before the war began.[10]

Instead, British resistance to aerial bombardment became an important psychological and practical resource, and the resiliency of the Home Front became a significant strength, since success in the war depended so crucially on uninterrupted industrial production.[11] Even Hitler was forced to admit early in 1941 that the effect of the bombing on British civilian morale had been relatively weak.[12] Indeed, the resiliency of the civilian population became an

[3] Constantine Fitzgibbon, *London's Burning* (London: Macdonald, 1971), p. 14.
[4] Ibid., p. 21. [5] Price, *Blitz*, p. 95.
[6] Angus Calder, *The People's War: Britain 1939–45* (London: Jonathan Cape, 1969), p. 226.
[7] Ibid., p. 188. [8] Ibid., p. 222. [9] Ibid., p. 169.
[10] Graham Greene, *Ministry of Fear* (New York: Viking, 1943), p. 128; Calder, *People's War*, p. 223.
[11] David Morgan and Mary Evans, *The Battle for Britain: Citizenship and Ideology in the Second World War* (London: Routledge, 1993), p. 38.
[12] Price, *Blitz*, p. 129.

important propaganda point, particularly in the campaign to draw the United States into the war, and the slogan of the day, immortalised as the title of a famous General Post Office (GPO) Film Unit short subject, became *Britain Can Take It!*[13] At least in its early stages, then, World War II was very much the People's War, in which, as Churchill put it in 1940, 'The fronts are everywhere. The trenches are dug in the towns and the streets.'[14] And since the main focus of struggle in this war was the morale of the people, cultural products – speeches, poems, films and songs – that expressed, reflected and reinforced that morale played an important role in the war effort.

It was partly by means of such cultural efforts that a series of stinging defeats was transformed into a story of successful resistance. Beginning with the mass evacuation of British troops from Dunkirk in June 1940 and extending to the end of the Blitz in May 1941, the populace steadily absorbed bad news, military setbacks, blackout, rationing and aerial bombardment. Though the dreaded invasion of Great Britain itself never materialised, and though the Luftwaffe was successfully turned back in the Battle of Britain, the ability of German bombers to attack continuously by night seemed to exemplify the desperately defensive and isolated position of the country. In practical terms, civilians were organised into an army of air-raid wardens, fire-watchers and fire fighters that ultimately numbered around 2 million.[15] Determined labour under difficult conditions also helped keep industrial production up to the necessary levels: the Ministry of Home Security estimated that the average bombed-out worker lost only six days of work.[16] But practical resistance of this kind was sustained by a popular mood, a general sense of solidarity and determination, so strong it is sometimes credited not just with carrying the UK through the war but also with transforming its political life immediately afterwards.

The most effective expressions of this mood, by general estimation, were the speeches of Churchill, the radio broadcasts of J. B. Priestley and Edward R. Murrow and the films produced by the Crown Film Unit. If, as Angus Calder insists, these remain 'more impressive as literary and artistic productions than almost all independently conceived poems, prose and artworks which address the Battle [of Britain] and the Blitz',[17] it is because they draw on and express two

[13] James Chapman, *The British at War: Cinema, State and Propaganda, 1939–1945* (London: Tauris, 1998), p. 98. See also Calder, *People's War*, p. 174.

[14] David Cannadine, ed., *Blood, Toil, Tears and Sweat: The Speeches of Winston Churchill* (Boston: Houghton Mifflin, 1989), p. 181. For the genesis of the term 'People's War', see Calder, *People's War*, p. 138.

[15] Tom Harrisson, *Living through the Blitz* (London: Collins, 1976), p. 38.

[16] Calder, *People's War*, p. 220.

[17] Angus Calder, *The Myth of the Blitz* (London: Jonathan Cape, 1991), p. 180.

key elements of the popular mood of the time. These can be seen most vividly in another frequently praised artwork of this period, the film *In Which We Serve*, which was released to tremendous acclaim in 1942. Rather improbably, this film immortalises a defeat, the British withdrawal from Crete, and the sinking of a battleship, the survivors of which spend the bulk of the movie gripping bits of floating wreckage. But it was part of the British ability to sustain its courage at this time that its citizens could be seen to take the very worst. Though Churchill solemnly lectured his people after Dunkirk that 'Wars are not won by evacuations', the almost miraculous ability of the British Expeditionary Force to escape and regroup after being trapped virtually without defences did expose 'a victory inside this deliverance'.[18] *In Which We Serve* also defied common sense by casting Noel Coward, hardly noted for his military resolve, as commander and hero, and though his performance can seem stiff and paternalistic to viewers now, the sight of this spectacle of elegance covered with grease, bobbing in the water along with his sailors, conveyed a powerful message at the time. These scenes offered such a vivid image of class levelling that even Pudovkin praised them.[19]

A stoic resistance that made mere survival into victory and solidarity across class lines thus became the main sustaining elements of a popular self conception that was the UK's chief cultural response to the war. In expressing it, Churchill, Priestley and the writers and directors of the Crown Film Unit self-consciously drew on reserves from the British cultural past, a habit that self-reflexively emphasised survival and solidarity, regardless of particular content. Churchill spoke in a voice adapted from past British orators – Cromwell, Chatham, Pitt, Macaulay, Disraeli and Gladstone – but his phrases became famous because they really did express a popular wish, turned by events into a popular will. He bridged this gap between times in part by moving between literary registers, combining 'great flights of oratory with sudden swoops into the intimate and the conversational'.[20] An exact cinematic equivalent was offered by the Crown Film Unit in the short film *Words for Battle*, which combined extracts from Camden, Milton, Blake, Browning and Kipling with Churchill's speeches and, somewhat improbably, the Gettysburg Address. These readings, delivered by Laurence Olivier, are illustrated by a montage of wartime scenes, backed by Handel's 'Water Music'.[21]

[18] Cannadine, *Blood, Toil, Tears and Sweat*, p. 160.
[19] Chapman, *British at War*, p. 186.
[20] Harold Nicolson, quoted in Cannadine, *Blood, Toil, Tears and Sweat*, pp. 2–3. See also Calder, *People's War*, pp. 91, 93 and 96.
[21] Chapman, *British at War*, p. 239. See also Anthony Aldgate and Jeffrey Richards, *Britain Can Take It: The British Cinema in World War II* (Oxford: Blackwell, 1986), p. 222.

Contemporary reviews of *Words for Battle* were actually a little sour, and the film does certainly seem grandiloquent at present, but another of the short Crown Film Unit productions of this time seems to sum up in a single instant nearly everything most exemplary in the culture of the war. *Listen to Britain* is a montage of the UK in 1941–2, linking together Spitfires and country lanes. Its most famous and perhaps its most expressive effect is a single cut from Bud Flanagan singing in a factory canteen to Dame Myra Hess performing Mozart at the National Gallery.[22] The spatial and cultural distance between music hall and Mozart is bridged as the cut is accomplished across a single chord, begun by Flanagan, picked up by Hess and Mozart. Though the message of solidarity across class lines may seem an obvious one, it is underscored by certain subtleties, including the fact that both Flanagan and Hess were Jewish and could not therefore have performed in Germany at all.[23] And the visual cut itself is not dissolved by the segue in the soundtrack, so that the distance covered between the canteen and the National Gallery remains and must, in fact, be accentuated to allow the segue to make its point.

In creating this paradoxical moment, Humphrey Jennings, the director responsible for the film, has adapted an avant-garde effect, the montage, to the patriotic purposes of the time. Trained by the GPO Film Unit, with a strong association with British Surrealism, Jennings brought a set of techniques publicly associated with Modernism to the making of what were after all short propaganda films.[24] But the association of the avant-garde, with its insistence on discontinuity and incongruity in film style, with the war effort, which required an emphasis on continuity over time and public solidarity, reflected in itself one of the main characteristics of the People's War. Particularly for civilians, the war itself was a surreal event, violently disrupting ordinary life and juxtaposing incongruous sights and sounds, but this very disruption also carried with it, many observers agreed, new opportunities for social cohesion. In the Crown Film Unit's longest film, *Fires Were Started*, to take a fictionalised example, the need to fight back against incendiary bombardment and the death and homelessness it causes brings together a socially mixed group of Englishmen, who live together in the alternate home of the fire station.[25] The

22 Chapman, *British at War*, p. 169. 23 Calder, *Myth*, p. 238.

24 Aldgate and Richards, *Britain Can Take It*, pp. 220–1; Chapman, *British at War*, p. 166. See also Robert Murphy, *British Cinema and the Second World War* (London: Continuum, 2000), p. 125.

25 For discussions of *Fires Were Started*, see Murphy, *British Cinema*, p. 144, and Chapman, *British at War*, pp. 174–6.

chord sustained across a cut may be taken, therefore, as an apt aesthetic reflection of the new connections that war, with its defeats and interruptions, made both necessary and possible.

It is a very real question whether there is any literature of this time that manages quite the same combination of aesthetic distinction with popular appeal and effect, of technical inventiveness with social responsibility. Though Andrew Sinclair maintains that the war years were 'the *anni mirabiles* of a national culture', it is not usually suggested that this is an especially distinguished period for British literature.[26] It is commonly asserted that Churchill pre-empted the role of inspiration and exhortation usually played by novelists or poets and that there was relatively little room for criticism in a war so commonly felt to be both just and unavoidable.[27] Simply in its physical effects alone, the war was a difficult time for literature. Rationing ultimately limited publishers to 40 per cent of the paper they had used before the war, and bombs destroyed 20 million books in publishers' warehouses, 5 million in a single night alone when the stocks of Hutchinsons, Blackwoods, Longmans, Collins, Eyre & Spottiswoode, Ward Lock and Sampson Low were destroyed by fire.[28] By 1945, the number of new books published annually fell from a pre-war high of about 17,000 to 6,747, of which 1,246 were fiction.[29] War fears led to what Robert Hewison calls 'a grand slaughter of magazines' in 1939–40, as the *Cornhill*, *Criterion*, *Fact*, *London Mercury*, *New Stories*, *New Verse*, *Purpose*, *Seven*, *Twentieth-Century Verse*, *Wales*, *Welsh Review* and *Voice of Scotland* all ceased publication.[30] After 25 May 1940, it was also illegal to start a new magazine.[31]

The effect of these depredations on the actual reading and writing of literature, however, is more difficult to determine. Tom Harrisson, for example, flatly asserts that both the occasion and the desire for reading declined during the Blitz, a moment, Brian Howard maintained, when fewer people wished to read than at any time since 'the invention of novels'.[32] And yet, book sales actually increased, despite paper rationing, and some maintained that the long hours of fretful waiting made reading especially necessary. Sales of poetry, according to Linda Shires, increased dramatically.[33] It is certainly

26 Andrew Sinclair, *War Like a Wasp: The Lost Decade of the 'Forties* (London: Hamish Hamilton, 1989), p. 9.
27 See, for example, Morgan and Evans, *Battle for Britain*, pp. 90–1.
28 Robert Hewison, *Under Siege: Literary Life in London 1939–45* (London: Methuen, 1988), pp. 24–5, 35–7. See also Calder, *People's War*, pp. 511–12.
29 Hewison, *Under Siege*, pp. 86, 94. 30 Ibid., p. 12. 31 Ibid., p. 90.
32 Harrisson, *Living through the Blitz*, p. 103; Hewison, *Under Siege*, p. 30.
33 Linda M. Shires, *British Poetry of World War II* (London: Macmillan, 1985), p. 15.

the case that there was a loud public demand for patriotic poetry, which, if the frequent query 'Where are the war poets?' is to be credited, went largely unfulfilled.

There were, in fact, a good many quick and superficial responses to the war, Dunkirk stories published as early as the beginning of 1941, accounts of the Blitz issued well before the bombs had stopped falling.[34] There was enough of this kind of literature to move Tom Harrisson to denounce it as 'a cataract of tripe' in 1941.[35] In time, there were far more estimable literary responses to the war as well, enough certainly to give at least some substance to Andrew Sinclair's claim for this period as an especially rich one in British literary history. It is far harder to credit, however, Sinclair's claim that there was a good deal of literary experiment in this period,[36] for what seems most conspicuously missing from the roster of World War II literature is not poetry or fiction per se but the kind of radical innovation in poetry and fiction that is so characteristic of the period during and immediately after World War I. What the second war did not produce was a publication like *Blast*, in which polemical response to the war issued in typographical and formal terms that were utterly new. As Cyril Connolly put it rather disconsolately in 1940, 'I am not conscious of any particular awakening or renaissance or discovery of new forms or fresh language being made.'[37]

In short, it is rather difficult to find much literature that reflects in formal terms the considerable attack on complacency and convention constituted by the war. The works that responded to this challenge were apt to do so in ways very similar to those of *Listen to Britain*, with a paradoxical mixture of discontinuity and convention sustained, idiosyncrasy and common appeal. In poetry, there is a model to be found in H. D.'s wartime trilogy, where the very title of the first book, *The Walls Do Not Fall*, is contradicted in its opening pages: 'ruin opens / the tomb, the temple . . . the shrine lies open to the sky . . . the sealed room / open to the air.'[38] This odd sense of the ruin of the city as a necessary prelude to literary and perhaps spiritual creativity is echoed in Elizabeth Bowen's commentary on the stories in her collection *The Demon Lover*: 'Walls went down; and we felt, if not knew, each other. We all

[34] Hewison, *Under Siege*, p. 42.

[35] Quoted in Sebastian D. G. Knowles, *A Purgatorial Flame: Seven British Writers in the Second World War* (Philadelphia: University of Pennsylvania Press, 1990), p. xiii.

[36] Sinclair, *War Like a Wasp*, p. 11.

[37] Quoted in Shires, *British Poetry*, p. 17.

[38] H. D., *Trilogy* (New York: New Directions, 1998), p. 3. See the discussion by Susan H. S. Graham, '"We have a secret. We are alive": H. D.'s *Trilogy* as a Response to War', *Texas Studies in Literature and Language*, 44, 2 (2002), 165.

lived in a state of lucid abnormality.'[39] Bowen reflects here a relatively homely truth about this period of rampant homelessness, that when the physical walls went down so too did a certain 'English reserve',[40] perhaps even some of the conventional British class system. There is a good deal of dispute now about the most extreme claim, characteristic of Priestley's broadcasts, that Britain 'is being bombed and burned into democracy'.[41] But there can be little dispute that, as Angus Calder puts it, wartime experiences drew 'together people who would previously have had nothing polite to say to each other'.[42] But Bowen most resembles H. D. in looking beyond camaraderie to the 'lucid abnormality' of a time when the walls come down. Even the most documentary of wartime accounts have a certain surreal quality, since it was not uncommon for the bombs to produce crazy juxtapositions, turning the inside out by revealing the interiors behind the walls. Thus it is not at all strange that the most compelling of wartime film documentaries should have been made by a director long associated with Surrealism, or that most memorable British art of this period has a strongly Gothic quality. But Bowen and H. D. both go well beyond this sort of documentary Surrealism, to include strong elements of the mythological and the uncanny in their wartime works, mingling in each case the temptation and the threat of the otherworldly. In this way they, and a few other writers of the time, take the characteristic mixed emotions of this period and make them into enduring literature.

The difficulty of doing so seems far greater for poets, who were, for various reasons, the focus of the public demand for serviceable war literature. 'Wars', the owner of London's largest bookshop blandly observed in 1940, 'usually do create an interest in poetry.'[43] Unfortunately, the interest created by World War II seems to have been for the poetry of World War I, and not that of Wilfred Owen or Isaac Rosenberg, but rather that of Rupert Brooke. The demand for 'war poets' was essentially a demand for uplifting songs of commitment, which would have been rather difficult to produce at this time even if more poets had been willing. Military hostilities in this war were dispersed over the entire globe and were rather frequently fought out by mechanised forces that did not easily give rise to romantic identification. But the chief difference of this war was that so much of it was fought out on the everyday territory of home, where an

[39] Elizabeth Bowen, *The Demon Lover* (London: Jonathan Cape, 1945), p. 218.

[40] Calder, *People's War*, p. 178. [41] Quoted in ibid., p. 163.

[42] Ibid., p. 181. It is part of the claim of this book that such togetherness did not reach the heights claimed by Priestley.

[43] Ibid., p. 517.

act of heroism might amount to getting to work though one's flat was reduced to rubble. This is one reason why the battlefield poets of this war, Alun Lewis, Sidney Keyes, Keith Douglas, no matter what their respective merits might be as poets, add so little to the world's stock of innovative literature, because it was the civilian experience of war that was so characteristically new in this case.

If this meant that one former model of the war poet, derived from World War I, was passé, it also meant that another, derived from the Spanish Civil War, was virtually unacceptable. There was relatively little meaningful opposition to this war in any case, with C. Day Lewis's grumpy willingness to 'defend the bad against the worse' as perhaps the most committed literary critique.[44] But it must have been especially difficult to question basic war aims while most of the casualties were civilians, one's friends, family and potential readers. If, then, there were few war poets, it was because being a war poet at this time meant not just writing on a particular subject, but also finding a wholly new approach congruent with the quite different terms of this particular war.

Of course, there was an uninterrupted supply of pulp poetry, exemplified perhaps by Alice Duer Miller's *The White Cliffs*, which sold over 300,000 copies in the United States alone, and there were poets who attempted to fill the gap left by the death of Newbolt by sounding Drake's drum.[45] For a brief time, Henry Treece, Norman MacCaig and a few others were banded together as poets of the 'New Apocalypse', but the influence of the group did not last much past mid-war and the poetry produced by it turned out to have a strictly temporary appeal.[46] In some respects, the attempts of the Auden group to speak to the moment were no more successful, Stephen Spender's ode, 'Destruction and Resurrection: England Burning', being an especially embarrassing example: 'Coursers, draw on with your avenging hooves / The sullen barbarian marauder and his followers, to divide by lot / Crucified light.'[47] In fact, the characteristic tone of the Auden group, a tone of exhortation backed by what Calder calls 'large, confident generalizations',[48] seemed more seriously outmoded than any other. It may make sense, therefore, that only

[44] C. Day Lewis, 'Where Are the War Poets?' *Penguin New Writing* 3 (Harmondsworth: Penguin, 1941), p. 114.

[45] Calder, *Myth*, pp. 149, 210. Calder does grant that Miller's poem is competently written.

[46] For typical assessments, see Calder, *People's War*, p. 520 and Hewison, *Under Siege*, pp. 126–9.

[47] Stephen Spender, 'Destruction and Resurrection: England Burning', in H. S. Ingham, ed., *Fire and Water: An Anthology by Members of the NFS* (London: Lindsay Drummond, 1942), p. 14.

[48] Calder, *People's War*, p. 514.

the most loosely affiliated poet of the group seemed to thrive at this time and to contradict almost single-handed Randall Swingler's verdict that the war 'has put an end to that literary generation'.[49]

Autumn Journal, a verse diary of 1938 by Louis MacNeice, is generally considered the finest poetic version of the paralysed despair of the time around Munich, but MacNeice also wrote a fair number of shorter poems during the early war years. Through much of the Blitz, MacNeice worked for the BBC, for which he wrote a number of radio scripts promoting the theme of British resistance to the bombing.[50] He also provided a regular London Letter to the American journal *Common Sense*, in which he described, in terms quite similar to those of the Crown Unit film shorts, the aftermath of the air raids. In one of these letters, the massive fires acquire a peculiar, quite literally seductive, beauty: 'These fires were a wedding of power with a feminine sensuous beauty . . . a yellow liquid power – a kind of Virgin Birth – which is sheer destruction.'[51] Some of this same fascination grips the poems MacNeice wrote at this time, particularly 'Brother Fire', in which the fire becomes a dog, slavering and crunching at the human buildings it burns, and 'The Trolls', which personifies the fires as 'Halfwit demons who rape and slobber'.[52] Even at their most alien, however, the fires call to something familiar in the poet, until they seem both 'enemy and image of ourselves', with a destructiveness that is part of the natural world though it 'wills us dead' ('Brother Fire'). That destructiveness is part of poetry as well, and it affects these poems at the visceral level of sound itself: 'though cotted in a grille of sizzling air' ('Brother Fire'). Here MacNeice marvels at the power of the fire and mimics it at the same time, slavering and crunching his way through the consonants as if unleashed himself.

Of the other short poems written during the Blitz, only those by Roy Fuller manage to articulate a comparably complex response. Posted to North Africa as a mechanic with the Navy's Fleet Air Arm, Fuller wrote some of the most uncommon poems of the war, in that they have far more to do with the unfamiliar flora and fauna of Africa than with combat. Before being called up, though, Fuller also produced some of the most interesting poetic expressions of the People's War, including 'First Winter of War' and 'Soliloquy in an Air-Raid', the first of which remained uncollected until 1973. The common wartime

49 Quoted in Shires, *British Poetry*, p. 3.
50 Peter McDonald, *Louis MacNeice: The Poet in His Contexts* (Oxford: Clarendon Press, 1991), p. 118.
51 Quoted in Edna Longley, *Louis MacNeice: A Study* (London: Faber & Faber, 1988), p. 87.
52 Louis MacNeice, *Collected Poems* (London: Faber & Faber, 1979), pp. 196, 198.

feeling of helplessness before history is personified as an uncanny alter ego in the last stanza of 'First Winter of War':

> It is dark at twelve: I walk down the up escalator
> And see that hooded figure before me
> Ascending motionless upon a certain step.
> As I try to pass, it will stab me with a year.[53]

The almost comic urban homeliness of the metaphor of the escalator somehow makes the inevitable arrival of the Grim Reaper more horrible rather than less so. 'Soliloquy in an Air-Raid'[54] is less successful because it attempts to adapt Auden's 'Spain' to the later conditions of a different war. In fact, Fuller uses Auden's characteristic rhythms, appropriately enough, to express doubts about his own ability to meet the war in words: 'Inside the poets the words are changed to desire, / And formulations of feeling are lost in action.' So the soliloquy in an air-raid becomes the soliloquy of an air-raid, as *'the old life'* speaks *in propria persona* and the *'new life'* issues its challenges in return, very much the way Spain itself takes over Auden's propaganda poem of a few years before. But the staleness of language before the power of the air-raids is part of the subject of the poem, which manages fitfully to contradict itself by finding powerful images: 'the winter heavens, seen all day alone, assume the colour of aircraft'.

The most considerable poetic responses to the Blitz, however, were produced by older poets whose affiliation with London was quite voluntary. H. D.'s *Trilogy* was very positively received when it was first published in 1944, but it is hardly ever included in contemporary discussions of wartime poetry.[55] Yet it contains some of the most economically vivid images of blitzed London that can be found in the poetry of the period: 'another sliced wall / where poor utensils show / like rare objects in a museum'.[56] Furthermore, these intense glimpses into other private worlds are included in a more general aesthetic, wherein the destruction of boundaries frees the imagination to roam an ambiguous territory between the historical and the mythological: 'like a ghost / we entered a house through a wall; / then still not knowing / whether (like the wall) / we were there or not-there'.[57] The particular mythological realm into which the poet steps through this ruined wall is a fairly private one, and for

[53] Roy Fuller, *New and Collected Poems 1934–84* (London: Secker & Warburg, 1985), p. 34. This poem is included with those published in *The Middle of a War* (1942), though it was not in the original volume. See Neil Powell, *Roy Fuller: Writer and Society* (Manchester: Carcanet Press, 1995), p. 68.
[54] Fuller, *Collected Poems*, pp. 41–2. [55] Graham, 'H. D.'s *Trilogy*', p. 179.
[56] H. D., *Trilogy*, p. 4. [57] Ibid., p. 83.

vast tracts of its considerable length, *Trilogy* does succeed in being hermetic. But the notion that the bombs had opened a way to apocalyptic knowledge of some kind was general in the literature of this period, and there is no better description of the dual effect of the devastation than this from H. D.'s memoir, *Within the Walls*: 'though our houses and our minds have been sliced open by the attacks of the enemy overhead, that, overhead is as well the great drift of stars, and those stars found an entrance into the shattered house of life'.[58]

A similar cosmic irony is evoked in what is almost universally considered the single piece of formal literature to rival Churchill in expressing the mood of wartime Britain: T. S. Eliot's 'Little Gidding'. In fact, Eliot's terms are so close to those of Churchill that it is sometimes rather critically supposed that these are purposeful echoes. As Angus Calder suggests, '"History is now and England" chimes with Churchill's "this was their finest hour". The folding "into one party" of past factions suggests Churchill's mighty, triumphant coalition.'[59] In fact, the successive quartets added to 'Burnt Norton' throughout the war years were generally received as appropriate responses to, if not precisely appropriate comments on, particular developments in the war,[60] so that the invidious choice between a historical and a spiritual reading need not arise: they were topical precisely because they saw the events of the People's War as the sort of break in ordinary existence that opens it to the extra-ordinary. In this way, the *Quartets* also come to resemble the projects of the Crown Film Unit, wherein the dislocations of the war produce an everyday surreality, an accidental association of unlike things, that stands in formally for the forced unity of the war years.

Thus it is not simply argued in 'Little Gidding' that war has united all England in a single party, but that the British are a people 'United in the strife which divided them'.[61] This state is neither a bland uniformity nor an automatic continuity, but a paradoxical condition in which actual strife raises community to a higher, tenser level. The harmony of Bud Flanagan and Dame Myra Hess, to take the example of *Listen to Britain*, can only appear when the walls between them are blown down. The same destruction introduces the present to a ghostly version of its future, much like the 'hooded figure' that Fuller confronts on his escalator. 'See, now they vanish, / The faces and places, with the self which, as it could, loved them, / To become renewed, transfigured,

58 H. D., *Within the Walls* (Iowa City: Windhover, 1993), p. 25. Quoted in Graham, 'H. D.'s *Trilogy*', p. 194.
59 Calder, *Myth*, p. 148. 60 Knowles, *Purgatorial Flame*, p. 101.
61 T. S. Eliot, *Collected Poems, 1909–1962* (New York: Harcourt Brace, 1963), p. 206.

in another pattern.'[62] Timeless patterns only appear, in other words, when history interrupts itself and the present, with all the inescapable power of the here and now, is shifted for a moment to one side.

The most famous such moment, perhaps the most famous single moment in the literature of the Blitz, is the meeting with the 'familiar compound ghost' that occurs in Part II of 'Little Gidding'. What is most remarkable in this context, however, is how much this celebrated vision resembles other poetic confrontations with ghosts in bombed-out buildings, particularly those in *Trilogy*. This sense of the dead past superimposed with a vision of some unknown future, of 'meeting nowhere, no before and after', seems to have been very common at the time, and Eliot's somewhat grandiose superimpositions, such as the 'dark dove with the flickering tongue' that stands in for the German bombers, seem less egregious in context than when read alone. In fact, Eliot's ghostly double, with his home amid the bombed-out ruins, would be quite at home in many of the key fictional texts of this time.

Wartime experience, according to Lyndsey Stonebridge, 'both threatens and provokes narrative'.[63] The convergence of these two mutually opposed forces, the break in continuity that is virtually synonymous with war itself and the demand that narrative make some sense of things, results in a literature of short forms. The short documentary account, of the kind that appeared under the general rubric 'The Way We Live Now' in *Penguin New Writing* is the most common, and perhaps the least demanding, of these forms to appear during the war. As Rod Mengham suggests, such accounts simply set down a quick impressionistic record for later understanding, putting off the whole problem of shaping events that defy understanding.[64] Thus there was also a vogue for the short story at this time, and certain of the most interesting writers of fiction, such as William Sansom, worked only in this form. For a time at least, in the first few years of the war, it must have been impossible to write a contemporary story with a convincing conclusion, since the general sense in the UK was of life held in abeyance. All fiction, in a sense, should have been titled *Between the Acts*, or it might, as Mengham suggests, have taken its cue from *Four Quartets* and made contingency itself part of a formal pattern.

There were, of course, a great many journalistic wartime accounts, published quickly and without any self-consciousness about contingency or

62 Eliot, *Collected Poems*, p. 205.

63 Lyndsey Stonebridge, 'Bombs and Roses: the Writing of Anxiety in Henry Green's *Caught*', in Rod Mengham and N. H. Reeve, eds., *The Fiction of the 1940s: Stories of Survival* (Hampshire: Palgrave, 2001), p. 48.

64 Rod Mengham, 'Broken Glass', in Mengham and Reeve, *Fiction of the 1940s*, p. 126.

novelistic form. Diaries, true-life accounts and thinly fictionalised stories of warfare, the Blitz and the Fire Service, were published in some numbers even at the very beginning of the war.[65] Perhaps the most famous and the most considerable of these is Richard Hillary's *The Last Enemy*, which recounts Hillary's training and brief war service, during which he was seriously burned, and his convalescence during the Blitz. John Strachey's *Post D*, subtitled 'Some Experiences of an Air-Raid Warden', is just as thinly fictionalised and technically unambitious as the subtitle suggests, but the modesty of these quasi-documentary accounts is part of the polemical point they seek to make. As the main character of *Post D* maintains in his closing 'invocation to Hitler': 'You have encountered the unemphatic and the unassuming. It is not that they have done anything, nor ever can do anything, that you need fear – except one thing; they have survived.'[66] J. B. Priestley's novel of factory life in an aircraft plant, *Daylight on Saturday*, confesses the limits of its ambitions by ending with a list of the characters, 'to name only those we have met, and ignoring the thousands we do not know although we share their life and time'.[67] Simply to record the 'vast blurred stream of humanity' seems enough for fiction under the threat of obliteration by war.

Yet there were a few novels published in these years that also attempted to render the civilian experience of war in more thoroughly formal terms. One of the most disturbing of these is James Hanley's *No Directions*, published in 1943. Set entirely in a single building, the inhabitants of which are isolated from the outside world by blackout and air-raids, *No Directions* manages to make the unremitting darkness of these wartime nights almost palpable, in part by reducing its characters to disembodied voices. Often they cannot tell one another apart, which means that the hapless reader is usually even more confused. But the characters are also indistinguishable for more fundamental reasons: 'Being alone don't count any more, nobody can be alone any more, see?'[68] The camaraderie celebrated in films like *Britain Can Take It* appears here as the coercive togetherness of the air-raid shelter and the reduction of the individual to nothing before the fall of the bombs. The only courageous responses possible to this sort of anonymity are likely to seem a little crazed,

65 Hewison, *Under Siege*, pp. 42–3.

66 John Strachey, *Digging for Mrs Miller* (New York: Random House, 1941). This is the American edition of *Post D*.

67 J. B. Priestley, *Daylight on Saturday* (New York: Harper, 1943), p. 280. The following quotation comes from the same passage.

68 James Hanley, *No Directions* (London: Nicholson & Watson, 1943), p. 10. For a brief discussion of the characters, see Alan Munton, *English Fiction of World War II* (London: Faber & Faber, 1989), pp. 41–2.

like the dogged insistence of one of the characters that his huge painting must be dragged down into the basement shelter along with all the tenants.

Precisely the opposite response is to be found in another 1943 novel often praised for its picture of wartime conditions, Graham Greene's *Ministry of Fear*. Greene's characters frequently find that 'sometimes it is more difficult to make a scene than to die',[69] and the colourless protagonist of this novel really wants nothing more than to merge into the general dimness of the civilian bunkers. As is usually the case in Greene, though, accident will not allow its victims to die an inoffensive death but forces them to live an improbable life, and the role of accident in this case is played by the bombs: 'Blast is an odd thing; it is just as likely to have the appearance of an embarrassing dream as of man's serious vengeance on man, landing you naked in the street or exposing you in your bed or on your lavatory seat to the neighbours' gaze.'[70] The surreal tumbling about visited on Arthur Rowe does not kill him, but it does tear open his private life and expose it to the machinations of others in ways he finds almost as painful as death. Like Hanley, Greene explores the negative side of the wartime truism that 'nobody can be alone any more'.

If Arthur Rowe's rather indistinguishable name is meant to signify this loss of individuality in the war, its effect is uncannily compounded by another 1943 novel, in which the main character is named Richard Roe precisely for this reason. Henry Green's *Caught* is one of a number of works about the Auxiliary and National Fire Services, and it has been seen as a very close novelistic equivalent of the Crown Film Unit's *Fires Were Started*, which featured Green's fellow writer William Sansom in a key role.[71] The enforced anonymity of war service is suggested by Roe's name, the equal and opposite lack of privacy by the odd way his name combines with that of his sub-officer, Pye, to make the Greek word for fire. The ability of what Greene calls 'Blast' to open one's secrets to the public air is represented here by the coincidence that Pye's sister is incarcerated in a mental hospital for attempting to kidnap Roe's son. This book also makes the dark of the blackout into a disruptive psychic force, one so powerful that it causes Pye to doubt his own memories and almost lose his sanity. Life in the fire service is a paradoxical amalgam of rigid routine, lashed together by mindlessly niggling rules, and the utter chaos and confusion of the fires, and Pye's inability to mind the rules while under the surreal spell of the blackout ultimately undoes him. Roe, for his part, ends the novel by delivering one of the most affecting accounts of the Blitz, strained

[69] Greene, *Ministry of Fear*, p. 54. [70] Ibid., p. 23.
[71] Stonebridge, 'Bombs and Roses', p. 49.

as it is between the ordinary daily life of his sister, to whom he tells his story, and his own half-suppressed recollections, which arise in parentheses to give the lie to all his attempts to tame them into narrative. This conclusion, in which Green self-reflexively dramatises his own attempts to tell the story of the great fires, is the best fictional illustration of the paradox Stonebridge identifies, whereby the war provokes the desire to tell and disables it at the same time.

What Green and Greene add to the standard wartime accounts is a faint, unhinging intimation of guilt, which is in part the civilian's inability ever to suffer enough and in part the novelist's constitutional separation from participation in the events to be described. Surely the most complex exploration of such feelings, though, is to be found in the wartime fiction of Elizabeth Bowen. Where most war accounts concentrate on uplift, Bowen gives, in the words of Henry Reed, the 'subtly degrading effects of war . . . that feeling of the deterioration of spirit which, when the tumult, and the shouting, and the self-deception subside, is seen to be the war's residue'.[72] Bowen acquired some of her material as Eliot did, working as an air-raid warden, work that she credits with giving her stories a sensory fidelity to this peculiar time. But there is also a strongly hallucinatory quality to Bowen's wartime stories, and sometimes the presence of actual ghosts, who seem to come accusing the living of betrayal and faithlessness. In her comment on *The Demon Lover*, Bowen accounts for these hallucinations, these visitations, as defences against the war, as a spiritual element driven out of a mechanised life.[73] But some of the most vivid of the ghosts in these stories, particularly the one in 'The Demon Lover' itself, are clearly unpaid debts to the past, which suggests a much more complex relationship between realism and hallucination, fidelity and faithlessness, comradeship and guilt.

These relationships are most fully explored in Bowen's novel of this period, *The Heat of the Day*, which appeared in 1948. The main events in the fiction are very clearly synchronised with the chief turning-points of the war, in response to Bowen's stated aim of writing a present-day historical novel. But the plot of the novel is also rather haltingly doled out, with major revelations such as the treason of Robert Kelway held back and then blurted out all at once. And the main relationship in the book ends, as Bowen herself puts it, 'in mid air', as Kelway simply disappears off the roof of his lover's temporary flat.[74]

72 Quoted in Heather Bryant Jordan, *How Will the Heart Endure: Elizabeth Bowen and the Landscape of War* (Ann Arbor: University of Michigan Press, 1992), p. 130.

73 Bowen, *Demon Lover*, p. 219.

74 Elizabeth Bowen, *The Heat of the Day* (New York: Penguin, 1962), p. 301.

Kelway himself is so unconvincing a character that even his lover catches herself wondering if he might be 'fictitious'.[75]

On one level, the artificial, almost papery quality of the fiction is itself reflective of the history of the time, expressed in the way all these characters are dislodged by the Blitz and thus dislocated within their own lives. When the 'walls went down', as Bowen puts it, the ability to maintain life as a convincing story also collapsed. But the collapse of the walls also seems to make it more difficult to maintain one's loyalty. As a traitor, Kelway is, in Maud Ellmann's words, 'a "leak" in human form who peddles secrets to the enemy',[76] a breach in the human walls of citizenship and loyalty. For Stella, who loves him, he presents another kind of collapse as well, the collapse of the wall between good and evil, since he is clearly wrong though personally so appealing, while his ghostly double, the offensive Harrison, is clearly on the right side, while also being a deeply dubious personality. According to many accounts of Bowen's life, she acquired this insight too through personal service, working for the Ministry of Information writing 'secret reports' on Irish attitudes towards the war.[77] The complex of loyalties surrounding this writing must also penetrate *The Demon Lover* and *The Heat of the Day*, and not just at the level of plot, where it is often hard to distinguish between the good and the true, but also in the very material of the fiction, which frequently seems haunted by the knowledge that it is possible to write truly and faithlessly all at once.

Literature thus brings to the wartime situation a complexity of doubt that Churchill and the Crown Film Unit could not and probably should not have brought, that was not widely possible in the UK until the Allies had themselves inflicted 600,000 civilian deaths on Germany, bringing a degree of destruction to cities such as Hamburg and Dresden that did at least approach pre-war predictions. British literature has recorded its own ruins in a fair number of literary and cultural forms, and though it is hard to think of a literary example with anything like the influence of Churchill's speeches or the formal originality of the Crown Unit films, it does seem that there is in a very few literary works of this time a unique acknowledgement of the 'subtly degrading effects of the war', even on the righteous.

75 Ibid., p. 97.

76 Maud Ellmann, 'Elizabeth Bowen: the Shadowy Fifth', in Mengham and Reeve, *Fiction of the 1940s*, p. 2.

77 Karen Schneider, *Loving Arms: British Women Writing World War II* (Lexington: University Press of Kentucky, 1997), p. 75. See also Ellmann, 'Elizabeth Bowen', p. 15.

FOUR

*

POST-WAR CULTURES, 1945–1970

25

Culture, class and education

KEN HIRSCHKOP

We think of the post-war period as a rising time: rising standards of living, rising rates of literacy (fuelled by the guarantee of secondary state education until fifteen) and 'The Rise of the Provincials' – as it was called by Malcolm Bradbury – into the ranks of the cultural and intellectual elite.[1] Most of all, the post-war period appears to us as the moment when capitalism finally hits its stride. It had promised, since its inception, steady progress towards a more prosperous, more secure, and – from the mid-nineteenth century onwards – fairer society. But the progress and the assurances were always upset by periodic catastrophes it seemed unable to escape: the great depressions of the 1870s and the 1930s, the brutal inter-capitalist wars that sprung up regularly from 1800 to the middle of the twentieth century, the revolutions and murderous counter-revolutions that punctured the self-image of civilised Europe.

From 1945 onwards, things were different. Keynesian economic policies used state expenditure to avoid dramatic economic crises; the welfare state's panoply of new benefits and public institutions, by stealing socialism's thunder, kept the lid on class conflict; and the twin facts of the Common Market and the domination of Europe by the Cold War ensured there would be no further inter-capitalist armed conflict. As a result of these arrangements, British social life acquired a distinctive rhythm and feel, which structured the sense of what social life was fundamentally like for three generations. So much so that for anyone born too late to have experienced the war first-hand, the social world as such assumed: politics without periodic wars or revolutionary moments; an everyday life structured around domestic consumerism and the relative absence of absolute poverty; an emphasis on individual attainment heavily dependent on educational achievement; and communications that, as

[1] See Malcolm Bradbury, 'The Rise of the Provincials', *Antioch Review*, 16 (1956), pp. 469–77.

Raymond Williams once pointed out, made more drama available on screen each week than previous generations saw in a lifetime.[2]

For once, the steady, undramatic progress capitalism had promised seemed to be put within the reach of a majority of the population. This democratisation of progress, and the advent of a mass media – principally television and recorded music – that didn't mind who tuned in, suggested to some that class distinctions were disappearing, or that the working class was undergoing 'embourgeoisement'. It was not only that the grossest aspects of inequality were mitigated by Keynesian economics and the welfare state, it was also that 'classless' forms of experience – embodied in new consumer objects, new kinds of mass culture, new kinds of places to live, as well as new types of occupation – seemed to be emerging, such that even figures on the Left such as Richard Hoggart and Stuart Hall pointed to a 'cultural classlessness' on the horizon.[3] Part and parcel of this was the growing importance of education to the economy and to the social structure more generally. Many of the new occupational types – what's been called the 'new middle class' of managers, new-style professionals, welfare-state employees and the like – depended on formal education in a way that hadn't been true of either older manual or older middle-class forms of work (excepting the traditional professions). Formal education hadn't always had a direct tie to social power or prestige; many of the most powerful in the British polity had seen no need to attend university. Therefore this new synchronisation between social position and what could – hypothetically, at least – be learned by anyone in a classroom had significant consequences for the wider culture.

The post-war period featured a number of significant cultural initiatives, such as the creation of the Arts Council, the 1951 Festival of Britain, the expansion and transformation of the BBC's provision, and the inauguration of independent television (independent in the same sense as 'independent schools'). But the crucial and most controversial initiative was launched during the war: the Education Act of 1944, which guaranteed free state education until fifteen (albeit in a tiered, socially divisive school system), and brought the previously independent religious and grammar schools into the state system. It is hardly an accident that T. S. Eliot's *Notes Toward the Definition of Culture*, an otherwise assured disquisition on the social arrangements best suited to the maintenance

2 Raymond Williams, 'Drama in a Dramatised Society: an Inaugural Lecture' (Cambridge University Press, 1975), p. 5.

3 Richard Hoggart, 'Speaking to Each Other', in Norman MacKenzie, ed., *Conviction* (London: MacGibbon & Kee, 1958), pp. 121–38; Stuart Hall, 'A Sense of Classlessness', *Universities and Left Review*, 5 (1958), pp. 26–32.

of culture, loses its composure precisely in the chapter entitled 'Notes on Education and Culture', which one otherwise admiring reviewer fairly described as a mere rationalisation of prejudices.[4] Eliot's book, published in 1948, the year in which he received the Nobel Prize for Literature, staked the health and well-being of culture on the preservation of classes. Sometimes, as in that final chapter, this was expressed as mere contempt for the idea of equality of opportunity. But the central argument of the text was more nuanced, if equally backward-looking.

To Eliot it seemed that the threat to social class in Britain came not from social revolution, but from the new centrality of education. Education replaced the idea of inherited power and prestige with the concept of the trained expert and the elite, who ruled by virtue of superior talent, honed and proven by formal educational achievement. While an educated elite had its uses and perhaps represented a useful freshening up of the old class apparatus, such elites were only appropriate when the object in view was something amenable to rational planning. 'Culture', however, 'is the one thing that we cannot deliberately aim at' and attempts to improve or build upon it by means of education or the creation of quasi-state institutions were doomed.[5]

Failure to acknowledge this flowed from a confusion about the meaning of the term 'culture' itself, Eliot argued. For 'culture' could refer to the development of an individual, a group or class, or a whole society, and the kind of thing it referred to in each case was different. In particular, the high culture that Eliot saw as the patrimony and responsibility of the upper classes had to be distinguished from the culture of the society as a whole: the former was conscious, and embodied in the usual array of finer arts; the latter was unconscious, consisting of the beliefs that informed the unconscious, intuitive behaviour of people within the society. Culture as a specific field, the arts traditionally understood, was therefore related to but distinct from culture as – in a phrase that later becomes crucial – 'a whole way of life'. In truth, it seems Eliot thought of the latter as effectively a series of rituals essential to the identity of a people, which he summoned up in a notorious and hackneyed list of English tribal rites: Derby Day, Henley Regatta, Cowes, the twelfth of August, FA cup finals, and the rest.

Eliot thought the cultural policy of the post-war state was confused on this issue; it assumed that to bring culture into the ambit of the masses it

[4] T. S. Eliot, *Notes Toward the Definition of Culture* (London: Faber & Faber, 1948); the review is Raymond Williams, 'Second Thoughts I – T. S. Eliot on Culture', *Essays in Criticism*, 6, 3 (1956), p. 307.

[5] T. S. Eliot, *Notes*, p. 19.

had to make them participate in the essentially class-bound culture enjoyed by the minority, rather than letting them enjoy their rituals in peace. Yet the real danger was not a mass desertion of cup finals in favour of poetry readings – the Education Act specified that only one-quarter of all secondary students would be able to attend the academically orientated grammar schools – but a new minority, an educated elite whose cultural capital was acquired through conscious learning and research. However well educated and elitist this talented minority might be, it would, in the end

> consist solely of individuals whose only common bond will be their professional interest: with no social cohesion, with no social continuity. They will be united only by a part, and that the most conscious part, of their personalities.[6]

Elites could bring new ideas into the cultivated world of the propertied classes, but these consciously developed innovations would have to be digested into an intuitively held and transmitted way of life. Because culture was both conscious invention and unconscious behaviour, it could only be effectively transmitted only by 'groups of families persisting, from generation to generation, each in the same way of life'.[7] That a 'whole way of life' was here transmuted into the 'same way of life' should come as no surprise. In a famous overblown phrase Eliot claimed that making class the guarantor of culture ensured 'piety towards the dead, however obscure, and a solicitude for the unborn, however remote':[8] this was his way of reminding us what he had argued some forty years earlier in 'Tradition and the Individual Talent' – that culture stands as a patterning above the vagaries of historical change, incapable of 'progress'.[9] In this sense, culture and education had distinctive, irreconcilable relations to time, which is why, in the end, the educated would have to give way to the continuity ensured by great families.

An argument against progress as such was bound to fail in the post-war world, and Eliot's passed into the history books as soon as it was made. But the terms of his case remained influential, in large part because they depended on and echoed familiar assumptions about the relationship between culture and class. Eliot had wanted to show that culture depended on the maintenance of class; but his argument turns equally on the idea that class depends on the maintenance of culture. One could easily argue that members of a political, cultural or economic elite are simply ruling-class people who have taken an

[6] Ibid., p. 47. [7] Ibid., p. 48. [8] Ibid., p. 44.

[9] See 'Tradition and the Individual Talent', in *Selected Prose of T. S. Eliot* (London: Faber & Faber, 1975), p. 38. The exact claim is that 'the whole of the literature of Europe from Homer . . . has a simultaneous existence and composes a simultaneous order'.

alternative route to the same destination. But Eliot, in keeping with his source, the theory of elites developed by Karl Mannheim, insisted that the essence of class is *inherited* authority and privilege. And what had to be inherited – because it could only be passed on via the family – was a web of unconscious beliefs and behaviours, solidified in rituals and made conscious in art. Class required property, but its essence in these terms was cultural and moral.

1948 was also the year in which the dying George Orwell published his last major work, the novel *Nineteen Eighty-Four*. Orwell's political and social beliefs could hardly be more distant from Eliot's, and he was in every respect a shrewder and more intelligent social critic. His socio-cultural commentary, however, shares an architecture with Eliot's, and they are united by a conception of culture that leaves education to one side. In Orwell's long wartime essay 'The Lion and the Unicorn', Eliot's tripartite structure of ruling class, English mass and new elite recurs, albeit with a different political colouring.[10]

Orwell was just as keen as Eliot to identify the rituals or experiences that define a popular English way of life, and, though he was more systematic in his enumeration of English traits (hostility to philosophy, respect for the law, gentleness and lack of militarism, devotion to private liberty, etc.), he was likewise partial to evocative lists of distinctively English objects and experiences: 'solid breakfasts and gloomy Sundays, smoky towns and winding roads, green fields and red pillar-boxes'.[11] This timeless England sits beneath the veneer of social change:

> In whatever shape England emerges from the war, it will be deeply tinged with the characteristics that I have spoken of earlier. The intellectuals who hope to see it Russianised or Germanised will be disappointed. The gentleness, the hypocrisy, the thoughtlessness, the reverence for law and the hatred of uniforms will remain, along with the suet puddings and the misty skies.[12]

This England ('England your England') finds expression throughout the range of social activity, and though its constituency is primarily the working-class majority, it encompasses large sections of the new middle classes as well. In relation to this culture the ruling class are not so much an active opposition – they in fact share most of these 'English' traits – as an obstacle. Orwell's famous characterisation of the English polity as a 'family with the wrong members

[10] George Orwell, *The Lion and the Unicorn – Socialism and the English Genius* (London: Secker & Warburg, 1941); quotations are from the version published in *The Complete Works of George Orwell, Vol. XII: A Patriot After All 1940–41*, ed. Peter Davison (London: Secker & Warburg, 1998). Davison's editorial note points out that in the second half of 1949 Orwell named this text as one of four works he did not wish to see reprinted.

[11] Ibid., p. 393. [12] Ibid., pp. 408–9.

in control' condemned the ruling class for holding England back.[13] The facts of class were grim, but they were also antiquated, and the point of socialism would be to create political arrangements that would fit a culture that had evolved beneath it. 'The past is fighting the future', Orwell claimed, and in this context social revolution is no more than 'the task of bringing the real England to the surface'. 'By revolution', he said, 'we become more ourselves, not less.'[14]

There was, of course, one group outside this charmed circle: the intellectuals, condemned not only for the wrong-headedness of their policies, but also for their cosmopolitan distance from the English virtues. The 'Europeanised' intelligentsia are the negative, empty image of the English people: their 'sniggering . . . at patriotism and physical courage', their 'persistent effort to chip away English morale' threatens domestic resistance to the German war effort.[15] Orwell was notoriously splenetic about the organised Left in Britain, and he reserved his most vicious language for them. But the heart of his argument is not about necessary political change, for in most respects the programme described in 'The Lion and the Unicorn' and elsewhere (nationalisation of industry and finance, progressive decolonisation and so on) coincides with that of the political Left. The adrenalin-producing difference is that the Left intelligentsia regards these political changes as the point of revolution, whereas Orwell sees them as a means to bring society up to date with its evolving culture.[16]

English politics on the surface; English culture below. But how could one reasonably claim that class as a social principle was antiquated, a merely political superstructure, when it so definitively and comprehensively shaped the everyday culture of English life? The answer was the appearance in England of something new: 'people of indeterminate social class':

> The place to look for the germs of the future England is in the light-industry areas and along the arterial roads. In Slough, Dagenham, Barnet, Letchworth, Hayes – everywhere, indeed, on the outskirts of great towns – the old pattern is gradually changing into something new . . . There are wide gradations of income, but it is the same kind of life that is being lived at different levels, in labour-saving flats or council houses, along the concrete roads and in the

[13] Ibid., p. 401. [14] Ibid., p. 432. [15] Ibid., p. 428.

[16] In this respect, Orwell embodies a strikingly contradictory version of what Francis Mulhern has dubbed 'metaculture'. The latter is culture which invokes itself as a generality in order to make a claim for a social authority greater than that of politics; see Mulhern, *Culture/Metaculture* (London and New York: Routledge, 2000). Orwell was, by his own definition, a political writer. At the same time, he made culture the bulwark of progressive socialist politics, in some sense against politics itself.

naked democracy of the swimming-pools. It is a rather restless, cultureless life, centring round tinned food, *Picture Post*, the radio and the internal combustion engine.[17]

This new group – composed of 'the technicians and the higher-paid skilled workers, the airmen and their mechanics, the radio experts, film producers, popular journalists and industrial chemists' – would play a large role in post-war cultural debate, and new suburbs like Slough and Surbiton were taken as signifiers of a way of life indecipherable in the old terms of class analysis. But the 'class that isn't a class' and the places it inhabited were interesting precisely because they seemed to demand a new method of study.

When Orwell said that 'the old distinction between Right and Left broke down when *Picture Post* was first published', he was claiming that English society had subtly but comprehensively reorganised itself.[18] To understand 'the condition of England' in the 1930s he had gone to Wigan Pier, where he lived, spoke with, and observed the industrial working class. By the 1940s he was convinced that the newsagent was the best place from which to scan English culture, because '[p]robably the contents of these shops is the best available indication of what the mass of the English people really feels and thinks'.[19] Class had depended on dramatic distinctions in habitat, leisure, manners and clothing; the new classlessness softened the edges of these while offering a classless mass culture in its place. The inhabitants of Slough and Dagenham, rather than the leaders of the politicised working class, would carry English culture into the future.

In his political criticism Orwell could make this case with a degree of optimism: the fiction told a darker story. George Bowling, the insurance-selling hero of *Coming Up for Air* (1939), lives in precisely the sort of mass-produced suburb that was redrawing the class landscape of England. Equally distant from the antiquated culture of old England and the political rhetoric of the Left Book Club, Bowling's reminiscences of an older, different England coexist uneasily in the novel with foreboding about the war with Germany waiting just over the horizon. At the conclusion of *Coming Up for Air*, Bowling decides to travel to that different England by car rather than in his mind, in the shape of a visit to the place of his childhood, Lower Binfield. In this case, of course, the past turns out not to be another country, but the same modernising England Bowling already inhabits: he finds 'Lower Binfield swollen into a kind of

17 Orwell, 'The Lion and the Unicorn', p. 408.
18 Ibid., p. 418.
19 George Orwell, 'Boys' Weeklies', in *Inside the Whale and Other Essays* (London: Victor Gollancz, 1940). Cited from publication in *The Complete Works, Vol. XII*, p. 88.

Dagenham', prone to a kind of mass cultural levelling, and when his visit ends with the accidental dropping of an RAF bomb, he's forced to the sober acknowledgement that 'the old life's finished, and to go about looking for it is a waste of time'.[20] The plotting of the novel suggests this change is forced and violent, the invasion of a way of life for which Bowling feels a spontaneous affection by the 'new kind of men from eastern Europe, the stream-lined men who think in slogans and talk in bullets'.[21] At a deeper level, however, it is not Fascism that overwhelms England, but the kind of modernity – undramatic, technically advanced, 'classless' – represented by Bowling himself, a modernity that has transformed sleepy Lower Binfield and for which the bomb provides only punctuation.

A wartime later, and Orwell is writing about the classless Winston Smith in *Nineteen Eighty-Four*, who begins with a distrust of political rhetoric at least the equal of Bowling's, and ends up thinking in slogans and ready to take the bullet from Big Brother. Like Bowling, Smith is drawn to reminiscence of an earlier and happier life and at first glance he shares the middling decency that defines his precursor. But *Nineteen Eighty-Four* plots a different, far simpler social structure onto the future of England. The new class of office-workers, now all 'employed' as cogs in a boundaryless state bureaucracy, dominates the novel entirely, with contrast provided only by the mass of the 'proles', the latter furnishing an island on which the entire past of England – all the rituals, objects and attitudes beloved of Orwell – has been marooned. In 'The Lion and the Unicorn', Orwell had prophesied the emergence of English men and women who would maintain recognisably English cultural virtues while shedding the visible signs of class distinction. But in *Nineteen Eighty-Four* the classless Smith's sceptical Englishness is no match for the stream-lined men of his time. Engaged in the mass production of culture himself (his job is to rewrite the past when the Party demands it), he has only memories and individual dissent to anchor his resistance to the pervasive re-educational efforts of the all-powerful Party. The kind of culture that could serve as a bulwark against totalitarianism is found only among the proles, who, like the people from the past Smith recalls, are still 'governed by private loyalties which they did not question'.[22] Echoing

[20] George Orwell, *Coming up for Air* (London: Secker & Warburg, 1939). Quotations from the edition published as *The Complete Works, Vol. VII: Coming up for Air* (London: Secker & Warburg, 1986), pp. 222, 237.

[21] Ibid., pp. 168–9.

[22] George Orwell, *Nineteen Eighty-four: A Novel* (London: Secker & Warburg, 1949). Quotations from the edition published as *The Complete Works, Vol. IX: Nineteen Eighty-Four* (London: Secker & Warburg, 1987), p. 172.

Eliot's *Notes, Nineteen Eighty-Four* represents culture as depending on 'groups of families persisting, from generation to generation, each in the same way of life', with the difference that these groups of families live on council estates and drop their aitches. Early on, Winston Smith is compelled to acknowledge that 'the future belonged to the proles'.[23] In which case – given that the working class is here defined by its solid, unbending attachment to an antiquated way of life – there is no future in the qualitative sense at all.

As it turned out, men from Eastern Europe did arrive in England during and after the war, but they were of a type Orwell welcomed rather than feared. When the Hungarian Arthur Koestler announced his arrival in the United Kingdom with the publication of *Darkness at Noon* (1940), Orwell was quick to contrast the political shrewdness of continental Europeans with the blindness of his compatriots. In an essay devoted to Koestler written in 1944, Orwell concluded that the only political writing in English that was worth anything had been translated from a continental European language.[24] The reason was quite simple: these writers had experienced Fascism or Communism at first hand – 'In Europe, during the past decade and more, things have been happening to middle-class people which in England do not even happen to the working class.'[25]

Britain was already host to a substantial group of émigré Central and East European intellectuals (Isaiah Berlin, Bronislaw Malinowski, Ludwig Wittgenstein, Melanie Klein, to name just a few), who had leavened the national culture with theoretical acumen and continental faith in the intellectual vocation. The war brought others (Koestler, Karl Popper, Ernest Gellner, Isaac Deutscher), with varying political sympathies. Orwell's comment if anything underplayed the difference in perspective the émigrés brought with them. Most were Jewish, and had left on account of rising anti-Semitism and a narrowing sense of what a 'national' culture amounted to. All had seen, or could see coming, the direct repression of cultural life by the state, rather than by the barriers posed by class. Their presence added more than a dash of cosmopolitanism to English debates about culture and class: it focused attention on the roles of the state and of the 'engaged' intellectual, and introduced geopolitics into the heart of discussion.

23 Ibid., p. 229.

24 Orwell, 'Arthur Koestler', in *Critical Essays* (London: Secker & Warburg, 1946). Quotations below are from the edition in *The Complete Works, Vol. XVI: I Have Tried to Tell the Truth* (London: Secker & Warburg, 1998), pp. 392–402.

25 Ibid., p. 393.

As one of the victorious Allies, and the home of a native social democratic tradition hostile to Communism, England was assigned a key role in the developing Cold War. The founding and funding of the new intellectual journal *Encounter*, with Stephen Spender as editor, by the US Central Intelligence Agency was only the most egregious of attempts to ensure European intellectuals were won to the US side. *The God that Failed*, a collection of essays edited by the Labour politician Richard Crossman, united native English hostility to Soviet Communism with testimony from European writers who had seen the error of their formerly Communist ways: its contributors included Spender, Koestler, Ignazio Silone and André Gide.[26]

In the minds of many, however, polemic such as this was only one element of the broader debate that the struggle against Fascism in Europe had engendered, a debate on the role of 'commitment' in literature and culture and the responsibility of intellectuals. Here the leading figure was, as in continental Europe, Jean-Paul Sartre, whose works were rapidly translated after the war (*What is Literature?*, his most explicit statement of the issues, was available in English from 1950, a mere two years after its publication in France).[27] The engagement – or lack of it – with the struggle against Fascism and Stalinism had posed political choices that were irreducible to questions of class allegiance, and for writers keen to establish and enhance the presence of the working class culturally, they provided a sharp reminder of the ambiguity of the state in modern society.

But although Sartre (and Albert Camus) were notable and influential, the more profound opening to the continent depended on the rise of Khrushchev in the Soviet Union, the repression of workers in Berlin in 1953 and the invasion of Hungary by the Soviet Union in 1956. These events effectively split the Communist movement and separated most of its most prominent intellectuals from Party discipline. What would become the New Left drew much of its intellectual firepower from socialist writers who felt little or no allegiance to Stalinist definitions of commitment, and from the 1950s onwards it drew inspiration from the works of continental socialist and Communist intellectuals, now available in translation. The chance encounter of a wartime émigré with a translator led to the English publication of Georg Lukács's *Studies in European Realism* as early as 1950, but what has proved to be in retrospect the most important translation – of selections made from Antonio Gramsci's

[26] Richard Crossman, ed., *The God that Failed: Six Studies in Communism* (London: Hamish Hamilton, 1950).

[27] Jean-Paul Sartre, *What is Literature?*, trans. Bernard Frechtman (London: Methuen, 1950).

prison notebooks – had to wait until 1957, after the Khrushchevite thaw had loosened the Communist apparatus.[28]

Continental writing could, of course, provide only one element of a new cultural orientation: the more significant part had to come from a renewed attempt to establish the cultural pertinence of the English working class. Richard Hoggart, educated at university before the war, and an adult-education tutor after it, had noticed the new 'cultural classlessness' that attracted Orwell's attention, although he nominated *Woman*, not the *Picture Post* as 'the first truly classless journal of the new Britain'.[29] Unlike Orwell, however, Hoggart was in essence a member of this new social stratum, having grown up in a working-class family in the north of England and ended up as staff for the expansion in educational provision. He was therefore aware, in a way Orwell was not, that although 'all classes are on the move', 'one class is most strikingly moving, emotionally and physically'.[30] But that class was not therefore replaced by the new squadrons of technicians and white-collar workers living in the new suburbs ringing London: it moved, and carried its cultural baggage with it. Hoggart was as interested as Orwell in what was on the shelves at the newsagent's, but he did not identify the contents of what was there with the consciousness of the new class. The new mass culture, embodied in new magazines and papers, recorded music, and a culture of milk bars and youth sociability, was aimed at a working class which had native cultural resources of its own. The result was therefore an amalgamation, and one not without conflict, of older and newer structures.

Hoggart's analysis of this restructuring was initially to be called *The Abuses of Literacy*, and it was to consist of a critical discussion of the contents of the new media and their reception by an 'older' English working class.[31] But Hoggart could not count on an audience which had the same experience of class mobility as himself and could draw on his knowledge of certain forms of working-class culture. He was therefore asked to produce a first half which would describe and analyse this culture for readers more or less unaware of it. In the end, the book – retitled *The Uses of Literacy* at the behest of

[28] Georg Lukács, *Studies in European Realism*, trans. Edith Bone (London: Hillway Publishing, 1950). The émigré was Chimen Abramsky, later Professor of Jewish Studies at University College London; Antonio Gramsci, *'The Modern Prince' and Other Writings*, trans. Louis Marks (London: Lawrence & Wishart, 1957). On the translation of Gramsci into English and the UK, see David Forgacs, 'Gramsci and Marxism in Britain', *New Left Review*, 176 (1989), pp. 70–88.

[29] Hoggart, 'Speaking to Each Other', pp. 121, 122.

[30] Ibid., p. 122.

[31] Hoggart, *A Sort of Clowning: Life and Times, Volume II, 1940–1959* (London: Chatto & Windus, 1990), pp. 140–5.

the publisher's lawyers – consisted of a passionate rendition of working-class culture and all its virtues and vices, and an account of the forces besieging it from the newagent's.[32]

This was no longer a listing of characteristic objects and scenes, in the manner of Eliot and Orwell. Hoggart instead sought to describe 'one fairly homogeneous group of working-class people' and tried to 'evoke the atmosphere, the quality, of their lives by describing their setting and their attitudes'.[33] The effort was self-confessedly autobiographical and presented as almost a memoir in the present tense. A chapter called 'Landscape with Figures' set out the family home and sketched in the neighbourhood. Those that followed sought to describe typical people, places and activities (club-singing, for example), as well as the typical structure of a working-class life for men and women. The prose style certainly owed much to the novelistic tradition Hoggart had been trained to analyse, and this was emphasised by the presentation of class as a moral–geographical category: it pointed to the way of life of people living in a particular area and the attitudes embodied in it. Work therefore appeared as a brutal necessity and a source of income, but not as part of the geography itself; conversely, the class itself appeared as a social group rather than as something made conscious and institutionalised in trade unions or friendly societies.

But the book's most significant novelistic feature was its strong aestheticising impulse. Hoggart had been trained as a Leavisite literary critic, and he acquired that tradition's stylistic and moral preferences. But the Leavises' case rested on the distinction between a self-consciously minority culture and the mass civilisation beyond it. Hoggart's masterstroke was to write about the class he came from in terms that would evoke the 'rightness' and organic quality of its own mode of life. A typical example:

> There are varieties of light he [a working-class child] will know: the sun forcing its way down as far as the ground floor windows on a very sunny afternoon, the foggy grey of November over the slates and chimneys, the misty evenings of March when the gangs congregate in the watery yellow light of the kicked and scratched gas lamp. Or the smells: the beer-and-Woodbine smell of the men on Saturday nights, the cheap-powder-and-cream smell of his grown-up sisters, fish-and-chips, the fresh starchiness of new clothes at Whitsun, the pervasive aura of urine – dog, cat and human. Most attractive of all, a scene with noise, light and smell – between eleven and twelve on a Sunday morning, when all doors are open and all steps occupied; the roast beef gives out its flavour from almost every house, the wirelesses mix their noises with each

32 Richard Hoggart, *The Uses of Literacy* (London: Chatto & Windus, 1957).

33 Ibid., p. 19.

> other, you can hear families talking or laughing or quarrelling. But there is little quarrelling just now; over almost all is a sense of ease, recreation and good fortune to come.[34]

Eliot had said whereas the ordinary man 'falls in love, or reads Spinoza, and these two experiences have nothing to do with each other, or with the noise of the typewriter or the smell of cooking; in the mind of the poet these experiences are always forming new wholes'.[35] Hoggart underscores the point, by presenting working-class life as a balanced concatenation of sounds and smells, which fit together as a way of life with a 'peculiarly gripping wholeness' and dignity.[36]

This aesthetic intention shaped the very attitudes Hoggart sought to portray. Orwell, in keeping with his political interests, had described the attitudes of the common people in terms of militarism, respect for law and so forth. Hoggart, however, wanted to preserve what he felt was the distinctively concrete shape of working-class life and its concomitant distance from public, political ideologies; a controversial position, which I discuss below. The attitudes he extracts from the class he examines are therefore named in their own idiom: 'putting up with things', ''aving a good time while y'can', 'we are all in the same boat', and so on. By embedding attitudes directly into a scene and an immediate style of speech, Hoggart made it less easy to endow them with political significance. But it's likely that the ultimate aim of this procedure was to preserve the literary qualities of the way of life he was celebrating, stressing it as a concrete whole in which even spoken commitments could not be abstracted as ideologies.

What followed was an account of the assault on this way of life by the commercial culture of the 1950s. The print media, music, television and social culture aimed at Orwell's indefinable class was striving to twist and distort the attitudes Hoggart had described and, in the process, wrench apart a culture that made sense on its own terms. Working-class tolerance became 'anything goes': 'not so much a charitable allowance for human frailty and the difficulties of ordinary lives, as a weakness, a ceaseless leaking-away of the will-to-decide on matters outside the immediately touchable orbit'.[37] Group pride in working-class life became an absurd apotheosis of the 'little man' and unthinking hatred of highbrows ('made to seem big because everything is scaled down to his measure').[38] 'Living in the present' became 'progressivism', an obsession with youth and up-to-dateness, which tends naturally to the 'shiny barbarism' of

[34] Ibid., p. 56. [35] T. S. Eliot, 'The Metaphysical Poets', in *Selected Prose*, p. 64.
[36] Hoggart, *The Uses of Literacy*, p. 59. [37] Ibid., p. 147. [38] Ibid., p. 150.

the new commodity world.[39] These new attitudes were promoted by both the substance of the new mass culture and its form, which seemed to Hoggart abstracted from the routines of working-class life. The separateness of the cinema and the milk bar, their decoupling as dedicated consumer practices, was part and parcel of a new way of life, bereft of the moral resources of the old.

Hoggart's principal point, however, was that one could not understand what English people really think and feel by reading the magazines they read: working-class culture, in the form he described it, had a resistant solidity, a stubbornness and rootedness that prevented the wholesale adoption of new 'Modernist' attitudes. But in characterising the struggle as resistance to an alien force, Hoggart sundered working-class culture itself from the educational reforms that were bent on transforming it. Culture in his description depended on being embedded in a way of life that, however complex and formal, was dependable and reproducible. The problem was not that Hoggart left no room for the working class to advance, but that he had made it impossible in principle for their culture to advance. That working-class culture was entirely disjoint, in form and substance, from formal education was underlined by what is in many ways the most striking and well-written chapter in the book, 'Unbent Springs: a Note on the Uprooted and the Anxious', which detailed the acute isolation suffered by scholarship boys who went on to university. Hoggart's experience would seem to have borne out Eliot's argument: the scholarship boy who enters the elite without belonging to its 'native' class finds himself with knowledge and technique, but no culture.

Hoggart's book generated a swift and excited reaction. This was in large part because Hoggart was able to present working-class life as a complex and stylised whole, but also because he had addressed the new rhythm and culture of everyday life in a direct, if defensive way. The principal criticism levelled then and since was that Hoggart had, despite his best efforts, romanticised the earlier form of working-class culture. Like every tale of decline and degeneration, the old had an integrity, while the new appeared merely disparate and fragmentary. The most detailed and significant critique of Hoggart had to wait for the second wave of the feminist movement and for Carolyn Steedman in particular, whose *Landscape for a Good Woman* took direct aim at Hoggart's sharp distinction between culture and consumer desire.[40] The desire for things after the war

[39] Ibid., pp. 157–60.
[40] Carolyn Steedman, *Landscape for a Good Woman: A Story of Two Lives* (London: Virago, 1986).

could not, she argued, be interpreted merely as an affront to a solidaristic working-class culture. For women in particular, often the explicit addressees of the call for a new, commodity-led domesticity, the distinction between family and economics was not as clear-cut, not a simple binary of value and desire, as Hoggart had led us to believe.

At the time, however, the most significant response came from the emerging New Left, which immediately recognised the significance of the debate Hoggart had opened up. In an essay published in the collection *Conviction*, one year after *Uses*, Hoggart made the question of the new culture more open. Rather than bemoan the anonymity of the mass media, he instead asked his readers to consider the new 'cultural classlessness' seriously, as a possible route to a better society than the one that had existed before. Even a neutral analysis, however, would not be easy. 'It is easier', Hoggart remarked, 'to see a hole in a shoe than to assess the outlook encouraged by the television set which the emancipated worker has bought and turned his eyes to.'[41] But this engagement with the changes wrought by contemporary culture was precisely what intrigued the writers gathered around the newly founded *Universities and Left Review*. Although explicitly political in orientation, the editors of the journal aimed for 'a principled critique of the quality of contemporary life'.[42] They accordingly devoted a substantial part of their second issue to a symposium on *The Uses of Literacy*.[43]

The lead review was by Raymond Williams, like Hoggart the child of a working-class family who had gone to university and then become a tutor in adult education. Hoggart and Williams were to become the twin inspirations for a new critique of contemporary life; though they did not meet for many years, they entered into a dialogue in print by reviewing each other's publications.[44] Williams's piece in the critical symposium, 'Working-Class Culture', was in many respects a preview or précis of his own *Culture and Society 1780–1950*, the second blast of the new cultural criticism.[45] In the main

41 Hoggart, 'Speaking to Each Other', pp. 123–4.

42 'Editorial', *Universities and Left Review*, 4 (1958), p. 3.

43 *Universities and Left Review*, 1, 2 (1957), pp. 29–40. It included critical reviews by Raymond Williams, Alan Lovell, John McLeish and Gwyn Illtyd Lewis.

44 See Raymond Williams, 'Fiction and the Writing Public' (a review of *The Uses of Literacy*), *Essays in Criticism*, 7, 4 (1957), pp. 422–8; and Richard Hoggart, 'An Important Book' (a review of *Culture and Society 1780–1950*), *Essays in Criticism*, 9, 2 (1959), pp. 171–9. Responses to Hoggart's review, and a reply from Williams, were published as 'A Critical Forum: Culture and Society', *Essays in Criticism*, 9, 4 (1959), pp. 425–37.

45 Raymond Williams, 'Working-Class Culture', *Universities and Left Review*, 1, 2 (1957), pp. 29–32.

he welcomed Hoggart's detailed, first-hand description of working-class life. But Williams saw risks in trying to define working-class culture and risks in Hoggart's project, and the risks took him to the centre of the argument he was about to make at length in *Culture and Society*.

Since 1950 Williams had been looking at the history of 'The Idea of Culture' (as he named his first article on the topic).[46] In examining this history, he discovered that the concept had begun with a general frame of reference, indicating the process of cultivating human abilities and values. In the nineteenth century the term had become the lever for a critique of the new industrial society, the means by which social thinkers could make a qualitative assessment of the striking changes before them. Over the course of the century, however, the reference to a total critique was lost, and the word became a term referring only to specialised kinds of activity – commonly known as the arts – which were held to embody values necessarily absent from the society at large. As a result, 'culture' referred both to a 'whole way of life' in a fairly neutral anthropological sense (adopted by Eliot) and to a range of specialised and specially valued activities.

If one judged 'working-class culture' according to the latter definition, it would be found wanting, for people 'excluded from the mainstream by the pressures of a class society' would not produce their share of fine art.[47] Perhaps more damagingly, this way of thinking assumed that 'mainstream' literary culture could be comfortably identified as bourgeois, which Williams maintained it was not. To define the working class in more anthropological terms, however, risked cutting it off from the creative and critical elements of the ideal in exactly the way Eliot had done. Hoggart had detailed working-class life anthropologically, but had endowed it with value by pressing it into the organicist mould of Eliot's literary tradition.

At the same time, Williams resisted the argument that modern commercial culture was the culture of the working class. For one thing, the techniques of mass culture, which required large capital resources 'passed naturally into the hands of the commercial bourgeoisie, so that their use became, and has remained, characteristically capitalist in methods of production and distribution'.[48] For another, the new commercial culture was, as Hoggart and Orwell had both recognised, classless in many respects, aiming to enlist middle- and upper-class consumers as eagerly as working-class ones.

[46] Raymond Williams, 'The Idea of Culture', *Essays in Criticism*, 3, 3 (1953), pp. 239–66.
[47] Williams, 'Working-Class Culture', p. 29. [48] Ibid., p. 30.

Published at the same time as his review of Hoggart, Williams's *Culture and Society* laid out the solution in terms worth quoting in full:

> We may now see what is properly meant by 'working-class culture'. It is not proletarian art, or council houses, or a particular use of language; it is, rather, the basic collective idea, and the institutions, manners, habits of thought and intentions which proceed from this. Bourgeois culture, similarly, is the basic individualist idea and the institutions, manners, habits of thought and intentions which proceed from that. In our culture as a whole, there is both a constant interaction between these ways of life and an area which can properly be described as common to or underlying both. The working class, because of its position, has not, since the Industrial Revolution, produced a culture in the narrower sense. The culture which it has produced, and which it is important to recognize, is the collective democratic institution, whether in the trade unions, the cooperative movement or a political party. Working-class culture, in the stage through which it has been passing, is primarily social (in that it has created institutions) rather than individual (in particular intellectual or imaginative work). When it is considered in context, it can be seen as a very remarkable creative achievement.[49]

The problem of working-class culture could only be solved by returning to the origins of the 'the idea of culture'. Culture had become a term of minority contempt in the writing of Leavis and Eliot, but this had to be understood as only the faint and distorted echo of the term's original, critical social application. In the 'Conclusion' to *Culture and Society*, from which the above is drawn, the working class is cast as the critical force that will revive the broad aspirations of the 'culture and society' tradition. But to recognise this one had to make fundamental adjustments in the term's semantic force-field.

In particular, one had to undo the damage done by the split between the anthropological sense of culture as a whole way of life, and the use of the term to designate specifically artistic activity. In the phrase Williams coined (and used as a title for another article of 1958), 'culture is ordinary': 'both the most ordinary common meanings and the finest individual meanings'.[50] When the creative, active element of culture was narrowed to the individualised efforts of writers and artists, the social side of it was maintained, but only in the form of mutely accepted, unthinkingly repeated values and rituals. The trick was

[49] Raymond Williams, *Culture and Society 1780–1950* (London: Chatto & Windus, 1958), p. 327.

[50] Raymond Williams, 'Culture is Ordinary', in MacKenzie, *Conviction*, p. 75.

to understand a 'whole way of life' as itself developmental, the progressive discovery and consolidation of meanings, and to acknowledge that the project of 'culture' could therefore be realised only if the way of life itself was radically democratised.

In conversation with Hoggart, Williams suggested that his belief in a 'high working-class tradition' of culture-as-politics stemmed from a family and neighbourhood devoted to education and political activism with equal enthusiasm.[51] The autobiographical opening of essays like 'Culture is Ordinary' – '[t]o grow up in that family was to see the shaping of minds: the learning of new skills, the shifting of new relationships, the emergence of different language and ideas' – lent credence to that interpretation.[52] The autobiographical rhetoric, however, disguises a deeper shift. For Williams describes education not only as a fundamental support of culture but as the model for its structure: in his writings, culture is educational in form and intention, both 'the slow learning of shapes, purposes and meanings', and 'the making of new observations, comparisons and meanings . . . which are offered and tested'.[53] What is passed on 'from generation to generation' of the working class is a cultural tradition, but one defined by an inner impulse to move forward in an open, progressive, self-transforming manner.

Working-class culture was this impulse, this tradition, *and*, crucially, its blockage by the society it inhabited. Although Williams saw it as grounded in 'primary affections and allegiances, in family and neighbourhood', just as Hoggart had, he regarded the solidarity developed there as something unsettled and unsettling, an impulse to organise which came from frustrations visited on working-class imagination, and which knew that imagination could only be set loose by radically democratising the society beyond it.[54] Progress was the watchword of the post-war order, but blockage and resistance is the dominant theme of its cultural criticism, the 'stalemate state' as it was described by the editor of *Conviction*.[55] The post-war rhetoric that assured everybody they had never had it so good, and they would soon have it even better, depended on the renunciation of wider cultural aspirations. Education and the new labour market it served was to be the visible incarnation of this new progress, but it was education severed from the primary loyalties, education as mere expertise and training for an 'elite'. It was not the kind of culture-driving education Hoggart

[51] Richard Hoggart and Raymond Williams, 'Working-Class Attitudes', *New Left Review*, 1 (1961), pp. 26–30.

[52] Williams, 'Culture is Ordinary', p. 75. [53] Ibid.

[54] Williams, 'Working-Class Culture', p. 31.

[55] Norman MacKenzie, 'After the Stalemate State', in *Conviction*, p. 7.

and Williams had in mind when they taught for the Workers' Educational Association.

In effect, Hoggart and Williams prised open an argument that, in the end, snapped shut. The emergence of a New Left inspired by them and determined to come to grips with the post-war world set the stage for a further analysis, to which Williams contributed with the publication of *The Long Revolution* and Hoggart by setting up a Centre for Contemporary Cultural Studies at the University of Birmingham.[56] But 'cultural classlessness' became a means of evading wider cultural change rather than initiating it, and it became clear soon enough that the new media would serve as entertainment for the majority while education continued to serve a minority. In the face of this decoupling, older certainties reasserted themselves. Education as such (rather than private education in particular) became one more badge of middle-classness; debate on popular culture turned back to the question of whether it was – on its own, so to speak – healthy or debilitating, or, in the language that came to predominate, 'ideological' or 'subversive'. The argument that working-class culture was to be found in its own institutions, in, so to speak, the university of politics, dropped from sight. Post-war progress, torn from the structures that might have given it life, became the empty promise of something new.

[56] Williams, *The Long Revolution* (London: Chatto & Windus, 1961).

26

Post-war broadcast drama

KEITH WILLIAMS

Broadcasting was just as responsible as cinema, if not more so, for opening up the established theatrical tradition to mass audiences, firstly on radio as what J. C. Trewin dubbed 'the National Theatre of the Air', then on television as potentially 'The Largest Theatre in the World', in Shaun Sutton's famous phrase. Simultaneously, drama also underwent its own radical transformation within these new media. They served not just to revitalise older genres, but to open genuinely new creative possibilities for dramatic form. It is the leading contours of such innovations and their evolving social and cultural significance which this essay endeavours to sketch.

By 1945 BBC radio had built up a listenership with the necessary habits and skills to broadcast some four hundred plays annually, in addition to 'microphone serials', *Dick Barton Special Agent* becoming the most popular. Of broadcast genres, serialisation and the series are arguably the most distinctive, with television developing radio's pattern. Radio's principal narrative and 'textural' techniques, genres and methods were pioneered in pre-war drama and features by 'producer–directors' and writers such as Lance Sieveking, Tyrone Guthrie, Olive Shapley and D. G. Bridson. These developed a 'radiophonic' space–time fluidity comparable to cinema's, through montage, association or superimposition of acoustic images, by fade-ups/outs, 'dissolves' and so on, cross-cutting between locations for simultaneity and dramatic contrast, breaking down conventional scenes into 'shots', 'zooms' and 'close-ups'. Radio's 'basic grammar' borrowed terminology from film, music and psychology as much as the stage.[1]

All this resulted from experimentation and debate about the 'stuff of radio' as Sieveking called it. It took time to free the medium from mere theatricality, or conventional drama 'by means of radio', and carve out its inherent creative forms, judgable on their own terms. Key technological advances such as the

[1] See John Drakakis, ed., *British Radio Drama* (Cambridge University Press, 1981), p. 7.

Dramatic Control Panel (introduced in 1928) allowed simultaneous orchestration of dialogue and sound, from different studios, into one intertextual weave, or dialogic rhythm. Radiophonic form was also enhanced after magnetic tape became widespread in the 1950s. Taping arguably forfeited the live transmission's intimacy, but opened a treasure house of edited natural or artificial sound (the BBC's Radiophonic Workshop began in 1958). The 'authenticity' of Bill Naughton's northern working-class features was influenced by taping colloquial speech, but also, though very differently, Beckett and Pinter's 'non-naturalistic' drama. Stereophony, VHF and, most recently, digital transmission have added qualitative contributions, too.

Early broadcasting coincided with Modernist literary foregrounding of voice and consciousness, ambiguity of 'presence', language and textuality in general. Radio gradually discovered a distinctive capacity for staging interiority, through versions of stream of consciousness/interior monologue, switching between mimesis of perception into psychological processes. This inevitably involved tensions with the microphone as ultra-naturalistic 'ear on the wall' device, for straight transmission of acoustic realities elsewhere.

Though perhaps no other medium brings words into closer focus, radio was potentially handicapped by lack of literal vision. One solution was stated by L. Du Garde Peach – 'Where there is nothing to look at there must be something to think about'[2] – i.e. 'prosthetic' enhancement of the auditory sense by techno-poetic means. Radio, ideally, stimulated listeners' imaginative inner vision. Performance through the ether was actualised by suggestion in a 'theatre of the mind', unhampered by set locations and specific props. Paradoxically, radio aimed at a form of visualisation, alternative to, yet symbiotic with, the development of film and television.[3] Nevertheless, 'blindness' is its perennially self-referential trope. Sightless characters and narrators evoke audiences' inner vision by proxy, along with disembodied and displaced speech of all kinds, from memories and séances, to telephone calls, tapings and voice-mail. Typically, the Third Programme's feature series *The Inward Eye* began in 1948 with scripts from deaf–blind writer R. C. Scriven, who became a radio mainstay.

Post-war BBC radio was divided into the Home Service, and the Light and Third Programmes. However, Director General William Haley intended this to be a cross-fertilising 'ecology', carrying on the Reithian brief to 'Inform, Educate and Entertain', rather than rigid social–intellectual stratification, even

2 Quoted in Asa Briggs, *A History of Broadcasting in the United Kingdom*, 5 vols., new edn (London: Oxford University Press, 1995), vol. II, *The Golden Age of Wireless*, p. 166.

3 See Tim Crook, *Radio Drama: Theory and Practice* (London: Routledge, 1999), pp. 25–6 and 53–69.

if, to an extent, that was the net result. The specialist Third Programme arguably presumed an educated minority audience, but many of its programmes transferred to the Home Service and even to the Light Programme. 1948 figures show listeners far from segregated.[4] 1955 ratings still regularly peaked at 6.75 million for the Home Service's *Saturday Night Theatre*. Consequently, the 'golden age', when radiophonic forms blossomed but retained mass audiences (later haemorrhaging under competition from BBC and commercial television), cannot simply be discredited as nostalgic myth. The best dramas today can still match if not surpass those of the 1940s and 50s (winners of the annual Giles Cooper Award and BBC Young Playwrights' Festivals prove this),[5] but circumstances of programme-making and relationship with audience were unique to this cultural moment.

The Third Programme expanded airtime for a diversity of challenging drama and helped redefine what radio was about. Until the early 1950s, specially written scripts remained relatively rare, the Drama Department confining itself mainly to stage adaptations and classic novels by Dickens, Hardy, Austen and so on. The Third Programme extended this to contemporary texts, such as Giles Cooper's epochal dramatisation of *Lord of the Flies* (August 1955). Receptiveness to 'Angry' and Absurdist theatre accelerated when Martin Esslin finally replaced Val Gielgud, long-serving Department Head, in 1963. The Home Service generally carried more 'popular' and accessible programming. Despite allegations that the Third Programme was a 'highbrow' ghetto (still haunting Radio 3, its successor), interaction between them probably prevented Home Service drama from declining into mediocrity (an anxiety frequently voiced by radio veterans in the fifties). BBC radio was reorganised again after its internal report 'Broadcasting in the Seventies', though on a model which finally conceded it couldn't compete with television's scale of output and that 'cultural fragmentation' was inevitable.

Cooper was representative of the 'golden age'. His *Mathry Beacon* won the Prix Italia in 1956 and a 1962 festival was dedicated to his work. Scripts by novelists Dorothy L. Sayers and Susan Hill squared the circle of aesthetic quality and popular appeal. Though Louis MacNeice and Dylan Thomas were also crucial figures, both cut their radiophonic teeth during the war in the Features department rather than in Drama. MacNeice employed a highly parabolic

[4] See Kate Whitehead, *The Third Programme: A Literary History* (Oxford: Clarendon Press, 1989), p. 57.

[5] These include talents as diverse as dramatists Tim Pepler (*Song of the Forest* (1990)), Tom Stoppard (*In the Native State* (1991)), reggae-poet Benjamin Zephaniah (*Hurricane Dub*) and novelist Jeanette Winterson (*Static*; both 1988), as well as film-maker Anthony Minghella's *Cigarettes and Chocolate* (1998).

range of modes (testifying to radio's power for 'visualising' abstractions over optical media). These drew on the orality of medieval and classical drama, folktale, saga and myth, as well as incorporating Modernist influences like Expressionism and 1930s 'Audenesque'. MacNeice also engaged with popular and contemporary forms such as pantomime and zany broadcast comedies like *ITMA* and *The Goons*. His critical writings show crucial understanding that broadcast verse plays were written to be realised through the 'ear', rather than pored over by the 'eye'. Lyricism had to stretch audiences without forfeiting comprehensibility, in keeping with radio's 'middlebrow' tendencies as a culturally progressive, democratic medium. MacNeice's 1946 quest drama, *The Dark Tower* (redolent of the soul-searching of the war's aftermath) is acknowledged as a key moment. Against music by Britten, MacNeice's blind seer commented chorically on the temptations Roland encounters, emphasising the symbolic and interior nature of the dragon he slays, just as reformist Britain acknowledged complicity in Fascism's rise, as well as glorying in its defeat. *The Dark Tower* was first broadcast (despite misgivings about formal 'difficulty') on the Home Service. Although richly allusive, its dream-like narrative flow is not impeded by its intertextual freight. However, until his death in 1963, MacNeice's plays (at least two per year) were predominantly on the Third Programme.

Unlike Drama's formal conservatism, Features (under Lawrence Gilliam) had a highly creative relationship with the 1930s documentary movement. Its programmes were based on factual material or explicitly topical issues, but largely free from either plot mechanics or Griersonian film's mimetic obligations. This made Features the more technically innovative, until finally remerged with Drama in 1964. Producer Douglas Cleverdon distinguished them more by the theatrical and technological methodologies they derived from than by subjects or themes.[6] Many seminal programmes, though recognisably dramatic fictions, such as MacNeice's *Christopher Columbus* (October 1942) and Dylan Thomas's 'play for voices', the Italia Prize-winning *Under Milk Wood* (January 1954), were also produced as features. Thomas's episodic structural precedents lay in the social cross-sections, presenting an aural 'day-in-the-life' of places, institutions or events through a montage of speech, sounds and music (including his own *Return Journey* (June 1947)). *Milk Wood* evoked inner vision in a complex layered 'polyphony', through extra-diegetic framing voices and blind 'Captain Cat' (eavesdropper on both living and dead), as well as dreams, thoughts and dialogue of 'Llareggub's' townsfolk. Thomas

[6] See Douglas Cleverdon, *The Growth of Milk Wood* (London: Dent, 1969), p. 17.

assimilated numerous Modernist techniques, most notably Joyce's 'comedy of the unconscious', from 'Circe' in *Ulysses*; the interrogative narrators of 'Ithaca'; the euphonic wordplay of *Finnegans Wake*. *Milk Wood* also realised possibilities from 'unstageable' Symbolist scripts by Ibsen and Strindberg (*Peer Gynt*, *A Dream Play*). It had massive and ongoing impact on radio's parameters, as well as being adapted into other media.

An influential fusion of the feature with 'living newspaper' form was the first 'radio ballad', by producer Charles Parker and folksingers Ewan MacColl and Peggy Seeger. *The Ballad of John Axon* (1958) orchestrated actuality recording, narration and music to dramatise a train wreck prevented from disaster by self-sacrifice. The form proved flexible enough for a whole range of topics (even explaining brake failure in song) and ran until 1963. Its method was revived by director Peter Cheeseman in the 1970s 'Stoke documentaries'. Features also fed back into stage avant-gardism. Theatre Workshop's seminal *Oh What a Lovely War* (1963) was inspired by Charles Chilton's *The Long Trail* (1961–2). These programmes historicised the experience of ordinary soldiers through field recordings of Great War songs, their sentimentality bestowing an ironic bite. Joan Littlewood's 'alienating' pierrot-show format was also indebted to music-hall star Bud Flanagan's narration. Features also prompted television docu-drama. Jeremy Sandford's first crack at the issue underlying *Cathy Come Home* was *Homeless People* (1964), a largely verbatim montage of interviews. Innovative feature-making continued, as exemplified by the work of Piers Plowright and Kate Rowland. The latter's 1997 *From Salford to Jericho* (in Radio 4's New Drama slot), interwove monologues by Manchester street-sleepers with Simon Armitage's verse and musical effects.

The Third Programme staked its credentials on broadcasting Sartre's *Huis Clos* in October 1946, banned on the British stage. Though Gielgud missed the chance of premiering *Godot* in 1955, Beckett's radiophonic potential was quickly recognised by his new assistant, Donald MacWhinnie. The medium's aurality, its creation of environmental 'soundscapes', proved especially suited to existential explorations of consciousness and deconstructions of subjectivity. There is a distinctive 'metaradio' in Beckett's early plays *All that Fall* (1957), *Embers* (1959) and *Words and Music* (1962). *Fall* was not only Beckett's first in English; its intricate counterpointing between dialogue and effects spawned the Radiophonic Workshop. Naturalistic sound ('[I]*mmediately exaggerated*' noises of trains, sheep, the blind husband's stick, etc.) was cued to undercut itself. 'Mrs Rooney' seems aware she and her recollected milieu exist only in and through communication. They are radiophonic illusions, absent presences whose 'ether-reality' is a spectral effect of mediation between transmitter and ear. *Fall* was stereophonically remade in the seventies. *Krapp's Last Tape* (1958) may also have been inspired by Beckett's experience in radio.

Similarly, the ways in where language destabilises through ambiguity took on a broadcast dimension in Pinter's drama. His charging of pauses and silence, as well as tension between speaker's tones and meanings, endowing inconsequential dialogue with psychologically unsettling subtexts, quickly found radiophonic form in *A Slight Ache* (July 1959), *A Night Out* and *The Dwarfs* (March and December 1960). As well as characters' struggles for (now aural) space, Pinter devised disturbing themes of imperilled vision, producing a steady radio output into the seventies. Symptomatic of radio's new adventurousness (which finally put an end to the anachronistic theatre censorship enforced by the Lord Chamberlain), Pinter's *Landscape* was broadcast to a national audience in 1968, after being refused a stage licence.

The BBC, like the rest of Britain's cultural institutions, was shifting, ditching taboos. In April 1975, Radio 4's Monday Play was its first explicit lesbian drama, Jill Hyem's *Now She Laughs, Now She Cries*, preceded by warnings about 'family listening'. For those who tuned in, radio now disseminated avant-gardism much more widely than fringe theatres, premiering Henry Reed's influential translations of Brecht. 'New Wavers' John Arden and Tom Stoppard led simultaneous stage and radio careers, including adaptations of the latter's Postmodern comedies, alongside original scripts, such as *If You're Glad I'll be Frank* (February 1966). Stoppard's *Artist Descending a Staircase* (1972) centred on a blind girl's perceptions in 'Duchampesque' counterpart to his Surrealist mystery, *After Magritte*.

Contemporary novelists also rose to radio's challenge, as Muriel Spark's 1971 collection *Voices at Play* testifies. Fay Weldon (*Polaris* (1978)), Rhys Adrian (*Watching the Plays Together* (1982) and *Outpatient* (1985)), Don Haworth (*Episode on a Thursday Evening* (1978) and *Daybreak* (1984)), Jonathan Raban and Howard Barker showed that younger talents remained committed to innovative radio writing. Raban's *Will You Accept the Call?* (March 1977) twisted the 'unseen voice' trope telephonically, as if listeners were receiving a call from a madman. Barker's *Scenes from an Execution* (October 1984) is a model of sightless 'visualisation', evoking the Venetian milieu of the artist Galactia.

In the nineties, *The Adoption Papers*, by African–Scots poet Jackie Kay, exemplified how fluid interweaving of past and present voices remained radio's imaginative stuff and showed that its possibilities could be pushed in unexpected directions so long as new writers discovered a hospitable home in the medium, despite relative lack of exposure. At the turn of the century, the most touching and controversial play of recent times remained Lee Hall's

Spoonface Steinberg (Radio 4, January 1997). A seven-year-old autistic girl ponders the burdens of cancer and generational memory of the Holocaust, transcending them through an obsession with Maria Callas.

Despite erosions of audience and of painstaking listening habits, individual radio programmes might still reach hundreds of thousands. They were more than just aural prototypes for the visual media (BBC 2's adaptation of *Spoonface* (1999) failed because its radiophonic qualities proved untranslatable). What J. L. Styan wrote about radio in 1960 was still relevant (and might be enhanced by the potentials of digital broadcasting). Its 'unique power upon the ear . . . can embrace subjects film and theatre may never approach. Its subtle and mercurial manipulation of sounds and words, allied to its quality of immediacy and intimacy with the listener, give it possibilities of development that await only the right dramatist.'[7]

Television might have taken over as principal source for what Raymond Williams called 'constant dramatic representation as a daily habit and need',[8] generated by broadcasting, but strands such as Radio 4's Friday, Saturday and Afternoon Play, Classic Serials, as well as Radio 3's Sunday Feature and continuing experimental dramas, kept a distinctive tradition diverse and far from socially irrelevant. The BBC remained virtually the sole broadcaster of original radio drama in the UK, though with some interesting stirrings on the Internet, such as Independent Radio Productions' 'Play of the Month', which began in 1997.

By 1949, Britons already possessed over 90,000 television receivers, approximately three times pre-war numbers. Even more than for radio, the leading question was how to balance entertainment function with edification, achieving reach without 'dumbing down'. This guiding principle was encapsulated by Huw Wheldon (BBC Managing Director, 1968–75): 'to make the good popular and the popular good'. If writers had been concerned about the wireless's cultural rivalry, they now confronted an even more levelling medium, combining its pervasiveness with cinema's visual fascinations. Television drama had become essential to what veteran producer Tony Garnett called television's 'ecology', vital to the nation's cultural and political health,[9] enabling playwrights to explore issues before audiences unprecedented, paradoxically, in both vastness and social atomisation.

[7] J. L. Styan, *The Elements of Drama* (Cambridge University Press, 1960), p. 287.

[8] Raymond Williams, *Drama in a Dramatised Society: An Inaugural Lecture* (Cambridge University Press, 1974), p. 10.

[9] See Tony Garnett, 'Contexts', in Jonathan Bignell, Stephen Lacey and Madeleine Macmurragh-Kavanagh, eds., *British Television Drama: Past, Present and Future* (Basingstoke: Palgrave, 2000), pp. 11–23, esp. pp. 15–16.

The question of television content was also particularly controversial, because of its ambiguous mirroring of the viewer's private situation.[10] According to John Ellis, television reflects or undermines assumed normality. Like Freud's *Unheimlich* (literally '*un*homely'), it can disturb by representing what is repressed in domestic situations.[11] This affords dramatic power, but also obligations, as a corporate product within a mass-communications framework. Consequently, television's vitality consists precisely in creative tension between programme-making and viewers' expectations. At best, it engages the widest audiences without causing them to switch off through excessively shocking subjects, or incomprehensibly experimental form.

Regular television broadcasting began in 1936. Its first specially written play was J. Bissell Thomas's *Underground Murder Mystery* (1937), though most (usually 10–20 minutes) were adapted stage and sometimes radio hits, as in *Theatre Parade*. There were occasional live theatre excerpts (as, famously, from John Osborne's *Look Back in Anger* in 1956). Though early television was studio-bound, some specifically 'televisual' innovation nonetheless took place. By the turn of the century research had unearthed a whole range of pioneering programmes,[12] exploding the myth that all pre-war television was static, with an 'aesthetic' of mere necessity.

When transmission resumed on 7 June 1946, television still only covered the south-east, reaching the midlands and north only in 1949 and 51, and, thereafter, spreading to the rest of Britain. There was also undeniable metropolitan bias in a cultural sense. Drama head Robert McDermot aimed to make specially written material 50 per cent of output. However, the staple pattern of West End successes didn't really alter until his successor Michael Barry. Nevertheless, minority pioneering progressed. Alec Coppel's *I Killed the Count* (March 1948) incorporated *Rashomon*-like 'flashbacks'. Wells's *Time Machine* (January 1949) was visualised by Robert Barr eleven years before Hollywood. Stephen Harrison's adaptation of *Rope* (January 1950) deployed close-ups making characters' reactions as psychologically telling as actions and dialogue. A major landmark was Nigel Kneale's serial *The Quatermass Experiment* (July–August 1953), beginning his partnership with producer Rudolph Cartier, who fundamentally shaped British television. *Quatermass* established a national taste for original television drama, especially after its climax when

10 A recent satirical twist to this is the discomforting pleasure of watching the BBC's television-addicted *Royle Family*.

11 See John Ellis, *Visible Fictions* (London: Routledge & Kegan Paul, 1982), p. 167.

12 See, for example, Jason Jacobs, *Intimate Screen: Early British Television* (Oxford University Press, 2000).

alien life-form metamorphoses from astronaut host. 1955 launched the prototypical police series *Dixon of Dock Green* (brainchild of Ted Willis), which helped spawn the more grittily realistic *Z Cars*. Made in co-operation with Lancashire police, its fast cutting and close shooting rendered *Z Cars* one of the most innovative early sixties' dramas, apprenticing a whole generation of programme-makers.[13]

Television underwent similar emancipation from theatrical and literary traditions and its possibilities were equally linked with technical developments. At first, reception of *both* sound and vision seemed dramatic enough. Virtually all programmes were performed live for direct transmission, as inherited from radio,[14] except for occasional filmed inserts. This gave little opportunity for camera movement and dynamic editing, arguably perpetuating 'fourth-wall' naturalism. Plays were theatrically structured in 'long takes', rather than neatly intercut scenes or shots, with talk predominating over visuality. Later, stage dramas from Shakepeare's histories to Aeschylus' *Oresteia* proved eminently televisual, once a suitable word–image economy was worked out. A more intimate than panoramic form, television's strength lies in registering microscopic changes in expression and so on. Actors' performances were 'scaled down', even more so than for cinema. On the other hand, like cinema, television shifts diegetically in space and time, more expensively than radio, but more convincingly than on stage.

Despite live television's logistical *and* artistic restrictions, great things were still achievable within its parameters, as in the 1954 two-hour adaptation of *Nineteen Eighty-Four* (another Kneale–Cartier product). It was prescient of the BBC to fix on Orwell's satire about the coming power of media-saturated 'hyperreality'. The production used 'meta-televisual' devices, most notably screens-within-the-screen, anticipating more critically self-reflexive practices to come. Kneale later reworked Orwell's themes after television had penetrated much deeper into everyday life. The dystopia of *The Year of the Sex Olympics* (BBC2 July 1968) didn't need state terror: it numbed away discontent and passion through desensitising spectacle. A group of rebels leave for an island apparently beyond its reach. However, foreshadowing today's 'reality' shows (as well as Dennis Potter's posthumous serial, *Cold Lazarus*) *they* are set up as the ultimate, twenty-four-hour, voyeuristic thrill.

[13] Early scripts were by Troy Kennedy Martin, Elwyn Jones, John Hopkins, Allan Prior and Alan Plater; directors included Shaun Sutton, John McGrath and Ken Loach.

[14] As late as 1975, the BBC still regularly broadcast a live drama series, *The Eleventh Hour* (there was an even later one from Pebble Mill in 1983, which attempted to make an experimental 'non-naturalistic' virtue out of liveness).

Fusion with film gave fluidity and pace to early American cop shows and westerns. Things evolved differently here, where investment in studio facilities made film a luxury for scenes unshootable by other means. It was a long time before post-production benefits open to cinema, including montage construction, were exploitable.[15] However, some argue the shift to film as a technological and aesthetic framework tipped the creative balance away from writers, towards directors. Though it's debatable whether the studio play was more than just an evolutionary phase *qua* aesthetic, it could still allow contemporary stage experiments to be shared with larger audiences.

The Garnett–Loach use of 16mm film cameras (see below) had a revolutionary impact for a number of related developments: the abandonment of continuous for edited and, therefore, cinematic diegesis. This movement simultaneously helped television map a regionalism of culture, politics and class literally 'outside' both West End tradition and studio metropolitanism. Many dramas were subsequently also based on location, although 35mm became prevalent. Over the following decades the one-off play declined, but its descendant was the one-off film, often co-produced for both screening and transmission. This growing media symbiosis was exemplified by the groundbreaking *Film on 4* series, followed by the BBC's *Screen 2* in the 1990s. Videotaping also did not become usual until the late sixties, enabling multiple camera viewpoints to be deployed simultaneously, though, unlike film, output could be immediately selected and linked by a 'vision mixer'. Handheld and digital cameras became ever cheaper and more portable than old outside-broadcast units. Equally, post-production sped up with electronic editing (rather than 'cutting and splicing'), bringing an expanding host of visual wonders, and, latterly, merging film and video methods in practice.

Despite the fact that television plays, more so than theatre or even radio, were *collectively* produced, the writer's role and status was a key factor. Television also had a harder struggle establishing serious cultural credentials. It therefore needed a version of Michel Foucault's 'author function'. Promoting writers was a frontline defence against accusations of terminal vacuousness. Authored drama was also 'licensed' to say what could not be said in other programme formats. Unlike news reporting, it was less constrained by corporate balance or factual accuracy. Like the feature in its heyday, the single play was regarded as the genre allowing greatest creative scope and freedom

[15] For recent overviews of the evolutionary symbiosis between the two media, see John Hill and Martin McLoone, eds., *Big Picture, Small Screen: The Relations Between Film and Television* (University of Luton Press, 1997) and Jane Stokes, *On Screen Rivals: Cinema and Television in the United States and Britain* (Basingstoke: Macmillan, 1999).

of expression. It was a principal means of entry for new dramatic talents[16] and a laboratory for established writers. As television's most prestigious format,[17] the single play also has the longest tradition of critical study (as in H. Thomas's *Armchair Theatre* (1959)). This made it the initial locus for exploring notions of 'quality programming' and the medium's formal capabilities, though critical attention gradually encompassed television's other genres and aspects of its production and reception contexts.

Competition from the Independent Television Network (opening in 1955)[18] stimulated specifically televisual quality, as well as the breaking down of class, linguistic and regional bias, bringing drama into the street. ITV's adoption of grittily working-class characters and settings was partly due to popular American imports, but also catalysed the rise of single plays, under umbrella titles or 'strands'. By 1962 there were over three hundred hours of drama per year, 9 per cent of BBC output, especially after it poached Sydney Newman as its new Drama head. BBC2 (transmitting from 1964) increased this further.

ABC (making drama for Midland Weekend) was particularly groundbreaking, commissioning new writers for its flagship *Armchair Theatre* (an interpretation Musset never dreamt of). Influenced by *Playhouse 90* (to which top American writers contributed socially conscious scripts), *Armchair*'s 'agitational contemporaneity' changed television's look and style for ever. A shrewd Canadian, production head Newman recognised television's fundamental parameters as a 'mass-medium', but also what was achievable within them. Given inherited cultural inequalities, majority British audiences had little experience of theatre, but plenty of cinema. To be relevant, Newman believed, programmes needed to comment on the world familiar to most, in accessible yet challenging forms aligned with the 'Angry' revolution against polite convention. He built up creative nuclei of writers, producers and directors in a kind of 'studio system', investing in talents such as Alun Owen (*Lena, O My Lena* (September 1960), about a Liverpool student and a factory girl), Ted

16 Robert Holles estimated that 80 per cent came into television by this route in the 1960s and 70s. (His 'Independent Television and the Single Play' is quoted in David Self, *Television Drama: An Introduction* (Basingstoke: Macmillan, 1984), p. 7.)

17 'At the top are the aristocrats of the single play, then come those who work on the prestige serials, followed by the manufacturers of popular series, with soap opera labourers languishing at the bottom. Somewhere in the middle – the equivalent of skilled plumbers, perhaps, or electrical engineers – are those who make dramatisations and adaptations.' Hugh Whitemore, 'Word into Image: Reflections on the Television Dramatist', in Frank Pike, ed., *Ah! Mischief: The Writer and Television* (London: Faber & Faber, 1982), p. 101.

18 British commercial television was introduced by the Conservative Government's 1954 Television Act. Regulation and programme planning was the responsibility of the Independent Television (later 'Broadcasting') Authority. The IBA granted regional franchises to companies making programmes for their area and/or the network as a whole.

Willis (*Hot Summer Night* (May 1959)) and Mordecai Richler (*The Apprenticeship of Duddy Kravitz* (July 1961)).

Though denounced as a 'downmarket Sam Goldwyn', Newman transplanted this populism-with-commitment to the BBC. Under his auspices, some of television's leading partnerships were forged: Owen with Ted Kotcheff; Dennis Potter with Kenith Trodd; Jeremy Sandford and Jim Allen with Tony Garnett and Ken Loach. He initiated *Quatermass*'s phenomenal successor, *Doctor Who*, and *Dr Finlay's Casebook* (from A. J. Cronin's stories), but, most importantly for the sixties' 'New Wave', introduced *The Wednesday Play* slot.[19] This, and its successor, *Play for Today* (BBC1 1970–84), presented some of television's most outstanding drama, breaking taboos and highlighting problems of homelessness, poverty, unemployment, single parenthood, addiction, domestic violence, labour exploitation, bureaucratic ineptitude, political careerism and so on. It became a byword for controversial drama, provoking parliamentary questions, upsetting mandarins, outraging tabloids and self-selecting pressure groups. *The Wednesday Play* also established a canon for television's equivalent 'golden age', predominantly realist and left-of-centre. However, though regarded as the 'kitchen-sink' era, critical historicisation has reinstated other modes and subjects from the 1960s and 70s, such as explorations of fantasy and subjectivism by, for example, David Mercer and Dennis Potter. It is even arguable that its classic docu-dramas were less naturalist than modernist (with a small 'm'), probing televisual form and engaging with the contemporary.[20]

The *Wednesday Play*'s impact is still epitomised by Sandford's *Cathy Come Home* (first shown in 1966). This spotlighted the plight of urban families and led to the formation of the charity for the homeless, Shelter. Other highlights included Potter's *Vote, Vote, Vote for Nigel Barton* and Nell Dunn's *Up the Junction* (July and November 1965). The latter was particularly notorious for 'permissive' sex and abortion, from a female, working-class perspective (also starring *Cathy*'s Carol White). Allen's *The Lump* (February 1967) dramatised industrial conflict and malpractice in building. Mercer's *In Two Minds* (March 1967) sharpened debate on social attitudes to women and schizophrenia. *Play for Today* kept the pace with Allen's *Rank and File* and Sandford's *Edna the Inebriate Woman* (May and October 1971). The latter mapped a still Orwellian underworld of destitution through Patricia Hayes's virtuoso performance. Mike Leigh's *Abigail's Party* (November 1977) satirised consumer aspirations which would underpin popular support for Thatcherism. It also

19 *The Wednesday Play* eventually subdivided into two strands, *Festival*, which presented classical pieces, old and contemporary, and *First Night*, devoted to new writers.

20 See 'Editors' Introduction to Part II', in Bignell, et al., eds., *British Television Drama*, p. 88.

pushed realist improvisation into expressionistic caricature. Potter's *Blue Remembered Hills* (January 1979) used adults playing children to defamiliarise how tribal prejudice and cruelty are handed down. But some dramas proved too problematic for 'today'. Potter's *Brimstone and Treacle* and Roy Minton's *Scum*, though radically different in mode, were both removed from the schedules in 1976 and 1977, because they included rape scenes.

In April 1979, *The South Bank Show* transmitted 'The Rise and Fall of the Single Play', as though the 'golden age' were indeed over. However, many programme-makers believe this was due more to the decline of liberal working practices and the creative possibilities they opened, than the end of quality television as such. There was no real fall in BBC drama in the seventies, though ITV's output declined somewhat. Pressure for longer packages from schedulers and advertisers did create a surge of period and novel-based serials, though some (e.g. BBC2's *I Claudius* and Frederic Raphael's *The Glittering Prizes* (September–December and January–February 1976, respectively) are classics of their genre. Moreover, keeping the challenging single drama alive (as play or television 'film') was picked up by Channel 4 in November 1982, with its founding brief to 'encourage innovation and experiment', as a platform for independent production companies.[21] This undoubtedly reinvigorated ITV and BBC output in turn. Reasons for the single play's decline are complex, but the one-off production became increasingly anomalous when television policy was dictated by cost and ratings. Nevertheless, managements supported it as a safeguard of public service commitment to creativity. This made the single play a characteristically British form, as a critical space for rethinking television's ethics and relationship with audience.

The Pilkington Committee's report (1960) reinforced this paradigm of quality. Because success was not judged solely by financial performance, ITV differed from corporate cultures in other industries, at least until the Thatcherite Broadcasting Act of 1990 prioritised a franchise bidding system. Similarly, the BBC's gradual shift from paternalistically educating audiences through programme types and levels, to a market-driven model of consumers exercising free choice, risks patronising assumptions about what the public can cope with.[22] It may foster 'cultural pluralism', with broadcasting reflecting society's composition, rather than moulding it, but whether it safeguards quality

[21] Channel 4 is a subsidiary of the IBA, financed by regional advertising slots, which mainly buys or commissions programmes from ITV companies and, most importantly, other independent sources.

[22] For detailed historicisation of these shifts, see (among others) Ien Ang's *Desperately Seeking the Audience* (London: Routledge, 1991).

drama is debatable. Hence allegations by programme-makers that the 1990s 'managerial revolution' of Director General John Birt undermined creative autonomy by concentrating decision-making in executive hands. Reduction in challenging drama has also been attributed to the narrowing of debate in the media during the Thatcher era. The BBC's vaunted independence came under political pressure over issues such as its reporting of the 1984 miners' strike and the 'shoot to kill' documentary, *Death on the Rock* (1988).

Television's earliest series was the 1938 'romcom' *Ann and Harold*. Within their own genre, the best have been as challenging and creative as the single play. There were once clear formal boundaries. Series comprised separate plays (by one or more writers) about recurring characters, locations and/or institutions, each narratively self-contained, whereas serials (as in cinematic and radio predecessors) used 'cliff-hangers' for episodic tension (their theoretically unending form is soap-opera.) However, hybridisation eroded this. Greater narrative length builds texture, situations or characters (Dennis Potter's *Pennies from Heaven* afforded equivalent density to a novel). From the 1970s, much original drama deployed serial format, often picking up the single play's critical realist convictions. *Days of Hope* (BBC1 September–October 1975) is regarded as paradigmatic of the Allen–Loach–Garnett school of programme-making. It dramatised idealisms and interpersonal/social conflicts in a Yorkshire family against the backdrops of the Great War and General Strike, sparking off a *Screen* debate about documentary drama.[23] The same impulse permeated series such as Tony Marchant's *Holding On* (1998) and Paul Abbot's serial *State of Play* (ITV 2003). The former used a cross-section of characters, in synchronic and intersecting storylines, to represent media-saturated London as the locus of a critique of social alienation, during New Labour's uneasy accommodation with Thatcherism's free-market legacy.

There is a third segmental form: the 'anthology' of plays, thematically linked. The outstanding example remains *The Boys from the Blackstuff* (BBC2 October–November 1982). Alan Bleasdale reconvened his one-off pilot's Scouse tarmac gang, each episode developing an individual in their milieu, to be viewed intrinsically, or cross-referenced. 'Yosser' Hughes's family split and breakdown was perhaps the most memorable televisual moment of the 1980s, not least for its manic catchphrase – 'Gissajob, I could do that!' Other episodes similarly mixed black comedy and social satire, striking a national chord as unemployment peaked around 4 million. Bleasdale's ten-part *GBH* (Channel 4

[23] For extended discussion of *Days of Hope* and its impact, see Paul Madden, 'Jim Allen', in George W. Brandt, ed., *British Television Drama* (Cambridge University Press, 1981), pp. 36–55, esp. pp. 48–52.

June–July 1991) moved beyond critical realism, with probing flashbacks to 'Michael Murray's' traumatic childhood, and into Surrealism, when the militant council leader is mobbed by costumed science fiction conventioneers. Bleasdale earlier made a controversial historical foray with his Western Front serial *The Monocled Mutineer* (BBC1 August–September 1986), another kind of 'faction', i.e., plays based on, or incorporating, specific actualities.

Television realism is sometimes compared to the 'escapism' of costume drama. However, the sternest political critics couldn't deny topicality to Andrew Davies's 2002 serialisation of Trollope's *The Way We Live Now*. Davies (who cut his teeth on the *Wednesday Play*) created an allegory of recent market scandals. Similarly, soap-operas, once denigrated as 'feminine', industrial imports, thrived (the homegrown original was the *Grove Family* (1954–7)). In the 1980s, Britain's first independently produced soap, Phil Redmond's *Brookside* for Channel 4, was genuinely innovative, setting a trend for 'relevant' contemporary issues, though its formula finally became melodramatically overblown and campy self-referential. But critics erred in not regarding soap as drama, because, as Graham Greene said of another medium, masterpieces may be unwritable in 'complete ignorance of popular taste'. As with *Z Cars*, it's worth noting how many now illustrious talents were apprenticed to the discipline of writing for *Coronation Street*. Arguably, from the nineties soap became as much of a *via regia* into serious television as the single play once was, especially for female writers, including Kay Mellor (*Band of Gold*), Lynda La Plante (several series of *Prime Suspect*) and Debbie Horsfield (*The Riff-Raff Element* and *Cutting It*). Their work developed in reaction against stereotyping (sometimes from first-hand experience as actresses) and the dearth of strong female leads, often drawing on soap's 'domestic' traditions, as well as popular thrillers.

As for television modes, there were broadly two complementary tendencies, both evolving against early studio-bound theatricality – documentary realism and 'non-naturalism', the latter heralded by Troy Kennedy Martin's seminal manifesto 'Nats Go Home'.[24] Documentary drama has roots in pre-war theatre, film and the radio feature, but its origins as specifically televisual mode lay in the paradox of making topical fictions compete for impact with what Jean Baudrillard calls the 'hyperreality' of current events in a news medium which (more than any other before) appeared to present their facts 'unmediated'. Plays on burning social issues date back to Reginald Beckwith's borstal drama

[24] Troy Kennedy Martin 'Nats Go Home: First Statement of a New Drama for Television', *Encore*, 11, 2 (1964), pp. 21–33.

Boys in Brown (July 1947). Programmes by Colin Morris and Gilchrist Calder were classified 'documentaries', because of working methods and themes like delinquency (*The Wharf Road Mob* (March 1957)) and interrogation procedures (*Who, Me?* (October 1959)). Sixties' and seventies' strands refined this into a distinctive form, so that, as Jonathan Raban put it, 'Their plays made news because they were made *like* news.'[25] Significantly, 16mm blimped cameras were deployed on *Cathy*. These had, hitherto, been reserved for news, or the graininess of documentary film, so that Loach and Garnett deliberately aimed at equivalent 'claiming of the real'. Hence this pre-association shaped the parameters of television social realism. Subsequent documentary plays were similarly not mimetic of unprocessed reality, but the conventions by which screen journalism constructs it, superadding drama's empathy and narrative drive. As Barry Hanson commented, this made *Cathy*, arguably, 'the first dramatic political statement on television in terms of form and content, congruent with its channel of communication'.[26]

Documentary plays often used unknowns (such as Carol White and Ray Brookes as *Cathy*'s ill-fated couple), with improvisation over pre-scripting, as well as location action, to maximise their 'reality effect'. Classically, a narrative of fictional particularity typified a general situation, to make a case for reform through galvanising opinion.[27] But such formal borrowings tend to deconstruct generic boundaries in practice. Ethically as well as aesthetically, good docu-drama at the turn of the century continued to make claims on the real while avoiding crude propagandising. It might still depend on simulating other modes of factual representation, but critiqued them from the inside, as in Chris Morris's *Brass Eye* 'mockumentary' (2001), parodying media fomentation of hysteria about paedophilia.

A distinction also developed between topical docu-drama and faction.[28] Again, Cartier produced a landmark with Felix Lutzkendorf's *Lee Oswald – Assassin* (BBC 'Play of the Month', March 1966). Writer–director Peter Watkins's *Culloden* applied the same principle to the historical past, as if a news team had been at the Jacobite defeat (BBC1 December 1964). Watkins's *The War Game*

[25] Jonathan Raban, '*Leeds-United!*: Drama Making News', *Radio Times* (7 November 1974), p. 82. For more recent discussion of docudrama see (among others): Madeleine Macmurragh-Kavanagh '"Drama Into News": Strategies of Intervention in *The Wednesday Play*', *Screen*, 38, 3 (1997), pp. 247–59); also her 'The BBC and the Birth of *The Wednesday Play* (1962–1966): Institutional Containment Versus "Agitational Contemporaneity"', *Historical Journal of Film, Radio and Television*, 17, 3 (1997), pp. 367–81.

[26] Barry Hanson '1970s Regional Variations', in Bignell, et. al., eds., *British Television Drama*, pp. 58–63, esp. p. 59.

[27] See David Edgar 'Documentary Drama', in Pike, ed., *Ah! Mischief*, p. 20.

[28] For this distinction, see Self, *Television Drama*, p. 17.

(made in 1965, but controversially banned for twenty years) similarly combined amateurs and *verité* techniques for hypothetical nuclear attack.

Non-naturalism also eschewed the 'boxed set' studio play's inadequate realism, but at the opposite formal pole to mimesis. As on radio, from the early sixties' BBC (and later Channel 4) productions of Beckett focused on deconstructing the characteristics of small screen dimensionality and presence. The vicarious intimacy of close-up transforms into surreal visual synecdoche in *Not I*, television's talking heads dilated to a nameless, logorrhoeic orifice. Similarly, *Happy Days* narrows in on what remains of 'Winnie', as she sinks into existential predicament. Beckett deliberately uncoupled soundtrack and image (reversing television's staple dependency on synchronised dialogue), as Krapp listens to recordings of earlier selves, and in the disembodied speech of *Eh, Joe*.

Potter, a first-generation specialised television dramatist, managed, in a 'Postmodern' way, to root his work in lessons from the avant-gardism of Beckett, Joyce and Brecht, and in popular culture. As he wrote,

> The best non-naturalist drama, in its very structure *dis*orientates the viewer smack in the middle of the orientation process which television perpetually uses. It disrupts the patterns that are endemic to television and upsets or exposes the narrative styles of so many of the other allegedly non-fiction programmes. It shows the frame in the picture when most television is busy showing the picture in the frame.[29]

Potter's serial *Pennies from Heaven* (BBC1 March–April 1978) featured 'lip-synching' to saccharine, yet strangely metaphysical thirties songs. Fantasies and discontents were projected by radical dissociation of the word–image relationship at the medium's discursive core, creating a 'stretch of tension between sound and picture'.[30] This counterpointed Hollywood idealism with the reality of Depression life. Characters were transported 'over the rainbow', but circumstances remained in focus. *Pennies* also employed colour-separation overlay (CSO), an innovation from video-editing and forerunner of computer-generated imagery. CSO creates a 'layering' effect, superimposing images against backgrounds or 'inserting' characters into other discourses, to place 'Arthur' into a songsheet cover, or his wife into a magazine advertisement. The result was stunning visual 'intertextuality', multiple frames within one picture, including state-of-the-art animated graphics.

29 Dennis Potter, 'Realism and Non-Naturalism 2', *The Official Programme of the Edinburgh International Television Festival 1977*, August 1977, p. 36.

30 For Potter's 'stretch of tension', see David Cook, *Dennis Potter: A Life on Screen*, 2nd edn (Manchester University Press, 1998), p. 13.

However, it's unfair to restrict discussion of non-naturalism to formal innovation and deny any distinctive social or psychological critique. As a result of their dialogue with popular cultural forms, Potter's dramas offer some kind of ideological analysis of gendered subjectivity and modes of consumption. He deployed equivalent visual and aural intertexts in *The Singing Detective* (1986), especially hard-boiled *noir* fiction and the films springing from it. These frame 'Marlow's' attempt to solve his life-mystery, simultaneously with the viewer's. There is comparable multi-generic parody in serials of Fay Weldon's fictions, notably *Life and Loves of a She-Devil* (BBC2 October 1986). Docu-drama, advertising, soap opera, Gothic and science fiction drove its feminist critique. Oddly, 'magic realist' intertexuality with Arthurian romance is missing from Jeanette Winterson's otherwise brilliant adaptation of her novel, *Oranges Are Not the Only Fruit* (BBC2 January 1990). *Detective*'s metafictionality also implied television voyeurism itself. This intensified in Potter's *Blackeyes* (BBC2 November–December 1989) as well as the Cartier–Kneale futurism of his *Cold Lazarus*, a rare 1998 BBC/Channel 4 co-production, about a cryogenic head, whose memories are broadcast as virtual reality for global audiences detached from authentic sensory and emotional experience.

Television drama was both reflective of cultural change and an agent of it, though research showed ongoing under-representation of women and ethnic minorities in broadcasting, as writers, producers, subjects and in critical discourse. Irene Shubik was exceptional as a producer responsible for entire showcase strands, *The Wednesday Play* and *Play for Today*. By the mid-nineties women still only constituted 15 per cent of television's workforce, though (for particular programming) the target majority of audiences. Revisionist analysis of the 'golden age' canon also unearthed intriguing discrepancies between ratings for female-authored *Wednesday Plays* (sixteen out of 176) and their lack of critical standing, because of gender-biased aesthetics.[31] Single parents were shown as victims of the system, but dramatisation of women as a whole could be narrow, even misogynistic. Male-authored docu-dramas, referring to 'public' contexts of social injustice, received prestigious film treatment; while plays referring to women's 'private' experience were (with the exception of *Up the Junction*) relegated to studio production. Nonetheless, audiences may have responded to dissenting messages about gender roles, even if subtextually 'coded'. Barrister Nemone Lethbridge's trilogy, *The Portsmouth Defence*, *The Little Master Mind* and *An Officer of the Court* (1966–7) attacked the legal

[31] See Madeleine MacMurragh Kavanagh, 'Too Secret for Words: Coded Dissent in Female-Authored *Wednesday Plays*, in Bignell, et. al., eds., *British Television Drama*, pp. 150–61.

system's patriarchal bias by such means. It was a measure of how far television drama had come that La Plante could confront police procedures and 'canteen culture' head on in *Prime Suspect* (1990). Hyem battled to incorporate 'unfeminine' realism into *Tenko*'s depiction of women prisoners of war (BBC1 1981–2) (including same-sex relationships, as she had on radio), opening the gates for depicting other issues more dispassionately in subsequent serials. Nevertheless, despite her vast experience of broadcasting, Weldon's serialisation of her novel *Life and Loves of a She-Devil* was turned down by the BBC as 'too cruel', though Ted Whitehead's eventually won a 1987 BAFTA.

In broadcasting, whoever pays the piper calls the tune, especially in international co-productions. Its future will probably continue to be shaped by both economic and technical parameters, with rising audience expectations, but its cultural health has always been determined by a (not altogether foreseeable) complex of factors. New cable and satellite networks have to date done disappointingly little to stimulate dramatic innovation, generally just retransmitting classic material on subscription channels. This raises the question of how popular audiences can be sustained for quality drama when fragmented by programming beamed from outside national boundaries, so that individuals are increasingly unlikely to stumble fortuitously across plays expanding tastes or broadening minds. The Davies Committee called digital the 'fourth broadcasting revolution', following radio, monochrome and then colour television. Its multi-channelling, technical superiority and 'interactivity' promises much, although it seems less likely to deliver if governments allow means of dissemination to concentrate in global media empires.

However, there seems, as yet, no end to need for the low-tech element of some kind of script, and 'big names' are still advertised, though many writers feel, at best, ambivalent about their experience. Some, like Beckett, safeguarded creative autonomy by directing, or even, like Potter, producing, their work (with Pennies From Heaven Ltd, from 1980). It's undoubtedly consoling that their *auteurial* ranking in broadcast credits is where the director's would be in cinema, perhaps because television's earliest roots stem from theatrical traditions. Authored drama's licence has also allowed some radical interventions in post-war culture.[32] The best scripts have been written with some technical understanding of broadcasting's radiophonic or televisual nature, for collaborators who realise them maximally within its parameters. Playwrights

[32] See Carl Gardner and John Wyver, 'The Single Play: from Reithian Reverence to Cost-Accounting and Censorship', *Official Programme of the Edinburgh Television Festival* (1980), p. 51.

have traded traditional textual control for the enhanced expressive possibilities of auditory and/or visual effects. There is every likelihood that future dramas may be cultural 'events' and talking points, rather than merging into a consensual flow from speaker and screen, if ongoing managerial commitment matches creative interests. But this won't happen if a 'mixed' ecology becomes dominated by cost-effective programming, based on prescriptive formulas and squeezing challenging drama out of the schedules. The danger is not so much direct censorship as the political context of production policy.

27

Drama and the new theatre companies

TREVOR R. GRIFFITHS

> For the most part the British theatre does not take into account the fact that we have had a World War since 1939, and that everything in the world has changed – values, ways of living, ideals, hopes and fears. As I see it, our theatre is far too often pre-war, safe and easy-going in what it offers, and lacking in the stimulation that will attract fresh audiences.[1]

Thus, in 1955, the young Peter Hall voiced a widespread dissatisfaction with the state of British theatre. The post-war period has often been characterised as one of stagnation in British drama, redeemed by high-quality productions, with actors like Olivier, Gielgud and Richardson gracing the stage in revivals designed by Motley and photographed by Cecil Beaton. American musicals such as *Oklahoma!* and the plays of Tennessee Williams and Arthur Miller had a raw power and theatricality that was lacking in British theatre writing, while Giraudoux and Anouilh offered a Gallic intellectual stimulation absent from the home-grown product. There is some truth in this aesthetic judgement but it ignores crucial economic factors: new work often fails to attract audiences because of fear of the unknown, lack of bankable stars or critical hostility to experimentation. Revivals, stars and imports all carry with them some guarantee against economic failure: what has succeeded before can be expected to succeed again.

In the immediate post-war period of economic austerity in order to pay for World War II and the implementation of the welfare state, the economic situation fuelled managerial conservatism: theatre capacity was limited due to wartime destruction; production costs had risen and were rising massively; and plays were staying in theatres longer. The average length of a run was three times greater than it had been pre-war, so there were far fewer

[1] *Cambridge Evening News*, 20 April 1955, quoted in Stephen Fay, *Power Play: The Life and Times of Peter Hall* (London: Hodder & Stoughton, 1995), pp. 84–5.

opportunities for new productions.[2] Economic considerations were clearly highly influential in the conservative tenor of the West End but with many theatres effectively controlled by Binkie Beaumont of the management company H. M. Tennent, there was little room for work that was not to his taste.[3]

Established writers continued to produce polished accounts of middle-class problems within limited realist frameworks, whether in courtroom dramas, drawing-room comedies, psychological thrillers, or farces. Successful plays, whatever their ostensible genre, tended, as the picture spreads in the monthly magazine *Theatre World* demonstrate, to be located in a world of panelled drawing rooms serviced by eccentric servants. When Tennent's did produce new work, they took great care to maximise their chances of recouping their investment. For example, N. C. Hunter was 'an entirely unknown dramatist' when they staged *Waters of the Moon* in 1951 with 'a cast-list normally lavished by this management on "dressy" Oscar Wilde revivals, and including two actress Dames'. Hunter reminded critics of Chekhov; Tennents were rewarded with an eighteen-month run and his next play, *A Day by the Sea*, boasted three knights and a Dame.[4]

Even the more adventurous dramatists worked within broadly realist frameworks. In *An Inspector Calls* (1945), J. B. Priestley, a campaigner against many aspects of the theatrical status quo, subverted the conventions of the detective thriller to accommodate an oppositional reading. Priestley reveals Edwardian values as fraudulent, and a supposedly golden age as one of hypocrisy that contributed to the political and social failings of the thirties. Writing just in advance of the creation of the welfare state, Priestley demands that his audience care for others or share the fate of his characters. Terence Rattigan also used the Edwardian period to probe social hypocrisy in *The Winslow Boy* (1946). Rattigan, a closet homosexual, excelled at quiet understatement in both situation and the expression of emotion that permitted the distillation of emotional subtext into the apparently banal. His theatrical conservativism meant his reputation slumped in the late fifties, but latterly his work has been evaluated more positively.[5]

2 John Pick, *The West End: Mismanagement and Snobbery* (Eastbourne: Offord, 1983), p. 151.

3 Richard Huggett, *Binkie Beaumont, Eminence Grise of the West End Theatre 1933–1973* (London: Hodder & Stoughton, 1984), is the standard biography.

4 Audrey Williamson, *Contemporary Theatre* (London: Rockliff, 1956), p. 37.

5 For Priestley, see Judith Cook, *Priestley* (London: Bloomsbury, 1997); for Rattigan, see Geoffrey Wansell, *Terence Rattigan* (London: Fourth Estate, 1995), B. A. Young, *The Rattigan Version* (London: Hamish Hamilton, 1986).

Poetic drama briefly appeared to offer an alternative to routine West End fare and the drabness of post-war life. Ronald Duncan, who was to become an unhappy co-founder of the English Stage Company, achieved some success, while Christopher Fry impressed audiences and critics with his exuberant verse, but he retreated from the theatre for several years after 1956.[6] Post-war T. S. Eliot continued to ignore the example he had set with *Sweeney Agonistes* (1926), the rhythms of which anticipate Harold Pinter. In *The Cocktail Party* (Edinburgh Festival 1949), Eliot, drawing on the *Alcestis* of Euripides, mixes drawing-room comedy with aspects of the thriller to create Christian propaganda. Unfortunately his plays became increasingly prosaic and, although his publishing company Faber was to publish both John Osborne and Samuel Beckett, he was unable to find a consistently effective theatrical form to deliver his precarious combinations of ancient Greek and Christian elements.

Farces and thrillers remained a staple of the West End. Colin Morris's *Reluctant Heroes* (1950), a National Service farce, starred Brian Rix who brought it into the Whitehall Theatre, initiating a series of 'Whitehall Farces' that continued the Aldwych traditions of the twenties and thirties.[7] By the end of the period, the thriller moved into the realms of parody and self-consciousness in works like Tom Stoppard's *The Real Inspector Hound* (1968) and Anthony Shaffer's *Sleuth* (1970),[8] but there were already strong comic elements in such plays as Agatha Christie's *The Mousetrap* (1952), the longest-running play of all time, having celebrated its fiftieth anniversary in 2002. Christie herself, by far the most successful thriller writer of the period, thought that *The Mousetrap* was 'the sort of play you can take anyone to. It is not really frightening. It is not really horrible. It is not really a farce but it has a little bit of all these things and perhaps that satisfies a lot of different people.'[9] The critic Harold Hobson described the play as 'a parable of the social outlook of our times'[10] and it does touch on issues of nature and nurture, social responsibility, the politics of sexual identity, and child abuse. Unfortunately, however, it remains inert beneath the generic paraphernalia of cross-purposes, suspicion and the traditional demand for closure and restoration of order.

[6] For poetic drama, see Glenda Leeming, *Poetic Drama* (Basingstoke: Macmillan, 1989), pp. 155 ff; on Fry's reaction to 1956 see Dan Rebellato, *1956 and All That: The Making of Modern British Drama* (London: Routledge, 1999), p. 227, n. 2.

[7] See Leslie Smith, *Modern British Farce* (Basingstoke: Macmillan, 1989).

[8] Marvin Carlson, *Deathtraps: The Postmodern Comedy Thriller* (Bloomington: Indiana University Press, 1993), passim.

[9] Peter Saunders, *The Mousetrap Story*, [1992], privately printed. p. 92.

[10] Ibid., p. 7; Dominic Shellard, *Harold Hobson: Witness and Judge* (Keele University Press, 1995), is the fullest account of Hobson's career.

Although wartime experiments with state subsidies for the arts through the Council for the Encouragement of Music and the Arts (CEMA) led to the creation of the Arts Council in 1945, it took some time to develop an arts-funding infrastructure that would encourage experimental work. In the immediate post-war world, non-commercial theatres that attempted to break away from the formulas of West End theatre with new works by unestablished writers played a vital role in compensating for the lack of opportunities elsewhere, but these 'fringe' ventures were short-lived as they succumbed to the adverse economic climate.[11] Representative works included the Pirandellian *Exercise Bowler* by 'T. Atkinson' (Arts, 1946) in which 'a third-rate long-running play with a tired cast expressing trite and utterly false sentiments about the war' is interrupted by three soldiers who re-enact their experiences,[12] Madelaine Bingham's *The Man From the Ministry*, about the housing shortage (Services' Sunday Society 1946), Richard Llewellyn's *Noose* (Services' Sunday Society 1947), 'an underworld story' that included a highly realistic raid on a nightclub,[13] and plays about India (Harry Ballam, *That Equal Sky*, Boltons, 1947), artificial insemination (Dan Sutherland, *Breach of Marriage*, Torch, 1948) and the Berlin airlift (Lionel Birch and Lorna Hay, *The Compelled People*, New Lindsey, 1949).

London Unity Theatre, a well-established left-wing amateur theatre company, attempted to capitalise on the post-war mood of reconstruction by turning professional in 1945 under the leadership of the dramatist Ted Willis. Unity's theatre was too small to generate enough income to support the company without subsidy or sponsorship, but neither the fledgling Arts Council nor the Trade Union movement supported the venture and London Unity reverted amid great acrimony to amateur status.[14] A Scottish professional Unity company fared better initially: Glasgow Unity toured Ena Lamont Stewart's *Men Should Weep* (1947) to Edinburgh and London and their production of Robert McLeish's *The Gorbals Story* (1946) reached London in 1948. Alan Dent pointed out how different it was from standard West End fare: 'Playgoers who are – as they should be, a little weary of the Mayfair Story, the Chelsea Story and the Home Counties Story – should go see Mr McLeish's play and get a profound shock and a strange thrill. For this is Glasgow, the slummy swarming core of it, presented with honesty, frankness and verisimilitude.'[15] The company

11 J. C. Trewin, *Drama 1945–1950* (London: Longmans Green/British Council, 1951), pp. 41–3, Kitty Black, *Upper Circle* (London: Methuen, 1984), pp. 139–40, Norman Marshall, *The Other Theatre* (London: John Lehmann, 1947).

12 *Theatre World*, June 1946. 13 *Theatre World*, May 1947.

14 Colin Chambers, *The Story of Unity Theatre* (London: Lawrence & Wishart, 1989), pp. 263–78.

15 Oscar Lewenstein, *Kicking against the Pricks* (London: Nick Hern, 1994), p. 74.

eventually succumbed in 1951, having inadvertently started the Edinburgh Festival Fringe in 1947 when, uninvited, it made its own unofficial visit to the first International Festival, at the cost of its Arts Council support.[16] As these failures demonstrate, there was no lack of innovative aspiration in this period but economic conditions continued to thwart attempts to develop more permanent ventures.

The career of John Whiting, perhaps the most innovative dramatist of the early fifties, is indicative of the problems faced by young writers. Whiting's Napoleonic Wars comedy *A Penny for a Song* (1951), directed by Peter Brook, had a short run at the Haymarket, while *Saint's Day* (1951), the winning entry in the Festival of Britain playwriting competition (judged by the director Alec Clunes and the playwrights Peter Ustinov and Christopher Fry) was excoriated by the critics, although it was defended by many theatrical professionals. Tennent's produced *Marching Song* to respectful notices and modest box office in 1954, but *The Gates of Summer* (1956) did not reach London, and it was only when Peter Hall, who had directed undergraduate productions of Whiting's plays, commissioned him to adapt *The Devils* (1961), from Aldous Huxley's *The Devils of Loudun* for the Royal Shakespeare Company (RSC), that he achieved any great success. Whiting's was an idiosyncratic talent and even his admirers admit to structural problems in much of his work, but he could clearly have benefited from the kinds of support that would be available later, including the annual award named after him that the Arts Council inaugurated in 1965, two years after his death, and given to a play 'in which the writing is of special quality', 'of relevance and importance to contemporary life' and 'of potential value to British theatre'.[17]

As the social, economic and political changes of the post-war period worked through in the mid-fifties, a dominant theatre of conservative form, social affirmation and social consolidation began to accommodate a theatre of social and cultural dissent. However erroneously, myth has chosen the opening night of John Osborne's *Look Back in Anger* in 1956 to mark a rebirth of British theatre.[18] In fact, the whole process was much more complex and many other important factors contributed to it. Although Samuel Beckett would create ever more minimal plays, the 1955 British premier of Beckett's *Waiting for Godot*, directed

16 Chambers, *Unity Theatre*, pp. 282–3.

17 Quoted from the criteria for the 2000 John Whiting award supplied by Jemima Lee, Arts Council of England. For Whiting see Simon Trussler, *The Plays of John Whiting: An Assessment* (London: Victor Gollancz, 1972), Eric Salmon, *The Dark Journey: John Whiting as Dramatist* (London: Barrie & Jenkins, 1979), Charles Duff, *The Lost Summer: The Heyday of the West End Theatre* (London: Nick Hern, 1995), pp. 171–82.

18 See Rebellato, *1956 and All That*, for a demolition of the traditional position.

by Peter Hall, was a revelation of how much theatre could actually do without while still remaining entertaining and how profound insights could be delivered through comic routines. Beckett stripped away the accretions of naturalistic settings and characterisation to create an utterance tortured by memory and reduced to a strategy to ward off acknowledging the pain of existence. He coupled this with intensely theatrical images of humanity at the margins of existence: the characters in a bare landscape in *Godot*, Hamm in his wheelchair, his parents in dustbins in *Endgame* (1957), the solitary Krapp and his tapes in *Krapp's Last Tape* (1958), Winnie sinking into her mound in *Happy Days* (1961) or the disembodied mouth in *Not I* (1972) refusing to accept the first-person singular.

Bertolt Brecht became increasingly important in the UK in the fifties as the influential critic Kenneth Tynan[19] championed him in the *Observer* and more of his works were staged. In 1955 Joan Littlewood played Mother Courage but 1956 saw Oscar Lewenstein stage *Threepenny Opera* in February, RADA offer *The Caucasian Chalk Circle* in July, the Berliner Ensemble make its first visit to the UK in August and the English Stage Company (ESC) open what was then called *The Good Woman of Setzuan* in October (with Osborne in the cast; the 'Brechtian' qualities of *The Entertainer* and *Luther* are not a coincidence).[20] The increasing availability of Brecht's work played a major part in creating a new sense of dramatic and theatrical possibility and books by Martin Esslin and John Willett, both published in 1959, attempted to explain his practice to a wider public.[21]

Littlewood, the co-founder of Theatre Workshop, was committed to using popular forms to try to address local audiences, to creating an ensemble company and to developing plays through the active involvement of the company.[22] She used improvisation to develop Brendan Behan's *The Quare Fellow* (1956) and *The Hostage* (1958) and Shelagh Delaney's *A Taste of Honey* (1958) into major works. The matter-of-fact treatment of bastardy, promiscuity, inter-racial sex and homosexuality in *A Taste of Honey* opens up new territory for the drama of the period and, unusually, the play centres on the women, not the men.

19 See Kathleen Tynan, *The Life of Kenneth Tynan* (London: Weidenfeld & Nicolson, 1987), pp. 85–6, 117–18 and passim and Tynan's reviews in, e.g., *Tynan on Theatre* (Harmondsworth: Penguin, 1964).

20 See Nicholas Jacobs and Prudence Ohlsen, comps. and eds., *Bertolt Brecht in Britain*, TQ Publications, 1977.

21 John Willett, *Brecht: A Study from Eight Aspects* (London: Methuen, 1959), and Martin Esslin, *Brecht: A Choice of Evils* (London: Eyre & Spottiswoode, 1959).

22 See Howard Goorney, *The Theatre Workshop Story* (London: Eyre Methuen, 1981), for the fullest account of the company.

Littlewood used an on-stage jazz group to provide mood-setting music for a sequence of scenes structured almost cinematically and achieved a liberating fluidity in production.

In comparison to the works of Littlewood, Beckett and Brecht, *Look Back in Anger* is, as Osborne himself noted, 'a formal, rather old-fashioned play':[23] three acts, a small cast and a single realistic set, even if the actual location in a one-roomed flat was itself unusual. It was the third production of the ESC at the Royal Court, a rather unlikely coalition tortuously brought together by chance, expediency and a shared interest in developing new writing.[24] George Devine, the ESC's Artistic Director, sought plays from established novelists but the company also advertised for new plays. They received 675 and staged one of them, *Look Back in Anger*. It was recognised as a significant new work, even by those who did not like it. Tynan points out that Osborne had succeeded in staging an aspect of life that had been significantly absent from the theatre: the play

> presents post-war youth as it really is, with special emphasis on the non-U intelligentsia who live in bed-sitters . . . All the qualities are there, qualities one had despaired of ever seeing on the stage – the drift towards anarchy, the instinctive leftishness, the automatic rejection of 'official' attitudes, the surrealist sense of humour . . . , the casual promiscuity, the sense of lacking a crusade worth fighting for, and, underlying all these, the determination that no one who dies shall go unmourned.[25]

Although Osborne's autobiography suggests that the play is a barely fictionalised account of his own first marriage,[26] it voices class and generational antagonisms that had been submerged beneath a cosy political consensus and the growth of a consumer society. Jimmy's lament about the lack of decent political causes reflects this and Alison is, as Jimmy says, a trophy of the class war. The key factor in the play's success was that Osborne had created in Jimmy a character of 'evident and blazing vitality'.[27] Irving Wardle quotes an unnamed playwright who had read the play before it was staged: 'Well. It's very excitingly written, but you can't put that on in a theatre! People won't

[23] Quoted in Christopher Innes, *Modern British Drama 1890–1990* (Cambridge University Press, 1992), p. 103.

[24] Philip Roberts, *The Royal Court Theatre and the Modern Stage* (Cambridge University Press, 1999), pp. 1–44, gives a comprehensive account of the genesis of the company.

[25] Tynan, *Tynan on Theatre*, p. 42.

[26] John Osborne, *A Better Class of Person* (London: Faber & Faber, 1981), pp. 238–53.

[27] Tynan, *Tynan on Theatre*, p. 41. See Rebellato, *1956 and All That*, p. 26, on the importance of 'vitality'.

stand for being shouted at like that, it's not what they go the theatre for.'[28] As it turned out, it was. Osborne's energetic writing seemed particularly exciting compared to the more muted qualities of a writer like Rattigan who was unfairly seen as an exemplar of theatrical conservatism. At the first night of *Look Back in Anger*, which Rattigan disliked intensely, he told a reporter that Osborne 'was saying "Look, Ma, I'm not Terence Rattigan."'[29] Rattigan and Fry were the most noteworthy writers who were eclipsed by the success of the ESC. However, Rodney Ackland, a significant talent rediscovered in the nineties, Wynyard Browne, Bridget Boland, Lesley Storm and Enid Bagnold, whose *The Chalk Garden* (1955) Tynan had described as probably 'the finest artificial comedy to have flowed from an English (as opposed to an Irish) pen since the death of Congreve', are among those who deserve greater attention than they have generally received from later critics.[30]

Earlier attempts to create something like the ESC had failed because the inherent risks of any theatrical venture are compounded by a focus on new writing. The ESC spread the risk with a mixed economy of French drama (including Beckett and the Absurdists), classics such as *Lysistrata* (1958), and productions aimed at commercial success (e.g. Noel Coward's Feydeau adaptation, *Look After Lulu*, 1959), supported by subsidy and rights income. In 1956, aided by George Fearon's brilliant coinage of the phrase 'Angry Young Men'[31] and a televised extract, *Look Back* attracted great attention but *The County Wife* generated much more business. An Arts Council grant and income from transfers and rights tipped the balance in favour of survival as they would in many subsequent years.[32] Devine championed the 'right to fail', ensuring that productions could be given a reasonably extended run despite poor box office if other income balanced the books. The greatest beneficiary of this policy was John Arden, an uncompromising dramatist whose political vision and epic dramaturgy never found a large audience. His early productions played to a box office of 25 per cent (*Live Like Pigs*, 1958),

28 Irving Wardle, *The Theatres of George Devine* (London: Jonathan Cape, 1978), p. 180.
29 Dominic Shellard, *British Theatre Since the War* (New Haven: Yale University Press, 1999), p. 53.
30 See Duff, *The Lost Summer*, pp. 139–68; for Ackland and pp. 63–94 for Browne; Rebellato, *1956 and All That*, pp. 131–5, for Boland; Susan Bennett, 'New Plays and Women's Voices in the 1950s' in Elaine Aston and Janelle Reinelt, eds., *The Cambridge Companion to Modern British Women Playwrights* (Cambridge University Press, 2000), 38–52, pp. 41–50 for Bagnold and Storm. Tynan is quoted from Anne Sebba, *Enid Bagnold* (London: Weidenfeld & Nicolson, 1986), p. 196.
31 Roberts, *The Royal Court Theatre and the Modern Stage*, p. 48.
32 Richard Findlater, ed., *At The Royal Court* (Charlbury: Amber Lane, 1981), p. 246.

21 per cent (*Serjeant Musgrave's Dance*, 1959) and 12 per cent (*The Happy Haven*, 1960).[33]

As part of its mission to encourage new writing the ESC ran a Writers' Group from 1958 for two years. Arden, Arnold Wesker, Edward Bond, Wole Soyinka and Ann Jellicoe were among the participants.[34] In her first play *The Sport of My Mad Mother* (1958) Jellicoe anticipated many of the concerns of later feminist writers with her exploration of matriarchy and of fragmenting language. *The Knack* (1961) was very successful in presenting patriarchal struggles for domination between three men and used ritual patterns, movement and arbitrary language of the kind familiar in improvisation to energise the work. The ESC also wanted to encourage regional theatres so Wesker's largely autobiographical trilogy (*Chicken Soup with Barley*, 1958, *Roots*, 1959, and *I'm Talking About Jerusalem*, 1960) arrived at the Court via a deal with the newly opened Belgrade, Coventry. *Roots* was praised for its presentation of Beattie Bryant's emancipation from the competing claims of her rural roots and her socialist boyfriend–mentor. One of the main objections to the majority of pre-1956 theatre was its concentration on only a very small fraction of the population, the upper-middle classes and the professions. In the trilogy, Wesker extended the social territory gained by Osborne into a working-class world of council flats and tied cottages, East End Jewish socialists and Suffolk labourers. In *The Kitchen* (1959) the increasingly frenetic activity as the workers prepare meals acts as a hostile presentation of the workings of capitalism. Wesker's *Chips with Everything* (1962), like John McGrath's *Events While Guarding the Bofors Gun* (1966), presented the class tensions and indignities of National Service without resorting to the farce conventions often associated with plays about conscription.

Harold Pinter's early plays unsettled audiences by appearing to engage the traditional mechanisms of the thriller before frustrating traditional expectations of disclosure and resolution. Harold Hobson's favourable review of *The Room* (1957) at the National Student Drama Festival led a new producer, Michael Codron, to stage *The Birthday Party* in 1958. Greeted with critical incomprehension, this story of two outsiders who destroy the fragile equilibrium of a seaside boarding house had folded before Hobson again came to the rescue with a glowing review in the *Sunday Times*. Although Irving Wardle subsequently regretted coining the term 'comedy of menace' to describe the work of Pinter, N. F. Simpson, David Campton and Nigel Dennis,[35] it does reflect the

33 Ibid., pp. 246–7.
34 William Gaskill, *A Sense of Direction* (London: Faber & Faber, 1988), p. 37.
35 *Encore*, September 1958.

way in which Pinter uses a rhetoric composed of the banal and the clichéd to create sinister scenarios of immanent doom. Pinter's work has been explained (away?) in terms of, for example, its ritual patterns, its debts to Judaism, psychoanalytical theories, rituals, game-playing, use of phatic language, archetype and stereotype.[36] While all or some of these approaches may provide insights into, for example, the Oedipal relationship between Stanley and Meg in *The Birthday Party*, the placatory strategies of two hit-men in *The Dumb Waiter* (1960) or the behaviour of the wildly dysfunctional family in *The Homecoming* (1964) when the absent son returns with his inscrutable wife, audiences soon learned to enjoy their inability to pin Pinter's works down to one definitive meaning and the absence of an authorial *raisonneur* to explain the inexplicable and offer final reassurance.

Osborne may have made the theatre fashionable again, but Beckett, Littlewood and Brecht offered approaches to creating theatre that liberated the imagination from traditional subjects and dramatic forms. Arts Council support meant that the material conditions of production and reception were now more favourable to challenging the moribund, but, conversely, its absence compromised Theatre Workshop's aim of running an ensemble-based community theatre because of the need to transfer successful productions to the West End to sustain the company financially. By 1956 the working through of the 1944 Education Act had created an 'educated and upwardly mobile fraction of the middle class' who had 'every reason to welcome an attack on the ethos and credentials of the established middle class, which seemed to be sustaining extremes of wealth and poverty, stifling creativity by despising those without the right accent, and endangering the world by obscuring the reality of the international situation'.[37] This group were now heavily represented among practitioners of theatre and its audiences.

Some of the twenty new theatres built after 1958 actively championed new writing[38] and even theatre shapes were subject to change: Stephen Joseph, a tireless proponent of theatre-in-the-round, established the Library Theatre at Scarborough in 1956, which, in its various subsequent incarnations and latterly under the artistic leadership of Alan Ayckbourn, was one of the two

[36] See, e.g. Susan Hollis Merritt, *Pinter in Play* (Durham, NC: Duke University Press, 1990) for a comprehensive account of critical approaches to Pinter.

[37] Alan Sinfield, 'The Theatre and its Audiences', in Alan Sinfield, ed., *Society and Literature 1945–1970* (London: Methuen, 1983), pp. 173–97. See also Michelene Wandor, *Look Back in Gender* (London: Methuen, 1987), and Stephen Lacey, *British Realist Theatre* (London: Routledge, 1995), for important studies of this period.

[38] George Rowell and Anthony Jackson, *The Repertory Movement* (Cambridge University Press, 1984), pp. 89, 193–4.

major theatres-in-the-round established in this period. The other is the Stoke Victoria (1962), where Peter Cheeseman created a theatre with a distinctive local emphasis, often with plays by Peter Terson. Terson's best-known play *Zigger Zagger* (1967), written for the National Youth Theatre, is notable for its use of the massed ranks of the company in stylised scenes of football crowds.[39]

By the early sixties the number of outlets for new writing had begun to expand substantially. The success of the ESC was matched in 1960 by Peter Hall's decision to commit the RSC to new writing and a London base as well as to Shakespeare and Stratford, and in 1963 by the long-awaited creation of a National Theatre, with Olivier as its director and Tynan as its literary manager.[40] The new producers Michael White and Michael Codron facilitated the careers of dramatists such as Pinter, Joe Orton, John Mortimer, Charles Wood and Tom Stoppard, while the agent Peggy Ramsay championed writers as varied as Howard Brenton and Robert Bolt.[41]

Cold War suspicion and fear of totalitarian power, fuelled by Britain's Suez débâcle and the Soviet invasion of Hungary, both in 1956, permeate many plays of the period. Like Stanley in *The Birthday Party*, Sir Thomas More in Bolt's *A Man for All Seasons* (1960) cannot escape the implacable outsiders who insist that he comply with their demands. Bolt said that using 'the historical form' in *A Man for All Seasons* 'gave me the courage to drive away from the naturalistic form, a courage I lacked when dealing with my own times'[42] and he described his approach to the story of More, the politician who was a casualty of Henry VIII's dynastic politics, as bastardised Brecht. His most obviously Brechtian device is the Common Man, a composite character who plays a number of what would otherwise have been individual small parts and acts as scene-setter and chorus.

The sense of helplessness in the face of uncontrollable forces links characters from the scapegoat tramp in David Rudkin's *Afore Night Come* (RSC, 1962), or the businessman in Bolt's *Gentle Jack* (1963) who is offered the powers of the

[39] For Joseph, Ayckbourn and Cheeseman see Stephen Joseph, *Theatre in the Round* (London: Barrie & Rockliff, 1967), Paul Allen, *Alan Ayckbourn: Grinning at the Edge* (London: Methuen, 2000). See also Shellard, *British Theatre*, p. 129, Rowell and Jackson, *The Repertory Movement*, pp. 150–6.

[40] See John Elsom and Nicholas Tomalin, *The History of the National Theatre* (London: Jonathan Cape, 1978), Sally Beauman, *The Royal Shakespeare Company* (Oxford University Press, 1982), Fay, *Power Play*, pp. 132–93, Kathleen Tynan, *Life of Kenneth Tynan*, particularly pp. 215–29.

[41] For Ramsay, see Colin Chambers, *Peggy: The Life of Margaret Ramsay, Play Agent* (London: Nick Hern, 1997). See James Inverne, *The Impresarios* (London: Oberon, 2000), for White (pp. 134–43, 227–8) and Codron (pp. 158–65, 228–30). See also Michael White, *Empty Seats* (London: Hamish Hamilton, 1984).

[42] Adrian Turner, *Robert Bolt: Scenes from Two Lives* (London: Hutchinson, 1998), p. 161.

god Pan, to the Inca Atahuallpa and the Spaniard Pizzaro in Peter Shaffer's *The Royal Hunt of the Sun* (National, 1964), a spectacular epic about the Spanish conquest of Peru. It also links such otherwise apparently disparate works as Theatre Workshop's *Oh What A Lovely War* (1963) and Stoppard's first success, *Rosencrantz and Guildenstern are Dead* (1966). In the aftermath of the Cuban Missile Crisis (1962), which appeared likely to trigger a third world war, *Oh What A Lovely War* used period songs, improvisation and historical research to create an ironic condemnation of the industrial slaughter of World War I in the form of a seaside pierrot show. Stoppard's play focuses on two attendant lords from *Hamlet*, presented initially in a world like that of *Waiting for Godot* or Pinter's *The Dumb Waiter* (1960), who are forced to deal with the increasingly irrational demands of the action of Shakespeare's play without ever fully understanding their situation.[43]

Although the West End farceur Ray Cooney developed topical frameworks such as the defection of ballet dancers in *Chase Me Comrade!* (1964; Rudolph Nureyev defected from the USSR in 1961) or Middle Eastern James Bond-style intrigue in *Bang Bang Beirut; or, Stand by Your Bedouin* (with Tony Hilton, 1967), Joe Orton claimed new ground for the genre with *Loot* (1965) and *What the Butler Saw* (1969). The industry that grew up after Orton's sensational death, at the hands of his long-term lover Kenneth Halliwell, has tended to obscure the merits of his works[44] but, as Martin Esslin suggested, he democratised the comedy of manners and inverted the traditional generic patterns of farce and the thriller to create worlds in which the triumph of misrule replaces the anticipated resolution of misunderstandings and the restoration of order.[45]

The campaign against pre-censorship of drama gained strength throughout this period culminating in 1968 in the abolition of the Lord Chamberlain's power to ban plays or to insist on radical changes to them. Bans on exploring political, sexual and religious topics led to a certain infantilising of drama and to a barter system where, for example, a certain number of expletives of one kind could sometimes be substituted for a certain number of others. As in the case of Rattigan, censorship may have encouraged writers to develop subtle subtexts and covert systems of euphemism, but it meant that whole areas of life were taboo. In 1957, following the publication of the Wolfenden Report,

43 See Ira Nadel, *Double Act: A Life of Tom Stoppard* (London: Methuen, 2002), for a full biographical account of his career.

44 See Simon Shepherd, *Because We're Queers* (London: Gay Men's Press, 1989) for a critique of that industry.

45 Martin Esslin, 'Joe Orton: the Comedy of (Ill) Manners', in C. W. E. Bigsby, ed., *Contemporary English Drama* (London: Edward Arnold, 1981), pp. 95–107.

the Lord Chamberlain instructed his readers to modify the previous ban on plays dealing with homosexuality in order to allow those that 'made a serious and sincere attempt to deal with the subject'.[46] However, his difficulties with the sexually explicit continued throughout the sixties and dramatists became increasingly determined to tackle political issues. The Lord Chamberlain tried to ban *US* (1966), a controversial devised play about the Vietnam War, derived from the RSC's Artaudian Theatre of Cruelty season mounted at LAMDA in 1964 under the aegis of Peter Brook and Charles Marowitz, because of its perceived danger to the so-called 'special relationship' between the USA and the UK.[47] When politics and (homo)sexuality were mixed, as in the case of Osborne's *A Patriot for Me* (1966) and Edward Bond's *Saved* (1965) and *Early Morning* (1968), the Royal Court had to resort to legal subterfuges to stage them.[48]

Saved, set in a contemporary working-class environment, outraged some critics because of a scene in which a baby in a pram is stoned to death. Bond argues that capitalism effaces institutionalised state violence, while condemning those who commit individual violent acts, and that the bombing of civilians is as reprehensible as killing a baby. Unfortunately the spare naturalistic style of *Saved* means that there is no room to make the comparison within the narrative. In *Narrow Road to the Deep North* (Coventry 1968), Bond abandoned contemporary settings for Brechtian parable, staging both his analysis and the narrative from which it emerges.

Politically, 1968 was noted for worldwide agitation against the state, whether capitalist or Communist, with the *évènements* of May in France, the Prague Spring and anti-Vietnam War protest in the USA and Britain.[49] In theatrical terms the end of pre-censorship led to greater freedom for dramatists to explore political and sexual issues. The further expansion of higher education and the creation of new universities in the sixties, a growth of subsidy and the emerging structures of alternative theatre and touring also encouraged new writing. The year 1968 saw Jim Haynes, who had opened the Traverse Theatre in Edinburgh in 1963, establish the Arts Lab in London and Thelma Holt and Charles Marowitz open their first Open Space theatre. The establishment of the London listings magazine *Time Out*, also in 1968, offered new opportunities

[46] Shellard, *British Theatre*, p. 59.

[47] Nicholas de Jongh, *Politics, Prudery and Perversions: The Censoring of the English Stage, 1901–1968* (London: Methuen, 2000), pp. 148–55.

[48] Roberts, *The Royal Court Theatre and the Modern Stage*, pp. 103, 108–13; de Jongh, *Politics, Prudery and Perversions*, pp. 121–9, 214–44.

[49] Tariq Ali and Susan Watkins, *1968: Marching in the Streets* (London: Bloomsbury, 1998), passim.

for publicising, reviewing and disseminating news about fringe productions. Ed Berman started Interaction's lunchtime theatre in 1968 and played an important role in creating infrastructures to support writing by black, women and gay writers. Prior to the establishment of the Women's Theatre Group and Gay Sweatshop as a result of Berman's seasons, there were relatively few successful plays on gay or lesbian topics. Exceptions include Charles Dyer's *Staircase* (1966) about a male homosexual hairdresser and Frank Marcus's *The Killing of Sister George* (1966), about a lesbian radio star. Black British writers were also largely neglected, although Barry Reckord achieved some success with *Skyvers* (1963), which deals with issues of social exclusion in the context of a failing London school. However, for Berman's 1970 'Black and White Power' season the director Roland Rees discovered a major writer in Mustapha Matura.[50]

The early careers of three writers who were beginning to establish themselves at the end of the sixties are indicative of the ways in which the opportunities for new writing had expanded. Howard Brenton had a Sunday night staging at the Royal Court and a production at Nottingham in 1966. In 1969 he had plays staged by the Brighton Combination, the University of Bradford Drama Group, the Royal Court Upstairs and Portable Theatre (at one of the new London venues, the Oval House). He was awarded an Arts Council bursary and won the John Whiting Award in the same year; *Wesley* was staged in a Methodist chapel in Bradford in 1970 and *Fruit* in a double bill at the Theatre Upstairs with David Hare's *Whatever Happened to Blake*. Brenton met Hare, co-founder of Portable Theatre with Tony Bicât, when he was the only person in the audience for an early Portable Theatre production. Hare's early success *Slag* (1970) was first staged at the Hampstead Theatre Club (founded in 1959) before a revival at the Royal Court where he was successively Literary Manager and Resident Dramatist from 1969–71. Trevor Griffiths's *The Wages of Thin* (1969) and *Occupations* (1970) were first staged at the Stables Theatre Club in Manchester. Hare and Brenton's early careers show that the Royal Court remained an important proving ground but there were now also potential financial rewards in the form of the John Whiting and George Devine awards, bursaries and support for commissions from the Arts Council. Regional theatres, university drama groups, new touring companies, venues such as Hampstead, and new spaces that not been originally designed for theatre such as the Oval House all actively encouraged new writing.

[50] See Roland Rees, *Fringe First* (London: Oberon, 1992), pp. 19–26; Catherine Itzin, *Stages in the Revolution* (London: Methuen, 1980).

By 1970 dramatists were confidently using a wide variety of forms with great freedom. In Alan Ayckbourn's *How the Other Half Loves* (1969) the set simultaneously represents the homes of the boss and his wife and his subordinate and his wife as they each entertain another couple to dinner on separate occasions. This simultaneous staging permits the dramatist to develop radical forms of ironic juxtaposition within the very fabric of the set itself. This established one of the main threads of Ayckbourn's practice in which the collision of discourses is dramatised through the collisions of time and space on the stage.[51] Peter Nichols's *A Day in the Death of Joe Egg* (Glasgow Citizens' Theatre, 1967), an autobiographical account of a couple dealing with challenges posed by their seriously handicapped daughter, uses narrators, stand-up comic routines and parody to enrich his dramaturgy, refusing to treat the situation as simply tragic. His ironic juxtaposition of comic routines and human suffering was extended in *The National Health* (National Theatre at the Old Vic, 1969), where the grim realities of hospital existence are counterpointed by scenes from a romanticised television soap opera like the then-popular *Emergency Ward Ten*. Similarly Peter Barnes's *The Ruling Class* (Nottingham Playhouse, 1968), a forceful attack on the establishment and the hereditary principle, attempted 'to create by means of soliloquy, rhetoric, formalised ritual, slapstick, song and dances, a comic theatre of contrasting moods and opposites, where everything is simultaneously tragic and ridiculous'.[52] This could stand as a programme note for much of the most interesting new writing of the period, with its emphasis on the use of popular forms to interrogate conventional pieties. Alan Bennett's *Forty Years On* (1968) uses the format of a boarding-school house play to offer a pastiche history and critique of Britain in the twentieth century. David Storey's *In Celebration* (1969), where the return of grown-up sons to celebrate their parents' fortieth wedding anniversary leads to Ibsenite recriminations, and *The Contractor* (1969), notable for the erection and dismantling of a wedding marquee on stage, belie their apparently naturalistic form by relegating the celebrations to the interval and, in *The Contractor*, by actually staging the work of putting up the tent.

While Heathcote Williams's *AC/DC* (1970) epitomises many aspects of the new counter-culture, with its three hippies, two schizophrenics, a freewheeling fragmentary linguistic energy and an on-stage trepanning, Christopher Hampton's *The Philanthropist* (also 1970) is a literate, playful modern academic comedy of middle-class disillusionments. In the same year, David Mercer was

[51] See Allen, *Alan Ayckbourn*, pp. 108 ff. and 122 ff.

[52] Trevor R. Griffiths and Carole Woddis, *Theatre Guide*, 2nd edn (London: Bloomsbury, 1991), p. 23.

exploring heady mixes of R. D. Laing and Marx while John McGrath's *Random Happenings in the Hebrides*, influenced by his experience of Paris in May 1968, began to develop the political analysis that was to characterise his later work with the 7:84 company.

It has long been recognised that the more extravagant claims for a revolutionary change in British theatre in the mid-fifties are a mixture of wishful hoping and propaganda. However, despite powerful continuities between the late forties and the late sixties, the British theatre in 1970 was significantly different from that of 1945, in terms of its economic and social organisation, its aesthetics, its politics and its institutions. In 1945 there was no national theatre; by 1970 there were two national companies. In 1945 all plays had to be submitted for censorship before they could be staged; by 1970 they did not. Although by 1945 the wartime CEMA had become the Arts Council, its influence was minimal compared to 1970. In 1945 the ESC did not exist and economic factors militated strongly against the success of ventures committed to new writing; by 1970 the ESC was securely established and there was a developed infrastructure of fringe theatres, commissions and touring companies committed to nurturing new writing. In 1945 it was hard to escape realism and the middle classes; by 1970 Brecht, Littlewood, Pinter and Beckett had opened up a new world of dramatic possibilities.

28

Modernism and anti-Modernism in British poetry

KEITH TUMA AND NATE DORWARD

The most far-reaching changes in the character and self-understanding of British poetry in the post-war era were set in motion in the 1950s, with the advent of a group of writers who were quickly dubbed 'The Movement' – names include Philip Larkin, Donald Davie, Kingsley Amis, D. J. Enright, Robert Conquest, Elizabeth Jennings, John Holloway, John Wain and Thom Gunn. Despite the collective name, the Movement was only a loose affiliation of writers, and whatever sense of group identity and common purpose these writers shared in the 1950s largely dissolved as they pursued increasingly divergent paths in later decades. But the Movement remains crucial to recent literary history because in the 1950s the writers associated with it reimagined and promoted discourses of national identity in order to make of necessity (the reduced role of Britain in world politics) a virtue. This involved complex, sometimes contradictory and provisional adaptations of an argument that set an English poetry and a tradition of Englishness in poetry over and against cosmopolitan Modernisms identified as non-native – an opposition that is at the root of divisions in British poetry that continue to influence the production and critical evaluation of poetry in the present. From our retrospective position it is possible to see Modernist and anti-Modernist discourses in post-war England as existing in a symbiotic relationship; though too much focus on them can leave important middle ground neglected, the questions the Movement raised about Modernism are among the most important literary legacies of the 1950s.

The Movement's identification and promotion as a group was achieved through a well-timed wave of publicity, a history documented by the scholar Blake Morrison.[1] Some of the first book publication of Movement poets came

We would like to thank Peter Middleton and Peter Robinson for their responses to a draft of this essay.

[1] Blake Morrison, *The Movement: English Poetry and Fiction of the 1950s* (Oxford University Press, 1980).

from the small Oxford-based Fantasy Press, but it was the poets' decision to look beyond the coterie culture of little magazines which had sustained previous generations of poets that enabled them to emerge into notoriety with nearly unprecedented speed. Movement poets courted an academic audience by publishing in journals such as F. W. Bateson's *Essays in Criticism*, an academic journal, which, like its forerunner *Scrutiny*, took recent poetry as a legitimate subject of study for a professionalised literary criticism. But they also pursued publication in weeklies such as the *Spectator* and received important radio exposure on the BBC via John Lehmann's show *New Soundings* and John Wain's *First Reading*. The poets were first publicly identified as a group and indirectly bestowed their oddly generic name in J. D. Scott's (unsigned) 1 October 1954 *Spectator* article, 'In the Movement'. The article was quickly followed up by the publication of two group anthologies: D. J. Enright's *Poets of the 1950s* (1955), and the defining anthology, Robert Conquest's *New Lines* (1956) – at once the moment of greatest success for the Movement and the point from which its always-provisional coherence as a group began to unravel.

Critics such as Blake Morrison and Alan Sinfield have analysed the local contexts of the Movement, demonstrating how the writing was responsive to the values of a lower-middle class as these were promoted by the post-war Labour Government and the consensus politics of the 1950s.[2] Hopes for social mobility competed with disappointed adjustment to the persistence of class-divisions. Movement poets were also acutely conscious of and often anxious about the audience for contemporary poetry. For some Movement writers poetry was an invitation to participate in shared cultural ideals of civility and urbanity. Dismissing by implication a range of poetic postures available as the legacy of Romantic agonism, Parnassian elitism, and avant-garde criticality, Donald Davie stressed the importance of a neo-Augustan 'contract' between reader and writer. Movement writers often imagined their audience in terms of the 'discriminating' or 'common reader' that older critics such as F. R. Leavis posited, in hopes of mounting a defence against the onslaughts of a mass culture. Their readers were to be much as they themselves were, neither a vanguard nor the brutalised masses but men and women aspiring to the earnest literacy of the educated middle class. But a number of Movement writers, such as Larkin and Amis, were at times more willing to reach beyond the 'discriminating' reader to court a broader public, whose tastes Leavis himself would have regarded as philistine. In either case, the poets of the Movement

[2] Ibid.; Alan Sinfield, *Literature, Politics and Culture in Postwar Britain* (Oxford: Basil Blackwell, 1989).

were suspicious of or hostile to the 'difficulty' of Modernist predecessors, which they saw as having put poetry's audience at risk. Meanwhile, factors such as expanded access to and growth in higher education in Britain (especially in the 1960s), the introduction of state support for the arts (in the 1950s), and the expansion of paperback publishing suggested an opportunity to build a larger audience for poetry.

Though his work does not always speak for the Movement as a whole, Davie's criticism of the time provides a useful index to the preoccupations behind the writing collected in *New Lines*. Davie's *Purity of Diction in English Verse* (1952) concerns the poetry of the seventeenth, eighteenth and nineteenth centuries but is also a manifesto for Movement aesthetic principles and a polemic concerning the audience for modern poetry. In this book Davie distinguishes between poets such as Gerard Manley Hopkins, who 'could have found a place for every word in the language if only he could have written enough poems',[3] and poets such as Oliver Goldsmith, whose diction is more self-consciously restricted. Davie argues on behalf of a 'chaste diction in poetry', the chosen medium of poets who understand that they are 'writing in a web of responsibilities', 'responsible to past masters for conserving the genres and the decorum which they have evolved'.[4] An Arnoldian tone of the centre is desirable if poetry is to be 'central to the language, conversational not colloquial, poetic not poetical', and reflect a 'valuable urbanity, a civilized moderation and elegance'.[5] Davie acknowledges that the modern poet has 'greater freedom of choice' than the poets from earlier centuries he admires (primarily eighteenth-century poets such as Cowper, Pope, Johnson and hymn-writers such as Wesley and Watts); but for Davie this freedom is 'part and parcel of [the modern poet's] isolated position in his civilization'.[6] Davie's proposal is that a chaster diction and a more 'responsible' attitude towards the tradition will restore poetry to an importance it has lost.

Davie's ideals are a useful guide, but in *New Lines* they alternately reinforce or strain against another tendency in the Movement, a sometimes bitter debunking of high culture as it allegedly reproduced rarefied and effete values, snobbery and privilege – high culture as aristocratic culture. The poetry in *New Lines* is overtly 'traditional', cast in the form of the brief lyric, making use of tightly controlled form, rhyme and metre rather than free verse. At the same time, Movement writers distrusted writing that seemed to them too 'literary': not only rejecting the rhetorical excess of 1940s neo-Romanticism,

3 Donald Davie, *Purity of Diction in English Verse* (1952; rpt. with postscript, London: Routledge, 1967), p. 5.

4 Ibid., pp. 26, 16. 5 Ibid., p. 27. 6 Ibid., p. 10.

they also abandoned much of the conventional territory of the lyric tradition – both Wain and Amis, for instance, contributed poems ridiculing the genre of nature poetry ('Reason for Not Writing Orthodox Nature Poetry' and 'Here Is Where').[7] Movement writing used a plain idiom, conversational in tone and sometimes pointedly low and unliterary (e.g. Larkin's 'Toads' or Amis's 'Something Nasty in the Bookshop'),[8] but more often decorous and urbane. Its characteristic voice has often been described as 'ironic', though this irony was a matter of its self-consciously deflationary tone, rather than the kinds of structural poetic irony valued by the New Criticism. The poems are prone to aphorism and to asides to an implied reader; they often develop by means of logical argumentation or via a move from anecdote to a moral proposition (often stoical cold comfort). Such an emphasis on discursiveness within a lyrical form is reminiscent of the work of the seventeenth-century Metaphysicals and – in Wain's work in particular – of William Empson's modern development of that style; but it also bears comparison with currents in British philosophy of the period. Suspicion of metaphysical claims and confidence in the resources of plain, everyday language are among the values they share with influential philosophers such as Wittgenstein, Ayer and Austin. In George Orwell they had one important model of an older writer who applied some of those same values to cultural criticism.

The Movement's views of poetry and poetic vocation now seem unambitious; at the time, though, their poems and aesthetic ideals were often presented as a necessary and ethical response to economic and geopolitical developments in the post-war world. Davie put the argument histrionically in poems like 'Creon's Mouse', which advocated a 'self-induced and stubborn loss of nerve', and 'Rejoinder to a Critic', which rather oddly saw the bombing of Hiroshima as the result of intemperate passion and asked rhetorically: 'How dare we now be anything but numb?'[9] This emphasis on the 'moral' and the 'moderate' was also a polemical attack on Modernism and on the neo-Romantic poetry of the 1940s, poetries whose moral failings were conveniently symbolised by the figures of the American poet Ezra Pound (with his anti-Semitism and his turn to Italian Fascism) and the British poet Dylan Thomas (who drank himself to death in his thirties). The critique of 'hyperbolic and highly metaphorical language' in *Purity of Diction* implicitly targeted 1940s poetic styles, but its most notorious attack is on Anglo-American Modernism,

7 Robert Conquest, ed., *New Lines* (London: Macmillan, 1956), pp. 83–4, 47–8.
8 Ibid., pp. 26–8, 46–7.
9 Donald Davie, *Collected Poems*, ed. Neil Powell (Manchester: Carcanet Press, 2002), pp. 17, 67–8.

in Davie's claim that 'the development from Imagism in poetry to fascism in politics is clear and unbroken'.[10]

The Movement did not invent anti-Modernism; rather, it manipulated an existing discourse in which 'Englishness' had long figured as the opposite term to 'Modernism'. As Charles Harrison writes in an essay on British avant-garde painters of the 1930s: 'To adopt a cosmopolitan position is . . . to view the culture of British art with a critical regard and thus to step outside the business-as-normal of the insular art world . . . [M]odernism itself was still seen as an exotic commodity in the British art world of the 1920s and early 1930s.'[11] It is not that Modernism was unknown in Britain in those earlier decades, but rather that – despite the existence of many British writers and artists working in Modernist or Modernist-inflected modes – Modernism remained for many something foreign. The rhetorical counterbalance to a cosmopolitan Modernist discourse is a native English genius whose attributes are enumerated by Harrison in connection with the visual arts but are also pertinent to literature: 'an attachment to the landscape, an empirical regard, a romanticism towards the past, a sense of moderation sometimes associated with virtuous amateurism . . . and, most important of all, a determined individuality'.[12] The pastoralism evident in such a self-image is often given a bitter spin by the Movement, redolent of its 1950s context: a nostalgia for a national culture and native landscape that are in the process of decay; a defensive insularity memorably encapsulated in Larkin's scoffing in an interview at the idea of reading foreign authors: '*Foreign* poetry? *No!*'[13] As Harrison's phrase 'empirical regard' suggests, 'empiricism' was one key nexus of ideas of Englishness: a commonsense emphasis on the unmediated experience of an autonomous, coherent self able to represent self and world in language in principle transparent; a corresponding scepticism concerning metaphysical claims and openly rhetorical or opaque uses of language.[14] Here again one notes continuities between the Movement's distrust of Modernist styles and the hostility of ordinary-language philosophy to the 'jargon' of continental philosophy.

The Movement's assiduous promotional campaign succeeded in attracting much discussion, both favourable and unfavourable, and the appearance of

[10] Davie, *Purity of Diction*, pp. 18, 99.

[11] Charles Harrison, 'England's Climate', in Brian Allen, ed., *Towards a Modern Art World* (New Haven and London: Yale University Press, 1995), pp. 207–25; quotation from p. 211.

[12] Ibid., pp. 215–16.

[13] Philip Larkin, 'A Conversation with Ian Hamilton', in Anthony Thwaite, ed., *Further Requirements: Interviews, Broadcasts, Statements and Book Reviews* (London: Faber & Faber, 2001), pp. 19–26; quotation from p. 25.

[14] See Antony Easthope, *Englishness and National Culture* (London and New York: Routledge, 1999).

New Lines even prompted a riposte in the shape of Dannie Abse and Howard Sergeant's *Mavericks* (1957), an anthology of contemporary poets excluded from the other book. But the most decisive response to *New Lines* came some years later, with A. Alvarez's 1962 Penguin anthology *The New Poetry*.[15] Though the selection included several Movement poets, Alvarez's preface, subtitled 'Beyond the Gentility Principle', was sharply critical of the Movement's limitations. For Alvarez, the twentieth century delivered two crucial shocks to traditional humanism that were insufficiently recognised by Movement writers: the first was Freud's discovery of the unconscious; the second was the unprecedented violence of a century that saw two world wars, the Holocaust and the development of the atom bomb. These two shocks were for Alvarez essentially the same: the revelation of the savagery and madness that lie at the heart of man. Alvarez was trying to articulate an Existentialist or Absurdist poetics (he was among the first critics to understand Samuel Beckett's importance); but in *The New Poetry* his preference turns out to be for an Expressionist poetry articulating personal crisis and despair, exemplified by American 'Confessional' poetry. The book's selection of British poetry is prefaced by generous selections from Robert Lowell and John Berryman; in the second edition, Anne Sexton and Sylvia Plath were added (including Plath's notorious 'Daddy', which neatly fulfilled Alvarez's agenda through its appropriation of Holocaust imagery).[16]

Alvarez's favoured author among the British contributors to *The New Poetry* was Ted Hughes. Like Alvarez, Hughes was preoccupied with the legacy of psychological and cultural damage inflicted by both world wars: each of Hughes's early books contains poems about World War I, and Hughes was an early advocate of the posthumously published work of World War II soldier–poet Keith Douglas. But the central mode of Hughes's work is an anti-sentimental revision of an English tradition of nature poetry. His immediate twentieth-century precursor was the D. H. Lawrence of *Birds, Beasts and Flowers*, but Lawrence's quirky wit and use of the mock-dialogue to convey the quiddity of animals and plants is absent from Hughes's harsher and blunter rhetoric, which conjures up and celebrates with grim relish the malevolence and violence of the natural world. Lurid and visceral images insist on the carnality of the mind and on the otherness of nature: when in 'Thrushes', for instance, he calls the birds 'More coiled steel than living',[17] the figure points simultaneously to the

15 A. Alvarez, ed., *The New Poetry* (Harmondsworth: Penguin, 1962).
16 A. Alvarez, ed., *The New Poetry*, 2nd edn (Harmondsworth: Penguin, 1966), pp. 64–6.
17 Ted Hughes, *Selected Poems, 1957–1981* (London: Faber & Faber, 1982), p. 57.

inhuman dimensions of both the man-made and natural worlds. Such similes have their risks, however: in his less successful work, the anthropocentric metaphors and similes can suggest the reductiveness of a cartoonish bestiary. In Hughes's most famous book, *Crow* (1970), a series of poems about an avian trickster figure, he embraced just such a cartoon.

Hughes's exaltation of a predatory animal world is pitched explicitly against the rationality and self-consciousness of civilised humankind, as if morality is frail or irrelevant beside the Hobbesian imperatives of survival. Though in his earlier poems he does not address life in Britain in the 1950s by overtly commenting on contemporary social conditions, this sense of the decadence of modern civilisation bears comparison with the Movement's nostalgia and sense of Britain's cultural decline. An early Hughes poem, 'The Retired Colonel', is untypical of his work but revealing:

> And what if his sort should vanish?
> The rabble starlings roar upon
> Trafalgar. The man-eating British lion
> By a pimply age brought down.[18]

Such macho nostalgia forms an important subtext to his sense of animal instinct as superior to (Christian) morality and to the rational, 'civilised' mind. Consider the closing lines from 'Hawk Roosting' – one of Hughes's most controversial poems for its apparent glorification of the hawk's brute power and violence:

> My eye has permitted no change.
> I am going to keep things like this.[19]

The hawk's boast of his control over an unchanging world, when juxtaposed with the lament for the colonel whose era is past, suggests that Hughes's assertion of a permanent, primordial perspective is indirectly a response to the fact of British decline and impotence – an escapist fantasy grounded in a deeply conservative view of cultural history.

From the perspective of younger, more cosmopolitan writers, the emergence of Alvarez and Hughes did not importantly reshape the contours of post-war British poetry. In 1983, for instance, the poet–critic Andrew Crozier argued that 'our sense of the situation of poetry today is conditioned by the arguments of 1956–66'.[20] Crozier's essay is a critique of the circumscribed nature

[18] Ibid., p. 50. [19] Ibid., p. 43.

[20] Andrew Crozier, 'Thrills and Frills: Poetry as Figures of Empirical Lyricism', in Alan Sinfield, ed., *Society and Literature, 1945–1970* (London: Methuen, 1983), pp. 199–233; quotation from p. 220–1.

of the contemporary British poetry canon, which then had as its chief figures Larkin, Hughes and the Irish poet Seamus Heaney. One of Crozier's most provocative gestures is to insist that Larkin and Hughes, poets usually 'perceived as antithetical, the one tame and insular, the other barbaric and invoking elemental powers', in fact share several key aesthetic assumptions that have come to define the post-war canon.[21] He sums these up in a later essay: 'the enunciation . . . of an empirical subject, and a textual insistence on figures of rhetoric as the discernible sign of the poetic'.[22] For Crozier, such an aesthetic weakens poetry's capacity to register the world outside the self, external particulars becoming at worst mere accessories to the poet–speaker's egotism – as the poet Charles Tomlinson acidly put it in a 1957 review of *New Lines*, to his 'mental conceit of himself'.[23] The world is wilfully banalised, only to be reanimated by a luxuriance of rhetorical devices. A poet such as Larkin was (as Crozier shows) highly various and subtle in his range of rhetorical devices, but the history of mainstream poetry shows a progressive stylistic thinning-out, settling down eventually on metaphor and simile as the quintessential guarantees of the poetic.

Crozier's account is a polemical one, and thus cannot explain the profile and reputation of a number of poets in this period working at a distance from the shifts in literary taste and politics marked by *New Lines* and *The New Poetry*. Alvarez's anthology, however much it served to consolidate a poetic 'mainstream' style (in its second edition (1966) it became a bestseller of the decade), contained several poets working at a markedly critical slant to such a style. Geoffrey Hill is a particularly interesting inclusion from this perspective. Among Hill's early poetic models were the American poet–critics Allen Tate and John Crowe Ransom, who were mentors to Alvarez's pantheon of Lowell and Berryman. Such influences place Hill in a particular Modernist lineage – one might call it 'post-Eliotic' – and a Modernist 'crisis of the word' is central to Hill's work. Hill's anxious preoccupation with the question of the poet's ethical responsibilities is informed by a sense of the inherent treacherousness and inertia of language itself, and in particular by a sense of how deeply language has been tainted by the violence of human history, especially the atrocities of both world wars (a further point of contact with Alvarez). Such a sense of taint echoes religious concepts of original sin – Hill's prose writings

[21] Ibid., p. 202.

[22] Andrew Crozier, 'Resting on Laurels', in Alistair Davies and Alan Sinfield, eds., *British Culture of the Postwar: An Introduction to Literature and Society, 1945–1999* (London and New York: Routledge, 2000), pp. 192–204; quotation from p. 193.

[23] Cited in Crozier in Sinfield, ed., 'Thrills and Frills', p. 215.

work in knotty dialogue with theological concepts and terminology. But it is also a response specific to the post-World War II moment, one also found in European authors such as Paul Celan. For Hill, art's claims to autonomy or to being a token of civilisation need to be subjected to disillusioned, sometimes agonised scrutiny.

Hill's early work approaches such concerns with a mixture of ceremonial elegy and cutting ironies. Here, for example, is 'Drake's Drum', from the sequence 'Metamorphoses' (1959):

> Those varied dead. The undiscerning sea
> Shelves and dissolves their flesh as it burns spray
>
> Who do not shriek like gulls nor dolphins ride
> Crouched under spume to England's erect side
>
> Though there a soaked sleeve lolls or shoe patrols
> Tide-padded thick shallows, squats in choked pools
>
> Neither our designed wreaths nor used words
> Sink to their melted ears and melted hearts.[24]

Like Eliot, Hill appropriates other works' titles to position the writing with self-conscious irony within cultural and literary history. The high-culture reference to Ovid's *Metamorphoses* bumps up against the allusion to a once-popular late-Victorian poem, Sir Henry Newbolt's thumpingly patriotic 'Drake's Drum'. Hill's poem is charged with a distrust of its own ability to memorialise the dead, and of the way that the dead have been memorialised in past poetry. The impure diction registers points of maximum pressure: the first line, for instance, yokes together a dignified commonplace (the sea's erasure of the particularities of human existences into a common mortality) and a parodic aestheticism (as if the speaker were absurdly appreciating the corpses' aesthetic variety and complaining about the sea's lack of critical discernment). The next stanzas dispose of Ovid and Newbolt's consolatory myths: of the metamorphic persistence of life (according to seafaring lore, gulls are the souls of dead sailors), the power of poetry (the poet Arion, facing drowning, sang a dirge and was saved by a dolphin which carried him off to Corinth), and of patriotic myth (Newbolt's poem claims that beating the drum of Sir Francis Drake will summon his spirit to repel an invasion of England's shores). The final couplet questions the value of poetic rhetoric: a eulogy aims to melt the hearts of the living; the dead, now out of reach, are only 'melted' in that their

[24] Geoffrey Hill, *Collected Poems* (Harmondsworth: Penguin, 1985), p. 35.

memories are manipulated like wax by the skilful rhetorician for his own ends. Though written before *The New Poetry* appeared, it is as if the poem delivers an anticipatory critique of Alvarez's histrionic rhetoric.

The New Poetry's inclusion of Hill, and other poets such as Charles Tomlinson and Christopher Middleton working in recognisably Modernist veins, begins to complicate our picture of the 1950s and early 1960s. There were also many other, often older poets active in this period who fell outside the chronological or aesthetic boundaries of Alvarez's book, though shifts of taste and literary power often meant that their careers were in eclipse. Modernist poets of an earlier generation such as Hugh MacDiarmid, David Jones, Lynette Roberts and Basil Bunting were still writing; the last three all wrote major long poems responsive to the experience of World War II: Jones's *The Anathemata* (1952), Roberts's *Gods with Stainless Ears* (1951), and Bunting's *The Spoils* (1951). Several poets associated with 1940s neo-Romanticism were still active, such as Kathleen Raine, David Gascoyne and George Barker; Barker even achieved a *succès de scandale* with the BBC broadcast of *The True Confessions of George Barker*, with its swaggering sexual frankness. W. S. Graham's opaque Apocalyptic idiom of the 1940s had by the time of *The Nightfishing* (1955) developed into a wholly distinctive style, and that book's title poem is one of the decade's finest and most ambitious long poems, a lyrical meditation on the rhythms and mysteries of being. Other 1940s writers dropped from sight: Nicholas Moore, for instance, virtually ceased writing and publishing after his selected poems, *Recollections of the Gala*, appeared in 1950, and was only to return to poetry again in the late 1960s in the more receptive climate of the small-press scene of the time.

While it is important to understand the ways in which an anti-Modernist poetry seemed to have the upper hand during much of the period under discussion, we need to see both Modernist and anti-Modernist poetry as in many ways part of a larger whole, at once linked and divided by their preoccupations with a number of common aesthetic issues. Perhaps the closest approach to such a perspective within the period itself came in Donald Davie's second critical book, *Articulate Energy: An Enquiry into the Syntax of English Poetry* (1955), a transitional book still within the ambit of Movement aesthetics but less polemical, more pluralist than *Purity of Diction*; the book demonstrates a growing, if critical, involvement with Modernist aesthetics that would become explicit with his next book, *Ezra Pound: Poet as Sculptor* (1964). *Articulate Energy* identifies the 'decisive innovation' that gives us a modern poetry as a 'change of attitude toward poetic syntax': '*What is common to all modern poetry is the assertion or the assumption (most often the latter) that syntax in poetry is wholly different from syntax as understood by logicians and grammarians*.'[25] Davie argues that even when post-Symbolist poetries adhere to conventional syntactic forms these are in a sense hollowed-out: treated (as he says) 'like music' or 'like mathematics'.[26] His exposition of such ideas is careful and often sympathetic, but in the end for Davie they imply a disastrous, almost decadent loss of faith in the ability of language to represent experience and convey the poet's meaning. He instead defends what he calls 'authentic syntax' – that is, a form of mimesis: he especially values, for instance, syntax's ability to 'mim[e] a movement of the mind or of fate', and, fearing that 'The tendency of all symbolist theories is to make the world of poetry more autonomous', argues for poetry that retains 'the reek of the human'.[27]

Davie's book thus makes explicit certain tacit assumptions lying behind this period's divisions between Modernism and anti-Modernism. The pluralism of Davie's survey is unable to dislodge the starkly posed oppositions that structure his argument. In terms he borrows from philosopher Susanne Langer he sees the poet as choosing between 'expression' and 'expressiveness', between insisting upon authorial power over language and ceding control to the signifier.[28] It is as if Davie feels these tendencies are divergent or even mutually exclusive, rather than the necessarily interlocking components of any poetic utterance. By contrast, a later writer such as the contemporary poet–critic Denise Riley has spoken of her desire to 'revive some of the dialectic as a quite modest mutuality between the great dictator Language and the writer, even if the boss [i. e. language] inevitably retains the upper hand'. Elsewhere she says, in words that get to the heart of the binary set forth by Davie: 'It's neither that affect may be "conveyed in" words nor that in a coldly reductive manner it is "really only" words – but that in a full and exuberant sense, sensibility *is* words.'[29]

Both Davie's and Riley's arguments remind us – although with (respectively) an anxious and a more optimistic spin – that the words of the poem are rooted in affective and social values that transcend poetry, a fact that helps us understand the consequences of what otherwise might seem to be only aesthetic choices. Careful examination of poems of this period reveals a range of response to questions of whether to mimic the qualities of everyday speech or to work at a tangent to them; of whether to emphasise the enunciating 'I' or to displace

[25] Donald Davie, *Articulate Energy: An Enquiry into the Syntax of English Poetry* (1955; rpt. New York: Harcourt, Brace, 1958), p. 148.
[26] Ibid., pp. 85, 91. [27] Ibid., pp. 158, 161.
[28] Susanne Langer, quoted in Davie, *Articulate Energy*, p. 17.
[29] Denise Riley, *The Words of Selves: Identification, Solidarity, Irony* (Stanford University Press, 2000), pp. 68, 36.

it; of whether and how to engage with traditional metrics, syntax and form – all these decisions suggesting the poets' different ways of understanding human agency as it shapes and is shaped by the social and historical medium of language. Consider, for instance, passages from poems by Roberts and then Graham, which borrow equally from Modernist and 1940s aesthetics:

I, rimmeled, awake before the dressing sun:
Alone I, pent up incinerator, serf of satellite gloom
Cower around my cradled self; find crape-plume
In a work-basket cast into swaddling clothes
Forcipated from my mind after the foetal fall:

Rising ashly, challenge blood to curb – compose –
Martial mortal, face a red mourning alone.[30]

Yes as alike as entirely
You my father I see
That high Greenock tenement
And whole shipyarded front.[31]

In both these passages syntax is pushed out of shape in order to shift a personal pronoun into an unusually precarious position, perhaps out of a distrust of poetic egotism similar to Crozier's and Tomlinson's. In Roberts's lines the pronoun 'I' is immediately introduced, and then isolated by a comma – it is indeed an 'Alone I', who in this extraordinarily winding, tortuous sentence goes from the extremes of despair and self-division (at this point in the narrative the speaker has endured a miscarriage and the absence of a lover) to a new resolve as she 'Ris[es] ashly' like a phoenix. Graham's lines are an address to a family member, and the speech-like informality of the opening 'Yes' and the simple diction (only the coinage 'shipyarded' is out of the ordinary) give them a markedly different tone from Roberts's stricken bardic voice. But Graham's ambiguous syntax and lineation retard the pace of reading, pulling words apart from one another: we are led to see meaning as emerging in the poem rather than as something pre-existing and carried by it. The first line, for instance, is barely under way before Graham essays a different wording, leaving both possibilities side by side: likeness *and* identity. It is as if in these lines Graham is questioning distinctions between subject and object, self and environment, present and memory. Subject and object are withheld until line 2, at which point

30 Lynette Roberts *Gods with Stainless Ears* (London: Faber & Faber, 1951), p. 38.
31 W. S. Graham, 'To My Father' (1949), *Collected Poems, 1942–1977* (London and Boston: Faber & Faber, 1979), p. 85.

all the pronouns are crammed together in a single line, with 'You' occupying the place where one might ordinarily find an adjective. 'I see' – ordinarily the most masterful of assertions – is instead like a hinge: the lineation tempts one into reading line 2 as a contorted version of 'I see you, my father', but at the turn of the line, with (at last) a syntactically unbroken run of words, the poem finally permits an unobstructed view of a scene.

Syntax is no less scrupulously and self-consciously employed in the openings of two well-known poems by Movement writers Thom Gunn and Philip Larkin, though to very different ends:

> Across the open countryside,
> Into the walls of rain I ride.
> It beats my cheek, drenches my knees,
> But I am being what I please.[32]

> Once I am sure there's nothing going on
> I step inside, letting the door thud shut.[33]

The withholding of subject and verb in Gunn's first sentence is comparable to Graham's use of suspension, but here the syntactic inversions, heavy rhyme and regular rhythm are recognizably part of an older, canonical tradition of verse syntax, and Gunn exploits them to shunt an assertive pronoun and verb – 'I ride' – to the sentence's point of maximum emphasis and closure. This play of suspension and resolution assists in underlining the tensions between formality and freedom that are the subject of this and many another poem of Gunn's. The next couplet functions to balance the first, complementing assertive *doing* ('I ride') with a strangely assertive 'being', the hypnotically parallel syntax and repetitive possessives and pronouns enfolding the self *in* itself (a premonition of the cyclist's 'Vision of his Death') – a point reinforced by the repeated long 'e's that give the couplet the sound of tautology.

The opening of 'Church Going' is far closer to the textures of conversational English than Gunn. Larkin's lines again contain a brief suspension, but the inclusion of the first-person pronoun in the suspended clause ('Once I am sure . . .') serves to downplay syntactic tension. One could easily imagine the lines placed in reverse order, but Larkin's arrangement is in the service of understated comedy – the speaker sneaking in 'when nothing's going on' (a telling paraphrasis for 'when no service is in progress'), the 'I' who at last

[32] Thom Gunn, 'The Unsettled Motorcyclist's Vision of his Death' (1957), *Collected Poems* (London and Boston: Faber & Faber, 1993), p. 54.

[33] Philip Larkin, 'Church Going' (1955), *Collected Poems*, ed. Anthony Thwaite (London: Faber & Faber, 1988), p. 97.

takes action – 'I step inside' – embarrassed by the door's loud closing. Such deflationary comedy and arch philistinism are part of a larger rhetorical structure which builds from this opening to the final resonant and enveloping cadences: 'A serious house on serious earth it is, / In whose blent air all our compulsions meet, / Are recognised, and robed as destinies.' As the poem moves from anecdote to summary statement the speaker imagines a representative man of the future, the 'he' who recognises the dignity of religious traditions passing away; meanwhile, the poem's language preserves that dignity in a secular form, by lending him the authority of traditions of public, quasi-liturgical oratory.

Similar attempts at closer analysis could be performed with the work of many of the successors to the Movement, though arguably little of this body of work is as compellingly realised as the best Movement verse. In the early 1960s, the Movement's most direct successor was 'The Group', a similarly blandly named set of writers who emerged from a regular writing workshop conducted by Philip Hobsbaum, and whose poems were gathered in *A Group Anthology* (1963). Poets associated with the Group include Alan Brownjohn, Peter Porter, George MacBeth (who was to be highly influential through his poetry programming at the BBC), Edward Lucie-Smith and Adrian Mitchell. For the most part these poets shared the Movement's suspicion of Modernist form and high seriousness – one of Porter's later books is entitled *The Cost of Seriousness* (1978). Loquacious where Larkin is terse, Porter's poetry is indebted to the Roman and Augustan satirists (he is a noted translator of the Latin epigrammatist Martial) but also often explicitly debunks the pretensions of his learning: 'Kierkegaard was a commuter too, can I come and smell you . . .'[34] Brownjohn's poetry can be equally prolix but has strains of earnestness and a tonal irony more akin to Movement poetry. The most idiosyncratic and possibly finest poet in the Group was Peter Redgrove, whose work has been linked with the poetry of Ted Hughes for its neo-Expressionism and investment in archetypal psychology, though Redgrove's poetry and his prose collaborations with Penelope Shuttle have more sympathetically explored feminine archetypes in human psychology. Alvarez's most direct heir was the poet–critic Ian Hamilton, founder of *The Review*, one of the most influential journals of the time and famous for the harshness of its reviews. Hamilton's primary enthusiasms were for the American writers Alvarez had espoused, such as Lowell and Berryman; his own verse deals with confessional

34 Peter Porter, 'Nine Points of the Law', in *Collected Poems* (Oxford University Press, 1983), pp. 67–71; quotation from p. 69.

themes with tight-lipped stylisation. Other poets active in the 1960s – names include Rosemary Tonks, C. H. Sisson, and Stevie Smith – do not belong to these tendencies in post-Movement verse, nor to the diverse modes of 'counter-culture' poetry to which we now turn.

In the 1960s, rhetoric linking Movement poets with conservative and academic values was common. This rhetoric is strident in Michael Horovitz's 1969 anthology *Children of Albion: Poetry of the Underground*, which happily announces the end of the Movement.[35] Horovitz's evidence was the poetry of David Chaloner, Andrew Crozier, Ian Hamilton Finlay, Roy Fisher, Lee Harwood, John James, Tom Pickard, Tom Raworth, Carlyle Reedy, Anselm Hollo and Gael Turnbull, among others who went on to less notable accomplishment (it is nothing if not an exasperating grab-bag of a book). Horovitz's 'Afterwords' manifesto exudes a spirit of wilful enthusiasm that will seem poignant, naïve, optimistic or bewildered depending on one's view of the 'underground' or 'counter-culture' that emerged in the decade. William Blake and Allen Ginsberg are iconic figures for him, as they were for much of the counter-culture for their promotion of an idea of the poet as prophet or revolutionary; European avant-gardists from Rimbaud to Mayakovsky and American Modernists are praised in a hymn to an international and transatlantic experimentalism that promised to liberate British poetry from 'the demands of immured Academe' and other ills associated with the Movement.[36]

If Horowitz's book now seems period-bound, its description of important changes in poetry retains a basic truth. Poets were indeed rejecting the 'prescription of "craft"' for 'process, the direct dictates of the writing in hand',[37] and despite the Movement's fears that Modernism had destroyed the audience for modern poetry, Modernist techniques and styles were being recognisably drawn on and reimagined by the counter-culture. The eminently accessible poems of the popular poet Adrian Henri, for instance, use modes of collage and parataxis borrowed from Dada and Surrealism. Poetry readings in clubs and cafes and at venues such as the Morden Tower in Newcastle were pushing poetry beyond 'the dusty iambic grooves of book (society) culture'[38] into the centre of a new youth culture. If select poets such as Dylan Thomas, Larkin and Sir John Betjeman still sold well, the poetry readings of the middle to late 1960s gathered sizable audiences for a newer poetry and for poetry as *event*. The improvisational aesthetic of jazz and, in the work of the Liverpool poets (Henri, Brian Patten and Roger McGough), the energies of rock 'n' roll were

[35] Michael Horovitz, 'Afterwords', in Michael Horovitz, ed., *Children of Albion: Poetry of the Underground in Great Britain* (Harmondsworth: Penguin, 1969), p. 317.
[36] Ibid., p. 318. [37] Ibid., p. 320. [38] Ibid., p. 329.

resources as poets rejected older forms of high culture. Other forms of cross-artform fertilisation were evident in the work of Bob Cobbing and Ian Hamilton Finlay, both associated with the international 'concrete poetry' movement of the time but developing almost diametrically opposed aesthetics – Cobbing's practice opening onto a 'sound poetry' tradition harking back to Dada and Kurt Schwitters; Finlay's onto sculpture, installation and land art. Poetry was to be briefly at the centre of a revolution of everyday life reinventing social and sexual codes and offering resistance to Cold War politics in Vietnam and elsewhere. Anarchic and collectivist energies were evident not only in the modes of poetic facture and performance but also in the proliferation of do-it-yourself small-press magazines and books, patterned after similar activity in the United States. Magazines were published not only in London but also in cities throughout Britain; some of them, like Jon Silkin's *Stand* or John Riley and Tim Longville's *Grosseteste Review*, were to have a long life. Small presses flourished, including Ferry, Fulcrum, Goliard, Grosseteste, Trigram, Wild Hawthorn and Writers Forum.

The internationalism of 1960s counter-culture was a challenge to the Movement's 'little-englandism', its effort to consolidate English identity and secure its position at the moral and political centre of post-imperial British culture; but this was only half the story. In this period regional identities and traditions were also being reimagined, often by merging local with Modernist traditions. This was not altogether a new development; internationalism and regionalism had coexisted, for instance, in the work of the Scottish Modernist Hugh MacDiarmid. What was different in the 1960s is that regional identities *within England* also began to be more manifest. Roy Fisher's long poem *City* (1962) appropriates and collages together a range of available modes, from Eliotic monologue to Objectivist lyric to Surrealism to descriptive prose, in its meditations on alienation and the urban decay and renewal of Birmingham. The example of William Carlos Williams and other Modernists inspired poets such as Tom Pickard (in Newcastle) and Tom Leonard (in Glasgow) in their effort to create a poetry out of the working-class dialects they spoke and heard. 'Englishness' itself was being refashioned in the work of the poets associated with the worksheet *The English Intelligencer* – J. H. Prynne, Andrew Crozier, Peter Riley and many others – in a collective endeavour indebted to the emphasis on history and place as the grounds of being and knowledge in the work of Charles Olson and other New American poets.

But there was no more important figure in the merger of local, regional traditions and Modernism than the Northumbrian poet Basil Bunting, whose greatest poem, *Briggflatts*, was published in 1966 by Fulcrum. The poem is autobiography in the impersonal Modernist mode, the poet's life merging with a host of historical figures. Bunting's poem is every bit as deserving of an adjective like 'post-imperial' as is Movement work, but in its celebration of Northumbrian culture and its description of the wanderings of the poet, it reads the history of empire as fact rather than occasion for commentary. The poem bypasses Movement irony and moralising: it finds a place for passages that are unabashedly sentimental and for others marked by a stoic disregard for time: 'Shepherds follow the links, / sweet turf studded with thrift . . . / silence by silence sits / and Then is diffused in Now.'[39] Bunting's verse technique suggests influences ranging from Persian classical poetry to the work of his mentor Pound; Eliot's *Four Quartets* may also have influenced his use of the sonata as a musical analogue for the poem's structure, in which motifs are stated and revisited in tones ranging from the heroic to the elegiac. The poem's dense weave of rhyme, alliteration and assonance, and its variation of syntax, line and stanza, are *sui generis*. When pressed to explain the poem's patterned music and layered symbols, Bunting often referred to the lacings and plaitings of the illuminations to the *Codex Lindisfarnensis*, the most famous of Northumbrian books, and his notes to the poem insist on a northern idiom that would be mangled by 'southrons'. Thus the poem tries to bespeak an Englishness that would be foreign to the Movement, a geography that includes Dublin, York and Orkney (and an interlude in Persia) and a history reaching back to the Vikings and beyond. It also voices – if sometimes regretfully – an ambitious idea of poetic vocation that is neither the Movement idea of the poet as common man aspiring to the public voice of the cultural commentator, nor the 'underground' idea of the poet as priest or revolutionary. Rather, the poet is the person who risks all in pursuit of precision of craft and in service to the traditions of bardic song:

Brief words are hard to find,
shapes to carve and discard:
Bloodaxe, king of York,
king of Dublin, king of Orkney.
Take no notice of tears;
letter the stone to stand
over love laid aside lest
insufferable happiness impede
flight to Stainmore,

[39] Basil Bunting, *Complete Poems*, ed. Richard Caddel (Oxford and New York: Oxford University Press, 1995), p. 61.

to trace
lark, mallet,
becks, flocks,
and axe knocks.[40]

When *Briggflatts* was published, many poets and critics were buoyed by the possibilities of Modernism in England. In an effort to name it as the crowning achievement of its era, Donald Davie was to go so far as to title a 1989 collection of his criticism *Under Briggflatts*. But Bunting was an old man by 1966 and wrote little after *Briggflatts*. The opening for Modernism that *Briggflatts* and other notable poetic achievements of the 1960s – Prynne's *The White Stones*, Fisher's *City*, Tom Raworth's *The Relation Ship* and Lee Harwood's *The White Room*, among many others – appeared to offer poetry in Britain would seem like ancient history just a decade later. The economic crises of the 1970s and the growing ideological backlash against 1960s counter-culture combined to put pressure on the Modernist small-press community, limiting opportunities for publishing and for critical discourse about what suddenly had become a marginal poetic practice; the increasing importance of identity politics in the period lent representational and autobiographical poetic modes new urgency. By the early 1980s, much of the Modernist small-press activity of the past decades could be written out of the record by a newly rejuvenated poetic mainstream, a process visible in miniature in Edward Lucie-Smith's new pessimism about the prospects of Modernism and small-press publishing in the 'Introduction' to the revised 1985 edition of his 1970 anthology *British Poetry since 1945*,[41] or in the flat assertion by Blake Morrison and Andrew Motion in the 'Introduction' to their *Penguin Book of Contemporary British Poetry* (1982) that for 'much of the 1960s and 70s . . . very little . . . seemed to be happening' in British poetry.[42] The history of this turn of the tide is the subject of Peter Middleton's essay later in this volume.

40 Ibid., p. 46.

41 Edward Lucie-Smith, ed., *British Poetry since 1945*, rev. edn (Harmondsworth: Penguin, 1985).

42 Blake Morrison and Andrew Motion, 'Introduction' to *The Penguin Book of Contemporary British Poetry*, ed. Blake Morrison and Andrew Motion (Harmondsworth: Penguin, 1982), p. 11.

29

Nation, region, place: devolving cultures

MORAG SHIACH

The years between 1945 and 1970 saw a significant increase in public funding for the arts. The Arts Council, the British Council, the British Film Institute and local authorities all invested increasingly in forms of creative production. This process of investment generated a series of complex questions about the relations between cultures and identities, with artists being asked to address an increasingly recalcitrant set of relationships between nation, region and metropolis. In order to capture the particular role of literature in this fraught engagement with questions of region, nation and identity, this chapter will begin with a discussion of the larger economic, political and cultural forces that made devolution such a pressing issue between 1945 and 1970. It will then consider the ways in which the cultural meanings of regionalism were theorised by key cultural figures of that period. Following an analysis of the role of cultural institutions in the creation and development of regional cultures, it will conclude with an analysis of specific aspects of literary production in Scotland, in Northern Ireland, in Wales and in English regions. In each case the aim will be to reach an understanding of the ways in which the literary imagination can respond to the linguistic and formal challenges of a reconfigured geographical and cultural identity.

This reconfiguration was characterised by Tom Nairn, in his reflection on the reinvigorated nationalisms operating within Britain since the war, as 'The Break-Up of Britain'.[1] Nairn argued that the movement towards devolution in this period was intimately connected to 'the long-term, irreversible degeneration of the Anglo-British state' (81). Nairn analyses nationalist movements in Scotland, in Wales, in Northern Ireland and in England, and suggests that they can be understood only in the context of a wide appreciation of the economic, historical and political situation of the post-war British state. For example,

1 Tom Nairn, *The Break-Up of Britain: Crisis and Neo-Nationalism*, 2nd edn (London: Verso, 1981). Further references given in parenthesis in the text.

after a detailed theorisation of the emergence and development of forms of Scottish nationalism since the eighteenth century, Nairn turns his attention to the economic role of Scotland in an age of multinational corporations and of the internationalisation of capital. His specific argument is about the capacity of the oil industry in Scotland to create critical forms of uneven economic development, so that 'something like the classical "development gap" was thrust upon Scotland' (175), but this quite particular reading is in turn situated by the observation that 'the political problem returned only with the post-World-War-II decline of the United Kingdom' (129).

Nairn explores the distinct character of different nationalist movements since 1945, but he also sees them as an inescapable part of a wider political and geographical adjustment. The creation of a European Union, he argues, would make it possible to transcend the imaginative and economic borders of the nation–state; 'the great capitalist process of integration, launched in the 1950s, would produce a United States of Europe well before the end of the century' (217). The declining global economic standing of Britain created spaces of disadvantage and of uneven development, thus giving rise to an understanding of the interests of different parts of Britain as quite distinct. And in this very process of disintegration, he argues, we can discern the very clear faultlines within the structure of the United Kingdom as it had developed since the eighteenth century: 'approaching its dissolution, the primal pattern becomes unexpectedly clear' (302).

For a number of cultural theorists and writers in the period, the distinctiveness of regional cultures was the key to cultural innovation and renewal. For example, the Northern Irish poet John Hewitt published an essay, 'Regionalism: the Last Chance' in 1947.[2] He argues that the culture of the region is the necessary mediation between the individual and the social. In a period when the nation is too complex to form the basis of a significant or substantial identification, Hewitt argues that 'a full recognition of the component regions will deepen and enrich the vitality of a nation' (122). He associates regionalism with emotional and intellectual rootedness, with continuity, and with individual loyalty to the social.

Similarly, T. S. Eliot advanced the case of the region in 1948 in his *Notes Toward the Definition of Culture*.[3] Eliot argues that 'it is important that man

[2] John Hewitt, 'Regionalism: the Last Chance', in *Ancestral Voices: The Selected Prose of John Hewitt*, ed. Tom Clyde (Belfast: Blackstaff Press, 1987), pp. 122–5.

[3] T. S. Eliot, 'Unity and Diversity: the Region', in *Notes Toward the Definition of Culture* (London: Faber & Faber, 1948), pp. 50–66. Further references given in parenthesis in the text.

should feel himself to be, not merely a citizen of a particular nation, but a citizen of a particular part of his country, with local loyalties' (52). He insists that each region must have its distinct local culture, which would then enrich the cultures of neighbouring regions. Yet Eliot is not, in the end, committed to these local cultures, but rather to their ability to enrich the central tradition of English literature: 'it is of great advantage for English culture to be constantly influenced from Scotland, Ireland and Wales' (55). The condescension that emerges in such a remark is a specific target of Raymond Williams's rather later essay on 'Region and Class in the Novel', where he points out the selectiveness of what is understood to be 'regional' and warns against any assumption that a cultural text cannot be both local and universal.[4] Williams asserts the critical importance of approaching the region neither as subordinate nor as provincial, but he also acknowledges that the capacity of regional writing to function within a large aesthetic and historical canvas is, in itself, historical: 'historically, in any case, regions and classes are only fully constituted when they fully declare themselves' (68).

The process of devolving culture happens in and through institutions. The key cultural institutions that supported the work of writers, ensured the dissemination of literary texts, and generated the critical categories through which literary work was assessed, developed distinctive regional characters in the years between 1945 and 1970. The Arts Council, the BBC and the universities all developed in ways that embedded aspects of local cultural production and constituted a challenge to the idea of one unified national culture: an idea that had, of course, been particularly significant during the war.

At the outbreak of war, the Council for the Encouragement of Music and the Arts (CEMA) was formed to ensure the development and the dissemination of key aspects of cultural production. CEMA was committed to ensuring that cultural practice was sustained and supported in all parts of the United Kingdom through support for local arts initiatives as well as for touring exhibitions and concerts. The Chairman of CEMA was John Maynard Keynes. At the end of the war, the success of this initiative was recognised by the formation of the Arts Council of Great Britain, once more with Keynes as its Chairman. The Arts Council inherited a structure that was explicitly committed to supporting the diversity of regional culture: a Scottish Committee and a Welsh

[4] Raymond Williams, 'Region and Class in the Novel', in Douglas Jefferson and Graham Martin, eds., *The Uses of Fiction: Essays on the Modern Novel in Honour of Arnold Kettle* (Milton Keynes: Open University Press, 1982), pp. 59–68. Further references given in parenthesis in the text.

Committee each had significant degrees of autonomy in funding decisions; while English regional offices administered local areas and represented their interests nationally. The impact of this devolved structure can be seen in the planning of the Festival of Arts, which was run by the Arts Council as part of the 1951 Festival of Britain. As reported in the Council's *Annual Report* of 1947–8 this 'would include not only London during the concentrated Summer Festival, but also a series of events at places, large and small all over the country, through which the cultural traditions and resources of the nation could be shown to their best advantage to visitors from abroad'.[5] In fact, over 18 million people were to visit over 2,000 local events during the Festival, which included twenty-two local arts festivals (including the Edinburgh International Festival, which had begun in 1947 with Arts Council support).

Having inherited a robustly regional structure, however, the Arts Council set about dismantling it. One historian of the Arts Council argues that regionalism was 'anathema to Keynes with his wish for centralism' and that this attitude led the Council away from regionalism from its inception.[6] Others have suggested a more complex set of pressures driving decision-making towards London, including an anxiety that regionalism meant a dilution of the pool of creative talent: a tendency some critics have denounced as the expression of 'a self-appointed and self-perpetuating metropolitan clique'.[7] Certainly, throughout the fifties, the Arts Council saw its role less as a matter of ensuring cultural access for all, and more in terms of a need to ensure minimum aesthetic standards in all the work it funded. Having inherited a structure of regional offices from CEMA, it dismantled these between 1953 and 1955, arguing that the cost of maintaining such local offices was excessive. Instead, peripatetic arts officers were to ensure that the interests of the regions were properly represented to the Council as a whole. This move was highly unpopular, as the Council itself was later to acknowledge: 'The closure of the regional offices was an unpopular move. Much local goodwill had been engendered by members of the Arts Council regional staffs; and their withdrawal was widely misinterpreted as evidence of the Arts Council's future intention of concentrating its funds on London at the expense of the provinces.'[8] Indeed,

5 The Arts Council of Great Britain, *Annual Report 1947–8* (London: Arts Council, 1948), p. 7.

6 Andrew Sinclair, *Arts and Cultures: The History of the 50 Years of the Arts Council of Great Britain* (London: Sinclair Stevenson, 1995), p. 63.

7 Geoff Mulgan and Ken Worpole, *Saturday Night or Sunday Morning? From Arts to Industry – New Forms of Cultural Policy* (London: Comedia Publishing, 1986), p. 20.

8 The Arts Council of Great Britain, *21st Annual Report 1965–66* (London: Arts Council, 1966), p. 22.

two regions simply refused to accept it, and the South Western Arts Association and the Midlands Arts Association were active from the mid-fifties.

Having begun in the immediate post-war period as a cultural body structurally committed to regionalism, by the early sixties the Arts Council had consolidated the bulk of decision-making, and of the cultural production it funded, in London. This process was to be dramatically reversed following the election of the Labour Government in 1964, and the appointment of Jennie Lee as the first Minister for the Arts in 1965. Over the next six years, funding for the Council trebled, and much of this additional funding was directed towards the regions. Regional Arts Associations were established across England, and in 1967 the Scottish and Welsh Committees of the Arts Council became national Councils in the own right. In the same period, it was decided to extend the remit of the Council beyond poetry and towards a broader range of literary output including novels, short stories, translations, and literary and cultural magazines.

Such financial and institutional support for writers increased also because of the expansion of the number of universities throughout Britain. In the first half of the sixties, the Universities of Essex, East Anglia, Kent, Lancaster, Sussex, Ulster, Warwick and York were all founded, and many other regional universities were created out of existing colleges. These universities provided halls and theatres for performances, new constituencies of readers, academic jobs for writers and a lively context of cultural debate with a regional as well as a national focus. The capacity of universities to support and develop writers can be seen, for example, in Belfast, where Queen's University supported a major cultural festival.

The third significant supporter of regional literary production in the period was the BBC, which was to provide employment, commissions and audiences for a wide range of writers. The BBC, like the Arts Council, had a significant degree of regionalism from its earliest days. Early radio transmission had depended on a network of radio stations in order to ensure coverage of most geographical regions of the UK: in 1922 there were stations in Aberdeen, Glasgow, Manchester, Cardiff, Birmingham, London, Newcastle and Plymouth, with a station in Belfast added shortly after. In the early 1930s these stations were, however, reorganised according to the BBC's 'regional scheme', which established a pattern of local and national broadcasting that gave increasing prominence to the output of the national programme. Then, with the outbreak of war in 1939, the fractious relationship between the BBC and its regions ceased, since the establishment of the 'Home Service' meant the end of all regional broadcasting for a substantial number of years. By 1945, however, a pattern of 'Home', 'Light' and 'Third' programmes once more left space for regional output: 'the justification for Regional services was that there was a recognisable need for the BBC to be seen to be catering for local life, culture and artistic talent'.[9] When television broadcasting resumed in 1946, the technical needs of geographical coverage also led to a reinforcement of a regional pattern of broadcasting, with stations distributed across London, the north, the midlands, Wales and the west country, and Scotland, and later being established in Northern Ireland in the fifties.

Regional broadcasting provided a platform, as well as an income, for a wide range of writers: Stan Barstow and Keith Waterhouse both submitted early work to the BBC, while in Northern Ireland, a series of cultural programmes increased and extended the audience for contemporary poetry, fiction and drama. In their submission to the Pilkington Committee on Broadcasting in 1960, the BBC stressed their continuing commitments to regional broadcasting structures, and these were indeed to find fuller expression in the sixties with the development first of BBC2, and then of local radio. The BBC was thus a central cultural provider, creating employment, generating commissions and ensuring a significant level of visibility for regional cultural production throughout the sixties.

Literatures of region and nation

Scottish literary production in the post-war period was significantly marked by writings and debates generated during the 'Scottish Renaissance' of the 1920s. The Renaissance was a period of self-conscious cultural renewal, based on innovative work in Scottish historical writing, formal and linguistic experimentation in literary writing and a broad commitment to a politics of Scottish Nationalism. The most prominent figure in this literary movement was Hugh MacDiarmid, whose poetic and polemical writings advocated a move 'from Burns to Dunbar'. MacDiarmid argued that the Old Scots of Robert Dunbar offered a significantly more vigorous and linguistic inheritance than what he saw as the debased Romanticism of Robert Burns. MacDiarmid worked to establish Lallans as a viable literary language. This version of Scots was not the spoken language of any group or region, but was constructed from historical texts and from scholarly research into the history of the language. It was, in that sense, 'artificial', but MacDiarmid believed that it had the capacity

9 W. H. McDowell, *A History of BBC Broadcasting in Scotland, 1923–1983* (Edinburgh University Press, 1992), p. 59.

to become a significant form of modern cultural expression, open to the innovations of European culture, but grounded in the history of a particular nation.

MacDiarmid's own literary output declined in the thirties, but in the immediate post-war period the impact of the 'Lallans Makars' who came in his wake was very significant. These poets included Robert Garioch, a drily comic poet; Douglas Young, with his Scottish renditions of classical literary texts, such as *The Puddocks* (1957); and Alexander Scott, who as well as being a prominent poet was also in 1948 the first lecturer in Scottish Literature to be appointed in any university in Scotland. One of the best-known poetic texts of this group is *Under the Eildon Tree*, by Sydney Goodsir Smith. Smith was not in fact born in Scotland, and he learned to write in Scots after systematic and detailed study of Scottish literary history. His series of elegies was published in 1948, and is an intriguing and inventive engagement with the legacy of Dunbar, with the traditions of love poetry developed in classical literature and with the linguistic and cultural idioms of Scotland. His linguistic tone can be captured in the following stanza, which, despite its innovations, is surely accessible to the reader of Standard English, equipped only with the additional knowledge that 'kenspeckle' means something like 'distinguished'. This information was, in fact, offered in an appendix to the text as originally published, so we can see that Smith at least aspired to attract a readership beyond those already familiar with Lallans.

> There's monie anither bard alive the day
>   In Scotland and the Isles
> Maist kenspeckle and renouned,
> Far-famed i their masterie,
> Aa maist dexterous and wurdie o makars –
>   But anerlie I, my queyne,
> Coud ever scrieve this leid o thee
> For anerlie I, excessive in aathing,
>   Wad eer commit
> The follie o loein you
> Til siccan a daft extremitie.[10]

Here we see Smith both playful and intense in his declaration of the excess of his love. His choice of words such as 'bard' and 'makar' places his text within a distinctively Scottish poetic tradition, while the poem as a whole

[10] Sydney Goodsir Smith, *Under the Eildon Tree: A Poem in XXIV Elegies* (Edinburgh, Serif Books, 1948), p. 14.

displays an inwardness with a wide range of classical and European literary traditions.

The literary output of these Lallans Makars was supported by a number of related cultural initiatives, in which the poet and critic Maurice Lindsay was to play a prominent role. Lindsay edited *Modern Scottish Poetry: Anthology of the Scottish Renaissance, 1920–1945*, whose publication in 1946 made the innovations and debates of that earlier period available to a significantly wider readership. He also founded the journal *Poetry Scotland*, whose publication between 1943 and 1949 provided an outlet for a wide range of poets writing in the Scots language. The simultaneous appearance of the journal *Scottish Arts and Letters* extended the range of voices and literary positions actively debating the linguistic and formal contours of what could be a distinctively Scottish literary culture.

The linguistic questions, and choices, facing Scottish writers in the post-war period were substantial. Some writers, such as Edwin Muir, chose to write in Standard Scottish English,[11] while others, such as Sorley Maclean, wrote in Gaelic. The various rural and urban versions of contemporary Scots were represented in a wide range of fictional writings, while Lallans continued to develop as a poetic language. The question of 'authenticity' in language gave way to a more sophisticated set of discussions about audience, representativeness and the formal resources of different linguistic traditions.

The relations between language and form were particularly pressing for poets writing in Gaelic who had a powerful sense of the need to sustain a minority language and to preserve its literary traditions, while also responding to the challenges and innovations of poetic Modernisms. Sorley Maclean decided at an early stage in his career to write only in Gaelic. His Symbolist writing with its strong sense of the poetic and cultural legacies of the traumas of Scottish history was a powerful model for later writers in Gaelic, including Derick Thomson and Donald MacAulay. Derick Thomson also played a key role in embedding literary writing in Gaelic within the overall literary culture of Scotland, founding the Gaelic Books Council in 1968 and (with Finlay J. MacDonald) setting up the Gaelic Quarterly, *Gairm*, in 1956.[12] Donald MacAulay was to be the editor of an important bilingual edition of the work of

[11] For discussion of the various linguistic traditions within Scotland, see John Corbett, *Language and Scottish Literature* (Edinburgh University Press, 1997).

[12] See Ronald I. M. Black, 'Gaelic Poetry in the Twentieth Century', in Cairns Craig, ed., *The History of Scottish Literature. Vol. IV: The Twentieth Century* (Aberdeen University Press, 1987), pp. 195–215.

post-war Gaelic writers, which stressed their modernity, and in particular the relationship to key Modernist figures such as Yeats, Pound and William Carlos Williams.[13] The publication of this volume in 1976 coincided historically with the appearance of Maclean's *Selected Poems*, also in a bilingual edition.[14]

For prose writers in this period, the demands of regionalism were at least as strong as those of nationalism. The effort to render the speech and the cultural experiences of post-war Scotland generated a series of novels that tried to capture the very particular voice of different Scottish regions. Thus, for example, Compton Mackenzie, in *Whisky Galore* (1947) represented the mores of the Western Isles, with strict Sabbath observance, a clear sense of social hierarchies and a shared moral code: 'They were a bit old-fashioned out here in the Islands.'[15] The novel is written largely in Standard English, although the representation of speech stresses the particularities of a regional accent, but it also includes phrases in Gaelic, which serve to underline the remoteness and the unfamiliarity of the culture depicted. The novel was highly successful, as indeed was its filmed version in 1949; an interesting collaboration between Mackenzie and Ealing Studios, who also made such a distinctive contribution to the representation of English regional identities in films such as *Passport to Pimlico* (1948). The ghost of the 'kailyard', that tradition of Scottish fiction that makes of the local the provincial, and makes of history a warmly remembered haze, still lingers in Mackenzie's novel. Its wartime setting places it robustly in its twentieth-century moment, but the strangeness of the mores so affectionately rendered do leave an uncomfortable excess of sentiment as well as a marked sense of separation from the lives depicted.

Muriel Spark's *The Prime of Miss Jean Brodie* (1961) was also later to be made into a film. Jean Brodie is a teacher in a private school in Edinburgh. She has a particular interest in, and a particular influence over, one group of girls, known to others at the school as 'the Brodie set'. Jean Brodie represents herself as daring and unconventional, and she shares her knowledge about art, about history, and about intimate aspects of her own life with the girls in an effort to cultivate in them a sort of distinction, or at least a sort of distinctiveness. The novel has a complex temporal structure, beginning in 1936 but also containing numerous proleptic passages in which we discover

[13] Donald MacAulay, ed., 'Foreword' to *Modern Scottish Gaelic Poems/Nua-bhàrdachd Ghàidhlig* (Edinburgh: Southside, 1976).

[14] Sorley MacLean/Somhairle MacGill-eain, *Spring Tide and Neap Tide: Selected Poems 1932–72/Reothairt is Contraigh: Taghadh de Dhàin 1932–72* (Edinburgh: Canongate, 1977).

[15] Compton Mackenzie, *Whisky Galore* (London: Chatto & Windus, 1947), p. 25.

the marked, sometimes comical and sometimes poignant, extent to which the future lives of all characters depart sharply from the futures Jean Brodie imagines for them. The novel is concerned with illusions and also with self-delusion, but it is also concerned importantly with Edinburgh. The ways in which Jean Brodie imagines distinction, the forms of delusion to which she is subject, and the social anxieties which haunt her, are all related to her identity as an unmarried, bourgeois, citizen of Edinburgh: 'in many ways Miss Brodie was an Edinburgh spinster of the deepest dye'.[16] And when she gives vent to her sense of the importance of subtle forms of cultural and social distinction, she is represented as an embodiment of Edinburgh itself: '"For those who like that sort of thing," said Miss Brodie in her best Edinburgh voice, "that is the sort of thing they like"' (37). Spark's novel is no caricature, however, and such critique is tempered by a sense of the very real limits, both historical and cultural, that make the struggle for distinctiveness we see in Jean Brodie admirable if also, simultaneously, impossible.

Jessie Kesson's novel *Glitter of Mica* (1963) seeks to capture the particularity of the rural culture of north-east Scotland in the early 1960s. Kesson was at this stage working for the BBC, making features programmes. The novel's central character, Hugh Riddell, a dairyman, is an angry, inarticulate and, ultimately, a dangerous man. The limits of his experience, and of his imagination, become a source of suffering, particularly as he interacts with his daughter Helen, who has had access to levels of education denied to him. The novel dwells on the frustration and the inarticulacy of Hugh, who, though he is to some extent admirable in his self-certainty, is at the same time dangerous in his inflexibility:

> Times he had felt like contradicting his daughter, Helen, when she came home from her work in a Youth Centre in the Town, with words on the tip of her tongue, like labels, ready to be stuck on to all human faults and frailties. As though the correct word for them could cure them. Words like Delinquency, Hereditary, Environment, Behaviour Patterns. Whiles he felt just like boring through that wall of words with which Helen had surrounded both herself and her vocation, and blowing them sky high with the anger that would be over him.[17]

The irony of the words to which Hugh takes exception here is substantial, particularly given the fact that in the following paragraph Hugh goes on to

[16] Muriel Spark, *The Prime of Miss Jean Brodie* (London: Macmillan, 1961), p. 31.
[17] Jessie Kesson, *Glitter of Mica* (London: Chatto & Windus, 1963), pp. 39–40.

muse over his murderous feelings towards his wife. Kesson's vision of rural life is bleak, stressing the frustrations, the limitations and the violence of its narrative world while also charting its demise, which is attributed to the disruptive economic and cultural effects of the war. Nonetheless, the novel does represent an imaginative achievement in its exploration of the local contours of particular lives: an achievement more fully realised in the revival of interest in Kesson's writing in the 1980s.

The achievement of distinctive forms of cultural production within Scotland in this period also took place in the theatre and in theatrical writing. In the immediate post-war period, Unity Theatre was established as a professional theatre company in Scotland, performing plays such as *The Gorbals Story* by Robert McLeish and *Men Should Weep*, by Ena Lamont Stewart, both of which explored aspects of contemporary life in urban Scotland. The Citizens' Theatre Company was founded in Glasgow in 1943, and in 1948 presented a very successful production of Sir David Lindsay's medieval play *Ane Satire of the Thrie Estaitis*, directed by Tyrone Guthrie, at the recently founded Edinburgh International Festival. The Royal Scottish Academy of Music and Drama was opened in Glasgow by James Bridie in 1950. A new theatre in Pitlochry was opened in 1951, and this was followed by new theatres in Perth and Dundee. The sixties saw further investment in the infrastructure of regional theatres, with the Traverse Theatre Club opening in Edinburgh in 1963, and quickly becoming a significant patron of new writing for the theatre, and the Royal Lyceum Theatre opening in Edinburgh in 1965. As one recent critic has argued, 'regional theatre flourished in this period on an unprecedented scale'.[18]

To write about Northern Ireland in terms either of regionalism or of nationalism raises difficult political and methodological questions. The creation of a separate political entity out of six counties in the north of Ireland was still a recent, and contested, historical process in 1945. The six counties themselves contained a diversity of regional cultures, and a range of languages including Standard English, Hiberno-English, Scots and Gaelic. The non-coincidence of the six counties and the older province of Ulster generated a further set of difficulties, with literary traditions and a sense of belonging frequently being experienced in terms of the older region. And even thinking of Northern Ireland as a region apart from the Irish Republic was impossible for many writers and critics who disputed the legitimacy of partition.

[18] Jen Harvie, 'Nationalizing the "Creative Industries"', *Contemporary Theatre Review*, 13, 1 (2003), pp. 15–32 (p. 20).

Added to these difficulties is the sense of the period from 1945 as a sort of cultural 'interregnum':

> Poets from the North of Ireland have recently dominated the Irish, and even the English, literary scene to such an extent that the long interval between the death of Yeats in 1939 and of Joyce in 1941 and the appearance of Seamus Heaney, Derek Mahon, Michael Longley, and James Simmons in the mid-sixties has tended to be looked upon as an interregnum.[19]

The forties and the fifties in this critical narrative seem like a period in which nothing of great significance was happening: at best a period of preparing for the cultural energies that would emerge so forcefully in the sixties.

Yet, the idea of 'regionalism' is clearly of some significance in this period. We have seen John Hewitt defend it forcefully in 1947, and it was a significant idea for many cultural institutions and writers in the period. The founding of the Ulster Folk and Transport Museum in 1958 was indeed an attempt to give some greater cultural and historical substance to the conception of this region: 'its creation was indicative of a confidence in the regional status of Northern Ireland within the United Kingdom'.[20] Northern Ireland did have its own government until 1972, but many of its cultural institutions were British in their origins. In its early years BBC Northern Ireland employed mainly English and Scots broadcasters,[21] while the Arts Council of Northern Ireland was founded on the model of the Arts Council of Great Britain. Also, the specificity of Northern Ireland would have been acutely felt at the end of a war in which Northern Ireland had been part of the allied forces while the Republic had remained neutral. In the sixties, this specificity was felt in rather different ways, as the formation of the Civil Rights Association in 1967 was followed by the arrival of British troops, creating a catastrophic escalation of violence and imposition of Direct Rule by Britain in 1972. The legitimacy of the political and cultural space of Northern Ireland was vigorously debated and contested throughout the period, but the very terms and forms of these debates can be seen as constituting a specifically regional culture.

The nature of literary and cultural production in Northern Ireland was the subject of *The Arts in Ulster: A Symposium*, which was published in 1951.[22]

[19] Seamus Deane, *A Short History of Irish Literature* (London: Hutchinson, 1986), p. 227.

[20] Richard Kirkland, *Literature and Culture in Northern Ireland since 1965: Moments of Danger* (London: Longman, 1996), p. 20.

[21] Jonathan Bardon, *Beyond the Studio: A History of BBC Northern Ireland* (Belfast: Blackstaff Press, 2000), chapter 1.

[22] Sam Hanna Bell, Nesca A. Robb, John Hewitt, eds., *The Arts in Ulster: A Symposium* (London: George G. Harrap, 1951).

Sam Hanna Bell begins this volume by stressing the key role of the BBC in supporting writing in Northern Ireland: 'Since 1945 practically every Ulster writer has contributed, at one time or another, to the Northern Ireland Region of the BBC' (20). This includes Louis MacNeice, whose poetic writing of the thirties and forties was of great importance for the following generation. Prose writers in the fifties created texts that were alert to the local while also reaching out to a more inclusive form of Symbolism that could capture the darker and despairing sense of a temporality that is uncertain and insecure. Thus both Sam Hanna Bell in *December Bride* (1951) and Brian Moore in *The Lonely Passion of Judith Hearne* (1955) give us heroines whose aspiration and frustrations point towards a more general metaphor for the contemporary. Cultural production in the fifties was also enhanced by innovations in theatrical production. For example, the formation of the Belfast Lyric Theatre in 1951 by Mary O'Malley and P. Pearse O'Malley created a space for the preservation and development of the tradition of poetic drama associated with W. B. Yeats. This in turn led to the creation of a literary journal, *Threshold*, in 1957, which was to provide a publishing outlet for a wide range of writers in the following years.

The upsurge of innovative poetic writing in the early sixties has been associated with the arrival of Philip Hobsbaum at Queen's University in 1962. Hobsbaum led a writers' group which included Seamus Heaney, Michael Longley, Seamus Deane and James Simmons, and engaged in animated discussions about critical and formal aspect of poetic writing. Each of these writers was to have a significant impact on writing in Northern Ireland from that moment on. James Simmons founded the journal *The Honest Ulsterman* in 1968; Michael Longley promoted writing in Northern Ireland through his work with the Arts Council; Seamus Deane established a prominent identity as a historian and critic of Irish writing, and Seamus Heaney's poetic output has made him one of the most important contemporary poets writing in English. The hallmarks of Heaney's style are his spareness of diction, his commitment to the particular qualities of different material forms, and his fascination with loss and with death. All can be seen in the following extract from 'Digging', published in *Death of a Naturalist* (1966)

> The cold smell of potato mould, the squelch and slap
> Of soggy peat, the curt cuts of an edge
> Through living roots awaken in my head.
> But I've no spade to follow men like them.

Between my finger and my thumb
The squat pen rests.
I'll dig with it.[23]

The sense of connection to, yet painful distance from, 'men like them' generates the compensatory image of poetic writing as a continuation of a particular local tradition of manual labour. But the poignancy of this poem consists in the sense that the pen is, finally, offering only an immaterial form of production, without the sounds and smells associated with cutting peat. The poet here gains his universality of vision at the expense of a direct and physical relation to a particular place.

Literary production in Wales between 1945 and 1970 was sharply divided between English-language and Welsh-language writing, with very little communication between the two traditions until the end of the period. Welsh literature situated itself in relation to a long national tradition of poetic writing, while Anglo-Welsh writing displayed more of a sense of regionalism in its reshaping of forms and narratives taken from English literary texts.

The earliest known poetic writing in Welsh dates back to the sixth century, and a continuous tradition of forms and techniques can be mapped from that moment up to the sixteenth century: 'a single expanding tradition, thematically and stylistically distinct from the rest of Europe'.[24] This poetic tradition was celebrated in, and sustained by, the Eisteddfod, a festival of Welsh culture that began in its modern form in the eighteenth century. For poets writing in Welsh in the twentieth century, however, the challenge was to find ways to connect this quite particular national tradition to the poetic innovations they saw in the various European and American Modernisms. Both T. H. Parry-Williams, who was Professor of Welsh at Aberystwyth, and D. Gwenallt Jones wrote with this consciousness of a larger European tradition; indeed Parry-Williams had studied for some time at the Sorbonne.

The most prominent representative of the cultural and national importance of the Welsh language in the fifties and sixties was the poet and critic, Saunders Lewis. Lewis was President of Plaid Cymru, a Welsh Nationalist political party, from 1926 to 1939, and was imprisoned for acts of militancy for this cause in 1936. In 1962 he broadcast a talk on the BBC, 'The Fate of the Language', in which he argued that the Welsh language was under threat, and that its survival

23 Seamus Heaney, *Death of a Naturalist* (London: Faber & Faber, 1966), p. 14.

24 *The Penguin Book of Welsh Verse*, trans. Anthony Conran in association with J. E. Caerwyn Williams (Harmondsworth: Penguin, 1967), p. 13.

was central to a vision of a viable national identity for Wales. The reaction to this talk was very significant, and led eventually to the formation of the Welsh Language Society, which worked actively to promote use of the language, and then to the passing of the Welsh Language Act in 1967, which gave clear legal status to Wales's bilingualism. Writing in Welsh also became available to English-speaking readers in this period through a series of translations. Gwyn Williams translated one volume entitled *Presenting Welsh Poetry* in 1959, and a second, *Medieval Welsh Lyrics* in 1965, while in 1967, *The Penguin Book of Welsh Verse* brought the long historical tradition of poetic writing in Welsh to a wide readership throughout Britain.

The sense of English-language writing from Wales as an identifiable Anglo-Welsh literature is a much more recent cultural phenomenon, with its origins in the early years of the twentieth century.[25] In its early years, the Anglo-Welsh tradition had little contact with writing in Welsh. The specific formal and thematic concerns of Anglo-Welsh writers were established through anthologies such as *Modern Welsh Voices*, edited by Keidrich Rhys in 1944, and *This World of Wales*, edited by Gerald Morgan in 1968, and in literary journals such as *Wales*, *The Anglo-Welsh Review* and *Poetry Wales*. David Jones and R. S. Thomas had a very significant poetic output in the early years of this period, but the writer whose work made the idiom of Anglo-Welsh poetry most widely known was Dylan Thomas. His *Collected Poems*, published in 1952, sold very well, while the broadcast of *Under Milk Wood* by the BBC in 1954 made his linguistic inventiveness and his anarchic energies available to an audience throughout the United Kingdom.[26]

Anglo-Welsh novels in this period showed a strong commitment to the detail of the local and the regional. Writers such as Michael Gareth Llewellyn and Richard Vaughan developed narratives that explored the cultural and linguistic particularity of their regions of Wales, the Vale of Glamorgan and Carmarthenshire respectively. Similarly, Raymond Williams's *Border Country* (1960) maps the intellectual and emotional movements of its central character Matthew Price between his life as a university lecturer in London and his family home in the Welsh borders. Williams's novel stresses both the visceral relationship Price has to the landscape and the spaces of his youth, but also the distance and the strangeness these now can only evoke: '"I've been away too long", he said, sitting down at the table. "I've forgotten it all, and I can't

[25] Roland Mathias, *Anglo-Welsh Literature: An Illustrated History* (Bridgend: Poetry Wales Press, 1987), chapter 12.

[26] Dylan Thomas, *Collected Poems 1934–52* (London: J. M. Dent, 1952).

bring myself back."'[27] Price returns to his family home because his father is dying, and his hesitant and often frustrated attempts to remember how to inhabit the social identity of his childhood are interspersed with episodes exploring the political and cultural history of his region. Finally, he returns to London, having understood something more about the displacements he has undergone through his education and his work. It is with sadness, but not with hopelessness or despair, that Price concludes his home can never be a substantial place of memory or identity for his children, 'Glynmawr, to them, was a name, a holiday in the country, no part of their ordinary world' (349).

In the late sixties, a more productive set of exchanges between writers in Welsh and in English began to develop. This process was encouraged by the work of Meic Stephens, who chaired the Literature Committee of the Welsh Arts Council following its creation in 1967. Stephens worked to present Welsh and English-language writing together, to promote debate between the two traditions and also to give writers in both languages access to Arts Council bursaries.

Within England, too, distinctive regional voices emerged between 1945 and 1970. These were largely associated with a new post-war generation of writers, such as the 'Angry Young Men' of the fifties. Writers such as John Osborne, Colin Wilson or Alan Sillitoe explored the new aspirations of a more prosperous and materially comfortable generation who felt restricted by the rigidity and the hierarchy of the social structure in which they were living. Arthur Seaton, Sillitoe's hero in *Saturday Night and Sunday Morning* (1958), does physically exhausting work in a factory in Nottingham and spends his weekends drinking heavily, with Saturday night 'a violent preamble to a prostrate Sabbath'.[28] The novel begins with Seaton's spectacular drunken fall down a flight of stairs, and follows his affair with a married woman, his violent physical assault and his return to work on the Monday. Seaton robustly refuses notions of prudence or forethought, insisting that the only reasonable response to relative prosperity is to enjoy spending. The speech, dress and cultural mores of a Nottingham working-class community are carefully rendered in the novel, including the impact of new cultural forms such as television, though Seaton's values and experiences are also offered as expressive of a broader historical moment of modernisation and change.

This insistence on the progressive and modern quality of a regional experience is challenged explicitly by other texts of the fifties. Kingsley Amis's *Lucky*

[27] Raymond Williams, *Border Country* (London: Chatto & Windus, 1960), p. 82.
[28] Alan Sillitoe, *Saturday Night and Sunday Morning* (London: W. H. Allen, 1958), p. 7.

Jim (1953), for example, makes the experience of life at a provincial university seem terrifyingly banal. Jim Dixon is struggling to establish himself as a scholar, and is continually frustrated by what he sees as the mediocrity, the moralism and the conformity of provincial life. In this novel London beckons tantalisingly, offering a counterpoint to all that Dixon finds so despicable about a provincial university and a regional community. Jim is lucky, finally, only because he is forced to escape.

In the sixties, further new voices emerged from different English regions. The expansion of secondary and higher education generated new writers who tried to reach different audiences. The 'Liverpool Poets', Adrian Henri, Roger McGough and Brian Patten, were part of this process. Their collection, *The Mersey Sound* (1967) used a contemporary popular idiom in the creation of poems that were often comic, frequently polemical, and always accessible:

> 'Song for a Beautiful Girl Petrol-Pump Attendant on the Motorway'
> I wanted your soft verges
> But you gave me the hard shoulder.[29]

The use of the motorway as a metaphorical resource for the representation of erotic desire here is absurd, but also emphatically contemporary. It also offers an insight into the ways in which the reconfiguration of the landscape of Britain by new modes of transport and new forms of community gave scope for the development and the dissemination of distinctive regional voices between 1945 and 1970.

[29] Adrian Henri, Roger McGough, Brian Patten, *The Mersey Sound*, Penguin Modern Poets 10 (Harmondsworth: Penguin, 1967), p. 20.

30

The sixties: realism and experiment

JOHN LUCAS

I

We have grown used to a way of telling the history. The 1950s, that decade of rationing, austerity, of dank deference and drab conformity, was replaced by the explosive energies of the 1960s, exuberant, experimental, enterprising. But this is History as Headlines: alliterative and casually associative. These or similar headlines can be glimpsed hovering over the cut-and-paste methods adopted by Martin Harrison, the curator of an exhibition mounted at the Barbican in 2002, TRANSITION: *The London Art Scene in the Fifties*. In the introductory essay to his splendid catalogue, Harrison reports the artist Richard Smith's feeling that living and working through the fifties was analogous to a journey from darkness to light. Harrison's exhibition becomes a step-by-step retracing of this journey. The first important painting is by David Bomberg, 'Evening in the City of London', painted in 1944, its slabs of red and umber, with the black of St Paul's brooding in the background, eloquent of a city broken and burnt by Nazi incendiary bombs. The last painting is by David Hockney. 'I'm in the Mood for Love', executed in 1961, wittily plays with the image of a wolf on the prowl against a phantasmagoric New York skyline. Sexual intercourse is not far off. Moreover, Hockney's work, while it undoubtedly owes something to Francis Bacon's ways of slathering paint on canvas, points in a quite different direction. Hockney is making clear that his paintings are not, in Harrison's words, 'literal representation of fact'. Now meaning is to be found in the marks made on canvas.

A year after he painted 'I'm in the Mood for Love' Hockney famously attended the ceremony at which he was to receive the RCA's gold medal dressed not in traditional academic gown but in gold-lamé jacket, his hair dyed blond. 'The event that crystallised the transition in British art', Harrison notes, 'also proclaimed the imminent revolution in society – and was literally dazzling.'[1]

Looking again at photographs of street scenes in the 1950s, it is impossible not to relive the sense of that time as one of cramping poverty. As G. S. Fraser put it in his poem, 'For Tilly, Sick, With Love', 'So little we had.' But he then immediately adds, 'and so gay, it is something to ponder.'[2] The outer world may have been drab, but the word doesn't do justice to much of the best imaginative energy of the 1950s. And there is another point. One of the most affecting works in Harrison's exhibition is a painting by John Berger, 'Scaffolding: Festival of Britain', executed in 1950. Harrison calls Berger's style gritty and direct, but this is to undersell the art that has gone into Berger's painting, in particular his choice of a viewpoint that forces us to look both up and down, to recognise, confront and vicariously experience something of the sheer effort that has gone into erecting and, still more, will go into climbing the scaffolding. And without wishing to press the point too hard, it is also apparent that the scaffolding has symbolic significance. A new decade – even a new era – is about to begin. The painting may not suggest an unguarded confidence in new styles of architecture, a change of heart, but nor is it merely a literal representation of fact.

Ten years later this almost Morrisian concern with work – 'the actual troublous life of every day, with toil of the hands and brain together' – was coming to seem *passé*, at all events in fiction.[3] There is an exception to this: the experience of women's work, especially work in the home. This is a matter I shall develop later. For the moment I want to note how writers who had begun in the 1950s either changed style in the next decade or struggled to stay true to their belief in the realism that had sustained them in their earlier work. For such writers the appearance in English of the work of Georg Lukács, especially his *Studies in European Realism* (1950) and, even more, *The Historical Novel* (1962), had an at least indirect impact. They may not all have read his words, though some certainly did, but his ideas were soon mediated through discussions of the art of fiction, and undoubtedly affected commentators, including reviewers in the more serious journals and broadsheets. In the first place, Lukács made a clear distinction between realism (good) and naturalism (bad). In the second, he argued for the importance to realism of the 'average'

1 Martin Harrison, *Transition: The London Art Scene in the Fifties* (London: Merrell in association with Barbican Art, 2002), p. 168.

2 Ian Fletcher and John Lucas, eds., *Poems of G. S. Fraser* (Leicester University Press, 1981), p. 149.

3 Stan Smith, *Edward Thomas* (London: Faber & Faber, 1986), p. 143.

hero, someone whose world-historical importance owed nothing to him or her being in any way exceptional. Lukács praises the fictions of Walter Scott, because his key protagonists are not kings or generals but 'ordinary' folk who, as it were, embody the energies and desires of the community, even the class, to which they belong. It was through the activities of such people that historical movement – progress – could be seen to operate. This was realism. Naturalism, on the other hand, was incapable of understanding movement. Its deeply pessimistic, even cynical, assumption was that individuals and societies are subject to laws over which they have no control, and which they are unable to affect. As Marx had famously observed, previous philosophers had only interpreted the world in different ways, while the point was to change it. But you cannot change a world that is perceived to be answerable only to 'natural' laws. Such a world – or anyway such a world view – cancels agency, denies the possibility of meaningful intervention.

In December 1954, David Sylvester had published in the journal *Encounter* an article called 'The Kitchen Sink'. Sylvester's intention was to discuss recent work by a number of British artists, but his title was soon appropriated by commentators who wanted to pin it onto writers of the period. By the end of the fifties, such novelists as Stan Barstow, Philip Callow, Sid Chaplin (whose *The Day of the Sardine* was much admired when it first appeared in 1961), Alan Sillitoe and David Storey were all routinely lumped together as representatives of 'kitchen-sink realism'. Realism here meant much the same as 'gritty and direct'. More particularly, it meant a close, intimate inspection of working-class lives. These lives were not seen as the expression of a larger cause. If attention had finally to be paid to the people who filled the novels of Callow and Sillitoe, it was not because the authors thought in terms of the class from which they both came as being the agents of change but because their characters, too, had lives to lead. The unlikely combination of D. H. Lawrence and Jack Kerouac prompted both novelists. Neither was especially interested in telling a story and the more the sixties went on the less interested they became. In section 9 of *Going to the Moon* (1968), Callow protests at the idea of a book cut away from its writer and asserts that he doesn't believe 'in fact and fiction, I don't believe in autobiography, poetry, philosophy, I don't believe in chapters, in a story'.[4] Sillitoe might well have said something similar. Both writers were irritated at being saddled with the kind of epithet which, they rightly felt, denied the individuality of their work in the interests of labelling them as marketable merchandise.

[4] Philip Callow, *Going to the Moon* (London: Alison & Busby, 1989), p. 44.

The label was especially unfair to Callow, a writer of remarkable originality. His trilogy *Another Flesh*, of which *Going to the Moon* is the first book (the others are *The Bliss Body* (1969) and *Flesh of Morning* (1971)) is one of the finest fictional achievements of the period, and, Lawrence apart, I know of no other writer who so exactly, unjudgementally, sensitively, evoked the shifting shallows and depths of the mostly working-class people he writes about. But because he rarely encased these people in a conventional story, and because his work resists any easy categorisation, his fiction has gone unremarked except by a discriminating few.

If Alan Sillitoe has fared better it is because the phenomenal success of *Saturday Night and Sunday Morning* has continued to ensure a certain marketability for his work, whereas Callow has for years now failed to find a major publisher for his fiction. In addition, for all his – ill-judged – refusal to accept editorial interventions, Sillitoe is more prepared to work within the conventions of plot structures than Callow. That he is uneasy with these is nevertheless apparent from their awkward carpentry. His few attempts at crime fiction have been particularly unsuccessful. Sillitoe's best novels are therefore those which allow him to concentrate on dialogue and what might be called the atmospherics of relationships, especially in the ambience of working-class Nottingham he knew so well as a boy and youth. They include *Key to the Door* (1961) and *The Death of William Posters* (1964). For the same reason his short stories are invariably successful, and among the best are those gathered together in *Guzman Go Home* (1968).

Stanley Middleton also writes about Nottingham, or 'Beechnall' as the place is known in his novels. Unlike Callow and Sillitoe, Middleton's concern is not so much with working-class as middle-class people. Also unlike them, he is at ease with plot. Not that his novels are elaborately constructed, at least in terms of story. But virtually all of them have as *donnée* some sort of crisis: a death, a breakdown in a relationship, an unexpected and unwelcome task to be undertaken. And by the end something has been learnt: a marriage patched together or loneliness more or less accepted, a professional career salvaged or its disappointed expectations confronted. Resolutions in Middleton's novels are at best provisional, hedged about by time passing, by the uncertainties that necessarily attach to personal relationships, by all that contingency means. This may make him seem low key. Yet Middleton is a major writer, and if the neglect of Callow is a disgrace, the downplaying of Middleton's importance in accounts of post-war British fiction is even more so. (Neither is represented in the 1971 *Penguin Companion to British and Commonwealth Literature*, edited by David Daiches.) During the 1960s, Middleton published no fewer than eight novels, and while this may seem to guarantee quantity over quality, the fact is that *Harris's Requiem* (1960), *A Serious Woman* (1961), *Him They Compelled* (1964 – the title is to be regretted) and *Wages of Virtue* (1969) are all possessed of that unfakable imaginative scrupulosity that testifies not to garrulity, still less unthinking facility, but to an unceasing, sceptical, disillusioned, but by no means cynical, curiosity about the inner and outer weather of people's lives.

A just comparison of Kingsley Amis's *Take A Girl Like You* (1960) with *A Serious Woman* is bound to find in favour of Middleton's novel. For while Amis writes with undeniable comic verve, his characters are, if not stereotypical, then near to pastiche. The men are mostly lecherous, vain, egotistical, the women mostly put-upon. *Take a Girl Like You* is in a sense a rewriting of Fielding for modern times, although Amis is certainly harder on Patrick Standish than Fielding can bring himself to be about Tom Jones. But Middleton's novel, which is told from the woman's point of view, is infinitely more subtle in its registering of the hurts of love. It is also weightier, with an almost Johnsonian gravity of understanding of hope's delusive mines. And its weave of dialogue, introspection and authorial commentary, especially between Dorothea (whether Middleton intends a glance at George Eliot I rather doubt) and her pompous schoolmaster father, is masterly. No better writing of its kind is to be found in any other fiction of the 1960s.

That kind may be the issue in trying to account for Middleton's comparative neglect. Provincial, middle-class, modest: the terms are as fatally opprobrious as they are intendedly descriptive. Thinking of Middleton's excellence, I think of Patrick Kavanagh's poem 'Epic', and of Homer's ghost who 'came whispering to my mind / He said: I made the Iliad from such / A local row. Gods make their own importance.'[5]

II

Set against local rows are the Big Issues. In the 1960s no issue seemed bigger than the possibility of nuclear annihilation. Nevil Shute had made nuclear war and its aftermath the occasion for his story of doomed lovers in *On The Beach* (1957), and it had been an absent presence in Golding's *Lord of the Flies* (1954); but on the whole novelists in the 1960s ignore the subject. Perhaps the resolution of the Cuban Missile Crisis marked an end of terror, or, more likely, the subject seemed intractable. An exception of a sort is provided by Angus Wilson's *The Old Men at the Zoo* (1961). In a 'Prefatory Note', Wilson says that

[5] Patrick Kavanagh, *Collected Poems* (London: Martin Brian & O'Keeffe, 1972), p. 136.

'The events described here as taking place in 1970–3 are utterly improbable. Our future is possibly brighter, probably more gloomy.' The events in question are those that hinge on plans to remove animals from Regent's Park Zoo at the time of nuclear war, against what the novel's protagonist calls 'a background of ruin and stench'.[6]

Wilson's novel is certainly exercised by fear of war but it is also, and more valuably, a satire on officialdom, on committee-men, on the English class system, its snobberies, bone-headed philistinism, as well as the social cruelty of the aristocracy, deference of middle-class placemen and so forth. *The Old Men at the Zoo* might be characterised as Dickensian in two ways. Its ambition is large. It is a report on contemporary England, rather as *Bleak House*, *Little Dorrit* and *Our Mutual Friend* can be thought of as reports on the 1850s and 1860s. The characters also, and I think not always intentionally, verge on the caricature. And this is equally true of Wilson's next novel, *Late Call* (1964). Here, Wilson's subject is new-town England (the building of Milton Keynes had only recently been begun) and the hopes for constructing a new, more generously inclusive, society than the one he had gone some way to anatomising in *The Old Men at the Zoo*. The central character of *Late Call*, Sylvia Calvert, had grown up in the days before World War I, and her son, Harold, now a headmaster of idealistic energies, is a product of the 1930s. Wilson rather impressively imagines the two generations' readiness to work for their vision of an England that can leave behind the literal and moral impoverishments of the first half of the twentieth century, and he does not sentimentalise or scant the difficulties of shaping new styles of architecture, as J. B. Priestley before him would have done.

Late Call is nevertheless unusual among the novels of the 1960s. Its optimism, although it chimes with the shift in political considerations that brought Harold Wilson's Labour Government to power in the year of its publication, is not shared by many other fictions of the period. Moreover, its account of the England on which it focuses feels almost doggedly referential. (Where, that is, it is not pastiche.) Wilson had made his reputation with two collections of short stories, both of which were notable for a satiric sharpness that bordered on the camp: as though Aldous Huxley had been crossed with Ronald Firbank. This sharpness continues to serve him well in his novels, up to and including *The Old Men at the Zoo*. But in *Late Call* it appears not merely fusty ('Dickensian' in its 'sketches' of comic types) but worrying, because the very people who ought to be part of his inclusive vision of the new England are reduced to farcical clichés: furniture-removal men and charladies as walk-on caricatures.

[6] Angus Wilson, *The Old Men at the Zoo* (London: Secker & Warburg, 1961), 'Prefatory Note'.

The trouble with this is that it runs clean counter to the novel's presumed intention. For all its generous wish to imagine and indeed discover a change of heart that can be expressive of new styles of architecture, *Late Call* is trapped in assumptions that seriously compromise its vision.

Nevertheless, Wilson deserves credit for not aligning himself with the cheap and shallow reports on a severely restricted England that characterise the fiction of Amis and his epigoni, for whom fictional resource hardens into an increasingly sterile series of observations on contemporary *mores*, or such few of them as the novelists in question were aware of. They should have got out more. Instead, they chose to demonstrate their good (i.e., superior) taste by a withdrawal, a wincing away from whatever seemed to them new – and therefore vulgar, crude, a betrayal of standards. The Amis who wrote *Take a Girl Like You* was after all the same Amis who would respond to plans of the Wilson Government for expanding higher education by announcing that more would mean worse. And his lament for the good old days was echoed by Philip Larkin who in 'Homage to a Government' (1969) attacked Wilson's decision to bring the troops home from east of Suez. 'Our children will not know it's a different country. / All we can hope to leave them now is money', Larkin's poem ends, as though to suggest that imperialism had been a moral obligation.[7]

Larkin chooses to forget the Suez fiasco of 1956 and had perhaps turned a deaf ear to Macmillan's 1961 declaration that a new wind was blowing through Africa. Oddly, though end of empire was a major issue of the 1960s, it did not much feature in the decade's fiction. Notable exceptions are V. S. Naipaul's *A House for Mr Biswas* (1961) and Paul Scott's *The Alien Sky*, *Staying On* and *The Raj Quartet*. This latter work was completed in the 1970s. *The Alien Sky* had first been published in 1958. But as that novel gained new readers and far more by way of serious attention when it was republished in 1967, so the *Quartet*, like Scott's best-known novel, *Staying On*, was conceived in, and belongs to, the decade.

Mention should also be made here of Robert Shaw's *The Sun Doctor* (1961). Shaw's novel, set in Angola, is a fable about the abuses of colonial power, its protagonist Dr Benjamin Halliday an emblem of interfering do-goodism, whose sense of personal failure is brought into ironic juxtaposition with official recognition of his work in 'helping' the strange Manda people. (He is granted a knighthood.) Shaw does not demonise Halliday; the man means well, and acts

[7] Philip Larkin, *High Windows* (London: Faber & Faber, 1974), p. 29.

in the best interests, as he thinks, of the Manda. But in imposing his views on them he as good as denies the propriety of their own cultural resources.

The Sun Doctor had the misfortune to appear in the same year as Naipaul's *A House for Mr Biswas*. So much has been written about this great novel that to attempt commentary on it here would be otiose. It is, however, worth noting that in a peculiarly ill-judged review *The Times* wrote of it as though it was the flesh of a Caribbean cricket crowd turned word: 'Less a book than an explosion! A riot of tropical creativeness with life running wild, people jam-packed and flowing over.'[8] Behind these words can be heard the clichés so beloved of BBC cricket commentators: fun-loving, colourful, sun (and rum) 'soaked' . . . There is nothing here to suggest the supreme artistry with which Naipaul so meticulously builds his sad, funny novel, nor of the scrupulous tact with which he gradually lays bare Mr Biswas's pathetic dignity, the unsentimental account of what is in effect double alienation. For Biswas is a Hindu in a culture dominated by the British and refracted through Afro-Caribbean circumstance. It would be crude to call Naipaul's novel 'anti-colonial' if by that is meant a programmatic critique of colonialism. On the other hand, *A House for Mr Biswas* is perhaps the greatest novel ever written about what might be called the soul of man under colonial influence, one that penetrates nearly every crevice of life.

Not that Mr Biswas is in any sense a 'case'. He is intensely realised in all his individuality, is indeed a triumph of that realism for which Erich Auerbach had spoken up in his enormously influential *Mimesis*, a book much read in both the 1950s and 60s. There, Auerbach had argued that the rise of realism could be found in 'the serious treatment of everyday reality, the rise of more extensive and socially inferior groups to the position of subject matter', together with 'the embedding of random persons and events in the general course of contemporary history, the fluid historical background'.[9] I have no means of knowing whether Naipaul had come across Auerbach and even if he had I don't suggest that his fictional concerns were in any way shaped by *Mimesis*. It is enough to say that Auerbach's thesis finds perhaps its most eloquent contemporary justification in *A House for Mr Biswas*.

Naipaul's novel contrasts sharply with those of Paul Scott, not merely because Naipaul is by far the better writer, but because Scott writes from the point of view of the white colonialists. To be sure, these are not by and large the important people. Scott's protagonists are for the most part what Kipling

[8] V. S. Naipaul, *A House for Mr Biswas* (London: Fontana, 1963), back cover.

[9] Eric Auerbach, *Mimesis: The Representation of Reality in Western Literature* (Princeton University Press, 1953), p. 473.

had called 'the mere, uncounted folk', tied to unrewarding jobs under, as the title of one novel says, an alien sky. His true subject is the pathos of those lesser administrators who are left behind after the events of 1947, bereft of purpose, unsure of their identity, dimly conscious of the possibility that they have wasted their lives, that the cause to which they had committed themselves has dissolved and in its disappearance left them without resource: dissolute in all senses of the word. Scott's novels may not be major contributions to the art of fiction, but they are certainly part of the story of the 1960s and could have been written in no other decade.

III

The same may hold for William Golding's fables, especially *Free Fall* (1959) and *The Spire* (1964). From the beginning, that is from *Lord of the Flies* (1954), Golding had been preoccupied with the deep recesses of what William Empson called the black heart of man. Empson found evidence for such blackness in the Christian story of the crucifixion, which for him embodied the evil of suffering wished on anyone who could be assured it proved the working of some larger plan. In the 1950s, and especially after the Hungarian Uprising of 1956, the wickedness of Stalin's and his successors' plans for the good of totalitarianism appalled many, including large numbers of those who had joined the Communist Party in the 1930s and 40s, when Communism seemed a bulwark against the spread of international Fascism. For others, the Nazi plans for purifying their race by exterminating Jews, as well as homosexuals, gipsies and the mentally ill, plans they put into operation with meticulous attention to detail, provided evidence beyond gainsaying of pure evil. No more lyric poetry after Auschwitz, Adorno said. But what art could be adequate to such wickedness? Not realism. And not merely because realistic fiction takes for granted human agency as implicated in, as in some way, the locus of change (where change suggests progress); but because the enormity of Nazi evil seemed to be beyond the scope of a form of art that had come to be looked on as descriptive rather than diagnostic. Even Hannah Arendt's famous attempt to identify evil as essentially banal (the work of pettifogging bureaucrats with limited imaginations) was not a usable concept for writers attempting to come to terms with an end to Enlightenment. Golding's fables revisit the Christian metaphysic, and in doing so give the lie to Angus Wilson's contention that the English novel could not deal with the idea of evil, although in arguing this in *The Wild Garden* (1963), essays based on a series of lectures he had given on fiction, Wilson forgot Dickens, for whom the black heart of man was, increasingly, a force to be recognised as operating at both individual and social levels.

It may be, though, that Wilson didn't so much forget as ignore this powerful element in Dickens's novels. As we have seen, what interested him were Dickens's powers of mimicry, his fascination with comic grotesques and his readiness to act as super-reporter: to tell the English about the country they lived in. These qualities were precisely what made Dickens suspect to most writers and critics in the 1950s and 60s. The law-giver on the art of fiction was widely granted to be Henry James and James more or less dismissed Dickens as a populariser incapable of sustained seriousness. Hence, F. R. Leavis's pronouncement that there was nothing for the mature mind in Dickens's novels. Hawthorne, whom James praised, was, however, a different matter. Long before the creation of American Studies departments in UK universities, Hawthorne was among those American writers eagerly read and discussed, his fables such as 'The Veil', 'Young Goodman Brown' and 'The Maypole of Merrymount', to say nothing of *The Scarlet Letter*, scrutinised for evidence of the Puritan, New England conscience, one in which evil was omni-present.

Whether Golding read Hawthorne as attentively as many of his contemporaries scarcely matters. It is enough to say that his own novels owe much to the climate created by the favourable reception of Hawthorne's fiction in post-war England. So does the applause with which they were greeted. Golding's account of the evil done by Sammy Mountjoy, the protagonist of *Free Fall*, assumes his capacity to choose freely. Sammy is entirely responsible for corrupting by seducing the innocent Beatrice. Once he has done this he loses freedom, becomes the deed's creature. Hence, the appearance of the Nazi camp-officer who tells Sammy that 'your nature compels you' to move on in evil, much as Macbeth decides he is so steeped in blood that 'Returning were as tedious as go o'er.' *Free Fall* became a much commented-on novel and it is notable that the Catholic critics Ian Gregor and Mark Kinkead-Weekes took it to be not only good but true. In contrast, Juliet Mitchell criticised what she saw as Golding's muddle in insisting on a freedom he never really examined but only posited. The unstated assumption behind her Marxist-influenced criticism is that there are determining forces in the construction of individuality as a result of which talk of freedom is a liberal–bourgeois mystification, amounting to denial of the actual forces at work within those social circumstances into which we all are born.

The force of Mitchell's criticism is not however entirely Marxist. It is also feminist. For implicit in her argument is her sense that for Golding women are symbols of incorruptible innocence until corrupted by men. Pincher Martin raped Mary. Sammy Mountjoy seduces Beatrice. The women's names are sufficiently indicative of their meaning in Golding's work. Women are passive until acted upon by men. And if this seems unduly stark it can be said that nowhere in Golding's fiction of the sixties period do we find a female character who in any way acts rather than being acted upon. In fact women are by and large absent from the novels. *The Spire* is about male hubris, and the fall of Father Jocelin's vast architectural folly, while it glances at the possible end awaiting humanist attempts to build ambitious social structures, also symbolises the toppling of power. It is therefore significant that *The Spire* should appear in 1964, two years after the publication of Doris Lessing's *The Golden Notebook*.

IV

Lessing had been a respected writer since her arrival in England in 1949. She brought with her the manuscript of a novel, *The Grass is Singing*, which rightly earned her much critical acclaim. But the reception of *The Golden Notebook* made Lessing not merely a hugely respected novelist, it gave her prominence among a new generation of women writers, most of them university-educated and keen to be active agents in their shaping of their lives. Their story cannot be separated from new energies that distinguish the history of the book in the 1960s. These showed themselves in a variety of ways. New publishers came into existence. Older publishers, under threat of losing their market position, employed new designers, brought out new imprints. Paperbacks became widely accepted as a reputable form of publishing, although that didn't prevent many from falling to pieces at the first attempt to open them. (Glued spines cracked and discharged salvoes of poorly printed paper.) New bookshops emerged: Bumpus, Better Books, Compendium in London, others equally good elsewhere throughout the UK. In many ways, indeed, the 1960s was the heyday of the book.

It was certainly a good time for *The Golden Notebook* to appear. To what degree Lessing's novel gave a new direction to women's fiction as opposed to leading the way such fiction was bound to take is difficult to determine. But there is no doubt that such fiction was remaking itself. Not so much in terms of manner as matter, although a tone of engagement replaced the observational comedy that had characterised much writing by well-regarded women novelists of the immediate post-war period. This may not at first seem true of Iris Murdoch, whose career began in the 1950s but who achieved new fame in the following decade with a series of novels that blend symbolism with highly convoluted plots in a manner presumably intended to draw attention to their own fictive status. Yet for all the differences between such novels as *A Severed Head* (1961), *An Unofficial Rose* (1962), *The Unicorn* (1963) and *The Italian Girl* (1964), each plays with the question of whether individual moral worth can survive falls from moral grace, which usually means taking turns on the sexual roundabout. As the poet Scott Kelly put it in his poem about Murdoch's novels, 'it's not if you're good in bed / that counts, but if in bed you can be good'.[10]

By comparison with Murdoch, Elizabeth Taylor, whose style was formed before the 1960s and not much affected by newer energies, may at a glance seem old-fashioned. But a closer inspection reveals her to be a novelist of enduring worth. Her studies of upper-middle-class life in southern England are best represented in the decade by *In A Summer Season* (1961) and *The Soul of Kindness* (1964), the sometimes bee-sting hurt of their comedies a world away from the directness of Lessing's fiction. This is in no sense to discount the value of Taylor's work. Within her two square inches of ivory she paints with a sharp exactness, and her rendering of male and female self-delusion is as precise as it is quietly ruthless. There is, for example, Dermot, the idle – indeed, kept – husband of *In A Summer Season*, whose pretence of education and cultural attainment, considerately though his wife tries to maintain it, is repeatedly exposed, as when he frowns over a letter from a friend of hers, written from France, and full of French phrases: '"I'm afraid I can only read simple things like 'Arc de Triomphe'" he told Kate.'[11] Dermot feels guilt, occasionally, because he does no work. In Taylor's fiction men should work and women keep house. Spinsterhood is mostly reserved for eccentrics. But in *The Soul of Kindness* the most powerful woman is Liz Corbett, running to fat, unbothered by her personal appearance, living for her art. Here, if anywhere, Taylor pays tribute to a phenomenon that runs through much fiction by women during the 1960s: that of the single, working woman. It seems proper that *The Golden Notebook* should appear at the beginning of the decade and that at its end, in 1969, Storm Jameson should publish the first volume of her autobiography, *Journey from the North*, in which she claims that 'The day in 1960 when I had the idea of writing these memoirs was also the day when I realized sharply that the kind of novel I have taught myself to write belongs to a past age.'[12] Although she overstates the case about the break point coming at the beginning of the

10 Scott Kelly, *Life All Round* (London: Pecten Press, 2001), p. 64.
11 Elizabeth Taylor, *In a Summer Season* (London: Peter Davies, 1961), p. 45.
12 Storm Jameson, *Journey from the North* (London: Collins & Harvill Press, 1969), 'Prefatory Note'.

decade, there can be no doubt that Jameson was alert to changes in direction of fiction written by women during the 1960s, and the importance of Lessing's contribution to this can hardly be over-estimated. For at the heart of *The Golden Notebook* is the question of how, or indeed whether, her protagonist, Anna, can resolve what she comes to perceive as conflicting demands upon her: as writer, lover, mother, demands that, as she tries to confront them, become increasingly peremptory. There can, in fact, be no satisfactory resolution of the conflicts which make up Anna's life. The last sentence of Lessing's great novel is as spare as it is hard: 'The two women kissed and separated.'[13] Each of the novel's five sections is sub-divided into sections from four Notebooks and each has as running title 'Free Women'. At the end, being free is as much of a problem as it has ever been. It brings women together, it separates them. Or rather, given that Lessing wants to explore the nature and extent of agency, of women's freedom to act, to choose, freedom to choose imposes an awareness of roads not taken, of possibilities, some alluring, resisted.

A year after the appearance of *The Golden Notebook*, Margaret Drabble published her first novel, *A Summer Bird-Cage*. It was quickly followed by *The Garrick Year* (1964), *The Millstone* (1965), *Jerusalem the Golden* (1967) and *The Waterfall* (1969). Drabble's heroines tend to be young graduates living in London, surrounded by left-leaning friends and acquaintances, all exercised by professional careers and the problems of personal relationships. Drabble's faux-naïf style, which I assume is intentional, allows her to maintain a wide-eyed receptivity to all that she or a particular heroine observes, so that there is a peculiar tension between, say, the innocent vulnerability of Rosamund Stacey, the protagonist of *The Millstone*, and her determination to take responsibility for her own life. When she discovers that she is pregnant by a man with whom she has only once had sex, she thinks that there is no reason why she shouldn't have a baby: 'It would serve me right, I thought, for having been born a woman in the first place. I couldn't pretend I wasn't a woman, could I, however much I might try from day to day to avoid the issue?'[14]

Avoiding the issue involves not merely avoiding sex but, for Rosamund, not taking herself seriously as a scholar. (She is supposed to be researching Elizabethan sonnet sequences, especially those of Samuel Daniels.) There is a difficulty here in that Rosamund never seems especially interested in her scholarly work, although I doubt we are meant to infer that she is a mere dilettante. It is more that Drabble fails to imagine Rosamund as a person

13 Dorris Lessing, *The Golden Notebook* (London: Michael Joseph, 1962).
14 Margaret Drabble, *The Millstone* (London: Weidenfeld & Nicolson, 1963), p. 16.

of intellectual curiosity and zeal. The contrast with Anna is thus stark, for Lessing's protagonist is a most powerful study of a writer for whom writing has become a frustrating incompletion of her life.

The professional women of Muriel Spark's fiction tend to operate at a lower level of activity. *The Girls of Slender Means* (1963), which looks back to the immediate post-war period of London, ironically evokes a past when 'all the nice people in England were poor, allowing for exceptions'.[15] As for *The Prime of Miss Jean Brodie*, this minor masterpiece combines a slightly camp, satiric coolness in narration with a ruthless contempt, however silkily sheathed, for liberal humanism. Spark is something of a Jansenist: her view of human nature is as dark as Golding's, her excoriation of Miss Brodie's belief that she has the right to control her chosen girl's lives is every bit as ruthless as Miss Brodie herself. Spark is *sui generis*. Nevertheless, the new spirit of hospitality to fiction, as to so much other writing in the 1960s, undoubtedly encouraged Spark's talent. And while her cat-and-mouse games with women's lives has nothing at all in common with Lessing's fiction, it may legitimately be thought of as a sceptical response to dreams of perfectability that sometimes seem to invade the writing of the decade.

Yet much of the decade's writing by women is more alert to the imperfections of present-day reality. Hence, perhaps, Edna O'Brien's *August is a Wicked Month* (1965), in which a married woman's desire for a sexual escapade leads to humiliation. The lover whom Ellen takes gives her a dose of clap: '"Well if you must be careless you've got to pay," the lady doctor said grimly as she probed first with a rubber-gloved finger and then with a cold metal instrument.'[16] O'Brien is drawing on the full meaning of the word 'careless'. Acting without forethought, being free of care, unstudied. By the time she wrote the novel, the pill had come on the market, and this led to lower numbers of unwanted pregnancies and higher numbers of the venereally infected. O'Brien's acutely judged novel – its tone exactly calibrated so as not to overdo the angst – neatly adumbrates some of the costs of the new freedom which women sought, and which they were encouraged to pursue. *August is a Wicked Month* ruefully lays open the fallacy of some cherished and much-vaunted illusions about new freedoms. Telling it from the woman's angle undercuts the wispier hopes of shared hedonism.

As though to confirm this sardonic understanding, the following year saw the publication of Jean Rhys's *Wide Sargasso Sea*. The story of how the

[15] Muriel Spark, *The Girls of Slender Means* (London: Macmillan, 1963), p. 1.
[16] Edna O'Brien, *August is a Wicked Month* (London: Jonathan Cape, 1965), p. 168.

appearance of the novel lifted Rhys from obscurity to fame has been well told by Carole Angier. Here, it needs to be said that for once in her life Rhys's timing was impeccable. Her retelling of the story of Rochester's mad wife from her own point of view not only helped to return *Jane Eyre* to prominence, but provided the perfect vehicle for reconstructing narratives from the point of view of the World's Wife (to borrow the title of Carol Anne Duffy's 1999 collection of poems, which, like so many feminist writings since 1966, finds voices for women whose for-the-most-part silent roles have been taken for granted in male narratives, whether fictive or otherwise). Yet while Rhys is almost certainly the onlie begetter of this particular way of reordering the world, we should note that it is characteristic of the decade in which E. P. Thompson, in his classic *The Making of the English Working Class* (1963), made it his business to write history 'from below', and famously announced his intention to free the poor stockinger from 'the enormous condescension of posterity'. Rhys's Antoinette is mostly passive, in the sense that she cannot control her own destiny. As Angier notes, like all Rhys's heroines she lives painfully 'and without plan from day to day', because her fate has been sealed.[17] But it is this very helplessness which makes her so sympathetic a figure, especially for women who continue to see in her an articulate image of trapped circumstance. And in this sense at least she is typical of those whose history was being made newly visible in the 1960s. Writing about such people no longer meant writing them off.

V

There is, then, an important element of transgressiveness in much fiction of the 1960s. It willingly steps beyond limits. From the Lady Chatterley trial to the publication in 1969 of Brigid Brophy's novel *In Transit* the decade might, in fact, be accounted for as one of overstepping bounds. Brophy subtitled her novel 'A trans-sexual adventure', and in it indulges wordplay and a kind of elision of modes in order to confuse categories not merely of sex and gender but of fictional types. *In Transit* is a virtual handbook of transgression or, to use another key word of the decade, liberation. It is also an example of literature at play, as where the protagonist considers that the reason authors of fictional narrative are held in disesteem is that they don't want to give in to the compulsion of narrative. They would rather indulge their facility with

[17] Carole Angier, *Jean Rhys: Life and Work* (London: André Deutsch, 1990), p. 179.

words. And so Brophy's hero/heroine runs 'my fingers through the fringes of para-printed matter', seeking there a pleasure to be found nowhere else.[18]

In drawing attention to the text as verbal construct Brophy not only pays obeisance to her fictional forebears Sterne and Joyce, both of whom assumed an iconic status for certain writers of the time, she also signals her kinship with the experimental energies of the decade. The releasing of these energies cannot be attributed only to the rediscovery of *Tristram Shandy*, nor the homage paid to *Finnegans Wake*. As already noted, the literary world of the 1960s was remarkable for an expansiveness, a readiness to welcome the new. Brophy's sideswipe at realism comes at the end of a decade which had been much influenced by a number of American novels that had between them made an almost programmatic assault on realism (rather as American abstract Expressionism was an assault on social realism in art). William Burroughs's *The Naked Lunch* had been published by the Olympia Press in Paris in 1959 and soon gained the status of underground classic. John Barth's *The Sot-Weed Factor* was published in the UK in 1961 and its debt to Sterne is manifest, not merely because it is ostensibly set in the eighteenth century, but because its bawdy tale is subject to endless digressions, interpolations of different narrative voices and mock-serious speculations on literature. Add that Samuel Beckett's *Trilogy* was published by John Calder in 1959 (Calder was one of the first of the new breed of independent publishers devoted to the cause of experimental writing), tip in the republication of Malcolm Lowry's *Under the Volcano* in 1962 (by Penguin) five years after its author's death so that it, too, took on the status of modern classic, stir with examples of the *nouvelle vague* by such writers as Natalie Sarraute and Marguerite Duras, not forgetting Günter Grass's *The Tin Drum* (first published in an English edition by 1962), and you have a heady brew that would certainly threaten the sobriety of English fiction.

Beckett's trilogy of novels, *Molloy*, *Malone Dies* and *The Unnamable* can indeed be read as charting the collapse of a certain kind of realism, in a movement towards an experimental prose that borders, like *Finnegans Wake*, on the unreadable. The first novel of the trilogy, *Molloy*, is a two-part narrative that is written partly in the style of a detective novel. Moran, the bourgeois protagonist of the novel's second half, is a detective who is employed, or otherwise enjoined, to track down Molloy, the vagabond protagonist of the first half. Anticipating Thomas Pynchon's experiments with the detective genre in 1966 in *The Crying of Lot 49*, Moran fails to locate or apprehend Molloy, but rather comes increasingly to resemble his quarry. As Moran's rambling search for

[18] Brigid Brophy, *In Transit, A Trans-sexual Adventure* (London: Macdonald, 1969), p. 80.

Molloy continues, he gradually loses his assurance, his command of style and form, and his narration disintegrates from brisk realism to the aimlessness of Molloy's threadbare, unparagraphed and meandering prose.

If this failure of the detective genre might suggest that the novel form is suffering a kind of breakdown here, a tilt towards ragged homelessness, then the following two novels of Beckett's trilogy take the erosion of realist narrative much further. *Malone Dies* charts the death of a bed-bound decrepit named Malone – as it happens, the author himself of a trilogy of stories. Malone starts off his narration with a kind of pale verve, setting out his storytelling agenda with a certain flourish. But he soon finds that the business of scribbling stories in a notebook loses its hold over him. 'It is so nice to know where you're going', as Beckett's narrator says of his best-laid plans, 'it almost rids you of the wish to go there.'[19] As the novel progresses towards the death of Malone, the stories that he writes as well as the story in which he stars gradually fall apart, suggesting that death is not only the end of this narrative but its ongoing condition, the substance of the narrative which the patchy plot barely fails to hide. *The Unnamable*, the final instalment of the trilogy, takes place in the deathly space that is left when the fictions of Molloy, Moran and Malone have collapsed. The narrator of the final novel of the trilogy, if such a stable figure can be said to exist, makes a gestural attempt to tell himself stories, but by now the very possibility of narration has worn away, leaving only a voice which is brutally confronted by the failure of its own language.

Beckett's trilogy, then, dramatises the failure after Auschwitz not only of lyric poetry, but of narrative fiction. The attempt to write stories leads Beckett ineluctably to *The Unnamable*, and to the excruciatingly stalled final line, 'I can't go on. I'll go on.'[20] Fiction after 1959 has to contend with the aporia to which Beckett's narrator brings the novel in this line – despite his admission that he doesn't know what the word aporia means.[21] But while the trilogy points to the end of a certain mode of narration, there is a complementary move here towards a new and experimental form of expression. As the fittings and the fixtures of the realist novel are eroded by the excoriating voice of the narrator who insists upon his unnamability, Beckett's fiction opens onto the voice of a new kind of author, whose way of going on is born from an exiled, silent cunning that is only shadowed forth in Joyce.

The two most significant English experimental writers of the decade are Christine Brooke-Rose and B. S. Johnson. Of the two, Brooke-Rose

[19] Samuel Beckett, *Molloy, Malone Dies, The Unnamable* (London: Calder, 1959), p. 20.
[20] Ibid., p. 382. [21] Ibid., p. 267.

undoubtedly owes more to French models. Frank Kermode is on record as saying that 'If we are ever to experience in English the serious *practice* of narrative as the French have developed it over the last few years, we shall have to attend to Christine Brooke-Rose.'[22] The novels of hers requiring attention are *Out* (1964), *Such* (1966) and *Between* (1968). Different though they are from each other they have certain features in common: a cool, forensic style of narration which I take to be that of uninvolved (pitiless?) objectivity, and which is conducted in the present tense (as though to defeat the expectations of conventional realism), a stylistic habit of indicating speech not by quotation marks but by a dash, or, even, asposiopesis; and a constant refusal to make clear whether we are reading a report on the world 'out there', or speculations of the narrator – whoever that may be. Brooke-Rose teases her readers into uncertainty. Johnson more aggressively confronts his with the writer's own doubts. After the initial success of *Travelling People* (1963), Johnson produced *Albert Angelo* (1964), *Trawl* (1966) and *The Unfortunates* (1969), as well as short stories and poems. *The Unfortunates* consisted of twenty-seven pamphlets inserted into a box, from which, with the exception of those called 'First' and 'Last', each is to be extracted and read in any order the reader happens to choose. But all the novels have experimental devices, including the grey and then black pages of *Travelling People* (heart attack followed by death) and the pages split into separate columns of *Albert Angelo*, to represent the narrator's different public and private personae (speech and thought.) *Albert Angelo* also contains a statement that reads like a *cri de cœur* and which begins the section called, significantly, 'Disintegration': ' – fuck all this lying look what I'm really trying to write about is writing not all this stuff about architecture . . . '[23]

Johnson believed that the realist novel had had its day. By temperament he was a battler against the odds. His finest gifts were for the comic, and he was an especially brilliant mimic. *Travelling People* is a tour de force. Different chapters use different styles: diary, film-script, epistolary novel. *Albert Angelo* drops in more-or-less literate letters from the schoolkids Albert teaches. *Trawl* ranges from the exact, unemotional observations of the narrator at sea to the turmoil of his inner life, where he is all at sea. In each novel Johnson tries something new. This willingness to experiment is without doubt an expression of the decade's best energies. It may be thought a tragedy for English fiction no less than for Johnson himself that in 1973 he killed himself.

22 Christina Brooke-Rose, *The Christina Brooke-Rose Omnibus* (Manchester: Carcanet Press, 1986), endorsement.

23 B. S. Johnson, *Albert Angelo* (London: Constable, 1964), p. 165.

31

'Voyaging in': colonialism and migration

SUSHEILA NASTA

The period immediately following World War II is now well known for the migration to the United Kingdom of a large number of writers and artists from a fast-declining empire. Lured to the once-imperial metropolis to find publishers and a wider audience for their work, many were to have a major impact on the face of British writing as the century progressed.[1] Yet, few attempts were made to include them in post-war accounts of British literary history.[2] Moreover, the pigeonholes that were eventually set up either excluded them on grounds of race, placing them neatly in separate national traditions, or partially assimilated them as the 'exotic' flowers of what came by the 1960s to be known as 'Commonwealth Literature': a so-called wave of 'new' writings in English from previously colonised areas but which were frequently reduced by well-meaning liberal critics to simply derivative or mimicking branches of the main.[3] There were, of course, several reasons for this. Not only had the critical

[1] See Simon Gikandi, *Maps of Englishness: Writing Identity in the Culture of Colonialism* (New York: Columbia University Press, 1996); Graham Huggan, *The Post-Colonial Exotic: Marketing the Margins* (London: Routledge, 2001), pp. 228–64.

[2] This lack of coherent coverage is discussed in Andrzej Gasiorek, *Post-War British Fiction: Realism and After* (London: Edward Arnold, 1995) and still continues in recent studies of English Literature such as Margaret Drabble, *Concise Companion to English Literature* (Oxford University Press, 1987). For examples of this silence, see Bryan Appleyard, *The Pleasures of Peace: Art and Imagination in Post-War Britain* (London: Faber & Faber, 1989); Bernard Bergonzi, *The Situation of the Novel* (London: Macmillan, 1970); David Lodge, *The Novelist at the Crossroads* (London: Routledge & Kegan Paul, 1971); Malcolm Bradbury and David Palmer, eds., *The Contemporary English Novel* (New York: Holmes and Meier, 1980); David Gervais, *Literary England: Versions of 'Englishness' in Modern Writing* (Cambridge University Press, 1993).

[3] See: William Walsh, *Commonwealth Literature* (Oxford University Press, 1973); Bruce King, ed., *Literatures of the World in English* (London: Routledge, 1974); Anna Rutherford, ed., *From Commonwealth to Post-Colonial* (Sydney: Dangaroo Press, 1992); Hena Maes-Jelinek, Kirsten Holst Petersen, Anna Rutherford, eds., *A Shaping of Connections: Commonwealth Literature Studies – Then and Now* (Sydney, Dangaroo, 1989); Sarah Lawson Welsh, 'New Wine in New Bottles: the Reception of West Indian Writing in Britain in the 1950s and 1960s', in Alison Donnell and Sarah Lawson Welsh, eds., *The Routledge Reader in Caribbean Literature* (London: Routledge, 1996), pp. 261–8; Gail Low, 'Finding the Centre: Publishing

temper of British writing become narrowly parochial (with a loss of interest in the cosmopolitanism characteristic of the Modernist movement earlier in the century), but it was still fuelled, even after Independence, by the lingering ideologies of a three-hundred-year imperial history, the divisive legacies of a manichean colonialist discourse which failed to accept that the formation of the nation was not only built on the culture of empire but also created by it. Domestic ideas of the national character had always been buoyed up by a process of exclusion, where what was British was defined in contradistinction to those it regarded to be the nation's 'others', whether at home or abroad.[4] Thus, while the lineage of what F. R. Leavis was to call the 'great tradition' had been liberally exported to the British colonies as part of the civilising mission of empire – an invented tradition which had itself originally been defined against the sense of alterity which colonisation brought with it – it was more difficult to come to terms with its hybridised return: to recognise, in short, the formation of alternative modernities written not only from within the European body, and which challenged some of its established premises.[5] While this myopia in the UK's literary historiography began to be addressed much later in the century with the advent of Postcolonial theory – a general move in critical thinking, influenced by Post-structuralist discourse analysis, and which sought by the mid-1980s to expose the heterogeneity of the nation's cultural archive – there nevertheless remains a general failure to recognise the extent to which the map of British literature has always been dependent on its long and mixed colonial past.[6]

Questions of empire, colonialism and migration have always been closely related. So, indeed, have questions of literature and the formation of national identities. Yet one of the most commonly held myths about Britain's immigrant history is that it *began* with the symbolic docking in Tilbury in June 1948 of the SS *Empire Windrush*, a moment that not only inaugurated the so-called 'black presence' in the UK but also marked the starting-point for the large-scale migrations from India, Pakistan and East Africa which were to follow in the

Commonwealth Writing in London', *Journal of Commonwealth Literature*, 37, 2 (2002), pp. 15–34.

4 Raphael Samuel, ed., *Patriotism: The Making and Unmaking of British National Identity. Vol. I: History and Politics* (London: Routledge, 1989); Alan Sinfield, *Society and Literature, 1945–70* (London: Methuen, 1983).

5 Susheila Nasta, *Home Truths: Fictions of the South Asian Diaspora in Britain* (Basingstoke: Palgrave, 2002), pp. 15–53.

6 Paul Gilroy, *There Ain't No Black in the Union Jack* (London: Routledge, 1987) and *The Black Atlantic: Modernity and Double Consciousness* (London: Verso, 1993). Also C. L. Innes, *A History of Black and Asian Writing in Britain, 1700–2000* (Cambridge University Press, 2002).

next three decades.[7] It cannot be doubted that the arrival of this boatload of four hundred and ninety-two expectant migrants from the West Indian islands – whose passengers were bound on a 'journey' not to a welcoming colonial motherland but to 'an illusion'– represents an iconic moment in post-war immigrant history.[8] But the frequent mythologisation of this arrival has also served to write over and disguise a number of more complex and contradictory pasts. For this inaugural moment not only marked a departure point for the growth of a tradition of black and migrant writing in the UK, a time when it is said the Empire's so-called colonial chickens came home to roost, but also coincided importantly with a waning sense of national confidence in Britannia's continuing prowess as an imperial power, a fear sparked by Indian Independence in 1947 and further exacerbated by the transformation of the Empire into the Commonwealth of Nations in 1948.[9]

It is well known that Britain has had a mixed migrant population for well over three hundred years, at least as long, that is, as the history of the Empire abroad. It is therefore worth remembering that Britain was historically as much the 'home' of the colonial encounter as were the colonies themselves, situated in the so-called peripheries. Hence, as many historians have now noted, the more visible presence in the UK of several generations of African, Caribbean and Asian 'immigrants' in the decades after World War II was not simply an effect of the residue of empire but the culmination of a long and more intimate relationship.[10] As Lyn Innes has demonstrated in *A History of Black and Asian Writing in Britain 1700–2000*, the presence of this racially mixed empire within had impacted for several generations on the nation's cultural and literary life, forming the backcloth to the publication of a substantial body of literary work, responsible well before 1945 for a number of productive international and transnational connections which were to have major ramifications later in the century.

[7] Peter Fryer, *Staying Power: The History of Black People in Britain* (London: Pluto Press, 1984); Rozina Visram, *Asians in Britain: Four Hundred Years of History* (London: Pluto Press, 2002); Mike Phillips and Trevor Phillips, *Windrush: The Irresistible Rise of Multi-Racial Britain* (London: HarperCollins, 1998); James Procter, ed., *Writing Black Britain* (Manchester University Press, 2000).

[8] Donald Hinds, *Journey to an Illusion: A Study of West Indians in Britain* (London: Heinemann, 1966).

[9] Aubrey Menen provides a satirical analysis of this in his collection, *Dead Man in a Silver Market: An Autobiographical Essay on National Pride* (London: Chatto & Windus, 1954), pp. 8–11.

[10] Fryer, *Staying Power*; Visram, *Asians in Britain*; also Antoinette Burton, *At the Heart of Empire: Indians and the Colonial Encounter in Late Victorian Britain* (Berkeley: University of California Press, 1998).

The effects on the imagination of the nation were not, however, always obvious ones. At a crucial moment during World War II, to take one example, Sir Winston Churchill delivered a famous speech to the House of Commons to rouse the patriotic spirit of the British nation. In his speech he quoted liberally from a sonnet entitled, 'If We Must Die', by a then little-known Jamaican émigré poet and novelist, Claude McKay.[11] While Churchill was clearly intending to bolster the morale of British troops to rise up to the challenge of war and not surrender their 'precious blood' by dying 'like hogs penned in an inglorious spot', McKay's 1919 poem was originally written as a call to resist the continuing violations of human rights inflicted on the black descendants of the Atlantic slave trade in the United States.[12] A leading light in the Harlem Renaissance, McKay had emigrated to the USA from Jamaica in 1912, and, unlike many other colonial artists and intellectuals who settled in the UK prior to the end of World War II, McKay was only to spend a brief and disillusioned spell in the country he had once imagined to be his spiritual and intellectual homeland. However, Churchill's appropriation and subsequent translation of these lines by a Caribbean émigré into one of the sustaining narratives of the nation's patriotic memory following the defeat of Germany in 1945 is not only interesting for its obvious ironies (the source and original purpose of the poem have seldom been noted or attributed), but is also indicative of a number of significant questions that need to be addressed in this chapter. For while it is now common knowledge that many colonials were enlisted to fight for the nation in both world wars, the intellectual impact that these once imperial subjects have made on the cultural history of the nation is frequently elided.

If we consider the literary landscape prior to 1948, it soon becomes clear that London was not only the 'heart' of empire but also 'home' to a number of students, writers and intellectuals who were to play an important, if not always acknowledged, role in shaping the nation's cultural history.[13] The influential cross-cultural relationship between the Irish poet W. B. Yeats, the American Ezra Pound and the Nobel Prize-winning Bengali poet Rabrindranath Tagore in the first part of the century is well known. But many other individuals who migrated to Britain from 1910 onwards were to become notable contributors to literary life. Figures such as the New Zealander Katherine Mansfield, the

[11] Claude McKay, *Selected Poems* (New York, 1953); see also Paula Burnett, *The Penguin Book of Caribbean Verse in English* (Harmondsworth: Penguin, 1986), pp. 144, 402, who discusses Churchill's use of the poem in the House of Commons and its original publication in 1919. See also Fryer, *Staying Power*, p. 319.

[12] Claude McKay, 'If We Must Die', in Paula Burnett, *Caribbean Verse*, p. 144.

[13] This history is documented in detail in Innes, *History of Black and Asian Writing.*

Jamaican poet and playwright Una Marson, the white creole Dominican Jean Rhys, the Indian novelists Mulk Raj Anand, Raja Rao and G. V. Desani, as well as the Trinidadian C. L. R. James, were all drawn in different ways to a received 'idea' of England, inculcated through the shared language of a colonial education. Their histories, however, were also global ones and many were enabled by the culturally mixed nature of their colonial experience to express a vision which both resisted and assimilated, critiquing from within the dominant epistemologies of a Western modernity which traditionally had sought to exclude them. Jean Rhys's early novel of exile, *Voyage in the Dark* (1934) – a work which looks forward in illuminating ways to her later interrogation in *Wide Sargasso Sea* (1966) of the inherited imperial discourse underpinning Charlotte Brontë's creation of Bertha, the mad creole woman in the attic in *Jane Eyre* – is not only already highly self-conscious about its subversive translation of a number of Western Modernist strategies but also manipulates them to express a world suspended in the spaces that both separate and conjoin her colonial past and metropolitan present; a mulatto reality that cannot be contained by either.[14]

Similarly, C. L. R. James, who passaged to the UK from Trinidad in 1932 and who is perhaps one of the most distinguished writers of both the pre- and post-war periods, was fully cognisant of the extent to which Western European thought had determined his thinking, acknowledging that it would be Caliban's intimate knowledge of Prospero's library that would lift the mask of his colonial relation. As he explains in *Beyond a Boundary* (1963), an impressive autobiographical work which not only details the background to his arrival in the UK but explores the philosophical, historical and literary background to the substantial interventions James was to effect in all of his published works, 'To establish his own identity, Caliban . . . must himself pioneer into regions Caesar never knew.'[15] Moreover, in James's view, the encounter with British history and Western literature was a necessary prerequisite to the evolution of an anti-colonial aesthetic which could begin to reshape the architecture of the master's house. This was a perspective already apparent in his first novel of yard life, *Minty Alley* (1936), and is most clearly elucidated, perhaps, in the radical philosophy driving his historical and political works culminating in *Beyond a Boundary*, with its perceptive cultural analysis of the quintessentially 'English'

14 In *Jean Rhys: The West Indian Novels* (New York University Press, 1986), Teresa O'Connor discusses Jean Rhys's early short stories and novels from this perspective as does Helen Carr, *Jean Rhys* (Plymouth: Northcote House, 1996), pp. 21–40.

15 C. L. R. James, *Beyond a Boundary* (London: Serpent's Tail, 1983), p. xxi (first published London: Stanley Paul/ Hutchinson, 1963).

game of cricket. In his published works, James straddles several genres, appearing as political essayist, philosopher, literary critic, historian, playwright and novelist.[16] Like many others from the Caribbean who followed on in the post-war period, James was keen from the outset to open up a series of broader global dialogues, to establish connections between the shared language of Prospero and Caliban, the creolised modernities of his Caribbean past and the parallel, but differently located modernities of other so-called 'outsiders' within the Euro-American tradition. Like Jean Rhys and Claude McKay, James's perspective was one which existed both within and outside the dominant tradition of the Western canon, providing a mobility of mind and a doubling of consciousness which was to create a unique vantage-point for a second generation of black writers in Britain in the years to come. Although he migrated to the United States before the outbreak of war in 1939, C. L. R. James was to return in 1953 and spent the majority of his remaining years living and working in Britain until his death in 1989.

One of the significant features of C. L. R. James's work, as with others such as Mulk Raj Anand, was that it spoke to a number of different cultural constituencies whether at home or abroad, often drawing links between the seemingly oppositional categories that separated them. Both writers, like many others in the inter-war years, were initially attracted to Marxism as a form of 'tri-continental' anti-colonial resistance, a means to combat the inequalities of their colonial relation and to move beyond the limitations of a narrow monolithic vision.[17] Thus, while Anand's first novel, *Untouchable* (1935), has most frequently been located, like many of his later socially realist fictions, as one of the founding works of the burgeoning 'nationalist' tradition of Indian writing in English, it is clear with hindsight that his multiple perspective not only gave voice and a place to subaltern characters not previously visible in English fiction but also sought from an early stage to challenge the West's narrow view of its own civility. As is apparent, too, in *Across the Black Waters* (1940) – a later novel which exposes Britain's exploitative enlisting of Indian sepoys to cross to *Villayet* [England] as cannon fodder during World

[16] C. L. R. James published several major historical and literary studies (see bibliography). He was involved during this period with the Pan-African movement and figures such as Jomo Kenyatta and Nkrumah who were to become key players in African politics later in the century. See Innes, *History of Black and Asian Writing*, pp. 175–9; also Simon Gikandi, *Writing in Limbo: Modernism and Caribbean Literature* (New York: Cornell University Press, 1992), pp. 42–56.

[17] Early versions of this 'tri-continental' vision, a term used by Robert Young to account for this transnational history in *Postcolonialism* (Oxford: Blackwell, 2001), were also evident in the works of early critics in the 1930s such as Cedric Dover, author of the novel *Half-Caste* (London: Secker & Warburg, 1937).

War I – so-called 'barbarism' was generated as much from within as without, the inevitable product of a Western modernity that had led to a series of repetitive atrocities worldwide. As Anand makes plain in *Conversations in Bloomsbury* (1981), a memoir of discussions he shared with many of the Bloomsbury Group including T. S. Eliot, Aldous Huxley, Virginia Woolf, Leonard Woolf, E. M. Forster and Edith Sitwell, he was clearly conscious, like C. L. R. James, of both the attractions and the pitfalls of anti-colonial resistance; the limitations of forever holding up a mirror of opposites, universally in conflict, rather than as 'mutual deformations' and 'creative reformations' of each other.[18] Interestingly, the mixed cultural trajectories evident in the work of early migrant colonials such as Anand and Raja Rao (another elder statesman of the so-called nationalist period in the Indian novel in English but who, in fact, was writing in France and the UK at this time) can be fruitfully compared to a number of later writers from the subcontinent who were to become key players in the definition of a genre of postcolonial and diasporic South Asian fictions by the end of the century.[19]

Anand returned to India, after more than twenty years in the UK, before Independence in 1947. However, many others such as Tambimuttu, the Ceylonese poet and editor from 1939–51 of *Poetry London*, stayed on until well after the war and continued to play a significant role in British intellectual life, intervening in and shaping many of its cultural institutions. Major British poets such as George Barker, Stephen Spender, Gavin Ewart, Dylan Thomas, Kathleen Raine and Lawrence Durrell were first published in the pages of *Poetry London*, and it was another Indian colonial, Krishna Menon, a lawyer, editor and key campaigner for Independence in 1947, who was to launch figures such as Naomi Mitchison with Bodley Head and later, as founding editor of Pelican Books, bring George Bernard Shaw, Roger Fry and H. G. Wells to a wider audience. Others, such as Una Marson, the Jamaican poet and political radical who is frequently seen as one of the feminist 'foremothers' of a tradition of black women's writing in the UK, or Attia Hosain, an Indian exile of aristocratic background, whose short stories and novel, *Sunlight on a Broken Column* (1961), were to place the realities of Muslim women's lives at the centre of the narrative of dislocation associated with Partition, became active

18 This develops an argument used by Bryan Cheyette in 'Venetian Spaces: Old–New Literatures and the Ambivalent Use of Jewish History', in Susheila Nasta, ed., *Reading the 'New' Literatures in a Postcolonial Era* (Cambridge: Brewer, 2000), p. 69. It is further explored in Nasta, *Home Truths*.

19 The background to the emergence of a diasporic tradition of writers with South Asian origins such as Salman Rushdie, Bharati Mukherjee, V. S. Naipaul et al. is elaborated on in Nasta, *Home Truths*.

with the BBC as producers and contributed alongside figures such as George Orwell to the literary content of its programmes. The important BBC literary review *Caribbean Voices* was first broadcast in 1943 as a result of Marson's initial direction and later, under the more well-known editorship of Henry Swanzy and V. S. Naipaul, was to play a seminal role in attracting writers to the UK in the 1950s, making London a West Indian literary capital. Significantly, too, it was a writer such as G. V. Desani, whose iconoclastic novel *All About H. Hatterr* – written during the war and published with much critical acclaim in 1948 – who was to become an acknowledged precursor for Salman Rushdie and the episodic and picaresque narratives of a later generation of Postcolonial writers in Britain. For Desani's inspired creation in this subversive novel of the mixed-race and orphaned, H. Hatterr was not only an early and prophetic representation of the migrant as a universal Everyman figure – a cosmopolitan and hybrid voyeur who comes to dominate the content of much late twentieth-century Postmodernist and Postcolonial fiction – but was also demonstrably an example of an inventive form of textual insurrection, a parodic mode of writing which implicitly questioned its own biases. And although Desani, like Jean Rhys earlier, was to disappear from public attention for several years, their narratives were to become formative models in the strategies many others were to adopt in challenging the dominance of Western orthodoxies and writing back to empire later in the century.[20]

The UK was already well established then, prior to *Windrush*, as an important literary crossroads for the larger-scale migrations which were to follow on. For not only did London retain its attraction as the beckoning cultural heart of the colonial motherland, but it also became an international publishing capital. As Diana Athill, one of the most influential literary editors of the post-war period recounts, there was a general mood in the 1950s and 1960s of an idealism combined with a guilt at Britain's imperial past.[21] In tandem with a general post-war boom in the publishing industry, this situation created a favourable milieu for writers from the new Commonwealth nations, a history that is reflected in early contributions to literary journals such as the *London Magazine* and *Lilliput* as well as by review coverage in national newspapers during the 1950s and 60s. Between 1952 and 1967 alone, over one hundred and thirty-seven novels by West Indians were published in the UK, including many

[20] Diana Athill, *stet* (London: Granta Books, 2000); B. Ashcroft, G. Griffiths, Helen Tiffin, eds., *The Empire Writes Back: Theory and Practice in Post-Colonial Literatures* (London: Routledge, 1989).

[21] Athill, *stet*, p. 102.

anthologies, volumes of short stories and plays.[22] The formative Heinemann African Writers Series was launched in 1962 and many now highly distinguished postcolonial writers were first published by London houses such as Faber & Faber, André Deutsch, Jonathan Cape and Allen Wingate. This extension of the international reach of the publishing industry was also to provide crucial publishing opportunities for a number of Caribbean, African and South Asian writers resident in the UK at the time.[23] In fact, as Athill – who played a major role along with Francis Wyndham in rescuing Jean Rhys from oblivion and publishing the then little-known Trinidadian colonial, V. S. Naipaul, tells us – it was probably easier in some ways during this period 'for a black writer to get his book accepted by a London publisher than it was for a young white person'.[24]

Despite, however, the initial enthusiasm shown by publishers and some enlightened reviewers who wished to extend the narrow parameters of English reading, the reception of these writers in the UK became an increasingly contradictory one. For while many were keen to signal the 'new blood' these artists were contributing to the perceived dullness of the post-war literary scene at home, their comments were frequently barbed by a patronising paternalism which did not look much further than the immediately surface preoccupations of what were seen to be the predictable concerns of these 'outsiders' with questions of history, exilic versions of childhood or the representation of emergent national identities in what was for many an era of independence.[25] Placed firmly, therefore, outside the protected boundaries of the established canon, many were only seen to be worth commenting on for the exotic novelty of their themes, their naturalistic subject-matter, the naïve authenticity of their uses of vernacular forms of English, or their otherwise realistic sociological portraits of the UK's new immigrant communities. Seldom were critics willing to provide in-depth discussions of the innate literary quality of such works,

[22] Kenneth Ramchand, *The West Indian Novel and Its Background* (London: Faber & Faber, 1970), pp. 3–6; also Rhonda Cobham, 'The Background', in Bruce King, ed., *West Indian Literature* (London: Macmillan, 1979), pp. 9–30.

[23] Anne Walmsley, *The Caribbean Artists' Movement 1966–72* (London: New Beacon, 1992), pp. 1–35, and Gail Low, 'In Pursuit of Publishing: Heinemann's African Writers Series', *Wasafiri*, 37 (Winter 2002), pp. 31–6.

[24] Athill, *stet*, p. 102.

[25] David Dabydeen, 'West Indian Writers in Britain', in Ferdinand Dennis, Naseem Khan, eds., *Voices of the Crossing* (London: Serpent's Tail, 2000), pp. 59–77. See also, Sarah Lawson Welsh, '(Un)belonging Citizens, Unmapped Territory: Black Immigration and British Identity in the Post-1945 period', in Stuart Murray, ed., *Not on Any Map: Essays on Postcoloniality and Cultural Nationalism* (Exeter University Press, 1997), pp. 43–8.

their self-conscious innovations with language and form or the fact that the majority of these so-called writers from 'elsewhere' were centrally involved in a commonly felt need to discover alternative discursive strategies to reshape the dominant epistemological borders of the English canon. While, as we shall see later, individual approaches varied, it was the need to create a new architecture for the imagination, a language for rather than against identity, which was to become a key issue of political, historical and literary contestation in the years to follow, as these writers strove to find new frames and more fitting aesthetic correlatives to house their diverse and syncretic cultural backgrounds.

The paradoxical nature of this widespread failure to accommodate this burgeoning tradition of new writing within the closely guarded parameters of the British canon was heightened as the large-scale migrations from the Caribbean, South Asia and Africa began to visibly colonise the UK in reverse and to threaten the commonly held myth of England as a green and pleasant land. Moreover, the initially welcoming atmosphere of the Nationality Act of 1948 – an open-door policy that had explicitly invited citizens from *all* of the UK's colonies into the country to relieve the labour shortages after the war – began to shift to the expression of a fierce domestic nationalism, an exclusionary discourse, which focused, after the imposition of the Immigration Acts of the 1960s, on race as the prime determinant in restricting free access to the subjects of the UK's ex-colonies. By 1968, with Enoch Powell's notorious 'rivers of blood' speech, the UK's non-white immigrant populations began to be seen as the dark side of the nation's consciousness, second-class citizens who were not only a physical reminder of its waning imperial power, but a body of alien people who had come to pollute the realm.[26]

While many writers from the white dominions were also, in fact, to settle in the UK during this period, including Doris Lessing (novelist, Rhodesia/Zimbabwe), Peter Porter (poet, Australia) and Fleur Adcock (poet, New Zealand), by far the largest 'group' came from the West Indian islands, along with several individuals from the Asian subcontinent and Africa. Among those from the subcontinent were the poet Dom Moraes and the novelists Kamala Markandaya and Farukh Dhondy, as well as the already well-established Bengali philosopher and historian Nirad Chaudhuri, author of *Autobiography of an Unknown Indian* (1951). Wole Soyinka (Nigeria) and Ngugi wa'Thiongo (Kenya) were both students in the UK during the 1960s and identified early

[26] Gikandi, *Maps of Englishness*, p. 86.

in their careers, like many others, with the anti-colonialist stance of the Martinican psychoanalyst, Frantz Fanon, in *The Wretched of the Earth* (1968), as well as a general desire to break away from the literary manacles of a colonial past. While both Ngugi and Soyinka were to return to their native lands before political events made exile abroad inevitable, others from Africa such as Buchi Emecheta (Nigeria) and Abdulrazak Gurnah (Zanzibar) arrived later and made their homes in the UK. And although some, as we have already seen, had been resident there since well before 1945, or indeed were born there (like Aubrey Menen, a widely published novelist, journalist and broadcaster who was of mixed Irish and Indian descent), it was the West Indian 'group' who were to have the most immediate impact on reshaping the contours of British writing and transforming the former imperial centre's sense of itself. For their arrival not only initiated an important movement in Caribbean literary history but also laid the foundations for a tradition of black and Postcolonial writing which was to consolidate itself in the UK during the 1970s.[27]

Unlike those individuals who settled in the UK before the war, these writers did not come alone. Commonly referred to, therefore, as the *Windrush* generation, they came, in fact, from a variety of different island regions, with different literary agendas, different racial, cultural and class backgrounds and at different times. While accounts by writers of their individual reasons for departure vary, they all shared the need to 'get out', to escape the 'philistinism' of the West Indian middle classes and to discover a metropolitan reading public for their work.[28] Virtually every West Indian writer – with few major exceptions apart from Derek Walcott – crossed the Atlantic to the UK in the period between 1948 and 1970. Attracted by the opportunity for recognition offered by the weekly broadcasts of the BBC *Caribbean Voices* programme, many were encouraged by the early success of Edgar Mittelholzer (Guyana), George Lamming (Barbados) and Sam Selvon (Trinidad), who all succeeded in getting their first novels published soon after their arrival. And while some, such as Andrew Salkey (Jamaica) and John Figueroa (Jamaica), Wilson Harris (Guyana), James Berry (Jamaica) and E. A. Markham (Montserrat), arrived as ordinary immigrants, others, like V. S. Naipaul (Trinidad), his brother Shiva Naipaul, E. R. Braithwaite (Jamaica), Kamau Brathwaite (Barbados), Stuart Hall (Jamaica), Beryl Gilroy (Guyana) and Merle Hodge (Trinidad), came initially as students on prestigious island scholarships. And although

[27] Walmsley, *Caribbean Artists' Movement*, pp. 1–32; Procter, *Writing Black Britain*, pp. i–xii.
[28] George Lamming, *The Pleasures of Exile* (London: Michael Joseph, 1960), p. 41.

a few individuals, such as the poet and historian Kamau Brathwaite and George Lamming, later returned or migrated elsewhere, the majority stayed on in the UK and produced a substantial body of work in the decades to come.

Due to the now well-documented effects of growing up under the influence of a divisive colonial education system – a situation where, as the young V. S. Naipaul put it, 'the language was mine' but 'the tradition was not' – these writers were both intimate with and separate from British culture.[29] In fact, as George Lamming noted, it was only after arrival in the UK that a firm sense of a West Indian cultural identity was born, as islanders began to meet and read each other's work for the first time. Ironically, perhaps, it was through the encounter with London that it became possible to inscribe a more fully realised picture of the world back home – to depict the complex background to a history of racial admixture, cultural dislocation and economic exploitation – and to define a Caribbean consciousness within a British context. Escape from the islands was frequently seen as an important step in the process of decolonisation, exile not beginning but ending with departure and representing a turning-point in what had previously been a negative cycle of fragmentation and diaspora. However, if departure enabled in one sense the end of 'exile', it also produced its own difficulties as these artists fought for survival in a city whose streets were not paved with gold, and sought to negotiate their ambivalent location both within and outside British society.[30] In a memorial tribute to Sam Selvon delivered in 1994, George Lamming attempted to reconstruct the atmosphere of the early days he shared with him both on the boat journey to England, and later, as young writers struggling to earn a living with the BBC. 'Can you imagine', he says, 'waking up one morning and discovering a stranger asleep on the sofa of your living room?' This was the situation many English people found themselves in when 'they awoke' to find these 'people', once comrades on World War II battlefields, now strangers and post-war immigrants, metaphorically asleep in their houses. On 'the one hand the sleeper on the sofa was absolutely sure through imperial tutelage that he was at home, on the other the native Englishman was completely mystified by this unknown interloper'.[31]

[29] V. S. Naipaul, 'Jasmine', in *The Overcrowded Barracoon* (London: André Deutsch, 1972), p. 27 (this essay first appeared in the *Times Literary Supplement*, 4 June 1964.

[30] Jan Carew in *The Fulcrums of Change* (New Jersey: Africa World Press, 1988), pp. 91–108, suggests, among others, that exile for the Caribbean writer was a force for cultural survival and creativity rather than a repetition of an ancient history of dislocation.

[31] George Lamming, 'The Coldest Spring in Fifty Years', *Kunapipi*, 20, 1 (1998), pp. 4–10.

Many fictional and non-fictional accounts have documented this important phase in the history of West Indian writing.[32] For not only was it a period, as George Lamming notes in *The Pleasures of Exile*, when the category 'West Indian' formerly understood as a 'geographical term' assumed 'cultural significance', but it was also the most formative period in the Caribbean literary renaissance. First novels such as Sam Selvon's *A Brighter Sun* (1952), George Lamming's *In the Castle of My Skin* (1953), and even V. S. Naipaul's early and satiric social comedies such as *Miguel St* (1959) frequently focused on the themes of childhood and departure as a means of linking the emergent public histories of their respective islands with the private vision of the individual artist, coming to consciousness during a time of national and regional self-definition, setting trends for those who followed in the 1960s and 1970s.[33] In others, the question of a divided consciousness and the issue of cultural location are explored through the disorientating experiences of exile in the metropolis. While Sam Selvon's pioneering London work *The Lonely Londoners* (1956) was emblematic in its literary translation of a pluralist Trinidadian aesthetic into the ironically constituted monolith of a 'black' colony in the heart of the city, there were many others, such as George Lamming's *The Emigrants* (1954), E. R. Braithwaite's *To Sir With Love* (1959), Andrew Salkey's *Escape to an Autumn Pavement* (1960), and V. S. Naipaul's *The Mimic Men* (1967), which deal in different ways with the dislocation and disillusion of the early immigrant experience. Few women writers, apart from Jean Rhys, whose ground-breaking novel *Wide Sargasso Sea* appeared in 1966, were published at this time, due mainly to the fact that the first wave of immigration to the UK from the Caribbean islands was largely male. This imbalance is often evident in the subject-matter of these works, where there is a notable absence of women and even successful love relationships, children or any organic social or family life.[34] This sense of something missing, combined with a desire to move beyond the masquerade of the colonial myth, had far-reaching effects on this first generation of

[32] Walmsley, *Caribbean Artists' Movement*; Lamming, *Pleasures of Exile*; Michael Gilkes, *The West Indian Novel* (Boston: Twayne, 1981); Donnell and Welsh, *Routledge Reader in Caribbean Literature* (London: Routledge, 1996).

[33] *Miguel St* (1959) was Naipaul's first-written but third-published novel; see V. S. Naipaul, *Finding the Centre* (London: André Deutsch, 1984). Many novels of childhood followed those by George Lamming and Sam Selvon including Michael Anthony, *The Year in San Fernando* (London: Heinemann, 1965); Jean Rhys, *Wide Sargasso Sea* (London: André Deutsch, 1966); Merle Hodge, *Crick Crack Monkey* (London: Heinemann, 1970).

[34] Women were writing at this time, as is evident from Una Marson and Louise Bennett. However, many, such as Beryl Gilroy, found it difficult to get their work published. Gilroy's novel of exile, *In Praise of Love and Children* (Leeds: Peepal Tree Press, 1996) was written in Britain in the 1960s but did not receive public attention until the late 1990s.

Caribbean writers. They searched, often in vain, for the solid world of a cultural metropolis which had grown up in their imaginations on artificial and dubious literary foundations. And although England frequently represented promise and expectation, a mythic quest for a metropolitan El Dorado, their experiences in the grey-world city were defined less by a sense of imaginative freedom than by the grim realities of living in an almost surreal metropolis frequently reduced to nothing more than colourless rooms in sordid boarding-houses.[35] As Sorbert, in Andrew Salkey's *Escape to An Autumn Pavement*, comes to realise, he has not inherited a language and culture from the British but rather a sense of the lack of one:

> I walk around London and I see statues of this one and the other . . . There's even Stonehenge.
>
> And do you know how I feel deep down? . . . I feel nothing. . . . We've been fed on the Mother Country myths. Its language. Its literature. Its Civics . . . What happened to me between African bondage and British hypocrisy. What?[36]

The sense, however, of living in limbo, in the twilight world of the once-imperial metropolis, was to bring about new imaginative and literary connections.[37] For while the painful forging of a Caribbean and a Black–British identity by confrontation with the myths of the mother-country are central themes in a large number of novels published at this time, the differences among writers about how such themes were to be mediated resulted in a number of significant critical interventions. For many of these discussions not only anticipated but also helped to map the ground for issues which were to become pivotal much later, as the West began to question the centrality of its own grand narratives with the advent of what came to be called postmodernity. The prime focus of the debates for this group of Caribbean writers abroad, however, centred on questions of syncretism, creolisation, Negritude, as well as the need to draw on the oral and folk traditions of indigenous sources. They were led initially by figures such as George Lamming, Kamau Brathwaite the Barbadian poet and, later, Wilson Harris. Many shared the need to overcome what V. S. Naipaul described in a 1958 essay as the problems of 'The Regional Barrier', while avoiding at the same time the dangers of being forever trapped in a derivative mimicry – a difficulty Naipaul was particularly concerned with in his early work.[38] They were also acutely aware of the problems involved

35 Sam Selvon, *El Dorado: West One* (Leeds: Peepal Tree Press, 1988).
36 Andrew Salkey, *Escape to an Autumn Pavement* (London: Hutchinson, 1960), p. 46.
37 Gikandi, *Writing in Limbo*.
38 V. S. Naipaul, 'The Regional Barrier', *Times Literary Supplement*, 15 August 1958, pp. 27–8.

in breaking out of a complex historical and psychic entanglement with a universe that had partially formed their vision, while side-stepping the pitfalls of a naïve counter-discourse that would leave them, like Sam Selvon's eponymous anti-hero, Moses, standing in the same spot.

Frequently, as in Lamming's work, such questions can only be addressed within the context of the Old World. For England was not only 'heritage' and 'place of welcome' but 'the name of a responsibility which may have coincided with the beginning of time'.[39] Moreover, for Lamming, as we saw with C. L. R. James earlier, the restaging of a meeting between Caliban and Prospero, on home ground, was not only a necessary stage in the evolution of a distinctively Caribbean sensibility, but became the basis for creating an alternative aesthetic which would enable a new entry-point into history. Lamming's life-long project to restore the full status of the Caribbean psyche into the historical cycle of the Black Atlantic figures in all of his major fictional and non-fictional works ranging from his classic portrait of a West Indian artist as a young man, *In the Castle of My Skin*, to later novels such as *Season of Adventure* (1970), *Water With Berries* (1971) and *Natives of My Person* (1972). While these books cover different moments in Caribbean history and are set in a variety of locations, they share a clear political agenda which seeks to disrupt the apparently smooth march of Western modernity by moving outside the linear shapes of the realist novel and interrupting what Lamming perceived to be its absolutist cultural boundaries. While there is no question that Lamming's political and intellectual stance was to make him a pioneering theorist of the postcolonial condition and a major influence on a later generation of Black–British writers, not all of his contemporaries at the time or subsequently shared his views.

By far the most internationally distinguished figure to emerge in this period was V. S. Naipaul, a Trinidadian of East Indian origin. Over the next five decades Naipaul was to present a substantially different political perspective and relationship to the canonical house of Englishness and his colonial background. Writing in an early travelogue, *The Middle Passage* (1962), that 'nothing was created in the West Indies', he fast developed a notorious reputation for an arrogant and dismissive attitude to newly emergent postcolonial societies which he regarded as 'second-hand' and 'restricted'.[40] Combined with what many perceived to be a dubious political perspective deriving from his desire as a 'thorough colonial' to become an acceptable part of the British establishment, his group of social comedies set in Trinidad – *The Mystic Masseur*

[39] Lamming, 'The Coldest Spring', pp. 5–7.

[40] V. S. Naipaul, *The Middle Passage* (London: André Deutsch, 1962), p. 29; also, *The Mimic Men* (London: André Deutsch, 1967).

(1957), *The Suffrage of Elvira* (1958) and *Miguel St* (1959) – were criticised for what Lamming was to call a 'castrated satire', the use of a distancing narrative voice which, unlike the intimate and sympathetic representation of the voices of ordinary, unlettered characters in Sam Selvon's Trinidadian and London fictions, ridiculed its subjects.[41] While Lamming was accurate in drawing attention to an important difference in tone and perspective between the two Trinidadian writers, his comments inadvertently set up polarities between the two which have subsequently been misleading. For although Selvon was to become a pioneer in his self-conscious creation of an idiomatic and oral literary voice which closed the gap between his narrators and his characters, modulating across the entire spectrum of the Caribbean linguistic scale, his major concern, like Naipaul's – whether in his so-called 'peasant' novels, *A Brighter Sun* (1952) and *Turn Again Tiger* (1958), or in his urban trickster and calypsonian 'ballads', *Ways of Sunlight* (1957), *The Lonely Londoners* or *The Housing Lark* (1960) – has been with defining and redefining a sense of form to create a fitting vehicle to house the voices of his fictional subjects.[42] Clearly Naipaul's writing was marked on the surface by an immediately accessible Augustan prose style which sought to repress his East Indian/Trinidadian heritage and attracted a Western readership. Clearly too, Naipaul's narrators often speak in Standard English and exist at an ironic distance from their subjects. Yet his classic novel of unaccommodated colonial man, *A House For Mr Biswas* (1961) which represents the culmination of the first phase of his writing career – the period in which, as he has put it, he was trying to record his reactions to the world by using 'borrowed forms' to define his subject – creolises the Dickensian model it draws on just as much as it attempts to make epic for the first time the life of an ordinary East Indian man based on Naipaul's would-be writer–journalist father. Moreover, as is evident from *The Mimic Men* (1968) onwards – a novel of exile set both in the Caribbean and London and which looks forward in its cyclical episodic style to Naipaul's confrontation with the colonial deceptions of language and the canonical house of 'Englishness' in *The Enigma of Arrival* (1987) – his subject, whether in his wide range of subsequent travel writings such as *An Area of Darkness* (1968), or, his histories like *The Loss of El Dorado* (1969) and, in his large output of subsequent fictions, has remained driven by an investigation into the passing away of empire and the desire to write and rewrite the self within the trauma of that history. And although Naipaul has

[41] Lamming, *Pleasures of Exile*, p. 224–5; see also, Nasta, *Home Truths*, pp. 93–132, for a full discussion of the ways in which Lamming placed Selvon and Naipaul on different sides of the Caribbean literary fence.

[42] Nasta, *Home Truths*, pp. 56–90.

consistently refused any identification with the 'group' of other West Indians who were in the UK during the period in which he established himself, his concern to extricate himself from the predetermined plot of an imperial history, combined with a relentless urge to write about unhousing while still remaining unhoused, has resulted in a career dedicated primarily to coming to terms with his background as a twice-born immigrant and the concurrent need to use the process of writing itself as a performative act of intervention and survival.[43]

Naipaul was the first writer of his generation to be the recipient in 1971 of the Booker Prize and has since been awarded many literary honours and accolades by a Western readership, including the David Cohen Prize for a life-time's work in British writing as well as the Nobel Prize in 2002. Sam Selvon, in contrast, has most frequently been heralded as the 'father' of black writing in Britain although he too, like many others of this period, was the recipient of a number of international literary awards.[44] The difference in the nature of their reception is instructive. For although Selvon has dealt equally in his fictions set in Trinidad with the processes of creolisation among the East Indian rural community, as well as with the existential dilemmas of middle-class Trinidadians in the period following Independence, it was his London short stories and novels which were to gain him the most significant critical attention in the UK. Yet such analyses have tended to focus less on Selvon's transnational sensibility as an artful alchemist of language, who, like G. V. Desani before him, hybridises the boundaries of the novel form and reinvents the city of London as a black city of words, than on his abilities to invert conventional racist stereotypes and make his trickster black characters central subjects in English fiction. While Selvon has often been praised for his humour, his naturalism and his pathos, as well as the subtleties of his flexible use of a modified form of the vernacular in works such as *Ways of Sunlight* and *The Lonely Londoners* – a picaresque mode, in which he not only revisions Dickens's London, invokes Dante's Inferno and makes epic the experiences of his ordinary immigrant characters who live in it – the focus by critics on questions of race and the sociological aspects of the early immigrant experience has often led to simplistic readings of his iconoclastic art. As is evident in novels such as *The Housing Lark* (1960) and *Moses Ascending* (1975) – a parodic sequel to *The Lonely Londoners*, and one which draws on *Robinson Crusoe* as one of the founding myths of European colonialism as well as many

43 Feroza Jussawalla, ed., *Conversations with V. S. Naipaul* (Jackson: University of Mississippi, 1997) for several discussions of this; also, V. S. Naipaul, *Letters Between a Father and Son* (London: Little, Brown, 1999) for comments on others writing at the time, pp. 239, 261.

44 Dabydeen, 'West Indian Writers in Britain', pp. 69–70, discusses the many mainstream literary awards these writers were awarded in Britain between 1950 and 1980.

other well-known literary intertexts – Selvon's use of language as well as his inventive strategies to shift the shapes of the English canon draw as much on an intimacy with the grand narratives of European modernity as they do on the orality of the trickster traditions of calypso, Carnival and Anancy folklore inherited from his multicultural Trinidadian past.

Questions of accommodation combined with the need to refashion the architecture of traditional literary forms to make present the realities of the New World experience continued to preoccupy many writers who followed on from this pioneering generation of now major novelists in the 1950s and extended to other genres and art-forms. With the formation of the Caribbean Artists' Movement (CAM) in 1968 a critical platform was established for the articulation of the views of an increasingly large community of vocal intellectuals, critics and artists who, by 1972, were responsible for shifting the terms of definition away from individual questions of exile and / or immigration to those of settlement and the establishment of a specifically Black–British and Caribbean aesthetic.[45] It was in this kind of context that the location of Jean Rhys's novel *Wide Sargasso Sea* (1966) was fiercely contested, as some critics argued that her racial background as a white West Indian creole excluded her from the realms of a specifically Caribbean tradition, a debate about Rhys's location as a writer which was to continue until well into the 1990s.[46] At the same time, other members of CAM, who now included Kamau Brathwaite, Andrew Salkey, Wilson Harris, John La Rose, Stuart Hall and C. L. R. James, were becoming increasingly aware of their global relationship with other black voices and cultural traditions, such as those from the Francophone Caribbean, Africa and the USA. In addition, connections were made between the improvisatory forms of African–American jazz, the artistic possibilities of vernacular speech and the mythical landscapes of visual artists such as the Guyanese painter, Aubrey Williams. Some of the lectures published in Wilson Harris's collection, *Tradition, the Writer and Society* (1967), were first delivered at CAM conferences, critical essays which not only outline the highly individualistic approach Harris was to adopt in his fiction but also long predate the theories of hybridity and syncretism common among Postcolonial theorists such as Homi Bhabha in the 1980s.[47] Like Lamming and Brathwaite, Harris viewed the conventional European novel of manners as a limiting and limited

45 Walmsley, *Caribbean Artists' Movement*, pp. 94–223.

46 For the controversies this debate caused, see Peter Hulme, 'The Place of *Wide Sargasso Sea*', *Wasafiri*, 20 (1994), pp. 5–11; Kamau Brathwaite's reply to Hulme, 'A Post-Cautionary Tale of the Helen of Our Wars', *Wasafiri*, 22 (1996), pp. 69–82.

47 Bart Moore Gilbert, *Postcolonial Theory: Contexts, Practices, Politics* (London: Verso, 1997), pp. 180–3.

genre inappropriate to the complex and constantly shifting nature of the Caribbean landscape and its multilayered histories. His view of the Caribbean as a paradigm for a modernity that has always enabled revolutionary shifts in perception and sensibility is evident from the outset in his fiction. Early works, such as the Guyana Quartet – which includes *The Palace of the Peacock* (1960), *The Far Journey of Oudin* (1961), *The Whole Armour* (1962) and *The Secret Ladder* (1963) – to some of his later works such as *The Four Banks of the River of Space* (1990), dramatise a vision that draws on myth, symbolism and a vast range of cultural sources from Amerindian histories to William Blake, Christian mysticism and Surrealism to quantum physics. Frequently seen as 'difficult' by many readers, he has consistently refused the chronology of a European sense of time, making the need to delve deeply into the Guyanese landscape a metaphor for the regeneration of the Caribbean psyche and its innate potential to consume both its own biases and its cross-cultural, literary and racial boundaries.

One consistent motif for this exploration and the ability to cross between several often contradictory worlds in Harris's work is the use of Anancy, symbol both of cultural survival and the transgressions of history. This West African spider figure, who appears in much Caribbean writing as a kind of Tiresias, is also central to Kamau Brathwaite's important poetic trilogy of the Middle Passage, *The Arrivants*. Originally published in three sections – *Rights of Passage* in 1967, followed swiftly by *Masks* and *Islands* in 1968 – this cycle established Brathwaite's reputation, alongside that of Derek Walcott, as one of the Caribbean's most innovative and distinguished poets. The poem employs a number of oral, performative techniques, ranging from the rhythm of the African drums in the opening sections to the incorporation of the syncopated rhythms of the blues and jazz in the later New World sections. Like Harris, Brathwaite's vision of the history of modernity and the Caribbean is one that highlights cross-cultural and diasporic connection. Combined, however, with a historical interest in creole cultures as a source for regeneration and the creation of what he was famously to term 'nation-language' in Caribbean literature, his poetry in later volumes (such as *Other Exiles* (1975) or *Mother Poem* (1977)) continues to give body to the fragmentations of Caribbean history through a restoration of the voices of a communal past.[48] Like Una Marson

[48] Kamau Brathwaite, *History of the Voice: The Development of Nation Language in Anglophone Caribbean Poetry* (London and Port of Spain: New Beacon, 1984). See also early critical essays in *Bim*: 'The New West Indian Novelists – 1', *Bim*, 8, 31 (1960), pp. 199–210; 'The New West Indian Novelists – 2', *Bim*, 8, 32 (1961), pp. 271–80; 'Jazz and the West Indian Novel – 1', *Bim*, 12, 44 (1967), pp. 275–84.

and Louise Bennett earlier, Brathwaite's focus was on performance and orality; although, as was evident in Sam Selvon's fiction, he combined this with a refashioning both of traditional poetic forms such as the Shakespearian iambic pentameter and the techniques of Modernist poets who had been early influences, such as T. S. Eliot. Other major poets such as James Berry, recipient of the Queen's Medal for Poetry and the editor in 1964 of one of the first anthologies of West Indian and Black–British poetry, *BlueFoot Traveller*, were to continue to develop this tradition, as in Berry's many published collections such as *Lucy's Letters and Loving* (1982). During the late 1970s and 1980s a large volume of Caribbean and Black–British poetry was published as figures such as E. A. Markham, Linton Kwesi Johnson, Grace Nichols, David Dabydeen, John Agard and Merle Collins began to publish material in a variety of genres and drawing on an eclectic range of literary forms. And while these works emerged in a different racial and political climate in the UK – a situation where, as one critic once put it, they had to fight to make visible the black in the Union Jack – their work continued to build on modernities established in the New World yet linked to the experience of colonialism, migration, exile and diaspora defined by writers such as C. L. R. James, in the earlier part of the century. As James was to make clear in 1984, the perspective of this new generation of black writers in the UK was to become increasingly significant in providing a 'new vision' and a unique insight into Western civilisation.[49] Moreover, as Professor Stuart Hall, one of the initial group of *Windrush* migrants, observed in a now oft-quoted essay on twentieth-century modernity in Britain written almost fifty years after their initial arrival: 'Now that, in the postmodern age, you all feel dispersed, I become centred. What I've thought of as dispersed and fragmented comes, paradoxically, to be the representative modern experience! This is coming home with a vengeance.'[50]

[49] C. L. R. James, 'Africans and Afro-Caribbeans: a Personal View', *Ten* 8, 16 (1984); rpt. in Procter, *Writing Black Britain*, pp. 60–3.

[50] Stuart Hall, 'Minimal Selves', in Lisa Appignanesi, ed., *Identity* (London: Institute of Contemporary Arts, Documents 6, 1987), pp. 25–6.

FIVE

*

TOWARDS THE MILLENNIUM, 1970–2000

32

The seventies and the cult of culture

TIM ARMSTRONG

In the post-war world, it is the late sixties and seventies which give birth to much of what we recognise as contemporary culture: a commodified counter-culture; identity politics; the celebration of popular culture and its recycling of materials; suspicion of authority and political process. The turbulent decade of the seventies is marked by a release and dissemination of energies which have their origins in the political rebellions of the sixties, and by a move towards culture itself as the ground of debate and resistance. This was a move reinforced theoretically by the 'New Left' with its emphasis on culture, increasingly broadly defined, as a site of contestation, and a shift towards notions of hegemony and false consciousness derived from Antonio Gramsci and Louis Althusser, rather than the 'Old Left' emphasis on class, labour and dialectics. The period also sees the rise of the discourse of Postmodernism itself as an analytic framework for contemporary historical faultlines.

At the same time, the seventies is a decade we associate with a number of cultural problems: kitsch, nostalgia, violence, paranoia and the origins of the radical conservatism of the eighties. Three strands will be highlighted in what follows: the anxiety associated with notions of cultural and personal freedom; the question of the representation of history when history's narratives seem to have been corrupted; and the issue of identity politics. The discussion will move fairly freely between a postmodernising American context which, in retrospect, seems to set the scene for cultural shifts elsewhere, and a British context in which a troubled sense of post-Suez shock, economic decline, and historical and geographical inheritance informs literature in distinctive ways.

Culture, commodification and violence

Begin 'the morning after the sixties'. The phrase is the title of a 1970 essay by Joan Didion which dwells on the distance of the world she knew in the

1950s.[1] It sounds two keynotes of seventies culture: a sense of trauma produced by disturbing events; and a nostalgia associated with rapid cultural change. In *The White Album* (1979), Didion chronicles student protest, Black Power, the Kennedy assassination, the musical apocalypse of the Doors, the Manson killings. For Americans the early seventies saw the continuation of the Vietnam War, Watergate, and Nixon's resignation. The year 1973 was one hinge point: Watergate; the OPEC-created oil crisis which led to the final breakdown of post-war economic stability; a CIA-sponsored coup in Chile. In the UK, 1971 set the scene for a decade of turmoil: the *Oz* trial, Angry Brigade bombings, the collapse and nationalisation of Rolls Royce; to be followed by the 1972 miners' strike, hyperinflation, labour struggle and recurrent political crisis. The seventies saw what to many was a dangerous breakdown of social order, both reinforced by and prompting urban decay and the middle-class flight to the suburbs. A pulse of catastrophic violence runs through the decade: mass killings in Uganda; the Khmer Rouge in Cambodia; the terrorism of the IRA and Red Army; the millenarianism of the Jonestown massacre; wars in Biafra, Angola, Israel, Cyprus, Nicaragua, Afghanistan and elsewhere. Violence pervades films of the period, whether the origins are nominally human (*The Godfather*, *Deliverance*, *Straw Dogs*), natural (*Jaws*), or accidental (the disaster film).

The historical turbulence of the seventies was matched by rapid social and cultural change. If the sixties saw social revolution, it was largely confined to particular groups: the young metropolitan bourgeoisie; African–Americans. The lives of most in the West remained relatively stable. It was the seventies which saw the dissemination and commercialisation of the freedoms associated with the previous decade (these included legal freedoms: legalisation of homosexual acts and abortion in the UK in 1967 and easier divorce in 1969; Civil Rights legislation in the USA). Attitudes to society, 'the Establishment', work, consumption, credit, sexuality, marriage, religion and drugs decisively shifted towards more anti-authoritarian, individualist and libertarian positions. One example of this shift was the widespread reaction against the 1971 imprisonment of Richard Neville, the editor of the satirical magazine *Oz*, for its 'Schoolkids' Issue'. Since *Oz*'s collages and cartoons were relatively tame compared to what was available in Soho, the trial – aimed at the 'underground' press rather than at pornography – suggested establishment hypocrisy; indeed, it led to the exposure of a network of bribery between police and the porn industry.

It is in this context that we need to see the idea of a 'counter-culture'; a culture predicated on opposition to official culture and its hierarchies, but with a

[1] Joan Didion, *The White Album* (New York: Simon & Schuster, 1979), pp. 205–8.

more coherent, commodified and institutional location than any earlier avant-garde. Two examples originating in the 1960s illustrate this process: in New York, the Factory, the studio established by Andy Warhol in 1963, produced artwork on haphazard collaborative principles; in his second Factory, established in 1968, Warhol established a more corporate stance with the studio as the site of a branded, de-personalised, and tantalisingly dissident (gay, political or 'Catholic') art. A second example is the Royal Court Theatre in London, which throughout the sixties and seventies offered an institutional space for provocative theatre, its aesthetic entering 'official' theatre when Howard Brenton's *Weapons of Happiness* was staged at the new National Theatre in 1976. But the period after 1970 all too often sees the depoliticisation and exploitation of the counter-cultural styles of the late sixties: Fluxus, agitprop and guerrilla theatre degenerate into the staged transgression of Alice Cooper.

This process of counter-cultural diffusion is closely related to the association of the 1970s, in popular memory, with a new flamboyance and the cultural extremes of kitsch: glam rock, progressive rock, disco, pornography, flares and heels, chopper bikes, the spa pool, *Love Story*, Rod McKuen, Pink Floyd. As described by Norbert Elias in 1935, kitsch is a product of the way in which, in industrialised consumer society, a heightened formalism is constantly threatened by its Decadence, creating an 'incessant interdependence of structure and disintegration'.[2] If the origins of the term lie in the ambivalence felt by artists for their clientele ('kitsch' as work to be sold to the ignorant), Elias suggests that in late capitalism the distance between elite and mass collapses into a more general kitsch style, conditioned by the leisure industries, and characterised by a charged emotionality, the very excessiveness of which is indicative of the covert pressures of social regimentation. It is one indication of this commercialised kitsch style that the seventies saw the flowering of the 'blockbuster' or 'event' novel, often linked to a film: bestsellers included *The Godfather*, *The Exorcist*, *Love Story*, *Jaws* and *The Thorn Birds*, as well as *Fear of Flying* and *Jonathan Livingstone Seagull*.[3] In the UK, headline-creating literary prizes (the Booker Prize, established 1969; the Whitbread, 1971) developed a more middlebrow version of the 'event' novel.

Elias also traces an alternation between a stress on form and the classics, on the one hand, and radicalism on the other. Seen in this light, seventies kitsch can be partly read as a palliative response to the radical pressures of

[2] Norbert Elias, 'The Kitsch Style and the Age of Kitsch' (1935), in *The Norbert Elias Reader*, ed. Johan Gouldblom and Stephen Mennell (Oxford: Blackwell, 1998), p. 28.

[3] See John Sutherland, *Bestsellers: Popular Fiction in the Seventies* (London: Routledge & Kegan Paul, 1981).

the 1960s, incorporating a nostalgia for an earlier mass culture already seen in films like *American Graffiti* (1973), with its homage to fifties music and movies. The supplanting of reality by the image in these texts signals a Postmodern turn in which popular culture exists in an intimate relation to 'high' culture – as in the songs, references to comic books and Hollywood film in *Gravity's Rainbow* (1973). This complex cultural nostalgia is explored in the recycling of Hollywood style in the early photography of Cindy Sherman, in Warhol's work in this period, and elsewhere.

The 'interdependence of structure and disintegration' also appears in the aesthetic violence apparent everywhere in seventies culture. From the point of view of the Left, increasingly extreme positions needed to be occupied in order to preserve a critique which might penetrate the surface of a culture which is notionally open and permissive, but which is understood (as in the theoretical work of Althusser) as an expression of false consciousness, a mirror-like self-representation which must be shattered. British drama constantly resorts to shock effects: in the wake of the abolition of the Lord Chamberlain's role as censor in 1968, itself partly prompted by the prosecution of the Royal Court for staging Edward Bond's *Saved* with its baby-stoning episode, the autonomy of dramatic culture was expressed in a series of assaults on the audience's gaze – a figure literalised in the eye-plucking of Bond's *Lear* (1971) and the eye-gouging of horses in Peter Shaffer's *Equus* (1973); culminating in the on-stage anal rape of Howard Brenton's *The Romans in Britain* (1980). Other examples can be constellated: UK television audiences would see the the Sex Pistols mouthing obscenities, and might buy their banned improvement of 'God Save the Queen'; readers would be shocked by coprophagia in *Gravity's Rainbow*, and by the Gothic domestic perversions of Ian McEwan's *First Love, Last Rites* (1975) and *The Cement Garden* (1978). The Australian novelist Thomas Keneally's *The Chant of Jimmie Blacksmith* (1972) would depict a massacre of a family enacted by an aboriginal rebel. In New York, the young Kathy Acker, inspired by Burroughs and Trocchi, would write mixtures of plagiarism and pornography. Punk's deformation of 'well-made' music and Acker's anti-art stance represent a response to historical crisis from which the utopian hopes of the 1968 student rebellions and movements like Fluxus are largely expunged.

Bond's *Lear* might be seen as a representative text here: a savage rewriting of Shakespeare's play as a drama of political enlightenment, it depicts a despotic king – we first see him executing a soldier – deposed by his daughters Bodice and Fontanelle, themselves killed by the peasant army led by Cordelia (in this play no relation to Lear, a revenger modelled on Stalin). The blinded Lear becomes an opponent of the regime who is able to use his legendary status in an attack on the giant Wall around the kingdom which he had started, symbolic of the military–industrial complex; in the final scene he is shot as he digs at the Wall. Declaring that 'violence just *is* the big problem in our society', Bond uses the apparent formlessness of the play to represent an aesthetic crisis in which *praxis* can only be extracted by the deformation of high art.[4] *Lear* deploys an anti-realist cartoonic grotesque directed at the dramatic medium itself and in this respect recalls the work of American writers like Burroughs and Vonnegut, painters like Philip Guston, and even John Ashbery, who in 'Daffy Duck in Hollywood' mixes dissonant cultural references: 'a mint-condition can / Off Rumford's Baking Powder, a celluloid earring, Speedy / Gonzales, the latest from Helen Topping Miller's fertile / Escritoire'. Such images combine to suggest an overloaded but inescapable allegory, in which symbols are heaped like commodities and the poet ultimately identifies with the process: 'we greet him who announces / The change as we would the change itself'. This is a kitsch aesthetic exploited rather than resisted.

The argument that hyper-stimulation characterises the popular and high art of the period – one only has to think of novels like William Gaddis's exorbitant masterpiece *J. R.* (1975) – has a particular relation to the stress on the self which is at the heart of seventies culture. Consider Didion's description of people operating 'on what I later recognised as dice theory . . . devoid of any logic save that of the dreamwork'.[5] Dice theory is associated with Luke Rhinehart cult novel *The Dice Man* (1974), in which the hero gives up his life to the throw of a dice – an act which conveys a sense of the possibilities and limits of freedom, including its attenuation into forms of indulgence and random violence. Rhinehart's novel enacts the perils of what the Frankfurt School labelled 'repressive desublimation': the pursuit of libidinous discharge at any cost; at the limit a 'liberation' of the self into a social space so unstructured that it appears free-floating (a situation described in John Ashbery's 1972 *Three Poems*: 'All its links severed with the worldly matrix from which it sprang, the soul feels that it is propelling itself forward at an ever-increasing speed. This very speed becomes a source of intoxication . . . ').[6] It is here that the freedoms attributed to the self become problematic: as Slavoj Žižek notes, the modern language of freedom operates in close partnership with the aggressive energies of the superego; it is your *duty* to embrace all experience; anything which

4 Edward Bond, June 1971, in Simon Trussler, ed., *New Theatre Voices of the Seventies: Sixteen Interviews from 'Theatre Quarterly' 1970–1980* (London: Eyre Methuen, 1981), p. 30.
5 Didion, *The White Album*, p. 18.
6 John Ashbery, *Three Poems* (1972; New York: Ecco Press, 1989), p. 70.

stands in the way of self-realisation will be destroyed.[7] The literary corollary of this critique is the fact that the reaction against established forms is often combined with a violence directed at the self in its limited ability to cope with its new freedoms – something visible in the early fiction of Martin Amis, whose *The Rachel Papers* (1974), *Dead Babies* (1975) and *Success* (1978) represent both a refreshingly adolescent reaction against the ethical and public focus of the English bourgeois novel and an often misogynistic assault on the autonomy of the objects of masculine desire. *The Rachel Papers* parodies the discourse of sexual liberation, sexual technique manuals and so on; offering a resistance to youth culture which nevertheless remains intoxicated by its freedoms.

Conspiracy and the poisoning of history

The characterisation of the seventies above – in terms of violence and a cultural uncertainty – risks simplification of a decade which begins with the continuation of a strong utopian element; after all, mass protest on such issues as nuclear disarmament and racism continued throughout the decade, and on the shelves of students one would find editions of Ivan Ilyich's *Deschooling Society* (1971), Paolo Freire's *Pedagogy of the Oppressed* (1972) and E. F. Schumacher's *Small is Beautiful* (1973). But even these critiques of corporate and professional culture, outside the Third World context, fed into a politics of personal liberation. Indeed, one of the distinctive features of seventies culture is the representation of politics as suspect, compromised by agencies whose agenda is hidden and powers of surveillance potentially huge. 'Paranoia' has become something of a cliché in descriptions of the seventies: what we need to remember is that it is a product of Cold War realities and a polity in which knowledge and expertise is compartmentalised and the surface of represented reality, even language itself, is infected. This leaves politics stranded between covert action mirroring state secrecy (terrorism) and the often uncertain politics of the personal; indeed, the period around 1970 saw a number of splits within radical circles in Europe and the Americas between direct-action groups and those adopting more liberal positions. This situation again leaves representation as the site of contestation. Perhaps the best example is the Angry Brigade, which created turmoil in the UK in 1971 with a series of bombs, arson attacks, and communiqués. Many of their interventions can be described as a politics of publicity: a May Day bomb at Biba, the trend-setting fashion store, accompanied by *Communiqué 8*; targets

[7] Slavoj Žižek, 'You May!' (1999), in Bran Nichol, ed., *Postmodernism and the Contemporary Novel: A Reader* (Edinburgh University Press, 2002), pp. 121–9.

including Judge Argyll, the judge of the *Oz* trial, and others connected only by being in the news (for example a pub which refused to serve workers on the M4 motorway).

Two very different texts could be taken as emblematic of the uncertainties bound up with this situation: Pynchon's *Gravity's Rainbow* and Graham Greene's *The Human Factor* (1978). The former, a classic of conspiracy and paranoia, hinges on the notion of a betrayed polity: the international military–industrial complex solidified at the end of World War II, the 'rocket-state', is only weakly opposed by the 'counter-force', a green alliance centred on respect for the everyday, the powers of nature, the body. The plot of *Gravity's Rainbow* hinges on surveillance: not simply the pursuit of the 'hero', Tyrone Slothrop, because of his connection to the V2 rocket, but also the suggestion that he has been tampered with in infancy in order to write that connection into his sexual responses, as well as the writing of surveillance and cybernetics into human response generally (for example the incestuous scientist Franz Pökler, whose daughter Ilse's annual appearances – it may be her or a substitute – are likened to the frame-based temporality of the cinema, and thus the disavowal of 'natural' time). Greene's late and most disillusioned Cold War novel *The Human Factor* may seem like an unlikely comparison, but it, too, investigates surveillance, games, self-monitoring, codes and reading. Everyone is a double agent; under suspicion as well as suspecting. The incomplete mythic structures suggested by names (the protagonist, obsessed with the security of his family, is Castle; a spy and fisherman is called Percival), as well as other intertextual references unified by the idea of the 'book code' (Trollope, Browning, Tolstoy, Conrad, the Bible), ultimately implicate literature in the claustrophobic systems of the Cold War.

Perhaps the most important aspect of seventies paranoia, in the wake of Kennedy's assassination, is the sense that history itself has been hijacked, and its narratives obscured. Michael Herr's *Dispatches* (1977), the best account of Vietnam produced by the 'New Journalism', describes history as a 'poisoned flower', polluted by official rhetoric: 'The spokesmen spoke in words that had no currency left as words, sentences with no hope of meaning in the sane world.' In the face of this 'psychotic vaudeville', the necessity for a counter-history becomes intense: 'Straight history, auto-revised history, history without handles, for all the books and articles and white papers, all the talk and miles of film, something wasn't answered, it wasn't even asked.'[8] Herr cannot order this 'secret history'. In the British context this suspicion may appear less

8 Michael Herr, *Dispatches* (1977; London: Picador, 1978), pp. 173, 46.

marked – after all, Anthony Powell continued his series of realist novels on upper-class political and cultural life *A Dance to the Music of Time* up to 1975 – but novels like John Berger's G. (Booker Prize, 1972) began a self-conscious revision of historical method; and theoretical writings by Stuart Hall, Germaine Greer, Judith Williamson and others in the field of cultural studies attempted to expose the underpinnings of bourgeois reality.

The sense of historical uncertainty and the tendency towards allegory in some of the texts discussed above raises an important set of questions about the politics of literature, related to Fredric Jameson's claim that the 1970s see the birth of a Postmodern aesthetic in which history becomes a depthless copy rather than lived experience. One of Jameson's test cases is American novelist E. L. Doctorow. If *The Book of Daniel* (1971) had returned to the historical outrage represented by the execution of the Rosenbergs, *Ragtime* (1975) shuffles 'real' historical figures like J. P. Morgan and Harry Houdini with invented characters in order to suggest the rhythms of the new century. This procedure was hardly new, but it is interesting that *Ragtime* meditates on the principle of reproducibility: in the 'movie books' made by the silhouette-artist Tateh; in Ford's factories; in the Victrola on which the boy plays the same record 'over and over again . . . as if to test the endurance of a duplicated event'.[9] For Jameson, *Ragtime* marks a shift to the representational (dis)orders of Postmodernism, in which history is produced as allegory; that is as a series of historical counters selected from a 'multitudinous photographic simulacrum', whose historical value is simply recycled as representation.[10] The fact that there is a *déjà vu* in Jameson's own description of the novel's version of the preterite tense – it echoes Sartre's description of Dos Passos's *USA* – means that his formulae share this tendency to vertiginous historical rewriting. But Jameson lacks Sartre's hope that the depiction of a 'closed' history will impel readers to assert their own agency.

In retrospect Jameson's formulae (dating from 1984) seem as much symptoms of a particular moment as a firm analysis of historical transition: after all, the 1980s was to see a return to historical fiction. His claims chime with the intellectual gymnastics of Tom Stoppard's plays *Jumpers* (1972) and *Travesties* (1974), in which historical figures are pasted together in resonant locales (Joyce and Tzara in Zurich); or other works which display a shift from historicity to allegory. English fiction of the seventies – against the background of the

9 E. L. Doctorow, *Ragtime* (1975; London: Picador, 1985), p. 91.

10 Fredric Jameson, *PostModernism, or, The Cultural Logic of Late Capitalism* (London: Verso, 1991), pp. 21–5.

continuation of a class-based realism in works like Beryl Bainbridge's *The Bottle Factory Outing* (1974) – often takes a plunge towards the metafictional or magical. Iris Murdoch's *The Sea, the Sea* (Booker Prize, 1978) ends with a preternatural event not previously seen in her writings; Muriel Spark's novels of the seventies depart from realism and experiment with genre and parody; and Jean Rhys's stories in *Sleep It Off Lady* (1976) memorably deal with states of dissociation expressed in terms of violence, the uncanny and textual fragmentation. The final story of the collection, an unsettling page-and-a-half, is emblematic: what is described as a historical return, a commentary on change, turns out to be a haunting in which the narrator slowly realises she is dead. Finally, William Golding's return to fiction after a twelve-year absence, with *Darkness Visible* (1979), produced a novel in which historical allegory is constantly signalled but can never be stabilised – a fact nicely inflected by the scene in which the novel's central incarnation of goodness, the biblically named Matthew (Matty) Seven, who has emerged miraculously from the fiery furnace of the Blitz, tears out the pages of his bible – effacing his own intertext. The seventies novel typically negotiates in this way between uncertainty and allegory, between what is hidden and what can be recovered as resonant fragment.

Gravity's Rainbow itself offers a good example of the excavation of heterogonous historical traces. As a historical novel, it evokes wartime London, pre-war Berlin, the Somme and other fragments of history including the 1960s, evading any Hegelian sense of history as an unfolding entity in favour of an unstable mixture of plots (involving multinationals, governments), shifts in the history of technology, and individual stories in which larger narratives are implicated in ways which can seem quite direct or strangely allegorical. The mysticism of *Gravity's Rainbow* can be treated in the light of Adorno's remark that 'Superstition is knowledge, because it sees together the ciphers of destruction scattered on the social surface; it is folly, because in all its death-wish it still clings to illusions'[11] – which is to say that Pynchon describes a situation in which no unified historical narrative based on an organic community can be provided; in which narratives compete and clash. The novel investigates the myths informing technological thinking, the way in which (as Gabriele Schwab puts it) 'the mutilated remains of individuality sound the retreat into perverted shapes of ancient archetypical mythologies, humanistic nostalgia, or the metaphysics of individuality'. But, as she adds, 'even those mythologies are generated as much by modern technologies and their modes of information as

11 Theodor Adorno, *Minima Moralia*, trans. E. F. N. Jephcott (London: New Left Books, 1974), p. 241.

by disowned or violated individual histories'.[12] In this sense, the switchboard which is *Gravity's Rainbow* represents the uncertainties of its own time.

Identity politics

If the politics of the state become suspect, what replaces them? It is the seventies which sees the flowering of identity politics; that is of a fragmented, issue-based politics which centres itself on the integrity of the self in relation to group affiliations (gender, race, handicap) and a dominant culture which is seen as wounding the self – rather than a politics based, for example, on an analysis of conflict between classes conceived as analytically prior. A stress on the self and its health is a recurrent feature as historicity is reconceived as trauma and political action seen as (at least in the first instance) therapeutic. The context here includes a range of counter-cultural texts on self-healing and lifestyle, from the *Whole Earth Catalogue* and *The Joy of Sex* to Carlos Castenada's books, as well as the liberation psychology of R. D. Laing's *The Divided Self* (1960) and other critiques of institutional thinking. It is certainly true that identity politics can spark mass action – the legacy of the 1969 Stonewall Riots, one of the foundation points of gay identity, included a march of 600,000 in Washington in 1987 – but such rights-based action is limited in focus and linked to a culture which must be celebrated and instantiated in the person.

One place where one can see the move to identity politics is in the African–American tradition. Black writing at the beginning of the decade includes both an experimental literature and largely forgotten radical writings – the anthology *Black Voices from Prison* (1970), and the prison writer George Jackson's *Soledad Brother* (1970) had a major impact. But the early seventies saw a shift towards the 'new generation' represented by Ishmael Reed, Nikki Giovanni, Michael S. Harper and others, with work characterised by a more allegorical impulse and a stress on the burdens of selfhood. Reed's *Mumbo Jumbo* (1972) rewrites black history as playful Manichean allegory and ends with the celebration of black culture as the grounds of resistance. A black feminism crystallised around Ntozake Shange's play *for colored girls who have considered suicide / when the rainbow is enuf* (1974), a work criticised for its attack on the myth of unity of black women and men in the face of racial oppression. But it is Toni Morrison's novels of the 1970s which, in retrospect, most clearly point

[12] Gabriele Schwab, 'Creative Paranoia and Frost Patterns of White Words', in Harold Bloom, ed., *Thomas Pynchon's 'Gravity's Rainbow'* (New York: Chelsea House, 1986), p. 105.

the way towards an identity politics in which trauma and cultural affirmation are more important than overt political impulse. *The Bluest Eye* (1970), *Sula* (1973) and *Song of Solomon* (1977) all investigate black history and community, with a stress on the fragmentation of black experience in urban life and the wounding effects of racism on the self. The latter novel gestures towards recovery through cultural recollection: a healing dependent on a hermeneutic pathway attached to a family history. In all Morrison's work there is an implied original state of cultural unity: not the concrete political solidarity proposed in *Soledad Brother*, but one located in the almost mythical cohesion of the slave experience and small Southern communities set up after slavery.

Feminism also moves towards a politics of identity. In the wake of the pioneering work of Simone de Beauvoir, Betty Friedan and others in the sixties, this was the decade of second-wave feminism's entry into mainstream culture, producing among other things an aesthetic aimed at extending earlier critique into the celebration and empowerment of women. Bestsellers like Germaine Greer's polemic *The Female Eunuch* (1971), Erica Jong's novel *Fear of Flying* (1973) and Adrienne Rich's poetry in *Diving into the Wreck* (1973) urged women to celebrate their sexuality and power. Writing of her 1973 novel *Small Changes*, Marge Piercy said that it was 'an attempt to produce in fiction the equivalent of a full experience in a consciousness-raising group for many women who would never go through the experience'.[13] This aesthetics has its roots deep in the American tradition in which sentimental identification is seen both as an enrichment of the self and as stimulating an impulse to self-renovation. What the seventies adds is a keen sense of the pragmatics of 'self-realisation', and the stress on trauma and healing we have noted. The lesbian identification increasingly espoused by Rich and others, extended at the end of the decade into the theorisation of black lesbianism, was part of this shift: one can only enter this politics by affirming an identity.

Other women's fiction of the period seems to suggest the uncertainties of any quest for self-knowledge. Margaret Atwood's novel *Surfacing* (1972) and Doris Lessing's three brilliant novels of the early seventies, *Briefing for a Descent into Hell* (1971), *The Summer before the Dark* (1973) and *The Memoirs of a Survivor* (1974), all deal with forms of dissociation and alienation, bordering on madness; describing traumatic disruptions of reality from which a new self might finally emerge. *Surfacing* enacts an ambiguous rite of passage which

[13] Marge Piercy, 'Mirror Images', in Gayle Kimball, ed., *Women's Culture: The Women's Renaissance of the Seventies* (Metuchen, NJ: Scarecrow Press, 1981), p. 192.

includes a ritual isolation as the protagonist returns to the Canadian island on a lake where her father has disappeared; a movement outside reason and language, even towards the animal; an encounter with death; rebirth and a hinted social reintegration. Atwood's work remains open and unstable in its notion of identity: the ending of *Surfacing* is equivocal, the tensions between language and the irrational not easily resolved. The work of Angela Carter in the seventies is similarly unsettling in its destabilisation of gender identity and its stress on the perversity of desire: *The Infernal Desire Machines of Doctor Hoffman* (1972) offers a sardonic commentary on the anarchic and pornographic thinking of Reich and others. The quasi-allegorical trans-sexual journey of *The Passion of New Eve* (1977) could even be described as an early Deconstruction of identity politics, as well as the 'masculine' libertarianism of the sixties, in its fluid progress through different positions on gender (misogyny, feminine separatism, biologism, camp) to an uncertain ending.

As the above suggests, apparent freedom can be linked to stress, since the culture of the self demands a constant self-monitoring; an internalised ethics aimed at self-optimisation. In *The Seventies Now: Culture as Surveillance*, Stephen Paul Miller points to a linkage between surveillance and self-surveillance: Nixon bugging himself as well as others. In the wider world, patterns of consumption are monitored with a new exactness; markets are discriminated; and consumers show a heightened awareness of the implication of identity in consumer choices. One could even fit Robert Pirsig's novel (or Thoreauvian essay) *Zen and the Art of Motorcycle Maintenance* (1974) into this pattern: not only for its weaving of an investigation of philosophical wholeness and ethics into mechanics; but for its approach to philosophy itself, which can resemble a consumer's guide in its mixture of Pragmatism, discrimination and reflexivity ('Is this the right philosophy for *me*?'). Self-surveillance is the culture demanded by consumer-based society.

Modernism / Postmodernism

So far, questions about the cultural divide represented by the seventies have remained latent. The 'dating' of the 'Postmodern turn' is notoriously difficult, since while some of its proposed determinants – new media, cybernetics – have a clear historical referent, more abstract references to the 'end of grand narratives' (the world-views of Freud, Marx, Christianity) take in a range of twentieth-century thought. While it is fair to say that the consensus places the cultural shift involved in the seventies, one can be clearer about the fact that the decade saw the development of the *discourse* of Postmodernism, with texts from Ihan Hassan's 'POSTModernism: A Paracritical Bibliography' (1971) to Jean-François Lyotard's *The Postmodern Condition* (1979) exploring, in the wake of post-Structuralism, the formal and sociological determinants of the Postmodern.

In literary terms, the late sixties and early seventies can be more easily characterised in terms of a re-engagement with Modernism than a clearly-defined Postmodernism. This is most clear in poetics, with a recovery of the Poundian tradition accompanying the decline of the Movement in the UK and the confessional mode in the USA. Two influential studies, Hugh Kenner's *The Pound Era* (1971) and Donald Davie's *Thomas Hardy and British Poetry* (1973), placed Pound – who died in the intervening year – at the centre of twentieth-century poetry, and the period saw the return to publication of a number of Modernist poets – George Oppen, after a gap of decades; Basil Bunting with *Briggflats* in 1966. Charles Olsen's influence also stimulated a re-engagement with Pound. The Spring 1971 issue of *TriQuarterly*, dedicated to 'Modern British Poets', included work from earlier Modernist poets like Bunting and Hugh MacDiarmid, and from younger poets including Lee Harwood, Ted Hughes, Tom Raworth, Charles Tomlinson and Gael Turnbull. The work of Jeremy Prynne and Veronica Forrest-Thomson, of Douglas Oliver, Iain Sinclair and Edwin Morgan returned to Modernism in its ludic and experimental modes (this was, in fact, the moment Lyotard was to label 'postmodern'), often espousing a radical formalism in which the humanistic 'seriousness' of Heaney's self-scrutiny is replaced by an intentionality invested in language. In the USA comparable work was to emerge from interchanges between the New York art scene and poetry in the mid- and late 1970s. Susan Howe's *Hinge Picture* (1974) represented a continuation in sculpturally arranged words of the tradition of Duchamp. L=A=N=G=U=A=G=E poetry belongs to the 1980s in its fullest development, but nevertheless has its origins in experimental work of the sixties.

Other late-Modernist work of importance includes that of the Scottish poet W. S. Graham, who, like Bunting, wrote from a dissident, alienated position, far from the metropolitan centre, in Cornwall – the assertion of a regional identity is, in fact, an important element of this Modernist revival. Graham's poems typically dwell on the dislocations and intimacies involved in writing and reading (one of his poems of the period returns teasingly to the phrase 'What is the language using us for?'); on poetry as an imagined community involving the living and the dead. In Ireland, a number of writers whose origins were in the pre-war world of Joyce and Beckett saw their careers revived: Brian Coffey's *Advent* (1975), for example, is one of the greatest late-Modernist long poems. Thomas Kinsella's progress from 'Nightwalker' (1968) to 'A Technical Supplement' (1976) might be described as a move from an ironic Modernist aesthetics to one of baroque excess, but still within a framework whose parameters are Modernist – for example in his engagement with Enlightenment thinkers like Diderot and Swift. In Australia, the work of Kenneth Slessor (d. 1971) served as a focus for poets like Robert Adamson, again working in a consciously regionalist version of Modernist tradition. In New Zealand, the work of the Catholic mystic James K. Baxter represented the first significant dialogue with Maori culture, though in forms borrowed from Robert Graves. And so on.

At the very least, this revival supports the argument that there is a lag between some of the cultural determinants of postmodernity and the literary work which might be related to them. Where the beginnings of a Postmodern trajectory are more visible is in the centrality of the category of space. In part we might attribute this to the breakdown of the colonial world-view (post-Suez; post-Vietnam) and various national mythologies of spatial experience; in part to the continuing penetration of space by capital. Space as an abstract, reworked category increasingly emerges as a concern in British and American writings and art (for example in the Land Art of Robert Smithson and Richard Long). Expanded forms of regional archaeology, mythography and geography unite otherwise disparate British texts of the period: Hughes's *Crow* (1970, expanded 1972), Geoffrey Hill's *Mercian Hymns* (1971), Allen Fisher's *Place* sequence (from 1974), and Sinclair's *Lud Heat* (1975). With connections to Long's documented walks and to Situationist mapping, Fisher's poem is a sprawling meditation on history and the lost rivers of London. Sinclair's Blakean poem-with-pictures centres on the geomythography of Hawksmoor's London churches. In this work, an analysis of space which is more typically Postmodern – concerned with praxis and textuality – begins to emerge.

The story of the end of the seventies is partly one of reaction, with the rise of new forms of conservatism in the politics of Thatcher and Reagan, and the waning of a subsidised counter-culture. Reagan sought to heal the trauma of Vietnam by a reassertion of American power, mapped onto a cultural nostalgia rooted in his own fifties film roles. In the UK, the Labour Party imploded and gave birth to the ideology of a 'classless' society in the splinter Social Democrat Party (SDP). The SDP, as Raphael Samuel has commented, can be seen as the inheritor of the reforms of the late sixties and seventies, marked both by a managerial and often narcissistic individualism and a determination to marginalise the union movements.[14] Both these developments, and parallel ones elsewhere (for example the success of a radical monetarist but socially liberal 'Labour' party in New Zealand in the 1980s) have their origins in the complexities of seventies culture. At the end of the nineties, a seventies revival in films like *Boogie Nights* and *Velvet Goldmine* continued to both celebrate and express suspicions of the decade's dangerous freedoms (pornography, drugs, easy money), suggesting that its cultural problematics are still with us.

[14] Raphael Samuel, *Island Stories: Unravelling Britain* (London: Verso, 1998), pp. 256–71.

33

Feminism and writing: the politics of culture

PATRICIA WAUGH

'Women are writing, and the air is heavy with expectation: What will they write that is new?' The expectations to which Kristeva refers in her seminal essay 'Women's Time' (1981) are the subject of this chapter.[1] The inauguration of 'women's time' had begun a decade before, but Kristeva saw that the time had also come to reflect upon some of the more metaphysical, as well as political, implications of women's entry into historical temporality. By 1981, the Women's Liberation Movement had splintered into a bewildering diversity of identity politics around issues of race, sexuality and class, but feminist writing had changed for all time the political and literary landscape. The burning issue thrown up by this maelstrom, however, was the question of what it is to be a *woman* and what is meant by *women's writing*. In the same year, 1981, Elaine Showalter's essay 'Feminist Criticism in the Wilderness' tempered Kristeva's utopian sense of expectation in suggesting that women's writing has always been, and will remain, essentially double-voiced: inevitably an articulation of both the muted and the dominant, the old and the new. Moreover, she implied that feminist re-visioning (to use Adrienne Rich's term) will require both an impulse towards, and resistance to, the concept of the feminine, to identity as *woman*. Showalter's essay performatively demonstrates her own undecidability. Proceeding in sections, each headed by citations from literary mothers, dead and alive, her argument develops in a mode of textual parallax, woven through and striated by a female chorus whose ghostly voices beckon towards unity and solidarity and simultaneously threaten to break into cacophony and difference. Her first voice, unmistakably refined, haute-bourgeois, but also dissident, rebellious, a voice struggling with the conundrum of whether it is worse to be locked out or worse to be *penned* in, is that of Virginia Woolf: 'A woman's writing is always feminine; at its best it is most feminine; the only difficulty lies in defining what we mean by feminine.' Within a paragraph or

[1] Julia Kristeva, 'Women's Time', *Signs*, 7, 1 (1981), p. 32.

two, Hélène Cixous takes up the dialogue from within second-wave feminism, insisting that it 'is impossible to define a feminine practice of writing, and this is an impossibility that will remain, for this practice will never be theorised, enclosed, encoded – which doesn't mean that it doesn't exist'.[2]

In the period 1970–2000, the terms of Woolf's and Cixous's imaginary exchange on female authorship dialectically frame most of the debates within feminist cultural politics. Second-wave feminism began with the Women's Liberation Movement in 1968 and, almost immediately, political activists and creative writers were pulled into the turbulent undertow and crosscurrents of this anxious dialogue on 'feminine' identity and female authorship. A political movement seeking equality and recognition of a gendered identity, feminism had ushered in 'women's time' but raised difficult questions about the meaning of woman. How might women affirm a feminine identity historically constructed through the very cultural and ideological formations which feminism as a movement was also seeking to challenge and dismantle? Despite the collective commitment to uncover a unified woman's voice, the idea of the 'feminine' seemed only sustainable, indeed, through modes of double-voicing, a femininity at once affirmative *and* negatory. To embrace unproblematically the concept of a 'woman's voice' as the belief that liberation from false consciousness might uncover a buried but authentic female self, might come dangerously close to reproducing that very patriarchal construction of femininity which feminists had set out to contest. But equally, any pre-emptive surgery, designed to liberate from the organic sexed body of woman a socially constructed and free-floating gender, might simply serve to facilitate yet another variety of reappropriation: of the 'feminine' as convenient cipher of marginality for a male avant-garde actively willing its own exclusion from bourgeois mores and positivist rationalities.

The Women's Movement grew out of the upsurge of counter-cultural and sub-cultural political activism of 1968 and developed alongside other radical movements such as Gay Liberation, the Civil Rights Movement and Black Power. The broad political context was initially one of grass-roots activism, with the goal for Women's Liberation of analysing the sources within patriarchal societies of women's oppression in order to overthrow such political orders and liberate not so much the 'feminine' as actual *women*. Early second-wave feminism attempted to ground its political practice by introducing the question of gender difference into those available radical discourses (Marxism,

[2] Elaine Showalter, 'Feminist Criticism in the Wilderness', *Critical Inquiry*, 8, 2 (Winter 1981); rpt. in Elaine Showalter, *The New Feminist Criticism: Essays on Women, Literature and Theory* (New York: Pantheon, 1985), pp. 247–8.

anarchism, Existentialism) which already offered foundational theorisations of self, society and nature.[3] Their impersonal and systematic accounts of oppression, however, proved inadequate for the specific task of defining women's 'experience' at the point of intersection between public and private identities and languages. Psychoanalysis seemed for a while to offer a way of complementing political theories by explaining personal resistances and obstacles to change: of why, for example, it seemed so difficult for human beings emotionally to accept a new order when the political conditions for change seemed propitious. Freud's observation that 'the data of conscious self-perception . . . have proved in every respect inadequate to fathom the profusion and complexity of the processes of the mind, to reveal their interconnections and so to recognise the determinants of their disturbances', suggested the limits to consciousness-raising and introduced a marked psychoanalytic orientation in feminist theory.[4] Psychoanalytic discourses provided further means of assault on the complacencies of a liberal humanism whose universal model of rational subjectivity had functioned to exclude women through their identification with a hysterical 'femininity' situated outside of but always threatening to disrupt a masculine order of logic and reason. But psychoanalysis also introduced its own problems. In contesting traditional constructions of subjectivity, psychoanalysis also hijacked those Enlightenment models of political agency which activist feminism seemed to require.

Almost inevitably, feminists turned to art and literature as a means of working through such contradictions and, more than any other political movement before 1970, feminism developed as a distinctively *cultural* politics. The power of symbolic representation and cultural embodiment in constructing and containing identities and subjectivities was recognised from the first as a definitive aspect of the new cultural politics. Feminist writers and critics embraced the utopian potential of art, its capacity not only to defamiliarise and expose sources of inequality, but also to imagine and construct worlds elsewhere. Art might serve as a vehicle for that epistemological interrogation, peculiar to the utopian mode of thought-experiment, which deduces from alternative premises the shape of a new and different and better world. Utopia in this mode

3 See Michèle Barrett, *Women's Oppression Today* (London: Verso, 1980); Rosalind Coward and John Ellis, *Language and Materialism* (London: Routledge & Kegan Paul, 1977); Juliet Mitchell, *Women's Estate* (Harmondsworth: Penguin, 1971); Sheila Rowbotham, *Hidden From History: Three Hundred Years of Women's Oppression and the Fight Against It* (London: Pluto Press, 1973).

4 Sigmund Freud, *An Outline of Psychoanalysis*, in *The Standard Edition of the Complete Psychological Works of Sigmund Freud*, trans. James Strachey, 24 vols. (London: Hogarth Press, 1951), XXIII, pp. 195–6.

is less a project to found a heaven on earth, than a means to evolve, through symbolic representation, a language of politics anchored in and constitutive of a fully human experience. Yet, although utopian in this sense, women's writing in the seventies was broadly realist in its commitment to the humanist exploration of women's situation and experience, though drawing on metafictional disruptions to explore the limitations of realism in fashioning new identities and imagining other worlds. Looking back on the early seventies activist search for a unified voice of woman, Offred, in *The Handmaid's Tale* (1986), wryly comments from her position within Atwood's futuristically conceived women's culture (a socio-biologically inspired fundamentalist theocracy): 'if Moira thought she could create Utopia by shutting herself in a women-only enclave she was mistaken. Men were just not going to go away. . . . You couldn't just ignore them.' It was crucially through the multivocality of literary representation that feminism might explore women's experience, assess the difficulties of trying to achieve social change, and thereby temper those totalising political discourses which theorised revolutionary change through the scientific analysis of monocausalities, such as economics or the laws of history: 'as if everything were available to us, as if there were no contingencies, no boundaries, as if we were free to shape and reshape the ever-expanding perimeters of our lives'.[5] Formal experiment was central to this process and from the problematised realisms of the seventies to the Postmodern fantastic of the eighties, and the Postcolonial hybridity of the nineties, women's writing produced an upsurge of technical and generic inventiveness propelled by the need, in Rachel Blau du Plessis's words, for women to 'break the sentence'; to create 'a rupture with the internalisation of the authorities and voices of dominance' and then to 'create that further rupture . . . breaking the sequence – the expected order'.[6]

In the seventies, therefore, 'the personal is political' became the resonant sound-bite encapsulation of a commitment to recover women's voices from 'between the acts' of world history. This archaeological practice would also involve an uncovering of buried relations between political practice and the domestic 'underworld' of women's experience, subsumed by and relegated to the margins within a patriarchal liberalism founded on the axiomatic separation of public and private. Liberalism, as a philosophy of 'freedom to' (in Isaiah Berlin's useful but problematic phrase), rests on a theory of justice (also and interestingly reinvigorated in the period by the political philosopher John

[5] Margaret Atwood, *The Handmaid's Tale* (London: Jonathan Cape, 1986), pp. 172, 225.

[6] Rachael Blau du Plessis, *Writing Beyond the Ending: New Strategies of Twentieth-Century Women Writers* (Bloomington: Indiana University Press, 1985).

Rawls) which requires a 'veil of ignorance': an assumption that if all citizens are to be given equal rights before the law, then the specific cultural situatedness of each subject should be regarded as a matter which lies outside any consideration of the legal constitution of the subject, properly the jurisdiction of the minimal state in its concern with the justice and liberty of all. Each citizen should be allowed to pursue his own (sic) freedom providing that the pursuit of private goods honour the liberty and freedom of others.[7] Feminists in the seventies drew on the Marxist recognition that within a system of capitalist exploitation, however, those 'others' may often be economically prevented from exercising their liberty and availing themselves of their liberal 'rights'. But they also recognised the inadequacy of Marxism itself in failing, like liberalism, to account for the specific construction of women's identity within a 'personal' space conveniently located outside of market relations as the sphere of the domestic or the 'natural' (biological). The exploration and representation of this space of women's 'experience' and the utopian attempt to imagine beyond current constraints became an abiding concern of women writers and of feminism as a *cultural* politics.

After important publications in the sixties and early seventies by Betty Friedan, Germaine Greer, Mary Ellmann and Kate Millett, the search was on for a mode of writing and rewriting which might liberate the woman's voice and interrogate her history of oppression.[8] The search was on to articulate Woolf's 'feminine' through a hermeneutics of suspicion which would come to interrogate all literary forms (realism, fantasy and science fiction, utopianism, Gothic, romance, crime fiction), cultural and political movements (the avant-garde, the tradition of radical and liberal dissent, socialism), and even to turn back self-reflexively on the fundamental tools of its own analysis: for the objects of knowledge (women, men, bodies, minds) come to be seen not so much as entities represented in language, but as artefacts constructed through and within discourse. For the question of enfranchisement, of securing a political voice, a representation, could no longer be regarded as a goal separable from the question of representation as a problem of the relation between form and meaning. To claim subjectivity simply within the terms of available discourses might be no more than to gain vocal representation through conformism

7 Isaiah Berlin, *Four Essays on Liberty* (Oxford University Press, 1969); John Rawls, *A Theory of Justice* (Oxford University Press, 1971).

8 Betty Friedan, *The Feminine Mystique* (Harmondsworth: Penguin, 1965); Germaine Greer, *The Female Eunuch* (London: Paladin, 1971); Mary Ellmann, *Thinking About Women* (New York: Harcourt Brace Jovanovitch, 1968); Kate Millett, *Sexual Politics* (New York: Doubleday, 1970).

to pre-existing categories or established identities.[9] If, as Audre Lorde put it, 'the master's tools will never dismantle the master's house', then second-wave feminism must proceed through an unprecedented and self-questioning cross-fertilisation between critical and creative writing, political activism and cultural discourse, which would dramatically problematise the search for that unified 'feminine' voice.[10] Not only must feminism engage with the profound differences in women's cultural situations, but also with the problem that, even allowing for such difference, the entry into a symbolic order entails that one's voice, unlike one's room, may never entirely be one's own. Feminism in the seventies was already caught between the modern and the Postmodern. A product of Enlightened modernity, drawing on its models of reason, justice and autonomous subjectivity, it was unavoidably caught up in the Postmodern in beginning to articulate issues of difference which would expose some of the most entrenched and disguised contradictions of Enlightenment thought. The existence, specifically, of sexual difference, not only challenged Enlightenment principles of universality and sameness, but also exposed the ways in which such principles are themselves contradicted in the construction of a public/private divide consigning women to the realm of the private. Identified through the space of domesticity, the feminine comes to carry all those associations of the affective, irrational and the corporeal which function to clarify the public demesne as one of logic, order, reason and masculinity.

Enlightenment might be crucial to feminism, but could not remain intact, and across the period, women writers grappled with those losses inevitably entailed in the quest for 're-vision': to write the feminine within the terms of post-Cartesian modernity is to risk abandonment of the sexed body as constitutive of difference; to turn the feminine into semiotic practice is equally to risk writing out real women. Either way, something is killed. Woolf herself, of course, was the first to talk of killing, of the feminine as 'Angel', before women could take up the pen and find their voice: 'had I not killed her she would have killed me . . . Whenever I felt the shadow of her wing or the radiance of her halo upon my page, I took up the inkpot and flung it at her. She died hard.'[11] Dying as an art has never more preoccupied women writers than when the question arises of what to put in place of the corpse. How to reinvent, reconstruct, rewrite; how to play Frankenstein to one's own monster without

9 See Jacques Derrida, 'Sending: On Representation', *Social Research*, 49, 2 (Summer 1982), p. 317.

10 Audre Lorde, *Sister Outsider: Essays and Speeches* (Freedom, California: Crossing Press, 1984), p. 110.

11 Virginia Woolf, 'Professions for Women', in Michèle Barrett, ed., *Virginia Woolf: Women and Writing* (Women's Press, 1979), p. 60.

reproducing Dr Frankenstein's potent mix of Romantic and Enlightenment masculine idealism? As Woolf saw, once the

> Angel was Dead: what then remained? You may say that what remained was a simple and common object – a young woman in a bedroom with an inkpot. In other words, now that she had rid herself of falsehood, that young woman had only to be herself. Ah but what was herself? I mean, what is a woman? I assure you, I do not know . . . These were two of the adventures of my professional life. The first – killing the Angel in the House – I think I solved. She died. But the second, telling the truth about my experiences as a body, I do not think I solved. I doubt that any woman has solved it yet.[12]

In 1931, Woolf had already hit on the abiding problem for theoretical feminism in the eighties: 'Can we imagine, or should we, a position that speaks in tropes and walks in sensible shoes?'[13] Without an identity grounded in 'experiences of the body', even one fractured by differences of race, class, sexuality and ethnicity, how might feminism survive, as a political movement of solidarity among women?

The 'movement' of course did not survive (the last conference of Women's Liberation in Britain was held in Birmingham in 1978) yet, by the eighties, feminism was respectably established within the academy and the broader world of literary publication. Major academic journals flourished in the eighties and nineties: *Signs* (launched in 1976), *m/f* (1978) and *Feminist Review* (1979). Independent feminist and women's presses, negotiating the terrain between the academic and the broader literary culture, were established at the same time: Virago in 1973, Onlywomen (1974), The Women's Press (1977), Sheba (1980) and Pandora (1981) and the seventies and eighties saw a 'woman-centred' publishing boom of unprecedented scale. By 1978, feminism had established itself as a broad cultural politics working on a plurality of fronts: academic, confessional, polemic, deconstructive, journalistic, literary and artistic. But the very discursive plurality wherein lies its capacity to avoid definitive capture has also thrown up difficulties for feminism as an activist movement. Factions and splinterings have occurred, not only across differences of class, race and sexuality, but at the interfaces of the popular and the academic and between earlier and later phases. Any account of such interrelationships within feminism, however, cannot afford to ignore the significance of shifting cultural contexts outside of feminism. There was a marked tendency in the eighties

[12] Ibid., pp. 60–1.

[13] Nancy Miller, 'The Text's Heroine: a Feminist Critic and Her Fiction', *Diacritics*, 12, 2 (1982), p. 53.

and nineties, for example, for Postmodern feminists to regard women's writing of the seventies as naïve and undertheorised, concerned to articulate a non-problematic feminine identity through expressive realist and confessional modes of writing. But this is to read that work purely within the frame of our own cultural preoccupations. As feminism strengthened itself within the academy, taking on the professionalised apparatus of scholarship and theory, personal and confessional discourses began to seem unsophisticated and lacking in rigour. Moreover, the personal and the confessional were appropriated in the nineties as powerful and effective media tools in the patriarchal hands of Western national governments and global superpowers seeking to control the political agenda through strategies of domestication and sentimentalisation. The Jerry Springer-style confession and the newsworthy eye-witness account have become ways of distracting attention from more fundamental issues concerning those relations of economics and power which finally underpin lifestyles and intimate relationships. It is not surprising that feminism in the eighties began to take flight from 'experience' and to develop a romance with those high theorists of Deconstruction for whom the 'subject' was only ever a position in discourse. But the situation was very different in the seventies. Consciousness-raising, confessional writing and the quest to find new forms in which to explore women's experience were practised in conjunction with a Marxist–feminist analysis of economic oppression and an existential critique of liberal exclusion and separation of the public and the private. Confession was part of an attempt to forge, for the very first time, the political solidarity of a woman-centred culture organised to subvert the patriarchal structures (political and economic) of the liberal state.

Tillie Olsen's *Silences*, for example, published in 1980, but written mainly in the sixties, was dedicated to uncovering and discovering 'our silenced people, century after century their beings consumed in the hard everyday essential work of maintaining human life. Their art, which still they made – as their other contributions – anonymous; refused respect, recognition, lost'.[14] Similarly, Shulamith Firestone, writing in 1971, insisted that the first task of feminism must be 'an exploration of strictly female reality' as a 'necessary step to correct the warp in a sexually biased culture. It is only after we have integrated the dark side of the moon into our worldview that we can begin to talk seriously of universal culture.'[15] Adrienne Rich's work celebrated the newly won opportunity to 'write directly and overtly as a woman, out of a woman's body and experience,

[14] Tillie Olsen, dedication to *Silences* (London: Virago, 1980).

[15] Shulamith Firestone, *The Dialectic of Sex: The Case for Feminist Revolution* (London: Women's Press, 1979), p. 167.

to take women's existence seriously as a theme and source for art, something I had been hungering to do, needing to do, all my writing life'.[16] Confession was the beginning of an attempt to articulate what Betty Friedan had called 'the problem with no name', that experience of femininity as negation, curtailment, lack, imprisonment, reduction: what Plath's Esther Greenwood experiences as 'the person in the bell jar, blank and stopped as a dead baby'. Or what a later sixties heroine, Margaret Atwood's Marian in *The Edible Woman*, internalises as hyperinflation, monstrosity, inchoateness, amorphousness, consummated in the iconic figure of the parturitional woman: 'swollen mass of flesh with a tiny pinhead, a shape that had made her think of a queen ant, bulging with the burdens of an entire society, a semi-person – or sometimes, she thought, several people, a cluster of hidden personalities that she didn't know at all'.[17]

It is simply too easy to homogenise this work and dismiss it as 'essentialist' and misguidedly and naïvely in search of a chimerical feminine identity. Since Woolf at least, women writers have explored the contradictoriness of female identity and recognised that the formulation of a unified 'woman's voice' is as risky a strategy as its dissolution into a fluid and free-floating semiosis. Writers of the late sixties and seventies were no exception: Muriel Spark's *The Driver's Seat* (1968) explored the contradictions of female authorship premised on the hystericisation of the female body through her character Lise who sets out to take over the 'driver's seat', to give authorship to her life by plotting her own (clean) murder. But in her author's vocal control over the verbal tense of the novel, and in its unnerving proleptic descriptions of her actual demise (raped and then murdered), is reflected a measure of all the agency we have, as ruthless narrative projection brings the future into the present and reminds us of those larger plots which frustrate our authorial desires and impulses to scriptoral autonomy. Novelists such as Atwood in *The Edible Woman* (1969) and *Lady Oracle* (1976) similarly experimented with shifts in narrative voice which teased out the complicated relations between writing and written selves, between the desire for a feminine voice and a deep internalised ambivalence towards the female body as a ripe fruit 'in various stages of growth and decay' and immanentised in a 'thick Sargasso sea of femininity'.[18] Margaret Drabble's *The Waterfall* (1969) used an unstable narrative voice to present a critical view of a love-affair through a first-person voice which

[16] Adrienne Rich, 'Toward a More Feminist Criticism', *Blood, Bread and Poetry* (London: Virago, 1986), p. 182.

[17] Sylvia Plath, *The Bell Jar* (London: Faber & Faber, 1964), p. 250; Margaret Atwood, *The Edible Woman* (London: Virago, 1982), p. 115.

[18] Atwood, *The Edible Woman*, p. 167.

alternates with a third-person romance narrative. Her protagonist Jane Grey comes to recognise how 'I split myself. I went underground' in order to avoid the direct vocalisation of an anger which she fears might annihilate everything, 'any word of mine . . . might shatter them all into fragments'.[19] Even Anita Brookner's ambivalent romances explored the split consciousnesses of women who can neither comfortably masquerade in the public world of ambition, efficiency and autonomy nor accept their feminine condition of self-effacement, dependency and silence. In *Look at Me* (1982), Brookner's writer–protagonist Fanny recognises her condition of femininity as a kind of illness, an iatrogenic disease identifiable through the charted representations of the melancholic who 'is very frightening, but the person she frightens most is herself. She is her own disease.' But though her writing is the search for an authentic voice, a way of entering the public world, Fanny recognises that it is also a way of saying 'look at me', of using voice narcissistically to attract gaze, just as her need for Nick on any terms is that 'his greatest gift . . . was that intermittent, speculative gaze'.[20] Given the problematic relationship between women and voice, it is hardly surprising that most of the great innovators in the use of free indirect discourse (the quintessential mode of double-voicing, and the perfect vehicle for mimicry, masquerade, subversion, satire, contested authority, intimacy, dialogism and irony) have been women writers: Jane Austen, Virginia Woolf, Margaret Atwood. In criticism, too, fascination with varieties of simulation: with 'strategy', for example, as in the self-consciously adopted positionality of Gayatri Spivak's 'strategic essentialism'; or with duplicitous masquerade as in Judith Butler's 'drag performances'; or with 'mimicry' as a form of reverse discourse in the writing of Luce Irigaray, can be viewed as varieties of what Susan Sontag in the sixties referred to as a discourse of 'camp', a subversive politics waged through the erotic pleasures of the (aesthetic) text. In this sense, cultural Postmodernism is more an elaboration and exaggeration of already available codes than an apocalyptic break with aesthetic tradition.[21]

Even in criticism, feminist writers such as Germaine Greer and Kate Millett used vocal play in the service of a cultural polemic arguably as slippery and polyphonic as any of the academic theory of the eighties. Both defied academic convention in producing confessional and polemical texts which repudiated the usual scholarly procedures of genuflection to authority, even-handed distribution of argument and counter-argument, and extensive citations and referencing. Instead, they claimed authorship as independent voices whose

19 Margaret Drabble, *The Waterfall* (Harmondsworth: Penguin, 1981), pp. 114, 51.
20 Anita Brookner, *Look at Me* (London: Triad/Granada, 1983), pp. 6, 84.
21 Susan Sontag, *Against Interpretation* (New York: Farrar, Straus & Giroux, 1966).

authority to speak for others arose from their boldness in contesting distinctions between the academic and the popular, the scholarly and the journalistic, and the literary and the critical. Texts such as *The Female Eunuch* (1970) combined the devices of popular oratory (denunciation, exhortation, *reductio ad absurdam*, mimicry and ridicule) with those more restrained and impersonal conventions of academic 'research' (factual citation, sociological analysis) and with the direct appeal of personal testimonial (intimate anecdotes and narrative reconstructions of experiences as a woman, elision of the split between the narrating and the narrated I) to induce a sense of shared intimacy with their readers, a rallying call to a 'we', a collective first person who must speak out and denounce the 'they' of oppression. There is no single voice of the 'real' Germaine Greer in *The Female Eunuch* but a playful orchestration of multiple voices creating a polyphonic re-vision of the political treatise.

Greer was also concerned, of course, to wrest the category of authorship from male control (at precisely the moment when male writers and critics were beginning to revel in the death of the author). Ironically, one mark of her success is reflected in the disproportionate number of academic 'celebrities' thrown up by feminism in the period. The marketing of female authorial 'voice' (even of voices who disclaim authorship and voice) has gathered strength from the time of de Beauvoir to that of Greer, Camille Paglia and Judith Butler, accompanied by dust-jacket photographs, 'centre-page' interviews and the kind of 'star' paraphernalia usually associated with pop-stars, actors and media-gurus.[22] So-called 'post-feminism' in the nineties has ridden on feminism's marketable back, and a new generation of women sages (Naomi Wolf, Natasha Walters, for example) are using remarkably similar aesthetic strategies in an attempt to create a supposedly third-wave collective 'we' in a move *against* their liberation mothers who are now subsumed into the 'they', the third-person vehicles of newly perceived oppressions.[23] Not surprisingly, post-feminists of the nineties share a vested interest with Postmodernists of the eighties in presenting their own positions and arguments as more sophisticated, more knowing, more theory-conscious than their predecessors, and in so doing have constructed a myth of early second-wave writing as naïvely confessional or unproblematically essentialist. But feminist critics and writers have always drawn on the aesthetic to resist what Lessing explicitly identified in *The Golden*

[22] See Lauren Berlant, *The Queen of America Goes to Washington City: Essays on Sex and Citizenship* (Durham and London: Duke University Press, 1997).

[23] Natasha Walter, *The New Feminism* (London: Little, Brown, 1998); Naomi Wolf, *Promiscuities: A Secret History of Female Desire* (London: Vintage, 1998).

Notebook (1962) as that intellectual form of patriarchal 'bullying' which favours the abstract and systematic over the fluid, the material and the contingent.

In the 'Preface' to the novel, Lessing justified her commitment to the Lukácsian ideal of humanist character and to the writing of fiction as a means of exploring contingent experience, the 'raw feel' of being a woman or a man living in the late twentieth century:

> The way to deal with the problem of 'subjectivity', that shocking business of being preoccupied with the tiny individual who is at the same time caught up in such an explosion of terrible and marvellous possibilities, is to see him as a microcosm and in this way to break through the personal, the subjective, making the personal general, as indeed life always does, transforming a private experience . . . into something larger: growing up is after all only the understanding that one's unique experience is what everyone shares.

But Lessing's problem is whether conventional realism can any longer express the complex fragmentariness of late modernity in terms which neither reduce social experience to particularised flashes of insular personal emotion, nor subsume the particular into the generalised impersonality of the rationalised discourses of social science and political theory. Initially, Anna Wulf, the writer, tries to work her way through the problem and overcome her writer's block by separating herself out into distinct voices, one for each of the four notebooks, convinced that if the essence of neurosis is conflict, then dividing up, separating out the voices, is the way to stay sane. But in the final, golden notebook, she begins to break down and to experience a complete dissolution of the voices into each other and into those of other characters. Recognising that 'the cruelty and the spite and the I I I of Saul and Anna were part of the logic of war', she becomes part of Saul, part of an Algerian soldier; part of an African nationalist; she experiences her room (like Woolf before her) not simply as an objective correlative for her own sense of ego but as an aspect of herself as a transitional object.[24] For Lessing, only *immersion* in the cacophonous vocal chorus which is the 'small personal voice' of the late twentieth century offers a way of breaking through to new political identities, for, as Martha Quest observes in *The Four-Gated City* (1969), 'when people open up a new area in themselves, start doing something new, then it must be clumsy and raw, like a baby trying to walk'.[25] After the completion of *The Golden Notebook*, Lessing said in an interview that she had 'floated away from the personal . . . I don't

[24] Doris Lessing, *The Golden Notebook* (St Albans: Panther, 1973), pp. 7, 568.
[25] Doris Lessing, *The Four-Gated City* (St Albans: Granada/Panther, 1972), p. 195.

believe anymore that I have a thought. There is a thought around.'[26] But this is not some mode of post-Structuralism *avant la lettre*: it is simply one of the ways in which, throughout the century, and particularly in the contemporary period, women writers have tried to expand and explore a semiotic feminine subjectivity without abandoning the category of women's experience and the concept of a personal voice.

So if there are discernible shifts and phases in second-wave feminism from the so-called 'personal' to the so-called 'postmodern', we should not be too rigid in our attempts at categorisation, nor assume that there is only one way to be personal, one way to be Postmodern. A preferable option might be to see various phases characterised by a rhetorical 'dominant', but each drawing on aesthetic strategies and thematic preoccupations which persist through the period. How might these phases be characterised? First, a pre-theorised and ambivalent phase beginning in the sixties and involving writers such as Iris Murdoch, Doris Lessing, Sylvia Plath, Simone de Beauvoir and Muriel Spark; second, a phase of explicitly 'writing as a woman' and involving, above all, a quest to reconcile the collective with the personal voice, to explore the reverberations of 'the personal is political' as in the continuing work of Lessing, Greer, Millett, Rich, in *écriture féminine* and the 'middle-ground' or metafictionalised realism of writers such as Margaret Drabble, Anita Brookner and early Margaret Atwood; and third, a phase of explicit engagement with the challenges of Deconstruction, Postmodernism and Postcolonialism, the moment when feminism enters fully what Showalter describes as the 'wilderness': the moment of theory and proliferation of difference, as women writers turn self-consciously and deliberately to the parodic and the fantastic, to masquerade and monstrosity, as in the works of Fay Weldon, Angela Carter, Jeanette Winterson, in later Atwood and in Caryl Churchill's writing of the eighties and nineties. The rhetorical dominance of this phase has now begun to wane, and it seems that feminism has embarked upon a moment of Hegelian synthesis, working over the expressive realist thesis of the early years and the antithetical deconstructions of the eighties and early nineties, to return to a reconsideration of experience, rights, subjectivities, in the context of a new era of globalisation and multiculturalism and in response to new threats from biotechnologies and the rejuvenated discourses of socio-biology.[27]

[26] Jonah Raskin, 'Doris Lessing at Stony Brook: an Interview', in Paul Schleuter, ed., *A Small Personal Voice* (New York: Vintage, 1972), p. 173.

[27] See Seyla Benhabib, *Critique, Norm and Utopia* (New York: Columbia, 1996); Chantal Mouffe, *The Return of the Political* (London: Verso, 1993); Sylvia Walby, *Gender Transformation* (London: Routledge, 1997).

Viewed from this perspective, one of the most fascinating aspects of the writing of radical women who began their careers before but continued writing in the sixties and seventies (de Beauvoir, Murdoch, Lessing), is their attempt to sustain universalist or transcendent modes of representation while reconciling them with a sense of identity as perspectival and radically situated in specific bodies. Each interrogates a grand narrative but finds it wanting *from the woman's point of view*: Communism for Lessing, liberalism for Murdoch and Existentialism for de Beauvoir. Each of them longs to write a 'book powered with an intellectual or moral passion strong enough to create order, to create a new way of looking at life'.[28] Of the three, Iris Murdoch might seem the least interested in a feminist perspective on cultural politics, reflecting on her preference for writing

> about things on the whole where it doesn't matter whether you're male or female, in which case you'd better be male, because a man represents ordinary human beings, unfortunately as things stand at the moment, whereas a woman is always a woman! . . . It's a freer world that you are in as a man than a woman.[29]

But de Beauvoir, too, announced in the 'Preface' to *The Second Sex* (published in France in 1949) that 'enough ink has been spilled in quarrelling over feminism, now practically over, and perhaps we should say no more about it'.[30] And Lessing herself never revised her opinion that we should 'stop talking about men and women writers. Our whole language, the way we think, is set up for putting things into departments. We've got far more in common with each other than what separates us.'[31]

But as humanists who profoundly challenge the assumptions of humanism from within, all three are still relevant to a feminism now trying to negotiate its way out of the impasses of the Postmodern. What unites them as writers is their search for a model of self-reflexive consciousness as an opening out into the world which proceeds from a radical embeddedness in which the 'body' is not simply a text overwritten by culture, but a situation through which we experience our very subjectivity: for 'the body is not a thing, it is a situation . . . it is the instrument of our grasp on the world'.[32] Despite

28 Lessing, *The Golden Notebook*, p. 61.

29 Iris Murdoch, in *Recontres avec Iris Murdoch* (Caen, France: Centre de Recherches de Littérature et Linguistique des Pays de Langue Anglaise, 1978), p. 82. Author's translation.

30 Simone de Beauvoir, *The Second Sex* (1949), trans. H. M. Parshley (Harmondsworth: Penguin, 1972), p. xix.

31 Doris Lessing, in Earl G. Ingersoll, ed., *Putting the Questions Differently: Interviews with Doris Lessing 1964–94* (London: Flamingo, 1996), pp. 61–2.

32 de Beauvoir, *The Second Sex*, p. 34.

Murdoch's shared ambivalence about writing as a woman and her famous preference for male narrators, she too uses her fiction to demonstrate the negative consequences for human flourishing of scientific liberalism's acceptance of the logical positivist separation of facts and values (the so-called 'naturalistic fallacy'). She develops an alternative vision of the human where each of us is situated as an embodied but self-reflexive consciousness engaging a world which never presents itself simply as neutral 'facts'. In this world, goodness ever escapes the frantic egomaniacal fantasies and desires of her loquacious male artist–narrators and enchanters, and is more often to be discovered in the muted and tacit responses of those women characters or 'feminised' males who, accepting the contingent, the brute materiality of the world, serve (often self-sacrificially) as the means to expose the seductive egotism of masculine desire in its will to absorb the world and the 'other' into self-projected and crystalline schemes. Accordingly, good art is that which tempers a will to transcendence with an acceptance of immanence and, as 'the most educational thing we have', art is valuable because of its 'pierced nature . . . its limitless connection with ordinary life, even its defencelessness against its client'.[33] Art is a means of countering what Lessing has also described as the thinning of language against the density of experience.

De Beauvoir, too, insists on our radical embodiment. Biological facts are woefully insufficient as a justification for the 'hierarchy of the sexes', but nevertheless, if our situated bodies are still, fundamentally, the 'instrument of our grasp on the world' then 'the world is bound to seem a very different thing when apprehended in one manner or another'.[34] But for women, held merely as bodies within the defining gaze of the male, experience has been forcefully limited to an immanence precluding that projection forth into the full existence of participation in the universal. Like Murdoch, and unlike Sartre, she rejects the Hegelian concept of a subjectivity ever premised on the objectification of the 'other', and calls for an 'ethics of ambiguity' which would recognise that 'equivalent centre of self' (George Eliot's term) and allow for one's own ambiguous positioning as both subject and object. Though de Beauvoir retained a horror of the female body and a fear of being regarded as 'just a woman', and though she refrains from the kind of critique of liberal universalism central to Murdoch's writing, she, too, offers a thoroughgoing critique of those Cartesian assumptions which have been instrumental in separating a feminised body from a masculinised model of mind. Like Woolf, all three

[33] Iris Murdoch, *The Fire and the Sun: Why Plato Banished the Artists* (Oxford University Press, 1977), p. 86.

[34] de Beauvoir, *The Second Sex*, p. 33.

women writers of this generation recognise the ways in which a specifically female body has been required to carry the negative projections of a culture founded upon an inadequate and discriminatory idea of reason. To tell 'the truth about one's experience as a body', is to begin to transgress a propriety which has served to patrol a defensively constructed rationalism purporting to be universal but actually arising from a fear and loathing of the corporeal body.

Indeed, though the nineties seemed to be the 'decade of the body' in cultural and literary studies (though declared as the decade of the brain by Bill Clinton), the problem of the body has been central to feminism throughout the century. Yet, viewed from the perspective of the writing examined above, the Postmodern body begins to look curiously complicit with the Cartesian project. For if gender is a 'free-floating artifice, with the consequence that man and masculinity might just as easily signify a female body as a male one, and women and feminine a male body as easily as a feminine one' then the body, paradoxically, and as in the *Discourse on Method*, ceases to matter and, as matter, becomes expendable in the very construction of subjectivity.[35] Judith Butler's theoretical project began with the familiar insistence that it is 'wrong to assume that there is a category of "women" that simply needs to be filled in with various components of race, class, age, ethnicity and sexuality in order to become complete', reiterating the idea that the meaning of woman and of the feminine must always be indeterminate.[36] But she goes much further than this in claiming that the sexed body is itself always an imitation which actually produces what it claims to imitate. For Butler's performative body is entirely *disembodied*:

> Within speech-act theory a performative is that discursive practice that enacts or produces that which it names . . . the norm of sex takes hold to the extent that it is 'cited' as such a norm, but it also derives its power from the citations that it compels. The paradox of subjectivation (*assujetissement*) is precisely that the subject who would resist such norms is itself enabled, or not produced, by such norms.[37]

In the end, 'body matters' seems to mean that the body as matter does not matter: a Cartesian claim if ever there was one. But the body does matter and has certainly mattered to feminists and women writers throughout the

35 Judith Butler, *Gender Trouble: Feminism and the Subversion of Identity* (London and New York: Routledge, 1990), p. 6.
36 Ibid., p. 209.
37 Judith Butler, *Bodies That Matter: On the Discursive Limits of 'Sex'* (London and New York: Routledge, 1993), pp. 13, 15.

second wave. Even in the year 2000, Germaine Greer declared in *The Whole Woman* that 'a woman's body is the battlefield where she fights for liberation. It is through her body that oppression works, reifying her, sexualising her, victimising her, disabling her.'[38] Monstrous bodies, anorectic bodies, hybrid bodies, cyborg bodies, fantastic bodies, zombies (bodies without souls) fill the pages of women writers in the seventies and eighties (one thinks here of Atwood's *Edible Woman*, *Lady Oracle*, Muriel Spark's *The Public Image* (1968)and *The Hothouse by the East River* (1973), Fay Weldon's *Puffball* (1980) and *The Life and Loves of a She-Devil* (1983), Lessing's *Memoirs of a Survivor* (1974) and *The Fifth Child* (1988), Carter's *The Passion of New Eve* (1977) and *Nights at the Circus* (1984), Winterson's *Sexing the Cherry* (1989) and *Written on the Body* (1992) – the list is endless). In such Postmodern fictions, the monstrous body functions as a means to voice and overcome anxieties concerning not only dominant constructions of femininity as uncontrollability and irrationality, but also about the contingency of the material as a constant threat to the crystalline perfections of rationalistic philosophy. Carter's Fevvers, for example, in *Nights at the Circus*, poses the question to Walser, 'what is "natural" and "unnatural", sir?', while the text repeatedly and metafictionally raises the question whether she is fact or fiction. Walser himself ponders whether Fevver's freakishness lies in the fact that she is indeed a bodily 'freak' (paradigmatic object of the gaze) or whether her true freakishness lies in the power of her performance thus to convince her audience and thereby to turn the gaze to her own advantage. He reflects that if

> she were indeed a *lusus naturae*, a prodigy, then – she was no longer a wonder . . . no more the greatest *Aerialiste* in the world, but – a freak . . . a marvellous monster, an exemplary being denied the human privilege of flesh and blood, always the object of the observer, never the subject of sympathy, an alien creature forever estranged.[39]

At least Carter's own Postmodern fictional performance keeps us guessing about Fevver's real bodily condition and she is allowed to demonstrate her physical prowess in overcoming all those who would simply kill her into symbolic life (a warning to the reader to read the text as more than a Postmodern parable of an all-pervasive textuality). The status of the body in Postmodern feminist theory, however, threatens to dissolve entirely into an a priori condition of semiosis. In their evasive flight from the organismic to the metaphoric

[38] Germaine Greer, *The Whole Woman* (London: Anchor, 2000), p. 135.
[39] Angela Carter, *Nights at the Circus* (London: Vintage, 1994), p. 161.

body, critics such as Judith Butler and Donna Haraway seem perversely complicit with all those currently dominant scientific reductionisms which would also convert the human body into a 'lumbering robot', vehicle for the selfishly replicating genes, and have joined forces with the cognitive sciences and the burgeoning field of evolutionary psychology to revive a truly essentialist socio-biological thesis which first rallied against feminism with the publication of E. O. Wilson's book, *Sociobiology* in 1975.[40] Here, too, the body is 'written' through a coded text (the genome) endlessly replicating and re-cited. Like the Postmodern theorist, the scientist and bio-engineer have also become textual interpreters reading the book of nature written in three billion coded letters, an endless play of signifiers without authorial or cellular origin, and at once overwhelmingly determinist but available for specialised reinscription and re-engineering. Here, too, the virtual body is emancipated from its organic counterpart to become a fluid information flow, hovering between machine and information system, in a scientific picture of human selves as vast computer networks driven by information chips and available for upgrading, downloading and redesigning. Just as earlier Postmodern feminist theory courted the deconstructive motif of the body-without-organs, later versions have sought liberation through the cyborg. Like avant-garde versions of the 'feminine', the cyborg is another figure for the Postmodern textual sublime, of a utopian radical alterity which might escape entirely all those patriarchal myths of origins which have kept women penned in the cave, on the dark side of the moon. But the cyborg, a fantasy of biotechnical Big Science, simply repeats as a gesture of liberation those very patriarchal discourses (socio-biological, techno-scientific) deployed in the control of actual women.[41] One of the tasks awaiting feminist cultural politics in the new century is to recognise and respond fully to the global threat posed by the latest biotechnological sciences. The response will require a reconsideration of the extent to which Postmodern feminists, in their own evacuation of the organic body and panic flight from experience into the pleasures of the text, may have actually been complicit with this most recent flight from the human. But that would be to anticipate the feminist cultural politics of the first thirty years of the twenty-first century. The air still hangs heavy with expectation.

40 Richard Dawkins, *The Selfish Gene* (Oxford and New York: Oxford University Press, 1989), p. 20.

41 Donna Haraway, 'A Cyborg Manifesto: Science, Technology and Socialist–Feminism in the Late Twentieth Century', in *Simians, Cyborgs and Women: The Reinvention of Nature* (New York: Routledge, 1991), pp. 149–83.

34

The half-lives of literary fictions: genre fictions in the late twentieth century

SCOTT McCRACKEN

In the post-war period, the popularity of genre fictions grew in all media. The period 1970–2000 saw a proliferation of genres beyond the standard four – detective, romance, science fiction and horror – to include the 'blockbuster', the 'bonkbuster', the family saga, the 'sex and shopping' novel, 'chick-lit', 'new man' and 'lad' fiction as well as a revival of the popular memoir and the elevation of certain children's novels to bestselling status. Each of these was a distinct, if inevitably ephemeral, literary formation and each needs a proper contextualisation in terms of the moment of its emergence and decline. Despite a proliferation, and to some extent a hybridisation, of genres, the key popular forms of the late twentieth century remained the standard four. What follows offers a short history of those genres as well as of the key popular literary formations of the three decades. However, before embarking on a literary history of popular genre fiction in the last three decades of the century, it is useful to define just what an account of the recent, the fleeting and the contingent (to paraphrase Baudelaire) might entail.

For much of the century, literary criticism either did not think genre fiction worthy of discussion or simply ignored the vast mass of fiction bought by the reading public. By the end of the twentieth century two factors, the overwhelming dominance of the cultural industries that produced genre fictions in their hundreds and thousands (in all media) and the emergence of cultural studies in the UK and the USA, meant that even those institutions that formerly wished to bar the door had to recognise the force, if not always the significance, of popular fiction.[1] A plethora of cultural theories – Structuralist, post-Structuralist, feminist, Marxist and psychoanalytic – were deployed to try and grasp the sources of mass culture's power, its satisfactions and its disappointments.

[1] Thus in 1992, Terry Eagleton in his inaugural lecture as Warton Professor of English literature at Oxford University argued for the study of popular culture: 'The Crisis of Contemporary Culture', *New Left Review*, 196 (1992), p. 37.

Questions of genre were hardly absent in post-war criticism, but key texts such as Northrop Frye's *Anatomy of Criticism* (1957) and Hayden White's *Metahistory* (1974) continued to use the classical genres as their starting-points (although both included the oldest form of popular fiction, romance, in their discussions). Even in 1981, Fredric Jameson was unusual in recognising the clear dominance of popular genres over their historical forebears in the twentieth century:

> With the elimination of an institutionalized social status for the cultural producer and the opening of the work of art itself to commodification, the older generic specifications transformed into a brand-name system against which any authentic artistic expression must necessarily struggle. The older generic categories do not, for all that, die out, but persist in the half-life of the subliterary genres of mass culture, transformed into drugstore and airport paperback lines of gothics, mysteries, bestsellers and popular biographies, where they await the resurrection of their immemorial, archetypal resonance at the hands of a Frye or a[n Ernst] Bloch.[2]

The project described by Jameson defines the key critical question raised by twentieth-century genre fictions: how to maintain a critical position conscious of their status as commodities and, at the same time, seek to rescue them from rapid obscurity and establish their historical significance? As Jameson asks: 'what happens when plot falls into history, so to speak, and enters the force fields of modern societies?'[3] A literary history of popular fiction between 1970 and 2000 offers some answers to that question.

The post-war period saw the emergence of three tendencies that became more pronounced in the last decades of the century. Firstly, the dominance of publishing by fewer and fewer global corporations. Secondly, the influence of America on British popular culture; and thirdly, the importance of other media in the selling of fiction in the shape of film and television 'tie-ins'. John Sutherland sees the 1970s as the decade when the 'a vast bestseller machine emerged'.[4] One genre, the spy thriller, demonstrates all three tendencies. British spy thrillers made a significant contribution to the development of the genre, including the action thrillers of Ian Fleming and the more cerebral novels of John le Carré. But after World War II a key part of their success was to transplant the local existence of the detective hero onto the international

2 Fredric Jameson, *The Political Unconscious* (London: Methuen, 1981), p. 107.
3 Ibid., p. 130.
4 John Sutherland, *Reading the Decades: Fifty Years of the Nation's Bestselling Books* (London: BBC Worldwide, 2002), p. 83.

stage. Here the British spy was a trickster, less powerful than his counterparts in either the United States or the Soviet Union, but cleverer, and able to win respect for his experience and abilities. The genre's potential for political critique continued to be explored as late as Graham Greene's *The Human Factor* (1978). However, it was the American spy thriller that dominated the period of the Cold War and continued to dominate until the end of the century. While local politics would only ever be of interest to a local audience, the leading role of the United States on the world stage meant that its diplomacy, wars and intrigues were of interest to a global readership. This factor, combined with the economic dominance of the American cultural industries meant that, with a few exceptions, such as the James Bond series, it was American spy thrillers that reached an international cinema audience; an audience that was increasingly fascinated by the culture of the USA.

The United States was also the origin of the 'blockbuster', the defining popular genre of the 1970s. Sometimes described as 'airport' novels, partly after Arthur Hailey's 1968 novel and partly because airport bookstalls became one of the most important outlets for popular fiction, the genre involved tales of adventure or corporate greed packaged as thick paperbacks by writers such as Wilbur Smith and Harold Robbins. If novels such as Hailey's *Airport* or *Wheels* (1971) were typical, Colleen McCullough's romance *The Thorn Birds* (1977) also fitted the category.[5] An Australian family saga that explored an affair between a young woman and a Catholic priest, McCullough's novel was written with the sole aim of achieving large sales. Sex and money were the most successful formulae for the blockbuster. British authors who aimed at an international readership, for example Ken Follett and Jeffrey Archer, had to compete in a market dominated by the USA. Follett broke into the USA lists with *The Eye of the Needle* in 1978. Archer's first success was *Not a Penny More, Not a Penny Less* in 1975.[6] Both used the narrative framework of the thriller. Follett made it to the number one slot of the *New York Times* bestseller list by the end of the decade with *Triple*, while Archer had to wait until 1982 with *The Prodigal Daughter*.

British detective fiction of the 1970s still bore the legacy of the interwar period. Agatha Christie's last novels came out in the early part of the decade, a sign of the longevity not only of the author, but of the golden age of English detective fiction. Many British writers continued to write the classic 'whodunit', characterised by a retrospective narrative, where the crime has already

[5] Cora Kaplan, '*The Thorn Birds*: Fiction, Fantasy and Femininity', *Seachanges: Essays on Culture and Feminism* (London: Verso, 1986).

[6] See Sutherland, *Reading the Decades*, pp. 93, 126–8.

been committed. Colin Dexter's Inspector Morse, whose first outing was in 1975, was little changed from the inter-war period's urbane, amateur sleuths. At the same time, a harder edge crept in under the influence of the American thriller, where a 'hardboiled style', first borrowed by social realists (for example, Alan Sillitoe) in the 1950s, signified in Britain the rejection of the class-bound atmosphere of the golden age and a new engagement with urban life. The most successful British authors were Ruth Rendell and P. D. James, who incorporated elements of American social and psychological realism into the whodunit form.

In many ways, detective fiction exemplified the contradiction cultural theory found in popular culture at the end of the twentieth century. On the one hand, in critical debates about the politics of 'high' and 'low' culture, the predictability of the whodunit was seen as evidence of social and cultural conservatism. In this view, the solution negates the narrative's literariness.[7] Its repetition of the same story was an example of what Walter Benjamin had called the tendency to eternal return in modern culture: the return of a mythic structure through the production of apparently endless novelty that is, in fact, always the same.[8] On the other hand, Ernst Bloch saw the origins of the mystery story in myths of dark beginnings and unknown crimes, among which he includes the story of Eve's temptation and Oedipus.[9] While Bloch argued that the detective story preserved these mythic archetypes, he did not see them as unchanging. Modern popular fiction preserves the elements of hope present in earlier narrative forms. The desire to overcome all difficulties expressed by the heroes of popular tradition persisted in mass-market fiction. For Bloch, popular narrative always exceeds the commodity form through what he calls an ideological surplus: that persistent element in the cultural heritage that anticipates the possibility of a better future.[10] This idea of a surplus offers an explanation for the extraordinary productivity of the detective narrative into the late twentieth century. The continuing success of the English detective story as exemplified by Rendell, James or Dexter lay in its ability to preserve the cultural heritage of the past even while it engaged with the present.

7 See Franco Moretti, 'Clues', *Signs Taken for Wonders: Essays in the Sociology of Literary Forms* (London: New Left Books, 1983), p. 148.

8 Walter Benjamin, *The Arcades Project* (Cambridge, MA and London: Belknap Press of Harvard University Press, 1999), pp. 115–18, 544.

9 Ernst Bloch, 'A Philosophical View of the Detective Novel', *The Utopian Function of Art and Literature Selected Essays* (Cambridge, MA: MIT Press), pp. 255–61

10 Bloch, 'Ideas as Transformed Material', in Human Minds, or Problems in the Ideological Superstructure (Cultural Heritage)', *The Utopian Function of Art and Literature*, p. 46.

British romance fiction also preserved a distinctive national flavour. The towering figures in British romantic fiction from the 1970s through to the 1990s were Barbara Cartland and Catherine Cookson, each of whom wrote about opposite ends of the social spectrum. Where Cartland wrote historical romances of aristocratic life, Cookson developed a peculiarly British form of popular romance, depicting the lives of working-class heroines, often from her native Tyneside. In her work, the injuries of class were understood through the modality of gender.

Cookson was also a key author in the development of the 'family saga', a popular form that followed the lives and loves of a family over several generations, but used the emotional language of romance and intimacy characteristic of mass-market romance. It is, however, difficult to talk about romance authors of the period without reference to the kinds of collective work that went into producing mass-market fiction. The most successful authors, like Cookson and Cartland, relied on teams of researchers and editors who filled in background material and sorted out inconsistencies of style. As the authors got older, the teams became more and more important to the finished, branded, product. On the death of the American writer, Virginia Andrews, the team took over altogether.

Sales of formula romances in Britain were dominated by the Mills & Boon imprint, the sister company to Harlequin in the USA. Here the form was even more tightly defined and carefully edited. The background was always familiar to the time in which it was written and pitched so as not to upset contemporary social conventions. Between 1940 and 1970 the form reflected social changes, from the introduction of the welfare state, to the affluent society, to the changing position of women in society. Feminist critics have noted that as the Women's Movement took off and ideas of gender equality took hold, the market for romance fiction expanded.[11] From the 1970s, formula romance became a textual space in which the limits of women's social and sexual freedom could be explored.

In other ways, however, the narrative structure of mass-market romance remained constant between 1940 and 1980. The heroine was portrayed as isolated, misunderstood, or even abandoned, at the outset, at odds with her father or family. The key narrative events took place in archetypal fantasy settings: in kitchens, womb-like hideaways or the bedroom. The possibilities inherent in the genre lay not so much in narrative innovation, but in the

[11] Ann Rosalind Jones, 'Mills and Boon meets Feminism', in Jean Radford, ed., *The Progress of Romance: The Politics of Popular Fiction* (London: Routledge & Kegan Paul, 1986).

representation of what the heroine lacked, a narrative technique designed to prompt the reader to fantasy. As feminist appropriations of psychoanalytic criticism suggested, the opposed positions of hero and heroine created a space in which the reader could insert herself, so that she was, temporarily, beyond an essentialised gender identity.[12] But this licensed fantasy never extended to a transformation of what femininity meant. The genre's development in the 1970s was as much a matter of obscuring real historical changes in gender relations as exploring the possibility of new constellations. It was as if genre fiction's function was to offer the possibility of an alternative way of life, without ever defining what that might actually be.

The genre that took accelerated social change as its reason for being was science fiction. In the first half of the twentieth century, science fiction was largely an extension of a more general popular enthusiasm for science and technology. Its distinctive orientation was towards the future, so that the genre became a medium for processing the experience of rapid change as new inventions like the motorcar, radio, cinema, television, space rockets and computers followed one another in bewildering succession. Utopian preoccupations in the post-war period were largely related to an enthusiasm for space travel and an orientation towards futures improved by technological progress. Dystopian visions speculated on the problems thrown up by technology, whether the moral dilemmas of robotics (as in the work of Isaac Asimov) or, most commonly, the horrors that might follow a nuclear war. Throughout the twentieth century, American science fiction dominated, although Arthur C. Clarke and John Wyndham established a distinctive British tradition, and the British-born Australian Nevil Shute's *On the Beach* (1957) formed a notable contribution to the body of work that envisioned the end of the human species following a nuclear apocalypse. Clarke's work helped to establish some of the main themes for a tradition of space literature that was to continue until the end of the twentieth century: the exploration and colonisation of space; and encounters with alien species.

The background to British science fiction in the 1970s was the emergence of the 'New Wave' novelists Michael Moorcock, J. G. Ballard and Brian Aldiss in the 1960s. These authors all continued to publish over the next three decades. Ballard was the most prominent. His novel *Crash* (1973) set the darker tone that was to predominate as the post-war enthusiasm for an economy fuelled by mass consumption began to fade in the wake of the oil crisis. The novel

[12] For a longer version of this argument, see Scott McCracken, *Pulp: Reading Popular Fiction* (Manchester University Press, 1998), chapter 3, 'Romance'.

was a grisly account of an obsession with car crashes, in which the sexual attractions of power and speed were compared with their consequences for a humanity transformed both physically and psychologically. While the theme of the encounter between humanity and machine is at least as old as the industrial revolution, the last three decades of the twentieth century saw an increasing preoccupation with changing ideas of what it means to be human, provoked by computing and biotechnology.

An important new development in the genre from the 1960s on was the emergence of feminist science fiction. Earlier examples in the century had included Charlotte Perkins Gilman's *Herland* (1915), while Virginia Woolf's *Orlando* (1928) was an unorthodox approach to time travel as well as an exploration of the limits of gender. At the end of the century, North American writers Ursula Le Guin, Marge Piercy and Joanna Russ, the Canadian Margaret Atwood and the British writer Gwyneth Jones all used the form to imagine dystopian worlds, in which gender divisions were sharpened, or utopian worlds, in which new kinds of gendered relationship come into play.

By the 1970s, horror fiction, a direct descendant of a Gothic tradition that extended back to the eighteenth century, had become the literary genre most difficult to disentangle from film. It was a staple of Hollywood productions for much of the century, but in its last three decades there were successive waves of horror movies, aimed largely at teenagers and audiences in their twenties. Written fiction provided a substantial bank of material on which directors could draw, most notably the work of Stephen King, whose first novels were published in the 1970s. But cult authors, published in short print-runs, formed a significant part of Gothic fiction in the period. Gothic's relationship to the unconventional and the macabre made it a natural ally of counter-cultural and sub-cultural movements. For example, Ann Rice's homoerotic novel *Interview with a Vampire* was published in 1976, attained a growing cult status for more than ten years, but did not succeed in becoming a bestseller until the release of the film in 1994.

Partly because of the influence of Hollywood, it had already become difficult to define a distinctively British horror tradition by the 1970s. An author like Dennis Wheatley already seemed dated and parochial, his fictions more appropriate to the suburban fears of the 1950s and 60s. The only successful period of British film, the low-budget Hammer productions, largely based on adaptations of nineteenth-century Gothic tales like *Dracula* and *Frankenstein*, eventually achieved cult status, but never really challenged Hollywood. Even James Herbert, who set his novels in British locations (his first, *Rats* was published in 1974), mimicked a technique common to a transatlantic Gothic style dominated by Hollywood. Clive Barker moved to the United States to write books and to direct films, part of a movement from Alfred Hitchcock onwards for British directors to move west. The fact that one of the most successful horror/science fiction sequences, the *Alien* films, were begun (in 1979) in Hollywood by a British director, Ridley Scott, only underlines the difficulty of disentangling a national tradition, particularly at a time when the genre's youthful audience was so influenced by American culture.

The 1980s saw a shift away from the narrative structure of the blockbuster towards a more epigrammatic style exemplified by writers like Jackie Collins. Collins specialised in short terse sentences and a montage of short narrative sections, a style mimetic of the film industry that supplied the context for her fiction. With Collins as its queen, the decade gave rise to the 'bonkbuster' and the 'sex and shopping novel'. In Britain, Jilly Cooper's *Rivals* was one of many that celebrated sexual adventurism and the eighties' culture of consumerism. The 'sex and shopping' novel seemed to epitomise the politics of Thatcherism and Reaganism. Perhaps the most self-conscious example was Julie Burchill's *Ambition* (1989), which was, at least in part, an ironic comment on the genre's rampant individualism and underlying violence.

Excess was also the watchword of detective fiction in the 1980s. The descriptions of murders became more graphic and the murders themselves became more plentiful. A popular development was the advent of the serial-killer novel. Pioneered by American writers Thomas Harris and Patricia Cornwell, this was later adopted by, among others, Manchester writer Val McDiarmid. Attention shifted from the clues left by the murderer to the body of the victim. Cornwell's detective Kay Scarpetta was both forensic scientist and detective, equally at home with the scalpel and the gun. The detective's identity became more flexible in other ways as well. If the early twentieth century established the detective as the embodiment of the modern, self-reflexive individual, the social changes of the 1960s produced a slew of new detective personalities in the 1970s and 1980s. Just as feminism, civil rights and lesbian and gay rights in Britain were heavily influenced by the new social movements in the United States, so the most influential new detectives were American. Whereas Cornwell's Scarpetta flirted with (but did not actually adopt) a lesbian identity, in Britain the new detectives had a more marginal existence.

In romance fiction, the 1980s saw the consolidation of the family saga as the most popular form of romance. Barbara Taylor Bradford's *A Woman of Substance* (1979) gave rise to numerous imitators; but the form was also adopted by novelists like the Chilean Isabel Allende, who worked on the boundary between the literary fictions of magical realism and popular women's fiction. In the family saga, a form of historical novel that puts women at its centre, the change in the position of women over two or three generations registered both the difficulties and the gains for women during periods of rapid social and political change.

Under pressure from other more explicit genres, the famed prudery of women's romance fiction broke down, and emotional openness was matched by detailed sexual encounters. However, as feminist critics in the decade demonstrated, the possibilities offered by the formula romance seldom involved simple identification. The text could be used to compensate for an otherwise unsatisfactory existence,[13] but it also allowed an exploration of women's fears of male violence and permitted a fantasy of revenge.[14] The inevitable convergence between heroine and hero at the narrative's end posited the utopian possibility of perfect understanding between the genders; but the closure, like the solution to the murder mystery, was seldom satisfactory. The ideal speech situation in which the hero declared his love and the heroine revealed hers was never as powerful or convincing as the misunderstandings that were the real substance of the genre. Such misunderstandings meant that a bestselling romantic novelist, like Danielle Steel, was almost able to match Stephen King's record in fiction sales.

While J. G. Ballard was clearly a precursor, the history of science fiction from the 1980s onwards was dominated by the (largely North American) 'cyberpunk' movement, for which a key influence was the work of Philip K. Dick. Cyberpunk emerged as the imaginative corollary of new computer technologies and the new fictional possibilities offered by the internet. For Fredric Jameson this new type of science fiction was 'fully as much an expression of transnational corporate realities as . . . of global paranoia itself'.[15] Cyberpunk anticipated the new global economic order after the fall of the Berlin Wall in 1989 and then offered a fictional landscape in which its opportunities and its pitfalls could be imagined. Its roots can be found in the post-apocalyptic literature that followed World War II and in a fascination with the interaction between humanity and technology already established in the nineteenth century. In cyberpunk, the fragmentation of the political sphere and the near-disappearance of public space on the one hand were contrasted

[13] Janice Radway, *Reading the Romance: Women, Patriarchy and Popular Literature* (Chapel Hill and London: North Carolina University Press, 1984), p. 95.

[14] See Tania Modleski, *Living with a Vengeance: Mass-Produced Fantasies for Women* (London: Methuen, 1982).

[15] Fredric Jameson, *Postmodernism, or the Cultural Logic of Late Capitalism*, (London: Verso, 1991), p. 38.

with a counter-public sphere represented by alternative communities. These bore recognisable signs of the youth sub-cultures of the West since the 1960s. In William Gibson's work, new technologies were extrapolated from current developments, but their use exposed the social contradictions of an increasingly divided society. Gibson depicts the new myths and mysticisms that seep into the gaps and fractures of a fragmented social body, confounding the belief that historical progress and rationality are intertwined.

Horror fiction in the 1980s was dominated by Stephen King, whose work in turn dominated popular fiction as a whole; but he was unusual in being virtually the only horror novelist to reach the bestseller list consistently. The secret behind his sales, 300 million copies by 2000, was a symbiotic relationship with cinema. The skilful translation of his texts into film expanded his popularity beyond anything the publishing industry had known before.[16] Alternative horror fiction continued to be sold, but as cult fiction, in short print-runs. Ann Rice's 'Vampire Chronicles' were more typical of the genre. King's work, by contrast, used the Gothic as a hook to write thrillers and adventure stories that incorporated an element of the supernatural. Some of his work was highly regarded by critics: in particular, *Misery* (1987), which explored the relationship between a popular novelist and his (largely female) audience, realised in the Gothic figure of Annie Wilkes, who kidnaps and tortures him until he writes the novel she desires. By the end of the decade King had become a brand name he tried unsuccessfully to escape, assuming pseudonyms such as Richard Bachman. In the 1990s, a novel with his name on it sold whatever its quality.

In the UK, it was Angela Carter's brilliant literary fictions that did most to develop the tradition of female Gothic, a form that did not translate so well into film. Carter's work successfully extended feminist insights into fantastic worlds where gendered identity lost its solidity. In this she led the way, later followed by Fay Weldon in a more populist mode with novels that included *The Life and Loves of a She-Devil* (1983).

The 1990s saw a less harsh political climate and the demise of the 'sex and shopping novel' in favour of 'lifestyle' narratives. The light comedy that would come to dominate the decade's popular fiction began as a newspaper column, *Bridget Jones's Diary* by Helen Fielding. The success of Fielding's novel gave rise to a wave of novels, described as 'chick lit', appealing to a new demographic category: young, single professional women. A complementary category catered

[16] Sutherland, *Reading the Decades*, p. 157.

for men and included novels such as Nick Hornby's *About a Boy* and Tony Parsons's *Man and Boy*. Whatever the gender of their main character, the novels all owed much to formula romance, opening up that market to male readers. Men's fiction by writers such as Hornby and Parsons took on some of the language of emotion formerly found in women's romance. If the new man showed an admirable ability to wear his heart on his sleeve (even if it was the sleeve of his football shirt), the effect in sales was to reach a bigger audience of both men and women.

Thrillers were popular in the decade, but had to adapt to the end of the Cold War. John le Carré was one of the first to explore the rapidly changing geography of international relations. Interestingly, the function of the international thriller became clearer at a time of greater political uncertainty. The right-wing American writer Tom Clancy achieved his best sales in this decade by mapping the limits and the possibilities of American power in fantasy situations, some of which, like his vision of an aircraft flown by a terrorist into the Capitol, were later to be realised. The imaginative basis for a world dominated by a single hegemony, albeit one besieged by multiple threats, was sketched out in a series of thrillers, in which the protagonist, Jack Ryan, goes from military commander to President.

British detective fiction persisted in the face of the new challenge of the American legal thriller, the most successful examples of which were written by John Grisham. Writers like P. D. James and Ruth Rendell continued to be successful and were joined by Minette Walters, who incorporated grisly scenes into the English tradition. However, the problematic definition of Englishness towards the end of the century caused problems for a genre that requires a clear sense of place in order to define the detective's identity. Ethnic and geographical locations were essential to the American detective, so that the popular hero or heroine engaged with modernity through a distinctively local or community-based identity. The hegemony of the English detective, essentially derived from an inter-war concept of Englishness, limited the development of a detective identity formed by England's provincial cities. Exceptions in fiction (television was more open to crime series based outside London) included Val McDiarmid's novels, set in Manchester, and Ian Rankin's Rebus series, set in Edinburgh. Of these, the latter series was the more successful, drawing on a tradition of Scottish Gothic and aided by a resurgent nationalism. The lack of comparable examples in England pointed again to the difficulty of establishing alternative points of reference in the face of American popular culture.

In romance, the end of the century saw an attempt by the publishers to rejuvenate the genre in the face of a culture where frank discussions of sexuality had become the norm. However, in the 1990s, its appeal remained, at least for older readers. With consumer culture's increasing emphasis on youth, romance offered an alternative world to those excluded from an embodied ideal of sexual health. Its utopian promise became as much a Proustian resurrection of lost moments as the hope of future fulfilment. Several writers followed Isabel Allende in employing the family saga to tell national or ethnic histories. For the Chinese–American writer Amy Tan this involved fiction, but, writing from Britain, the Chinese exile Jung Chang, in *Wild Swans, Three Daughters of China* (1991), used the same narrative structure to tell her family history before and after the Chinese Revolution. Catherine Cookson's work continued to dominate the British market up until her death, but numerous authors, for example Josephine Cox, who wrote about North-West England, followed in her footsteps.

Cyberpunk continued to be the dominant trend in science fiction in the 1990s. William Gibson's *Virtual Light* (1994) depicted a world in which the nation–state has all but collapsed and large corporations dominate. British science fiction of the 1990s also offered alternative worlds engendered by new computer, medical or biological technologies. Jeff Noon's Manchester in *Vurt* (1993) did for Manchester what *Virtual Light* did for San Francisco. Drug culture provided the background here for a society where hybrid creatures and hallucinatory experiences exist in a decaying urban environment. Gwyneth Jones wrote a series of novels that use the familiar trope of alien encounter to explore organic technologies, where machines are grown rather than made. The author Iain M. Banks wrote a successful series of novels in a more traditional 'space-ship' mode. However, even here, the moral dilemma that structured the narratives was whether or not to interfere in other planetary cultures. Writing as Iain Banks, his earthbound novels, for example *The Wasp Factory* and *Complicity*, while not strictly speaking science fiction, explored the Postmodern theme of confused or fungible identities. Whether the subject-matter was the interface between consciousness and machine, mechanism and living organism, or human and alien bodies, the common theme in late twentieth-century science fiction was the permeability of the boundaries that constitute human identities.

The scope permitted to science fiction allowed it to be perhaps the most innovative of all popular forms. It was, at one and the same time, remarkably successful in terms of quantities of sales, and able to maintain some of the features of the avant-garde: its short print-runs and magazine culture allowed it to be experimental in a way that sustained its vibrancy. Contemporaneously, the impact of technology on everyday life at the end of the twentieth century intensified and, as a result, not only was science fiction a staple of film and television productions, but almost all popular fictions represented some aspect of daily life mediated through email, mobile-phone calls, and the internet. Science fiction became just one of the genres that explored such 'virtual worlds'.

Writers in the USA remained the dominant influence on horror fiction in the 1990s. While some British writers stood out, they were outside the mainstream of popular culture. Print was subordinate to the new media. Film, television and, increasingly, computer games adopted and developed popular genres. All were subject to intense commercial pressures, often resulting in a standard product. Yet the persistence of horror was not just about the success of the same. Popular texts appealed to their audience's real needs, hopes and fears and those audiences read for the differences and deviations from the standard structure as much as the familiarity of its conventions. Horror offered an extreme version of the dialectic between the familiar and the unfamiliar that was a part of all genre fictions. Its continuing dependence on short print-runs and small, specialised audiences meant that it was able to keep some of its freshness. Predominantly aimed at a younger audience, horror's conventions were continually revised so as to defamiliarise its formal devices for each new generation of readers. Only by such defamiliarisation could it produce a (temporarily) indefinable monstrosity designed to explore the limits of identity and the anxieties and pleasures induced by its breakdown. As a genre it was unusually productive of meaning. Its mode was excessive on a number of levels. As Judith Halberstam argued in the mid-1990s, monstrosity can be as desirable in its capacity to transform identity as it is horrific in its ability to destroy.[17] Consequently, new authors, such as the American Poppy Z. Brite, were still emerging to write counter-cultural Gothic fiction at the end of the decade.

A genre that occupied a kind of halfway house between science fiction and horror was fantasy fiction. Often related in form to older romance narratives, twentieth-century fantasy had its origins in children's fiction. C. S. Lewis's 'Narnia' series quickly achieved the status of a children's classic. Tolkien's *Lord of the Rings* had an even wider appeal and became an originary text for the 'sword and sorcery' genre. Here narratives that seemed to echo medieval romance were able to cross over into texts that were closer to science fiction or the Gothic landscapes of horror fiction. Terry Pratchett's comic fantasies,

[17] See Judith Halberstam, *Skin Shows: Gothic Horror and the Technology of Monsters* (Durham, NC: Duke University Press, 1995).

which take place in the imaginary 'Discworld' were the most successful example of the genre. The 'Harry Potter' series, only just begun at the end of the century, demonstrated the continuing appeal of stories of magic for children, but the extent of its success in book sales was also indicative of the new role marketing played in every aspect of the publishing industry. In this respect, it was difficult to judge the success of J. K. Rowling relative to earlier children's fiction, because her novels were subject to a marketing campaign unprecedented for a children's (or, indeed, any previous) work of fiction.

One consequence was to create the conditions where, as with Phillip Pullman's fantasy sequence, the *His Dark Materials* trilogy, children's fiction crossed over into the adult market. The interpenetration of children's writing and adult fiction was indicative of a larger process whereby narrative and commodification became inextricable by the end of the century.[18] Children as young as two years old were subject to targeted picture books and television programming. Successful sales or viewing figures offered marketing opportunities for a range of spin-offs, toys, games, films, stage-shows, food products and so on. On the other hand, adults brought up in a media culture already well entrenched in the 1970s maintained an affection for recognisable fantasy worlds and were prepared to buy fiction that took such worlds seriously, rather than consigning them to either the 'degraded' realm of mass culture or a separate (and trivialised) world of childhood.

In conclusion, the 'half-life' identified by Jameson might be seen to refer to the persistence in branded fiction of the genre's original significance for its audience, including the promise of fulfilment denied by everyday life. Like fairy tales in an earlier age, popular genres offered the hope of something better.[19] In this respect, twentieth-century genres were related to earlier genres and to the particular historical moments that gave rise to them. They retained traces of those moments and of the contract of hope struck between those literary forms and their audiences. One important function of popular fiction was to act as a storehouse or reservoir of the stories that constitute a cultural heritage.[20] But, unlike the literary novel, which abolishes genre in its playfulness with literary form, popular genres solidified into a recognisable shape that can be identified or 'branded' in the marketplace; and this was the case even where

[18] The argument repeated in Sutherland that the success of Rowling and Pullman was because their narratives dealt with 'big metaphysical questions about good and evil, the meaning of life and the human condition' is unconvincing (p. 153).

[19] Ernst Bloch, 'Better Castles in the Sky at the Country Fair and Circus, in Fairy Tales and Colportage', *The Utopian Function of Art and Literature*, pp. 167–85.

[20] For a full account of cultural heritage, see Ernst Bloch, 'Ideas as Transformed Material', pp. 18–71.

the brand was identified not so much by an identifiable narrative form but by the author's name: a 'John Grisham', a 'Danielle Steel' or a 'Stephen King'.

From one point of view, 'branding' might be seen to reduce the significance of genre fiction to the mere confirmation of market society: the most favourable conditions for commodity exchange. Nowhere was that process better exemplified than in mass-market, formula romance, where the same plot was recycled endlessly. But to accept this perspective uncritically would be to ignore commodity culture's failure to deliver on its promise: the sense present in all commercial culture that something is missing.[21] It was in the contradiction between mass culture's attempt to satisfy that yearning and its failure to achieve fulfilment that popular genres thrived. Cultural theory's preoccupation with mass culture in the late twentieth century can perhaps be seen as a contradictory response to, on the one hand, the sense of the power of mass culture in everyday life and, on the other, an equal sense that, despite its pervasive influence, popular texts might gesture towards an as yet undefined alternative, what Ernst Bloch had called the 'Not-Yet-Become'.[22]

As important as the different forms taken by popular fiction was the audience (or market) to which those forms appealed. All popular genres or branded authors had in common a contract with a particular audience, so that meaning was established through familiarity and recognition. That contract was mediated through the economic conditions in which genre fictions flourished: the production, distribution and consumption of hundreds of thousands of paperback novels that could more easily find a market position because they conformed to a modern generic type. When, from the 1970s onwards, older genre distinctions began to break down, bestsellers were often hybrid genres, which, as with the blockbuster, 'sex and shopping' or 'lifestyle' novel, reflected the cultural formations of the moment. But generic forms did not themselves disappear. They simply proliferated and became more ephemeral.

Towards the end of the century this process intensified. In the 1990s, ever-bigger companies operating across the cultural industries acquired many of the small independent publishers specialising in fiction. If British publishing in the 1970s could still be described as a 'cottage industry',[23] by 2000 it was hardly British. Of the five biggest publishing firms only two were based in the UK, two belonged to the German Bertelsmann and one, HarperCollins, was

[21] Theodor Adorno and Ernst Bloch, 'Something's Missing: a Discussion between Ernst Bloch and Theodor Adorno on the Contradictions of Utopian Longing', *The Utopian Function of Art and Literature*.

[22] For a full account of this concept, see Ernst Bloch, *The Principle of Hope*, 3 vols. (Oxford: Blackwell, 1986).

[23] Alison Baverstock, *How to Market Books* (London: Kogan Page, 2000), p. 1.

part of Rupert Murdoch's global empire.[24] At the same time, book chains, but also airport outlets and supermarkets, supplanted independent bookshops and focused on fewer titles, promoting them ever more aggressively. This increased the profile of genre fiction as familiar products that fit into past patterns of sales (at the end of the century internet sales still held an insignificant share of the market and it was difficult to predict their future). But it also created the conditions where new, ephemeral genres could spring up and older literary forms could be given new life. In this respect, the divide between 'literary' and 'popular' fictions started to narrow, not least because they were being produced, distributed and consumed in ways that were increasingly similar.

At the more literary end of the scale there was a vogue for well-written memoirs that developed out of the long-standing demand for popular biographies. Here the new market conditions meant that publications receiving good reviews in the (very limited) literary press might, with the promotion of the publishers, be pushed at a rate equal to bestselling titles and achieve high sales.[25] This then encouraged publishers to look for similar material until the vogue declined. At the other end of the literary spectrum, there was the extraordinary phenomenon of popular biographies of personalities so young that the stories of their lives were virtually without content. These were published in such rapid succession about the same person that hardly anything had happened between one point in the life-narrative and the next. This genre acted as a kind of blank canvas for fantasies that could be projected onto celebrity figures, the blander the better, to allow full scope for fantasy.

However, against the cynical process where publishers desperately try to hold on to a fleeting readership must be opposed the situation of the reader at the end of century, and the importance of what has been called the 'text in use'.[26] Popular fictions cannot be divorced from the social contexts in which they were read. One of the reasons genre fiction was able to escape its commodity form was because, as a response to the moment, it had to relate to the everyday context of the reader. Paradoxically, its ephemeral nature was the key to its ability to exceed its form. Being in tune with fashion rendered it semi-invisible, enabling it to fade into banality, boredom and thence a fantasy that exceeds the limited situations of the reader.[27] The everyday contexts in

[24] Ibid., p. 2.

[25] Typical examples were Frank McCourt's *Angela's Ashes* (1996) and Lorna Sage's *Bad Blood* (2000).

[26] See Helen Taylor, 'Romantic Readers', in Helen Carr, ed., *From My Guy to Sci-Fi: Genre and Women's Writing in the Postmodern World* (London: Pandora, 1989), p. 66.

[27] 'The dream of colportage is never again to be trapped by the routine of daily life', Bloch, 'Better Castles in the Sky', p. 183.

which it was consumed were periods of non-times, time that escapes quantification – the railway journey, the airport wait, the holiday – as opposed to the valued time legitimated by the cultural institutions that support high art – universities, galleries, museums, libraries. Thus, popular fiction had a mimetic as well as a utopian function. It mimicked the banality of modern existence even as it offered the stimulation that took the reader beyond it. As Umberto Eco commented of pornography, boredom is as essential as sensation to the structure of popular genres.

Thus, even in an age saturated by commodity culture, the small gap for innovation opened up by popular texts was a crack that permitted its audience to see another world than the one in which they lived. Without that vision, it can be argued, the popular genres of the late twentieth century would never have achieved their success. Popular fiction at the end of the twentieth century continued to occupy a contradictory place in culture. On the one hand, the grid of control that Theodor Adorno first identified in the cultural industries of the 1940s persisted in representing the new as the ever the same.[28] On the other, it offered an enormous resource of old and new cultural forms, one which could be endlessly exploited by high art and literary fiction. In that respect, late twentieth-century genre fiction still had the capacity to offer hope in the midst of homogeneity and blandness.

[28] T. W. Adorno and M. Horkheimer, *Dialectic of Enlightenment* (London: Verso, 1979).

35

Theatre and politics

SIMON SHEPHERD

It is the run-up to Christmas 2001. A community centre in Homerton, in the East End of London, is hosting a series of acts by a range of performing artists. A man in a beard and long coat steps into the empty space. His extended arm begins slowly to trace a wide arc. In his hand he holds a small sleigh. Behind him there appears a projection of the twin towers in New York. The traditional image of Christmas blurs with the more recent image of another event, the terrorist attack of 11 September. Santa's sleigh flies on.

Was this performance political? It touched a hot political topic, but did it take a position on it? Did it need to? Could it remain playful and enigmatic and yet be political? Was its effectiveness dwarfed by the thing it referred to? What precisely was the relationship between this piece of theatre and the politics of the event? Is that relationship political?

I

As he surveyed the contemporary scene in 1982, the playwright David Edgar was clear about the connection of theatre and politics. He defined it as 'the project of explaining public events in a privatized way'[1]. The key word perhaps is 'explaining'. So, for example, John Arden and Margaretta d'Arcy's *Island of the Mighty* from 1972 could be said to use the story of Arthur's reign in the sixth century to explain what life in the modern UK felt like. With its oppositions of Roman and Celtic, reason and magic, male and female, central and marginal the play images a state that, with its war in Ireland, its industrial disputes, its counter-culture, seemed to be desperately hanging on to dreams of lost empire in order not to face its own disintegration. In the next year, 1973, that process of disintegration was helped on its way by *The Cheviot, the Stag and the Black, Black Oil*, by John McGrath and 7:84 theatre company. The play explained how

[1] David Edgar, 'Viewpoint: Politics and Performance', *TLS* (10 September 1982), p. 969.

the discovery and exploitation of North Sea oil fitted into the historical scheme of systematic English repression and robbery of the Scots, and destruction of their culture and language. Playing to Scottish audiences, the company did English landowners as cartoons, sang folksongs and spoke Gaelic, and showed their own real feelings about the political issues.

The theatrical project of explaining public events usually involved mobilising private emotions. Often it did so with an abrasively sardonic view of the time in which the audience lives. Thus Howard Brenton and David Hare's *Brassneck* (1973) ends with a wealthy social gathering. The entertainment is a strip show which comes to an end with the stripper shooting up and then raising the heroin hypodermic in a form of salute – to a new source of profit for the ruling class. When the audience toasts the 'last days' of capitalism, the gesture might have been recognised by some other inhabitants of a UK that is organised by the routines of consumption and drug-dealing, a world where the body is also viewed as an object for sex. In Mark Ravenhill's *Shopping and Fucking* (1996) the action relentlessly insists on the brutality, greed and dehumanisation that constitute contemporary life. Just over twenty years apart, the plays agree on their image of the modern UK.

But *Brassneck*, looking forward shockingly, predicts the growth of drug-dealing as a planned diversification by a class whose sources of wealth are drying up. The staging works like a polemical argument, and is pleasurable because of that. The last scene is set in a plush strip club, with a flashing sign saying 'The Lower Depths Club'. The stripper discards mayoral then masonic robes. After the toast the whole lot descends. This labelling is a deliberate part of the texture of the play, and its politics. The stage is felt to be occupied by people who are distanced. Their toast to capitalism salutes one system among others – with the clear implication that an opposed system, say socialism, would be less violent and more fully human. The mid-nineties world of *Shopping and Fucking* works similarly, for the stage is also made to glisten, now like a shop window, even while human interaction is shot through with illness and violence. Here, though, capitalism is not a system promulgated by one class but is all-pervasive.

Where the two plays differ most noticeably is that *Brassneck* offers its closing image as the outcome of a particular historical process. At its start, in 1945, there is the destitute Alfred Bagley. Then scene by scene his acquisition of wealth and power is shown, the staging points, as it were, of a history. It was a dramatic method that came to characterise a decade of plays. Not all were structured as a forward movement. Howard Brenton's *Churchill Play* (1974) is set in a concentration camp ten years in the future, but, through its play-within-the-play, it reaches back, again, to World War II's myths of heroism. If for Osborne's Jimmy Porter the Spanish Civil War of the mid-thirties was a crucial focus, the next generation of fictions looked back to the ideals of nation of the world war period, in order to unpick them.

These chronicle plays, with their effort to describe, and explain the causes of, contemporary life in England are generally known as 'state-of-the-nation' plays. The characteristic tone is cynical, the plays confront their art-theatre audience with the demolition of liberal middle ground. A favourite character is the man who rejects a socialist parent, or the NCO who has contempt as much for the officer class above him as the enemy. It is as if the voice of the small-shopkeeping class, wise to the failures of socialism, has arrived to speak for England – as indeed she did in the person of Margaret Thatcher.

By the 1990s, however cynical and prescient their vision, state-of-the-nation plays were regarded as outmoded. Their attempt to chronicle social change was seen as naïve. For the more fashionable intellectual position now espoused a belief in relativism. Through a selective attention to the work of such philosophers as Foucault and Lyotard, a generation of students thought that they learnt that power was constituted not as a monolith but as a set of micro-negotiations and that attempts to make sense of society through overarching grand narratives were misleading. The explanatory interlocking of private behaviours and larger social changes was associated with unfashionable philosophies such as Marxism, now proved ineffectual by the overthrow of Communist regimes in Eastern Europe. State-of-the-nation dramaturgy no longer seemed credible.

While the political issues themselves remain very similar – the sense of a competitive, greedy, sexploitative, racist society – the instrument for thinking about them changed. For part of the work of the dramaturgy is not so much to imitate the feeling of life in the modern UK as to demonstrate an awareness of how properly to think about this life. Let's look at two plays which deal with racism and Fascism.

David Edgar's *Destiny* (1976) sought to explain the contemporary growth of Fascism. Beginning in 1947, in India, with the ending of British rule, it tracks forward to 1970, following three figures, a Colonel, Major Rolfe and Sergeant Turner. Each confronts a UK that is changed: rougher, more depressed, more directionless. The Colonel simply dies, taking with him his form of wealthy gentle conservatism. Rolfe embraces a Fascist contempt for both the wealthy complacence and the national decline, and ends up in the City of London. Turner, running a small shop, is the figure who gets most attention, in that the play argues that his class is most susceptible to the Fascist message. Using the vehicle of an election in the west midlands the play makes its characters illustrate the range of causes which lead people to support or reject Fascism. As Edgar acknowledged, he was more or less writing from a diagram of social types. This is particularly apparent in the right-wing political meeting depicted in Act 2, where, as each character speaks, another position is demonstrated.

With this way of writing about British Fascism we can compare Roy Williams's 2002 play *Sing Yer Heart Out for the Lads*. It is set entirely in a south-west London pub during an England–Germany football game, which is on the television. Most of the characters are male, and involved with the pub football team. They are mixed in terms of race and age, but their social class is similar. The play's crisis develops from a revelation by the landlady's son that he has had his mobile phone stolen. This develops into a confrontation which shapes itself along racial lines. While a crowd gathers outside the pub, some of the lads inside remain glued to the match. The stage image can be interpreted as a sardonic reflection on the effect of television as distraction away from threatening social issues.

But the football match enables a consideration of the matter of race and identity. One of the black lads distances himself from his brother by joining in with the racist abuse of the German team. The shifting to and fro of loyalties and prejudice is sustained by the mode of writing, which is not broken into formal scenes and which follows the apparently haphazard rhythms of conversation, punctuated both by the televised match and by irruptions from outside. Conceived in this way the play moves forward not so much as an action but as reaction to stimulus from elsewhere. Politics is not defined in terms of elections but as a set of personal positions in relation largely to race. Yet, despite this, Williams's play is not so far removed from Edgar's. Each play demolishes the possibility of a liberal middle way, and the pub has its own ideologue, Alan, a racist with an articulate version of English history. As much as any character in the 'explaining' plays of the seventies, Alan offers a perspective on the state of the nation.

But the dramaturgy feels very different. Edgar's long scene of a political meeting is typical of its period. Meeting scenes were a favourite of seventies' political drama because they could open the play out to an audience in a way which felt both involving and risky. At the same time they could be used somewhat schematically to illustrate positions. And alongside the explanation there is also an attempt to mobilise emotion – *Destiny* has a famous scene in which at a normal-looking party Hitler's portrait is suddenly uncovered and the partygoers' clothing is transformed into uniform. *Sing Yer Heart* conspicuously avoids big effects – its scene of a stabbing is sudden and unmotivated. Its typically nineties dramaturgy has the conversation, and especially the anecdote, replacing the scenic unit. And the conversation is layered, cutting together the responses to the match with dialogue elsewhere in the pub. That layering is focused by the favourite nineties stage prop, the mobile phone, which enables a character to be concentrating on and talking into two different spaces at the same time, not being fully present for any one audience. It's a mode of writing which not only apparently imitates the texture of fast, shapeless lives but also refuses to give a sense of the author shaping scenes to pursue an argument. And it can therefore appear 'unpolitical'.

But the idea of the 'political' here is tied up with the state-of-the-nation play, an effect of its dramaturgy – what could be called a quality of politicality. But this quality does not guarantee that the play will work politically on its audience: Peter Womack notes that the schematic nature of *Destiny* makes it like an illustrated talk, so 'depoliticizing the theatrical occasion'.[2] A different sort of political play may well thus aim to appear 'unpolitical'.

State-of-the-nation plays, then, sought to produce an understanding which demolished cosy myths of England. They did so in a way which announced that they were seriously political: they generated politicality. Nineties plays disavow politicality while still being caught into the same sense of what contemporary life feels like. Instead, they enact the non-viability of being 'political'. But the generation of politicality, or its denial, does not itself guarantee that the play works in a politically productive way on its audience . . . nor on the company that puts the play on.

II

Bradford, July 1975. On stage a show about industrial politics by David Edgar. Suddenly one of the performers stops performing and goes on strike, announcing that as a gay man he has suffered harassment from his co-workers. Taking control over the text of the show, the actor enables a hitherto silenced voice to be heard.

This action was characteristic of its time, firstly in that it accused those who assumed their control over the political agenda and its artworks of perpetrating a heterosexual male regime. Secondly, when the actor interferes with the script artistic control is moved from the author to those who make the show. And following from this action, thirdly, attention is drawn to those in whose name the show is made. To concentrate on playwrights alone, as this chapter has done

[2] Peter Womack, 'Post-War Theatre and the State', in Simon Shepherd and Peter Womack, *English Drama: A Cultural History* (Oxford: Blackwell, 1996), p. 321.

so far, is to take a political position in that much of the dramatic production of the last three decades regarded itself as political because of its mode of work. That mode of work broadened the creative base, effacing distinctions between writers, designers and actors – and indeed administrators and stage managers. The individual author is replaced by a creative company, even a collective. And to the extent that a company seeks to express the concerns of a defined group (working-class women, say, or tenants in Salford), the author is not so much replaced by, but becomes a mouthpiece for, a community.

For a decade or so from the mid-1970s political theatre tended to be associated with the names of companies rather than writers. The tensions made themselves felt in such episodes as that when the female members of 7:84 accused the company's main author, John McGrath, of prejudice against women, and did so in the letters page of a feminist magazine. Political theatre companies opposed themselves to a theatre world that was organised around profiteering and perpetuated a value system centred on heterosexual white males, whether it was the West End or subsidised regional rep. These companies lived by touring, necessarily, but touring was also a political imperative. John McGrath outlines this most famously in his book *A Good Night Out* (1981), which celebrates both the effectiveness and dynamism of a form of theatre that takes itself to communities whose values, and entertainments, differ from those of middle-class theatre audiences.

The touring company linked up communities who were geographically disparate but socially similar. North West Spanner devised its shows in relation to the urban problems of Lancashire but then played to other urban working-class audiences. When an audience is able to recognise its life in the story of another's it is enabled to develop a broader perspective, seeing itself not just as isolated victims but as a class. By the same logic audiences also became addressed as a race or sex. The company's address to its audience was given authority because the company members demonstrably shared the race and sex of the audience: Black Theatre Co-op, Temba and Tara Arts emerged from and played to black and Asian audiences; feminist groups such as the Women's Theatre Group would habitually insist on the community of audience with performers by playing women-only gigs. The politics of these companies were less evident in aesthetic innovation than in the wresting of creative control from white males. For the Women's Playhouse Trust in 1984 the important work was to revive a play by the 1690s playwright Aphra Behn; meanwhile the more innovatory antics of the women's clowning group, Cunning Stunts, were dismissed by a (female) regional arts officer as 'finger up the nose humour'.

Most of these companies were generically referred to as 'political theatre' groups. But in the late seventies that adjective was having its meaning contested. Feminists argued that the 'personal is political' and from here logically followed a refusal of the politics of parliamentary parties and formal institutions, to concentrate on the lives and causes of the minoritised, the grass roots, the thing that could be defined against dominant groups as 'community'. In the early eighties much political work in the theatre was focused on the creation, paradoxically, of 'non-political' community plays. Ann Jellicoe walked out of success in the London theatre to set up the Colway Theatre Trust in Dorset in 1979. For Jellicoe community was geographically defined. The participation in an artwork, she felt, especially for people facing change, enabled a 'spiritual' transformation. Dramatic effectiveness has less to do with images made than with their mode of production. The show involves a large number, across a wide age-range, interacting with an audience either known to them or treated as if known to them. Its work is to produce a sense of inclusivity, showing how many are involved, offering points for recognition, making a coherent entity of something that is otherwise amorphous and threatened by outside forces.

Jellicoe's sort of play was, however, criticised for masking the differences in power and wealth that actually existed. Graham Woodruff, in 1989, opposed against geographical community two different entities: community of interest and the working class as agent of change. Abstract debates about the definition of 'community' were underpinned by the more concrete, and therefore graspable, practices with which a company interacted with a community. The touring show relied upon local organisers providing the venue and, through local networks, the audience: the 'community' becomes apparent in these arrangements. John McGrath describes the importance of villagers helping the company to unpack the touring van. Steve Gooch tells how he was smuggled into the Dagenham car plant by trade unionists in order to research *The Motor Show*.

In Jellicoe's work the town becomes the company that mounts a show; in McGrath's work the show is already rehearsed by the company before the van is unpacked in the village. At issue is the difference between the company as an entity indistinguishable from a community and as an entity that galvanises the community into a consciousness of itself. It was the active negotiation of this issue which led to innovations in aesthetic form and developments in the role of the company. Based in Birmingham, Banner Theatre of Actuality made shows commissioned by trade unions. Their mode of work in, say, *Dr Healey's Casebook* (1977), which was done for the National Union of Public Employees, was to interview those in poorly paid jobs, such as school dinner-ladies, and to take their photographs. The performers then delivered an edited version of this text, against a projection of its real speaker. The performance makes present, without subsuming, the particularity of those whose voice is all too often not heard. In *Healey* this reality was further underlined by playing civil servants and Healey himself (then Chancellor of the Exchequer) as cartoon figures.

In a show by Welfare State International the dinner-lady might end up playing a part, or at least making something and processing. The company set up community projects in relation to a performance, famously involving about 10,000 people in various organisations in making, and then processing with, lanterns in *Glasgow All Lit Up!* (1990). This mode of work claims to encourage expression of the creativity, the dreams and desires, of the participants, in all their various forms. The display of the extent and variety of people's involvement is a large part of the show's power, offering the feeling of a genuinely communal image in a society where such images have become empty and false.

At the opposite pole, perhaps, Forced Entertainment see no community, staging instead only the disintegrated, a 'scrappy urban collective unconscious'[3]. This sense of the incomplete and provisional dictated their aesthetic. Company collaboration meant that theatre was defined as 'a space in which different visions, different sensibilities, different intentions could collide.'[4] But the company also described their work as deeply political – indeed it was precisely by engaging with the 'fractured ambiguous landscape' of the eighties and nineties that the work could break from what had hitherto been described as political theatre. Politics for them was in playing between 'real and phantasmatic, between the actual landscape and the media one'.[5] This need to engage with lives always irredeemably mediated became a dominant influence on many companies in the late eighties and nineties. Blast Theory explore political and ethical issues by creating environments in which audiences are moved around spaces, interrogated, interact with live and recorded video images. Mixed-reality and 'inhabited television' projects don't simply stage relations with media but with that entity referred to as 'the public'.

For Forced Entertainment in 1984–5, in Sheffield, the televised reports of the miners' strike seemed more real, they said, than the events they had seen earlier in the city. This is a rather different relation between theatre and trade union

[3] Tim Etchells, *Certain Fragments* (London: Routledge, 1999), p. 53.
[4] Ibid., p. 55. [5] Ibid., p. 19.

activism than that of Banner Theatre. Banner worked to stage the particular presence of the dinner-lady, Forced Entertainment staged their inability fully to realise that presence. For Banner the politics resided in the union's struggle for higher wages, for Forced Entertainment the politics resides in how they know their relationship to that struggle. One of the most successful groups of the nineties could be said to be replaying the melancholy but necessary truth that their company is not a community.

III

The differences between community dramas and other sorts of theatre were listed schematically by Baz Kershaw in 1983: democratic/hierarchic; celebration/presentation; ensemble/hire and fire; local/national and so on. Eugene van Erven similarly defines 'radical popular theatre': creates plays collectively, seeks non-theatre audiences, regards plays as non-permanent and so on . . . The chart that maps the differences between modes of theatre has a history, going back to Brecht's comparison of Dramatic and Epic theatres. In 1989 Howard Barker used a similar list to define 'Theatre of Catastrophe' against Humanist Theatre: 'art must be understood'/ 'art is a problem of understanding'; 'we celebrate our unity'/ 'we quarrel to love'; 'message is important'/ 'the play is important' and so on. These lists tend not to be retrospective summaries. Instead, they accompany emerging forms, and are one of the means by which a new form defines itself, marking its difference from the old, the dominant, the conservative. Mapping difference in this way has a polemical edge to it.

More often the formal contrasts presented by lists are mapped over time, presented as 'history'. In the *TLS* piece with which this chapter opened, Edgar spoke of a generation of playwrights, active in the 1970s, who shared a belief that the job of theatre was to analyse society's rottenness. By 1991, Gillian Hanna, of the feminist company Monstrous Regiment, referred to the 'political theatre movement' as dead. At the end of the century the director James Macdonald attacked the assumed superiority of those seventies' plays, with their state-of-the-nation speeches and their 'signposts indicating meaning'.[6]

The nineties had seen the arrival of new young playwrights, whose plays often prompted outraged reviews. But that outrage was itself the evidence which testified to the genuine novelty of this new voice. While a well-established

6 Quoted in Graham Saunders, *'Love Me or Kill Me': Sarah Kane and the Theatre of Extremes* (Manchester University Press, 2002), p. 9.

dramatist such as Harold Pinter was becoming more explicitly political in his pronouncements, his plays were nevertheless trapped into his established mode, decorously theatrical. It was the new voices, whatever their politics, that were associated with outrage. Once again, as in the days of Bond's *Saved* or Brenton's *Romans in Britain*, plays seemed to have an impact that went beyond the reviews pages. One of the favourite words applied to them was 'visceral', usually supported by journalists' accounts of their personal responses to images of brutalised sexual contact or bodily harm. This critical technique has the effect of placing the journalist not simply as a spectator, at the event, but as one whose own language becomes violent and personalised – a participant in the viscerality, a witness to the emergence of new 'brutalism', 'in-yer-face theatre'.

The difference between in-yer-face and state-of-the-nation is not, however, thoroughly clear. There are similar images of a national culture, similar analyses. Furthermore, it is difficult to see how the plays of, say, Anthony Neilson are any more new than the work of Blast Theory. But the theatre needed, perhaps, to find its equivalent of what the British art scene had already found in the early nineties – not so much a new art as new personalities, with highly marketable youth, bad habits and naïveté. And now, with an attendant apparatus which ensured the smooth transition of the outrageous into the ownable, outrage itself becomes quotation as journalism replays the sort of scandal that greeted *Saved*, for example, in 1965. But while similar concerns appear in plays, while even a 1980s concern with the impact of the media repeats the early sixties, the discourse by which we might make sense of this material – in journalism, commentary, criticism – has itself become more attuned to novelty and change, more fixated on mapping difference, rushing to invent new labels.

Mark Ravenhill's Robbie in *Shopping and Fucking* says, 'a long time ago there were big stories . . . But they all died . . . so now we're all making up our own stories.'[7] The line invokes J. F. Lyotard and his famous critique of grand narratives, those attempts to provide overarching explanations of fractured societies. But it also echoes one of the famous lines of Osborne's Jimmy Porter, similarly facing a world which was pointless, fatigued, ruthless. In echoing the line Ravenhill jokily aligns himself with another shockingly 'new' playwright, Osborne. But the repetition also suggests that there may still be a grand story to be told, of youth alienated in the commodity culture of capitalism. That textual nuance was, however, overlooked by most reviewers, who

[7] Mark Ravenhill, *Shopping and Fucking*, in *Plays: 1* (London: Methuen, 2001), p. 66.

instead concentrated on a moment which more adequately embodied the new viscerality. When Lulu auditions for a job in an ad agency she has to uncover her breasts and recite Chekhov. The image neatly suggests a polemical relationship between 'new' nineties drama and the values traditionally associated with a well-covered Chekhov. But it also suggests, more cynically, the trivialising of theatre writing in a world culturally dominated by advertising. That cynicism would have been recognised by any of the young dramatists of the seventies.

While the contrast between state-of-the-nation and nineties 'new' plays is thus perhaps more polemical than real, there is another contrast which has mapped theatrical politics and value. That contrast has already shaped this chapter. It is the one that emerges from the touring theatre of the late seventies and early eighties. As we have seen, touring had a political value, reaching out to the communities who did not normally go to the theatre, employing not arty, elite or classical forms but popular ones, seeking to provide 'a good night out', or a version of what this might be.

There are two elements to the touring ethos: one is an attempt to draw on new sources for theatrical language – the folk songs and stand-up routines of a culture associated with the popular; the other is a hostility to custom-built theatres which were seen as the property of the middle class, inhibiting in their very architecture the possibilities of radical theatre-making and interpretation – a view which persists into Baz Kershaw's eloquent *The Radical in Performance* (1999). The roots of that hostility go deep into the nineteenth century's marginalisation of artisan spectators. The 'happenings' of the sixties, Growtowski's 'poor' theatre and Brook's 'rough theatre' all reinforced the idea that high production values in traditional spaces would only produce inauthenticity. That same hostility characterises the emergence of what has variously been called Live Art, Performance Art and, more neatly, Performance. The form, emerging into pre-eminence in the seventies, looks back to visual art practices rather than theatrical ones, and foregrounds work in installations, non-theatrical spaces and site-specific events, such as a show under the M6 'spaghetti junction'. Set against theatre – even the visceral sort – performance is now often seen, polemically, as the only form which can break free of the compromises and conservatism that entrap theatre practice.

In tracing through these sets of contrasts we find that the phrase 'theatre and politics' can refer not only to theatre's relation to political issues or social groups but also to its relation to its own practices. One form of theatre practice will define itself, or be defined, against another. That act of definition has political purpose. Further, the word 'political' has its own career mapped by these acts of definition. Those associated with the 'political theatre movement' tended to apply the label to themselves, so 'political' came to describe the forms they used, forms which generate a sense of being political, politicality. As such they comprise one phase of theatre production in the last three decades. The problem, however, is that for some adherents of 'political theatre' this was the only way of being political. At a 1988 conference addressing the 'Crisis' in British theatre one speaker attacked the younger generation for being strong on protest but having no 'language of analysis' – not writing explaining plays. A tussle over whether leftist drama could or should embrace the 'culture of the image' is symptomatic: mapping word against image, analysis against protest, leftism against anarchism, establishing a checklist of the properly political.

Meanwhile, Forced Entertainment had for several years been doing their 'deeply political' plays with both word and image, without either analysis or protest. And for the mid-nineties dramatists, 'political' was a word that appeared in the wrong place on the map, already used, already worn out. So a reaction sets in, not so much to the notion of being political, but to the claims of theatre to be able to speak authoritatively to and for others. What comes to be resented is the fullness of such theatre. Tim Etchells, of Forced Entertainment, speaks of loving the moment 'where theatre regrets itself and refuses to speak';[8] the bare-breasted Lulu doing Chekhov is theatre embarrassed for itself. The desire is to make a theatre that will persistently say that theatre should regret itself. Because perhaps someone once before knew how theatre should be 'political'.

IV

In the mortuary the hospital orderlies lift up the naked corpse of a young woman by her ankles and wrists. They swing her to and fro to make her breasts wobble. They accidentally drop her. She comes round, they talk to her, she dies. They wash the body in blood and lower it into a large dustbin. Then they bring on a naked male corpse, wash it in blood, put it in the bin, add pips and stir. They make jam.

A soldier turns the man over, holding a revolver to his head. Then, weeping, rapes him. Finished, he pushes his gun up the man's arse, then withdraws and reminisces about the horrors of war. He puts his mouth over one of the man's eyes, sucks it out, bites it off and eats it. He does the same with the other eye.

[8] Etchells, *Certain Fragments*, p. 79

Each play created a sensation in the press. One was commissioned by the Royal Court, but turned down; the other was premiered at the Royal Court Theatre Upstairs. One was published by a relatively small 'arty' house in one edition, the other by a well-known play publisher in several editions. Almost twenty-five years separates the two plays. The first, *Lay By*, was collectively authored and dates from 1971. The other, *Blasted*, by Sarah Kane is from 1995. In between these two scenes the political theatre movement came to prominence and then faded away. At least three of the authors of *Lay By* became key writers of political-theatre plays, then went on to write for film and television. State-of-the-nation plays are one way of being political, *Lay By* and *Blasted* are others.

Some audiences watching *Lay By* will have been able to track its stage methods back to shows of the previous decade, in particular Peter Brook's Theatre of Cruelty season in 1964, based on the work of Artaud. To link *Blasted* with *Lay By* is to construct a long tradition of Artaudian work. It's a tradition that makes itself felt just as much around the edges of dominant theatre work as in the radically emergent. In the former case, as Peter Womack argues, Peter Shaffer's plays show a nervous desire to contain, or tidy up, that which is too abrasively theatrical, too present.[9] In the latter case, Artaud is also there in a self-conscious attempt to create a new theatre model for the eighties. Howard Barker's Theatre of Catastrophe takes an audience into a space beyond what is already accommodated, the 'carnival mania of the left' and the 'moral crusade of the right'. Skinner, the elderly lesbian 'witch' of *The Castle* (1985), has the rotting body of the man she murdered fixed to her front. Suddenly Krak, architect of the patriarchal castle, representative of reason and measure, kneels in front of her: 'Where's cunt's geometry? The thing has got no angles!'[10] Skinner is about to be worshipped. The big, often contradictory images, the shouting, the calculated unreason all work, like Artaud's Cruelty, to overwhelm everyday norms.

Isolated within the longer Artaudian tradition, the 'political theatre movement' claimed influences from Brecht, and, with groups such as Broadside Mobile Workers' Theatre, roots in the Workers' Theatre Movement. This Brechtian heritage underpins another attempt to make a theatre model for the eighties, Edward Bond's Rational Theatre, with its 'theatre events'. These again put pressure on an audience, as incidents which must be examined for themselves, not subsumed into a story. By these means theatre can 'make physical and imagistic what is ordinarily mundane: the silent scream is more

[9] Womack, 'Post-War Theatre and the State'.

[10] Howard Barker, *The Castle*, in *Collected Plays: Volume 1* (London: John Calder, 1990), p. 241.

than just another scream'.[11] With his silent scream, however, Bond recalls us to earlier work such as *Lear*, which, in its complex and productively rich violence, its Cruelty, works to resist the everyday inhumanity of a mechanised society.[12]

These attempts to remodel theatre practice are clearly politically directed. There are, however, a number of formal experiments which could be taken as more characteristic of this period, and more innovatory.

Women from different historical periods speak together at dinner. A dead woman tells of what she can see, back through history, speaking to her living partner on the stage by her. A domestic dialogue begins, two gunmen come through the door and kill everybody, the dialogue starts from the top again. The stage space developed by Caryl Churchill through the eighties and nineties was one that was no longer governed by assumed laws of space and time. By contrast, verbal language proceeded according to rules and patterns which diverged from those of daily conversation. A Churchill script will indicate meticulous structures of interruption or develop a language of its own: 'it was all a glamour amour amorphous fuss about nothing'.[13] Language is not so much spoken by the characters as speaking them, pulling them into its own patterns and rhythms.

The movement into this sort of writing can be seen in work by Tom Stoppard. Coming out of the late 1960s, his plays seem to circle around philosophical propositions about, for example, chance, perception, ethics. The dialogue calls attention to its own writtenness, with its wordplay, games, allusions and repetitions. This quality sets it apart from both the deliberately banal dialogue of stage realism and the apparently non-scripted Happenings of the preceding period. With characters who seem to be caught up into verbal structures, Stoppard's writing had clearly learnt from Beckett, and gone a step further. In *Travesties* (1974) the Dada poet Tristan Tzara first enters as a stereotypical Rumanian, and then re-enters as a more understated version; the author James Joyce conducts a whole scene in limericks. The pretext for these tricks is that we are watching the events as remembered by the central character. Remembered episodes, and realities, begin to blur together. The dialogue gets tangled up with the text of Wilde's *Importance of Being Earnest*, in which the central character appeared in his youth.

Described in this way Stoppard's work hardly seems to be 'political' as, say, state-of-the-nation plays are. But it can nevertheless be described as having

[11] Edward Bond quoted in *New Theatre Quarterly*, 1991.

[12] See Simon Shepherd, 'Drama in the Age of Television', in Shepherd and Womack, *English Drama: A Cultural History*, p. 372.

[13] Caryl Churchill, *The Skriker*, in *Plays: 3* (London: Nick Hern Books, 1998), p. 245.

a political effect. In the seventies Stoppard was famous for a personally articulated opposition to totalitarian Communism (as seen in his realist television play *Professional Foul* 1977). His stage plays make clear the position from which this opposition comes. In among the pastiche and verbal games of *Travesties* there is a narrative of the Russian Revolution of 1917: alongside the artistic revolutionaries Tzara and Joyce in Zurich is the social revolutionary Lenin. But the narrative of the social revolution comes to have the same status as all the other verbal tricks. While we could say that the 'totalitarian' heroics are thus undercut, we could also say that all realities are reduced to the same level and that the only clear position is an overarching literary knowingness. Assuming an ability to recognise literary allusions, this sort of writing can be seen as a reaction against the more democratised art of the early seventies. It panders to, and reproduces, cultural elitism.

The enjoyment is assisted by, early on, putting the verbal tricksiness within a secure framework for the spectator. At one point the dialogue keeps returning to the same two-line exchange. Stoppard wants the punctuations of these 'time slips' to be marked by light or sound, so that it is clear what is going on. With this effect we can contrast Caryl Churchill's *Heart's Desire* (1997). Three characters expect the arrival of their daughter/niece. As they talk, their dialogue keeps returning to the top and repeating itself. It is as if it tries out possible developments and then rejects them. These possibilities range from the colour of a garment to improbable entries through the door – murderous gunmen or a ten-foot bird. Gradually, through stopping and starting, the dialogue finds a satisfactory shape for itself as it approaches the moment of the daughter's arrival. But as it goes through its meticulously precise repetitions we also become aware of all the other possibilities, the rejected drafts, the wildly improbable directions that could, perhaps, be taken. What is being staged is not so much the characters' emotions about the arrival but the business of arriving at a satisfyingly complete 'realist' text. This too, however, is an impossibility. Because in establishing itself the text shows what has been rejected, what the stage is also capable of imagining. There is no point of secure arrival. Just as the daughter arrives and the father claims he now has his heart's desire, the whole play starts again from the top. And at the point he tries to say the line again, the play stops, starts again and ends.

So while Stoppard positions us securely to enjoy a highly worked literary text, Churchill explores the desire for completeness, with its fetishism of precise repetition and copying. She shows a desire for wholeness and 'arrival' which excludes play, metaphor and the improbable and unnecessary. This kind of dramatic writing is political insofar as it offers to explore and critique an audience's assumed relationship with the medium of drama and especially realist drama. But it is important to note that it can only offer to do this. Audiences can refuse such critique. In an earlier play Churchill had experienced that refusal. *Serious Money* (1987) is set among the dealers and bankers of the City of London. As a way of imaging the aggressive brilliance and speediness of this world, the play is written in rhyming couplets. Arguably this device also shows how enclosed this world is, how artificial and stagy, and so it can function as critique. But in performance in London whole rows of the auditorium were booked by City dealers and corporate hospitality. For the nominal subjects of the play their world had been appropriately glamorised by the savage verbal trickery.

From this ambivalent example let's look further at experiments with words on stage. Words can establish a reality that apparently supersedes, and renders illusory, other physical realities – the sex of a body, the dimensions of a space. Within the domain of storytelling this is common. But in the work of Noel Greig this is the convention of the show. A Greig script such as *Plague of Innocence* (1988) presents simply as a column of lines down the page. This form was developed by Greig in the face of debilitating cuts in support for touring theatre, so the text could be done by a solo performer if need be. When a group engages with it one of the techniques for distributing the voices is to invite performers to speak the lines that attract them. In this way the performers voluntarily take up with regard to the text a position based at deepest on their own desires.

Similar on the page is the appearance of Sarah Kane's *Crave* (1998). It has four nominal persons, but the text is so written that its implications will change according to the relationship between the voices. The link between written text and staged one is very open, with the written occasionally demanding impossible effects – such as live rats carrying away human feet (in *Cleansed*). This polemical – or poetic – challenge to staging is reminiscent of the German playwright Heiner Müller. With his work, too, Kane shares her method of making provisional what is spoken by a performer. One performer may inhabit several characterisations – and vice versa. Lines are thus not delivered by a coherent entity, like a character, but by something that can be called a 'speaking position', a voice which is not fixed in its relation to narrative or other voices.

These formal experiments have in common, first of all, an insistence that the stage is a place where impossible things concretely take place. And they need to do so, in order to make connections which are not otherwise available. Kane famously insisted on the interconnection between the rape in a Leeds hotel room and the war in Bosnia. When one of Churchill's agricultural labourers irons the ploughed field, woman's domestic labour, the conditions of her livelihood, and its history, merge. There is a politics to these impossible, metaphoric, images. So, too, there is to the language and its speaking. Within the fiction there might be an image of characters caught into the rhythms of language, its assumptions, its habits of operation – like an ideological machine. And within the production process there is a possible sense of collectivity, ownership, choice in relation to the spoken.

That sense of ownership in relation to the spoken takes us into a different area of innovation. In *The Fears and Miseries of Nixon's Reich* (1974) one performer 'pretends to be Nixon, pretending first to be Marilyn Monroe, then Tony Curtis' – while remaining himself.[14] For the director of this show, Albert Hunt, at the heart of theatre is not imitation or message but contradiction, between, for example, 'the real performer, physically *there*, and the parts he said he was playing'.[15] The theatre is serious, politically so, precisely because it is impossible, metaphoric, play-full. In 1991 the gay male drag company Bloolips collaborated with the lesbian company Split Britches to rework the film of Tennessee Williams's classic play, *A Streetcar Named Desire*, with its archetypally presented gender roles (Marlon Brando playing Stanley). The show was called *Belle Reprieve*. As a project it connects with and pushes further some of the issues we have noted before: the company collaboration rather than single author, the intervention into how communities were defining themselves (in the wake of lesbian 'separatism'), the reappraisal of a classic play in the light of new political interests, the opening up of realism to pastiche, metaphor and play. At one moment Lois Weaver, playing Stella, talks alone to the audience. Presenting as feminine and blonde, she describes Cassandra, the prophetess of ancient Troy who was destined never to be believed; and then she imagines herself as one of the soldiers in the wooden horse, in love with the 'blonde' Cassandra. Speaking as this soldier, feeling Cassandra's hands on her breasts, she is both male and female: 'Somebody stole my woman . . . filched her from history, and I'm here to get her back. I am a powerful warrior.' As she speaks she reveals a tight, strapless dress and begins to pose like Marilyn Monroe: 'I'm in here. Can't you see me? I'm having sex with the fortune teller that men don't believe.'[16] Stella, the lesbian performer, the mythic Cassandra, a Greek warrior in a horse and the 'sex object' Marilyn Monroe are all fused together. Characterisation is replaced by a multiple identity. The celebration of lesbian desire is simultaneously an act of political reclamation. Marilyn Monroe is

[14] Albert Hunt, *Hopes for Great Happenings* (London: Eyre Methuen, 1976), p. 101.
[15] Ibid., p. 103.
[16] Bette Bourne, Paul Shaw, Peggy Shaw, Lois Weaver, *Belle Reprieve: A Collaboration*, in Sue-Ellen Case, ed., *Split Britches* London: Routledge, 1996, p. 160.

re-inhabited but is no less sexy. This relationship with the audience is not that of instruction or cruelty.

In its most innovatory moments the theatre invited the audience into the space of play – which is impossible, contradictory and deeply desiring. And these moments were thoroughly political, where the business of politics is not separable from the working of desire.

36

Irish literature: tradition and modernity

RONAN McDONALD

Lamenting the erosion of traditional values, a disillusioned Irish politician is reputed to have complained that there was no sex in Ireland before television. The national television service was inaugurated in 1962. So, assuming that Philip Larkin was right in dating the beginning of sexual intercourse to 1963, sex came to Ireland a full year before it reached the United Kingdom. Sex was only one of the foreign arrivals that came to Ireland during the sixties. Under the expansionist polices of Taoiseach Sean Lemass and his economic adviser T. K. Whitaker, the protectionist strategies of the de Valera era were reversed and an open economy fuelled by international markets and foreign investment was nurtured. The resulting economic growth checked the emigration and unemployment of the forties and fifties, while the cities and towns of Ireland burgeoned around the new factories. Outside Belfast, Ireland had never really had an industrial revolution and the overwhelmingly rural nature of Irish life, when enlisted by nationalist ideology, often emerged as a pastoral ideal, with images of mystic landscapes and cosy homesteads. In literary terms, however, from Patrick Kavanagh's *The Great Hunger* (1942) to (perhaps belatedly) Martin McDonagh's *The Leenane Trilogy* (1995–7), it became a very familiar manoeuvre to debunk this ideal, and to depict repressive, materially impoverished communities, starved of meaningful spiritual and emotional sustenance. In 1971, though, for the first time in its history, more Irish people were living in towns than in the countryside.[1] Sooner or later, a crucial aspect of the Irish self-image would need fundamental reassessment.

The 1990s would see another economic boom, fuelled in part by the tax-breaks afforded to multinational companies and high-tech industry. As with the recent rise in fortunes, economic change in the Ireland of the sixties was quickly read in terms of a broader narrative, an outward sign of a fundamental change in the values and direction of the nation. At the same time, the impact

[1] Declan Kiberd, *Inventing Ireland* (London: Jonathan Cape, 1995), p. 567.

of other, well-rehearsed cultural and social transformations also came to Irish shores: the revolutions in technology, mass communications and travel, the rise of a specifically 'youth' culture, the increased availability of secondary and tertiary-level education, the impact of the second Vatican council on the Catholic Church, and so on. The idea that Irish society was moving away from insular, 'backward-looking' nationalism towards a new internationalist order became ever more dominant among media commentators. Sometimes, however, this has led to reductive, Manichean views of the transformations in Irish society, inadequate to complex realities. Deep-rooted problems in Irish life, such as those that led to the eruption of violence in the North, are explained away as a sign that certain sections of the country have insufficiently 'modernised'. Irish society came to be analysed in terms of a 'two-civilisation' model, between modernisers and traditionalists, the metropolitan East and the rural West or, as one commentator acidly put it, between 'nice people' and 'rednecks'.[2]

The best literature of the last thirty years has, unlike the worst journalism, troubled and confounded these binary social graphs. Along with the obligation to express the changes in Irish society, creative writing has also had to negotiate its own shifting relationships with state authority. With the new liberalism of the sixties, there were signs that the grip of censorship, for years a bane for serious Irish writers, was weakening, though it lingered long enough to affect the early careers of some of Ireland's best-known novelists. If sex came to Ireland in 1962, it had an early muse in Edna O'Brien, originally from rural Clare, and an active and often controversial novelist and short-story writer to the present day. Her early trilogy, *Country Girls* (1960), *The Girl with Green Eyes* (first published as *The Lonely Girl* in 1962) and *Girls in their Married Bliss* (1963), depicts the sexual discovery of young girls, and often their victimisation, by older and more experienced men, as they move from rural Ireland to Dublin and on to London. Narrating stories of adolescent female sexuality in conflict with a patriarchal Church and society, O'Brien's novels were promptly banned in Ireland. However, as well as being chronicles of the clash between youthful self-assertion and conservative authority, these novels also became arenas for that same clash.

Television and a new mass media gave a platform for liberal voices to argue against censorship in cases like that of O'Brien and of John McGahern, who lost his teaching job in 1965 when his novel *The Dark*, a story of troubled male

[2] Desmond Fennell, *Nice People and Rednecks: Ireland in the 1980s* (Dublin: Gill & Macmillan, 1986).

adolescence, was banned by the Irish Censorship Board. In the furore that followed, McGahern left the country, not to return for a decade. McGahern now enjoys the status of one of Ireland's leading novelists. Garlanded with literary awards and esteemed by critics, his novels are written in a meditative, intense, descriptive style and are mostly set in the rural County Longford of his upbringing. Given his early clash with authority, McGahern has avoided the cliché of the aging iconoclast: indeed, though he has charted the social changes in Ireland over his writing career, he has also revealed just how jaded the contrast between 'retarded tradition' and 'progressive modernity' has actually become. Never more so, perhaps, than in his novel *That They May Face the Rising Sun* (2002). The organic rhythms of the seasons and of farm life that dominate the story might indicate that, like the Ruttledges, who have returned from London in search of a quieter life, the novel nestles in the reassurance of rural continuity. But rather than enacting a callow evasion of history and politics, the novel intermixes psychological and social complexities. If McGahern's work excels at characterisation, it does not reduce context to mere 'background' but rather demonstrates the formation and deformation of social subjects by the forces of history.

Since realist fiction tends to foreground character and individual agency, it has sometimes been accused of inadequately engaging with politics and history. It gets so close to character and domestic life that the wider social forces in the formation of family and the individual supposedly fall out of focus. Another of Ireland's leading fiction writers who, like McGahern, tends to confound this notion is William Trevor. Perhaps it is not coincidental that both writers are masters of the short story, which relies on the wry sidelong look, the unstated and suggested more than the elaborately articulated. The short story has long thrived in Irish soil. Other leading practitioners (who have also published novels) include Bryan MacMahon, Mary Lavin, Benedict Kiely and, more recently, Julia O'Faoláin, Bernard MacLaverty and Colum MacCann. Trevor himself was born to a southern Protestant family in County Cork but has lived in England for many years and has a devoted international readership. Much of his work (especially his early work) is set outside of Ireland. Indeed, one of his virtues is his range, and he depicts small-town Ireland and middle-class suburban England with equally deft and often devastating acuity and understatement. In Ireland, his best-known work includes 'The Ballroom of Romance' (the title story of a 1972 collection), a poignant tale of emotional disappointment and compromise set in the rural west. Many of Trevor's stories depict the anomie and claustrophobia of small-town, rural Ireland – an Ireland to which, by implication, the Lemass–Whitaker economic revolution did not come quickly enough, nor go far enough. However, he has reacted with notable imaginative engagement to the outbreak of the Troubles in the North, specifically in a series of historical novels and politically accented short stories during the eighties.

In 1967 the Minister for Justice introduced legislation providing for the unbanning of books after twelve years and thousands of titles were freed to enter the Irish market. Gradually, 'liberal' Ireland won the battle against the censors, one of its many victories, to the point in the eighties and nineties when writers were far more likely to be feted and paraded by politicians and officials than banned, a celebrity status which held its own dangers for creativity. Indeed, one of the most notable factors in studying Irish literature in the last thirty-five years of the twentieth century is the reconfiguration of the artist's relationship to the state, from one of dissent to one of incorporation. One of the ways that a state on a modernising stint handles the (previously potent) force of tradition is to repackage it as 'heritage' – a point not lost on the packaging of Ireland as the 'land of writers' by the Irish tourist board. That said, on many levels the increased support for artists in the seventies and eighties was welcome and beneficial. A very important factor, not just in the development of new talent but also in raising consciousness of a specifically Irish publishing industry, was the establishment of a number of new publishing houses, many assisted by Arts Council grants. Previously, most Irish writers had been published in the UK.

Even more than poetry and fiction, drama and the theatre has benefited from increased state assistance, not just to large Dublin theatres like the Abbey and the Gate, but also to smaller ventures in the capital and to regional theatre throughout the country. With some exceptions, theatre in Ireland in the forties and fifties had been in something of a moribund condition, but the sixties and seventies saw the emergence of such towering, innovative talents as Brian Friel, Tom Murphy and Thomas Kilroy, who brought a new vitality and urgency to the Irish stage. State subsidy must be a major factor in explaining this resurgence in drama, though, as we shall see, the pressure of the Northern problem also led to important, formally experimental theatre. There has been the discernment of a further dramatic renaissance in the 1990s, with the arrival of younger playwrights such as Sebastian Barry, Marina Carr, Conor McPherson and Martin McDonagh.

In 1969, Minister for Finance Charles J. Haughey introduced measures which relieved artists and writers from paying income tax on their work, a policy which made Ireland a haven for foreign writers of bestsellers as much as for indigenous literary talent. In 1983, the Arts Council established *Aosdána*

('People of the arts'), a self-electing body of writers, artists and musicians, each of whom would be offered a governmental stipend. The Irish state had come a long way from its policy of censoring all but the most biddable writers. To be sure these developments provided useful material support to writers, but in another sense the embrace of the writer by the state could be bewildering and disabling. It had become customary in independent Ireland for literature to go against establishment winds; now, when the direction of these winds had so decisively changed, it was difficult to know where to sail. At least when the state was repressive and Philistine, the writer's role was clear. Perhaps this may explain why so much Irish writing of the last thirty years of the century was set in the forties and fifties.[3] Lacking the possibility of an oppositional stance in contemporary Ireland, many writers and especially film-makers returned to a period when the target was clearly defined, and where tales of restive youth overcoming an authoritarian and repressive Church and state readily offered themselves. A sample of some prominent examples from the nineties might include Frank McCourt's *Angela's Ashes* (1996), Brian Friel's *Dancing at Lughnasa* (1990) and Patrick McCabe's *The Butcher Boy* (1992). Significantly, all three of these texts have been made into high-profile films, perhaps an indication of the international penchant for images of Ireland as a locus of belated modernity.

Another of the ways that many Irish novelists have sought to negotiate their situation in a rapidly changing Irish society is to eschew membership of a tradition, or indeed of the 'nation', altogether. Denied the stance of opposition, and brave, enlightened dissent, there have been many strong assertions of autonomy and individuality in recent writing from the Republic, an insistence on the privacy of experience and the avoidance of a political role. In the south novelists like Dermot Bolger and Colm Tóibín have sought to deploy this strategy, arguing for the autonomy of the artist and dismissive of the suffocating pressures on Irish writers to speak of or to the nation. This is also, in part, a response and a disavowal of the Northern Troubles. Bolger decries the obsession with the North and Irish nationalism, kicking against what he perceives as a tired mythology, with little to say about the lives of the working-class Dublin communities of which he writes. He insists on the rights and responsibilities of writers like himself to express the problems and experiences of a modern, urban Ireland, of concrete and dual carriageways. Roddy Doyle is another novelist of urban Dublin, more upbeat and comic, less dystopian than Bolger, especially in his 'Barrytown' trilogy of novels (1989–91).

[3] See Joe Cleary, 'Modernization and Aesthetic Ideology in Contemporary Irish Culture', in Ray Ryan, ed., *Writing in the Irish Republic: Literature, Culture, Politics 1949–99* (Basingstoke: Palgrave Macmillan, 2002), pp. 105–29.

This mode brought Doyle huge commercial success, but he reached for graver subject-matter in *The Woman who Walked into Doors* (1996), which deals with domestic violence, or in the first in a historical trilogy, *A Star Called Henry* (1999), dealing with the Anglo-Irish War. There is a high preponderance of dialogue in Doyle's novels and an insistent urbanism, with a soundtrack of popular music and culture – these are novels vibrantly aware of a 'new' Ireland with its porous cultural borders. Yet at the same time, Doyle's work sounds familiar notes. His witty, fast-talking, garrulous Dubliners evoke Sean O'Casey and Brendan Behan. Furthermore, there may be an inverted pastoralism in his images of working-class Dublin, a transfer of 'wildness', whereby the rough landscapes of the west of Ireland are replaced by the vandalised stairwells and ragged horses of urban Dublin.

Given that the position of dissent was not so readily available in a new Ireland, now that the state has so closely befriended the artist, it may not be insignificant that one of the great heroes of many of the younger generation was Francis Stuart, the last surviving member of the Irish Renaissance, who held as an artistic credo the duty of the writer to oppose all consensus and, like Christ, to expect dishonour and disgrace. Stuart's *Black List, Section H* (1971) was both a memoir of the Irish revival and a justification for the author's time in Nazi Germany, from where he broadcast radio programmes during World War II. An alternative to this dissent and dishonour (if only by proxy) is exile, deracination and monastic integrity. Enter Samuel Beckett. From his eyrie in Paris, the old master was still crafting his 'fizzles' and 'stirrings' well into the eighties. Indeed, in his later years Irish topography and landscape seemed to resurface in his imagination (if they had ever really been submerged) in elliptical, autobiographical pieces such as the prose work *Company* (1980) or the dramaticule *That Time* (1976). Beckett's presence in late twentieth-century Irish literature is not simply measurable in terms of his direct influence, considerable though this is. He also became a sort of a mythic figure, the last of the great Modernists, living out his final years in splendid reclusion. It is striking how well-known Beckett's face is and how little known his voice. That deeply scored face, with those penetrating blue eyes, became, as it were, an emblem of artistic integrity and existential bravery. Irish writers, variously facing the pressure of political crisis in the North and the disorientating clashes of tradition and modernity throughout the island, could look enviously at the magisterial independence of the figure who carried the flame for an earlier generation of artists who steadfastly refused to compromise.

Beckett is a presiding influence on the literature of Ireland since 1970, not just in drama and fiction but also in poetry, as the work of Richard Murphy and Derek Mahon amply demonstrates. However, just as the development of world theatre in the second half of the twentieth century would have been inconceivable without Beckett's revolutionary dramaturgy, Irish theatre bears the heaviest traces of his influence. For instance, the prevalence of monologue and storytelling in so much Irish drama in this period, the most notable example being Brian Friel's masterpiece *Faith Healer* (1979), carries a strong echo of Beckett's compulsive talkers. The talk and idle blather that recurs in contemporary Irish theatre, the storytelling and inconsequential dialogue, often deployed as a means to keep 'awareness' at bay, are techniques enduringly associated with Beckett. If Conor MacPherson's West End hit *The Weir* (1997) evokes Synge's pub-talkers, it also demonstrates these Beckettian tendencies. Similarly the physicality, grotesquerie and comic pairings of Martin MacDonagh's work is reminiscent of Estragon and Vladimir. The shadowy, ethereal figures of Beckett's later work are also observable in a number of Irish plays. Witness the haunted memories and ghostly invocations of Frank McGuinness's *Observe the Sons of Ulster Marching Towards the Somme* (1986) and Sebastian Barry's *Steward of Christendom* (1995), for instance. Little wonder, then, that one critic can declare that the 'presiding genius of contemporary Irish drama, the ghostly founding father, is Samuel Beckett'.[4]

Outside drama, the Beckettian inflection colours a particular strain of stylised, cosmopolitan Irish fiction which sits more easily in a Modernist than a realist tradition. 'Despair young and never look back' was Beckett's Polonius-like advice to a young Aidan Higgins.[5] He has also been a large influence on John Banville and the Irish-language novelists Máirtín Ó Cadhain and Alan Titley. Banville takes from Beckett an exquisite aesthetic sense, wrought into a minimal, even cold, style, and a penchant for psychologically damaged first-person narrators. Banville is a 'literary' novelist who enjoys high international esteem for these stylistic qualities. His novels have a strongly European, Mandarin and allusive quality, exemplified by his tetralogy dealing with European scientists and mathematicians from Copernicus to Kepler, which raises philosophical questions about linkages between the scientific and the literary imagination. Later novels have sometimes been loosely drawn from more recent history – such as a notorious Dublin murder in *The Book of Evidence* (1989) or the later life of Anthony Blunt, the Cambridge spy, in *The Untouchable* (1997). Typically Banville's novels are narrated by a protagonist who is cultivated and alienated, ruminating on complex forms of guilt and betrayal and haunted

4 Anthony Roche, *Contemporary Irish Drama: From Beckett to McGuinness* (Dublin: Gill & Macmillan, 1994), p. 6.

5 Anthony Cronin, *Samuel Beckett: The Last Modernist* (London: HarperCollins, 1996), p. 565.

by demons and doppelgangers. The setting of some of his novels evokes the Irish Big House (a venerable genre which has remained extant in Irish fiction), but Banville's work, with all its richly allusive textuality, demonstrates that 'European' and 'Irish' do not exist as mutually exclusive categories.

Generally speaking, poets have tended to blur the tradition/modernity opposition more than writers of fiction, often finding in the past resonances with the present (or vice versa) and recognising that 'progress' often comes at a price. One of the leading poets from the Republic of Ireland, Thomas Kinsella, could scarcely be accused of reactionary sentiments or of poetic provincialism. His poetic forefathers are Eliot and Auden and, with his interest in Jungian archetypes, he belongs very much to a Modernist lineage, which probes the crises of selfhood in contemporary society. Kinsella has had a long career and his poetic range is broad. However, he has offered notable critiques of the consumerism and capitalism in modern Irish life. He has also written poignantly about the loss of the Irish language and about the 'dual tradition' of Gaelic–Irish and Anglo-Irish in Ireland. He is painfully aware of the fissures and discontinuities of Irish history and, perhaps in a gesture of healing, has written highly regarded translations of old Irish poetry and myth such as *The Táin* (1969) and, with Seán Ó Tuama, *An Duanaire: Poems of the Dispossessed 1600–1900* (1981).

Translation, not just of Irish texts but of many European and classical plays and poems, has been one of the defining features of Irish writing in the last thirty years of the century. However, Irish-language writers have by no means reached consensus on how to greet translation to English. Nuala NíDhomhnail has reached an admiring English language audience through the translations of her poetry by other leading poets like Paul Muldoon and Ciaran Carson. However, 'Biddy Jenkinson', though highly regarded in Irish-language circles, has refused to allow her work to be translated, mistrustful of the inevitable loss inherent in the process. There are some who feel that a culture of translation reinforces the idea of Irish as a foreign language within Ireland. The gifted bilingual poet Michael Hartnett initially wrote English poetry and translations of Irish work but for many years after *A Farewell to English* (1975) dedicated himself to writing solely in Irish in an effort to embrace the language more seriously than the gesture of translation allows. To approach the range and richness of Irish language poetry since 1970 would need more scope than is afforded by this *History*, but would include Máire Mac an tSaoi, Seán O Ríordáin, Michael Davitt, Cathail O'Searcaigh and numerous others.

The outbreak of the Troubles in 1969 both undermined and reinforced the rush towards modernity in Ireland. In the Republic, it was an uncomfortable reminder that the history is a nightmare not as easily evaded as many of the Dublin liberal establishment would wish to believe. On the other hand, here was good reason to distance modern 'Ireland' from the past, from outmoded Romanticism and nationalism, and it may in part explain the disavowal of nationalism by writers such as Bolger and Tóibín. Ideas of liberalism, secularism and pluralism were at once punctured and inflated by the Troubles.

In the North it was different and the implications of political strife bore down with unavoidable urgency. While there have been hundreds of 'thrillers' about the troubles, many of dubious quality, there have also been some very notable achievements in fiction, such as Benedict Kiely's *Proxopera* (1977) or Bernard MacLaverty's *Cal* (1983), along with a wealth of short stories. However, the major literary engagements with the Troubles have been in the fields of drama and poetry. Within these forms, the creative dilemma has often been to avoid on the one hand an isolated, apolitical artiness and on the other a coarse agitprop. If there are pressures on playwrights and poets to address themselves to the 'situation', there is a corresponding need to develop techniques of refraction. In other words, distancing strategies are often developed that strive to present the Troubles and its various complexities in a fresh light. The central danger of all writing about the Troubles is the danger of cliché. If we see cliché as the tired use of language, a use that calcifies and deadens imagination, then it is the verbal equivalent of tribal entrenchment, a spasmodic reflex towards the familiar and the reassuring, the instinct to go with the grain.

Since the early days of the Abbey theatre, there has been an abiding intimacy between drama and politics in Ireland. It is appropriate, then, that the most notable cultural attempt to contribute to a resolution of the political crisis in the North came from a dramatic movement. The Field Day Theatre Company, founded in 1980, overtly sought to find ways of reimagining and reenacting entrenched political positions, of discovering a mythic 'fifth province' in Ireland, beyond the hackneyed historical roles and established stereotypes about the Troubles. Field Day sought to probe deeper than conventional, realist forms had allowed and initiated a drama of ideas, which would not baulk from history plays and experimental forms. With Field Day the creative and the critical were always in close alignment. Some of its directors, for instance Seamus Deane, Seamus Heaney and Tom Paulin, were critics as well as poets and the movement became a broader cultural phenomenon, publishing critical pamphlets by leading intellectuals.

Inside and outside Field Day, a politicised drama strove for a more daring, more formally innovative theatrical register. A number of dramatists, including

Brian Friel, Thomas Kilroy, Stewart Parker and Frank McGuinness, addressed the Troubles in these terms, at once distanced from the object of concern but at the same time seeking to sound some of its deepest structural strata. Departures from naturalism have been commonplace: the divided stage in Brian Friel's *The Freedom of the City* (1973) and in Frank McGuinness's *Observe the Sons of Ulster Marching Towards the Somme* (1985), the treatment of language and style as themes in themselves in Friel's *Translations* (1980) and in Stewart Parker's *Northern Star* (1984), or the use of multiple-role acting to blur divisions between imagination and reality in Marie Jones's *A Night in November* (1995) and Owen McCafferty's *Mojo Mickybo* (1997). Marie Jones is the most prominent figure to have emerged from Charabanc Theatre Company, a women's theatre movement set up in Belfast in 1983, initially to provide work for five unemployed actors. Operating at the same time as Field Day, Charabanc also addressed issues of social strife and political division but with a very different sort of theatrical practice. Like Field Day, the movement went on tours around Ireland and abroad. Charabanc staged a number of plays, utilising improvisation, collaborative writing, and popular, inclusive forms, including street songs and multiple-role acting.

Another significant strain in Northern Irish theatre, associated (though not exclusively) with Field Day is the history play (or its cousin, the memory play) where questions of identity and tribe, of colonialism and political domination, of violence and betrayal, issues central to the Troubles, can be examined in a less blurred and contentious context. In other words the dual and perhaps paradoxical function of the history play is to gain critical distance from the constricting confusions of the actual situation, while at the same time approaching an understanding of the conflict by plumbing its historical origins. Throwing light on the past, it was hoped, might illuminate current schisms; ancestral voices, the ghosts of the past, might dispel the atavistic antagonisms of the present. One of the finest of these plays is Friel's *Translations* (1980), the first Field Day production. Set in pre-Famine Donegal, during the ordnance survey mapping of the country, the play probes issues of language, community, identity and colonialism. However, in depicting a society lured by the promises of modernity, but not fully alert to its costs, the play also bears the traces of a very contemporary condition. Other history plays of the eighties include Friel's *Making History* (1988), McGuinness's *Observe the Sons of Ulster Marching Towards the Somme* (1985), Christina Reid's *Tea in a China Cup* (1983) (which could also be classified as domestic drama and a memory play), Stewart Parker's *Northern Star* (1984) and Tom Kilroy's *Double Cross* (1986).

Northern Ireland has also produced a number of internationally renowned poets, though what has become known as the 'renaissance' in Northern poetry can be dated back to the sixties, before the Troubles proper started. It is difficult to use broad brush-strokes to describe so large and diverse a group, but it is safe to venture that themes of identity, of place, of history and its ongoing legacies, of the role of the writer at a time of political crisis have a persistent centrality. Poets from both cultural traditions in the North are well represented in this upsurge, though the extent to which individual poets see themselves as mouthpieces for the religious and cultural traditions of their birth tends to vary. In general, the older poets have shown less Postmodern unease about deploying a fixity of treatment on issues of place and origin. John Hewitt was aware of himself as belonging to the non-conformist, radical tradition and was greatly interested in Ulster regionalism. In 1970 he co-published a collection, *The Planter and the Gael*, along with John Montague who, also interested in the evocative power of place, tribe and ancestral memory, played the native to Hewitt's settler. Montague has lived in New York and Paris and alongside his interest in community and locale, he brings a consciously cosmopolitan, anti-puritanical sensibility to bear on his critique of modern society. He seeks to reconcile, then, the local and the cosmopolitan, the rural and the urban, tradition and modernity, and in this he strikes a keynote of much Irish poetry over the last thirty years of the century.

Another Northern poet interested in the relationship between history and geography is Seamus Heaney. Heaney, who won the Nobel Prize in 1995, is Ireland's best-known living poet. His early collections, *Death of a Naturalist* (1966) and *Door into the Dark* (1969), reflect on his childhood experiences in rural Derry, and are marked by vivid depictions of the sounds, smells, tastes and textures of farm life and its environs. 'Digging', the much-anthologised first poem of *Death of a Naturalist*, treats the poet's ambivalent, guilty feelings about his vocation and involves an extended conceit whereby his passive, onanistic act of writing is finally brought into reassuring analogy with his father's and grandfather's actual 'digging' (and fertilisation): 'Between my finger and my thumb / The squat pen rests. / I'll dig with it.'[6] Excavation, as a metaphor and a theme, has abided in Heaney's work and surfaces in his more political poems of the mid-seventies, especially in the volume *North* (1975), which answered those critics who chided him for not engaging with the political situation in the province. Since then, both inside and outside poetry, Heaney has articulated

[6] Seamus Heaney, *New Selected Poems 1966–1987* (London: Faber & Faber, 1990), p. 2.

the difficulties of being a writer in time of political trouble, a difficulty he feels with particular pointedness. On the one hand, unless the poet is content to be a merely decorative irrelevancy, he or she must have a public role. At a time when language has calcified, when the available vehicles of communication seem shrivelled and public discourse inseparable from journalistic cliché (a condition memorably described in Heaney's poem 'Whatever You Say, Say Nothing'), the poet's duty is not to provide lyrical distraction but to search for new imaginative possibilities, new ways of conceiving identity, myth, history. Mindful of this imperative, however, the poet must avoid becoming swamped by politics or allowing the last atrocity to dictate subject-matter. The opposite danger to being the detached poet is to fall into the role of propagandist. In order to find a way of negotiating these opposing perils, Heaney's poetry needs a distancing mechanism. He finds it in the Danish 'Bog People', those Iron Age victims of ritual sacrifice, whose bodies have been preserved in the Danish bogs. By aestheticising these preserved remains and poetically contemplating their fate, Heaney asserts a linkage between these historic brutalities and the current tribal violence in the North of Ireland. Yet while suggesting the analogy, Heaney also draws back from the blandishments of myth by asserting the particularity of the suffering individual and by critiquing his own voyeuristic poetic urges.

The second half of *North* offers more overtly political poems, but finishes with 'Exposure', a beautiful, guilty meditation on Heaney's departure from Northern Ireland. In *Station Island* (1984), Heaney intensifies his characteristic mode of self-critique. In the title poem, set in the context of a religious pilgrimage, the poet encounters figures from his own life and from literary history, who are given their own voices and who offer occasional advice and frequent rebukes to the poet–pilgrim. Many of these upbraid the poet for his use of myth or for his tendency to poeticise and lyricise violence. *The Haw Lantern* (1987), *Seeing Things* (1991) and *The Spirit Level* (1996) continue the restive yet affirming spirit of Heaney's poetic ethos. They tend to be less geographically fixed or rooted in place than his early work: often the journey and movement are used as a means of showing how the outlandish and the banal, the mythic and mundane, are often a matter of perspective rather than fixed meaning. But this avowal of looking at things anew, of trying to crack open the sediments of familiarity and cliché, is charged with political and historical significance and is deeply allied to Heaney's belief in the redemptive powers of poetry and language.

Other Northern poets have also mused poetically over the problem of addressing the Troubles without coarsening their poetic voice. And other poets have felt the guilt of leaving the situation behind, just as Heaney mused about his move to Dublin in the early seventies. As Derek Mahon puts it:

Perhaps if I'd stayed behind
And lived it bomb by bomb
I might have grown up at last
And learnt what is meant by home.[7]

Born in Belfast to a middle-class Protestant family, Mahon is often concerned with 'home' and 'identity' but in a more fractious, uneasy way than Hewitt is. In some of his most memorable work, Mahon is drawn to those without a home, the marginal, the displaced, the rejected: those forgotten by history. In 'A Disused Shed in County Wexford', from *The Snow Party* (1975), widely regarded as one of the greatest Irish poems of the late twentieth century, Mahon uses the startlingly original conceit of mushrooms in an abandoned shed, straining for the light, to articulate the condition of disinherited and forgotten peoples. If Mahon is concerned with 'home' and 'identity' (notions usually associated with tradition), his poems, marked as they are by a vocabulary of yearning, are equally concerned with the future and the past. Moreover, like his heroes Samuel Beckett and Louis MacNeice, his work has a strikingly European and internationalist reach.

Michael Longley is a contemporary of Mahon and Heaney and is also one of the leading lights of the Northern group. He published his first volume in 1969 but has had a late flowering in the 1990s with *Gorse Fires* (1991) and *The Ghost Orchid* (1995). Like Mahon, he comes from a Protestant background but his is a very different voice. His interests straddle the immediate and the mythic, the domestic and the classical, the familial and the foreign. Among the former, he has written some very moving poetry about his father, including 'Wounds' (from *An Exploded View* (1973), a poem which links his father's involvement in World War I with the Troubles). Often Longley's response to the political strife has been one of immediate human sympathy for the suffering, a poetic concentration on the magnitude of loss, rather than mythic distancing or an attempt to probe the origins of the violence.

Any notion that the Northern Irish poets who came of age in the sixties would overshadow the next generation has been thoroughly scotched by the emergence of such original and urgent voices as Paul Muldoon, Ciaran Carson and Medbh McGuckian. Muldoon in particular has won huge international attention for his endlessly inventive, witty, associative facility with

[7] Derek Mahon, *Poems 1962–78* (Oxford, 1979), p. 58.

language, his delight in poetic ironies and his rich and promiscuously allusive reach across cultures and traditions. 'Postmodern' is a term often used to describe Muldoon's work and he revels in a resistance to fixity and origin. However, his work, for all its hallucinations and pyrotechnics, is not without serious moral purpose or depth of emotion as, for instance, in his wonderful 'Incantata', an elegy after the death of a former lover, published in *The Annals of Chile* (1994). Like Muldoon, Ciaran Carson has an interest in the Irish language – an interest that confounds superficial oppositions between tradition and modernity. Carson is also steeped in Irish traditional music and mythology yet, again troubling the opposition, he is a profoundly modern and urban poet with a keen ear for demotic speech patterns and a sense of the associative and non-rational powers of language. Medbh McGuckian, like Carson, hails from Belfast. Along with Muldoon she has sometimes been accused of difficulty and obscurity. But, if her work resists immediate interpretation, she nonetheless produces rhythms, phrases and images of arresting lyricism, beauty and richness, which offer their own insights and epiphanies. Her settings, often domestic, are depicted in an intense, dense and intimate lyrical voice, rich in unexpected and cerebral conceits and suffused with the strange, magical and unsettling.

While many male Irish poets struggle with themes of national and political identity, with tradition, colonialism and contesting public voices, McGuckian has the added pressure and conflict of writing as a woman and a mother – an identity and an experience historically marginalised within the Irish poetic tradition. There have been numerous women writers who in their different ways have articulated these dilemmas and have sought to renegotiate the relationship between Ireland, nationality and masculinity. Poets like Eavan Boland and Nuala ní Dhomnaill and dramatists like Anne Devlin and Christina Reid have explicitly questioned the old political binaries between nationalist and unionist, Ireland and the UK, and tried to insert women's experience into the equation. Boland has described the problems of operating within a tradition where women have been the objects rather than the authors of poetry, functioning simply as images, emblems and metaphors. This is a familiar dilemma for women writers, but the problem is twisted further in Ireland, a country which has itself long been figured and mythologised as a woman (the figures of 'Cathleen ní Houlihan', 'The Poor Old Woman' and numerous other incarnations), which in turn becomes endlessly idealised in the Irish poetic tradition. As Boland puts it, 'However much my powers of expression made my mind as a human being the subject of the poem, my life as a woman remained obdurately the object of it.'[8] If Boland has been criticised for importing the language of the university seminar too forcefully into her poems, she has refreshed poetry by bringing it into neglected corners of experience and domestic life, while remaining alert to the wider forces of history, politics and barbarism.

Throughout Ireland there has been an outpouring of poetry, fiction and drama by women writers since 1970, the richness and variety of which resists convenient categorisation as 'Women's Writing'. By constructive assaults on the poetic past, by bending its idioms, rewriting its mythologies and reshaping its subject-matter, Boland and other women poets are intervening in the dialectic between tradition and modernity, not by abnegating the history in the search for an illusory tabula rasa, but by reshaping current relations between past and present. Tradition, then, operates not so much as an inherited authority as a fluid, enabling source of identities, possibilities and self-invention. And gender is no longer destiny. Irish literature since 1970 has often undertaken comparable reconsiderations of the relationship between past and present, the bequests of nationhood and the promises of modernity. The two have often been put into false opposition and false hierarchy. Early in the twentieth century, Yeats and the Irish Literary Revivalists saw Ireland as the haven for an ancient, spiritual idealism, a salutary antidote to the 'filthy modern tide' of science, empiricism and middle-class mercantilism. The elite of the new Irish state adopted a similar model but infused it with a devotional, Catholic colouring. Some of the euphoria generated by the economic booms, new internationalism and by the rhetoric of 'progress' in Irish society simply *inverts* this model – whereas previously pure Ireland needed to be defended against foreign corruption (the justification behind the Draconian censorship laws), now it is the traditional, with all its associations of Irish nationalism, the rural west, the Catholic Church and so on, which needs to be spurned. The best Irish writing and cultural commentary of the last thirty years of the century, such as that produced by Field Day, has often set its teeth against such reductive binary logic. The problem according to this thinking may not be tradition or modernity in itself, but rather the inability to consider these two as other than locked in deadly antagonism. Could 'tradition' (often 'invented' after all) not itself be an aspect of modernity? Or could the search for the 'new' not itself be one of the very oldest searches?

8 Eavan Boland, *Object Lessons: The Life of the Woman and the Poet in Our Time* (New York: Norton, 1995), p. 28.

37

Scottish literature: Second Renaissance

GERARD CARRUTHERS

Robert Crawford has argued that 'Scotland needs not the pursuit of some elusive *echt*-Scottishness, but requires many reminders of its protean and plural past, present and future.'[1] Indeed, in literary and cultural terms, Scotland during the last three decades of the twentieth century has increasingly found a series of 'usable' pasts and presents as it has divested itself of a former desire for an organic unity in national identity; one that rested on an over-wrought perception of the country's ever fragmenting history within the context of a hopelessly marginalising British superstate. In creative literature, as elsewhere, this liberation from the aggrieved pursuit of an ideally coherent nation has resulted in a much greater inclusiveness of the various historical and cultural component parts of 'Scottishness' and an experimentation that can be both suitably iconoclastic and re-evaluative.

One of the most striking voices to emerge since the first publication of his work in 1968 is that of Tom Leonard who sounds a mischievously scandalising note in his poster-poem, 'Makars' Society': 'GRAN' MEETIN' THE NICHT TAE DECIDE THE SPELLIN' O' THIS POSTER'.[2] Leonard is one of a group of writers who have brought Glasgow and the west of Scotland to the centre of the Scottish literary stage for the first time in any critical mass. Leonard, Alasdair Gray, James Kelman, Liz Lochhead and others formed enduring personal associations in creative writing seminars run by Philip Hobsbaum, the English poet and academic, who was already well known as a supporter of 'regional' writing in Ulster when he arrived to work at the University of Glasgow. The outpouring of cultural confidence in the west of Scotland from the late 1960s is trumpeted in 'Makars' Society' where Leonard mocks the over-prescriptive

[1] Robert Crawford, 'Dedefining Scotland', in Susan Bassnett, ed., *Studying British Cultures* (London and New York: Routledge, 1997), p. 92.

[2] Tom Leonard, *Intimate Voices 1965–1983* (Newcastle upon Tyne: Galloping Dog Press, 1984), p. 53.

nature of the Scots-language purists who had been unleashed on Scotland in the wake of Hugh MacDiarmid's successful creative revival of the language from the 1920s. Leonard goes on the offensive, satirising linguistic ossification, as, for many purist Scots activists, his Glaswegian parlance was (and remains) a somewhat debased dialect associated with the working classes and an area of ethnic hotchpotch. His concern to tap into the potential of his local language is analogous to the linguistic freedom practised by MacDiarmid forty-five years earlier during the so-called Scottish Renaissance. Leonard celebrates the expressive excitement of the Glasgow 'patois' in poems where unselfconscious speakers enthusiastically discourse on football, work and sexual attraction. At his subtly aggressive best, Leonard brings such 'naturalism' into collision with the attitudinal biases in the cultural firmament. His most famous poetic sequence, 'Unrelated Incidents', conjugates notions of reality, truth and linguistic propriety in confrontational fashion so that, for instance, the six o'clock news is surreally introduced in a 'coarse' working-class Glaswegian voice. One of the myths rehearsed by Leonard is that of west-of-Scotland, male, working-class inarticulacy:

'A Summer's Day'
yir eyes ur
eh
a mean yir

pirrit this wey
ah a thingk yir
byewitfl like ehm

fact
fact a thingk yir
ach a luvyi thahts

thahts
jist thi wey it iz like
thahts ehm
aw ther iz ti say[3]

Here the anti-formal playfulness of resisted metaphor, the image from Shakespeare's poem marking the 'high cultural' expression that is unavailable to the speaker and which the author sets down in his title in ironic juxtaposition,

[3] Ibid., p. 41.

and the fourteen-line layout of the poem, that produces a parodic form of the sonnet, asks questions about the 'reserved' emotional power of literature. Alongside this interrogation of the ownership of language, the piece is marked by the strong influence on Leonard's work of expressively minimalist and concrete forms of poetry as pioneered by William Carlos Williams.

In drawing upon the wry form-bending and vernacular phonetic freedom that was engendered by the most radical American and European poetry of the 1960s, Leonard exemplifies the much larger frame of literary reference with which Scottish writers from the 1970s increasingly feel comfortable. Hobsbaum's colleague in the English Literature department at Glasgow University, Edwin Morgan, is the figure who has most consistently interacted with and encouraged younger Scottish writers over the last thirty years of the twentieth century. His cosmopolitan influence may prove as significant in Scottish literary history as the galvanising nationalist presence of MacDiarmid in the early part of the century. Morgan, poet, dramatist, translator and academic, became in 2000 the Poet Laureate of Glasgow, an official civic post designed especially for him. The irony of a gay, middle-class man holding such a position in Glasgow's 'no mean city' is delicious, although an even larger one, perhaps, is that the metropolis's stereotypically parochial image is contradicted by its production and honouring of a poet marked so deeply by his reading in Anglo-Saxon, Russian, American, French, Czech and German literatures among others. As with Leonard, whom Morgan greatly encouraged in his early writing, 1968 might be seen as a watershed year since this is when Morgan's collection, *The Second Life*, was published. The title refers obliquely to Morgan's sexual orientation: homosexuality had only become legal in the UK the previous year. Having already written around a dozen volumes of poetry and as a man approaching fifty, Morgan, in his compressed title, alludes both to his previously long-hidden personal life and his present, hoped-for new beginning in a more open society. Morgan, however, did not publicly avow his homosexuality until the late 1980s and *The Second Life* is also masterfully reserved even as it frames some of the most playfully tender love-poems to have come out of Scotland. 'One cigarette', for example, is universal in its theme of parted lovers and peddles a somewhat disarming metaphysical conceit where a cigarette stands for the relationship of the two. Traditional cinematic connotations of the romance of smoking obfuscate (as the smoke of the cigarette in the lover's home literally obfuscates) the socially illicit nature of the intense and long love affair actually being addressed here. The charming poignancy of the poem is inviting but encrypts within it a sad longing that is much deeper and more wry than the unaware reader suspects:

No smoke without you, my fire.
After you left,
your cigarette glowed on in my ashtray
and sent up a long thread of such quiet grey
I smiled to wonder who would believe its signal
of so much love.[4]

Morgan is a highly ambidextrous poet as he handles both old and new technologies. He is centrally inspired in whole collections, such as *Instamatic Poems* (1972) and *From Glasgow to Saturn* (1973), by scientific innovation, and in *Sonnets from Scotland* (1984) and *Demon* (1999) by venerably old forms and ideas. For Morgan, a poet of astonishingly various output through a prolific fifty-year period, where human life has been and where it is going are things both uncertain and to be warmly, intimately explored. His sonnet, 'The Picts', typically circumscribes the wonder that he finds everywhere as he reconsiders one of the rather tired mythical foundation ethnicities of Scotland: 'Names as from outer space, names without roots: / Bes, son of Nanammovvezz; Bliesblituth'.[5] Morgan's sheer delight in words is the cornerstone of his human sympathy for life both real and mythical. We see a particularly nice example of this where his talent as a mimic is to the fore while contemplating the brief sojourn of Gerard Manley Hopkins as a priest in Glasgow:

He blessed them, frowned, beat on his hands. The load
of coal-black darkness clattering on his head
half-crushed, half-fed the bluely burning need
that trudged him back along North Woodside Road.[6]

Poised in everything that he does, Morgan's sense of sound is also as often deployed for fun, as in 'The Loch Ness Monster's Song' (though even here with implicit questions about the functions of prosody) as for sonorous effect:

Sssnnnwhuffffll?
Hnwhuffl hhnnwfl hnfl hnfl
Gdroblboblhobngbl gbl gl g g g g glbgl.
Drublhaflabhaflubhafgabhaflhafl fl fl –[7]

Following the publication of *The Second Life* Morgan became the modern Scottish poet most frequently taught in schools and universities, though he was

4 Edwin Morgan, *Collected Poems* (Manchester: Carcanet Press, 1990), p. 186.
5 Ibid., p. 440. 6 'G. M. Hopkins in Glasgow' in ibid., p. 445.
7 Morgan, *Collected Poems*, p. 248.

closely followed in this popularity by three others, all of whom had been publishing for at least twenty years before the high watermark of their recognition during the seventies. Norman MacCaig went from being a rather excitably surreal poet of the New Apocalypse movement during the forties, producing work that he strenuously tried to disown until the end of his life, to a writer coolly sceptical of large visionary impulses, though nonetheless frequently and flagrantly foregrounding the quirks and complexities of subjective perception. Scotland's most accomplished practitioner of free verse from the 1960s to the 1980s, MacCaig specialises in describing the working of the self-centred human brain as it processes information from a hyperactive world and the poet's own hyperactive image memory-bank. The collections *A World of Difference* (1983), *A Man in My Position* (1969) and *Voice-Over* (1988) contain MacCaig's most accomplished work and as the titles of all of these indicate he is a poet keen to signal the artificial nature of the poet's utterance. Writers 'writing about writing' is, of course, a very widespread contemporary idiom, but it derives especial purchase in the Scottish context where MacCaig is highly conscious of the national Calvinist mindset with its suspicion of profanely seductive narratives and images and the allure of nature.

Iain Crichton Smith is, like MacCaig, an agnostic who retains a somewhat Calvinistic outlook upon the world. Smith was brought up on Lewis, island fortress of Free-Church Presbyterianism, a religion and a culture that he came to associate with the rebarbative denial of life and art. As with MacCaig though, who similarly rejects the Puritanism strongly present in the historic Scottish Protestant mindset, Smith constantly worries over the tension between the luxuriant amplitude of art and the perhaps superior clear-sightedness of harshly realistic Calvinism:

> The meagre furniture appals me here,
> the props of rock, of heather, and of sea,
> the constancy
> of ruined walls and nettles. A humming bee
> is smartly burning round an absent pier.
>
> Life without art, the minimum. I hear
> A sermon tolling, for your theatre is
> the fire of grace,
> hypothesis of hell, a judging face
> looming from storm towards boats and sea-drenched gear[8]

[8] Iain Crichton Smith, *A Life* (Manchester: Carcanet Press, 1983), p. 11.

Which is the more accurately descriptive, Smith asks, enamelled art or minimalist, eagerly conclusive Calvinism? Like Morgan and MacCaig a highly prolific writer for more than forty years, Smith, in his verse, constantly returns to questions regarding the validity of poetry's exuberantly descriptive order in the face of a transient, disappointing and brutal world. Throughout he does so with a leavening of defiant humour, a quality alongside his observation of the tenderness of human love that prevents acquiescence to the idea that expression is completely futile. Plagued by periodic bouts of disabling depression, Smith himself found love late in life and produced his finest work in thirty years in *The Leaf and the Marble* (1998), inspired by his wife and in which he reaches the conclusion that 'When everything trembles, only love holds it together.'[9]

Our fourth among the best-known Scottish poets from the seventies to the end of the century, George Mackay Brown, is, in his ideas, perhaps, the most direct descendent of the first Scottish Renaissance. Tutored by Edwin Muir at Newbattle Abbey, Mackay Brown endorses his teacher's critique of the fatal blight of Calvinism upon the Scottish imagination. Attempting to redress a denuded sacramental consciousness, he emphasises cyclical and universal patterns as he writes about nature and the rural life of his native Orkney. Admired for his tender and direct powers of description in both poetry and fiction, Mackay Brown presents landscapes and humanscapes where propitious and adverse circumstances and goodness and sin sit side by side, not necessarily comfortably but allowing always the possibility for God's grace to be received.

If Mackay Brown represents the most recognisable continuation of the cultural agenda of the literary generation previous to his own, Ian Hamilton Finlay and Kenneth White mark the most heterogeneous energies in Scottish poetry of the later twentieth century. Hamilton Finlay, visual artist as well as poet, has since 1969 established a base for the housing of many of his 'concrete' poems executed on wood, stone and other materials at his home in Dunsyre, Lanarkshire, one of the most remarkable sites of literary holdings in Scotland. Like Hamilton Finlay, Kenneth White has been much more lauded abroad than in his own country (rather provocatively, he is entirely omitted from *The New Penguin Book of Scottish Verse* (2000)).[10] A professor at the Sorbonne who took French citizenship in 1979, his verse spans Whitmanesque and Eastern mystical sensibilities in a formation of thought and expression that he labels 'geopoetics'. Having written a substantial corpus of poetry in both French and

9 Iain Crichton Smith, *The Leaf and the Marble* (Manchester: Carcanet Press, 1998), p. 23.
10 Robert Crawford and Mick Imlah, eds., *The New Penguin Book of Scottish Verse* (Harmondsworth: Penguin, 2000).

English from the 1960s, White's impact in Britain was only truly registered with the summative collection *The Bird Path* (1989) that accumulated for White a vastly increased group of admirers, as well as, it must be added, drawing the attention of many sceptical of his lyrical effusiveness.

Alongside Tom Leonard, two other Anglophone Scottish poets of his generation stand out in both their widespread popularity and their positive critical reception: Douglas Dunn and Liz Lochhead. Dunn can, of course, be claimed to be an important 'English' urban poet in his treatment of Hull, where he lived from 1966 until the 1980s, and in his professional and personal relationship with Philip Larkin (the two were colleagues at Hull University library). Working in the University of St Andrews, where he became a Professor of English, and involved in a flourishing creative writing programme, Dunn has been a particularly strong encourager of a new generation of writers. A striking fact of the Scottish literary scene from the sixties onwards is that, for all the country's much vaunted tradition of autodidact poets, figures such as Hobsbaum, Morgan and Dunn have influenced and associated themselves with much of the best new poetry from the universities. The hallmark of Dunn's work is a technical panache where internal rhyme and a meticulous syntax complement a visual brilliance. His reflections upon the past and contemporary cultural state of Scotland are particularly notable in his collection, *St Kilda's Parliament* (1981). Like Morgan, Leonard and Dunn, Liz Lochhead might be seen as essentially an urban poet as she deals with the experience of women enduring domestic tedium and enjoying moments of mental liberation in the Glasgow setting. Her *Memo for Spring* (1972) represented a very sharp contribution to the growing awareness of feminist issues combined with a warm sense of irony. At the turn of the century her poetry remains widely taught in schools and universities in Scotland, even though since the 1980s Lochhead's greatest importance has been as a dramatist and a theatrical director.

Among the most contemporary generation of Scottish poets is to be found a grouping that was called 'The Informationists', though this term in seeming somewhat contrived to observers outside the group has tended to be used with decreasing frequency. Robert Crawford, David Kinloch, W. N. Herbert and Richard Price are all writers who can be seen responding to the Postmodern information overload and out of this condition framing poems that are both sceptical and lyrical as they attest to the difficulty in defining the relationship of the individual to any solid cultural centre, perhaps especially a national one. At the same time each of these writers has sought to invest in his national culture, Crawford constantly worrying away at how inclusive Scotland might ideally be; Kinloch essaying ancient and modern links that might be made between Scotland and Europe; Herbert, somewhat the heir to MacDiarmid, the most technically gifted poet writing in Scots at the turn of the century, as well as the most fiercely intellectual of the grouping, as he works through a difficult language, quite often involving startling neologisms, and as he addresses a national past full of both failure and still latent opportunity (his collaboration with Crawford, *Sharawaggi* (1990), is a highly amusing and thoughtful rehearsal of many of the linguistic and intellectual energies traditionally associated with Scotland); and Price an important proselytiser for the most cosmopolitan links being made between the poetry of numerous cultures from west to east (among many other important publishing ventures, Price was a founding co-editor of the influential periodical *Verse* along with Crawford and Kinloch). Don Paterson is perhaps the most painstaking formal craftsman among the current generation of Scottish poets as his *Nil Nil* (1993) demonstrates; its polished, unpretentious phrasing accompanies an assemblage of reflections upon 'real' life and art. Carol Ann Duffy and Kathleen Jamie are perhaps at present the two Scottish poets most feted outside their native country, the latter even being touted as a possible British poet laureate when the position was vacant in the late 1990s. Both poets are obviously interested in the complexities of modern gender and sexual transactions, their writings extending, in the case of Duffy, into contemplation of awkward liminal spaces in the mind (see especially *The Other Country* (1990)) and, in the case of Jamie, into a mythical and even mystical terrain that poses questions about the best terms that might be found to describe individual action (see, especially, *The Autonomous Region* (1993)).

The anthology, *Dream State: The New Scottish Poets* (1994) gathered up something of the particularly intense though diffuse energy of Scottish poets over the previous decade that had been a particularly strong feature in a raft of small magazines such as *Cencrastus*, *Chapman*, *The Dark Horse*, *Edinburgh Review*, *Gairfish*, *Lines Review*, *New Writing Scotland*, *Northwords* and *Poetry Scotland*.[11] *Dream State* displays the potent combination of realism and spirituality found in the verse of John Burnside. Alan Riach appears with his sharp eye for landscape that often shifts through the lens of human feeling. Robert Alan Jamieson features with his accents of Shetland and a narrative control that carries the reader through often strange, alienated experience with a deceptive facility. The questioning of how seriously modernity ought to be seen as a problem,

11 Daniel O'Rourke ed. *Dream State: The New Scottish Poets* (Edinburgh: Polygon, 1994).

rather than simply lived, is a cheerfully complex site of enquiry in the work of Iain Bamforth; Maud Sulter, born and brought up in Glasgow, has written powerfully about her status as a black woman, though her poetry is arguably more directly influenced by her experiences of living in London and New York. At the turn of the century, Sulter's career has become predominantly that of visual artist and it looks as though poetry has outlived its usefulness for her. Of all the poets in the anthology, Angela McSeveney is perhaps the most accessible of Scotland's late twentieth-century poets, with her spare style and riotous humour, though her work is no less intellectually engaging than that of the others.

It is interesting that Scotland's predominant poetic language is English (perhaps Scots–English) and that, despite the best efforts of magazines like *Lallans*, writing in Scots is very much a minority activity (the most notable of recent poets in Scots besides Leonard and Herbert being Alison Kermack). Gaelic verse, on the other hand, continues to flourish much more evenly in spite of the fall in the number of Gaelic speakers during the twentieth century to around 60,000 (though this number is now steadily rising again among devotees in the cities) out of a population of around 5 million. Gaelic poetry has perhaps suffered particularly from a time-lapse, its greatest poet of the twentieth century, Sorley MacLean, writing his best work in the 1940s and 50s, though not really finding a large Scottish and international audience until the 1970s. The promotion of Gaelic verse owes most to Derick Thomson, founder of a magazine of remarkably consistent quality, *Gairm*. Thomson is himself a poet who began publishing in the 1940s and who, from the 1970s, has continued to be one of the most innovative of Gaelic poets.[12]

Scotland's most critically and popularly acclaimed writer since at least Robert Louis Stevenson is Muriel Spark, but she occupies a somewhat ambivalent position in the contemporary Scottish literary pantheon. Her only serious competitor for the title of Scotland's 'senior' living novelist, Robin Jenkins, has said of Spark that it would be 'very difficult to get any real Scottish person accepting her as a Scottish writer'.[13] Jenkins here speaks for the generation immediately following the Scottish Renaissance that saw native subject-matter as a crucial ingredient for his nation's writers. Jenkins's own writing from the 1950s meditates powerfully on definitions of good and evil in the context of the Calvinist *Weltanschauung* of Scotland. In this regard his

[12] Notable among the contemporary Gaels are Aonghas MacNeacail (b. 1942), Myles Campbell (b. 1944), Christopher Whyte (b. 1952), Mary Montgomery (b. 1955), Meg Bateman (b. 1959), Roddy Gorman (b. 1960) and Anne Frater (b. 1967).

[13] See Inga Agustdottir's interview with Robin Jenkins in *In Scotland*, 1 (Autumn 1999), p. 13.

best post-1970 work, *Fergus Lamont* (1979), a reworking of James Hogg's *Private Memoirs and Confessions of a Justified Sinner* (1824) in a twentieth-century urban setting, *The Awakening of George Darroch* (1985), powerfully reimagining the atmosphere surrounding the important cultural watershed of the Disruption of the Church of Scotland in 1843, and *Just Duffy* (1988), featuring an intellectually muscular protagonist motivated by a crusade for good where his idealism may, in fact, be dangerous arrogance, make for some of the most culturally ambiguous fiction to have been produced in late twentieth-century Scotland. Jenkins's remark about Spark, therefore, sits somewhat strangely when we consider her fictional essays pinpointing the difficulty of moral discernment and meaningful pattern in human life. The novel that Spark herself believes to be her finest, *The Driver's Seat* (1970), presents a woman whose feelings of her raging isolation in a modern city (she may be living in London though we are never sure) cause her to contrive the details of her own death so that she appears the innocent victim of a murder. In this way the central character creates the image of a violently dramatic story so as to counterpoint her brutally meaningless life. *Not to Disturb* (1971) offers the techniques of the *roman nouveau* with an anagogic slant. A blend of Gothic, 'whodunit' and Elizabethan theatrical scenarios oversees the predictable deaths of the protagonists in a love triangle 'in the library' of a manorial house in Geneva and this generic inevitability lampoons the Calvinist doctrine of predestination. *The Only Problem* (1984), set in France, essays the existence of suffering with special reference to the Book of Job. *Symposium* (1990) deals with blackmail and murder centred on a Caledonian locus and has a demonstrably mad character claim that in Scotland 'people are more capable of perpetrating good or evil than anywhere else'.[14] The diffuse geographical co-ordinates of Spark's fiction would seem to make for the feature that attracts Jenkins's hostility. However, her recurrent concerns with the problems of moral and spiritual identity and her frequent recourse to the ethical and cultural atmosphere of Scotland, even when mocking this as in *Symposium*, makes Spark highly pertinent within her national context.

If Alasdair Gray and James Kelman have been the two most feted Scottish writers of fiction during this period, two other figures likewise from the west of Scotland, George Friel and, most especially, William McIlvanney, also stand out during this time. Friel's *Mr Alfred MA* (1972) represents the culmination in the career of a writer of extraordinary stylistic range who can simultaneously encompass the sparest narrative voice and a wryly strange and ornate

[14] Muriel Spark, *Symposium* (London: Constable, 1990), p. 159.

language that points to the influence of James Joyce more than on any other Scottish writer of the twentieth century. No slavish imitator, Friel, in *Mr Alfred MA*, juxtaposes a late Modernist aesthetic with the perennial Scottish interest in education to show the difficult life of its eponymous schoolteacher in a rough urban development leavened, though not redeemed, by his love of poetry. The novel's narrative frame, with its intense attention to the usages of language within different groupings, points to the foreclosed social systems against which no single individual, however well-intentioned, can hope to prevail. No more than half a dozen Scottish novels since have demonstrated the sheer facility with language apparent in *Mr Alfred MA*. William McIlvanney, like Friel a former schoolteacher, is Scotland's most sensitive documenter of the shifting class culture of the country from 1950 to 2000. His first novel, *Remedy is None* (1966), sees the exploration of a pattern, class migration, to which McIlvanney returns, as Charlie, the central protagonist, turns his back on his university studies, newly available to someone of his background, to wreak violent havoc upon his dysfunctional working-class family. The novel somewhat flew in the face of the contemporary optimism in the UK as the Robins report was greatly widening access to universities during this time. The difficulty of belonging in a Scotland characterised by an increasingly amorphous social system is dealt with in a dazzling display of character focalisation in McIlvanney's finest work, *Docherty* (1975), a historical novel beginning in the early twentieth century that explores the frequently thrown up pattern in Scottish fiction as well as real life (the examples of James Boswell and Robert Louis Stevenson are often cited) of conflict between father and son. From the perspective of the maturing boy, Conn Docherty, we see the simultaneously harsh and community-minded mining town of Graithnock, a fictional place modelled on McIlvanney's native Kilmarnock in Ayrshire. Existing in a family heritage of some complexity, where understated Irish immigration in the deep past has played its historical part, Conn both feels for and is sometimes repelled (though more by the situation than the person) by his father, a man of physical prowess and mental dignity whose life is often circumscribed by forces of capitalist control that do not allow his virtues free and full scope. McIlvanney somewhat surprised and even disappointed many of his admirers with his turn to 'detective' novels, *Laidlaw* (1978), *The Papers of Tony Veitch* (1983) and *Strange Loyalties* (1991). All of these certainly belong to the genre of crime-writing, but their central character, the Glasgow detective Jack Laidlaw, an inhabitant originally of Graithnock, is more than usually reflective about the moral existence of both the individuals he encounters and their location within communities of varying degrees of coherence. His job, as much as that of policeman, is to expose failures that are institutional and cultural as well as personal in the area of disrespect for human dignity. Both the metaphorical exuberance and the fine calibration of anthropological lens that McIlvanney has been lauded for throughout his career are to the fore in *The Kiln* (1996), which again picks up the Docherty family-saga, this time with Tom Docherty, the son of Conn. Two real historical personages overarch the novel, those of Kilmarnock-educated Alexander Fleming and Margaret Thatcher, as the cultural terrain of Britain from 1955 (the year of Fleming's death and the birth-year of western youth-culture with the advent of rock 'n' roll) to 1990s post-Thatcherite society is essayed. Obliquely what is signalled is the supposed end of a society, especially the kind of Scottish society from which Fleming comes, where the 'lad o' pairts' is motivated by the desire to do some great good such as invent penicillin, and the enshrining of a different kind of personal striving where brutal economic individualism is the primary motivation. *The Kiln*, however, is no mere lament for a supposed golden age of idealism. It acknowledges, as Tom Docherty goes to university, becomes a successful writer and suffers deeply from a failed marriage, that both loss and gain (in terms of personal freedom and integrity for someone of a background like that of the Docherty family) are involved in a radically changed attitudinal world across forty years. The metaphor of the kiln, as we see Tom in his final summer before commencing his studies at work in the local brick-making factory, both points to Tom's formation by family and community materials and is deliberately all too claustrophobic a symbol for someone who has choices to make that are very specific to him in situations that his forebears have never experienced. Finely nuanced with regard to the treatment of class, community, family and gender, *The Kiln*, simultaneously lyrical and sardonic and with a beautifully paced cross-cutting structure, is among the very best Scottish historical novels of the twentieth century.

James Kelman is the Scottish writer most lauded by the literary establishment during the last twenty years of the century, having won an unprecedented string of British writing prizes presided over by the publishing and academic industries, most notably the Booker Prize for 1994 with his novel, *How Late it Was, How Late*. This is a remarkable achievement when one considers the trajectory of Kelman's career. A defining moment for his work was the establishment in 1978 of 'The Print Studio Press, Glasgow', an intellectually loose but highly inter-supportive collective of writers helping finance publication of each other's work (each participant made an initial contribution of £25 to the project) and promoting public readings among the group. Under these auspices, Kelman's *Short Tales from the Nightshift* (1978) appeared. The hallmark of these pieces, sawn-off short stories, is a spare narrative style and subject-content, where urban myths, small everyday pleasures and petty injustices are conveyed very directly, though with the potential to resonate in the alert reader's mind as he or she is implicitly invited to contemplate the underplayed macroeconomic context of these situations (such as the politics of the labour system). *Not Not While the Giro* was published in 1983, by which time Kelman had found an Edinburgh imprint with Polygon, the most adventurous publishing house in Scotland during the final quarter of the twentieth century; the text gathers up some of his earlier material and provides more extensive short stories where his naturalistic method is again apparent. Notoriously, this naturalism includes mundane slabs of urban working-class, post-industrial reality, the recording of the heaps of expletives casually spoken by some people of this background and a sympathetically focalised narrative voice so that there is often little distinction between the *mentality* of character and narrator. The challenge for the reader, most especially the middle-class reader, is to sympathise with such 'uneventful' life, which was so strangely unfamiliar to readers in the early 1980s as *Not Not While the Giro* made a huge and uneasy impact. There is an interesting paradox with regard to the reception of his supposedly 'urban' fiction that Kelman has himself expressed, most especially within his national context: 'There's an odd thing about the way people approach art in this country. Scotland's broad left is happy with social realism; unless you're doing social realism they get a bit worried, and can't really handle you, like they can, say, William McIlvanney.'[15] Kelman's puritanical naturalism, shorn of descriptive language in general, is stark, but this alienation effect circumscribes an existential aesthetic where the reader's failed expectations of a 'story' challenge the received 'bourgeois' view of the world in general, as a place that is coherently eventful and interesting. The title-story of his first major collection brings into collision the realms of the uneventful (though the central protagonist whose life may be described in this way is suffering from the degradation of the massive structural unemployment as overseen and even guided by the Thatcher Government, and here, for Kelman, lies the deeply embedded 'story') and the idea of a grand, Hamlet-like 'literary' angst. In the grim humour of the scenario, the double negative of the title marks out the limited space inhabited by its materially and morally impoverished central character who resists suicide ('to be or not to be') while the thin sustenance of his dole-cheque continues to arrive.

[15] See Kathleen Jamie, 'The Voice of the Oppressed', in *Scotland on Sunday*, 19th February 1999.

Kelman's first novel, *The Busconductor Hines* (1984), gives an extended view of an intelligent man economically marginalised. We see Rab Hines, fiercely humorous and iconoclastic, on the verge of losing his job on the buses (conducted under demeaning terms of employment), and with seemingly looming marital unhappiness (Rab and his wife share a very tender relationship, but, in her aspirations for the family to better its living conditions she can never entirely sympathise with Rab and his Kafkaesque sensibility as he refuses compliance in the face of authority). The novel ends with a deliberate inconclusiveness, where the reader has probably expected some definite outcomes for a character that is amusing and intelligent.

The novel *A Chancer* (1985) provides a more difficult-to-fathom character as it follows the drifting gambler Tammas, who is secretive about his physical movements and his motivations. Questions are posed through this infuriating character as to whether the isolation and disconnectedness seemingly inherent in so much modern living is entirely unavoidable. *A Disaffection* (1989) sees Kelman having recourse to that favourite theme in Scottish culture, education. Patrick Doyle attempts to speak to his pupils at his comprehensive school with a profound philosophical eloquence as well as in a frank, generally uncensored, fashion to which they respond in intelligent and earthy kind. Given the complex enmeshing of Doyle's interior monologues and the 'reality' he experiences we are never entirely sure of the status of the classroom exchanges. Do they represent actually stunning pedagogical results, or are they fantasies in Doyle's mind? Related to this situation, it is around this time that, in common with many other commentators, Kelman becomes interested in the ideas of the Scottish Enlightenment, most especially as channelled through the work of George Davie.[16] Davie's reinterpretation of the Enlightenment in Scotland (previously, in the mindset of the Scottish Renaissance movement of the early twentieth century, a cultural villain to rival the Reformation, in its channelling of Anglo-centric and bourgeois mores) located within it the educational ethic of the 'democratic intellect'. Here knowledge was to be kept as coherent, or as 'generalist' as possible, rather than 'specialist', the supposed educational model favoured in England, in being made available to the widest possible community. *How Late it Was, How Late* (1994) follows the tortuous peregrinations around the city of a man blinded after a weekend drinking-bout, dirty and degraded as he attempts to make some kind of sense of his situation and to eke out a very basic survival as he collides with the police and the social security system. With its wry acknowledgment of James Joyce, the novel

[16] George Davie, *The Democratic Intellect* (Edinburgh University Press, 1961).

brilliantly performs the typical Kelman strategy of juxtaposing received literary models with undignified, even rebarbative, subject-matter that challenges the comfort of its familiar resonances. If the novel is Kelman's *Ulysses*, *Translated Accounts* (2001) is somewhat akin to his *Finnegans Wake* in that it has been seen in diffuse terms by critics as Kelman's most difficult novel, either because it explores with such a nightmarish resonance the labyrinthine powers at work exercising control over our political and linguistic domains, or because it is an all too subjective and somewhat messily paranoid view of the world.

Alasdair Gray's *Lanark* (1981) has been praised by the critical establishment more than any single Scottish work of the last half of the twentieth century. *Lanark* was begun in the 1950s and parts of it were intermittently published in various periodicals down to the 1970s. It was not, however, until after a period of almost thirty years that Gray felt he had achieved the necessary blend of fantasy and *Bildungsroman*, and sought publication of the full novel. The book alternates between the Kafkaesque situation of a man called Lanark, who suffers from 'dragonhide' and who is then plunged into the surreal world of the Institute where he is to be uncertainly cured or rehabilitated, and the charting of the bungled rites of passage of working-class Duncan Thaw, as he moves through art school, failed relationships and mental and physical illness. It becomes apparent that the two spheres inhabited by Lanark and Thaw can be read as reflections of one another where the aesthetic obsession and excruciating sensitivity of Thaw have produced a world of dystopian fantasy. Gray's mainstay profession as working painter through many of the years taken to produce his novel is apparent throughout in its gallery of Surrealism, caricature, allegory and colourful symbolism, a riotous, overloaded assembly that marks out one of the most darkly playful of Postmodern novels. Notable among Gray's other fiction are the novels *1982, Janine* (1984), a narrative that is encompassed by the alternately clear-sighted and diseased reflections during one night by Jock McLeish, a character of energetic neurosis provocatively exemplary of Scotland, and *Something Leather* (1990), a collision of antiquarian reconstruction (as it purports to deal with the newly discovered papers of a nineteenth-century public health inspector) and satirical sexual fetishism, so that public and private spheres as in *Lanark* chafe uncomfortably and comically against each other.

The map of contemporary Scottish writing is highly contoured and, indeed, contorted in a way that would displease anyone eager to impose some sense of smooth national unity upon it. Since 2001, Leonard, Kelman and Gray have shared a chair in creative writing at the University of Glasgow, confirming for some the dominance of the urban, alienated, working-class voice. By contrast with the first part of the twentieth century, it is in fiction now that the Scots language is most noticeable. Recent striking usages are to be found in the industrial novel *Swing Hammer Swing* (1992) by Jeff Torrington, in that seminal novel for the 'chemical generation', Irvine Welsh's *Trainspotting* (1993), and in Duncan McLean's *Bunker Man* (1995), a novel that replays the 'Jekyll and Hyde' syndrome in a study of macho, working-class aggression. Even in drama, perennially the Cinderella genre of Scottish literature and of the arts in Scotland more generally, Scots has been more potently present than in poetry. This is the case in the most successful Scottish plays of the last thirty years of the century, John Byrne's *The Slab Boys* trilogy (1978, 1979 and 1982) and Liz Lochhead's *Mary Queen of Scots Got Her Head Chopped Off* (1987). Two further writers (connected to some extent with the Print Studio Press grouping of Leonard, Kelman and Gray), Carl MacDougal and Bernard MacLaverty, have been substantially successful in the eyes of both critics and readers generally. MacDougal's finest novel, perhaps, is *The Casanova Papers* (1996) where a recently bereaved Glasgow journalist travels to Paris in an attempt to unlock the secrets of papers by the eighteenth-century lover and finds all kinds of startling self-confrontations. MacLaverty, Ulsterman happily resident in Glasgow since the early seventies and during the period of his highly successful novels that have dealt with the Catholic ethos and the troubles of his Irish background, is a seemingly ill-fitting point on the modern Scottish literary map. His *Grace Notes* (1997) spans the cultural locations of Glasgow, Ulster and the Highlands and finds excruciating modern emotional tensions in all of these places, and is also that work which most gloriously confirms the recent interest in an axis of Scots–Irish writing.

Assorted areas of less currently resonant but indisputable quality are to be found in modern Scottish fiction. Allan Massie is an exceptional writer of literary historical fiction by any standards. Ronald Frame is a slightly unfashionable writer of 'middle-class' fiction who dwells upon human relationships with an icy prose style and a tolerant eye. George Mackay Brown's fiction of the seventies and eighties retains a large readership; his *Magnus* (1973) draws upon the saga literature of Orkney and espouses a vision of religious spirituality that might seem to belong to a previous age but is a novel still widely taught and admired in Scotland. Alan Spence brings a sardonic, Buddhist-inflected eye to bear upon the mores of his native country. Where do expatriate, 'incomer' and Scots-by-descent writers fit in to whatever it is that they are supposed to be fitting in with? Such a catchment would include such 'British' notables as Leila Aboulela, Elspeth Barker, William Boyd, Sian Hayton, Candia McWilliam and Emma Tennant.

Women's writing and gay and lesbian writing are as vibrant in Scotland as anywhere. Janice Galloway and A. L. Kennedy are shrewd observers of sexual politics as well as possessing many other features that diffusely relate their work to numerous aspects of the Scottish and international cultural firmament in all its dislocated modern sensibility. Fiction by Thomas Healy, Christopher Whyte, Jackie Kay and Ali Smith has a readership extending well beyond both sexual and national boundaries. Frank Kuppner, Iain Banks, Alan Warner and Andrew O'Hagan, are, along with Irvine Welsh, those literary writers who appeal most to the notoriously expanding 'youth' sector. Shifting demographics are a fact of life in Scottish culture as much as anywhere else, ensuring that the writing of the nation is best seen as a palimpsest. If there has indeed been a 'second renaissance' in contemporary Scottish writing then this has comprised an increasingly 'denationalised' body of work, but one of entangled roots in keeping with the full complexity of Western cultural modernity.

38

Towards devolution: new Welsh writing

JANE AARON

Wales is a small country, with two linguistic cultures, which, as a nation, has survived into the third millennium by the skin of its teeth. About a quarter of its 2.75 million inhabitants – only 5 per cent of the UK population as a whole – were not born in Wales, and accordingly are unlikely to have a strong sense of allegiance to it. While two-thirds of Scots identify themselves as Scottish as opposed to British, in a 1999 survey only 43 per cent of Welsh respondents saw themselves as Welsh first and foremost. [1] Apart from a brief period of industrial prosperity during the early years of the twentieth century, it has remained one of the poorest areas in the UK, its household incomes at 10 per cent below those of the UK generally, and its output per head, in terms of GDP, currently standing at about 82 per cent of the UK average.[2] Since its Anglo-Norman conquest in the thirteenth century, it has had few national institutions to mark its distinctiveness, apart from an indigenous language in steep decline during the twentieth century: the figures for Welsh-language speakers dropped from 54.4 per cent of the Welsh population in 1891 to 18.7 per cent in 1991.[3] The long struggle to save the language from extinction in itself causes internal division in Wales, with some of the non-Welsh speaking majority seeing little purpose in spending scarce resources on keeping alive a culture they have already lost. These obstacles to the development of a confident national identity manifested themselves in the Welsh Devolution Referendum of 1 March 1979, in which 80 per cent of the voters registered a 'No' vote for Wales on its national saint's day. Yet in 1997, a massive 30 per cent swing in favour of at least a measure of Welsh autonomy won the second Devolution Referendum for the 'Yes' voters, albeit by a very narrow majority. Furthermore, the 1991 Census figures showed, for the first time, a halt in the decline of the Welsh language, with a gain of 5,000

[1] Graham Day, *Making Sense of Wales: A Sociological Perspective* (Cardiff: University of Wales Press, 2002), p. 254.
[2] Ibid., p. 260.
[3] John May, *Reference Wales* (Cardiff: University of Wales Press, 1994), pp. 67–8.

in the number of its speakers since 1981, and a loss of only 0.2 per cent in terms of the population as a whole. And the granting in March 1999 of Objective 1 status in the European Union to virtually the whole of the western half of Wales has brought increased hopes of Welsh economic recovery. During the last thirty years of the twentieth century, therefore, the pattern of Welsh politics has changed in a manner which would suggest a renewed determination among Welsh people to survive as a distinct entity. These changes in the construction of Welsh identity have been wrought as much in the cultural as the political field, and – as this chapter will show – as much in Wales's English-language literature as in its indigenous Welsh-language culture.

But why should the world at large be interested in the cultural wrangles of this minute proportion of its inhabitants? To any reader of literature whose interests include the ways in which a resurgent culture struggles to construct a new, necessarily hybridised, national identity after the experience of colonisation, or to resist the homogenising tendencies of global capitalist culture, the answer to that question should be apparent enough. The complexity and contentiousness of the national question in Wales means that its cultural process often appears – and indeed, to its participants, often feels like – a claustrophobically self-enclosed dispute, focused on its own innards, and fought in isolation. Yet the questions raised by that debate – what needs to be preserved to make identity meaningful, what value should be placed on community, history or cultural heritage, how far is it possible, or even desirable, to refigure a self-consciousness forged under the dominion of a non-indigenous culture – all these are issues of central concern to large tracts of the world's population. A seminal text in the developing understanding of the matter of Wales made precisely that point in 1970: at the close of *The Welsh Extremist: Welsh Politics, Literature and Society*, Ned Thomas emphasised the similarities between the Welsh situation and that of other groups worldwide whose identities had been suppressed.[4] And Raymond Williams, returning to Wales in 1981 to find that the mass of the population shared his own ambivalent and contradictory sense of Welsh identity, remarked that such internal divisiveness should but equip Welsh people the better to understand the equivalent situation of increasing numbers of the world's inhabitants.[5] Between 1970 and 1981, however, those contradictions in Welsh identity had manifested themselves politically in a

4 Ned Thomas, *The Welsh Extremist: Modern Welsh Politics, Literature and Society* (1970; new edn, Talybont: Y Lolfa, 1990), pp. 121–2.

5 Raymond Williams in interview with Terry Eagleton, 'The Politics of Hope: an Interview', in Terry Eagleton, ed., *Raymond Williams: Critical Perspectives* (Cambridge: Polity Press, 1989), p. 182.

manner which imperilled the likelihood of Wales's continuing existence as a distinct voice; they also featured as starkly oppositional formations within its English-language culture.

Writers of the 1970s in Wales were polarised by their differing attitudes towards, firstly, the activities of Welsh-language supporters and, secondly, the social heritage of Welsh industrialism. Following the teachings of the founder of the Welsh Nationalist Party, Saunders Lewis, by whom he had been personally influenced, R. S. Thomas, the strongest player on the pro-Welsh-language side, and indeed one of the dominant figures in Welsh culture generally for at least four decades before his death in 2000, denounced industrialism as the destroyer of indigenous Welshness, and the cause of his own lack of Welsh as a first language. In 'It Hurts Him to Think' (1974), for example, the poet presents himself as 'born into the squalor' of English-speaking industrialists, as they came 'burrowing / in the corpse of a nation / for its congealed blood', so that he 'sucked their speech / in with my mother's / infected milk'.[6] For another group of writers, however, the Wales that came into being through the industrial revolution, and had historically played a distinguished role in the evolution of British and international socialism, in itself constituted a Welshman's proudest heritage, one which was also by now endangered. Novelists and short-story writers like Ron Berry and Alun Richards continued the tradition of Welsh social-realist fiction first established in the 1930s. Welsh identity, in their work, is marked by a radicalism arising primarily out of class rather than cultural consciousness; the fate of the Welsh language is largely an irrelevance, and its supporters at times become the object of aggressive ridicule. In Alun Richards's *Home to an Empty House* (1973), for example, a character scoffs at the 'sneak-and-run schoolmasters rubbing out road signs with green paint',[7] a reference to the Welsh Language Movement's campaign to inscribe Welsh place-names on signposts, which resulted in numerous fines and prison sentences in the early 1970s. But for R. S. Thomas, and a group of like-minded English-language writers, like the poets Harri Webb, Raymond Garlick and John Tripp and the novelist Emyr Humphreys, the law-breaking activities of the Welsh Language Movement represented one of the few sources of hope for the future. Unlike Thomas, however, Webb, Garlick, Tripp and Humphreys all in different ways sought to bridge the division between industrial English-speaking Wales and the rural Welsh-speaking heartlands, and understood their

[6] R. S. Thomas, 'It Hurts Him to Think', *What is a Welshman?* (1974), *Collected Poems 1945–1990* (London: Dent, 1993; new edn, London: Phoenix, 1995), p. 262.

[7] Alun Richards, *Home to an Empty House* (Llandysul: Gwasg Gomer, 1973), p. 175.

mission as English-language writers to be precisely that of healing the rift between Wales's two linguistic cultures.[8] Tripp and Webb in particular sought to resurrect the edifices of Welsh cultural identity for their English-speaking audience, while at the same time emphasising and appreciating their own origins in the industrial communities of Wales; both cultures 'couple arms in a spurt of spirit' in their verses.[9]

In 1979, however, the Welsh population as a whole was not ready to endorse such attempts at cultural recognition. For those writers who had espoused the pro-Welsh language cause, the results of the 1979 Devolution Referendum in which the 'Yes' voters failed to gain more than 20 per cent of the vote was devastating. 'It's a tragedy, what happened on March 1st . . . and you can't expect your poets to be the same again', said John Tripp.[10] *Salt of the Earth* (1985), the first post '79 novel Emyr Humphreys published in his 'Land of the Living' sequence, is set in the Wales of the 1930s but its characters' references to the fatal 'serf mentality' of the Welsh reflect the Referendum trauma, and parallel the sentiments of Welsh-language novelists and poets, like Angharad Tomos or Gerallt Lloyd Owen, who also felt that the results of the 1979 Referendum had given them good reason to fear that contemporary Wales was more afraid of freedom than of death itself.[11] 'This country / of failure'[12] is similarly mourned in R. S. Thomas's post-1979 poems. In 'Perspectives' he sees modern Wales as a nation fallen into autumnal decline, whose only promise of spring relies on borrowing artificial – and, to Wales, destructive – energies from England.[13] For Thomas, the English-language speakers of Wales constituted in particular 'the lost'. While Welsh-language speakers still had the ancient tongue to fight for, their monoglot brethren had become 'exiles within / our own country', eating 'our bread / at a pre-empted table'; 'We have our signposts / but they are in another tongue.'[14] It was feared that Welsh writers in English, after '79,

8 See Raymond Garlick, *An Introduction to Anglo-Welsh Literature* (Cardiff: University of Wales Press, 1971), pp. 83–4.

9 John Tripp, 'Henry VIII, of Ignoble Memory', in *The Loss of Ancestry*, rpt in John Ormond, ed., *Selected Poems* (Bridgend: Seren Press, 1989), pp. 38–9.

10 John Tripp in interview with Nigel Jenkins, *Planet*, 60 (1987), p. 42.

11 Emyr Humphreys, *Salt of the Earth* (London: Dent, 1985), p. 205. The 'Land of the Living' novel sequence also includes *National Winner* (London: Hodder & Stoughton, 1971); *Flesh and Blood* (London: Hodder & Stoughton, 1974); *The Best of Friends* (London: Hodder & Stoughton, 1978); *An Absolute Hero* (London: Dent, 1986); *Open Secrets* (London: Dent, 1988) and *Bonds of Attachment* (London: Macmillan, 1991), all of which have been reprinted by the University of Wales Press.

12 R. S. Thomas, 'The Bush', from *Later Poems* (1983), *Collected Poems 1945–1990*, London: J. M. Dent, 1993; Phoenix edn, 1995), p. 422.

13 Thomas, 'Perspectives', *Later Poems*, *Collected Poems*, p. 403.

14 Thomas, 'The Lost', in *No Truce with the Furies* (Newcastle upon Tyne: Bloodaxe, 1995), p. 14.

would give up the struggle of upholding and defending an amorphous identity which dared not stake its claim to independent life, and turn towards England for their subject matter. Indeed, in 1985 Harri Webb described Welsh writers in English as lost to their country to such a degree that their work had become of little account. 'I don't believe that writing in English about Wales matters very much any more', he said: 'Anglo-Welsh literature is, more or less, a load of rubbish. It has only marginal relevance to Wales now.'[15]

Yet, looking back at this period with hindsight it is evident that the majority English-speaking communities of Wales cannot have been as 'lost' to their country during the inter-referendum years as these devastated campaigners of the 1979 Referendum believed. The 30 per cent swing which, by a narrow margin, won the second, 1997, Welsh Devolution Referendum for the 'Yes' voters was more marked in English-speaking South Wales than it was in the majority Welsh-speaking communities of the north and west. Neath Port Talbot's percentage of 'Yes' voters (66.3 per cent) was the highest in Wales, greater than that of Gwynedd (63.9 per cent) or Carmarthen (65.3 per cent), and the numbers of pro-devolutionary voters in the South Wales valleys generally, with Rhondda Cynon Taf at 58.5 per cent and Merthyr Tydfil at 57.9 per cent, were commensurate with West Wales Ceredigion's at 58.5 per cent. Compared to south, west and mid Glamorgan's average of 17.3 per cent 'Yes' voters in 1979, these figures stand as evidence that a change of attitude of major political significance took place in the predominantly English-speaking communities of Wales during the 1980s and 1990s. That such a fundamental shift should not in any way be reflected in the English-language culture of Wales during those same years would be strange indeed. It would contradict the Marxist categorisation of literature as part of that superstructure which reflects social change, and records, if it does not initiate, the emergence of new alignments. Rather, what can be recognised as taking place in the English-language culture of Wales during the 1980s was the development of new formations which appeared initially to be unrelated, or marginal, to the matter of Wales debate, but which served in effect to broaden the demographic representativeness of Welsh culture.

First and foremost, the 1980s saw the emergence of a feminist Welsh voice, at first most apparent in poetry. At the time when Gillian Clarke, Hilary Llewellyn-Williams and others first started to publish their work, many saw them as but the mouthpieces of an internationalist women's movement, with little to offer Wales except an indictment of the patriarchal element in its

[15] Harri Webb, *Western Mail* interview, 2 April 1985.

traditions. By the turn of the century, however, a number of critics have recognised that the work of these writers functioned so as to make room for women within a male-dominated Welsh culture which had previously seemed reluctant to include the feminine.[16] While Clarke's seminal 'Letter from a far country', for example, did indeed put on record the manner in which women in Wales had historically been subordinated, it also stressed the fact that Wales had always been the land of our mothers as well as fathers; as a country and as a social construct, it had always been shaped by female as well as male forces.[17] When these poets rewrote Welsh myth from the point of view of its female characters, as in Hilary Llewellyn-Williams's 'The song of Blodeuwedd on a May morning';[18] or gave voice to Dafydd ap Gwilym's hitherto silent lovers, as in Clarke's 'Dyddgu replies to Dafydd';[19] or recreated the enthusiasms of those numerous female converts who helped to bring about the Welsh Nonconformist revivals, as in Ruth Bidgood's 'Banquet',[20] they were making Welshness a concept with which more women could identify. The death-throes of the sexual double-standard in Wales were also celebrated in such texts as Penny Windsor's two collections *Dangerous Women* (1987) and *Like Oranges* (1989),[21] both published by the Welsh feminist publishers Honno Press, which since its establishment in 1987 has done much to further women's writing in Wales. Women novelists also undertook the task of reclaiming Welsh culture for women: Mary Jones's *Resistance* (1985) sympathetically interpellated the Welsh-language movement from the point of view of an initially alienated English-speaking female incomer;[22] and Siân James's *Storm at Arberth* (1994) resurrected the power of the Celtic mother–goddesses in a modern comedy.[23] By inserting women's perspectives into Welsh writing in English, such texts helped to create a Wales for which, in 1997, women could vote without feeling

[16] See, for example, M. Wynn Thomas, 'Staying to Mind Things: Gillian Clarke's Early Poetry', in Menna Elfyn, ed., *Trying the Line: A Volume of Tribute to Gillian Clarke* (Llandysul: Gwasg Gomer, 1997), pp. 44–68; or Jeremy Hooker, 'Ceridwen's Daughters: Welsh Women Poets and the Uses of Tradition', *Welsh Writing in English*, 1 (1995), pp. 128–44.

[17] Gillian Clarke, *Letter from a Far Country* (Manchester: Carcanet Press, 1982), pp. 7–18.

[18] Hilary Llewellyn-Williams, 'The Song of Blodeuwedd on a May morning', *The Tree Calendar* (Bridgend: Poetry Wales Press, 1987), pp. 45–6.

[19] Gillian Clarke, 'Dyddgu replies to Dafydd', *The Sundial* (Llandysul: Gwasg Gomer, 1978), p. 20.

[20] Ruth Bidgood, 'Banquet', *Kindred* (Bridgend: Poetry Wales Press, 1986), pp. 10–11.

[21] Penny Windsor, *Dangerous Women* (Dinas Powys: Honno Press, 1987) and *Like Oranges* (Dinas Powys: Honno Press, 1989).

[22] Mary Jones, *Resistance* (Belfast: Blackstaff Press, 1985). For an interpretation of this novel, see M. Wynn Thomas, *Internal Difference: Literature in Twentieth-Century Wales* (Cardiff: University of Wales Press, 1992), pp. 156–63.

[23] Siân James, *Storm at Arberth* (Bridgend: Seren Books, 1994).

alienated; they were no longer required to choose between loyalty to their gender or to their nation. Far from distracting attention from the needs of Wales, therefore, or attacking the already fragile concept of Welshness from an alien perspective, these writers were rather expanding the idea of Wales to make it more inclusive of the female half of the populace.

Another omnipresent concern of women writers in 1980s Wales, and one not unconnected with the emphasis on women's experience and the construction of Welsh female identity, was eco-politics: the importance of safeguarding the fragile balance of natural life was a theme central to such collections as Sheenagh Pugh's *Earth Studies and Other Voyages* (1982),[24] and Christine Evans's *Cometary Phases* (1989).[25] In the works of Evans, Llewellyn-Williams, Bidgood and Clarke, this concern was evoked primarily in reflective poems on the rural Welsh landscape in which all four poets chose to make their homes, though none of them had been reared there. The 'new nature' poetry (as Gillian Clarke termed it)[26] which they produced was imbued with a scientific respect for, and fascination with, the interconnected patterning of living cycles. Traditional Welsh ways of life which had hitherto worked in close connection with such patterns were respected in these poems for having a wisdom of their own, more pertinent than ever in the modern 1980s context of accumulating warheads and nuclear threat. When Jean Earle, for example, describes the act of cleaning her step, 'rubbing with bluestone in the old way', as 'My scour against the world's indifference / To important symbols – the common roof, / Likeness of patterns,[27] the mundane and stereotypically female domestic task becomes imbued with a spirit of resistance in the face of contemporary negligence which has the effect of endearing readers to that 'common roof' under which the bluestone was traditionally employed – that is, working- or peasant-class Wales, with its old values now treasured in a new light. Similarly, when Ruth Bidgood, in such poems as 'Heol y Mwyn (Mine Road)' and 'Slate-quarry, Penceulan', reminds us (with an intensity which no doubt came from the fact that she, like Earle, was reared in the coal-mining villages of South Wales) of the threatening hollows carved out by defunct industries under the sunny surface of the Welsh landscape, she too is evoking a particularly Welsh historical resistance to the exploitative forces which undermine the security of

24 Sheenagh Pugh, *Earth Studies and Other Voyages* (Bridgend: Poetry Wales Press, 1982).
25 Christine Evans, *Cometary Phases* (Bridgend: Seren Books, 1989).
26 Gillian Clarke, 'Beginning with Bendigeidfran', in Jane Aaron, Teresa Rees, Sandra Betts and Moira Vincentelli, eds., *Our Sisters' Land: The Changing Identities of Women in Wales* (Cardiff: University of Wales Press, 1994), p. 291.
27 Jean Earle, 'Visiting Light', *Visiting Light* (Bridgend: Poetry Wales Press, 1987); p. 11.

both human life and nature.[28] In fiction too, Glenda Beagan in such short stories as 'Shining Stones' from her collection *The Medlar Tree* (1992),[29] or Catherine Merriman in her novel *State of Desire* (1996),[30] in which the protagonist plays a central role in her community's fight against a local open-cast mine, show women calling upon traditional Welsh values of community and respect for nature to resist contemporary threats to the environment.

The association of green values with the peace movement, and in particular the Greenham Common campaign – started as it was in September 1981 by Anne Pettit from her small-holding in South Wales – is also strongly present in the work of these writers. Throughout the 1980s the peace camp at Greenham served as a potent symbol for many Welsh women, English- and Welsh-speaking alike; there is barely a Welsh woman poet of this era who does not have a Greenham poem in her *œuvre*. Not only women writers but many male artists too, gave their primary political allegiance to peace and ecological movements in 1980s Wales. Tony Curtis, in his poem series 'The Deerslayers' and poetry collection *War Voices*, explores the dehumanising consequences of purposeless destructions of natural life, and the defilements of war.[31] Robert Minhinnick, founder of Friends of the Earth Cymru, incorporated that movement's politics into such literary works as his poetry collection *Life Sentences* (1983) and volume of essays *Badlands* (1996).[32] The success of CND Cymru in making Wales the first Nuclear Free Zone in Europe in 1982 was commemorated in the work of various poets: Nigel Jenkins, for example, celebrates in his poetry CND activity at Brawdy, a military base in rural Pembrokeshire where attempts were made to establish a Greenham Common-style peace camp.[33] This green image of Wales was markedly successful in the important task of drawing many of the numerous immigrants who settled in rural Wales during the 1980s into political sympathy with the indigenous people of the area. Having come to Wales for its greenness, they identified with the political concept of a green Wales, demonstrating the truth of the maxim 'small is beautiful', at that time propagated by Plaid Cymru. The official support which the Green Party in Cardiganshire and North Pembrokeshire gave Plaid

[28] Ruth Bidgood, 'Heol y Mwyn (Mine Road)', *Lighting Candles* (Bridgend: Poetry Wales Press, 1982), p. 64, and 'Slate-quarry, Penceulan', *Kindred*, p. 49.

[29] Glenda Beagan, *The Medlar Tree* (Bridgend: Seren Books, 1992).

[30] Catherine Merriman, *State of Desire* (London: Macmillan, 1996).

[31] Tony Curtis, 'The Deerslayers', *Selected Poems 1970–1985* (Bridgend: Poetry Wales Press, 1986), pp. 7–72; *War Voices* (Bridgend: Seren Books, 1995).

[32] Robert Minhinnick, *Life Sentences* (Bridgend: Poetry Wales Press, 1983) and *Badlands* (Bridgend: Seren Books, 1996).

[33] Nigel Jenkins, 'Brawdy', in Nigel Jenkins and Menna Elfyn, eds., *Glas-Nos: Poems for Peace/Cerddi dros Heddwch* (Machynlleth: CND Cymru, 1987), pp. 34–5. .

Cymru candidate Cynog Dafis helped to win him a parliamentary seat in the 1992 general election, and set the pattern for an integration of political interests which did much to encourage green-minded incomers to vote 'Yes' for Wales in 1997. Once again, therefore, the preoccupation of the representative Welsh writer in English with issues not apparently directly related to Wales – in this case, with green and peace politics – worked ultimately not to divert attention from Welsh needs but to expand the concept of Welshness so that a new and numerically significant group of voters could experience their concerns as incorporated within it.

This new coalition of interests was, of course, unintentionally much fortified by the impact on Wales of Margaret Thatcher, and her monetary and neo-imperialist politics. The 1982 Falklands War, in which a number of Welsh soldiers were killed, was a grim reminder of British imperialism, and of Wales's ambivalent relation to it. The ironies of that war – that Welsh soldiers should die fighting a people within whom were numbered the descendents of Patagonians who had gone to Argentina in the first place in order to escape the pressures of English cultural colonialism in nineteenth-century Wales – exacerbated anti-imperialist feelings in Wales. In his 'Elegy for the Welsh Dead, in the Falkland Islands, 1982', Tony Conran drew attention to these ironies by evoking the sixth-century Welsh poem, *Y Gododdin*, in which Aneirin mourned those who died fighting the Anglo-Saxon invaders at Catraeth.[34] The poem served as a reminder of the manner in which Wales's history had been one of resistance to invasion, of defeat and subsequent colonisation, rather than of imperialism, and functioned to unite those antagonised by the neo-imperialism of the Thatcher regime more strongly with Wales as a more sinned against than sinning alternative. Through his fine and influential translations into English of classical Welsh-language poetry, and through the series of original poetry collections he published in the early nineties, Conran strove to create in his readers a sense of Welsh citizenship, through reminding them of the intricate politics of their past, not least the 1979 Referendum vote which he describes as 'a green force aborted'.[35]

The dire consequences of not having voted for at least a measure of devolution in 1979 were, however, most effectively brought home to the Welsh

[34] Tony Conran, 'Elegy for the Welsh Dead, in the Falkland Islands, 1982', *Blodeuwedd* (Bridgend: Poetry Wales Press, 1988), p. 15.

[35] Tony Conran, 'Referendum', *All Hallows: A Symphony in 3 Movements* (Llandysul: Gomer Press, 1995), p. 24. See also his *The Penguin Book of Welsh Verse* (Harmondsworth: Penguin, 1967); *Castles: Variations on an original theme* (Llandysul: Gomer Press, 1993) and *A Gwynedd Symphony* (Llandysul: Gomer Press, 1999), first performed in 1996.

population at large by the pit closures that preceded and followed the miners' strike of 1984–5. Anger at the rapid and wide-scale destruction of Wales's heavy industries lessened any sense of fellow-feeling with an English populace which bafflingly kept voting back into power a Tory government apparently intent on bringing Wales to its knees. Both the anger and the resilience of the South Wales industrial communities in the face of these successive onslaughts were sympathetically represented by the poets, novelists and dramatists of the 1980s. The Red Poets' Society, with its stated aims of 'turning the world on its head with Welsh socialist poetry',[36] was formed, and toured its performance poetry productions around the pubs and clubs of South Wales, aided in the popularity stakes by its links with an emergent and angry English-language Welsh pop music culture (Patrick Jones, the brother of the Manic Street Preachers' lyricist Nicky Wire, publishes with the Red Poets' Society). In his Merthyr dialect poems, Mike Jenkins, the editor of Red Poets' Society's pamphlet series, employed the characteristic accent of South Wales in a manner which both voiced the region's grievances, once again, as in the 1920s and 30s, bereft of its occupation and plunged into unemployment, and emphasised the difference between the people of the South Wales valleys and their Whitehall rulers. They may ostensibly be speaking the same language – English – but the valleys people do so with such a difference that they are marked as 'other' as soon as they open their mouths.[37]

The 1984–5 strike featured in such novels as Roger Granelli's *Dark Edge* (1997), while Chris Meredith's 1988 novel *Shifts*, on the 1977 closures at the steelworks in Ebbw Vale, fleshed out the manifold social consequences of the demise of the heavy industries of Wales.[38] For all their primary concern with portraying the impact of industrial closures and the miners' strike on the predominantly male workforce, both of these novels also reflected the manner in which economic change affected female as well as male experience. Jude, the central female character of *Shifts*, goes through changes which finally persuade her that she has to define herself, without tying her identity to that of either her husband or her lover. Accordingly she serves as representative of that generation of valleys women who the historian Gwyn Alf Williams described as experiencing 'shifts' in their lives of revolutionary proportions, as the collapse of the heavy industries affected the gendered patterns of employment, and as the second wave of the feminist movement made its impact

36 *Red Poets' Society*, I (1993), title page.

37 See Mike Jenkins, *Graffiti Narratives: Poems 'n' Stories* (Aberystwyth: Planet, 1994).

38 Roger Granelli, *Dark Edge* (Bridgend: Seren Books, 1997); Christopher Meredith, *Shifts* (Bridgend: Seren Books, 1988).

felt.[39] Similarly, Susan, the heroine of *Dark Edge*, represents the 1980s generation of valleys women who won more than they had initially bargained for as a consequence of their activity in support of the miners' strike. Defying her policeman husband, Susan joins the women's support groups, and this move out of the confinement of her increasingly violent marriage eventually gives her the strength to leave her husband. Her politicisation as a result of the strike becomes a feminist as well as a socialist awakening.

Commenting on the emergence of feminist attitudes among women involved in the 1984–5 miners' strike, the Postcolonial theorist Homi K. Bhabha cites their characteristic movement, from traditional, trade-union and male-focused socialism to a socialism now including feminism, as a definitive example of 'the hybrid moment of political change'. 'The transformational value of change', Bhabha suggests, 'lies in the rearticulation, or translation, of elements that are *neither the One* (unitary working class) *nor the Other* (the politics of gender) *but something else besides*, which contests the terms and territories of both.' 'What does a working woman put first?' he asks, 'Which of her identities is the one that determines her political choices?'[40] In Wales, women's recorded responses to their involvement in the strike's support groups indicate that yet another term must be added to their ongoing negotiation of values and identities during this period: nationalist, as well as feminist and socialist, allegiances were reanimated by the strike.[41] Both *Shifts* and *Dark Edge* also suggest that Welsh working-class males, as well as their female counterparts, were similarly made more aware of their nationalist allegiances through their involvement in the strike. The central male character of each novel determines at the close 'to make another attempt to learn the language that should have been his by right', as a 'sign-post' of the political change that he is undergoing.[42] 'How we knew ourselves / Was how we laboured' says Robert Minhinnick of the South Whalian identity in his 1983 poem 'Smith's Garage';[43] but these post 1984–5 fictions show Welsh men and women attempting to get to know themselves through their national rather than work identities. Their decision to learn Welsh make both Keith and Edwin representative of a popular

[39] See Gwyn A. Williams, speech to the Women's Institute, reported in *Western Mail* (24 April 1987), and quoted in Teresa Rees, 'Changing Patterns of Women's Work in Wales: Some Myths Explored', *Contemporary Wales*, 2 (1988), pp. 126–7.

[40] Homi K. Bhabha, 'The Commitment to Theory', *The Location of Culture* (London and New York: Routledge, 1994), p. 28.

[41] See, for example, the oral testimonies recorded in Jill Miller, *You Can't Kill the Spirit: Women in a Welsh Mining Valley* (London: Women's Press, 1986).

[42] Granelli, *Dark Edge*, p. 185; see also Meredith, *Shifts*, p. 213.

[43] Robert Minhinnick, 'Smith's Garage', *Life Sentences* (Bridgend: Poetry Wales Press, 1983), p. 7.

movement within the valleys communities of their generation. The 1970s and 80s saw the establishment, by grass-roots demand, of Welsh-language primary and secondary schools, and adult learning classes, throughout the valleys: between the 1981 and 1991 census dates the numbers of Welsh speakers in south and mid Glamorgan, and in Islwyn in Gwent, went up for the first time in the twentieth century.

These fictions illustrate the manner in which, pre-1997, 'hybrid moments of political change' led – in the South Wales valleys in particular – to a shift in popular attitudes towards the Welsh language issue, making it a force which could now serve to unite, rather than as hitherto to divide, the south and north of west Wales. By the close of the 1980s, the sharpest concerns were not the old divisions between Wales's two linguistic cultures, but the repeated humiliations that Wales had undergone during the Thatcher years, humiliations that also served as a reminder of the exploitative manner in which the Welsh workforce had also been abused during earlier epochs of the twentieth century. A new breed of dramatists also began to flesh out the ills of contemporary Wales, staging the cultural effects of the attrition of the heavy industries, and making more overt the felt need for a specifically Welsh cultural and political solution to Welsh problems. Ed Thomas illustrated in his play *House of America* (1988) the appalling consequences on his generation of unemployment, and the loss of past identity patterns based on work. In their alienation, his characters elaborate an escapist fantasy world in which they inhabit the Beat America of Jack Kerouac, with what Thomas shows to be disastrous effects for their sense of reality.[44] Looking elsewhere to other cultures for solace can only lead ultimately to an increased despair with the realities of the here and now in Wales. That 'here and now' also featured interestingly in Ian Rowlands's one-act monologue *Marriage of Convenience*, first performed in 1996, in which a Rhondda inhabitant reflects on his divided upbringing, educated by his dead father's choice in a Welsh-language school but living under the rule of a new step-father alienated by the revival of the language in the valleys. The boy manipulates the step-father into physically abusing him, in his mother's presence, for his Welsh language cultural and political allegiances, and thereby wins the domestic stand-off, as his mother is sufficiently angered to insist that the step-father leaves the next day.[45] The son has won his battle through accepting blows, just as it could be said that Wales won her modicum of

44 Edward Thomas, *House of America* (1988) in *Three Plays* (Bridgend: Seren Books, 1994), pp. 13–100.

45 Ian Rowlands, 'Marriage of Convenience' (1996) in David Adams, ed., *One Man, One Voice* (Cardiff: Parthian Books, 2001), pp. 83–115.

freedom in 1997 through the fact that enough of her people were sufficiently antagonised by the blows Wales received during the Thatcher years to vote for her greater independence. In 1997 it was clear to just enough of the Welsh voters that such a step-father as the English administration had proved itself to be could no longer be trusted to rule the roost at home for the best.

Ed Thomas and Ian Rowlands are both bilingual writers, who contributed in the 1990s to the two linguistic cultures of Wales, and were not alone in so doing. Bilingual poets also emerged, like Gwyneth Lewis, whose work in both languages often evokes the pains but also the energising pleasures of standing on an edge, between two cultures.[46] Macaronic texts – for example, Peter Finch's experimental wordplay poems – in which Welsh words and phrases feature, without translation, alongside the English, started to be published;[47] because of the increased emphasis on learning Welsh, it could now be assumed that English-speaking audiences in Wales would have sufficient knowledge of the language to make some sense of them. Welsh and English language literature also more frequently appeared side by side in the same bilingual texts, with new anthologies including both English- and Welsh-language poetry,[48] and some Welsh-language poets, like Menna Elfyn, making a point of publishing editions of their work in which English-language translations appeared alongside the Welsh originals.[49]

These developments suggested a greater capacity to recognise, accept and celebrate, as cultural richness, the previously divisive elements within Welsh society. The long-established ethnic minority and mixed-race populations of South Wales also found literary representation in the 1990s. Dannie Abse, in his autobiographical prose in particular, continued to reflect upon the experience of the Jewish community in Wales;[50] and in 1995 Leonora Brito's short-story collection *dat's love* gave literary voice to the Black communities of Cardiff's

[46] Gwyneth Lewis's publications include *Parables and Faxes* (Newcastle upon Tyne: Bloodaxe Books, 1995), *Zero Gravity* (Newcastle upon Tyne: Bloodaxe Books, 1998), and three Welsh-language poetry collections, *Sonedau Redsa* (Llandysul: Gwasg Gomer, 1990); *Cyfrif Un ac Un yn Dri* (Felindre, Abertawe: Cyhoeddiadau Barddas, 1996) and *Y Llofrudd Iaith* (Felindre, Abertawe: Cyhoeddiadau Barddas, 1999).

[47] Peter Finch, 'St David's Hall', or 'Dydi'r Haf: ex-Dafydd ap Gwilym', in *Food* (Bridgend: Seren Books, 2001), pp. 23 and 61.

[48] See, for example, Jenkins and Elfyn, eds., *Glas-Nos: Poems for Peace/Cerddi dros Heddwch* and Amy Wack and Grahame Davies, eds., *Oxygen: New Poets from Wales/ Beirdd Newydd o Gymru* (Bridgend: Seren Books, 2000).

[49] Menna Elfyn's bilingual poetry collections include *Eucalyptus* (Llandysul: Gwasg Gomer, 1995), *Cell Angel* (Newcastle upon Tyne: Bloodaxe Books, 1996) and *Cusan Dyn Dall/ Blind Man's Kiss* (Tarset, Northumberland: Bloodaxe Books, 2001).

[50] Dannie Abse, *There Was a Young Man from Cardiff* (Harmondsworth: Penguin, 1991).

Tiger Bay area, threatened as that community was by the redevelopment of the docklands.[51] Similarly, on the stage Afshan Malik dramatised the negotiation of Asian and Welsh identities.[52] Since 1997, this development has been yet more marked with the poet Catherine Fisher, for example, including in her poetry collection *Altered States* (1999) a moving series of sonnets on the landing on the mudbanks off Newport of her Irish forebears, in flight from the Famine,[53] while Merthyr novelist Desmond Barry portrays in his novel *A Bloody Good Friday*, the long-established Irish contingent of the Merthyr population.[54] Trezza Azzopardi's novel *The Hiding Place*, on the Maltese community of Tiger Bay in the 1950s,[55] was followed by Charlotte Williams's *Sugar and Slate* (2002), the fullest exploration to date of such conflicting ethnic identities in Wales, intertwining as it does the histories of Williams's Afro-Caribbean father's people and those of her Welsh mother from the slate-quarrying communities of North Wales.[56] At the close of this autobiographical volume, Williams opts for Welshness out of the array of possible ethnicities available to her precisely because Wales is so diverse, 'as mixed up as I was', she says: 'I like it because it is fragmented, because there is a loud bawling row raging, because its inner pain is coming to terms with its differences and its divisions, because it realises it can't hold on to the myth of sameness, past or present.'[57]

Since 1997, another previously submerged minority culture contributed its voice to this ongoing 'row' and presented its difference more confidently in Welsh writing. Roger Williams's dramas of gay lifestyles in Cardiff[58] were followed by John Sam Jones's tellingly entitled short-story collection, *Welsh Boys Too* (2000);[59] and Gillian Brightmore's 'blue' vignettes of Welsh lesbian lives[60] by the more assertive lesbian fictions of Pembrokeshire-born Sarah Waters – though, significantly perhaps, none of Sarah Waters's novels is located in Wales or features Welsh characters.[61] However, Stevie Davies's temporally multi-layered novel *Impassioned Clay* (2000) very positively portrays as one of its central protagonists a seventeenth-century Welsh lesbian; and Erica Wooff's

[51] Leonora Brito, *dat's love* (Bridgend: Seren Books, 1995).
[52] Afshan Malik, 'Safar', in *New Welsh Drama* (Cardiff: Parthian Books, 1998), pp. 15–74.
[53] Catherine Fisher, 'Estuary Poems', *Altered States* (Bridgend: Seren Books, 1999), pp. 49–62.
[54] Desmond Barry, *A Bloody Good Friday* (London: Jonathan Cape, 2002).
[55] Trezza Azzopardi, *The Hiding Place* (London: Picador, 2000).
[56] Charlotte Williams, *Sugar and Slate* (Aberystwyth: Planet, 2002).
[57] Ibid., pp. 169 and 191.
[58] Roger Williams, 'Gulp', in *New Welsh Drama* (Cardiff: Parthian Books, 1998), pp. 75–198.
[59] John Sam Jones, *Welsh Boys Too* (Cardiff: Parthian Books, 2000).
[60] Gillian Brightmore, 'Blue Sisters', *The Works*, 1 (1988), pp. 80–3.
[61] Sarah Waters, *Tipping the Velvet* (London: Virago, 1998), *Affinity* (London: Virago, 1999) and *Fingersmith* (London: Virago, 2002).

Mud Puppy presents lesbianism as a taken-for-granted facet of Welsh life in contemporary working-class Newport.[62]

By their consciousness-raising activities in imaging and reflecting upon the political and cultural changes which took place during the inter-referendum years, all these new developments in Welsh writing in English contributed to the 1997 result. They helped to bring together the previously battling Welsh tribes, not to form some kind of bland conformity, in which the various cultures would have but a contributionist relation to one another, but to encounter, record and negotiate that diversity which is modern Wales at the end of the twentieth century. The writers may have appeared to work deviously, often pursuing concerns and goals which seemed unrelated to Welsh needs, but those concerns succeeded in drawing in new adherents to an expanded and more inclusive image of Wales, in which a more varied and heterogeneous percentage of the Welsh population could feel they had a stake. Their writing contributed to the construction of that more expansive image of Wales which finally in 1997 persuaded sufficient of the Welsh to vote it into being as a nation with a more autonomous existence, and increased hopes for future developments. As such, their work in its relation to its social context serves as an interesting example of cultural affect in the production of national identity and the resistance to global homogenisation.

62 Stevie Davies, *Impassioned Clay* (London: Women's Press, 2000); Erica Wooff, *Mud Puppy* (London: Women's Press, 2002).

39

British–Jewish writing and the turn towards diaspora

BRYAN CHEYETTE

The internal chronology of British–Jewish literature extends back to the eighteenth century and is therefore difficult to incorporate into recent theories of multiculturalism which focus mainly on the post-war period.[1] For this reason, British–Jewish writing is for the most part excluded from the received historiography of post-war literature in Britain.[2] The widespread orthodoxy in the 1960s and 70s concerning the parochialism of British culture – having supposedly rejected the cosmopolitan Modernist tradition of the first half of the century – has led to the assumption that 'new' postcolonial literatures reinvigorated a moribund and hopelessly provincial national tradition. It is in these terms that the belief in the decline of the English novel has been related to the decline of British imperial power and a subsequent loss of a sense of national futurity.[3] The historical longevity of British–Jewish writing, however, helps to qualify postcolonialism as a master signifier in relation to other minority literatures in post-war Britain. By overdetermining the supplementary role of 'new' immigrants to Britain's shores, other histories of migration are either foreshortened or written out altogether. The black/white paradigm of literary multiculturalism – essentially non-white writers contributing to white culture – clearly down-plays other 'comparative ethnic histories'.[4]

[1] A detailed chronology of British–Jewish Literature can be found in Bryan Cheyette, ed., *Contemporary Jewish Writing in Britain and Ireland: An Anthology* (Lincoln: University of Nebraska Press and London: Peter Halban, 1998), pp. xiii–lxxi. Accounts of British–Jewish writing and multiculturalism are included in Monika Fludernik, ed., *Diaspora and Multiculturalism: Common Traditions and New Developments* (Amsterdam and New York: Rodopi, 2003) and A. Robert Lee, ed., *Other Britain, Other British: Contemporary Multicultural Fiction* (London: Pluto Press, 1995).

[2] Dominic Head, *The Cambridge Introduction to Modern British Fiction, 1950–2000* (Cambridge University Press, 2002) is an exception to this rule.

[3] Steven Connor, *The English Novel in History 1950–1995* (London and New York: Routledge, 1996), chapter 4.

[4] Stephen May, 'Multiculturalism', in David Theo Goldberg and John Solomos, eds., *A Companion to Racial and Ethnic Studies* (Oxford: Blackwell, 2002), p. 130.

It is in the context of this conventional literary historiography that an understanding of contemporary British–Jewish writing might prove to be a useful corrective. After all, East European Jews migrating to Britain were the object of the earliest anti-immigration and naturalisation acts in the first half of the twentieth century and this legislation was extended in each decade from the 1960s onwards. Jewish immigrants anticipated their 'new' commonwealth counterparts in having to negotiate 'anti-alien' legislation by demonstrating that they were respectable and hard-working citizens who valued, above all else, religion, family and community.[5] Many pre-war British–Jewish writers, such as Louis Golding, succumbed to these assimilatory or conformist pressures which were focused primarily on Jews of East European origin living in the tenements of many of Britain's major cities. In stark contrast to such literary forebears, a post-war generation was to embrace class and ethnic differences and become part of an anti-assimilatory counter-culture. Colin MacInnes in his *England, Half English: A Polyphoto of the Fifties* (1961) captured something of this contemporary mood when he juxtaposed Bernard Kops's East End play *The Hamlet of Stepney Green* (1956) with accounts of British Jazz, Afro-Caribbean street life in Brixton and fifties youth culture. Writing at about the same time, George Steiner argued in a similar spirit that the supposed 'supremacy of the English language' should be decoupled from the presumed 'exemplary moral and institutional authority of English life' as the growth of 'African English, Australian English, the rich speech of West Indian and Anglo-Indian writers' demonstrate that the 'language taught and written on this island is no longer the inevitable authority or focus'.[6]

The demise of an assimilatory British–Jewish writing was marked by the death in 1958 at the age of sixty-two of Louis Golding, whom *The Times* in their obituary described accurately as an 'apt interpreter of British Jewry'.[7] As with Israel Zangwill at the end of the nineteenth century or Grace Aguilar in the Victorian era, Golding was a reassuring presence for the majoritarian culture as he was a willing mediator between a supposedly timeless Englishness and an ever more obeisant Anglo-Jewish community. As if to highlight the end of such apologetics, Brian Glanville in December 1958, three months after Golding's death, began a series of interviews in the London *Jewish Chronicle* with an emerging group of poets, dramatists and novelists under the heading

[5] David Cesarani and Tony Kushner, eds., *The Internment of Aliens in Twentieth-Century Britain* (London: Frank Cass, 1993).

[6] George Steiner, 'To Civilize Our Gentlemen' (1965), *Language and Silence: Essays 1958–1966* (London: Perguin, 1969), p. 82.

[7] 'Mr Louis Golding: Novels and Essays', *The Times*, 11 August 1958, p. 10.

'Young Jewish Writers and the Community'. The writers interviewed were Dannie Abse, Alexander Baron, Bernard Kops, Wolf Mankowitz, Peter Shaffer and Arnold Wesker. All refused any engagement with the established Anglo-Jewish community and referred instead (with Glanville's prompting) to Arthur Koestler's oft-stated belief that Jews in the diaspora would either assimilate completely or immigrate to the state of Israel.[8] Each writer rejected an implied mediating role between nation and community and instead spoke of an alternative East European Yiddish folk tradition (Kops and Mankowitz) or identified with British working-class culture (Baron and Wesker) or were entirely sceptical about writing in any identifiable tradition of Jewish literature (Abse and Shaffer).

Throughout the 1960s there was a series of similar interviews with other writers of the so-called 'new Elizabethan age of modern Jewish literature' which included Gerda Charles, Ruth Fainlight, Michael Hamburger, Dan Jacobson, Emanuel Litvinoff, Harold Pinter, Frederic Raphael, Bernice Rubens and Jon Silkin. These interviews 'On Being English and Jewish' were published in the *Jewish Quarterly*, founded in London in 1953 by Jacob Sonntag, a refugee from Bukovina and Vienna who settled in Britain in 1938. Fluent in Yiddish, Hebrew, Czech and German, Sonntag wanted his magazine to 'cultivate literary journalism in the best tradition of Central and Eastern Europe' as he belonged to the generation which 'looked for a synthesis between our Jewishness and our Europeanism, between our nationalism and our socialism, between the particular and the universal'.[9] Although it had a small circulation, the magazine was a unique space which brought together émigrés from Central Europe, such as George Steiner and Isaac Deutscher, translated the Yiddish and Hebrew cultures of Eastern Europe and the state of Israel, and also cultivated the 'new wave' of post-war British– and American–Jewish writing. Most importantly, the magazine acted as an alternative mediating space so that Jewish writers no longer needed to focus on nation and community but could, instead, engage extraterritorially with Jewish history and culture.

One key function of the journal, in its first three decades, was to preserve the vanished world of European Jewish culture. Each writer interviewed in

[8] Brian Glanville, 'Young Jewish Writers and the Community', *Jewish Chronicle*, 19 December 1958, p. 19; 26 December 1958, p. 13; 2 January 1959, p. 17; 9 January 1959; and 16 January 1959, p. 19. For the impact of Arthur Koestler's views on Jews and Zionism in the 1950s see David Cesarani, *Arthur Koestler: The Homeless Mind* (London: William Heineman, 1998), pp. 427–31.

[9] Natasha Lehrer, ed., *The Golden Chain: Fifty Years of the Jewish Quarterly* (London and Oregon: Vallentine Mitchell, 2003), p. vii. See also Jacob Sonntag, ed., *Caravan: A Jewish Quarterly Omnibus* (London and New York: Thomas Yoseloff, 1962), pp. 5–6.

the *Jewish Quarterly* spoke of the genocide of European Jewry as a central, albeit private, preoccupation. Abse, for instance, argued that 'Hitler has made me more of a Jew than Moses'; Baron that it was 'the master obsession of my life'; and Litvinoff that it 'completed' his education.[10] But the threat of nuclear armageddon during the Cold War meant that the Holocaust was often diminished in the 1960s as a 'small-scale trial run for a nuclear war', in the words of Al Alvarez.[11] As the historian Tony Kushner has noted, the genocide of European Jewry lacked any significant public recognition in Britain until the 1970s, in stark contrast both to the continent of Europe and the United States. The particularity of the Jewish fate, in the context of generalised apocalyptic fears, meant that television programmes, such as the 'Genocide' episode of Jeremy Isaacs's *World at War* (1975) series, had an extraordinary impact. But the Holocaust in the 1970s was not part of the school curriculum or of museum culture and plans to construct a national Holocaust memorial in Britain at this time were fiercely contested. This conspicuous absence was bound up with both celebratory national myths concerning World War II and what George Steiner has called the 'continuum of sanity, of liberal imagining, in British politics'.[12] Such liberal imagining also had a strong cultural and literary dimension as illustrated by the largely bemused response to the ground-breaking essays contained in Steiner's *Language and Silence: Essays 1958–1966* (1967) by colleagues in the English Department at Cambridge.

In his location of barbarism at the heart of Western humanism in *Language and Silence*, Steiner transformed himself into an accessible version of Walter Benjamin and Theodor Adorno. But it was precisely Steiner's importation of this strand of continental cultural pessimism into Britain in the 1960s that caused a great deal of unease. His essay, 'To Civilize Our Gentlemen' (1965), a critique of the discipline of English Literature, is believed to have cost him his professorship and examination rights at Cambridge. Steiner's isolation in the UK in the 1960s resulted in 1969 in his voluntary exile to Geneva. His sense of embattlement underscores his essays: 'Recently one of my [Cambridge] colleagues . . . inquired of me, with genuine bafflement, why someone trying to establish himself in an English literature faculty should refer so often to concentration camps; why they were in any way relevant.' Steiner, however,

[10] Jacob Sonntag, ed., *Jewish Perspectives: 25 Years of Jewish Writing* (London: Secker & Warburg, 1980), pp. 70, 85 and 100–1.

[11] Al Alvarez, 'The Literature of the Holocaust', cited in Mark Rawlinson, 'British Culture and the Holocaust', *Cambridge Quarterly*, 25, 1 (1996), p. 20.

[12] George Steiner, 'Book-Keeping of Torture', *Sunday Times*, 10 April 1988, cited in Tony Kushner, *The Holocaust and the Liberal Imagination: A Social and Cultural History* (Oxford and Cambridge, MA: Basil Blackwell, 1994), p. 19.

responded uncompromisingly and argued that as the humanities failed to be 'humane . . . before the holocaust', the discipline of English literature was not unlike its pre-war German counterpart in being a form of cultural nationalism which was therefore potentially just as inhumane.[13]

Such un-English preoccupations were replicated in the experiences of the 'new wave' of British–Jewish writers as summarised by the Cambridge-educated Frederic Raphael in a *Jewish Quarterly* interview: 'My Jewishness is the Jewishness of the disillusioned diaspora Jew, the Jewishness of loneliness . . . I do not believe in salvation, either through community or religion. Thus I am not English either, for I feel myself excluded from the community of Britons. I function within it, but I am not absorbed or satisfied by it.'[14] Along with Steiner's *Anno Domini* (1964), Alexander Baron's *Lowlife* (1963) and Emanuel Litvinoff's *The Lost European* (1960), Raphael's early fiction, *The Limits of Love* (1960) and *Lindmann* (1963), locates the Holocaust at the heart of British and European culture. In *The Limits of Love* it is the figure of Otto Kahane, a refugee from Dachau, who returns to haunt his relatives in Cricklewood and whose presence disrupts the false equilibrium of post-war Britain. *Lindmann* concerns the traumatised over-identification of a British civil servant, James Shepherd, with the eponymous Jewish survivor from the SS *Broda*, a ship full of illegal immigrants sunk off the Turkish coast in 1942. Lindmann / Shepherd live among the Afro-Caribbean community in London and, so, the plight of wartime European Jewish refugees on the SS *Broda*, forced to take to the seas due to the imposition of British immigrant quotas, echoes the history of the SS *Windrush*.

Raphael treats at length the unravelling of assimilatory liberal Englishness in *The Limits of Love*, where the child of successfully acculturated British Jews returns to the East End of London so as to rediscover the unremembered communist politics and poverty-stricken social conditions of an earlier generation. Such journeys of self-discovery were invariably isolated and dispiriting due to the destruction of much of the Jewish East End of London during the war. Brian Glanville, with typical asperity, dismissed the 'new wave' of British–Jewish writing as a literature which portrays 'an East End Jewish world which no longer exists, presented in terms of a tradition which was built up and died in Eastern Europe'.[15] This double loss, according to this lachrymose

13 Steiner, 'To Civilize Our Gentlemen', p. 88. See also Steiner's *Errata: An Examined Life* (London: Weidenfeld & Nicolson, 1997), pp. 91–2.

14 Sonntag, *Jewish Perspectives*, pp. 76–7.

15 Brian Glanville, 'The Anglo-Jewish Writer', cited in Colin Macinnes, *England, Half English: A Polyphoto of the Fifties* (Harmondsworth: Penguin, 1966), p. 77.

perspective, accounts for the decline of the 'new wave' of Jewish writers in Britain, such as Glanville himself, Alexander Baron, Gerda Charles, Bernard Kops and Emanuel Litvinoff, in stark contrast to the American 'new wave', which included Saul Bellow, Bernard Malamud and Philip Roth, who helped to transform post-war American literature.

The obliteration of the Jewish East End, compared to the abiding presence of New York's East Side, is a key factor here. As Emanuel Litvinoff notes in his *Journey Through a Small Planet* (1972), a memoir of his childhood in Bethnal Green, those who 'survived' the East End were 'moving eagerly into the universe of the future and had no wish to look back at the retreating past'. His book therefore finds it necessary to rehabilitate a once 'crowded East European Ghetto' and challenge a prevalent cultural amnesia. Revisiting Bethnal Green in the early 1970s, now largely populated by British–Asians, Litvinoff felt 'indescribably bereaved, a ghost haunting the irrecoverable past'. Rather than finding an easy identification with the 'new' commonwealth immigrants in London's East End, these post-war East End inhabitants were perceived by Litvinoff to have further eroded his past. His imaginative recreation of his childhood and adolescence is thus both an antidote to this sense of radical displacement and, like the proletarian memoirs of Simon Blumenfeld and William Goldman, a portrait of the nascent artist.[16]

By the end of *Journey Through a Small Planet*, Litvinoff writes his first youthful poem and is aware that 'things would never be the same again' as there had been a shift from the 'outer space' of his 'small planet' in East London to the 'inner space' of his ever-expanding consciousness.[17] This tension between outer and inner, the collective and the individual, assumed a variety of different forms in many British–Jewish writers who came to prominence in the 1970s. The distrust of all forms of collectivity, for instance, was first signalled by the poet Dannie Abse when he coedited *Mavericks* (1957) with Howard Sergeant as a counterblast to the *New Lines* (1956) anthology of Movement poets edited by Robert Conquest. As with *New Lines*, *Mavericks* contained nine poets which included Abse, Michael Hamburger and Jon Silkin. As Abse was to later remark: 'I felt in opposition to "the Movement" . . . There were also certain political undertones with the upraising of the English tradition. It was a feeling that . . . foreign poetry was no good . . . I didn't feel myself to be a Little Englander.' At the same time, Abse refused simply to promote an alternative grouping of

16 Emanuel Litvinoff, *Journey Through a Small Planet* (London: Michael Joseph, 1972), pp. 9–11, and Ken Worpole, *Dockers and Detectives* (London: Verso, 1983), chapter 5.

17 Litvinoff, *Journey Through a Small Planet*, p. 158.

Mavericks (beyond the anthology) but instead wrote within a series of competing identities which have been accurately summarised as 'British / Jewish, English / Welsh, seeker / sceptic, bourgeois / bohemian, poet / doctor'.[18] This rejection of a settled national or literary tradition, coupled with a creatively fragmented and sustaining set of identities, can be said to characterise much contemporary British–Jewish literature.

To be sure, other writers did stress more coherent and alternative literary canons which, in the words of Jon Silkin, amalgamated 'humanism and . . . cosmopolitanism, cautioned, as it were, by English and Jewish specifics'. Silkin, in particular, constructed the World War I poet Isaac Rosenberg as a literary forebear but argued that it was impossible 'to determine what emphasis to put upon the ethnic impulse and what on the radical' in his poetry. Instead he believed that 'for Rosenberg the two issues were in common. To be Jewish in England then was to be, in the main, working class.'[19] By the 1970s, however, Silkin was unusual in articulating a synthetic Jewish counter-culture expressed through the spontaneity of American poetry or the particular voice of English linguistic regionalism. Many Jewish writers in Britain tended to signify their oppositional stance by utilising marginalised aesthetic forms in their work such as the European literary Modernism of Eva Figes and Gabriel Josipovici, the Yiddish folk tradition of Bernard Kops and Wolf Mankowitz, and the use of Gothic and fable in the fiction of Dan Jacobson and Elaine Feinstein.

After the 1950s, mainstream cinematic and literary depictions of the working classes were no longer located in East London but instead moved further north: 'Nottingham, Rotherham, Liverpool, Blackpool; exotic, unknown and interchangeable'.[20] While Silkin successfully reclaimed an alternative Jewish literary tradition for himself, and located this in the radicalised north of England, other Jewish writers in Britain found it harder to resist the universalising cultural assimilation of the metropolitan liberal-Left. Wesker's inability to conform to the expectations of the liberal-Left in his role as artistic director of Centre 42 is symptomatic in this regard. Appointed artistic director of Centre 42 in 1960, Wesker utilised trade-union support in Britain to popularise the arts

[18] Daniel Hoffman, 'Way Out in the Centre', in Joseph Cohen, ed., *The Poetry of Dannie Abse: Critical Essays and Reminiscences* (London: Robson Books, 1983), p. 50 and Peter Lawson, 'Otherness and Affiliation: Anglo-Jewish Poetry from Isaac Rosenberg to Elaine Feinstein', unpublished PhD thesis, University of Southampton, (2002), p. 18.

[19] Jon Silkin, *Out of Battle: The Poetry of the Great War* (Oxford University Press, 1978), p. 263 and 'Anglo-Jewish Poetry', *Jewish Quarterly* (Spring 1967), pp. 22–4 cited in Lawson, 'Otherness and Affiliation', p. 145.

[20] Iain Sinclair, 'Introduction' to Alexander Baron, *The Lowlife* (London: Harvill Press, 2001), p. xi.

among a wide social grouping. Instead of promoting a particular working-class culture, however, Wesker aimed to make the 'best' of culture available to everyone. But this amalgam of high and low culture, a common feature of much 'new wave' Anglo-American Jewish literature, proved unpopular and Centre 42 collapsed in 1970.[21] Six years later Wesker produced his play *The Merchant* (1976) (later renamed *Shylock*) which is a comprehensive reworking of Shakespeare's *The Merchant of Venice* from Shylock's viewpoint. Wesker's shift from class (central to his *Trilogy* [1958–60]) to ethnicity as an organising principle was to resonate throughout the contemporary period. Wesker anticipated, in other words, the general fragmentation of culture and the location of identity outside of the nation–state and particular class formations.

Other 'new wave' Jewish writers also transformed the absence of a Jewish past and sustaining literary tradition into a virtue. As Peter Shaffer notes in his *Jewish Chronicle* interview: 'I think the last despairing call of a culture is to its past.'[22] Shaffer's plays can be said to be written against all forms of orthodoxy and absoluteness and they usually pit such orthodoxies against rather primitive or unsocialised free spirits (such as Walter Langer, Julian Cristoforou, Alan Strang and Mozart) who challenge a prevailing assimilatory conformism. But rather than merely celebrate such radical individualism, Harold Pinter's early work, in contrast to Shaffer's, is distinguished by an overriding uncertainty concerning his characters' recent history. In *The Birthday Party* (1958), for instance, Goldberg simultaneously articulates Englishness and Jewishness as unreal identities which incorporate contrived and illusory memories of the past. He extols repeatedly the virtues of 'a little Austin, tea in Fullers, a library book from Boots' in a self-conscious parody of a nostalgic Englishness.[23] Goldberg's underlying menace goes hand in hand with his sentimentality, as can be seen in relation to the blatant self-contradictions concerning his Anglo-Jewish upbringing (not least in the doubt surrounding his forename). Pinter, through Goldberg (whom he has often played), exposes equally Englishness and Jewishness as specious fabrications; mirror-images of each other insofar as they both incorporate absurdly idealised versions of community.

There was a marked increase in the 1970s in the visibility of British–Jewish women writers, who challenged English liberal verities from a less masculine, more intimate, perspective. The domestic novel or play was often an appropriate form in which to challenge these verities given that the trajectory of poor

21 Robert Hewison, *Too Much: Art and Society in the Sixties, 1960–75* (London: Methuen, 1986), pp. 17–23.

22 'Young Jewish Writers and the Community', *Jewish Chronicle*, 26 December 1958, p. 13.

23 Harold Pinter, *The Birthday Party* (London: Faber & Faber, 1993 edn), p. 86.

immigrant Jews was meant to be away from the ghettoes and into the suburbs. That bit of the Anglo-Jewish story which does not fit into a narrative of liberal self-improvement and embourgeoisement can be said to be the subject of much British–Jewish writing. The fiction of Bernice Rubens, for instance, concerns the disabling nature of family and communal expectations which tend to emotionally cripple her characters. Norman Zweck, in the Booker Prize-winning *The Elected Member* (1969), is condemned to a partial existence by his parents. The novel takes as its epigraph a statement from R. D. Laing – 'If patients are disturbed, their families are very disturbing' – as Norman has been 'elected' to bear the burden of his family's fervent craving for social betterment. Rubens's use of grotesque realism has been rightly compared with the paintings of Francis Bacon and Lucien Freud and her fiction of the 1960s and 70s has been aptly described as 'short bursts of madness, tightly controlled, and superficially logical, mingling comic horror with appalled ordinariness'.[24]

By the 1970s, the critique of English liberal values, and the rejection of national and communal forms of identification, resulted in the location of much British–Jewish writing in a diasporic realm. To a large extent, as John Sutherland has noted, the international theme of many novelists after the 1970s is directly related to the economics of post-war publishing.[25] The conditions were ripe for a significant number of Jewish writers in Britain, such as Ruth Fainlight, Eva Figes, Dan Jacobson and Gabriel Josipovici, to embrace a more expansive literary culture, especially American and European literary forms. As Steven Connor has noted, there are a large number of post-war English 'novel-sequences' which are an 'exercise in world-making' and offer a 'working simulacrum of the real'.[26] But it is salutary to compare such exercises in 'world-making' with the word of British–Jewish writers in the 1970s who had neither an established version of the past to rewrite nor a stable sense of place in which to locate a novel-sequence. Emanuel Litvinoff's *Faces of Terror* (1973–8) trilogy, for instance, moves from London's East End to the impact of the Russian Revolution and the horrors of Stalinism. His novel-sequence is built around the extended diaspora of powerless and power-obsessed East European revolutionaries.

Rather than grounding his narrative in generational continuity, Litvinoff builds his trilogy around uncontrollable revolutionary change and thus varies it considerably from the novel-sequences which assume stable and linear 'fictions

24 Michael Woolf, 'Negotiating the Self: Jewish Fiction in Britain Since 1945', in Lee, *Other Britain, Other British*, pp. 135–7.

25 John Sutherland, *Fiction and the Fiction Industry* (London: Athlone Press, 1978), cited in Connor, *The English Novel in History*, p. 85.

26 Connor, *The English Novel in History*, p. 136.

of history' which encompass both the colonial and the postcolonial.[27] It was not a coincidence that Litvinoff's trilogy, centred around political extremism, was published in a decade in which political iconoclasm and organised terrorism came to the fore. Muriel Spark's surprisingly unmediated narrator in *The Takeover* (1976), initially subtitled 'A Parable of the Pagan Seventies', has been taken as a representative view of the 1970s, which is said to be characterised by 'a complete mutation not merely to be defined as the collapse of the capitalist system, or a global recession, but such a sea-change in the nature of reality as could not have been envisaged by Karl Marx or Sigmund Freud'. It is typical of Spark's narrator to evoke, merely to negate, two (Jewish) revolutionaries who had once changed the 'nature of reality' but whose power is now confined to the past. *The Takeover*, set between 1973 and 1975, dates this 'sea-change' in reality to the October 1973 war and subsequent 'oil trauma' and thus associates the origins of an apocalyptic shift in thinking with the Arab–Israeli conflict.[28]

Echoing her earlier *The Mandelbaum Gate* (1965), the Middle East again becomes the source of all chaos and leads to a world spun out of control and terminally in crisis. Crucially, in *The Takeover* and *The Mandelbaum Gate*, Spark emphasises a distinctly feminine spirituality so as to enable her heroines to challenge patriarchal authority of all kinds. At the end of *The Takeover*, Maggie Radcliffe's reversion to the status of a moon-lit gypsy proves to be the perfect balance between the two extremes of unbounded spirituality and anarchic materialism. Her return to an originary state of nature in reaction to the unreality of modern life recalls the feminised lunar paganism in Spark's short story, 'The Gentile Jewesses' (1963). As a Catholic convert, Spark is an atypical Jewish writer although a number of representative British–Jewish authors, such as Naomi Jacob and G. B. Stern, converted to Anglicanism or Catholicism. But Spark's sense of herself as 'an exile in heart and mind' and her refusal to settle on any one period, place or identity is not unlike many of her British–Jewish contemporaries who, similarly, have a diasporic reach and unsettled sense of time and locale.[29]

Along with Spark, Elaine Feinstein was a key figure who, from the 1960s onwards, articulated a diasporic Jewish identity in her fiction and poetry. As with the most accomplished British–Jewish writers, Feinstein defined her poetry

27 Bernard Bergonzi, *The Situation of the Novel* (London and Basingstoke: Macmillan, 1979 edn), chapter 8.

28 Muriel Spark, *The Takeover* (Harmondsworth: Penguin, 1978), pp. 90–1 and 99.

29 Muriel Spark, 'What Images Return', in Karl Miller, ed., *Memoirs of a Modern Scotland* (London: Faber & Faber, 1970), pp. 151–2. See also Bryan Cheyette, *Muriel Spark: Writers and their Work* (Plymouth: Northcote House, 2000).

and prose in opposition to indigenous English literary forms and discovered her poetic and fictional voice in both European and American traditions. When her early novels were characterised as a species of contemporary 'Gothic' – along with fiction by Angela Carter, J. G. Ballard and Emma Tennant – she was quick to differentiate herself from what she thought of as this 'steely rejection of humanism, a fashionable resistance to compassion which I believe is as much a luxury of our English innocence as the euphoria of the flower generation'.[30] Her career as a writer has precisely gone beyond such easy anti-humanism by evoking a Central European humanist tradition. In this she contrasts ironically with those émigré Jewish women writers, such as Ruth Prawer Jhabvala and Eva Figes, who had direct experience of Nazi Germany but who take comfort from such 'English innocence' in their fiction and memoirs. Only after she became the translator of the poetry of Marina Tsvetayeva in 1971, and later, of Margarita Aliger, Yunna Moritz and Bella Akhmadulina in 1976, did Feinstein discover her voice as a 'European' writer. Unlike Silkin, who located Rosenberg as an indigenous literary forebear, Feinstein located her female literary ancestors in Eastern Europe.

Feinstein's poem 'Exile' (1971) speaks of the 'mist of invisible / English power' and one response to such power was precisely to circumvent it by exploring cultural realms which did not mystify her sense of self. She taught English Literature at Essex in the late 1960s although her poetry was defined in opposition to an influential group of Essex University poets (including Lee Harwood and Tom Pickard). While her fiction is mainly situated in a European historical context, her poetry tends to assert a solitary first-person voice which she took initially from American Black Mountain poetry. In an important exchange with Charles Olson in 1959, Feinstein discusses the importance of 'phrasing' in poetry and, as Ruth Padel has argued, she subsequently learned to 'take risks with space and voice', whether it be the search for an imaginative geography or the painful intimacy of the domestic sphere.[31] It is the tension between her poetry and prose, the inward confessional voice and the outward search for a lost European past, which characterises Feinstein's *œuvre*. Her poetry and fiction, that is, need a liberating extraterritoriality so as to eclipse the parochial representations and received images of a naturalised Englishness. For this reason, the diasporic turn of Feinstein's work marks a key development

[30] Cited in Peter Conradi, 'Elaine Feinstein: Life and Novels', *Literary Review* (April 1982), pp. 24–5.

[31] Ruth Padel, 'Imports in England's Lane', *TLS*, 16 November 1990, p. 1248, and Ralph Maud, ed., *Selected Letters of Charles Olson* (Berkeley: University of California Press, 2000), pp. 264–6, cited in Lawson, 'Otherness and Affiliation', p. 190.

in the history of late twentieth-century Jewish writing in Britain as it constructs a European Jewish past as a source of literary and cultural inheritance and not merely as a site of victimhood. Her novel *The Border* (1984) explores the tensions in her work through the figure of Walter Benjamin –'a Marxist who is not a materialist' – a character depicted as a 'mystical' synthesising figure fixed within the borders of history while embodying the many fissures which are writ large in the novel.[32]

By the 1980s, the Holocaust had become a visible part of British culture, to the extent that it was possible to write extensively on the Holocaust in British poetry and fiction without including any British–Jewish authors. The Americanisation of the Holocaust in the 1980s and 90s, and its relative absence in Britain in the 1970s, accounts to a large extent for the marked appropriation of this history in much mainstream British writing, such as Martin Amis's *Time's Arrow* (1991), D. M. Thomas's *The White Hotel* (1981) and Geoffrey Hill's *Collected Poems* (1985).[33] From a postcolonial perspective, Salman Rushdie's influential essay 'Imaginary Homelands' (1982) invokes 'the Jews' in calling for an alternative cultural and political tradition of migration and displacement to replace the 'narrowly defined cultural frontiers' of India and England.[34] It was at this time of literary expansiveness (in response to Thatcherite narrowness) that a new generation of British–Jewish writers in the 1980s began to express with confidence a multiplicity of identities in their work. The most significant writer in this regard was undoubtedly Clive Sinclair, who in 1983 was declared, along with Rushdie, one of the twenty 'Best of Young British Novelists' by *Granta* and was particularly grouped with Amis and Ian McEwan as one of a clutch of 'new nasties'.

Sinclair has been rightly described as instigating a 'quiet but profound revolution' in British–Jewish letters.[35] His two early collections of short stories, *Hearts of Gold* (1979) (which won a Somerset Maugham Award) and *Bedbugs* (1982), pointedly attempted to 'write fiction that owes nothing to any English antecedents' and he has, therefore, located his imagined histories as a Jew in Israel, the United States and Eastern Europe. He describes his fiction as a self-consciously failed 'attempt to distill the essence of other places. To make myself

[32] Elaine Feinstein, *The Border* (London: Hutchinson, 1984) p. 57.

[33] Sue Vice, *Holocaust Fiction* (London and New York: Routledge, 2000), and Jon Harris, 'An Elegy for Myself: British Poetry and the Holocaust', *English*, 41, 171 (Autumn 1992), pp. 213–32.

[34] Salman Rushdie, *Imaginary Homelands: Essays and Criticism 1981–1991* (London: Granta Books, 1991), pp. 20–1.

[35] Tony Lerman, '"Diaspora Blues": Real or Imagined', *Jewish Quarterly*, 128 (Winter 1987), pp. 11–12.

temporarily at home'. Sinclair's cautious 'homeless logic' is worth noting as he is well aware of a too easy appropriation of other histories and cultures.[36] His knowing conflation of selfhood with nationhood in his fiction is, on one level, the necessary solipsistic response of an author who displaces the national culture of his birth-place onto a useful fiction. For the post-holocaust writer, however, such aestheticised 'imaginary homelands' cannot be constituted by words alone as the traumatic past is no longer transfigured easily by art. It is the tension between history and the imaginary which is the subject of much of Sinclair's diasporic fiction.

His first two novels, *Blood Libels* (1985) and *Cosmetic Effects* (1989), are personal histories which have national consequences. Following the megalomaniacal storyteller of 'Ashkenazia' (1982) – who thinks that he can breath life into Europe's 'skeletons' – *Augustus Rex* (1992) sets out to make ironic the supposedly unlimited power of the writer as figured in August Strindberg's death-defying art. In this way, Sinclair is able to question the limits of an extraterritorial writing displaced from time and space. His Chekhov-inspired collection of novellas and stories, *The Lady With the Laptop* (1996), continues to invent purely imaginary national homelands – such as 'Ishmalaya' in his novella, 'The Iceman Cometh' – while simultaneously subjecting his aestheticised diaspora to the contingencies of history. *Meet the Wife* (2002) continues to play with the boundaries between life and death, past and present, in a bid both to assert the power of artistry and also to acknowledge the insurmountable borders which the aesthetic cannot surpass.

The 1980s and 1990s saw a revival of Jewish literature in Britain which took two main forms. Accomplished Jewish writers in a wide range of genres, such as Anita Brookner, Dan Jacobson, Gabriel Josipovici and Harold Pinter, began to validate Jewish themes in their work, often for the first time. The trajectory of these writers is worth noting. Dan Jacobson, for instance, began by writing naturalistic novels such as *The Trap* (1955) and *A Dance in the Sun* (1956) but eventually moved towards fabular fictions, most notably *The Rape of Tamar* (1970) which was turned into the stage play *Yonadab* (1985) by Peter Shaffer. Jacobson's move from realism to biblically inspired myth–history culminated in *The God-Fearer* (1992) which constructs an other-history where the dominant proselytising religion in Europe is no longer Christianity but Judaism. That Judaism could now be understood as a determining aspect of European

36 '"On the Edge of the Imagination": Clive Sinclair interviewed by Bryan Cheyette', *Jewish Quarterly*, 3–4 (1984), pp. 26–29. See also the entry on Sinclair in *World Authors: 1985–1990* (New York: H. W. Wilson, 1995), pp. 818–20, and Clive Sinclair, *Diaspora Blues: A View of Israel* (London: Heinemann, 1987).

culture was, in part, a response to the impact of German and French thinkers on British culture as both of these European modern and Postmodern cultural and philosophical traditions engaged influentially with Judaic thinking. The Modernist fiction of Josipovici, for example, has moved from the exilic cosmopolitanism of his early work, such as *Migrations* (1977), to a more explicitly Judaic inflection of the world in his later fiction *The Big Glass* (1991) and *In a Hotel Garden* (1993).[37]

Pinter's *Ashes to Ashes* (1996) and Brookner's *The Latecomers* (1988) and *A Family Romance* (1993) reinvested established canonical forms with an engagement with versions of European Jewishness. As John Skinner has argued, although Brookner writes 'stylistically' as an English 'insider' her predominantly female protagonists are 'mentally, if not ethnically, outsiders'.[38] Her characters' multiple positions – as neither insiders nor outsiders, neither Jewish nor English – can, in this regard, be related to the dramatis personae of Pinter's plays, who are similarly situated in an indeterminate 'no man's land'. At this time a range of literary genres were imbued with a specifically Jewish perspective. Howard Jacobson rewrote the campus novel in *Coming from Behind* (1983) and also Judaised the fiction of Thomas Hardy and Charles Dickens in *Peeping Tom* (1984) and *The Mighty Walzer* (1999). Simon Louvish's Scottish–Israeli version of magic realism in his novel-sequence – ranging from *The Therapy of Avram Blok* (1985) to *The Days of Miracles and Wonders* (1997) – is an endlessly fluid account of cyclical political and historical conflict in the Middle East and elsewhere. Reminiscent of Kops's *The Hamlet of Stepney Green*, Alan Isler combines New York Yiddish humour with Shakespeare's Hamlet in his *The Prince of West End Avenue* (1994).

Along with the game-playing of much British–Jewish literature in relation to canonical figures and received genres, there was an astonishing growth in the 1990s in the number of memoirs and auto/biographical texts which engaged with the Jewish past and a range of possible Jewish identities. That which was repressed in post-war British culture has returned at the end of the century in an astonishing wave of books, which lie somewhere between fiction and memoir, such as Linda Grant's *Remind Me Who I Am, Again* (1998), Louise Kehoe's *In this Dark House: A Memoir* (1995) and Anne Karpf's *The War After:*

[37] Bryan Cheyette and Laura Marcus, eds., *Modernity, Culture and 'the Jew'* (Cambridge: Polity Press, and Stanford University Press, 1998) and Monika Fludernik, *Echoes and Mirrorings: Gabriel Josipovici* (Frankfurt am Main: Peter Lang, 2000).

[38] John Skinner, *The Fictions of Anita Brookner* (London: Macmillan, 1992), p. 6, and Louise Sylvester, 'Troping the Other: Anita Brookner's Jews', *English*, 50, 196 (Spring 2001), pp. 47–58.

Living With the Holocaust (1996). While it is worth noting the number of women writing in this mode, as David Brauner has argued, the return to history at this time was not gender-specific and there were equally significant excursions into the Jewish past in the work of male writers, such as Dan Jacobson's *Heschel's Kingdom* (1998), Howard Jacobson's *Roots Schmoots: Journeys Among the Jews* (1993) and Theo Richmond's *Konin: A Quest* (1995).[39] The search for authenticity in these self-conscious voyages into the past is clearly related to the playfulness of contemporary fiction. Howard Jacobson's comically empty characterisation of Jewishness as the 'other' to Englishness in his early fiction was matched, for instance, by a comprehensive account of the myriad versions of diasporic and national Jewishness in his *Roots Schmoots*.

Supposedly authentic journeys into history and knowingly inauthentic Jewish fictions continue to vie with each other as one among many versions of ethnicity in Britain. The liberal appropriation of Jewish experience reached its climax in Margaret Drabble's *The Radiant Way* (1987), in which Esther Breuer, whose Jewish family immigrated to England before the war, becomes one of Drabble's three representative voices on the condition of post-war England. At the same time, there has been a shift from a liberal to a postcolonial appropriation of Jewishness in Anita Desai's *Baumgartner's Bombay* (1988) and Caryl Phillips's *The Nature of Blood* (1997). Ruth Prawer Jhabvala's traumatised silence about her past was in part the subject of Desai's novel.[40] Zadie Smith's *The Autograph Man* (2002), which won the *Jewish Quarterly* fiction prize, signalled an extreme blurring of ethnic boundaries in the figure of her Judaeo-Chinese protagonist, Alex-Li Tandem. The ersatz Kabbalism and Buddhism of *The Autograph Man* followed the mix of North London black, Jewish and Asian ethnicities in *White Teeth* (2000).

By the end of the century, a range of authors, such as Ruth Fainlight, Alan Isler, Elena Lappin, Will Self, Jonathan Treitel (aka Jonathan Tel) and Jonathan Wilson, can all in part be designated as Anglo-American Jewish writers whose fluid national selves have informed the multiple contexts for much of their fiction and poetry. In stark contrast to such plural identities, A. S. Byatt, in her edition of *The Oxford Book of English Short Stories* (1998), drew the boundaries of Englishness so tight, as Clive Sinclair noted, as to exclude all non-English authors.[41] The boundarilessness of contemporary diasporic literature and the

39 David Brauner, *Post-War Jewish Fiction: Ambivalence, Self-Explanation and Transatlantic Connections* (Basingstoke and New York: Palgrave, 2001), chapter 4.

40 Judy Newman, *The Ballastic Bard: Postcolonial Fictions* (London and New York: Arnold, 1995) p. 30.

41 Clive Sinclair, 'England – that Sinking Feeling', *Guardian*, 25 April 1998, p. 8.

boundedness of national discourse continue to play off each other. This tension was perfectly expressed in *Rodinsky's Room* (1999) by Rachel Lichtenstein and Iain Sinclair, which combines competing accounts of East End Jewish history and culture with the archival reclamation of many authors, such as Alexander Baron and Emanuel Litvinoff, who are currently lost to the canon of British literature. Amy Levy and Isaac Rosenberg, curtailed voices from an earlier period, were also remade in the fiction and poetry of Elaine Feinstein and Clive Sinclair and have been republished in a variety of forms. The ability of British–Jewish writers to refuse the opposition of nation and exile, authenticity and inauthenticity, indicates the extent to which they successfully challenge a conservative multiculturalism which mistakenly valorises closed cultures, roots and traditions.

40

Fiction and postmodernity

JULIAN MURPHET

Hegel's designation of America as 'the land of the future'[1] has been echoed by the conspicuous 'Americanocentrism' of Postmodernism – in Fredric Jameson's words, the 'the first specifically North American global style'.[2] This marks a reversal of imperial fortunes. Where once the literary forms of the British Empire (the novel paramount among them) had been disseminated across the Anglophone world as so many instruction manuals for bourgeois subjectivity, now the 'frivolous' forms of US culture are eroding the last of those underpinnings of the Victorian era, and helping to establish a decentred, consumerist subjectivity. This feature of Postmodernism is one reason why there have been so few British defenders of that aesthetic, and why titles such as *The Illusions of Postmodernism*, *What's Wrong with Postmodernism* and *Against Postmodernism* characterise British contributions to the debate.[3] Yet a sober assessment of the facts is not necessarily apologia; and we will conclude this chapter with a quick discussion of the irresistible economics of that same 'cultural imperialism' as it literally swallowed up British publishing in the late twentieth century.

There is at any rate the sense that Postmodernism came to the United Kingdom as a pre-packaged phenomenon. Whereas the likes of Pynchon, Barthelme, Coover and Gass had launched a literary campaign against an imposing international style, the British Postmodernists had not only the American example, but also the rising tide of continental theory before them. The two 'posts' (-Modernism and -Structuralism) were, by the late 1970s,

1 G. W. F. Hegel, *Philosophy and History* (New York: Dover, 1956), p. 86.

2 Fredric Jameson, *Postmodernism, or The Cultural Logic of Late Capitalism* (London: Verso, 1991), p. xx.

3 Terry Eagleton, *The Illusions of Postmodernism* (Oxford: Blackwell, 1996); Christopher Norris, *What's Wrong with Postmodernism: Critical Theory and the Ends of Philosophy* (London: Harvester Wheatsheaf, 1990); Alex Callinicos, *Against Postmodernism: A Marxist Critique* (Cambridge: Polity Press, 1989).

achieved realities, and, since both took the act of writing particularly seriously, served as convenient bulwarks whence to assail the literary establishment. Peter Ackroyd and Julian Barnes donned the mantle of French theory to decry the parochialism and unreflexiveness of post-war English writing; while Martin Amis and Salman Rushdie fused a generational distemper with the exciting new liberties of pan-American literature to declare the existing conventions moribund, and their own fictions properly international. That so much of the work should already have been done does not lessen the significance of these declarations, but by this stage it was going to be odd if they were not made. Postmodernism was imported to the UK, then, with a canon and a body of significant intellectual manifestos behind it; and as such, it was perhaps heralded with rather less enthusiasm than that with which Pound had greeted Marinetti in London many years earlier.

And here we meet the greatest of the ironies about British Postmodernism. For while a version of Modernism may have flourished in London, it was hardly an 'English' phenomenon. As Perry Anderson has put it, 'England, the pioneer of capitalist industrialisation and master of the world market for a century, . . . [scarcely generated any Modernist movement at all]: beach-head for Eliot and Pound, offshore to Joyce, it produced virtually no significant native movement of a Modernist type in the first decades of the century – unlike Germany or Italy, France or Russia, Holland or America.'[4] The likely fortunes of a cultural movement predicated on the supersession of a moment in some sense locally 'missed' do not seem especially auspicious. Postmodernism would thus be the second instance of a globally dominant set of cultural forms and styles, introduced from without and generating local derivations, while the established English mode of writing – liberal–humanist realism – carried on regardless.

These ironies assume a different status, however, if we cease to think of either Modernism or Postmodernism as 'optional' aesthetic strategies, but as inevitable responses to spreading changes in the world economy. The radical thrust of Jameson's conceptualisation of both these 'cultural dominants' is that they are to be understood as cultural symptoms arising from shifts in the regime of capital accumulation.[5] In that sense, the local tradition of 'Realism' emerged from the UK's establishment of an integrated national system

[4] Perry Anderson, 'Marshall Berman: Modernity and Revolution' (1983), *A Zone of Engagement* (London: Verso, 1992), p. 32.

[5] See *Postmodernism*, but also *The Cultural Turn: Selected Writings on Postmodernism* (London: Verso, 1998); and *The Seeds of Time* (New York: Columbia University Press, 1994).

of industrialisation and joint-stock companies; 'Modernism', meanwhile, was the contradictory cultural reflex to an imperial system of monopoly accumulation. The postulate of America as the epicentre of a still later shattering of forms and values in 'postmodernity' then looks more reasonable. It is not that, 'overnight' as Virginia Woolf might have put it, human character 'changed on or about December 1973', but that a new and supremely powerful cultural dominant had been installed via the global reach of the interlaced products of the USA's military–industrial complex and 'Culture Industry'. The logic of this dominant is unlike earlier ones, particularly in its aggressive equation of an essentially 'abstract' culture with commerce itself[6] – the disappearance of any gap between economics on the one hand and 'the arts' on the other. Once the Modernist shibboleth of the 'purely aesthetic' had been shattered, it was impossible to reinvent; and not only in the United States, but any culture redefined by its products. Jameson's *résumé* of consequences at the level of cultural form is well known: a flattening of earlier semantic depths; a 'waning of affect' from the content of the work; a fragmenting of the subject-position of the work's address; a new and aggressive accent on social space in the work; and a 'textualisation' of its relationship to history, which can henceforth only be represented as pastiche.

The larger economic and social processes of Postmodernism, however, had less immediate influence on British reaction to the canonical forms of Modernism, than did the realisation of their logic at the level of the political: namely, the election of Margaret Thatcher's Conservative Government in May 1979 – the abrupt break from decades of Keynesian corporatism; privatisation; assaults on organised labour; and the tell-tale declaration that society did not exist. Britain required this peculiar free-market mediator in order to learn the larger lessons emanating from America since the early 1970s. British Postmodernism, with a few significant exceptions, is a product of the Thatcher–Major years and their Blairite aftermath, a response at the levels of form and content to an 'Americanisation' of values and practices.

Farewell to pastoral

One of the chief advantages of the American scene as an incubator of Postmodernism was its characteristic 'flatness'. The built environment itself is

6 See Perry Anderson, 'Force and Consent', *New Left Review*, 17 (September/October, 2002): pp. 24–5.

a constantly transforming one, where planned obsolescence and billboard semiosis are incessantly restructuring urban space. 'Learning from Las Vegas' was the slogan of architects exhausted with the stringent formalisms of late Modernism.[7] British space was always less amenable to this kind of amnesia: the odd 'New Town' such as Milton Keynes aside, built space in the archipelago has long been a gradual and additive affair, a congeries of evolving historical styles, expressive of their periods, often lying cheek by jowl on the high streets. While the twentieth century has accelerated the speed of development in the cities, the social space of the UK is still a palimpsest of historical stylistic layers. To that extent, Postmodernism as an aesthetic in which 'the past as "referent" finds itself gradually bracketed, and then effaced altogether, leaving us with nothing but texts'[8] must hit some kind of material barrier on the UK side of the Atlantic. Nevertheless, it is also the case that much of the postmodernisation of space in the UK occurs under the aegis of the tourism business, or the 'Heritage Industry'. The effectiveness of various historical spaces as barriers to the inexorable sway of global homogenisation is waning as those very buffers are marketed as 'leisure' commodities.

As an 'adviser to the elite' tells an entrepreneur in Julian Barnes's *England, England* (1998),

> You – we – England – my client – is – are a nation of great age, great history, great accumulated wisdom. Social and cultural history – stacks of it, reams of it – eminently marketable, never more so than in the current climate . . . *We are already what others may hope to become*. This isn't self-pity, this is the strength of our position, our glory, our product placement. We are the new pioneers. We must sell our past to other nations as their future![9]

The narrative that springs from this revelation concerns itself with the construction and operation of a virtual England, 'England, England,' on the Isle of Wight, whose inhabitants become the costumed employees of a theme park of cultural clichés. 'England' is reduced to a simulacrum of the 'Fifty Quintessences of Englishness': Royal Family, Big Ben, Manchester United Football Club, and so on. The wish-fulfilment of the text is that this travesty of 'Englishness' might be sequestered and removed to an island holiday resort,

7 Robert Venturi, Denise Scott Brown, Steven Izenour, *Learning from Las Vegas* (Cambridge, MA: MIT Press, 1972).

8 Jameson, *Postmodernism*, p. 18.

9 Julian Barnes, *England, England* (London: Jonathan Cape, 1998), pp. 39–40. Further references given in parenthesis in the text.

allowing England itself, cowering between the European tiger economies of Scotland, Wales and Ireland, to revert to its own authentic mode – which is nothing other than *pastoral*:

> Common land was re-established; fields and farms grew smaller; hedgerows were replanted. Butterflies again justified the thickness of old butterfly books; migratory birds which for generations had passed swiftly over the toxic isle now stayed longer, and some decided to settle. (255)

This utopia is a perfectly English reaction to global postmodernisation: an ironic nostalgia-mode stripped of all signs of modernity, positing a 'real cliché' of pastures unravaged by capitalism.

Pastoral, then, persists as a potent ideological wish under the cool surfaces of the Postmodern UK; yet, as Barnes makes clear, it cannot be represented as such without an overlay of irony or an elaborately prepared defence against easy charges of Romanticism. Graham Swift has attempted to explore the afterlife of pastoral in two rather different ways in his novels *Waterland* (1983) and *Last Orders* (1996). The first of these recalls Thomas Hardy's revulsion from the myths of pastoral in his Wessex novels, via a hypnotic evocation of the Norfolk Fens, 'an unrelieved and monotonous flatness'. This landscape is a man-made one, a simulacrum of 'Natural' space, 'which, of all landscapes, approximated to Nothing': a kind of non-pastoral that calls it forth negatively. This is one of those Foucauldian 'heterotopias',[10] neither urban nor wilderness proper, that so much present-day fiction has reverted to in order to sidestep the immense representational challenge of contemporary urban life, and draw the social map on an altogether more human and 'knowable' scale. That this is perforce a Postmodern symptom is made plain not only by the scholarly encyclopaedism of the book's contents, but by the many literary antecedents it inevitably 'quotes': Hardy, Melville, Brontë, Faulkner. Faulkner is also the touchstone of Swift's later novel, *Last Orders*, which cannibalises the form of *As I Lay Dying* (1930) to make an ironic claim for some last moment of pastoral innocence in the hopfields of Kent, 'the Garden of England'. It is in these 'fields and woods and hedges and orchards' that Jack Dodds and his wife Amy first meet, but the love and child they conceive there are botched and translate into a life-sentence of compromise and failure. If there is any authentic passion in the novel, it is between Amy and Jack's best friend Ray; this latter affect will have nowhere to realise itself but in the back of a camper van trundling over the motorways of the post-war era – pastoral inverted. In a final and desperate

[10] Michel Foucault, 'Different Spaces', trans. Robert Hurley, *Essential Works of Foucault 1954–1984. Volume II: Aesthetics*, ed. James D. Faubion (London: Penguin, 2000), pp. 175–85.

act of displacement, it is only in the antipodes of Australia that any semblance of pastoral consummation will be able, belatedly, to take place.

These attempts to rework and displace the function of pastoral within Postmodern British fiction nevertheless fail the stringent demands of a much earlier work. Britain's great inaugural contribution to Postmodernist fiction, J. G. Ballard's *Crash* (1973), had already announced the *extinction* of that mode, in a manner that left little room for poignant reanimations. *Crash*, which is both response to and argument with the Romanticism of the American Beat writers, posits a world stripped of the elements of pastoral. All that is left are the crude remnants evinced in a typical clause: 'an abandoned car lying in the rust-stained grass on the lower slopes of the reservoir embankment'.[11] The crucial second aspect of Ballard's concrete-and-steel universe is that, along with Nature, history is also erased from the texture of everyday life. There is no sense of Britain as a durable social or cultural entity. This double negation under the concrete carapace leaves Ballard only the last-ditch option of a techno-sexual 'perverse', where the erogenous zones of the body and the technical spaces of automobile interiors meld in a numbed, postmodernised Futurism: 'These unions of torn genitalia and sections of car body and instrument panel formed a series of disturbing modules, units in a new currency of pain and desire' (134). Onto these 'modules' are projected the objectivised fantasies of the American culture industry: movie stars, car chases, carnage. So it is that the novel's own Dean Moriarty, Vaughan, pursues his deviant course towards a car-crash apotheosis with Elizabeth Taylor, a concrete flyover, and a cine-camera – not from the impulse of some 'inner' psychology, but from the multi-layered promptings of technicolour American spectacles.[12]

The epochal shifts of which Ballard's text was the harbinger can be distilled into the standard features of cultural Postmodernism: a two-dimensional, de-naturalised world; a hollowed-out subjectivity and affectless voice; a prosthetic, technological object-world; and an imaginative prostration before the culture industry. Indeed, the only key element missing is that element of 'pastiche' in which the voices of the past are paraded as so many available styles in Malraux's 'imaginary museum' and delivered up for present-day delectation; Ballard's hostility towards historicism being very much a function of his assumed prophetic role, itself a vestige of a more-or-less 'Modernist' vocation. By the time that many of these lessons had been absorbed, a new generation

[11] J. G. Ballard, *Crash* (London: Vintage, 1995), p. 79. Further references given in parenthesis in the text.

[12] See here the discussion in Guy Debord, *Society of the Spectacle* (Black and Red: Detroit, 1983).

was at hand to dispense with even that vestigial Modernism. It is not that the apocalyptic note itself was missing from the works of Martin Amis and others, but that the tone in which it was sounded had become a hoarse, comic bray. The existential horror of Ballard's anti-pastoral segued into a generalised moral disgust at the tenor of the times – a sense that something had been lost, something that could only be represented through pastiche.

Old and new

A. S. Byatt's novel *Possession: A Romance* (1990) has justly been vaunted for its bravura displays of period pastiche; and this ties it to a notable stream of Postmodern British fiction, which by reanimating styles from the literary tradition, explores the relation of that tradition to the fate of language and literary culture in the contemporary era. Because the novel is principally an academic one, its interest is as much in who can claim to 'possess' the treasures of the past, as in what it might be to be possessed by them. The two contemporary English protagonists, Roland Michell and Maud Bailey, each respectively (and respectfully) researching the works of Victorian poets Randolph Ash and Christabel LaMotte, come up against a villainous force in the form of American institutional money and 'theory'. Byatt's conflation of theory with money, and both with the juggernaut of American academia, suggests a parochial defence of painstaking English empiricism: an empiricism and respect for detail which are amply confirmed by her own astonishingly accomplished mock-ups of the manuscripts of Ash and LaMotte. In good romance fashion, the narrative is resolved in favour of the English tradition by the supremely unlikely stroke of having Maud Bailey turn out to be the literal descendant of the two Victorian poets. Thus cultural 'possession' is trumped by legal possession and inheritance, as self-consciously 'novelistic' a tactic as can be imagined, underscored by the presiding trope of ventriloquism. Claims over the past are legitimised by common law and style simultaneously; the spectre of American theoretical finance capital is exorcised by a fine native regard for, and pastiche of, the tradition itself.

Julian Barnes's formally ingenious novel, *Flaubert's Parrot* (1984), raises the issue of pastiche through the device of a narrator, Geoffery Braithwaite, obsessed with the style of Flaubert, to the point that it has become a fetish. This fetish, and its narrative reconfiguration as a quest for the 'real' parrot of *Un cœur simple*, occupies a critical place in the psychology of Braithwaite, masking as it does the traumatic wound of his wife's infidelity and suicide. The key strategy is Barnes's focus on the emergence of that prototypical feature of

High Modernism, the 'disappearance' of the artist from his work, in Flaubert's fictional prose. 'Contemporary critics who pompously reclassify all novels and plays and poems as texts – the author to the guillotine! – shouldn't skip lightly over Flaubert. A century before them he was preparing texts and denying the significance of his own personality.'[13] This erasure, which in the era of High Modernism was a constitutive and formal one, is significantly recast here by the fact that, in Braithwaite's case, it is an act of denial. All the scintillating Flaubertian maxims – about style as 'the flesh of thought itself... When a line is good, it ceases to belong to any school. A line of prose must be as immutable as a line of poetry. If you happen to write well, you are accused of lacking ideas' (160) – are traduced as indices of a merely personal neurosis. There can be no authentic 'style' in the Postmodern; the voice you adopt is a borrowed armature. Flaubert is the fossilised shell in which Braithwaite's vulnerable invertebrate takes up residence.

Martin Amis has generally been taken as the poster-boy of a mature British Postmodernism, deferential above all to the stylistics of his own adopted literary fathers, Nabokov and Saul Bellow. Oddly, however, Amis's England, reviewed through these American lenses, assumes the style of Dickensian vigour – repackaged in what Iain Sinclair has called 'style journalism: fashions, lingos, indoor sport, the entropy catalogue'.[14] And repackaged, too, in the acute self-consciousness of a very Postmodern authorial reflexiveness, or 'metafiction'; a tactic which keeps the narrators of both *Money* (1984) and *London Fields* (1989) not only noisily in the narrative foreground, but in explicit power relationships with 'Martin Amis' or 'M.A.' himself. Yet it is the Victorian gusto with which the characters of John Self and Keith Talent are unleashed onto the page that best defines Amis's Postmodern relationship with 'Englishness'. For these are characters only in the sense that they have already become caricatures and grotesques. Their monstrosity is an effect derived from the distension of two-dimensional stereotypes to their inflatable limits. John Self, the gargantuan hero of *Money*, is the sum of every cliché of 'yuppiedom' and a very familiar middle-class fantasy of the London working class. The latter's residual 'authenticity' (pubs, gangsters, prostitutes, pornography) is exploded into ironic shards by the former's American demi-urge (deals, movie stars, charge accounts, *money*) – so that, in the end, John Self is exposed as a mere stooge in a rather obvious American fraud. Thus the odd sense that, unlike Bret Easton Ellis's narrator in *American Psycho* (1990), Self

[13] Julian Barnes, *Flaubert's Parrot* (London: Picador, 1985), p. 98. Further references given in parenthesis in the text.

[14] Iain Sinclair, Review of Martin Amis's *The Information*, in the *Independent* (25 March 1995).

is ultimately redeemable. Our appalled reaction throughout the book at his depravity is retroactively modulated into a nostalgic sympathy for the very qualities of 'laddish' self-indulgence which now stand revealed as signs of innocence before the inexorable sway of American capital. This ambivalence of the anti-heroic Self, caught somewhere between a knowing satire and a nostalgic affection, is realised anew in the Keith Talent of *London Fields*.

On the one hand, Amis inherits a European notion of 'literature', emancipated from parochial habits of representation, seeking release in sheer effects of style, and inflected by an American ease with colloquialisms, vulgarity and violence: Malcolm Bradbury is right to say that Amis's discourse is 'extravagantly inventive, word-spinning, culturally acquisitive'.[15] Yet on the other hand, Amis, in need of some durable source of cultural value, is unable to find it in Europe (Fascism, in *Time's Arrow* (1991), Bolshevism, in *Koba the Dread* (2002)) or America, and so is driven to prospect for it in the degraded stereotypes of 'England' itself. Thus the whole business of metafictional and formal ingenuity, and the exaggeratedly masculine ease of style, are compensations for the fact that it is still only Dickensian 'low life' that emerges from his work with any kind of verve. The rest is perhaps only cleverness, 'talent'. It is surely a formal embarrassment that, in the struggle against his father, Modernism and 'English Literature', Amis should principally have given us a very Victorian characterology; an embarrassment that he confesses:

> The moment I set eyes on him I thought Keith Talent was an anachronistic kind of character. I thought that time and inflation and the new demographics would have mopped him up by now or sent him somewhere else: to the North, or at least to the suburbs. Not so. The streets were full of jokers, dodgers, jack-the-lads and willie-the-dips – whole crews of Keith . . . Fagin himself would have nothing to do with them. He'd be horrified.[16]

Another logical response to the Postmodern crisis of representation has been to seize onto those very 'new demographics' of which Amis writes, and mine them for more original resources, not only of character, but of voice, tone and formal construction as well. As Jameson has stressed, 'demographics' itself constitutes a vital Postmodern preoccupation.[17] That the epic process of Third World emigration should have 'come home' to the old seat of empire itself, and inscribed itself there in a force-field of distinct and intermingled ethno-religious communities, is a profoundly Postmodern fact.

[15] Malcolm Bradbury, *The Modern British Novel 1878–2001* (London: Penguin, 2001), p. 479.
[16] Martin Amis, *London Fields* (London: Penguin, 1990), p. 134.
[17] See especially Jameson, *Postmodernism*, pp. 356–64.

Hanif Kureishi's first novel, *The Buddha of Suburbia* (1990), rejoins the tradition of youth-and-race literature begun by Colin MacInnes in the 1950s, and saturates it with the period imaginary of the 1970s. He presents a ready-made set of cultural and style references in which known 'subcultures' have taken shape.[18] Kureishi's first-person narrator, Karim Amir, has a fragmented identity: his hybrid ethnicity (paternal 'Indianness' and maternal 'Englishness') is experienced as domestic gloom, while his generational affiliation with the new youth cultures of the 1970s is felt as a vital self-realisation and escape from suburbia. The patchy tale that unfurls is meant to do two things at once: chart the difficult emergence of a 'self' in Karim; and ultimately unmask this very construct as a sham, a reactionary Postmodern collage. In the novel's painfully allegorical final scene, Karim's father's engagement to a Thatcherite entrepreneur becomes a literal celebration of Thatcher's election as Prime Minister. Karim's alignment with these new materialist forces tells heavily against him. His musing, 'I could think about the past and what I'd been through as I'd struggled to locate myself and learn what the heart is. Perhaps in the future I would live more deeply',[19] must be received with a lethal undercurrent of irony, since Thatcher's epoch was to unleash those social forces least conducive to 'depth'. Kureishi's Postmodern fable refuses ethnic essentialisms and endorses instead the far greater power of commodified style and glamour to rewire 'youth' subjectivity into malleable subcultures. Yet there is the suspicion throughout that the author himself is as compromised by this immersion in the signs and practices of the subculture as his impressionable narrator. What we have in effect is an exhilarating pastiche of the dead languages of the recent past: glam, punk, and New Age-ism.

It was the work of Salman Rushdie, and particularly *The Satanic Verses* (1988), that most vividly sought to reimagine England through the optics and practices of a new generation of immigrants. *The Satanic Verses*, the great and durable masterpiece of British Postmodernism, also enjoys a similar stature as a work of Indian fiction, and as a global cultural and political icon. Rushdie at his peak was the liveliest exponent in the British tradition of what he himself calls (after Bakhtin) 'carnivalesque literature', a mode that posits human agents as 'masked strangers, . . . beastly, devilish, miraculous beings, dream-encrusted, protean, multiform, wonderful'.[20] It is a tradition not without significant roots in just that Dickensian substratum we have seen nourishing Martin Amis's

[18] Dick Hebdige, *Subculture: The Meaning of Style* (London: Methuen, 1979).

[19] Hanif Kureishi, *The Buddha of Suburbia* (New York: Penguin, 1990), pp. 283–4.

[20] Salman Rushdie, Review of Robert Coover's *Pinnochio in Venice*, in the *Independent on Sunday* (28 April 1991).

fiction, but in Rushdie's hands this resource is framed dynamically within a competing media space. At the novel's end, all the major protagonists gather at a party at Shepperton studios where a musical version of *Our Mutual Friend* – *The Chums* – is being shot. The fakery and flimsiness of the sets, and the risible quality of the songs, serve as a pretext in which to present a crucial passage whose 'Postmodernism' consists in the sheer number of embedded quotation marks we are to acknowledge and somehow negotiate as we read:

> Now, in Rex-Harrisonian speech-song, she addresses an invisible Foreigner. 'And How Do You Like London? – "Aynormaymong rich?" – Enormously Rich, we say. Our English adverbs do Not terminate in Mong. – And Do You Find, Sir, Many Evidences of our British Constitution in the Streets of the World's Metropolis, London, Londres, London? – I would say,' she adds, still Podsnapping, 'that there is in the Englishman a combination of qualities, a modesty, an independence, a responsibility, a repose, which one would seek in vain among the Nations of the Earth.'[21]

Such critical reframing of the not-yet-dead Dickensian language, the nesting of so many distinct levels of irony and media reference, dismantles the solidity of the scene without sacrificing the humour of the whole performance (an English woman is unbuttoning her blouse in a sexual advance to an Indian man), or its urgent postcolonial politics. What is most striking about Rushdie's achievement throughout *The Satanic Verses* is this ability to maintain so many distinct registers, narrative lines and symbols within a narrative discourse capacious and flexible enough to accommodate all of them.

The techniques of 'magical realism' that Rushdie adopted from Günter Grass, Garcia Marquez and others are really little more than the formal co-ordinates on which can be spun such phantasmagoric and luminous passages as this evocation of London through the focal lens of Gibreel Farishta in his guise as the Archangel:

> When you looked through an angel's eyes you saw essences instead of surfaces, you saw the decay of the soul blistering and bubbling on the skins of people in the street, you saw the generosity of certain spirits resting on their shoulders in the form of birds. As he roamed the metamorphosed city he saw bat-winged imps sitting on the corners of buildings made of deceits and glimpsed goblins oozing wormily through the broken tilework of public urinals for men.
>
> (321)

[21] Salman Rushdie, *The Satanic Verses* (London: Vintage, 1998), p. 424. Further references given in parenthesis in the text.

This Archangel, cohabiting the three major religions and the three temporal modalities all at once, is one of the more omniscient focalisers in the history of the novel as a form. What it produces is this sensuous penetration of reified surfaces and the disclosure of occluded essences: a pre-modern epistemology issued as Postmodern prophecy. In the narrative, Farishta, a jovial film actor, becomes the redemptive Archangel; while his companion on a fatal aeroplane flight, Saladin Chamchawala, a radio actor, transmogrifies into a cloven-hoofed devil. Between them, they manage to attract most of the British fantasies about South Asians, and wear them on their bodies like the projections of mass entertainment (the industry in which they both work). But more than that, they *see* the city from their fantastic vantage-points as a Balkanised space of racial and religious differences, erupting into flash-points of riot and political upheaval. All that had been reified in Amis and Kureishi, and that is again, differently, in Zadie Smith's Rushdie-inspired but overly schematic *White Teeth* (2000), is jolted into convulsive life by Rushdie's unparalleled dynamism. Thanks to a narrative inventiveness and a cosmic ambition rarely matched in British fiction, Rushdie is able to make protean again cultural fragments fossilised by the inertia of overuse. *The Satanic Verses* is our own *Ulysses* – a mock-epic allegory of postcolonial Britain.

If Rushdie had adopted carnivalesque magic–realist techniques to prod ancient Islamic and Postmodern English codes into productive collision, Angela Carter more modestly sought to assimilate a carnivalesque mode to tease away at the 'legitimacy' of British establishment culture. A central tenet of Postmodern theory is the collapse of the distinction between 'high' and 'low' cultural forms, and Carter makes this proposition into a comic rationale for exploding inert cultural pretensions in her fiction, without sacrificing the richness and strength of the venerated 'tradition'. So it is that the Bard, in her final and best novel *Wise Children* (1991), sits uneasily at the helm of a dynasty (both familial and abstractly cultural) riven by competing strains of legitimacy and illegitimacy. As in a Shakespearian comedy, identical twins proliferate and questions of legitimacy abound. Melchior Hazard, a noted Shakespearian actor, and father of the ex-hoofer narrator Dora Chance and her twin sister Nora, refuses to acknowledge his patrimony of such low-cultural illegitimates; but the trend of twentieth-century culture away from the classics inevitably forces both halves of the family into collaboration, first in a musical revue (*What? You Will?* – in which Melchior plays the Bard), and later in an appalling Hollywood production of *A Midsummer Night's Dream*. Further generations of the dynasty enter television and are subsumed by game-show crassness, while the old man sells his face and voice for scotch commercials. However, the clear indicators of decline are countered by a sign of revival: a camp reclaiming of the forgotten film of the *Dream*, signalling at once that neither the familial high–low fusion, nor Shakespeare himself, has been quite forgotten. Value here is located in the ongoing interpenetration of high and low since the Elizabethan stage itself; it prompts the realisation that the construction of Shakespeare into an icon of the establishment was a Victorian deformation. 'Shakespeare' is only what any given performance makes of him; and so it is with patriarchy and paternity itself. '"Father" is a hypothesis', says Dora, echoing Joyce's line about paternity as a legal fiction.[22] There is no legitimacy that is not internally corrupted by the engulfing shadow of its antithesis; no product of civilisation that is not, at the same time, a product of buffoonery and 'barbarism'.

Carter's medium for handling these paradoxes is the oldest of novelistic devices, the confessional, memoir-writing first-person voice; in this case an amiable pastiche of a working-class London woman of her mother's generation, a survival from the 1920s and 30s. It is this voice that is left with the task of resolving the various irresolvable tensions, straddling the idioms of both the East End music hall and the high strains of Elizabethan iambic pentameter. It is the voice, that it to say, of the *actress*, the lower-class vehicle through which high culture invariably speaks; a kind of radical schizophrenia whose only safety valve is that of humour. The question is, however, to what extent this voice speaks to us at all; how far this pastiche manages to overcome its stylistic and formal origins in the vanished cultural past. The polyphonies of Rushdie, or the self-conscious hyperboles of Amis, look distinctly more honest than, say, this rendition of a tense family moment:

> Then he spotted the photo of little Tiff in the silver frame that we keep on the breakfast-room mantlepiece and the waterworks started up again. I felt quite sorry for the poor kid. 'Kid', I say. He's all of thirty-five; he'll be pushing forty in no time. All the same, his stock in trade is boyish charm. God knows what he'll do when he loses that. But we were all a-tremble, all anxiety; what the fuck was going on? So Nora bunged his cassette in the VCR sharpish.
>
> (10)

The novel's voice is little more than this weak assemblage of 'class idioms', clichés and archaisms, pumped up into an energy that is insincere in its self-vaunted nostalgia, 'the vice of the aged' (10).

22 Angela Carter, *Wise Children* (London: Vintage, 1992), p. 223. Further references given in parenthesis in the text.

Time, space, history

Ian McEwan assumes a much less self-consciously Postmodernist stance than these writers. Instead, his Postmodernism springs from the peculiar attitude he adopts towards narrative time and the aesthetics of the 'moment'. The Modernists had embraced a wide spectrum of notions about the moment, but speaking at a very general level, it can be said that for all of them (except Woolf) the 'thing itself', the moment in its unimpeded immediacy and density, was inaccessible to experience or conscious reflection. This is not so for McEwan, the unrivalled master of the 'fateful moment' – that extraordinary event which, in its horror and intensity, is the nugget of the Real around which the rest of narrative time circulates. The disappearance of the daughter (*The Child in Time*, 1987), the apparition of the black dogs (*Black Dogs*, 1992), the horrific ballooning accident (*Enduring Love*, 1997), the rape of a young woman (*Atonement*, 2001): these are the fateful moments which succeed in transcending time itself, so profoundly embedded do they become in the psyches of their witnesses. Typically, these witnesses are divided into opposing camps of rational 'explanation' and spiritual 'apprehensiveness', and often enough the central protagonist is split down the middle in this way. The upsurge of something that can only be described as evil opens up loopholes in the fourth dimension. McEwan holds these ajar to allow for a degree of conceptual abstraction absent from most of his fellow English Postmodernists:

> 'There's a whole supermarket of theories [on time] these days. You can take your pick . . . But whatever time is, the commonsense, everyday version of it as linear, regular, absolute, marching from left to right, from the past through the present to the future, is either nonsense or a tiny fraction of the truth. . . . There is no absolute, generally recognised "now" – but you know all this.'[23]

Yet this scepticism only serves to confirm the immense, haunting power of McEwan's own 'nows' as his faultless, impersonal prose incarnates them on the page. They are multi-temporal, but always integral and complete. We may hazard a speculation, that in such intensities, the initial Modernist formulation of Baudelaire is properly postmodernised: now the 'transient, the fleeting, the contingent' is no longer in *opposition* to 'the eternal and immutable', but both have been fused into the self-same impulse – the enactment of a literary quantum theory.

[23] Ian McEwan, *A Child in Time* (London: Vintage, 1992), pp. 117–18. Further references given in parenthesis in the text.

One thing that emerges from these events is the power of place to retain eventful imprints. After Stephen Lewis, in *The Child in Time*, experiences his extraordinary *déja-vu* on the North Downs, it occurs to him that 'the loudness . . . of this particular location had its origins outside his own existence' (56–7). Later he discovers that this location was where the question of his own possible abortion was raised and settled, immediately after the war (and how often World War II serves McEwan as the procrustean bed of his trans-temporal moments).

Michèle Roberts's novel *In The Red Kitchen* (1990) explores this potential for place to 'mediate' distinct historical periods, but interestingly departs from the tendency to dualise the temporal locations between which most Postmodern novels flicker. While there is a certain familiarity about the primary alternation between the story of a contemporary woman writer, and that of the Victorian medium Flora Milk whose birthplace in the East End she now occupies – an alternation reaching moments of recognition in the titular basement kitchen – Roberts significantly expands the horizon of trans-historical mediumship by incorporating a third dimension, that of ancient Egypt. In that interwoven strand of the novel, the daughter of a Pharaoh makes an irresistible rise to power, ultimately becoming consort to her dead father, and a man and Pharaoh herself. 'And day after day I erect my self in granite, in limestone. Incorruptible, undecayed.'[24] The clear analogy here is between architecture and language, both of which serve to perpetuate the memory and afterlife of the dead: 'Words mean life. The absence of words means death: being forgotten by men for all eternity' (24). Roberts seeks to incarnate forgotten beings, women, in language freighted with the melancholy acceptance of death and oblivion. The kingdom of ancient Egypt is no mere arbitrary selection for amplification here; but whether its incorporation is successful is questionable, since the novel tends to fall apart into four incommensurable voices, tied together only by the verbal modulation of King Hat into Hattie King, the name of the contemporary narrator.

The notion that space itself bears the traces of time's convulsions is also a presumption of Peter Ackroyd and Iain Sinclair. Peter Ackroyd has made a career out of the reanimation of Britain's, and more particularly London's manifold and discontinuous pasts. His sense of the great metropolis as one enormous organism is made perfectly clear in his 'non-fiction' triumph, *London* (2001), a biography of the city. Yet if it is an organism, it is one with the

[24] Michèle Roberts, *In the Red Kitchen* (London: Vintage, 1993), p. 114. Further references given in parenthesis in the text.

power both to shed and to retain its skins. In his most successful work of fiction, *Hawksmoor* (1984), two of these historical layers come into uncanny contact: the London of the late seventeenth century, and of the present day. Denis Donoghue has argued that Ackroyd 'links events, real or imagined, by likeness and not by chronology. He sets aside the official privilege of sequence, cause and effect, and produces a simultaneous concatenation of likenesses and differences, regardless of temporal impediments.'[25] This is an apt description of a literary method that works without any narrative urgency, despite the formal scaffolding of the detective story; but through folds in time, wherein the trans-historical elements stand revealed: an imperishable lumpenproletariat, eerie children's songs, omnipresent dust, and, again, the irrational upsurge of evil. Ackroyd's amazing talent for period ventriloquism ensures that our dissatisfactions with the contemporary parts of the novel are compensated for by a simple pleasure in well-executed pastiche. This pastiche works overtime to locate authenticity and lyrical intensity in the past, and associates these values with the anti-Enlightenment esoterics of the architect Dyer himself, a sexless and curmudgeonly Satanist. Ackroyd's Postmodernism is a reaction against the guiding ethos of the modern era, a reversion to a crypto-magical world-view of Neolithic origins. This mysticism, in the context of Thatcher's reactionary policies, suggests a rather conservative nationalism (most evident in his books *English Music* (1992) and *Albion* (2002)), where 'Englishness' is defined as a local, telluric genius, the poor are 'always with us', and the labours of critical ratiocination remain fruitless and wan.

Surface similarities aside, there are important differences between this reactionary Postmodernism and the far more flexible and satirical work of Ackroyd's contemporary, Iain Sinclair. While Sinclair, too, dabbles in the imponderable energies of leylines, and declares (and performs) an utter inability with cohesive narrative form, his textual experiments are charged with precisely the novelistic polyphonies that are absent from Ackroyd's fast-frozen period pastiches. It has been in the development of a style unique in its supercharged and multi-tiered acidity – a sentence-form able to negotiate sudden shifts in register between a turgid melancholia, a savage social satire, an arcane textual knowingness, a theoretical *nous*, and a self-ironising comic deflation – that Sinclair has asserted his valid claim to pre-eminence in the field of contemporary letters. His 'fiction' books (the boundaries are never very stable), which include the obsessive 'Baroque Realist' figure of Sinclair himself, are arranged

[25] Denis Donoghue, review of *Hawksmoor*, *New York Times Book Review* (17 January 1988), p. 40.

according to principles far removed from those of classical unity. A chain of inspired associations is detonated around the typical narrative strategy of a walk, undertaken as a frantic quest for historical residues and stains. These clues will, if assembled aright, restore the portentous meaning of lost time.

History itself, particularly its infamous passages and obscured episodes, incarnate in the very stones of the city, is the nourishing content of this wonderfully elastic form, and as Sinclair trawls over London, his rhetorical net snares an unholy catch: the Ripper murders, bodies in the Thames, strange happenings on disused railway lines, the radon vaults of London hospitals, lumpens living in abandoned hulks. Into this mix is added the literary tracings of many writers: Blake and Swedenborg, Conrad, Wilde, Eliot, Lewis Carroll, a host of obscure historians, poets and guidebook writers, Stephen J. Hawking, Peter Ackroyd and Sinclair himself. We are obliged to acknowledge these texts as cryptic co-ordinates to the social space of London itself. As with any genuine enthusiast, *everything* is grist to the mill. Chance formations, such as the acronym formed by the names of the Ripper's victims, or a stray graffito, become irrefutable evidence of a cosmic conspiracy. There is no attempt at aesthetic unity; only the refraction of a city's malign history through the opaque lens of a habitual *flâneur*. The city's contemporary deformation through speculation on the real-estate market, the gentrification of the East End and the erosion of services amid a rising homeless population, is the peculiar matrix of many of Sinclair's rambles.

As the notion of 'organic form' undergoes radical decomposition in his texts, what emerges are scintillating fragments, alluring and pregnant phrases. As if to show how threadbare Martin Amis's caricatures truly are, Sinclair's own drip with the menace of a genuine *grimoire*:

> Jon Kay. How had this prohibited life-form survived? What miracle had preserved him to rebuke these dark days? Some deathbat brushed its wing against his face. He was too far gone to be affected by mere memory. Electrical connections twitched and sparked. Red cells perished as a septic tide rushed into his cheek. Memory, for him, was a form of sympathetic jaundice. Veins collapsed (like landslides) in his mollusc eyes. He poured with sweat and clawed at his palpitating belly.[26]

There has been no prose like this in English since Wyndham Lewis. Like Lewis, Sinclair reserves a level of authorial discourse far above his satirised subjects, subjecting them to the merciless dissections of a stylistic scalpel unwilling to

[26] Iain Sinclair, *Downriver* (London: Granta, 2000), p. 332.

distinguish between human and animal, animal and machine. The sheer figural energy of a passage such as this, with its manic dislocations of scale undergirded by crazily mixed metaphors, achieves more than caricature – it attains to an autonomous aesthetics of style, predicated on literary effects elsewhere unavailable in Postmodern culture. This stylistic kinesis belongs under the aegis of Modernism itself: Iain Sinclair is a Modernist *manqué*, writing in and against a Postmodern age. His vital importance to this age is to have kept alive the reality of Modernism as a labour towards ends other than pastiche, trickery, or play – the end of style. His is a unique and dyspeptic accent amid the messages of a media culture, an accent with strong political urges. 'He did', we are told by the character Joblard, 'float some bravado subtext about considering his book a failure if the Widow [Thatcher] clung on to power one year after its publication; but this was, I assume, a joke of sorts' (384). The assumption is perhaps misguided. Mrs Thatcher was deposed within the predicted year.

Conclusion

Sinclair's exceptionalism must be related directly to his association with one of the very few remaining significant independent publishing houses in Britain, Granta Books. For in the 1980s and 1990s, a discernable process of 'dumbing down' in mainstream fiction went hand in hand with an extraordinary chain of mergers and buy-outs, signalling the end of the great tradition of British independent publishing. In the words of Steven Connor, 'Increasingly, publishing houses found themselves either part of large publishing conglomerates, which demanded high-volume sales from every unit of production, or part of multinational companies, whose publishing sections were only a small part of a range of different activities.'[27] And as André Schiffrin concludes, 'This has left little room for books with new, controversial ideas or challenging literary voices.'[28] Indeed, since most of the British independents were swallowed by gigantic media corporations in the 1980s, the quality of literature coming out of the UK has noticeably altered. Acutely aware of the long-term diminution in the readership of avowedly literary fiction, and of the attendant rise of the genres, subgenres and mass-market paperbacks, writers have adjusted the scope and manner of their works accordingly. According to Malcolm

[27] Steven Connor, *The English Novel in History, 1950–1995* (London: Routledge, 1996), pp. 17–18.

[28] André Schiffrin, *The Business of Books* (London: Verso, 2000), p. 7.

Bradbury, 'Experimental Post-Modernism adapted to the marketplace; political issues softened into relationship narratives. Fiction had its big talents, but was settling towards a mainstream, often commercial fin-de-siècle.'[29]

A more positive aspect of these momentous changes in the nature of publishing has been the generation of entirely new forms out of the market research undertaken by these firms in the quest for new markets. 'Gay fiction', 'Gen X' fiction, 'Lad Lit', 'Chick Lit' emerged as viable literary categories during the 1990s; categories which swiftly became forms, canons, celebrities and cover styles. At their best, these novels (such as those by Alan Hollinghurst and Jeanette Winterson) transcended genre altogether, showing that women's, gay and lesbian histories were profoundly embedded in the social history of Britain, and adding a significant new dimension to the representation of its social space. Hollinghurst's juxtaposition of contemporary 'cottaging' and an unearthed Roman baths in mid-London, in *The Swimming Pool Library* (1988), remains emblematic. However, these were exceptions. The infiltration of what in America is called 'ID politics' into the business of publishing and the production of literature is a markedly Postmodern symptom, since it recognises and reinforces the fragmentation of the marketplace into so many 'lifestyles', and incontestably presents this astute commercial logic as a mode of democratisation. Yet by accepting the splintering of the mythical 'reading public' into a series of tribes and identities, the industry directly assisted the latent trend towards a cultural horizon in which 'literary fiction' was just one more minority taste, no nearer to representing the 'dialect of the tribe' than any other, and indeed *false* to the extent that it pretended to do so. This, added to the appropriation and dissemination of the great works of Modernist literature as 'classics' (mainly for university literature programmes), gives rise to a situation in which the scandal of the modern, its rebarbative and unapologetic elitism, is diffused in what Brecht might have called a 'plebeianisation' of taste.

This is where we leave the present survey, acknowledging real imaginative gains and necessary turning points, alongside hard economic logic and a downward-tending spiral of literary standards. At its worst, British Postmodernism has been an inert reworking of tricks and tropes developed elsewhere and for different reasons. However, the best of Postmodernism was given lasting form by Salman Rushdie's superlative performance – to the letter, throughout and in the aftermath of his great English novel – of his own

29 Malcolm Bradbury, *The Times* (18 December 1999).

definition of language: 'Language is courage: the ability to conceive a thought, to speak it, and by doing so to make it true' (281). British Postmodernism's greatest achievements have been a vindication of that kind of courage; a testimony to the intermittent truth-making power of the literary act in an age of untruth.[30]

[30] The reference to courage has as one of its contexts the so-called Rushdie affair. See p. 747 of this volume

41

Postcolonial fictions

TIM WOODS

The 1990s saw the rise and rise of Postcolonial studies. Writers like Salman Rushdie, Arundhati Roy and Zadie Smith became bestselling authors, while most university English departments energetically addressed the discourse known as Postcolonial theory in their undergraduate degrees. This ascendancy reflected the burgeoning growth in quantity and cultural importance of Anglophone literatures from countries other than Britain in the second half of the twentieth century that challenged the construction of the 'English literary canon'. The somewhat moribund areas of academic literary study previously known as 'Commonwealth Studies', 'New Literatures in English', 'World Literature in English', were revivified as 'Postcolonial Literatures'.

Yet even as new life was breathed into this body of academic study, debates occurred about whether this was in fact a homogeneous 'body' of study. Although the term 'Postcolonial' has become the most widely accepted designation for this group of literatures, an extended and sophisticated debate about the usefulness of even the term 'Postcolonial' has emerged in the last decades of the century. 'Postcolonial' might at first appear to be a 'period specific' designation, namely to refer to literature written *after* colonialism when nations gained their independence from colonising powers, usually from the 1950s onwards. However, this has been recognised as a problematic periodisation, since it fails to take into account the fact that even after independence, literatures from such countries still manifested the effects of 'neo-colonialism', or the lingering vestigial cultural remains of the imperial / colonial powers with all their negative and positive effects. For instance, this line of argument has led to pressures to change Departments of English in African universities to Departments of African Studies, as happened in Kenya under Ngugi wa Thiong'o's influence, thus eschewing the value of the English literary cultural tradition to the culture of that particular country. There have been vigorous debates over the efficacy of continuing to write in the 'colonial tongue' (English, French, Portuguese) instead of indigenous languages. Ngugi, for example, has abandoned writing in English in favour of his native tongue of Kikuyu, choosing to translate his writings into English as a later, second procedure.

Another problem is that 'Postcolonialism' as a term lends itself to very broad use. Australians and Canadians sometimes claim to live in postcolonial societies, but many would refuse them the label because their literature is dominated by European immigrants, and is therefore a literature of privilege rather than of protest. According to the usual Postcolonial paradigm only literature written by native peoples in Canada and Australia would truly qualify. Indeed, Australian, New Zealand and Canadian writings have generally had significant literary histories in the English language since their respective independences, although there have been anti-colonial works within these traditions. The transplanted culture of English imperialism always had to deal with stronger indigenous cultures in India and Africa, while it dominated or destroyed those in Australia, New Zealand, Canada and the Caribbean. Nevertheless, debates in this period about cultural marginality, ethnic centres and social peripheries signalled the emergence of indigenous writers, writing informed by cultural and linguistic traditions that have for many hundreds of years been obscured. Maori, Aboriginal and Native Canadian writing and their respective cultural and linguistic influences have begun to be treated seriously, especially with various writers winning Booker Prizes (Keri Hulme's *The Bone People* in 1985, and Michael Ondaatje's *The English Patient* in 1992), and other indigenous voices gaining an international readership, such as the Aboriginal novelists Mudrooroo and Sally Morgan. Yet it is still the English traditions that dominate in these countries and abroad, with writers like Margaret Atwood and Peter Carey exerting a large influence in the UK, albeit in a self-reflexive style that looks seriously at their cultural vantage-point.

Still other critics have used the term 'Postcolonial' to refer to forms of cultural production that are oppositional to colonialism, that is, *anti*-colonial in orientation. This embraces those texts produced during the colonial period construing them as 'Postcolonial', making a distinction between those that contest and those that are complicit with colonial ideologies (often a revisionist historiography). It could also be argued that this way of defining a whole era of writing as 'Postcolonial' is itself Eurocentric, in that it singles out the colonial experience as the most important fact about the countries involved. While it can readily be acknowledged that this experience has had many powerful influences, it is not necessarily the framework within which writers from – say – India, who have a long history of precolonial literature, wish to be viewed. One of the most popular and widely read of modern Indian writers – R. K. Narayan – displays a remarkable indifference to the historical experience of colonialism, a fact which results in his being often overlooked by Postcolonial scholars. The inclusion of the term 'colonial' in reference to any writing from Africa or Asia might be considered questionable, since some perceive this term to perpetuate the legacy of an era that most would prefer to consign to oblivion. Does it make sense to refer to Canadian writing as Postcolonial when its most marked influences come from the USA? Is Indian writing Postcolonial when it derives influences from cultural sources much older than the advent of the British raj?

A further approach investigates literature that is 'hybrid', a term most closely associated with the work of Homi Bhabha, which has become an important concept in Postcolonial theory, referring to the creation of transcultural forms within the colonial zones. In particular, it refers to the integration, cross-pollination or mingling of cultural signs and practices from the colonising and the colonised cultures. The assimilation and adaptation of cultural practices, the cross-fertilisation of cultures, can be seen as positive, enriching and dynamic, as well as oppressive. 'Hybridity' is also a useful concept for helping to break down the false sense that colonised cultures – or colonising cultures for that matter – are monolithic, or have essential, unchanging features.

Much of the academic interpretative framework for the analysis of this literature and its cultural impact derives from the work of three hugely influential theorists – Edward Said, Gayatri Spivak and Homi Bhabha – and one whose influence often goes unacknowledged – Frantz Fanon. Initially, the appearance of Edward Said's *Orientalism* (1978) was a key moment in the development of colonial discourse analysis. Said's polemical book outlined the ways in which the West objectified, in fact *constructed*, the Orient in its discursive practices in the arts and social sciences. Said's principal contribution to Postcolonial theory was the way he opened up the close interconnection between different sorts of cultural and representational texts and the formation of power structures, demonstrating the subtle and complex connections between systems of knowledge and strategies of domination and control. The other two figures who form what Robert Young has impishly termed the 'holy trinity' of Postcolonial theory are Homi Bhabha and Gayatri Spivak. While there are significant differences between the work of all three theorists, they nevertheless share the conviction that colonialism and imperialism are projects that construct identity. Decisively influenced by psychoanalysis and Post-structuralism, Bhabha has sought to show how cultural identity emerges in a contradictory and ambivalent space, which makes any claims for cultural 'purity' in essentialist theories unsustainable. Hybridity, Bhabha argues, subverts the narratives of colonial power and dominant cultures.[1] The series of inclusions and exclusions on which a dominant culture is premised are deconstructed by the very entry of the formerly excluded subjects into the mainstream discourse. However, one must guard against hybridity becoming a dehistoricising gesture, dislocating writing from its geographical, linguistic and historical features. Gayatri Spivak has been most influential in questioning whether the entire enterprise of 'Postcolonial studies' is itself fundamentally flawed. In asking the question 'Can the subaltern speak?', she has argued that no subaltern identity can be entirely outside the discourse of the coloniser since the subaltern subject's perspective cannot be separated from the dominant discourse that provides the language and concepts with which the subaltern speaks.[2] Even the existence of Postcolonial theory testifies to the dominant mode of discourse in which the voice of the marginalised subject is heard.

Although it has provided many of the conceptual and interpretative frameworks for discussions of Postcolonial fictions, Postcolonial theory is arguably a discourse that is distinct from Postcolonial fiction. Postcolonial theory has often proved to be about the West's view of the 'other', or how European views have influenced Third World writers, rather than actually about the writings from these new nations themselves. In fact, theory has sometimes been guilty of homogenising the Third World as an idealised movement of resistance to imperialism, demonising a European literary and cultural tradition against which the Empire is implicitly or openly rebelling. There are clearly instances where Postcolonial fiction is responding to ideas and debates originating in Postcolonial theory, but usually the fiction is responding to more pressing political issues, a point made forcefully by Aijaz Ahmad.[3] Indeed, it is a moot point as to whether the theory has driven the fiction or whether the fiction has driven the theorisation. Nevertheless, broadly speaking, Postcolonial writing has effected a new agenda in discussions of cultural value, and placed a new urgency on discussions of such issues as aboriginality, revisionist historiography, mappings, migrancy, landscape and language, oral and scribal traditions, responses to European texts (counter-discourses), gender mythologies, discovery and settlement, nationalisms, multiculturalism and cultural division.

[1] Homi K. Bhabha, *The Location of Culture* (London: Routledge, 1994), pp. 38–9.

[2] Gayatri Spivak, 'Can the Subaltern Speak?', in Cary Nelson and Lawrence Grossberg, eds., *Marxism and the Interpretation of Culture* (London: Macmillan, 1988), pp. 271–313.

[3] Aijaz Ahmad, 'The Politics of Literary Postcoloniality', *Race and Class*, 36, 3 (1995), pp. 1–20.

In a now well-worn phrase, Postcolonial literature has sought to 'write back against the empire'.[4] So, for example, the Nigerian novelist Chinua Achebe's early fiction sought to rewrite the African perspective of Nigeria after hundreds of years of colonial rule, in which people's cultures, histories and religions were routinely denigrated and dismissed. These novelists present the missing or excluded cultural histories of their peoples, such as Ngugi's novels about the Gikuyu during the transition from colony to independent Kenya in *The River Between* (1965), or novels by Elechi Amadi and Ayi Kwei Armah that seek to present indigenous life before colonialism in West Africa. Some of these writers also specifically engage with the aesthetic representations of European novelists, such as Achebe's engagement with Joseph Conrad and Joyce Cary, seeking to forge a national consciousness through the development of new cultural forms. The generic adaptation that has emerged in Postcolonial writing has often been responsible for constructing new or hybrid genres from oral traditions, such as Amos Tutuola's *The Palm-Wine Drinkard* (1952) or Maxine Hong Kingston's *The Woman Warrior* (1976). Furthermore, a host of Postcolonial writers such as Patrick White, Jean Rhys, Wilson Harris, George Lamming and Margaret Atwood have rewritten particular works from the English literary 'canon' with the intention of restructuring 'realities' from a Postcolonial perspective. This approach to representing hidden or obscured cultural histories has been termed 'decolonising fictions'.[5] However, the task of these writers has not been merely to find a non-repressive alternative to imperialist and colonialist discourse, but to resist repeating the repressive discursive structures in their new modes of writing. In writing back against the Empire, these fictions from the 'periphery' have been profoundly instrumental in forcing the 'centre' to rethink and reconceptualise central aspects of Enlightenment thought, such as concepts of history, issues of nationhood, and the constructions of race, ethnicity and subjectivity. Constructions of a national culture go hand-in-hand with definitions of new citizenship, new subjectivities and new social and political identities.

This inevitably has an impact on other nations when people begin to emigrate and effect transcultural changes. The 1970s and 1980s saw the full flowering of the 'other' voice in British literature, which produced a sustained and concerted challenge to English literary traditions and forms. The UK has a number of writers living within it whose cultural backgrounds derive from

4 Bill Ashcroft, Gareth Griffiths and Helen Tiffin, *The Empire Writes Back: Theory and Practice in Post-colonial Literatures* (London: Routledge, 1989).

5 Diana Brydon and Helen Tiffin, *Decolonising Fictions* (Sydney and Hebden Bridge: Dangaroo, 1993).

one-time colonies – the West Indies, areas of Africa like South Africa, Nigeria or Kenya, or from areas on the Indian subcontinent like India and Pakistan. It is difficult to imagine the contemporary British writing scene without writers like Buchi Emecheta, Hanif Kureishi, Kazuo Ishiguro, Timothy Mo, V. S. Naipaul, Ben Okri, Caryl Phillips, Salman Rushdie, Zadie Smith and Meera Syal, all of whom produce fictions that interrogate not only the colonial legacies in their cultural homelands, but also question and explore the implications of multiculturalism in the UK, or the cultural, social and political effects of being non-British and non-white within a contemporary pluralist society. Their fictions demonstrate a specific ambivalence towards the UK, and configure a subjectivity that is 'in-between' cultures, or interstitial. Ishiguro, for example, regards himself as an international writer, although his themes of memory, temporal dislocation and emotional estrangement haunt his novels as characters move through identities and drift between unconnected places. For this group of writers, an ever-present and urgent question is: what constitutes a 'homeland'? To what country does a writer belong if he or she has emigrated? How does one take account of an 'exilic consciousness'? Often suffering 'ghettoisation' in the 'new country', these groups are influenced by their previous migrant or diasporic histories, and for them 'home' often acts as an 'imagined' place. Salman Rushdie writes about his own diasporic stance: 'Writers in my position, exiles or emigrants or expatriates . . . will, in short, create fictions, not actual cities or villages, but invisible ones, imaginary homelands.'[6] This 'imaginary homeland' often acts as an orientation, a sense of origin, a concept of stability or security, and the border-crossing that has gone on allows the writer a place for upsetting structures and patterns.

For a central historical fact of colonisation was the voluntary or forcible removal of people from one country to another. As a result of increasing internationalisation, massive immigration and the ease with which national borders can now be crossed, a great diaspora emerged in the latter half of the twentieth century. Add to these destabilising fictions the ongoing debates about the tortured distinction between a federation of states and the preservation of state integrity, and a spectre is haunting the UK – the spectre of national identity. All the powers of Old Europe have entered into the holy alliance of the European Union to exorcise this spectre: Prime Minister and Chancellor, Romano Prodi and Javier Solana, Benelux archipelago and Iberian peninsula, French Eurocrats and German businessmen. Yet the spectre of identity refuses to go away

[6] Salman Rushdie, 'Imaginary Homelands', *Essays and Criticism 1981–1991* (London: Granta, 1992), p. 10.

as the UK agonises about its vestigial imperial importance, the preservation of sterling as a currency, or the impact of Brussels's bureaucratic diktats on the manufacture and standardisation of 'Cheddar cheese'. The crisis of 'identity politics' thus dominates the UK. Do we want to become a multicultural society? Do we already have one? How can diversity-within-unity be made to work politically and culturally? The heterogeneity of British cultural life is the focus of Zadie Smith's powerful début novel *White Teeth* (2000), as she charts the cross-cultural fusion of life in modern-day London in all its most rudimentary forms:

> This has been the century of strangers, brown, yellow and white. This has been the century of the great immigrant experiment. It is only this late in the day that you can walk into a playground and find Isaac Leung by the fish pond, Danny Rahman in the football cage, Quang O'Rourke bouncing a basketball, and Irie Jones humming a tune. Children with first and last names on a direct collision course. Names that secrete within them mass exodus, cramped boats and planes, cold arrivals, medical checks. It is only this late in the day, and possibly only in Willesden, that you can find best friends Sita and Sharon, constantly mistaken for each other because Sita is white (her mother liked the name) and Sharon is Pakistani (her mother thought it best – less trouble). Yet, despite all the mixing up, despite the fact that we have finally slipped into each other's lives with reasonable comfort (like a man returning to his lover's bed after a midnight walk), despite all this, it is still hard to admit that there is no one more English than the Indian, no one more Indian than the English.[7]

Following the shenanigans and involvements of the teenagers Irie Jones and Magid and Millat Iqbal, the novel resists easy categorisation, which is part of Smith's point about British multicultural experience and its restless hybridity.

Such 'in-between' lives are the stuff of British diasporic literatures which frequently manifest the consciousnesses of those who are acculturated but not fully assimilated in foreign lands, and these works resist easy compartmentalisation within national literary traditions. Diasporic groups have developed their own distinctive cultures which preserve and often extend their originary cultures, as they modify (and are modified by) indigenous cultures with which they come into contact.[8] There are clear distinctions between an internationalised cultural elite, immigrants who feel exiled, and those raised abroad who have nevertheless retained or developed a renewed sense of ethnicity. In the UK, for example, there are clear distinctions between Africans, British West

[7] Zadie Smith, *White Teeth* (2000; London: Penguin, 2001), pp. 326–7.
[8] See Avtar Brah, *Cartographies of Diaspora: Contesting Identities* (London: Routledge, 1996).

Indians, Black Britons or Indians; and a significant manifestation of a diasporic consciousness is the participation in several groups without feeling fully at home. Diasporic concerns feature in a wide variety of British Postcolonial fiction, such as the films and fiction of Hanif Kureishi. In Kureishi's first novel, *The Buddha of Suburbia* (1990), Karim, the protagonist, defines himself as 'having emerged from two old histories'.[9] To a large extent, the stories of Karim and most of the characters in this novel have been affected by history, especially the history of colonisation. The prejudices and preconceptions to which many of the characters are subject are rooted in issues connected with power, ideology and historical representation. London, historically the heart of the former British Empire, becomes the object of desire for many characters who strive to move from the margins to its centre. Such immigrant fiction acts as a witness to an imperialism-in-reverse as the New Commonwealth citizens colonise London's and other metropolitan cities' spaces. Karim, a British Indian adolescent, and Haroon, his Indian father, start a sort of pilgrimage from the suburbs to downtown London, from the geographical but also social periphery to the centre. Despite their enthusiasm, they are constantly reminded of their inability to be considered authentic Englishmen. After many years of 'trying to be more of an Englishman' (21), Haroon realises that it is more profitable for him to become a caricature of himself and to play up to English people's stereotyped ideas concerning his Indian identity. These constant admonitions teach him that English identity is a privilege that he can never attain. In a moment of insight, Karim realises that

> they never let him forget they thought him a nigger, a slave, a lower being. And we pursued English roses as we pursued England; by possessing these prizes, this kindness and beauty, we stared defiantly into the eye of the Empire and all its self-regard . . . We became part of England and yet proudly stood outside it. (227)

Kureishi pursues these themes in *The Black Album* (1995), where from the very outset, in a conversation between the protagonist Shahid and the spokesman for Islamic purity, Riaz, the issue of 'losing oneself in England'[10] is raised. The condition of the exile runs throughout the novel, and it portrays the intensity of the fragmentation and collapse of domestic unity and 'community' when confronted with unrelenting, pitiless racial hatred. Similarly, Joan Riley's *The Unbelonging* (1985) charts the agonising diasporic consciousness of

9 Hanif Kureishi, *The Buddha of Suburbia* (London: Penguin, 1991), p. 3. Further references given in parenthesis in the text.

10 Hanif Kureishi, *The Black Album* (London: Faber & Faber, 1995), p. 7.

Hyacinth, an eleven-year-old Black–British exile sent from Jamaica to join her father in England. This fractured childhood scenario is far from a typical childhood experience. In this extreme portrayal, Riley documents the psychological displacement for these children whose literal inhabitation of a divided self becomes worsened by racism and social insult and parental physical and psychological abuse. Hyacinth struggles to find a self between this Scylla and Charybdis of insult and abuse, carrying the traumatic residue of her abused childhood into adulthood. With no foundation to enter into adulthood and bottling her father's crimes up inside her, Hyacinth's silence results in a core of unhealed pain, obstructing her future ability to have male–female relationships. Her fear to disclose her father's abuse, the hatred of her blackness, and the hostility of the British society, all keep her chained to her childhood memories of Jamaica and to a false domicile in the imagination. This has grave repercussions on her conception of what constitutes one's abode; and 'home' is a concept that is split between 'belonging' and 'forgetting'.

Redefining what constitutes Englishness is also the central aspect of Timothy Mo's novel *Sour Sweet* (1982), which deals with the immigration of a Chinese family to England. Set in the 1960s, *Sour Sweet* revolves around Chen, his wife Lily, their son, and his sister-in-law, Mui, all of whom come to terms with a strange land, its people and their customs in different ways, and often through prejudice and misunderstanding. The family moves to England and buys a restaurant, and Chen becomes inadvertently involved with Triads. Mo's narrative concerns the cultural encounter between the Chinese family and the English. When Chen worked as a waiter, he was constantly amazed at the idiosyncracies of the English, such as the English habit of endeavouring to escape without paying the restaurant bill. The waiters have less difficulty in understanding the antagonistic behaviour of typical English customers, described as: 'loud and rowdy behaviour . . . including fencing with chopsticks and wearing inverted rice bowls on the head like brittle skull-caps, writing odd things on lavatory walls, and mixing the food on their plates in a disgusting way before putting soya sauce on everything'.[11] In spite of such socially patronising attitudes, the restaurant proprietor prefers English patrons to Chinese because they 'consumed expensive and unsuitable wines as well as beer with their meal and did not share the irritating obsessions of the Chinese customers with their totally unreasonable insistence that a meal be made up of fresh materials . . . '[12] In this comical way, Mo satirises the English lack of culinary sophistication. Mo's satirical perspective on English mores and manners eventually leads to

[11] Timothy Mo, *Sour Sweet* (London: Vintage, 1982), p. 29. [12] Ibid., p. 29.

a redefinition of the notion of Englishness. Hanif Kureishi echoes Mo when he presents this appeal in the essay 'The Rainbow Sign': 'It is the British, the white British, who have to learn that being British isn't what it was. Now it is a more complex thing, involving new elements. So there must be a fresh way of seeing Britain and the choices it faces: and a new way of being British after all this time.'[13]

In such a mélange and transgression of cultural boundaries, clearly the lines drawn to demarcate writers from one culture or another are confusing. For example, of those who write in English, Anita Desai is regarded as a Postcolonial writer, though she is half German. Ngugi wa Thiong'o is included even though he now writes primarily in Kikuyu. The South African novelist André Brink writes in Afrikaans, until recently the language bitterly identified with the repressive brutality of the apartheid regime. Bharati Mukherjee specifically rejects the label 'Indian–American', though she is an immigrant from India, and Rushdie prefers to be thought of as a sort of multinational hybrid (though he has, on occasion, used the label 'Postcolonial' in his own writing). Hanif Kureishi is more English than Pakistani in his outlook, and many Caribbean-born writers living in England are now classed as 'Black–British.' 'Black–British' itself is a term that is used to encompass an entire racialised group in Britain including those of Asian ancestry.[14] What determines when you are too acculturated to be counted as Postcolonial: where you were born? how long you've lived abroad? your subject matter? These and similar questions have been the object of constant debate since the SS *Empire Windrush* docked in Tilbury in June 1948, marking the beginnings of a 'Black British past'. Since then, a range of novels have sought to explore the immigrant's experience in the UK, from George Lamming's *The Emigrants* (1954), Sam Selvon's *The Lonely Londoners* (1956), Edward Braithwaite's *To Sir With Love* (1957), to Buchi Emecheta's *Second-Class Citizen* (1975) and Timothy Mo's *Sour Sweet* (1982). Among its other preoccupations, Salman Rushdie's *The Satanic Verses* (1988) also deals with the immigrant experience in Britain. Celebrating impurity, intermingling and mongrelisation, immigrant 'otherness' in the novel is undermined by cultural hybridity. In fact, Homi Bhabha developed the term 'hybridity' to capture the sense that many writers have of belonging to *both* cultures. Bhabha's discussion of hybridity also occurs in terms of 'mimicry', in which a mimic is a hybrid figure inasmuch as he or she reflects or appears to adopt the qualities and values of colonial authority.

[13] Hanif Kureishi, *'My Beautiful Laundrette' and 'The Rainbow Sign'* (London: Faber & Faber, 1986), p. 38.

[14] See Heidi Safia Mirza, ed., *Black British Feminism* (London: Routledge, 1997).

Bhabha's salient example of hybridity is Salman Rushdie, who rejects the older paradigm of 'exile' which was meaningful to earlier generations of emigrants, in favour of accepting a new blend of cultures as a positive synthesis. Rushdie's adopted position and perspective of the migrant writer, which he regards as fertile territory for a writer to occupy, allows him to be inside and outside the British culture he has depicted. Rushdie has proved to be one of the central figures in discussions of British Postcolonial fiction, especially with regard to debates concerning the forms and concepts of history, nations and nationhood. These issues emerged with the advent of European modernity and imperialism, and were specifically used to justify the project of colonialism itself.[15] European nations 'possessed' history, while others did not. Validated by their history and nationhood, European nations regarded colonial subjects as historyless and nationless 'others'. Although *Midnight's Children* (1981) appears to chart the association of a personal and a national history in the figure of Saleem Sinai, he turns out to be an unreliable narrator and factual errors occur in his narrative. Rather than being simply slipshod writing, this points to a tension between conceptions of history as a series of verifiable facts and history as an act of narration. For Rushdie, history is a kind of fiction. Saleem maintains that reality and truth are not ascertainable and that they are the constructs of imagination, experience and language:

> Memory's truth, because memory has its own special kind. It selects, eliminates, alters, exaggerates, minimizes, glorifies, and vilifies also; but in the end it creates its own reality, its heterogeneous but usually coherent version of events; and no sane human being ever trusts someone else's version more than his own.[16]

The 'truth' of a story lies in its telling and the selection of events from memory. *Midnight's Children* uses these debates about memory and history as a launching pad for an attack on the allied issues of nationhood and nationalism. Linked as it is to contemporary theories of the nation, the novel specifically endorses Benedict Anderson's concept of the nation as an 'imagined political community'. *Midnight's Children* demonstrates that different members of that community imagine different versions of it. Confronting the concept of narrative 'truth' head on, Saleem Sinai's unreliable narration causes us to be thoroughly sceptical about the very act of narration itself. Problematising as it does the *authority* of historical knowledge rather than dispensing with history

[15] See Partha Chatterjee, *Nationalist Thought and the Colonial World* (London: Zed Books, 1986).
[16] Salman Rushdie, *Midnight's Children* (London: Picador, 1982), p. 211.

altogether, history and nation emerge as suspect and contested concepts. That contestation came to a singularly ugly conclusion when the *fatwah* was issued by the Ayatollah on Rushdie's life upon the publication of *The Satanic Verses* (1988). This brought into the open with a jolt the persistent intolerances of different readerships, and opened a huge can of worms about the nature of censorship, freedom of speech, the laws concerning religious blasphemy, and the politics of literary adaptation. That the publication of a novel could be the impetus for a state-sponsored and religion-inspired call for assassination brought home to the world in a most extreme manner that cultural histories are different and that these cultural differences are still the cause of considerable misinterpretation. Rushdie has always made cynicism and satire a mainstay of his fiction, but different cultural perspectives determine what is acceptable or not. One person's irony is another person's profanity. In this respect, one of the strengths of multiculturalism is also one of its greatest risks.

Rushdie's writing also raises another vexed issue: the connection of Postcolonial literatures with Postmodernism. Many critics have rejected any linkage between the vitality and challenges of Postcolonial literatures with the Anglo-European notions of exhaustion and the end of history, and the connections with Postmodern eclecticism. Many Postcolonial writers regard Postmodernism as a mere distraction from the urgent issues of daily politics in their respective nations. But this does not entirely explain the whole story. For example, a self-consciously traditionally written novel like Vikram Seth's *A Suitable Boy*, in clear contrast to the metafictional games of Rushdie's fiction, but making deliberate use of older literary manners and forms, might be regarded as characteristically Postmodern. Others would argue that a relationship does exist between Postmodernism and Postcolonialism. For Postcolonial literatures clearly share some strategies with Postmodernism, like a movement away from realist representation, the hybridisation of forms, an interrogation of the forces at work in constructing subjectivities. In fact, many 'Postcolonial' writers search out models from the past and adapt them to local customs and experiences, such as Derek Walcott's *Omeros* (1990), or J. M. Coetzee's *Foe* (1986). Coetzee's importance to the development of contemporary British fiction is now widely agreed. Winning an unprecedented two Booker Prizes (1983 and 1999), his work addresses some of the key critical issues of our time: the relationship between Postmodernism and Postcolonialism, the role of history in the novel, and he repeatedly returns to how the author can combine an ethical and political consciousness with a commitment to the novel as a work of fiction. Largely responding to the particular form of colonial violence systematised as apartheid, Coetzee's fiction has nevertheless been regarded by some as an oblique rather than overt challenge. *Foe* is a typical example of this ambiguity. In a finely nuanced recasting of Daniel Defoe's *Robinson Crusoe*, Coetzee's principal dilemma is how to approach the colonised 'other' in Friday, the character whose history has been silenced by colonial violence: his tongue appears to have been cut out. In a style highly conscious of its own textuality, the novel opens up the double operation that associates literary and historical colonialism. Yet *Foe* is no lame articulation of this racial silencing: it is also a delicate probing of the politics of voicing the 'other'. Arguably the principal protagonist, Susan Barton, seeks to control Friday through her attempts to 'liberate' him, as her narrative gradually situates him in 'her' history. In addressing whether the subaltern has a voice, Coetzee raises questions about the Western master narratives concerning authority and authorship, gender, ethnicity and access to language. *Foe* seems self-consciously to acknowledge the impossibility of fictional narrative to heal the breaches caused by social violence. Yet for all its self-conscious literary allusions and textual knowing, *Foe* is not entirely representative of Coetzee's fiction: most of his other books confront colonial violence in more overt ways. With varying stylistic departures in each of his novels, Coetzee's fiction offers a brooding self-consciousness that is keenly aware of the dangers of self-enclosed textual play. Yet for all his suspicions of Western master narratives and his investigations of textual subversions, Coetzee has been widely criticised for establishing a position that has affinities with a broader political revision of history, a Postcolonial counter-narrative of historical alterity rather than a Postmodern narrative of allegorical destabilisation. Nevertheless, Coetzee's stature within the domain of Postcolonial literature lies partly in his ability to speak to a wider global community on issues of race, commodification, fiction and history, while at the same time continuing to offer a very specific discursive intervention in the context of apartheid. Dominic Head maintains that Coetzee's fiction presents Western readers with continual challenges to preconceptions about the *value* of fiction in a postcolonial context, since he 'gestures continually towards newly conceived political identities, through fictions which are themselves pointed acts of hybridity'.[17]

A distinctive late twentieth-century refashioning of the insider / outsider perspective has occurred in the work of writers like Caryl Phillips, Fred D'Aguiar, David Dabydeen, Hanif Kureishi and Abdulrazak Gurnah. Whereas the first generation of immigrants like Selvon, Lamming and Braithwaite tended to address themselves, albeit perhaps unconsciously, to a white British middle-class

[17] Dominic Head, *J. M. Coetzee* (Cambridge University Press, 1997), p. 20.

readership, the current generation address a readership *produced* by forty years of 'cultural diversity', attuned to issues of internationalism, cosmopolitanism, national identity and transculturation. Indeed, the 1980s and 1990s saw a wave of novels discovering or inventing a personal identity. These fictions frequently utilise variable time-scales and multiple locations to structure their narratives, as migrants travel backwards and forwards either in the mind or in physical space, to reflect the puzzlement of the protagonists as they attempt to fathom out their hybrid existences. Caryl Phillips's fiction explicitly deals with the history of the 'black presence' in the UK, especially depicting the historical context of the slave-trade voyages, the first immigrant arrivals, and the 1960s Powellite 'rivers of blood' racism. *The Final Passage* (1985), retelling the Caribbean emigration to the UK in the late 1950s, explicitly echoes the 'middle passage' of slaves across the Atlantic; while *Crossing the River* (1993) addresses the issues of displacement and dislocation from different temporal and spatial perspectives and presents a brilliantly coherent vision of two and a half centuries of the African diaspora. These ideas are further amplified in his collection of essays entitled *A New World Order* (2001), which concerns multiculturalism in the UK, the influence of the 'Black Atlantic' on British West Indian cultural consciousness, and the particularities and paradoxes of being 'Black–British' at the beginning of the twenty-first century. Phillips is largely concerned with the negative and positive effects of lacking a 'home':

> A twenty-first century world. A world in which it is impossible to resist the claims of the migrant, the asylum seeker, or the refugee. I watch them. The old static order in which one people speaks down to another, lesser, people is dead. The colonial, or Postcolonial, model has collapsed. In its place we have a new world order in which there will seem to be one global conversation with limited participation open to all, and full participation available to none. In this new world order nobody will feel fully at home.[18]

Postcolonial literature is all too often identified with the past and with history. But in this focus, it cannot shut out the future. In the face of dejected and fatuous laments over the decline of British culture, Phillips's novels are part of an ongoing cultural transformation of the UK brought about by its diverse and multicultural British subjects. This transformation insists, to quote Stuart Hall, that 'we all speak from a particular place, out of a particular history . . . without being contained by that position as *ethnic* artists'.[19] Although one needs to be

[18] Caryl Phillips, *A New World Order* (London: Secker & Warburg, 2001), p. 5.

[19] Stuart Hall, 'New Ethnicities' (1988), in James Procter, ed., *Writing Black Britain, 1948–1998: An Interdisciplinary Anthology* (Manchester University Press, 2000), pp. 265–75.

careful about establishing an exoticism and perpetuating a covert Orientalism in one's attention to these writings from alternative cultures and perspectives, it is nevertheless the emergence of something new, something different, from out of the cross-cultural fusions, the hybrid interminglings and the intergeneric coalescences, that makes Postcolonial fiction exciting and valuable. Furthermore, it relativises the significance of our respective cultures, showing that

> We are all, in that sense, *ethnically* located and our ethnic identities are crucial to our subjective sense of who we are. But this is also a recognition that this is not an ethnicity which is doomed to survive, as Englishness has, only by marginalising, dispossessing, displacing and forgetting other ethnicities. This precisely is the politics of ethnicity predicated on difference and diversity.[20]

Self-consciously recognising our own situatedness, with all the caveats that accompany that recognition, goes some way to building and fostering the aspiration to a politics of inclusive social democratic citizenship.

[20] Ibid., p. 273.

42

Writing lives

ALISON LIGHT

Personality-culture

Biography and autobiography have flourished in the last thirty years of the twentieth century. Both are stacked high in book shops and are among the books most borrowed from the public library. A glance at a current list of bestselling non-fiction reveals that six out of ten hardback bestsellers and eight out of ten paperback are either biography or autobiography. 'Celebrity' lives abound – the autobiographies of reformed villains and alcoholic footballers, rags to riches tales of pop stars or the scandalous accounts of high society (Andrew Morton's biography of the Princess of Wales, *Diana: Her True Story* sold millions worldwide after its publication in 1992); equally popular, however, are the painstakingly researched and weighty lives of writers and artists, scientists and politicians – 'literary biographies' – which together with the 'literary memoir' form part of what publishers now call 'literary non-fiction', a more elevated mix of specialist subject and trade publisher (among the surprise successes was Stella Tillyard's *Aristocrats*, published in 1994, which followed the lives of the four Lennox sisters in late eighteenth-century England and Ireland, and Claire Tomalin's *Samuel Pepys: The Unequalled Self*, which won the Whitbread Prize in 2001, and was a bestseller).

Not surprisingly, biographers are the first to claim the supremacy of their own sphere. Indeed, according to one of its main practitioners, Richard Holmes, literary biography is 'arguably the most successful, and intellectually stimulating, literary form which has held a general readership in Britain' since the 1960s. Yet 'the rise to power of a new literary genre' may have as much to do with the new economics of publishing and with wider cultural shifts as with any narrowly literary developments or innovations. 1971 saw the first Whitbread Book Award for Biography (it went to Michael Meyer's *Henrik Ibsen*), but the growth of a prize culture, like the chart-positions of books, is itself a phenomenon of the last thirty years of the century (the best known, the Man

Booker Prize for fiction was established in 1969 and new prizes continue to proliferate). Massive advances are paid to the superstar literary biographers, such as Peter Ackroyd, Michael Holroyd, Victoria Glendinning (Ackroyd received an advance of £650,000 to write biographies of Dickens and Blake), but arguably they owe as much to the conglomeration of publishing companies into vast multinational, even global corporations as to the popularity of the genre. As smaller booksellers and publishers go to the wall and chain-bookstores dominate, 'niche publishing' aimed at specific segments of the readers' market has become the way for publishers to ensure sales (Blake Publishing, for instance, specialises in the lives of 'hard men' and criminal autobiographers). Biography and autobiography may now be big business but their sales come at a price.

In his account of his novelist–father, *Experience* (2000), Martin Amis has complained that 'what everyone has in them, these days, is not a novel but a memoir'. Amis blames the autobiographical impulse in particular on 'the age of mass loquacity', a personality-culture in which everyone can fancy themselves as famous ('karaoke fame'). In the 1990s, magazines like *Hello* or *OK!* took over from women's magazines, displaying the weddings, houses and clothes of footballers or fashion models and inviting the reader into 'celebrity' lives; 'reality television', like the influential 'Big Brother' series in the late 1990s and after, helped to create 'ordinary' celebrity; the interview or profile became the model for British journalism, serious newspaper columnists on the broadsheets added their pictures to their bylines (as if we needed to see their homely faces) and even the stuffy *Times Literary Supplement* drastically changed its policy for the first time since its inception in 1902 and in 1974 abolished the anonymity of its contributors. The highbrow *London Review of Books*, like the *TLS*, routinely carries memoir on its commentary pages while the review pages of the broadsheets are increasingly concentrated upon what the Saturday *Guardian* calls 'Lives and Letters'. Ours is a culture of confession where television chat shows follow the popular model of therapy as de-repression and the search for total candour is paramount. Yet behind the sincerity of the autobiographer or biographer frequently lurks the virtual presence of a ghost-writer or publicist (in 2003, Hillary Clinton, the wife of the former US President, published her memoirs of their troubled marriage as part of her own campaign strategy). Where personalities are brands, where 'merchandising' and promoting applies as much to authors as their books, the pervasiveness of biography and autobiography in the bestsellers seems inevitable. All that is solid melts into PR.

There is plenty of evidence to suggest that we live in a culture obsessed with the contents and the shape of other people's lives. What this means is less clear. For some critics the popularity of biography and autobiography is an effect of an increasingly aggressive individualism in Europe and the West where politics, history and social life are now seen through the optic of the personal, a symptom of a shamelessly competitive and privatised culture, in which, in Margaret Thatcher's best-known aphorism, 'there is no such thing as society, only individuals and their families'. Yet if there has been – as it seems – a biographical turn in literary culture since the 1970s, it might equally be read as an attempt at compensation, a way of creating *ad hoc* communities in the absence of sustaining ones, of making those temporary affiliations and identifications which are one of the marks of 'postmodern' living. For its champions, biography and autobiography offer the vestiges of a common culture fashioned out of the random mix of different lives, a raft of humanist values in a floating world. Indeed, biography and autobiography are vaunted as the only literature left for the common reader. What Amis so dismissively calls 'mass loquacity' can also be registered more generously: there are now far more people who believe their lives count as history and who think they deserve to be listened to.

Within the universities until comparatively recently, biography and autobiography smacked too much of bellettrism and the marketplace. Between the wars the relatively new discipline of English literature, keen to establish its rigour, and to free the subject from the shades of the amateurism which had made it the province of women and adult learners, eschewed biographical approaches to works. In Cambridge, I. A. Richards's stress on attending to 'the words on the page', like T. S. Eliot's aesthetics of 'impersonality', kept the author at arm's length. In the USA, Richards's and Eliot's influence could be discerned in the 'New Criticism' of the 1940s (which found its way back to the UK in the decades after the war). In their *Theory of Literature* (1949), René Wellek and Austin Warren argued for the centrality of the literary work as a self-contained, autonomous structure, examined for its 'tension', irony' or 'paradoxes', cut off from the author: 'No biographical evidence', they wrote decisively, 'can change or influence critical evaluation.'[1]

Yet since the late 1960s there has been a dramatic sea-change, not least in the academy. Biography and autobiography have become acceptable objects of study – this chapter is itself a sign of the times in acknowledging them both as 'genres' – and biographical approaches within criticism are no longer seen as wholly dubious. In addition, if the period since 1970 has been marked

[1] René Wellek and Austin Warren, *Theory of Literature* (Harmondsworth: Peguin, 1980), p. 74.

by an expansion in a biographical culture, it has also seen, within literary studies, the intense theorisation of those ways of thinking about human beings and their histories which seek to undermine the ideas of selfhood and of authority (and indeed of the literary), upon which so much biography and autobiography relies. Paradoxically, the biographical turn of the last thirty-odd years of the century and 'the deconstructive turn' have gone hand in hand, despite apparently pulling in opposite directions.

Expansion and critique

The 1970s were particularly sympathetic to biographical and autobiographical writing. A new emphasis on personal identity in the political movements of the day, on the importance of self-exploration as being at the heart of programmes for social and sexual transformation, inspired those who felt themselves to be outside the mainstream of literary culture, in particular women and gays, working-class and Black–British writers. Writing and publishing biography and autobiography were central to asserting a group presence within British culture, challenging the official records of the national past. The act of telling a lifestory was invested with a political power: 'finding a voice', feeling 'entitled' to have one's story listened to or read, was itself felt to be emancipating – self-representation a primary act of political representation. While such a 'cultural politics' originally depended on the creation of small, independent publishers and bookshops, pamphlets and magazines, many of which no longer exist, the impact on mainstream publishing has been considerable, not least in creating new constituencies of readers and markets.

In the UK, as in the USA, the Women's Liberation and the gay movements generated many lifestories and novels which emphasised the process of 'consciousness-raising' and which bore a resemblance to the 'conversion narratives' or spiritual autobiographies of nineteenth-century socialists for whom the discovery of politics was the revelation on the road to Damascus. Many stories emphasised a growth into a shared recognition of collective oppression – Sheila Rowbotham's *Woman's Consciousness, Man's World* (1973), a political analysis of contemporary society, opens with an autobiographical 'journey' in this way. The moment of commitment to politics is frequently seen as the birth of a new identity, in which sexuality and individuality were to be freely expressed. Such stories often involved a new sexually explicit writing by women – Kate Millett's autobiography *Flying* (1974) celebrated erotic pleasure between women as did Verena Stefan's memoir *Shedding* (1975), where lesbianism is the heroine's liberation from the impasse of heterosexuality, while Erica Jong's

Fear of Flying (1974) teased its readers in the search for 'the zipless fuck'. The feminist presses, of which Virago was the most successful, promoted 'woman-centred' writing, assuming that reading about other women's lives encouraged self-esteem, and a sense of 'agency'. The first Virago Press book, Mary Chamberlain's *Fenwomen* in 1973, looked at women's lives in East Anglia; in 1978 the first in the Modern Classics series was Antonia White's autobiographical fiction *Frost in May* (1933), and the first reprinted non-fiction classic, Vera Brittain's autobiography *Testament of Youth* (1933), which ends with her espousal of feminism after World War I; in 1977 Virago reprinted the testimonies by women members of the Co-operative Guild collected in *Life as We Have Known It*, first published in 1931 by Leonard and Virginia Woolf's Hogarth Press. Virago also published a number of new biographies of female political figures such as Cathy Porter's life of Alexandra Kollontai (1980) and Alice Wexler's *Emma Goldman* (1984).

The liberalisation of the law and the lifting of censorship allowed for an increased candour in autobiography from the late 1960s – J. R. Ackerley's *My Father and Myself* (1968) openly discussed his homosexuality, while the television version of Quentin Crisp's *The Naked Civil Servant* (1968) brought homosexual persecution home to millions of British viewers when it was screened in the mid-seventies; Radclyffe Hall's once-banned *The Well of Loneliness* (1928) was reprinted by Transworld Publishers in 1968. An openly gay subculture produced a plethora of 'coming out' stories, characteristically telling of self-acceptance through the public declaration of one's sexuality – one anthology, *Walking After Midnight* (1989), collected testimonies from the Hall-Carpenter Archives and the London Gay Men's Oral History Group. Autobiographical novels and accounts from well-known figures like James Baldwin and Edmund White – or Christopher Isherwood's frank autobiography, *Christopher and His Kind* (1976) – indicated a climate of broader tolerance.

Autobiography and biography were also crucial forms for historians. The new social history of the 1970s – local history, regional history, labour history and family history – aimed to present an alternative 'history from below', offering the perspectives and experiences of those who might otherwise be 'hidden from history'. New works appeared – May Hobbs's *Born to Struggle* (1973), Winifred Foley's *A Child in the Forest* (1974), for instance – which put the experiences of the working classes on the literary map; older works were republished and critical studies began to uncover the history of literacy. The Workers' Federation of Writers and Community Publishers, formed in 1976, functioned as an umbrella-organisation giving people greater access to publishing in their locality (Queenspark books in Brighton, Centerprise in Hackney,

Bristol Broadsides, for instance) and included many lifestories in their publications. The first volume of a bibliography of working-class autobiography was published in 1985.[2] From the mid-1970s, 'oral history', namely, 'the interviewing of eye-witness participants in the events of the past for the purposes of historical reconstruction'[3] developed into an international movement of historians (the first international conference was held at Essex University in 1979), pioneering work on the role of subjectivity in history and on the difficulties as well as the validity of drawing on memories and personal experiences. The collecting and archiving of testimonies within university centres and sound archives became an established practice: in 1981 the Mass-Observation project (set up in 1937 as a way of analysing English society from inside) was housed at Sussex University with a new panel of over four hundred correspondents recording everyday life in Britain.

The publishing of black writers in the UK also drew sustenance from the USA, from the Civil Rights and Black Power movements, in particular, *The Autobiography of Malcolm X* (1965), published within months of his assassination. It traced his life from poor orphan to criminal to prison inmate, to reborn visionary and spokesman for the Nation of Islam, following the shape of a spiritual autobiography; *Soledad Brother: The Prison Letters of George Jackson* (Penguin (1971) with an introduction by Jean Genet) and the autobiography of his fellow-activist, Angela Davis, *With Freedom on my Mind* (1974) were also influential here, as was Alex Haley's bestselling *Roots: The Saga of an American Family* (1976) which encouraged many to explore their pasts. In Britain autobiographical novels like those of Sam Selvon or George Lamming had described life for immigrants in the Britain of the 1950s and 60s; the 1970s and 80s saw a new outpouring of autobiographical novels and poetry, especially by women, among them the novels of Nigerian-born Buchi Emecheta, *In the Ditch* (1972), *Second-Class Citizen* (1977) and her autobiography, *Head Above Water* (1986), the poetry of British–Caribbeans, Amryl Johnson and Valerie Bloom and the Guyana-born Grace Nichols, whose first volume *i is a long-memoried woman* won the Commonwealth Prize in 1983. Among autobiographies, the African–American Maya Angelou's five-volume sequence, beginning with *I Know Why the Caged Bird Sings* (1969), tracing her growth as a person and an artist, her recovery from rape and abuse as the victim of racism, offered a harrowing and triumphant journey through chaos to self-discovery. 'Lost' texts

[2] John Burnett, David Vincent and David Mayall, eds., *The Autobiography of the Working Class: An Annotated Critical Bibliography* (Brighton: Harvester, 1985).

[3] Robert Perks and Alistair Thomson, 'Introduction', to Perks and Thomson, eds., *The Oral History Reader* (London: Routledge, 1998) p. ix.

were reprinted including the memoirs of Mary Seacole, a Jamaican Creole woman – 'doctress', hotelier and merchant' – a bestseller in 1857, reprinted in 1984, which gave an instantly recognisable and wry observation of racial prejudice in London. *The Heart of the Race: Black Women's Lives in Britain* (1985) used autobiography collectively to place individual lives in the wider social and historical contexts, while the writers in the anthology *Let It Be Told* (1985) placed their emphasis upon 'creating strong self-images'[4]. The use of the term 'Black' was a deliberately oppositional, political category meant to unite different groups within the British diaspora in a collective claim to recognition.

From the late 1950s, 'confessional' poetry – Allen Ginsberg's *Howl* (1956), Robert Lowell's *Life Studies* (1959), Anne Sexton's *To Bedlam and Part Way Back* (1960), John Berryman's 77 *Dream Songs* (1964), Sylvia Plath's *Ariel* (1965) – spoke powerfully to readers about states of inner trauma, of extreme dislocation, breakdown and suicidal feelings. The idea of self-exploration as a political as well as personal necessity was further boosted in the period by the popularisation of psychology and of forms of therapy which were frequently meant to encourage a kind of de-repression, or release from the oppressive social structures in the self. Herbert Marcuse's *One-Dimensional Man* (1964), the work of Wilhelm Reich, and, in particular in the UK, the anti-psychiatry movement, especially the writings of R. D. Laing, drawing on Sartre's Existentialism, made a powerful impact: Laing's *The Divided Self*, published in paperback in 1965, was reprinted many times throughout the 1970s. Such ideas – for example of an 'inner self' imprisoned by society – caught the mood of those youth-centred cultures of music, drugs and poetry which also aimed at laying the self bare ('letting it all hang out'). Sexual freedom as political radicalism or a good in itself is a theme of many accounts, though few had the dramatist Joe Orton's exuberant faith in fucking as a force for change (his diaries were not published in full until 1986).

Writing about sex as the key to the self informed literary biography (the idea of 'the homosexual personality' shaped Edel's Henry James and George Painter's Proust in the early 1960s). Michael Holroyd's *Lytton Strachey* (1967–8) and Quentin Bell's biography of his aunt Virginia Woolf, in 1972, captured the sexually progressive mood of the day. Strachey's homosexuality, Woolf's feminism and the revelation of her sexual abuse as a child stimulated a revival of interest in 'Bloomsbury', newly congenial to the readers of the more 'permissive' 1970s, but also offered lives in which sexual experiences were seen as central

[4] *The Heart of the Race: Black Women's Lives in Britain*, ed. Beverley Bryan, Stella Dadzie and Suzanne Scafe (London: Virago, 1985). Lauretta Ngcobo, *Let It Be Told: Black Women Writers in Britain* (London: Virago, 1988), p. 1.

to the interior life and to creativity (as did Bertrand Russell's *Autobiography* in 1967–8). A post-Freudian insistence on the sexual as a key to the inner sanctum of the self still informs much biography – Diane Middlebrook's life of the confessional poet *Anne Sexton* (1991) used confidential records from her psychiatrist; Andrew Motion's biography of Philip Larkin (1993) exposed Larkin's penchant for pornography. If one of the deep pleasures of biography (which harks back to the religious idea of the model life) lies in discipleship, then the discovery that one's mentors are fallible may allow the reader gratifying feelings of infantile triumph as well as disappointment.

Bell's biography also prefigured another shift. As a family member he had special access to unpublished material – diaries, letters, memoirs – manuscripts which were eventually made available to scholars in the Berg Collection at the New York Public Library in the USA. The feminist championing of Woolf and new kinds of textual scholarship took off at the same time within the American academy. These kinds of collections became increasingly important in the period and biography gradually came to demand an intensely professional level of scholarship; not only the locating of private papers or the interviewing of friends and family, but the scrutinising of unpublished drafts and manuscripts (or 'holographs'), frequently to be found in (American) university research centres and libraries. This kind of historical research, combined with psychological interpretation and literary criticism, underpins Richard Ellmann's *James Joyce* (1959 but paperbacked in 1965), and Leon Edel's five-volume life of Henry James (1953–72). In Britain in the 1970s and 1980s the new universities and polytechnics saw the development of a more driven and professionalised academic-research culture (the PhD was relatively unimportant before the 1980s), together with an ever-increasing student and graduate reading public for whom biography offered informative, serious reading with an educative import. Scholars would need substantial commissions from publishers to pursue work which might take several years or research grants and awards from inside the academy.

From the 1970s, a steady stream of critical studies of biography and autobiography began to make claims for their literary status. Again the US academy took the lead (Leon Edel published his critical essays on biography, *Writing Lives* in 1965), James Olney's *Metaphors of the Self: The Meaning of Autobiography* (1972) examined autobiography in an attempt to 'secure added territory for Literature', through a series of key texts (including those of Montaigne, Darwin, Newman and Jung), offering images of wholeness and of 'the mature and integral self'. Like biography, autobiography was praised as a branch of humanist enquiry, relying on the capacities of authors (usually male) whose 'transcendent self-awareness' could convey an interior life, continuous and unique to the individual and yet communicable to others. The aim was to arrive at some form of 'self-realisation' since, in the grand words of another American critic, 'we perceive a noble life task in the cultivation of our individuality'.[5] Underlying such critical accounts, as in Richard Ellmann's biographies, was the search for a meaning and a unity in a human life which mirrored the ideals of a liberal democracy (Ellmann's 'amiable humanism' played down political radicalism, for example, and idealised both Yeats and Joyce as dedicated family men).[6]

In Britain, the establishing of the J. R. Ackerley prize for autobiography in 1982 was a sign of its new acceptability as a literary genre: Edward Blishen, Angelica Garnett and Jenny Diski have been among its winners. Autobiography (though not biography) was similarly approved by its inclusion in the 1983 edition of the influential *Penguin Guide to English Literature for the Modern Period*, edited by Boris Ford (one of the original contributors to F. R. Leavis's *Scrutiny* magazine in the 1930s). Autobiography's potential for offering 'clues to our own uneasy quest for identity' imbued it with seriousness; its relation to the sacrament of confession – for 'self-reflection and self-recreation' – gave it a moral purpose, and the writer's search for 'authenticity of being' underwrote its authority. Autobiography may increase our understanding of 'the process of individuation' – a term which suggested the influence of Jungian psychology (Jung's autobiography *Memories, Dreams and Reflections* was published in 1963 but paperbacked in 1977) – but perhaps, nonetheless, 'identity' was 'forever unknowable?'[7]

The quest motif also informs *Footsteps* (1985), Richard Holmes's autobiographical discussion of biography, and the perils and excitements of a 'Romantic biographer' (like others in the period he is untroubled by the unconscious masculinity of many of his terms – the heroic pursuit, the hunting of his quarry, and so on). Like the Freudian, the Romantic biographer looks for the true self of its subject in the early life, but the appeal of the literary or artistic life (or that of the great scientist) also lies in the idea of its having been 'self-created', its originality and individuality both assured from birth and yet continuously

5 Karl Weintraub, *The Value of the Individual: Self and Circumstance in Autobiography* (University of Chicago Press, 1978), p. 13.

6 See Patrick Parrinder's nuanced entry for Ellmann in Margaretta Jolly, ed., *The Encyclopedia of Life Writing*, 2 vols. (London: Fitzroy Dearborn, 2001), I, p. 298.

7 Peter Abbs, 'The Quest for Identity', *The Penguin Guide to English Literature for the Modern Period* (Harmondsworth: Penguin, 1983), p. 521.

reinvented. Holmes's *Shelley: The Pursuit* (1974) and his two volumes of *Coleridge* (1989, 1998), Peter Ackroyd's *Blake* (1995), Andrew Motion's *Keats* (1997), to take a handful of examples, in their different ways each evoke the Romantic longing for a life and a self which could be emancipated from the world, freed by their work from the mess of history, politics, traditions and ossified personal relations. For such biographers, biography is itself a species of romance, fuelled by the utopian desire to evoke a transcendent, yet coherent personality, shaped by, and yet bigger than, the circumstances in which it found itself.

By the late 1980s, however, as literary biography and autobiography began to boom, many of its assumptions were coming under attack. Marxism has a long history of distrusting the 'bourgeois individualism' of biographical approaches. The early 1970s saw the reinstating of Marxist cultural criticism which was in effect profoundly anti-biographical. Works from the 1930s were reprinted, such as Walter Benjamin's *Understanding Brecht* (1973), which included his essay on 'The Author as Producer'; contemporary theorists elaborated the relations between art and ideology and attacked the idea of the free, autonomous individual – Louis Althusser's *Lenin and Philosophy* (1971), for example, and Pierre Macherey's *A Theory of Literary Production* (originally 1970, but translated from the French in 1978). Such work, according to Terry Eagleton, one of its most committed proponents, in *Criticism and Ideology* (1976) and in *Marxism and Literary Criticism* (1976), insisted upon 'the artist as a worker rooted in a particular history with particular materials at his disposal' and militated against 'the Romantic notion of the author as *creator* – as the God-like figure who mysteriously conjures his handiwork out of nothing'.[8] It posed an uncomfortable challenge to those for whom the idea of representing one's self or one's experiences in writing was believed to be crucial to a 'people's history'.[9] It also argued against the 'transparency' of the work of art, suggesting that a literary 'text' (a word which denoted layering, fabrication and interconnection, rather than originality) might more usefully be read for its gaps, silences and inherent contradictions, as for reflecting any conscious intention on the part of its author.

The limitations and delusions of biography and autobiography were taken to task in the 1980s as new theories began to percolate. Elizabeth Wilson's *Mirror Writing* (1982) queried the Romanticism of much gay politics; Ronald Fraser's *In Search of a Past* (1984) brought the techniques of the oral historian to

8 Terry Eagleton, *Marxism and Literary Theory*, p. 68.

9 See the debates in Raphael Samuel, ed., *People's History and Socialist Theory* (London: Routledge, 1981).

bear on his childhood, interviewing family servants and interweaving extracts from his own psychoanalysis, attempting a more historicised account of 'the self'; Carolyn Steedman's *Landscape for a Good Woman: A Story of Two Lives* (1986) called into question the conventional assumptions of working-class biography and of feminism by looking at her mother's and her own life. Wilson, Fraser and Steedman all turned to psychoanalysis for a rejection of the idea that life-writing expressed an already-given 'identity'. From 1973, *The Pelican Freud Library* had made key works, and especially those on sexuality, available in paperback and by the early 1980s the work of the French psychoanalyst Jacques Lacan had filtered through British feminism, a rereading of Freud in the light of new linguistic theories which insisted that the human subject was always barred from self-knowledge by the unconscious or by language itself. 'Subjectivity' was processive and unfinished, endlessly redefined and ultimately unstable: 'Lacan's human subject', as his translators bluntly put it, 'is the obverse of the humanist's.'[10]

Finally, Roland Barthes's essay 'The Death of the Author' (published in 1968 but not translated in the UK until 1977), became the best-known of the post-Structuralist attacks on the 'prestige of the individual' and on the banality and inadequacy of seeking the explanation of a work in the author (which in effect merely elevated the critic at the author's expense). Barthes's aim was to liberate a work into its multiple readings (while 'the Death of the Author' has been much pilloried, Barthes's equal insistence on the birth of the reader gets less attention). Barthes argued that the self was the product of writing rather than the cause of it: language speaks and acts through writers, thus the idea of agency was at best a sleight of hand.[11] In his own autobiography or anti-autobiography, *Roland Barthes by Roland Barthes* (1975) – whose epigraph reads 'It must all be considered as if spoken by a character in a novel' – he experimented with an alternative to chronology, using titled fragments alphabetically arranged, photographs and recurring themes to conjure the terrain of his subjective experience – 'an image-repertoire', making his 'self' a text, shifting and mobile and unresolved. Barthes's final work, *Camera Lucida* (1980), interleaved reflections on photography, history and subjectivity with a threnody on the death of his mother.

10 Juliet Mitchell and Jacqueline Rose, 'Introduction' to Lacan's work, in *Feminine Sexuality* (Basingstoke: Macmillan, 1982), p. 5.

11 Two other key post-Structuralist essays are relevant here: Michel Foucault, 'What is an Author?' (1969), rpt. in Donald F. Bouchard, ed., *Language, Counter-Memory, Practice* (Oxford: Blackwell, 1977) and Paul de Man, 'Autobiography as De-Facement' (1979), reprinted in *The Rhetoric of Romanticism* (New York: Columbia University Press, 1984).

Life-writing in the age of deconstruction

In 1994 the critic Lorna Sage maintained that 'biography has long escaped the reflexiveness that afflicts serious fiction'.[12] On the contrary, we might argue that reflexiveness is now the norm but that – and here Sage would be right – it need not much disturb the reader. Since Peter Ackroyd's *Dickens* (1990) caused a minor sensation on the literary scene by including fictional dialogue between biographer and subject, biographers regularly confuse the boundaries between themselves and their subjects and reflect on the nature of biography, especially where the subject, like Sylvia Plath, has generated a considerable mythology around her: Janet Malcolm incorporated her views of past biographers of Plath and their possessiveness in *The Silent Woman* (1993) while Jacqueline Rose's *The Haunting of Sylvia Plath* (1992) rigorously deconstructed biographical reductions of Plath's work. As the bio-pic *Sylvia* (2003) suggested, however, a knowingness about sources (the scriptwriters were as aware of Ted Hughes's *Birthday Letters*, published in 1998, as of the many biographies of Plath) need not diminish the need for ancestor-worship or for the reassuring romance of blighted genius. The glut of literary biographies has also led to an acceptance of the idea of comparative biography – 'a Charlotte Brontë for the 90s' – rather than the definitive text for all time; the reader of multiple versions may be building a social history or acquiring archival knowledge. In *Bloomsbury Pie* (1997) Regina Marler looked back affectionately over the creation of the 'Bloomsbury Group' and its heritage, while Lucasta Miller examined the literary cult of the Haworth Parsonage in *The Brontë Myth* (2001).

Since the 1980s novelistic experiments have pointed to the fictitiousness of biography and the strategies of the biographer – Julian Barnes's *Flaubert's Parrot* and William Golding's *The Paper Men*, both published in 1984, Alison Lurie's *The Truth About Lorin Jones* (1988) and A. S. Byatt's novel *Possession*, which won the Booker prize in 1990, are cases in point. Fictional accounts of true lives – the *biographie romancée* – proliferate, among them, Julia Blackburn's *Daisy Bates in the Desert* (1994) and her account of Napoleon's life on Elba, or Janice Galloway's novelistic life of Clara Schumann (2002). Travel writing has long afforded opportunities for self-reflection – Bruce Chatwin's *What Am I Doing Here?* (1989) combined stories, profiles and travelogues, while in *Skating to Antartica* (1997), Jenny Diski used the travel motif to explore a 'journey' into the white space of depression. The nineties have seen 'biographies' of

[12] Lorna Sage, 'Surviving in the Wrong', *Times Literary Supplement*, 4 November 1994, p. 3.

commodities and of creatures like Mark Kurlansky's *Cod: A Biography of the Fish that Changed the World* (1997); of domestic objects, like those in Penelope Lively's autobiography *A House Unlocked* (2001), where furniture and mementos are numinous with the past and with lost selves (ours is a devoted museum culture). Such mixes and experiments stretch the limits of the form but also remind us that biographical and autobiographical writing has always overflowed its containers.

Within autobiography, the 'literary memoir' became the new publishing success of the 1990s, usually by a recognised writer, and suggesting a work more carefully composed than the random table-talk of politicians or statesmen. Mid-life memoirs reflecting on ambivalent relations to parents or the death of a parent, as with Blake Morrison's *And When Did You Last See Your Father?* (1993), or the experience of abusive and wretched childhoods as in Angela Ashworth's *Once in a House on Fire* (1998), or Lorna Sage's witty *Bad Blood* (2000), have crossed new boundaries in making public what have usually been seen as intensely private emotions. Frank McCourt's memoir of his impoverished Irish childhood, *Angela's Ashes* (1996), resulted in international celebrity and a Hollywood film. An unprecedented number of narratives about illness, bereavement or disability – 'pathography' as cultural critics have called it, 'sick lit', in publishers' more cynical jargon – have seized *fin-de-siècle* readers. Since Susan Sontag's *Illness as Metaphor* (1978), writers have used their struggles with the medical establishment to explore the cultural construction of illness (and especially the mythologising of AIDS), and to experiment with the forms of life-writing. Thom Gunn's *The Man with Night Sweats* (1992), his first full collection of poetry published in England for ten years, contributed to the commemorative role of AIDS writing; the film-maker Derek Jarman, in his journals *Modern Nature* (1991) and *At Your Own Risk: A Saint's Testament* (1992), threw down the gauntlet to heterosexuals, celebrating casual sex despite being HIV positive. Illness diaries – Elisa Segrave's *The Diary of a Breast* (1995), Ruth Picardie's *Before I Say Goodbye* (1998) and John Diamond's *C: Because Cowards Get Cancer Too* (1998) – both journalists who chronicled their illnesses in their newspaper columns – constituted another blurring of private and public. Such narratives frequently act as advocates on the part of the sick or disabled – Hollywood took up the cause of cerebral-palsy sufferers in its film version of the Irish painter–writer Christy Brown's autobiography, *My Left Foot* (1982); in *Iris* (1998) John Bayley gave a portrait of a marriage and a biography of his wife, the novelist Iris Murdoch, through the charting of her Alzheimer's. Illness narratives may appeal in a society where the body is a commodity and fears of aging abound, they may be symptoms of a 'culture of narcissism' or sharp shocks to its complacency. Celebrity memoirs of depression, alcoholism, drug abuse, eating disorders as in Spice Girl Geri Halliwell's battle with bulimia, *If Only* (1999), stress the ubiquity of suffering and seem a kind of levelling of celebrity or an antidote to its apparent shallowness. Illness charges the story with urgency and immediacy: regaining narrative control can be tantamount to an assertion of full identity. For others the loss of surety, or the challenge of ontological questions, as raised by Gillian Rose's philosophical exploration of her cancer in *Love's Work* (1997), compel both writer and reader.

Much autobiography has been founded on the notion of confession, but in the late twentieth century such a concept proves inadequate when the writer is the witness to and victim of traumatic events, like World War II, the Holocaust or the nuclear bomb, which 'overwhelm our ability to assimilate them and which exceed our capacity to understand'.[13] Such traumatic histories cannot simply be incorporated into narratives since they may only be known by a gap or 'collapse of understanding' but it is these incoherences and suspensions which come to carry the most significance. The idea of the 'witness', testifying (as in a court of law) to something he or she has not yet made sense of, suggests the reader is involved in a special kind of listening.[14] Primo Levi's *If This Is A Man* (1979) was originally written in 1947 when no one wanted to listen; survivor's memoirs, and the memoirs of second-generation growing – Eva Hoffman's *Lost in Translation: Life in a New Language* (1989), Anne Karpf's *The War After: Living with the Holocaust* (1996) – find forms for communicating both the belatedness of such suffering and its ultimate ineffability.

An account of suffering seems to guarantee the truth of the account and to give it ethical weight; others have chosen fiction, however, because of anxieties about the reliability of memory (Louis Begley's 1991 novel *Wartime Lies* adopted this strategy). The publication of *Fragments: Memories of a Childhood 1939–1948* by Binjamin Wilkomirksi in 1996, purporting to be the recovered memories of a child-survivor of the Nazi death camps, first lauded for its brave testimony, then attacked for being a fake, reveals how much 'authenticity' is always an effect of writing. For some, Wilkomirski (or Bruno Doessekker, a musician who spent the war in Switzerland) exhibits a pathological identification with the victims of the Holocaust, which suggests how much post-war Europeans have absorbed the Holocaust into their own unconscious life and repertoires of fantasy. When autobiography is not seen as truth-telling (since

13 Linda Anderson, *Autobiography* (London: Routledge, 2001), p. 127.

14 See Naomi Rosh White, 'Marking Absences: Holocaust Testimony and History', in Perks and Thomson, eds., *The Oral History Reader*, pp. 172–82.

one can always give false witness) but as the psychological history of the narrator, a 'case history' (Rousseau's *Confessions* are a study in paranoia), it is nevertheless clearly the product of a particular time and place. Yet the ethical dilemmas posed are not easily resolved (like those 'docudramas' which mix real footage with invention). Such 'fakes' trouble our attachments not only to writing but to history, to the idea of facts as events beyond the purely subjective. Within the universities, questions about the politics and ethics of memory – 'memory studies' – is now a growing area alongside oral history.[15] The writings of George Perec, especially *W or History of Childhood* (1975; translated 1996), or of W. G. Sebald, whose last novel, *Austerlitz* (2001), assumed the fallibility of all the evidence offered the reader – of the narrator, of eyewitness accounts, of photography – and offered elaborate, meditative perambulations as to how our memories are constructed, suggest the possibility of being 'post-autobiographical'.

A reflexiveness about national history and the place of biography has informed the attempts of a *New Dictionary of National Biography* to be more inclusive (and is a sign, surely, of the impact of those earlier oppositional politics around class, gender and race). Begun in 1992 and due to be published in 2004, the *New DNB* is another indicator of the huge investment in Britain in a biographical culture (supported by government via grants to the British Academy, it will also include likenesses chosen in collaboration with the National Portrait Gallery). Group entries, discussions of popular reputations (the myth of Robin Hood or Jack the Ripper), and a broad view of nationality – 'the Scots who built the Scandinavian economies and the Welsh who built the Russian' – strain at the limits of a narrative of any shared or continuous national history. According to its first editor, its electronic version should eventually accelerate 'the end of national reference works': 'it will be a suitable epitaph – some might say a lament – for the 1,500 years of the formation of the autochthonous United Kingdom'.[16]

Global migration, the movement of refugees and exiles, the existence of second- and third-generation immigrant communities in the UK, have challenged unitary models of national identity. Contemporary 'postcolonial' writers explore the bittersweet feelings which these mixed attachments and complex losses involve, as well as the experience of racism and of religious,

[15] See, for example, the overviews and discussion in two publications edited by Susannah Radstone and Katharine Hodgkin, *Contested Pasts: the Politics of Memory* (London: Routledge, 2003), and *Regimes of Memory* (London: Routledge, 2003).

[16] H. C. Matthew, 'Leslie Stephen and the *New Dictionary of National Biography*', Leslie Stephen Lecture, 25 October 1995, Cambridge University Press, p. 28 and pp. 36–7.

sexual and generational divisions within their communities – witness Yasmin Alibhai-Brown's account in *No Place Like Home* (1995) or the autobiographical fictions and essays of Hanif Kureishi, Zadie Smith and Monica Ali (whose 2003 novel about the Bangladeshi community in London's East End, *Brick Lane*, has been attacked by some of its members). The autobiographies of intellectuals and academics – the Palestinian Edward Said's *Out of Place: A Memoir* (1999), for example, or, less well known, Ien Ang's *On Not Speaking Chinese: Living Between Asia and the West* (2001) – propose multiple, 'hybrid' or transnational identities for those who grow up and move between poly-ethnic societies. 'The diasporic intellectual' now writes as well as problematises auto/biographical forms, reflecting on his or her 'situatedness' and on the new 'psycho-geography' of global capitalism. Ang's final chapter tries to imagine a life 'beyond identities'.

The wheel, it seems, has come full circle and far from being the poor relations of literary study, biography and autobiography are now key players. In the 1990s, several academic conferences discussed 'the art' or 'the poetics' of biography; academics now regularly write biographies and publish with trade publishers without being dismissed from their jobs for dilettantism. In 1999, Sussex University launched an MA in Life History Research and in 2001 Richard Holmes was appointed to the first chair in Biographical Studies at East Anglia. A new historicism has entered literary criticism and the current passion for the publishing of writerly ephemera – notebooks, drafts, unfinished memoirs and so on – may be indicative of an age which 'responds gratefully to the factual, the lived, leaving more formal literary arts to be felt as elitist'.[17] Research grants are increasingly tied to work on authorial papermines (like the masses to be seamed at the Harry Ransom Research Center at Austin, Texas) and they tend to generate work which is biographically informed. The painstaking chronologising of the evolution of a work in the life of the author need not interfere with ideas of intention, originality or genius.

For post-Structuralists, biography is always in danger of being 'fundamentally reactionary, conservative, perpetually accommodating new models of man, new theories of the inner self, into a personality-oriented cultural mainstream'.[18] The much-vaunted distinction between 'literary biography' and lower forms, is illusory: all biography is by definition 'celebrity' biography, since it singles out individuals; all biographers are unethical, believing they know better about their subjects than the subjects themselves, routinely ignoring their wishes. For all its fancy footwork, literary biography merely displays

[17] Barbara Everett, 'Alphabeted', *London Review of Books*, 7 August 2003, p. 6.

[18] Jurgen Schlaeger, 'Biography: Cult as Culture', in John Batchelor, ed., *The Art of Literary Biography* (Oxford University Press, 1995), p. 63.

in more sophisticated form – 'the unified subject of modern liberal ideology successfully allegorising their own history'.[19] On the other hand, the term 'life-writing' which has recently gained currency, though it comes less loaded with literary baggage, can also tend to assume that such writing is inherently a democratic creative act simply because every individual is capable of doing it.

If it is true that in the culture of the West the belief in the self as the 'hungry recipient of experience and a source of active self-determination has waned',[20] reading biography or autobiography must seem perverse, a kind of denial, a wild display of hope, or a deeply nostalgic pleasure. Readers still relish those Dick Whittington stories of the rise to fame and fortune from humble beginnings; stories of the artist's coming of age, of the doomed genius, rebel or outsider. Writers still want 'to set the record straight' about themselves and their lives (witness the preface to Muriel Spark's *Curriculum Vitae* in 1992), if only, as Doris Lessing puts it, in 'self-defence', since 'writers are like pegs to hang people's fantasies on'.[21] Ultimately it is hard to know how many readers are prepared to accept that both biography and autobiography are performances, that diaries and letters are not truth-tellers but always have an implied reader, knowingly or not; that memory is not to be relied upon, that evidence is never impartial, that writing expresses us. Perhaps the illusion of a coherent self is lovable and vital and enabling; perhaps the need to tell lifestories and impose continuity is a deep and irrevocable human impulse (like that of language), if only because such order is ultimately unattainable. Whether it is possible to live the illusion of individuality lightly, to be only temporarily attached to the idea of origin or place, to see the self or selves we inhabit, as mobile and multiple, and 'minimal',[22] to remain sceptical but not traumatised as the moderns were by this new sense of the contingency and indeterminacy of our identities – these are political questions as much as they are literary ones. The lives we write and read in the twenty-first century make new subjects of us all.

19 Anderson, *Autobiography*, p. 20.
20 Steven Connor, 'Romanticism, Modernity and Biography', BBC Radio 3, 28 October 1997 (text from his personal website).
21 Doris Lessing, *Under My Skin* (London: HarperCollins, 1994), p. 14.
22 Stuart Hall, 'Minimal Selves', in *The Real Me: PostModernism and the Question of Identity* (London: Institute of Contemporary Arts, 1987).

43

Poetry after 1970

PETER MIDDLETON

George Barker replied mischievously to a questionnaire sent to poets by the magazine *Agenda* in 1989: 'You kindly invite me to make "a few remarks about the state of poetry in England and Ireland" or something such. I have only one remark which is that I have been seeking far and wide for this fabulous mastodon and in several years only glimpsed it once and I think it was called a Tony Harrison.'[1] Is the idea of an English or a British poetry really extinct, and if not, can it be embodied in representative poets such as Tony Harrison (or other influential figures such as Simon Armitage, Carol Ann Duffy, Jenny Joseph, Andrew Motion, J. H. Prynne, Tom Raworth or Denise Riley)? Many poets and editors appear to think not, and to agree with the poet Michael Schmidt (who would seem to be in a unique position to judge, having created the leading independent poetry press, Carcanet, and edited the most influential poetry review, *PN Review*): 'I detect no coherence in the poetry scene, readership, approaches, or anything else in Britain.' Throughout the past thirty years there has been a pervasive insistence on singularity, typified by this remark from Geoffrey Hill: 'I've not found that anybody's expectations have led me to qualify or modify my own work.'[2] Some poets regret this. Lee Harwood says: 'I once believed in the idea of a community of artists, I think mainly because [of] that whole sixties' euphoria, but reality contradicted that fairy tale.'[3] But many poets appear comfortable with what Glyn Maxwell calls (perhaps misleadingly) his 'complete ignorance of and independence from all movements, schools, ideas and theories'.[4] There are good reasons why poets and critics believe that British poetry between 1970 and 2000 lacks any unity, that poets are autonomous creators, and that to call a

[1] George Barker, 'The State of Poetry', *Agenda*, 27, 3 (1989), p. 6.

[2] Geoffrey Hill interview in John Haffenden, *Viewpoints: Poets in Conversation* (London: Faber & Faber, 1981), p. 81.

[3] Lee Harwood interview, in Peterjon Skelt, *Prospect Into Breath: Interviews with North and South Writers* (Twickenham and Wakefield: North and South, 1991), p. 75.

[4] Glyn Maxwell, 'Out of the Rain', *Poetry Review*, 84, 1 (1994), p. 91.

poet British is merely to refer to passport data. The sheer diversity of what has been called British poetry certainly discourages unifying generalisations: it could include poems for children, popular-song lyrics, poems from local poetry groups, occasional poems such as elegies and praise-songs, and poems written by poets living not in the UK but in Ireland, America, Australia and even central Europe, as well as British poems written not in English but in Gaelic, Irish, Punjabi, Urdu, Welsh and other languages. Some poems don't use ordinary language at all, replacing it with abstract shapes, stone or air as part or even all of their lexis. Consider the implications of Bob Cobbing's ecumenical perspective:

> It is a mistake to think of poetry as just a branch of literature; it is also a branch of the performing arts and has much in common with music, dance and the graphic arts. There is, therefore, so much more to poetry than is normally 'allowed' for in the publishing and broadcasting media; and there is potentially so much more to the performance of poetry than is demonstrated by 'performance poetry.'[5]

It is also a mistake to think of poetry as an agreed-upon category of aesthetic value; there are no criteria for what makes a successful poem that do not have significant groups of intellectually credible dissidents. But the main reason why there appears to be 'no coherence in the poetry scene' is a division between two kinds of poetry, neither of which has an accepted name, that could with considerable cause be called Postmodernist and Modernist.

The Postmodernists have been in the ascendant for most of the period, and well-represented in a series of influential, commercially published anthologies of what Simon Armitage and Robert Crawford call 'this cluster of islands' in their preface to *The Penguin Book of Poetry from Britain and Ireland* (1998), and Paul Keegan, also trying to avoid difficulties about poetry and national identity, calls this 'archipelago' in *The New Penguin Book of English Verse* (2000) (they include: *British Poetry Since 1945* (1970), *The Oxford Book of Contemporary Verse: 1945–1980* (1980), *The Penguin Book of Contemporary British Poetry* (1982), *The Hutchinson Book of Post-War British Poets* (1989), *The New Poetry* (1993), *The Firebox: Poetry in Britain and Ireland after 1945* (1998), and *The Bloodaxe Book of 20th-Century Poetry* (2000)). Andrew Motion and Blake Morrison were among the first to call these poets Postmodern. In the introduction to their *Penguin Book of Contemporary British Poetry*, they imply that this is because it is reflexive, 'registering the degree to which the poem is an invention', and capable of

[5] Bob Cobbing, 'Preface', in Bob Cobbing and Lawrence Upton, eds., *Word Score Utterance: Choreography in Verbal and Visual Poetry* (London: Writers' Forum, 1998), p. 2.

'drawing attention to the problem of perception'.[6] This is Postmodernism as play, as withdrawal from political ideologies and commitment, and as the treatment of history and identity as style. Nevertheless it is a very different, much less radical Postmodernism than that in fiction or the visual arts, and often looks less modern than the Modernists. Anne Stevenson articulates this outlook very accurately:

> I think we who are writing now should think of ourselves as having come to the end of a period we call Modernist. Postmodernism is a weak coda to a turbulent movement that in itself was a coda to Romanticism. To truly make it new, we must look around for constants that transcend fashion and the human itch to experiment.[7]

This conservatism could be called insularity.

The general omission from these anthologies of poetry by immigrants, poetry emerging from new social movements, especially feminism, poetry in dialogue with European (with the limited exception of Eastern Europe), American and other cultures, and the absence of second-wave Modernist poetry also tells us that the terms by which the poetries of the past few decades might be categorised or evaluated are ideologically charged. This Modernist poetry is much harder to find. Anthologies have been fewer, several were published in France and America, and even those that were published by commercial presses have been quick to go out of print (anthologies of Modernist poetry include: *The New British Poetry: 1969–1988* (1988), *A Various Art* (1990), *Conductors of Chaos: A Poetry Anthology* (1996), *Other: British and Irish Poetry Since 1970* (1999), *Foil: Defining Poetry: 1985–2000* (2000)). Here is an entirely different archipelago. Only one anthology since Edward Lucie-Smith's *British Poetry Since 1945* (1970), Keith Tuma's *Anthology of Twentieth-Century British and Irish Poetry* (2001), published in America, shows the full range of what have otherwise been alternate universes of poetry. The Modernists write in a continuing tradition that includes Surrealism, High Modernist writers like Gertrude Stein, James Joyce, Mina Loy, Hilda Doolittle and both European and American Modernists. These poets also have difficulty naming themselves. Are they 'avant-garde' (an adjective not much liked by anyone), or 'underground' (even more disliked), 'linguistically innovative' or 'second-wave' Modernist?' Their poetry retains the Modernist belief that the poem is capable of challenging

6 Blake Morrison and Andrew Motion, eds., *The Penguin Book of Contemporary British Poetry* (Harmondsworth: Penguin, 1982), p. 19.

7 Anne Stevenson, 'A Few Words for the New Century', in W. N. Herbert and Matthew Hollis, eds., *Strong Words: Modern Poets on Modern Poetry* (Newcastle upon Tyne: Bloodaxe, 2000), p. 183.

the public sphere, investigating history and science, making discoveries, and is alert to the insights of literary theorists and identity politics. It recognises that language is already in play as the scene of desire and the field of the 'other', that it can be found, fragmented, neologistic, philosophical, and can show subjectivity in the process of emergence and deconstruction. They don't think experimentation is an itch.

This deep and sometimes hostile division between two kinds of poetry is complex in practice and has a history that is still unwritten. The clearest glimpses of it can be seen in the poetry magazines (such as *Agenda*, *Akros*, *Angel Exhaust*, *Infolio*, *Iron*, *Outposts*, *PN Review*, *Pages*, *Parataxis*, *Poetry Information*, *Poetry Review*, *Prospice*, *Reality Studios*, *Second Aeon*, *South*, *Spanner*, *Stand*, *Temenos*, *The Many Review*, *The Rialto* and others) which have been the mainstay of ambitious literary poetry. Anthologies are almost always latecomers. Here in the poetry journals the supposedly antagonistic types of poetry occasionally coexist in the same issue, suggesting that some of the divisions might be better understood as the result of a dialogue rather than mutual exclusion, and that exclusion in the anthologies, which has had a marked effect on popular knowledge of poetry, has had political and cultural causes beyond those active in the literary world. Magazines offer the nearest thing to a public sphere for poems by providing a discursive and sometimes visual environment that enables the poems to generate a conversation among themselves and with other poetries, and in doing so to address the wider public culture. It is also in the magazines that readers are trained to read new poetry by learning from the values and interpretations offered in prose commentaries and reviews as well as the juxtaposition of poems in illuminating clusters.

Two issues emerge again and again in these magazines: money and modernity. There has been little profit in poetry publishing (Oxford University Press closed down their entire list in the early nineties), and poetry lists were at best loss-leaders for mainstream publishers, unless like Penguin they were reprinting selections (the first *Penguin Modern Poets* series of twenty-six volumes was highly influential) or creating anthologies, or like Faber they were also able to produce school texts (such as editions of Seamus Heaney, Ted Hughes and Philip Larkin). Poets' incomes, publishing profiles, and careers increasingly depended on forms of state funding from institutions such as the Arts Council and the British Council, and this in turn depended on the influential discursive support radiating from the review pages of the broadsheets and weeklies. It was a system readily controlled by coteries and entrepreneurial individuals, and very sensitive to the demand for readily accessible poetry requiring little or no special knowledge or advanced reading techniques. There were two consequences of this economy. It created an environment in which the personal lyric increasingly became dominant, because its subtle blend of self-performance, intersection of personal and cultural memory, and foregrounding of the modulations of national identity (from English to archipelago) most readily matched those demands; and it excluded almost all the Modernists who then had to create their own poetic economy.

The dependence on funding is the result of wider cultural and social change that has rendered almost all poetry economically marginal. Poetry has not been the literary form in which the culture or the nation finds self-consciousness, and almost no poems have become central to the age in the way a considerable number of novels and films have done. Wendy Cope observed the ebbing of poetry's significance as part of the public sphere, and wrote in 1992: 'it's easy to forget, if one moves in poetry circles, that the names of most poets are unknown to most people. As a teacher, I had colleagues who had never heard of Larkin or Heaney. And I still meet educated people who wouldn't think of reading recent poetry.'[8] No British poet has anywhere near the equivalent cultural status of a considerable number of novelists both popular, such as Helen Fielding and Nick Hornby, and literary, such as Doris Lessing or Salman Rushdie (although Nobel Prize-winning poet Seamus Heaney may be a partial exception). It wasn't that poets didn't write the poems. It is not difficult to produce a list of poems that might have achieved such importance (a short list would include: David Dabydeen's 'Coolie Odyssey', Carol Ann Duffy's 'Foreign', Allen Fisher's 'Banda', Tony Harrison's 'V', Seamus Heaney's Bog poems, Geoffrey Hill's *Mercian Hymns*, Linton Kwesi Johnson's 'Inglan is a Bitch', Barry MacSweeney's *Odes*, Andrew Motion's 'Anne Frank Huis', Douglas Oliver's 'The Infant and the Pearl', J. H. Prynne's *Wound Response*, or Denise Riley's 'Affections Must Not'), but, with the exception of 'V', none of them gained the kind of media circulation that made a number of novels essential points of reference for political and cultural debate. Nor has British poetry done the cultural work of the visual arts, which have managed to maintain a balance, however uneasy, between the resistances to interpretation of a continuing Modernism and the demands of publicly funded institutions to ensure accessibility. There is no Tate Modern for poetry.

We ought perhaps to ask how poetry survived at all, given the growing scale and rapidity of certain cultural changes which might have seemed ready to supersede it. How did it retain some public presence when science, not literature, was increasingly the authoritative form of social knowledge and

[8] Wendy Cope, [no title], *Poetry Review*, 81, 4 (Winter 1991–2), p. 49.

offered the only legitimating methodologies for the establishment of fact and truth? Poetry also lost even more of the leisure time it had already conceded to radio and cinema to the conquering arts of television and the computer game. It might still have been able to claim a significant corner if popular music had not then surrounded most of what was left of its imaginative space with visceral sound annexed to the lyric poem made so compelling that it would be rock-music anthems which created the main articulation of political desires and utopian hopes for several generations of young people. Those readers and writers who might formerly have turned to poetry for personal or political expression (admittedly few even before this era) were now likely to immerse themselves in the music scene. Not that all the rock lyrics or mixed-media poetry were merely non-cognitive forms of pleasure; poetry flourished within this world too, and its influence reached deep into text-based verse as well. A full history of the poetry of this period would read the lyrics of David Bowie, Polystyrene and the Manic Street Preachers both within their own performative context and as an environment for poetry, which did survive and flourish despite these encroachments ('I think it's true to say that there have never been so many opportunities for poets to publish', says Paul Hyland in a book of advice to aspirants).[9] Very large numbers of people submit entries to the main poetry prizes (in 1990 the Peterloo Poets press offered a thousand pound prize sponsored by Marks & Spencer, for instance, neatly underlining the social status of poetry), the number of independent presses and small magazines has remained buoyant over the whole cycle despite sharp ups and downs, and more poets than ever before are managing to make a living out of poetry, and even in a few cases become celebrities. But poetry has had to adapt to survive.

Most poetry published by the commercial presses during the past thirty years makes the voice of the poet explicit. This voice can range from the overheard intimacy of Selima Hill's exasperated cry, 'I know I ought to love you / but it's hopeless',[10] to the semi-impersonal, representative self of the Irish poet looking for a new order of inspiration in Seamus Heaney's 'North': 'I returned to a long strand / the hammered curve of a bay, / and found only the secular / powers of the Atlantic thundering.'[11] Sometimes the voice doesn't announce itself, but signs itself everywhere in its poetic observations,

9 Paul Hyland, *Getting into Poetry: A Readers' and Writers' Guide to the Poetry Scene* (Newcastle upon Tyne: Bloodaxe, 1992), p. 60.

10 Selima Hill, 'I Know I Ought To Love You', in Sean O'Brien, ed., *The Firebox: Poetry in Britain and Ireland After 1945* (London: Picador, 1998), p. 306.

11 Seamus Heaney, 'North', *North* (London: Faber & Faber, 1975), p. 19.

as in William Scammell's poem about a shop selling hand-made paper: 'The wiring looped up in the corner / is the scribbled ghost of Hokusai, / the rafters Dürer's signature' – and the conceits are the poet's own scribbled signature.[12] This voice is almost always charming and witty as it confides secrets, admits to vulnerability (Carol Ann Duffy: 'I see our gestures endlessly repeated as / you turn to yours the way you used / to turn to me'),[13] and offers local perspectives on the world we know but haven't seen exactly this way. The statements and expressions of the poem are direct utterances of an 'I' who is tacitly assumed to be the author, unless it is clearly signalled that a persona is speaking, as in Craig Raine's 'A Martian Sends a Postcard Home' or David Dabydeen's 'Turner', or Carol Ann Duffy's 'You Jane'. In this latter poem the working-class man begins his self-portrait vividly – 'At night I fart a guinness smell against the wife' – with a statement of his actions that looks beyond dialogic speech to expressive self-accounting, and it is this that makes all these costume-drama poems biographical versions of the personal poem, however fictionalised. In place of generic poetic attributes of the lover, satirist, sensitive soul and so forth, the contemporary poet will go out of the way to provide authenticating detail that encourages a reader to trust the writer and identify with the emotions and dilemmas figured in the voice of the poem. Tony Harrison's poem 'August 1945', about the contrast between the joy in Britain at VJ day and the new reality of atomic warfare, relies on the authenticity of memories such as this: 'The morning after kids like me helped spray / hissing upholstery spring wire that still glowed / and cobbles boiling with black gas tar for VJ.'[14] The degree to which a poem makes possible both emotional empathy and conscious identification is a measure of its value, as Sheenagh Pugh explains in relation to her choice of a poem for a fund-raising anthology: 'It makes me feel like crying my eyes out, which is part of what I want from a poem. I've no time for what Gillian Clarke calls "clever young man poems", which make you think "how clever that poet is", rather than "how profound", or "how moving".'[15] The anti-intellectualism of this is widely shared, and the gender stereotyping reveals how readily poetic commitments can be caught up into class, race and gender conflicts as pennants for one side or another.

[12] William Scammell, 'Bleeding Heart Yard', in O'Brien, ed., *The Firebox*, p. 232.

[13] Carol Ann Duffy, 'Where We Came In', *Standing Female Nude* (London: Anvil Press, 1985), p. 24.

[14] Tony Harrison, 'Sonnets for August 1945', *The Gaze of the Gorgon* (Newcastle upon Tyne: Bloodaxe, 1992), p. 9.

[15] Owen Burt and Christine Jones, eds., *Voices at the Door: An Anthology of Favourite Poems* (Cardiff: University of Wales Press, 1995), p. 214.

Readers are discouraged from wondering why they need all this confessional detail about the lives of people who are strangers to them. The personal poem encourages identification based on the exchange of personal details which are a guarantee of authenticity, like the watermark in a banknote, and each such transaction is offered as proof that personal identity remains valuable, and can be the ground from which the individual's judgements (these poems always offer judgements) can be heard in the public sphere. Tony Harrison's poem 'Durham', about a clandestine visit to a lover in that city where he sees and hears many signs of government power, whether a motorcade or helicopters hunting escaped prisoners, almost makes this role of the personal poem explicit, by representing the illicit sex as 'love's anti-bodies in the sick, / sick body politic', implying that the poem is an anti-body to the suppression of the personal voice by the political sphere.[16] No wonder that the poet Denise Riley, one of the very few poets to write poems that are read across the divisions in contemporary poetry (like Roy Fisher, W. S. Graham, Christopher Middleton and Edwin Morgan), and the author of a key study of the representation of the self in poetry, asks: 'This / representing yourself, desperate to get it right, / as if you could, is that the aim of the writing?'[17]

There are several objections to treating this as the only paradigm for poetry. As Christopher Middleton said in a lecture in 1978: 'To recapture poetic reality in a tottering world, we may have to revise, once more, the idea of a poem as an expression of the "contents" of a subjectivity.'[18] The ethics of communication often fails in our culture, and many supposedly individual gestures are the creation of advertising or state policy. Freedom of speech may be a basic right, but for most people it is largely theoretical, merely permission to speak aloud rather than an opportunity guaranteed by the State to everyone that they will be able to publicise their thoughts. Our utterances, especially those which are personal, like Andrew Motion's elegy based on an account of his experiences of the Thames where his friend died, 'Fresh Water', are in fact rarely heard as public speech outside the sphere of poetry.[19] Many modern thinkers have argued that the self is variously constructed in language, the field of desire or by ideology, and although such theories of writing are conflicted and sometimes

[16] Tony Harrison, 'Durham', *Selected Poems* (Harmondsworth: Penguin, 1985), p. 69.

[17] Denise Riley, 'A Shortened Set', *Mop Mop Georgette: New and Selected Poems, 1986–1993* (London: Reality Street, 1993), p. 17. See also: Denise Riley, *The Words of Selves: Identification, Solidarity, Irony* (Stanford University Press, 2000).

[18] Christopher Middleton, 'Reflections on a Viking Prow', *Selected Writings* (London: Paladin, 1990), p. 283.

[19] Andrew Motion, 'Fresh Water', *Selected Poems* (London: Faber & Faber, 1998), p. 144.

contradictory, they derive from lived forms of modernity which encompass us all. The personal poem also has a restricted semantic repertoire, achieving its ends by rigorous suppression of many aspects of language, writing and material production which can contribute to meaning. Words and structure in these poems are made to look as natural as possible, as if this were just a reasonable, articulate person talking confidingly to the reader in what is usually a flatly informational mode. Sentences are completed, phonemes neatly clipped, page layout's contribution to meaning is minimised, and etymological, sonic, idiomatic and other effects, largely ignored. Continuity of the time of the poem's utterance is everything, so each sentence follows its predecessor with clear narrative and syllogistic force. The poet must seem to speak the language of the poem, not be spoken by it, and the speaking should reveal a communicable interiority, not the intransigent exteriority that many modern writers have testified to.

Division between different Modernist currents was not the likely outcome of the poetry landscape at the start of the period. Around 1970 there was a widely shared excitement at the achievements of modernity which seemed to have led to détente between the 'Children of Albion', as Michael Horovitz called his new Modernists, and the anti-Modernists of the Movement (whom Blake Morrison aptly describes as aspiring to 'the unity and order of pre-Modernism').[20] Most of the large commercial publishers still had poetry lists, and a few of the independent or semi-independent presses like Cape Goliard, Fulcrum and Trigram were producing high-quality books of poetry by both American and British writers. This was also an exceptionally internationalist moment, when European and American poetry, especially the work of Paul Celan, the French Surrealists such as Tristan Tzara and René Char, and the Black Mountain poets Robert Creeley and Charles Olson, was being translated, published and discussed widely in the UK. Public readings at the Albert Hall and many local venues were not only popular; they were often integrated into fervent political occasions of opposition to the Vietnam War or alliance with new social movements. Poetry appeared to be about to step onto centre stage of the public sphere.

This was not to be. Instead of a broad and vital national poetry culture, a balkanisation set in that has homologies with the political schisms of the period, especially the enduring split between the Left and the Centre of British politics, and the rise of an autonomous right-wing populism under

20 Blake Morrison, *The Movement: English Poetry and Fiction of the 1950s* (London: Methuen, 1980), p. 211.

Margaret Thatcher. Jeremy Prynne's confident use of the collective pronoun 'we' as an invitation to ethical transformation in *The White Stones* (1969) had disappeared by the time he wrote *News of Warring Clans* (1977), whose title is ironically appropriate to this period of history. The developing cracks in the foundations of British poetry that would tear it apart are already just visible in *The White Stones*, as they are in two other books from that time which also show the same struggle to break with the hold of Movement ideas: Ted Hughes's *Crow* (1970), and Geoffrey Hill's *Mercian Hymns* (1971). Where Hill implies that we are all Offas now, brutal and morally opportunist, Hughes's sequence makes us identify reluctantly with a demi-urge, Crow (the English pet-lovers' superman who does turn out to be a bird after all), who does battle with words that betray, bomb and escape him, as if he were fighting an Armageddon against the Modernists of the Sign. It has not worn well. Its misogyny, its lack of an internal narrative or thematic structure, and the unresolved tension between linguistic suspicion and the confident, functional language of its expression, leave it deeply compromised, and its verbal delight in destruction more a precursor to a 'Shoot-em-up' game than a deconstructive critique of modern belief. Prynne's *The White Stones* is more wary of the lures of such myths ('A Charm against too Many Apples' or 'The Ideal Star-Fighter' read like prebuttals of some of Hughes's more extreme counter-Edenic myth-making). There is a sharp pathos in the attempt to share judgements and propositions about the state of the nation, which despite managing to sustain hard-won clarities for a brief interlude ('The night is young and limitless our greed'; or 'quality / became the name you have, / like some anthem to the absent forces of nature'), are soon compelled to acknowledge that this is a time when one experiences 'mere words splitting like glass into the / air'.[21] The violent decline of the country depicted in all three books was not mere rhetorical and poetic exaggeration. Britain in the seventies was politically unstable, as government shifted back and forth between the two major political parties, world economic conditions worsened and the aspirations manifested in the phenomena of the 'Sixties' and in the new social movements were repeatedly baulked. Much of the success of poets such as Hughes, Heaney and Harrison would depend upon widespread baffled rage at the resultant injustice and the persistence of a 'them and [ʌz]' culture (as Harrison cleverly points out with his use of a phonetic symbol that reminds 'us' of the intellectual sophistication of people who don't use standard English). Popular and high art cultures of this

[21] J. H. Prynne, *Poems* (South Fremantle and Newcastle upon Tyne: Fremantle Arts Centre Press and Bloodaxe, 1999), pp. 88, 54, 79.

decade showed many signs of the internal strains that eventually led to Margaret Thatcher's election on a platform of individualism, reduced government and indifference to social inequality.

Soon after Margaret Thatcher's election, a younger generation of poets, led by Andrew Motion, James Fenton and Craig Raine, challenged the earlier hegemony of Hill and Hughes with the most polemical anthology of hegemonic poetry since A. Alvarez's *The New Poetry* of twenty years before, *The Penguin Book of Contemporary British Poetry* (1982). Morrison and Motion talk cautiously of a new movement 'antipathetic to the production of a candidly personal poetry'. They place Seamus Heaney at the head of this new group (and recognise explicitly the great influence of Irish and Scottish poets in this period: Douglas Dunn, Derek Mahon, Paul Muldoon, Medbh McGuckian and Tom Paulin among others), whose poetic stance is 'the attitude of the anthropologist or alien invader or remembering exile . . . not inhabitants of their own lives so much as intrigued observers . . . not poets working in a confessional white heat but dramatists and story-tellers'. In fact these poets will continue to draw on memory and other autobiographical resources of the personal lyric while extrapolating its subjectivities to historical and imagined personae. What they do challenge is the muscular sincerity of their elders, by deconstructing the stance of so much British verse, its unjustified homiletic metaphorising. They were making explicit a stance already apparent in much of the poetry of the seventies, as is evident in the mood of disenchantment with the modern world that reconciles itself in a wry stance of superiority, so evident in the poems Paul Keegan chooses to represent the seventies in *The New Penguin Book of English Verse* (another anthology that mysteriously eradicates all traces of post-war Modernism).

There was something wilful about the Morrison and Motion anthology's narrow conspectus that was deeply damaging, whatever its good intentions.[22] Its diagnosis of the problems with earlier poetry would have been much more valuable if it had gone on to consider the contribution of feminist poets, black writers, or the avant-garde to poetry. Its refusal to do this is prefigured in the trope of the alien Martian who misapprehends the truth about culture. Outsiders were not to be trusted in the home of British poetry, a populist sentiment much in tune with the times.

For women poets who were also feminist, the anthology confirmed their politics. The expansive cultural situation in 1970 had been a largely masculine

[22] Both editors could be said to have made subsequent amends. Morrison has published extensively on gender issues related to his family history, and Motion has worked hard for many enterprises which aim to widen both knowledge of and participation in poetry.

invention; it was not auspicious for women writers. One of the most promising of younger poets of the previous decade, Sylvia Plath, had committed suicide, and whatever the many underlying causes, it was hard not to believe that her difficulty achieving recognition in the UK had not had some part to play in her terminal depression. Many important women writers, who might have been poetic mentors to women poets, had been rendered largely invisible by either the academy or the publishing world. Second-wave feminism was highly attuned to the significance of cultural practice, and therefore placed poetry in a much more prominent position than might have been expected of a political movement. Marginalised women poets of the past were republished and celebrated, new anthologies of women poets appeared, and literary institutions were gradually transformed from largely male preserves. Anne Stevenson imagines how the well-entrenched male poets might have felt about such changes in her poem 'From the men of letters' (1982):

> We live
> decently rehoused
> in the storeys of a time.
>
> When they throw their arms
> around our words
> and weep
>
> we are horribly embarrassed.
> How will their experience
> forgive our tall books?[23]

It is worth underlining that the need for change applied as much to the independent presses of the marginalised poetry networks as to the hegemonic ones. Several feminist presses were set up (Onlywomen Press, Virago, and the Women's Press were the most prominent) and published widely circulated single editions of contemporary women poets, as well as anthologies. Close ties between text and politics gave them considerable cultural authority with their readerships. Lilian Mohin's anthology *One Foot on the Mountain* (1979) brought together poetry by activists like Sheila Rowbotham, writers like Judith Kazantzis and Michèle Roberts who have gone on to become well-known poets, and feminists whose work has taken them in other directions. Stef Pixner captured some of the spirit of the period in her poem, 'High Heeled Sneakers', which begins: 'I dreamed Simone de Beauvoir and i / were climbing

[23] Anne Stevenson, *The Collected Poems 1955–1995* (Oxford University Press, 1996), p. 86.

a mountain eating crepes.' Caroline Halliday's brilliant poem 'November, '77' bears the weight of self-examination, political hopes and struggles over identity in a series of narratives that record the work of areas of feminist activism such as women's refuges and the dangers of coming out.[24] Notably absent from this anthology were the more Modernist women poets who have found themselves neglected both by the feminists who wanted a poetry in which the role of language in the production of identity would not be worked into the forms of expression, anthologists of women poets such as Fleur Adcock, Jeni Couzyn and Carol Rumens, and also by their male counterparts. Not until Maggie O'Sullivan's *Out of Everywhere* (1996) did it begin to become possible to gauge the full achievement of such poets as Anna Mendelssohn (aka Grace Lake), Geraldine Monk, Wendy Mulford, Carlyle Reedy, Denise Riley and others.[25] By the nineties, women poets were enjoying much more support, and several women poets emerged whose work, although aware of feminism, and still drawing on the legacy of personal poetics, doesn't foreground the politics (Kate Clanchy, Wendy Cope, Helen Dunmore, Sophie Hannah, and Jo Shapcott for instance), a situation reflected in anthologies like Couzyn's *Bloodaxe Book of Contemporary Women Poets* (1992). The Modernist poets have also been more visible over the last decade of the century, and had more opportunity to develop their literary experimentation in other directions than identity politics: Caroline Bergvall has developed and taught 'performance writing'; Geraldine Monk has worked with improvised music; and Maggie O'Sullivan has consolidated an impressive body of sound poetry that is also one of the most original engagements with English pastoral.

Black poetry has also made a large contribution to the shaping of British poetry over the past thirty years, one whose full extent has still not been measured. White British racism and insularity has hindered recognition of the work of black poets and hearing the complexity of identity in the collective noun in lines such as these from E. A. Markham's poem 'New Year 1982': 'We sort out which are ours / / and sigh with relief when the names / prove foreign, difficult to say: we always knew / it couldn't happen here. We take our cue from newsreaders.'[26] James Berry says, 'I have come to believe that exclusivity in poetry has been cultivated', and sees his own activities as poet and teacher as a contribution to changing this. The tendency of white editors has been

[24] Lilian Mohin, *One Foot on the Mountain: An Anthology of British Feminist Poetry 1969–1979* (London: Onlywomen Press, 1979), pp. 222, 61.

[25] Maggie O'Sullivan, *Out of Everywhere: Linguistically Innovative Poetry by Women in North America and the UK* (London and Saxmundham: Reality Street Editions, 1996).

[26] E. A. Markham, *Human Rites: Selected Poems 1970–1982* (London: Anvil Press, 1984), p. 78.

to fail to see differences between black poets, as Fred D'Aguiar notes.[27] A well-meaning anthology introduction to Grace Nichols – 'Nichols combines salty humour with pithy observations on love and life in England, while incorporating a mythic–historical dimension in her treatment of blackness and womanhood'[28] – demonstrates just how much such caveats may still be needed. Black poets in Britain have faced many external pressures on their poetry as identity politics waxed and waned, as the competing popularity of reggae music made any page-based poetry look too white, and as genealogical ties to Africa, the Caribbean and North America made the UK and its capital London seem 'like a parent / Home from which to rebel' and travel elsewhere.[29] Discrimination, poverty and alienation have done their work, making literary representation often as difficult as achieving political representation. David Dabydeen's satirical swipe in 'Coolie Odyssey' at the iconic status of Tony Harrison and Seamus Heaney because of their poetics of roots, or D'Aguiar's turning away from the UK to write a verse novel about American slavery, or D. S. Marriott's reimagining of the presence of slave ships in the British colonies of the West Indies, as well as the migration westward to America of all three writers, points up a continuing difficulty for black poets.

Orature has played an important part in Black poetry. John Agard's clever and witty exposure of the oppressions associated with the teaching and maintenance of Standard English in schools, universities and the media – 'Dem accuse me of assault on de Oxford dictionary / imagine a concise peaceful man like me' – relies on both writing and audible pronunciation for its full force. Grace Nichols's poem 'Thoughts drifting through the fat black woman's head while having a full bubble bath', which repeats the pseudo-scientific word used by anthropologists, 'steatopygous', until its absurdity becomes apparent and her conclusion, 'steatopygous me', gains a new ostensive definition through the presence of the author as referent.[30] D'Aguiar's point about diversity is also a reminder that there are several distinct forms of cultural 'blackness' emergent in poetry during this period. The young poet Khalid Hakim suggests that his own obliquity to standard English may appear to have an avant-garde torque: 'same w/ that L=A=N =G=W =I=G =E textualitie guff they starrid afecting me owt of wat i doo – what *do* i do – a lone popular polemick against the cors of poetick *use* & transmishon sins the Renaisance. Im caerful

[27] Fred D'Aguiar, 'Black British Poetry', in Gillian Allnutt, et al., eds., *The New British Poetry: 1968–1988* (London: Paladin, 1988), p. 4.
[28] O'Brien, ed., *The Firebox*, p. 375.
[29] E. A. Markham, 'Hinterland', in Markham, ed., *Hinterland: Caribbean Poetry from the West Indies and Britain* (Newcastle upon Tyne: Bloodaxe, 1989), p. 209.
[30] Grace Nichols, *The Fat Black Woman's Poems* (London: Virago, 1984), p.15.

of my conformist streek.'[31] But the usual categories of British, traditional or avant-garde start to break down when seen in the mirrors of ethnic identity.

Avant-garde poets are even less of a cohesive group, and cannot be represented by a single poetics or shared history. They have necessarily had to create support networks based usually around performance venues and small presses, but none have worked so collectively in their poetic composition that they could accurately be called a school. Behind the most visible groupings of poets linked to London, Cambridge, Newcastle, Glasgow, Cork and other cities are complexities of practice and poetics. Two of these groups will have to represent the diversity.

A group of poets, whose connections were routed through Cambridge as both place and university, began publishing in earnest during the seventies with several independent presses – Ferry Press, Grosseteste and Street Editions – and were eventually represented by the anthology *A Various Art* (1992) (although representation failed the women poets). They shared a strong commitment to careful meditation on the ethical responsibilities and phenomenology of the rituals of ordinary life that promote individuation. Andrew Crozier doesn't think this is an easy or retiring option: 'no one / can escape the ordeal of being with everything else/ in the world',[32] and Peter Riley insists that this requires emotional work: 'Unable to sustain love we succumb to the strata' of 'chaos and sameness'.[33] Poetic form centres on a discursive free verse that is acutely aware of the nuances of stanzaic form, but always insists on the dominance of idiomatic direction rather than metrical determinations. Sometimes it seems as if they might have written verse within the Movement and its successors, if it were not for their deep mistrust of self-display and the deceptions of self-expression. If this meant sacrificing accessibility so be it. In J. H. Prynne's work this can entail the use of the specialist vocabularies of the new policy-makers, the scientists and other experts, as in 'Cool as a Mountain Stream' from *Wound Response*, which takes the slogan for menthol cigarettes as the title of a poem which reflects on the radiant central image of Walt Whitman's 'Song of Myself', the moment when Whitman undergoes an erotic annunciation that will confer the power of a poetic science to perceive and express the entire natural world. Prynne works the language and the reader's expectations very hard by adding a number of devices for producing meaning. Sentences begin

[31] Khaled Hakim, 'Letter to Antin', in Nicholas Johnson, ed., *Foil: Defining Poetry 1985–2000* (Buckfastleigh, Devon: Etruscan Books, 2000), p. 47.
[32] Andrew Crozier, 'The Life Class', *All Where Each Is* (London: Allardyce Barnett, 1985), p. 139.
[33] Peter Riley, *Tracks and Mineshafts* (Matlock: Grosseteste Press, 1983), p. 76.

with the expectation of an idiomatic or standard resolution only to swerve off in another direction: 'soft hair mute against / what we say' leaves behind a Cheshire cat grin of some such phrase as 'the skin' ('beast of virtue' leaves the word 'burden' grinning out at the reader). Words carry their full weight of variant meanings and etymological connections ('vane', 'roots', 'mount', 'hard rock' and so on). Syntax retains a haunting awareness of what authoritative statement and authorial sincerity sound like, yet the fragmentation of sense compels this communicative bond to question itself repeatedly. Almost every line ending invites the reader to decide how to interpret its significance. This expectation of care in reading has been a defining feature of these poets. In his poem 'Czargrad', John Riley asks: 'how make you hear is to say / how shall I hear. how shall I hear? say it or how / hear exactly what was heard / in the ruins'. To write poetry is to hold to 'the poem as life: a denial / of accident'.[34]

London's avant-garde poetry (still under-represented in anthologies, although *The New British Poetry*, *Floating Capital*, and *Conductors of Chaos* give a partial idea of it) has been more heterogeneous, linked by belief in the value of radical innovation and diversity, as well as cross-overs into other media. Tom Raworth, for example, whose early books of poetry are gorgeously illustrated by Barry Flanagan, Jim Dine, Joe Brainard and others, displays a sense of irony, suspicion of bourgeois pieties and critique of ideological language similar to that of J. H. Prynne, but with very different results. He mistrusts the position from which ethical insight is dispensed, and prefers wit to wisdom. He was one of a few metropolitan poets who created a nucleus of inspiration for succeeding generations. Bob Cobbing, Lee Harwood and Eric Mottram (who edited *Poetry Review* between 1971 and 1976), were catalysts and mentors for avant-garde poets either based in London, or oriented towards it. Although their poetry often made large intellectual, emotional and aesthetic demands on readers, several had no higher education at all (compare the largely Oxbridge backgrounds of the hegemonic poets of that decade), and therefore freed themselves of the anti-intellectualism that has bedevilled British culture in the twentieth century. Their presses (Aloes, Anti-Copyright Bluff Books, Magenta, Pirate Press, Sixpack, Writers' Forum and others) produced extremely distinctive hand-produced books, using coloured typefaces, drawings and complex typographical layouts to distinguish these works from the highly standardised productions of the commercial presses. All of the poets worked broadly within a Modernist American and British heritage, although their degree of freedom within it varied widely. Allen Fisher's *Place* sequence

[34] Ibid., pp. 32, 37.

was as influenced by Situationism as by Olson, while Bill Griffiths drew on Anglo-Saxon alliterative verse metrics and Romanticism rather than the contemporary Americans. Cris Cheek, Maggie O'Sullivan and others worked with Bob Cobbing and other sound and visual artists. These poets were often committed to projects rather than single poems, and in Allen Fisher's case this could extend over a decade and several long works, and encompass visual and investigative practices. *Unpolished Mirrors* (1983) offered a radical's history of London in the form of monologues by visionary figures, and then *Brixton Fractals* (1985) introduced a combinatorial structure to a series of narratives and encounters between characters who experience London's position at the crossroads of the state, new scientific knowledges and urban living.

During the eighties this London network of poets tended towards a harsh, urban language that acknowledged the late industrial landscape of the city, previously only intermittently recognised in poetry such as that of Roy Fisher or the Glasgow poets. Gilbert Adair, Adrian Clarke, Andrew Duncan, Ken Edwards, Frances Presley, Gavin Selerie, Robert Sheppard, Hazel Smith and others produced consistently experimental work, much of which still remains uncollected. Out of this ferment emerged a distinctive body of poetry whose influence remains much greater than its relative lack of visibility might seem to warrant. A similar shift took place in the work of some of the younger contemporaries of the Cambridge poets, in the work of Rod Mengham, Drew Milne, John Wilkinson and others. They, too, felt the need to respond to the ideological saturation of public language during the eighties and early nineties. Performance was important to all these poets, and was the foundation of one of the most impressive achievements to emerge from this period, the poetry of Maggie O'Sullivan, who developed a distinctive style of writing that invites a dual response based on both silent reading and hearing her perform. 'Hill Figures', a poem that responds to the predatory vision of nature made so well known by Ted Hughes, for example, is enigmatic on first reading, but its production of meaning becomes much more evident when read alongside the memory of her reading the poem, because then the puns ('Crow-Shade' / 'Crocheted'; 'plumb' / 'plum'; 'Oth' / 'Oath' / 'O the'; 'superates' / 'super eights' / 'suppurates' for instance) are heard as fields of echoing vocabulary whose various meanings then crochet themselves into patterns. On the page the Joycean-style neologism 'vasish' is baffling. When read aloud its components of 'vase,' 'vas' (a duct, hence the word 'vasiform'), and 'vanish' are all audible and like parapraxes that conflate two words in ordinary conversation, the word balances its vase of meanings quite deftly. O'Sullivan's performative style differs from the norm of a naturalised cantabile typical of many writers of the personal lyric (such as Jackie Kay's confiding conversational voice). Hers is one of the most effective of a range of performative techniques which are also part of the recent history of poetry.

During the last decade of the twentieth century the divisions in poetry began to diminish. Writers of the personal poem began to break away from some of the enduring constraints of good taste and tradition that had proved such unreliable companions, by emulating the growing vogue for stand-up comedy. Such humour became a means of remaining sincere and yet questioning the importance of authenticity, and therefore beginning to open up the foundations of the personal lyric to transformation. Whole careers have been built on this comic turn: Simon Armitage, Polly Clarke, Wendy Cope, James Fenton, Kathleen Jamie, Craig Raine, Hugo Williams and others have explored the rhetorics of wit, and some poets have taken these new skills into children's writing (John Agard, Jackie Kay, Christopher Reid and Kit Wright, for instance). Children's poetry itself has been undergoing considerable change recently that may herald better teaching of the possible range of poetry and the alternatives to a poetry of unquestioned self-expression. The new children's poets are exemplified by Tony Mitton, winner of a Smarties Award for *The Red and White Spotted Handkerchief* (2000), who writes poems whose innovative use of metre and rhyme works with a potentially radical questioning of the premises of the personal lyric. 'Puzzled Pea' from *Plum* might be addressed to the child who was baffled about the pleasures of sadness and identification: 'although like the others, / I'm a plain, green pea, / they are all *them*, / while I'm *me*.'[35]

Two anthologies appeared in the early nineties which further pointed to a shift away from rigid division. Bloodaxe, a publisher of poetry which has become as significant as Carcanet Press, published a collection of *The New Poetry* edited by Michael Hulse, David Kennedy and David Morley. Their thoughtful effort to take the measure of recent poetry was soon followed by a different, more ambitious attempt to create a stir about new poetry. In 1993, three poetry editors from Faber, Harvill and Secker devised a plan to promote twenty younger poets under the name New Generation Poets or New Gen as it became known. Once again Modernists were excluded, but this time some black and feminist poets were part of the heavily advertised bookshop displays and reading tours. This had an unintended consequence: the hidden management of poetry promotion was made more visible than it had ever been. These two developments, despite the control exercised by

[35] Tony Mitton, *Plum* (London: Scholastic Press, 1988), p. 84.

cultural mandarins, did begin to open up the field and, for example, show how important narrative had become in the work of a number of writers, notably Peter Reading, and bring forward writers such as John Ash, Peter Didsbury and Robert Crawford, whose poetry shows the influence of avant-garde ideas as well as the previous generation of Motion and Morrison, as it moved away from the comforting landmarks of expressive authenticity and poetic anecdote. Parallel developments appeared among younger avant-garde poets. A number of the poets in Nicholas Johnson's shrewdly chosen collection of younger writers, *Foil*, write in ways that suggest a new openness (Andrew Brewerton, Nicholas Johnson, Helen Macdonald, David Rees and Aaron Williamson, for instance) to a wide range of poetic resources, no longer treating allegiance to one or another form as a prerequisite for integrity. Divisions continue but the sectarianism that sustains them may be ebbing.[36]

[36] Many of the important essays to which I refer remain uncollected and can only be found in the poetry magazines of the period. This is particularly true of work by the avant-garde poets. Readers interested in the background to this poetry should look at *Angel Exhaust*, *fragmente*, *Grosseteste Review*, *Object Permanence*, *Poetry Information*, *Parataxis*, *Reality Studios*, *The Gig*, and *The Many Review*. Copies can usually be found in the Arts Council Poetry Library, London, and the Poetry/Rare Books Collection, University of Buffalo, State University of New York.

44

Ending the century: literature and digital technology

ROGER LUCKHURST

To combine questions of 'endism', literature and technology is a particularly risky endeavour. There is always the chance of making the mistake of repeating the overheated millennial rhetoric of much 1990s cultural theory on these issues. Having survived the millennium bug, the armfuls of handbooks on cyborgs and how to become posthuman, and sullenly acknowledged (despite what Jean Baudrillard promised) that the year 2000 really did take place, there is still the lure of that minatory discourse on the 'fate' of literature in this end-time. To be dragged into the noisy declamations of the prophets of the end or new beginning of the book is to lose critical distance just when it is most needed. Then again, precisely how is distance to be attained when it is evident that the Third Industrial Revolution – the digital one – is still only just starting to unfold? The history of technology is littered with unpredictable trajectories and wholly unforeseen applications, and given the accelerated cycles of technological innovation and obsolescence, the transience of current forms of digital technology is always painfully clear. Speed of change is something that, as Leo Marx has observed, encourages technological determinism, a mode of thought that 'invests technologies with enough power to drive history'.[1] With all these risks, any claim to authoritative statement can often seem to be just a symptom of the technoculture it had hoped to master.

'Increasingly', Friedrich Kittler claims, 'data flows once confined to books and later to records and films are disappearing into black holes and boxes that, as artificial intelligences, are bidding us farewell on their way to nameless high commands. In this situation we are left only with reminiscences.'[2] The heightened rhetoric and the casual paranoid ascription of motive to digital machines

[1] Leo Marx and Merritt Roe Smith, 'Introduction' to Marx and Smith eds., *Does Technology Drive History? The Dilemma of Technological Determinism* (Cambridge, MA: MIT Press, 1994), p. xiv.

[2] Friedrich Kittler, *Gramophone, Film, Typewriter*, trans. Geoffrey Winthrop-Young and Michael Wutz (Stanford University Press, 1999), p. xxxix.

here is typical of much writing on the subject. Kittler, however, signals in his second sentence that the history of technology might act as some kind of resource; that it might explain how some of the more apocalyptic visions of the digitised world emerge. Cultural historians of technology have reminded us that such media are not, in Carolyn Marvin's words, 'fixed natural objects', but are 'constructed complexes of habits, beliefs, and procedures embedded in elaborate cultural codes of communication'.[3] They require as much attention to human subjectivity and interaction as to technical blueprints.

In this spirit, histories have examined how the capitalist West has, since the mid-nineteenth century, experienced the extension of technology into everyday life as profoundly traumatic. We owe the very idea of psychological trauma and the legal definition of 'nervous shock' to the arrival of the railways. As Wolfgang Schivelbusch has argued, not only did the railway place its bourgeois travellers inside a 'machine ensemble' for the first time (extending machinic organisation beyond the factories of the First Industrial Revolution), the medical language of 'railway spine' and 'traumatic neurosis' also attempted to find a diagnostic language for the unforeseen psychical effects of the new technology.[4] Modes of reading and the very forms of literature were also profoundly affected, as numerous critics have noted.[5] The shock effect was similarly implanted at the mythic origin of cinema. Placing one technology inside another, the Lumière brothers' 1895 film *Arrival of a Train at the Station* (from which the first audiences allegedly ran screaming) inaugurated what Tom Gunning has called 'the cinema of attractions, which envisioned cinema as a series of visual shocks'.[6] This argument follows Walter Benjamin's proposal that, in cinema, 'perception in the form of shocks was established as a formal principle'.[7] Cinema was only part of Benjamin's larger view of the modernity of the technologised environs of the city, in which film, traffic signals, conveyor belts, newspapers and crowd flows constituted a saturated space of 'shocks and collisions' in which 'technology has subjected the human sensorium to a complex

[3] Carolyn Marvin, *When Old Technologies Were New: Thinking about Electric Communication in the Late Nineteenth Century* (Oxford University Press, 1988), p. 8.

[4] Wolfgang Schivelbusch, *The Railway Journey: The Industrialization of Time and Space in the Nineteenth Century* (New York: Berg, 1986).

[5] See, for instance, Nicholas Daly, 'Railway Novels: Sensation Fiction and the Modernization of the Senses', *ELH*, 66 (1999), pp. 461–87 and Laura Marcus, 'Oedipus Express: Trains, Trauma and Detective Fiction', *New Formations*, 41 (2000), pp. 173–88.

[6] Tom Gunning, 'An Aesthetic of Astonishment: Early Film and the (In)credulous Spectator', in Leo Braudy and Marshall Cohen, eds., *Film Theory and Criticism: An Introductory Reader*, 5th edn (Oxford University Press, 1999), p. 820.

[7] Walter Benjamin, 'On Some Motifs in Baudelaire', *Illuminations*, trans. Harry Zohn (London: Fontana, 1973), p. 171.

kind of training'.[8] This is a quintessential Modernist inversion: technologies assumed to be what Martin Heidegger termed 'at hand', passive instruments for the extension of human power, in fact come to routinise and programme the human. As for the moderns, so for the Postmoderns: on the question concerning technology, at least, the argument reads like a continuous intensification of the same logic of Heideggerian 'Enframing'. For Jean-François Lyotard, Postmodern techno-science ensures that 'the human race even has to "de-humanise" itself . . . so as to rise to the new complexity, so as to become tele-graphic'.[9] The trauma of this reduction to transmissible informational bits is marked out for Lyotard by the ghosts of those excluded or abandoned to the outside of the system, leaving to the philosopher only 'the anguish of a mind haunted by a familiar and unknown guest which is agitating it'.[10] This latter-day invocation of the ghostly is entirely in keeping with a history of electrical technologies. They have been persistently shadowed by an imaginary of spectres. Because Victorian gramophones astonished by preserving the voices of the dead, and telegraphy and telephony could apparently help to connect this world to the next, it is no surprise that contemporary fantasies of cyberspace imagine it as populated by the uploaded dead and spiritual machines.[11]

If traumatic shock or being spooked has become a standard response to ever newer modes of technologisation, it is hardly surprising that initial responses are in so many ways exorbitant. In the 1990s the West developed a new language of rage-states, nearly always to do with angers erupting at dysfunctional technological interfaces – road-rage, air-rage, desk-rage. When it comes to computers, some argue that there is a 'digital dialectic' that can hold together the opposing positions of the 'network idealists' and the 'naïve realists' who defend lost human integrity.[12] This is to give too much coherence to what is a wildly oscillating set of extremes. Sven Birkets, in *The Gutenberg Elegies*, was inconsolable over the 'millennial transformation of society' effected by computers. 'The printed word is part of a vestigial order that we are moving away from', he opined.[13] Birkets elided the apparent permanence, stability and sequential logic of the printed book with every worthwhile aspect

8 Ibid.

9 Jean-François Lyotard, *The Inhuman: Reflections on Time Today*, trans. Rachel Bowlby and Geoffrey Bennington (Cambridge: Polity Press, 1991), p. 53.

10 Ibid., p. 2.

11 For a history of the spectres haunting these technologies, see Erik Davis, *TechGnosis: Myth, Magic and Mysticism in the Age of Information* (London: Serpent's Tail, 1999).

12 Michael Heim, 'The Cyberspace Dialectic', in Peter Lunenfeld, ed., *The Digital Dialectic: New Essays on New Media* (Cambridge, MA: MIT Press, 1999), pp. 25–45.

13 Sven Birkets, *The Gutenberg Elegies: The Fate of Reading in an Electronic Age* (London: Faber & Faber, 1994), pp. 5 and 118.

of human culture, so that the arrival of the computer heralded evanescence, the end of history, and even the end of 'differentiations of subjective individualism'.[14] Computer visionaries, meanwhile, either began to use 'humanist' as a term of abuse for the Luddite denial of what George Landow called 'a revolution in human thought', or actively celebrated precisely the end of Birkets's limited human subject.[15] The idea of 'being digital' (to quote Nicholas Negroponte's 1996 manifesto title) prompted the emergence of one of the more radical groups of idealists, the Extropy Institute. The Extropians keep an updated 'transhumanist declaration' on their web-site. 'We see humanity as a transitory stage in the evolutionary development of intelligence', they proclaim. 'We advocate using science to accelerate our move from human to a transhuman or posthuman condition.'[16] Members of the Institute include some of the leading American writers and researchers on computing, artificial intelligence and digital life. Somewhere in the middle, cultural commentary on the digital world often slewed uncomfortably between these extremes. Scott Bukatman's *Terminal Identity,* for instance, could only comment on (rather than control) its own 'intriguingly hyperbolic' argument, one premised on the view that 'technology and the human are no longer dichotomous'.[17] It was often unclear from the book whether this was to be mourned or embraced: perhaps, in the wake of Jean Baudrillard's influential style of deadpan apocalypticism about the hyper-real, this was the point.

Although I have merely *described* these exorbitant responses, description nevertheless has some value as inoculation. In what follows, I want to eschew millennialism as far as possible and pursue a more modest aim. I want to sketch out a taxonomy of the literature that has responded directly to the new possibilities of various digital environments. This is a nascent discourse, in an extremely early stage of development: taxonomic ordering helps organise this very recent history, and allows some sense of proportion on claims about its allegedly revolutionary impact.

Tony Feldman, in the midst of frantic cycles of innovation, has provided an immensely useful way of orienting oneself in this field by distinguishing between *offline* digital media and *networked* media. Offline media include audio Compact Discs, CD-ROMs and latterly DVDs; they exist in 'stand-alone

[14] Ibid., p. 131.

[15] George P. Landow, *Hypertext 2.0: The Convergence of Contemporary Literary Theory and Technology* (Baltimore: Johns Hopkins University Press, 1997), p. 2.

[16] 'Extropian Principles 3.0: A Transhumanist Declaration', <www.extropy.org/ideas/principles.html,> paragraph 1.

[17] Scott Bukatman, *Terminal Identity: The Virtual Subject in Postmodern Science Fiction* (Durham, NC: Duke University Press, 1993), pp. 17 and 5.

physical form, palpable to the real world and dominated by developments in optical disc technology'.[18] Offline media were also the first digital software to emerge: CD-ROMs appeared in 1985, with standard conventions on formatting only agreed in 1990. As Feldman recalls, 'multimedia' was the buzz-word of the early 1990s, yet this technology was largely conceived as limited circulation, high-cost storage devices for large corporations or public institutions like libraries. This was before the rapid expansion of the home-computing market from about 1992: the number of machines out in the world that could actually read CD-ROMs leapt from about 6,000 in 1986 to 25 million in 1994. Home computing finally realised the idea of networking machines together in a concrete and widely available way. Although histories of the internet trace its origins back to the American defence department ARPAnet linkage of academic mainframe computers in the late 1960s, and the primitive bulletin-board systems that ran from the 1970s,[19] it is worth recalling that protocols for transferring data, translating text and locating other computers by their URL (universal resource locator) were only agreed in 1993. In the same year Vice-President Al Gore launched the American Government plan for the National Information Infrastructure, and tried to popularise the term 'information superhighway'.[20] The World Wide Web, designed at the European Laboratory for Particle Physics, was also launched in 1993. The first graphical interface, Netscape, appeared in 1995. Internet sites increased from 300,000 in 1990 to 72 million by 2000. Even these attempts at what might be called the Statistical Sublime fail to capture that networks invoke a wholly different digital imaginary from offline forms. Transmitted media are 'abstract and invisible', and the engagement ranges, Feldman observes, 'from largely non-interactive broadcasting systems . . . to heavily switched systems which provide uniquely one-to-one routeing of information'.[21]

A superficial view of these developments might see a movement from closed offline systems to open networked ones. Yet this trajectory fails to consider the heavily capitalised interests of multinational corporations in these developments. An audio CD is a tangible and controllable commodity that can resell analogue records in an allegedly 'superior' (random access, endlessly replayable) format. A file that encodes music into universally transferable informational bits that can be sent globally across a network, however, represents

18 Tony Feldman, *An Introduction to Digital Media* (London: Routledge, 1997), p. 35.

19 See, for instance, Katie Hafner and Matthew Lyon, *When Wizards Stay up Late: The Origins of the Internet* (New York: Touchstone, 1996).

20 For jaundiced commentary, see Rob Latham, *Consuming Youth: Vampires, Cyborgs and the Culture of Consumption* (University of Chicago Press, 2002), particularly chapter 5.

21 Feldman, *An Introduction to Digital Media*, p. 35.

a dangerous loss of proprietorial control and therefore of surplus value. The history of these technologies constantly stages a struggle between the maxim (held by hackers, cyberians, crypto-anarchists and other digital libertarian groups) that 'information wants to be free' and various attempts to contain digital information within closed, commodified and copyrighted forms. This materialist view cuts across the rather more idealist claims made on behalf of digital media, as we shall see.

Digital literature can be understood along this axis of closed to open access. The earliest forms of hypertext fiction were closed CD-ROMs in the late-1980s; the mid-1990s saw the emergence of internet fictions that minimally exploited the idea of networks; the late-1990s has seen the development of 'open-source' novels, increasing numbers of open and searchable on-line archives of non-copyrighted literature, and an increase in the extent of the interactive subculture of 'fanfic'. As I fill out this trajectory in more detail, however, I want to remain strongly sceptical about claims for any notion of a developing literary democracy through digitisation.

Most discussions of early hypertext fiction at some point signal that Michael Joyce's *afternoon, a story* (1987) is both the founding text and the legitimating instance of the genre. It was, Janet Murray asserts, 'the first narrative to lay claim to the digital environment as a home for serious literature in new formats'.[22] *afternoon* is a hypertext in the sense that the reader is presented with a short opening piece of text presented in a window, with a 'tool bar' of options beneath it. How you answer – clicking on yes or no or using 'Enter' as a default in an attempt to 'turn the page' – determines the sequence of textual fragments to which you may be 'linked'. The 539 different screens of text are hyperlinked by visually unmarked 'hot-words' on each screen, but the pathways through are gated, and only allow certain routes to open up after a predetermined sequence of screens has been visited. From this format of links between screens of poeticised prose a necessarily elusive, fragmented story emerges around the sentence to which the reader is constantly returned: 'I want to say that I have seen my son die this morning.' There are more exhaustive accounts of the phenomenological 'reader-response' to *afternoon* available – these have actually been integral to the high profile of Joyce's text.[23]

22 Janet H. Murray, *Hamlet on the Holodeck: The Future of Narrative in Cyberspace* (New York: Free Press, 1997), p. 58.

23 See Jane Yellowlees Douglas, '"How Do I Stop This Thing?": Closure and Indeterminacy in Interactive Narratives', in George Landow, ed., *Hyper/Text/Theory* (Baltimore: Johns Hopkins University Press, 1994), pp. 159–88.

Given the limits of the programme and the frustratingly restricted interactions that *afternoon* allows, the disjunction between the experience of reading these early hypertexts and the theoretical claims made on their behalf is all the more striking. Joyce himself called it 'a revolutionary artistic medium' because it allegedly dismantles the authority of the author, and obviates any distinction between reading and writing, since each reader's choice 'creates' the text.[24] Jay David Bolter, the coiner of the dramatic term 'the late age of print' and the co-designer of the Storyspace program on which *afternoon* was composed, similarly noted that in hypertext formats the 'reader calls forth his or her own text out of the network, and each such text belongs to one reader and one particular act of reading'.[25] Aggressive claims about the form were also articulated by George Landow. His view was that hypertext would 'produce effects on our culture, particularly on our literature, education, criticism, and scholarship, just as radical as those produced by Gutenberg's movable type'.[26] If print was linear, hierarchical, oppressive and the protected preserve of elite humanists, then electronic text uniformly promised to be multi-linear, laterally networked, democratic and interactive. In a move that precisely dates his intervention, the radicalism of hypertext is entirely elided with the rhetoric of revolution that surrounded post-Structuralist theory in the Anglo-American academy in the late 1980s and early 1990s. Hypertext was not only an 'embarrassingly literal embodiment' of Roland Barthes's idea of the 'death of the author', but also somehow of Derridean textuality, Deleuzian rhizomatics, Bakhtinian multivocality *and* Kristevan intertextuality all at the same time.[27] Paradoxically, Landow found that *afternoon* was 'high Modernist' – 'difficult' and 'hieratic' – as opposed to the emerging feminist hypertext fictions of Shelley Jackson or Carolyn Guyer (texts that, inevitably for Landow, literalised *écriture féminine*).[28]

afternoon contains a metafictional level of commentary on its own strategy, either in direct clues for the frustrated reader ('You merely need to backtrack, or

24 Michael Joyce, *Of Two Minds: Hypertext Pedagogy and Poetics* (Ann Arbor: University of Michigan Press, 1995), p. 20.

25 Jay David Bolter, *Writing Space: The Computer, Hypertext, and the History of Writing* (Hillsdale, NJ: Lawrence Erlbaum, 1991), p. 6. His 'Introduction' famously begins by pronouncing: 'Today we are living in the late age of print. The evidence of senescence, if not senility, is all around us', p. 2. This phrase casts a long shadow: see, for instance, Elizabeth Bergmann Loizeaux and Neil Frestat, eds., *Reimagining Textuality: Textual Studies in the Late Age of Print* (Madison: University of Wisconsin Press, 2002).

26 Landow, *Hypertext 2.0*, p. 21.

27 Ibid., p. 32.

28 Ibid., p. 204. Carolyn Guyer's hypertext, *Quibbling*, was issued by Eastgate Systems in 1992. Shelley Jackson's *Patchwork Girl*, also from Eastgate, was published in 1995. Jackson has since co-written *Lasting Image* with Michael Joyce (2000).

take other paths. Usually the silent characters yield what the investigator needs to know' one chunk heavily nudges), or via citations of literary precedents, with Jorge Luis Borges's 'Garden of Forking Paths' (1941) and Julio Cortazar's *Hop-Scotch* (1966) prominent points of reference. As Bolter observes, sounding like an electronic Paul de Man, *afternoon* 'is about the problem of its own reading'.[29] *afternoon* itself and the commentary around it relies heavily on prior print precedents like the generative fictions of the Oulipo movement, the *nouveau roman*, or post-Structuralist textual 'play', and this undermines the claims made for a ruptural break, or else actively recycles prior rhetorics of revolution.[30] But this is as nothing to the way that the idealisation of democratic open-access and co-creativity grates against closed assertions of ownership. Joyce argues that 'each alternative reading will cause the text itself to degrade or reform, so that no successive reading will ever again substantially parallel a traversal of the initial master text'.[31] Having placed the Eastgate Systems CD-ROM in your drive, however, the first screen is in fact the License Agreement that sternly warns 'You MAY NOT . . . modify, translate, reverse engineer, decompile, disassemble, create derivative works based upon, or copy the program or accompanying documentation.' Hypertextual openness is here prefaced and fatally contained by its own legal limit.

As the move is made from closed offline literary objects to the open system of the network, tensions like this increase rather than decline. It was inevitable that William Gibson, the science-fiction writer who coined the term 'cyberspace' and developed the densely metaphoric language to imagine this 'consensual hallucination' in his 1984 novel, *Neuromancer,* would experiment with new possibilities of digital writing.[32] In 1992, Gibson released his prose poem 'Agrippa: A Book of the Dead' in diskette form. This was a mournful text, written after his father's death, focusing on the faded images of a family photograph album to structure fragile memories. Digitisation allowed form to follow content: the reader could only read the text once, because as it scrolled up the screen, it also erased itself. The play with ephemeral human memory used the digital format inventively, although 'Agrippa' equally invited

[29] Bolter, *Writing Space*, p. 127. De Man proclaimed that 'any narrative is primarily the allegory of its own reading' in *Allegories of Reading: Figural Language in Rousseau, Nietzsche, Rilke and Proust* (New Haven: Yale University Press, 1979), p. 76.

[30] For discussion of Oulipo linguistic and situational generative fictions, see Bruce Morrisette, 'Post-Modern Generative Fiction: Novel and Film', *Critical Inquiry*, 2 (1975), pp. 253–62.

[31] Joyce, *Of Two Minds*, pp. 139–40.

[32] William Gibson, *Neuromancer* (London: Grafton, 1993), p. 67.

reflections on the ephemerality of the fetishised commodity form, at some level possibly satirising notions of ownership. The demand for Gibson's text, though, was eventually its downfall: it was made available on the internet for a day as a 'download', and the very hackers and 'console cowboys' Gibson's cyberpunk fictions of the 1980s had helped create rapidly cracked the self-destructing element of the text. Hundreds of internet sites now host a static version of Gibson's 'Agrippa'. These sites are more permanent, in fact, than the book version of the piece that was published with sensitive type that faded after exposure to light – a book that left the acquisitive Gibson collector with the paradox of a tangible yet unreadable object.

'Agrippa' neatly bridges closed and open digital forms, and its fate is also instructive. The move from commercial diskette to endless replication on the internet might exemplify the view that information wants to be free, and that the Web instantiates the possibility of democratic access. Yet this move also destroys a central element of the initial form of 'Agrippa' – a passingness that in the end can only be reintroduced by reverting to book form. The book reappears at the end of this story, rather than being superseded at the beginning: a forceful reminder that the institution of literature has not thus far been essentially changed by the advent of digital culture, whatever the revolutionaries assert.

The philosopher Jacques Derrida has argued that the institution of literature cannot be meaningful without 'a positive law implying the author's rights, the identification of the signatory, of the corpus, names, titles, the distinction between the original and the copy'.[33] Although a particular strand of Derrida's writing – most typically, the double-columned, 'morsellated' text *Glas* – has been championed by hypertext advocates, Derrida's understanding of the material supports of literature points up a number of constraints that writing about digital fiction, particularly on the open networks of the internet, has not yet addressed.

Geoff Ryman's 'novel' *253* was first uploaded on the internet in 1996.[34] It is very much a generative fiction in that Ryman sets himself strict limits within which to compose. 253 is the number of seats available on a London Underground train, including the driver's seat. Each seat is occupied, with no one standing (this is a clear sign that we are dealing with fantasy). Each person is given a single screen, in which their outward appearance and inward thoughts

[33] Jacques Derrida, 'No Apocalypse, Not Now (Full Speed Ahead, Seven Missiles, Seven Missives)', *Diacritics*, 14, 2 (1984), p. 26.

[34] <http://www.ryman-novel.com>

are described in 253 words. Any connection to other people riding on the train is marked by a hypertext link: Ryman ensures a relatively high level of interconnections, with co-workers, rivals, lovers, husbands and wives all travelling on the same train. The reader can thus choose to read linearly, through the train carriages, or is invited to follow the hot-links to other travellers, thus working around the text by lateral association. Ryman understands that lateral reading is always oriented against the conventionally linear: a 'map' of each carriage, of the train as a whole, allows readers to reorient themselves quickly at any point. The main menu page also includes a link to *253? Why 253?* – explanatory pages that guarantee a quick comprehension of the rules of the game.

Ryman's fiction is presented with whimsy rather than any claims to radicalism. Advertisements border the main business of the character screens, often gently mocking the idea of the electronic novel ('End literary embarrassment forever . . . Just imagine the boss's face when you tell him "I've read *253*, the novel for the internet"'), but also undercutting the claims made for interactive fiction by inviting readers to randomise the text of *253* ('Become a writer in your spare time! . . . Earn big £££££!!!!!'). He also understands that it is narrative that binds readers into literary texts rather than random lateral movements, so that after the 253 characters are described, a narrative section, 'The End of the Line', revisits significant people as the train crashes through the buffers, killing all those left on board.

Some internet reviews regarded the 1998 book version of *253* (subtitled *The Print Remix*) as a betrayal of the original version.[35] Yet the internet *253* makes no breach with the institution of literature that the book form suddenly reinstates: on the internet, the proper name of the author remains a rigid designator of authority (the way of finding the site in the first place, in fact), and the reader makes only minimal interventions within a strictly circumscribed set of possibilities. Perhaps most obviously, *253* is really an *intranet* fiction – it links only within its own borders, within the frame of its own corpus, its own name, its own title. A properly internet text invites connections outside itself, clicks moving laterally across a diversity of sites, rapidly losing track of the connections. If this kind of associative 'net-surfing' is the typical engagement with the World Wide Web as it currently stands, this is what the paratextual framing and the restrictive 'author-function' of literature

[35] Geoff Ryman, *253: The Print Remix* (London: Flamingo, 1998). For negative reviews see, for instance, Chris Mitchell, 'Mind the Gap', *Spike Magazine*, March 1998, <http://www.spikemagazine.com/0398_253.htm>

cannot allow.[36] These apparati ensure that *253* remains fundamentally a closed form.

This is the contradiction at the heart of Douglas Rushkoff's 'open-source' web novel, *Exit Strategy*. Rushkoff is a professional electronic frontiersman: he published *Cyberia: Life in the Trenches of Cyberspace* in 1994, becoming as a result a syndicated journalist on these topics. *Cyberia* reported on the attempts of a number of radical groups to maintain the anarchistic and libertarian spirit of the early internet; *Exit Strategy* was written in the wake of the 1998–9 market boom, in which the internet was at the centre of an astounding capitalisation by banks, investment funds and venture capitalists (the bubble burst in March 2000). At the moment when commercial usage of the internet overtook non-profit-making usage and some feared the irreversible capitalist containment of the Web, the Open Source Initiative was launched in February 1998 with the aim of maintaining the ideals of 'freeware' – program code shared openly for mutual design and development, and without profit.[37] Rushkoff launched *Exit Strategy* as a literary contribution to these open-source ideals: 'The story I wrote is merely the starting place for what I hope will be a lively interaction between all of us.'[38] The novel is a heavy-handed satire of the internet boom – the lead character is transposed from hacker roots into dotcom madness, hallucinating capitalists turning into literal bulls as the bull-market in technology zooms towards its inevitable crash. The text stages a struggle between hackers and the apotheosis of capitalist consumerism on the Web: the Synapticom company, which claims to have developed a way of injecting seratonin into the internet user when they press the 'Buy' button. The open-source aspect of the novel developed from Rushkoff's invitation that readers might submit explanatory footnotes to the main body of the text. Using a basic mode of science fictional estrangement, the premise is that this text is a manuscript discovered in the twenty-third century that requires anthropological annotation of the strange objects and opaque rituals that dominate this barely comprehensible hyper-capitalist society. It works to a certain extent (Microsoft packages are annotated as having an 'outlandishly cumbersome code . . . designed to necessitate the purchase of faster computer

36 I am referring here to Gerard Genette, *Paratexts: Thresholds of Interpretation*, trans. Jane E. Lewin (Cambridge University Press, 1997) and Michel Foucault's discussion of the author-function in 'What is an Author?' in *The Foucault Reader* (Harmondsworth: Penguin, 1986), pp. 101–20.

37 See the 'History of the OSI' at <www.opensource.org/docs/history.php>

38 See Douglas Rushkoff, 'A Word of Introduction', www.yil.com/features/rushkoff. *Exit Strategy* was later published in book form (New York: Soft Skull Press, 2002).

chips' and Attention Deficit Disorder as 'a diagnosis used to describe young men whose brains had developed resistance to corporate programming'),[39] but it never loses, or wants to lose, its hierarchical formation in which footnotes are submitted, screened and selected by Rushkoff, and then run under the main text on screen in smaller print in a separate dialogue box. The further reduction of footnotes in the book version to the two hundred best contributions only amplifies the distortions at work in this allegedly democratic exercise: just as Rushkoff thanks his rabbi and points to the Talmud as a model of interactive exegesis, so some annotations are rewarded with selection largely, it seems, for their distinctly anti-Palestinian views. Efforts to get this bug out of the open-source *Exit Strategy* code would be difficult, one suspects. The language of open-network access again meets a limit.

As the 1990s progressed, the phenomenon of 'fanfic' (fiction written by fans, centred mainly on characters from popular television series) increasingly served as a place where commentators could argue that a genuinely open, interactive and democratic writing was developing. Fan culture has been marked out by cultural-studies discourse as an active and subversive appropriation and refunctioning of mass cultural forms. Writing in 1992, Henry Jenkins argued that fans were abjected by most critics because of their 'violation of dominant cultural hierarchies', most particularly their status as 'undisciplined rogue readers'.[40] As late as 1997, Constance Penley emphasised that *Star Trek* fan-fiction writers seemed to relish their sub-cultural obscurity by deliberately using low-tech forms of publication – samizdat photocopied or even mimeographed copies circulated by mail – as if marking out their work from heavily capitalised production values of the television and film industry.[41] Neither Jenkins nor Penley anticipated how the self-publication possibilities and instant global reach of the internet would result in the huge increase in the cultural visibility of this field. Sites like fanfiction.net are hubs for a large array of writing, with clusters developing around *The X-Files* and *Buffy the Vampire Slayer* as much as *Star Trek*. Camille Bacon-Smith has hyperbolically argued that as science fiction is meant to predict the future so interactive science fiction fandom like this predicts the future of (electronic) community in America.[42]

39 Rushkoff, *Exit Strategy* (book version), pp. 30 and 142.

40 Henry Jenkins, *Textual Poachers: Television Fans and Participatory Culture* (London: Routledge, 1992), pp. 17 and 18.

41 Constance Penley, *NASA/Trek Popular Science and Sex in America* (London: Verso, 1997).

42 Camille Bacon-Smith, *Science Fiction Culture* (Philadelphia: University of Pennsylvania Press, 2000).

To the suspicion of some, much energy has been expended on discussing one particular type of fanfic: slash fiction.[43] These are narratives built around erotic encounters, initially between Kirk/Spock, in which the captain and his Vulcan aide finally explore the sexual subtext of their relationship. The conventions of the K/S genre have been strictly established since they first appeared in *Star Trek* fandom in the early 1970s. A narrative scenario is generally taken from the source text, but any homosocial bonding is queered towards a halting confession of love, a phase of confused and anxious struggle with normative repressions, and concluded by an abandonment to ecstatic sexual and affective union. A jargon has emerged that identifies different aspects of this basic plot of male-to-male slash: angst, romance, comedy, h/c (hurt/comfort), AU (alternate universe – a licence to change basic premises of the originating show), and so on. The initial subculture fascinated critics because slash was composed mainly by heterosexual women, usually under obvious pseudonyms. For Penley, the reiterated plot structure rewrites romance through the utopian potentials inherent in science fiction. The m/m coupling explores new possibilities and romantic ideals for a resensitised heterosexual masculinity.

There has been some disagreement over how to interpret this complex cross-gendered/sexual writing – it is, after all, a perfect instance of the Queer Theory view of sexual identity as an 'open mesh of possibilities, gaps, overlaps, dissonances and resonances'.[44] This complexity has intensified with the move to the internet – a small subculture, usually treated through ethnographic models of participant observation, has now exploded in a myriad directions, with numerous hubs like Slash Online to help the browser search through hundreds of thousands of stories. Couplings of Mulder/Krycek from *The X-Files* continue the angsty K/S model, but are now combined with galleries of digitally manipulated soft-porn clasps of the two on some sites. *Buffy*'s team of angst-ridden teenagers has allowed endlessly inventive couplings: the vampiric premise is, of course, inherently perverse. As one fan writer observes, 'The creator of the Buffy universe admits that there's sexual tension between every character and every other character. Fans have taken this pronouncement to heart.'[45]

43 For reservations about the importance of slash fiction, see Will Brooker, *Using the Force: Creativity, Community and Star Wars Fans* (London: Continuum, 2002), particularly chapter 7.

44 Eve Kosofsky Sedgwick, *Tendencies* (London: Routledge, 1994), p. 8. For a reading of slash fiction that contests Penley, see Matt Hills, *Fan Cultures* (London: Routledge, 2002), pp. 101–3.

45 'Mosca', 'Buffyverse' http://mosca.freeservers.com/fanfic/buffyrecs.html, opening paragraph.

In the broadest, ethnographic sense this is literature – a lot of it poorly conceived and composed, some of it remarkable in its full-scale intricate plotting and affect. It does not seem helpful, however, simply to erase boundaries and elide this cultural activity with Literature (as an institution of the corpus and the proper name), or claim that this kind of participatory writing is the future of literary culture. Fan fiction might promise that stream of anonymous, unbounded discourse dreamt of by Michel Foucault, were it not that its very dependence recalls all the means by which Foucault describes how 'the production of discourse is at once controlled, selected, organised and redistributed by a certain number of procedures'.[46] Slash fiction develops within the interstices of mass cultural production, each tale usually prefaced by a legalistic acknowledgement of the corporate ownership of the characters and appealing to the law of 'fair use'. These legal disclaimers have developed in the wake of some aggressive attempts by copyright owners to stamp out 'slashed' versions of their characters (the author of 'The Vampire Chronicles', Anne Rice, is notorious in this regard). Queered subversion is a tolerated form, then, and internet technology in fact makes this cultural activity *easier* to police than older *samizdat* forms, given the impressive panoptical reach of the newer search engines.

It is precisely the reactive and fugitive nature of slash fiction that has resulted in much of the attention from Cultural Studies, I suspect: it embodies Michel de Certeau's well-tried formulations about the subversive 'poaching' tactics of the powerless against the strategies of dominant culture and power.[47] The digital version of slash fiction also connects immediately to the extensive writing on how telepresence can disconnect sexual identity from bodily constraint, the screen becoming 'the new location for our fantasies, both erotic and intellectual', and where people 'become authors not only of text but of themselves, constructing new selves through social interaction'.[48] Pursuing the question of the 'literariness' of slash fiction seems a completely misplaced understanding of the kinds of cultural, identitarian work the genre undertakes.

This partial and selective account plots out some of the key points along the axis of digital literature, from offline to networked forms. I have focused particularly on narrative forms: a consideration of poetry would, I think, require a very different trajectory across these technologies. Writing by critics

[46] Michel Foucault, 'The Order of Discourse', in Robert Young, ed., *Untying the Text: A Post-Structuralist Reader* (London: Routledge & Kegan Paul, 1981), p. 52.

[47] Michel de Certeau, *The Practice of Everyday Life*, trans. Steven Rendell (Berkeley: University of California Press, 1984). Both Jenkins and Penley use de Certeau's model.

[48] Sherry Turkle, *Life on the Screen: Identity in the Age of the Internet* (London: Phoenix, 1997), pp. 26 and 12. See also Rosanne Allucquere Stone, *The War Between Desire and Technology at the Close of the Mechanical Age* (Cambridge, MA: MIT Press, 1995).

like Peter Middleton has begun to suggest how computer connectivity and the transversal 'surfing' of the internet might transform the syntactical compressions and metaphorical yokings typical of poetics – even at some distance from the computer screen.[49] Given the limits of space here, though, I will conclude with three general observations.

It remains an unexamined conviction of digital literature and its advocates that participatory openness, the merging of the roles of writer and reader, is the only proper destination for literature. Apart from the repeated ways in which the current practice of digital textuality fails to sustain this rhetoric, I have seen no argument that works through exactly why participatory, 'writing back' models are to be given automatic privilege. I am suspicious of these appeals for different reasons: they can risk reviving a pre-critical model of the expressivist subject, and in so doing, they dismiss a raft of other, complex modes of engagement with cultural forms as somehow 'passive'. They also coexist uneasily with political claims about the digital revival of participatory democracy just when the electoral history of the late twentieth century demonstrates a markedly growing democratic deficit. A much more carefully situated reading of the value and purposes of participatory literature needs to be developed.

Second, discussions of digital literature – this one included – risk technological determinism by focusing almost exclusively on the formal innovations of the texts. Readers in this field have to endure lengthy, static, old-fashioned print descriptions of the technological wizardry of anti-linear, de-hierarchising hypertext, to the exclusion of almost everything else. While we are promised that this material offers a radical new kind of reading and a bright, utopian future, the actual content of many of these fictions often significantly centres on narratives of trauma and loss. The fragmented, evasive and circling screens of Joyce's *afternoon* ask to be read on one level as representing mimetically the shocked state of the father, who has witnessed and possibly caused the death of his own son and estranged wife. The pivotal image of Shelley Jackson's *Patchwork Girl* is of the scar ('If you want to see me whole, you will have to sew me together yourself'), and while George Landow as always celebrates the technology of the text, he does little but cite the evocative suggestion by one of his students that the hypertext link might be understood as a 'textual trauma', where the disjunctive leap disorders and disaggregates as much as liberates.[50] Death and the ephemerality of family memory drives Gibson's 'Agrippa'; the

[49] Peter Middleton, 'The New Memoryism: How Computers Change the Way We Read', *New Formations*, 50 (2003), pp. 57–74.

[50] Jeffrey Pack cited in Landow, *Hypertext 2.0*, p. 203.

decisions made by the passengers in Ryman's *253* determine whether or not they will die in the train crash. Slash fiction favours narratives of 'angst' or 'hurt/comfort', playing out scenarios that are about exposure to, and possible resolution of, various types of traumatic sexual encounter. Even the most ardent advocates of hypertext tellingly use examples of mourning and loss: Landow suggests *In Memoriam* is a perfect text for multimedia technology, because Tennyson's mourning already constructs 'an antilinear poetry of fragments', while Janet Murray develops at length a hypothetical hypertext that might explore from different angles the apparently inexplicable suicide of a young man ('Only after viewing all the stories, after repeating the mourning process from each of several viewpoints, would we feel a larger catharsis').[51] Michael Joyce, contemplating the move from offline to networked digital technology, has latterly confessed: 'The truth is that the web puts me at a loss and I do not know why.'[52]

For me, what these instances allegorise, often against the grain of confident techno-utopian statement, is the felt trauma of technology change. In this sense, it is continuous with the theorisation of shock developed for the rise of the railway, the cinema and urban modernity. Indeed, many of the texts in question figure the traumatic impact through prior technologies: the car accident in *afternoon,* the train crash in *253*. Gibson's 'Agrippa' lovingly works over the decaying materiality of the photograph album put together by his father, memories organised around 'the revealed grace / of the mechanism' – whether the camera, his father's gun, an umbrella, or the changing technologies of a small Canadian town. Digital media evidently need to cannibalise prior technological forms – this is what Jay David Bolter and Richard Grusin have termed 'remediation', a strategy whereby 'they honor, rival, and revise linear-perspective painting, photography, film, television, and print'.[53] There is no sudden rupture introduced by the advent of digital technology: indeed, these early instances of electronic literature insistently figure the form through older technologies. Some of the more nuanced literary criticism about the digital age has suggested that it is the complex overlapping of new digital forms with 'the continued presence of older, less advanced storage and communication technologies' that produces an 'intermedial ecology'. Precisely because

[51] Landow, *Hypertext 2.0*, p. 54, and Murray, *Hamlet on the Holodeck*, p. 178.

[52] Michael Joyce, *Othermindedness: The Emergence of Network Culture* (Ann Arbor: University of Michigan Press, 2000), p. 59.

[53] Jay David Bolter and Richard Grusin, *Remediation: Understanding New Media* (Cambridge, MA: MIT Press, 1999), p. 15.

of the complexity of this environment, it is suggested, 'the novel remains the one medium that allows the historical effects of media differentiation to be remarked'.[54]

This could be the insight from which to develop an argument that a notable strand of recent novelistic discourse has responded to technologically saturated culture in its own inventive and appropriative ways through a mutation in the complexity and over-determination of plotting and the rapid and often bewildering shifting between real and virtual worlds. The work of Thomas Pynchon or Don DeLillo are common points of reference, since both have been long engaged in twisting the technology of print into new forms as post-war American culture became increasingly saturated in military, industrial and media technologies. One could also point to writers such as Gary Indiana, whose 'novels' (if that is what they are) of the late 1990s, *Resentment* and *Three Month Fever,* find a breathless, helter-skelter style of hysterical telegraphese to reflect pitilessly on the televisual mediation of everyday life in contemporary America.[55] Science-fiction writers, perhaps unsurprisingly in a genre devoted to exploring the cultural impacts of technology, have also opened a rich seam. Tellingly, this has been mined less through computer-based or digital forms, than in a renaissance of the novel. Jeff Noon pushed successive works towards various forms of digitally (and chemically) inspired ways of disassembling and reassembling text, culminating in *Cobralingus.*[56] It is significant, though, that he has returned to the novel, as if acknowledging the greater plasticity of the form. Indeed, some of the most inventive responses are wrapped inside what look initially like unreconstructed regressions to ancient 1930s space opera plots. Ken Macleod's extraordinary quartet, written between 1995 and 2000, moves between a fragmented London and a New Mars at the other end of the universe, populated by the uploaded dead and Artificial Intelligences campaigning for 'human' rights. Macleod abandons linear plotting across the quartet for a kind of compaction that abandons sequence for simultaneity, a complexification of form precisely related to his exploration of the utopian and

54 Joesph Tabbi and Michael Wutz, 'Introduction' to Tabbi and Wutz, eds., *Reading Matters: Narratives in the New Media Ecology* (Ithaca: Cornell University Press, 1997), pp. 9 and 18.

55 Gary Indiana, *Resentment* (London: Quartet, 1998) and *Three-Month Fever* (London: HarperCollins, 1999).

56 Jeff Noon, *Cobralingus* (Hove: Codex, 2001). The 'Instructions' inform the reader: 'The Cobralingus Engine makes use of the Metamorphiction process. This process imagines text to be a signal, which can be passed through various FILTER GATES, each of which has a specific effect upon the language', p. 13. The computing metaphor is continued throughout the collection.

dystopian possibilities of digital and machinic life in a political economy traced genealogically from the 1970s to the far future.[57] In the slightly staid-looking virtual worlds of cyberpunk fiction (so very 1980s), updates have included Pat Cadigan's cynical cybercop Doré Konstantin, who has a few sober reminders that the essence of virtual reality in the future will be the tireless ingenuity of advertisers, con-men and rip-off businesses solely dedicated to maximising 'billable time' online.[58]

But my third and final observation might be to ask, somewhat perversely, whether it is literature that is really the best place to ponder the impacts of digital technology. It is striking that literary culture has not produced a significant avant-garde response to this technology in the spirit of the Modernist ones that stretched from Italian Futurist celebrations of mechanical speed to William Burroughs's cut-ups in the 1950s, a technique designed to frustrate the inhuman efficiencies of cybernetics. The lack of a digital equivalent might say something about the much-debated fate of the avant-garde; it might say something about the 'drastic decline of literary fiction's cultural currency'.[59] But it might also be the case that different cultural forms are more profoundly affected by, and therefore necessarily more responsive to, digitisation. Photography, for instance, has been so bound up in theories of indexicality, of the photographic image as the physical yet ghostly trace of the object itself, that the digitisation of the image into endlessly manipulable bits has necessitated a basic reconception of photographic theory and practice.[60] In textual terms, too, the internet – through its storage capacities, global reach and potential ability to link any site to another – evidently energises some discourses more than others. It has given new impetus to marginal or 'subjugated knowledges', ranging from anti-globalisation protesters and counter-hegemonic news agencies to New Age hubs like SpiritWeb.[61] Conspiracy-theory sites have blossomed, perhaps because the paranoid connection of everything to everything else matches the

[57] Ken Macleod, *The Star Fraction, The Stone Canal, The Cassini Division, The Sky Road* (London: Orbit, 1995, 1996, 1998, 2000).

[58] Pat Cadigan, *Tea From an Empty Cup* (New York: Tor, 1998) and *Dervish is Digital* (London: Macmillan, 2000).

[59] Tabbi and Wutz, 'Introduction', p. 18.

[60] See, for instance, W. J. T. Mitchell, *The Reconfigured Eye* (Cambridge, MA: MIT Press, 1994) and Hubertus v Amelunxen, et al., *Photography after Photography: Memory and Representation in the Digital Age* (Amsterdam: G + B Arts, 1996).

[61] For discussion of internet political activism, see Tiziana Terranova, 'Demonstrating the Globe: Virtual Action and the Network Society', in David Holmes, ed., *Virtual Globalization: Virtual Spaces / Tourist Spaces* (London: Routledge, 2001), pp. 57–75. New Age fascination with technologies (before the rise of the World Wide Web) is discussed by Andrew Ross, *Strange Weather: Culture, Science and Technology in the Age of Limits* (London: Verso, 1991).

illimitable connectivity of the internet itself. The lack of hierarchy in a flattened network, the difficulty of determining boundaries or authorising frameworks, and the dislocation of *site* from *place* more acutely effect discourses premised on truth-claims than any kind of fiction. Nevertheless, these impacts have been strikingly explored in some novelistic remediations in recent years – perhaps most interestingly in those novelists experimenting with blurring the boundaries between fictive and factual discourse, like Gary Indiana's mock memoir of Gianni Versace's killer in *Three Month Fever* or Don DeLillo's highly self-conscious attempt to locate novel-writing as a privileged mode of composing post-war history in *Underworld*. If hypertext fictions have yet to convince that they can grasp, immanently, the implications of digital technologies for cultural production, this can only be good news for the future of the novel. Always novel, intrinsically of the *new*, this is not a form likely to face demise in any immediate future, whatever the apocalyptic pronouncements made in its name.

Select bibliography

Part 1. Writing modernity

Ackerman, Robert. *J. G. Frazer: His Life and Work.* Cambridge University Press, 1987.

Anderson, Amanda, and Joseph Valente. *Disciplinarity at the Fin de Siècle.* Princeton University Press, 2002.

Ardis, Ann L. *Modernism and Cultural Conflict, 1880–1922.* Cambridge University Press, 2002.

Ardis, Ann L., and Leslie W. Lewis, eds. *Women's Experience of Modernity, 1875–1945.* Baltimore and London: Johns Hopkins University Press, 2002.

Arnold, A. James. *Modernism and Negritude: The Poetry and Politics of Aimé Cesaire.* Cambridge, MA: Harvard University Press, 1981.

Asad, Talal, ed. *Anthropology and the Colonial Encounter.* Ithaca: Cornell University Press, 1973.

Ashcroft, Bill, Gareth Griffiths and Helen Tiffin. *The Empire Writes Back: Theory and Practice in Post-Colonial Literatures.* London: Routledge, 1989.

Beer, Gillian. *Open Fields: Science in Cultural Encounter.* Oxford: Clarendon Press, 1996.

Bhabha, Homi. *The Location of Culture.* London: Routledge, 1994.

Boehmer, Elleke. *Colonial and Postcolonial Literature: Migrant Metaphors*, rev. edn. Oxford University Press, 2004.

Empire, the National and the Postcolonial 1880–1920. Oxford University Press, 2002.

Empire Writing: An Anthology of Colonial Literature 1870–1920. Oxford University Press, 1998.

Boos, Florence S., and Carole G. Silver, eds. *Socialism and the Literary Artistry of William Morris.* Columbia: University of Missouri Press, 1990.

Booth, Howard J., and Nigel Rigby, eds. *Modernism and Empire.* Manchester University Press, 2000.

Brack, O. M., Jr., ed. *Twilight of Dawn: Studies in English Literature in Transition.* Tucson: Arizona State University Press, 1987.

Brake, Laurel. *Subjugated Knowledges: Journalism, Gender, and Literature in the Nineteenth Century.* London: Macmillan, 1994.

Brantlinger, Patrick. *Rule of Darkness: British Literature and Imperialism 1830–1914.* Ithaca: Cornell University Press, 1988.

Burdett, Carolyn. *Olive Schreiner and the Progress of Feminism: Evolution, Gender, Empire.* New York: Palgrave, 2001.

Burton, Antoinette. *At the Heart of Empire: Indians and the Colonial Encounter in Late Victorian Britain*. Berkeley: University of California Press, 1998.

Carter, Paul. *Living in a New Country: History, Travelling and Language*. London: Faber & Faber, 1992.

Cevasco, G. A., ed. *The 1890s: An Encyclopedia of British Literature, Art, and Culture*. New York: Garland, 1993.

Cheng, Vincent. *Joyce, Race and Empire*. Cambridge University Press, 1995.

Chrisman, Laura. *Rereading the Imperial Romance: British Imperialism and South African Resistance in Haggard, Schreiner Plaati*. Oxford University Press, 2000.

Collini, Stefan. *English Pasts: Essays in History and Culture*. Oxford University Press, 1999.

Crawford, Robert. *The Savage and the City*. Oxford: Clarendon Press, 1987.

Cullingford, Elizabeth. *Yeats, Ireland and Fascism*. London: Macmillan, 1984.

Dellamora, Richard, ed. *Victorian Sexual Dissidence*. University of Chicago Press, 1999.

Demastes, William W., and Katherine E. Kelly, eds. *British Playwrights, 1880–1956: A Research and Production Sourcebook*. Westport, CT, and London: Greenwood, 1996.

Dettmar, Kevin J. H., and Stephen Watt, eds. *Marketing Modernism: Self-Promotion, Canonization, Rereading*. Ann Arbor: University of Michigan Press, 1996.

Dowling, Linda. *The Vulgarization of Art: The Victorians and Aesthetic Democracy*. Charlottesville: University Press of Virginia, 1996.

Felski, Rita. *The Gender of Modernity*. Cambridge, MA: Harvard University Press, 1995.

First, Ruth, and Ann Scott. *Olive Schreiner*. London: Women's Press, 1989.

Flint, Kate. *The Woman Reader, 1837–1914*. Oxford: Clarendon Press, 1993.

Fraser, Robert, ed. *Sir James Frazer and the Literary Imagination: Essays in Affinity and Influence*. Basingstoke: Macmillan, 1990.

Gagnier, Regenia. *Idylls of the Marketplace: Oscar Wilde and the Victorian Public*. Stanford University Press, 1986.

The Insatiability of Human Wants: Economics and Aesthetics in Market Society. University of Chicago Press, 2000.

Subjectivities: A History of Self-Representation in Britain 1832–1920. New York: Oxford University Press, 1991.

Gates, Joanna. *Elizabeth Robins, 1862–1951: Actress, Novelist, Feminist*. Tuscaloosa, AL: University of Alabama Press, 1994.

Gibbons, Tom. *Rooms in the Darwin Hotel: Studies in English Literary Criticism and Ideas 1880–1920*. Nedlands, WA: University of Western Australia Press, 1973.

Gikandi, Simon. *Maps of Englishness: Writing Identity in the Cultures of Colonialism*. New York: Columbia University Press, 1996.

Green, Martin. *The English Novel in the Twentieth Century*. London: Routledge & Kegan Paul, 1984.

Greenslade, William. *Degeneration, Culture and the Novel 1880–1940*. Cambridge University Press, 1994.

Hapgood, Lynne, and Nancy L. Paxton, eds. *Outside Modernism: In Pursuit of the English Novel*. Basingstoke: Macmillan, 2000.

Harlow, Barbara, and Mia Carter, eds. *Imperialism and Orientalism: A Documentary Sourcebook*. Oxford: Blackwell, 1999.

Harris, Jose. *Private Lives, Public Spirit 1870–1914*. Harmondsworth: Penguin, 1993.

Heilmann, Ann. *New Woman Fiction: Women Writing First-Wave Feminism*. London: Macmillan; New York: St Martin's Press, 2000.

Heilmann, Ann, ed. *The Late-Victorian Marriage Question: A Collection of Key New Woman Texts*. London: Routledge / Thoemmes Press, 1998.

Herbert, Christopher. *Culture and Anomie: Ethnographic Imagination in the Nineteenth Century*. Chicago and London: University of Chicago Press, 1991.

Hobsbawm, Eric. *The Age of Empire 1875–1914*. Harmondsworth: Penguin, 1987.

Howe, Stephen. *Anti-colonialism in British Politics: The Left and the End of Empire 1928–1964*. Oxford: Clarendon Press, 1993.

Hughes, H. Stuart. *Consciousness and Society: The Reorientation of European Social Thought 1890–1930*. London: MacGibbon & Kee, 1959.

Hurley, Kelly. *The Gothic Body: Sexuality, Materialism, and Degeneration at the Fin de Siècle*. Cambridge University Press, 1996.

Hyam, Ronald. *Britain's Imperial Century 1815–1914: A Study of Empire and Expansion*. London: Macmillan, 1993.

Innes, C. L. *A History of Black and Asian Writing in Britain, 1700–2000*. Cambridge University Press, 2002.

Jackson, Holbrook. *The Eighteen Nineties: A Review of Art and Ideas at the Close of the Nineteenth Century*. New York: Mitchell Kennerley, 1914.

Jameson, Fredric. 'Modernism and Imperialism'. In *Nationalism, Colonialism and Literature*. Minneapolis: University of Minnesota Press, 1990.

The Political Unconscious: Narrative as a Socially Symbolic Act. Ithaca: Cornell University Press, 1981.

Jayawardena, Kumari. *The White Woman's Other Burden*. London: Routledge, 1995.

Kaplan, Carola M., and Anne B. Simpson, eds. *Seeing Double: Revisioning Edwardian and Modernist Literature*. Basingstoke: Macmillan, 1996.

Keating, Peter, ed. *Into Unknown England 1860–1913: Selections from the Social Explorers*. Manchester University Press, 1976.

Working-Class Stories of the 1890s. New York: Barnes and Noble, 1971.

Kelly, Katherine E., ed. *Modern Drama by Women 1880s–1930s: An International Anthology*. London and New York: Routledge, 1996.

Kern, Stephen. *The Culture of Time and Space: 1880–1918*. Cambridge, MA: Harvard University Press, 1983.

Kolakowski, Leszek. *Positivist Philosophy: From Hume to the Vienna Circle*, trans. Norbert Guterman. Harmondsworth: Penguin, 1972.

Laird, Holly. *Women Coauthors*. Urbana and Chicago: University of Illinois Press, 2000.

Lawrence, Karen R., ed. *Decolonizing Tradition*. Urbana: University of Illinois Press, 1992.

Transcultural Joyce. Cambridge University Press, 1998.

Leavis, F. R. *Two Cultures? The Significance of C. P. Snow*. London: Chatto & Windus, 1962.

Ledger, Sally. *The New Woman: Fiction and Feminism at the Fin de Siècle*. Manchester University Press, 1997.

Letwin, Shirley Robin. *The Pursuit of Certainty*. London: Cambridge University Press, 1965.

Lightman, Bernard, ed. *Victorian Science in Context*. Chicago and London: University of Chicago Press, 1997.

London, Bette. *Writing Double: Women's Literary Partnerships*. Ithaca and London: Cornell University Press, 1999.

Martin, Wallace. *'The New Age' Under Orage: Chapters in English Cultural History*. Manchester University Press, 1967.
Matthews, Steven. *Modernism*. Contexts Series. London: Arnold, 2004.
McAleer, Joseph. *Popular Reading and Publishing in Britain, 1914–50*. Oxford: Clarendon Press, 1992.
McClure, John A. *Kipling and Conrad: The Colonial Fiction*. Cambridge, MA: Harvard University Press, 1981.
McDonald, Gail. *Learning to Be Modern: Pound, Eliot, and the American University*. Oxford University Press, 1993.
McGuinness, Patrick. *Symbolism, Decadence and the Fin de Siècle: French and European Perspectives*. University of Exeter Press, 2000.
Morton, Peter. *The Vital Science: Biology and the Literary Imagination 1860–1900*. London: Allen & Unwin, 1984.
Nolan, Emer. *James Joyce and Nationalism*. London: Routledge, 1995.
Parker, W. H. *Mackinder: Geography as an Aid to Statecraft*. Oxford: Clarendon Press, 1982.
Parrinder, Patrick. *Authors and Authority: English and American Criticism 1750–1990*. Basingstoke: Macmillan; New York: Columbia University Press, 1991.
Parry, Benita. *Conrad and Imperialism*. London: Macmillan, 1983.
Delusions and Discoveries: Studies on India in the British Imagination 1880–1930. London: Allen Lane, 1972.
Philips, Kathy. *Virginia Woolf against Empire*. Knoxville: University of Tennessee Press, 1994.
Pick, Daniel. *Faces of Degeneration*. Cambridge University Press, 1989.
Pocock, Tom. *Rider Haggard and the Lost Empire*. London: Weidenfeld & Nicolson, 1993.
Powell, Kerry. *Women and Victorian Theatre*. Cambridge University Press, 1997.
Pratt, Mary Louise. *Imperial Eyes: Travel Writing and Transculturation*. London: Routledge, 1992.
Pykett, Lynn. *Engendering Fictions: The English Novel in the Early Twentieth Century*. London: Edward Arnold, 1995.
Rainey, Lawrence. *Institutions of Modernism: Literary Elites and Public Culture*. New Haven: Yale University Press, 1998.
Reade, Brian, ed. *Sexual Heretics: Male Homosexuality in English Literature from 1850 to 1900: An Anthology*. London: Routledge & Kegan Paul, 1970.
Richards, David. *Masks of Difference*. Cambridge University Press, 1995.
Richards, Thomas. *The Imperial Archive: Knowledge and the Fantasy of Empire*. London and New York: Verso, 1993.
Richardson, Angelique, and Chris Willis, eds. *The New Woman in Fiction and Fact: Fin-de-Siècle Feminisms*. London: Palgrave, 2001.
Robbins, Bruce. *Secular Vocations: Intellectuals, Professionalism, and Culture*. London and New York: Verso, 1993.
Rose, Jonathan. *The Intellectual Life of the British Working Classes*. New Haven: Yale University Press, 2001.
Said, Edward. *Culture and Imperialism*. London: Chatto & Windus, 1993.
Orientalism. London: Routledge & Kegan Paul, 1978.
Sambrook, James, ed. *Pre-Raphaelitism: A Collection of Critical Essays*. University of Chicago Press, 1974.

Schaffer, Talia. *The Forgotten Female Aesthetes: Literary Culture in Late-Victorian England*. Charlottesville and London: University Press of Virginia, 2000.

Schaffer, Talia, and Kathy Psomiades, eds. *Women and British Aestheticism*. Charlottesville and London: University Press of Virginia, 1999.

Schneer, Jonathan. *London 1900: The Imperial Metropolis*. London and New Haven: Yale University Press, 1999.

Sedgwick, Eve Kosofsky. *Between Men: English Literature and Male Homosocial Desire*. New York: Columbia University Press, 1985.

Shand-Tucci, Douglass. *Boston Bohemia 1881–1900. Ralph Adams Cram: Life and Architecture.* Amherst: University of Massachusetts Press, 1995.

Showalter, Elaine. *Sexual Anarchy: Gender and Cutlure at the Fin de Siècle*. New York: Viking Penguin, 1990.

Spurr, David. *The Rhetoric of Empire*. Durham, NC and London: Duke University Press, 1993.

Stevens, Hugh, and Caroline Howlett, eds. *Modernist Sexualities*. Manchester University Press, 2000.

Stokes, John. *In the Nineties*. University of Chicago Press, 1989.

Teich, Mikulas, and Roy Porter, eds. *Fin de Siècle and Its Legacy*. Cambridge University Press, 1990.

Thomas, Nicholas. *Colonialism's Culture: Anthropology, Travel and Governance*. Cambridge: Polity Press, 1994.

Thornton, R. K. R. *The Decadent Dilemma*. London: Edward Arnold, 1983.

Vickery, John B. *The Literary Impact of 'The Golden Bough'*, Princeton University Press, 1973.

Werskey, Gary. *The Visible College: A Collective Biography of British Scientists and Socialists of the 1930s*. London: Free Association, 1988.

Williams, Raymond. *The Country and the City*. Oxford and New York: Oxford University Press, 1973.

The Politics of Modernism: Against the New Conformists. Ed. Tony Pinkney. London: Verso, 1989.

Part 2. The emerging avant-garde

Ackroyd, Peter. *T. S. Eliot*. London: Abacus, 1984.

Barry, Iris. 'The Ezra Pound Period', *Bookman* (October 1931), 159–71.

Baudelaire, Charles. *The Painter of Modern Life and Other Essays*, ed. Jonathan Mayne. London: Phaidon Press, 1964.

Beckett, Jane, and Deborah Cherry. 'Reconceptualizing Vorticism: Women, Modernity, Modernism'. In Paul Edwards, ed., *Blast: Vorticism 1914–1918*. Aldershot: Ashgate, 2000, pp. 59–72.

Bell-Villada, Gene H. *Art for Art's Sake and Literary Life: How Politics and Markets Helped Shape the Ideology and Culture of Aestheticism, 1790–1990*. Lincoln, Nebraska: University of Nebraska Press, 1996.

Bergonzi, Bernard. *Heroes' Twilight: A Study of the Literature of the Great War*. 2nd edn. Basingstoke: Macmillan, 1980.

Booth, Allyson. *Postcards from the Trenches: Negotiating the Spaces Between Modernism and the First World War*. New York: Oxford University Press, 1996.

Bourdieu, Pierre. *The Rules of Art: Genesis and Structure of the Literary Field*, trans. Susan Emanuel. Stanford University Press, 1992.

Brooker, Peter. *Bohemia in London. The Social Scene of Early Modernism*. London: Palgrave 2004.

Brown, Marilyn R. *Gypsies and Other Bohemians: The Myth of the Artist in Nineteenth-Century France*. Ann Arbor: UMI Research Press, 1985.

Buitenhuis, Peter. *The Great War of Words: British, American, and Canadian Propaganda and Fiction, 1914–1933*. Vancouver: University of British Columbia Press, 1987.

Bullen, J. B., ed. *Post-Impressionists in England*. London: Routledge, 1988.

Bürger, Peter. *The Decline of Modernism*, trans. Nicholas Walker. University Park: Pennsylvania State University Press, 1992.

Theory of the Avant-Garde, trans. Michael Shaw. Minneapolis: University of Minnesota Press, 1984.

Caesar, Adrian. *Taking it like a Man: Suffering, Sexuality and the War Poets*. Manchester University Press, 1993.

Calinescu, Matei. *Five Faces of Modernity: Modernism, Avant-Garde, Decadence, Kitsch, Postmodernism*. Durham, N. C. Duke University Press, 1987.

Carabine, Keith. *The Life and the Art: A Study of Conrad's 'Under Western Eyes'*. Amsterdam and Atlanta, GA: Rodopi, 1996.

Cardinal, Agnès, Dorothy Goldman and Judith Hattaway, eds. *Women's Writing on the First World War*. Oxford University Press, 1999.

Carpenter, Humphrey. *A Serious Character: The Life of Ezra Pound*. London: Faber, 1988.

Caserio, Robert L. *The Novel in England 1900–1950: History and Theory*. New York and London: Twayne and Prentice Hall, 1999.

Cecil, Hugh. *The Flower of Battle: British Fiction Writers of the First World War*. London: Secker & Warburg, 1995.

Cianci, Giovanni. 'D. H. Lawrence and Futurism/Vorticism'. *Arbeiten aus Anglistik und Amerikanistik*, 8, 1 (1983), 41–53.

'Futurism and the English Avant-Garde: the Early Pound between Imagism and Vorticism'. *Arbeiten aus Anglistik und Amerikanistik*, 6, 1 (1981), 3–39.

'Futurism and its Impact on Vorticism'. *ICSAC Cahier 8* (December 1998), 83–101.

Clements, Patricia. *Baudelaire and the English Tradition*. Princeton University Press, 1985.

Cole, Sarah. *Modernism, male friendship, and the First World War*. Cambridge University Press, 2003.

Cookson, William, ed. *Ezra Pound. Selected Prose 1909–1965*. London: Faber & Faber, 1973.

Cooperman, Stanley. *World War I and The American Novel*. Baltimore: Johns Hopkins University Press, 1967.

Cork, Richard. *Art Beyond the Gallery*. New Haven and London: Yale University Press, 1985.

Modern Art in the Common Culture. New Haven and London: Yale University Press, 1996.

Dahlhaus, Carl. *Between Romanticism and Modernism*, trans. Mary Whittall. Berkeley and Los Angeles: University of California Press, 1980.

Daly, Nicholas. *Modernism, Romance and the Fin de Siècle: Popular Fiction and British Culture, 1880–1914*. Cambridge University Press, 1999.

David, Hugh. *The Fitzrovians: A Portrait of Bohemian Society 1900–55*. London: Michael Joseph, 1988.

Davie, Donald. *Studies in Ezra Pound*. Cheadle: Carcarnet Press, 1991.

Donald, James, Anne Friedberg and Laura Marcus, eds. *Close Up 1927–1933: Cinema and Modernism*. London: Cassell, 1998.

Edwards, Paul, ed. *Blast: Vorticism 1914–1918* Aldershot: Ashgate, 2000.

'Lewis's Myth of the Artist: From Bohemia to the Underground'. In *Volcanic Heaven: Essays on Wyndham Lewis's Painting and Writing*. Santa Rosa: Black Sparrow Press, 1996, pp. 25–39.

Eksteins, Modris. *Rites of Spring: The Great War and the Birth of the Modern Age*. Boston: Houghton Mifflin, 1989.

Eliot, T. S. *Inventions of the March Hare: Poems 1909–1917*, ed. Christopher Ricks. London: Faber & Faber, 1996.

The Letters of T. S. Eliot. Vol. 1, 1898–1922. London: Faber & Faber, 1988.

Flint, F. S. 'Book of the Week', *The New Age*, 11 February, 1909, 327–8.

Fogel, Aaron. *Coercion to Speak: Conrad's Poetics of Dialogue*. Cambridge, MA: Harvard University Press, 1985.

Foot, Michael. *H. G.: The History of Mr Wells*. Washington, DC: Counterpoint, 1995.

Ford, Ford Madox. *The Soul of London*. 1905; London: Everyman, 1995.

Garafola, Lynn. *Diaghilev's Ballets Russes*. Oxford University Press, 1989.

Gilbert, Sandra M., and Susan Gubar. *No Man's Land: The Place of the Woman Writer in the Twentieth Century*. Vol. II: *Sexchanges*. New Haven: Yale University Press, 1989.

Gioè, Valerio, 'Futurism in England: a Bibliography'. *Bulletin of Bibliography*, 44, 3 (September 1987), 172–88.

Gluck, Mary. 'Theorizing the Cultural Roots of the Bohemian Artist'. *Modernism / Modernity*, 7, 3 (2000) 351–378.

Goldring, Douglas. *South Lodge*. London: Constable, 1943.

Graña, César. *Bohemian Versus Bourgeois: French Society and the French Man of Letters in the Nineteenth Century*. New York: Basic Books, 1964.

Green, Martin. *Seven Types of Adventure Tale: An Etiology of A Major Genre*. University Park. Pennsylvania State University Press, 1991.

Grigoriev, S. I. *The Diaghilev Ballet, 1909–1929*. London: Penguin Books, 1960.

Hall, Donald. 'The Art of Poetry, V. Ezra Pound: an Interview'. *Paris Review*, 28 (1962), 22–51.

Hampson, Robert. 'Travellers, Dreamers, and Visitors: Ford and Fantasy'. In Robert Hampson and Tony Davenport, eds., *Ford Madox Ford: A Reappraisal*. Amsterdam and New York: Rodopi, 2002, pp. 31–57.

Harrison, Charles. *English Art and Modernism, 1900–1939*. Bloomington: University of Indiana Press, 1981.

Hibberd, Dominic. *Harold Monro: Poet of the New Age*. Houndmills: Palgrave, 2001.

Hutchins, Patricia. *Ezra Pound's Kensington*. London: Faber & Faber, 1965.

Huyssen, Andreas. *After the Great Divide: Modernism, Mass Culture, Postmodernism*. Bloomington: Indiana University Press, 1986.

Hynes, Samuel. *The Edwardian Turn of Mind*. Princeton University Press, 1968.

A War Imagined: The First World War and English Culture. New York: Atheneum, 1991.

Innes, Christopher. 'Modernism in Drama'. In Michael Levenson, ed., *The Cambridge Companion to Modernism*. Cambridge University Press, 1999, pp. 30–56.

Johnson, John H. *English Poetry of the First World War: A Study in the Evolution of Lyric and Narrative Form*. Princeton University Press, 1964.

Joannou, Maroula. 'The Angel of Freedom: Dora Marsden and the Transformation of *The Freewoman* into *The Egoist*'. *Women's History Review*, 11, 4 (2002), 596–611.

Kadlec, David. 'Pound, *Blast*, and Syndicalism'. *ELH*, 60, 4 (Winter 1993), 1015–31.

Kahn, Nosheen. *Women's Poetry of the First World War*. Lexington: University of Kentucky, 1988.

Kemp, Sandra, Charlotte Mitchell and David Trotter, eds. *The Oxford Companion to Edwardian Fiction*. Oxford University Press, 1997.

Kennedy, Dennis. *Granville Barker and the Dream of Theatre*. Cambridge University Press, 1985.

Kenner, Hugh. *A Sinking Island: The Modern English Writers*. London: Barrie & Jenkins, 1988.

'D. P. Remembered', *Paideuma*, 2, 3 (Winter 1973), 485–493.

Kolocotroni, Vassiliki, Jane Goldman and Olga Taxidou, eds. *Modernism: An Anthology of Sources and Documents*. Edinburgh University Press, 1998.

Lacoue-Labarthe, Philippe. *Musica Ficta (Figures of Wagner)*, trans. Felicia McCarren. Stanford University Press, 1994.

Larson, Jill. *Ethics and Narrative in the English Novel 1880–1914*. Cambridge University Press, 2001.

Lee, Hermione. *Virginia Woolf*. London: Vintage, 1997.

Levitine, George. *The Dawn of Bohemianism: The Barbu Rebellion and Primitivism in Neoclassical France*. University Park: Pennsylvania State University Press, 1978.

Lewis, Wyndham. *Blasting and Bombardiering*. London: John Calder, 1982.

'Introduction' to 'Wyndham Lewis and Vorticism'. London: Tate Gallery, 1956.

ed. *Blast 1*. 1914; Santa Rosa: Black Sparrow, 1997.

ed. *Blast 2*. 1915; Santa Barbara: Black Sparrow, 1981.

Lyon, Janet. 'Militant Discourse, Strange Bedfellows: Suffragettes and Vorticists before the War'. *Differences*, 4, 2 (1992), 100–31.

Marinetti, F. T. *Marinetti: Selected Writings*, ed. R. W. Flint. New York: Farrar, Straus & Giroux, 1972.

Mason, R. B. 'Missing the Boat: the Failures of Harold Monro and the Poetry Bookshop'. *The Antigonish Review*, 81–2 (Spring–Summer 1990), 53–8.

Materer, Timothy. 'Make it Sell! Ezra Pound Advertises Modernism'. In Kevin J. H. Dettmar and Stephen Watt, eds., *Marketing Modernisms: Self-Promotion, Canonization, Rereading*. Ann Arbor: University of Michigan Press, 1996, pp. 17–36.

Matz, Jesse. *Literary Impressionism and Modernist Aesthetics*. Cambridge University Press, 2001.

McClure, John. *Late Imperial Romance*. London and New York: Verso–New Left Books, 1994.

Meisel, Martin. *Shaw and the Nineteenth-Century Theater*. Princeton University Press, 1963.

Morrison, Mark. *The Public Face of Modernism: Little Magazines, Audiences, and Reception 1905–1920*. Madison: University of Wisconsin Press, 2001.

Morrison, Mark. 'Marketing British Modernism: *The Egoist* and Counter-Public Spheres'. *Twentieth-Century Literature*, 43, 4 (Winter 1997), 439–69.

Nicholls, Peter. *Modernisms: A Literary Guide*. Berkeley and Los Angeles: University of California Press, 1995.

Norris, Margot. *Writing War in the Twentieth Century*. Charlottesville: University of Virginia Press, 2000.

North, Michael. *Reading 1922: A Return to the Scene of the Modern*. New York: Oxford University Press, 1999.

Onions, John. *English Fiction and Drama of the Great War, 1918–39*. Basingstoke: Macmillan, 1990.

Orel, Harold. *Popular Fiction in England, 1914–1918*. Hemel Hempstead: Harvester Wheatsheaf, 1992.

Ouditt, Sharon. *Fighting Forces, Writing Women: Identity and Ideology in the First World War*. London: Routledge, 1994.

Paige, D. D., ed. *Selected Letters of Ezra Pound*. New York: New Directions, 1971.

Parrinder, Patrick. *Shadows of the Future: H. G. Wells, Science Fiction, and Prophecy*. Syracuse University Press, 1995.

Perloff, Marjorie. *The Futurist Moment: Avant-Garde, Avant-Guerre, and the Language of Rupture*. University of Chicago Press, 1986.

Pick, Daniel. *War Machine: The Rationalisation of Slaughter in the Modern Age*. New Haven: Yale University Press, 1993.

Pound, Ezra. *Certain Radio Speeches*, ed. William Levy. Rotterdam: Cold Turkey Press, 1975.

Pound, Omar, and A. Walton Litz, eds. *Gaudier-Brzeska: A Memoir*. New York: New Directions, 1970.

Literary Essays, ed. T. S. Eliot. London: Faber & Faber, 1960.

'Status Rerum', *Poetry* (January 1913), 123–7.

Ezra Pound and Dorothy Shakespear: Their Letters 1909–1914. London: Faber & Faber, 1984.

Priestley, J. B. *The Edwardians*. New York and Evanston: Harper & Row, 1970.

Radford, Jean. *Dorothy Richardson*. London: Harvester, 1991.

Rainey, Lawrence. *Institutions of Modernism: Literary Elites and Public Culture*. New Haven and London: Yale University Press, 1998.

Raitt, Suzanne, and Trudi Tate, eds. *Women's Fiction and the Great War*. Oxford University Press, 1997.

Reilly, Catherine W. *English Poetry of the First World War: A Bibliography*. London: George Prior, 1978.

Reynolds, Paige. 'Chaos Invading Concept: *Blast* as a Native Theory of Promotional Culture'. *Twentieth-Century Literature*, 46, 2, 238–68.

Robins, Anna Gruetzner. *Modern Art in Britain 1910–1914*. London: Merrell Holbertson in association with Barbican Art Gallery, 1997.

Ruthven, K. K. *A Guide to Ezra Pound's Personae (1926)*. Berkeley and Los Angeles: University of California Press, 1969.

Saunders, Max. *Ford Madox Ford: A Dual Life*. 2 vols. Vol. 1: *The World Before the War*. Oxford and New York: Oxford University Press, 1996.

Seigel, Jerrold. *Bohemian Paris: Culture, Politics, and the Boundaries of Bourgeois Life, 1830–1930*. New York: Penguin Books, 1986.

Sherry, Vincent. *Ezra Pound, Wyndham Lewis, and Radical Modernism*. New York: Oxford University Press, 1993.

The Great War and the Language of Modernism. New York: Oxford University Press, 2003.

Silkin, Jon. *Out of Battle: The Poetry of the Great War*. London: Oxford University Press, 1972.

Smith, Angela K. *The Second Battlefield: Women, Modernism and the First World War*. Manchester University Press, 2000.

Starkie, Enid. *From Gautier to Eliot: The Influence of France on English Literature, 1851–1939*. London: Hutchinson University Library, 1960.

Stead, C. K. *The New Poetic: Yeats to Eliot*. Harmondsworth: Penguin, 1967.

Pound, Yeats, Eliot and the Modernist Movement. London: Macmillan, 1986.

Stock, Noel. *The Life of Ezra Pound*. London: Penguin, 1970.

Symons, Arthur. *The Café Royal And Other Essays*. London: Beaumont Press, 1924.

Symons, Julian, ed. *The Essential Wyndham Lewis*. London: André Deutsch, 1989.

Tate, Trudi. *Modernism, History, and the First World War*. Manchester University Press, 1998.

Taylor, Georgina. *H. D. and the Public Sphere of Modernist Women Writers, 1913–1946: Talking Women*. Oxford University Press, 2001.

Temple, Ruth Zabriskie. *The Critic's Alchemy: A Study of the Introduction of French Symbolism into England*. New York: Twayne, 1953.

Tickner, Lisa. *Modern Life and Modern Subjects: British Art in the Early Twentieth Century*. New Haven and London: Yale University Press, 2000.

Tillyard, S. K. *The Impact of Modernism 1900–1920: Early Modernism and the Arts and Crafts Movement in Edwardian England*. London: Routledge, 1988.

Tuma, Keith. 'Wyndham Lewis, *Blast*, and Popular Culture'. *ELH*, 54, 2 (Summer 1987), 403–19.

Wees, W. C. *Vorticism and the English Avant-Garde*. Manchester University Press, 1972.

Weiss, Jeffrey. *The Popular Culture of Modern Art: Picasso, Duchamp, and Avant-Gardism*. New Haven: Yale University Press, 1994.

White, Andrea. *Joseph Conrad and the Adventure Tradition: Constructing and Deconstructing the Imperial Subject*. Cambridge University Press, 1993.

Wilhelm, J. J. *Ezra Pound in London and Paris*. University Park and London: Pennsylvania State University Press, 1990.

Wilson, Edmund. *Axel's Castle: A Study of the Imaginative Literature of 1870–1930*. New York: Charles Scribner's Sons, 1931.

Witemeyer, Hugh. *The Poetry of Ezra Pound: Forms and Renewal, 1908–1920*. Berkeley and Los Angeles: University of California Press, 1969.

Wollen, Peter. 'Out of the Past: Fashion/Orientalism/The Body'. In *Raiding the Icebox: Reflections on Twentieth-Century Culture*. Bloomington: Indiana University Press, 1993, pp. 1–34.

Woolf, Virginia. *A Woman's Essays*, ed. Rachel Bowlby. London: Penguin, 1992.

Worth, Katharine. *The Irish Drama of Europe from Yeats to Beckett*. London: Athlone, 1986.

Part 3. Modernism and its aftermath, 1918–1945

Abel, Elizabeth. *Virginia Woolf and the Fictions of Psychoanalysis*. University of Chicago Press, 1989.

Accardi, Bernard, et al., eds. *Recent Studies in Myths and Literature, 1970–1990*. New York: Greenwood, 1991.

Agate, James. *A Short View of the English Stage*. London: Jenkins, 1926.

Aldgate, Anthony, and Jeffrey Richards. *Britain Can Take It: The British Cinema in the Second World War*. Oxford: Blackwell, 1986.

Anderson, Linda. *Autobiography*. London: Routledge, 2000.

Women and Autobiography in the Twentieth Century. London: Prentice Hall, 1997.

Antze, Paul, and Michael Lambek. *Tense Past: Cultural Essays in Trauma and Memory*. London: Routledge, 1996.

Armstrong, Tim. *Modernism, Technology and the Body: A Cultural Study*. Cambridge University Press, 1998.

Ayers, David. *English Literature of the 1920s*. Edinburgh University Press, 1999.

Backscheider, Paula. *Reflections on Biography*. Oxford University Press, 2001.

Baker, Robert S. *The Dark Historic Page: Social Satire and Historicism in the Novels of Aldous Huxley 1921–1939*. Madison: University of Wisconsin Press, 1982.

Baldick, Chris. *The Social Mission of English Criticism, 1848–1932*. Oxford: Clarendon Press, 1983.

Barthes, Roland. 'The Death of the Author'. In *Image: Music: Text*, trans. and ed. Stephen Heath. London: Fontana / Collins, 1977.

Bason, Fred. *Gallery Unreserved*. London: John Heritage, 1931.

Batchelor, John, ed. *The Art of Literary Biography*. Oxford University Press, 1995.

Batchelor, John and Chris Pawling. *Narrating the Thirties. A Decade in the Making: 1930 to the Present*. Basingstoke: Macmillan, 1996.

Baxendale, John and Chris Pawling. *Narrating the Thirties: A Decade in the Making*. Basingstoke: Macmillan, 1996.

Beaty, Frederick L. *The Ironic World of Evelyn Waugh: A Study of Eight Novels*. DeKalb: Northern Illinois University Press, 1994.

Beauman, Nicola. *A Very Great Profession: The Women's Novel 1914–39*. London: Virago, 1983.

Bell, Michael. *Literature, Modernism and Myth: Belief and Responsibility in the Twentieth Century*. Cambridge University Press, 1997.

Bell, Michael and Peter Poellner, eds. *Myth and the Making of Modernity*. Amsterdam and Atlanta, GA: Rodopi, 1998.

Bergonzi, Bernard. *Reading the Thirties: Texts and Contexts*. London: Macmillan, 1978.

Bergstrom, Janet, ed. *Endless Night: Cinema and Psychoanalysis, Parallel Histories*. Berkeley and Los Angeles: University of California Press, 1999.

Bersani, Leo. *The Culture of Redemption*. Cambridge, MA: Harvard University Press, 1990.

Billingham, Peter, ed. *Theatre of Conscience 1939–1959*. London: Routledge Harwood, 2001.

Birch, M. J. 'The Popular Fiction Industry: Market, Formula, Ideology'. *Journal of Popular Culture*, 21, 3 (Winter 1987), 79–102.

Birkerts, Sven. 'Biography and the Dissolving Self'. In *Readings*. St Paul, Minnesota: Graywolf Press, 1999, 91–5.

Bloom, Clive. *Bestsellers: Popular Fiction Since 1900*. Basingstoke: Palgrave Macmillan, 2002.

Blumenberg, Hans. *Work on Myth*. Trans. Robert M. Wallace. Cambridge, MA, and London: MIT Press, 1985.

Boll, Theophilus E. M. 'May Sinclair and the Medico-Psychological Clinic of London'. *The Proceedings of the American Philosophical Society*, 106, 4 (1962), 310–26.

Bolton, Jonathan. *Personal Landscapes: British Poets in Egypt during the World War*. New York: St Martin's Press, 1997.
Bowser, Eileen. *The Transformation of Cinema, 1908–1915*. New York: Scribner's, 1990.
Bradbury, Malcolm. 'The Modern Comic Novel in the 1920s: Lewis, Huxley, and Waugh'. In *Possibilities: Essays on the State of the Novel*. London and Oxford University Press, 1973, pp. 140–63.
Bradshaw, David. 'The Best of Companions: J. W. N. Sullivan, Aldous Huxley, and the New Physics'. *Review of English Studies*, 47, 186 (May 1996), 188–206; 47, 187 (August 1996), 352–68.
Brendon, Piers. *Dark Valley: A Panorama of the 1930s*. London: Pimlico, 2001.
Brooks, Cleanth. *Modern Poetry and the Tradition*. Chapel Hill: University of North Carolina Press, 1939.
Burch, Noel. *Life to those Shadows*, trans. Ben Brewster. Berkeley and Los Angeles: University of California Press, 1990.
Burdett, Charles and Derek Duncan. *Cultural Encounters: European Travel Writing in the 1930s*. Oxford: Berghahn, 2002.
Burkdall, Thomas L. *Joycean Frames: Film and the Fiction of James Joyce*. New York and London: Routledge, 2001.
Bush, Ronald. *T. S. Eliot: A Study of Character and Style*. New York: Oxford University Press, 1984.
Butler, William V. *The Durable Desperadoes*. London: Macmillan, 1973.
Caesar, Adrian. *Dividing Lines: Poetry, Class and Ideology in the 1930s*. Manchester University Press, 1991.
Calder, Angus. *The Myth of the Blitz*. London: Jonathan Cape, 1991.
The People's War: Britain 1939–45. London: Pimlico, 1992.
Cannadine, David, ed. *Blood, Toil, Tears and Sweat: The Speeches of Winston Churchill*. Boston: Houghton Mifflin, 1989.
Caruth, Cathy. *Trauma: Explorations in Memory*. Baltimore: Johns Hopkins University Press, 1995.
Unclaimed Experience: Trauma, Narrative, and History. Baltimore: Johns Hopkins University Press, 1996.
Cavell, Stanley. *The World Viewed: Reflections on the Ontology of Film*. Cambridge, MA: Harvard University Press, 1979.
Cawelti, John G. *Adventure, Mystery, and Romance: Formula Stories as Art and Popular Culture*. Chicago and London: University of Chicago Press, 1976.
Chambers, Colins. *The Story of Unity Theatre*. London and New York: Lawrence & Wishart, 1989.
Chapman, James. *The British at War: Cinema, State and Propaganda. 1939–1945*. London: Tauris, 1998.
Chapman, Robert T. *Wyndham Lewis: Fictions and Satires*. London: Vision Press, 1973.
Charney, Leo, and Vanessa R. Schwartz. *Cinema and the Invention of Modern Life*. Berkeley and Los Angeles: University of California Press, 1995.
Charney, Leo. *Empty Moments: Cinema, Modernity and Drift*. Durham, NC: Duke University Press, 1998.
Chatman, Seymour. *Story and Discourse: Narrative Structure in Fiction*. Ithaca: Cornell University Press, 1978.

Chothia, Jean. *English Drama of the Early Modern Period 1890–1940*. London: Longman, 1996.

Christie, Ian. *The Last Machine: Early Cinema and the Birth of the Modern World*. London: BBC/BFI, 1994.

Clarke, Jon, Margot Heinemann, David Margolies and Carol Snee. *Culture and Crisis in Britain in the 1930s*. London: Lawrence & Wishart, 1979.

Clum, John. *Acting Gay: Male Homosexuality in Modern Drama*. New York: Columbia University Press, 1992.

Coates, Paul. *Film at the Intersection of High and Mass Culture*. Cambridge University Press, 1994.

Cockburn, Claud. *Bestseller: The Books that Everyone Read 1900–1939*. Harmondsworth: Penguin, 1975.

Cohen, Keith. *Film and Fiction: The Dynamics of Exchange*. New Haven and London: Yale University Press, 1999.

Colletta, Lisa. *Dark Humor and Social Satire in the Modern British Novel*. Basingstoke: Palgrave Macmillan, 2003.

Conrad, Peter. *Modern Times, Modern Places: Life and Art in the Twentieth Century*. London: Thames & Hudson, 1998.

Coope, Lawrence. *Myth*. London: Routledge, 1997.

Costello, Donald P. *The Serpent's Eye: Shaw and the Cinema*. University of Notre Dame Press, 1965.

Croft, Andy. *Red Letter Days: British Fiction in the 1930s*. London: Lawrence & Wishart, 1990.

Cunningham, Valentine. *British Writers of the Thirties*. Oxford University Press, 1988.

Danius, Sara. *The Senses of Modernism: Technology, Perception, and Aesthetics*. Ithaca: Cornell University Press, 2002.

Davies, Andrew. *Other Theatres: The Development of Alternative and Experimental Theatre in Britain*. London: Macmillan, 1987.

Davis, Jim, and and Victor Emeljanow. '"Wistful Remembrancer": the Historiographical Problem of Macqueen-Popery', in *New Theatre Quarterly*, 17, 4 (2001), 299–309.

Davy, Charles, ed. *Footnotes to the Film*. London: Lovat Dickinson, 1938.

Day, Gary, ed. *Literature and Culture in Modern Britain*, 3 vols. Vol. II: *1930–1955*. Harlow: Longman, 1997.

de Jongh, Nicholas. *Not in front of The Audience*. London: Routledge, 1992.

Politics, Prudery and Perversions: The Censoring of the English Stage 1901–1968. London: Methuen, 2000.

Dean, Basil. *The Theatre at War*. London: Harrap, 1956.

Deane, Patrick, ed. *History in Our Hands: A Critical Anthology of Writings on Literature, Culture and Politics from the 1930s*. London and New York: Leicester University Press, 1998.

Deeney, John. 'Censoring the Uncensored: *Children in Uniform*'. *New Theatre Quarterly*, 16, 3 (August 2000), 219–26.

Denning, Michael. *Cover Stories: Narrative and Ideology in the British Spy Thriller*. London: Routledge & Kegan Paul, 1987.

Derrida, Jacques. *Texts and Discussions with Jacques Derrida: The Ear of the Other*, ed. Christie McDonald. Lincoln: University of Nebraska Press, 1988.

Diemert, Brian. *Graham Greene's Thrillers and the 1930s*. Montreal and London: McGill–Queen's University Press, 1996.

Donald, James. *Imagining the Modern City*. London: Athlone, 1999.

Donald, James, Anne Friedberg and Laura Marcus, *Close Up 1927–1933: Cinema and Modernism*. London: Cassell, 1998.

Doubrovsky, Serge, Jacques Lecarme and Philippe Lejeune, eds. *Autofictions et Cie*. Paris: Université Paris X, 1993.

Edmunds, Susan. *Out of Line: History, Psychoanalysis and Montage in H. D.'s Long Poems*. Stanford University Press, 1994.

Edwards, Paul. *Wyndham Lewis: Painter and Writer.* New Haven and London: Yale University Press, 2000.

Eliot, T. S. 'Tradition and the Individual Talent'. In *Selected Essays*, 3rd enlarged edn. London: Faber & Faber, 1951, pp. 13–22.

Ellis, David. *Literary Lives: Biography and the Search for Understanding*. Edinburgh University Press, 2000.

Ellmann, Richard. 'Freud and Literary Biography'. In Peregrine Hordern, ed., *Freud and the Humanities*. Oxford University Press, 1985.

Ellwood, Robert. *The Politics of Myth: A Study of C. G. Jung, Mircea Eliade, and Joseph Campbell*. Albany: State University of New York Press, 1999.

Elsaesser, Thomas, ed. *Early Cinema: Space, Frame, Narrative*. London: British Film Institute, 1981.

Empson, William. *Using Biography*. London: Chatto & Windus; Hogarth Press, 1984.

English, James F. *Comic Transactions: Literature, Humor, and the Politics of Community in Twentieth-Century Britain*. Ithaca and London: Cornell University Press, 1994.

Eysteinsson, Astradur. *The Concept of Modernism*. Ithaca: Cornell University Press, 1990.

Felber, Lynette. *Literary Liaisons: Auto/Biographical Appropriations in Modernist Women's Fiction*. DeKalb, Ill.: Northern Illinois University Press, 2002.

Felman, Shoshana, and Dori Laub. *Testimony: Crises of Witnessing in Literature, Psychoanalysis, and History*. New York: Routledge, 1992.

Findlater, Richard. *Banned*. London: Panther, 1968.

The Unholy Trade. London: Gollancz, 1952.

Finney, Brian. *The Inner I: British Literary Autobiography of the Twentieth Century*. London: Faber & Faber, 1985.

Firchow, Peter. *Aldous Huxley: Satirist and Novelist*. Minneapolis: University of Minnesota Press, 1972.

Fitzgibbon, Constantine. *London's Burning*. London: Macdonald, 1971.

Foucault, Michel. 'What is an Author?' (1969). In *Language, Counter-Memory, Practice*. ed. Donald F. Bouchard. Oxford: Blackwell, 1977.

Fowler, Bridget. *The Alienated Reader: Women and Popular Romantic Literature in the Twentieth Century.* Hemel Hempstead: Harvester Wheatsheaf, 1991.

France, Peter, and William St Clair, eds. *Mapping Lives: The Uses of Biography*. Oxford University Press, 2002.

Fraser, Robert, ed. *Sir James Frazer and the Literary Imagination*. London: Macmillan, 1990.

Frayling, Christopher. *Things to Come*. London: British Film Institute, 1995.

Freshwater, Helen. 'Suppressed Desire: Inscriptions of Lesbianism in the British Theatre of the 1930s'. *New Theatre Quarterly*, 17, 4 (2001), 310–18.

Friedberg, Anne. *Window Shopping: Cinema and the Postmodern*. Berkeley: University of California Press, 1993.

Frye, Northrop. *Anatomy of Criticism: Four Essays*. Princeton University Press, 1957.

Fussell, Paul. *The Great War and Modern Memory*. Oxford University Press, 1975.

Wartime: Understanding and Behavior in the Second World War. Oxford University Press, 1989.

Gagnier, Regenia. *Subjectivities: A History of Self-Representation in Britain, 1832–1920*. New York and Oxford: Oxford University Press, 1991.

Gale, Maggie B. 'From Fame to Obscurity: in Search of Clemence Dane'. In Maggie B. Gale and Viv Gardner, eds., *Women, Theatre and Performance: New Histories, New Historiographies*. Manchester University Press, 2000, pp. 121–41.

West End Women: Women on the London Stage 1918–1962. London: Routledge, 1996.

Garnett. Robert R. *From Grimes to Brideshead: The Early Novels of Evelyn Waugh*. London and Toronto: Associated University Presses, 1990.

Gascoyne, David. *A Short Survey of Surrealism*. Preface by Dawn Ades. Intro. Michel Remy. London: Enitharmon Press, 2000.

Gasset, José Ortega y. 'The Dehumanization of Art'. In *The Dehumanization of Art and Notes on the Novel*, trans. Helene Weyl. Princeton University Press, 1948, pp. 3–54.

Genette, Gérard. *Narrative Discourse: An Essay in Method*, trans. Jane E. Lewin. Ithaca: Cornell University Press, 1980.

Gevirtz, Susan. *Narrative's Journey: The Fiction and Film Writing of Dorothy Richardson*, New York: Peter Lang, 1996.

Gilbert, Sandra, and Susan Gubar. *No Man's Land: The Place of the Woman Writer in the Twentieth Century*, Vol. 1: *The War of the Words*. London: Yale University Press, 1988.

Gilmore, L. *The Limits of Autobiography: Trauma and Testimony*. Ithaca, : Cornell University Press, 2001.

Gindin, James. *British Fiction in the 1930s*. London: Macmillan, 1992.

Gittings, Robert. *The Nature of Biography*. London: Heinemann, 1978.

Gloversmith, Frank, ed. *Class, Culture and Social Change: A New View of the 1930s*. Brighton: Harvester Press, 1980.

Godfrey, Phillip. *Back Stage*. London: Harrap, 1933.

Goldie, David. *A Critical Difference: T. S. Eliot and John Middleton Murry in English Literary Criticism, 1919–1928*. Oxford: Clarendon Press, 1998.

Gooding, Mel. 'A Selection of British Texts on Surrealism'. In Alexander Robertson, Michel Remy, Mel Gooding, Terry Friedman, eds., *Surrealism in Britain in the Thirties: Angels of Anarchy and Machines for Making Clouds*. Exhibition Catalogue, Leeds Art Galleries, 1986.

Goodstone, Tony, ed. *The Pulps: Fifty Years of American Pop Culture*. New York: Chelsea House, 1970.

Gould, Eric. *Mythical Intentions in Modern Literature*. Princeton University Press, 1981.

Gould, Warwick, and Thomas F. Staley, eds. *Writing the Lives of Writers*. London and New York: Macmillan and St Martin's Press, 1998.

Graham, Desmond, ed. *Poetry of the Second World War: An International Anthology*. London: Chatto & Windus, 1995.

Graham, Susan H. S. 'We Have a Secret. We Are Alive': H. D.'s *Trilogy* as a Response to War'. *Texas Studies in Literature and Language*, 44, 2 (2002), 161–210.

Greenblatt, Stephen J. *Three Modern Satirists: Waugh, Orwell, and Huxley.* New Haven and London: Yale University Press, 1965.

Hamilton, Cicely. *The Old Vic*. London: Jonathan Cape, 1926.

Harrison, Charles. *English Art and Modernism, 1900–1939*. 2nd edn. New Haven and London: Yale University Press, 1994.

Harrisson, Tom. *Living through the Blitz*. London: Collins, 1976.

Hartley, Jenny. *Millions Like Us: British Women's Fiction of the Second World War.* London: Virago, 1997.

Heidegger, Martin. *Being and Time*, trans. John Macquarrie and Edward Robinson. New York: Harper & Row, 1962.

Hendry, J. F., and Henry Treece, eds. *The New Apocalypse*. London: Fortune Press, 1939.

The White Horseman. London: Routledge, 1941.

Herman, Judith. *Trauma and Recovery*. New York: Basic Books, 1992.

Hewison, Robert. *Under Siege: Literary Life in London 1939–45*. London: Methuen, 1988.

Higson, Andrew, ed. *Young and Innocent: The Cinema in Britain 1896–1930*. University of Exeter Press, 2002.

Hinshelwood, Robert. 'Psychoanalysis in Britain: Points of Cultural Access, 1893–1918'. *The International Journal of Psychoanalysis*, 76, 1 (February 1995), 135–51.

Hoffman, F. J. 'From Surrealism to the Apocalypse: a Development in Twentieth-Century Irrationalism'. *English Literary History*, 15 (1948), 147–65.

Holland, Steve. *The Mushroom Jungle: A History of Postwar Paperback Publishing.* Westbury: Zeon Books, 1993.

Holsinger, M. Paul, and Mary Anne Schofield, eds. *Visions of War: World War II in Popular Literature and Culture*. Bowling Green: Popular Press, 1992.

Hudson, Lytton. *The Twentieth-Century Drama*. London: Harrap, 1946.

Huggett, Richard. *Binkie Beaumont: Eminence Grise of the West End Theatre 1933–1973*. London: Hodder & Stoughton, 1989.

Husserl, Edmund. *On the Phenomenology of the Consciousness of Internal Time*, trans. John Barnett Brough. Dordrecht: Kluwer, 1991.

Hynes, Samuel. *The Soldier's Tale: Bearing Witness to Modern War.* London: Pimlico, 1998.

Hynes, Samuel. *The Auden Generation: Literature and Politics in England in the 1930s.* London: Bodley Head, 1976.

Jackaman, Rob. *The Course of English Surrealist Poetry since the 1930s*. Lampeter: Edwin Mellen Press, 1989.

Rose, Jacqueline. *Why War? Psychoanalysis, Politics and the Return to Melanie Klein.* Oxford University Press, 1993.

Jameson, Fredric. *Fables of Aggression: Wyndham Lewis, The Modernist as Fascist.* Berkeley, Los Angeles and London: University of California Press, 1979.

Jolly, Margaretta, ed., *Encyclopedia of Life Writing: Autobiographical and Biographical Forms*, 2 vols. London: Fitzroy Dearborn, 2001.

Jones, Ernest. 'Reminiscent Notes on the Early History of Psycho-Analysis in English-Speaking Countries'. *The International Journal of Psychoanalysis*, 26 (1945), 8–10.

Jordan, Heather Bryant. *How Will the Heart Endure: Elizabeth Bowen and the Landscape of War.* Ann Arbor: University of Michigan Press, 1992.

Keating, H. R. F., ed. *Whodunit? A Guide to Crime, Suspense and Spy Fiction*. London: Windward, 1982.

Kenner, Hugh. *The Pound Era*. Berkeley: University of California Press, 1971.

The Romantic Image. London: Routledge, 2002.

The Sense of an Ending: Studies in the Theory of Fiction. New York: Oxford University Press, 1966.

Kermode, Frank. *History and Value*. Oxford: Clarendon Press, 1988.

Kern, Stephen. *The Culture of Time and Space, 1880–1918*, Cambridge, MA: Harvard University Press, 1983.

Kerrigan, John. 'Checklist of the Publications of Hugh Sykes Davies'. *Jacket*, 20 (December 2002), http://jacketmagazine.com/20/hsd-check.html.

King, Michael, ed. *H. D. Woman and Poet*. Orono, ME: National Poetry Foundation, 1986.

Kirkham, Pat, and David Thoms, eds. *War Culture: Social Change and Changing Experience in World War Two*. London: Lawrence & Wishart, 1995.

Klein, Holger, ed. *The Second World War in Fiction*. London: Macmillan, 1984.

Knowles, Dorothy. *The Censor, the Drama and the Film: 1900–1934*. London: George Allen & Unwin, 1934.

Knowles, Sebastian D. G. *A Purgatorial Flame: Seven British Writers in the Second World War*. Philadelphia: University of Pennsylvania Press, 1990.

Koselleck, Reinhart. *Futures Past: The Semantics of Historical Time*, trans. Keith Tribe. Cambridge, MA: MIT Press, 1985.

Kracauer, Siegfried. *From Caligari to Hitler: A Psychological History of the German Cinema*. Princeton University Press, 1947.

The Mass Ornament: Weimar Essays. Cambridge, MA: Harvard University Press, 1995.

Langbaum, Robert. *The Poetry of Experience: The Dramatic Monologue in Modern Literary Tradition*. New York: Norton, 1957.

Lant, Antonia. *Blackout: Reinventing Women for Wartime British Cinema*. Princeton University Press, 1991.

Leavis, F. R. *New Bearings in English Poetry: A Study of the Contemporary Situation*. London: Chatto & Windus, 1932.

Lejeune, Philippe. *Le pacte autobiographique*. Paris: Editions du Seuil, 1975.

Lentricchia, Frank. *Modernist Quartet*. Cambridge University Press, 1994.

Levy, Silvano, ed. *Surrealism: Surrealist Visuality*. Keele University Press, 1997.

Leys, Ruth. 'Traumatic Cures: Shell Shock, Janet, and the Question of Memory', *Critical Inquiry*, 20 (1994), 623–62.

Light, Alison. *Forever England: Femininity, Literature and Conservatism Between the Wars*. London: Routledge, 1991.

Longley, Edna. *Louis MacNeice: A Study*. London: Faber & Faber, 1988.

MacDermott, Norman. *Everymania: The History of the Everyman Theatre Hampstead 1920–1926*. London: Society for Theatre Research, 1975.

MacKillop, I. D. *F. R. Leavis: A Life in Criticism*. London: Allen Lane, 1995.

Mander, Raymond and Joe Mitchenson. *The Theatres of London*. London: Rupert Hart-Davis, 1961.

Marcus, Laura, *Virginia Woolf*. 2nd edn. Plymouth: Northcote House, 2004.

Auto/biographical Discourses. Manchester University Press, 1994.

ed. *Mass-Observation as Poetics and Science, New Formations* no. 44 (Autumn 2001).

Marcus, Steven. *Freud and the Culture of Psychoanalysis*. Boston: Allen & Unwin, 1984.

Marshall, Norman. *The Other Theatre*. London: John Lehmann, 1948.

Martin, Linda Wagner. *Telling Women's Lives. The New Biography*. New Brunswick, NJ: Rutgers University Press, 1994.

Matthews, J. H. 'Surrealism in England'. *Comparative Literature Studies*, 1 (1964), 55–72.

Matthews, Stephen, and Williams. Keith, *Rewriting the Thirties: Modernism and After*. London: Longman, 1937.

McAleer, Joseph. *Passion's Fortune: The Story of Mills & Boon*. Oxford University Press, 1999.

Popular Reading and Publishing in Britain 1914–1950. Oxford: Clarendon Press, 1992.

McDonald, Peter. *Louis MacNeice: The Poet in His Contexts*. Oxford: Clarendon Press, 1991.

McLaine, Ian. *Ministry of Morale*. London: George Allen & Unwin, 1979.

McMillan, Dougauld. *Transition: The History of a Literary Era 1927–1938*. London: Calder & Boyars, 1975.

Meckier, Jerome. *Aldous Huxley: Satire and Structure*. London: Chatto & Windus, 1969.

Meisel, Perry, and Walter Kendrick, eds. *Bloomsbury/Freud: The Letters of James and Alix Strachey*. London: Chatto & Windus, 1986.

Meletinsky, Eleazar M. *The Poetics of Myth*, trans. Guy Lanoue and Alexandre Sadetsky. New York and London: Routledge, 2000.

Mellor, David, ed. *A Paradise Lost: The Neo-Romantic Imagination in Britain 1935–55*. London: Lund Humphries, 1987.

Mendelson, Edward. *Early Auden*. London: Faber & Faber, 1981.

Mengham, Rod. *The Idiom of the Time: The Writings of Henry Green*. Cambridge University Press, 1983.

Mengham, Rod, and N. H. Reeve. *The Fiction of the 1940s: Stories of Survival*. Basingstoke: Palgrave, 2001.

Micale, Mark S., and Paul Lerner. *Traumatic Pasts: History, Psychiatry, and Trauma in the Modern Age, 1870–1930*. Cambridge University Press, 2001.

Miller, Tyrus. *Late Modernism: Politics, Fiction, and the Arts between the World Wars*. Berkeley, Los Angeles and London: University of California Press, 1999.

Minow-Pinkney, Makiko. *Virginia Woolf and the Problem of the Subject*. Brighton: Harvester Press, 1987.

Montefiore, Janet. *Men and Women Writers of the 1930s: The Dangerous Flood of History*. London: Routledge, 1996.

Mooneyham, Laura. 'Comedy among the Modernists: P. G. Wodehouse and the Anachronism of Comic Form'. *Twentieth-Century Literature*, 40, 1 (Spring 1994), 114–38.

Morgan, David, and Mary Evans, eds. *The Battle for Britain: Citizenship and Ideology in the Second World War*. London: Routledge, 1993.

Morgan, Fidelis, ed. *The Years Between: Plays by Women on the London Stage 1900–1950*. London: Virago, 1994.

Morpurgo, J. E. *Allen Lane: King Penguin. A Biography*. London: Hutchinson, 1979.

Mulhern, Francis. *The Moment of 'Scrutiny'*. London: New Left Books, 1979.

Munton, Alan. *English Fiction of the Second World War*. London: Faber & Faber, 1989.

Murphet, Julian, and Lydia Rainford. *Literature and Visual Technologies: Writing after Cinema*. Basingstoke: Palgrave Macmillan, 2003.

Murphy, Robert. *British Cinema and the Second World War*. London: Continuum, 2000.

Nalbantian, Suzanne. *Aesthetic Autobiography: From Life to Art in Marcel Proust, James Joyce, Virginia Woolf and Anaïs Nin*. Basingstoke: Macmillan, 1994.
Nicholson, Steve. *British Theatre and the Red Peril: The Portrayal of Communism 1917–1945*. Exeter University Press, 1999.
The Censorship of British Drama 1900–1968. 3 vols. Vol. I: *1900–1932*. Exeter University Press, 2003.
North, Michael. *The Dialect of Modernism: Race, Language and Twentieth-Century Literature*. Oxford University Press, 1994.
Olney, James. *Metaphors of Self: The Meaning of Autobiography*. Princeton University Press, 1972.
Ouditt, Sharon. *Fighting Forces, Writing Women: Identity and Ideology in the First World War*. London: Routledge, 1994.
Parke, Catherine. *Biography: Writing Lives*. New York and London: Routledge, 2002.
Parsons, Deborah. *Streetwalking the Metropolis*. Oxford University Press, 2000.
Pascal, Roy. *Design and Truth in Autobiography*. London: Routledge & Kegan Paul, 1960.
Patey, Douglas Lane. *The Life of Evelyn Waugh: A Critical Biography*. Oxford: Blackwell, 1998.
Pellizzi, Camillo. *The English Drama: The Last Great Phase*. London: Macmillan, 1935.
Perrino, Mark. *The Poetics of Mockery: Wyndham Lewis's 'The Apes of God' and the Popularization of Modernism*. Leeds: W. S. Maney for the Modern Humanities Research Association, 1995.
Peters Corbett, David. *The Modernity of English Art 1914–1930*. Manchester University Press, 1997.
Phillips, Adam. *Equalities*. London: Faber & Faber, 2002.
Pick, John. *The State and The Arts*. London: Offord, 1983.
Piette, Adam. *Imagination at War: British Fiction and Poetry 1939–45*. London and Basingstoke: Macmillan, 1995.
Pippin, Robert B. *Modernism as a Philosophical Problem: On the Dissatisfactions of European High Culture*. Oxford: Blackwell, 1991.
Plain, Gill. *Twentieth-century Crime Fiction: Gender, Sexuality and the Body*. Edinburgh University Press, 2001.
Women's Fiction of the Second World War: Gender, Power and Resistance. Edinburgh University Press, 1996.
Pogson, Reg. *Theatre Between the Wars (1919–1939)*. Clevedon: Triangle Press, 1947.
Pope, Macqueen. *The Footlights Flickered*. London: Herbert Jenkins, 1959.
Poster, Jem. *The Thirties Poets*. Buckingham: Open University Press, 1993.
Powell, Neil. *Roy Fuller: Writer and Society*. Manchester: Carcanet Press, 1995.
Prawer, S. S. *Caligari's Children*. Oxford University Press, 1980.
Price, Alfred. *Blitz on Britain 1939–45*. Stroud: Sutton, 2000.
Priestley, J. B. *The Plays of J. B. Priestly: Vol. III*. London: Heinemann, 1950.
Theatre Outlook. London: Nicholson and Watson, 1947.
Quinn, Patrick, ed. *Recharting the Thirties*. London: Associated University Presses, 1996.
Raitt, Suzanne. *May Sinclair: A Modern Victorian*. Oxford University Press, 2000.
Rapp, Dean. 'The Reception of Freud by the British Press: General Interest and Literary Magazines, 1920–1925'. *Journal of the History of the Behavioral Sciences*, 24 (April 1988), 191–201.

Rawlinson, Mark. *British Writing of the Second World War*. Oxford: Clarendon Press, 2000.

Ray, Paul C. *The Surrealist Movement in England*. Ithaca and London: Cornell University Press, 1971.

Read, Herbert, ed. *Surrealism*. London: Faber & Faber, 1936.

Rebellato, Dan. *1956 and All That: The Making of Modern Drama*. London: Routledge, 1999.

Reeve, N. H. *The Novels of Rex Warner*. Basingstoke: Macmillan, 1989.

Remy, Michel. *Surrealism in Britain*. Aldershot: Ashgate, 1999.

'Surrealism in England' (chronology). In *A Salute to British Surrealism*. Colchester: The Minories, 1985.

Ricoeur, Paul. *Time and Narrative*. 3 vols. Trans. Kathleen McLaughlin and David Pellauer. University of Chicago Press, 1984–8.

Roazen, Paul. *The Historiography of Psychoanalysis*. New Brunswick and London: Transaction, 2001.

Robinson, David. *Das Cabinet des Dr Caligari*. London: British Film Institute, 1997.

Rose, Jonathan. *The Intellectual Life of the British Working Classes*. New Haven and London: Yale University Press, 2001.

Rosemont, Penelope, ed., *Surrealist Women: An International Anthology*. Austin : University of Texas, 1998.

Rosenfeld, Alvin. *Imagining Hitler*. Bloomington: Indiana University Press, 1985.

Ross, Robert H. *The Georgian Revolt 1911–1922*. Carbondale: Southern Illinois University Press, 1965.

Russell, Bertrand. *The ABC of Relativity*. New York: Harper & Brother, 1925.

Ruthven, K. K. *Myth*. London: Methuen, 1976.

Samuel, Raphael, Ewan MacColl and Stuart Cosgrove. *Theatres of the Left*. London: Routledge & Kegan Paul, 1985.

Sandison, G. *Theatre Ownership in Britain*. London: Federation of Theatre Unions, 1953.

Saunders, Max. *Ford Madox Ford: A Dual Life*. 2 vols. Vol. II, *The After-War World*. Oxford University Press, 1996.

'Reflections on Impressionist Autobiography: James, Conrad and Ford'. *Conrad, James, Ford, and Other Relations*; 'Joseph Conrad: Eastern and Western Perspectives' series, ed. Wieslaw Krajka. Lublin/Columbia University Press, 2003.

Scarfe, Francis. *Auden and After: The Liberation of Poetry 193–1941*. London: Routledge, 1942.

Schleifer, Ronald. *Modernism and Time: The Logic of Abundance in Literature, Science, and Culture 1880–1930*. Cambridge University Press, 2000.

Schneider, Karen. *Loving Arms: British Women Writing the Second World War*. Lexington: University Press of Kentucky, 1997.

Schultz, William. *Cassirer and Langer on Myth: An Introduction*. New York: Garland, 2000.

Segal, Hanna. 'A Psycho-Analytical Approach to Aesthetics'. In *New Directions in Psychoanalysis: The Significance of Infant Conflict in the Pattern of Adult Behaviour* (1955), ed. Melanie Klein, Paula Heimann, R. E. Money-Kyrle. London: Karnac, 1985, pp. 384–405.

Segal, Robert A., ed. *Jung on Mythology*. London: Routledge, 1998.

Shelden, Michael. *Orwell: The Authorised Biography*. London: Heinemann, 1991.

Shellard, Dominic, ed. *Theatre in The 1950s*. Sheffield Academic Press, 2000.

Shires, Linda M. *British Poetry of the Second World War*. London: Macmillan, 1985.
Short, Ernest. *Sixty Years of Theatre*. London: Eyre & Spottiswoode, 1951.
Short, Kenneth, ed. *Film and Radio Propaganda in World War II*. London: Croom Helm, 1983.
Theatrical Cavalcade. London: Eyre & Spottiswoode, 1942.
Shulman, Robert. *The Power of Political Art: The 1930s Literary Left Reconsidered*. Chapel Hill and London: University of North Carolina Press, 2000.
Sinclair, Andrew. *War Like a Wasp: The Lost Decade of the 'Forties*. London: Hamish Hamilton, 1989.
Sinfield, Alan. *Out on Stage: Lesbian and Gay Theatre in the Twentieth Century*. New Haven: Yale University Press, 1999.
Sitney, P. Adams. *Modernist Montage: The Obscurity of Vision in Cinema and Literature*. New York: Columbia, 1990.
Spengemann, William. *The Forms of Autobiography*. New Haven and London: Yale University Press, 1980.
Spiegel, Alan. *Fiction and the Camera Eye: Visual Consciousness in Film and the Modern Novel*. Charlottesville: University Press of Virginia, 1976.
Stafford, David. *The Silent Game: The Real World of Imaginary Spies*. Toronto: Lester & Orpen Dennys, 1988.
Stanford, Derek. *Inside the Forties: Literary Memoirs 1937–1957*. London: Sidgwick & Jackson, 1977.
Stanford Friedman, Susan. *Analyzing Freud: Letters of H. D., Bryher, and their Circle*. New York: New Directions, 2002.
Stanley, Liz. *The Autobiographical I*. Manchester University Press, 1995.
Stansky, Peter, and William Abrahams. *London's Burning: Life, Death and Art in the Second World War*. London: Constable, 1994.
Stevenson, John and Chris Cook. *Britain in the Depression: Society and Politics, 1929–1939*. Harlow: Longman, 1977; 1994.
Stevenson, Randall. *The British Novel Since the Thirties*. London: Batsford, 1986.
Stewart, Victoria. *Women's Autobiography*. Basingstoke: Palgrave, 2003.
Stonebridge, Lyndsey. *The Destructive Element: British Psychoanalysis and Modernism*. Basingstoke: Macmillan, 1998.
Stourac, R., and K. McCreery. *Theatre as a Weapon*. London: Routledge and Kegan Paul, 1986.
Strenski, Ivan. *Four Theories of Myth in Twentieth-Century History: Cassirer, Eliade, Lévi-Strauss and Malinowski*. Basingstoke: Macmillan, 1987.
Symons, Julian. *Bloody Murder. From the Detective Story to the Crime Novel: A History*. London: Pan, 1994.
The Thirties: A Dream Revolved. London: Faber & Faber, 1975.
Swindells, Julia, ed. *The Uses of Autobiography*. London: Taylor & Francis, 1995.
Terdiman, Richard. *Present Past: Modernity and the Memory Crisis*. Ithaca: Cornell University Press, 1993.
Thorpe, André. *Britain in the 1930s: The Deceptive Decade*. Oxford and Cambridge, MA: Blackwell, 1992.
Timms, Edward, and Naomi Segal, eds. *Freud in Exile, Psychoanalysis and its Vicissitudes*. New Haven: Yale University Press, 1988.

Timms, Edward, and Peter Collier, eds. *Visions and Blueprints: Avant-Garde Culture and Radical Politics in Early Twentieth Century Europe*. Manchester University Press, 1988.

Tindall, William York. *Forces in Modern British Literature 1885–1946*. 1947; New York: Arno Press, 1980.

Tolley, A. T. *The Poetry of the Forties*. Manchester University Press, 1985.

Trewin, J. C. *The Gay Twenties*. London: Macdonald, 1958.

The Turbulent Thirties. London: Macdonald, 1960.

Trewin, J. C., and Wendy. *The Arts Theatre London: 1927–1981*. London: Society for Theatre Research, 1986.

Trotter, David. *The English Novel in History 1895–1920*. London: Routledge, 1993.

Valentine, Kylie. *Psychoanalysis, Psychiatry and Modernist Literature*. Basingstoke: Palgrave Macmillan, 2003.

Van Druten, John. 'The Sex Play'. *Theatre Arts Monthly*, 11 January 1927, 23–7.

Vice, Sue. *Holocaust Fiction*. London: Routledge, 2000.

Vickery, John. *The Literary Impact of 'The Golden Bough'*. Princeton University Press, 1973.

Walker, Stephen F. *Jung and the Jungians on Myth: An Introduction*. New York and London: Routledge, 2002.

Wasserstein, Bernard. *Britain and the Jews of Europe, 1939–1945*. London: Clarendon Press, 1979.

Watts, Carol. *Dorothy Richardson*. Plymouth: Northcote House, 1995.

Wilis, J. H. *Leonard and Virginia Woolf as Publishers: The Hogarth Press, 1917–41*. Charlottesville and London: University Press of Virginia, 1992.

Williams, Keith, and Steven Matthews. *Rewriting the Thirties: Modernism and After*. Harlow: Longman, 1997.

Williams, Keith. *British Writers and the Media 1930–45*. Basingstoke: Macmillan, 1996.

Williams, Linda Ruth. *Sex in the Head: Visions of Femininity and Film in D. H. Lawrence*. Hemel Hempstead: Harvester Wheatsheaf, 1993.

Wilson, Edmund. *Axel's Castle: A Study in the Imaginative Literature of 1870–1930*. New York: Scribner, 1931.

Winter, Jay. *Sites of Memory, Sites of Mourning*. Cambridge University Press, 1995.

Wood, Michael. *America at the Movies: or, 'Santa Maria, it had slipped my mind'*. New York: Basic Books, 1975.

Woolf, Virginia. 'The New Biography' (1927), in *The Essays of Virginia Woolf*, vol. IV, ed. Andrew McNeillie. London: Hogarth Press, 1994, pp. 473–80.

Young, Alan. *Dada and After: Extremist Modernism and English Literature*. Manchester University Press, 1981.

Zischler, Hanns. *Kafka Goes to the Movies*, trans. Susan. H. Gillespie. University of Chicago Press, 1993.

Part 4. Post-war cultures: 1945–1970

Acheson, James and Romana Huk. *Contemporary British Poetry: Essays in Theory and Criticism*. Albany: State University of New York Press, 1996.

Allen, Paul. *Alan Ayckbourn: Grinning at the Edge*. London: Methuen, 2000.

Anand, M. R. *Conversations in Bloomsbury*. London: Wildwood House, 1981.

Anderson, Perry. 'Components of the National Culture', *New Left Review*, 50 (1968), 3–57.
Archer, Robin, et al. *Out of Apathy: Voices of the New Left Thirty Years On*. London and New York: Verso, 1989.
Beauman, Sally. *The Royal Shakespeare Company*. Oxford University Press, 1982.
Belbin, David, and John Lucas, eds. *Stanley Middleton at Eighty*. Nottingham: Five Leaves Publications, 1999.
Bergonzi, Bernard. *Wartime and Aftermath: English Literature and Its Background, 1939–1960*. Oxford University Press, 1993.
Bignell, Jonathan, Stephen Lacey and Madeleine Macmurragh-Kavanagh, eds. *British Television Drama: Past, Present and Future*. Basingstoke: Palgrave, 2000.
Blake, A., L. Ghandi and S. Thomas. *England Through Colonial Eyes in Twentieth Century Fiction*. Basingstoke: Palgrave, 2001.
Booth, H. J., and N. Rigby, eds. *Modernism and Empire*. Manchester University Press, 2000.
Bradbury, Malcolm, ed. *The Novel Today*. Glasgow: Fontana, 1977.
Brooke-Rose, Christine. *Invisible Author: Last Essays*. Columbus: Ohio State University, 1994.
Brunsdon, Charlotte, Julie D'Acci and Lynn Spigel, eds. *Feminist Television Criticism: A Reader*. Oxford University Press, 1997.
Buhle, Paul. *C. L. R. James: The Artist as Revolutionary*. London: Verso, 1988.
Caughie, John. *Television Drama: Realism, Modernism, and British Culture*. Oxford University Press, 2000.
Chambers, Colin. *Peggy: The Life of Margaret Ramsay, Play Agent*. London: Nick Hern, 1997.
The Story of Unity Theatre. London: Lawrence & Wishart, 1989.
Cohen, R. *Frontiers of Identity: The British and the Others*. London: Longman, 1994.
Conekin, Becky E. *'The Autobiography of a Nation': The 1951 Festival of Britain*. (Manchester University Press, 2003.
Conradi, Peter. *Iris Murdoch: A Life*. London: HarperCollins, 2001.
Corbett, John. *Language and Scottish Literature*. Edinburgh University Press, 1997.
Corcoran, Neil. *English Poetry Since 1940*. London and New York: Longman, 1993.
Craig, Cairns, ed. *The History of Scottish Literature*. 4 vols. Vol. IV: *The Twentieth Century* Aberdeen University Press, 1987.
Crook, Tim. *Radio Drama: Theory and Practice*. London: Routledge, 1999.
Crozier, Andrew. 'Resting on Laurels'. In Alistair Davies and Alan Sinfield, eds., *British Culture of the Postwar: An Introduction to Literature and Society, 1945–1999*. London: Routledge, 2000, pp. 192–204.
'Thrills and Frills: Poetry as Figures of Empirical Lyricism'. In Alan Sinfield, ed., *Society and Literature, 1945–1970*. London: Methuen, 1983, pp. 199–233.
Dabydeen, David, ed. *The Black Presence in English Literature*. Manchester University Press, 1983.
Davie, Donald. *Articulate Energy: An Enquiry into the Syntax of English Poetry*. 1955; rpt. New York: Harcourt, Brace, 1958.
Purity of Diction in English Verse. 1952 rpt. with postscript, London: Routledge, 1967.
Thomas Hardy and British Poetry. London: Routledge, 1973.
Under Briggflatts: A History of Poetry in Great Britain, 1960–1988. Manchester: Carcanet Press, 1989.
Day-Lewis, Sean. *Talk of Drama: Views of the Television Dramatist Now and Then*. Luton: John Libbey Press, 1998.

Deane, Seamus. *A Short History of Irish Literature*. London: Hutchinson, 1986.

Dekker, George, ed. *Donald Davie and the Responsibilities of Literature*. Manchester: Carcanet Press, 1983.

Dennis, F., and N. Khan, eds. *Voices of the Crossing: The Impact on Britain of Writers From Asia, the Caribbean and Africa*. London: Serpent's Tail, 2000.

Dover, C. *Feathers in the Arrow: An Approach for Coloured Writers and Readers*. Bombay: Padma Publications, 1947.

Drakakis, John, ed. *British Radio Drama*. Cambridge University Press, 1981.

Duff, Charles. *The Lost Summer: The Heyday of the West End Theatre*. London: Nick Hern, 1995.

Duncan, Andrew. *The Failure of Conservatism in Modern British Poetry*. Cambridge: Salt Publishing, 2003.

Dyer, Geoff, ed. *John Berger: Selected Essays*. London: Bloomsbury, 2001.

Easthope, Antony. *Englishness and National Culture*. London and New York: Routledge, 1999.

Eliot, T. S. *Notes Toward the Definition of Culture*. London: Faber & Faber, 1948.

Elsom, John, and Nicholas Tomalin. *The History of the National Theatre*. London: Jonathan Cape, 1978.

Fay, Stephen. *Power Play: The Life and Times of Peter Hall*. London: Hodder & Stoughton, 1995.

Forrest-Thomson, Veronica. *Poetic Artifice: A Theory of Twentieth-Century Poetry*. Manchester University Press, 1978.

Fryer, Peter *Staying Power: The History of Black People in Britain*. London: Pluto Press, 1984.

Gasiorek, A. *Post-War British Fiction: Realism and After*. London: Edward Arnold, 1995.

Gaskill, William. *A Sense of Direction*. London: Faber & Faber, 1988.

George, R. M. *The Politics of Home: Postcolonial Relocations and Twentieth-Century Fiction*. Cambridge University Press, 1996.

Giddings, Robert, and Keith Selby. *The Classic Serial on Television and Radio*. Basingstoke: Palgrave, 2001.

Gikandi, Simon *Maps of Englishness: Writing Identity in the Culture of Colonialism*. New York: Columbia University Press, 1996.

Gilroy, Paul *The Black Atlantic: Modernity and Double Consciousness*. London: Verso, 1993.

Goode, John. 'Character in the Novel'. In *Collected Essays*. Keele University Press, 1995.

Goorney, Howard. *The Theatre Workshop Story*. London: Eyre Methuen, 1981.

Griffiths, Trevor R., and Margaret Llewellyn-Jones, eds. *British and Irish Women Dramatists Since 1958*. Buckingam: Open University Press, 1993.

Guralnick, Elissa S. *Sight Unseen: Beckett, Pinter, Stoppard and Other Contemporary Dramatists on Radio*. Athens, OH: Ohio University Press, 1996.

Halio, Jay, ed. *British Novelists Since 1960*. Vol. XIV Detroit: Gale Research, 1983.

Hall, Stuart, and Paddy Whannel. *The Popular Arts*. London: Hutchinson Educational, 1964.

Harris, W. *Tradition, the Writer and Society*. London: New Beacon, 1967.

Harrison, Charles. 'England's Climate'. In *Towards a Modern Art World*, ed. Brian Allen. New Haven and London: Yale University Press, 1995, pp. 207–25.

Hatzioulou, Elizabeth. *John Wain: Life and Work*. Oxford: Pisces Press, 1997.

Hewison, Robert. *Too Much: Art and Society in the Sixties*. London: Methuen, 1986.

Higgin, Gurth. *Symptoms of Tomorrow: Letters from a Sociologist on the Present State of Society*. London: Plume Press/Ward Lock, 1973.
Higgins, John. *Raymond Williams: Literature, Marxism and Cultural Materialism*. London and New York: Routledge, 1999.
Hoggart, Richard. *A Sort of Clowning: Life and Times 1940–1959*. London: Chatto & Windus, 1990.
The Uses of Literacy. London: Chatto & Windus, 1957.
Huggett, Richard. *Binkie Beaumont, Eminence Grise of the West End Theatre 1933–1973*, London: Hodder & Stoughton, 1984.
Innes, C. L. *A History of Black and Asian Writing in Britain, 1700–2000*. Cambridge University Press, 2002.
Jacobs, Jason. *Intimate Screen: Early British Television*. Oxford University Press, 2000.
Jacobs, Nicholas, and Prudence Ohlsen, eds., *Bertolt Brecht in Britain*. London: TQ Publications, 1977.
Johnson, Deborah. *Iris Murdoch*. Hassocks: Harvester Press, 1987.
Johnston, Dafydd. *A Guide to Welsh Literature*. 6 vols. Vol. VI: *c.1900–1996*. Cardiff: University of Wales Press, 1998.
Joseph, Stephen. *Theatre in the Round*. London: Barrie & Rockliff, 1967.
Kenny, Michael. *The First New Left: British Intellectuals After Stalin*. London: Lawrence & Wishart, 1995.
King, Bruce. *The Oxford English Literary History*. 13 vols. Vol. XIII: *1948–2000: The Internationalization of English Literature*. Oxford University Press, 2004.
Kirkland, Richard. *Literature and Culture in Northern Ireland since 1965: Moments of Danger*. London: Longman, 1996.
Koestler, Arthur. *Darkness at Noon*, Trans. Daphne Hardy. London: Jonathan Cape, 1940.
Lahr, J. *Prick Up Your Ears*. London: Penguin, 1980.
Lamming, George. *The Pleasures of Exile*. London: Michael Joseph, 1960.
Lee, A. R., ed. *Other Britain: Other British*. London: Pluto Press, 1995.
Lewis, Peter, ed. *Radio Drama*. London: Longman, 1981.
Lodge, David. *The Novelist at the Crossroads*. London: Routledge and Kegan Paul, 1971.
Lucas, John. *Moderns and Contemporaries: Novelists, Poets, Critics*. Hassocks: Harvester Press, 1985.
MacKenzie, Norman, ed. *Conviction*. London: MacGibbon & Kee, 1958.
Marshall, Norman. *The Other Theatre*. London: John Lehmann, 1947.
Marwick, Arthur. *British Society Since 1945*. Harmondsworth: Penguin, 1982.
Maslen, Elizabeth. *Doris Lessing*. Plymouth: Northcote House, 1994.
Mathias, Roland. *Anglo-Welsh Literature: An Illustrated History*. Bridgend: Poetry Wales Press, 1987.
Millington, Bob, and Robin Nelson. *Boys from the Blackstuff: The Making of a Television Drama*. London: Comedia, 1986.
Morrison, Blake. *The Movement: English Poetry and Fiction of the 1950s*. Oxford University Press, 1980.
Mulhern, Francis. *Culture/Metaculture*. London and New York: Routledge, 2000.
Nadel, Ira. *Double Act: A Life of Tom Stoppard*. London: Methuen, 2002.
Nairn, Tom. *The Break-Up of Britain: Crisis and Neo-Nationalism*. London: New Left Books, 1977.

Nasta, Susheila *Home Truths: Fictions of the South Asian Diaspora in Britain*. Basingstoke: Palgrave, 2002.

Nelson, R. *TV Drama in Transition: Forms, Values and Cultural Change*. London: Macmillan, 1997.

Nixon, R. *London Calling: V. S. Naipaul, Postcolonial Mandarin*. Oxford University Press, 1992.

Nuttall, Jeff. *Bomb Culture*. London: MacGibbon & Kee, 1968.

O'Connor, Alan, ed. *Raymond Williams on Television: Selected Writings*. London: Routledge, 1989.

Paget, Derek. *No Other Way to Tell It: Dramadoc/Docudrama on Television*. Manchester University Press, 1998.

True Stories: Documentary Drama on Radio, Screen and Stage. Manchester University Press, 1990.

Phillips, Mike, and Trevor Phillips. *Windrush: The Irresistible Rise of Multi-Racial Britain*. London: HarperCollins, 1998.

Rebellato, Dan. *1956 and All That: The Making of Modern British Drama*. London: Routledge, 1999.

Riley, Denise. *The Words of Selves: Identification, Solidarity, Irony*. Stanford University Press, 2000.

Roberts, Philip. *The Royal Court Theatre and the Modern Stage*. Cambridge University Press, 1999.

Rodger, Ian. *Radio Drama*. London: Macmillan, 1982.

Rowell, George, and Anthony Jackson. *The Repertory Movement*. Cambridge University Press, 1984.

Said, E. *Culture and Imperialism*. London: Chatto & Windus, 1993.

Samuel, Raphael ed. *Patriotism: The Making and Unmaking of British National Identity*. 3 vols. Vol. 1: *History and Politics*. London: Routledge, 1989.

Sandhu, S. *London Calling*. London: HarperCollins, 2003.

Schmidt, Michael, and Grevel Lindop, eds. *British Poetry Since 1960: A Critical Survey*. Manchester: Carcanet Press, 1972.

Self, David. *Television Drama: An Introduction*. Basingstoke: Macmillan, 1984.

Shellard, Dominic. *British Theatre Since the War*. New Haven: Yale University Press, 1999.

Sinclair, Andrew. *Arts and Cultures: The History of the Fifty Years of the Arts Council of Great Britain*. London: Sinclair Stevenson, 1995.

Sinfield, Alan. *Literature, Politics and Culture in Postwar Britain*. Oxford: Blackwell, 1989.

Sinfield, Alan, ed. *Society and Literature, 1945–70*. London: Methuen, 1983.

Snow, C. P. *The Two Cultures and the Scientific Revolution*. Cambridge University Press, 1959.

Steedman, Carolyn. *Landscape for a Good Woman: A Story of Two Lives*. London: Virago, 1986.

Stokes, Jane. *On Screen Rivals: Cinema and Television in the United States and Britain*. Basingstoke: Macmillan, 1999.

Taylor, John Russell. *Anger and After*, rev. edn. Harmondsworth: Penguin, 1963.

The Second Wave: British Drama for the Seventies. London: Methuen, 1971.

Thompson, E. P. 'The Peculiarity of the English' (1965). In *The Poverty of Theory and Other Essays*. London: Merlin Press, 1978.

Trewin, J. C. *Drama 1945–1950*. London: Longmans Green/British Council, 1951.

Trotter, David. *The Making of the Reader: Language and Subjectivity in Modern American, English, and Irish Poetry.* London: Macmillan, 1984.
Tuma, Keith. *Fishing by Obstinate Isles: Modern and Postmodern British Poetry and American Readers*. Evanston, IL: Northwestern University Press, 1998.
Turner, Adrian. *Robert Bolt: Scenes from Two Lives*. London: Hutchinson, 1998.
Tynan, Kenneth. *Tynan on Theatre*, Harmondsworth: Penguin, 1964.
Vahimagi, Tise. *British Television: An Illustrated Guide*, 2nd edn, Oxford University Press / British Film Institute, 1996.
Visram, Rozina. *Asians in Britain: Four Hundred Years of History*. London: Pluto Press, 2002.
Wain, John. *Dear Shadows: Portraits from Memory*. London: John Murray, 1986.
Walmsley, A. *The Caribbean Artists' Movement 1966–1972*. London: New Beacon, 1992.
Wansell, Geoffrey. *Terence Rattigan*. London: Fourth Estate, 1995.
Wardle, Irving. *The Theatres of George Devine*. London: Jonathan Cape, 1978.
Weatherhead, A. Kingsley. *The British Dissonance: Essays on Ten Contemporary Poets.* Columbia and London: University of Missouri Press, 1983.
Whitehead, Kate. *The Third Programme: A Literary History*. Oxford: Clarendon Press, 1989.
Williams, Raymond. *Culture and Society 1780–1950*. London: Chatto & Windus, 1958.
The Long Revolution. London: Chatto & Windus, 1961.
'Working-Class Culture', *Universities and Left Review*, 1, 2 (1957), 29–32.
Young, Robert *Postcolonialism: An Historical Introduction.* Oxford: Blackwell, 2001.

Part 5. Towards the millennium, 1970–2000

Aaron, Jane, Teresa Rees, Sandra Betts and Moira Vincentelli, eds. *Our Sisters' Land: The Changing Identities of Women in Wales*. Cardiff: University of Wales Press, 1994.
Acheson, James, and Romana Huk, eds. *Contemporary British Poetry: Essays in Theory and Criticism*. Albany: State University of New York Press, 1996.
Adam, Ian and Helen Tiffin, eds. *Past the Last Post: Theorizing Post-Colonialism and Post-Modernism*. Hemel Hempstead: Harvester, 1991.
Adams, Sam, ed., *Seeing Wales Whole: Essays in the Literature of Wales*. Cardiff: University of Wales Press, 1998.
Adorno, T. W., and M. Horkheimer. *Dialectic of Enlightenment*. London: Verso, 1979.
Ahmad, Aijaz. 'The Politics of Literary Postcoloniality'. *Race and Class*, 36, 3 (1995), 1–20.
Allnutt, Gillian, Fred D'Aguiar, Ken Edwards and Eric Mottram, eds. *The New British Poetry: 1968–1988*. London: Paladin, 1988.
Anderson, Linda, ed. *Plotting Change: Contemporary Women's Fiction*. London: Edward Arnold, 1990.
Ansorge, Peter. *Disrupting the Spectacle: Five Years of Experimental and Fringe Theatre in Britain*. London: Pitman, 1975.
Arden, John. *To Present the Pretence: Essays on the Theatre and its Public*. London: Eyre Methuen, 1977.
Armitage, Simon, and Robert Crawford, eds. *The Penguin Book of Poetry from Britain and Ireland*. Harmondsworth: Penguin, 1998.

Ashcroft, Bill, Gareth Griffiths and Helen Tiffin, eds. *The Empire Writes Back: Theory and Practice in Post-colonial Literatures*. London: Routledge, 1989.

Assiter, Alison. *Enlightened Women: Modernist Feminism in a Postmodern Age*. London and New York: Routledge, 1996.

Aston, Elaine. *An Introduction to Feminism and Theatre*. London: Routledge, 1995.

Backscheider, Paula R. *Reflections on Biography*. Oxford University Press, 1999.

Barker, Francis, Peter Hulme and Margaret Iversen, eds. *Colonial Discourse/Postcolonial Theory*. Manchester University Press, 1994.

Barker, Howard. *Arguments for a Theatre*. Manchester University Press, 1993.

Barrett, Michèle. *Women's Oppression Today: Problems in Marxist Feminist Analysis*. London: Verso, 1980.

Barry, Peter. *Contemporary British Poetry and the City*. Manchester University Press, 2000.

Batchelor, John, ed. *The Art of Literary Biography*. Oxford University Press, 1995.

Bennett, T., ed. *Popular Fiction*. London: Routledge, 1990.

Bhabha, Homi K. *The Location of Culture*. London and New York: Routledge, 1994.

Nation and Narration. London: Routledge, 1991.

Bianchi, Tony. 'Aztecs in Troedrhiwgwair: Recent Fictions in Wales'. In Ian Bell ed., *Peripheral Visions: Images of Nationhood in Contemporary British Fiction*. Cardiff: University of Wales Press, 1995, pp. 44–76.

Birke, Lynda. *Feminism and the Biological Body*. Edinburgh University Press, 1999.

Birkets, Sven. *The Gutenberg Elegies: The Fate of Reading in an Electronic Age*. London: Faber & Faber, 1994.

Blau du Plessis, R., and A. Snitow. *The Feminist Memoir Project: Voices from the Women's Liberation Movement*. New York: Three Rivers Press, 1998.

Bloch, Ernst. *The Utopian Function of Art and Literature: Selected Essays*. Cambridge, MA: MIT Press, 1988.

Blom, Mattias Bolkéus. *Stories of Old: The Imaginative West and the Crisis of Historical Symbology in the 1970s*. Uppsala: Acta Universitatis Upsaliensis, 1999.

Bold, Alan. *Modern Scottish Literature*. Longman: Harlow, 1984.

Bolger, Dermot, ed. *Druids, Dudes and Beauty Queens: The Changing Face of Irish Theatre*. Dublin: New Island Press, 2001.

Bolter, Jay David. *Writing Space: The Computer, Hypertext, and the History of Writing*. Hillsdale, NJ: Lawrence Erlbaum, 1991.

Booth, Martin. *British Poetry 1964–1984: Driving Through the Barricades*. London: Routledge & Kegan Paul, 1985.

Botting, F. *Gothic*. London: Routledge, 1996.

Bradoitti, Rosi. *Patterns of Dissonance: A Study of Women in Contemporary Philosophy*. Cambridge: Polity Press, 1991.

Brah, Avtar. *Cartographies of Diaspora: Contesting Identities*. London: Routledge, 1996.

Brauner, David. *Post-War Jewish Fiction: Ambivalence, Self-Explanation and Transatlantic Connections*. Basingstoke and New York: Palgrave, 2001.

Braunstein, Peter, and Michael William Doyle, eds. *Imagine Nation: The American Counterculture of the 1960s and 70s*. New York: Routledge, 2002.

Brown, Terence. *Ireland: A Social and Cultural History 1922–1985*. 2nd edn. London: Fontana, 1985.

Brown, Tony, and Russell Stephens. *Nations and Relations: Writing across the British Isles*. Cardiff: New Welsh Review, 2000.

Brydon, Diana, and Helen Tiffin. *Decolonising Fictions*. Sydney and Hebden Bridge: Dangaroo, 1993.

Bukatman, Scott. *Terminal Identity: The Virtual Subject in Postmodern Science Fiction*. Durham, NC: Duke University Press, 1993.

Burnett, John, David Vincent and David Mayall, eds. *The Autobiography of the Working Class: An Annotated Critical Bibliography*. 3 vols. Vol. III. Brighton: Harvester Press, 1989.

Bush, Clive. *Out of Dissent: A Study of Five Contemporary British Poets*. London: Talus, 1997.

Caddel, Richard, and Peter Quartermain, eds. *Other: British and Irish Poetry Since 1970*. Hanover, NH: Wesleyan University Press, 1999.

Campbell, Matthew, ed. *The Cambridge Companion to Contemporary Irish Poetry*. Cambridge University Press, 2003.

Carr, Helen, ed. *From My Guy to Sci-Fi: Genre and Women's Writing in the Postmodern World*. London: Pandora, 1989.

Carruthers, Gerard, David Goldie, and Alastair Renfrew, eds. *Beyond Scotland: New Contexts for Twentieth-Century Scottish Literature*. Amsterdam and New York : Rodopi, 2004.

Case, Sue-Ellen, and Janelle Reinelt, eds. *The Performance of Power: Theatrical Discourse and Politics*. University of Iowa Press, 1991.

Castells, Manuel. *The Rise of the Network Society*. Oxford: Blackwell, 1996.

Cawelti, J. G. *Adventure, Mystery and Romance: Formula Stories as Art and Popular Culture*. Chicago University Press, 1976.

Cesarani, David. *Arthur Koestler: The Homeless Mind*. London: William Heinemann, 1998.

Charles, Gerda, ed. *Modern Jewish Stories*. London: Faber & Faber, 1963.

Chatterjee, Partha. *Nationalist Thought and the Colonial World*. London: Zed Books, 1986.

Cheyette, Bryan. *Muriel Spark: Writers and Their Work*. Plymouth: Northcote House, 2000.

Cheyette, Bryan, ed. *Contemporary Jewish Writing in Britain and Ireland: An Anthology*. Lincoln, NB: University of Nebraska Press and London: Peter Halban, 1998.

Cheyette, Bryan, and Laura Marcus, eds. *Modernity, Culture and 'the Jew'*. Cambridge: Polity Press, and Stanford University Press, 1998.

Christianson, Aileen, and Alison Lumsden, eds. *Contemporary Scottish Women Writers*. Edinburgh University Press, 2000.

Cleary, Joe. *Literature, Partition and the Nation State: Culture and Conflict in Ireland, Israel and Palestine*. Cambridge University Press, 2002.

Connolly, Claire, ed. *Theorizing Ireland*. Basingstoke: Palgrave, 2003.

Connor, Steven, *Postmodernist Culture: An Introduction to Theories of the Postmodern*. 2nd edn. Oxford: Blackwell, 1997.

The English Novel in History, 1950–1995. London: Routledge, 1997.

Conran, Anthony. *The Cost of Strangeness: Essays on the English Poets of Wales*. Llandysul: Gomer Press, 1982.

Frontiers in Anglo-Welsh Poetry. Cardiff: University of Wales Press, 1997.

Corbett, John. *Language and Scottish Literature*. Edinburgh University Press, 1997.

Corcoran, Neil. *After Yeats and Joyce: Reading Modern Irish Literature*. Oxford University Press, 1997.

English Poetry Since 1940. London: Longman, 1993.

Couser, G. Thomas. *Recovering Bodies: Illness, Disability and Life Writing*. Madison: University of Wisconsin Press, 1997.

Craig, Cairns. *The Modern Scottish Novel: Narrative and the National Imagination*. Edinburgh University Press, 1999.

Out of History: Narrative Paradigms in Scottish and British Culture. Edinburgh: Polygon, 1996.

Craig, Cairns, ed. *The History of Scottish Literature*. 4 vols. Vol. IV: *The Twentieth Century*. Aberdeen University Press, 1987.

Craig, Sandy, ed. *Dreams and Deconstructions: Alternative Theatre in Britain*. Ambergate: Amber Lane Press, 1980.

Crawford, Robert. *Literature in Twentieth-Century Scotland: A Bibliography*. London : British Council, 1995.

Crozier, Andrew, and Tim Longville, eds. *A Various Art*. London: Paladin, 1990.

Curtis, Tony, ed. *Wales: The Imagined Nation: Essays in Cultural and National Identity*. Bridgend: Poetry Wales Press, 1986.

Davie, Donald. *Under Briggflatts: A History of Poetry in Great Britain 1960–1988*. University of Chicago Press, 1989.

Davies, Grahame. 'Resident Aliens: R. S. Thomas and the Anti-Modern Movement'. *Welsh Writing in English: A Yearbook of Critical Essays*, 7 (2001–2), 50–77.

Davies, Hazel Walford, ed., *State of Play: Four Playwrights from Wales*. Llandysul: Gomer Press, 1998.

Davies, James A. '"Two Strikes and You're Out": 1926 and 1984 in Welsh Industrial Fiction'. In H. Gustav Klaus and Stephen Knight, eds. *British Industrial Fictions*. Cardiff: University of Wales Press, 2000, pp. 137–47.

Davies, Jason Walford. 'Allusions to Welsh Literature in the Writing of R. S. Thomas'. *Welsh Writing in English: A Yearbook of Critical Essays*, 1 (1995), 75–127.

De Beauvoir, Simone. *The Second Sex* (1949), Trans. H. M. Parshley. Harmondsworth: Penguin, 1972.

De Lauretis, Teresa. *Technologies of Gender: Essays on Theory, Film and Fiction*. Bloomington: Indiana University Press, 1987.

Deane, Seamus. *Celtic Revivals: Essays in Irish Literature 1880–1980*. London: Faber & Faber, 1985.

Deane, Seamus, gen. ed. *The Field Day Anthology of Irish Writing*. 3 vols. Vol. III. Derry: Field Day, 1991.

Deane, Seamus, *Nationalism, Colonialism, and Literature*. Minneapolis: University of Minnesota Press, 1990.

Devine, Thomas. *The Scottish Nation 1700–2000*. Penguin: London, 1999.

Donaldson, Ian, Peter Read and James Walter, eds. *Shaping Lives: Reflections on Biography*. Canberra: Australian National University, 1992.

Du Gay, Paul, Jessica Evans and Peter Redman, eds. *Identity: A Reader*. London: Sage, 2000.

Duncan, Andrew. *The Failure of Conservatism in Modern British Poetry*. Cambridge: Salt, 2003.

Eagleton, Terry. 'The Crisis of Contemporary Culture'. *New Left Review*, 196 (1992), 29–44.

Echols, Alice. *Shaky Ground: The Sixties and its Aftershocks*. New York: Columbia University Press, 2002.

Eddershaw, Margaret. *Performing Brecht: Forty Years of British Performances*. London: Routledge, 1996.

Elias, Norbert. 'The Kitsch Style and the Age of Kitsch' (1935). In Johan Gouldblom and Stephen Mennell, eds., *The Norbert Elias Reader*. Oxford: Blackwell, 1998.

Ellmann, Mary. *Thinking About Women*. New York: Harcourt, 1968.

Fazzini, Marco. *Crossings: Essays on Contemporary Scottish Poetry and Hybridity*. Venice: Supernova, 2000.

Feldman, Tony. *An Introduction to Digital Media*. London: Routledge, 1997.

Felski, Rita. *Beyond Feminist Aesthetics: Feminist Literature and Social Change*. London: Hutchinson Radius, 1989.

Finlay, Richard J. *Modern Scotland: 1914–2000*. London: Profile, 2003.

Firestone, Shulamith. *The Dialectic of Sex: The Case for Feminist Revolution*. London: Women's Press, 1979.

Fludernik, Monika. *Echoes and Mirrorings: Gabriel Josipovici*. Frankfurt am Main: Peter Lang, 2000.

Fludernik, Monika, ed. *Diaspora and Multiculturalism: Common Traditions and New Developments*. Amsterdam and New York: Rodopi, 2003.

Frum, David. *How We Go Here. The Seventies: The Decade that Brought You Modern Life (For Better or Worse)*. New York: Basic Books, 2000.

Fuchs, Elinor. *The Death of Character: Perspectives on Theater After Modernism*. Bloomington: Indiana University Press, 1996.

Gibbons, Luke. *Transformations in Irish Culture*. Cork University Press, 1996.

Gifford, Douglas, and Dorothy McMillan, eds. *A History of Scottish Women's Writing*. Edinburgh University Press, 1997.

Gifford, Douglas, Sarah Dunnigan, Alan MacGillivray and Beth Dickson, eds. *Scottish Literature in English and Scots*. Edinburgh University Press, 2002.

Gilroy, Paul. *The Black Atlantic: Modernity and Double Consciousness*. London: Verso, 1993.

Gooch, Steve. *All Together Now: An Alternative View of Theatre and Community*. London: Methuen, 1984.

Görtschacher, Wolfgang. *Little Magazine Profiles: The Little Magazines in Great Britain 1939–1993*. University of Salzburg Press, 1993.

Gramich, Katie, and Andrew Hiscock, eds. *Dangerous Diversity: The Changing Faces of Wales*. Cardiff: University of Wales Press, 1998.

Greer, Germaine. *The Female Eunuch*. London: Paladin, 1971.

Hafner, Katie, and Matthew Lyon. *When Wizards Stay up Late: The Origins of the Internet*. New York: Touchstone, 1996.

Hagemann, Susanne ed. *Studies in Scottish Fiction: 1945 to the Present*. Frankfurt am Main: Peter Lang, 1996.

Hall, Stuart. 'New Ethnicities' (1988). In James Procter ed., *Writing Black Britain, 1948–1998: An Interdisciplinary Anthology*. Manchester University Press, 2000, pp. 265– 75.

Hampson, Robert, and Peter Barry, eds. *New British Poetries: The Scope of the Possible*. Manchester University Press, 1993.

Harte, Liam, and Michael Parker, eds. *Contemporary Irish Fiction: Themes, Tropes, Theories*. Basingstoke: Macmillan, 2000.

Harvie, Christopher. *No Gods and Precious Few Heroes*. Edinburgh University Press, 1998.

Head, Dominic. *The Cambridge Introduction to Modern British Fiction, 1950–2000*. Cambridge University Press, 2002.

Holderness, Graham, ed. *The Politics of Theatre and Drama*. London: Macmillan, 1992.

Holmes, Richard. *Footsteps: Adventures of a Romantic Biographer*. Harmondsworth: Penguin, 1986.

Homberger, Eric, and John Charmley, eds. *The Troubled Face of Biography*. London: Macmillan, 1988.

Hooker, Jeremy. *Imagining Wales: A View of Modern Welsh Writing in English*. Cardiff: University of Wales Press, 2001.

'Ceridwen's Daughters: Welsh Women Poets and the Uses of Tradition'. *Welsh Writing in English: A Yearbook of Critical Essays*, 1 (1995), 128–44.

Huk, Romana. *Assembling Alternatives: Reading Postmodern Poetries Transnationally*. Middletown, CT.: Wesleyan University Press, 2003.

Hunt, Albert. *Hopes for Great Happenings*. London: Eyre Methuen, 1976.

Itzin, Catherine. *Stages in the Revolution: Political Theatre in Britain since 1968*. London: Eyre Methuen, 1980.

Jameson, Fredric. *The Political Unconscious*. London: Methuen, 1981.

Postmodernism, or The Cultural Logic of Late Capitalism. London: Verso, 1991.

JanMohammed, Abdul. *Manichean Aesthetics: The Politics of Literature in Colonial Africa*. Amherst: University of Massachusetts Press, 1983.

Jones, Glyn. *The Dragon Has Two Tongues: Essays on Anglo-Welsh Writers and Writing*. 1968; Cardiff: University of Wales Press, 2000.

Jones, Peter, and Michael Schmidt, eds. *British Poetry Since 1970: A Critical Survey*. Manchester: Carcanet Press, 1980.

Jordan, Eamonn, ed. *Theatre Stuff: Critical Essays on Contemporary Irish Theatre*. Dublin: Carysfort Press, 2000.

Joyce, Michael. *Of Two Minds: Hypertext Pedagogy and Poetics*. Ann Arbor: University of Michigan Press, 1995.

Othermindedness: The Emergence of Network Culture. Ann Arbor: University of Michigan Press, 2000.

Halberstam Judith, *Skin Shows: Gothic Horror and the Technology of Monsters*. Durham, NC: Duke University Press, 1995.

Kaplan, Cora. *Seachanges: Essays on Culture and Feminism*. London: Verso, 1986.

Kennedy, David. *New Relations: The Refashioning of British Poetry 1980–1994*. Bridgend: Poetry Wales Press, 1996.

Kerbel, Sorrel, ed. *Jewish Writers of the Twentieth Century*. London and New York: Fitzroy Dearborn, 2003.

Kershaw, Baz. *The Politics of Performance*. London: Routledge, 1992.

The Radical in Performance. London: Routledge, 1999.

Kiberd, Declan. *Inventing Ireland*. London: Jonathan Cape, 1995.

Irish Classics. London: Granta, 2001.

Kirkland, Richard. *Literature and Culture in Ireland since 1965: Moments of Danger*. Harlow: Longman, 1996.

Knight, Stephen. *Form and Ideology in Crime Fiction*. London: Macmillan, 1980.

'The Voices of Glamorgan: Gwyn Thomas's Colonial Fiction'. *Welsh Writing in English: A Yearbook of Critical Essays*, 7 (2001–2), 16–34.

Kreitman, Morris, ed. *Jewish Short Stories of Today*. London: Faber & Faber, 1938.

Landow, George. *Hypertext 2.0: The Convergence of Contemporary Literary Theory and Technology*. Baltimore: Johns Hopkins University Press, 1997.

Landow, George, ed. *Hyper/Text/Theory*. Baltimore: Johns Hopkins University Press, 1994.

Lane, Richard, et al., eds. *Contemporary British Fiction*. Cambridge: Polity Press 2003.

Lavender, Andrew. 'Turns and Transformations.' In Colin Chambers and Vera Gottlieb, eds., *Theatre in a Cool Climate*. Oxford: Amber Lane Press, 1999.

Peter Lawson. *Singers of the Diaspora: Anglo-Jewish Poetry from Isaac Rosenberg to Elaine Feinstein*. London and Oregon: Vallentine Mitchell, 2005.

Lawson, Peter, ed. *Passionate Renewal: Jewish Poetry in Britain since 1945*. Nottingham: Five Leaves, 2001.

Leader, Zachary, ed., *On Modern British Fiction*. Oxford University Press, 2002

Lee, A. Robert, ed. *Other Britain, Other British: Contemporary Multicultural Fiction*. London: Pluto Press, 1995.

Lehrer, Natasha, ed. *The Golden Chain: Fifty Years of the Jewish Quarterly*. London and Oregon: Vallentine Mitchell, 2003.

Litvinoff, Emanuel, ed. *The Penguin Book of Jewish Short Stories*. Harmondsworth: Penguin, 1979.

Loizeaux, Elizabeth Bergmann, and Neil Frestat, eds. *Reimagining Textuality: Textual Studies in the Late Age of Print*. Madison: University of Wisconsin Press, 2002.

Longley, Edna. *The Living Stream: Literature and Revisionism in Ireland*. Newcastle: Bloodaxe, 1994.

Poetry in the Wars. Newcastle: Bloodaxe, 1986.

Lorde, Audre. *Sister Outsider: Essays and Speeches*, Freedom, CA: Crossing Press, 1984.

Lunenfeld, Peter, ed. *The Digital Dialectic: New Essays on New Media*. Cambridge, MA: MIT Press, 1999.

Lyotard, Jean-François. *The Inhuman: Reflections on Time Today*, trans. Rachel Bowlby and Geoffrey Bennington. Cambridge: Polity Press, 1991.

Malzahn, Manfred. *Aspects of Identity: The Contemporary Scottish Novel 1978–81*. Frankfurt am Main: Peter Lang, 1984.

McCarthy, Conor. *Modernisation, Crisis and Culture in Ireland, 1969–1992*. Dublin: Four Courts Press, 2000.

McCracken, Scott. *Pulp: Reading Popular Fiction*. Manchester University Press, 1998.

McDonald, Peter. *Mistaken Identities: Poetry and Northern Ireland*. Oxford: Clarendon Press, 1997.

McGrath, John. *The Bone Won't Break: On Theatre and Hope in Hard Times*. London: Methuen, 1990.

A Good Night Out. London: Methuen, 1981.

McHale, Brian. *Postmodernist Fiction*. London: Methuen, 1987.

Middleton, Peter. 'The New Memoryism: How Computers Change the Way We Read'. *New Formations*, 50 (2003), 57–74.

Middleton, Peter and Tim Woods. *Literatures of Memory: History, Time and Space in Postwar Writing*. Manchester University Press. 2000.

Miller, Stephen Paul. *The Seventies Now: Culture as Surveillance*. Durham, NC, and London: Duke University Press, 1999.

Mirza, Heidi Safia, ed. *Black British Feminism*. London: Routledge, 1997.

Mitchell, Juliet. *Psychoanalysis and Feminism*. Harmondsworth: Penguin, 1974.

Modleski, Tania. *Living with a Vengeance: Mass-Produced Fantasies for Women*. London: Methuen, 1982.

Moi, Toril. *Sexual/Textual Politics: Feminist Literary Theory*. London: Penguin, 1985.

Monterrey, Tómas, ed. *Contemporary Scottish Literature 1970–2000*. La Laguna, Canary Isles: Universidad de la Laguna, 2000.

Moretti, F. *Signs Taken for Wonders: Essays in the Sociology of Literary Forms*. London: New Left Books, 1983.

Morrison, Blake, and Andrew Motion, eds. *The Penguin Book of Contemporary British Poetry*. Harmondsworth: Penguin, 1982.

Murray, Janet H. *Hamlet on the Holodeck: The Future of Narrative in Cyberspace*. New York: Free Press, 1997.

Nicol, Bran, ed. *Postmodernism and the Contemporary Novel*: Edinburgh University Press, 2002.

Nicholson, Colin. *Poem, Purpose and Place: Shaping Identity in Contemporary Scottish Verse*. Edinburgh: Polygon, 1992.

O'Donoghue, Bernard. *Seamus Heaney and the Language of Poetry*. Hemel Hempstead: Harvester Wheatsheaf, 1994.

Olney, James. *Metaphors of the Self: The Meaning of Autobiography*. Princeton University Press, 1972.

Pawling, C., ed. *Popular Fiction and Social Change*. London: Macmillan, 1984.

Peach, Linden. *The Contemporary Irish Novel: Critical Readings*. Basingstoke: Palgrave Macmillan, 2004.

Perks, Robert, and Alistair Thomson, eds. *The Oral History Reader*. London: Routledge, 1998.

Plummer, Ken. *Telling Sexual Stories: Power, Change and Social Worlds*. London: Routledge, 1995.

Prentki, Tim. 'Cop-out, Cop-in: Carnival as Political Theatre'. *New Theatre Quarterly*, 6 (1990).

Quayson, Ato. *Postcolonialism: Theory, Practice or Process?* Cambridge University Press, 2000.

Raban, Jonathan. *The Society of the Poem*. London: Harrap, 1971.

Radford, Jean, ed. *The Progress of Romance: The Politics of Popular Fiction*. London: Routledge & Kegan Paul, 1986.

Radstone, Susannah, and Katharine Hodgkin. *Contested Pasts: The Politics of Memory*. London: Routledge, 2003.

Radway, Janice. *Reading the Romance: Women, Patriarchy and Popular Literature*. Chapel Hill and London: North Carolina University Press, 1984.

Rebellato, Dan. 'Introduction'. In Mark Ravenhill, *Plays: 1*. London: Methuen, 2001.

Reinelt, Janelle, ed. *Crucibles of Crisis: Performing Social Change*. Ann Arbor: University of Michigan Press, 1996.

Reinelt, Janelle, and Joseph Roach, eds. *Critical Theory and Performance*. Ann Arbor: University of Michigan Press, 1992.

Riley, Denise, ed. *Poets on Writing: Britain, 1970–1991*. London: Macmillan, 1992.

Roberts, Neil. *A Companion to Twentieth-Century Poetry*. Oxford: Blackwell, 2003.

Narrative and Voice in Postwar Poetry. London: Addison Wesley Longman, 1999.

Roche, Anthony. *Contemporary Irish Drama: From Beckett to McGuinness*. Dublin: Gill & Macmillan, 1994.

Ryan, Ray. *Ireland and Scotland: Literature and Culture, State and Nation, 1966–2000*. Oxford University Press, 2002.

Ryan, Ray, ed. *Writing in the Irish Republic: Literature, Culture, Politics 1949–99*. Basingstoke: Palgrave, 2002.

Sage, Lorna. *Women in the House of Fiction: Post-War Women Novelists*. London: Macmillan, 1992.

Said, Edward. *Orientalism*. London: Penguin, 1978.

Samuel, Raphael, ed. *People's History and Socialist Theory*. London: Routledge, 1981.

Sewell, Frank. *Modern Irish Poetry: A New Alhambra*. Oxford University Press, 2000.

Shepherd, Simon, and Mick Wallis. *Drama, Theatre, Performance*. London: Routledge, 2004.

Studying Plays. London: Edward Arnold, 2002.

Shepherd, Simon, and Peter Womack. *English Drama: A Cultural History*. Oxford: Blackwell, 1996.

Sheppard, Robert. 'Artifice and the Everyday World: Poetry in the 1970s'. In Bart Moore-Gilbert, ed. *The Arts in the 1970s: Cultural Closure?* London: Routledge, 1994.

Showalter, Elaine. *A Literature of their Own: British Women Novelists from Bront to Lessing*. Princeton University Press, 1977.

Skelt, Peterjon. *Prospect Into Breath: Interviews with North and South Writers*. Twickenham and Wakefield: North and South, 1991.

Smith, Dai. *Aneurin Bevan and the World of South Wales*. Cardiff: University of Wales Press, 1995.

Smyth, Gerry. *The Novel and the Nation: Studies in the New Irish Fiction*. London: Pluto Press, 1997.

Sonntag, Jacob, ed. *Caravan: A Jewish Quarterly Omnibus*. London and New York: Thomas Yoseloff, 1962.

Jewish Perspectives: Twenty-five Years of Jewish Writing. London: Secker & Warburg, 1980.

Spivak, Gayatri. 'Can the Subaltern Speak?' In Cary Nelson and Lawrence Grossberg, eds. *Marxism and the Interpretation of Culture*. London: Macmillan, 1988, pp. 271–313.

Stevenson, Randall, *The Oxford English Literary History, vol. XII, 1960–2000*. Oxford University Press, 2004.

Stone, Rosanne Allucquere. *The War Between Desire and Technology at the Close of the Mechanical Age*. Cambridge, MA: MIT Press, 1995.

Sturrock, John. *The Language of Autobiography: Studies in the First Person Singular*. Cambridge University Press, 1993.

Sutherland, John. *Reading the Decades: Fifty Years of the Nation's Bestselling Books*. London: BBC Worldwide, 2002.

Suvin, Darko. *Positions and Presuppositions in Science Fiction*. Kent State University Press, 1988.

Tabbi, Joseph, and Michael Wutz, eds. *Reading Matters: Narratives in the New Media Ecology*. Ithaca: Cornell University Press, 1997.

Taylor, Anne-Marie, ed. *Staging Wales: Welsh Theatre, 1979–1997*. Cardiff: University of Wales Press, 1997.

Thomas, M. Wynn. *Corresponding Cultures: The Two Literatures of Wales*. Cardiff: University of Wales Press, 1999.

Internal Difference: Literature in Twentieth-Century Wales. Cardiff: University of Wales Press, 1992.

'Emyr Humphreys: Regional Novelist?' In K. D. Snell, ed., *The Regional Novel in Britain and Ireland, 1800–1990*. Cambridge University Press, 1998, pp. 201–20.

Thomas, Ned. *The Welsh Extremist: Modern Welsh Politics, Literature and Society*. 1971; new edn. Talybont: Lolfa Press, 1994.

Trussler, Simon, ed. *New Theatre Voices of the Seventies: Sixteen Interviews from 'Theatre Quarterly' 1970–1980*. London: Eyre Methuen, 1981.

Tuma, Keith, ed. *Anthology of Twentieth-Century British and Irish Poetry*. New York and Oxford: Oxford University Press, 2001.

Fishing by Obstinate Isles: Modern and Postmodern British Poetry and American Readers. Evanston, IL: Northwestern University Press, 1998.

Turkle, Sherry. *Life on the Screen: Identity in the Age of the Internet*. London: Phoenix, 1997.

van Erven, Eugene. *Radical People's Theatre*. Bloomington and Indianapolis: Indiana University Press, 1988.

Vice, Sue. *Holocaust Fiction*. London and New York: Routledge, 2000.

Walker, Marshall. *Scottish Literature Since 1707*. London and New York: Longman, 1996.

Wallace, Gavin, and Randall Stevenson, eds. *The Scottish Novel Since the Seventies: New Visions, Old Dreams*. Edinburgh University Press, 1993.

Watson, Roderick. *The Literature of Scotland*. Basingstoke: Macmillan, 1984.

Waugh, Patricia. *Feminine Fictions: Revisiting the Postmodern*. London and New York: Routledge, 1989.

Weedon, Chris. *Feminism, Theory and the Politics of Difference*. Oxford: Blackwell, 1999.

Weintraub, Karl. *The Value of the Individual: Self and Circumstance in Autobiography*. University of Chicago Press, 1978.

Werlock, Abby H. P., ed. *British Women Writing Fiction*. Tuscaloosa: University of Alabama Press, 2000.

Whyte, Christopher ed., *Gendering the Nation*. Edinburgh University Press, 1995.

Williams, Raymond. 'Welsh Culture'. In *Resources of Hope: Culture, Democracy, Socialism*. London: Verso, 1989.

The Welsh Industrial Novel. Cardiff University Press, 1979, rpt. in *Problems in Materialism and Culture*. London: Verso, 1980, pp. 213–29.

Wills, Clair. *Improprieties: Politics and Sexuality in Northern Irish Poetry*. Oxford: Clarendon Press, 1993.

Wolff, Janet. *Resident Alien: Feminist Cultural Criticism*. Cambridge : Polity Press, 1995.

Woodruff, Graham. 'Community, Class and Control: a View of Community Plays'. *New Theatre Quarterly*, 5, 20 (1989).

Worpole, Ken. *Dockers and Detectives*. London: Verso, 1983.

Young, Robert. *White Mythologies: Writing, History and the West*. London: Routledge, 1990.

Index